MARIA THERESA

Maria Theresa

THE HABSBURG EMPRESS
IN HER TIME

BARBARA
STOLLBERG-RILINGER

TRANSLATED BY ROBERT SAVAGE

PRINCETON UNIVERSITY PRESS

PRINCETON & OXFORD

Published by Princeton University Press
41 William Street, Princeton, New Jersey 08540
99 Banbury Road, Oxford OX2 6JX

press.princeton.edu

GPSR Authorized Representative: Easy Access System Europe - Mustamäe tee 50,
10621 Tallinn, Estonia, gpsr.requests@easproject.com

First paperback printing, 2025
Paperback ISBN 9780691202709

The Library of Congress has cataloged the cloth edition of this book as follows:

Names: Stollberg-Rilinger, Barbara, author. | Savage, Robert (Robert Ian), translator.
Title: Maria Theresa : the Habsburg empress in her time / Barbara Stollberg-Rilinger ;
    translated by Robert Savage. Other titles: Maria Theresia. English
Description: Princeton : Princeton University Press, 2021. | Includes bibliographical
    references and index.
Identifiers: LCCN 2020038369 (print) | LCCN 2020038370 (ebook) |
    ISBN 9780691179063 (hardback) | ISBN 9780691219851 (ebook)
Subjects: LCSH: Maria Theresa, Empress of Austria, 1717–1780. | Austria—Kings
    and rulers—Biography. | Austria—History—Maria Theresa, 1740–1780.
Classification: LCC DB71 .S7613 2021 (print) | LCC DB71 (ebook) |
    DDC 943.6/032–dc23
LC record available at https://lccn.loc.gov/2020038369
LC ebook record available at https://lccn.loc.gov/2020038370

British Library Cataloging-in-Publication Data is available

Editorial: Priya Nelson and Thalia Leaf
Production Editorial: Kathleen Cioffi
Jacket/Cover Design: Pamela L. Schnitter
Production: Danielle Amatucci
Publicity: Maria Whelan and Amy Stewart

The translation of this work was funded by Geisteswissenschaften International—
Translation Funding for Humanities and Social Sciences from Germany, a joint
initiative of the Fritz Thyssen Foundation, the German Federal Foreign Office, the
collecting society VG WORT and the Börsenverein des Deutschen Buchhandels
(German Publishers & Booksellers Association).

This book has been composed in Arno

Printed in the United States of America

CONTENTS

TRANSLATOR'S NOTE

WHEREVER POSSIBLE, I have used commonly recognized English spellings for both place names and persons ("Cologne" not "Köln," "Charles V" not "Karl V"). The term "Empire" is capitalized only when referring to the historic polity of the Holy Roman Empire. In order to avoid confronting readers with a welter of German terms, I have consistently provided English translations for the many titles, honorifics, and offices mentioned in the text: "Court Chamber," not "Hofkammer," "lord high steward," not "Obersthofmeister," and so on. A list of the most important such terms, along with their English translations, is provided below.

Allerhöchstes Erzhaus = All-Highest Archducal House
Chiffrenkanzlei = Secret Cipher Chancellery
Conferenz in Internis = Domestic Conference
Erbländer = (Habsburg) hereditary lands
Erzhaus = Archducal House
Erzkanzler = Imperial Archchancellor
Grundherr = landlord
(Haupt-)Deputation = (Chief) Deputation
Hauptsiegelamt = Office of the Great Seal
Hofbaudirektor = court building director
Hofkammer(rat) = Court Chamber, court chamber councillor
Hofkanzlei = Court Chancellery
Hofkanzler = court chancellor
Hofkonferenz = Court Conference
Hofkontrolamt = Office of Court Finances
Hofkriegsrat = Court War Council, court war councillor

Hofrat = Court Council, court councillor
Hofrechenkammer = Court Audit Office
Hofzahlamt = Court Treasury
Kammerfourier = quartermaster
Kreisamt = Circle Office
Kreishauptmann = circle captain
Kriegszahlmeister = paymaster of the forces
Kurfürst = prince-elector, elector
Landeshauptmann = captain of territorial estates
Landstände = territorial estates, provincial estates
Landtag = territorial diet, provincial diet
Leibgarde = lifeguards
Ober-Erblandtürhüter = supreme custodian of the patrimonial lands
Oberjägermeister = grand master of the hunt
Obersthofmarschall = grand marshal of the court
Obersthofmeister = lord high steward
Obersthofmeisterin = chief lady-in-waiting
Oberstkämmerer = lord high chamberlain
Oberstkanzler = lord high chancellor
Oberste Justizstelle = Supreme Judiciary
Policeyhofkommission = Police Commission
Prinzipalkommissar = Principal Commissioner
Reichshofrat = Imperial Aulic Council, imperial aulic councillor
Reichs(hof)kanzlei = Imperial (Court) Chancellery
Reichskammergericht = Imperial Chamber Court
Reichskreise = imperial circles
Reichsmarschall = imperial marshal
Reichspostmeister = imperial postmaster
Reichstag = Imperial Diet
Reichsverband = imperial confederation
Ritterstube = Knights' Room
Staatskanzlei = State Chancellery
Staatskanzler = state chancellor
Staatsrat = State Council

Statthalter = governor or viceregent
Untertanen = subjects
Wachtstube = Guards' Room
Wahltag = electoral diet

Map of Habsburg lands, 1740–1780

MARIA THERESA

1

Prologue

FIGURE 1. Maria Theresa monument on the Ringstrasse in Vienna. Sculptures by Caspar Zumbusch based on a design by Alfred von Arneth, 1888

Monumental History

The story of Maria Theresa, as it is usually told, reads like a fairy tale. Once upon a time there was a beautiful princess and young mother who inherited an enormous, rundown old empire and was immediately set upon by her many foes. She convinced a band of rough but valiant warriors to take up arms for her cause. With their help, she defended her ancestral throne, "fighting with dauntless spirit against the ravening horde of enemies that surrounded her, and emerging from the contest not always unscathed, . . . but happily in the end."[1] Three times she faced her most ruthless adversary and was forced to cede him her richest province. But fate turned these defeats to her advantage. For it was only thanks to this serious ordeal that she was able to dismiss the hidebound old men who had advised her father and so, with the help of the wise counsellors she appointed in their place, transform her ramshackle empire into a modern state. "Having been all but given up for lost, the state ultimately emerged victorious from the struggle that had threatened it with utter ruin."[2] This fairy-tale narrative filtered down to the last dregs of popular historical knowledge, the collectors' albums mass-produced by the advertising industry in the twentieth century: "From the very first day of her reign, the twenty-three-year-old showed that she was a born ruler. From the motley collection of lands she inherited, a true state grew under her hands."[3]

The suggestive power of this heroic narrative is difficult to resist. Over the course of the nineteenth century, it transformed Maria Theresa into *the* symbolic figurehead of Austrian statehood.[4] It is equally difficult to imagine a time when she was seen any differently. Shortly after 1800, one contemporary wrote: "I have often wondered how it came about that Maria Theresa, a woman of true greatness, could so easily have been forgotten."[5] During the revolutionary period from 1789 to 1848, it was hard to know what to make of her. Her son, Joseph II, had replaced her in public favor as the hero of the hour—the sober rationalist, despiser of court ceremony, and would-be revolutionary, even if he did not live to see much of the revolution himself. From this nadir in her public fortunes, she was catapulted to the opposite extreme as the nineteenth century progressed. Maria Theresa now grew into a national icon, the "ideal embodiment of Austrian greatness and beauty."[6] The more territories were forfeited by the Habsburg monarchy in the decades leading up to the First World War, the more imposing and glorious the empress was made to appear.

Her public image has been shaped to this day by two awe-inspiring monuments. The first is the gigantic memorial on the Ringstrasse in

Vienna featuring sculptures by Caspar von Zumbusch. Unveiled by Emperor Franz Joseph in 1888, it was unprecedented in both scale and expense.[7] It was accompanied by a commemorative volume designed to be read "by every family in the Austro-Hungarian monarchy, their friends and loved ones," as well as by soldiers and students.[8] The plan for the monument had been conceived after the defeat at Königgrätz in 1866. It would have been unseemly for Maria Theresa, as a woman, to be immortalized astride a warhorse, the pose in which Joseph II had been commemorated in 1807 or Prince Eugene in 1865; a different iconography conveying no less imperial an impression had to be found. The solution hit upon in the end brings to mind female allegories of good government: a larger-than-life Maria Theresa sits enthroned in majesty above the great men of her realm, who gather around the massive pedestal in the form of equestrian statues, sculptures, and half-reliefs. In her left hand she holds aloft the Pragmatic Sanction, a kind of constitutional charter for the Austrian monarchy; with her right hand she gestures toward spectators, her people. As she sits there in regal majesty, flanked by allegories of virtue, she appears less an individual historical personage than the patroness and mother of the state itself, a second *Magna Mater Austriae* towering far above the base reality of history. There was no place in this enormous ensemble for her husband, the Holy Roman emperor Francis I; nobody wanted to be reminded of that long-vanished empire. Maria Theresa instead finds herself surrounded by "great men who made history": generals, ministers, scholars, artists.[9]

The other, perhaps even more influential monument to Maria Theresa is the ten-volume biography by Alfred Ritter von Arneth, director of the State Archive and president of the Academy of Sciences in Vienna, who also came up with the idea for the memorial on the Ringstrasse. Without Arneth's immense work, which appeared between 1863 and 1879 and was buttressed by a myriad of primary source editions, the Maria Theresa renaissance in the last third of the nineteenth century could never have occurred. His biography is unsurpassed to this day in its exhaustiveness and sheer wealth of detail. A knight of the realm, von Arneth (1819–1897) epitomizes the scholar whose first loyalty lies with the state, a type that produced reams of national-heroic history writing in the nineteenth and early twentieth centuries. In 1848–49 he had sat in the first freely elected German parliament in Frankfurt as a representative of pan-German constitutionalism. He later became a member of the Lower Austrian provincial assembly. Over the second half of the century, his interests shifted away from parliament and toward archival and academic work, historical research, and academic politics, a move that secured him an all but unchallenged interpretive monopoly over the Theresian period.[10] While his biography is not entirely free of critical undertones, on the whole it attests to the same hero-worshiping attitude as the memorial on the Ringstrasse. "Grasping the vital essence of this exalted woman, her way of looking at the world, her views and opinions—this must be one of the worthiest tasks an Austrian historian could set himself." The motivation behind his archival research was, he wrote, the "ardent desire to see the real treasures retrieved from the archives by a trustworthy pair of hands and then, in a manner befitting so great a subject, turn them over to the people: as much to the glory of the Empress herself and her illustrious house as to the honor of our Fatherland."[11]

While the two monuments were still under construction, the Habsburg monarchy was losing its former greatness bit by bit. In 1859 it handed over Lombardy to the new Italian nation-state; Venetia followed in 1866, when it also suffered defeat at the hands of Prussia and left the German Confederation; the following year it had to accept Hungary's de facto independence; and in 1871 the foundation of the German Empire put an end to all hopes of a "Greater German" solution (that is, one that included Austria in the unified nation-state)—not to mention the nationalistically motivated secessionist movements in the Balkans and the deep economic upheavals of the fin de siècle. Amid these vicissitudes, a sense of hope and orientation for the future could be won by contemplating past crises that had been heroically overcome. The majesty of a memorial does not just elevate those it commemorates but also—and above all—those who erect it. Both memorials to Maria Theresa, one in bronze and the other in paper, are deluxe examples of monumental history in the sense of Friedrich Nietzsche's famous second Untimely Meditation, "On the Uses and Disadvantage of History for

Life" (1874). History writing is monumental, in Nietzsche's terms, if it places the past in the service of modern-day hopes and expectations: "history as a means against resignation." It teaches "that the greatness that once existed was in any event possible and may thus be possible again." Such history writing works by flattening out the differences between past and present: "the individuality of the past has to be forced into a general form and all its sharp angles and lines broken to pieces for the sake of the comparison."[12]

Nineteenth-century monumental history stands between us and the historical figure of Maria Theresa, preventing us from seeing her without distortion. Between her age, the ancien régime of the eighteenth century, and our own, so many revolutionary changes have taken place that it is difficult for us for to peer behind them. It is tempting to use her as an occasion for wish fulfillment, to project our own identity politics onto her majestic person, and to find it reflecting back at us our present-day concerns. In doing so, we all too easily forget that the polities ruled over by Maria Theresa—the Holy Roman Empire of the German Nation, with its ancient imperial dignity, and the patchwork of territories controlled by the "All-Highest Archducal House" (Allerhöchstes Erzhaus), that strange, nameless monarchy held together solely by dynastic allegiance—have long since ceased to exist. And their various successor states—the Austrian Empire of 1804, the Austro-Hungarian dual monarchy of 1867, the Prussian-led German Empire—did not long outlast them, swept away in the cataclysmic deluge of the First World War.

More was at stake in all these upheavals than just the redrawing and renaming of state borders. In the course of the nineteenth and especially the twentieth centuries, political structures were transformed beyond recognition. These deep, successive shocks were accompanied and cushioned from the outset, however, by narratives and symbols of continuity, which made it easier to overlook the chasms that had opened up between past and present. For has not Vienna remained the capital of Austria? Does not the head of state still reside in the old imperial palace, the Hofburg? Are we not therefore justified in concluding that Maria Theresa and her ministers were the creators of modern Austria?[13] Yet this is an optical illusion. There were as many different narratives of continuity—or discontinuity—as there were successor states to the old Habsburg monarchy. Apart from an Austrian history of Maria Theresa, a German, Hungarian, Czech, Slovak, Slovene, Serbian, Romanian, Belgian, or Italian version could also be told, each in monarchist, socialist, or liberal democratic variants. Maria Theresa would play a different role in each of these narratives.[14] It is not easy to keep such constructions of continuity at a distance, yet such is the intention of this book. And even if another approach is ventured, we should remain ever mindful that a postmodern, postnationalist perspective on Maria Theresa, three hundred years after her birth, is also one among many possible perspectives and has no claim to objective validity. The only difference is that here a perspective of foreignness has been deliberately adopted. Unlike in Nietzsche's monumental history, the chasms separating us from the eighteenth century will not be filled in, nor will Maria Theresa's rough edges be smoothed over. In short: no false intimacy with Maria Theresa will be presumed. The heroine shall be kept at arm's length.[15]

Male Fantasies

In large part, what makes the traditional story of Maria Theresa read so much like a fairytale is its unexpectedly happy ending—unexpected not least because the near-miraculous salvation of the monarchy was the work of a woman. Her eulogists already saw things this way at the time: "What could we do to combat dangers so numerous and so pressing? Such steadfastness, courage, and resolve . . . had not been expected of a woman, since even a male ruler seemed incapable of shouldering so heavy a burden."[16] Through her extraordinary mix of masculine heroism and feminine virtue, her "maternal majesty," Maria Theresa became a source of endless fascination.[17] She was known not only as an empress but also as a faithful wife and mother of sixteen. Sensational fertility and virile leadership, female and male perfection in a single person, made her an exceptional figure. She appeared exceptional even when compared with other famous female rulers of world history such as Cleopatra, Elizabeth I, or Catherine II. Whereas these other monarchs had neglected their roles as spouse and mother—they were unmarried, or childless, or sexually promiscuous, or all at once—Maria Theresa alone united wise governance, conjugal fidelity, impeccable morals, and teeming fecundity in her capacious bosom. She appeared, in other words, to be an exception among exceptions.[18]

For the eighteenth century, a period when the dynastic principle still largely held sway throughout Europe, there was nothing especially unusual about a female head of state. While a woman on the throne was perceived even then as less desirable, she was not yet a contradiction; the spheres of the public and the private, politics and the family were not yet categorically distinct. Maria Theresa's contemporaries already found it remarkable that a representative of the lesser sex could wield such power. But they did not regard her rule as entirely anomalous: she was "a woman, and a mother to her country, just as a prince can be a man and father to his country." Her rule proved that "the greatest of all the arts, that of governing kingdoms, is not beyond the soul of a lady."[19] What was extraordinary, in the eighteenth-century context, was less the fact that a woman held the scepter of power than that a monarch, whether male or female, took the task of government so seriously. Princes came in many forms—patrons of the arts, skirt-chasers, war heroes, family fathers, scholars, philosophers—and each prince could shape his everyday life as he saw fit. Very few approached the task of rule with the single-minded dedication of a Maria Theresa. She met the criteria of a conscientious ruler to a remarkable degree, far more than most other sovereigns of the time.

Maria Theresa's contemporaries already praised this as her "manliness of soul," her *virilità d'anima*.[20] Some even called her a "*Grand-Homme*";[21] "in the attractive body of a queen" she was "fully a king, in the most glorious, all-encompassing sense of the word."[22] Later historians reprised the theme, describing her as a "man filled with insight and vigor."[23] That a masculine soul could reside in a female body had long been a commonplace, albeit one used less to elevate women than to cast shame on men. Praising a woman for her manly bravery or resolution, her masculine courage or spirit, served above all as an indirect criticism of men—something that holds true even to this day, as when Margaret Thatcher or Angela Merkel is described as the "only man in the cabinet."[24]

It was in this sense that Frederick II wrote about the empress: "for once the Habsburgs have a man, and it is a woman."[25] Conversely, a pro-Habsburg pamphlet in the War of Succession scoffed that Frederick had "met his man" in a woman.[26] When a woman is said to be the better man, this casts a devastating judgment on all her male peers. The key point is that calling an exceptional woman like Maria Theresa a "real man" consolidates the sexual hierarchy rather than calling it into question. Such praise assumes that masculinity is a compliment and that the male sex is and remains superior.

Over the course of time, the idea of female rule came increasingly to be seen as a provocation and a paradox. This was not yet the case in the seventeenth and eighteenth centuries. In the Age of Reason, a clear distinction could still be made between physical constitution and political role, in keeping with the adage "Reason has no sex."[27] If, in the words of one contemporary, "queens . . . cease to be women as soon as they ascend the throne,"[28] then this was not to say that they instantly changed sex upon coming to power, only that their gender was immaterial to their ability to govern. Differentiating in this way between physical and political existence was no longer possible in the nineteenth century: women now seemed to be ever more dominated by their flesh. For revolutionaries around 1800, female rule was a symptom of the decadent ancien régime, which tied the exercise of power to the vagaries of birth rather than to popular election and merit. Women were far more rigorously excluded from the new bourgeois sexual order than they had ever been from the aristocratic society of old. As the discipline of history gained in prestige as an instrument of national legitimation, its practitioners therefore regarded women as essentially irrelevant to their craft. For them, the highest object of history was politics—the realm of freedom and progress, an exclusively masculine domain. Women, by contrast, belonged to the realm of nature: the kingdom of necessity and fleshly reality, to which they were bound by the unchanging reproductive cycle. The medievalist Heinrich Finke summed up the point with unsurpassed clarity in 1913: "World history is the history of the human race, that is, the history of man and his development. Woman, and the history of her development, appear only incidentally. That is why only—or predominantly—the deeds of men are inscribed on the historical record."[29]

A female ruler like Maria Theresa could best be integrated into this worldview by being treated as the great exception that proved the rule. For a rule only properly takes shape once it has been transgressed; crossing a border first makes the border visible as such—provided that the exception remains just that. Normative orders are sustained by such exceptions. What has been said of exceptional women in art holds equally true for female rulers like Maria Theresa: they "received institutional recognition solely on the condition that they could be described as an exception or remained the exception."[30] As an exceptional woman, Maria Theresa posed no threat to established gender roles. On the contrary, she allowed historians to wax lyrical about her femininity, beauty, fertility, naturalness, charm, warmth, and devotion. "The harmony of woman and queen is what . . . lends Maria Theresa her incomparable appeal: the fact that she performed her life's work without the least detraction to her feminine being."[31] "Everything about her is instinctive, sprung from a rich temperament and a clever mind not given to reflection and abstraction, full of charm even when it is illogical and unsystematic."[32] Maria Theresa, her gentleman admirers found, did not rule by abstract reasoning; she acted naïvely, impelled by female intuition, with a "heart better educated than her head."[33] Her womanly essence was manifested in her "practical" and "natural domestic understanding," which was "utterly focused on the particulars." Ever "the loving, caring mother," she exuded "tact" and "feminine charm," "touching kindness and a certain reliance on support."[34] She always let "her mind follow her heart," and so on—the quotes extolling such stereotypically feminine virtues could be multiplied at will.[35] In a panegyric written for her two hundredth birthday in 1917, and reprinted as late as 1980 in an official commemorative volume, Hugo von Hofmannsthal elevated her to almost supernatural status, glorifying her enchanting persona and mystique. In his eyes, what made Maria Theresa one of a kind was the fusion in her person of two otherwise incompatible qualities: maternity and kingship. Hofmannsthal took the title *Magna Mater Austriae* literally, attributing to Maria Theresa a kind of political childbearing capacity:

"The demonically maternal side of her was decisive. She transferred her ability to animate a body, to bring into the world a being through whose veins flows the sensation of life and unity, onto the part of the world that had been entrusted to her care."[36] The act of state creation appeared as parturition, the Habsburg complex of territories as an animate being that, like her sixteen children, owed its existence to the maternal ruler.

But Maria Theresa's extraordinary combination of femininity and power also made her attractive to those who turned the gender hierarchy on its head by giving the woman the dominant sexual role. It is therefore unsurprising that Leopold von Sacher-Masoch idolized the empress. Inspired—or, rather, turned on—by the portrait *Maria Theresa as Sultana* (color plate 22), he imagined her as the heroine of an "erotic legend" and the "fairest of her sex," a woman whose "lust for power" had awakened early on "with truly demonic energy," causing not only her "bridegroom, intoxicated by his own happiness," but even her state chancellor, Kaunitz, "to obey her as her slaves."[37]

Maria Theresa's pronounced femininity cried out for a masculine counterpart. Nothing could have been easier than to stylize the lifelong conflict between her and her near-contemporary, the king of Prussia, as a battle between the sexes, thereby inscribing it into the timelessly universal, natural opposition between man and woman. This was the step taken, above all, by historians who advocated the so-called lesser German solution to the German Question, involving the unification of German territories under Prussian dominance and without the inclusion of Austria. For historians such as Ranke, Droysen, and Treitschke,[38] the masculine/feminine dichotomy served as a convenient binary code for ordering the world and the course of history: male Prussia versus female Austria, thrusting attack versus lackluster defense, the forces of progress versus the forces of inertia, Protestantism versus Catholicism, the future versus the past, decisive action versus indecisive vacillation, homogeneity versus heterogeneity, and so on. According to this template, Frederick II stood in relation to Maria Theresa as intellect to emotion, mind to heart, sterility to fertility, cold rationality to maternal warmth, tragic inner turmoil to imperturbable repose. Austrian culture was feminine, Prussian masculine. Everything fitted neatly into the eternal antagonism of man and woman.

The masculine/feminine binary could be adapted to suit changing circumstances. Depending on political exigency, the two sexes could either be presented as irreconcilable opposites—this was the Prussian, "lesser German" reading—or they could be depicted as counterpoles that needed each other to form a whole, as in the "greater German" account. Antithetical yet evenly matched in their "monumental greatness," Maria Theresa and Frederick II were transformed into something like the dream couple of "greater German" history, their romance sadly thwarted by an inimical fate. In 1925, writing in the book series *Die deutschen Führer*, German Leaders, Heinrich Kretschmayr imagined the greatness Germany might have achieved if only their parents had married them off to each other. He thought it a tragedy that "Prussia could become a state only at the cost of German unity." "Austria and Prussia had pushed each other to stellar achievements, to the honor of both," but Germany "had had to pay for their antagonism by all but irrevocably forgoing its unity."[39] Maria Theresa appeared not just as the greatest but also as "the most German woman of the time, perhaps of *all* time: open, true, warm-hearted, virtuous, an exemplary wife and mother," gushed the Bohemian-Austrian writer Richard von Kralik in 1916.[40] And in 1930 the German historian Willy Andreas invoked the higher unity of the German people in the contrast between Maria Theresa and Frederick II, South and North, Catholic and Protestant. Just as the opposition between man and woman was harmoniously resolved in matrimony, so too both sovereigns together constituted the essence of the era: "Not by chance does the period take its name from Frederick the Second and Maria Theresa."[41]

With Hitler's annexation of Austria in 1938, this kind of history writing came into vogue for obvious reasons. Four years later, when Heinrich Ritter von Srbik celebrated the longed-for "greater German *Volksreich*, born of the will of the nation and created by the deeds of one German genius," he found that the time had finally come to unite Maria Theresa and Frederick the Great "in the proud symphony of our entire nation." Their "opposing life principles," and the conflicting needs of the states they led, may have prevented them from building "the inner bridge to each other" during their own lifetimes. But this should not stop later generations from reclaiming them both as "the proud posses-sion of the people as a whole."[42] For Srbik, Maria Theresa was the ideal "embodiment of German womanhood": "German was her thinking and feeling, German her temperament, . . . German the loyalty and love she gave her pleasure-loving husband and her troop of children." She had "created a true state" along Prussian lines, one that was "essentially a German" state, "with a fixed chain of command and a soundly organized administration." The German culture she revitalized had "spilled out beyond the civilizational gradient of the monarchy towards the far east of Central Europe," extending "the soil of the German people" into Transylvania and the Banat. Nor should it be forgotten that "she was an instinctive enemy of Judaism." In short, "the creation of a woman who felt fully German and was conscious of her own Germanness," in whom "the old German imperial idea . . . lived on unperceived," could not be praised highly enough.[43]

Following the Second World War, the Austrian side gave up empha-sizing the higher unity of opposites, preferring instead to reidentify with just one of the two poles, the feminine-Theresian. In 1958 the writer Friedrich Heer described the empress in his essay "Humanitas austri-aca" as the embodiment of a specifically Austrian type that was "strongly conditioned by the feminine element" and characterized by its levity, humanity, and hostility to barren "abstraction." While *Homo austriacus* was inherently tolerant, the centuries-long policy of forced re-Catholicization pursued by the Habsburgs was decidedly un-Austrian. "In opposing Fredrick II, Maria Theresa fights against a very one-sided, strong-willed man, as well as against an Enlightenment in which she senses a masculine, willful, violently ideological element."[44] Now that establishing distance from National Socialist Germany had become the order of the day, the old antagonism between Maria Theresa and Fred-erick II took on new relevance: trustfulness, love, and benevolence on the one side, suspicion, violence, and ideological blindness on the other.

The sexual codification of the contrast between Austria and Prussia once again bore garish fruit. A particularly fine example is the descrip-tion of Vienna by Wilhelm Hausenstein, who argued for the "matriar-chal character of the Austrian Baroque empire."[45] In his reading, Maria

Theresa's maternal fertility and voluptuousness stood opposed to Frederick II's sterility and austerity. Hausenstein literally follows this idea step by step as he walks from the outskirts of the city toward the center. Vienna is the heart of the Habsburg monarchy, the city center is Baroque, and Viennese Baroque is archetypally feminine: "It could be said metaphorically that Viennese Baroque gives the appearance of striving to reach the center of Austrian culture named Maria Theresa. . . . Certainly, the Viennese Baroque is older than Maria Theresa, . . . but the history of Vienna still suggests to the observer a river destined to flow into this maternal delta." In contrast to "masculine-Baroque" cities such as Rome and Berlin, Vienna has no "powerfully ostentatious, clearly oriented Via triumphalis"; there reigns here "rather a deeply rooted law of gentle, non-axial agglomeration." In feminine-Baroque Vienna even sexual differences become blurred, such that "busts of men and women cannot always be told apart at first glance": Francis I is effeminate, while Maria Theresa strikes a pose of masculine command. "This strange contrast expresses something of Vienna's innermost essence: the axial element (man) seems overwhelmed by feminine abundance and force, and everything gathers in concentric circles around a central maternal figure." The topographical midpoint of this deeply female Vienna is the imperial palace, the Hofburg; its center, in turn, is the white and gold State Bedroom; and at the heart of the bedchamber lies the imperial matrimonial bed, the shrine awaiting Hausenstein at the end of his pilgrimage through the city. Maria Theresa's "heavy and luxurious bed of state, the bed of a majestic love," already preserved under Franz Joseph as a memorial to the empress, sets the author's fantasy aflame as "the most unconventional and special place in the Hofburg," the place where "this entire palace's being is rooted," "the pulsating heart of life in the Hofburg." The bed and its counterpart, the conjugal sarcophagus in the crypt, together form the "center of the dynasty, the summit of Austrian history": "Vienna's head and heart—in womanly form!"

For Maria Theresa historiography, as indeed for the discipline of history in Germany and Austria as a whole, 1945 did not mark a clean break with the past. Historians still clung to the perspective of obsequious subjects, writing about Maria Theresa in the lofty strains of panegyric.[46]

This tone was still resurfacing in the commemorative writings published on the occasion of the two hundredth anniversary of her death in 1980, when Hugo von Hofmannsthal's essay was reprinted. The uncontested dominance of the nationalist-conservative myth evidently made Maria Theresa uninteresting for other approaches. Even in a recent overview of the research literature, she is described as "perhaps the least controversial figure in Habsburg history"; her image, it is said, still tends "to be overly kitschy."[47] The feminist movement of the 1970s, which invented first the history of woman and then that of gender, was strikingly uninterested in Maria Theresa and initially made no attempt to enlist her for its cause. It almost sounded ironic when, writing in the feminist magazine *Emma* in 2010, Barbara Sichtermann reclaimed the empress as the model of an emancipated wife and mother who enjoyed autonomy in her marriage and struck an effortless balance between family and career.[48] First-generation feminist historians were more preoccupied with giving a voice to the invisible and downtrodden women in history. The "housewife empress," transfigured by generations of male historians into an exceptional figure, was hardly an obvious candidate for a new, emancipatory women's history, in stark contrast to her daughter Marie Antoinette. Feminists could do without this staid icon of national-conservative political history. Maria Theresa fitted no less awkwardly into the categories of feminist historians, intent on liberating women from their role as victims, than she had into those of traditional historians, who insisted that history was made exclusively by men.

At any rate, the lack of interest in Maria Theresa is conspicuous. It is significant that a number of recent research projects on the Habsburg monarchy in general, and the Viennese court in particular, end with her accession to the throne in 1740.[49] There has been moderate interest in her husband, Francis I, and in some of her top officials, aristocrats, and ministers,[50] as well as in selected topics such as frontier policy, religious policy, or cross-cultural contact with the Ottoman Empire[51]—but very little in the person of the empress-queen. The sole exception is representations of her in the visual media, which have been intensively discussed by art historians.[52] Until the three hundredth anniversary of her birth in 2017, no scholarly biography in German had been published since the jubilee year of 1917, which saw the appearance of Eugen Guglia's two-volume work.[53] This left the field open to French and British historians, who were less contaminated by nationalist mythmaking,[54] as well as authors of popular nonfiction, who promised readers a glimpse through the Hofburg keyhole with titles like "Children, Church and Corset."[55]

The fact that the younger generation of historians has previously steered clear of Maria Theresa has ensured that her broader public image is still shaped to a remarkable degree by the viewpoint of nineteenth- and twentieth-century Austrian historians. As presented by these men, Maria Theresa is either particularly feminine or particularly masculine, authentically Austrian or *echt deutsch*. She is the heroine who prevailed against the superior force of her enemies and defended right against might. She is the "empress of Austria" who relegated her husband—no less eminent a figure than the Holy Roman emperor—to the role of helpmate. She is the respectably bourgeois housewife-empress who put an end to aristocratic dominance at court and its stuffy ceremonial. She is the resolute founder of a modern, bureaucratic administration that did away with privilege and patronage. And, finally, she is the queen of hearts, a monarch who loved her people as her own children and was loved by them in turn, gladly lending an ear to the lowliest of her subjects.[56] In somewhat exaggerated form, those are the stereotypes that any biography of Maria Theresa must confront today.

An Extraordinary Ordinary Case

It is high time, then, for the figure of Maria Theresa to be historicized and contemplated in its foreignness. Yet it would be naïve to think that we are now finally in a position to tell her *true* story. Arneth's monumental biography is by no means wrong—on the contrary, it has yet to be surpassed in its exhaustiveness and wealth of descriptive detail. Anyone looking for a painstaking account of diplomatic negotiations in times of war and peace could do no better than consult his masterpiece. Yet biographical narrative cannot be handled in the same way today as in Arneth's time—unless, that is, a deliberately novelistic approach is attempted.[57]

To be sure, the genre of biography is no longer treated with the suspicion or even contempt that it was shown in the 1970s. As we have become increasingly aware of the constructive achievement of the narrator and the suggestive power of narrative, historical narrative, including the narration of individual lives, has long since been rehabilitated as a legitimate form of historical knowledge. When strict deconstructionists refer to the "biographical illusion," this is no objection to the genre as such. It goes without saying that a life is not intrinsically a story but is first shaped into one at the hands of a storyteller.

Yet historians today can no longer retroactively transform a multifaceted, contingent plethora of historical events into an unambiguous, unidirectional narrative. They can no longer present themselves as omniscient narrators, tacitly purporting to arrive at timelessly valid psychological truths through introspection and divining their subject's motives through direct empathy. Such an approach necessarily results in anachronistic misinterpretations—such as the one that imputes the feelings of a nineteenth-century middle-class mother to a ruler like Maria Theresa. It would be better to start off by acknowledging that the era we are seeking to recreate was structurally different to our own. We can then ask which of these differences are "noteworthy and meaningful" for understanding our cast of characters.[58] For when it comes to historical understanding, foreignness is not a barrier but a necessary starting point. Historical understanding cannot be had free of charge; it demands determined hermeneutic effort. For instance: what did people take for granted back then; which conceptual categories did they apply; which social distinctions did they make; what was the unspoken logic underlying their actions; on which expectations, rules, and conventions did they orient their behavior; what stock of common knowledge could they draw on; which habitualized routines did they employ; how did they typically express their feelings; what limits were set to their actions? Potentially, all these things were fundamentally different from what appears self-evident to us today, and the gap separating "now" from "then" needs to be gauged as precisely as possible.

There is no need for the figure being investigated in this way to be "representative" in a sociological sense. Microhistorians speak of "extraordinary normality," a paradoxical concept that is relevant in this context.[59] Exceptions are usually far better documented than regular cases, those which "go without saying." Yet precisely a case that is rare, unusual, and abnormal allows us to draw conclusions about what is considered normal and self-evident, which it always presupposes as its background. The individual person and the general structure inform each other rather than standing starkly opposed. Microhistorians have used this argument since the 1980s to justify the broader historical relevance and value of their unusual individual case studies, which mostly concern marginalized "little people." What holds true of figures like the completely unknown miller Menocchio applies just as much to famous historical personages such as Maria Theresa. She too was a thoroughly unusual exception, and yet her story reveals a great deal about the rules and norms that made her exceptional in the first place. In this case, however, the challenge is precisely the opposite of that faced by microhistorians: Maria Theresa has no need to be awakened to historical life; she must instead be retrieved from the various historiographical projections that have been superimposed on her over time.

A biography does not simply tell itself. It is up to the author to establish its narrative structure and continuity. I have followed three principles in this biography. First I have attempted to avoid the illusion of omniscience as well as the "natural complicity" of the biographer with her subject.[60] I have instead juxtaposed multiple perspectives and modes of perception in the belief that variety and even incompatibility in source perspectives, far from representing an obstacle that the narrator ought to eliminate, are what first give a narrative its richness.[61] Second, I have attempted to combine narrative and analytic elements throughout, switching between close-up and wide-angle, microscopic and macroscopic approaches to the subject. Third, I have adopted a distancing, "ethnological" gaze that seeks to avoid any false intimacy with my heroine.[62] This includes letting the alien-sounding, prickly language of the primary sources be heard as often as possible. The goal is to understand Maria Theresa in her time—and, conversely, to disclose her time *pars pro toto* through Maria Theresa.

baptized by the name of Maria Theresa Walburga Amalia Christine.[1]
According to the court calendar, the birth took place in the sixth year of
the imperial reign of Charles VI and the fourteenth year of his rule in
Spain. Over three thousand years had passed since "the first foundations
of the city of Vienna were laid"; it was the 505th year since "the imperial
fortress was first built" and the thirty-fourth "following the relief of the
determined siege by the Turkish army and their expulsion from these
parts."[2] Preparations for the arrival of the child had long been underway.
In January, subjects in Habsburg lands from Milan to Silesia had already
begun gathering in their parish churches to pray for a happy birth and
healthy successor. Processions were held to beseech the Mother of God
for her benign intercession.[3] By April, arrangements had been made for
the newborn's household and wet nurses engaged. Overall responsibility for the child, the office of aya, had been assigned to a high-ranking
matron at court.[4]

The institutional matrix into which the child was born was old, august, and awe inspiring: the glorious Archducal House of Austria, the
Holy Roman Empire, and not least the one true Catholic Church, which
had successfully withstood the siege of Protestant heresy. All these institutions laid claim, more or less plausibly, to an ancient and venerable
lineage. While the House of Habsburg, the mightiest of all the imperial
estates, no longer traced its ancestry back to the biblical patriarch Noah
or to Hector, the hero of ancient Troy, it still claimed descent from
Eticho, an Alsatian vassal of the seventh-century Frankish king Childe-
bert.[5] The Roman-German imperial title, which the house had held
continuously since the fifteenth century, had been inherited from the
queen Augustus via Charlemagne. Lastly, the Catholic Church, founded
by Christ himself, had proceeded in uninterrupted succession from the
apostle Peter to the current pontiff, Clement XI, the child's godfather.
In all three cases, the institution in question derived its authority from
the principle of a centuries-long, seemingly unbroken transmission of
power from one incumbent to the next. Even at the time, admittedly,
these impressive continuities did not always stand up to critical scrutiny.
But that was beside the point, so long as the primordial longevity and
sanctity of the dynasty, the imperial throne, and the Roman church

were constantly invoked and experienced in ritual form. This is precisely what occurred in the rite of baptism, which was at once a family celebration, an act of state, and a religious sacrament, a display of social hierarchy, political power, and sacral dignity. Through holy artifacts, ancient words, and ritual gestures, through the whole complex ceremonial arrangement, and not least through the names it was given, the newborn infant was assigned a place in a preexisting order and symbolically connected with its oldest traditions.

To ensure that everything went according to plan, details of the baptismal site and ceremony had been discussed and decided beforehand in a special conference attended by the highest court officials.[6] The baptism was held, not in a public church or the court chapel, but in the imperial state apartment of the Hofburg, the Knights' Room (*Ritterstube*), which had been carefully refurbished for the occasion. The room was decked out with gold- and silver-threaded silk tapestries, illuminated with numerous crystal chandeliers, and furnished with a canopy, an altar, and a baptismal font. The Knights' Room was located on the first floor of the Hofburg, in the so-called Leopoldine Wing, an elongated, strictly geometrical structure that had been built on to the old castle in the 1660s to meet increased ceremonial demands. More castle than palace, the Hofburg was in essence a rambling old sixteenth-century pile in the middle of an equally labyrinthine Vienna, hemmed in by the city's medieval fortifications.[7] Even in the days of Emperor Leopold I, it had struck visitors as "not especially stately, and fairly cramped for so mighty . . . a potentate."[8] Although it continued to be extended and modernized in the eighteenth century—in 1717 a new wing was added to house the Imperial Chancellery (*Reichskanzlei*)—it failed to satisfy contemporary tastes, which demanded symmetrical forms, sweeping visual axes, an imposingly grand central staircase, and above all extensive, geometrically laid out gardens.

Yet the imperial court, which still claimed to be the highest-ranking secular court in all Christendom, set greater store on preserving tradition than on aping the latest courtly fashions from hostile France. This was no less true of the ceremonial with which the newborn infant was received into the world. It remained essentially the same Burgundian-Spanish

FIGURE 3. The Hofburg in Vienna. Detail from the bird's-eye view by Josef Daniel Huber, *Scenographie oder Geometrisch Perspect. Abbildung der Kayl. Königl. Haubt- u. Residenz Stadt Wien in Oesterreich*, 1773

ritual that had first been introduced to the Austrian court by Ferdinand I in 1527. This order stipulated that courtiers could only ever approach the royal couple after bending a knee three times. It regulated such matters as who had access to which rooms and who could serve the emperor when he dined alone. Hallowed by age, the ceremonial was inflexible, solemn, and exclusive, and it distanced the ruling family from the rest of the world—quite unlike the French court at the same time, where almost anyone was allowed access to royalty so long as they were cleanly and properly attired.[9]

Maria Theresa's baptism also followed this strict ceremonial order. Proceedings played out exclusively within the walls of the Hofburg. On the evening of the delivery, a solemn procession, accompanied by drums and trumpets, made its way from the empress's bedchamber to the baptismal room. It was led by cavaliers and members of the Lower Austrian territorial estates (*Landstände*), the imperial chamberlains, and privy counsellors, all "in precious campaign dress." Then came the papal nuncio and Venetian ambassador pacing side by side, since each refused to cede precedence to the other. They were followed by the emperor in Spanish court dress, shimmering with gold and silver brocade and with red feathers in his hat, the two widows of the former emperors Leopold I and Joseph I, both still in mourning, and finally the aya with the newborn "Most Serene Archduchess," lying bejeweled on a cushion of white Atlas silk. The deceased emperors' daughters, the heads of the female court household, and countless court ladies, ministers' wives, and noblewomen from the city brought up the rear. At the entrance to the Knights' Room, the mewling infant was handed over to Liechtenstein, the lord high steward (*Obersthofmeister*), who bore her into the room amid trumpet fanfares and drumbeats. There the bishop of Vienna, assisted by a gallery of senior prelates, administered the sacrament of baptism. After the Ambrosian song of praise, a closing prayer, and the bishop's blessing, the entire company withdrew in orderly procession to their apartments.

The two imperial widows and no less august a personage than Pope Clement XI, represented by his nuncio, stood godparents to the child. The choice of godfather was doubly significant: with the supreme head of Christendom, the child not only gained the highest-ranking godfather Catholic Europe had to offer, the baptism also provided a welcome opportunity to strengthen the far from ironclad political alliance with the Holy See. In the War of the Spanish Succession, this same pope had stood on the opposing side; now they needed each other to make common cause against the Turks.[10] Before the birth, the Court Conference (*Hofkonferenz*: an informal committee of top court officials, whom the emperor advised to appoint him in all matters of state) had also deliberated on the choice of godfather in the event of a son and heir apparent. Only high-ranking Catholic potentates such as the kings of France, Portugal, or Poland had come into consideration; the Elector Palatine and Duke of Lorraine had also been discussed as fallback candidates—almost all of them relatives of the house. In the end the choice had fallen on the

of age. Solemnities at the imperial court marking the birth of a daughter were considerably less elaborate than those heralding the arrival of a son.[19] But even if it was "only" a daughter, any birth in the royal family—provided the infant was not so frail as to place its survival in doubt—was a joyous occasion of profound dynastic and political import. The news was immediately proclaimed far and wide. As befitted so strictly hierarchical a society, the manner in which this occurred was finely graded: on the one hand according to the child's sex, on the other depending on the rank and closeness of the addressee. The people of Vienna were the first to hear about it. If a son was born, particularly a firstborn, the public was notified with cannon fire, a triple volley from the guards, as well as a blaze of trumpets, drums, and pealing bells. In the event of a daughter, as in this case, the military signals were omitted and only church bells rang out the glad tidings. Maria Theresa later modified this custom, ordering cannons to be fired upon the birth of her daughters as well.[20] How the news was brought to other courts also varied by degree. It was simplest to inform foreign emissaries in a face-to-face audience so that they could then relay the news in writing to their courts. A more labor-intensive method, which therefore conveyed greater esteem, was to dispatch a courier to a foreign court with written notification. And the most considerate means of all was to send a chamberlain to bear the news in person to the other court. In this way, closely related, amiably disposed, or allied courts could be assured of the emperor's particular regard and the sociopolitical network of relations could be drawn more tightly. For their part, addressees responded with no less finely graded messages of congratulation and perhaps also gifts. A large part of communication between courts consisted of such reciprocal "notifications" and "compliments," tangible and intangible gifts and countergifts. Births and baptisms, but also New Year's greetings, marriages, birthdays and name days, victories in battle, successfully overcome illnesses or deaths, all provided an opportunity to cement relationships through displays of mutual goodwill. Baptisms were occasions for gift-giving on a lavish scale. Mother and child received costly symbolic gifts from godparents and from emissaries of other courts, mostly jewelry, diamond-encrusted tobacco boxes, and portraits, which then called for gifts in return. The entire chamber personnel, physicians, midwives, and so on received presents of money, chains, and medallions at a value precisely calibrated to their position in the court hierarchy.

The reading public outside the capital could learn about the dynastic event from printed newspapers. The *Wienerische Diarium*, brought out by the court-appointed publisher Ghelen, was one of the oldest periodicals in Europe. Still in circulation today as the *Wiener Zeitung*, it regularly appeared several times a week from 1703 onward.[21] This early newspaper reported on the latest wars, events at court, catastrophes, and sensations of all kinds, although it was far from what we would understand today by a critical press. There was still no firm distinction between a court-sanctioned public relations agency and a privately organized newspaper business. The *Wienerische Diarium* enjoyed a monopoly on information. Anyone granted the right to call himself "Book Printer and Publisher by Appointment to the Court" was spared the need to have his products monitored and censored by the authorities. He was hardly likely to risk having the privilege revoked through insubordinate or inappropriate reporting. Those who bought and consumed these newspapers wanted above all to read their own names in its pages and had no interest in critical undertones. For anyone interested in finding out what the educated, well-to-do Viennese public was supposed to know about events at court, the *Wienerische Diarium* is thus an exceptional source. It reported on the birth of Maria Theresa in the most obsequious and deferential manner, drawing its information from a separately printed text entitled *Description of the most happy delivery of Her Majesty the Reigning Queen on May 13, 1717 and thereafter the most magnificent ceremony of baptism performed here in the imperial castle.* This text, issued by the "Imp[erial] Court Press," was a court report dictated to the press by the Lord High Steward's Office.

For commoners in the various lands ruled by the dynasty, the sphere of temporal power was as shimmeringly otherworldly and remote as the sphere of celestial power, which was reflected in the regal "terrestrial gods" (*Erdengötter*). If they received any word of events at court then it was principally through their priest, who exhorted them from the pulpit to give thanks for the newborn archduchess and offer prayers for her health. Communication on the occasion of the birth was thus not limited to the world below. The infant's parents and relatives likewise thanked the Mother of God, the most important heavenly intercessor, for the happy delivery. Gratitude was expressed not only in prayers but also in gifts such as religious foundations. On the day of Maria Theresa's birth, the widowed empress Wilhelmina Amalia ceremoniously laid the foundation stone for a church for the Salesian nuns on the Rennweg in Vienna, not least "to make the birthday . . . even more worthy of remembrance."[22] In Catholic princely houses, moreover, it was customary to donate "a silver image of the same weight as the newborn prince" to the Mother of God, or to some other saint to whom such an offering had been pledged.[23] The gift's value increased still further in the case of imperial children, such as following the birth of the firstborn prince Leopold and that of his sister.[24] On June 6, 1717, an imperial chamberlain set out for the pilgrimage church at Mariazell "that he might thereafter, in the name of their Reigning Imp[erial] Majesties, lay down their recently pledged offering, . . . a child worked of pure gold, at the miraculous icon of the Virgin."[25] The massive gold figure was publicly displayed in front of the chapel grille before being set before the altar at a solemn high Mass the next day. An inscription recorded that it had been given in return for the heaven-sent gift, which the parents had literally balanced out in gold.[26]

Theatrum Europaeum

The rituals at the Habsburg court convey a one-sided impression. The world into which Maria Theresa was born in 1717 was by no means as static and unchanging as they suggest. On the contrary, it was in a state of considerable flux.

Europe's unity consisted—to put it paradoxically—in its discord. The Europe of potentates, the *Theatrum Europaeum*, had for centuries been racked by ongoing armed conflict. What the eighteenth century called "Europe" was largely shaped by the permanent competitive rivalry among intermarrying dynasties. Europe's borders were those of a kinship system that integrated the high aristocracy throughout all Latin Christendom. In effect, Europe was a single marriage market, the sum of all the territories whose ruling families looked to each other for eligible partners. European royalty, the *société des princes*, consisted of all the families which potentially came into consideration whenever dynastic marriage projects were on the cards: the houses of Habsburg and Bourbon, the Stuarts and the Oranges, the Guelphs and the Wettins, the Hohenzollerns and the Wittelsbachs, the Savoys and the Lorraines, but also the Romanovs (to name only the most important). To contemporary observers, nothing so clearly revealed Russia's metamorphosis into a European power as the marriage negotiations conducted in the 1720s between Tsar Peter and the House of Bourbon. Following the Peace of Westphalia, Europe was not yet a system of sovereign states. This is an anachronistic view that mistakes the theory of international law for the practice. Rather, sovereignty was still a matter of social status.[27] Sovereigns were monarchs, princes, dynastic overlords whose rule was reproduced through inheritance. To a large extent, politics was still a family enterprise. Actors were primarily concerned with accruing fame, status, glory, and honor for their aristocratic house. Yet family ties do not always make for peace and harmony—quite the opposite. The dynasties found themselves in a state of permanent rivalry. Their relationship was structurally bellicose rather than peaceful. There were no long-term stable alliances, no fixed confessional or ideological camps; everything could shift from one moment to the next. This was especially apparent during the period between the Peace of Westphalia and the French Revolution. Most military conflicts arose from disputes over succession. The more closely the dynasties were knitted together through intermarriage, the more easily they could get caught up in competing inheritance claims.

At the beginning of the eighteenth century, a long and ruinously expensive war had been fought over the gigantic inheritance of the Spanish crown (1701–1713/14). When the congenitally unfit King Charles II died, childless and heirless, in 1700, the Austrian Habsburgs and French Bourbons (among others) disputed the succession, launching a twelve-year conflict that brought the Spanish global empire of the Golden Age to its knees.[28] The two dynasties had traditionally vied for dominance in Europe yet were linked at the same time through multiple intermarriages. This made it extremely difficult to sort out the various succession claims. On his deathbed, Charles II had named Philip of Anjou, the grandson of the French king, his heir. England, the Netherlands, and the Holy Roman Empire responded by forming a Grand Alliance, fearing that Louis XIV would otherwise gain hegemony over the continent. Almost all the European potentates, including the pope, were embroiled either directly or indirectly in the ensuing conflict, which spilled out over several theaters of war. For the Spanish inheritance encompassed not only Spain itself but, even more important, half of Italy as well: the Kingdom of Naples, the Duchy of Milan, Sardinia, and Sicily. It additionally included the southern Netherlands, roughly equivalent to today's Belgium, as well as the vast Spanish colonies in the New World. For a time, Archduke Charles of Austria, Maria Theresa's father, held court in Barcelona as King Charles III of Spain, but after a long and bloody campaign he eventually had to renounce the throne in favor of the French candidate, Philip of Anjou. During the war he had succeeded his brother Joseph as holy Roman emperor, and his allies were not prepared to accept so great a concentration of power in the hands of a single ruler, whether Habsburg or Bourbon. As compensation he received the southern Netherlands, the Kingdom of Naples, the island of Sardinia, and the duchies of Milan and Mantua—a solution that neither he nor the new Spanish king found acceptable, paving the way for further conflict in the decades to come. In the War of the Spanish Succession, the increasing global entanglement of European power interests already made itself felt. The war was equally a commercial and colonial showdown between the French, on the one side, and the British, Dutch, and Portuguese, on the other. At stake was the Atlantic trade in slaves, cloth, and tobacco, with state-authorized privateers roving the high seas in search of booty. Other conflict zones included the Spanish, French, and British colonies on the American Atlantic coast from the Caribbean to Newfoundland. Indigenous people were also drawn into the conflict as combatants and victims; from an American perspective it has even been called the Second French and Indian War.

The new order that emerged from the war, concluded after a series of long and complex negotiations in Utrecht, Rastatt, and Baden in 1713–14, was neither complete—Charles VI and Philip of Spain had not yet made peace—nor lasting: a fresh campaign for the Italian territories broke out against the new Spanish king only a few years later. The lesson that small to middling potentates could draw from these peace treaties was that they could always count on serving as pawns to be exchanged or sacrificed in the games of the great powers. These top-tier sovereigns acted in accordance with the informal principle of *convenance*, or the balance of power. They tacitly agreed to coordinate their interests to ensure that no single state surpassed the rest in power and prestige. It was above all England that promoted and profited from this maxim by establishing itself as a kind of arbiter over the distribution of power in Europe. This also played into the hands of the new king, George I, simultaneously elector of Brunswick-Lüneburg, who ascended the English throne in 1714 and thereby established the far from incontestable succession of the Hanoverian line.[29] England emerged as the biggest winner from the War of the Spanish Succession. It would go on to become an unrivaled trading power and, increasingly, a model for elites of other nations in questions of social conduct, intellectual fashion, and material lifestyle. For France, on the other hand, the "classical" era of its unchallenged predominance in matters of taste gradually came to an end following the death of Louis XIV in 1715.

Charles VI learned his lesson from the experience of the war, making provisions designed to safeguard his dynasty from future conflict. A dynastic law was drafted to ensure a clear and orderly succession to the Habsburg throne, regardless of future contingencies. If no male heir was forthcoming, the king's lands were neither to be dismembered nor fall prey to other dynasties. This concern was not unfounded, since Charles was still childless at the time and his late brother, Joseph I, had sired only daughters. In 1713, the year of the Peace of Utrecht, Charles VI therefore proclaimed a new succession law. If he died without a son, his daughters, then the daughters of Joseph I, and finally the sisters of Charles and Joseph (or their direct descendants) would inherit the throne. The novelty of this arrangement was not the subsidiary female right of succession, which had existed before in the House of Habsburg. In 1703 the king's father, Leopold I, had already regulated the succession between his sons Joseph and Charles in such a way as to prevent his lands being broken up after his death. What was new in this *Pactum mutuae successionis* was that Charles now gave priority to his *own* daughters over the daughters of his brother, Joseph I. Furthermore, the regulation was now to be enshrined as an eternal, irrevocably binding law for all the lands of the House of Austria. That is why Charles, drawing on a late Roman legal concept, gave it the name *sanctio pragmatica*, Pragmatic Sanction: an inviolable law commanding absolute authority.[30]

Yet proclaiming such a law was one thing, ensuring that it was universally recognized was another. To this end, Charles called on the estates of all his dominions to give their solemn and explicit assent to the decree. The estates, consisting of the established noble families, clerical corporations and cities, took themselves to embody their respective lands and traditionally expected to be consulted on all important matters concerning the community as whole. That is what now happened in the *Erbländer*—the Austrian hereditary lands—as well as in Bohemia, Hungary, and the Italian territories. In addition, Charles relied on the support of the Imperial Diet (*Reichstag*), where the totality of the Empire's princes and estates were represented. Like all emperors, Charles had been elected to occupy the imperial throne after his predecessor's death. Although he ranked as the Empire's supreme overlord, this did not stop the Empire's princes from treating him as a kind of first among equals, demanding certain concessions in exchange for their vote. The emperor therefore not only had to deal with the Imperial Diet as a collective body on this matter, he also had to negotiate individually with the most powerful imperial princes. The prince-electors of Saxony and Bavaria withheld their support in the Imperial Diet since, as his in-laws, they had no wish to relinquish their own inheritance claims. By contrast, Charles succeeded in securing the consent of the Prussian king, Frederick William I, in return for imperial backing in his own succession dispute over Jülich-Berg. Yet even that was not enough–too many interests of other European powers were affected by the new inheritance law, too many rival claims had to be denied. For the rest of his reign, the emperor was kept busy making concessions on all sides to have the Pragmatic Sanction accepted throughout Europe: in Spain, Russia, England, Denmark, and the United Netherlands. All these solemn declarations would prove worthless after his death.

The other great theme of Charles VI's reign was his willingness to take up the fight against the Habsburgs' longstanding enemies, the Turks. In 1714 the ever-simmering conflict had once again boiled over into open military confrontation. On the same day that Maria Theresa came into the world, the imperial field-marshal Prince Eugene of Savoy, renowned throughout Europe for his military prowess, set out once again for the southeast border of Hungary to take to the field against the sultan's troops. The skulls and bones of thousands of unburied soldiers still littered the battlefield near Zenta, where Prince Eugene had celebrated a famous victory in 1697.[31] His new campaign was equally successful. On July 19 he laid siege to Belgrade with an army of 70,000 men, on August 16 he took the city; and only a year later, on July 21, 1718, he concluded peace with the sultan in the Serbian town of Passarowitz. Like the Treaty of Karlowitz that had ended the Great Turkish War in 1699, the terms of this new treaty were highly unfavorable to the Ottomans. The Habsburgs extended their hegemony further southeast. The perennial threat in the southeastern marchlands of the Habsburg Empire appeared to have been banished for good; traumatic memories of the two Ottoman sieges of Vienna, in 1529 and 1683, seemed to have been laid to rest. Yet this was an illusion. Barely twenty years later, the emperor joined with his ally Russia to launch a new offensive against the Turks, but this time success would prove elusive. Eventually, in the Peace of Belgrade of 1739, he was forced to relinquish almost all his gains from the previous war. And so it was to remain: Maria Theresa never waged war against the Ottomans, although the specter of the Turkish threat continued to haunt Europe for some time to come.

Back Stage and Front Stage

Little is known about Maria Theresa's childhood. After the baptism she largely disappears from the sources, besides some affectionate remarks in her father's diary[32] and several portraits from her infancy (see color plate 2).[33] Very few composition exercises, educational records, or descriptions of her at this age have survived. This created a void that the bourgeois historical imagination was all too eager to fill: Maria Theresa, we are told, grew up in "a good Austrian, good Viennese-German middle-class family environment."[34] When the children "saw their parents, the atmosphere was informal, just like in a middle-class household. In this respect, the court in Vienna was different from most other courts, even those of the petty German princes. The language and tone heard in the private imperial chambers was also unstuffy and familial."[35] The image of unforced "coziness"[36] projected here was entirely in keeping with the ideal of the nineteenth-century bourgeois nuclear family. Yet even if their father spoke lovingly of his daughters and addressed them with Viennese pet names, life at the imperial court was no more relaxed than it was at other German courts. If anything, the opposite was the case.[37] Admittedly, there was a sharp contrast between the highly formal front stage and the more informal back stage of life at court. Children generally had no business appearing on the front stage. As soon as they failed to abide by the prevailing strict standards of physical discipline, they were an unwanted nuisance. Maria Theresa and her two younger sisters, Maria Anna (born 1718) and Maria Amalia (born 1724), therefore grew up largely separated from their parents and court society, entrusted to the care of their aya, their nannies, and their own dedicated chamber personnel. In winter they lived at the Hofburg; in summer they decamped to the palais "Favorita," twenty minutes away by foot, the small summer residence that today houses the Theresianum boarding school. It is telling that Maria Theresa reserved the name of "Mama" for her second aya, Countess Fuchs, who took on the position in 1728 at the age of fifty-four. She continued to call her by this name until the countess's death in 1754, when she was accorded the unprecedented honor of burial in the Habsburg family crypt in the Capuchin monastery. Maria Theresa was closer to her aya than to anyone else, with the possible exception of her husband—certainly closer than to her own mother, who reportedly felt slighted as a result. When the countess passed away, it was said of her: "It would be difficult to find an example of such boundless and perfect confidence as that enjoyed by this blessed lady from both their imperial Majesties," Maria Theresa and her husband.[38] Such blatant favoritism would normally have made her a target of resentment and envy at court. It is remarkable that "no one, almost without exception, begrudged her this grace and favor."[39] This suggests that she must have been extremely clever as well as likable.

Maria Theresa rarely appeared on the front stage as a young girl. In the ceremonial protocols chronicling all the external details of daily life at court, her presence is explicitly noted in such cases. Thus we read that on April 28, 1728 the eleven-year-old archduchess "wore court dress for the first time" on the occasion of a gala held in honor of her mother's birthday, when the court was in Graz to receive the homage of the Styrian estates.[40] Not by chance, this was also the year of her first communion, since religious and courtly rites of passage went hand in hand. The first state portrait of the heiress dates from the same period (see fig. 2). It shows her in a sumptuous dress embroidered with pearls and with an ermine-lined archducal mantle draped over her right arm. The basket of flowers and the blossoms gathered in her lap allude to her beauty, youth, and virginity. The silk portière behind her and the archducal crown on the red velvet cushion to the left identify the picture as an example of classical state portraiture: the girl who gazes at the viewer with an air of cool detachment is next in line to the Austrian throne.

Maria Theresa would also put in an appearance at court on her birthday. One entry in the ceremonial records from May 13, 1729 states: "The most gracious Infanta and Archduchess Maria Theresa marks her auspicious birthday by feasting thirteen poor maidens . . . and for that reason the nobility appeared in gala."[41] A year later "Her Archducal Highness feasted and distributed gifts to fourteen poor maidens at Laxenburg, one for each year of the age she has now most happily attained,"[42] and she spent the evening before her fifteenth birthday entertaining "fifteen poor maidens . . . as is her annual custom."[43] This custom represented a ritual and symbolic form of benevolence practiced at many courts at the time. The girls, chosen by age and number to match the age of the princess, served *partes pro toto* as objects for the royal virtue of *caritas*. This occurred in the context of a gala day, when the entire court was summoned to the imperial apartment in prescribed festive dress so that the little archduchess might have an audience as she symbolically dispensed largesse to her less fortunate coevals.

A princess was only an asset for a dynasty if she lived long enough to be married off. This was far from assured. Only around one in two children survived into puberty at the time, regardless of social class. Concern for the princess's welfare had both a medical and a religious dimension. Nannies hand-picked for their health, strength, and piety were entrusted with her physical wellbeing from the beginning. The aya was initially given sole responsibility for inculcating the correct religious attitude in her charges, later joined by a Jesuit priest who acted as their confessor and spiritual guide. Maria Theresa and her sisters were accustomed from an early age to the unbending external and internal discipline that would later be required of them at court, receiving the physical and spiritual conditioning that impressed onlookers as the innate mark of nobility. They followed a strict regimen in everything they did, not least in the punctilious observation of religious duties, a form of training that was at once spiritual and physical. By learning to assume an air of reverent concentration and to perform the correct gestures at daily Mass, the children took on the aristocratic bearing that communicated their natural superiority. Learning to be a devout Catholic and how to behave properly at court had less to do with adopting a body of knowledge than with acquiring the right deportment. Nobody was better equipped to teach this than the Jesuits. Having pioneered new methods of self-control and spiritual supervision, from the late sixteenth century they enjoyed an unrivaled reputation in Catholic Europe as educators, including of dynastic pupils.

In second place after religion came the classical aristocratic techniques for training the body. Young royals learned to cut a fine figure at the various court entertainments such as the theater, dancing, and hunting. If reports of contemporary observers are to be believed, Maria Theresa carried off her public performances with aplomb. Her extraordinary musical talent and fine singing voice were widely attested.[44] One of the imperial court's favorite pastimes was rehearsing plays with musical, dramatic, and balletic elements and then putting them on before a court audience. These pieces were written and composed by prominent court artists such as Pietro Metastasio, Johann Adolph Hasse, or Antonio Caldara, and the noble dilettantes studied them with great perfectionism. At the tender age of seven, Maria Theresa was already appearing with her younger sister as a dancer in the opera *Euristeo*, and at eighteen she performed the leading role in the musical drama *Le grazie vendicate*, which she herself had commissioned for her mother's birthday.[45] During the rehearsal period, Metastasio enthused to his brother about the "skill, docility, and winsomeness of these exalted princesses," cautiously adding that his judgment was unclouded by the social eminence of these ladies.[46] It was not until she ascended the throne that Maria Theresa somewhat reluctantly gave up her theatrical career. She had planned to appear in *Ipermestra*, a musical drama that had been written and composed for her by Metastasio and Hasse in 1744. Rehearsals had already gotten underway when her advisers persuaded her to quit the production on the grounds that it ill became her dignity as a sovereign.

Nobody else was put off by such qualms. On the contrary, singing, dancing, and acting were encouraged as promoting the cultivation of courtly manners. They provided good training for what court life later demanded in general of the "most serene lords and ladies": the permanent staging of themselves, a skill that presupposed physical discipline and an adroit public presence. Theatrical performances at court were like plays within a play. Here actors could learn how to perform a role until role play itself became second nature to them. Contemporaries were aware of the structural affinity between life at court and theatrical performance.[47] It was not by chance that *theatrum*, translated into German as *Schau-Platz*, showplace, was the era's metaphor of choice. Yet the metaphor became increasingly discredited during Maria Theresa's lifetime. It eventually fell victim, toward the end of the century, to a new vogue for spontaneity, authenticity, and freedom from affectation.

Courtly Curriculum

Children born into the high nobility attended formal lessons from the age of seven. They no longer spent all their time sequestered in the "ladies' chamber." The children's education was now taken in hand by men as well. When Maria Theresa was thirteen, word got around—as one foreign traveler reported—that "especially the elder [of the two arch-duchesses] possesses a keen intellect and understanding."[48] She received tuition from priests and distinguished court scholars[49]: the Jesuits Michael Pachter and Franz Xaver Vogel instructed her in the Catholic religion; Johann Franz Keller and Gottfried Philipp Spannagl, the court librarian, in Latin, geography, and history; the court mathematician and astronomer Johann Marinoni in arithmetic and geometry;[50] a certain Johann Franz Chièvre in the modern languages Italian and French. The Jesuits made her stick to a strict timetable that gave every activity in her waking life—primarily spiritual exercises, but also occasional recreational pursuits—its assigned place.

Not much is known about the content of her lessons, let alone which books she was set to read. Only her history lessons have been preserved in the instructional manuals composed for her by her teacher.[51] Spannagl had written an outline of history in question-and-answer-format for "the two most serene highnesses, Maria Theresa and Maria Anna." Modeled on the curriculum taught at Austrian Jesuit colleges, it took history to mean "a narrative of the most remarkable things that have come to pass from the beginning of the universe to the present day." It was essentially a commented list of rulers based on information taken from Holy Scripture as well as ancient and medieval historians. This was intricately woven together to produce a linear sequence, starting with the biblical patriarchs and continuing via Alexander, Augustus, and Charlemagne all the way to the Habsburg emperors. One or two females cropped up in this series of rulers as well. The legendary builder of Babylon, Semiramis, was presented as "a woman who surpassed all men as well as all women in virtue and courage."[52] What the archduchesses were taught was still essentially the early medieval Christian conception of salvific history, beginning with the creation of the universe; lingering on the four ancient world empires of the Assyrians, Persians, Greeks, and Romans; and then jumping ahead to the Habsburgs and finally Maria Theresa's own father. For the Holy Roman Empire of the German Nation understood itself to be the continuation of the Roman empire, the fourth kingdom that had once appeared in a dream to the prophet Daniel. The redeemer had lived and died at the start of this last kingdom; once that kingdom fell, the world would end along with it. The two young archduchesses dutifully learned all the key information by heart, writing their answers in an uneven childish hand that can still be read today.[53] Even if Maria Theresa went on to forget all these names and events, one thing presumably stuck in her memory: the history of the world had been ordained by God for his own glory and for the salvation of humankind, and it represented an orderly chain in which her own family had been assigned an extremely prominent position.

Later, it was frequently maintained that Maria Theresa's father had failed to prepare her for her role as heir to the House of Austria. She herself justified her relative ignorance by claiming "that it never pleased my father to involve me when he attended to foreign or domestic affairs, nor to inform me about them."[54] Needless to say, as a daughter she was denied the opportunity to undertake a grand tour of the royal residences of Europe, as was customary for sons of the nobility. Yet besides the fact that she was never instructed in jurisprudence, her canon of subjects was not so very different from that of an archduke. When modern historians assert that the Jesuits "stuffed her brain with useless odds and ends of information from antiquated texts,"[55] or simply that her education was "absurd,"[56] they apply an anachronistic standard. After all, the pedagogical program for male princes in Catholic houses was essentially the same. It was based on the curriculum of Jesuit schools, the *Ratio studiorum* from the year 1599, which was entirely dedicated to the ancient authorities. This is shown not least in the curriculum assigned to prince heir Francis Stephen of Lorraine, nine years Maria Theresa's senior and educated at the Viennese court around the same time: Aristotle's logic, physics, and metaphysics, Quintilian's rhetoric, the theology of Thomas of Aquinas, Justinian's Institutes. Quite in the spirit of the late Scholastic tradition, students were still expected to study the canonic texts and memorize summaries of the material in question and answer format.[57] The pedagogical revolution that encouraged children to experiment, think, and judge for themselves, rather than imbibing the timelessly valid knowledge of the ancients, was still some decades away.[58] And the young Francis Stephen also learned nothing of the new methods and disciplines that had revolutionized the culture of knowledge several decades earlier—the metaphysics of Descartes; the natural law of Hobbes, Locke, and Pufendorf; or the experimental physics of Galilei or Newton, for example.

So far as language training was concerned, the princess's curriculum was also fundamentally no different from that of a male prince: French, Italian, Spanish, and Latin were the languages spoken at the Viennese court, but to different extents and for different purposes. French was the language most commonly used at courts in Europe; Spanish—or more precisely, Castilian—was the tongue of the Habsburg ancestral lands; Italian was not only the language of important Habsburg territories but also that of the literary and musical culture favored at court in Vienna; Latin was still the lingua franca of scholars and clerics as well as the administrative language in Hungary. Maria Theresa corresponded in French and German, sometimes also in Italian; she could speak and write with proficiency in all three languages. There were many other languages spoken in her polyglot empire that she was unable to speak: Hungarian, Czech, Dutch, Serbian, Croatian, or Romanian. Her first language was German, but not because it was the language spoken to her by her mother. She picked it up from her nanny instead, with the result that she always spoke German in Viennese dialect. "Even the Empress talked in vulgar Austrian jargon," the daughter of her lady-in-waiting later recalled, adding, "At the time it could be said of most upper-class Viennese what a poet says of himself: 'I speak Italian like Dante, / Latin like Cicero, / English like Pope and Thomson, / Greek like Demosthenes, / French like Diderot, / And German–like my nanny.'"[59] German was what the common people spoke. It was neither the language of the nobility nor a scholarly language, and it was certainly not a respectable literary idiom. The bureaucracy cultivated an inelegant, pedantic jargon, peppered with Latin phrases, which did nothing to make German more appealing.[60] That changed only gradually. When Maria Theresa later used several languages, this not only allowed her to communicate with people from different geographical backgrounds, it also catered to differences in social class. Letters to family members were generally written in French, messages to bourgeois officials in German.

Dynastic Chess Moves

A royal daughter traditionally became the focus of her parents' attention once she could function as a piece on the dynastic chessboard. By expanding the dynasty's kinship network through an advantageous marriage, she could increase the political and symbolic capital of the house. On the other hand, such unions did not come cheap: it was expected that daughters would be wed with all the pomp befitting their station, including countless presents for guests. This could be a problem if a ruling couple had too many daughters. Frederick William of Prussia, the father of Frederick II, remarked with typical bluntness upon the birth of his sixth daughter, Luise Ulrike: "they should be drowned or packed off to a nunnery, they won't all get a man."[61]

Maria Theresa's parents did not have this problem. On the contrary, as heiress presumptive to the Habsburg throne she was the most eligible match in all Europe, even if the imperial couple still held out hope for a son for some time to come.[62] The pool of prospective grooms was fairly limited. The opening move was made by the queen of Spain, Elisabeth Farnese, who ruled on behalf of her mentally ill husband. For a time, she pursued the plan to reunite the Spanish dynasty with the Habsburgs by marrying off her two sons to the two daughters of Charles VI. In 1725 she declared herself prepared to accept the Pragmatic Sanction in return. Relations soon soured, however, and the match came to nothing. The Habsburgs had traditionally favored marriages between close relatives. For centuries marriages between first cousins, or between uncles and nieces, had been nothing out of the ordinary. It therefore seemed only fitting—not to mention in the interests of Habsburg unity—that two female cousins of Maria Theresa should now regard her as a potential bride for their eldest son. Both were daughters of Emperor Joseph I. One, Maria Josepha, was married to Elector Frederick August II of Saxony, the other, Maria Amalia, to Elector Karl Albrecht of Bavaria. Both had been disinherited through the Pragmatic Sanction, and they were both keen to reverse the setback by marrying their son to the Habsburg heiress. The Bavarian faction enjoyed the support of prominent figures at the Viennese court, including Prince Eugene. Joseph I's widow,

Amalia, also found it desirable that one of her grandsons should marry
Maria Theresa. Canon law prohibited marriage between relatives up to
and including the fourth degree. Yet this was not an insoluble problem;
providing marriage dispensations had long been a lucrative source of
income for the Holy See. Neither of the proposals went ahead, however,
as the emperor had long set his heart on a different plan.

Francis Stephen, a prince from the House of Lorraine, won the hand
of the heiress in the end, despite the fact that as second son he had not
initially come into consideration as a suitor. His father Leopold, Duke
of Lorraine, had long intended his firstborn son, Leopold Clement, to
marry her instead. The Lorraine dynasty belonged to the upper echelon of European nobility, having ties with both Habsburgs and Bourbons. One of Francis Stephen's great-grandmothers was the Habsburg
Anne d'Autriche, the mother of Louis XIV; one of his grandmothers
was Elisabeth Charlotte of the Palatinate, the Sun King's sister-in-law,
while the other was the sister of Emperor Leopold I (see Genealogical
Chart, p. 1024). To be related to two hostile houses was far from unusual. Indeed, if anything it was the norm, a consequence of the rapidly
shifting dynastic alliances that were a necessary survival strategy for
less powerful houses. The territories controlled by the family, the
Duchy of Lorraine and the Duchy of Bar, lay in the perennially contested border regions between France and the Empire. Although the
dukes owed allegiance to both the emperor and the king of France,
they had managed to preserve a certain degree of autonomy, even requiring their subjects to address them as *Altesse Royale*, Royal Highness. Their lands had a complicated and ambivalent status that their
overbearing neighbors had often been tempted to simplify by force of
arms. Louis XIV had occupied the lands for decades, while the Duke
of Lorraine resided at the Habsburg court, fighting as a general in
Habsburg service against the Turks. This conflict, among many others,
was eventually settled in the Treaty of Rijswijk of 1697. The duke was
given back his lands, and the successor to the throne, Leopold, was
married a year later to the daughter of the French prince Philip of
Orléans. Thirteen children issued from the union including Francis
Stephen, born in 1708.

It is characteristic of the political logic of the time that dynasties treated the lands they had inherited, amalgamated, and conquered like any other family asset. Each house was constantly on the lookout for opportunities to increase and round out its territorial holdings. As soon as it became apparent that somewhere a line would die out without a male heir, or that an elective principality was about to fall vacant, these lands were eyed with keen interest by the European courts and became the object of fervent dynastic calculations. Each contending party rushed to the archives to track down possible inheritance claims and dig up ancient titular rights. In the case of elective principalities—the Kingdom of Poland or the imperial bishoprics, for example—aspirants would attempt to sway the electors in their favor by showering them with gifts and promises. At the same time, rulers weighed up the possibility of territorial exchanges if a particular land was needed to fill a gap in their collection. The small territories of petty potentates or ecclesiastical princes could easily become bargaining chips in the hands of the great and powerful. In short, European governments and dynasties regarded their lands (and the people who inhabited them) as disposable pieces in a highly complex game where the advantage lay with whichever sovereign could keep one move ahead of his opponents.

While minor actors could make plans to improve their position, the fate of their lands largely depended on the schemes of others. So it was with the Duchy of Lorraine, which had already been eyed as a bargaining chip in the War of the Spanish Succession.[63] But Duke Leopold, a grandson of Emperor Ferdinand III and grandnephew of Louis XIV who had grown up at the court in Vienna, had extremely ambitious plans for the prince heir, Leopold Clement, whom he had carefully groomed for his future role as ruler. He had not only composed moral exhortations and general maxims for his son's benefit; he had also written up his observations about the most important people at the Viennese court so that his negotiators could more easily work the patronage networks there.

His secret plans were already far advanced; a first, inconspicuous meeting between the prince and the emperor on the latter's journey to his belated coronation in Bohemia had already been arranged, when

Leopold Clement died suddenly of smallpox in June 1723. For the duke, this was only a temporary setback. Within a week it had been decided that his younger son, Francis Stephen, would take his brother's place. The ambassador from Lorraine informed the emperor in an audience of the prince's death, and having received the imperial condolences, smoothly shifted the conversation to the second son: he too was very handsome, cut a fine figure, and had been brought up to revere the emperor. The duke would await the emperor's bidding with the deepest submission.[64] These hints clearly sufficed to steer the emperor onto the right track. At any rate, within less than a week Francis Stephen had replaced his brother as a marriage candidate and the most important piece in the Duke of Lorraine's chess game. In his late brother's stead, he immediately made his way incognito to Bohemia on the pretext of visiting the Duchy of Teschen, recently acquired by his father. The real reason for the trip was to be presented to the emperor and so prosecute his father's ambitious yet still secret plans for a match with Maria Theresa. Everything at this first meeting, the prince was given to understand, depended on him making a good impression on his prospective parents-in-law. The circumstances were auspicious. All he needed to do was focus on winning them over and living up to their expectations. He would then be allowed to make regular appearances at court.[65]

In this he was evidently successful. In Prague, where the imperial family was staying for Charles's coronation as king of Bohemia, the fifteen-year-old prince appeared for the first time before the empress and her five- and six-year-old daughters on August 14, 1723. The following day he was ceremoniously inducted into the Order of the Golden Fleece, securing him a permanent place in the court ceremonial.[66] A little later Charles VI wrote to Francis Stephen's father that he was very much taken with the prince heir, revealing that he had long harbored the wish for the two families to become one.[67] The exact date should not be fixed yet, nor should the arrangement be made public. The emperor thus kept an escape route open, and the Duke of Lorraine could not be certain that his plans would not be wrecked by changing circumstances. All the same, on December 22, 1723, Francis Stephen set out incognito for Vienna with a small entourage. He was received by the imperial couple and moved into the apartment in the Hofburg formerly occupied by the imperial widow, Eleanor.[68] For more than five years— until 1729—he lived there like a poor relative, valued by the emperor as a hunting companion but treated by courtiers with condescension or even disdain, particularly by those who had other marriage plans in mind for the heiress.[69]

Throughout all this period his father oversaw his education from afar. Members of his retinue were expected to provide regular updates on Francis Stephen's progress in German grammar and religious discipline, his health, his diligence, and his conduct at court. Evidently his internal and external bearing, his *conduite*, more than once fell short. His Jesuit confessor Assel noted that the prince was "tall, strong, handsome, and very friendly," he was also not unresponsive to the religious sentiments imparted to him by the priest, and he was subject to "no violent or dangerous passions." His behavior at daily divine service and his fasting discipline left much to be desired, however, and for some time he had shown an unfortunate tendency to use bad language and throw tantrums at his tutors, treating them disrespectfully even in the presence of others. His lessons bored him and he was unable to restrain his irritation, but nobody dared reprimand him.[70] This illustrates what made the education of noblemen more difficult than that of other children: they were expected to take orders from teachers they knew to be their social inferiors, their servants, and their future subjects—a structural contradiction that inevitably interfered with the children's duty to obey their teachers and their teachers' duty to do the royal family's bidding.

The sources reveal nothing about what contact Francis Stephen had with his future bride, the little archduchess nine years his junior. Looking back as a widow some fifty years later, she recalled having been instantly smitten: "He was the sole object of all my deeds and my affections from the age of six to this day."[71] Such statements cannot be understood without the experiences of the intervening five decades. In hindsight, her early childhood appeared as the prelude to an exemplary marriage. Furthermore, her letters to her grown-up children were intended to present their parents' marriage as the model of a perfect partnership. This is not to deny these memories any basis in fact. Yet there are no documents from the time corroborating their budding romance, neither from Maria Theresa nor from Francis Stephen. Instead, the correspondence of his tutors is interspersed with vague complaints about minor and major scandals. In 1725, for example, the seventeen-year-old was reported to have amused himself in an unseemly manner and been overly familiar with married and unmarried ladies (*trop familier avec les Dames ou Demoiselles*). That could displease the emperor, who was sensitive on this point.[72] In September 1726 an unspecified incident took place that, it was hoped, would not come to the emperor's attention even though it was already the talk of the town. Despite such episodes, which tended to be judged more harshly by his confessors than by his noble companions, Francis Stephen clearly gained the sympathy of Charles VI, who frequently invited him to join him on the hunt. As the emperor's hopes for a male son of his own faded, he increasingly came to regard the Prince of Lorraine as his successor. He did not go so far as to attempt to have the prince-electors crown him King of the Romans, which would have established his claim as the future holy Roman emperor. But at least the rival marriage plans hatched by the two daughters of the late emperor Joseph and their mother, the imperial widow Amalia, could be thwarted.[73]

For the time being, however, the Habsburg-Lorraine marriage proposal remained a closely guarded secret. The emperor avoided presenting Francis Stephen as his daughter's betrothed, his *amant déclaré et futur époux*,[74] well aware that so close a connection between Lorraine and Habsburg would be taken as an affront by the French court. It was therefore opportune that in March 1729 Francis Stephen was made Duke of Lorraine and could return to govern his lands.[75] Yet his stay there was a brief one. Not unusually for the time, his father had bequeathed him nothing but debts. The land had suffered a great deal from frequent French occupations and troop movements, as well as from the exorbitant lifestyle of the ducal household. Francis Stephen now made himself doubly unpopular through his drastic measures to restore the public finances: with the nobility by revoking the expensive privileges and pensions bestowed on them by his father, and with the people by introducing new tolls and taxes. The new duke was seen in his own country as a distant and impersonal foreigner who had imported unwelcome customs from abroad. His identification with the lands he had inherited should not be imagined as having been terribly heartfelt. At any rate, he soon set off on another tour of Europe, never to return. In 1732 he arrived in Vienna and was appointed viceregent (*Statthalter*) of the Kingdom of Hungary by Charles VI. He subsequently took up residence in Pressburg, today's Bratislava, not far from the imperial capital.

The emperor had not been acting out of consideration for his future son-in-law's wishes when he created this prominent position for him. Nor was Francis Stephen involved in the plans for an exchange of territories that came to a head shortly afterwards, in 1733, ultimately costing him his own duchy. The Polish throne had recently fallen vacant. Poland was an elective monarchy, and the throne thus became the object of Europe-wide dynastic haggling. A new war of succession had been brewing for some time. It finally broke out following the death of Augustus II the Strong, elector of Saxony and king of Poland. The Polish parliament initially elected the Polish magnate Stanislaus Leszczyński, whose daughter was married to the king of France. The rival candidate was Frederick Augustus of Saxony, a son-in-law to Emperor Joseph I, who had secured the support of Charles VI by finally recognizing the Pragmatic Sanction. Since the European powers were not prepared to leave the decision about so important a throne to the electorate, the only body authorized to choose a successor, war became all but inevitable. The front line ran between France and Spain, on the one hand, and Saxony, the emperor, and Russia, on the other; England and the Netherlands kept out of the conflict. The war soon took a disastrous turn for the emperor: French troops poured into Lorraine while Spanish soldiers conquered Naples and Sicily. The emperor was forced to sue for peace. What ensued resembled a complicated game of musical chairs. Stanislaus Leszczyński renounced his claim to the Polish throne (although not the royal title that went along with it) and gained the Duchy of Lorraine in return, which was to fall upon his death to his daughter, the queen of France, and her heirs. The emperor forfeited the Kingdom of Naples and Sicily, receiving in return the consent of the French and Spanish kings to the Pragmatic Sanction. The Duke of

Lorraine was to receive financial compensation for the loss of his ancestral lands as well as the Grand Duchy of Tuscany, an imperial fiefdom that would become his upon the death of the last Medici. The great powers in Paris and Vienna thus hammered out their compromise at the expense of Francis Stephen, only asking him for his opinion once the deal had already been brokered. While the duke put up a show of resistance, in the end he could only wring a few concessions in his favor.[76] In February 1737 he signed the formal notice of renunciation, and in March 1737 his mother and siblings, taking with them their retainers and all their worldly goods, were made to leave the duchy that had been in the family's possession since the eleventh century. This was the price the Duke of Lorraine had to pay for the hand of the Habsburg heiress.

The Wedding

Preparations for the wedding commenced in late 1735, after the preliminaries of the peace treaty had been concluded in Vienna in October 1735 but before Francis Stephen had formally renounced his ancestral lands.[77] The emperor summoned his highest officials to a conference to clarify "how much money was needed, where it was to be found, and how the wedding could be arranged as economically as possible with the appropriate decorum." His advisers pleaded "the calamitous and penurious times we live in now, when the direst need and poverty prevail everywhere," and proposed that the wedding be pushed forward to the Carnival season, when there would be all kinds of festivities anyway and expenses could be spared.[78] The emperor was unconvinced and decreed that an opera—the most lavish of all courtly entertainments—would have to be put on for the occasion. At the wedding of his daughter and heir, he simply could not afford to give the impression that he was pinching his pennies.

The emperor expected the money to be provided by the Upper and Lower Austrian estates, since on such joyous occasions "the Imp[erial] hereditary lands" tended "to make a substantial *donativum*"—a voluntary contribution—"to show their loyalty and devotion." The counselors were worried, however, that this would not be enough, since in their experience the estates could be relied on to deliver at most half the sum asked of them by the crown. At the previous wedding, for example, they had coughed up only 242,000 of the requested 400,000 guilders. The Court Chamber (*Hofkammer*), it was feared, would end up having to foot most of the bill. This detail shines a spotlight on premodern government and state finances in general. The traditional *donativum* from the estates was officially considered a voluntary gift, not a compulsory tax. Yet this was a symbolic fiction on both sides. The estates—not commoners but nobles and aldermen who identified themselves with "the land" itself–demonstrated their time-honored freedom, their "liberty," by appearing to offer their contributions as voluntary tokens of their esteem. Yet they were actually asked to contribute a precisely calculated sum. It was impossible for them to refuse payment outright; at most, they could delay or surreptitiously reduce it. The fiction of a voluntary arrangement equally prevented the ruler from formally insisting that the sum be paid in full, let alone threatening punishment in the event that funds were withheld. In other words, mutual expectations between the prince and the estates rested on a body of unwritten and informal customary law. This law demanded that both sides respect it as a point of honor rather than because they were compelled to do so; this was how relations between autonomous rulers were supposed to work. Other contributions from the estates proceeded on similar lines to the *donativum* for Maria Theresa's wedding. This was one of the deeper reasons for the parlous state of imperial finances. Radical measures would be needed to change all this, as would be seen a decade later.

After the question of costs had been thrown to the winds, a papal dispensation for consanguineous marriage arranged, and the ceremonial formalities settled in advance, the courtship could officially commence. On January 31, 1736, Francis Stephen asked the emperor for his eldest daughter's hand in marriage.[79] The petition was not submitted in private or spontaneously; it was framed as a "solemnity," recorded in writing, and brought to public attention in a printed record.[80] Every ceremonial detail merited the closest attention, nothing was considered too trivial to be left to chance. By being conducted as a "solemnity"— that is, a formal ceremony confirmed by numerous witnesses—the whole procedure was validated as a mutually binding pact. For this to happen, the suit of marriage had to be clearly distinguished from everyday life at court and symbolically marked as such. The suitor, arrayed in gala dress, moved with his entire retinue—couriers, lackeys, pages, cavaliers, chamberlains, and nobles from Lorraine—in a solemn procession through the Hofburg from the imperial chamberlain's room to the emperor. Their route took them past the imperial lifeguards posted in the Guards' Room (*Wachtstube*) and the Knights' Room to the first antechamber, where the duke was greeted by the three highest court officials. He was then ushered through the second antechamber and the privy counselors' chamber up to the imperial retirade, or retreat, the secular Holy of Holies, as it were, the most central and exclusive place in the Hofburg. The emperor received him "with particular affection" before the door to the retirade, only one wing of which was open, led him inside, and stayed with him there for some time with the door closed: a display of perfect intimacy calculated to generate the greatest possible amount of publicity among the assembled court. What played out inside the emperor's private quarters was brought to the center of attention precisely by remaining concealed from public view. "Having been asked for his Most Serene daughter's hand in marriage," the emperor accompanied the groom out of the retirade and farewelled him at the threshold "with another tender compliment." There the groom was again received by the highest-ranking imperial courtiers and escorted part of the way back. With his entire retinue he then proceeded through the corridor known as the "comptroller's passage" (*Controlorgang*) over to the Ladies' Wing, where the empress awaited him. There he once again traversed the ceremonial suite of rooms and was received by the highest office-bearers—the exact mirror image of before. The door to the audience chamber was again half-open; inside they were awaited by the mistress of the robes (*Obristhofmeisterin*) and the aya, Countess Fuchs. The empress was standing at her table, Maria Theresa to her left. As the duke approached the empress, he twice "bent his knee in reverence," but before he could make the third reverence prescribed by Spanish court ceremonial, the empress took a step "towards him in welcome"—a sign of particular favor and intimacy. A brief exchange of

formalities preceded the address to the bride, who, "having first looked
to Her Majesty her mother, and received a sign from her, was given a
priceless diamond-set portrait from His Royal Highness, together with
a tender kiss on the hand."[81] A few pleasantries were exchanged; then
the groom and his entourage withdrew in the same spectacular fashion.
No detail of the procedure was accidental or insignificant. Even the fact
that the door to the ladies' apartment was left ajar, and that Maria Theresa accepted the engagement gift and the suitor's kiss only after a cue
from her mother, was of symbolic importance. "A number of people"
had been specially "positioned there to record the correctness of the
public compliments paid by His Royal Highness [the Duke of Lorraine]
in accordance with official protocol." Such independent verification was
necessary, as the courtship was meant to have the status of a binding
ritual, and a ritual can only achieve its expected effect if it is performed
exactly according to script and before witnesses. The same held true of
the ensuing "Act of Renunciation," the solemn declaration that Maria
Theresa and Francis Stephen would renounce their claim to the throne
in the event of a son being born to the emperor and empress.[82] If their
wealthy daughter was going to marry an ex-monarch suspended precari-
ously between two thrones, then the condition was that they themselves
would retain ultimate control over their lands.

But first a matrimonial contract had to be drawn up.[83] It was no different in structure from what was customary in other classes when a
marriage—that is, a large-scale transfer of goods between families and
generations—had been decided on. It stipulated what both sides would
bring to the union and what each would keep if predeceased by the
other. First of all, there was the bridal dowry and the bridegroom's
equivalent countergift, the so-called *Widerlag*, which differed from that
of other estates only in the sums involved: both parties contributed
150,000 guilders. In addition, the contract contained an exhaustive in-
ventory of all their movable goods. Maria Theresa's residence in the
event of her widowhood was also noted, with both Commercy in Lorraine and Siena in the Grand Duchy of Tuscany coming into consideration; at this stage, Francis Stephen had not yet formally renounced
Lorraine. Finally, the contract stipulated how any children issuing from

the marriage were to be provided for, particularly if one of their parents was to remarry.

After these highly formal preliminaries, Francis Stephen returned to his Pressburg residence to resume his position as governor, although he was away for less than a fortnight. A minimal symbolic period of separation had to elapse between the proposal of marriage and its consummation, or *Beylager*. We have this brief separation to thank for three handwritten letters from Maria Theresa to her fiancé. Written over three consecutive days, they are the earliest surviving sources composed by Maria Theresa. They also grant us a first glimpse into her existence outside the confines of court ceremony. They are among the most famous personal statements she ever made. The three short letters were written in response to letters from her fiancé, now lost. She addresses him formally as "Most Serene Duke, Beloved Groom" and generally sticks to the conventions of polite discourse: "It is good that the absence is not long, and it is to be wished that a more constant companionship might obtain in future"; or: "in replying from the heart to your dear letter, so obliging and so complimentary, I wish you a happy journey and fine weather." The letters all conclude the same way: "Your loving and most faithful bride, Maria Theresa." In a French postscript to the first letter, however, she strikes a quite different, more playful, and more loving tone than in the cumbersome and stiff German text: "*j'etois en peine comme une pauvre chienne*"—she longed for his news like a poor dog. She then signs off again with "*adieu mäusl, je vous embrasse de tout mon coeur, menagez vous bien, adieu caro viso, je suis la votre sponsia dilectissima* [adieu little mouse, I embrace you with all my heart, farewell, adieu dear face, I am your most loving bride]."[84]

The contrast between the stiff formality of the courtship ritual and the intimate tone of the letter once again goes to show that there were two different spheres at court, a formal front stage and an informal back stage. From the viewpoint of national-bourgeois historiography, these two spheres stood in relation to each other as appearance to reality, falsehood to truth, hypocrisy to authenticity. In the letters sent by the young bride, historians sought to grasp the "real," innermost essence of her personality. This viewpoint still strikes us as highly plausible, since court ceremonial has come to seem utterly alien to us while the ideal of the autonomous individual remains central to our modern value system. Yet it is one-sided and incomplete; if anything, it hinders our understanding of premodern relations at court. The ritual of courtship and the bridal letters do not belong to separate universes. Front stage and back stage were two sides of the same coin. From an early age, Maria Theresa had been accustomed to moving back and forth between these two stages and to switching effortlessly between two different modes of behavior. These early letters bear eloquent testimony to this skill.

The actual "copulation," the wedding ceremony, was held on February 12, 1736.[85] Unlike royal weddings today, the proceedings took place out of sight of the general public within the Hofburg, which had been carefully cordoned off for the occasion: "*Notandum* that from noon on the day of the copulation until the same hour the next day, all entrances to the imperial, palatial, and court church were closed, and to that end Imp[erial] chamberlains, stewards, officers of the guards, and common soldiers were posted there."[86] The marriage, like the courtship before it, was solemnized before a congregation made up entirely of courtiers. Commoners experienced it only indirectly, through the acoustic symbolism of cannon fire, gun salutes, drumming, and trumpet fanfares.

It was not until the afternoon of the wedding day that the bridegroom was finally brought by stagecoach from Pressburg. The high nobility gathered in magnificent gala dress in the antechamber to the imperial apartment. The groom's personal retinue assembled in the lord high chamberlain's apartment, where Francis Stephen was disrobed by his attendants and then dressed in a silver-white coat-dress, the collar of the Golden Fleece, and a white plumed hat; even his stockings and shoes were white. At the invitation of the imperial quartermaster (*Kammerfourier*), he made his way in stately procession, preceded by his cavaliers and officers, to the imperial retirade, where he was awaited by his bride (likewise decked out in white and adorned with priceless jewelry), her parents, and the hierarchically arrayed court household.[87] After an exchange of ceremonial pleasantries, the entire company proceeded, again in strict hierarchical order, through the Guards' Room and Knights' Room, lined with hartschiers (house guards) and trabants (lifeguards), before entering a covered passageway that took them to the Augustinian Church, the site of the ceremony.

According to Catholic dogma, marriage was (and still is) a sacrament bestowed on each other by the bride and groom; there was no need for a priest to officiate. The principle that marriage was brought about solely through the will of the espoused couple had been enshrined in canon law since the thirteenth century. A marriage was manifested in ritual form through the wedding vow, the exchange of rings, and *commixtio carnalis*, "carnal conjunction." According to canon law, neither sacerdotal blessing nor parental consent was strictly necessary. But such theological niceties bore little relation to social reality. In fact, marriages were arranged by the two families concerned, all the more so if important economic and political interests were at stake. How the royal wedding was conducted neatly expressed this tension between the freely voiced consent required of the bride de jure and the parents' de facto authority over their daughter. After the papal nuncio had first read the marriage vow to the bridegroom in Latin and received the reply, *volo*, "I consent," Maria Theresa was asked whether she wished to take Francis Stephen of Lorraine to be her husband. "Whereat she, having previously turned with a deep reverence to their Imp[erial] M[ajesties], the Emperor and her Imp[erial] Mother, and been given a sign from them indicating their most gracious permission, likewise replied with *volo*."[88] This symbolic gesture of submission to the parental will had also played a key role in the courtship scene. Once again, everything was painstakingly recorded and even disclosed in full to readers of the *Wienerische Diarium*. A ruling dynasty could not allow the autonomous will of the daughter to dictate her choice of a husband, not even symbolically.

Rings were exchanged, the nuncio gave the marriage the Church's blessing and intoned the Te Deum, drums and trumpets were sounded, the city guard released an artillery salvo, and sixty canons positioned on bastions all around the city were fired off for the first time. Enveloped in a cocoon of sound, the procession left the church in the same order as before, returning via the wide staircase and the wooden passageway to the castle and the imperial retirade. That evening, a public banquet was held at which, in accordance with Spanish court ceremonial, only

FIGURE 5. Wedding of Maria Theresa and Francis Stephen of Lorraine in the Augustinian Church in Vienna on February 12, 1736. Copperplate engraving by Elias Böck, 1736

the imperial couple, the newlyweds, and the three other members of the imperial family ate and drank, while they were attended by all of court society and ritually served by the highest court officials (color plate 3).[89] Finally, again in accordance with archaic custom, the entire wedding party led the newlyweds to their apartment for the consummation. The guests then withdrew, leaving the couple to be undressed by Maria Theresa's parents before they climbed into the matrimonial bed. In this way, her parents gave their symbolic blessing to the "carnal conjunction" in which the sacrament culminated.[90] The following day there was a wedding Mass that ministers, privy counselors, and chamberlains were now permitted to attend. A great gala was proclaimed, and the opera written especially for the occasion by the court poet, Metastasio, received its first performance.[91] The third day coincided with Carnival, so the festivities were concluded with a masked ball. By Ash Wednesday it was all over. Not long afterwards, the couple placed a golden heart set with diamonds before the miraculous image of Our Lady at the church of pilgrimage at Mariazell to secure Mary's support for a happy and fruitful marriage.

Yet the wedding did not proceed as harmoniously as appearances might suggest.[92] In the lead-up to the ceremony, the nuncio had already quarreled with the Archbishop of Vienna over precedence. The archbishop stayed away, refusing to yield to the papal delegate. Even more unfortunate was the fact that no single member of the House of Lorraine could officially be involved in the festivities. Francis Stephen's brother Charles was physically present in the background as a spectator, but only incognito. For ceremonial purposes he was considered absent and was effectively ignored. His was hardly a unique case. The presence of the bridegroom's family at the imperial court confronted the lord high steward with almost insurmountable difficulties. The cause was a structural problem that was characteristic of the entire epoch: an increasing split between those who were recognized as sovereigns and those denied entry to that exclusive club. The title of royalty made all the difference.[93] Like all princes who had not been anointed and legitimized as "crowned heads," the dukes of Lorraine had a status problem. While they asserted the right to be treated and addressed as Royal Highnesses, the other, "genuine" kings generally refused to concede this title to them. The supreme goal of all uncrowned princes was therefore to get their hands on a royal title. Only then could they lay claim to the majesty befitting a true sovereign. Some—the electors of Brandenburg, for example—achieved this goal; others, including the dukes of Lorraine, were less successful. As distant descendants of the crusader Charles II of Anjou, the Lorraine dynasty clung to the phantom title of "king of Jerusalem," notwithstanding the fact that the last remnants of that kingdom had been conquered by the Mamluks at the end of the thirteenth century. The other sovereigns, taking their cue from the pope, refused to recognize the claim and denied the House of Lorraine the *honores regii*, royal honors. If the Lothringians did not wish to feel slighted, they had only two options: either they could completely avoid crossing paths with the nuncio and the royal ambassadors, or they could reside at court incognito. Needless to say, the second option was ruled out for Francis Stephen following his marriage. The problem became particularly acute once Maria Theresa had taken the throne as queen of Hungary and Bohemia, an unequivocally higher position than that held by her own husband. She then had to decide whether she would rather have the nuncio or her husband at her side on any given state occasion, since it was impossible for both of them to be in the room at the same time.[94] This was the price that had to be paid by the biggest fish in the pond of European royalty for having married a dynastic minnow.

The Court Cosmos

Marriage fundamentally changed a woman's status, regardless of social class. Maria Theresa was now no longer archduchess of Austria but duchess of Lorraine and, from October 1737, when the last of the Medicis passed away, grand duchess of Tuscany as well. In all stations of life, it was customary for a wife to leave her parents and set up a new home with her husband or join his parental household. Yet because Francis Stephen was in the process of giving up his inherited realm without having yet received a new one in exchange, Maria Theresa continued living with him in her parents' home—an utterly remarkable constellation. From now on, Maria Theresa was treated at the Viennese court as the wife of a foreign sovereign. Like her husband, she was addressed as *Votre Altesse Royale*, "Your Royal Highness," thereby maintaining the fiction that Lorraine was still a sovereign monarchy when in fact it had definitively surrendered its autonomy.[95] Maria Theresa's new status as a wife required her to move into the "Lothringian" rooms and to receive a Lothringian retinue comprising some thirty people, from the first lady of the court to the heater of the rooms.[96]

The imperial court was an immense social and economic cosmos revolving around the ruling family.[97] Impressed observers noted that "so numerous a court of such splendor and magnificence could not easily be found elsewhere," so far as the pedigree of the court nobility and the sheer number of fixed ranks were concerned.[98] In sum, this cosmos consisted of around two thousand people who, although varying greatly in status, were united in their common desire to take advantage of their connections at court. It is impossible to give a precise figure, however, as there were different degrees of affiliation. As befitted a noble household—and unlike in a modern organization such as a government agency or commercial enterprise—there were closer or more distant circles around the imperial family: relatives, servants, noble, clerical and middle-class officials, visitors, and petitioners; there were those who lived under the same roof as the ruling family and those who served them from time to time; there were salaried and unsalaried office-bearers. The borders of the court world were porous at the edges.

At the heart of the court was the sprawling court household (*Hofstaat*), responsible for services in the kitchen and the cellar, the chambers and the stables.[99] The nobility claimed the age-old privilege of personally performing these services on special ceremonial occasions, so demonstrating in symbolic-ritual form their direct access to the throne, their attachment and devotion to the imperial *familia*. At all other times they delegated these duties to their respective staffs. The lord high steward (*Obersthofmeister*) held the top supervisory position over the entire court and was responsible for the "organization of the organization."[100] The grand marshal (*Obersthofmarschall*) presided as judge over all the court personnel while the lord high chamberlain (*Oberstkämmerer*) oversaw table and room service. They were joined in the upper echelon of court service by the master of the horse (*Oberststallmeister*), the master of the hunt (*Oberstjägermeister*), and the chief falconer (*Oberstfalkenmeister*). Together, they commanded armies of man- and maidservants encompassing pages and ladies-in-waiting, court clerics and scholars, court artists and artisans, doorkeepers and upholsterers, cooks and confectioners, heralds, hartschiers and trabants, lackeys, heyducks, couriers and sedan bearers, musicians, singers, dancing and fencing masters, chamber attendants and gardeners, coachmen and grooms, fodderers and quartermasters, secretaries and interpreters, scribes and paymasters, inspectors, comptrollers and expeditors, and so on and so forth in a seemingly unending series–all carefully organized into staffs and ranked from top to bottom: from keeper of the silver plate to scullery wench, from castellan to regimental servant, from court chaplain to chapel washerwoman, from master of the hunt to kennel boy. The extent of specialization in handicrafts was truly astonishing: there was the maker of mathematical instruments, the compass maker, the barometer maker and clock maker, the gemstone driller, the bone carver, the crystal cutter and mirror maker, the court gilder, the gold and pearl embroiderer and button maker. The court household was so vast and unwieldy in large part because every higher office-bearer was entitled to servants of his own. Even the court priests had their own table-setter, who in turn was assisted by an underling. Services for the high and mighty were specialized to the point of absurdity: the bonnet stitcher was responsible solely for attaching Maria Theresa's bonnet to her regal head, there were maids whose working lives were devoted to ironing her lace underwear,[101] and if any task remained to be performed in the ladies' chamber for which there was no designated functionary, a "supernumerary manservant" or "supernumerary maid of the ladies' chamber" could always be found.[102]

Together, all these functionaries made up the court household, the servants attached to the royal family. A fundamental class barrier separated the office-holding nobles from the nonnoble court staff. Yet noble and (high-ranking) nonnoble court officials alike drew salaries from the Court Chamber and were listed in the annual Imperial Court and Honors Calendar; they had all sworn an oath of fealty to the ruler and pledged him their lifelong service. The extent to which this was a personal bond between master and servant rather than an impersonal, functional obligation is shown by the fact that it was nullified by the ruler's death and had to be established anew by his successor.

Besides those who stood on official pay lists, there were also unsalaried members of the court household who resided only temporarily at court. These included the two to three hundred imperial chamberlains. Bearers of this honorific title only had to serve four weeks a year and spent the rest of their time far from the court somewhere in the hereditary lands. Yet the title was still extremely valuable, for the chamberlains theoretically enjoyed unlimited access to the court, symbolically demonstrated by the coveted golden key they wore on their belt. Many other people stayed at court in an unofficial capacity for shorter or longer periods: relatives of the ruling house, scions of the high imperial nobility, young lords stopping by on their grand tour, and also, it should not be forgotten, the permanent embassies of foreign powers. Every passing nobleman sought an audience with the imperial family, if only to be able to report later on, like Charles de Montesquieu in 1728: "I had the honor of kissing the hand of the emperor and the empress."[103] There was a self-strengthening dynamic to the social attractiveness of the court: the more aristocrats flocked there, the more they added to its luster. For the great powers of Europe tacitly competed with each other, not just for the best architects, painters, and sculptors, the most virtuosic composers, musicians, and singers, but equally for the finest princes and princesses, lords and ladies they could entice to their courts. Even if the court at Vienna was less materially opulent than Versailles, in social terms it was considered to be the most glamorous in all Europe. Nowhere else were so many and such high-ranking nobles assembled in so confined a space. Their presence there "uncommonly magnified its glory."[104]

Yet the court was not just a vastly extended dynastic family; it was at the same time the pilot house of a sprawling empire. The sphere of politics had gradually evolved from the sphere of the household, the *oikos*, yet it still followed a similar social logic. Both—the economy of the court and the economy of the country—belonged together. This is what was meant when a king characterized himself as the father of his country or a queen as its mother. A prince's rule over his subjects resembled his dominion in the family circle over his wife, children, and servants, or at least the same language and concepts were used to talk about both. The Viennese court was—or was meant to be—the place where the strings of government over the various lands were drawn together, where resources were centrally administered, where law was pronounced in the name of the sovereign, where armies were marshaled and commanded, where emissaries of foreign powers advocated the interests of their principals—in other words, the center of what the eighteenth century began to call a "state," with its various court chancelleries, court chamber, war council, and countless other commissions and advisory bodies. It was a thicket of institutions that had been growing rampant for centuries, choked with half-dead branches and fresh shoots, impenetrable to outsiders with its multiply overlapping powers, rivalries, and special privileges.[105] This dense network, populated by armies of lettered and unlettered personnel, had been incessantly ramifying since the Middle Ages. When new offices were introduced, the old ones were not simply abolished but allowed to linger on with the same title, rank, and in many cases also remuneration as before. The top officials, for their part, oversaw a seemingly endless number of servants, secretaries, copyists, clerks, draftsmen, expeditors, and registrars. The Viennese court was ultimately not just the place where the Habsburg sovereign ruled over his numerous ancestral lands, but also his seat of residence as emperor and head of the Holy Roman Empire of the German Nation, as supreme judge and paramount feudal overlord. There were separate institutions for these functions as well, the Imperial Aulic Council (*Reichshofrat*) and the Imperial Court Chancellery (*Reichshofkanzlei*).[106] Above them all, finally, had been set up an informal gathering of the ruler's closest advisers, the Court Conference. It was consulted on all matters of importance, whether these affected the house and the dynasty, the lands, the Empire, or relations with foreign powers. All these entities were difficult to disentangle. The court was not a bureaucratic apparatus with well-defined powers, clear chains of command, and fixed career paths. What characterized it instead was that economic, legal, political, and religious functions were closely intertwined and obeyed one and the same social logic. That logic was one of personal patronage.

The Logic of Favor

People from all walks of life looked to the court to further their own interests, whether they had their eye on the office of First Keeper of the Silverware, a prestigious seat on the Imperial Aulic Council, or an appointment as washerwoman; for "His Majesty's Grace extends from the most august personages at court all the way to the humblest lackey or coachman."[107] The court was the center of an all-encompassing system of patronage and gift-giving. It was the needle's eye through which ran the threads distributing the material and immaterial resources of the Habsburg territories. A critic of the court such as the Frankfurt merchant Johann Michael von Loen spoke disdainfully of "the countless mass of high- and lowborn beggars who flock to the imperial court from all the ends of the earth. . . . Everyone entreats the Imperial Majesty for his grace and favor."[108]

Such "beggars" at the imperial table vied for different kinds of favors. First, there were material goods, ranging from pensions, emoluments, and annuities to specific gifts: a cast-off dress for a lady-in-waiting, a diamond-set portrait of the emperor for a distinguished guest from abroad, a landed estate for a long-serving lord high steward. Second, there were various posts to be distributed: secular offices in the court household, in justice and administration, in military and diplomatic service, but also ecclesiastical sinecures—or at least the prospect that such offices and sinecures would be granted in future. Third, people came to the court in the hope of securing privileges and freedoms: prerogatives of one kind or another, whether concessions for every imaginable activity or exemptions from duties and charges. Yet the goods available at court were not just material ones; there were also symbolic goods on offer. These could and did command steep prices. To receive a chamberlain's key or the title of privy councillor, to acquire a patent of nobility, to be inducted into the Honor Guard, the Order of the Starry Cross, or the Order of the Golden Fleece: such distinctions, preferments, and honorary titles increased the glory of the recipient's own house and were available only at the imperial court, nowhere else.

Among the most important of the symbolic goods that nobles could acquire there was noble habitus. For the imperial court was also a highly exclusive finishing school. Living at court as pages and ladies-in-waiting, the sons and daughters of noble families in the hereditary lands learned everything they needed to know about fitting into an aristocratic milieu, from graceful comportment to genteel conversation, anything that could not be picked up from books but had to become second nature. Apart from convent schools, there were hardly any other places where noble Catholic daughters could be educated in a manner befitting their high rank.[109] Most of them entered court service at the age of eighteen and stayed there until marriage. This often came about through direct intervention and required the permission of the imperial family. For young noblemen, marrying an imperial lady-in-waiting was a highly advantageous career move. The court was thus also the most prominent marriage market in the hereditary lands and indeed the entire Empire.

More than that, it was the most important site for making social contact with fellow aristocrats.

For all these reasons, it was vitally important to be present at court in person, at least for a time.[110] The court was the place where fortunes were made, regardless of rank and occupation. Yet the logic of court service was ambivalent: for all the opportunities for material and social advancement, the risk of failure was considerable. The number of those competing for goods was great, and the rules according to which goods were distributed were not formalized. The social cosmos of the court rested on personal relations instead. All the available positions, preferments, perquisites, and privileges seemed to flow directly or indirectly from the emperor's hand; they were gifts freely bestowed by the "All-Highest Majesty," obliging the beneficiary to lasting gratitude and loyalty.

The most valuable resource in this society was the ruler's personal favor. It provided access to all other resources, yet it was scarce, fickle, and ephemeral. The elemental characteristic of the court as a social system was therefore its high instability and its limited predictability. What typifies favor, in contrast to justice, is that it is freely given and can be retracted at any moment. That made service at court risky, and it was all the riskier the higher up in the social hierarchy one perched. Precisely for the nobility, such service could be fraught with financial peril. While the common servants at court as well as middle-ranking officials generally drew a fixed salary that guaranteed them a decent standard of living, the salaries of higher noble office-holders were relatively modest. It was also rare for them to be paid regularly or punctually. As a result, the higher one stood in the hierarchy, the less one could rely on a secure income. Monarchs were reluctant to set the time and rate at which they compensated nobles for their services. Charles VI preferred giving a trusted old official a diamond-set portrait valued at 15,000 guilders rather than permanently raising his fixed annual salary of just 2,000 guilders.[111] This allowed his gift to appear as a one-off favor, an expression of regal munificence and personal friendship, rather than as a payment to which the recipient had a regular claim or legal entitlement. Most noble office-holders were therefore forced to draw on their own private revenues to finance their official expenses, in the vague hope of being amply recompensed at some future date. They were further required to maintain themselves in all the trappings of office: clothing, decoration, silver tableware, horses, coaches, servants. The higher their position, the more important it was that they not fall behind their peers in pomp and ostentation. Luxury spending was not left to individual discretion. Anyone who wanted to appear on gala days had to adhere to a strict dress code appropriate "to the decor of the most exalted court."[112] As a consequence, the costs of high office could be exorbitant.

If nobles nonetheless chose to bear the expense, rather than leading a more comfortable and less ruinous life on their country estates, then there were two main reasons for this. On the one hand, the court, as the center of all splendor and magnificence, was simply *the* place to be for anyone with ambitions of climbing to the top of the social ladder. It was where the music was playing, both literally and figuratively. The imperial court reflected something of its glory on all who gathered there to bask in it; this alone was worth the price of entry. On the other hand, the profligate life at court had its own economic rationality. All the contacts that could be made there, all the honors that could be awarded in full public view, represented a form of socio-symbolic capital that—it was hoped—would one day generate material interest, whether in the form of an advantageous marriage, lucrative assets, or plum sinecures for the courtier and his descendants. This long-term, intergenerational strategy called for a very high initial financial outlay and deep reserves of patience. The prince attached the high nobility to his service precisely by taking his time to give them something in return. It was not only the gifts themselves that motivated the courtier to offer his services but also the expectation of such gifts. This system was not immune to disappointment; it entailed a high level of risk for the courtier. It was almost a cliché that injustice sprouted rapidly at court while goodwill could take years to bear fruit. As one critic sardonically remarked: "The brevity of human life may be much to blame that great lords never get around to giving active proof of their gratitude. This is the conclusion that must be drawn, at any rate, when it is said in praise of someone who had served until he was old, lame, poor, and finally dead: had he only lived longer, he would have been richly rewarded."[113]

The sovereign's favor was not only capricious and unpredictable, it was also a fundamentally scarce social resource. Favor rested on personal proximity, inclination, and trust. It therefore could not be dispensed to everyone in equal measure. Every ruler relied on intermediaries to channel his favors and commands, and this dependence, paradoxically enough, only increased with his power.[114] Conversely, anyone wishing to profit, directly or indirectly, from the sovereign's grace and favor needed someone to speak on his behalf. This explains the ubiquitous power of personal relations, which extended outward from the court to span the entire country and beyond, forming a network between European courts. Personal relations structured the hierarchically ordered society both horizontally, through kinship and friendship—at the time another word for kinship by marriage—and vertically, through patronage and clientelism. The court was the narrow social funnel through which all other goods were allocated and distributed. Access was the key to making a fortune, and access was not to be had without the advocacy of those who already enjoyed it. This meant making as many connections and cultivating them as assiduously as possible. It also meant accumulating social capital in the hope that it would one day pay dividends.

Interpersonal relations were fundamentally different at court than in a bureaucratic organization, where—at least notionally—positions are awarded to suitable people in accordance with transparent formal procedures. The exact opposite was the case at court: people were rewarded with suitable positions. When a post fell vacant, it was not publicly advertised and filled with the applicant who best met the selection criteria; such candidates already stood at the ready with their justified expectations and network of influential advocates. This held true, not just of the court household, but also of the administrative and judicial authorities all the way up to the Imperial Aulic Council. Even when an office was tied to certain prior achievements, such as a high judicial posting requiring academic credentials, this qualification constituted a necessary but insufficient condition for the position. Without advocacy, without access, and without credit, even the best qualified candidate did not stand a chance.

The first question was, accordingly: How could aspiring courtiers gain a foothold at court? They first had to be the relative or client of someone already established there. Which led to the next question: How did they then find their way in this new world? How were they expected to behave? Having arrived at court, they needed comprehensive information to help them navigate its treacherous shoals: who could be trusted, who should be avoided, who should be flattered, who could be ignored? And above all: who could be useful? An initial point of orientation was provided by the annual court and state calendar, which listed all current office-holders along with their rank.[115] Yet this was not enough, since the formal court hierarchy was not identical with informal structures of influence. It was therefore necessary to study constellations of friendship and enmity, to identify the various factions and coalitions at court, and to distinguish those who wielded real power from those who merely looked on from the sidelines. Once one had identified who stood in favor with their superiors or even with the ruler himself, the next step was to carefully analyze their strengths and weaknesses of character, their potential interests and future moves, their usefulness and trustworthiness—in short, to calculate their value for one's own advancement. One then needed to "bow and scrape" to be admitted to their presence and subsequently win their favor through all manner of services, compliments, and pleasantries—material and immaterial "insinuations," in the parlance of the day—before once again seeking access to persons of even greater influence, and so on in an endless bid to make others the instruments of one's own fortune.[116]

It is not by chance that the keywords of courtly logic, "interest" and "credit," are concepts that to this day carry both a moral and an economic meaning. Conduct at court conformed to an economics of honor,[117] and personal contacts were its currency. To have credit meant to be found trustworthy, to enjoy the esteem and hence protection of others. One could never accumulate enough of this capital, since it was impossible to calculate developments at court in advance. As a consequence, time had to be invested in cultivating relationships, contacts had to be nurtured and put to work so that social capital could generate interest. There were fluctuations and reversals of fortune, *hausses* and *baisses*. Those who already stood in favor attracted even more of it, whereas those known to have lost the patronage of the high and mighty were shunned by all. Interest—striving for one's own advantage—and credit—striving to win the trust of others—stood in tension with each other. In order to gain credit, to acquire the reputation of an *homme sure*, a reliable person, one had to conceal one's own interest as much as possible. All social interactions were therefore strategic in nature: it was vitally important that one appear to be trustworthy—not necessarily be it.

Broker of Imperial Patronage

The system for bestowing grace and favor was not limited to life at court; it also encompassed the hereditary lands and the Empire, even extending to relations between European courts. As the emperor's daughter, as next in line to the throne, and as wife to the new Grand Duke of Tuscany, Maria Theresa played an important role in this patronage network. When the last of the Medicis died on July 9, 1737, Francis Stephen inherited the territory in accordance with the deal brokered by his father-in-law. It was hardly to be expected that he would immediately identify with the position; he was also off campaigning at the time, leading an army in the war against the Turks. He therefore initially appointed a governor to rule in his stead. A year passed before he and his wife made their way to Tuscany to inaugurate their reign formally and in person. On December 17, 1738, they set out accompanied by a retinue of 453 people, 39 coaches, and 21 baggage wagons.[118] The traditional journey took them in several stages to Florence, where in January 1739 they were ritually welcomed at inordinate expense by dignitaries, estates, and corporations, received their oath of homage, and confirmed the land's traditional freedoms and privileges in return. Citizens erected a triumphal arch just for the royal couple's entry; operas, contests, and fireworks displays were organized; noble youths put on a historic football match; the Jewish community constructed a *cuccagna*, an ornamental pyramid made out of food; medals were struck and distributed among the people; songs of praise were composed; and all the festivities were documented in large-format copperplate engravings—in short, the hosts spared no expense in celebrating the guests and themselves in the form of a Baroque spectacle with all the trimmings, and not just in Florence but subsequently in Livorno and Siena as well.[119]

The official tour's purpose was to recognize the new ruling couple, the legitimacy of their succession, and the sovereign status of their princely realm. All this was far from self-evident, especially in a case such as this one—hence the need to generate and demonstrate new loyalties in ritual form. Premodern rule was not a generalized, abstract relationship between the ruler and the subject population but a personal commitment between the prince and his dynasty, on the one hand, and, on the other, the ensconced noble families, ecclesiastical corporations, and civic elites. In Tuscany the change in dynasty meant that the kind of social bonds that were normally tended and handed down from one generation to the next, involving the provision of material and symbolic goods in exchange for services and loyalties, were almost entirely absent. In the eyes of contemporaries, a good prince or a good princess was one who showered blessings on the country, particularly at the start of their reign. "Doing good deeds to well-disposed persons of credit has always been one of the great arts of kingship," wrote the Venetian emissary Zeno in 1740.[120] These good deeds came in the form of favors to trustworthy and loyal high-ranking individuals, those *persone di credito e ben affette* whose lasting inclination and support it was particularly important for a foreign monarch to secure: privileges, exemptions, and concessions; pensions and offices; honorary titles and promotions within the social hierarchy. They did not entail beneficence toward the subject population at large. Maria Theresa's Italian correspondence from the period after the journey shows how she fulfilled the role of the good princess in just this sense.

Because she complained in retrospect that her father had never adequately prepared her for her role as regent, and that the situation confronting her after his death had taken her by surprise, later historians concluded that before this point in time—as befitted a woman, in their eyes—political expectations and experiences had been completely foreign to her. As her biographer Arneth asserted, "Nothing whatsoever had been done to initiate her into . . . state affairs" before her corona-tion.[121] And another biographer, Eugen Guglia, writing in 1917, empa-thetically imagined that the empress later "looked back on this time, when she needed only to be a wife and daughter, as a lost paradise," for "her hopes . . . were in the first instance conjugal and maternal."[122] In 1925 Heinrich Kretschmayr commented of Francis Stephen's spell as grand duke and commander in the Turkish war: "There is nothing to suggest that Francis's wife showed her concern about all this in any other capacity than as a wife, daughter, and mother."[123] And Edward Crankshaw, writing in 1969, imagined her "relaxed enjoyment on sub-mitting herself to her husband's will."[124] On closer inspection, such judgments prove to be the projections of later historians who not only had clear ideas about inherent female submissiveness but also under-stood politics to be primarily a matter of warfare and treaty-making. This blinded them to the logic specific to dynastic activity. If we exam-ine Maria Theresa's correspondence from her time as Grand Duchess of Tuscany, however, we see that she was doing precisely what the era took politics to mean.

When Maria Theresa herself claimed in hindsight that "as long as the emperor was alive, no one so much as looked at me, nor did anyone come to visit me," her memory was playing tricks on her.[125] In fact, she maintained contacts with noble families and ecclesiastical worthies in Italy and Lorraine, received representatives of foreign powers, peddled influence in the Habsburg patronage system, and made recommenda-tions for official appointments. Her correspondence, directed by her secretary, Wolfscron, makes this quite clear. Along with the usual holi-day and New Year's greetings, condolence letters, messages of congratu-lation on her accession to power and the birth of her first child, expres-sions of thanks for gifts, and diplomatic credentials, she also frequently received letters of solicitation that were addressed to her as ruler of Tuscany, or which asked her to put in a good word with the emperor or empress.[126] As wife of the new grand duke and daughter of the emperor, Maria Theresa occupied key positions in the Habsburg trust network and could provide access to all the symbolic and social capital the court had to offer. The official correspondence she conducted at the time shows how the system of favor and patronage functioned and just how far it reached.

Two or three examples may suffice to illustrate this. On September 25, 1739 her aunt Maria Elisabeth, Governor-General of the Habsburg Netherlands, wrote from Brussels to ask her "beloved niece and sister" Maria Theresa to "be so kind as to arrange an audience" with the emperor for the young Count Hohenlohe-Schillingsfürst "by means of my friendly letter of introduction," for the young man was "a close relative of my First Lady in Waiting." Maria Theresa replied in equally mannerly prose that she had received the count and been given the letter in question. She assured her aunt of her "ever constant, faithful, and undiminished affection" and made known that, "in view of your kind recommendation, which I am only too happy to relay, as well as on account of the close kinship obtaining between your First Lady in Waiting and the aforementioned Count, everything shall be done during his stay here, and on all other occasions, to assure him of my particular regard and favor."[127]

Several intermediary steps were necessary for a young nobleman—let alone someone not of noble birth—to be admitted to court. In this case, the young Hohenlohe had the good fortune to be a relative of the first lady in waiting of the aunt of the emperor's daughter. Had he been a nobody, he could not have hoped for such support. Grace and favor were bestowed in highly targeted ways within the context of the gift economy at court. We can observe this with some precision because even unanswered letters soliciting for pensions, regimental commands, or financial support were carefully filed in Maria Theresa's record office. Thus, the Discalced Carmelites' plea for financial assistance in rebuilding their derelict monastery fell on deaf ears and was not even dignified with a response. Secretary Wolfscron instead noted conscientiously that "the petition of the Barefoot Carmelites at Florence for a contribution towards restoring their ruined monastery . . . remained unanswered at [Maria Theresa's] most gracious behest."[128]

"Great" politics was structurally no different from "petty" politics. The procedure for filling even the highest offices in Christendom was fundamentally the same as the process by which pensions, military regiments, or positions were doled out at court. There were simply more contestants in the game, and the stakes were considerably higher when cardinals' hats, episcopal sees, or the papacy itself were up for grabs. Here, too, examples can be found in Maria Theresa's correspondence. Thus, on January 6, 1738 Prince Joseph of Hesse, canon at the Cathedral of Augsburg, requested her "intercession in my favor, so that in any future vacancy of the bishopric, my name may be considered before all others."[129] This was typical: influential advocates were not sought out once a post fell vacant but well in advance of an anticipated opening. This required cultivating an extremely obsequious mode of expression. The cathedral canon had, he wrote, "been greatly comforted to learn" that Maria Theresa "harbored the most benign intention to take a gracious part in furthering my person and interest." That is why he "most fervently and humbly beseech[ed]" her to speak on his behalf to the empress, who, in turn, would intercede for him with the emperor. By this circuitous route he hoped the emperor would "hasten to send the letter of recommendation" to the dean of Augsburg Cathedral "for the promotion of my person, that I might eventually come to feel its desired effect." The canon placed his spiritual services at her disposal in return: "For my part I will not neglect or cease to implore the Almighty to grant you long-lasting, undisturbed health and the Grand Duke all desirable well-being, to provide you with the solace of an heir to the throne, and to include the Most Serene House of Austria in my daily mass." Maria Theresa suggestively replied that she would be glad if the recommendation she had made to her mother on his behalf had its intended effect. In the event, the petitioner got what he wanted: when the Prince-Bishop of Augsburg passed away two years later, the diocesan chapter elected the Hessian prince as his successor. It is impossible to say how much he owed Maria Theresa for his good fortune, and he himself could not be sure. Yet this very uncertainty was at the foundation of the system of obligations operating at court.[130] The extent to which influence had been exerted in favor of (or against) a candidate was always a matter of conjecture, since several influential persons were usually approached for their support well in advance of the hour when it was needed. The petitioner could therefore never be absolutely sure whether any particular request for support had made a difference. If his efforts eventually met with success, this obligated him to general and long-term gratitude toward everyone he had approached to intercede on his behalf. If he was unsuccessful, blame could not be clearly assigned; it was always possible that his intercessors had pleaded his case but been unable to carry the day. The system of court patronage generally worked in favor of those who wielded influence, increasing the power of the already powerful: success reaped them debts of gratitude, while failure did not necessarily reflect badly on them.

Such a long-term debt of gratitude increased in value for the intercessor with the influence and importance of the vacant position and the wealth of the associated resources. Nothing surpassed the papacy in this respect.[131] That the imperial house had a massive influence on who was elected pope—or, more precisely, on the cardinals who voted in the election—was common knowledge. In 1739, when an impending vacancy of the Holy See became apparent, the emperor's daughter was involved in these machinations as well. Ever since Pope Clement XII had fallen seriously ill, Vienna had been preoccupied with the question of his successor.[132] In October 1739 a special envoy was sent to Rome, where French and Spanish agents were already at work.[133] When Clement XII died on February 6, 1740, an Austro-French and a Spanish party stood opposed to each other in the College of Cardinals. The conclave to elect a new pontiff was no longer deserving of that name; there could be no talk of cardinals meeting under lock and key (con-clavis). The envoys of the great powers wandered in and out of the Sistine Chapel as they pleased. During the eventful, dramatic, and spectacularly long forty-day conclave, at which numerous candidates were treated as *papabile* and no fewer than three electors passed away, the brother of Cardinal Pompeo Aldrovandi petitioned Maria Theresa for a "recommendation" to the emperor. As her secretary noted in the register of her correspondence, she did not answer in writing "owing to the importance of the matter" but made the imperial answer known to the petitioner in person through a middleman. In the end, Aldrovandi narrowly lost the vote. A compromise candidate was elected instead, the

Archbishop of Bologna, Lorenzo Lambertini, who went on to rule for almost twenty years under the name of Benedict XIV. The defeated Aldrovandi nonetheless wrote to Maria Theresa to express his thanks for her support, while the imperial envoy sought to justify himself to her for his lack of success. Yet despite the costly influence-peddling on all sides, Maria Theresa ultimately ascribed the result of the papal election to "the inspiration of the Holy Spirit," which on this occasion had unfortunately disappointed the hopes placed in it by the Austrian contingent.

These examples show Maria Theresa playing the classic role of intermediary in the imperial patronage system: as heiress presumptive, she had the ear of the emperor. Later, as regent of the hereditary lands and especially as empress, she could no longer perform this role herself. A sovereign overlord was supposed to stand *above* such networks; rulers cultivated an aura of strict impartiality and universal justice. This required them to have a general overview, yet such an overview was fictitious—all the more so the further their rule extended. Every ruler therefore necessarily relied on intermediaries. Compared with what awaited Maria Theresa in 1740, her previous political activity may seem trivial, and this role was indeed different from the business of governing in her own right. Yet the fact that she was directly involved in the dynastic clientele system, as was only to be expected of an emperor's daughter and grand duke's wife, certainly helped prepare her for her later political duties. When she began ruling the Austrian hereditary lands, she was already at home in the sphere of "micropolitics."[134] The change was thus by no means as abrupt as she herself presented it in retrospect. If her childhood is compared with the education of male heirs to the throne, who were usually explicitly initiated into the business of governing, it is true that her father had left her unprepared for the role of regent. It is not true, however, when one takes into account that she grew into the role of courtly politics—which was a politics of networking—like any other high-born wife.

That said, Maria Theresa did not have an easy time at court in the early years of her marriage. As a daughter, even one who potentially stood to inherit the throne, she had to put up with being treated like a child by her father's ministers. Symptomatic of this is the way the elderly court chancellor, Philipp Ludwig von Sinzendorf, dealt with her. Sinzendorf was perhaps the most influential man at court, a member of the inner sanctum around the emperor, the Privy Court Conference. Contemporaries were unanimous in describing him as an experienced hand in foreign policy but self-interested and avaricious, disloyal, and cunning. It was an open secret that he stood in the pay of foreign powers—a practice that was far from unusual at the time—and deliberately threw a veil over his affairs, reveling in an atmosphere of strategic chaos; yet he evidently enjoyed the emperor's blind trust and was therefore indispensable to the Lorraine faction at court.[135] A significant detail shows how he sought to put Maria Theresa in her place: the question of the language in which her official correspondence was conducted. Maria Theresa preferred writing in Italian and French, but this "contravened the archducal style of writing and was therefore to cease forthwith pending further orders from His Excellency the Lord High Court Chancellor."[136] Sinzendorf went over her head, ordering her rivate secretary, Wolfscron, to write solely in German and Latin. Maria Theresa continued her Italian and French correspondence undeterred, even though the secretary repeatedly reminded her of "the instructions given by His Excellency the Lord High Court Chancellor."[137] By insisting on her preferred style, she gave a first indication that she refused to be intimidated, not even by the all-powerful old minister, but would stick to her guns with remarkable steadfastness and resolve.

The Hapless Husband

Yet there was one problem over which she had no control: many felt she had married the wrong man. The more courtiers warmed to the princess, the darker was the portrait they painted of her husband. It was a pity, they said, that so formidable a woman should be married to such a man.[138] Francis Stephen of Lorraine was seen as weak, lazy, timid, indecisive, and completely unfit to cope with the tasks entrusted in him by the emperor. His brother Charles judged that, while he might be an honorable man, he was "raised with the naivety of a child" and was treated as such "by both the emperor and the ministers." He was totally reliant on Count Sinzendorf, "who goes behind his back." He was "unloved" in the country, in fact "hated in many cases," which his brother put down to his ironic, unserious manner.[139] Another observer, the aulic councillor Christoph Ludwig Seckendorff, wrote at the end of 1737 that Francis Stephen had "all Austrians as [his] enemies"; his parents-in-law were "displeased" with him and he with them; only Maria Theresa stuck up for him.[140] Just how much he was belittled at court is shown by a malicious anonymous satire produced for the Carnival of 1738. Francis Stephen is presented there as "Arlequin Enfant, Statue et Perroquet," that is to say: a childish, stiff buffoon who parrots back whatever others say to him.[141]

It is easy to see why Francis Stephen had such a hard time at court. He lacked everything that counted in the world of the nobility. As a plaything of more powerful interests, he had been forced to relinquish status, honor, his ancestral lands, and the very name of his house; he had unwillingly betrayed the time-honored attachment to place that lay at the heart of a nobleman's sense of self. His consolation prize, the Grand Duchy of Tuscany, he owed not to any conquests of his own but to the charity of others. The military glory that might have made up for a good deal of his misfortune stubbornly eluded him. Having been placed in overall charge of the war against the Ottomans by Charles VI in 1738, he returned in ill health following a series of humiliating setbacks, never again to be entrusted with a position of high command. His hapless campaign contributed to the loss of almost all the territory earlier recovered by Prince Eugene in Bosnia, Serbia, and Wallachia (including Belgrade). In the eyes of contemporaries, this last, disastrous Turkish war was a permanent blight on the House of Habsburg, and they were only too happy to shift the blame onto a "foreigner" like Francis Stephen of Lorraine. Everything seemed to tell against him. His talent for running an efficient household was interpreted as money-grubbing miserliness. He was said to have given out only cheap presents at his wedding; as a rule, "all Lothringian gifts were bad."[142] In a normative system that took demonstrative liberality and profligate expenditure as an index of social power, this was a damning judgment. To add insult to injury, he even lacked the necessary success between the sheets: while siring one daughter after another, he seemed unable to produce a boy who might one day inherit Charles VI's throne. Maria Elizabeth was born on February 5, 1737, Maria Anna on October 6, 1738,[143] Maria Carolina on January 12, 1740. As public hopes rose ever higher with each pregnancy, so too the sighs of disappointment became ever more audible with each delivery.[144] All this was blamed on Francis Stephen, particularly by those at court who had always viewed the heir to the Bavarian throne as the better match. Courtiers mercilessly noted every weakness of the landless outsider, who was entirely dependent on his father-in-law's beneficence and was now not even fulfilling his most basic conjugal duty. This contempt was reflected in the rumors that circulated about him at court, which continued to dog his reputation until the end of his life and beyond: the all-powerful cabinet secretary Bartenstein—himself an ennobled parvenu—"had told him to his face . . . that, after the emperor had done him the favor of giving him his daughter, he would have to yield to the emperor's will in everything."[145]

In the first years of their marriage, the couple was thus in an unenviable situation. But so too was the court, the dynasty, and the monarchy as a whole. Courtiers had every reason to be cynical, as evidenced by the maliciously perceptive satire from the 1738 Carnival season cited earlier, penned by an anonymous author—most likely a member of the French embassy—who was intimately acquainted with internal affairs at court.[146] The short text consists of a list of *dramatis personae* and captions actors and events at court with the titles of French comedies popular at the time. To wit, the war against the Turks: *Le Naufrage*—shipwrecked; money for the next campaign: *L'Inconnu*—unknown; the imperial treasury: *Le Banqueroutier*—bankrupt; decisions at court: *Le je ne scai quoi*—not a clue; the people of Vienna: *Muet par crainte*—struck dumb with fear. And finally, the author includes a famous tragedy among all the comedies: the Pragmatic Sanction—*Medea*, who murders her own children.[147] That would prove to be prophetic.

PLATE 1. Reliquary with a nail from Christ's cross, c. 1650, from the imperial treasury in Vienna

PLATE 2. Maria Theresa as a small child with a doll. Artist unknown, Convent of the
Sisters of St. Elisabeth, Klagenfurt

PLATE 3. Public table on the occasion of Maria Theresa's marriage to Francis Stephen of Lorraine in 1736. Attributed to the workshop of Martin van Meytens. Seated at table (from left): Archduchesses Maria Anna and Maria Magdalena (sisters of Charles VI), Emperor Charles VI, Empress Elisabeth Christine, Maria Theresa, and Francis Stephen

PLATE 4. Maria Theresa is crowned queen of Hungary in Pressburg in 1741.
From a series of ceremonial paintings by Franz Moessmer and Wenzel Pohl,
commissioned by Maria Theresa for the Hungarian Court Chancellery,
1769–70

PLATE 5. Ladies' Carousel in the Winter Riding School on January 2, 1743.
Workshop of Martin van Meytens, 1769–70

PLATE 6. Emperor Francis Stephen in his coronation regalia.
Wenzel Pohl, 1755

PLATE 7. Joseph at the age of three, depicted as heir in Hungarian attire.
Workshop of Martin van Meytens, 1744

PLATE 8. Portraits of Maria Theresa and Francis
Stephen on Holíč faience, mid-1800s

3

The War of Succession

FIGURE 6. A hussar cuts down a Prussian
soldier. Table clock, mid-eighteenth century.

A Change of Rule

On October 20, 1740, Charles VI passed away after a brief illness. He was
only fifty-five years old.[1] The death of a ruler was always a neuralgic
moment in hereditary monarchies, one that could lead to territorial partitions, prompt the estates to demand greater political participation, or
trigger intervention from foreign rivals. The dangers were especially
great on this occasion, for it had long been obvious that the Habsburg

territories were mired in serious military and financial difficulties. When Maria Theresa's father died, two inheritances fell vacant that had for some time been eyed with keen interest at European courts: rule over his numerous lands, on the one hand, and the elected office of holy Roman emperor, on the other. These two entities—the hereditary lands and the Empire—were quite distinct. Maria Theresa stood to inherit the Habsburg lands, but she could not be elected empress.

The monarchy she inherited was one without a name. The "hereditary lands" (*Erbländer*) was a vague coverall term for the patchwork of territories that the "All-Highest Archducal House" (*Allerhöchstes Erzhaus*), the Austrian branch of the Habsburg dynasty, had accumulated over time through war, inheritance, and marriage (see map, p. xv). Their heartlands—the "Austrian" or "German" hereditary lands, in the narrow sense of the term—consisted of the two archduchies above and below the Enns River (Upper and Lower Austria[2]); the duchies of Styria, Carinthia, and Carniola (Inner Austria); the county of Tyrol, including the Vorarlberg, the county of Gorizia, Inner Istria, and the Adriatic port city of Trieste; and finally an array of old landholdings scattered in the Breisgau and in Swabia (Further Austria). Most of these core territories belonged to the Holy Roman Empire, even if numerous privileges and exemptions guaranteed their special status. The majority of Habsburg territories, however, the hereditary lands in the broader sense, lay outside the Empire or were affiliated with it only loosely: the Lands of the Bohemian Crown (Bohemia, Moravia, Silesia) and the ancient Lands of the Crown of St. Stephen (Hungary, Croatia, Slavonia, Dalmatia), including the regions of Transylvania and the Banat won back from the Turks. In addition, there was a clutch of Italian principalities—the duchies of Milan, Mantua, Parma, and Piacenza—and finally the Southern (or Catholic) Netherlands, roughly equivalent to today's Belgium. The Grand Duchy of Tuscany had been brought into the marriage by Francis Stephen. The Pragmatic Sanction was intended to prevent the hereditary lands from fracturing upon the death of Charles VI. After all, they had nothing in common besides the ruling dynasty. The fact that they did not even have a proper name is telling. Around six million people lived in the Austrian lands and Bohemia alone. The entire dominion encompassed a landmass of around 730,000 square kilometers, by far the greater part of which lay outside the Holy Roman Empire.[3] Yet any attempt to represent the geographical extent of the lands of the House of Austria by drawing lines on a map is bound to be misleading. For in suggesting the existence of clear-cut borders and contiguous territorial states, such cartographical exercises conceal the highly intricate and at times murky power relations in those lands.

Whereas the principle of dynastic succession held sway in all these territories, Roman kingship or emperorship was based on the principle of free election by a small, exclusive group of prince-electors.[4] And while Charles VI had had to pay a high political price for securing the dynastic succession, he had barely given a thought to nominating a successor to the imperial throne, not even bothering to have his son-in-law Francis Stephen elected king of the Romans (and hence emperor-elect) in good time, as would normally have been the case. The Holy Roman German Empire, with the emperor at its helm, was an extremely complex political construct. Its various, highly disparate parts were held together by a series of common institutions, above all the Imperial Diet and the supreme imperial courts.[5] Since 1483 the prince-electors, supposedly acting on behalf of the entire Empire, had always backed the Habsburg candidate—the previous emperor's son, grandson, or brother—to be their new overlord. Yet this was no mere formality, for on each occasion their votes had to be coaxed from them with lucrative privileges, promises, and presents.

Now that the emperor had died without a male heir and without having arranged the election of a successor, all bets were off. A woman could inherit rule, but she could not be elected head of the Empire. Although this was nowhere formally spelled out in black and white, the idea of a holy Roman empress seemed inconceivable at the time. As Johann Jakob Moser, the leading expert on imperial law, tersely stated: "A woman is excluded from the imperial title neither by imperial law nor by imperial custom, yet she would be ill-advised ever to entertain hopes of it." And this despite the fact that in times gone by, "the imperial government, . . . partly on account of the emperor's minority, partly due to his absence," had occasionally been steered by women.[6]

Although hardly unknown, "petticoat government" was considered a problem in premodern Europe. In the early modern period, as in the Middle Ages before it, women had been viewed as inferior and hence also subordinate to men on account of their weaker minds and bodies. Each of the three higher faculties of learning at the time—theology, medicine, and law—lent theoretical support to this assumption. Admittedly, some scholars set out to demonstrate the unique virtues of individual "strong women," *mulieres fortes*, adducing evidence from history and the Bible. Yet these were scholarly games designed to give authors an opportunity to flaunt their erudition. Orthodox opinion held that female rule was a monstrous affront to the divine, natural, and human order.[7] What was feared was "domestic gynocracy" (*gynaecocratia domestica*), the upending of expected relations between men and women in marriage, household, and the family; its forbidding prototype was Xanthippe, the shrewish wife of Socrates. Things were somewhat different in the case of "political gynocracy" (*gynaecocratia politica*), a subject of lively scholarly debate. From a political point of view, many argued that it was an "affliction on the state," an abomination.[8] From a juristic viewpoint, however, they were forced to concede that female rule could in many cases be perfectly legitimate. There were several different possibilities. The most common was for a widow to act as regent for her son until he came of age or for a princess to rule on behalf of her absent husband. It was less common for women to rule in their own right, as was the case with imperial abbesses, elected by an all-female collegiate chapter. Finally, a daughter could inherit her father's throne provided this was permitted under domestic dynastic law, as it was in Austria. Yet female succession only came about if the male line had been extinguished or interrupted. In other words, if Maria Theresa had given birth to a son while her father was still alive then he would have been next in line to the throne, and she would have ruled on his behalf only until he had attained his majority. But Maria Theresa, despite producing three daughters in quick succession, had so far frustrated the hopes placed in her for a male child. Charles VI thus died not just without a son but without any male grandchildren as well, resulting in what was called an "interruption in the male line." This is why Maria Theresa inherited rule in accordance with the Pragmatic Sanction—an outcome that, while formally unobjectionable, was still politically tricky.[9]

In the marriage between Maria Theresa and Francis Stephen, the sexual hierarchy had been upended since the emperor's death, at the latest.[10] Francis Stephen of Lorraine inherited nothing from his father-in-law. Maria Theresa, balancing two European crowns on her head, now ruled over a vast and sprawling empire; the man at her side was a mere grand duke. This state of affairs was highly irregular, to say the least, in the eyes of a society that cared more for lineage, rank, and status than almost anything else. Once Maria Theresa had inherited the kingdoms of Hungary and Bohemia, the title of "crowned head" separated her from her consort. Yet this constituted the key symbolic difference between European potentates; through their coronation and anointment, kings were elevated into a social stratosphere that placed them far above mere princes. In this marriage, then, gender and power relations were sharply at odds. Put differently, the House of Austria was a *gynaecocratia domestica*: the woman, not the man, called the shots.

Maria Theresa herself was keenly aware of the problem. On ceremonial occasions at the Viennese court, her consort's lesser standing had been clear from the first, causing endless headaches for the lord high steward.[11] That the situation had been immeasurably complicated by her accession to the throne could already be seen from the way it disrupted conventional spatial arrangements. Following the death of Charles VI, Maria Theresa and Francis Stephen moved into the state apartments in the so-called Leopoldine Wing, symbolically manifesting her newly acquired status. As was customary in residential palaces, here too there was a gentlemen's wing and a ladies' wing. These were designed to mirror each other, ensuring that the same ceremonial rules of access could be observed in audiences with the ruling couple: respects were paid first to the ruler, then to his wife, both times in the same form.[12] The gentlemen's wing was traditionally the place for performing grand acts of state, such as accepting homage from the territorial estates (*Landstände*) or receiving foreign ambassadors. In her role as wife, Maria Theresa followed tradition in having her private quarters in the ladies' wing. Yet in her role as ruler, she emulated her male forebears in receiving the traditional homage of the estates in the gentlemen's wing.[13] This meant that Francis Stephen either had to vacate his own rooms for the occasion or make do with the subordinate place usually assigned the royal consort, a simple chair to Maria Theresa's left. Nothing could have more conspicuously advertised the reversal of gender roles to a public that had internalized the grammar of court ceremonial. Nobody could escape this grammar; it ineluctably conveyed its symbolic messages, whether intended or not. This is why Maria Theresa took such pains to secure her husband a higher rank that would resolve these ceremonial dissonances.[14]

Although female rule was not uncommon in premodern times (at least in dynastic polities) and occurred in various forms, it seldom went uncontested. Every form of "gynocracy" was an open invitation to relatives or neighbors to register their rival claims to power, on the pretext that women were constitutionally unfit to govern. Whoever wished to assert his own ambitions against a female ruler could easily draw support from conventional wisdom about the lesser, weaker sex. So too here. The Viennese court poet Zeno registered "*voci tumultuanti*," seditious voices, who claimed that it sullied the honor of the land to be ruled by a woman. The public interest required that a German prince succeed to the throne.[15] This amounted to an open show of support for the claim to the Habsburg inheritance asserted by Karl Albrecht, elector of Bavaria. Court society had long been split between Lothringian and Bavarian factions. The Bavarian elector was married to a daughter of Emperor Joseph I, making the imperial widow Amalia his mother-in-law and hence the natural head of the Bavarian faction at the court in Vienna.[16] To be sure, Maria Theresa had been nominated successor to her father in line with the Pragmatic Sanction. She herself was unshaken in her belief that assuming this inheritance was her sacred duty to God, the House of Habsburg, and the hereditary lands. Yet it was a moot question whether her subjects would consent to be ruled by a woman, or whether other European powers would feel duty-bound to respect the new succession law.

The late emperor's corpse was still lying in state in the Knights' Room of the Hofburg[17] when unrest broke out not far from the capital. Many commoners evidently regarded Maria Theresa's succession to the throne as illegitimate and therefore regarded the throne as still unoccupied.[18] The situation was already tense: bad weather had destroyed that year's vintage and pushed up food prices. Poor harvests were often the occasion for popular unrest, since, given the subsistence conditions under which so many were living at the time, rising prices quickly led to famine. Two destabilizing factors came together here. The ruler's death was a moment when the existing order of things appeared to have been suspended, emboldening disgruntled subjects to air their grievances. On this occasion, public anger was centered on the copious game that the hunting-mad emperor had lovingly tended and protected during his lifetime. These animals were the exclusive preserve of the court, and they grazed on peasants' fields and gardens with impunity. Noble hunting privileges had long been a source of popular resentment and had led to frequent disturbances in the past, not just in Austria. Such displays of discontent regularly accompanied royal successions, sometimes even escalating into open insurrection. Hunting, that courtly pleasure *par excellence*, was the perfect symbol for the indifference of pampered courtiers to the everyday hardships faced by their social inferiors.[19] Simmering anger boiled over into open rebellion the moment the scepter of power passed from one ruler to the next. Peasants trespassed on the imperial hunting grounds and slaughtered game in prodigious quantities, even though poachers were severely punished. To defuse the outbreak of insubordination, Maria Theresa had no choice but to have game animals shot in large numbers by her court hunters.[20] Discontent about the irregular succession hardly helped soothe inflamed tempers. All the more importance was therefore now attached to the traditional rites for transferring power.

With the ruler's death, all obligations of service and fealty traditionally lapsed as well, since these were regarded as personal relations that had to be renewed each time a new ruler came to the throne. A series of transitional rituals ensured that this difficult threshold was safely crossed and that, with each change of incumbent, the order remained essentially the same. Solemn oaths needed to be sworn on different levels of the social hierarchy to guarantee the new ruler's legitimacy in the public eye as well as to forge new personal loyalties. Accordingly, ministers and courtiers were not the only ones who had to take an oath of office to their new monarch; the troops were called on to pledge their allegiance as well, and the estates of all the hereditary lands likewise owed her their homage. In most lands this was simply delivered to emissaries or avowed in writing. The signal exception was the homage given by the estates of Lower Austria, which Maria Theresa—like her forebears—received with great ceremony in the Hofburg. This took place as early as November 22, 1740, impelled by a sense of urgency arising from the volatile political situation.[21]

In Austria this ritual was functionally equivalent to a coronation, which remained the prerogative of monarchies. The archducal hat was specially transported for the occasion in a solemn procession from Klosterneuburg to Vienna, allowing the Archduchess Maria Theresa to receive homage in all the finery of her dynastic insignia. Klosterneuburg was the sacral center of the Archducal House; there too the skull of Leopold, the sainted family patriarch, was preserved as a relic, imbuing the nearby archducal hat with its sanctifying power. This "hat"—like the "electoral hats" worn by the prince-electors—was shaped like a crown, even though it could not be called by that name. Like a crown, it embodied rulership over the land, which remained unchanged as it passed from one ruler to the next. Maria Theresa's ancestor, Rudolf IV of Habsburg, had appropriated the insignia in the fourteenth century, together with a series of other imposing prerogatives and the self-proclaimed title of archduke, by means of a fake imperial document, the *Privilegium Maius*, because he lacked the status of a prince-elector and therefore felt appreciably neglected in the hierarchy of the Empire.[22]

A cycle of lavishly produced, large-format copperplates bore testimony to the various stages in the solemn act of investiture that now took place. The course of events had been carefully planned in advance.[23] It began with a grand public procession and ceremonious High Mass to the Holy Spirit in the Stephansdom, the Cathedral of St. Stephen in Vienna. This was followed by the mutually binding pact in the Knights' Room of the Hofburg: first the new regent promised to protect the rights and freedoms of the province, then the territorial estates raised their hands to swear the oath of allegiance before kissing her proffered hand in order of rank. The Te Deum Laudamus was sung in the court chapel before the proceedings came to a close with an open banquet, where the ruling couple were served at table by nobles holding hereditary territorial offices.

The ritual sequence traditionally repeated on all such occasions had multiple meanings: not only was the new ruler inducted into the given order, but this order itself was enveloped in an aura of timelessness and inevitability. Not least, everyone who participated in the ceremony was confirmed in their more-or-less privileged positions. The order in which people were placed in the procession, in the church, and at table represented a kind of ritualized tableau of the territorial hierarchy, consolidated by the presence of countless spectators. Even these commoners were by no means simply passive onlookers. They were traditionally given coins, wine, and other gifts, and thereby symbolically included in the feast at the end of the ritual. Yet the very ritual that was intended to provide institutional support for the change of dynast was also the site where protesters could be sure to attract attention. The regime was by no means as invulnerable as the elaborate theatrics would suggest. Neither the series of lavish images produced to commemorate the ceremony nor the official description in the *Wienerische Diarium* gives any inkling of the fury of the assembled crowd, which culminated in the windows of a particularly reviled court war councillor (*Hofkriegsrat*) being smashed in and a street fight breaking out between rioters and the city watch. In the end, a regiment of dragoons had to be called in to restore the peace.[24]

Yet all this was only a minor disturbance compared with what was to come. It soon became apparent that all the arrangements made by Charles VI to safeguard his inheritance after his death had not been worth the paper they were written on. While most European monarchs, including the Prussian king, observed the formalities of congratulating Maria Theresa, the French court brooded over how she should be addressed—a sign that her new status had not been accepted unconditionally.[25] The elector of Bavaria refused to recognize Maria Theresa from the outset and submitted a complaint to Vienna formally protesting her accession to the throne.[26] Karl Albrecht of Bavaria already had a prepared legal argument to hand, making the case for why he himself should rule over all the Habsburg lands. From documents dating back some two centuries, the marriage contract and testament of Emperor Ferdinand I from 1543 and 1546, respectively, he had his court archivist derive his legal entitlement to the entire estate. These documents stipulated, however, that the House of Wittelsbach would only inherit the Habsburg estate in the event that the house were to die out completely (and not just its male line). The fact that Karl Albrecht had solemnly foresworn all inheritance claims to the Archducal House when he married the emperor's daughter did not prevent him from now proclaiming it his right, indeed his sacred duty toward his descendants, to take over Charles VI's inheritance. At the same time, he also registered his claim to be elected emperor, an honor that had already been twice bestowed on the House of Wittelsbach in the Late Middle Ages. The vacancy of the imperial throne appeared to offer his family a welcome, long overdue opportunity to attain to the dignity befitting its venerable historic status. For in contrast to his colleagues in the electoral college from Berlin, Dresden, and Hannover, the Bavarian elector had not yet succeeded in acquiring a European royal crown, and hence in gaining the international stature he craved as a true sovereign. He had not completely thought through his strategy for attaining this ambitious goal, however; he lacked the necessary troops, funds, and diplomatic preparations to overcome potential opposition. Without foreign—in this case primarily French—support, it was unthinkable that his plans would ever come to fruition. Yet Karl Albrecht had so far been unable to win over the irenic French chief minister, Cardinal Fleury.

Maria Theresa curtly dismissed the Bavarian elector's claim to her inheritance. The Bavarian emissary in Vienna was invited to see with his own eyes that the original documents failed to support the claims made on their behalf. Not only was Maria Theresa determined to defend the Habsburg inheritance against the Bavarian pretender, she also expected that her husband would continue the tradition of the House of Habsburg supplying an emperor. As a preliminary to this objective, but also to reinstate the gender hierarchy at the Viennese court (and not "to place the burden of government on stronger shoulders than her own," as nineteenth-century historians would have it[27]), she appointed Francis Stephen coregent in November. She also made him grand master of the Order of the Golden Fleece and transferred to him the electoral vote to which she was entitled as Queen of Bohemia but which, as a woman, she was unable to exercise herself at the upcoming imperial election.[28] Francis Stephen's nomination as coregent was a balancing act. On the one hand, Maria Theresa adapted to the expectations of her environment, making a concession to the conventions of the gender hierarchy in order to solve formal problems such as managing electoral votes and establishing precedence at court. On the other hand, she made unmistakably clear that she intended to relinquish none of her sovereignty. Count Sylva-Tarouca, one of her closest confidants, remarked that the decision to make Francis Stephen coregent "depended solely on the will of the Queen, who reigns over all and can choose to be assisted by whomever she pleases; this co-regency is nothing other than a means of support, something like a first minister."[29]

The elector of Mainz, who as imperial archchancellor was responsible for calling the election, had invited Francis Stephen to the electoral diet in Frankfurt immediately after the death of Charles VI.[30] This move now proved to have been premature. The electors of Bavaria and Saxony lodged an official protest. August III, elector of Saxony and king of Poland, nursed hopes of his own for parts of the inheritance and the title of emperor. Now it was disputed whether a woman could inherit the Bohemian electorship in the first place, let alone transfer it to her husband. Neither the Golden Bull, the old imperial charter, nor the Pragmatic Sanction had foreseen this contingency. As Grand Duke of Tuscany, it was argued, Francis Stephen did not qualify as an elector and was not even entitled to a regular seat at the Imperial Diet. When Maria Theresa nonetheless sent an emissary to the election in Frankfurt, the other prince-electors refused him all official recognition, quarters, or contact—an unprecedented public affront.[31]

Yet while all interested parties were still busily sending emissaries to each other's courts to sound out support for their schemes, another newcomer to the throne was creating new facts on the ground. On

December 16, 1740, the recently crowned King of Prussia, Frederick II, seized the opportunity to march with his troops into Silesia. The invasion was not entirely unexpected. As early as 1738, the imperial emissary had reported from Berlin to Vienna on Crown Prince Frederick's passion for the military, warning that he intended to begin his reign with a bang: "*Son principe est de commencer par un coup d'éclat.*"[32] Frederick, only five years older than the twenty-three-year-old Maria Theresa, had previously drawn attention to himself as a musically and intellectually gifted aesthete who surrounded himself in his salon with the most provocative writers, freethinking scholars, and fashionable artists of his day. Now that he was finally rid of his tyrannical father, he was eager for the "rendezvous with fame" opened up for him by the Habsburg monarchy's weakness.[33] The circumstances could hardly have been more propitious: his father had bequeathed him overflowing state coffers and a large, highly modern army. Frederick justified his incursion into the neighboring Duchy of Silesia, one of the most prosperous territories of the Habsburg monarchy, not only by pleading the old and legitimate claims of his house, which he quickly ensured were set out in a legal defense, but also by brazenly presenting himself as a friend in need to the vulnerable heiress. It had been necessary to preempt other powers, which "secretly harbor plans to appropriate a part of the inheritance for themselves. . . . My sole concern is for the perpetuation and true advantage of the House of Austria."[34] In exquisitely courteous prose, Frederick avowed the greatest affection for his "dear sister"(*Madame Ma Soeur*) and commended himself to her as her staunchest ally, the kind of caring and protective older brother she had never had. His march on her territory had, he assured her, been guided by the "purest intentions" and the "sincerest esteem."[35] He magnanimously offered his aid against any future attack from abroad and his vote for the election of her husband, along with a loan of two million guilders. All he asked in thanks for everything he had done for the glory of the Archducal House was that Silesia be ceded in its entirety to Prussia. Ignoring his honeyed words, Maria Theresa soberly informed her ambassador "that we neither can nor wish to trust in such assurances; for how is it possible to attack one's neighbor on the grounds that he sees no need to accept one's assistance?"[36] In her official explanation, she categorically rejected Frederick's offer and permitted herself the ironic remark that if he intended by such means to preserve the constitution of the Empire and the welfare of Europe, she was interested to know what it would look like should he ever set out to destroy them. She did not need his help to secure her rightful inheritance, she added, since this was the duty of the entire Empire. No war had ever been launched to force a prince to accept the offer of money and support, and she had not the slightest intention of beginning her reign by having her territories partitioned.[37]

Frederick's campaign in Silesia was a brief and one-sided affair.[38] The Silesian estates, which had only recently paid homage to Maria Theresa, were ill equipped to defend themselves. Apart from a handful of fortresses, Frederick had taken over the entire province within two months. Meanwhile, the Austrian supreme commander Neipperg had not even set out from Vienna. In keeping with military tradition, the general waited until the start of April to launch his campaign, slowly leading his army into Silesia. The decisive encounter took place there on April 10 near the town of Mollwitz, southeast of Breslau. No one had expected the army of the cocky Prussian upstart to hold its own against the Austrian heavyweights. Unlike their opponents, however, the Prussian infantry had been drilled to take turns automatically charging and firing in rows, undismayed by the bodies falling to their left and right. All the same, even the Prussian king doubted his troops' success; on the advice of his generals, he was whisked away to safety before the battle was over. Yet victory went to the last side left standing with their flags on the battlefield, and at Mollwitz this was the Prussians—although the Austrians also claimed victory and ordered the Te Deum to be sung in churches.[39] For his part, Frederick ordained a thanksgiving service, pointedly setting a reading from St. Paul's first epistle to Timothy: "But I suffer not a woman to teach, nor to usurp authority over the man."

The defeat at Mollwitz prompted other interested parties to enter the fray and claim their own piece of the Habsburg pie.[40] In May and June of 1741, a coalition formed against Maria Theresa. Each partner had its own agenda. Queen Elisabeth of Spain, holding the reins of government for her husband, saw a golden opportunity to win back Tuscany and perhaps also take over the Upper Italian duchies of Parma and Piacenza. At the French court the ambitious Marshal Belle-Isle prevailed against the less hawkish Prime Minister Fleury with a carefully planned policy aimed at dismembering the entire Habsburg estate, dividing the spoils among the remaining powers in Europe, and in this way permanently eliminating the Habsburgs as rivals to the House of Bourbon and incumbents of the imperial throne. The Bavarian and Saxon plans likewise foresaw carving up almost all of Maria Theresa's inheritance, leaving her Hungary at most. Meanwhile, in Frankfurt, where envoys of the prince-electors had convened to elect a new emperor, the French were gradually helping to put together a majority in favor of Karl Albrecht of Bavaria.[41] All Maria Theresa's hopes of securing support against Prussia from her French, English, Dutch, Russian, or Saxon-Polish allies were dashed: France, Bavaria and Spain presented a united front, and in September, Saxony-Poland joined the ranks of her opponents. Through all this time, the English emissary in Vienna sought to play a mediating role and advised her to sue for peace. Great Britain was already fighting a war at sea with Spain, feared French intervention, and had no desire to add Prussia to its list of enemies.

Pressure mounted on Maria Theresa to sacrifice parts of Silesia, or at least find some other minor territory that could be sacrificed in its stead. Most of her ministers recommended this course. Her husband, too, thought she should cut her losses and bring the war with Frederick to a speedy end. But Maria Theresa remained unconvinced. As she wrote to the Bohemian court chancellor, Count Philipp Kinsky, one of the few who encouraged her to stand her ground, she was only pretending to agree to the concessions urged on her by her ministers. In fact, it was her "firm resolve never to give up any part of Silesia. . . . God preserve me from ever contemplating such a thing."[42] She saw it as her historic duty toward the dynasty and as her God-given mission to hold on to the inheritance of her forebears, not releasing the smallest parcel of land from her grip. Depending on their perspective, historians have described this stance as one of unwavering determination[43] or foolish obstinacy.[44] Whichever the case may be, in the end she had no option but to come to terms with Frederick II. For the elector of Bavaria and

Marshal Belle-Isle had by now invaded the Austrian heartland, and she needed all the troops at her disposal for its defense. Not until the beginning of September did she declare herself prepared—albeit with the greatest reluctance—to make a few concessions: "*Placet* [I agree], as there is no alternative, but with the greatest anguish," she noted in the margins of a ministerial proposal,[45] and she complained to Court Chancellor Sinzendorff that the entire matter had been foisted on her against her will.[46] Yet her negotiating position had dramatically deteriorated in the meantime; Frederick had now joined forces with France, Saxony, and Bavaria.[47] In October 1741 she concluded an armistice with the Prussians that compelled her to abandon Lower Silesia.[48] They even staged a fake siege of the fortress of Neisse so that Frederick's allies would be unaware that he was about to desert them.[49] Frederick changed his mind a little later, broke the truce, and once again threw in his lot with Maria Theresa's enemies.

On August 15, 1741, French troops began crossing the Rhine and joining up with their Bavarian allies. Under the personal leadership of Karl Albrecht, elector of Bavaria, the combined army marched into the land above the Enns. Here, too, events moved on apace.[50] The forces mustered by the territory proved no match for their opponents and were sent home in disarray, while the Austrian troops retreated before the advancing enemy. In August the imperial widow Amalia personally presented Maria Theresa with a list of demands from her Bavarian son-in-law.[51] Spanish troops opened another theater of war in Upper Italy. On September 15 Karl Albrecht entered the Upper Austrian capital of Linz, where the estates solemnly received him as their new liege lord and bowed down before him in homage. In Vienna preparations for a siege began in earnest. The only land to which Maria Theresa could turn for succor in her plight was the Kingdom of Hungary.

Loyal and Disloyal Hungarians

Throughout this flurry of events, from June to October 1741, Maria Theresa was away from Vienna in her residence in Pressburg (Poszony in Hungarian, now the Slovakian capital of Bratislava). She had come there to assume the reins of power in person.[52] Pressburg was the "most Austrian" city in Hungary, situated only half a day's journey down the Danube at the westernmost edge of the great kingdom. The investiture ceremony in Pressburg took a dramatic course. To this day, it plays a key role in the standard hagiographical account of Maria Theresa.

The Habsburgs' relations with Hungary had always been tense. The fact that Maria Theresa had been addressed since her father's death as Queen of Hungary, rather than as Archduchess of Austria, had less to do with any special preference for this country on her part—she rarely stayed in Pressburg—than with the fact that the Hungarian royal title was the most valuable at her disposal. The title of *Rex Hungariae* was associated with rule over a sprawling collection of territories symbolically united by the crown of the eleventh-century St. Stephen, revered as the founder of the Christian Kingdom of Hungary. Along with the Hungarian heartland, these included the subordinate kingdoms of Slavonia, Dalmatia, and Croatia in the south, as well as the separate realms of Transylvania and the Banat in the southeast. After these territories had been wrested from Ottoman suzerainty, it had been thought prudent not to integrate them into the Kingdom of Hungary but to administer them directly from Vienna instead. Taken together, these lands covered an area roughly equivalent in size to almost all the other hereditary lands combined (see map, p. xv).[53] The region was essentially rural in character and had been hard hit by war. Members of distinct linguistic communities lived cheek by jowl in the villages: Magyars, Croats, Serbs, Slovaks, Wallachs, Swabians, Saxons, Ruthenians, Greeks, and "Gypsies." Unlike in the hereditary lands, there was also enormous religious diversity: alongside Catholics, there were Lutherans, Calvinists, Greek Orthodox and Uniate Christians, Jews, even Antitrinitarians, Sabbatists, and various other small religious groups. The population was split along these ethnoreligious and linguistic lines; in many villages different groups lived side by side without ever intermingling, intermarrying, or establishing common political institutions and forums.

The peasants were mostly serfs of noble landlords (*Grundherren*), who ruled them without any notable checks to their power. The nobility did not constitute a single homogeneous class, however, but was deeply fissured. Two hundred or so extremely wealthy magnate families—the Batthyánys, Pálffys, Eszterházys, or Nádasdys—moved in a different sphere to the numerous lesser nobles, who enjoyed certain privileges but otherwise led lives similar to the peasantry. In the thinly populated regions bordering the Ottoman Empire, the so-called military frontier, armed free peasants lived in fortified villages. There were few towns to speak of; trade was dominated by Austrian merchants. The Hungarian heartland was divided into counties. These were districts self-administered by the local nobles, who were responsible for collecting taxes, levying troops, and much else besides. Each county was headed by a major landowner representing the crown—not just an appointed office-holder but a ruler in his own right.

The Kingdom of Hungary was a monarchy held in check by estates, and in this sense it corresponded to the traditional type of political constitution prevalent in Europe at the time. The political unity of what was called Hungary was first produced by territorial diets (*Landtage*). From time to time the king summoned the estates of the realm to assemble as a body in order to negotiate with them in traditional, ritualistic form—initially upon his accession to the throne, then whenever he needed troops, money, or both, or when he wanted to encroach in some way on the customary rights of the land. The kingdom's estates, *status et ordines*, were possessed of sovereign rights, and the king needed their permission to draw on the economic resources of the land. In Hungary these estates were, on the one hand, the supreme religious and secular dignitaries along with the heads of families belonging to the higher nobility (the Upper House) and, on the other, the deputies of the lesser nobility and free cities, who were elected in county assemblies (the Lower House). When they convened for a diet, the king's representative began by ceremoniously announcing what he wanted from them. The estates then conferred separately in their respective chambers (or around two tables) before reuniting to decide on a joint resolution, which they finally presented to the king.[54] In return for their concessions, the estates were confirmed in their possession of all possible collective privileges and liberties—mostly at the expense of their own subjects. Something like this was the norm in all early modern European monarchies. The relationship between the territorial overlords and the estates was conceived as a contract based on mutual rights and obligations, not as a relation of one-sided dominance. The land's unity derived from the estates' claim to represent the land as a whole, and this in a twofold sense: they conspicuously embodied the land by assembling at diets in ritual, hierarchically ordered form, and at the same time they produced the land as a political entity insofar as the resolutions they negotiated and concluded with the ruler were binding for all inhabitants. Because the Habsburg overlords, mindful of the ongoing conflict with the Turks on their doorstep, had been forced to grant sweeping concessions to the estates, this corporative constitution had stronger roots in Hungary than in many other European monarchies.

For the older Austrian national historiography, which saw Hungary as the fault line between Christian civilization and "oriental barbarism," between Europe and Asia, the Habsburgs had liberated and brought peace to the land by pushing back the Ottomans.[55] This was a distorted view, to put it mildly. In fact, the fronts were by no means as clear cut as this account suggests. In Hungary, as in other lands, the partly Protestant nobility held the foreign-based, Catholic ruling dynasty in no greater affection than the Muslim sultan it had replaced. The relationship of the estates to the Habsburgs had always vacillated between strategic alliance, covert opposition, and outright resistance.[56] The coalitions were complex and shifting: some cooperated with the Habsburgs against the Turks, others—the so-called malcontents—with the Turks and the French against the Habsburgs. The Hungarian estates were repeatedly able to exploit the friction between these three great powers to their own advantage.

The expulsion of their Muslim suzerains in the Turkish wars had created a power vacuum in the reconquered territories that both the Habsburgs and their noble opponents were eager to fill. With Turkish and French support, Francis II Rákoczi, a scion of one of Hungary's wealthiest families whose ancestors had served in high office under the Ottomans, had succeeded in uniting the estates against the Austrians. Once Maria Theresa's father, Charles VI, had finally put down the rebellion, he wisely refrained from attempting—as his predecessors had done—to impose a strict policy of centralization and Catholicization on the entire country. In the Peace of Szátmár (1711), he had instead promised never to rule Hungary in the same way as the other hereditary lands. This was the price for having his hereditary claim to the throne recognized by the estates. For how one became King of Hungary, whether by being elected by the estates or through inheritance, had long been unclear and contentious. According to conventional wisdom, it was still the medieval inauguration rite of unction and coronation that made someone king, whereas the Habsburgs bore the title even before the ritual to signal their hereditary right to the crown.

When Maria Theresa came to power, she depended for her very existence on the support of the Hungarian estates. The latter used the change of monarch as an opportunity to redefine their relationship with the crown. The setting for the showdown was the traditional coronation diet, where the ruler and the estates came together to make the kingdom's constitution vividly present. The diet climaxed in the coronation of the new king: by affirming their reciprocal rights and obligations, the king and the estates here validated in symbolic-ritual form what had previously been negotiated in the diet. This was particularly relevant in 1741, when the factual recognition of the Pragmatic Sanction by Hungary and the repudiation of the Bavarian claim were at stake.

On January 21, 1741, Maria Theresa called her first diet.[57] On May 18, the Hungarian estates assembled in Pressburg for the festive opening session, where the most senior bishop in the Empire, the *Primas* or primate, delivered the royal proposition. The estates withdrew to engage in at times heated debate about how they would respond, including what counterdemands they would raise. They then sent a delegation to Vienna to congratulate Maria Theresa on the birth of her son and heir Joseph on March 13 and to invite her to attend the diet in person. On June 19 Maria Theresa, accompanied by her husband and a large retinue, sailed down the Danube on a flotilla of royal barges and was ritually greeted the next day by dignitaries awaiting her at the Hungarian border. She donned Hungarian dress in a specially erected pavilion before being led into the city—a ritual change of clothing that, as was typical in premodern times, demonstrated she was switching kingship roles. All the details had been precisely worked out in advance. The *adventus*, the ceremonial arrival of the new ruler, was a ritual that drew on ancient traditions and had been customary in Europe since the Late Middle Ages. Staged with great pageantry, it symbolized reciprocal relations between a new ruler and the estates.[58]

On June 21 the diet met as a whole in the presence of Maria Theresa, who briefly and formulaically addressed the estates in elegant Latin, as observers noted, before the proposition was read out on her behalf.[59] Its content was unsurprising: the queen pledged in advance that she would affirm the land's customary freedoms, take the coronation oath in the traditional form, and have a new palatine elected. Although the palatine was officially the crown's representative, he was drawn from the native magnates and acted on their behalf. His office had been vacant for years while Francis Stephen officiated as Habsburg governor, a source of simmering resentment for the Hungarians. In return for her concessions, Maria Theresa demanded the formation of a standing army as well as ongoing payment of the contributions this would require. The counterdemands put by the estates, however, went well beyond what Maria Theresa was prepared to concede. They included freedom from taxation for the nobility, separate government in perpetuity for Hungary, the incorporation of Transylvania into Hungary as a separate administrative district, a monopoly on Hungarian offices and sinecures for the native nobility, and the queen's regular personal attendance at diets. Francis Stephen's coregency in Hungary also proved highly contentious. Negotiations among the estates were tumultuous. Habsburg partisans in the Upper Chamber, where many nobles and courtiers from the "German" hereditary lands had a seat and voice, faced stiff opposition from the Lower Chamber. Maria Theresa refused to accept the additional conditions, which would have imposed massive restrictions on her ability to mobilize the land's resources and to integrate it more closely with the other hereditary lands. For this question went to the crux of the matter: how could the Habsburg outsider gain access to the land's riches, both to meet her pressing military needs and to provide her own clientele with lucrative Hungarian offices and sinecures?

The key issues of dispute were still unresolved when the coronation went ahead on the preassigned date of June 25. Maria Theresa had largely had her way in the wording of the oath and the document, although she had been forced to make a written undertaking that she would give due consideration to the estates' wishes in further negotiations.[60] Real dissent was thus provisionally set aside in order that the medieval coronation ritual might be celebrated in traditional form and a show of festive concord put on for the public.

The ritual of royal investiture placed every new Hungarian king in a line stretching back to St. Stephen.[61] Places, objects, words, and gestures connected him directly with the mythic-sacral origin of the monarchy. The link was made at the moment the candidate for coronation had bestowed on him the first king's hallowed insignia. The symbolism of the Christian ruler as defender of the faith pervaded the entire ritual, which at the same time affirmed the "freedom" of the Hungarian political nation under its self-elected king. The entire spectacle was designed to appeal to the patriotism of the Hungarian nobility and present the new queen as one of their own. On the day of her coronation, Maria Theresa, dressed in sumptuous Hungarian attire and resplendent in her jewelry, was fetched from her residence, the formidable medieval castle at Pressburg, and led in solemn procession to St. Martin's Cathedral. All the Austrian nobles who held Hungarian offices, together with their wives and daughters, had likewise been instructed to wear Hungarian dress. Steps had been taken to ensure that the royal insignia were carried in the procession by Hungarian barons, not Viennese courtiers.[62] Civilian militias lined the way, keeping at bay the crowds of onlookers hoping for a glimpse of the spectacle, whose presence was absolutely crucial to the success of the ritual. Hungary's most senior clergy awaited the queen in the coronation church, along with the papal nuncio, the archbishop of Vienna, and the Venetian ambassador. The archbishop of Gran, the kingdom's primate, officiated at the investiture ritual, which in many respects resembled an imperial coronation. The scenery was framed by the Hungarian imperial marshal with his sword drawn, the palatine, and ten counts bearing the flags of the ten ancient Hungarian territories. The candidate had to kneel on the lowest step to the altar, symbolizing that in order to be raised high, she first had to abase herself. The primate ritually exhorted her to rule with virtue. The insignia of St. Stephen were then placed on the altar: crown, sword, mantle, orb, and scepter, all sacral objects representing the kingdom's suprapersonal longevity and unity in material form. The candidate had to kiss the proffered cross, place two fingers on the book of gospels, and take the coronation oath. The prescribed prayers were then offered and the litany of saints sung, before the primate anointed the candidate on her right shoulder and chest with consecrated oil. Anointment had been the sacral high point of Christian regal investitures since the Early Middle Ages; as a counterpart to episcopal consecration, it made the king the Lord's anointed, *rex et sacerdos*—a sacral, almost sacerdotal dignity that was not ordinarily extended to women. The candidate then took her seat on the throne and was clad in the mantle of St. Stephen. Great emphasis was placed throughout on Maria Theresa not being "crowned as a king's wife, but as herself a king," as the ceremonial protocol states.[63] During High Mass she knelt once more, to receive the bared sword, and having been enjoined to defeat "the enemies of the people of Israel,"[64] she was fitted out with crown, scepter, and imperial orb. With that the performative act making her king of Hungary was at an end. She was acclaimed by all present as *rex et domina noster*, a finely balanced formula that had been previously decided in this exact wording by the diet.[65] Drums, trumpets, and cannon fire resounded and the Te Deum was sung.

Following the Mass, the newly crowned monarch, still in full regalia, proceeded on foot to the Franciscan church. On her way there, covered by a baldachin and with the sword borne before her, she stopped off to pay her ritual obeisance at the statue of the victorious Virgin Mary. The epithet "victorious" recalls the circumstances under which Maria Theresa's grandfather, Leopold I, had commissioned the statue in 1675 after having expelled the Protestants from those parts of the realm.[66] In the Franciscan church she asserted her regal authority for the first time by knighting forty-eight nobles, thereby ritually demonstrating her suzerainty over Hungary. She then repeated her coronation oath on an open-air stage for the assembled populace before making her way to the coronation hill, a small, artificially elevated platform decorated in the colors of the land (see color plate 4). "At its foot she mounted a horse adorned with precious gemstones and pearls and galloped up the hill on her own, sword held aloft. To the jubilation of the people she dealt four strokes to the four corners of the world in cruciform, thereby showing that she would protect her kingdom from the enemy wheresoever he might appear."[67]

The fact that the person anointed King of Hungary and invested with the symbols of regal authority was a woman was exceptional and utterly without historical precedent. Even the horse ride was unorthodox; Maria Theresa had prepared for the occasion by taking riding lessons. In all this she was acting symbolically as *rex Hungariae*, not as *regina*, since she appeared in Pressburg not as the wife of a king but as a ruler in her own right. It was specifically noted in the ceremonial papers that she was "not coming as a royal spouse but to be crowned king, and all other matters pertaining to the coronation of a king should be observed."[68] Physical sex and legal gender were two quite different things here; by virtue of ritual fiction she was considered in this case to be a man. The frailties of her sex could be ignored when the rulership claims of the All-Highest Archducal House were at stake. Lord High Steward Khevenhüller trenchantly expressed the same point on another occasion: "In worldly ceremonies, no distinction can be made between the male and female sex, since majesty and supremacy apply to both in the same form and essence."[69]

As already mentioned, Maria Theresa was anointed on her right arm and on her chest in the sacral act of royal unction, just as the prophet Samuel had anointed King David in the Old Testament. At episcopal consecrations, too, the right hand was anointed in accordance with Roman liturgy, the same hand that would go on to administer the salvific sacraments. Even in this liturgically relevant detail, Maria Theresa was treated as a man, without regard for her natural sex.[70] Indeed, gender relations between herself and her husband had practically been turned on their head. Francis Stephen had been almost totally excluded from the coronation, as decided earlier at the diet. At the very spectacle where the institutional order of both the country and the Viennese court was staged with all pomp and ceremony, he had no formal role to play. At best he could view the proceedings informally, like any other common spectator.[71] Only at the very end, at the coronation banquet in the residence where dignitaries, magnates, ministers, and representatives of the estates dined at fifteen tables, was he allowed to make an official appearance and sit at the same table as his wife—albeit not directly to her right, as was customary for a ruling couple, but next to her sister, Archduchess Maria Anna. He thereby showed in almost humiliating fashion that he was an outsider to the Habsburg dynasty and had no say in Hungary–although, or rather precisely because, he had been the king's representative there until recently.

"The Queen thus commenced her reign to general approbation," concluded a contemporary account, even if it was to be regretted that "here and there the war slightly impeded the progress of affairs of state."[72] This was putting it mildly. Enemy troops had invested the hereditary lands; formal diplomatic protests from Bavaria and Spain had been lodged. The conflict with the Hungarian estates had also been concealed only temporarily behind a façade of consensus at the coronation ritual. Negotiations at the diet resumed with as much controversy as before. Besides the central questions of finances and offices, the estates also contested the amount of the "voluntary" traditional coronation gift— the Lower Chamber balked at even the relatively modest sum of a hundred thousand guilders—and the question of Francis Stephen's coregency in Hungary. The refractory estates contended that having two regents would leave the land doubly hard pressed. They expected to be dragged even further into the Habsburg inheritance conflicts if they gave their assent; above all, they feared that Lothringian as well as Austrian families would gain access to their country's offices, sinecures, and assets.[73] Overall, it was a question of securing the lasting independence of the Hungarian nobility against the impositions of Habsburg rule. When the estates finally drafted a formal answer to the royal proposition and delivered it to the queen on July 9, she reportedly burst into tears at their recalcitrance.[74] Maria Theresa gave the estates an essentially negative response. The diet reacted with outrage; many threatened to pack their bags and leave. At the same time, anonymous diatribes against Maria Theresa and the magnates who supported her began to appear in print. As punishment for lèse majesté, the palatine had them consigned to the flames by the public executioner.[75] Meanwhile, enemy armies were marching on Austria, and an attack on Vienna appeared imminent. All this did nothing to improve Maria Theresa's bargaining position. On August 30 the estates presented her with yet another hard-line resolution. At this critical juncture she decided against the advice of her ministers to change her strategy, calling the Hungarians to a general insurrection in defense of the realm. Having previously secured support from the most important magnates behind the scenes, she invited the combined estates to reconvene on September 11 in the castle, where she would present them with a new proposition.[76]

Maria Theresa staged this audience as a dramatic personal appeal. After the Hungarian court chancellor had informed the estates of the dangers threatening the realm, she herself took the unorthodox step of addressing them directly in Latin: the security of the crown, that of her own person and her children were at stake. She appealed to *virtutem et belligeram fidelitatem*, the manly courage and valor of the Hungarians, in the firm belief that they would not fail her in her hour of need. When she mentioned her children, the sources report that she was unable to hold back her tears. Moved by this image of persecuted innocence (*calamitosa innocentia*), the Hungarians cried out, "*Vitam et sanguinem!*", declaring their readiness to sacrifice their lives and shed their blood for her.[77] The primate improvised a speech characterizing the kingdom as one body and Maria Theresa as its soul, promising her all the help she needed against the enemy. The sources do not conceal that not everyone shared in this outpouring of emotion; on the contrary, angry words, threats, and curses were heard as well.[78]

Yet the scene was so clearly the stuff of legend that all dissonant undertones were soon suppressed. It appeared as a threefold triumph: of "persecuted innocence, rightful sovereignty, and feminine beauty."[79] The wild, impetuous, freedom-loving Hungarians, it was said, had been so enchanted by the irresistible allure of the imperiled, fair young mother that they had forgotten all their constitutional liberties and pledged her their flesh and blood. This was a story drawing on the full emotional register of a classic hero narrative: mortal danger for mother

and children, maternal pain and desperate courage, threatened innocence, chivalry and gallantry, the willingness to make sacrifices and look
death in the face, feminine beauty and masculine strength. The scene
was repeatedly retold, painted, and printed, and the European public
lapped it up. In England, where the story was received with "enthusiastic
pleasure,"[80] Hussar costumes immediately became all the rage: "fashionable Gentlemen" were now seen strolling through London "like warriors of the queen of Hungary," noted the *Female Spectator*.[81]

The transfiguration of the scene in the public imagination owed
much to Voltaire, the historian of his own time, who depicted it as
follows:

> The more the ruin of this Princess seemed inevitable, the more cour-
> age she exerted. In this distress she left Vienna, and threw herself into
> the arms of the Hungarians, who had been so severely treated by her
> father and by her ancestors. Having convened the four orders of the
> state at Pressburg, she appeared in the assembly holding her eldest
> son in her arms, almost yet in his cradle, and addressed herself to
> them in Latin. . . . "Abandoned by my friends, persecuted by my en-
> emies, attacked by my nearest relation, I have no resource left but in
> your fidelity, your courage, and my constancy. I commit to your
> hands the daughter and the son of your king, who expect of you their
> safety." At this speech the Palatines were greatly moved, and drawing
> their sabers, they all cried out, *Moriamur pro rege nostro* Maria The-
> resa: "Let us die for our king Maria Theresa." They always give the
> title of king to their queen; and never was there a princess more de-
> serving of this title. They wept when they took the oath to defend
> her; she alone appeared unmoved. . . . At that time she was with
> child, and it was not long since she had written to her mother-in-law,
> the Duchess of Lorraine, "I know not whether I will have a town left
> me to be brought to bed in."[82]

Voltaire's unerring instinct for the telling detail led him to add the presence of the newborn child. This fabricated detail is what first made the
scene perfect, turning Maria Theresa into a Madonnalike figure. And
this is exactly how she was portrayed, as the Mother of God with the

FIGURE 7. Queen Maria Theresa appeals to her Hungarian estates for help against her
enemies, June 1741. Etching by Bernhard Rode, 1779

Christ child, in countless variations in the period that followed (see figs. 7
and 8).[83] Even eyewitnesses were later to remember how moved they
were when a nurse came in bearing the little prince on a cushion. Everyone shed open tears, it was claimed.[84] In Voltaire's version of events,
Maria Theresa's fear that she would not even find a refuge for her impending confinement likewise recalls the story of the holy family. A
further hagiographical embellishment was added later, placing Maria
Theresa in the tradition of her ancestors and their struggle for the true
faith. She had, it was said, taken the same crucifix with her to Pressburg
that her forebear, Emperor Ferdinand II, had knelt before when he received a prophetic vision in 1619. He had heard the words *Non te de-
seram,* "I will not leave you!" coming from the cross.[85] The Madonna
scene accorded with the stereotypical view of the Hungarians as a nation of "most cruel, bloodthirsty, rebellious traitors,"[86] who, finally
tamed, had found their way back to their true, rightful, Catholic rulers.

Kaiserin Maria Theresia
Serie 609 Bild 5

GARTMANN SCHOKOLADE

FIGURE 8. Maria Theresa with the heir apparent at the Hungarian diet in 1741. Collectors' card from the series "Famous Women." Gartmann Cocoa Collectors' Album

But the story was also in keeping with the gender stereotype of the vulnerable, innocent, and above all beautiful young woman who throws herself on the mercy of savage warriors and transforms them into Christian knights through her heartfelt appeal for protection.

The episode was later elaborated still further for maximum emotional effect. It was told, for example, how Maria Theresa had secretly pinched the child she was cradling on her arm so that he would burst into tears and move the Hungarians to pity.[87] As her nineteenth-century biographer Alfred von Arneth demonstrated, the entire anecdote was apocryphal, since the infant heir to the throne was demonstrably brought only later from Vienna to Pressburg.[88] Yet even Arneth, like other biographers before and since, turned the scene into the stuff of hagiography. As always when the monarch's female psyche was concerned, the sober national historian plugged gaps in the historical record with figments of his own imagination. The dust of the archives was shaken off his otherwise solidly researched account and fantasy given free rein: "A melancholy earnest lay on her features as she slowly and majestically paced the rows of Hungarians.... Her magical gaze filled all who saw her with enthusiasm."[89] For Hungarian historians, too, the scene became a key moment in national history, since it allowed them to reconcile pride in their own national independence with pride in their affiliation to the Habsburg empire. When a constitutional compromise gave birth to the dual Austro-Hungarian monarchy in 1867, Maria Theresa was celebrated as its precursor and the dramatic audience at the diet of 1741 as a quasi-mythical primal scene that any school child could be expected to know.[90] Even on the colorful collectors' cards mass-produced by the chocolate and cigarette industry from the late nineteenth century onward, the best index of the popularization and mythologization of history, no motif involving Maria Theresa was so beloved and widespread as that of the mother with child surrounded by her devoted Hungarian subjects.[91]

In fact, opposition from the estates at the diet had been far from silenced by the queen's dramatic appeal. The assembly went on for a further six weeks following this supposedly watershed moment. On October 29, after meeting ninety times over a period of more than five months, the estates reconvened for a ceremonious final session. From the Habsburg point of view, the overall results were somewhat disappointing: while Francis Stephen was installed as coregent and the estates, having been guaranteed almost all the privileges to the extent requested, agreed to a tremendous levy of around a hundred thousand men, the actual delivery of troops proceeded sluggishly and incompletely.[92] The biggest winners were the Hungarian magnates who had supported the queen at the diet; they were rewarded with valuable gifts, military promotions, and appointments to court service.[93]

In the period that followed, Hungarian troops nonetheless formed a lynchpin in Maria Theresa's war effort. She continued her policy of harnessing the country's enormous potential to her ends by obligating the Hungarian nobility through symbolic signs of her favor.[94] In 1760, for example, she created a Hungarian lifeguard to protect the royal family. Its members also escorted the archdukes whenever they went on campaign and enjoyed privileged access to court apartments. After the Seven Years' War, when her financial need was even greater than in 1741, she established the Order of St. Stephen as a special source of prestige for the Hungarian aristocracy, hoping thereby to reduce the crushing state debt. In this she was only partly successful. The conflict between the crown and the Hungarian estates broke out again at the diet of

1764–65. This time the estates refused to pay the additional taxes demanded of them. Maria Theresa indefinitely deferred the diet and proceeded to implement reforms in favor of the peasants, on justice, education, and medicine without the consent of the estates, relying on the support of loyal office-holders from the native nobility.[95] She failed to uphold the commitment she had made in 1741 that she would regularly visit the old royal city of Buda and reside there. She never resided in the very comfortable, spacious, and modern castle built for her use, which dominates Castle Hill to this day. On the occasion of the controversial Pressburg Diet of 1764, while making a brief detour to Buda to inspect this ambitious and expensive building project, she ruefully admitted that "it was indeed quite ridiculous to erect such a magnificent building, and one so sumptuously decorated in the latest fashions, at such a place, when it was plain for all to see that the court never would nor could reside there."[96] By way of compensation, in 1771 she at least ordered one arm of the saintly King Stephen to be transferred from its resting place in Ragusa (today's Dubrovnik) to Buda, where she had the relic put on display in a purpose-built chapel.[97] In this way, the first Hungarian king himself came to reside in the old capital in her stead, if only *pars pro toto*, his miraculously preserved hand representing the power of the Hungarian monarchy to withstand the vicissitudes of time. Central control of Hungarian resources, meanwhile, was organized through the Hungarian Court Chancellery in Vienna.[98] In the imposing Baroque palace built by Fischer von Erlach in the Bankgasse, where this institution radiated the glory of the Hungarian monarchy (and today still houses the Hungarian embassy), Maria Theresa later hanged a series of seven large-format ceremonial paintings commemorating the Hungarian coronation.[99]

The Queen Is Naked

At the beginning of 1742 the situation for Maria Theresa looked dismal, despite the promise of Hungarian aid. The previous October the Upper Austrian estates had gathered in Linz to pay homage to Karl Albrecht of Bavaria as their new territorial overlord; in November he had entered

Prague in triumph and likewise been hailed by the estates there as the new king of Bohemia. On January 24 he was unanimously elected emperor by the electors in Frankfurt am Main at the instigation of the French Marshal Belle-Isle. Maria Theresa formally protested to the Imperial Diet that the election was invalid because, as the rightful Queen of Bohemia, she had not been allowed to cast her vote in accordance with the electoral rules stipulated in the Golden Bull, but her protest was ignored. Shortly thereafter, on February 12, the Bavarian's brother, the Elector and Archbishop of Cologne, crowned him emperor in Frankfurt am Main, where, as he himself proudly remarked, he was the cynosure of all eyes in the world.[100] The coronation followed medieval tradition but was staged with unprecedented splendor. A witness from Versailles noted: "This was a wonderful day for France. . . . To achieve this success, France had promised every willing prince a territory that would advantage him at the expense of the House of Austria, which was to be destroyed. This may cause some consternation in the Empire, used as people are to the rule of this house, especially the common folk, this slave of habit."[101] Yet events took a different course. The new emperor was forced to remain in Frankfurt, for his own country had in the meantime been largely occupied by Austrian troops. His residential city, Munich, capitulated just two days after the coronation. His lack of a secure power base, disguised only with the help of French troops and his Prussian and Saxon allies, was shown up by the fact that now, as Emperor Charles VII, he had to make do with a makeshift substitute court in Frankfurt.

The outlook for Maria Theresa was nonetheless bleak. After the Spanish fleet landed in Tuscany in November 1741, a new theater of war opened in Italy as fighting continued in Bohemia, Moravia, and Silesia. The new Russian tsarina Elizabeth, an ally of Maria Theresa's, was at war with Sweden and offered her no material aid. The Dutch Republic insisted on neutrality. And Maria Theresa's English allies repeatedly urged her to give ground and make peace with her enemies. For the English, the War of the Austrian Succession was only a sideshow in a far bigger geopolitical game. Even Francis Stephen drafted peace proposals offering concessions to Prussia and Bavaria in order to be rid of the French, but his wife was unrelenting.[102]

The traditional view of Prussian-German national historiography, which stylized the conflict as the opening round in a long-running duel between Maria Theresa and Frederick the Great, distorts the proportions and blinds us to the global dimension of the conflict. In reality there was not just one war but several, a bundle of interrelated military conflicts waged at varying intervals on a number of fronts in Europe and far beyond: not just in Silesia, Bohemia, and Bavaria, on the Rhine and the Main, in Lorraine and the Netherlands, in Italy and Provence, but in India and on the Atlantic as well. In the background stood a structural conflict of interests between the two Bourbon kingdoms of France and Spain, on the one hand, and the two "sea powers" Great Britain (in personal union with the Electorate of Hannover) and the Republic of the United Netherlands, on the other. England and France fought each other at sea for trade privileges and colonial possessions in southeast Asia and America. From the end of 1739, England was also at war with Spain.[103] As a result of this constellation, the English always appeared as natural allies to the Habsburgs in their ancient rivalry with the Bourbons, while the French court regularly sided with Habsburg enemies. But English politicians had no interest in having the conflict over the Habsburg succession drive ever more allies into the arms of their French adversaries. They therefore urged Maria Theresa to make concessions. Meanwhile, the help promised by England in the form of troops and subsidy payments had yet to arrive.[104]

As the loser in the ongoing conflict, Maria Theresa was the butt of cruel jokes. The European public poked fun at her spectacular misfortune with caricatures which drew their satirical point from the sexual connotations of warfare.[105] The struggle between potentates, just like the battle between the sexes, involved attack and defense, siege and subjection, victory and defeat. In war, as in love, everything ultimately came down to power or potency—*potentia*—and female resistance only whetted the male appetite for conquest. The war's sexual connotations were not lost on pamphleteers at the time. In the struggle for the Habsburg inheritance, the metaphor of military conquest as the overpowering of a weak woman by strong, virile men appeared to have become a reality. A series of illustrated fliers appeared on the liberal

FIGURE 9. Maria Theresa is stripped of her clothing. Anonymous Dutch broadsheet, c. 1742

English and Dutch print market depicting the military situation in terms of sexual conquest or even rape. The scenario of the beautiful young heiress stripped of her clothes, her honor, and her lands was gleefully staged in a number of more or less explicit variants.

In one we see Maria Theresa on a sofa, naked to the waist—the artistic motif of the falsely accused Susanna in the bath is here transposed to the boudoir—struggling in vain to fend off the unwanted advances of a cavalier kneeling to her right (the king of Prussia), while a cleric, the French minister, Cardinal Fleury, gropes her from the other side (fig. 9). Meanwhile, another gentleman caller—the elector of Bavaria— steals out the door with the crown and scepter, a second—the Spaniard—holds up an (Italian) stocking, and a third–presumably the Grand Pensionary of the United Netherlands–sits unperturbed beside him with a declaration of neutrality in his hand. A fourth figure lurks passively in the shadows—Francis Stephen, the impotent husband?— and laments the curse lying on the House of Austria.[106] The roles are reassigned on a second print (fig. 10), where Maria Theresa is shown

FIGURE 10. Maria Theresa is undressed. Anonymous broadsheet, c. 1742

standing at the center, stark naked, in the pose of the Medici Venus. A cardinal, glancing furtively around him, grasps the queen's right hand, which is covering her private parts, while the other gentlemen make off with various items of clothing: on the right, the Bavarian with the imperial crown and the Bohemian dress; beside him, a Prussian with the Moravian chemise and a Pole with the Silesian overskirt; on the left, two gentlemen with stockings from Milan and shoes from Parma.[107]

A third Dutch broadsheet is even more explicit in presenting the course of events as a rape scene (fig. 11). Maria Theresa is shown lying on the floor of her bedroom in front of her bed of state, legs splayed and bared to her upper thighs, in a torn, open bodice and short underskirts. One of the intruders, an impudent young Prussian dandy, the "Mof," is reaching for her skirt while a Frenchman and a Pole—"Waal" and "Polak"—squabble over booty behind his back; a fourth figure in the foreground to the right, the "Boer," identifiable as a Bavarian by the lion at his side, is already leaving the scene with his stolen treasure. Shoes, stockings, and an overturned chamber-pot lie scattered on the floor, along with a chest from which multiply sealed documents have been

EEN VROUW VAN EEDEL BLOET, WERD HIER BEROOFT VAN LANT, EN GOET.

FIGURE 11. *Een Vrouw van eedel Bloet.* Anonymous broadsheet, Netherlands, c. 1742

ripped. The little heir in his cradle is stretching out his arms for help. Yet salvation is at hand: armed troops are pouring in through the door to the right; one defender is already poised to bring his sword down on a fleeing thief. The caption to the image takes the side of the "lady of noble blood" who is being so flagrantly violated.[108] An English print in even coarser taste shows a team of physicians applying an enormous enema, various concoctions, and emetics to purge Maria Theresa of her worldly goods.[109] Others staged the war in more gallant form as an invitation to a dance,[110] or as a game of billiards played by princes.[111] The subtext of most of these images was unambiguously sexual in nature: the frail woman was shown succumbing to strong and powerful men. Even if the images made her cruel suitors look unattractive and were therefore likely to arouse sympathy for the innocent Queen, they still suggested that males were now forcefully reasserting their natural position of dominance in the sexual hierarchy. Victories to the Prussians,

Bavarians, and French had corrected the gender imbalance caused by female rule in the House of Habsburg.

Yet not for long. The tide turned once again. In July 1742 Frederick II (temporarily) deserted the ranks of Maria Theresa's enemies in the Peace of Berlin, brokered by England. In return, he retained the economically highly developed province of Silesia—an unprecedented achievement that immediately increased his territories by around a third and nearly doubled his subject populace. Following Prussian military successes in Bohemia, Maria Theresa felt constrained to sign away Silesia in order that she might now concentrate all her energies on the war against the Bavarians and the French. A little later Augustus of Saxony-Poland joined the Berlin peace accord. Enemy troops were driven out of Upper Austria and Bohemia, and Prague was recaptured toward the end of 1742. In Italy, too, Habsburg troops went on the offensive, emerging victorious from the battle of Campo Santo in February 1743. Reconquering the Kingdom of Naples from the Bourbons now appeared a distinct possibility. In the meantime, troops from the Netherlands, England, Hannover, and Hesse had come together in the so-called Pragmatic Army to support the Austrians against the French. By May 1743 Maria Theresa could enter the Bohemian capital, with all the pomp and pageantry befitting the occasion, to be crowned king of Bohemia. On her way back to Prague she learned that the Pragmatic Army had won a spectacular victory against the French at the battle of Dettingen on June 26.

Now the caricaturists, pamphleteers and balladeers turned the tables. The image of the disrobed Queen was reprised and directed against the "sham emperor" from Bavaria:

Einstmals sah ich ihr Porträt	Once I saw Her Highness
Als ob sie ein Kleid anhätt,	Depicted in a dress.
So aus allen ihren Landen,	From all the lands she owned
die sie hatte, was bestanden;	The royal dress was sewed;
Ihre Feinde standen schon,	Around her stood her foes
Jeder schnitt ein Trumm davon.	Who each snipped at her clothes.

Dass euch nicht die Scheer zerbricht!	May your shears not break! I thought.
Dacht' ich.—Alsbald, was geschicht?	And now I can report:
Kleider dieser Landesmutter	The clothes worn by Her Majesty
Haben ungarisch Unterfutter;	Are lined with fur from Hungary.
Nur des Königs Friedrichs Faust	Only King Frederick's fist
Hat ein Lock in Sack gezaust.	Punched a hole in their midst.
Was thut dieses wackre Weib?	Her body bared to public view
Sie hält was auf ihren Leib.	What does the good woman do?
Kann kein Loch in Kleidern leiden,	To mend the ugly slit
Sondern flickt es fein beizeiten;	She reaches for her sewing kit;
Wie haushaltisch ist sie doch,	Thriftily she finds a match,
Setzt ein bayrischen Fleck auf's Loch.	Covers it with a Bavarian patch.

The image of the queen stripped bare could be found even on medallions, media not only of triumphalist propaganda on the part of the ruling class but also of popular cultural memory. A satirical victory medallion, available in silver or copper, showed the well-known motif of the naked Maria Theresa between Cardinal Fleury and Charles VII, who is shown running off with a pair of hose under his arm. The reverse side made clear how dramatically the situation had changed in the queen's favor: Maria Theresa, now with the crown on her head, calls after the emperor, who is about to lose his own crown, "*Vous avez perdu*," or "You have lost," and "puts on the Bavarian hose."[112]

This change in military fortune needed to be exploited as quickly as possible to dispel any doubts about Maria Theresa's legitimacy as Queen of Bohemia. That was the purpose of her coronation in Prague's St. Vitus Cathedral on May 12, 1743. The ritual of investiture was anything but a "merely symbolic" display devoid of relevance for "real" power politics, as older historians maintained.[113] Maria Theresa's apparently disrespectful remark about the Crown of Wenceslas, which had been created by Emperor Charles IV in 1337 and consecrated to the Bohemian patron saint—that it looked like a "fool's cap"—has often been cited in just this sense.[114] It was taken to mean that Maria Theresa derided the medieval tradition of Bohemian kingship given tangible presence in the crown. It is hard to imagine, however, that Maria Theresa would have been so insensitive to the venerability and sanctity of the Bohemian crown, particularly considering how much her own legitimacy depended on it. Indeed, the golden Crown of Wenceslas looked no more anachronistic than the even older Crown of St. Stephen. In sharp contrast to her husband's later coronation as emperor, on this occasion her own sacral legitimation as crowned and divinely consecrated head of one of her most important hereditary lands was at stake—a dignity, moreover, which had to be defended in a situation of existential peril.

Just how crucial the coronation ceremony was still considered to be for monarchical status is demonstrated by the opposite case of Karl Albrecht of Bavaria. Unable to lay his hands on the Crown of Wenceslas, which was locked up in the imperial treasury in Vienna along with all the other Bohemian regal insignia, he had not been crowned in Prague and had to make do with the estates' homage instead.[115] Substituting an alternative crown was out of the question, since the correct execution of the ritual demanded that the "authentic" insignia be bestowed. They alone conveyed the mythical aura of St. Wenceslas and the divinely ordained continuity of Bohemian kingship. It is thus hardly surprising that the other prince-electors at the imperial election were unprepared either to recognize Karl Albrecht as king of Bohemia or to let him cast the Bohemian electoral vote.[116] Without anointment and coronation, the Bavarian's royal legitimacy was highly dubious; it lacked the seal of divine approval and had more than a whiff of violent usurpation about it.

It was therefore all the more important for Maria Theresa that her exclusive right to the Bohemian crown be affirmed as soon as possible through her coronation. Planning for the ceremony got underway immediately after the French retreat from Prague. It was intended to follow exactly the same course as her late father's coronation there twenty

FIGURE 12. Maria Theresa's coronation as king of Bohemia. In Johann Heinrich Ramhoffsky, *Drey Beschreibungen, Erstens: Des Königlichen Einzugs, welchen [...] Maria Theresia [...] in Dero Königliche drey Prager Städte gehalten, Andertens: Der Erb-Huldigung [...]; Drittens: [...] Königlich- Böhmischen Crönung*, Prague 1743

years earlier. No expense was spared for the coronation procession, with its massive cortège; a lavishly produced commemorative volume illuminated with large-format copperplates ensured that the event would be appropriately publicized in European court circles.[117] On the very day of the ceremony, news of victory over the Bavarians at Braunau arrived in Prague—a coincidence that, while perhaps a little manipulated, was still taken as a happy omen, "as a manifest decision by the most exalted judge, who . . . has cast direct judgment on the lawfulness of her [Maria Theresa's] right of succession."[118] The coronation itself, like its Hungarian and German counterparts, followed a pattern that had originated in medieval France before spreading throughout Europe. For this ceremony, as for the earlier one in Hungary, Maria Theresa was both compelled and empowered by ritual fiction to "change her sex," as she herself reportedly once put it.[119] As in Hungary, she became *rex et sacerdos* upon being anointed and defender of the faith upon receiving the sword. In the coronation laudes she was again addressed as *rex foemina* rather than as *regina*, and here too a woman was crowned king for the first time in the history of the realm. The contemporary loyalist press took up the motif with gusto, praising Maria Theresa in broadsheets and panegyrics as *foemineus princeps, mater,* and *masculus heros,* as "feminine prince, mother, and masculine hero" in one. Her first biographer repeated in 1747 "what so many writers and newspapers have been proclaiming for the last four years: in appearance a woman, in her heart a man, and a goddess in her surpassing grace."[120]

Following her coronation, Maria Theresa received the homage of the Bohemian estates, including those who had earlier bowed in "invalid homage" before the Bavarian, Charles VII.[121] Not a few Bohemian magnates and many knights were among them. Those who had lived solely off their Bohemian lands, neither holding high office nor receiving honors at the Viennese court, had been more inclined to throw in their lot with the Bavarian. In Bohemia as in Hungary, there was a sizeable contingent, drawn mainly from the lesser nobility, who were disaffected with Habsburg rule and looked forward to a greater degree of autonomy from a weak king. Furthermore, the Bavarian had put considerable pressure on the estates, threatening to punish them in the event of "disobedience." For all that, over half the Bohemian nobility had avoided pledging him their personal fealty, pleading illness as an excuse or sending a representative to pay homage in their stead. Some had even incurred Maria Theresa's displeasure by asking her for her permission to pay their homage to the Bavarian in writing. The Bohemian estates, like the Upper

Austrian estates in Linz, were now hauled before an "inquisition" charged with determining those who had been particularly disloyal to their queen. Yet the vast majority escaped punishment. Maria Theresa's acceptance of the estates' contrite homage in Prague (and also in Linz) could be understood as a demonstrative gesture of reconciliation.[122] By pardoning the renegades for their disloyalty, she obliged them to give all the more convincing proofs of their devotion in future. The credit she was willing to extend them was calculated to yield high returns in years to come, payable in the currency of political reliability. In the event, it did not take long for some of the former turncoats to regain high office, the Bohemian Kolowrat family being the most prominent example. And those who had demonstrated their unswerving loyalty to the Habsburgs were rewarded by being made privy councillors or chamberlains when she was crowned in Prague.[123]

Forced onto the defensive on all fronts in the summer of 1743, Charles VII found himself compelled to open negotiations with Maria Theresa. The Imperial Diet offered to mediate between queen and emperor.[124] The French, too, pondered how they might come to terms with their enemies following their spectacular defeat at the battle of Dettingen in June 1743. At the same time the "Pragmatic Army," led by George II of England, pulled out of the conflict in the Rhineland, much to Maria Theresa's bitter disappointment.[125] And in Italy she was forced to make considerable concessions to her ally, the king of Sardinia, to dissuade him from coming to terms with her opponents.[126] All the signs now pointed toward a diplomatic solution. Yet the queen rejected all offers to negotiate a settlement. She insisted on her duty to defend the sacred right of her dynasty, come what may. Now that the military situation was improving, this meant compensating for the loss of Silesia, which she had been forced to accept by treaty, through further conquests. She thus contemplated keeping Bavaria and compensating Charles VII at the cost of the Spaniards with the Dual Kingdom of Naples and Sicily, a plan that ran aground on English resistance.[127]

In the year following her coronation in Prague, Maria Theresa's situation deteriorated still further. In Italy Austrian troops prosecuted their war for the Kingdom of Naples on the neutral ground of the Papal

States, but a decisive victory eluded them. In the Habsburg Netherlands, the French opened a new, fourth theater of war in early 1744 and
now formally declared war as well, having previously only contributed
auxiliary troops to the Bavarians. Maria Theresa sought to persuade the
English and Dutch to launch an offensive against France, but to no avail.
Instead, in summer she sent her own troops over the Rhine under the
command of her brother-in-law, Charles of Lorraine. Meanwhile, Frederick II was busily hatching plans for a renewed intervention. He entered an alliance with the emperor, the Elector Palatine and the Landgrave of Hesse-Kassel—purportedly to defend the imperial constitution
and restore Charles VII to his ancestral land of Bavaria, but actually, as
recorded in a secret treaty, with the intention of annexing Bohemia.
Maria Theresa was not only at war with the elected and crowned head
of the Empire, she was now also acting in violation of imperial law by
allowing her foreign—Hungarian—troops to move through uninvolved
imperial territories and requisition supplies there. This offered the Prussian king a welcome pretext to present himself to the Empire as an up-
holder of justice and peace, a claim that was well received in some quarters of the Empire.[128] On July 29, 1744, he ordered sixty thousand men
to march into Electoral Saxony, officially as auxiliaries sent in support
of the emperor. Disasters now befell Maria Theresa on all sides: Prague
capitulated to the Prussians on September 16; Charles VII reconquered
Bavaria; the French invaded the Empire once more. The Dutch theater
had ground to a stalemate, and Austrian troops were forced to pull back
in Italy.

Maria Theresa staked everything on forging a grand coalition against
Prussia. By January 1745 she had succeeded. The Russian tsarina mobilized troops as Austria-Hungary, Saxony-Poland, Hannover-England,
and the Dutch Republic joined the Warsaw Alliance. Maria Theresa too
drew on a rhetoric of peace and justice to make an appeal to imperial
patriotism, for she as well could point out that the emperor—an illegitimate pretender, in her eyes—had summoned foreign troops into the
Empire who were likewise marauding through neutral territories. Moreover, in 1742, at the suggestion of Frederick II, Charles VII had already
contemplated strengthening his hand by unilaterally mediatizing a

number of free imperial cities and prince-bishoprics—Freising, Passau, Augsburg, Regensburg, Würzburg, Bamberg, Eichstätt, Salzburg—and incorporating them into his Bavarian territory. This would have signified a flagrant breach of the imperial constitution. Yet the crisis was averted when Charles VII died unexpectedly on January 20, 1745 at the age of forty-eight.

The new prince-Epector of Bavaria, Maximilian Joseph, was only seventeen at the time. In April 1745 he came to terms with Maria Theresa. Frederick II also made a peace overture but she rejected his offer, determined to win back Silesia. Yet her belief that this was still possible proved illusory. On June 4, 1745, the Prussians inflicted a crushing defeat on the Austrians at the battle of Hohenfriedberg. Shortly before, on May 11, a French army numbering 90,000 had defeated the Pragmatic Allies at Fontenoy on the Schelde River in a two-day-long engagement that incurred high casualties on both sides. The path to Flanders was now clear. The English withdrew from the conflict; they had more pressing concerns when in August 1745 the exiled Catholic pretender, Charles Stuart, landed in Scotland to lead an uprising against the king. The English emissary once again urged Maria Theresa to conclude a peace treaty with Frederick II, who offered her in return his vote for her husband's election to the imperial throne. Yet Maria Theresa refused to entertain the offer. She explained to the Venetian ambassador why she resisted and would continue to resist making peace with Prussia: it was not from obstinacy but from bitter experience; the king was not to be trusted.[129] The English emissary Robinson noted her indignant remark that "the Grand Duke is not so ambitious, as you imagine, of an empty honor, much less to enjoy it, under the tutelage of the king of Prussia. . . . The imperial crown! Is it compatible with the fatal deprivation of Silesia?"[130]

The question had become acutely relevant, since negotiations for the election of the new emperor were now underway.[131] In February the elector of Mainz had invited the other electors to Frankfurt, including the queen of Bohemia. The objection of her opponents that Maria Theresa, as a woman, was not entitled to the Bohemian vote, was thus peremptorily swept aside. This was hardly by chance, given that the Mainz elector, Friedrich Karl von Ostein, owed his status as the Empire's second highest-ranking dignitary to his connections in the Habsburg patronage network. A French attempt to set up the elector of Saxony as a rival candidate for the imperial election foundered on his lack of interest in the role. French pamphlets disputed that Francis Stephen, as a "foreign" interloper who ruled over Tuscany, even had the right to stand for election. They alleged that, through his election, the House of Habsburg was in effect seeking to make the imperial crown hereditary in the female line.[132] Such objections failed to resonate for the simple reason that there was no credible alternative to Francis Stephen. The disaster of the Wittelsbach reign had made clear that any aspirant to the imperial throne would need a strong and secure power base of his own. The negotiations prior to the election in Frankfurt were not about which candidate would be elected but the concessions he would have to make. In the end, Francis Stephen was elected emperor on September 13, 1745 with the votes of Mainz, Cologne, Trier, Bohemia, Saxony, Bavaria, and Hannover. The emissaries from Brandenburg and the Electoral Palatinate registered their protest in advance and left Frankfurt the day before the election to avoid having to bow to the majority decision. Maria Theresa took part only incognito in the solemn coronation of her husband in Frankfurt's Cathedral of St. Bartholomew on October 4, 1745; despite Francis Stephen's urgings, she refused to be crowned empress herself.[133] This would prove to be the only journey "into the Empire" she ever made.

It took a series of further military defeats—against the Prussians at Soor in September, against the Spanish in Lombardy, against the French in the southern Netherlands—before Maria Theresa finally gave up her embittered resistance and declared herself ready to extend an olive branch to Frederick II. On December 25, 1745 she reluctantly agreed to the Peace of Dresden and was thus forced to accept the loss of Silesia a second time. Yet the war was not yet over now that Bavaria and then Prussia had left the fray. Far from it: fighting not only continued in Italy and the Netherlands, new fronts opened up as well. Brussels, the capital of the Habsburg Netherlands, capitulated in February 1746; a number of other Flemish towns followed suit. By October the Austrian troops had lost their last fortresses there. Nonetheless, Maria Theresa adamantly rejected all peace overtures. When Philip V of Spain died in July and the Portuguese offered to broker a peace with Spain, she was not to be swayed. She instead had troops shipped from Italy to Provence to fight alongside the English against the French, with the aim of securing continued English support for her cause. England and France were still locked in a global struggle for supremacy at sea, a conflict in which the English had already notched up a series of spectacular naval victories. In the autumn of 1746 Austrian troops occupied the Republic of Genoa, a Spanish ally, before being ousted in a popular insurrection in December. Maria Theresa then made it her mission to reconquer the republic and punish the rebels. The year 1747 found her still undeterred, planning further campaigns for the new season even though her war-ravaged lands had completely exhausted their finances and were on the brink of economic ruin. A new universal head tax was introduced to provide relief. In the Netherlands, in Italy, and in southern France, the war dragged on.

Throughout these military conflicts, however, diplomatic contacts were always maintained through direct or indirect channels. The war was never total; all parties to the conflict were continuously testing the waters to ascertain how their political objectives might be attained through nonviolent means. Maria Theresa's ambassadors were also involved in this process, but they were continually thwarted by her inveterate refusal, even now, to budge from her demands. She insisted on having the Habsburg Netherlands and the Grand Duchy of Tuscany returned in their entirety, if Naples or Bavaria were no longer to be had. For a long time, she was unwilling to exchange a devastating war for a "bad" peace, notwithstanding all the disastrous consequences.

It therefore came as a great surprise to all concerned when in November 1747, after seven years of war, Maria Theresa suddenly changed her position. Lord High Chamberlain Khevenhüller recorded the spectacular volte-face in a diary entry from November 29, 1747:

But after the Empress had for some time been in an ill humor, since the misery of her troops, which indeed was deplorable and very great, had been described to her in the most moving terms, without any means of redress having been shown her, she resolved that she would need either to replenish her treasury or to make peace. . . . Finally she ordered us to submit to her our written opinion before church on the morrow with regard to the following question: whether she should nonetheless expose herself and her troops to the hazard of a campaign, or whether the time had now come to give her allies a clear notion of her predicament.[134]

She even composed an answer to this question herself on a note that she intended to read out to the ministers after they had voted but thought better of it once her "initial agitation" had subsided. The ministers were embarrassed and wished only for "an honorable exit"; the emperor, Khevenhüller noted with studied vagueness, "*ne faisoit pas trop bonne contenance en tout cela* [had not cut a terribly impressive figure in all this]."[135]

Maria Theresa had evidently arrived at the realistic insight that victory was impossible without far-reaching reforms to the entire military and fiscal system. With the support of her new minister Haugwitz, she now tackled the problem head on, showing as fierce a resolve as earlier when waging war. Yet now it was the turn of the French to hold fast to their favorable position; they were finally close to achieving their long-held goal of bringing the House of Austria to its knees, as the French emissary Saint-Sévérin was quoted as saying.[136] The war continued into early 1748 as negotiations got underway in Aachen. The French and English haggled out the preliminaries to the peace, presenting them to Maria Theresa—much to her outrage—as a fait accompli.[137] Yet in the end it was Maria Theresa who urged haste, eager for her troops to be withdrawn as swiftly as possible from the field. As Minister Anton Corfiz, Count Ulfeld, complained, nobody could imagine the empress's terrible impatience to get started with the much-needed internal reforms.[138] It was not until October 18, 1748, that the war between France on the one side and England and the Dutch Republic on the other was formally ended by the Peace of Aachen. A week later Maria Theresa acceded to the treaty with a heavy heart; the Spanish and Italian belligerents soon followed suit. After almost eight years of war against changing enemies, at an enormous cost in human life and resources, she had succeeded in defending the bulk of her inheritance, losing only Silesia, Glatz, and the three small Italian duchies of Parma, Piacenza, and Guastalla. Both the Pragmatic Sanction and Francis Stephen's claim to the imperial throne had now been recognized by all interested parties. Above all, the French were prepared to relinquish their Dutch conquests, which did nothing to make the Treaty of Aachen popular in France. For all that, Maria Theresa was deeply unhappy with the peace terms and felt herself humiliated in the eyes of the world, especially by the English. She ostentatiously refused to receive the English emissary when he tried to pay her the usual formal congratulatory visit upon the conclusion of peace, and she insisted on "making the whole world see that we participated only under duress in such a bad, inadequate work, already monstrous in its preliminaries and even worse in many of its particulars."[139]

Maria Theresa's biographer and admirer Alfred von Arneth showed considerable understanding for "the harrowing ordeal . . . which this high-minded woman had to endure in the depths of her soul," finding that "her compliance approached the limits of the tolerable."[140] Yet even he conceded that any evaluation of the war's outcome depended on the standard that was applied. Measured against the sacrosanct inheritance of the All-Highest Archducal House, Maria Theresa's rights had been trampled on and her sovereignty diminished. Yet measured against the ambitious plan originally devised by her opponents, which involved breaking up the entire conglomerate of Habsburg territories, measured too against the parlous state of the military and fiscal system when she first came to power, she had held up remarkably well. She was by no means the defenseless female menaced by strong men depicted in the satirical broadsheets from 1741. She was certainly free of any inclination to "lily-livered pacifism," as one biographer remarked of her approvingly in 1917, the year of the Great War.[141] Her use of war as an instrument of policy was by no means as defensive as she made it out to be in the memoranda published in her lifetime and in the apologetic writings she left behind for her descendants. Nineteenth-century national historians were only too happy to swallow this line, particularly as it confirmed the old historiographical cliché that the Habsburgs always preferred leaving warfare to others—bella gerant alii. The image of the beleaguered Queen stoutly defending hearth and home against her enemies largely owed its popularity to its sharp contrast with that of the martial, aggressive, risk-taking Prussian king, and seemed plausible not least because it fitted so neatly into the gender binary. Yet the image does justice neither to the context of the war in its full complexity nor to Maria Theresa's own stance toward it. Recent military history has done much to correct this anachronistic "soft focus portrait of the maternal baroque queen."[142]

It is true that the War of Succession was fought primarily to defend Maria Theresa's legitimate claim to the inheritance; in this she had both tradition and treaty law on her side. Yet for her, too, it was self-evident that conquerors could do as they pleased with the lands they subjugated. She too pursued expansionary goals when they suited her purposes and grasped military conquest as a legitimate opportunity to compensate for territorial losses: whether by acquiring the Electorate of Bavaria or wresting back the Duchy of Lorraine and the Kingdom of Naples—countries that had never belonged to her dynasty in the first place, which she had formally traded for others, or to which she had at some stage renounced her legal claim. After conquering Bavaria, Maria Theresa had herself hailed *Bavariae jure belli domina*, ruler of Bavaria by right of war.[143] Her dynasty's honor, fame, and greatness were the ultimate objectives in her system of values. In this she was no different from all the other princes and potentates of her age. The legitimacy of these objectives went unquestioned, legitimating breaches of contract, territorial exchanges, and military adventures. To these ends soldiers could be sacrificed without compunction. In a much-quoted letter to Philipp Joseph, Count Kinsky, from December 1741, Maria Theresa expressed herself on this point with all clarity: "I am resolved to stake everything, win or lose, on saving Bohemia. . . . I must hold the country and the soil, and for this all my armies, all Hungary shall be destroyed before I yield an inch of it. The critical moment is finally upon us; do not spare the country so that it may be preserved. . . . What the land cannot give of its own free will must be taken. You will say that I am cruel; that is true. But I know that all the cruelties I commit today to hold the country I shall one day be in a position to make good a hundredfold. And this I shall do. But for the present I close my heart to pity."[144]

In the heroic-aristocratic culture of the age, for a ruler to put his own life on the line was nothing out of the ordinary. Yet for the aristocracy this was a reciprocal arrangement–that too is made clear in the cited passage. The tacit expectation of noble families was that their sacrifices would be amply rewarded in the end with the spoils of war—lands, offices, sinecures, and the like. Commoners were never asked whether they saw things the same way. Their lives were simply not taken into consideration, while their welfare was identified without further ado with that of the dynasty. The metaphor of the commonwealth as one big family served this end: it was taken for granted that the children of the country would willingly lay down their lives for the "most mildly maternal Queen" or the "most mildly paternal King." And every potentate, needless to say, had God on their side. For Maria Theresa, too, the welfare and sacred rights of the All-Highest Archducal House were identical with that of the entire Roman-German Empire and all Christendom. When her brother-in-law, Charles of Lorraine, crossed the Rhine with his troops in the summer of 1744, she congratulated him on account of his "services to me, my dynasty, the German Empire, and all Christendom, in addition to the immortal fame you have already won for yourself."[145]

Waging War from Afar

The wars of the ancien régime need to be understood in aristocratic and dynastic categories, not in nationalist ones. They followed the imperatives of the stratified culture of the nobility. Maria Theresa was undoubtedly just as committed as her opponents to the traditional, heroic values of her time. This is shown not least in the question of military high command. The ideal ruler was still the warlord riding at the head of his troops. The commander clad in gleaming armor on his steed stood *pars pro toto* for the physical force on which all rule was ultimately based. That monarchs such as Frederick II of Prussia, George II of England, Charles XII of Sweden, or Karl Albrecht of Bavaria personally led their troops into battle was, to be sure, rather the exception than the rule— "great regents should not expose their sanctified persons to danger unless driven by the utmost need," it was argued by many,[146] yet such conduct was celebrated as the ideal embodiment of chivalrous values. Military commands continued to be the most coveted posts for scions of the high nobility and were all but obligatory for the second sons of a ruling dynasty. It was nothing out of the ordinary for the Habsburg heir Joseph to be assigned his own regimental command at the tender age of six. If a ruler wanted to present himself convincingly to the aristocracy as their supreme overlord, he could do no better than appear before them as a triumphant general. It was not by chance that monumental statues of rulers as mounted warriors had been all the rage among European potentates since Louis XIV.

For Maria Theresa, this posed a serious problem. Women were excluded from military service on account of their sex—even if there were many contemporary tales of disguised female soldiers, and even if artists rendered homage to the ancient myth of the Amazons. In a *Singspiel* by the Viennese court poet Metastasio, the heroine lamented the cruel fate that prevented her, as a woman, from marching off to war.[147] Maria Theresa herself complained about the disadvantages she suffered on account of her sex, experiencing her constantly recurring pregnancies as a burden that she tried as far as possible to ignore. "If I had not continually been heavy with child," she once wrote, "surely nobody would have prevented me from taking on this perfidious enemy [Frederick II] myself."[148] The Prussian emissary Podewils noted in 1747 what people were saying about her at court: "that she had for some time seriously contemplated assuming personal command of her armies. She takes pains to deny the frailties of her sex, and aspires to virtues that . . . women seldom possess. To have been born a woman appears to vex her."[149] She had, after all, already tried out a masculine role as *rex Hungariae* and *rex Bohemiae* and had at least symbolically wielded a sword on horseback. Little wonder, then, that she resented having to oversee the war from afar, relying in everything on stubborn and strong-willed commanders with whom she could communicate only through couriers and letters. It was a poor substitute when she sent Field Marshal Ludwig Andreas von Khevenhüller her portrait and that of her successor in order to be at least symbolically present on the battlefield (Fig. 13).[150]

FIGURE 13. Field Marshal Khevenhüller shows the troops the portrait of Maria Theresa.
Copperplate by Jan Caspar Philips

Appealing to soldiers' personal connection to the queen would, it was believed, increase their courage, dedication, and spirit of self-sacrifice. For this reason, she was also staged as *mater castrorum*, patroness of the camps. Metaphors and panegyrics drew on every conceivable mythological and biblical figure to associate the female ruler with military prowess: she was depicted as the union of Mars and Hera, as Pallas Athene, as the queen of Saba from the Old Testament, as Judith, as a female Siegfried.[151]

If Maria Theresa could not assume supreme command herself, she could at least ensure it stayed in her family. It did not go to her husband, however—at her insistence, he stayed by her side in Vienna.[152] She instead retained her unwavering confidence in her brother-in-law, Charles of Lorraine, notwithstanding his notoriously poor record as a commander. She likewise observed the rules of court patronage in all her other senior appointments to the army. Historians have frequently puzzled over this. Many have been tempted to attribute her loyalty to her susceptibility to the charms of an attractive in-law.[153] Yet that misses the point, ignoring the symbolic and social value accorded to high military command in an aristocratic society.

Maria Theresa evidently never doubted her own superior generalship. Every line of her numerous letters to her ministers and confidants betrays her growing impatience when faced with what she saw as the weakness, timidity, and irresolution of her commanders, her mounting frustration at her own forced inactivity. Although extraordinarily well-informed on all details of military operations, she was also painfully aware that it was out of the question for her to interfere directly in operational matters by issuing orders to her generals from afar. Time and again her letters to her commanders reveal just how hard she found it to keep her hands to herself. She continually exhorts them to "lose not a moment, not waste time, not let trivial matters detain" them,[154] to make "swift resolutions,"[155] to remain "undeterred," to be neither "fearful" nor "subdued,"[156] since nothing could be more damaging than "the prolonged inaction seen hitherto."[157] Most of her commanders saw things differently, preferring not to expose valuable resources and valuable soldiers to unnecessary risk. Their style of warfare tended to be more defensive in nature; open battles involving heavy casualties were avoided in favor of sieges to strategically important fortified positions. Maria Theresa had to put up with being told by her experienced commanders that she knew nothing about war. She nonetheless continued to press on them her often quite detailed strategic and tactical reflections. She even urged her husband—who, in June 1742, over her protests, had taken command in Bohemia—to take decisive action. She recommended that he adopt one of several meticulous plans of attack she set out before him, although she had no choice but to leave him with the decision.[158] Her skepticism about Francis Stephen's courage and resolution can be read between the lines: "In this life and in war, much must be ventured," she implored him. "I am full of courage. . . . Be not afraid!"[159]

Time and again she sought with great energy and tenacity, but also with growing bitterness, to assume control of the war effort from afar, which above all meant mobilizing new resources and keeping a closer eye on how the means already at her disposal were being deployed. She saw herself betrayed, blocked, deceived, and deserted on all sides. She personally oversaw details of recruitment, provisioning, clothing, and equipment, and was frequently irritated to see her instructions followed only sluggishly or not at all: "How is it possible that a matter I expressly ordered to be carried out and that occurs before my very eyes should not be followed through?"[160] At times there was no response to her written commands, and she then demanded to know "who was so lacking in respect and diligence that he failed to reply, so that he may step down from his post until he has learned to do his duty."[161] She expressed her sense of disillusionment to a trusted adviser, Privy Councillor Anton von Doblhoff: "All hands are asleep at the wheel, and if I did nothing to spur them on, nothing would get done."[162] "I have nobody working for me on whom I can depend other than you. . . . I am sick and tired of encountering nothing but difficulties, nothing but corruption."[163]

From the beginning the biggest problem was how to recruit, finance, and equip troops in sufficient numbers, and it grew dramatically worse the longer the war continued. Campaigns consumed hundreds of thousands of guilders each month.[164] Contributions fell short by millions; the money pledged by the estates in the hereditary lands trickled in slowly and incompletely, and those funds that did arrive seeped away along dark channels. In addition to the war taxes officially agreed to by the estates and the subventions provided by the allies, ever new burdens were imposed on the populace: special levies, extraordinary *dons gratuits*, maintenance fees, service contributions, payments in kind. Yet all this was still not enough to cover costs, making it necessary to take up credit with bankers and private individuals at home and abroad. At the same time, fresh troops were continually being sent into the field. Maria Theresa was therefore constantly entreating her ministers to come up with new sources of income. In early 1744 she wrote to Court Chancellor Ulfeld: "The army in Italy faces the utmost misery. . . . They are penniless until May. Truly my heart bleeds, can nothing be done for them?"[165] Or to Johann Franz, Count Dietrichstein, the president of the Court Chamber, in mid-1745: "Nothing more has happened in Italy, either. I demand to know where all the funds . . . are concealed or whether they have arrived. I want to inspect the records."[166] Her commands became ever more strident and threatening the less likely it seemed that military finances could be brought under control. The pay-master of the forces, she wrote to Dietrichstein, was to "make no cash payments without my express authorization, . . . and for this I will hold him personally accountable."[167] Or in August 1748: "I wish to be kept informed and on this point earnestly command that not a single penny shall be paid out, not a hundred guilders, without my signature, else the cashier, or whoever else gives out the money, shall pay for it with his head."[168] Lord High Steward Khevenhüller reports in his diary of Maria Theresa's tendency to lose her temper when confronted with the question of how new funds might be tapped for the armies: "*à quelle occasion* she burst into very heated expressions toward the lord high chancellor, who endured them with great fortitude and moderation."[169]

The problems that plagued the war effort were structural in kind, as Maria Theresa came increasingly to appreciate. Yet to understand her position during the war, it must be recalled that she never saw any actual fighting herself. The battlefields were far away. Even if she was kept regularly informed on current events by couriers, corresponded with commanders, and conferred with ministers on a weekly basis, her everyday life at court was only marginally affected. For those at court, the war was but one object among many that claimed their attention. Reading the diary of her lord high steward makes this strikingly clear. While Maria Theresa's overriding priority was undoubtedly to defend her inheritance, this does not mean that the war was the sole object of her concern in the first eight years of her reign. Her close confidant Sylva-Tarouca wrote about this time in retrospect: "At twenty-four or twenty-five years of age, Maria Theresa had many enemies, precious little money, and also little experience. . . . She depended entirely on her own resources, had to learn the ABC of governance, shouldered the workload of four, and yet somehow found the time to cheer us all by her presence. She rode almost too often, danced, played cards, talked, ate in company at both lunch and dinner, and went on many short excursions, not to mention bearing a child each year; so that back then she had as many reasons as today, if not more. . . . to shut herself off, and yet she still found the time to do all that, and do it well."[170] What Sylva-Tarouca neglects to mention is that she lost two of the seven children she bore during those seven years. One, Maria Carolina, died at the age of one on January 25, 1741, shortly after Frederick II's invasion of Silesia; the other, her tenth child, a daughter likewise called Carolina, was stillborn on September 17, 1748, shortly before the Peace of Aachen was concluded. Her beloved sister Marianna also died in childbirth on December 16, 1744, at just twenty-six years of age.

While all this was going on, the strictly ritualized life at court continued on its customary course: Maria Theresa attended daily church services, opened diets, presided over knighthood ceremonies, enfeoffed vassals, received foreign diplomats, heard petitioners, dined in public, gave soirees and masked balls, celebrated birthdays and name days, sent out invitations to hunting parties and sleigh rides, attended operas and comedies. In this "everyday" life at court that hardly merits the name, consisting as it did of a near-endless series of gala occasions,[171] the war registered only on the margins and in ceremonially subdued form: in parades, promotions, and postilions.

It began even before a regiment took to the field, with the consecration of flags in a solemn Mass. If taking place in Vienna itself, it was celebrated in the presence of the ruling family as a great social event to which all "the leading nobles" were invited. In the case of Prince Louis of Wolfenbüttel's infantry regiment, for example, the consecration was held in the Karlskirche, the Church of St. Charles in Vienna. Guests were then "most gallantly entertained in Prince Schwartzenberg's garden," after which a description appeared where nobles could see their names printed in illustrious company.[172] Parades for regiments that were about to set out on campaign or had just returned victorious from the field attracted similar attention. The troops' clothing, equipment, and perfectly symmetrical exercises were better suited to making a good impression on the parade ground than to the practical demands of warfare. The ever more ornate uniforms, the gleaming colors and gold and silver braids, the high caps tricked out with metal, the plumed feathers and magnificent saddle pads were quite unsuited to any military purpose.[173] Similarly, the drill books with their artificial evolutions were geared less to any actual movements on the battlefield than to public parades and maneuvers, run with clockwork precision and symmetry in accordance with the geometrical ideals of the time. Discipline and beauty were all but synonymous terms. Military drills served above all "to show the world what an army was capable of" and "enhance the commanding officer's reputation" by providing an "optically and acoustically impressive display."[174] The courtly public cast an appraising eye over these exercises and noted how "magnificently," "beautifully," or "marvelously" they came off.[175] Maria Theresa placed great value on seeing such maneuvers performed, sometimes lavishly entertaining the courtiers who gathered for the occasion from her private purse.[176] In summer 1754 she enthused to her friend Countess Trautson about recent maneuvers in Prague: "The eleventh infantry regiment and the third cavalry regiment marched past. Lobkowitz's cuirassiers were wonderful, Ghibert's dragoons no less so; I would like Joseph's [her son's] regiment to be adjusted in this way, blue and red, white shoulder straps, Württemberg red and black, like Savoy, all rather good. From the infantry it was Charles [of Lorraine] who bore the prize, as much for size as for beauty. . . . Brown one of the finest after Charles, all powdered and coiffed *également à la florent*, which looked odd but made an impact."[177]

Apart from regimental parades, war made its presence felt in the residential city primarily through news of victory. Whenever a successful siege or combat was announced, ritual celebrations were routinely held in Vienna and the other provincial capitals, as occurred on similar occasions for public rejoicing. These were finely graded, depending on how much significance was accorded the event.[178] After a messenger on horseback had first conveyed the news informally and discreetly, the same courier, or preferably a senior officer of the victorious troops, rode once more into town. It was determined beforehand how many trumpet-blowing postilions—two, four, six, eight, or even twelve—would ride ahead of him as he officially delivered the glad tidings. At the climax of the spectacle, the officer handed over the captured enemy flags to the queen and received a reward. Bells tolled, gun salutes were fired, court nobles were admitted to offer their congratulations and compliments, the Te Deum was sung in churches, and thanksgiving services were held throughout the land. Public jubilation was ordained for especially brilliant victories: citizens were told to illuminate their houses, victory coins were scattered among the crowds and wine donated. Media reports circulated alongside the celebrations: the *Wienerische Diarium* put out special editions, and foreign newspapers were supplied with accounts of the glorious battle.[179] News of defeat, by contrast, was conveyed with little fanfare and "hushed up as much as possible"[180]—a difficult endeavor if the enemy was not to be given an interpretive monopoly over events. Following the Marshal of Saxony's spectacular victory over Charles of Lorraine at Fontenoy, for example, the court issued a statement where "one or two circumstances had to be embellished somewhat in order to salvage the commander's reputation,"[181] although this could not prevent public expressions of discontent from breaking out on the streets of Vienna.

All her life, Maria Theresa took an enthusiastic interest in military exercises. "*Je suis toute militaire*," she once wrote to her son Ferdinand.[182] She had her sons raised in this martial spirit from an early age, believing that nothing more readily allowed a prince to bring credit to the monarchy and make a name for himself than military service.[183] Of all the tasks of government, military administration was said to interest her the most, and she held officers in the highest esteem.[184] As mentioned earlier, she had learned to ride a horse in preparation for galloping up the coronation hill in Pressburg, and she had thoroughly enjoyed the experience—much to the consternation of her lord high steward, who time and again warned his protégée of the health risks posed by riding, especially during pregnancy. The fact that she rode in a man's saddle, in particular, raised more than a few eyebrows at court (see color plate 23).[185] Riding allowed Maria Theresa to present herself in a male leadership role that was denied her in war. One substitute, albeit a feeble one, was provided by her appearance as a rococo Amazon at a sensational court entertainment, the "ladies' carousel" of January 1743. Carousels or horse ballets, a combination of dressage, tournament, and musical concert, had come into vogue in the early seventeenth century and were a highlight of Baroque court culture. When Maria Theresa was twelve, her father Charles VI had had a winter riding school built especially to that purpose in the Hofburg. Designed by Johann Bernhard Fischer von Erlach, it was the only element of the large castle complex to draw admiration from even the most sophisticated French travelers and was considered the finest riding hall in all Europe.[186] The carousel incorporated much that was characteristic of Baroque aristocratic culture: extravagant material display, chivalrous competition, geometrical aesthetics, precise choreography, virtuosic physical discipline, and above all, in a clear symbol of rule, the horse's complete and apparently effortless submission to the rider's will.[187]

It created a sensation when, in January 1743, "an uncommonly magnificent ladies' carousel, the like of which has never been seen before, nor been recorded in the annals of ancient or modern world history," was held "in the splendid royal riding school" (see color plate 5).[188] The "riders, marvelously attired as Amazon warriors," rode or drove in magnificent phaetons, the queen herself mounted at their head on a white steed. They competed to hit "Asiatic" or Mongol targets with their pistols or spears, or they tilted at dummies' heads with lances or swords.[189] All court society was in attendance, with several "townsfolk" being admitted to the gallery as well; guards were posted "to keep the inquisitive crowd at bay." All the "lady riders" were rewarded at the end with the most exquisite prizes, from diamond earrings to exotic tea services. It was a novelty for such a tournament to be contested solely by women, and the event attracted Europe-wide attention. Even the Parisian *Gazette de France* was forced to concede that this was the first spectacle of its kind in all Europe.[190] It was serendipitous that the repeatedly deferred performance finally went ahead just after Prague had been reconquered, giving it the appearance of a victory celebration. It had not originally been planned this way; Maria Theresa had been practicing for weeks with the Viennese "ladies of court and town" in the court riding school. In November Francis Stephen had already written to his brother reporting that nothing else was talked about at court.[191] Maria Theresa deliberately kept news of her latest pregnancy from getting out until after the performance lest she be prevented from participating. Later historians could not suppress their disapproval at such "excessive frivolity." Even her greatest admirer, Alfred von Arneth, found that such a *divertissement* "perhaps did not fully accord with the gravity of her situation."[192] Yet his judgment is anachronistic. For contemporaries, the court tournament and the "art of war" were of a piece, since both were subject to the same standards of aesthetic perfection. For Maria Theresa the carousel was among the most spectacular highlights of her reign. She subsequently specified that the motif be included in a cycle of large-format paintings she commissioned from her court painter Martin van Meytens.[193] This court spectacle carried an obvious political message. During a war fought against a coalition of male enemies, Maria Theresa was demonstrating to the public, both at home and abroad, her unprecedented sense of herself as a female warrior.

Waging War Up Close

From the nobility's point of view, war was a heroic, honorable affair promising fame and glory, an opportunity to showcase aristocratic virtues, and not least a high art, as expressed in aesthetically disciplined maneuvers and formally impeccable ceremonies. A classic of Baroque military science, Hanns Friedrich Fleming's "Perfect German Soldier" (*Der vollkommene teutsche Soldat*, 1729), took war to be practically the driving force behind a general refinement in conduct that had brought credit to the age: "Ceremonial is at its acme in our times; war itself has played a very great part in this." So-called war ceremonial or *decorum belli* extended to all areas of military praxis, from recruitment via marches, exercises, and parades, the exchange of prisoners, polite intercourse among rulers, generals, and officers, all the way to "battle formations, attacks, bombardments, and capitulations."[194] The strictly regimented geometrical order described by movements in space not only gratified the viewer's sense of aesthetic enjoyment; it also, and above all, exactly reproduced a social order that could only be imagined as hierarchically stratified. This was no different on the parade ground and the battlefield than at a court appearance or ambassadorial audience. The ceremonialization of war was a source of considerable pride to contemporaries. As one of the most recent accomplishments of international law, it was considered a hallmark of civilized nations: "Suchlike occurs only among nations which have grown accustomed to proceeding fairly in the *raison de guerre*, and have, through their particular statutes and regulations, habituated their militia to the ceremonial of war and *decoro belli*."[195]

Needless to say, the reality of war was quite different. The informal, dirty, utterly unceremonious, and unheroic everyday experience of warfare was as far removed from such regimented finery as the chaotic and unpredictable course of open battles. War in Maria Theresa's time was at once more and less than in the modern era. On the one hand, it was the normal state of affairs for many; the "trade" of soldiery was a way of life much like any other. On the other hand, war was never "total"—its effects were not felt everywhere to an equal extent. Everyday life was not dominated by events on the battlefield but by problems of troop recruitment, the transport of men and matériel, provisions, and financing. At the same time, diplomatic contacts were never entirely cut off, "even as the troops marched, sweated, froze, hungered, plundered, and sometimes even fought."[196] Ideally, the civilian population was spared as much as possible by the military, although this remained a pious wish for people living in the regions affected. Armies had been steadily growing since the seventeenth century and now numbered in the tens of thousands. Crisscrossing the country, they brought economic ruin wherever they went—not only to enemy territories but to their own lands and those of disinterested third parties as well. The underlying problem was a structural shortfall in matériel. Inadequate provisioning was not just a question of insufficient funds but also and especially one of logistics. Every soldier was entitled to a daily ration of two pounds of bread, so an army of fifty thousand needed to be supplied with some hundred thousand pounds of bread each day. All that grain had to be bought, stored, protected against vermin and rot as well as against mice, transported, ground, and baked; to this end troops had to bring along their own mills and ovens.[197] Transporting such equipment, along with the heavy artillery and munition, could not be done without thousands of horses, which in turn required enormous quantities of fodder.[198] The organizational frameworks and transport infrastructure of the time were simply unable to cope with such logistical demands. Hunger stalked the enormous armies as soon as they had left behind their supply points in the homeland and moved out of reach of their magazines. While war commissars requisitioned contributions and victuals from the local population, these were generally insufficient and soldiers were left largely to fend for themselves. If their salaries went unpaid, they had little choice but to resort to plunder. Ongoing substandard provisioning and inadequate shelter from the elements increased their susceptibility to disease. At least as many soldiers died on marches and in their winter quarters as on the battlefield. At the same time, the civilian population suffered from troop movements through their territory. The forced contributions and depredations affected seed stores and cost farmers their draft animals, leading to lower harvests in each succeeding year and ever more onerous contributions. In this way, the dreaded vicious cycle of the three heaven-sent plagues—war, famine, and pestilence—started spinning.

War primarily meant siege warfare.[199] Fortifications were dotted throughout Europe, although in the eighteenth century they rarely kept pace with ever more sophisticated siege techniques and the latest improvements to artillery. In the War of the Austrian Succession, a siege lasted twelve days on average before the fortress capitulated, unless a relief army arrived in time to put the besiegers to flight. Pitched battles, where infantries were arrayed in textbook fashion to charge at each other in extended rows of five, flanked by cavalry and exchanging fire at regular intervals, were avoided so as not to expose valuable line regiments to unnecessary risk. Standard nineteenth-century military histories maintained that the few great battles that actually took place determined the outcome of the war, yet this seems questionable. Who had won a given battle was often a matter of interpretation.[200] Generally speaking, the last side left standing on the battlefield was considered the victor. Yet capturing as many enemy flags as possible offered an alternative criterion, as did the number of fatalities, casualties, and prisoners. All this was frequently a bone of contention between the warring parties. Following the battle of Campo Santo on February 8, 1743, for example, both the Spanish and the Austrians claimed victory. The Austrians could point out that they had remained on the field overnight *en ordre de bataille*, but the Spanish passed off their withdrawal as an "entirely voluntary and orderly *retraite*."[201] Conversely, after the battle of Mollwitz the Austrians sang the Te Deum in thanksgiving for their supposed victory.[202] The result of the battle of Velletri in late August 1744 was likewise disputed.[203] It was thus not just the battle that had to be won, but also control over how it was reported and interpreted. After all, the political consequences of a battle depended to no small extent on how disastrous and demoralizing the outcome was perceived to be.

One of the acknowledged successes for the Habsburg side was the battle of Dettingen, a village on the River Main. On June 26, 1743 the Pragmatic Army of the British, Hanoverians, Austrians, and Hessians won a victory against numerically superior French forces—one of the few big, set-piece battles of the War of Succession, and certainly one of the bloodiest.[204] It lives on to this day in the collective memory of the English, at least, since George II personally led his troops into battle and George Frideric Handel composed a famous musical memorial to the king's military fame in his *Dettingen* Te Deum. The fighting began at nine in the morning and continued until well into the evening. The damage to nearby villages caused by foraging and plundering from the Pragmatic Army ran to 148,785 guilders and 4 kreutzer, according to accounts kept by the district of Aschaffenburg.[205] Around 35,000 men fought on the side of the allies, while the French forces numbered around 70,000, not all of whom actively participated in the combat. Total losses, including fatalities, serious injuries, and desertions, amounted to between 2,000 and 2,700 for the allies and 3,500 to 4,000 for the French. Serious injury was a fate worse than death: only a small minority of those who had an arm or leg amputated by the field surgeons survived to tell the tale. Not all the bodies of the dead and wounded were recovered; many were left lying on the battlefield and ransacked for valuables. Some three weeks after the fighting had come to an end, an order was issued "to bury the remaining human and animal corpses completely under the earth lest the hot weather lead to an outbreak of disease."[206] These precautions did nothing to prevent a subsequent outbreak of dysentery. Many who had not succumbed to their injuries or been drowned in the Main on their retreat fell victim to the epidemic. The Leipzig *Genealogical-Historical News* (*Genealogisch-historische Nachrichten*) printed an eyewitness report describing the fate of French captives:

It is impossible to give an adequate description of the misery endured by these poor wretches. Some had had a foot blown off, some both feet, others a hand or both arms; several went around with their heads split open; and who could give an account of all their injuries? . . . It was impossible to look on with dry eyes when they were lifted from the wagons and brought into the hospital, particularly when the surgeon dipped his finger in Rhenish brandy and poked around in the wounds before bandaging them with a wet cloth. When one of them died, he was sewn up in a bedsheet and buried outside the town in a field.[207]

Such descriptions were rare. Battles reports in newspapers and periodicals were dominated by tales of luck and misfortune, skill, courage, and valor on all sides. Adversaries were not dehumanized or demonized; they were respected for their military virtues and abilities. A far deeper division ran between persons of rank and common soldiers than between friend and foe. Social barriers remained standing long after the fronts between friend and enemy had shifted.

Pandurentheresl

War consumed a vast number of human lives. According to an admittedly unreliable source, the armies of the Habsburg monarchy totaled 143,438 men when the War of Succession began; by 1745 this number had climbed to 203,576, a figure that still appeared "almost laughably" small compared with the forces amassed by the French.[208] Soldiers were recruited in various ways. The traditional form was territorial defense (*Landesdefension*): troops were levied from the populace of any given territory, but they could be mobilized by the estates only in defense of their own land in an emergency and for short periods of time. They could also only be deployed in the territory itself.[209] Wars of expansion could not be prosecuted on such terms. From territorial defense, the so-called territorial recruitment system (*Landrekrutenstellung*) had evolved. Under this system, the estates of each territory were expected to provide a set number of recruits, although these could be replaced by financial contributions or recruits from abroad. Farmers, being deemed indispensable to agriculture, were exempted from territorial recruitment, as were Jews, "gypsies" and other foreign "nations." Soldiers were recruited largely from the classes below the peasantry on the social ladder: day laborers, farm hands, the poor and itinerant. Another possibility was for regiments to take recruitment into their own hands, particularly in neighboring imperial territories. Both forms of recruitment generally involved physical duress and the number of desertions was therefore notoriously high.

The largest source of troops for the Habsburg army was Bohemia and Hungary, and in Hungary particularly the military frontier, the region bordering the Ottoman Empire. So-called militia-peasants (*Wehrbauern*) had been settled there at the time of the Turkish wars. Subject to military administration, these men had originally been entrusted with defending the land against Ottoman incursions. Their whole lives were organized around their military usefulness. Once fear of the Turk had gradually subsided, they were increasingly deployed as militiamen in the Habsburgs' other wars. In the War of Succession, the Croatian military frontier alone yielded some 45,000 troops.[210] The frontiersmen were deployed as light troops in so-called petty warfare (*Kleiner Krieg*), where they typically scouted the terrain, provided cover to the main army, foraged, and picked off enemy convoys.[211] They wore their local attire rather than uniform and were reputed to be wild, reckless, ill-disciplined, dissolute, potentially mutinous, and excessively cruel. Their way of fighting was the dark underbelly of the heroic, honorable, ceremonially tamed combat celebrated by the elite, its disavowed yet indispensable shadow side. For Maria Theresa, these troops were of elemental significance. This is shown in exemplary fashion by her conduct toward the legendary Pandur commander, Baron Franz von der Trenck.

Right at the start of the War of Succession, on January 26, 1741, a call had gone out to all the Hungarian counties to provide cavalry to use in defense against the Prussians. Its great success had less to do with spontaneous enthusiasm for the young Queen than with the prospect of *praeda libera*, free booty, entertained by many an impoverished nobleman. The nobles who offered their services for the campaign had expressly been given license to loot and pillage.[212] One of the first to take up the call was Franz von der Trenck (1711–49), son of an East Prussian noble who had acquired extensive lands in Slavonia after the province was wrested back from Ottoman control. In May 1741, Trenck set out for Silesia with over a thousand cavalry he had raised himself. Stopping off in Vienna, they appeared before the monarch and the crowds in a parade replete with martial exoticism, bearing scimitars and daggers, clad in red Capuchin cloaks, and accompanied by Turkish military music.[213] The Viennese had never seen anything like it. The fascination exerted on the public by the Pandurs was highly ambivalent. Through their clothing, weaponry, and music, they symbolically shared in the "oriental" character of their home region. The primitive violence and cruelty attributed to everything that came from the Turkish borderlands now stood to benefit the All-Highest Archducal House and instill fear in its enemies. In the form of the Pandurs, the Viennese were suddenly confronted with a dangerous foreignness that they could nonetheless recognize and even welcome as their own. *Pandurenth'resl*, as Maria Theresa was now called in a popular song,[214] seemed to have domesticated the proverbial cruelty of the barbarian troops from the faraway country behind the mountains and exploited it for the just defense of her lands. Whether this reputation for cruelty was deserved is another matter. Death by impalement, for example, was presented as one of the Pandurs' more gruesome specialties. In fact it was the Habsburg field marshal, Joseph Frederick of Saxe-Hildburghausen, who as organizer of the military frontier under Charles VI had threatened anyone who betrayed his country or defected to the Turks with this form of punishment.[215]

Printers fostered the ambivalent fascination exerted by the wild frontiersmen and profited from it. The Augsburg publisher Martin Engelbrecht enjoyed considerable public success with his copperplate series on Maria Theresa's *milice étrangère*. It depicted a gallery of savages and cutthroats from the Turkish borderlands—Pandurs, Croats, Janissaries, Hussars, Hajduks, Wallachians, Tolpatches, and whatever other names they might go by: "Who else may be found in our German lands? / Are there Moors or even Chinese? / Behold the fashions of these foreign hands, / Whose face and bearing show them dauntless thieves!"[216]

Franz von der Trenck was the most colorful hero in this series. He had fought with the Russians in the last Turkish war and made a name for himself through his extraordinary cruelty, bravery, and lust for booty. He also later made good money with his *Remarkable Life and Deeds* (*Merckwürdige Leben und Thaten*), a more or less fictitious autobiography, cobbled together from anecdotes and plagiarized passages, that was eventually committed to the flames "by the executioner's hand."[217] Trenck, a warlord in today's terms, personified all the atrocities typically ascribed to the irregular forces from Hungary and the military frontier. His cousin and heir, the Prussian officer Friedrich von der Trenck, later remarked of him:

> In his eighteenth year he summarily beheaded an official on his father's estate for disobeying him and thereupon fled to Russia, where he was made major within three years on account of his extraordinary valor. This opportunity was afforded him by the Turkish war. I copy here nothing from his book, only what I was personally told by his comrades and enemies in Russia, to wit, that he often plunged single-handed into a pack of Tatars and on each occasion returned unharmed with a head, once even with three heads, a feat he made look effortless.[218]

He was reportedly court-martialed in Russia for striking a superior officer and sentenced to death, only to be pardoned and demoted. Returned to his father's estates in Slavonia, he found favor with the court in Vienna "by eradicating the robber bands." In fact, many "robbers" only switched sides: "in 1740 he established the first Pandur unit from pardoned robbers and his own subjects, with which he became famous and rich in the Austrian Wars of Succession. He delivered 22,000 prisoners of war to his empress along with contributions of 6 million and performed other meritorious services,"[219] wrote his Prussian cousin. Even taking into account Friedrich's hostility toward his cousin and his surely exaggerated figures, we are still left with the image of an old-style military entrepreneur and adventurer who raised troops on his own initiative and offered his services to his queen as a specialist in dirty "petty warfare" while remaining effectively a freebooter. All his ambition was

FIGURE 14. Pandur. From Martin Engelbrecht, *Théâtre de la malice étrangère. Schaubühne verschiedener in Teutschland bishero unbekannt gewester Soldaten von ausländischen Nationen*, Augsburg 1742–1744

directed at establishing an independent fiefdom in the Hungarian-Ottoman borderlands. In this he was aided by his innate propensity to physical violence. It was said of him that he secretly nurtured the "plan to be made sovereign prince of Slavonia,"[220] preferably with Ottoman support.[221] Such speculations were evidently made with historical antecedents in mind, anti-Habsburg bogeymen such as the Transylvanian prince Gabor Bethlen from the time of the Thirty Years' War.

In the course of the War of Succession, Trenck's Pandurs set tongues wagging as much through their military exploits as through their violent excesses toward the civilian population, but also toward their own people.[222] "The atrocities he committed made him feared even by soldiers," it was said.[223] Yet Trenck's troops were by no means alone in extorting contributions, torching villages, mistreating priests, desecrating churches, murdering peasants, and raping women. The sources are full of reports of such outrages being committed by troops from all sides. Still, light troops were dreaded far more than regular regiments. The diary of Abbot Marian Pusch, superior of the great and wealthy Benedictine Niederaltaich Abbey in Bavaria, conveys a vivid impression of the typical excesses. In 1742 opposing French and Austrian forces set up camp near the monastery on either side of the Danube. The monastery hosted the French generals until their precipitate withdrawal in August 1742, when it was turned over to the Austrian commanders: initially Ludwig Andreas von Khevenhüller and then in November 1742, for a short period, the brothers Francis Stephen and Charles of Lorraine. Trenck also wintered there in 1742–43.[224] The monastery additionally offered asylum to priests, deserters, and refugees, who kept the abbot well-informed about conditions in the surrounding area. Regular troops—whether friend or foe—laid waste to the fields, grazed the meadows, butchered the cattle, fished the ponds dry, and felled entire forests to build their fortifications. The abbot pointed out more than once that the allied French and even Bavarians had "plundered and pillaged with even greater abandon than the enemy himself."[225]

Yet far worse was repeatedly reported of the Croats, Hussars, and Pandurs: they set fire to houses and entire villages, even a hospital with the patients still inside;[226] they abused priests and hounded them naked through the streets, stripped churches of their valuables, trod the eucharist into the dust, spilled holy oil, donned priestly robes, and danced in them to the bagpipes.[227] Anyone who stood in their way was shot or stabbed; a female cook who resisted rape had her hand hacked off.[228] Those who concealed their money were tortured until they revealed its whereabouts. Sometimes even children were abducted or abused to get at their parents' savings.[229] Anyone who produced a writ of protection, procured at great expense from a commanding officer, was shown its worthlessness when their tormentors used it to wipe their backsides.[230] In light of such atrocities, Colonel von der Trenck by no means seemed the worst malefactor of them all; the Abbot of Niederaltaich even praised him on several occasions for "his fine command."[231] But what

FIGURE 15. Pandurs looting a Dutch village. Copperplate by Joseph van
Loo after Frans Breydel, 1746

Trenck's Pandurs did to the town of Cham in the Bavarian Forest in
1742, when its citizens failed to surrender soon enough for his liking,
made the usual excesses pale in comparison: "Everyone they found alive
there," the abbot writes, "young and old, was massacred in good Tatar
fashion, the whole town with its churches and monasteries wantonly
burned to the ground, the holy chalices and invaluable ecclesiastical
implements looted, and the sacred images and relics desecrated."[232]
    Particularly damaging to Trenck's reputation were reports that he
treated his own people with equal cruelty, paying no heed to differences
in rank and status. According to reports at court, "he was unspeakably
harsh to his officers; he often clapped them in irons to force them to
share their booty with him."[233] Then there was the story that "he sent
out divisions to kidnap young girls of thirteen to fourteen years of age,
even such of good family, and after raping them himself he tried to
marry them off to his officers."[234] He also bragged about his bad behavior in public, including at the table of Minister Ulfeld, and "spoke of his
robberies and depredations as if they were so many merry pranks."[235]
Even if he probably did not write them himself, Trenck's memoirs still
convey an impression of what was said about him by others. We read

there that "every officer . . . took as many girls as he pleased." Trenck himself claimed two fourteen-year-old virgins as prizes of war and "used them to his heart's content," such that by the end they had been "thoroughly broken in."[236] Such peccadilloes do not seem to have seriously affected how he has been judged by historians. The charge of *raptus et stuprum*—that is, rape—leveled against him by the Court War Council in Vienna was still being excused in the 1980s as a "pastoral idyll" with a "very young but clearly willing girl,"[237] or treated with barely disguised respect as an "amorous interlude" in the life of the lusty warrior.[238]

Trenck's reputation was well known to Maria Theresa, and it was not at all to her liking. Yet, in war, overriding consideration was given to success against the enemy, and Trenck had sufficiently distinguished himself in this regard for her to promote him, despite his reputation, first to lieutenant-colonel and then to colonel. His fall from grace began when he looted the Prussian king's tent at the battle of Soor on September 30, 1745. Soon after, rumors circulated that his greed for booty had prevented him from taking the king captive or even foiled an imminent Austrian victory. When these and similar accusations showed no sign of going away, Maria Theresa ordered a commission of inquiry. Trenck came to Vienna to mount his own defense, where he caused a stir through his improprieties and extravagances. In his trial before the Court War Council, he was accused of enriching himself at the expense of the army, mistreating his subordinates, and perpetrating outrages against the civilian population in Silesia and the hereditary lands. Among other things, he was alleged to have raped a miller's daughter and had a pregnant woman clubbed to death.[239] Before proceedings had even come to an end, he physically attacked the chairman, Court War Councillor Löwenwolde, and threatened to defenestrate him from the court building. He was then placed in chains and taken into custody. The trial concluded in August 1746 with a death sentence.

Court Chancellor Ulfeld and State Secretary Bartenstein urged Maria Theresa in the strongest possible terms to respect the independence of the judiciary and not pardon the criminal. Ulfeld explicitly praised the courage shown by the military judge, who had resisted pressure from the emperor in pronouncing the death sentence against Trenck. The law alone, not personal gratitude, had to be "the unshakeable guiding principle of any verdict."[240] Yet on account of "very powerful and noble protection,"[241] chiefly from Prince Charles of Lorraine and Francis Stephen himself, Maria Theresa demanded a retrial led by a commission under Field Marshal Königsegg. No friend of Trenck's, Königsegg was considered an exemplary, utterly incorruptible man of honor.[242] The appeal proceedings dragged on for over two years, and members of the commission were subjected to massive influence from Trenck's powerful patrons. When Maria Theresa ordered that the matter finally be brought to a decision, the members of the commission once again voted for the death sentence with only a single dissenting voice.[243] To Ulfeld's vehement disapproval, who warned that "justice was not to be trifled with,"[244] Prince Charles once again successfully interceded on behalf of the condemned. Maria Theresa overruled the commission's verdict, commuted the punishment to lifelong imprisonment, and further saw to it that the prisoner would be accommodated in a manner befitting his class. Trenck spent the last year of his life at Špilberk Castle near Brno. His incarceration should not be imagined as excessively harsh. The empress personally assigned him one ducat a day for his upkeep and permitted him paper, ink, and a manservant, who could enter and leave the fortress as he pleased.[245] On Sundays and holidays, Trenck attended Mass and dined with the fortress commander. When he fell ill, doctors, surgeons, and a priest were summoned to see to his physical and spiritual welfare. Maria Theresa personally approved his request that he be transferred to the Capuchin monastery in Brno and buried with full military honors. Yet nothing came of this, for a man who had forfeited all military offices and dignities was no longer entitled to such ceremonial privileges. Even the empress could not so easily defy military protocol.

It could hardly be denied that the orgies of violence, looting, arson, murder, and rape indulged in by the colonel and his Pandurs were reprehensible even by the standards of warfare; Maria Theresa was well aware of this. She was also determined to protect her subjects from such barbarities, issuing sharply worded edicts threatening to proceed mercilessly against the culprits: "the guilty cannot be punished enough: I do not regard a criminal as worthy of belonging in so venerable a corps as that charged with the defense of the lands."[246] The honor of the military itself required it, she wrote to a commander who had protested that the newly decreed criminal provisions were too severe. Not least, she feared that her subjects would be reduced to penury and driven to rebellion if their villages and livelihoods were destroyed. Yet the case of Trenck revealed a fundamental dilemma that confronted Maria Theresa on other occasions as well: the irreconcilability of abstract, universal norms and personal loyalty. Forced to choose between punishing a notorious war criminal and scourge of the countryside with the full force of the law, on the one hand, and demonstrating her personal gratitude to a decorated war hero, on the other, she opted for the latter.[247] "If he is judged solely by the rules of war, ... then it is certain that he has long merited the death sentence," she wrote to Privy Councillor Doblhoff, the official overseeing the case. Yet she went on to note that she had "dispensed with such [purely military] considerations. I hope that you will not join with the public in believing me to be on his side, nor lend an ear to such reports. They are utterly false; all the same, I cannot deny that I find it difficult to punish a man who has done great deeds on my behalf."[248]

Maria Theresa was faced with a structural problem. Pandurs and other irregular militia met the organizational needs of the military at the time, which required soldiers to show personal initiative. This had consequences for the motives of the commanders and their troops. As early as 1717 an English traveler described the imperial troops at the military frontier as "rather plunderers than soldiers; having no pay, they were practically forced into banditry."[249] The success of the royal call to arms in Hungary, which explicitly gave soldiers license to loot and pillage, was based on the same principle. Maria Theresa knew that "greed for booty had done more to foster insurrection than all the rescripts from the chancellery."[250] It was therefore no wonder that, as Field Marshal Khevenhüller complained, many of the Hungarian insurgents "had taken to robbery, committed great excesses, and were completely lacking in discipline."[251]

In a hierarchically stratified society where the state did not yet enjoy a monopoly on violence, and where the use of physical force was still an aristocratic privilege rather than subject to efficient centralized control, the presence of arms among large sections of the populace was a notorious problem. Those who had access to weapons could potentially turn them against the authorities. Military prowess and freedom had always gone hand in hand; those who were in a position to defend themselves were also entitled to certain privileges. That is why the general insurrection in Hungary was greeted with the greatest skepticism by the Austrian ministers, and it also explains why Maria Theresa initially shied away from deploying the same means in Bohemia to drive out the French and Bavarian forces. On July 5, 1742, by contrast, Charles VII had proclaimed an edict calling on everyone in the French-occupied territories of Bohemia—mostly serfs—to take up arms against the Austrian troops. In return they would be freed from serfdom, retain possession of everything they looted, and receive a three-year remission from taxation. In addition, the emperor promised that they could freely elect their leaders.

This amounted to a frontal assault against the entire social order, not just against hereditary serfdom. As the Court Conference pithily remarked, "There is no land where a distinction is not made between lords and subjects, and to absolve the latter of their obligations to the former would lead to a lack of restraint on one side and discontent on the other, and would fly in the face of justice all round."[252] To the contemporary mind, justice and social harmony were necessarily bound up with class inequality. A situation where the general populace was armed to the teeth was hardly compatible with this vision of society. Charles VII's edict amounted to an invitation for the serfs to rise up against the social order. Such an outcome had to be avoided at all costs.

Charles VII's imperial decree was to be burned by the executioner in a symbolic-ritual act–a traditional rite of punishment normally reserved for the writings of heretics and libertines.[253] Such a display drastically demonstrated the authorities' punitive power while symbolically restoring the divinely ordained order threatened by the offending publication, which was to be destroyed *pars pro toto* by the cleansing power of the flames. Yet, in a handwritten letter to her husband, Maria Theresa objected to the edict being treated in this way: "I have my doubts regarding the executioner."[254] She asked that the decree still be burned, but not at the unworthy hands of an executioner. Executioners were considered to be dishonorable, that is, they fell under a social taboo that sullied the good name of all who came into contact with them, including (indirectly) the author of a text that passed through their hands. In Maria Theresa's eyes a royal edict—however reprehensible its contents—should not be punished in this way. Her reasoning is instructive: crowned heads owed each other respect under all circumstances. No such reservations applied to those of her Bohemian subjects who had already followed the edict and now bore the brunt of the sovereign's displeasure. Disloyal Bohemian villages were razed to the ground by a squad of two thousand cavalry.[255] A juror who had spread word of the edict was publicly executed and then quartered, as Francis Stephen reported from the field to Maria Theresa: "Yesterday, a juryman from a place not far from here was beheaded and afterwards quartered, to general revulsion, because after reading the said edicts in the presence of the judge he proceeded to publicize and disseminate them."[256]

The episode is significant. It reveals once again that the class divide separating potentates from their subjects ran far deeper than hostility between military adversaries. The boundary separating class from class was a categorical one. Defending it at all costs lay in the common interest of rulers everywhere. Moreover, dynasts were linked by multiple ties of blood and intermarriage. Karl Albrecht of Bavaria was ultimately the stepson of the imperial widow Amalia, who lived at the Viennese court, and his wife was Maria Theresa's cousin. It was therefore imperative that his honor not be tainted by the executioner—even though he himself had flouted all the rules of sovereign solidarity by proclaiming the edict in the first place. The edict itself was highly ambivalent: on the one hand it possessed imperial authority, to which respect was due in the interest of the shared hierarchical order; on the other, it incited rebellion against that very order. Faced with this dilemma, Maria Theresa decided to remain loyal to her fellow sovereign. She respected the man who had proclaimed the edict and punished those who followed it. Nonetheless, she herself resorted to the means of armed insurrection, and not just in the case of Hungary—something that her ministers viewed from the outset as fraught with risk—but also in Moravia and Silesia. In early 1742 she issued a proclamation to the populace there, holding out the prospect of booty and tax relief to those who successfully took up arms against the Prussian occupying forces.[257]

Enmity between potentates was always passing. War and peace alternated in swift succession, meaning that today's enemy could easily become tomorrow's ally. The rules of courtesy were therefore never entirely cast aside. The jurist Friedrich Karl von Moser described it as the height of "state gallantry" that the French king had given Maria Theresa thirty hunting dogs upon her accession to the throne even as he was plotting her downfall.[258] The rules of state gallantry even pertained for a time between the Viennese court and the king of Prussia, who had initially offered his services as a protector against Maria Theresa's enemies, albeit on terms bordering on impudence. The difference between an ally, who was compensated for his military support with lands, and an enemy, who willfully seized the lands for himself, was only one of degree. At any rate, Maria Theresa's husband was still corresponding on extremely cordial terms with Frederick II in September 1741, when an armistice was in the offing. He had visited the court in Berlin as a young man, been a guest at Frederick's wedding, and taken a liking to the then crown prince. He now referred to the war almost as a trifling concern: "Since matters in Silesia are turning out to the satisfaction of Your Majesty, I hope to be able to resume the correspondence that I regrettably interrupted during the time of troubles. . . . I doubt not that the friendly feelings which Your Majesty bore towards the queen and myself at the beginning of the war are unchanged. In this hope (in which I believe myself not to be mistaken), I trust that Your Majesty will endeavor to support the queen in the possession of her remaining lands, in order to find in her a true and steadfast ally."[259]

Relations between members of the high nobility were not much different in war than in peace. When great lords took to the field, courtly life continued on campaign. Noblemen could not do without their comforts, and they needed to be adequately represented. "The field postmaster and numerous postilions, the trumpeters and drummers, the many reserve horses arrayed in sumptuous saddlecloths, the cart horses bearing tents, the mules carrying the dinner services, a part of the royal household in the train, the kitchen, cellar, silver, chamber and baggage wagons, the regimental wagons, the Masters of the Hunt, the artillerymen, the various military craftsmen, carpenters, saddlers, blacksmiths etc."—all these not only had to be supplied and quartered but also placed in the correct hierarchical order to prevent conflicts over precedence from breaking out.[260] When George II of England personally took part in the campaign in Flanders, the transport train of his battalion increased by over a mile in length.[261] The noble officers, undeterred by sumptuary laws, strove to emulate him. When the duc de Harcourt set up camp in Niederaltaich Abbey in 1742, he brought with him six cooks, a sommelier, a pastry chef, a confectioner, a silver polisher, three kitchen hands, and a retinue of liveried servants, among others, as well as silver tableware weighing some fifteen hundred pounds.[262]

The social logic governing the demonstration of status did not cease to operate on the battlefield. That was equally true of how adversaries dealt with each other. In keeping with the self-image of the aristocracy, class equals were treated no differently in war than in peace. This gave warfare the appearance of a noble tournament. "If a commander puts up a stout defense of a fortress, he is praised to the skies on surrendering it to the enemy, invited to dine at table, and treated most handsomely. Even in war, acts of courtesy are shown. The greatest princes and generals, despite their mutual enmity, visit each other through their trumpeters, as privileged persons, and exchange compliments. At times they convey their condolences on account of injuries or fatalities. . . . They even inquire as to the whereabouts of each other's main tent, with the assurance that this area will be spared bombardment and cannon fire."[263] Later, in the Seven Years' War, Maria Theresa took pains to treat the Prince of Brunswick-Bevern, a relative on her mother's side of the family, in a manner befitting his high status. She received him at her audiences, hosted him at her table, showed him every conceivable attention, and finally even let him choose between entering her service or returning to his regiment without having to pay a ransom. The prince opted for the latter, perhaps on a point of honor or from religious considerations, as Khevenhüller speculated. Frederick II promptly returned the favor in kind by likewise sending back a captive officer without insisting on a ransom.[264] The abbot of Niederaltaich also reported on several occasions of such demonstrations of noble courtesy amid the horrors of war. Field Marshal Khevenhüller, for example, was full of admiration for the precision with which the French had fired off a single synchronous salvo from forty-nine cannons.[265] When a nephew of the French general Harcourt fell into Austrian hands, Khevenhüller sent him back soon afterwards on a richly attired steed while waiving the usual ransom demand. The French could not withhold their respect for the "enemy's fine and noble action."[266] When the Austrians captured the baggage of Prince Bourbon-Conti, a member of the French royal household, Prince Charles ordered that it be returned intact to "His Lord Cousin."[267] And after Francis Stephen had lodged for a few days in Niederaltaich Abbey in the winter of 1742–43, he expressed his gratitude on his departure with exquisite courtesy by presenting the abbot with a golden snuffbox worth 340 guilders and by giving the abbey's servants 25 "brand new Hungarian talers." Yet it had cost the abbey around 9,000 guilders to provision the army, and this at a time when the local populace, including the monks, were suffering from extreme hunger and had burned their last tools to avoid freezing to death.[268]

In short, there was very little to separate friend from foe, both with regard to the catastrophic impact of their campaigns on the civilian population and so far as fraternizing between noble officers was concerned. A class-specific sense of aristocratic solidarity, operating at the expense of commoners, transcended the shifting allegiances of war. Having transferred their loyalty from the dynasty to the fatherland, the middle-class patriots of the eighteenth century took an increasingly critical view of this international aristocratic elite.[269] Yet this gradual shift in values did not make itself felt until eight years later, when war broke out once again. For the time being, however, peace returned to the Austrian hereditary lands, and Maria Theresa finally had the opportunity to act on a few key lessons she had learned during the War of Succession.

4

Empress, Emperor, Empire

Huldigung des Heil. Röm. Reichs Stadt Franckfurt am Mayn, wie solche Ihro Römisch-Kayserliche Majestät den 11. October 1745. in Allerhöchster Person von dem Magistrat und Bürgerschafft allergnädigst eingenommen.

FIGURE 16. The burghers of Frankfurt pay homage to Emperor Francis I on the Römerberg, 1745. Copperplate by Johann Georg Fünck and W. C. Meyer

Imperial Coronation

Older persons, who were present at the coronation of Francis I, related that Maria Theresa, beautiful beyond measure, had looked on this solemnity from a balcony window of the Frauenstein house, close to the Römer. As her consort returned from the cathedral in his strange costume, and seemed to her, so to speak, like a ghost of Charlemagne, he had, as if in jest, raised both his hands, and shown her the imperial globe, the scepter, and the curious gloves, at which she had broken out into immoderate laughter, which served for the great delight and edification of the crowd, which was thus honored with a sight of the good and natural matrimonial understanding between the most exalted couple in Christendom. But when the empress, to greet her consort, waved her handkerchief and even shouted a loud vivat to him, the enthusiasm and exultation of the people was raised to the highest, so that there was no end to the cheers of joy.[1]

Goethe's famous account in *Dichtung und Wahrheit* (*Poetry and Truth*) was as influential in shaping the later image of Francis I's imperial coronation as it was in creating that of the ideal imperial couple. Goethe combines at least two key messages in this artfully constructed episode. On the one hand, he depicts the imperial coronation as an almost spectral staging of a long obsolete medieval ritual, which at the same time stands *pars pro toto* for the outdated imperial constitution. On the other, the ritual's bizarre anachronism is reflected in the intimate and ironic gestures exchanged by the royal couple, which relieve the coronation of its seriousness while at the same time showing them in their apparently unfeigned, unpretentious, and authentic "naturalness." Their ironic distance toward the ritual performance reduces the human distance separating them from their subjects, who enthusiastically cheer them on as people who are—to all appearances—just like them.[2] At the time Goethe wrote these words, the Holy Roman Empire of the German Nation no longer existed. His depiction is a romanticizing retrospective commentary. It points, however, to a genuine ambivalence in Maria Theresa's attitude to the Empire and the imperial throne.

The election and coronation of a Roman-German emperor stood at the symbolic heart of the imperial constitution. In this highly complex sequence of events, the majesty of empire was made tangibly present in ritual form. Such occasions had become quite rare by the eighteenth century; now, the "old Empire of Germany, almost choked to death by so many parchments, papers, and books, came alive again for a moment."[3] Maria Theresa's attitude to the coronation mirrored her approach to the Empire as a whole. On the one hand, she had pulled all the diplomatic strings at her disposal to assist her husband on his second run at the throne. On the other, unlike many of her predecessors, she declined to have herself crowned empress alongside him,[4] even though Francis Stephen disagreed and repeatedly urged her to change her mind.[5] To that end he had sent her a handwritten letter from his camp in Heidelberg, and when this proved unavailing, he had asked Court Chancellor Ulfeld to plead his case. He argued that the coronation would have a positive effect on public opinion throughout the Empire and would do nothing to detract from Maria Theresa's own regal dignity.[6] She replied that she would rather miss the ceremony, "much as I am reluctant to do so, than be crowned in my present state."[7] This reference to her pregnancy was scarcely credible, given her reputation for carrying on with her duties until just before confinement. Ulfeld reported back to Francis Stephen on his failed attempts to persuade her:

> Your Royal Highness knows very well what Her Majesty is like once she has set her mind on something, and she gave me no answer other than that she does not wish it. If she knew in advance that she would be ambushed, so to speak, and forced to play along as soon as she arrived in Frankfurt, she would surely stay away. I have done my best, at least, to find out why the queen sees the matter in this light, but without success, since she refuses to say another word about it.

She repeated, when pressed, that "the coronation was a mere comedy in which she wished to play no part."

Ulfeld added a cautious explanation of his own: "I can only suppose—at the risk of deceiving myself—that she perhaps holds the imperial crown in lower regard than the two masculine crowns [*couronnes masculines*] she already wears."[8] Francis Stephen was thinking much the same thing when he assured his wife that her coronation as empress would in no way detract from her regal status, her *quallité de Roy*. Yet this was precisely what displeased her about the traditional ritual: unlike the crowns of Hungary and Bohemia, which she held in her own name by right of inheritance, the imperial coronation would have made her subordinate to her husband.[9] For an empress had "no real majesty or sovereignty in her own right, but only by virtue of her spouse."[10] For

Maria Theresa, symbolically deferring to her husband in this way was out of the question. It was clear to all concerned that her refusal could only be understood as a demonstrative slight to the imperial office—and hence, indirectly, to its present incumbent. In the subsequent course of the coronation festivities, too, she made clear how little she thought of the ceremony, how wasteful she found the vast sums expended on it, and how eager she was to bring it all to a speedy conclusion and return to Vienna.

With that, she not only dismissed the imperial coronation as a tiresome formality, she also called her husband's attention to the power base to which he owed his position as emperor. It was symptomatic that he could barely cover the costs of his stately procession to Frankfurt—comprising some 440 attendants, 640 horses, and 91 carriages—from his own Tuscan revenues.[11] As emperor, too, he appeared throughout his reign to rely on subsidies from the hereditary lands (although this later turned out to be untrue). Through her refusal to have herself crowned empress, Maria Theresa demonstrated for all to see that she placed dynasty above Empire, as well as clarifying relations between herself and her husband and between the hereditary lands and the imperial confederation. She also used diplomatic ceremonial to ensure that her separate role as queen—or more precisely, as king—of two lands, her "masculine function," was kept permanently visible.[12] When foreign ambassadors attended their first and farewell audiences, they were initially received by Francis as emperor, then by Maria Theresa as empress, and then again on the following day by Maria Theresa, this time in her capacity as ruler of the hereditary lands. The explicit point was "to mark the dual representation of both Majesties."[13] As Khevenhüller remarked of these unorthodox ceremonial arrangements, the emperor felt, not unreasonably, that he had "suffered some loss of dignity" as a result. But they were needed "to draw out and consolidate . . . the unique *souveraineté* of the empress as queen." Given the possibility that the Archducal House might once again lose the imperial throne, as had happened before, it seemed inadvisable to neglect the hereditary royal honors.[14] At any rate, foreign emissaries were in no doubt as to where real power lay at the Viennese court. Sometimes

FIGURE 17. Maria Theresa as empress with the imperial crown.
Her left hand is pointing to a small portrait medallion of Francis
Stephen pinned to her chest; lying in the shadows in the
foreground on the left is the Bohemian crown. Copperplate by
Philipp Andreas Kilian, after Martin van Meyten

they even ignored the emperor's ceremonial precedence and simply by-passed him.[15]

While Maria Theresa may have scoffed at the age-old formalities of the "Holy Empire," characterizing the imperial crown as an "empty honor" and dismissing the coronation as a "farce," this did not prevent her from turning the office to her political advantage once it returned to her house and her husband.[16] In the years that followed, Maria Theresa succeeded somehow in squaring the circle: she managed to exploit the symbolic and political capital of the imperial title for herself and her family without thereby having to defer to her husband as emperor—with such success, in fact, that she is popularly remembered to this day as the real incumbent of the imperial throne and "empress of Austria"—although at that time there was no such title. No one was surprised or took offense when she was depicted in several portraits with the imperial crown, even though this amounted, strictly speaking, to a usurpation of her husband's authority.[17]

Francis I

Ever since his arrival at the Viennese court at the age of fifteen, Francis Stephen of Lorraine[18] had grown used to being patronized and treated with condescension. Apparently, the couple only felt at ease in the company of Countess Fuchs, Maria Theresa's old aya and later chief lady-in-waiting (*Obersthofmeisterin*), which explains why Francis Stephen held her in the highest regard as long as she lived.[19] Following his marriage to the heir, his precarious status at court had given rise to embarrassing problems of protocol; foreign ambassadors and especially the papal legate had therefore been constantly obliged to go out of his way at court.[20] At the coronations in Pressburg and Prague he had been treated as if he were invisible. His poor showing as supreme commander in the Turkish war and the War of Succession had been the talk of the town in Vienna. He reacted to all these slights and indignities by withdrawing as far as possible from the formal life of the court. Observers characterized him as loving and warm-hearted, humorous and intelligent, tolerant and unpretentious, averse to regal ostentation and melancholy in disposition.[21] He hated having to wear the stiffly pompous Spanish court dress in which he is shown in official portraits. The Prussian emissary Podewils observed that his deportment and posture left much to be desired, while his features were distorted into a grimace by his habit of pulling faces.[22] He was uneasy with public appearances, mumbled when giving formal addresses, and swallowed his final syllables.[23] Ceremonial formalities were anathema to him, yet when they could not be avoided he submitted to them without demur. He took the same attitude to religious ceremonies as to political ones: while accepting their necessity, he saw no point in making a fuss about them. His writings to his children attest to a reflective and internalized personal religiosity, far removed from bigotry and fanaticism.[24] He had been admitted to a masonic lodge in his youth, whereas his wife relentlessly persecuted Freemasonry as a hotbed of sedition and superstition, ordering the first Viennese lodge to be dissolved.[25]

In contrast to Maria Theresa, Francis Stephen was generally diffident and reserved in his dealings with others. Witnesses also consistently reported that he avoided quarreling with her at all costs. Later, when his son Leopold took the reins of power in Tuscany, he bade him farewell with the following sage advice: courtesy, affability, and placidity (*politesse, complaisance et douceur*) would get one further than an imperious tone (*le ton de maitre*); inner repose (*tranquilleté chez soi*) was more important than authority. On matters of no importance it was best to give ground. Particularly in marriage, one should learn to compromise and make allowances for the other's temperament (*humeur*). A wife should regard her husband as her true friend, not as her lord and master. In his eyes the ideal marriage was characterized by "sincere friendship and perfect trust between husband and wife."[26] In general, he counselled his son to try and see things from other people's point of view and remain ever vigilant toward himself, since we ourselves are our own worst enemies; self-love can easily open the way to flattery and self-deception.[27] Many of these maxims were clearly the fruit of his years of experience with his formidable and combative spouse, although whether he adopted them by inclination or necessity remains a moot point. At any rate, their personalities struck most observers as complementary. He rarely responded in kind to Maria Theresa's frequent flare-ups. On the whole, he seems to have treated her with prudent forbearance, no doubt anticipating that resistance would be futile anyway. From the galling necessity of subordination to his wife, he evidently succeeded in fashioning the virtue of voluntary self-restraint. Yet his unwillingness to stand up to her only marginalized him further at court.

The fact that Francis Stephen had now risen to the highest secular office in all Christendom did nothing to alter this constellation—quite the contrary. Everyone knew that this position had come his way solely through his marriage to the Habsburg heir, hence that he owed it purely to Charles VI's favor rather than to his own dynastic pedigree. Maria Theresa herself continually reminded him of it, although she never left him in any doubt about her love and passion for him.[28] A "trustworthy source" informed emissary Podewils how on one occasion, during a court conference, she had "commanded him in no uncertain terms to hold his tongue, admonishing him not to interfere in matters he knew nothing about."[29] On the other hand, the lord high steward once noted her refusal to reach a decision in the emperor's absence.[30] Yet the general perception at court was different. Even if he won a great deal of sympathy over time on account of his sincerity, affability, and domestic virtues, he was still considered far too weak-willed and indolent to be willing or able to stand up to his temperamental spouse. But that was precisely what was expected of him as husband. Khevenhüller, who otherwise thought highly of him, blamed him for his own inferior status at court: especially in the first years of his reign, it was "entirely up to him to take the rudder in his own hands. Only, besides being not naturally very diligent, but slow and indecisive, he also lacked the requisite *fermeté* to resist the over-heated *vivacités* of his wife."[31] Francis Stephen himself was evidently under no illusions so far as his reputation was concerned. He disclosed to Podewils that he knew the Prussian king thought him powerless, though he claimed not to hold it against him.[32] The continued affronts at court nonetheless seemed to get under his skin. On more than one occasion, Khevenhüller noted in his journal that the emperor was suffering from bouts of melancholy.[33]

Francis Stephen appears to have been largely excluded from the court patronage system. His sporadic attempts to exploit his closeness to the queen to intercede on others' behalf generally backfired, particularly if Maria Theresa suspected his would-be protégés of having a malign influence on him. Courtiers took note whenever his rare efforts at protection ended in failure. According to one story, he had sought in vain to secure a certain young Count of Lippe a position as adjutant general in the army. When the young man was subsequently evicted from his apartments by the lord high chamberlain, the emperor took the extraordinary step of sending the young man a written apology along with a valuable gift.[34] According to the logic of court patronage, to provide so clear an admission of one's own impotence was unforgivable. It was likewise unbecoming, to say the least, for Francis Stephen to apologize to a courtier for giving offense, as he did when writing to the lord high chamberlain to seek his forgiveness for his short temper and rudeness.[35] He did the same to State Chancellor Kaunitz on at least one occasion, notwithstanding the frosty relations between the two. The emperor's apology was composed in his own idiosyncratic orthography: "*Ma vivasite fig mir Regt an et je vous dret ne lavoyre pas fay pour bocoup.*" That is to say, "My lively temper got the better of me, and I greatly regret not having acted otherwise." It is entirely characteristic of Maria Theresa's relationship with her husband, but also with her close confidant Kaunitz, that she saw fit to forward the sentence—now in linguistically correct form— to the insulted Chancellor with an apologetic commentary of her own: "By revealing his heartfelt remorse and regret about his earlier outburst," the emperor's letter "must be a true consolation to me, all the more so as he arrived at it through his own reflection."[36] Maria Theresa liked to dominate her husband and talk about him behind his back, albeit always with the best of intentions and with his best interests—or what she took to be his best interests—at heart.[37] Needless to say, this was hardly in keeping with his imperial status and did much to undermine his standing at court. Yet Francis Stephen himself was of the view that one could never debase oneself through politeness, modesty, and restraint.[38] For a ruler, he contended, the same principles applied in this respect as for an ordinary man of honor. In a dispute with Count Königsegg, for example, he vehemently defended the view that even sovereigns should never be permitted to violate the aristocratic norms of tact, délicatesse, and loyalty to kin, not even when higher political reasons seemed to require it. As Khevenhüller noted in his diary, the emperor became quite agitated, exclaiming: "I know the duties of a sovereign better than you, being one myself, and shall always maintain that the qualities of an *honnête homme* are as essential for a sovereign as for a private person."[39]

Francis Stephen was clearly unhappy with the demands placed on him as the highest-ranking regent in Europe.[40] As time went on he increasingly avoided court appearances and retreated to his private palace in the Wallnergasse, where he surrounded himself with a coterie of Lothringian compatriots and relatives.[41] A peaceful, secluded home life was of the utmost importance, he advised his son, otherwise the court could easily become a "purgatory in this world."[42] Gala days caused him acute discomfort. On one occasion, the English emissary Robinson reports, the emperor sat listlessly in a corner during a court festivity and told the ladies who were about to rise in his honor: "Pay no heed to me, for I shall stay here till the court is gone. The Empress and my children are the court," he added, "I am only a simple individual."[43] By the lights of courtiers such as Khevenhüller, this was an intolerable act of self-degradation. For all that he respected his master, the lord high chamberlain felt that he repeatedly demeaned himself with intimacies and harmless pleasures that were beneath the dignity of his office.[44] Francis Stephen devoted much of his time to hunting, billiards, cards, and ball games, as well as to collecting medallions, minerals, works of art, and curios. In all this he was scarcely different from many other princes of the time. What really set him apart in the eyes of observers was his Midas touch, whether at the card table, in his financial speculations, or in his economic management of his own territory, the Grand Duchy of Tuscany. He left millions to his heirs; boxes filled with cash kept turning up everywhere after his death.[45] All this was more in keeping with the image of an industrious and well-off nobleman than with that of a ruler. The idea of the *particulier*, the private individual, is often brought up in connection with Francis Stephen's lifestyle, but it tells only half the story.

In fact, Francis Stephen was actively involved in the business of government in Vienna. Along with Maria Theresa, he regularly took part in the Court Conference, long the most influential, albeit barely formalized, advisory and decision-making body in the monarchy. Convened several times a week in the rooms of State Chancellor Ulfeld, it was attended by the six most important ministers of the crown.[46] According to some observers, he participated only for form's sake and without enthusiasm, having no genuine interest in government and no understanding of imperial affairs, in particular.[47] But this view is belied by his habit of keeping detailed notes about every session he attended, written in his illegible handwriting and inimitable orthography.[48] This is hardly a sign of bored ignorance. If he steered clear of politics, this had more to do with the strength of his opponents. For Francis Stephen found himself in permanent political opposition to his wife and her favored councillors, first Bartenstein and later Kaunitz.[49] The indispensable cabinet secretary Bartenstein, who also set the tone in matters concerning the Empire, had always been hostile to the Lothringian faction at court. Rumor had it that he had directly advised Maria Theresa to deny her husband influence on government.[50] The steady stream of papers that he and Kaunitz produced on all important political questions was almost exclusively directed to the empress, hardly ever to the emperor.[51]

To many observers, the empress and emperor appeared to form the nuclei of two opposing "parties" at the Viennese court. In stark contrast to his wife, Francis Stephen tended not to be vindictive and advocated restoring friendly relations with Prussia. In 1749, when Maria Theresa demanded that all her conference ministers give their opinions on the reorganization of her foreign policy following the War of Succession, the emperor himself contributed a memorandum on the topic. With the Prussian king, he argued, we should be good neighbors, approaching him in a spirit of conciliation. Our all too understandable grievances should not be aired in public, and he should not be opposed in matters of indifference to the imperial house: in short, he should be given no excuse to renew hostilities. The utmost caution was required in dealing with the French court; it could never be trusted, since its intention was always "to prize us away from our natural allies," England and the Netherlands. Kaunitz's plan to estrange France from Prussia had to be regarded "as a perennial chimera."[52] Emissary Podewils was correct in signaling to his superior in Potsdam that the emperor was well disposed to the Prussian court. Prussia's enemies therefore "always made sure to sow discord between the empress and her husband for fear that the latter, who is unwilling to lend them an ear, might gain influence over the empress and eventually open her eyes to their intrigues."[53] Following the restructuring of the European alliance system in 1756—not a chimera after all—the political schism between the couple deepened still further. Francis Stephen mistrusted the alliance with France, which Kaunitz regarded as his crowning foreign policy achievement. Francis Stephen never forgave the French for the loss of his ancestral homeland, the Duchy of Lorraine, and remained suspicious of their intentions. Maria Theresa, by contrast, supported by her francophile and, from 1753, all-powerful state chancellor, hoped to make the alliance even stronger. These were irreconcilable positions. Lord High Chamberlain Khevenhüller, who felt equally attached to both emperor and empress, vented his frustration in 1757: "We have two lords, the emperor and the empress. Both desire to rule, and although the former directs the military, and also (to a certain extent) the finance system, or at least nothing important can easily get done in these two branches of government without his knowledge and consent, he is nonetheless too easy-going to bear such a heavy burden."[54]

Francis Stephen was thus evidently not so much uninterested in policy as placed at a structural disadvantage in relation to his wife. He was also personally averse to conflict. For better or worse, he preferred to accept her position of dominance and not squander his energies on fruitless opposition. His submissiveness was interpreted by most contemporaries, and even more so by later historians, as a sign of weakness, incapacity, irresolution, or even indolence. Clearly, he could not be forgiven for accepting the reversal of customary gender roles without apparent protest. For a long time the widespread contempt in which he was held led scholars to neglect his role as emperor. Yet there are other reasons why so little is known of his activities to this day. There is evidence that his papers were systematically, albeit incompletely, removed from the archives after his death. It is quite possible that Maria Theresa herself had the files destroyed to prevent details of her own domestic quarrels from coming to light.[55]

Imperial Politics

The reasons why historians have tended to neglect Emperor Francis I are more fundamental and structural in nature, however. They have to do with the lack of interest traditionally shown in the imperial confederation as a whole. The fact that the Holy Roman Empire of the German Nation ceased to exist in 1806, and that after 1804 the last emperor, Francis II, now only styled himself emperor of Austria, meant that this early modern "Old Empire" hardly played a role in either Prusso-German or Austrian historiography. Whether intent on glorifying the

Austro-Hungarian dual monarchy or the German Reich, those wanting to tell a coherent, linear success story about how the "modern" states of the nineteenth and twentieth century came into being found the Old Empire an anachronistic impediment. What counted was the imperial grandeur and glory of the Middle Ages; the early modern empire, by contrast, seemed but a pale shadow of its former self, an empty shell that the Austrian and Prusso-German states had smashed and put behind them at some stage in the eighteenth century. This view has since undergone drastic revision, in German historiography even more so than in Austria.[56] In Germany the Old Empire has experienced something of a renaissance since the 1980s; many historians now hold it up as the model of a functioning, proto-parliamentary state governed by rule of law. Yet that also fails to do justice to this strange political construct. In the eighteenth century the imperial confederation proved ill equipped to contain the extraordinary dynamism and growing antagonism of its key players within its rickety institutional framework. Even Friedrich Karl von Schönborn, whose family numbered among the confederation's main pillars of support, argued as early as 1736 that "our imperial system has been woven in such a way that it has to be patched up in Vienna every so often, [so that] I, an imperial vice-chancellor of many years' standing, fail to see how this beggars' cloak can last much longer."[57] The Empire's structural problems, on the one hand, and Francis I's subordination to his dominant and subsequently mythicized wife, on the other, meant that historians long felt little inclination to investigate the Viennese court's relationship to the Empire at the time of Maria Theresa.[58]

Following the political fiasco of Charles VII, the imperial confederation was in a state of permanent crisis. The Wittelsbach intermezzo had done lasting damage to the institution's standing and exacerbated the structural crisis afflicting the Empire.[59] As head of the Empire, Charles VII had felt little compunction in treating the ecclesiastical principalities of his surroundings as so many pawns to be disposed of as he saw fit, thereby abandoning basic principles of imperial law. Yet the other belligerent powers in the Empire—Prussia as well as Austria—had also appealed to imperial patriotism; for as long as it was expedient, each had claimed to be fighting in defense of the "old German freedom."[60] Ultimately it was impossible to determine who really had imperial law on their side. For the imperial constitution was not a systematic, self-contained whole but an extremely complex, internally contradictory network of highly diverse agreements, privileges, and legal traditions. Positive laws and treaties formed only "small islands in the sea of common-law tradition."[61] What went by the name of imperial constitutional law—*Reichsstaatsrecht* or *Ius publicum Romano-Germanicum*—had evolved over the centuries and sedimented into a number of heterogeneous layers. Conflicting interpretations were always possible, and no one could successfully claim an exclusive right to decide upon their respective merits. Imperial law provided all sides with ammunition for their rhetoric of self-justification, which could be dropped again once circumstances changed. The Empire's complicated order was poorly suited to dealing with large-scale conflicts such as the War of the Austrian Succession. When the emperor himself was a party to the conflict, he could hardly act as a neutral arbiter.

In the eighteenth century tensions mounted within the imperial confederation as the chasm deepened between the handful of great powers and the many bit players in the Empire. The Peace of Westphalia of 1648 had preserved the formal order but left little room for adapting to changing circumstances. As a result, formal and informal conduct drifted further and further apart. This was especially evident whenever a new emperor was elected and crowned: the emissaries sent by the great German princes faithfully observed the old order down to the finest ritual details and invoked "the sacred bond between the head and the limbs," but their masters, blithely ignoring this continually reaffirmed bond, pursued quite a different political course back at their courts. There was a good deal of structural hypocrisy on all sides, since it was a self-evident yet barely acknowledged truth that imperial tradition and European alliance politics were all but incompatible.[62]

To be sure, the relationship between the Empire and the Habsburg hereditary lands had been complicated and opaque since well before the eighteenth century. This can be seen even at the level of linguistic usage. From an Austrian perspective, "the Empire" lay outside the hereditary lands; its key sites and institutions were to be found in Frankfurt, Mainz,

Regensburg, or Wetzlar. People spoke of traveling "to the Empire" or of *étrangers de l'empire*, foreigners from the Empire[63]—even though the Habsburgs had occupied the imperial throne for centuries and their "German" ancestral lands indisputably belonged to the Empire (something that was far less clear-cut in the case of Bohemia and the Southern Netherlands). On the other hand, on the basis of a successful imperial forgery, the *Privilegium Maius*, these same hereditary lands enjoyed a range of privileges that from the fourteenth century separated them from the rest of the Empire. Above all, they were subject neither to imperial jurisdiction nor to imperial taxes. They were also exempt from the stipulation of the Westphalian Peace that a prince of the Empire was not allowed to change the confessional relations in his lands as they pertained in the so-called status quo year (*Normaljahr*) of 1624. The peace conference had ultimately failed to reach consensus regarding the extent to which the House of Habsburg was bound by the rules of confessional tolerance.[64] Despite its exceptional status, over the centuries the Archducal House had largely succeeded in causing the Holy Roman Empire to be identified with the Habsburg empire in the public mind. This was due not least to the defensive wars which the Habsburgs had fought against the Ottomans. Jointly financed by the imperial estates, these had had a strongly unifying effect on the imperial confederation. Throughout all the internal conflicts and interconfessional confrontations, a series of common institutions had been forged and consolidated that justified speaking of the Empire as a single political entity, imagined metaphorically as a body made up of head and limbs. The unity of the whole depended on a number of factors: the dignity of the emperor as supreme feudal overlord and highest judge; the standing of the elector of Mainz as ex-officio archchancellor of the Empire and of the Electoral College (*Kurkolleg*) as a whole; the authority of the two highest imperial lawcourts; the integrative power of the Imperial Diet; and the system for tax collection and military coordination administered by the Imperial Circles (*Reichskreise*).[65] All these institutions by no means functioned equally well at all times; above all, they did not operate in isolation from the power relations prevailing at the time. Whereas lesser cogs of the Empire—cities, prince-abbots and prince-bishops, counts or imperial knights with their small or even miniscule territories—had an existential stake in the proper functioning of imperial institutions, great princes saw them as either irksome fetters or useful instruments for furthering their own interests. By the time of Francis Stephen's accession to the throne, trust in the imperial confederation had already been seriously eroded.

Ruling the Empire and ruling the hereditary lands were two quite different things. They followed different logics and demanded different political strategies. As supreme head of the Empire, the emperor had to deal with a number of other great princes, some of whom were themselves kings of countries outside the Empire—Brandenburg in Prussia, Saxony in Poland, Hannover in England. Unable to force such potentates to do his bidding, the emperor needed to find consensus to get things done. Yet the emperor could generally rely on the support of a number of lesser princes and lords, knights, and cities to advance the interests of his own house. While the office of emperor did not bestow any sovereign powers on its incumbent, it still came with considerable advantages. It elevated him both symbolically and instrumentally above every other prince in the Empire and in Europe. The Habsburgs had profited from this preeminence for centuries, since the imperial court had in practice been identical with the court of the Archducal House. The imperial office had come to appear as a "self-evident attribute" of the House of Habsburg,[66] even if individual candidates always had to make fresh concessions to electors to win the crown. Doubts about the usefulness of the office for the Archducal House had never arisen. The Wittelsbach interlude from 1742 to 1745 changed all that, shaking previously unquestioned assumptions and causing the relationship between the hereditary lands and the imperial office to appear in the cold light of rational calculation and sober cost-benefit analysis. Such considerations shaped Maria Theresa's pragmatic approach to the imperial throne, which she no longer took for granted as a traditional family asset. It was a means to an end, nothing more, and its fitness for purpose needed to be weighed against the associated costs. Just how useful it actually was for the All-Highest Archducal House was the subject of intense debate following Francis Stephen's coronation.[67] "It can hardly be denied," Imperial Vice-Chancellor Colloredo argued, "that the Roman Empire shares a common bond with the Archducal Austrian hereditary lands, [and] that the prosperity of one largely depends on that of the other. . . . As soon as the compact between the Archducal House and the Empire fell into disorder, both sides suffered a marked deterioration in their affairs." It could still be assumed, however, that "the Most Serene Archducal House is strong enough to resist any of its most powerful enemies on its own, if need be, and that in future the Empire would continue to call on it for protection at any time." In Colloredo's view, then, the Empire relied far more on the Archducal House than vice versa; indeed, the former could not exist without the latter. Still, it could hardly be doubted that the imperial confederation benefited the Archducal House in many ways.[68]

The emperor's position in the imperial confederation rested on the fact that he was its highest lord and supreme judge. He formed the symbolic keystone, so to speak, of the entire confederation; as its consecrated, divinely ordained head, he was the reference point from which all legitimate order was ultimately derived.[69] Over time the prince-electors had bound the emperor to the formal consent of the imperial estates in all important decisions, yet he retained a range of opportunities denied other princes in the Empire. In the first place, the imperial court was an unrivaled source of symbolic capital; incontestably, it was still the foremost secular court in Christian Europe.[70] Only the emperor could promote courtiers to higher ranks within the aristocracy, fill important imperial offices, dispense special privileges, and grant valuable ceremonial advantages. He could influence who received plush benefices in the imperial church, and he had the final say on processes in the Aulic Council. All this assured the imperial court a central position in European princely society.[71]

Through the Wittelsbach intermezzo, this position and its associated resources had temporarily slipped from the grasp of the Archducal House. In the process, the Habsburg patronage system had been brought into serious disorder. Because the Habsburg court had been factually identical with the imperial court for the previous three centuries, imperial and Habsburg clients could no longer be separated. While imperial offices were formally distinct from offices in the hereditary lands, informally they formed a single pool of resources that could be drawn on to provide for Habsburg clients and buy off potential rivals. While it was not unusual for political conflicts to interfere with border-transcending aristocratic patronage networks, which then had to be recalibrated once peace returned, this was a novelty at the imperial court. The Empire had not seen a change of dynasty for over three hundred years. Yet now the offices and honors of Empire—imperial vice-chancellor, delegates to the Imperial Diet, aulic councillors, judges of the Imperial Chamber Court (*Reichskammergericht*), imperial chamberlains, and so forth—needed to be filled by Charles VII with his creatures, unless the old office-bearers had personally sworn him their fealty. For the imperial offices were still characterized by personal loyalty toward whichever emperor was on the throne at the time; officials were not yet the servants of an anonymous state, for all that they were nominally obliged to work for the common good. Maria Theresa had never formally recognized the Wittelsbach's claim to the throne. In her eyes, the throne had remained vacant, and the Imperial Diet and Aulic Council had never validly convened during the interregnum.[72] She therefore also ignored the promotions in office and rank made by Charles VII as emperor. In 1743, on the occasion of her Bohemian coronation, she ordered every chamberlain who had attained to this honor "under the pseudo-emperor" to be struck from the list—"a misfortune," as her lord high chamberlain remarked with some sympathy, "that befell many who had accepted such positions almost against their will amidst the general confusion of the time."[73] Now, in 1745, there were sweeping changes to court personnel. Many positions were refilled with superannuated officials who had served under Maria Theresa's father. Those who had accepted positions under Charles VII were in disgrace and had to start all over again.

Following the election and coronation of Francis I, the Imperial Diet had returned from Frankfurt to Regensburg and the Aulic Council was newly convened in the Hofburg. The *status quo ante bellum* appeared to have been restored and everything put right from a Habsburg perspective. Vienna was once again the highest-ranking court in Christendom, allowing a new order of precedence at court (*Hofrangordnung*) to be decreed at last.[74] Stephen now no longer had a lower status than his wife, sparing him further ceremonial humiliation. Foreign ambassadors were no longer forced to give him a wide berth at court to avoid conflicts of priority, and he also no longer had to sit to his wife's left.[75] Indeed, as queen of Bohemia and archduchess of Austria, Maria Theresa was now her husband's vassal in the imperial feudal system. She had to be formally reinstated in her possession of the hereditary lands and her electoral vote, and she was even willing to kneel before the imperial throne to do so (although this humiliation was spared her in the end).[76] Yet this was only one side of the coin. The venerable imperial confederation was characterized by a specific ambiguity.[77] On the formal level, the various legal titles—here: wife to the emperor on the one hand, sovereign queen on the other—were painstakingly kept apart in court ceremony and on paper, and were the objects of an arcane body of imperial law. Yet, on the informal level, all these titles could be brought together in the service of one and the same dynastic political strategy. It would therefore be misleading to say that Francis I pursued an "imperial policy" independently of his wife and the dynastic interests of the Archducal House. An imperial policy worthy of the name would have entailed strengthening the imperial confederation and heeding the demands for institutional reform coming from all sides. Imperial policy in this strict sense did not exist during the reign of Francis I.[78] The formal separation of roles between the emperor as head of the Empire and his wife as ruler of the hereditary lands could not disguise the fact that imperial policy was a means to a dynastic end. Maria Theresa, not the emperor, "decided on the direction of policy in Vienna."[79]

Immediately after the coronation, the imperial office was again harnessed to dynastic ends, if anything more energetically than ever before. This was made easier by the fact that the elector of Mainz and imperial archchancellor, who stood opposite the emperor at the apex of the entire imperial confederation, had since 1743 been a "creature" of the House of Habsburg, Johann Friedrich Karl, Count Ostein (1696–1763).[80] His representative at the imperial court was Rudolph, Count Colloredo (1706–88), the scion of a noble family richly endowed with lands in Bohemia. As imperial vice-chancellor he was formally responsible for overseeing all matters concerning the Empire from his office in

Vienna. His rise to high office had been meteoric. Having previously held the post on an acting basis under Maria Theresa's father, his appointment was now renewed by Francis I. He owed his position more to the influence of his father-in-law, the conference minister Starhemberg, than to his own merits. In the judgment of Lord High Chamberlain Khevenhüller, who could not stand the man, he had wormed his way into the office "against the queen's will through various tricks of the clever old man."[81] The powerful conference secretary Bartenstein had already had a hand in Colloredo's early career and went on to help him draft written submissions. Colloredo himself was considered a man of very modest talents: self-regarding, without any great political ambition, and unversed in the subtleties of imperial law. He did not bother reading the documents that were put before him,[82] and "had difficulty expressing himself in conferences and in public owing to an innate timidity and *mauvaise honte* [shyness]."[83] He was, however, peerless in everything that made a true cavalier. He had fallen out of favor with Maria Theresa owing to his many gallant affairs.[84]

In theory, the areas for which the Empire and the hereditary lands were responsible were clearly divided between the Imperial Chancellery and the State Chancellery, respectively.[85] In practice, however, the two power centers competed against each other. When the wily and ambitious Kaunitz—alongside Bartenstein, Maria Theresa's closest confidant—became state chancellor in 1753,[86] the political momentum shifted more and more from the Imperial Chancellery to the State Chancellery. Kaunitz, who disparaged imperial institutions and harbored a personal animosity toward Imperial Vice-Chancellor Colloredo, increasingly sidelined the Imperial Chancellery by placing one of his intimates there and cutting it off from the stream of government documents.[87] This was decisive in creating a situation where it was no longer possible to speak of an imperial policy in the strict sense, one that differed in its objectives from the policy toward the hereditary lands.

Among the familiars and clients of the House of Habsburg to have held key imperial positions under Maria Theresa's father and now be reinstated under Francis I were the former president of the Imperial Aulic Council, Johann Wilhelm, Count Wurmbrand (1670–1750), and his successor, Ferdinand Bonaventura, Count Harrach (1708–78). The Aulic Council was the most important consultative body of the emperor in his capacity as supreme judge and overlord, a cross between law court and imperial advisory council. Its function was to both keep the peace and uphold the law in a general sense and also to grant special favors and privileges of all kinds.[88] The Aulic Council had its seat in the imperial residence, where the emperor maintained a permanent symbolic presence in the form of his portrait. Although he was entitled to cast the deciding vote at every trial, the proceedings were in fact run by committees composed half of noble and half of nonnoble members. As the highest court in the realm—along with the Imperial Chamber Court in Wetzlar, which during Francis I's reign was crippled by gridlock and corruption scandals[89]—the Imperial Aulic Council was the Empire's central organ for conflict resolution. It heard cases between the imperial estates, but it also provided the emperor's subjects with a means for seeking legal redress from the authorities. This opportunity was seized by many; far more trials were brought before the few councillors than they could possibly bring to a verdict. Thousands of outstanding cases had accumulated over time, and hundreds more were added to them each year.[90] In countless cases, earlier emperors had successfully tasked commissions with resolving the conflict, and in certain spectacular cases they had even deposed territorial princes or town councils due to mismanagement or tyranny. Yet under Francis I the Imperial Aulic Council—the most precious "jewel of imperial dignity"[91]—was beset by crisis. Its authority had long been threatened by parties to the conflict taking frequent recourse to the Imperial Diet.[92] Now the number of cases brought before the court fell into steep decline.[93] The Protestants had always accused the court of confessional partisanship. The same line was now taken by all the Habsburgs' political enemies, including the Prussian emissary Fürst: "All Germany knows how little this court can be trusted to see justice done in the absence of support in high places. Passion, ignorance, and interest are rife here, with only a few exceptions; the supreme law is the emperor's will."[94] The noble councillors were "callow youths" who used the court as a springboard for their own careers, while many learned councillors were "venal souls," badly paid yet forced to keep up appearances and therefore dependent on gifts from litigants.[95] This criticism may have been exaggerated for polemical effect, but it could not be dismissed out of hand. In the 1750s and 1760s the number of cases appearing before the Aulic Council reached a new low—a sure sign that trust in the emperor's impartiality among imperial estates and ordinary subjects alike had all but vanished.[96]

Loyal Clients

The forum at which the emperor traditionally met and negotiated with the imperial estates as a collective was the Imperial Diet. Originally a grand ceremonious occasion for bringing together the Empire as a whole in all its representative finery, it had since become a fairly lackluster institution that convened permanently in Regensburg. For a long time, only envoys had gathered there, primarily to exchange information and maintain informal networks, but also occasionally to draft formal resolutions or even—very rarely—pass imperial laws.[97] The emperor himself, like the other princes, no longer appeared there in the eighteenth century. For the imperial court, the Imperial Diet was above all the center of its client network and a reservoir of allies against its enemies in the Empire.[98] The growing antagonism between Prussia and Habsburg was faithfully reproduced among the envoys in Regensburg. The Imperial Diet had a bad press in Europe owing to its notorious disputes over ceremonial protocol and its unwieldy procedural mechanisms. The French parliamentary president Montesquieu, who had visited Regensburg on a tour of Europe, noted in his travel account that most envoys at the diet were personages of no importance who "seek only ease or whatever perquisites they can extract from the court in Vienna."[99] Writing in the 1780s, the Habsburg envoy Trautmannsdorff summed up his years of experience: "Most issues that come before the attention of the Imperial Diet are utterly insignificant and of indifference to the All-Highest Imperial Court."[100]

Yet this was not the whole truth. The House of Habsburg had three different means at its disposal for swaying diet proceedings in its favor. The emperor himself was represented by the principal commissioner

(*Prinzipalkommissar*), who maintained a palatial imperial surrogate court in St. Emmeram's Abbey. Maria Theresa was represented as queen of Bohemia and archduchess of Austria by envoys in the Council of Electors (*Kurfürstenrat*) and Council of Princes (*Fürstenrat*), respectively. Moreover, hers was the highest-ranking secular voice in the Council of Princes, entitling her envoy to chair every second session. Princes from the hereditary lands as well as other Habsburg clients, especially prince-bishops, were also represented in the Council of Princes in large numbers. The opportunities for Habsburg influence on the Imperial Diet were thus many and varied, yet these were offset by the equally considerable influence exerted by their opponents, particularly the king of Prussia. Frederick II likewise not only had a vote in the Council of Electors but also controlled several seats in the Council of Princes. The lesser and middling courts in the Empire thus had to be wooed, and in this regard possession of the imperial throne conferred a distinct advantage. Imperial Vice-Chancellor Colloredo, whom Maria Theresa had asked for his opinion on the matter in the Court Conference in 1749, maintained that it was not difficult to win over princes of the Empire (and their households) for Habsburg ends, "since the smaller courts, or the ministries of the larger ones, are known to be always seeking and asking for favors from the imperial court." Such opportunities were there to be exploited. All that was needed to gain a useful client was the promise of exemption from military service or of advancement in imperial service. Gaining indirect influence over high officials need not cost much, either: it was enough to bestow "modest pensions of a few thousand guilders on ministers serving at the courts of imperial princes."[101] This was traditionally how the imperial court was able to secure a majority in the Imperial Diet.

The Archducal House's most important clients in the Empire were undoubtedly the prince-bishops, many of whom sat in the Imperial Diet. It was a unique feature of the imperial constitution that archbishops and bishops of imperial bishoprics, along with abbots and abbesses of imperial monasteries, simultaneously exercised secular authority over their territories and were thus entitled to a seat and vote at the Imperial Diet.[102] The prince-bishops notoriously suffered from existential angst, surrounded as they often were by more powerful neighbors looking for any pretext to incorporate their tiny *territoriuncula* into their own principalities. This danger came not only from Protestant princes but also from their fellow Catholics; the Wittelsbach emperor, Charles VII, had made grand plans to shore up his fragile power base in just this way. Here the Habsburg Archducal House, which had traditionally presented itself as the champion of the imperial church, offered itself as a refuge, since it appeared to be the only Catholic dynasty large and powerful enough to have no need to secularize neighboring ecclesiastic territories. What was crucial was that the prince-bishops were voted into their positions rather than inheriting them like other princes. The great Catholic dynasties—Habsburg and Wittelsbach, but also the houses of Electoral Saxony, Electoral Palatinate, and Württemberg, newly returned to the Catholic fold—thus competed with each other to influence these elections, and perhaps even install their own sons and daughters on a bishop's or abbess's throne. This rivalry kept the client system in perpetual motion. The emperor enjoyed the advantage of being present at each such election through his envoy: because the office in question was a dual one, both ecclesiastical and secular, whoever won the election had to be subsequently invested by the emperor with the powers of secular lordship over his or her territory. The vote itself, however, lay by canon law with the respective ecclesiastical chapter. These canons or canonesses generally came from the territorial landed aristocracy, and their votes did not come cheap—they were bought not only with privileges, offices, and benefices for themselves and their families but also simply with cash handouts. They therefore had a vested interest in keeping their voting rights free from outside interference.

How Maria Theresa dealt with these structural conditions and strategically used her influence on the imperial church whenever a vacancy appeared, or might be expected to appear, says a great deal about her relationship to the imperial constitution. Whether in Eichstätt[103] or Ellwangen,[104] in Würzburg,[105] Bamberg,[106] Speyer,[107] in nearby Salzburg[108] or—most important—in an ecclesiastical electorate such as Trier,[109] her goal at all times was for "loyalty to the All-Highest Archducal House to be consolidated and the number of those well-disposed towards it thereby increased."[110] This meant ensuring that a candidate was elected *ex gremio*, that is, from the circle of the collegiate chapter and hence from the territorial aristocracy, not from one of the great long-established princely dynasties, which were to be prevented from accruing even more power in the Empire. The House of Wittelsbach was the Archducal House's fiercest competitor on this terrain. Influence already needed to be exercised in electing the episcopal representative, the coadjutor, who in most cases enjoyed the right of succession.

Throughout all this, a dual strategy of "public discourse" and "secret activity" had to be pursued, as Imperial Vice-Chancellor Colloredo once bluntly put it.[111] The imperial court had at all costs to avoid the impression that it threatened the lofty principle of free elections in prince-bishoprics. Otherwise, there was always the danger that canons would dig in their collective heels, and in their zeal to defend their right to vote as they pleased, end up electing the very candidate opposed by the Habsburgs. The Archducal House also placed great value on not jeopardizing future relations with any candidates. When the next prince-bishop of Bamberg was due to be elected in July 1753, for example, the elector of Bavaria endorsed a canon, Adam Friedrich, Count Seinsheim, whose father was minister at his court. The rival candidate favored by the imperial house was the seventy-four-year-old dean of the cathedral, Franz Konrad, Count Stadion. Patronage relations on both sides were something of an open secret.[112] The election of a reliable candidate was especially important to the Viennese court on this occasion, since the Bishopric of Bamberg lay in the imperial circle (*Reichskreis*) of Franconia and had as its neighbor the principality of Brandenburg-Ansbach, which Frederick II of Prussia had his eye on at the time. The rivalry between Prussia and Austria was thus reflected on a smaller scale in the Franconian circle. In this case, as always, the imperial court struck the lofty rhetorical tone of liberty and patriotism: "In this, as in all other elections, our sincere wish and sole desire is that canonic electoral freedoms be preserved and a prince elected who upholds German patriotic principles," the Habsburg envoy to the election was instructed. The "fundamental rule" he should observe was "to conduct himself in such a way that whosoever is elected will feel convinced that they owe us a debt of gratitude. If Count Stadion carries the day, we expect . . . his thanks, but Seinsheim should be given no cause for suspecting us of having placed any obstacle in his path."[113] The strategy paid off. Stadion was duly elected prince-bishop but died not long thereafter, in 1757. Seinsheim succeeded him and proved a staunch supporter of the emperor in the Seven Years' War, albeit with catastrophic results for the principality's civilian population. In other cases, the choice was between several candidates who were each part of the Archducal House's patronage network. It was then all the more important that the successful candidate be left feeling that he had been elected with imperial support. The envoy should therefore "inconspicuously seek to find out where the majority lies and then act in such a way" that the winner "offers us his thanks and feels beholden to us."[114]

Imperial influence on ecclesiastical principalities could be a valuable political commodity. In 1763, for example, Antonia of Saxony expected Maria Theresa to throw her weight behind the election of her nephew Albert as coadjutor to the Master of the Teutonic Order. This was the unspoken favor in return for the Saxon vote in the upcoming election of Joseph as king. On this occasion Maria Theresa did not mince her words in explaining how the body of electors was to be dealt with: "I will arrange everything, and then the chapter must be made ready. These gentlemen are starting to take a haughty tone. I am incensed by what just happened in the chapters in Westphalia and Liège.[115] It shows that things must be managed in such a way that they do not believe they are being made to do anything against their will but think they are free to choose." This was important not least because Maria Theresa had plans for her youngest son Maximilian to join the clergy: "When the time comes I will ask him [the new grand master] to make my youngest son coadjutor."[116] Albert of Saxony later decided to forego an ecclesiastical career and became Maria Theresa's son-in-law instead. Antonia's nephew Clemens Wenzeslaus, on the other hand, scooped up a handful of important benefices with imperial backing after giving up his career in imperial military service. In 1763 he became bishop of Freising and Regensburg, in 1768 prince-bishop of Augsburg, and finally, as the climax of his ecclesiastical career, prince-elector and archbishop of Trier. The fact that he was also prince-abbot of Prüm and prince-provost of Ellwangen may have been of negligible political importance, but it brought him welcome additional income. By contrast, when Antonia of Saxony lobbied six years later for her youngest son, the sixteen-year-old Anton, to be installed on the bishop's throne in Liège, despite a distinct cooling in her relations with the imperial throne, Maria Theresa fobbed her off with the official line that she was powerless to interfere with the election process.[117] With her own son Maximilian, the imperial strategy for dealing with vacancies in the church also paid handsome dividends. In 1780 he was elected grand master of the Teutonic Order—not without significant financial outlay—as well as coadjutant of the Prince-Bishopric of Münster and Archbishopric of Cologne. This not only did much to counter Prussian influence in northwest Germany, it also cleared the way for Maximilian to become prince-bishop of Münster and elector-archbishop of Cologne upon his mother's death in 1784.[118]

All these cases show that Maria Theresa knew exactly how to operate the complex machinery of the imperial constitution, proclaiming her respect for imperial liberties on the outside while surreptitiously doing quid pro quo deals on the inside. To be sure, the electoral freedom asserted by the cathedral chapters was no mere façade; what mattered was simply knowing how to exploit it to one's advantage. If the empress was unable or unwilling to secure victory for a particular candidate, she could always evade her petitioners by pleading the principle of electoral freedom. Electoral freedom made it possible to conceal where real influence had been brought to bear, but it also allowed claims to be made on the successful candidate's gratitude even where there were no grounds for it. In this way, the extraordinarily lucrative benefices of the imperial church served as a reservoir for the Habsburg patronage network. They were also particularly valuable for the Archducal House because they eliminated the need to draw on the resources of its own hereditary lands.

Another key position in the imperial constitution that the imperial house could exploit for its own ends was that of Principal Commissioner (*Prinzipalkommissar*) at the Imperial Diet in Regensburg. How Maria Theresa used the diet to further her own domestic policy is revealed in exemplary fashion by the story of Principal Commissioner Alexander Ferdinand von Thurn and Taxis (1739–73).[119] The Thurn and Taxis family had enjoyed a hereditary monopoly over the imperial postal service for centuries. The postal service was so integral a component in the Habsburg patronage system that Emperor Leopold I had elevated the family to princely rank in 1695. Not the least reason why their loyalty lay dear to the Habsburgs' heart was because it meant that letters sent within the Empire could be systematically monitored, intercepted, and spied on. A network of secret bureaus had been set up under Maria Theresa's father, the so-called black cabinets (*cabinets noirs*), which allowed incoming mail to be opened, read, resealed, and then forwarded as required.[120] Close connections between the office of imperial postmaster (*Reichspostmeister*) and the imperial administration were highly advantageous to both sides. According to the logic of a stratified hierarchical society, such connections were based on family loyalties going back generations. The Wittelsbach intermezzo therefore seriously disrupted the long-term strategies of both families.

For Maria Theresa, it represented an act of gross disloyalty when in 1742 Alexander Ferdinand, changing his colors with the times, offered the Wittelsbach "pseudo-emperor," Charles VII, a dragoon regiment for the War of the Austrian Succession, subsequently accepting from him the post of principal commissioner at the Imperial Diet, the "foremost and noblest distinction in the Empire . . . that Your Imperial Majesty has it in Your power to bestow."[121] The principal commissioner stood in for the emperor in the full sense of the term: he presented himself and was treated by others as if he were the emperor himself. The office accordingly brought him immense prestige, although it called for ostentatious expenditure that exceeded his meager salary almost tenfold. In addition, Charles VII had the office of imperial postmaster upgraded to a princely fief granted directly by the throne. For the Thurn and Taxis family, this meant a vast increase in their symbolic capital as well as the promise of further rapid advancement in the feudal hierarchy. They could hardly have foreseen that the new emperor's reign would be so brief.

Maria Theresa reacted to the betrayal with outrage, seeking to force Alexander Ferdinand into giving up the principal commissariat by ordering him to be detained in Brussels, where he was staying at the time, although this was prevented through the intercession of the elector of Mainz.[122] After three months under house arrest the prince was set free. When Charles VII died, it was imperative that the office of imperial postmaster be returned to the House of Habsburg so that the invaluable system of communications might be brought back under their control. Yet since the imperial post was a hereditary fief, it could not simply be taken from the House of Thurn and Taxis. Maria Theresa therefore deployed the strategy of magnanimous forgiveness in this case as well. The prince of Thurn and Taxis was initially allowed to marry a princess from the House of Lorraine in 1745; a little later he was named privy councillor to the empress and two days later received the same title in the name of the emperor as well. When in 1748 the principal commissariat again fell vacant following the voluntary resignation of the previous incumbent, the emperor reassigned the prestigious (albeit costly) office to Prince Alexander Ferdinand. It was to remain in the hands of the Thurn and Taxis family until the Empire's downfall, but that was not all. In 1749 Alexander Ferdinand was inducted into the highly exclusive Order of the Golden Fleece, ensuring him privileged access to the court.[123] Promoting the status and honor of his family was to remain an important element in the Habsburg patronage system, for several reasons. First, hardly anyone else was both willing and able to meet the enormous costs that the office entailed. Second, the imperial postal system was an invaluable instrument of communication and control that the House of Habsburg could ill afford to relinquish. And third, the imperial postmaster was himself an influential patron who could bind his clientele in the Empire's southwest more tightly to the Archducal House, a pressing need in light of the ongoing power struggle with Prussia.

It is not hard to guess what Prince Alexander Ferdinand expected in return. He needed the support of the Habsburgs to defend his increasingly contested postal monopoly in the Empire, on the one hand, and to complete his family's ascent to the uppermost echelons of the social hierarchy, on the other. For his family found itself in a frustratingly indeterminate position so far as its status was concerned. Although it had been elevated to princely rank in 1695, it had no territories to rule over

and hence lacked a seat and voice at the Council of Princes in the Imperial Diet. The long-established imperial princes took it as an affront that
the emperor had imposed on them a principal commissioner whom
they were expected to approach on bended knee, despite him being
their social inferior. At the same time, they did all they could to resist
accepting a titular prince like Thurn and Taxis into their ranks. It was
generally taken as an embarrassing violation of the hierarchical order
that Alexander Ferdinand represented the emperor in the Imperial Diet
despite lacking the qualifications to sit there himself. This flagrantly contradicted the logic of so rigidly stratified a society. Everything had to be
done to allow the Thurn and Taxis family a "solemn introduction" into
the College of Princes in the Diet. This goal had the highest political
priority for Maria Theresa.

Alexander Ferdinand was considered lazy and incompetent in the
affairs of imperial politics; he was said to weigh *moins que zéro* (less than
nothing).[124] But this was beside the point. The real work was done with
great skill and success from 1745 onward by his representative, Deputy
Commissioner Carl Joseph von Palm. This second-generation middle-
class parvenu had already distinguished himself under Charles VI, and
then under Maria Theresa herself, through his many diplomatic services, and had even rebuffed an overture from Charles VII by pleading
his allegiance to the Archducal House.[125] As a loyal, hardworking, experienced, and ambitious diplomat, Palm did not always get on with his
indolent superior. Palm was troubled by Alexander Ferdinand's close
ties to opponents of the House of Habsburg and complained about his
frequent and long absences from the Imperial Diet. Conflict between
Palm and the prince of Thurn and Taxis also periodically broke out over
questions of ceremonial protocol, a perennial bone of contention in
Regensburg. The fact that their wives could hardly stand each other
made the relationship even more fraught. Against this background it is
unsurprising that the highly motivated and successful Palm should
sooner or later have fallen victim to intrigue. For all his competence, he
had neglected a fundamental rule of courtly prudence: always make
allowances for the envy of one's rivals rather than relying on one's own
professional qualities. It would have been in his own interest not to have

drawn attention to his achievements, or better yet to have ascribed them to others.[126] He clearly also lacked the necessary pliancy; he was accused of "stubborn self-regard."[127] At any rate, Thurn and Taxis became convinced that Palm was plotting against his admission into the Council of Princes, although there is no evidence for this in the sources.[128] The author of the allegation seems to have been a highly industrious and ambitious postal functionary called Lilien, who would distinguish himself soon after by expanding the system of *cabinets noirs*.[129] In any event, Thurn and Taxis threatened to resign from the office of principal commissioner if Palm was not removed from the Diet. Palm, secure in the knowledge of his irreproachable loyalty and generally acknowledged services to the Archducal House, was incensed and traveled to Vienna to lay his fate at the feet of both their majesties.[130] This presented them with an extremely awkward situation, given that Palm's merits were recognized even by his opponents.[131] Yet Maria Theresa acted in keeping with the norms of hierarchical society. She decided in favor of the prince and dismissed the blameless middle-class official from her service. Deeply wounded, Palm retired to his country estates and never again took up imperial office. Thurn und Taxis, backed by Maria Theresa, shortly afterward secured his long-awaited introduction to the Council of Princes.[132]

The story is significant for what it reveals about the priorities of the empress-queen. First, it shows how imperial policy was Habsburg domestic policy pursued with imperial means, not a policy directed at the Empire as a political whole. Second, Maria Theresa was the key decision-maker in all this. She was the one to whom competing parties directed their entreaties and appeals; the emperor got involved, if at all, then only at a later date.[133] And third, when it came to imperial politics, the bearer of a hereditary office who was related to her by marriage counted more for Maria Theresa—despite his record of disloyalty—than a reliable and hardworking yet ultimately expendable servant. In this case, it was more rational for her to follow the hierarchical logic of the imperial confederation than the logic of individual merit. In so doing, she applied to the Empire the same traditional strategy that she was seeking at the same time to overcome in the hereditary lands, where she was determined to establish an entirely new system.

5

Reforms

FIGURE 18. Imperial performing clock
(*Kayserliche Vorstellungsuhr*), made by
the Knaus brothers in Darmstadt.
Vienna, Hofburg, Office of the President

The Machinery of State

In October 1750 Ludwig VIII, Landgrave of Hesse-Darmstadt, sent a remarkable gift to Schönbrunn palace to congratulate the imperial couple on a double jubilee—the tenth anniversary of Maria Theresa's accession to the throne in the hereditary lands and the fifth anniversary of Francis Stephen's coronation as emperor. The gift in question was a silver machine almost two meters high and weighing over one hundred kilograms, a gigantic, intricately worked ornamental clock teeming with rocailles, figurines, and symbols of rule. The highlight of this marvel of technical ingenuity, which can still be admired today in the representational rooms of the president of Austria (fig. 18),[1] is an ornately framed stage, positioned directly beneath the clock face at the center. Once the clock has been wound up, the stage becomes the setting for a complicated performance with musical accompaniment. Against the background of a triumphalist architecture, the emperor and empress enter from the right and left, respectively, to be offered the insignia of rule by representatives of three realms: Francis receives the imperial crown, Maria Theresa the crowns of Hungary and Bohemia. Disaster looms in the form of a demon of discord and hatred, who ominously emerges from dark clouds gathering over the couple's heads. Yet divine help is at hand; from the other side of the sky, the archangel Michael comes fluttering down to drive out the diabolical spirit with his flaming sword. Finally, Clio, the muse of history, puts in an appearance, emblazoning the words "Vivant Franciscus et Theresia" on the sky in golden letters as laurel wreaths descend on the imperial couple and triumphal fanfares ring out. It all resembles an extremely elaborate, courtly Baroque version of the scenic displays featured on the tower clocks of many cities: the Frauenkirche in Nuremberg, for example, where the clockwork mechanism makes the seven electors step out and circle the golden figure of the emperor at noon each day.

This stupendous timepiece, built by the Hessian court clockmakers Ludwig and Friedrich Knaus at their landgrave's behest, was a sign of devotion to the imperial house the likes of which had never been seen before. The "imperial performing clock" (*Kaiserliche Vorstellungsuhr*), dedicated entirely to the glory of the House of Habsburg, was unsurpassed in its originality, its sheer size and expense—its cost was estimated at around 80,000 guilders—and above all its extraordinary horological workmanship and precision. The landgrave's motives were not entirely selfless, however. He hoped that, in return, Maria Theresa would cancel "house debts" to the value of 300,000 guilders dating back to the

Thirty Years' War about a hundred years before. He instructed his envoy to raise the matter with her when presenting her with the clock, albeit to no avail. At least his costly gift was subsequently rewarded with an imperial regimental command, whereas his court clockmaker was left seriously out of pocket.[2] Later still, the clock was transferred to the Hofburg treasury, where it was occasionally showed off to visiting dignitaries.[3]

Mechanical marvels such as the "imperial performing clock" fascinated contemporaries in general and the ruling couple in particular. Francis Stephen kept a cabinet of physical and mathematical curiosities featuring an assortment of valuable astronomical clocks and automata. He later appointed Friedrich Knaus, the maker of the performing clock, to be court mechanic for this cabinet. Among other things, Knaus built a "writing machine" and presented it to the emperor on his fifteenth jubilee: an automaton in a globe-shaped container, crowned by a silver female finger that could inscribe graceful letters on a board with feather and ink.[4] Francis Stephen's connoisseurship and patronage helped make Vienna a center for European horology. The court attracted a number of gifted scholars and machine-makers, mostly clerics or lay brothers who constructed astronomical clocks in monasteries and donated their masterpieces to the imperial couple (and were rewarded for their efforts with pensions and gifts).[5] Maria Theresa shared her husband's enthusiasm for such "mathematical artifices" and "ingenious machines" and owned several extraordinary astronomical showpiece clocks.[6] As a student she had been taught the fundamentals of physics and geometry by court mathematician Marinoni, head of the observatory and director of the Vienna Academy for Geometry and Military Science. Lord High Chamberlain Khevenhüller records her demonstrating bizarre automata to court society on several occasions. In 1745, for example, he mentions three marvelous machines in human form that appeared to move and act of their own accord. Maria Theresa invited the machine maker who had shown these *hommes-machines* at Vienna's old market to Schönbrunn and had him build a special booth there so he could present them to the court.[7]

Even more remarkable, perhaps, were the works constructed for the imperial court in his leisure hours by the Hungarian court chamber councillor Wolfgang von Kempelen. He constructed an astonishing variety of mechanical instruments, from water fountains in the park at Schönbrunn to a mechanically adjustable couch designed for use by the immobile, arthritic empress in her old age.[8] His masterpiece, however, was his chess-playing "Turk," unveiled at court to great applause in 1769. The chess player involved an element of trickery, for the automaton concealed a man who directed its movements from inside. Yet Kempelen was initially able to prevent word of his deception from getting out. The fact that his audience believed it possible for a machine to reproduce so complex a feat of human ingenuity shows the extraordinary faith they placed in the machine builder's art. Mechanical models were expected to be able to imitate—and hence make comprehensible—every process that transpired in the physical world. If the model of an astronomical clock could be used to infer the motions of celestial bodies, then why should it not be possible to use mechanical models to fathom the inner workings of living organisms? Like automata, these moved of their own accord without any apparent external motive force. In the seventeenth century the natural sciences had lastingly "mechanized" the way people viewed the natural world, teaching them to understand the entire material universe as built on laws of mechanical causality. The whole cosmos appeared as a kind of clockwork mechanism, wisely constructed by a divine clockmaker according to unchanging natural laws. Having once been wound up, it could be relied on to keep running smoothly and evenly until the end of time, dispensing with the need to believe in miracles or posit hidden purposes. While this mechanistic worldview did not go unchallenged, it long remained dominant, and it contributed to the enormous fascination exerted by these man-made automata: from astronomical clocks simulating the motions of the heavens and mechanically driven figurines on cathedral and town hall towers all the way to the colorful, seemingly autonomous puppets featured at fairground Punch and Judy shows.

If the "imperial performing clock" strikes us as bizarre today, then this is perhaps because it was so many things in one: symbol of rule and lavish gift of homage, decorative object and intricately worked piece of silverware, precision timepiece and toy for grownups with hints of the fairground attraction. Yet at the time the spheres of scientific inquiry, courtly entertainment, artistic production, and artisanal manufacture were not yet distinct. Scientific experiments were often performed as spectacles in aristocratic salons or town squares. The culture of knowledge as a whole was undergoing a profound transition. The greatest technological breakthroughs resulted from the confluence of traditional speculative erudition and common craftsmanship, "high" mathematics and "low" mechanics. The experimental sciences were not yet firmly established at the universities; the new way of doing research was barely professionalized and methodologically standardized. It tended to be carried out at courts, in monasteries and workshops, in learned societies and academies. Anyone with an active interest, even women and children, could get involved.

New mechanical instruments played a key role in all this. The clock, the most obvious paradigm for a self-operating machine, was the period's metaphor of choice and its guiding epistemic model. No less a figure than René Descartes had brought it to philosophical preeminence. In the eighteenth century the idea of machinery was in vogue across all domains of knowledge. People spoke of the "animal" or "human machine" when referring to a living body, for example. Besides physics, medicine, and theology, the machine metaphor entered political discourse as well. This was hardly surprising: human communities had been compared to living organisms since antiquity. If the body could be regarded as a machine, so too could the body politic. And if the theory of the commonwealth was now presented *more geometrico*, claiming for itself quasi-mathematical certainty, then nothing seemed more natural than to take the clock as a model and metaphor for the state as well.[9] Indeed, Thomas Hobbes had already based his strictly materialistic and mechanistic theory of the state on this very metaphor.[10]

In German lands the ideal of the princely state as a "well-made machine" owed its prominence to Johann Heinrich Gottlob Justi, an enterprising polymath from Thuringia who in the early 1750s had launched a career in Vienna that proved as meteoric as it was short lived. Having studied law and the still novel discipline of cameralistics in Lutheran Wittenberg, Justi was appointed to the Theresianum, the academy for young noblemen founded by Maria Theresa in 1746—although not before hastily converting to Catholicism.[11] Justi is remembered today as the great systematist of Austrian cameralistics. From the mid-seventeenth century, this branch of knowledge had concerned itself with investigating how the royal treasury could be most efficiently and sustainably replenished through the targeted exploitation of all conceivable sources of revenue, not least by stimulating economic activity and introducing a well-designed tax system.[12] Justi was the first to work through such questions in a strictly systematic sequence, which he adopted from the then-celebrated philosopher Christian Wolff. Through his efforts, cameralistics linked up with *the* fashionable eighteenth-century German philosophy, natural law theory. This was concerned with the foundations of human order in all its forms, from marriage and family through civil society to international law.[13] Justi's textbook on public economy (1754) satisfied the new demands of cameralistics as a scientific discipline and was widely read, including by Maria Theresa's ministers, who ordered it to be distributed to local authorities for the instruction of government officials.[14]

In his inaugural lecture at the Theresianum, Justi was already teaching that the state should be regarded as a machine whose effects depended solely on the systematic coordination of all its actions: "The great organization of the commonwealth is a machine, whereby all the parts, all the cogs, all the springs must fit together."[15] The regent, he wrote, "must be the artificer, the primum mobile or soul, so to speak, who sets everything in motion."[16] That is why absolute monarchy was the optimal form of government. One man (or one woman) was needed to oversee the machinery of state and ensure that all its component parts were operating smoothly. Nonetheless, the regent could not be expected to have all the details at his fingertips; he had to rely on reports submitted by his ministers and servants. He should also "be neither his own state chancellor, nor his supreme justice, nor his war minister, nor his president of finances."[17] His sole task was to examine whether their recommendations were "in keeping with the outlined plan of government and the ultimate objectives of the state." Yet this presupposed that the state had already been set in perfect order. Therein lay the first task of a wise regent, with Justi himself providing the necessary advice in his lectures and writings. Once the machine had been constructed on a rational and systematic basis, all that was needed was to supervise its regular operations: "The machine will run by itself and show all the forces and actions of which it is capable."[18]

The highest and most general principle by which the regent was enjoined to build the machine of state was its "ultimate purpose," the "strength and felicity of the state. As soon as an ultimate purpose has been given, all that is arbitrary in the order falls away, and everything must be arranged in accordance with this final end. All regulations which contribute but little, if anything, to this ultimate purpose stand in the way of good order, even if . . . they could be deemed orderly in a different setting." The "ultimate purpose" of "strength and felicity"— how exactly this was to be defined could be left to the regent's discretion—served as an absolute standard against which all time-honored conventions, traditions, customs, privileges and liberties would have to be assessed. "What enormous scope there is here for making a thousand observations about state institutions in their political and religious constitutions, which, once they are seen from this point of view, stand revealed as nothing more than fine and well-ordered disorders. Nonetheless, this is a most delicate subject; and nothing is more dangerous than tackling deeply rooted prejudices."[19]

Justi knew what he was talking about. In the early 1750s he had observed firsthand how Maria Theresa and her minister Friedrich Wilhelm von Haugwitz had fought in the teeth of fierce resistance to implement a "new system" of public administration in the hereditary lands. Justi's ideal of a machine of state was more inspired by Haugwitz's reform agenda than the other way around, since his writings arose only after the great reformist coup of 1748–49. And it is doubtful whether this coup was impelled by any such abstract theoretical program. Yet Justi— along with many other contemporary authors—interpreted the wave of reforms as a methodical campaign aimed at transforming public administration into a fully unified, hierarchically structured system of means and ends, one in which each element had to justify itself through its contribution to the "final purpose," and no part was permitted to pursue its own agenda and special interests. Justi, along with the many political scientists who followed in his wake, essentially did nothing more than bring the multitude of old and new state functions into a systematic conceptual framework. They treated the state as if it were a philosophical doctrine that permitted all individual theorems to be derived from a few universal axioms: a "system." This pet phrase of the reformers originated in philosophy and had very little to do with the actual practice of government and administration. Yet the idea of system, together with the image of clockwork uniformity and regularity that informed it, had an extraordinary suggestive force. These were immediately plausible phrases that justified doing away with powerful and long-held traditions. They shaped and polarized public debate on reform policy in the second half of the century.

Old Customs

The hereditary lands were anything but a well-made timepiece; they were not even a single entity, let alone an efficiently organized state. To Justi and his fellow reformers, they presented an impenetrable tangle of competing lordships and authorities, a jumble of countless offices, councils, and committees that differed, moreover, from one land (or group of lands) to the next. Since the sixteenth century, institutions had proliferated, merged, split off, and expanded as lands were partitioned and reapportioned through the lottery of inheritance. There was no clear-cut division of powers. Instead, responsibility for justice, the military, finance, foreign relations, and dynastic affairs was spread over many hands, giving rise to endless jurisdictional disputes. Such confusion within the individual lands was replicated in Vienna, where all the cogs in the machinery of state were supposedly set in motion and superintended by the monarch.

Yet what the new mechanistic view of statecraft decried as sheer disorder had its own logic, and this logic had long been pursued by the Habsburg dynasty to its advantage. There was no clear and straightforward conflict between the interests of the monarchy and those of the estates. Historians have long told far too simple a tale of their

relationship: here the monarchy's struggle to build up a modern centralized state, there the determined (and illegitimate) resistance put up by
the powerful privileged estates. Put differently, the *public* state interest,
represented by the king or queen, was supposedly opposed at every step
of the way by *private* special interests, represented by the great noble
families of the Habsburg territories. This public-private dualism is a
nineteenth-century anachronism. Things were far more complicated.
The ruling dynasty, after all, had initially been only one among many
noble families, albeit elevated above the rest through sacral consecration. It had taken centuries for the Habsburgs to establish their dominance over their many rivals for power in the nobility. Defensive wars
against both the Ottomans and Louis XIV had helped secure their supremacy, as had the defeat of Protestantism in Bohemia and Austria and
the successful policy of re-Catholicization pursued after the Thirty
Years' War. Yet perhaps the most important factor behind the consolida-
tion of their rule was that the Habsburgs had been able to draw the other
great noble families into a finely spun web of mutual obligations and
services. The entire political order rested on the principle of quid pro
quo. Magnate families in the hereditary lands ruled uncontested over
their own subjects on their enormous estates, but they also occupied
the top positions at court, in the central authorities, in the military, and
in the church. These positions were vast in number. The common social
logic uniting the noble families (and not just them) with their Habsburg
overlords was one of house and family. What mattered most was preserving and promoting one's "lineage, rank, and name" from one generation to the next;[20] everything else was merely a means to that end.
According to this logic, gaining preferment for family members took
precedence over any abstract goals of state. Vacancies had to be found
for people, not people for vacancies. This social logic determined the
structure of all institutions from top to bottom.

Above all, it shaped the relationship between the individual hereditary lands and the monarch. Ever since the Late Middle Ages, a "land"
had defined itself as a political entity via the territorial estates, made up
of noble families, clerical corporations, and towns. As we have already
seen in the case of Hungary, estates convened at territorial diets at more

or less regular intervals to voice their grievances and haggle over taxes with the crown's representative.[21] Yet because the subsidies agreed to by the estates were hardly ever paid on time and in full, and were never sufficient anyway, the increasingly indebted crown was forced to mortgage ever more sources of revenue (such as mines and customs duties) to the estates. Estate corporations were dominated by the landed nobility, which traditionally also controlled the office of captain (*Landeshauptmann*) or marshal (*Landmarschall*) and filled all the important posts at court. Both sides in this relationship—the Archducal House and the great families—depended on each other and worked to their mutual advantage. Yet various factors gradually tilted the scales in favor of the ruling dynasty, particularly the benefits that came with the imperial throne and victories against the Ottomans, which brought them enormous tracts of land in the east. It became ever more attractive for noble families to cultivate good relations with the Archducal House. This can be inferred not least from changes in how the estates in the hereditary lands represented themselves. From around 1700 they increasingly chose to erect monuments to the emperor or pay him some other form of symbolic homage, basking in the light of his ever-increasing glory.[22] On the other hand, the Archducal House was equally reliant on the magnates. Without their support and the wealth of resources at their disposal, governing the lands would have been impossible.

Rulers at the time, including Maria Theresa at the start of her reign, had two basic revenue streams: *cameralia* and *contributionalia*. *Cameralia* consisted of all the income that flowed to the ruling house from its own lands, the crown domains, as well as from various regalian rights and prerogatives: monopolies on mining, minting, and customs; levies and fees; and indirect taxes on a wide range of commodities, from a surcharge on beer to the so-called "meat shilling" (*Fleischkreuzer*). *Contributionalia*, on the other hand, were occasional taxes that the crown had to request each time from provincial estates. Such contributions, which went mainly toward financing wars, were negotiated at territorial diets. Neither side could easily disregard the unwritten rule of acquiescence—when the crown asked for their help, the "most obedient estates" could hardly refuse it. Yet the key point was that these taxes never really came under the crown's control. Having agreed to contribute a fixed sum, the estates then took matters into their own hands. They exacted it from their own subjects, administered it, and in large part also spent it on raising and equipping the troops they sent into the field for the Habsburg supreme commander, although not just for him. The concept of "state revenue" is misleading here. There was nothing like a budget or balancing of books for the entire state. No one at court had an overview of the monarchy's net income and expenditure.

The authorities that collected and disbursed contributions from the estates were the chancelleries of the respective lands. Each land (or group of lands) had its own government office in Vienna with a history of its own. There were court chancelleries for Austria, Bohemia, and Hungary, one for Transylvania, one for the Italian territories, and another for the Habsburg Netherlands. The Imperial Court Chancellery, charged with administering the affairs of the Empire, also played its own distinct role.[23] The court chancelleries were not just responsible for the finances of the corresponding territory; they were equally law courts, government authorities, and in some cases foreign offices as well. The heads of these chancelleries were Janus faced, since the chancellors, while remunerated by the crown, represented both the crown to the land and the land to the crown—not to mention the interests of their own families.[24] They were hinges connecting both sides. The Hungarian and Bohemian court chancelleries were in the hands of powerful magnate families, making them more rivals to the crown than its instruments. From the end of the seventeenth century, they resided in Vienna in opulent Baroque palaces that were representative in two respects: they embodied the autonomy of these lands while at the same time ostentatiously demonstrating the wealth and self-confidence of the chancellors (and their families) who lived there.[25] Thus the Hungarian court chancellors—during Maria Theresa's reign, men from the magnate families Batthyány, Nádasdy, Pálffy, and Esterházy—resided in a luxurious palace in the Bankgasse, built to designs by the great Baroque architect Johann Bernhard Fischer von Erlach. The same architect designed the imposing palace in the Wipplingerstraße, where the Bohemian Court Chancellery was housed when Maria Theresa came to the throne. The Austrian court chancellor resided in a palace on the Ballhausplatz designed by Johann Lukas von Hildebrandt. Just as official buildings and family palaces could not easily be separated, so too there was no clear distinction between assets that came with the office and the great families' private wealth. The top positions brought their incumbents far more income from the perquisites of office and other, informal sources than the official figures on treasury salary lists reveal.

On the other hand, there were very few central authorities that merited the name and bore responsibility for all the hereditary lands, including Hungary—let alone the Dutch and Italian lands, which had always been separately administered and continued to be so under Maria Theresa. The oldest source of institutional unity for the bundle of territories making up the hereditary lands was the Court Chamber, where all the cameral revenue flowing in from Prague, Pressburg, Brno, Breslau, Graz, and Innsbruck was supposed to end up.[26] But the flow of funds had long since slowed to a trickle. At the start of the century the Habsburgs had relinquished many sources of income as capital stock to the City Bank of Vienna (*Wiener Stadt-Banco*), a semimunicipal, semigovernmental credit agency controlled by a court deputation that now administered around half the cameral revenue. The Court Chamber, established in 1527, was cumbersome and ineffective in comparison.[27] Its political weight was inversely proportionate to its size. Between 1682 and 1728 the number of Court Chamber councillors had risen from ten to sixty-eight, even as they presided over a shrinking pool of resources. Central meetings and a central accounting system were nonexistent. Instead there was a welter of special committees and taskforces. No one had an overview of the whole. It is also significant that the Court Chamber, the only central fiscal authority in the entire monarchy, was quartered outside the Hofburg in the relatively humble Questenberghaus in the Johannesgasse. The contrast with the far grander addresses of the territorial chancelleries was revealing.

The Court Chamber offers a vivid example of how Maria Theresa tackled the structural problems that the War of Succession had so glaringly exposed. She set about reorganizing it before the war was even over. At the start of her reign, she ordered that all promotions and new appointments to the chamber council be suspended. Instead she asked Count Starhemberg, financial adviser to her late father, for his assessment of the situation. He was forthright in his criticism and proposed a long list of far-reaching reforms. Another paper, submitted on January 26, 1745 by the president of the chamber council, Count Dietrichstein, sheds further light on the structural problems bedeviling the Court Chamber.[28] Both men agreed that personnel would have to be reduced to cut costs. Yet the president warned that excessive cuts could jeopardize the chamber's operations. This was a particular concern "if future appointments are to be made without regard to recommendations or other external motives, but based solely on the qualities and experience required for the function or office." He thus implicitly acknowledged that personal connections and "external motives," not suitability for office, had previously determined appointments. But if officials were now expected to perform to the highest professional standards, it was all the more imperative that as many young people as possible be admitted to the chamber. Until now cameralistics had not been taught at universities but could be learned only "through long practice and training." This in turn had made it necessary for candidates to grow into their positions over time. At the beginning they had been prepared to accept a meager salary on the unspoken assumption that they would later be promoted to a more adequately remunerated position. Yet since coming to the throne Maria Theresa had robbed them of this justified expectation: "It is easy to imagine what lamentations, complaints, and frustrations this postponement [of promotions and new appointments] has caused since it was adopted . . . several years ago. In part, it has also led to a backlog of unfinished work, for which the officials are hardly to blame." As a result of this freeze, the chamber's subaltern functionaries were now paid half as much as those of other departments; they were worse off even than the lackeys at court, who at least benefited from free accommodation and clothing. What made this even harder to bear was the fact that the Court Chamber was the only department "dedicated solely to serving the royal interest, which it has to defend against the polity and the military, thereby incurring enmity on all sides."[29]

The Court Chamber's low wages and poor standing were mutually reinforcing and had fatal consequences. According to the logic of the time, for an office to command authority it needed to be headed by officials of appropriately high rank. All high-ranking councils consisted of a bench of lords and a bench of knights or scholars; in other words, they were staffed half by hereditary nobility and half by (ennobled) scholars. The chair was always drawn from the lords' bench. But low pay made positions on the Court Chamber unattractive for grandees, leading the president to warn "that the more respectable families will not aspire to serve there, but will turn instead to political and provincial services." Another report, written by the vice-president of the chamber, also arrived at the conclusion that "respectable families" would have to be induced to take a stronger interest in joining the lords' bench, "it being well known how attacks are leveled at the chamber from all sides, which the high standing of noble families with their adherents can resist much more effectively, supporting the chamber to a far greater extent, than other councilors."[30] In other words, when it came to collecting and administering cameral revenue, the monarchy was at least as reliant on the cooperation of noble families as the other way around.

Having received these and other written responses, Maria Theresa finally stipulated at the end of August 1745—in the form of a *Handbillet*, a handwritten note expressing the sovereign's will—how she wanted the Court Chamber to operate in future.[31] Overriding the objections of the chamber president, she drastically reduced the number of councillors while increasing their salaries, although these were not to exceed a *numerus fixus*, a fixed upper limit. All special committees were to be abolished and replaced by plenary sessions, which were to be held at least four times a week and from which nobody could absent themselves without her permission. If anyone put forward a dissenting opinion in the course of these deliberations, it was to be "recorded in writing, so that the time should not be passed in needless chatter." Individual councillors were to be granted administrative oversight over specific lands but were to be shuffled every two years, so that "their hangers-on in these lands will not develop too strong an attachment to such permanent representatives, as is currently the case." Matters relating to coinage and mining were removed from the Court Chamber's oversight, tasks unrelated to its core business of accountancy eliminated. In future, a ledger containing all items of income and expenditure was to be kept and an annual report presented to the empress. The many office-holders deprived of their functions by the reform were allowed, however, to retain their former rank and salary—a significant concession. "So that they may still have something to do," they were to work their way through old, neglected accounts. For every position that fell vacant, from chamber councillor to the lowliest gate keeper, the names of the "youngest and fittest" candidates were to be submitted to Maria Theresa herself for approval. She concluded by warning "that no one should profit directly or indirectly from his office, that everyone, from first to last and regardless of income, should not only refrain from self-enrichment but also refuse all gifts, under pain of dismissal." She was relying on the chamber president to "make a concerted effort to expedite these new arrangements."

The chamber councillors conferred among themselves before presenting the queen with a written response. It stated that "the directive regarding the chamber most graciously issued by Your Royal Majesty is worthy of Your God-given supreme talents and enlightened mind and can only be praised and venerated with the deepest respect." Every effort would be made to ensure it was implemented without delay. This encomium was directly followed by a long list of suggested changes. Such a combination of abject servility in form with undaunted persistence in content was nothing out of the ordinary. Maria Theresa dismissed all such objections with marginal comments such as "My resolution was clear: no changes or exceptions are to be made; my resolution stands."[32] A little later, on September 13, 1745, she confirmed the reforms to the Court Chamber, essentially unchanged, in a new handwritten note.[33]

While this was not the only administrative reform she embarked on before the end of the War of Succession, it is particularly well-suited to highlighting several key features of her regime at the time: her fixed resolve to stay the course once she had made a decision; her immunity to flattery; her determination to overcome resistance from all quarters; her reluctance to engage in lengthy deliberations aimed at reaching consensus, dismissed as "needless chatter"; her clear-sighted assessment of the peers of the realm; but also her realistic willingness to make allowances for their sensitivities. The reorganization of the Court Chamber was also typical in that it by no means represented the opening move in a systematic and methodical long-term reform process, as might be assumed. Quite the contrary: the Court Chamber was restructured again barely four years later, only to be reduced to complete insignificance soon afterward by a further wave of reforms.[34]

A New System

The War of Succession had laid bare the monarchy's structural weaknesses for all to see. The dynasty was deeply indebted to the estates and commanded few resources of its own; high office-holders were divided in their loyalties; contributions to the war chest trickled in slowly or not at all; troops were lacking in discipline. An immediate and effective response to future threats seemed out of the question. Even before the war was over, a provisional reorganization of the military had therefore been taken in hand.[35] Yet it was obvious that root and branch reform would be required. Among conference ministers, there was only limited imagination for what this might entail. A promising Silesian administrator stepped into the breach. In an ambitious memorandum, he offered his services to Maria Theresa by tying his own personal career prospects, for better or worse, to the interests of the dynasty.

Friedrich Wilhelm von Haugwitz (1702–65) was the scion of a noble Protestant family with lands in Glogau and Liegnitz. His father had served in the Saxon and later imperial army and was made a count in 1733. The son paid a visit to Lorraine on his Grand Tour—a canny career move, given that the Duke of Lorraine, Francis Stephen, was Duke of Troppau in Silesia at the time. Haugwitz converted to Catholicism in Lunéville and was appointed chamberlain to the court of Lorraine. Returned to Silesia, he entered administrative service in Breslau in 1725 and quickly climbed the ranks.[36] His marriage into the influential Silesian noble family, Nostitz, did nothing to harm his prospects. Many of its members occupied high positions at court in Vienna, including

Maria Theresa's former aya, Countess Fuchs. After his homeland had been conquered by Prussia, the queen made Haugwitz administrative president in rump Silesia. In this capacity he soon brought his plans to her attention. He proposed sweeping reforms to the finance system on the Prussian model, aimed at doing away with the barriers to absolute rule put up by the estates—first in Silesia, then in the other hereditary lands and in the monarchy as a whole.[37]

Haugwitz struck a new tone. He represented the ideal type of a princely servant who owed his rise and pledged his allegiance solely to the ruling dynasty. Like Maria Theresa herself, he regarded Habsburg rule as a God-given mandate that could, and indeed should, be defended by all means necessary.[38] His "new system" consisted, put briefly, in withdrawing authority for matters relating to administration, finance, and the military from the territorial estates and centralizing it in the hands of the monarch. Among other things, this involved revoking the separation of *contributionalia* and *cameralia* and building up an administrative apparatus at the regional and local level that would be beholden only to the center. It meant, in other words, transforming the proceeds derived from a wide variety of resources into actual state income by fully converting them into monetary form and ensuring that these monies were collected, administered, and disbursed by state officials. In the process, noble families from the hereditary lands were to shoulder the financial burden for defending their land alongside ordinary subjects, who had previously been made to bear these costs largely on their own. This approach concealed a radical change in perspective: noble families were thereby demoted from partners in rule to subjects, albeit highly privileged ones; the ruling dynasty, by contrast, appeared as a neutral third party, elevated far above both the estates and the common populace. A foreign observer summarized the changes by saying that one could now "no longer fully tell, as before, the difference between a lord and his vassals."[39] Such, at any rate, was the spirit of the new system over which Haugwitz presided as its supposedly disinterested guardian. Maria Theresa rewarded him with her unwavering confidence, seeing him as her only reliable ally against the squabbling, selfish aristocrats who surrounded her. She characterized him in retrospect as a man who was "honorable, disinterested, without predispositions, and with neither ambition nor hangers-on, who supported what was good because he saw it to be so, magnanimous, selfless and devoted to his monarch, unprejudiced, a man of great ability and industry and untiring diligence, not afraid to come into the open or to draw on himself the unjust hatred of interested parties."[40] This accords with the ideal image of a minister: a ruler had need of "a disinterested man . . . who seeks only the best for his sovereign and his country, never blinded by ambition nor lured by special interests to veer from this path."[41] Yet such conduct contravened the axioms of courtly prudence and was accordingly rare. A courtier normally could not afford to orient himself exclusively to his master's interest so long as he remained unsure of royal favor. A career at court simply could not function without access to a social network of mutual gratitude and obligation.

Haugwitz followed a different game plan, betting everything he had on a single card: the queen. It is misleading for later historians to stylize him as a modern bureaucrat and sworn enemy of the nobility.[42] Rather than serving an abstract state power, he pledged his allegiance to the hallowed dynasty, convinced of its divine right to rule. A nobleman himself, he pursued his personal career interests like everyone else, albeit with a significantly different strategy from most of his fellows: at the risk of incurring the hatred of other nobles, he had the courage to rely solely on the ruler's patronage. The strategy paid off. He acquired a large estate in Moravia, rose to become a count of the realm, and was made supreme custodian of the patrimonial lands (*Ober-Erblandtürhüter*) in Moravia. Khevenhüller retrospectively saw in him the man who had caused "the entire system of our internal constitution to be shaken up and turned upside down," but conceded that he had, "notwithstanding his confused and generally also overheated and violent temperament," always been *amis des ses amis*, a friend to his friends. In other words, Haugwitz too looked after his own, exploiting his access to the monarch to play clientelist politics and find positions in the Moravian administration for his favorites.[43] Maliciously, Khevenhüller went on to note that Haugwitz had "gladly helped every *particulier*, thereby proving of greater use to the *singulis* than to the *publico et complexo*, to which he rather dealt the first deathblow, whereupon the dire condition of the lands at the time was exacerbated by others and has unfortunately deteriorated to this hour, almost beyond hope of remission."[44] It is hardly coincidental that the picture of Haugwitz painted here by Khevenhüller is the exact opposite of the one by which he is remembered today: that provided by Maria Theresa herself. Among his peers he was considered far from disinterested; on the contrary, he was known to be an assiduous networker. In their eyes, he was not the brilliant financial reformer and architect of the new system but a dangerous maverick whose unpremeditated actions had plunged the state into chaos. Following Haugwitz's death in 1765, Khevenhüller noted that the minister was "by nature not very hardworking, slow, and indecisive"; he had "always maneuvered ineptly in his duties of office, and made a hash of everything"; even in his domestic affairs, he "had no inkling of the true state of his finances and often lacked the cash" to pay his suppliers—and this even though the empress was constantly topping up his annual salary of over fifty thousand guilders with large cash gifts.[45] In short, the great political economist was a miserable manager of his own money. Yet Haugwitz was hardly alone among his peers in squandering vast sums on formal gardens and silverware, on horses, hounds, and the hunt.

Understandably, other courtiers were infuriated by Haugwitz's success in convincing Maria Theresa that he lacked any ambition of his own. They recognized that Haugwitz, in his own way, was exploiting the logic of patronage to further his career. His strategy was risky but paid handsome dividends. He relied unconditionally on Maria Theresa's "all-highest protection," just as she placed her trust in him. Only because he enjoyed her unstinting confidence and support could he afford to make enemies and incite envy at court, flouting all the rules of aristocratic decorum. Many foreign observers who respected Haugwitz and his system saw things the same way: "He would long since have fallen without his princess's favor."[46] In short, Haugwitz unconditionally hitched his interest to that of the Archducal House to initiate reforms that flew in the face of conventional social logic.

He could only do so because a brief window of opportunity had opened up for him following the War of Succession. No one, not even the estates, could deny the disastrousness of the situation. Fears that the Prussians would make further advances had not yet abated, and the Ottoman threat was liable to flare up again at any moment. Haugwitz could argue that Prussia posed a clear and present danger to the entire commonwealth and "the holy Catholic religion." While he acknowledged that a Christian ruler had a duty to respect the time-honored privileges of the estates, he could point out that an appropriate contribution from the estates to the common defense was in their own interests if they wished to avoid being overrun by the enemy and thereby losing all their precious liberties.[47]

Nonetheless, the new system had to be implemented with extreme caution.[48] Even in rump Silesia, where Haugwitz first embarked on his reforms, the introduction of a new, more equitable distribution of taxes during the war had led to "lamentations without end." Prince Liechtenstein, a member of the Viennese court aristocracy whose landholdings were among those affected, demanded to be exempted from the regulations; others sought to achieve the same objective by bribing royal officials.[49] The task of "tax rectification" was dogged by a thousand obstacles but was eventually pushed through in its essentials, despite numerous concessions to vested interests. At any rate, it was enough of a success for Maria Theresa to regard it as a model for the other hereditary lands. In 1747 she sent Haugwitz to Carinthia and Carniola. His mission there, as in Silesia, was to place tax administration in the hands of new royal agencies, to separate the contribution from the domestic budget of the territorial estates, and to ensure that the tax burden was spread more evenly. The royal authorities still needed to collaborate with the estates-based institutions, however. Even as they proclaimed the new system to the populace, they were dependent on the same local grandees whose interests they threatened.[50] Resistance was particularly fierce in Carinthia, which is why the royal edict there sounded an almost threatening note: "If the estates" were not prepared to contribute to "a means truly adequate for preserving the land," the monarch would find herself compelled "to give them a very different constitution that may be less to their liking."[51]

It was clear that the nobility in the hereditary lands, and thus also the highest office-holders in Vienna, would put up fierce resistance if the new system were to be implemented in all of Austria and Bohemia; the experiments in rump Silesia, Carinthia, and Carniola had given them due warning. In the autumn of 1747 Haugwitz advised the monarch to proceed "with the utmost care and great caution."[52] To take the wind out of the sails of the expected opposition, conference ministers were first informed individually and in secret about the proposals and then asked for their written opinion on Haugwitz's reform plan. This plan was prefaced by estimates of the sums required to maintain a standing army of 108,000 men, the current extent of crown income and liabilities, and hence the contributions the provinces would have to pay to make up the difference. Based on these rough figures, Haugwitz proposed making the estates pay a net contribution of 14 million guilders over the following ten years—a significant increase. In return, the estates would be relieved of all additional obligations over the same period. Above all, they would no longer be required to administer and disburse these funds themselves, meaning that the costly provisioning of troops would also be taken off their hands. Centralization of military affairs was expected, not least, to result in improvements to troop discipline, since more regular pay and supplies would spare soldiers the need to pillage. The total sum was payable in installments based on a valuation of all immovable property, with noble estates taxed at 1 percent and ordinary farms at 2 percent of their estimated worth.

On January 29, 1748, "the regrettable new dispensation of the lands" was discussed in the presence of the empress and emperor at a momentous Privy Court Conference.[53] All the conference ministers—besides Haugwitz, these were Harrach, Kinsky, Ulfeld, Colloredo, and Sallaburg—saw the need for the estates to contribute the sum calculated by Haugwitz, yet they fretted over details, voiced objections, raised concerns, and warned of losing people's trust through precipitate action. Only Friedrich August von Harrach, the Bohemian court chancellor, put forward a comprehensive counterproposal.[54] He argued that even more money could be squeezed from the territorial estates provided that they themselves were assigned responsibility for the entire financial administration, including cameral revenue and City Bank funds. He also recommended abolishing indirect taxes as impediments to trade. With that he practically turned Haugwitz's system on its head. Haugwitz did not mince his words in his reply. He was personally familiar with the selfishness of the estates, he said, and knew "that the best way to imperil a land was to give its estates a free hand." Not only had they "misspent and squandered millions," they could even be held largely accountable for the loss of Silesia.[55] His grand plan had to be carried out "in all its parts, without exception," since the need for an adequate defense force "must be blindingly obvious to any rational human being." Yet neither the liberties of the estates nor the rights of the empress should suffer injury in the process. It would therefore first be necessary to "set out the entire matter to the lands as graciously as possible" and listen to what they had to say in response.[56]

The minutes record that Maria Theresa, having heard all the opinions of her ministers, asked Harrach whether he was prepared to put this system to the Bohemian and Lower Austrian estates. He replied that he "could not, nor did he believe that anyone else would be so bold as to do so."[57] Kinsky, Harrach's predecessor as Bohemian court chancellor, excused himself with "another obligation" when asked the same question. Yet it seemed that Maria Theresa had already made up her mind. She insisted that Harrach put the system to the estates, but prudently advised him to present it "as a project rather than as a decree." According to the minutes, the emperor exhorted ministers at the end "that, after the empress has so clearly and unmistakably expressed her all-highest will, every man should place his duty above his personal opinion, neither secretly nor openly seeking to obstruct the plan in any way."[58] Maria Theresa scrawled on the protocol: "*Placet*, and it is only too true that the matter took this course; in fifty years, no one will believe that these were the ministers whom I alone created."[59]

There were good reasons for her outrage. Harrach's open insubordination was extremely unusual and violated every norm of courtly conduct. The ruler's personal authority was ordinarily secured from assault by the unwritten rules of courtesy and the written rules of ceremonial. By directly refusing to obey her in the presence of others, Harrach blatantly contravened these rules. News of the unprecedented scene spread quickly at court, even reaching the ears of foreign emissaries. Podewils reported to his king in Potsdam: "He [Harrach] became vexed with the empress, who told him he had evidently forgotten he was addressing his sovereign."[60] Maria Theresa reacted only indirectly to Harrach's continued resistance, informing State Chancellor Ulfeld that he should "speak plainly with him." She decided against writing a letter directly to Harrach, let alone meeting with him, on the grounds that she wanted to give him no opportunity to offend her again. She instead wrote to Ulfeld: "I regret that Harrach wants to abandon himself. I will give him ten days to come around to obeying his lady [the empress] as a loyal subject." But if he proved unrelenting, there was nothing for it but to remove him from court for a year. Only his absence would shield him from the suspicion that he was actively involved in undermining her plan. "Whatever happens, I stand by my resolution; whoever cannot obey me may do as he pleases, but he shall no longer appear here and before my sight." She crossed out this harsh final sentence before sending the letter to Ulfeld.[61] Harrach then resigned from the post of marshal of Lower Austria, which he was holding on his brother's behalf, and withdrew "with great ostentation" to his Bohemian estates to conduct himself "passively in this whole business" and "avoid any suspicion that he was indirectly working against it."[62] He was back by July, however, a move that was interpreted at court as a sign of weakness; the otherwise "so skillful man had proved far more yielding than some had initially supposed, and thereby suffered considerable damage to the credit, esteem, and reputation he had enjoyed hitherto."[63]

In the meantime, Haugwitz and the other imperial commissioners brought the general plan before the delegations from the individual estates: first in Moravia, then in Bohemia, in Lower and Upper Austria, in Styria, Carinthia, Carniola, and Tyrol. The sovereign did not put in a personal appearance on these occasions, as was customary at Lower Austrian diets and as she had already done in Hungary in 1741. The initial phase in Moravia gave Maria Theresa "particular satisfaction."[64] The two estate functionaries whom she held accountable for the satisfactory outcome of negotiations there were rewarded on the spot with plum positions.[65] In Bohemia, too, everything ran smoothly; in Lower and Upper Austria the estates bowed to the inevitable and passed the "decennial recess." Representatives of the Styrian and Carniolan estates, by contrast, agreed to pay the taxes for three years only rather than ten, while in Carinthia they gave their assent only to withdraw it. Yet Maria Theresa was adamant that Haugwitz's system should be "uniformly implemented in every single land."[66] In Carinthia she pushed through the new system by royal fiat, *jure regio*, without the estates' consent.

This was a significant exception to the rule. In dealings with the territories—not just in the Habsburg empire, and not just in the eighteenth century—it was far more common for the estates to comply eventually with their sovereign's requests. At most they put up indirect resistance, such as delaying payments on various pretexts. They generally shied away from the kind of open, potentially violent conflicts that had broken out in the previous century, the age of Protestant noble revolt, knowing that these could only end in disaster. Instead, territorial diets were typically the setting for a performance of free choice. The sovereign and the estates were both operating on an unspoken agreement. The estates presented their concessions as voluntary, even if refusal was never really an option. The sovereign played along with the charade on the understanding that she would get her own way in the end, thereby allowing the estates to preserve their dignity. This was advantageous for both sides. The Prussian emissary astutely described the underlying logic: "The estates saw themselves compelled to concede of their own volition what no longer stood in their power, that they might preserve at least the shadow of their old liberty."[67] Just how tenaciously the estates clung to the semblance of that liberty is shown by the fact that during the 1748 summer recess, Maria Theresa explicitly promised them that the new taxation system would be described in the official publications as "freely consented."[68] It is equally characteristic that the Lower Austrian diet convened in its usual form in 1749 in Vienna, even though the previous year it had approved taxes for the next ten years. However, Maria Theresa underestimated the need felt by the estates to maintain (albeit in symbolic form) their old role as partners in power. She made her traditional personal appearance at the ceremonious opening session yet absented herself from the no less traditional public Mass of the Holy Spirit, "because she ... found it unseemly to beseech the

Holy Spirit for guidance in a matter that was already over and done with, believing that, after approval had already been granted for so many years . . . by the closed recess, the spiritual function that was customary on such occasions would be out of place and unfitting." Khevenhüller, to whom we owe this report, adds that this reflection would strike an unprejudiced mind as perfectly justified. Given the widespread discontent with the reform, however, the omission of the solemn Mass had "most naturally given rise to much improper criticism, . . . to the extent that in public antechambers there was constant and shameless talk of how the Empress herself recognizes that the Holy Spirit has nothing to do with the current new arrangements."[69]

Meanwhile, unconsecrated by the Holy Spirit, the establishment of the new "main system" (*Hauptsystem*) continued on its rocky course. In each land, a "deputation" was established with responsibility for contribution payments, cameral revenue, and the military. It was set above the existing (or soon to be established) district offices of territorial administration (*Kreisämter*). Deputations had the status of "authorities representing the all-highest person" and were equal in standing, prestige, and dignity to governorships. The old chancelleries had to be bypassed to prevent them holding up or sabotaging the entire operation. For that reason, deputations were accountable to the sovereign alone; all their reports had to be directly submitted to her "all-highest hands." Administration of treasury debts, which were to be paid off (with interest) at regular intervals, was now placed in the hands of the financially savvy emperor.[70] All the threads would come together at a special weekly court committee, personally chaired by the imperial couple. This committee, called the Chief Deputation (*Hauptdeputation*), sat for the first time in August 1748.[71] On November 1, 1748, immediately after the War of Succession had been concluded by the Peace of Aachen, the new "military, cameral, and debt system" officially came into force.

Yet Haugwitz was far from satisfied with what had been achieved. While his new handpicked officials, most of them strangers to the lands where they had been deployed, prepared to roll out the system, he produced one memorandum after another to ensure that this "salutary work, so beneficial to the lands, may be consolidated in such a way that the staunchly resolute, all-highest zeal shown on its behalf may not be frustrated but may share in the most fruitful effects to be expected therefrom."[72] It disturbed him that all kinds of powers still lay with the Court Chamber and that the empress's edicts were still issued via the court chancelleries. Moreover, the Chief Deputation was only an informal committee, not an established agency. It became ever more apparent that the new institutions could not simply act without regard for the old ones but would have to deal with resistance at all levels, not only among ministers but from subaltern officials as well. The entire "machine" threatened to grind to a shuddering halt.[73] Not unreasonably, Haugwitz saw intrigues being hatched against his system wherever he looked. Jealous of his success, the other heads of office, the *Capi*, were eagerly anticipating the collapse of the system "like the Jews their messiah," he wrote.[74] His tone became increasingly shrill. Whereas the previous year he had still spoken of estate privileges as a sanctuary worth preserving, now he decried his opponents' arrogance, ambition, and selfishness. "Multifarious attacks" and "deceitful insinuations" were being brought before the monarch's "hallowed eyes" from all sides; only by exercising the utmost "vigilance" and "keenest attention" would she be able to protect herself from them.[75] Ultimately, her sovereign authority was at stake. With mounting determination, Haugwitz fought to bring the entire administration of Habsburg lands under his sole control. Only in his hands, he believed, could it be made to run like clockwork. With the benefit of historical hindsight, such hopes can only be described as delusional. This is not how reforms to complex institutions work even today, and it is certainly not how they worked back then.

Fearing his enemies' intrigues, Haugwitz secretly, and in direct consultation with the emperor and empress, drafted plans for improving the system. Given he only had a few senior officials on his side, notably Ulfeld and Bartenstein, the Court Conference was sidelined. It therefore almost resembled a coup d'état when, on May 2, 1749, the empress dispatched handbillets to the relevant officials informing them that the Bohemian and Austrian Court Chancelleries had been abolished and two new agencies established in their stead, a supreme judicial and an administrative agency.[76] This sweeping reorganization came at Haugwitz's request. He himself was placed in charge of the new central administrative bureau, which had responsibility for all the Bohemian and Austrian hereditary lands and oversight of the individual territorial deputations. Emulating the Prussian model, it was named Directorium in Publicis et Cameralibus. To demonstrate its importance, the Directory moved into the palace formerly occupied by the Bohemian Court Chancellery. A more magnificent address could hardly be imagined; later, a chapel was built in this "directorial palace" dedicated, tellingly, to St. Theresa.[77] The territorial deputations, for their part, were renamed "representations and chambers" (*Repräsentationen und Kammern*), emphasizing the fact that they represented the sovereign in the full, immediate sense of the term. The new Directory was assigned most of the powers held by the old chancelleries and the Court Chamber, with the important exception of their judicial functions. The various judicial powers that had been a particular bone of contention in the past were now to be united in the *Oberste Justizstelle*, the future supreme judiciary for all legal proceedings in the hereditary lands. The new order thus amounted to a fundamental separation of the justice and administration systems.[78]

Nobody had expected a "revolution of this kind."[79] In both form and content, Maria Theresa's *démarche* of May 2 was perceived as both unprecedented and shocking. It upset deeply rooted assumptions in three key respects. First, the peremptory abolition of long-established institutions was highly unusual. Hallowed by tradition, such institutions had come to be regarded as almost sacrosanct. Those affected by the reforms felt that their positions, ranks, and titles were theirs by right. This explains why most of them were formally retained even when new arrangements had made them redundant. The world of the ancien régime was full of such titles that had outlived their purpose. It was a source of immense irritation to contemporaries that things should now suddenly be different for the two court chancelleries. Second, particular umbrage was taken at the fact that the coup had been prepared in secret, without consultation with conference ministers, and by "a cabal of lightweights" at that, "ill-equipped to take on so important a matter."[80] Although Maria Theresa's good intentions were not called into question, she was said to have been led astray by dishonorable schemers who did not truly have the glory of the Archducal House at heart. Khevenhüller expressed his dismay that "so illustrious a regent as our lady" did not confer with the experts beforehand and so prevent irreparable damage. Finally, it was significant for her unorthodox course of action that Maria Theresa had chosen a handbillet for her purpose rather than a formal ceremonial decree. Princely handbillets—those brief and informal letters personally signed by the sovereign—were ambiguous in their symbolic effects. On the one hand they were taken as signs of particular trust and closeness among those from the same social background. On the other, depending on context, they could serve to indicate a particularly harsh assertion of autocratic will, or even an attitude of insulting condescension. A contemporary textbook for aspiring chancellery officials at Vienna's Ritterakademie (Academy for Knights) even described handbillets as a means by which a regent could make a lower-ranking recipient "feel how indifferently and neglectfully one wants to treat him."[81] Regardless of how the recipients—Harrach, Seilern, Ulfeld, and Haugwitz himself—may have interpreted the letters in this case, by choosing this form of address Maria Theresa demonstrated that her decision was not the outcome of a collegial process but the expression of her supreme sovereign will. As such, it had to be obeyed unconditionally.[82]

Earlier historians saw in Haugwitz's work the birth pangs of the modern state. Depending on viewpoint, they celebrated or—in Bohemia's case—denounced it for spelling an end to national independence. The Kingdom of Bohemia and the "German" hereditary lands were indeed combined into a single administrative unit at the level of central organization, while the separate chancelleries for Hungary, Italy, and the Netherlands were left intact. Yet the Directory's responsibilities were confined to the individual lands, just as before. And on the whole, the work was less rationally and systematically planned than Haugwitz, along with many later historians, made out. The old Court War Council survived, for example; and against Haugwitz's recommendation the Court Chamber, which had undergone fundamental reform only a few years earlier, was not formally dissolved, despite now being stripped of most of its remaining powers. And the separation of justice and administration—a substantial constitutional innovation from a modern point of view—originally did not have the central programmatic importance ascribed to it later (in the sense of the liberal principle of a division of powers). It was more a necessary consequence of the other arrangements that the remaining powers were now pooled in a Supreme Judiciary (*Oberste Justizstelle*).

The image of the new state to be produced by the reforms was shaped not least by novel archival practices. In setting up the new central agencies, Maria Theresa ordered the creation of a central archive for the Archducal House. It is difficult to overestimate the long-term impact of this constitutive political act. Archiving acted as a means for controlling and regulating access to legally relevant documents; it was as much the condition as the symbol of stable political authority and efficacy.[83] Put bluntly, there could be no state without a state archive. In cases of dispute, legal claims or claims to power needed to be supported by documentation. In this respect, the Archducal House was in a sorry condition indeed.[84] Even when Maria Theresa came to power, it had taken some time to hunt down the relevant document refuting the Wittelsbach claim to the throne. The most important "house writings" lay mixed up in two sealed boxes in the "treasure vault" at the Hofburg in Vienna,[85] but not just there; much else was stored in the cellars of residences formerly occupied by individual lines of the house, in Prague, Innsbruck, and Graz. Careful preservation and systematic classification were signally absent. Bartenstein received a firsthand glimpse of the chaos when he tackled the question of archiving for the first time and could not even locate the files from the talks leading up to the Peace of Westphalia: "The original minutes of the protracted negotiations preceding the Westphalian Peace, kept by the imperial ambassador, were sold on the Tandelmarkt here and then sent by the old Count Wackerbarth to Dresden, where they were destroyed by fire over twenty years ago."[86] To eliminate this chaos and for the first time collect all the important documents of the Archducal House, Maria Theresa issued a decree on September 13, 1749, ordering a "house and state archive" to be set up, subject to Haugwitz's Directory. Over the following years, the newly appointed archivist, Rosenthal, brought together thousands of documents from Austria, Bohemia, and Hungary. The archives of the two dissolved court chancelleries were affected by this restructuring and hence taken out of the hands of the territorial estates. The files were culled as well as gathered in one place, and it was said that Haugwitz threw out whole cartloads of Bohemian files.[87]

The new house and state archive was conceived primarily as an "arsenal for defending the rights of the Archducal House," a place where argumentative weapons for future political conflicts would be stored ready for use. Yet its long-term effects went far beyond this. By ordering the scattered written records of the various lands and institutions to be sifted through and brought together in a central location, Maria Theresa invented a unified tradition for these lands. The archivist was commissioned to write a "diplomatic history" of the hereditary lands, which he never got around to finishing. But future generations of historians represented the histories of these lands as partial histories of a whole that had always existed in embryonic form. By causing territorial records to be brought together in a central archive in Vienna, Maria Theresa retroactively created unity where none had existed before.

Why was there not more resistance to the new system? Haugwitz's reform had to be socially cushioned at court; there could be no clear losers in the upper echelons of the aristocracy. The creation of the Supreme Judiciary had the desirable side effect that former members of the two court chancelleries could be furnished there with new titles and salaries befitting their status. Maria Theresa had approached Harrach to direct the Supreme Judiciary, although he turned down the offer.[88] She instead found another solution for him: at his request, he was made president of the new Domestic Conference (*Conferenz in internis*), a committee designed to replace the informal Chief Deputation. He presumably found the role attractive because it would place him above Haugwitz, who was to send him, Harrach, all the minutes of the Directory "not just for approval but also for censorship."[89] Khevenhüller interpreted this to mean that Harrach would have the "honor of performing the role of a Prime Minister for internal affairs".[90] In fact, the Domestic Conference turned out to be a kind of phantom institution that no longer had any function of its own following the establishment of the Directory and therefore fell into unmourned oblivion upon Harrach's death. At least this measure allowed Harrach to save face and emerge from an affair that he alone had openly attacked with his personal honor intact. He nonetheless staged a dramatic departure when the Bohemian Court Chancellery was dissolved. In Khevenhüller's account, Harrach had "bade farewell in such moving turns of phrase, summoning all his native eloquence, that almost everyone around him wept and he himself was heartbroken, so that he was in no condition to conclude his speech but, holding back his tears, had to break off abruptly and retire to his cabinet to give them free course."[91] He fell ill not long afterwards and died at the age of just fifty-three. Many at court were convinced that this devastating episode had hastened his demise.[92]

Harrach was far from alone in despising Haugwitz and regarding his reforms as a sure path to ruin. Harrach's view was shared not just by men like Khevenhüller, for whom even the slightest relaxation of the court dress code portended total anarchy. Foreign observers noted that the reforms were universally rejected: all *ministri principali* condemned the plan, wrote the Venetian emissary; there was general discontent, Podewils reported. If that is the case, it seems all the more astonishing and puzzling that resistance to Haugwitz's system was not more successful. That the two most prominent opponents, Kinsky and Harrach, died in quick succession certainly played a role,[93] but it does not explain why no one else took up their cause. In order to understand this, we need to examine the mechanisms of communication at court more closely.

The sovereign's favor was the eye of the needle through which everyone at court sought to attain their objectives. This made it less likely that potential opponents would join forces against the ruler. Courtiers were used to acting in line with personal and family career strategies; they were not (or were no longer) accustomed to pursuing a collective political goal. When forced to choose, maintaining good relations with the sovereign seemed more important than risking everything in defense of common class interests. A further factor played a part: a sovereign's prestige was a valuable resource for everyone at court, since their own privileged status derived from the ruler's "all-highest" authority.[94] Members of court therefore had a personal interest in demonstrating their obeisance. The honor and dignity of the "all-highest person" depended not least on the symbolic forms that governed her interactions with others. The former's "honor" always depended on the "deference" of the latter. A plethora of written and unwritten rules at court ensured that this functioned as smoothly as possible, elevating the sovereign person above everyone else and protecting her from slights and indignities. Because all parties had an interest in upholding the sovereign's authority, visible communication rarely deviated from protestations of devotion, consensus, and harmony. There was simply no legitimate, generally recognized avenue for open dissent. Furthermore, finding ways of expressing disagreement with the sovereign was not easy, since the rules protecting her authority ensured that communications always ran along tightly controlled channels.

As conflict with opponents to the reform loomed, Maria Theresa took advantage of these rules of courtly conduct to isolate and thereby contain resistance. One such "divide and rule" tactic she used with great skill was that of differentiated secrecy. In early 1748 no attempt was made to keep Haugwitz's plan completely secret—this would have been impossible anyway. Instead, the plan was separately and confidentially shared with individual conference ministers, each of whom had to assume it was intended for his eyes only. This made it less likely that they would jointly resist. Similarly, Haugwitz took care that negotiations with representatives of the lands concerning the introduction of the main system were conducted separately, and with the utmost discretion, so that the lands would not make common cause against it.[95]

More dangerous opponents like Harrach who openly threatened sovereign authority were denied access to the "all-highest person," no longer allowed to kiss her hand, or even banished from her presence. Thus, Maria Theresa not only forced Harrach to leave the court after he had affronted her in a conference session in January 1748; he was also denied an opportunity to react personally to his dismissal, which was conveyed to Ulfeld with the instruction that he pass on the message. Communication through third parties was a standard way to preserve royal authority. In other cases, too, Maria Theresa used middlemen to threaten a loss of patronage or hold out the possibility of clemency. Khevenhüller tells of such a case in August 1748.[96] His great-uncle, Philipp Joseph von Rosenberg-Orsini, a man from the Bohemian high nobility who had already suffered a setback to his career under Charles VI owing to various *étourderies*, lapses in judgment,[97] had been excessively "garrulous" and had evidently given the impression of sympathizing with opponents to the reform. Maria Theresa told Khevenhüller "to pay him [his uncle] a disagreeable compliment," in other words, to issue him a stern warning. In self-justification, Rosenberg sent his nephew a letter, clearly intended for the eyes of the queen, containing a detailed depiction of how Harrach had sought in vain to win him over.[98] Apparently mollified by this account, Maria Theresa let Rosenberg know she would forget about what had happened and harbor no further ill will toward him; but he would be well advised to "draw lessons for the future" from the matter. He should also understand that she had been particularly lenient in admonishing him through his nephew and not "through a more unpleasant channel."[99] This regal communication strategy had another advantageous side effect. The messages of warning that Maria Theresa conveyed through third parties to potential opponents were intended not just for their recipients but also, indirectly, for the messengers themselves. They were thereby marked as her trusted familiars and at the same time coopted into her service, making it very difficult for them to express solidarity with the message's recipients.

Threats to withdraw patronage from potential opponents were matched, on the other side, by demonstrative rewards for cooperative high-ranked individuals, such as the estate functionaries in Moravia or earlier in Hungary. Taken together, all these communicative strategies prevented courtiers from openly siding with a dangerous renegade like Harrach; at most, protest was limited to grumbling behind closed doors. Dissent that was never aired in public but circulated clandestinely instead, dissent that could not be ascribed to any one individual but was only rumored to exist, dissent that, above all, could not be perceived as a collective form of protest—such inconspicuous dissent could not have a significant social impact. This is why Harrach, for all the covert sympathy he attracted, remained isolated in his resistance. Indeed, Maria Theresa was determined to make an example of him. Everyone would see what happened to someone who opposed her so openly. This, however, acted as a disincentive. Finding someone willing to accept the office of Lower Austrian marshal left vacant by Harrach proved extremely difficult. Nobody wanted to be placed in the situation of potentially having to articulate the grievances of the estates.[100]

For all these reasons, there was no concerted resistance at court to Haugwitz's "main system." The fact that the system was nonetheless not a resounding and lasting success had other causes, which had more to do with local conditions and the nature of the system itself. Opponents to the reform predicted—not without reason—that the innovations proposed by Haugwitz, once introduced, would develop their own dynamic. The consequences were unforeseeable, "considering that—once the spirit of novelty takes over—it does not easily come to rest, but tends to spread ever further and pile up one confusion after the other."[101] That was exactly what happened. Haugwitz found himself forced to tinker continuously with his system. On the one hand, the Directorium in Publicis et Cameralibus expanded under his leadership and accumulated ever more powers. On the other, Haugwitz simultaneously created a number of other court committees alongside the Directory.[102] These constant additions produced a welter of new offices that he himself found increasingly difficult to oversee. Even the historians who admire him most are prepared to concede that Haugwitz had less talent for administration than for reform. At any rate, the system failed to pass the test for which it had originally been designed: after the next great war, which began in 1756, lasted seven years, consumed far more resources than its predecessor, and left the monarchy even more hopelessly mired in debt, it was largely dismantled and replaced by a new system. Ironically, the same fate he had once devised for Harrach now befell Haugwitz himself—in 1760 he was neutralized by being reassigned to a prestigious but useless position. Maria Theresa transferred her patronage to a new favorite, who had already made his first grand appearance in the Court Conference in Haugwitz's time and impressed everyone: the Moravian Count Wenzel Anton Kaunitz-Rietberg.[103]

"I Am No Longer What I Was . . ."

By the end of the War of Succession, the atmosphere at court in Vienna and the mood of the empress herself had altered perceptibly. The most concise account of this shift was provided by the Prussian emissary Podewils, a keen-eyed if not exactly impartial observer. Evaluating people's characters and discerning their hidden motives was a matter of vital importance for all courtiers; for an emissary, it went to the heart of his mission. Some brought this art to a pinnacle of perfection, Podewils among them. Frederick II had sent him to Vienna in 1745, following the Peace of Dresden, to repair broken trust and fathom the political intentions of the empress. The young Pomeranian cavalier—he was still only twenty-seven when he began his four-year mission—carried out the task to the great satisfaction of his king. Yet the arduous mission ruined his already poor health; he suffered a stroke at the age of just thirty-one, had to be recalled, and spent the rest of his life in retirement on his Pomeranian estate. Shunned by most of the Viennese court for obvious reasons and received only to formal audiences by Maria Theresa, he was forced to rely on third- or fourth-hand sources of information. Nonetheless, he was still able to deliver a series of richly detailed character portraits, several of which have already been cited here.

In a report to his king from January 1747, Podewils described the change he observed in Maria Theresa as a dramatic reversal in fortune. She had finally allowed her mask to fall and shown her true face:

When she ascended the throne, she knew the secret of winning everyone's love and admiration. . . . By showing only her good side—innocent, generous, charitable, popular, courageous, and noble—she quickly won the hearts of her subjects. . . . She publicly displayed her spiritual strength, bore her misfortune with resolution, and tried to instill her own courage into her subjects. I heard only words of praise for this empress. People lauded her to the skies. Everyone considered themselves fortunate. The estates gave her all they could to meet her needs. The people bore their taxes without complaint. . . . People deified her.

Yet then came the fateful turnaround:

> The queen could not restrain herself for long. Misfortune increases
> both the delight in being loved and the desire for it. The reversals she
> suffered at the onset of her reign brought out this mood in her. The
> successes of her policy after the Peace of Breslau [1745] caused it to
> subside. Slowly but surely, she reassumed her natural character. . . .
> She listened to advice only grudgingly, brooked no opposition,
> sought to arouse fear rather than love, fancied herself as proud as her
> ancestors, treated many with arrogance, showed herself vengeful and
> intransigent, and often heard with impatience the grievances brought
> to her ears. . . . So great a change elicited no less marked a reaction
> from her subjects, who began to protest the taxes they had to pay and
> expressed great discontent on every score.[104]

Podewils was telling a story about the emotional bond between ruler and
ruled: the misfortunes of war won the queen her subjects' hearts while
at the same time making her dependent on their love. Striving to be
loved, she made herself lovable in turn. Yet as the end of the war approached, she no longer had need of their affection and consequently
lost it through her high-handed actions. This interpretation reveals remarkable psychological insight into the dynamics of interpersonal relations, even if the tale of Maria Theresa's malicious dissimulation is surely
a concession to Frederick II's expectations—diplomats tried, after all, to
tell their masters what they wanted to hear. At any rate, the idea that estates and subjects had enthusiastically offered their contribution at the
start of the war was pure fantasy; as we have seen, there had been considerable popular unrest even when Maria Theresa came to the throne.
Yet in representing the general shift in opinion, Podewils was in agreement with many other internal and external observers. Much of what he
reports about the early years of Maria Theresa's reign he would have been
told by his informants in Vienna. The report undoubtedly follows a narrative template that was circulating at the Viennese court at the time,
which he simply spiced up a little for his audience in Potsdam.

There is a great deal of evidence to suggest that the mood at court
and among the public at large worsened as the reforms threatened to

PLATE 9. Portrait of Maria Theresa by Jean-Étienne Liotard, 1762

PLATE 10. Count Wenzel Anton Kaunitz-Rietberg in Spanish coat dress.
Workshop of Martin van Meytens, 1749–50

PLATE 11. Maria Theresa inducts Count Karl Friedrich Hatzfeld into the Order of
St. Stephen, 1764. Workshop of Martin van Meytens

PLATE 12. *The Battle of Hochkirch*, 1758. Johann Christian Brand, after 1769 (detail)

PLATE 13. Ornamental target with an allegory of Victoria, probably commemorating the Austrian victory over Prussia at the Battle of Hochkirch in 1758, Freistadt/Upper Austria. Mühlviertel Castle Museum

PLATE 14. The imperial family. Workshop of Martin van Meytens, after 1754

PLATE 15. Marie Antoinette, Ferdinand, and Maximilian dance the pastoral ballet *Il trinfo d'amore* in celebration of Joseph II's second wedding. Workshop of Martin van Meytens, 1765

PLATE 16. Entry into Vienna of Isabella of Parma, 1760. From the cycle of ceremonial paintings commemorating Joseph II's first wedding. Workshop of Martin van Meytens

put already high annual taxes on a permanent footing. We have already discussed the nobility's animosity toward Haugwitz. Common subjects saw just as little cause to welcome his innovations. As always with reforms from above, they feared—not without reason—that they would bear the brunt of the increased tax burden. Haugwitz's house had to be guarded by cuirassiers after a mob smashed its windows in the summer of 1748, allegedly spurred on by "grandees."[105] Demonstrations of divine displeasure were not wanting: in August a storm of unprecedented duration and violence damaged the Karlskirche; in October Hungary and Moravia were devastated by plagues of locusts; in June 1749 an earthquake lasting several minutes rocked Vienna.[106] Anyone so inclined could read these as signs of an impending apocalypse that could only be averted through a change in policy. God had clearly withheld his blessing from the reforms.

Multiple sources attest to Maria Theresa's own deteriorating mood. Observers found her much changed and *degoutée de tout*, sick of everything and everyone around her.[107] The crown had become an unbearable burden for her, it was said. Just as the war had ended and the pressure on her had begun to ease, her universally admired vitality appeared to give way to deep depression. There were a few possible explanations for this. She had experienced the peace agreement as a defeat and act of treachery from her allies. The implementation of the reform policy met with immense difficulties and tested her resolve. To make matters worse, in September 1748 she was delivered of a stillborn baby.[108] Her mother, the imperial widow Elisabeth Christine, died in December 1750, although she had lived in seclusion in the Hetzendorff convent for some time and her relationship with her daughter had always been distanced. It is difficult to gauge what effect these events had on Maria Theresa's emotional state. At any rate, her general unpopularity at this stage—the resentment of her courtiers and animosity of the nobility as well as popular discontent with her rule, so far as it came to her attention— seemed to trouble her much more than the objectively far greater difficulties she had confronted at the beginning of her reign. Then she had been dealing primarily with external attacks (for all that her foreign enemies had sympathizers at court in Vienna), whereas now she was under fire from her own people. It had become "intolerably painful" for her to put up with the "I will not say hatred—but ungratefulness" on all sides, she wrote in 1750. And five years later: anyone unaware of the "poor disposition" that God had given her could not conceive how much she took to heart the dwindling affection and ingratitude of her subjects.[109]

Her correspondence with Count Silva-Tarouca also conveys her despondent state of mind.[110] Tarouca (1691–1771), an old nobleman from an impoverished Portuguese family, had been in imperial service since 1716. He had already served in the Turkish war under Prince Eugene and had officiated since 1740 as president of the Council of the Netherlands. He was thus responsible for the correspondence between Vienna and the administration in Brussels. In 1744 he was made Knight of the Golden Fleece; in the same year, Maria Theresa appointed him court building director (*Hofbaudirektor*) and entrusted him with her pet project, the extensive renovation of Schönbrunn.[111] In 1750 she also placed him in charge of the Italian Council. Khevenhüller, who likewise held him in high regard and extended him his friendship, noted in 1753 that Tarouca's credit with Maria Theresa had "now risen so high that he can truly be considered the *ami de l'Imperatrice*. The empress has even made him a surrogate for Countess Fuchs, whose health deteriorates from day to day, and openly treats him as her most trusted friend. It is to him that she reveals her inmost self, while he for his part has her permission to bring up whatever subject he pleases, even if unrelated to her service."[112] Tarouca's relationship with the empress would later grow more distant under the influence of Kaunitz, who regarded him with antipathy from the first.[113]

It was to Tarouca that Maria Theresa complained about the *refroidissement... dans l'affection des Ses Sujets*, the cooling in her subjects' affections, seeking his advice on what she could do about it.[114] In reply, Tarouca pointed out how much she had changed since the early years of her reign. Back then, despite her many enemies, her lack of money, support, and experience, and the onerous demands of her work, she had always found time to relax and amuse herself, instead of withdrawing from company and confining herself to her cabinet. The empress shot off a handwritten reply: "I am no longer what I was, for me there are no more dissipations. I must dismiss all such thoughts. I try to get by as best I can and not let others notice anything amiss."[115]

This was the situation that Maria Theresa found herself in when she came to write the two great apologias defending herself against her critics, and presumably against her gnawing self-doubts as well: the first in 1750–51, the second in 1755–56. These "Political Testaments," as they were later called with reference to the genre of princely testaments, in general, and the *Testament politique* of her adversary Frederick II, in particular, are probably her two best known and most frequently cited autobiographical statements.[116] The original heading she gave the first text—"Instructions drawn up out of maternal solicitude for the special benefit of my posterity"—is misleading; the second bears no title. Admittedly, both texts are addressed to her children and are written in the familiar first person. But they contain no practical instructions beyond the stipulation that the new financial and administrative system be preserved unchanged at all costs, whatever false counsel may be offered to the contrary.[117] Instead of providing maxims for future conduct, both documents depict in detail the history of Maria Theresa's previous rule, including its desolate prehistory, with the explicit goal of making her children understand why she acted the way she did.

Neither text was written in her own hand. She also did not dictate them in full to a scribe but had them "drafted" by someone else, as is explicitly stated.[118] Both are composed in German, the language in which she usually corresponded with her officials, whereas she almost always wrote to family members in French. The later editor already surmised that Haugwitz played a key role in the genesis of the first "Political Testament."[119] It is indeed striking that many passages, at least in the first text, barely differ from Haugwitz's memoranda in both style and content. In addition, it is unlikely that Maria Theresa herself would have resorted to such obsequious phrases as *dienstersprießlich*, conducive to service. That the earlier text was ghostwritten by Haugwitz is further suggested by the numerous accompanying financial tables as well as by the fact that his own role as God-given savior is foregrounded with a certain obtrusiveness.[120] The second text from 1755–56 varies the theme of the first but is less systematically structured, has quite a different style, and already acknowledges the need for the reforms to be over-hauled and improved. It may therefore be assumed that Haugwitz did not play as central a role in drafting it.[121] In the end, however, the details of how the two texts came about are unimportant. What matters is that Maria Theresa explicitly presented herself as their author and thereby made them her own.

Her biographers, above all Alfred von Arneth, took their cue from these sources and identified to a considerable degree with their perspective. They quoted the texts as authentic documentary evidence of "how it really was," in Ranke's famous formulation.[122] In other words, Maria Theresa's apologia for the way she conducted herself in power, written to defend her reforms against attacks from present and future opponents, had a lasting impact on how the history of her time was viewed in Austria and beyond. In these two texts she succeeded to an extraordinary extent in shaping her own historical legacy. She did so in large part because the perspective adopted in these texts fits perfectly into the grand narrative of the emergence of the modern *Gesamtstaat* as the realization of a great idea. Yet historians today no longer tell the story of the reforms of 1748–49 as a struggle between good and evil, appropriating one of the two perspectives for themselves. They instead describe how the conflict was structured. The dispute sparked by the new system involved a fundamental conflict of norms: here the traditional norm of quid pro quo, based on the interdependence of the nobility and the ruling dynasty; there the norm of *raison d'état*, according to which the sovereign, freed from all particular interests and elevated far above nobles and ordinary subjects alike, impartially represents the interest of the whole. The monarchy's existential crisis afforded it a rare opportunity to do away with the traditional rules of aristocratic reciprocity and participation. Yet from the perspective of the estates and noble families, it was by no means obvious that permanently relinquishing control over their lands' resources and placing them at the disposal of the ruling dynasty was in their own best interest as well. The memoranda of 1750–51 and 1755–56 show that Maria Theresa was well aware of this conflict of norms. Above all, they show how she found the support she needed to break with tradition and persevere with her new course. Both texts tell a story of divine providence and resolutely overcome tribulations, of motherly love and childish ingratitude, of indefatigable toil for the common good, loyally devoted servants, and selfish adversaries.

The central self-legitimating argument is the idea that God has entrusted the Habsburg dynasty in general, and Maria Theresa in particular, with a sacred mission. Only the piety of her predecessors allowed them to retain divine support over the centuries and establish their undying glory.[123] God rewards and guides devout rulers. Those on whom he imposes the duty to rule, he also endows with the ability to rule well. Maria Theresa's chief maxim in times of need had always been "to trust only in God, whose almighty hand singled me out for this position without any doing or desire on my part and who would therefore also make me worthy . . . to discharge the tasks set before me."[124] But this also meant that "the greater the danger, the more marvelous was the help that came from God." So long as she acted according to his will, God would intervene to turn the tide of events in her favor. Thus, he himself "drew a line" by ending the lives of the reform opponents, Kinsky and Harrach, at just the right moment.[125] During the War of the Austrian Succession he turned the war to her advantage on three occasions, such that the salvation of her lands—a "blatant miracle"—was due "not to the art of weapons but solely to God's indulgence and support." She therefore had no doubt that he would at some stage "graciously assist" her house "in reconquering [Silesia] for the furtherance of his glory."[126] A quid pro quo relationship thus existed between the Almighty and the All-Highest Archducal House, with both sides working to each other's greater glory. Maria Theresa also attributed to God her own courage and steadfastness, her even temper and self-assurance under pressure. He alone gave her the strength she needed "to undertake so great and onerous a work, such as none of my predecessors dared launch."[127] Her unswerving identification with the Almighty allowed Maria Theresa to abase herself before God and to raise herself not only above her opponents but also above her own forebears, whose system of rule she self-consciously broke with. For all her declarations of filial devotion to her late father, she made it perfectly clear that he had bequeathed her nothing but entrenched malpractice, crippling debt, cowardly commanders, and shameless ministers, but no resources to assist her in the arduous task of rectifying these problems.

The second pillar of Maria Theresa's strategy of self-justification was the rhetoric of selfless motherly love. For this she could draw on the age-old metaphor of the ruling couple as the father and mother of their subjects and the land as an extended family. Ever since Augustus had stylized himself as *pater patriae*, at the latest, paternalism had been the central legitimizing motif of monarchical rule. As mother to a vast brood of children, Maria Theresa could effectively intensify this topos by explicitly placing her maternal love for her subjects over her love for her own offspring: "Dearly as I love my family and children, so that I spare no effort, trouble, care, or labor for their sakes, yet I would always have put the general welfare of my dominions above them had I been convinced in my conscience that . . . their welfare demanded it, seeing that I am the general and first mother of the said dominions."[128] Paradoxically, then, the topos of maternal devotion served to elevate her own rule far above the interests of her family: the welfare of her lands was so dear to her that, if necessary, she "should not merely have been willing to submit and abrogate my authority entirely to them [the estates], I should rather myself have diminished and renounced or limited it for my successors, because I should always have placed the welfare and prosperity of the lands before my own or that of my family and children."[129] This was deliberately written in the subjunctive mood. In fact, Maria Theresa was intent on showing that the interest of her dynasty was identical with that of the lands as a whole (she does not speak of an abstract "state"), in stark contrast to the selfishness of the estates and especially her own ministers, who had "often displayed only half-hearted regard for the general welfare and the interests of the crown" and had obstructed them with "contradiction and disputation."[130] The legitimacy of high office-holders is contested with the argument that, riven by mutual "envy, ill will, and calumny,"[131] they had squabbled incessantly among themselves and eyed each other with deep distrust, since each was only looking out for himself. A good ruler therefore had to acquire an overview of the situation with her own eyes, gain firsthand "experience," acquire "personal knowledge of the nature of [her] dominions."[132] She herself would have been overwhelmed by the conflicting advice she received from all quarters had she not "taken the utmost pains to acquaint [her]self through firsthand observation with the real state of affairs."[133] Only the sovereign had the well-being of her ordinary subjects at heart, only she could protect them from the capricious overreach of their lords and ensure that "the poor, and especially the unfree population, not suffer at the hands of the rich and their overlords."[134] Peasants should not have to suffer from the excesses of the military, nor should they be burdened with additional exactions—not least because they would then be unable "to pay their assigned quota of contributions."[135]

In short, all the measures taken by Maria Theresa's government were but "means for consolidating the monarchy and preserving it for [her] posterity."[136] With that, the hierarchy of means and ends was ultimately reinstated. Faith in the dynasty's divine mission, as inherited from her father through the Pragmatic Sanction, was the cornerstone of Maria Theresa's self-understanding and her bulwark against the challenges that confronted her on all sides. That is why her apologia was addressed solely to her posterity: they alone—not her ministers or even her subjects—needed to be convinced of the correctness of her decisions.

Change of Favorites

By the time Maria Theresa came to write her second apologia in 1755–56, it was already apparent that the reforms stood in need of improvement.[137] Haugwitz's system was destined not to survive the next large-scale conflict. This was due not just to the shortcomings of the system itself, and the difficulties posed by its implementation, but also to gradual yet fundamental changes in the constellation at court in the early 1750s. One man did more than anyone else to drive this transformation and then anchor it institutionally, restructuring key committees to suit his purposes: the highly ambitious Wenzel Anton, Count Kaunitz-Rietberg. Haugwitz was not his only victim; he engineered Johann Christoph von Bartenstein's fall from power as well. For decades the most important political adviser to the imperial house and closest

confidant of Charles VI, Bartenstein had been regarded by Maria Theresa during the War of Succession as "the soul of the tepid corps
here"[138]—loyal, hard-working, and reliable, the man who had revealed
her mission in its "true light" and bore primary responsibility for saving
the monarchy.[139] In many respects Bartenstein was the antithesis of
both Haugwitz and Kaunitz: a scholarly middle-class climber, a foreign
interloper in the aristocratic milieu of the Viennese court.[140]

Bartenstein was the talented son of a far-flung, strictly Lutheran pro-
fessorial dynasty from Strasbourg. He had begun his university studies
at the ripe age of twelve and concluded them at twenty-one as "doctor
of both laws," civil and ecclesiastical. In his youth he had kept company
with the intellectual aristocracy of his time; he had visited the learned
monks at the famous Abbey of St. Maurus in Paris and been introduced
to the elderly Gottfried Wilhelm Leibniz, corresponding with him until
Leibniz's death. His goal was not a scholarly career, however, but service
at court. Keenly aware of his extraordinary gifts, he had set his eyes on
the top from the first, making contact with the imperial court through
intermediaries. Pride in his superior abilities led him to look down on
those who had acquired their positions through what he called the
"casus genitivus and dativus"—in other words, through birth or gift-
giving. Yet, to his frustration he was forced to recognize that his Lutheran faith stood in the way of a career at the Viennese court. Far from
indifferent in matters of religion, he long wrestled with his conscience
before deciding in 1716 to convert to Catholicism.[141] It nonetheless took
him over a decade to rise to the Austrian Court Chancellery and eventually, in 1727, become state secretary (Staatsreferendar) and minute taker
(Protokollführer) to the Court Conference. Although not himself a
member of this exclusively noble colloquy, his unrivaled expertise and
support from the crown allowed him to direct business there and, above
all, control foreign policy, the so-called affairs of state (Staatssachen).
With that, he had attained the most that a middle-class official could
hope to achieve at the imperial court, and he played his cards well. He
had made himself indispensable to Charles VI through his indefatigable
labors on the emperor's behalf, as well as through his towering intellect
and unerring judgment. A voracious reader blessed with an excellent

memory, he was often the only one to penetrate the complicated affairs of state—and he took care to ensure that he remained the only one. He alone was the institutional memory of the Austrian Court Chancellery at a time when files had not yet been systematically archived. He had already dominated the Court Conference and Court Chancellery under Maria Theresa's father and was therefore a thorn in the side of other courtiers. When they were heard complaining that Charles VI preferred to take advice from "little people" rather than from worthy long-serving ministers, it was primarily the "subaltern matador" Bartenstein they had in mind. He was also rumored to have deceived the emperor and given him false advice.[142] In 1747 Podewils gave a detailed depiction of him as a "diminutive, pedantic schoolmaster," undoubtedly gifted with intellect and a prodigious memory but of limited political judgment. Those who envied his success with the ruling house interpreted it as the fruit of excessive ambition, flattery, and "feigned moderation." What persons of rank found unforgivable was that Bartenstein had the audacity to style himself their equal or even their superior, turning the social hierarchy on its head. Never one to suffer fools gladly, he was even known to interrupt his interlocutor mid-sentence. On the basis of his influence with theArchducal House, "everyone was forced to approach him on bended knee. People of the highest rank, imperial princes, generals, ministers, put in regular appearances to pay him their obeisance."[143] Khevenhüller, for one, secretly detested him but was anxious to ensure that "he does not turn against me."[144] Many clearly found it hard to stomach that Bartenstein made no attempt to imitate a courtly, elegant manner, which would have made him an object of general ridicule, but instead flaunted his bone-dry erudition with unruffled self-assurance.

Given that he had opposed her marriage to Francis Stephen, Maria Theresa's relationship with Bartenstein was initially cool. Yet in wartime conditions he quickly became as indispensable to her as he had once been to her father. His influence rose still higher following a first organizational restructuring of "affairs of state". When the old court chancellor, Sinzendorf, who had willingly deferred to Bartenstein, died in 1742, Maria Theresa split off the department of the Austrian Court Chancellery responsible for foreign correspondence and made it an independent bureau for the Archducal House's entire foreign policy, the Court and State Chancellery (*Hof- und Staatskanzlei*).[145] The man she appointed state chancellor, Anton Corfiz, Count Ulfeld (1699–1769), was a convert and an experienced diplomat whose Danish father had served as a general under Charles VI. Ulfeld was considered gruff, coarse, and dull witted but virtuous and unselfish. It spoke in his favor that his mother was a Sinzendorf by birth, but also that he had no intention of imposing his own plans on the State Chancellery. Considerably less intelligent than his secretary, yet also less smug, he let Bartenstein have his way and posed no threat to his dominance. The rumor therefore went around that Bartenstein had installed him in the position. Each profited from the other: Ulfeld was Bartenstein's patron, Bartenstein Ulfeld's political "oracle."[146]

During the war years, the industrious secretary produced an unending stream of memoranda for the State Chancellery. He was said to be infatuated with his own prose, notorious for its circumlocutory pedantry,[147] although his written proposals almost always met with Maria Theresa's approval.[148] Just how much Bartenstein was aware of his own indispensability is shown by an episode from 1748, the year of reform. When Maria Theresa approached him to head a commission for introducing the new financial system to the hereditary lands, he refused point blank. "The empress, who was not in a good mood to begin with, took offense and replied with angry words that she would turn to others instead. Bartenstein . . . countered with most unseemly protestations of the services he had rendered to the crown, provoking such an outburst that it could be heard almost word for word . . . all the way to the emperor's second retirada." Khevenhüller noted this with barely concealed satisfaction, since it was his task to soothe the irate empress: Bartenstein had "vented his spleen in muddle-headed madness and no longer knew what he was saying."[149]

Personal missions were not to Bartenstein's taste; he had never served as envoy or acquired the airs and graces of the courtier. His medium was writing. His great influence on the government had to do with the importance of written communication for the way decisions were made at the Viennese court. This is strikingly apparent from the way the Privy

Court Conference conducted its business. The conference was made up of the heads of the most important central court departments (Court Chamber, Court War Council, Court Chancelleries, Court Marshal's Office); its role in implementing Haugwitz's system has already been discussed at length. It convened every Monday, occasionally more often. Sometimes the empress and emperor were in personal attendance, sometimes not. Each member brought with him only a single secretary. As a central advisory body, such as gradually developed in all European monarchies, the conference was institutionalized only to a limited extent. It had neither specific responsibilities nor positions nor offices; it stood neither in the court calendar nor in the court treasury list. It served as a forum for discussing all the important questions of the day, from war and peace via the appropriate ceremonial for dynastic marriages to the principles of a princely education. The decision-making process in the conference was structured by a specific interplay of written and verbal communication that was entirely oriented to the sovereign.

Maria Theresa communicated with her conference ministers, as with all her other officials, "on the basis of the age-old constitution of the Most Serene Archducal House." Items placed on the conference's agenda were drawn up in writing and her decisions were made in writing.[150] No later than one day before a meeting, *Deliberations-Puncta*— items submitted for the conference's deliberation by one of the ministers—were communicated to the chair in writing. Sometimes Maria Theresa would ask the conference secretary to pose a question to the ministers in advance of the meeting and have each provide her with his written opinion. This had the effect of canalizing communications: each minister addressed his remarks to her, not to his colleagues, so her advisers' opinions were concealed from each other unless she chose to circulate them. During the meeting, "a vote was taken on every single *punctum deliberandum* after hearing from the office that was chiefly affected."[151] In other words, position papers were read out rather than the issue being thrown open to discussion. Finally, "the conclusion was reached."[152] How exactly this occurred remains something of a mystery. We should not assume that decisions were arrived at by a majority.

Instead they were almost certainly—like almost all decision-making procedures at the time—formed through rough consensus. The monarch herself always had the final say. But prolonged deliberative procedures were anathema to Maria Theresa; as we have seen, she dismissed them as "needless chatter."[153] She wanted dissenting opinions to be noted in writing but not discussed at length and, above all, not subsequently aired "in public." The perfect minister would deferentially express his opinion in conference but relent if the sovereign's decision went against him.[154]

Sessions were protocoled by the secretaries of the chancelleries which would later be responsible for implementing the ruler's decisions. For foreign affairs this was usually the State Chancellery, in other words Bartenstein. In his chancellery, the individual minutes were collated and a report composed, the so-called presentation (*Vortrag*) to the monarch. It was written on sheets folded lengthwise, with the left column left free for commentary indicating her approval, amendments, or rejection. Strictly speaking, this presentation had to be resubmitted to all the conference members so they could assure themselves that it accorded with what had been discussed and agreed on in the meeting.[155] At the end, Maria Theresa made her decision or resolution by writing her *placet* (with or without additional modifications) in the margin of the page (fig. 19). Only time-honored administrative customs, not clearly defined responsibilities or formal procedural rules, thus ensured a certain stabilization of the decision-making process.[156] The unspoken norm was still that of the old European tradition, according to which the final decision lay with the divinely authorized ruler, but always through consensus and in consultation with the grandees of the realm. Nowhere was it stipulated who exactly was to be consulted or how exactly consensus should be reached.

Coordination of the entire process lay with the Court Conference secretary—again Bartenstein. The title of "secretary" is to be understood in the literal sense; he was a keeper of secrets. Not by chance was the gathering called the *Privy* Court Conference. There was no stigma attached to secrecy. On the contrary, it was a perfectly legitimate means of exercising power that served to structure communication, not hinder

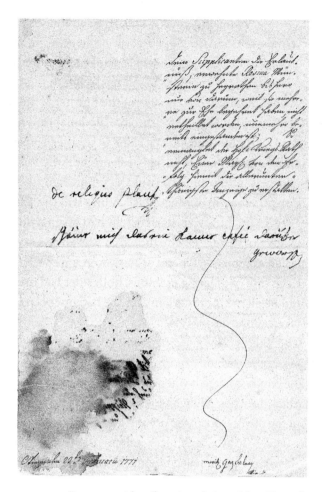

FIGURE 19. Document with coffee stain and, above, Maria Theresa's
handwritten comment: *de reliquo placet*. In the middle: *embarrassed
to have spilled a cup of coffee*, 1771

it.[157] Discretion was the cardinal virtue of the princely servant, induction into the circle of cognoscenti the most valuable distinction that
could be bestowed on him, as symbolized in the coveted title of privy
councillor (*Geheimer Rat*). Particularly in affairs of state, but also in
domestic affairs, secrecy was "the soul of everything."[158]

The fact that the Court Conference mostly conducted its business in
writing gave the secretary, as director of proceedings, discreet

possibilities for asserting influence. As his rivals in the Court Conference observed, Bartenstein developed a *belle methode* to "engineer" imperial resolutions to his liking: "he would convene meetings without making known what was to be discussed beforehand; then, after the conference, he would immediately submit the finished written reports for her *placet* without having previously circulated them among conference ministers."[159] Bartenstein himself came to see the problems inherent in such an arrangement once he had been ousted: when submissions were compiled, dissenting opinions could be suppressed and the sovereign's decisions thereby manipulated.[160] While still the all-powerful chancellery secretary, however, Bartenstein had given a different account of the advisory process. The monarch was always perfectly informed, since all arguments, for and against, were given a fair hearing: "because, in the case of differing opinions, both sides had their say, Her Majesty could be all the more certain that she had not been misguided by any mistaken supposition."[161]

Once Maria Theresa had given her handwritten *placet*, it was impossible to make any changes and expose instances of manipulation or deception. First, the empress hated it when anyone volunteered a private opinion after she had given her "all-highest resolution."[162] And second, she was loath to incur the displeasure of the powerful and (in his own mind) infallible Bartenstein.[163] In Khevenhüller's judgment, the same held true of "the lords" themselves, who relied too much on Bartenstein to challenge his "dominance." They were aware of the secretary's machinations, he thought, but since they "could not very well do anything to redress the situation (so as not to antagonize the secretary), they have no real confidence in the conference itself and seek out here and there opinions from other people, who cannot know the full context of their affairs. They are therefore always susceptible to error and irresolution."[164]

Even if this observation was colored by Khevenhüller's violent antipathy toward Bartenstein, it is still a remarkable indication of how the Privy Court Conference and its documentation procedures (which operated similarly in many other offices) were regarded at court. What such committees lacked in transparency and open debate, they made up for in paperwork. Secrecy served less to create a protected space within which all members could speak freely and disagreement could be aired without loss of face than to conceal the decision-making process from individual members of the committee themselves. This led to a situation where the Court Conference slowly but surely lost the ability to fulfill its original function: openly discussing proposals and measures, weighing up arguments for and against, and providing the monarch with informed advice. Ministers no longer referred important questions to the conference, preferring to take matters into their own hands.[165] Under such conditions, formal documentation procedures all but guaranteed their own informal erosion.

In effect, anyone seeking to influence the political decision-making process at the center had to bypass Bartenstein and his Court Conference. They were forced to turn instead to the second key figure in Maria Theresa's immediate environment, her personal cabinet secretary Ignaz Freiherr von Koch (1697–1763).[166] Although "of no extraction"[167]—he came from a middle-class background and was not ennobled by Maria Theresa until 1748—Koch had already managed Prince Eugene's private correspondence before becoming one of the most influential officials at court under Charles VI. From 1742 he was the eye of the needle through which almost all written requests and submissions to the monarch had to pass. "His task consists in informing her of the petitions and memoranda she receives and then passing them on to the relevant department with the decision of Her Imperial Majesty. He also places before the princess all papers requiring her signature and deals with her personal correspondence. To this end he works with her every morning," the Prussian emissary wrote. "Anyone seeking a position or favor is sure to approach him."[168] Koch was the most important broker of sovereign patronage at court. Even Khevenhüller used him when he had a delicate matter to broach. Haugwitz, too, essentially owed him his access to the empress.[169] Amazingly for someone in his position, Koch was not universally hated. The perceptive Podewils put this down to his modesty, which concealed his influence and at the same time made it easier for the court nobility to tolerate him. At any rate, both Maria Theresa and the court nobles considered him to be a man of incomparable discretion, "uncommonly honest, Christian, and not given to intrigue."[170] For the same reason he was appointed head of Maria Theresa's tentacular espionage apparatus, the Secret Cipher Chancellery (*Chiffrenkanzlei*).[171]

Koch was also the man who made it possible for the ambitious Kaunitz to circumvent the Court Conference, oust Bartenstein from the State Chancellery, and eventually replace Haugwitz as well. In the 1750s, in both foreign "affairs of state" and the administration of the hereditary lands, Kaunitz gradually edged out the former favorites and replaced the old systems with new ones of his own devising. He was to become the most influential figure at court for the rest of Maria Theresa's reign and beyond. Wenzel Anton von Kaunitz-Rietberg (1711–1794) came from an old Bohemian noble family which had come under the protection of the powerful Dietrichstein family during the Bohemian Revolt of 1618 and had since distinguished itself through its Catholic orthodoxy and staunch dynastic loyalty. His grandfather had been imperial vice chancellor and had risen to become imperial count, plunging the family's Moravian estates into debt in the process.[172] His father was captain of territorial estates in Moravia and had married a Westphalian notable, Imperial Countess Rietberg. Of their sixteen children, Wenzel Anton was the only surviving son. To him alone thus fell the task of restoring his family to its former glory. His father subjected him to a strict education and sent him off to study law at the University of Leipzig, a renowned center of the Protestant German Enlightenment— with great success, it was reported. As befitted a young knight, Wenzel Anton then set off on the Grand Tour, which took him via Berlin, Brussels, Cologne, Frankfurt, and Munich to Venice, Rome, Naples, Florence, Milan, Genoa, Turin, and finally Paris. Returned to Vienna, he entered the Imperial Aulic Council in 1735, considered a career springboard. Soon after he married the granddaughter of the powerful conference minister, Gundaker Thomas von Starhemberg. Maria Theresa used him for various assignments during the war, including as envoy to Turin, where he made a name for himself in 1742 through his astute memoranda on the system of foreign affairs. Yet his career did not quite take off. He was offered a number of more prestigious diplomatic missions but had to turn them down, lacking the means needed to represent the sovereign with the appropriate diplomatic finery. He eventually gained

Maria Theresa's particular favor through his successful involvement in the peace negotiations in Aachen in 1748. He began there to argue that the Archducal House would have to break with its traditional allies and draw France to its side if it ever wanted to win back Silesia.[173] His intelligence secured him entry into the exclusive circle of the Court Conference, where discussions took place in January 1749 about the overall political situation in Europe and the future course of the monarchy's foreign policy. Even on his first appearance, he made an impression through his extraordinary eloquence and cleverness.[174] Maria Theresa already held him in high esteem at the time as her most important and valued adviser, the *"seule ressource pour ma ministère."*[175] In 1750 she sent him as ambassador to Paris, where he was charged with placing Habsburg-Bourbon relations on a new footing.

Yet Kaunitz was difficult. A ponderous perfectionist and stickler for detail, narcissistic, vain, and pretentious, he thought of himself as a connoisseur of exquisite taste, collected paintings, dressed in the latest fashions even as an old man, took pride in his horsemanship, and flaunted his elegant command of four languages (see color plate 10). In Paris he styled himself a freethinker, reading Voltaire's works, subscribing to Diderot's epoch-making *Encyclopédie*, and collecting erotic literature.[176] Through his access to Madame Geoffrin's famous salon, frequented by the most fashionable *philosophes* of the day, he could consider himself the member of an exclusive club of self-proclaimed Enlightenment luminaries. Other emissaries found, however, that he did not keep house in the manner expected of an imperial representative, and they sneered at his habit of mixing with nouveau riche upstarts, a habit they attributed to his miserliness and his thirst for recognition.[177] Above all, they mocked his fastidious concern with his own body, his *galanterie vis-à-vis de lui-même*, his bizarre rules of hygiene and diet.[178] He came across as cold, unemotional, and inscrutable in company; he kept his opinions close to his chest and preferred to hold his tongue rather than express disagreement. No one liked him, although his keen intellect and wide-ranging knowledge were widely admired. The contrast between his *génie supérieur* and his many tics and extravagances did not escape Maria Theresa (or the Prussian king, for that matter). Khevenhüller reports that he spent a long time with her discussing Kaunitz's character, which "gave rise to various reflections on the contradictions of human nature."[179] To some extent, the pretentious Kaunitz must have irritated the modest Francis Stephen, not to mention the jealous ministers, who could barely conceal their antipathy toward him.[180]

During his ambassadorship in Paris from 1750 to 1752, Kaunitz was in constant correspondence with Cabinet Secretary Koch. From him he received word of all the deliberations in the Court Conference, and he deliberately went behind Bartenstein's back in his efforts to cultivate the empress. He had his sights set on the State Chancellery, that is, control of foreign policy. As mentioned earlier, in 1742 Maria Theresa had already split off this department from the Austrian Court Chancellery and made it an independent central bureau for "domestic, court, and state affairs."[181] It had since assumed responsibility for both the Archducal House's relations with foreign powers and all dynastic private matters such as marriages and inheritances—tellingly, since foreign policy was still in large part based on relations between dynasties. The State Chancellery was formally led by Ulfeld, although real power lay with Bartenstein. It was clear that Kaunitz, twenty years Bartenstein's junior and every bit as ambitious, would not be able to work with the self-righteous secretary if he wanted to make a career for himself in state affairs. Yet Maria Theresa was known for clinging all the more doggedly to her long-serving advisers the more they came under attack, and she harbored a deep distrust of people of ambition and interest. Driving Bartenstein out of office was therefore no easy matter and called for particular skill. How Kaunitz succeeded in deposing the old chancellery secretary is a textbook study of courtly ingenuity such as might have appeared in the famous Pocket Oracle of the Jesuit Balthasar Gracián, a kind of handbook for the prudent courtier.[182] For Kaunitz, what mattered most was to cloak his own ambition, arranging things in such a way that he achieved his objectives at the monarch's behest.

Maria Theresa had long been dissatisfied with the uncouth and ungainly Ulfeld as state chancellor—on one occasion she had been heard calling him an ass[183]—and planned to replace him with the young Kaunitz. But the situation had to be carefully managed to avoid loss of face. The death of Lord High Steward Königsegg in December 1751 was therefore timely; it cleared the way for Ulfeld to be relieved of his position with his honor intact. Maria Theresa seized the opportunity to have Koch offer Kaunitz the position of state chancellor. Kaunitz's reply to Koch, intended for the eyes of the queen, is a masterpiece of courtly dissimulation.[184] Kaunitz began by hinting at the limited financial means associated with the position, making it seem not particularly attractive. He then volunteered an apparently ruthlessly self-critical account of his own "physical and spiritual defects," *mes vices de corps et d'âme*, which supposedly made him unfit for the office. While his powers of apprehension were excellent, he had a terrible memory. He also had an aversion to talking about topics on which he had not previously formed clear ideas in accordance with the "natural order of things." On such occasions he could still express himself in both speech and writing with fluency and ease, but this proved a more taxing ordeal for him than for anyone else. The petty minutiae of business were also a torment to him; he would much rather devote himself to the great, essential questions. The state chancellor currently had to concern himself with all the details if the "machine" was not to come to a standstill. Things could be simplified, Kaunitz suggested, by employing subaltern officials to deal with routine processes, thereby freeing the chancellor to concentrate on the operations of the whole. The sad truth that emerged from Kaunitz's depiction of his own character was in every respect the opposite of how Bartenstein ran the chancellery. Even though, as he went on to write, the empress's offer naturally appealed to his ambitions and interests, he ought not to think of himself in this case and would have to decline it, since he was both unable and unworthy to fill the position.

Yet then, in the very same letter, he sketched a plan outlining how the State Chancellery would have to be reorganized—and Bartenstein removed—for him to take it on. The necessary new foreign policy system he described there was unmistakably informed by the idea of a rationally constructed, automatic clockwork mechanism.[185] The message was clear to anyone reading the letter: all of Kaunitz's self-professed defects were actually strengths, while all the strengths on which Bartenstein so prided himself were in fact structural weaknesses. If Kaunitz appeared to be the wrong man for the job, then this was only because the whole system had been poorly designed in the first place. The system would therefore have to be reformed in such a way that it would suit a man of Kaunitz's talents and abilities. This was the conclusion that Maria Theresa would inevitably draw from the letter without Kaunitz having to spell it out. By arguing that he was not jockeying for power but was prepared, however reluctantly, to take in hand the necessary reorganization, he was effectively dictating his terms to the empress. At the same time, his letter showed him to be a man of the utmost honesty, a selfless man of honor who placed the welfare of the Archducal House before his own personal interests. The most important lesson in Gracián's manual of dissimulation, after all, was to avoid being *seen* to dissimulate.[186]

The strategy paid off. When Kaunitz returned to Vienna in early 1753, Maria Theresa reshuffled many of the key positions at court. Ulfeld was made lord high steward, leaving the post of state chancellor free for Kaunitz.[187] Bartenstein lost the post of chancellery secretary—because "both geniuses would not easily be able to get along"[188]—and instead became vice chancellor of the Directorium in Publicis et Cameralibus and conference minister as well, an unprecedented honor for someone from a nonaristocratic background. When Ulfeld and Bartenstein learned of the plan at the end of October 1752, they sought in vain to avert their fate. Bartenstein addressed a letter to Maria Theresa setting out his services to the monarchy, insisting on his indispensability, and declaring himself willing to take orders from the new state chancellor in future.[189] Maria Theresa tried to persuade Kaunitz to let Bartenstein continue working in the State Chancellery, in however subordinate a role, but to no avail. Her failure to change his mind sheds light on her dependence on the new minister. Ulfeld was also far from overjoyed at his future "promotion" to lord high steward, venting his frustration to the empress in "coarse words" and demanding significant financial compensation.

The reshuffle, which Maria Theresa had wisely kept secret for as long as possible, broke with time-honored conventions at court. A bearer of high office could usually expect to keep his position until death, provided he was not found guilty of some serious offense. Deposing two such longstanding servants—Bartenstein had been in office since 1726—signified a public humiliation and left Maria Theresa open to the charge of unpredictable harshness and ingratitude. For these were in fact "demotions," not "promotions," as Khevenhüller wrote. To be sure, everything was done to disguise this fact. Bartenstein's letter of appointment was fulsome in its praise,[190] while Ulfeld's investiture as lord high steward was performed with the greatest possible "solemnity" and "decorum"; all the high officials, privy councillors, and chamberlains had to show up in Spanish coat dress. Ulfeld nonetheless experienced the whole episode as a serious blow to his honor and struggled to maintain his composure as he stammered out his official words of thanks; "one could not help noticing that he was heartbroken."[191]

A blow of this magnitude could only be lessened through extraordinary generosity. Those who bore the brunt of it were determined to recoup in financial capital what they had lost in its symbolic equivalent. In recompense, and also to ease her own troubled conscience, Maria Theresa was prepared to make exorbitant financial sacrifices. Ulfeld received an incredible 100,000 guilders as a gift. As compensation for the loss of his quarters at court, he received a further lump sum sufficient to purchase a representative palace. There was even a rumor that the empress had taken on 160,000 guilders of his debt.[192] Bartenstein received the same payout as Ulfeld and an increased salary for the rest of his life—not just for him but for his three sons as well. The other courtiers were none too pleased; such displays of imperial largesse considerably dampened their glee at Bartenstein's downfall. Yet that was not all. There were additional outlays for the new State Chancellor and his numerous newly appointed colleagues. The fact that Maria Theresa was prepared to spend such vast sums, despite the ongoing financial misery, shows how deeply she remained beholden to the social logic of quid pro quo governing life at court. She was unable to escape the norm that a sovereign ought to be generous. On the contrary, being a particularly magnanimous, gracious sovereign was entirely in keeping with her self-image. Courtiers knew how to exploit this to their own advantage. Maria Theresa complained bitterly to Khevenhüller at seeing her gifts "disparaged, as it were, when any impartial temperament would have to give them full acknowledgement. . . . *Elle avoit le coeur si gros* [she was so great-hearted], as one says, that she openly avowed her perplexity to me."[193] In the conflict between economic rationality and aristocratic norms, Maria Theresa decided in this case—as almost always—for the latter. But this did not spare her criticism from court society. There were serious concerns, after all, about appointing the opaque and capricious Kaunitz as state chancellor with considerably expanded powers.[194] To Khevenhüller, she explained that she could simply no longer stand Ulfeld and would therefore have to try Kaunitz instead, although she foresaw many disagreements—particularly from the emperor—and Kaunitz's poor health and idiosyncrasies promised but a brief tenure.[195] This supposition, perhaps intended only to appease Khevenhüller, would prove to be mistaken.

Once installed in office, Kaunitz immediately set about implementing his plans, reorganizing the State Chancellery along French lines for the sake of increased prestige, as Khevenhüller sardonically noted. At his behest "there was created . . . an entirely new State Chancellery or Bureau des affaires étrangères, staffed by personnel of his choosing."[196] Kaunitz was the first state chancellor who systematically filled all positions with his own personnel, mostly from a middle-class background, in the process setting down strict performance criteria to realize his ideal of a professional, hierarchically structured central administration.[197] Gradually he took over all the responsibilities of "foreign" policy that had previously been spread over various departments. He thus competed with the imperial vice chancellor on his own terrain—in other words, even the Empire was increasingly treated as a foreign realm. In 1755 he removed power over relations with the Ottomans from the Court War Council[198] and in 1757 he likewise assimilated the Italian and Dutch councils. The omnicompetent Court Conference, which Kaunitz had chaired since 1753, became increasingly obsolete, gradually forfeiting its central importance. The overall trend, which has been described in historical hindsight as a decisive "change of system" resulting in the establishment of a new kind of "foreign ministry," appeared to critics at the time as a creeping ministerial despotism.[199] Even Maria

Theresa, for all that she admired his abilities, came to find Kaunitz domineering and uncontrollable. In 1757 Ulfeld "reproached her in a letter with letting the all-powerful state chancellor usurp her authority, such that a great deal is done and decreed without Your Majesty's knowledge, much less authorization. . . . Little by little, all its powers have been stripped from the conference." Maria Theresa replied, "This is all too true and I can no longer do anything about it."[200]

Another New System

Kaunitz's ambition was not confined to the field of foreign affairs. A little later, during the war, he moved to impose his own agenda on the domestic administration as well. Haugwitz's revolutionary new system had failed to deliver what it had promised. It had not turned the administration of the hereditary lands into a well-oiled machine whose parts functioned automatically according to the laws of mechanical causality. Yet once the decision had been made to treat the entire bureaucracy like a machine, without regard for tradition, there was nothing to stop it being taken apart and reassembled once it had proven defective. And this came to seem ever more necessary.

From early on, Bartenstein had analyzed the successes and failures of Haugwitz's reform with an acute and pitiless eye. He continued to submit a flood of memoranda in his new position, justifying his candor with his incontestable concern for the good of the Archducal House. Although he had initially approved of Haugwitz's measures, even advising the monarch to prohibit criticism of the system once it came into effect,[201] he offered her a frank assessment of the reform in two lengthy memoranda submitted before the war, in 1753 and 1756.[202] Earlier historians generally judged Haugwitz to have been a brilliant reformer but a poor manager of his own system. The system worked well enough in peacetime, they argued, but the war exposed its shortcomings and placed it under intolerable strain. Bartenstein's memoranda show that these defects were apparent long before the outbreak of the new conflict. While conceding that the reform had regularized supplies to the army and improved the overall military situation, Bartenstein decried the bewildering complexity of the entire administrative apparatus, inadequacies in the system's implementation, and its lack of acceptance among all sections of the population. Serious errors had been made. Several new court committees had been established in competition with the General Directory, counteracting the effects of centralization. The separation of justice and administration had doubled the number of offices, increased personnel, and multiplied costs. The Directory was bogged down in trivialities, nobody had a clear overview, the tide of paperwork rose ever higher. Above all, the tax burden had not been reduced. The estates were unanimous in their complaints, and no one saw the reform as a blessing. What had originally been touted as the system's chief merit, the elimination of particular estate interests by an impartial, professional bureaucracy dedicated only to the common good, now seemed its Achilles' heel. The whole reform had been rushed through without proper consultation. Officials were unfamiliar with the lands they administered and paid no heed to their peculiarities; territorial constitutions were trodden underfoot. Glaring errors in calculating tax liabilities had led to appalling injustices, both between the lands and among individual subjects. Since the estates had not been consulted, they refused to cooperate in implementing the system on the ground. In short, rather than making governance more predictable and taxation fairer, the reform had only added to the confusion.[203] The ideal of an administration that ran like clockwork had proved a mess in reality.

Kaunitz responded by putting in place a new series of administrative reforms. The first were instituted in 1760,[204] in the midst of the Seven Years' War, when he was jolted into an awareness that the grand plan of humiliating Prussia and winning back Silesia threatened to founder on the desolate state of finances and an unwieldy bureaucracy. In a December 1760 memorandum he described the situation confronting the monarchy as so chaotic that Maria Theresa agreed to set up a new central consultative committee for internal affairs (parallel to the State Chancellery for foreign affairs), a *conseil d'état* or State Council (*Staatsrat*). In Kaunitz's plan this council would oversee everything, "surveiller à tout": administration, finances, trade, religion, justice, police—in short, *le sisteme universel de l'état*. It would ensure that now, once and for all, the foundations would be laid for a thriving monarchy, so that "the spirit of order and interconnection may spread to all other areas of the government."[205] It was unmistakably Justi's ideal of the machine that Kaunitz was setting before the monarch's eyes here, with its suggestion of technical perfectibility. The new council's cardinal rule was that members would be barred from holding any other office, allowing them to remain completely impartial and devote themselves exclusively to their central task. There was to be only one exception to this rule: the state chancellor, Kaunitz himself. It is not difficult to see how this committee would be the means by which he hoped to steer the complete reorganization of internal affairs.

Faced with a bleak military situation, Maria Theresa allowed herself to be quickly persuaded: "I await with great anticipation the beginning of this new State Council as the salvation of my hereditary lands, and a balm to my spirit and conscience," she wrote beneath the memorandum.[206] The new State Council convened for the first time in January 1761. Initially made up of six members and a secretary,[207] it sat twice a week in the residence. The emperor and empress regularly attended in person. Haugwitz, who saw his life's work placed at risk, was appointed to the council as a face-saving gesture.

The internal constitution of the State Council provided the template for the spirit of orderliness that Kaunitz envisaged would then sweep through all branches of government.[208] Kaunitz was animated by the rationalist belief that it should be possible to arrive through free discussion at the one and only correct answer to every political question. For this to happen, however, certain conditions would have to be in place that were rarely found in the social cosmos of the ancien régime. The State Council, for Kaunitz a "simple and pure institute" such as existed in no other monarchy on earth, was meant to offer such a free space for rational truth-seeking.[209] He personally drew up its formal standing orders in the form of a written constitution. This already marked a significant difference from the old Court Conference, and indeed from most other monarchical advisory committees of the traditional kind, which operated according to informally established rules.[210] The essence of this constitution consisted in the independence of its members and their *libertas votorum*, their freedom to vote as they saw fit. The chairmanship of the sovereign herself, the status and titular authority of the councillors as well as the choice of meeting place—*coram throno*, before the throne, as it were—ensured that the council was duly respected in the courtly environment. Membership was fixed, competing loyalties were ruled out. The only blemish to its otherwise flawless complexion was the fact that Kaunitz made himself an exception.[211]

The State Council's procedural rules were its standout feature. Nothing was to be discussed at meetings that had not been brought to members' attention well in advance; everything was to be scrupulously minuted and approved by each member. Everyone was to give his opinion in turn on each agenda item. Remarkably, they did so against the hierarchical order, proceeding from the youngest knight to the oldest lord. In all other situations the opposite held true: the highest-ranking member was the first to give his opinion, influencing votes to come through the social weight of his voice. From now on things would be done differently. Councillors would be guided solely by the matter at hand and would not be swayed by social considerations, respect, and conformism.[212] Discussions would resume when new substantive arguments arose; if no clear judgment was still forthcoming, the matter would be held in abeyance for as long as it took to gather new information. In general, expert advice played a central role. The State Council would not only be supplied with information by the relevant authorities, it would also attentively examine all "writing delivered into the all-highest hands," suggestions for improvement, complaints, and memoranda, regardless of who may have written them. Its responsibilities extended to all internal affairs concerning the "German hereditary lands" (including Bohemia). It was also charged with overseeing the implementation of any measures it inspired. Nonetheless, it was to decide nothing on its own and never interfere in administrative practice. The State Council was there solely "to find out the truth" and advise the monarch, who alone was authorized to make the final decision. Importantly, however, the "final all-highest resolution" would only be made once "all circumstances and doubts . . . have been sufficiently clarified and exhausted."[213] With this stipulation, the sovereign pledged to refrain from casting judgment until she had been thoroughly briefed on the matter under consideration. To be sure, free discussion came to an end with her ruling. But in true Enlightenment fashion, Kaunitz was confident that the monarch would always yield to the force of the better argument, since nobody could have a greater interest in the welfare of her lands.

The State Council was a rationalistic artifice that was doomed to failure. It quickly became swamped by the sheer mass of agenda items. Changes to its procedural rules soon proved necessary. The exact order in which opinions were heard, for example, was constantly being revised.[214] Criticism of its work continued up until Maria Theresa's death; the State Council was and remained its own topic of discussion.[215]

Yet it was also Kaunitz's central instrument for once again overhauling the entire administration of the state. What is remarkable is how this second round of reforms came about.[216] Kaunitz introduced a distinctive new political style. Rather than following in Haugwitz's footsteps and secretly plotting a coup d'état, he ordered an open and comprehensive review of existing arrangements. At the second meeting of the State Council in late January 1761, he was already inviting debate on the principles underlying his proposed reforms. A few days later, an imperial handwritten letter sent to all ten heads of the German hereditary lands and several other senior officials, including Bartenstein, posed the question: "On which fundamental rules should the entire system of the state and its internal constitution be based?"[217] Haugwitz defended his own system. Many sharply criticized it yet cautioned against abandoning the system in wartime, recommending minor improvements instead. Some also suggested that Kaunitz had drawn his abstract truths from books and had not the faintest idea about real-world problems. The debate dragged on into the autumn of 1761 and resulted, after much heated debate, in a package of reforms that came into effect on January 1, 1762.[218] A compromise between Kaunitz's ideas and the wishes of the territorial chiefs, its end effect was largely to overturn the reforms of 1748–49. One fundamental principle of the "new system" was revoked: having been brought together for the first time under Haugwitz, financial administration and general administration of the lands were now split apart again. The most striking change was that the Directorium in

Publicis et Cameralibus, Haugwitz's proud central Directory, was completely dismantled. The rump agency, renamed Bohemian-Austrian Court Chancellery, was stripped of its taxation powers. Finances were completely reorganized in line with the ideas of Ludwig von Zinzendorf, one of Kaunitz's young political protégés.[219] In the process, what Haugwitz had joined together was put asunder and redistributed among various authorities: the General Treasury (*Generalkasse*), the Court Chamber, the City Bank (*Stadtbanco*), and the Court Audit Office (*Hofrechenkammer*) were now responsible for revenue, administration, expenditure, and control of state finances, giving rise to recurrent boundary disputes. Only the separation of judiciary and administration was retained, although many in the provinces had spoken out against it. In any event, the entire restructuring did not last long. Barely three years later, in 1764–65, the reform was reformed once more, and the story did not end even there.[220]

The Legacy of Reform

The reforms of 1748–49 were long considered the birth hour of "the Austrian core state,"[221] "the most important step on the path to overcoming the medieval polity."[222] They shaped the image of Maria Theresa as a successful architect of the nation-state, a kind of housewife writ large who had "set her imperial household in order."[223] Maria Theresa and Haugwitz, it was argued, had done nothing less than "establish a new state."[224] What came afterwards was regarded as continuing and perfecting Haugwitz's reforms,[225] or occasionally regretted as detracting from his heroic state-building endeavors. Historians today are inclined to take a far more sober view. There was no logical evolution of an abstract idea of the state toward the inherent goal of its realization, as suggested by the statist mythology of the nineteenth and early twentieth century, which saw in nation-states the "ideas of God."[226] It is difficult today to hold up the nation-state as the goal and culmination of all history. Skepticism toward state bureaucracies and similar institutions has also grown. We now know that no organization has ever functioned exactly as prescribed by its statutes and as it sought to present itself to the outside world, and we are more aware of the inertia stemming from routinized procedures and informal detours.[227] Deeply rooted customs and conventions cannot simply be eliminated by imperial fiat.

All this allows us to see Maria Theresa's reform policy in a new light. First, the many measures adopted were neither strictly systematic nor free of contradiction. Second, they were not logical steps on the path to a preconceived goal. Third, little is known about how the reforms were implemented in the provinces and the manner in which local officials dealt with them. And fourth, their salutary effects on the populace were more often asserted than actually demonstrated.[228]

This is not to say, of course, that the reform policy changed nothing—only that it did not achieve what it set out to achieve. The measures undoubtedly had at least two effects. On the one hand, each new reform multiplied the number of offices and increased the associated costs. On the other, the volume of paperwork grew exponentially.[229] Whereas the Bohemian and Austrian Court Chancellery left behind around 2,000 fascicles of archival material for the period between 1527 and 1748, the figure for the half century from 1748 to 1792 is around 5,500 fascicles. In other words, around three times as many documents were produced in these last five decades than in the previous two centuries.[230] Yet these were merely the outwardly visible and quantifiable changes. Something else is crucial. Haugwitz's reforms signaled a break with the past because they released a transformational dynamic that would generate its own accelerating momentum in the years to come. Once the smooth functioning of a machine had been identified as a model of good governance, once statecraft had been grasped as a kind of technical performance, a continuous pressure for self-perfection built up, triggering an avalanche of paperwork. The reforms spawned problems that called for new, similar reforms, which in turn produced similar problems, and so on. All the measures were similar in the astonishingly optimistic expectation that the reorganization of central government agencies promised a solution to every problem. The rationalist model of the state as a machine suggested that it was possible, working from the center, to set in motion a causal-mechanistic chain reaction that would reach all the way to the outermost cogs of the state. It is therefore unsurprising that complaints about the defects of the various "new systems" tended to be strikingly similar: confusion caused by overlapping powers, lack of transparency, excessive documentation, increasing complexity, and dogged local resistance.

Yet the perspective of central rule was limited in a specific way. The queen remained ensconced in her residence like an unmoved mover and hardly ever left the center of her lands. Her rule still largely rested on personal presence; it was she who allowed petitioners to approach her rather than making her way to them. Yet this model of rule proved incapable of addressing the novel challenges with which Maria Theresa found herself confronted over the course of her reign. According to the ideal of the time, she alone should survey everything, yet at the same time she found herself removed from everyone else and ever more reliant on the eyes of others. To her dying day, she never resolved this paradox of power.[231]

6

Body Politics

FIGURE 20. Maria Theresa as a young queen. One of many official state portraits
from the studio of court painter Martin van Meytens, 1744

Beauty

In the European ancien régime, the sovereign's body was a political object of paramount importance. For one thing, it stood at the center of the sociosymbolic order: the ruler's physical body represented the immortal political body of his realm, of which he was simultaneously the head.[1] His corporeality served as a political metaphor, pointing beyond itself in several key respects. Command over one's own body was considered the precondition for ruling over others. Impotence was a symbol and index of political powerlessness, while sexual excess denoted tyranny. Yet the sovereign's body was the subject of political discourse in a literal as well as metaphorical sense. So long as rule rested on birthright and was passed on in quasi-natural fashion from the ruling couple to their offspring, the condition of their bodies—their beauty and integrity, their hygiene and discipline, their health and, above all, their fertility—played an absolutely central role. The dynastic transfer of power through birth had its advantages and disadvantages. On the one hand, it allowed succession to the throne to appear as a natural process, one that defied the arbitrary scheming of fallible mortals. On the other, it left the dynasty exposed to the accident of birth, to what Thomas Hobbes called a "natural lottery."[2] For if the ruler's body failed to meet the demands placed on it, if it was sick, feebleminded, sterile, or infirm, it jeopardized the continuity and acceptance of dynastic rule and encouraged rival claimants to the throne. This was especially the case when the body in question was deemed weak and unfit to rule merely on account of its sex. It was all the more important, then, for Maria Theresa to make up for this undeniable natural "defect" in other ways: through her beauty and her extraordinary fecundity.[3]

The ruler's beauty is an ancient topos. It can already be found in Old Testament psalms and is still encountered in fairy tales today.[4] The king is the handsomest man, the queen the fairest lady in all the realm. They can hardly be otherwise, precisely because they are king and queen. In a well-ordered, legible world, the visible exterior reliably reflects the invisible interior. Beauty was ascribed an indicative value: it was the sign of divine blessing, virtue, and purity. To be sure, Christian theologians warned against false appearances, the beautiful surface gnawed at from within by the canker of sin. Yet this did little to detract from beauty's suggestive force. This connection, too, was soberly analyzed by Thomas Hobbes, the great theorist of power. For Hobbes, power is "what quality soever maketh a man beloved, or feared of many, or the reputation of such quality." Among the qualities which procure the love of others, he includes beauty: "Forme is power, . . . being the promise of Good."[5] In much the same vein, the Austrian magnate Prince Liechtenstein advised his son that, when choosing a wife, he should look for a fine figure alongside virtue, chastity, and piety, since princes "are honored and beloved [on account of their] well-proportioned figures and physiognomies."[6] In other words, beauty was a virtue in rulers, endowing them with charisma and endearing them to their subjects.

The queen's beauty was therefore a powerful source of political legitimacy, evoked all the more insistently the more Maria Theresa's precarious inheritance came under attack. Everyone who set eyes on Maria Theresa in the first years of her reign, not just her partisans, remarked on her beauty. Even those who had not seen her personally relayed this reputation, right up to the nineteenth- and twentieth-century historians who lauded her as a "model of consummate femininity."[7] Her beauty and grace, her literally spellbinding appearance, were taken to justify the universal love of her subjects, and especially the Hungarians' willingness to take up arms in her defense.[8]

Descriptions of her beauty had a topical character. The lawyer Christian Gottlieb Richter, who clothed his paean to Maria Theresa (1745) in Old Testamentary dress, drew on the Song of Songs (1: 8–10) when singing her praises: "How beautiful is the daughter of Charles VI in her regal finery! Her jewelry and earrings are of gems from the Orient. How lovely her figure, how rosy her cheeks! She is the fairest among women."[9] Maria Theresa's beauty was a synonym for her monarchical grandeur; it made visible her royal status, the innate majesty of her person. As the English emissary, Charles Hanbury Williams, wrote in 1753: "Her person was made to wear a crown and her mind to give luster to it. Her countenance is filled with sense, spirit, and sweetness, and all her motions accompanied with grace and dignity."[10] Even in 1755, when she had already given birth to thirteen children and put on a great deal of weight, the Prussian emissary Fürst noted that "the Empress is one of the most beautiful princesses in Europe: for all her vigils and confinements, she has kept her figure very well. She has a majestic yet friendly gaze, although willpower and self-control may play a part in this. One does not approach her without a deep sense of admiration."[11]

She herself took a more disillusioned view. Among intimates, she occasionally spoke of herself as "*la grosse Therese,*" fat Theresa.[12] Writing to Antonia of Saxony in October 1749, at the age of just thirty-two, she declared herself old and overweight; anyone who had not seen her in the last ten years would fail to recognize her.[13] And to her favorite lady-in-waiting, Trautson, she lamented in 1754: "Those who had not seen me in eight years could hardly get over how obese I had become. It must be quite remarkable; but to sugar the pill, they assured me they found my complexion fairer and much improved. Still, that does nothing to undo the first blow".[14] Yet even those who met her in the 1770s mostly described her as still beautiful, despite her considerable girth and the pockmarks left behind by an attack of smallpox.[15]

The vast majority of people encountered the ruler's beauty in ever new variations in countless representations. Maria Theresa was the subject of around a hundred large-format state portraits, in addition to an untold number of copperplate engravings, miniatures, coins, and medallions.[16] Her profile on the silver Maria Theresa thaler became iconic, not just in Europe but throughout the entire Arab world (and well into the twentieth century).[17] The different genres of portraiture served different ends and were tailored to different audiences. On the one hand, there were the great conventional state portraits from the court painter's studio, showing the sovereign resplendent in her jewelry and royal insignia, framed by curtains drawn to one side as if offering viewers a glimpse into the otherwise hidden *arcana imperii*, the secrets of empire. Putting rulership on display, these images had a representative function in the full sense of the word: they represented the absent sovereign in audience chambers or courtrooms, and as such they had to be treated with the same deference as if she were there in person.[18] On the other hand, there were more intimate portraits such as those by Jean-Étienne

Liotard, whom Maria Theresa held in particularly high regard (see color plate 9). These helped maintain relations with family members and intimates over distances in time and space,[19] in keeping with the sentimental aesthetic of the time: portraits had to be painted vividly and from nature, without undue formality. Miniature copies of such portraits were the gifts of choice between courts; they were deployed in finely calculated degrees of preciousness to demonstrate the value of the relationship. Ambassadors and emissaries generally received a tobacco box or ring with a diamond-encrusted miniature of the empress as a farewell present from Khevenhüller's hand, displaying them thereafter on ceremonial occasions as symbolic capital.[20] Beyond the court milieu, images of the empress were a common sight for simple subjects as well: on fans, faiences, and copperplates for the better-off (see color plate 8); on coins and medallions for everyone; and in Mariazell even on the antependium, the panel in front of the high altar.[21] In the eighteenth century, it was not unusual for peasants to have a portrait of the queen before their eyes on the wall or on their drinking vessels: "The picture of the queen of Hungary is honored everywhere."[22] The avowed aim was to stimulate feelings of love and awe among subjects, since "arousing emotions is the greatest art in a state by which kings can obtain anything."[23] The court strategically pursued this politics of images, even arranging for portraits to be produced and sold to the public.[24] The ruler's beauty was valuable political capital.

What exactly did contemporaries perceive as beautiful? What were the key criteria? What conveyed an impression of majesty? In 1749 the perceptive Podewils painted the following "picture" of Maria Theresa for his king:

> Her figure is of over rather than under medium stature. It was very fine before her marriage, but the numerous births she has undergone, combined with her corpulence, have made her extremely heavy. Nonetheless, she has an easy carriage and majestic posture. Her appearance is elegant even though she spoils it by the way she dresses.... She has a full, round face and a clear brow. Her pronounced eyebrows are, like her hair, blond, without any reddish sheen. Her eyes are large,

bright, and at the same time very gentle, all accented by their light-blue color. Her nose is small, neither curved nor turned up, the mouth a little large, but still pretty, the teeth white, the smile pleasant, the neck and throat well formed, and the arms and hands beautiful. Her complexion cannot be any less so, judging by what one can see, despite the scant care she has devoted to it. She usually has a high color. Her expression is open and cheerful, her way of addressing people friendly and graceful. One cannot deny that she is attractive.[25]

The description is oriented—here as in other depictions of the external appearance of court notables—to the age's prevailing guidelines for judging beauty. These were, first and foremost, an "easy carriage" and "majestic posture." In the handbooks for seemly conduct at court, a central maxim was to adopt "free, unforced, yet modest gestures"[26] and an upright gait as second nature, in unstated contrast to the stooped, cramped, unfree comportment of the rabble. Even at a masked ball, Maria Theresa could always be recognized, it was said, by her "free demarche," her sprightly gait, whereas disguised peasants immediately gave themselves away through the oafish clumsiness of their movements.[27] Zedler's Universal Lexicon enumerates no fewer than thirty criteria in its entry on "female beauty," many of which recur in Podewils's depiction. Signs of beauty included a clear brow, a small, straight nose, a small mouth, "coral-red lips," white, even teeth, "lovely and fiery eyes," a pleasant voice, and a "comely smile."[28] A direct gaze and open-mouthed smile, meanwhile, were not condoned for everyone and at all times; the hierarchy of status and sex determined who was allowed to look up and speak without prior invitation. Another essential criterion for beauty was white, unblemished, clear skin on the face, neck, cleavage, arms, and hands, showing that neither serious illness (such as smallpox or even syphilis) nor physical labor in the sun, wind, and rain had taken their toll. Reddish cheeks and lips further accentuated the whiteness of the complexion and indicated "plentiful blood," that is, a sanguine, vital temperament such as that ascribed to Maria Theresa.[29]

Beauty guaranteed health and fertility, and "everything depends on fertility."[30] For a woman on the throne, childlessness was a catastrophe, for it imperiled dynastic continuity and showed that God had withheld his blessing from her marriage. One of Maria Theresa's predecessors, Anna of Tyrol, wife of Emperor Matthias, had spent much of her life atoning for her supposed barrenness. Great fecundity in a ruling couple, by contrast, revealed that their rule was pleasing in God's sight; it was at once pledge and symbol of the fertility and prosperity of their lands.[31] An anonymous panegyrist, extolling the great affection in which Maria Theresa was held by her subjects, asserted in 1745 that "she is loved as a happy mother, and for showering blessings on the land through her children. Seated on her throne, she represents the goddess who brings forth successors of her kind."[32] Dynastic baptisms and weddings prompted a deluge of popular prints glorifying the imperial marriage: "Theresa's fertility is Emperor Francis's delight, the age's praise and fame, the joy of German hearts" (see below, figs. 35 and 36).[33] Copious offspring, it was said, increased the House of Habsburg's power, allied it to other ruling houses, and consolidated peace throughout Europe.[34] In short, the queen's body was the vital principle of the monarchy.[35]

Love and Libertinage

Procreation in marriage was fundamental to the stability of the entire social order. On it depended not just the continuity of the ruling dynasty but the exclusive transmission of rank, name, title, goods, and privileges at every level of a stratified society. This made it imperative that sexuality be kept under tight control. Yet the rules of what was permitted and prohibited *in puncto sexti*, that is, in matters relating to the sixth commandment, were by no means as straightforward as the injunction "Thou shalt not commit adultery" might suggest. This commandment was very simple and applied to everyone, regardless of class or gender. The strict moral norms of the church not only tied sex to marriage, they tolerated it exclusively for procreative purposes and in the only position deemed natural. It was certainly impermissible as a means to satisfy carnal longings. Princes, too, were admonished to resist the devil and avoid "forbidden lechery outside the marriage bed."[36] The unwritten social rules of the ancien régime, however, were far more complicated and differed markedly for men and women, the wed and unwed, the widowed, nobles, and commoners. They were strictest for highborn virgins, whose undefiled bodies and reputations were extremely valuable social assets and who therefore had the most to lose.[37] The value of virginity decreased drastically at the opposite end of the social spectrum. Those who had little to expect or inherit from their parents had correspondingly less to lose and therefore enjoyed greater sexual latitude. Destitute girls and women could acquire wealth and status by offering sexual services.

Conversely, the laxest standards were reserved for men from the upper class—or, rather, for such men different standards of behavior applied. Whereas Christian religion demanded conjugal fidelity from a noble head of household as a matter of course, the aristocratic system of norms suggested an altogether different code of conduct. Sexual as well as military conquest belonged to the habitus of the *honnête homme*. Seventeenth- and early eighteenth-century French literature set the tone, cultivating an art of seductive and passionate love (*amour passion*) outside the narrow bounds of wedlock. For princes to keep mistresses was the rule rather than the exception, even if this was not everywhere so openly advertised as in Versailles or Dresden. A range of sexual possibilities was open to noblemen. Adventures with married women from their own class were risky; it was safer and far more common for them to maintain lovers, or even wives, of lower social standing. The boundary between mistress and prostitute was a fluid one. The scale extended from one-off sexual services for ready cash, on the one hand, to long-lasting extramarital relations on the basis of financial support in the form of generous "gifts," on the other. There was a clear class dimension to sexual libertinism. It was a prerogative of the aristocratic male; middle-class husbands typically felt less self-assured and had more scruples about their philandering. And in the end one had to be able to afford an extramarital relationship—the longer-lasting and more exclusive, the pricier.

Allowances were also made for women of high status, provided they were married or, better still, widowed. The *dernier cri* in the early eighteenth century was a so-called *cicisbeo* in the Italian fashion, a (mostly

socially inferior and unmarried) permanent male companion of ambivalent status, possibly involving erotic services; the exact nature of the
relationship was deliberately left in the dark.[38] In this labyrinth of sexual
rules, the most universal and strictest norm was undoubtedly the formal
preservation of class barriers. It was one thing to support and sexually
exploit economically dependent women or men from a lower class, it
was quite another to marry them.[39]

Since marriages were arranged with family considerations foremost
in mind, with the aim of accumulating as much economic, social, and
symbolic capital as possible, any emotional attachment between the
couple could not be given much weight. On the contrary, infatuation
was considered the worst possible foundation for a good and lasting
marriage. Passionate love and marriage were almost mutually exclusive.[40] The ideal marriage was a rational economic partnership of convenience for the purposes of procreation, child-rearing, and the intergenerational transmission of status, title, and wealth; objective, stable,
mutually advantageous grounds for matrimony took priority. These
were not easily compatible with passionate love. Love was at best a consequence of marriage, not its foundation, and even then it was imagined
more as a kind of amiable companionship. Love, in the sense of a passionate erotic relationship, belonged outside the bonds of wedlock and
was the object of a sophisticated aristocratic culture of gallantry. Countless French-language novels, plays, and "schools of love," *écoles des
amants*, set down the rules by which feelings were expressed and acted
out in social reality.[41] Books taught the art of seduction, an elaborate
game of encouragement and repudiation, dissimulation, siege, and conquest. There were only two categories of woman in this literary universe: the coquettes, who "always say yes," and the precious, who "always say no." The former were to be secured in lasting possession, the
latter vanquished. For an ambitious *galant homme*, this was the ultimate
goal; the precious, as the name suggests, were deemed the more valuable prize.[42] The code of gallant love was ever-present, not just in novels
and comedies but also in operas, paintings, and sculptures; it dictated
how feelings were perceived, articulated, and interpreted in the social
universe of the upper classes.

The social semantics of love underwent a profound transformation in the second half of the eighteenth century. Influenced once again by novels, a different ideal of relations between the sexes came fairly suddenly into fashion. Against the culture of gallantry, associated with aristocracy and the court, bestselling authors such as Samuel Richardson and Jean-Jacques Rousseau now expounded a new, "sentimental" culture of feeling. For them, love was something altogether different. Their heroines were characterized by their chastity, respectability, *and* passion. Love—a sentiment at once virtuous, rational, and tender—was now to find an outlet in marriage. In the name of "nature," the intimacy and permanence of conjugal love was set against the ephemerality and frivolity of the gallant affair. The new culture of feeling polemically targeted the lax morals associated with life at court, which is not to say that it did not also exert a powerful spell on aristocratic (mostly female) readers. Nonetheless, a stereotypical set of binary opposites became entrenched over time: gallant love—sinful, insincere, and feigned—counted as aristocratic and French; sentimental love—natural, chaste, sincere, and authentic—was considered bourgeois and German (or rather English, since the most fashionable novels came from England).

This stereotype also left its mark on the ideas of later historians, including how they tackled the topic of love and marriage. It was a topic they tended to avoid, for several reasons. First, anything related to sexuality they regarded as a private matter, and hence unworthy of serious political history writing, even though procreation was at the heart of dynastic politics. Second, sexuality was surrounded by many more taboos in the nineteenth century than under the ancien régime, and the bourgeois moral code no longer permitted such matters to be discussed openly. Third, historians were keen to protect the great men and women of world history from the slander and innuendo of "court gossip." The great source editions were accordingly bowdlerized: Maria Theresa's correspondence with Marie Antoinette, for example, or Joseph and Leopold's exchange on problems concerning the consummation of marriage, or the erotic letters between Archduchess Maria Christina and Joseph's first wife, Isabella.[43] What was omitted by "high" historiography almost inevitably became the object of a complementary genre,

"Illustrated History of Morals" (*Illustrierte Sittengeschichte*), which drew all the more uncritically on contemporary erotic literature. A classic of the genre is the work of the socialist Eduard Fuchs, sold under the counter to male customers only during the late Wilhelmine era.[44] His *Illustrated History of Morals* was considered dangerously inflammatory for two reasons. On the one hand, the author's disgust at the "drone's life" of the aristocracy was illustrated in lavish, lurid detail. On the other, his critique of aristocratic immorality was at the same time a barely veiled polemic against the "moribund feudal absolutism" of his own time. The many gallant women he showed in a state of undress served to denounce the decadence of the nobility in general and his own political elite in particular.[45] It is therefore hardly surprising that establishment historians preferred to keep their distance from such titillating, subversive fare.

In the meantime, the interests of historians have undergone no less radical a transformation than have sexual mores. The history of the body and sexuality has long since advanced to the status of a respectable historical subdiscipline. All the same, for a variety of reasons it is not easy to reconstruct sexual relations at court. For one thing, people talked about such matters in terms very different from how they are discussed today, making many formulations difficult to decipher. In addition, the sources contain many rumors that simply cannot be trusted—they may well be true, but then again they may not. However, what matters is not so much what actually went on in the boudoir but rather the social logic, the unwritten rules, the symbolic code that held sway at the time. And about this unverifiable rumors can tell us a great deal. After all, gossip has a social function: rumormongers communicate implicitly about the social mores that are seen to have been traduced. How sexual affairs are written about in memoirs, travel reports, letters, and diaries therefore reveals much about the prevailing system of social norms.

What did this system look like in Vienna, at the Viennese court, and under Maria Theresa? During her father's reign, the residential city had been notorious as a hotbed of adultery, although it barely differed from other metropolises in this regard. "Life in Vienna is jolly, free, noisy, wanton, yet at the same time devout, serious, and natural. The people are lustful and amorous, but not to excess. They laugh and make merry, but do not break their heads trying to be sharp-witted and delicate. They eat and drink, they fast and daydream; they pray and curse, all according to time and occasion."[46] At the beginning of the century the English diplomat's wife, Lady Montagu, described it as "the establish'd custom for every lady to have two husbands, one that bears the Name, and another that performs the Dutys." The practice was so commonly tolerated, she claimed, that it amounted to a public insult for a lady to be invited with only one of her husbands.[47] This was no doubt an ironic exaggeration. Gallant affairs may have been commonplace, but they were rarely paraded in public. Yet the tone in which sexual matters were discussed even in the emperor's presence—so long as the empress was absent—was astonishingly crass. Maria Theresa's father seems to have been inordinately fond of such *polissoneries*, or ribald banter.[48] Friedrich August Harrach informed his brother of the double standards practiced by ladies at the Viennese court: while crude remarks could not be made in their company, *in natura* they demonstrated no such inhibitions about what they blushed to hear mentioned in polite conversation.[49] The degree of reprehensibility depended in large part on public knowledge of the affair. The guiding principle was *nisi caste, tamen caute*—if not chaste, then at least cautious. The Jesuit order, to which all court confessors belonged until the 1760s, had plenty of experience discussing moral exceptions to the rule. They were generally prepared to be lenient in applying ecclesiastical norms to their noble confessants, naturally absolving them from sin at the end. It was an occasion for satisfaction when a noblewoman on her deathbed "evinced all desirable signs of true remorse and Christian repentance" for a longstanding extramarital affair.[50]

Whenever someone pays lip service to morality yet violates its precepts in practice, the word "hypocrisy" springs to mind. Yet when it came to sexual norms at court, the situation was rather more complicated. There was a structurally conditioned, collective hypocrisy that went far beyond individual lapses: court society tacitly tolerated what was strictly forbidden under religious law. Violations of the sixth commandment were not just expected, they were even admired—depending, to be sure, on who committed them.

FIGURE 21. Kneeling nun. Martin van Meytens the Younger, c. 1731
(recto and verso of the same picture)

Those who claimed to be paragons of moral propriety were most susceptible to the charge of hypocrisy. The portrait of a nun who can be viewed from both sides makes the point shockingly explicit: from the front she presents an image of conventional piety, from the back one of sacrilegious obscenity (fig. 21). Through the contrast between the two, the picture itself embodies what it represents, a sanctimonious performance that exposes itself as such on being turned around. The remarkable portrait was painted by none other than Martin van Meytens, who as court painter went on to create most of Maria Theresa's state portraits and the best-known ceremonial canvases of her reign. The *Kneeling Nun* dates from 1731, when van Meytens was preparing to move from Stockholm to Vienna and enter imperial service.[51] He later had no need to paint such pictures, and he surely would not have been forgiven had he done so. Maria Theresa herself took offense at mythological nudes, covering them with wallpaper and advising her son Leopold when he moved into his new residence in Florence: "Try gradually to rid the palace of its nudes, above all in paintings. Make known your distaste for them and do not allow such works to be made in future."[52]

If Maria Theresa bemused or (depending on perspective) amused her court society in anything, then it was in her attitude to marriage, love, and libertinage. Unwilling to tolerate the prevailing collective double standards, she sought to implement a policy of strict sexual control such as existed at no other European court. This led to her acquiring the reputation of a prudish bigot among many of her contemporaries, while in the eyes of later historians it made her an "unfading paragon of German femininity"[53] and harbinger of middle-class morality.

Her own engagement and marriage were a remarkable exception. During the period of their betrothal, Maria Theresa and Francis Stephen had enjoyed an extraordinary level of personal intimacy. Not only had they grown up at the same court, they had already shown signs of mutual attraction during this lengthy informal courtship.[54] It was more normal for a royal couple to know each other only from their portraits and meet for the first time on their wedding day—and sometimes not even then: marriage ceremonies *per procuratorem*, at which one party was represented by an envoy, were commonplace. Even the circumstances surrounding this wedding were thus utterly unique. The same was true of the marriage itself. "It was not at all fashionable at the time to be a good father, a good head of household, a good husband."[55] Hardly any foreign emissary at the Viennese court failed to draw attention to the ruling couple's conspicuous affection for each other.[56] Maria Theresa's closest companions saw it no differently: one heart and one soul, *un Coeur et un Esprit*, as Count Tarouca called them in 1740.[57]

At once the site and symbol of this unusual intimacy was the couple's shared bedroom in the Hofburg, the point where their two long, symmetrically arranged suites joined up to offer them a maximum of seclusion and intimacy.[58] At Schönbrunn there was also a shared bedroom midway between the two apartments.[59] It was common elsewhere for a prince to visit his wife in her separate chamber from time to time, but not for them to spend the whole night together in the same bed: to do, in other words, "as the peasants do."[60] Even if Francis Stephen did not always sleep overnight in the common bedroom, sometimes preferring to stay in his own palace in the Wallnergasse or take hunting trips outside Vienna, this bedroom represented the intimacy of the royal couple's relationship to the outside world. The unusual sarcophagus that Maria Theresa had built for herself and her husband in the Capuchin Crypt in 1754 was like a petrified immortalization of the shared nuptial bed (see fig. 40).[61]

Maria Theresa apparently valued such proximity and intimacy more highly than her husband. She later communicated the same message to her daughter, Marie Antoinette: "It is regrettable that the king [Louis XVI of France] prefers not to sleep with you; I consider this point to be quite essential, not for having children, but for being more intimately connected, more at ease and familiar with each other, as in this way one can spend several hours together each day without disruption."[62] She periodically returned to this point until shortly before her death: "I would have wished you to have behaved in the German manner and treasured the sure intimacy that arises when two people are together."[63] The courtly environment appears not to have approved unconditionally of this unusual closeness between the imperial couple, interpreting it as a sign of female dominance. A story went the rounds that Rosières, a close companion of Francis Stephen, had advised him to sleep separately from his wife. That way he could keep her under his thumb and get whatever he wanted from her.[64] While it is unclear whether the anecdote is based on a real conversation, it vividly illustrates what people thought were appropriate relations between the sexes. Indeed, owing to conflict with Maria Theresa, Rosières left the court around the same time.[65]

Maria Theresa herself was well aware of the dangers presented by an all too close relationship with her husband. She later counseled her daughter Maria Christina not to exaggerate her loving devotion: "The more freedom you allow your husband, the less you expect his visits to be punctual and regular, the more attractive he will find you and the more he will desire you."[66] Maria Christina should beware of the intensity of her own affection, make herself scarce, and heed the rules of female restraint, since passionate infatuation was quick to fade. A lastingly happy marriage, her mother affirmed, was built on respect, compromise, trust, and friendship. The advice Maria Theresa gave her favorite daughter upon her marriage is particularly informative, since Maria Christina's situation was in many respects similar to her mother's. She was the only daughter allowed to marry the man of her choice, although

from a dynastic viewpoint the match was clearly unsuitable. Maria Theresa was therefore all the more adamant that she submit to her husband
and obey him in everything. "Your situation is in this respect just as
tricky as mine. Never let him feel your superiority—nothing is difficult
if one loves without losing one's head. So far as I am concerned, I can at
least be calm on this point."[67]

There are good reasons for doubting this. The fact that Maria Theresa, at least at the beginning of her marriage, showed every sign of passionate attachment to her husband and cherished him all her life as her
closest companion does not mean that she played a subordinate role in
the marriage, as wives were expected to do at the time and as she herself
was constantly exhorting her own daughters. At times her devotion to
her "adorable consort"[68] verged on dominance. She was reluctant to let
him out of her sight. When he left her to lead his troops into battle in
1744, she used all the means at her disposal to try and stop him, later
writing self-critically to her sister: "I was sick with anger and pain, and
I made mon vieux [a habitual term of endearment for her husband]
catch fever with my wickedness. . . . I fell back on our usual refuge, ca-
resses and tears; but what good are they after nine years of marriage;
they achieved nothing, although he is the best husband in the world. At
last I resorted to anger, which had the effect of making both of us fall
ill."[69] Such outbursts of temper did not always remain hidden from public view. Even so devoted a servant to the empress as Khevenhüller occasionally revealed his consternation at how Maria Theresa treated her
husband. That the rules governing relations between the sexes had been
turned on their head in this marriage was a structural problem about
which nothing could be done. Francis Stephen had to live with the fact
that he was the weaker partner at court. His structural inferiority was
perhaps never more visible than when Maria Theresa tried to veil it, for
the stance that she occasionally allowed herself toward him was forbidden everyone else. She watched with eagle eye that he was treated him
with due deference at court and never slighted in ceremonial details.
Right at the start of her reign, she had insisted in the face of bitter opposition that princes of the Empire bend their knee three times before
her husband.[70] He was only a duke at the time; yet long after being

crowned emperor, minor symbolic marks of disrespect continued to be registered: not receiving adequate recognition in a performance by the court poet, for example.[71] However severely Maria Theresa might sanction such signs of disrespect toward her husband, the structural problem remained that hers was a marriage that upset contemporary norms. Maria Theresa herself was keenly aware of the conflict between her roles as sovereign overlord and as dutiful spouse ("the wife is subordinate to her husband").[72]

Maria Theresa survived her husband by fifteen years and never got over the loss.[73] Throughout her long widowhood she carefully cultivated the memory of their loving partnership: "Ever since I was five years old, my heart belonged only to this incomparable groom."[74] The way in which she retrospectively transfigured their marriage would subsequently enter historical memory. Taking their cue from many contemporaries, historians viewed this idealized marital and family life as quintessentially German and bourgeois: "full of refinement and obedience, tradition and restraint."[75] Yet this is a misunderstanding. In everyday life at court, in her relationship with her children, in her marriage strategies, and in almost every other respect, Maria Theresa followed the aristocratic rules of her age. The mere fact that her marriage was in some ways unconventional for its time is not enough to make it "bourgeois." The very notion is anachronistic: it measures Maria Theresa against a new ideal of conjugal love that she herself could not have known. When nineteenth- and twentieth-century scholars characterized her marriage as "bourgeois," they did so in the unspoken wish to make the imperial couple crown witnesses for their own anti-aristocratic value system.[76]

The impression of familial intimacy in a cozy middle-class setting is underscored by two well-known gouaches by Maria Christina, who inherited her mother's artistic talent.[77] One picture shows Christmas celebrations with the emperor in dressing gown and nightcap (fig. 22b),[78] the other her sister-in-law Isabella in childbed, lovingly tended by Joseph II. It is easy to take these images as documentary evidence of bourgeois domesticity in the House of Habsburg from the early 1760s— but they are nothing of the sort. Instead, Maria Christine copied two genre paintings by the Dutch painter Cornelis Troost (c. 1697–1750) and

FIGURES 22A AND B. Bourgeois Saint Nicolas's Day celebrations in the House of Habsburg? Illustration 22a, above: copperplate by Jacobus Houbraken after Cornelis Troost. Illustration 22b, below: watercolor drawing by Archduchess Maria Christina

gave the characters her family members' features. The spatial arrangement, the middle-class interior, the positioning of the figures, and the unadorned, intimately contemplative atmosphere are all the Dutchman's work. Neither the Hofburg nor Schönbrunn nor the hunting chateau of Laxenburg ever looked anything remotely like this. The pictures perhaps show that Maria Christina was influenced by the Rousseauian ideal of simple and unaffected behavior; they reveal nothing about what the House of Habsburg was really like. Yet these images confirmed later historians in their fawning admiration for the imperial family. Goethe already accounted for Maria Theresa and Francis Stephen's popularity in these terms: "As the great are, after all, human beings, the citizen thinks them his equals when he wishes to love them, and this he can best do when he can picture them to himself as loving spouses, tender parents, devoted siblings, and true friends."[79]

Maria Theresa's views on the subject of marriage were contradictory. While demanding that her own children submit obediently to dynastic considerations and marry the candidates of her choice—there will be more to say about this later[80]—in other cases she could push through a marriage against the wishes of the families involved. This was not just the case with her alter ego, her daughter Maria Christina, but also with several of her ladies-in-waiting. The court was an important marriage market for nobles.[81] A lady-in-waiting had to receive Maria Theresa's permission to marry; in return, she enjoyed the privilege of a court wedding with the empress herself as matron of honor. A spectacular instance was that of Charlotte von Hager, who as a privy councillor's daughter was of noble stock but who enjoyed Maria Theresa's particular confidence as governess of her two oldest daughters.[82] She was already forty-two years old when she was advised—not least for health reasons (!)—to find herself a husband. The empress had selected the necessary bridegroom, the councillor and chamberlain Count Stella. But this candidate was not good enough for the father of the bride owing to his "known lower extraction," his insufficiently venerable pedigree, and he proposed Prince Johann Wilhelm Trautson instead. The empress had already considered this widower, the last of his line and from a house of the utmost distinction, but had rejected the idea as unworkable, "since the prince's humor appears unsympathetic to an old maid."[83] For Traut-son, this was clearly a *mésalliance* out of all keeping with his social class. His sister, Princess Maria Antonia Xaveria von Auersperg, was particu-larly incensed, even though the plan had been cautiously broached to her by her confessor "the way one tends to announce a death or some such unhappy circumstance." She nonetheless "refused to countenance [the marriage] for a long time but spoke quite openly against it, denying her two brothers . . . entry to the house and frequently weeping and wailing for the shame done her family by so unequal a union. There was even speculation the empress would bar her from court. In the end, means were found to appease her to some extent, particularly since the empress . . . spoke to her in tones that were partly threatening, partly mollifying." The bride was made to furnish proof of her noble ancestry. Yet Princess Auersperg was still not prepared to attend the wedding or host the ensuing feast. The wedding cannot have been entirely welcome to the groom either, for his two previous marriages had failed to pro-duce a male heir and his new bride was past childbearing age. He thus knowingly faced the extinction of his line. Maria Theresa had to offer significant material and financial inducements to win him over. Besides contributing the entire wedding costs, trousseau, and a dowry of three thousand guilders, she gave the bride such "magnificent" wedding gifts as diamond jewelry and five thousand ducats in gold, as well as an an-nual pension of some four thousand guilders. The distinctions show-ered on the groom were truly impressive: he was awarded the position of lord high steward (which had actually been promised to someone else), as well as a lifelong pension of eight thousand guilders each year and the expectation that he would be admitted to the Order of the Golden Fleece. On top of all that, the wedding was held in spectacular fashion in the imperial council chamber (*Ratsstube*), otherwise reserved for great state ceremonies. In other words, Maria Theresa was in a posi-tion to assert her will against social conventions and buy her aging lady-in-waiting a first-rate princely groom. From the bride's point of view, this was an excellent bargain; it cleared the way for further social ad-vancement, and nobody would have seen the marriage as in any way demeaning for her. To be sure, there was no mention of love in all this.

Chastity Campaign

The culture of gallantry was omnipresent at Maria Theresa's court. Her male ancestors had kept mistresses without any great fuss. Even Lord High Chamberlain Khevenhüller, who upheld relatively strict moral standards, took such behavior more or less for granted. In 1743 he noted in his diary his displeasure at the "strange adventures and amorous intrigues" then flourishing in the ball season, which were "given all too great an opportunity by the freedom afforded by masks," and at the tendency for paramours "to make less attempt at concealment than under the previous, very serious regime." What bothered him were not so much the affairs themselves, however, as the fact they were flaunted in public view.[84] Others made fun of Khevenhüller's "Christian innocence"; he was said to blush whenever the name of a dancer he was besotted with was mentioned in his hearing. He was nonetheless prepared to tolerate the "dalliances with ladies" indulged in by his male peers.[85] Imperial Vice-Chancellor Colloredo, for example, Nikolaus Esterházy, Friedrich August von Harrach, but also Kaunitz were well known for pursuing extramarital affairs.[86] Such behavior was not usually a bone of contention, unless debaucheries were brought to public attention or conflicts erupted, as when former lovers or natural children made exorbitant financial demands or a wife ran off with her lover.[87] Gallant affairs were certainly a prominent topic of salon conversation. The topic was attractive precisely because it was never known for sure how much truth lay in the rumors. The many Italian operas and French comedies dealing with erotic intrigues and suspicions, mix-ups and cover-ups provided additional fodder for the imagination. Audiences were fed a diet of Molière, Voltaire, Marivaux, and Le Sage, delighting in their subtle double entendres.[88] Plays bore such characteristic titles as *Les ruses de l'amour* (*The Tricks of Love*), *Le rival supposé* (*The Assumed Rival*), or *Le mari amant de sa femme* (*The Husband in Love with his Wife*).[89]

Maria Theresa grew ever more impatient with the erotic innuendo and titillating ambiguities or "equivocations" that were a staple of these comedies and operas. In the early years of her marriage and during the War of Succession, she herself had greatly enjoyed the *divertissements* of the annual ball season in January and February. She had visited the theater and masked balls—they belonged together and were held at the same venues—and had occasionally even caroused the night away. This began to change radically from 1747 onward, as she lost her taste for dance and theater and increasingly withdrew from public amusements.[90] At the same time, she launched an unprecedented campaign against the prevailing climate of dissolution—at the court, in Vienna, and in the monarchy as a whole.

A first sign of her growing irritation became apparent in 1747, when she had members of the Opera Banda, a troupe of Italian singers, expelled from the country "because they had behaved too brazenly throughout Carnival." Actresses, singers, and dancers were coveted trophies for "gallant" noblemen; as such, they were notorious for their supposedly loose morals and were regarded by Maria Theresa with particular suspicion. The two best singers in the opera, the Ricci sisters, were "quite abruptly removed from here, *par ordre supérieur*, after becoming overly familiar with a number of young cavaliers," the lord high chamberlain noted in 1752.[91] It was an honor for any Italian singer to be banished from Vienna by Maria Theresa, Casanova joked in his memoirs.[92] Yet she did not stop at such ad hoc measures; for the first time, she directed her grand marshal of the court to set up a committee for carrying out systematic inspections of *das Comicum*, everything related to the performance of comedy.[93] The pious Khevenhüller commented on this critically in his diary. He disapproved of Carnival balls at court and in the city in general, since masquerade was practically an invitation to vice. He therefore found the singers' extradition to be "very laudable" in itself, yet not consequential enough to do away with the malaise. The problem had to be tackled at its root: one could not allow such "dangerous entertainments" as masked balls and "free spectacles" while at the same time calling for "Christian retirement" at court.[94] Was it not Maria Theresa herself who had first allowed masquerades in Vienna, in contrast to her father? Since then the "exuberance of youth" had passed away, and she would have long since withdrawn her permission were it not for her husband, who was accustomed to such amusements from his time in Lorraine.

In the following winter (1747–48), when Maria Theresa "was not in a good mood anyway" owing to her contested reform policy,[95] she launched a new and far more rigorous campaign against the excesses of the Carnival season. She conferred a monopoly on holding masked balls to the new general intendant for the theater, Colonel Rocco de lo Presti, while prohibiting "any and every masquerade in private houses."[96] The only exceptions were balls for the high nobility held in the House at the Mehlgrube. Even public balls were now subject to entrance restrictions and military supervision.[97] At the same time, she established a new committee charged with "seeing that all clandestine gatherings are prevented and disrupted."[98] The committee's members evidently went about their work diligently, not only keeping an eye on public places but stopping coaches and searching private apartments as well. Those found guilty of illicit revelry would—it was rumored—face removal from office, banishment, imprisonment, or confinement to a monastery. Even the strait-laced Khevenhüller found this too much of a good thing. Masked revelers were arrested "at the slightest impropriety," including some who had been falsely accused; not even married couples were spared. The *commission de chasteté*, as it was ironically called, soon gained legendary status.[99] Courtiers found it hard to believe what was happening. Foreign emissaries reported the crackdown with amusement to their principals; the papal nuncio joked about it; "it was even openly ridiculed in foreign newspapers."[100] What caused the most amazement and consternation was the fact that Maria Theresa had apparently ordered everyone to be treated equally, "without regard to person" and "without excepting princes and privy councillors."[101] Her chastity drive promptly netted delinquents from the high nobility, including members of great families such as Sinzendorf, Starhemberg, or Trautson. This was the real scandal, whereas there was nothing shocking about moral crusades targeting ordinary subjects. Adultery had always been a criminal offense, even if it was rarely actively prosecuted and punished. Stricter moral policing of commoners alone would probably not have provoked an uproar; it would have been tolerated, albeit grudgingly, as the zealous piety of a Christian ruler. What caused genuine outrage was that Maria Theresa had broken with a tacit moral consensus among the aristocratic elite. It had always been taken for granted that grandees, unlike commoners, were exempt from governmental oversight in questions of morality. In France aristocrats were untouchable in this regard. Even serious offenses went unpunished, unless a head of family decided to discipline his wayward son with a royal arrest warrant, a *lettre de cachet*.[102] Now the rules of the game had changed. The all-embracing chastity campaign was the equivalent in the moral realm to what nobles in the hereditary lands were simultaneously faced with in the area of finance policy. After all, Haugwitz's tax reform was likewise seen as an unprecedented attack on aristocratic privilege. In both cases, Maria Theresa defied expectations that she would show solidarity with her aristocratic peers.

There are nonetheless grounds for doubting that persons of high status were policed in exactly the same way as ordinary subjects.[103] It is not easy to reconstruct what really happened to those caught behaving badly. Moreover, the so-called chastity commission has left few traces in the archives, leading some conscientious historians to doubt whether it ever existed. The label was a pejorative term applied to various successive committees. Such imprecision is hardly surprising when one considers the many changes in the Viennese central bureaucracy during these years. The "chastity commission" was probably identical with the Police Commission (*Policeyhofkommission*), formally established in 1749, to which twenty-three new police stations were assigned in January 1751, four in the inner city and nineteen in the outskirts. The Police Commission was explicitly given responsibility for crimes against morality from 1752; the following year it was subsumed under the newly established Lower Austrian Representation and Chamber.[104]

How the police commissioners went about their day-to-day work can only be adduced from the many anecdotes on the matter that found their way into memoirs, letters, and travel reports. Tales circulated of cunning cavaliers who duped, bribed, or simply beat up members of Maria Theresa's vice squad to avoid punishment. An English lord was said to have traveled through half Europe with a "small seraglio" of eight women, a personal physician and two "negroes." The Police Commission detained and interrogated him in Vienna, but in the end his quick wits saw him released without charge.[105] The Swabian journalist Wilhelm Wekhrlin told of a beautiful hostess who was arrested in her matrimonial home and spent six weeks in prison under suspicion of being a procuress. She refused to denounce her clients even when caned: the cavaliers who frequented her house of ill repute, fearing with good reason that she might incriminate them, had paid her five hundred ducats to keep her lips sealed.[106] And Podewils reported of a commissioner who attempted "to persuade the valet of a young nobleman to let him know when his master received female company." The valet told his master, who ordered him to give the commissioner a tip-off "for a designated hour. The commissioner turned up and indeed found him with a wench. The young man pretended to be terrified, begged him not to expose him, and offered him a hundred ducats. After prevaricating for a while, the commissioner took the money, but had barely left the room when the young man gave him a hundred blows with his stick and forced him to hand back the money. He dared not lodge a complaint."[107]

Although surely boastful and exaggerated, stories such as these reveal that the commission met with resistance on all sides. All who came into contact with it—cavaliers and valets, procuresses and their customers—joined forces to oppose it. The anecdotes also show why the empress's attempt to transcend class barriers in her pursuit of moral rectitude was doomed to failure. For the commissioners were easily corrupted by the rich and powerful even as they persecuted the weak with the full force of the law. This was the unanimous verdict of quite differently disposed observers, from the respectable Count Bark, who lived in Vienna for thirty-four years as Swedish emissary, to Giacomo Casanova, who was based there in the 1760s and was eventually thrown out of the country after all kinds of illicit adventures.[108] The empress compelled everyone to hypocrisy, it was said. She mixed up the innocent and the guilty, punished women far more harshly than men, and even interfered in the sacred realm of matrimony, bringing trouble and dishonor by denouncing wives to their husbands at the least sign of infidelity.[109] Above all, she was reproached with expending her sovereign powers on far too slight an object, as if "love [were] a greater crime than murder and betrayal of one's country."[110] Of the seven deadly sins, Casanova jested, the empress had decided to ignore six and persecute only fornication.[111] In short, the chastity campaign sullied Maria Theresa's good name in the eyes of even her greatest admirers and gained her the reputation of a prudish bigot. She had proved herself as petty in small matters, the Swedish emissary wrote, as she could be generous in large ones.[112] And even Alfred von Arneth permitted himself the mild criticism that she had interfered in matters "which were too trivial for one in her lofty position, or which a woman of her purity of character should better have kept at arm's length."[113]

Rumors

Contemporaries could find no other explanation for Maria Theresa's chastity campaign than her jealous possessiveness toward her husband. For this personal reason, claimed Podewils, she had set out to banish all gallantry from court.[114] She tried to remove her husband from the company of courtiers notorious for their dissolute ways, instructing Kheven-hüller "to oblige everyone, so far as possible, to amuse the emperor and yet ... keep him away from disreputable society."[115] Those whom she was unable or unwilling to remove from her inner circle, such as Kaunitz, she did her best to reform. She thus repeatedly exhorted Kaunitz to stop consorting with prostitutes—and he repeatedly ignored her.[116] There are conflicting reports about her husband's behavior in this regard.

Francis Stephen had been brought up strictly by his father. Duke Leopold of Lorraine aspired to be a devout Christian prince and had urged his sons in a handwritten instruction to obey the sixth commandment—something he had not always done himself.[117] No sin was more debasing than adultery, he taught them, since it dragged the sinner down to the level of wild beasts. In addition, God already punished fornication in this world with fatal diseases, bastard children, and loss of wealth and honor. The adulterer plunged virgins into despair, did untold harm to their families, and violated sacred oaths; he was *absolument contraire à l'honnethomme*—the polar opposite of a gentleman. And the sixth commandment applied all the more strictly to a sovereign. After all, adultery was punishable by death. Any ruler who imposed this punishment on his subjects despite meriting it himself was an even more wicked criminal.[118] God was the only judge an adulterous ruler had to fear, but most rulers paid no heed to divine judgment. If court rumor was to be believed, the duke's two sons, Francis Stephen and Charles, were no different. Francis Stephen was reputed a gallant lover; his brother, who had married Maria Theresa's sister Marianna in 1744 only to be left a widower in his first year of marriage, was known by some for his gallantry, by others for his "gross debauchery," whatever that may mean.[119] Among his posthumous papers, for example, there is a precise description of a sign language for exchanging gallant messages in society with the secret object of one's desire.[120] Maria Theresa was said to be not entirely unaware of these vices, but they did not seriously detract from the love she bore her husband or her affection for her brother-in-law.

Maria Theresa remained true to her husband. She "stood . . . untarnished before her age, and, what is more, before her surroundings, the women who served her," attested Caroline Pichler, daughter of her long-serving maid and reader, Charlotte Hieronymus.[121] This judgment is hardly surprising from the perspective of one of her greatest admirers, yet even more sober observers and critics such as the Prussian emissaries found no evidence that Maria Theresa did not live up to her own exacting moral standards. Had it been otherwise, they surely would not have hidden it from their principal. Caroline Pichler goes on to write: "This fidelity and love is all the more glorious when one considers that the former was by no means reciprocated as it ought to have been. Emperor Francis had various lovers, some of whom were common knowledge, others not. His wife knew all about them, she drew one of them to her cards table; she suffered on account of them, but she loved the fickle one with undiminished ardor until his death."[122] The sources do in fact contain numerous references to Francis Stephen's infidelities. There was widespread consensus that he was an *amoroso*, a lady's man. On the other hand, many at court wondered how it was even possible for him to conduct affairs without arousing the jealous attention of his wife and giving rise to public scandal. Her means of surveillance were far reaching; she had spies everywhere who hoped to curry favor by providing her with information. For his part, Francis Stephen tried to avoid conflict and was careful not to provoke his wife's hot temper. It is therefore uncertain whether he really had as many mistresses as is sometimes claimed.[123]

"The emperor is too closely watched," wrote the Prussian ambassador Fürst. "He would have no opportunity to be unfaithful to his wife, even if he did not love her as he does."[124] Podewils was also skeptical. In 1747 he reported that the emperor had previously been especially fond of Countess Colloredo, his wife's lady-in-waiting, Countess Pálffy, and several other ladies, and that he had secretly met with them for gallant suppers, "but the empress's jealousy made him proceed no further."[125] The rumor that he used his hunting trips to carry out affairs behind his wife's back was dismissed by Podewils as malicious gossip, spread by those who had an interest in sowing discord between the imperial couple. Given Francis Stephen's good-humored and peaceable nature and Maria Theresa's suspicious vigilance—"his weakness in this regard being known to her"—Podewils could not imagine that she would not have long since put a stop to his philandering if there had been any truth to the rumors.

There were doubtless many malicious, scarcely credible anecdotes circulating among Maria Theresa's enemies. One such example is found in a letter written by the Prussian king. In 1754, as a conciliatory gesture during an interval of peace, he sent the famous Italian singer, Astrua, from Berlin to the Habsburg court, where she performed for the ruling couple. The singer, Frederick reported to his sister Wilhelmine of Bayreuth, told him that the emperor had paid court to her and offered himself as her *cicisbeo*. Maria Theresa herself had commented on this with the words *passe pour celle-là*, meaning roughly "better her than someone else." Frederick took this ironically as a sign of Astrua's extraordinary reputation: even the empress, "the most jealous person in the world," had been won over by her charms.[126]

The most persistent rumor concerned *la belle princesse*, Maria Wilhelmina Josepha von Auersberg née Neipperg (1738–75), who had been introduced to court at the age of sixteen and was one of Maria Theresa's maids. Her mother was born a Khevenhüller, while her father, Field

Marshal Wilhelm Reinhard von Neipperg, had been Francis Stephen's tutor and remained a father figure to him until his death. In 1755, at the age of seventeen, the beautiful princess married the widower Johann Adam Joseph von Auersperg, whom the emperor had elevated to the rank of prince only a few years earlier.[127] In May 1756, when the empress had fallen pregnant yet again and for the last time, her husband frequently undertook *parties de plaisir* in the countryside, "principally occasioned by the young Princess von Auersperg, for whom the emperor had developed a particular affection since the previous Carnival season," noted Khevenhüller. Such attention "was taken for a sign of pronounced inclination" by the court, a signal honor that practically elevated the princess to the informal position of favorite.[128] Although Khevenhüller himself lent no credence to the rumor, he remarked with growing disapproval how the emperor fed the rumor mill by allowing the princess to accompany him on his hunting expeditions.[129] Couples were mostly kept separate on these and similar occasions, but it was an open secret that such segregation could be manipulated; Maria Theresa herself was no stranger to the practice.[130] In any event, court society relished the opportunity to observe and exchange comments on the emperor's sleigh rides, card games, and visits to the theater with his favorite, some thirty years his junior. Writing to her daughter Maria Christina, who had evidently broached the subject with her, Maria Theresa claimed that there was no truth to the Auersperg affair: "What you imagine is false. The fair princess has done nothing to annoy me; indeed, I find her uncommonly pleasant and good-natured. They see and entertain each other only at table."[131] For almost a decade, until Francis Stephen's death in 1765, Princess Auersperg remained his close companion.[132]

If Prince Charles-Joseph de Ligne's memoirs are to be believed,[133] Francis Stephen was not the princess's only lover. The witty and charming Prince de Ligne (1735–1814) was almost the perfect embodiment of the aristocratic libertine, war hero, and rococo cavalier. He stood in high favor with both Maria Theresa and Francis Stephen. As the eldest male offspring of a princely house with lands straddling France and the Empire, he shuttled effortlessly between the courts of Versailles, Vienna, and Berlin, racked up immense debts, fought valorously in several wars under the imperial banner, and composed hundreds of literary works on the side: fragments, comedies, fantasies, reflections, and *contes immoraux*, immoral tales. His father had kept him on a tight budget but introduced him to the Viennese court when he was just sixteen years old, immediately secured his appointment as chamberlain, then found him a position in his regiment and in 1755 married him advantageously, at the age of twenty, to a Liechtenstein. The young prince was a connoisseur of the erotic scene and maintained the usual gallant affairs, without boasting excessively of his conquests.[134] He claimed in his memoirs to have shared a mistress with the emperor for a time, the ravishing Princess Auersperg. The following anecdote gives an impression of the nonchalance with which he treated such affairs:

> At the time when I shared the attractions of the most beautiful woman in the world, the greatest lady in Vienna, with the then emperor, the good, excellent, reliable, lovable, as well as fair, honorable, and good-humored Francis I, the empress was fond of visiting the theater. On those occasions the emperor did not dare leave his lodge. One day, when he saw that she was obviously distracted, he slipped into the lodge that I always used to visit at the time. His mistress and I were startled at his appearance. But we knew that he loved us both. He asked me to tell him the name of the little play that was being performed. It was "Crispin, Rival to his Master." I could not bring myself to say it. He insisted. I told him, stammering half with embarrassment, half with laughter. . . . Then I fled as quickly as possible and left it to the lively imagination of my beautiful and charming companion to concoct a tale that might explain our embarrassment and my hasty departure to her crowned lover.[135]

The fiction on the stage unexpectedly mirrored the reality in the lodge, threatening to expose how the rival had usurped his master's prerogative. Whether the episode really happened this way is uncertain; we do know that this comedy was performed at court in 1756.[136]

There are other indications that Francis Stephen may have had affairs that never reached the ears of court gossips, and possibly remained hidden from Maria Theresa as well. The emperor showed a keen interest in the fate of a young Florentine called Franz d'Arbogars, an interest explicable only on the assumption that he was his natural son.[137] The young man attended the college (*Gymnasium*) in Kremsmünster Abbey from 1748, breaking off his studies in 1754 to enter the military. The emperor corresponded with the Tuscan government on the matter on several occasions, calling for it to attend more carefully to the young man's education. His efforts were in vain; the young man enlisted as an officer cadet, was taken prisoner by the Prussians in the battle of Leuthen, and died in the fortress of Glogau. A certain Anna Franziska d'Arbogars in Florence, presumably his mother, received from Francis Stephen a lifelong annuity of one hundred guilders.

Francis Stephen maintained an altogether different kind of relationship with a woman from his own class, Béatrice de Ligneville, daughter of the Duke of Mignano and widow of the Lothringian Leopold-Marc de Ligneville. After the premature death of her husband in 1734, she lived on one of her family estates near Naples and maintained an intensive correspondence with the ducal family of Lorraine in Nancy. Contemporaries evidently knew nothing of her lifelong, intimate relationship with Francis Stephen, which essentially unfolded in the medium of writing. It came to light only much later, when scattered fragments of their exchange were discovered.[138] The friendship presumably dated back to Francis Stephen's stay in Lunéville between 1729 and 1731. A reunion in Tuscany in 1739 is mentioned in the correspondence. The few surviving fragments show that Francis Stephen maintained the exchange over many years in the vain hope of seeing her again. As late as 1758 she was still planning a journey to Vienna that evidently never came about, notwithstanding his fervent entreaties.[139] The letters also give an insight into the high level of secrecy demanded by the correspondence. Given that the post was closely monitored, they could not simply be sent like any other article but had to be conveyed by trusted personal couriers. In addition, the letters were often unsigned; the lovers relied on recognizing each other by their handwriting. However passionate this relationship may have been, Francis Stephen took great pains to keep it hidden from his wife. This was difficult, but it was clearly not impossible.

Actual affairs were one thing; rumors about them were another, perhaps more serious problem, no matter how much truth there was in them. How Maria Theresa dealt with such rumors can be seen in another telling episode. In 1768, when Francis Stephen had already been dead for three years, a certain Fräulein Juliane von Schönbad, Schönau, or Schönbaden—the names in the records vary—turned up in Bordeaux. She claimed to be the natural daughter of the deceased emperor and a "lady of the first distinction."[140] She then made the mistake of fabricating two letters, supposedly written by Joseph II, attesting to her high pedigree. One of these she sent to Karl von Cobenzl, the imperial envoy in Brussels, the other to Charles III, king of Spain. The king was skeptical and had inquiries made with Joseph about the letter's authenticity. This led to the fraud being exposed. Upon being informed of what had happened,[141] Maria Theresa commissioned Charles of Lorraine, governor of the Habsburg Netherlands since 1741, to convey the young lady with the utmost discretion to Brussels and launch a thorough investigation. She was to be promised mercy if she revealed her parents' true identity. Patrice-François Neny, president of the Brussels council, whose brother Corneille Neny was Maria Theresa's privy cabinet secretary in Vienna, was placed in charge of the investigation, assisted by emissary Cobenzl. The girl arrived in Brussels in the summer of 1769; she was imprisoned in Fort Monterey and interrogated at length. While she admitted falsifying the letters, she insisted that her mother, whom she did not know herself, must have been the mistress of a very high-placed grandee. It had dawned on her that her father could have been none other than Francis Stephen when she was given his portrait by a mysterious visitor. Neny was distrustful, while Cobenzl tended to believe her story.

The interrogations lasted two months without getting to the bottom of the matter. Attempts to prevent the story leaking were so unsuccessful, meanwhile, that it was soon a topic of discussion at a soirée given by the papal nuncio. The Duchess of Arenberg and several other aristocratic ladies were so curious that they even attempted to infiltrate the fortress just to catch a glimpse of the mysterious stranger. The emperor's memory threatened to be compromised in the eyes of the world. Those charged with sorting out the mess disagreed about the best course of action. The girl had undoubtedly been guilty of fraud. Should she be confined to a nunnery in some remote corner of the hereditary lands or inconspicuously returned to France? Should gossipers be met with dignified silence or threatened with punishment? Cobenzl still believed the stranger's statements; after all, she had spoken with great "naturalness" (*ingenuité*). Perhaps he knew more about the matter than he cared to let on: many suspected him of being the mysterious father. At any rate, he thought it likely that she really was of high birth. In that case, the empress could neither deliver her to the criminal justice system nor simply set her free and send her back to France. A convent was the best solution—the further away, the better. Neny countered that, were word of this to get out, it would be widely taken as involuntary confirmation of her story. He advocated adopting an attitude of studied indifference and sending the prisoner back to Bordeaux with the help of the French authorities; this would arouse the least attention.

Kaunitz was also taken into the queen's confidence. Through his offices, Maria Theresa informed her servants in Brussels how she wished to proceed. Kaunitz let Cobenzl know that the girl's true parentage was immaterial. All that mattered was how the honor of the Archducal House could best be preserved. He ordered Neny to send all documents relating to the case as quickly as possible to Vienna, so that no trace of it was left in Brussels (without success, as it turned out—the materials can still be found among Neny's papers in Brussels). Maria Theresa decided to bring the stranger to the border and from there have her escorted to Bordeaux under French guard. Kaunitz put this request to the French minister Choiseul, who coolly remarked that there was no need for such an escort, since France had nothing against the honorable young lady. His use of the epithet *hônnete* infuriated Maria Theresa, since with this "perfidious insinuation" Choiseul showed that he believed the statements made by the girl under interrogation. In January 1770 the empress finally ordered that she be taken to the Dutch or French border, released with a hundred guilders, and threatened with life imprisonment if she ever dared show her face in Habsburg territory again. She vanishes from the historical record in Holland.[142] Rumors, however, lingered on for some time. A decade and a half later, in 1785, an anonymous exposé appeared in Vienna entitled "The Unknown Woman. A True Story," based on knowledge of the interrogation files.

The episode is significant for what it reveals about politics and morality in the ancien régime. The virulence of such affairs rested on the fact that the existence of natural children could be assumed at all times. So long as gallant affairs were taken for granted while simultaneously cloaked in secrecy, nothing was certain yet everything possible. At the same time, procreation was a supremely political affair. Natural sons and daughters could potentially make inheritance claims. Adventurers who exuded an air of worldly self-assurance—Fräulein von Schönbaden, for example—exploited this to extort hush money or demand protection from on high. In such a situation, everything came down to scandal management. The truth was irrelevant; what was essential was communication. Kaunitz had recognized this, Cobenzl had not.

How did Maria Theresa deal with dangers of this kind? She despised rumor-mongering in principle and repeatedly admonished her children never to spread gossip or rely on hearsay.[143] Moreover, she opted to place her trust in those who stood close to her, even at the risk of being let down. She once wrote to her son Ferdinand that, in case of doubt, she would rather be deceived than treat people distrustfully in advance.[144] It was part of her regal demeanor to remain serenely unperturbed by indiscretions, intrigues, and rumors of all kinds. Yet this was only one side of the coin. On the one hand, she needed to appear to float far above the realm of idle chatter; on the other, she, more than anyone else, needed to be kept extremely well informed. Maria Theresa was seized by an almost obsessive wish to "know everything."[145] This normative conflict required a carefully calibrated dual strategy; above all, it called for a well-organized secret communications system. Maria Theresa relied on absolutely trustworthy and discreet informants to keep her up to date on the latest developments, gauge the danger of rumors, and, if necessary, take action against them, while she herself could maintain an air of sovereign disinterest. Kaunitz was one such confidant, as were cabinet secretaries such as Ignaz Koch and Corneille Neny.

Even when it came to her husband's infidelity, Maria Theresa seems to have pursued just such a dual strategy. At any rate, she did her utmost to give the impression that she paid no heed to the rumors and was not the jealous type, although she was clearly not very successful in this regard. She likewise urged her daughters not to limit their husbands' freedom or make them feel distrusted. As she candidly explained to her favorite daughter, Maria Christina, with whom she identified in many ways:

> Guard against jealousy towards your husband, it will only drive him away from you. Do not bring up the matter even in jest; jokes easily give rise to recriminations, a bitter tone creeps in, mutual respect and attraction suffer as a result, and suddenly one feels the poison of aversion. The greater the trust you place in your husband, the fewer constraints you impose upon him, the more you will be secure in his love and loyalty.[146]

And she once wrote to Mercy-Argeneau, the envoy sent to chaperone her daughter Marie-Antoinette in Paris:

> If one only knew who these infamous windbags are who want to drive the king [Louis XVI of France] into amorous adventures—the harshest punishment would be only too merited. On the other hand, I cannot wish to see my daughter drawn in and exposed before the king and the public. To my way of thinking, the wife has nothing else to do than patiently accept her husband's misdemeanors, and she has no right to take them ill of him.[147]

Displays of jealousy were also not in keeping with Maria Theresa's ideas of wifely decorum. Above all, revealing such weakness, and thereby first drawing public attention to it, was incompatible with her image of herself as a ruler. If she and her husband never came to blows on this point (so far as we are aware), then this is not necessarily because there were no affairs to disturb their domestic harmony, but because she chose to maintain an attitude of sovereign disregard and forgiveness. Her innermost feelings in such a situation remained carefully concealed from the outside world.

Disciplining Subjects

Quite different standards applied to commoners *in puncto sexti*. They were made to bear the brunt of the matron-in-chief's chastity campaign. Behavior she was forced to tolerate in her own husband and was unable, despite all her threats of punishment, to suppress among noble cavaliers, was persecuted all the more relentlessly when indulged in by ordinary subjects.

In itself, surveillance of marriage and sexuality was nothing new. It long predated Maria Theresa's "chastity commission" but had traditionally been a matter for the Church. Since the High Middle Ages, marriage—as one of the sacraments—had fallen under the purview of canon law and the ecclesiastical courts. It was therefore a new and unorthodox move for Maria Theresa to bring sexual mores under the supervision of the police (*Policey*). This word, unlike its modern equivalent, did not designate a state crime-fighting organ but the entire internal order of the community itself: the polity. Since the late Middle Ages, police matters had been expanding inexorably. Ever more objects were regulated by the authorities in the interests of a "well-instituted polity": weights, measures, and foodstuffs were checked, presales and profiteering prohibited, midwives and apothecaries monitored, fire prevention and urban sanitation measures put in place, the blamelessly poor and invalids provided with support, vagabonds and foreign beggars kept at bay, "boisterous peasants" disciplined, and so on. One of the police's classic responsibilities was ensuring that Sundays and holidays were kept holy and that blasphemy, gambling, and carousing were held in check, since a Christian government had to prevent God imposing collective punishment on the land for the sins of the few. It was also important to ensure that on occasions calling for ostentatious expenditure and display—at baptisms, weddings, and funerals—everyone adhered to the standards set for their class, lest the divinely ordained order become blurred. Over the centuries police ordinances regulating such matters had become ever longer and more complex to keep pace with changing social dynamics. This is not to say that they had become any more efficient. In the eighteenth century, authorities began to harbor growing doubts about the meaningfulness of many police laws. They came to realize, for example, that limiting luxury consumption among wealthy subjects and scrupulously policing class boundaries was not just a futile undertaking, it also served no useful purpose.

Maria Theresa came to much the same realization. Yet while relaxing sumptuary laws (albeit with some hesitation), she at the same time introduced new police regulations targeting the ordinary populace. These included crackdowns on speech critical of the authorities and on offenses against sexual morality. In a memorandum he sent to Maria Theresa on taking up his position at the Theresianum in Vienna, Johann Heinrich Gottlob Justi, the great pioneer of *Policeywissenschaft*, or "police science," had already proclaimed "supervision of morals" to be a key police task. His ambitious program, envisaging nothing less than the "happiness of the state," demanded that "a) all virtues be encouraged . . . and b) all vices punished, particularly those that violate public decency and cause public offense."[148] In the same spirit, Haugwitz's newly established Directory took on the task of improving the police regime in the hereditary lands.[149] The new territorial chambers were given responsibility for enforcing the police laws, along with the aforementioned new Police Commission in Lower Austria and the capital, Vienna. In 1751 no fewer than twenty-three local police stations were set up in Lower Austria and subordinated to this commission.[150] A little later, the Directory added one essential point to the commission's agenda: "targeted surveillance to identify and prosecute all public offenses."[151] The commission was to appoint "a number of vigilant officials" to conduct investigations on its behalf. Only "trusted judges or otherwise reliable people" were to be called to this delicate office, ensuring that no one fell unfairly under a cloud of suspicion. In general, the commission was to proceed with the utmost caution and discretion to avoid drawing undue attention to its activities. So long as a moral offense had not yet been publicized, officials were to act against it discreetly; had it already become the talk of the town, however, they were to punish it with the full force of the law. The empress herself asked to be kept up to date on the progress of their investigations; the Police Commission had to submit weekly protocols for her perusal.

In the individual hereditary lands, police matters were placed in the hands of the newly established Representations and Chambers. In 1750 Maria Theresa decreed that policing functions there should be taken over by specially appointed superintendents. Those selected for the job should be "capable and watchful, not learned men." They should pay regular visits to "taverns, cafés, and gambling houses" and keep their eyes and ears open.[152] To stimulate their interest in uncovering moral offenses, they were promised one third to one half of any fines imposed in place of a regular salary. Each police superintendent had to swear an oath to exercise his office without fear or favor. This new initiative to monitor public morals met with both eager assent and difficulties from the territorial bureaucracies. The Styrian Representation in Graz, for example, responded enthusiastically to the directive from Vienna, proposing many ideas of its own.[153] It found *one* police superintendent to be far too few, recommending a three-headed police commission for Styria alone. In addition, local officials drew up a compendious agenda containing twenty-six points. These included such classic police matters as the supervision of players, street performers, dancers, and wayfarers, as well as control of "prohibited games, night revelries, tumults, assemblies and mobs." Particular attention should be paid to suspicious houses and "encounters between those of the opposite sex."[154] Three names were put forward for the commission: two middle-class officials and a certain Count Auersperg. The nobleman had been chosen deliberately, "partly for increased prestige and operational effectiveness, partly so that in aristocratic gatherings the necessary inspections may be undertaken."[155] Officials thus correctly assumed that the nobility would not be spared scrutiny, but they found that such surveillance could only be carried out by fellow nobles, in accordance with the old precept that each could only be judged by his own. Although Maria Theresa turned down the proposal to create a special Police Commission for Styria, she did allow several police superintendents to be appointed. They were given the more dignified title of "police commissaires" and their ranks later swelled through the appointment of subcommissaires.[156] It may be assumed that they were not police spies; their activities appear to have been known to the wider populace.[157]

Yet this service proved extremely unpopular. Not everyone nominated for the task by civic magistrates was keen to be used as an informer. Respectable citizens feared for their reputations if they were seen moonlighting in places of ill repute. A case in point was the retired Inner Austrian government draftsman and commissioner for wards of state, Dr Ludwig Piccardi, sometime author of the treatise *Mary's All-Hallowed Heart*. He lodged a written complaint: he had "never frequented" the sinister sites he was supposed to monitor and had no intention of doing so in future. His position as rector of the Brotherhood of the Purification of Mary—a sodality that counted both their Supreme Majesties among its members—prohibited him from "setting a bad example to others, or at least provoking their outrage," by being seen to visit "such suspicious houses."[158] In short, the policing of public morals proved easier in theory than in practice. If respectable citizens were unwilling to take part, and only those enticed by payments for denunciation could be recruited to spy on their fellows, then the kind of clean, just, and impartial campaign that Maria Theresa had in mind was hardly possible. This did nothing to diminish the rigor with which the morality police went after men and, especially, women who had come to their attention owing to their habitually promiscuous way of life.

Those suspected of such offenses were threatened with a spell in the workhouse, imprisonment,[159] or deportation. In the so-called *Wasserschübe*, offenders were periodically shipped via the Danube and Tisza to the outermost periphery of the Habsburg empire: to Temesvár in the Banat, near the Turkish border.[160] Under Maria Theresa deportation became a means of choice for punishing "women of easy virtue." This strategy achieved several objectives at once. A public nuisance was removed from sight and the few local prisons and workhouses were relieved of excess inmates. At the same time, it was expected that offending women would be reeducated to perform socially useful work, contribute to colonizing the thinly settled Banat, and increase the Catholic share of the population. Moral, confessional, political, and economic goals appeared to dovetail beautifully here. In Temesvár the women would live in "pleasant dwellings" with plenty of fresh air; they would be kept clean and properly clothed. Proceeds from manual labor—weaving and knitting stockings—would allow them to defray their own transport and accommodation expenses.

The first deportation, consisting entirely of females, is attested for the summer of 1744: forty-nine women, most of them unwed, had been conveyed to Temesvár by September. Within two years twenty were dead and one had fled. The second consignment of twenty-eight women arrived in December of the same year: thirteen died and five escaped within a year. The death rates show that the salubrious living conditions imagined by Maria Theresa looked rather different on the ground. The territorial government of the Banat was overwhelmed. As District President Engelshofen complained to Vienna, there was not enough space for the women, who lived crushed together in great squalor, almost eaten alive by vermin and ravaged by swift-spreading disease. Under such conditions, there could be no talk of useful labor or even education. Mortality rates were somewhat lower for later deportations. The whole project nonetheless proved "unprofitable"—on the contrary, it was a significant drain on state coffers.[161] Yet Maria Theresa held fast to the goal of moral improvement, which in her view outweighed all economic cost-benefit considerations. The hope that deportation might have a deterrent effect no doubt also played a role. In 1753 the semiofficial *Wienerische Diarium* reported that "early in the morning a number of men and women were deported by water to the Banat, and some to Temesvár, on account of their deplorable and idle way of life."[162]

Over the following years deportations to Temesvár were expanded to include additional groups: male criminals, vagabonds, "gypsies," young men and old, people from the German, Hungarian, and Italian hereditary lands—anyone deemed undesirable or a menace to society was rounded up, generally between one hundred and two hundred people at a time. Government officials in the provinces clearly grew used to exporting their disciplinary problems to the furthest corners of the empire.[163] Needless to say, this did nothing to improve the situation in Temesvár. Although Maria Theresa again sought to have only women deported, the practice of mixed deportations, once introduced, became firmly established. Officials increasingly endeavored to classify the deportees into various categories and differentiate their treatment accordingly. Only a small number of hardened female delinquents would be temporarily or permanently housed in the women's prison, the *Weiberstockhaus*, while a larger number were consigned to the workhouse. The majority, however, could settle freely in the Banat, either working as maidservants or marrying and setting up their own household. This third group consisted mostly of girls and women who had been detained for committing adultery, procuring sexual services, or otherwise behaving immorally. Despite concerted attempts to categorize them, the deportees were treated in highly unsystematic fashion. No coherent system dictated whether they were incarcerated at all and, if so, for how long and under what conditions.[164] Yet the policy of resettlement was an abject failure: most women exiled to the Banat found neither a position nor a husband, returning as quickly as possible to their homelands. The authorities were powerless to intervene; to prevent the women from returning, it was said, they would have to lock them up or establish a military cordon at the Hungarian border.[165] The Lower Austrian government and the territorial administration in the Banat blamed each other for the horrendous conditions. Reports were drafted and proposals submitted, but, due to the prohibitive costs involved, nothing ever came of them. One report on workhouse conditions met with an indignant response from the empress. Maria Theresa found that the institution lacked everything needed to fulfill its intended function.[166]

Yet although the program demonstrably failed to meet all its original objectives, Maria Theresa clung "almost counter-factually to the meaningfulness of deportations."[167] The tide only turned after Joseph, now emperor and coregent alongside his mother, toured Hungary and the Banat in May 1768 and surveyed conditions for himself. Joseph returned to Vienna convinced "that deportation is a pointless, deleterious, and, in my view, unconscionable form of punishment." He backed up this stand with a long series of almost irrefutable arguments: deportation was arbitrarily imposed, failed to act as a deterrent, and improved nobody. Deportees found no work in the Banat, either perishing miserably from sickness and privation or resorting to crime in order to survive.

Young women had even been known to be sold by Rascians (i.e., Serbs) to the Turks.[168] Swayed by Joseph's impassioned appeal, Kaunitz threw his support behind him in the State Council, finding that "after learning the truth of the matter, it would indeed weigh heavily on our conscience if this unjust and harsh procedure were not immediately and permanently discontinued."[169] All this was still not enough to persuade Maria Theresa. She initially wanted to suspend deportations for two years before making a final decision. Yet in this case, Joseph had his way. The last deportation to Temesvár took place in October 1768.

The empress was not always so harsh and uncompromising as in her approach to notorious "women of easy virtue" and other "riffraff." In October 1755 she issued two decrees intended to benefit unwed women who had been seduced, impregnated, and then abandoned by their lovers. In this case, she acted less out of regard for the welfare of the "stricken women" than for the souls of their unbaptized children. In their helplessness and fear of public exposure, such women had to be kept from murdering their newborn infants.[170] Maria Theresa was acting in response to the "currently fashionable cruel vice of infanticide" which had increasingly come to public attention. Her aim was to save the children by depriving their young mothers of any motives for keeping their pregnancy a secret. To that end, a series of preventive measures was put in place. The authorities and courts were instructed to be lenient and discreet in punishing women for bearing children out of wedlock, or better yet, to let them off with a caution. They were certainly not to be fined, let alone exposed—as had long been customary—to public opprobrium. Midwives were not to alert the authorities to extramarital pregnancies but secretly assist such women when they went into labor. The courts were to see to it that fathers and relatives provided maintenance. The parish should offer basic support to destitute mothers and their offspring. In the event of infanticide, the child's father, along with any family members who had contributed to hushing up the pregnancy or refused to help in the delivery, were threatened with severe punishment. To prevent fallen women from "growing faint-hearted" for fear of shame, the empress was willing—as stated in the decree—to let those "whose honor has not been redeemed by their lovers through matrimony, but who have otherwise conducted themselves respectably, and who cannot be shown to have concealed their pregnancy, be given a certificate restoring them to a state of honor," waiving the fees normally required for such a formal dispensation.[171] When it came to saving the souls of newborns, Maria Theresa was clearly prepared to put her morality campaign on ice. Two and a half decades later, in the 1780s, the topic of infanticide sparked a debate on fundamental judicial principles. The Palatine Academy received around four hundred submissions in response to its prize question on how infanticide might be prevented. The theme was dramatized by the Sturm und Drang movement— Faust's Gretchen!—and became a touchstone for enlightened and philanthropic legislators.[172] With her decree from 1755, Maria Theresa was thus a quarter-century ahead of her time.

Births

Between 1737 and 1756, her twenty-first and her fortieth year, Maria Theresa brought sixteen children into the world.[173] She thus spent most of the first two decades of her marriage in a state of pregnancy. Her first three children were born before she came to the throne, all of them daughters: Maria Elisabeth on February 5, 1737; Maria Anna on October 6, 1738; and Maria Carolina on January 12, 1740. Two of them died in infancy: the first at the age of three, the third shortly after her first birthday. The heir apparent, Joseph, was born after Maria Theresa's accession to the throne, at the start of the War of Succession, on March 13, 1741. The next six children were also born during the war: Maria Christina on May 13, 1742; another girl, again baptized Maria Elisabeth, on August 13, 1743; a second son, Charles Joseph, on February 1, 1745; Maria Amalia on February 26, 1746; Peter Leopold on May 5, 1747; and on September 17, 1748, shortly before the Treaty of Aachen, a little girl, again named Maria Carolina, who did not survive the birth. Five children were born in the ensuing period of peace: Johanna Gabriele on February 4, 1750; Maria Josepha on March 11, 1751; a third Maria Carolina on August 13, 1752; Ferdinand on June 1, 1754; and Maria Antonia (or Marie Antoinette) on November 2, 1755, a day after the earthquake of Lisbon. The last child, Maximilian Francis, entered the world on December 8, 1756, shortly after the outbreak of another war that was destined to last a further six years. Over the following years, Maria Theresa had to look on as three more of her children died before reaching adulthood: Charles Joseph died in 1761 at the age of sixteen, Johanna Gabriele in 1762 at twelve, and Maria Josepha in 1767, likewise at sixteen. All the rest—ten out of sixteen children—outlived their mother. Given the infant mortality rates at the time across all levels of society, this was a disproportionately high number. Maria Theresa's tally of pregnancies, by contrast, was far from unusual. Her daughter Maria Carolina, for example, later queen of Naples, had eighteen children, all but four of whom predeceased her.

The ruler's body was a public body, never more so than when that body was pregnant: the happiness and continued existence of the house, indeed the entire monarchy, depended on her fertility. A royal pregnancy was therefore announced to the public as a joyful event. This occurred indirectly at first, when she was borne to church around the beginning of the fourth month in a majestic, silk-hung litter. This form of conveyance had a symbolic, ritual meaning rather than serving any practical purpose: the queen had changed her public status and was now officially "with child." By putting her own fertility on display, she embodied a thriving, divinely blessed dynasty. The litter was a public signal taken up and proclaimed to the world at large by the *Wienerische Diarium*. The public declaration of a royal pregnancy was common practice: "Whenever the wives of princes fall pregnant, the news is everywhere made public, with reports appearing from month to month on how the pregnancy is advancing. . . . This is announced to other courts, since she then receives the congratulations of foreigners as well as—through her deputies—those of her own subjects, particularly the imperial and territorial estates".[174] When Maria Theresa withheld news of her fifth pregnancy for longer than usual so she could take part in the spectacular ladies' carousel, this was widely held against her.[175]

It could be hard to tell whether or not a woman was pregnant. Only once she felt her unborn child moving inside her, around the fourth or fifth month, could she be sure. In itself, discontinued menstruation was not a sure sign. According to learned opinion, it could have many causes: a blockage in the bloodstream, for example, or the presence of a nonhuman growth, also called a "moonchild" or "mola." The fruit growing in the mother's womb was only considered to be a living human organism once she became aware of its movements.[176] Maria Theresa thus wrote to her son Ferdinand when his wife felt the first fetal stirrings of her pregnancy: "You are now father to a little living creature which you will see four months from now." Until that point she had always referred to "the fruit" (la fruit), now she spoke of "the child" (l'enfant).[177]

In the context of court society, pregnancy was also marked by the queen submitting to bloodletting on three separate occasions during her term, each reported to the public by the Wienerische Diarium. There were both medical and social reasons for this. Physicians at the time saw bloodletting as a universal remedy. It unclogged the blood, removed harmful particles, and even seemed to promise an easier conception.[178] In accordance with ancient doctrine, health was regarded as the right mixture—complexio or temperamentum—of the four bodily humors: blood, phlegm, black bile, and yellow bile. Pregnancy upset the balance of humors. Physicians taught that menstrual blood regularly flushed harmful substances out of the system. During pregnancy, it was assumed, this blood was needed to nourish the fetus, meaning that it could no longer continue cleansing the body.[179] Nausea and vomiting during the first months were seen as resulting from a buildup of superfluous blood, since the fruit did not need much blood in the first phases of its gestation. Regular bloodletting was thus necessary as a substitute for the suspended monthly emissions, particularly in a woman of a "sanguinary disposition" such as Maria Theresa.[180] After she came to power, each such bloodletting was generally celebrated with a gala day, as also occurred on birthdays, name days, and other solemn occasions. These usually took place three times during the pregnancy: at the beginning, in the middle, and near the end.[181] Festively attired courtiers gathered around the empress to congratulate her on her successful treatment and celebrate it with various entertainments. Even when Maria Theresa gave no public notification of her bloodletting, everyone with rights of access still showed up in gala dress to offer her their good wishes.[182]

She was expected to take good care of herself. For a pregnant woman, danger lurked everywhere, above all for the health of the child. In October 1740, for example, Maria Theresa was forbidden from approaching her father's deathbed for fear of exposing her unborn baby to harm.[183] It was thought that a terrifying or frightening sight could make a literal impression on the viewer, causing, in the case of pregnant women, damage to the fetus. A court decree from August 27, 1773 sternly reiterated that "beggars afflicted with terrible deformities" were to be moved on, since their presence "often has unfortunate consequences with respect to pregnant women and deliveries."[184] Even the official manual for midwifery from 1774 states that, after receiving traumatic impressions, women bear children "on whose bodies the signs of their fatal accident have clearly been perceived."[185] Windows in birthing rooms were therefore normally draped with cloth: not to prevent outsiders from looking in but, conversely, to prevent the pregnant woman from looking out and endangering both herself and her child.

Maria Theresa, for her part, was not so easily impressed. She bore her many pregnancies and confinements with remarkable fortitude. After giving birth to Joseph, she reportedly wished that she were back in her sixth month of pregnancy.[186] And in early 1745 she wrote to her personal physician, "Although I am now nine months pregnant, I am feeling fit as a fiddle."[187] As much as possible, she always sought to preserve her daily routine. Those around her, deeply troubled by her reckless conduct, feared *les fausses couches*, miscarriages. Any excessive movement, especially riding, dancing, or driving rapidly over bumpy streets, was considered dangerous. Time after time, Maria Theresa's refusal to make the slightest concession in this regard attracted disapproving comment.[188] This only changed after her sister Marianna died in her first childbed in 1744, and above all when she herself was delivered of a stillborn child in 1748. She blamed the fatality on a coach ride to Holíč she had undertaken shortly before the delivery. "Do not follow my example, for I have always been only too fortunate in bearing children, more than I deserved," she wrote to her sister shortly before the latter came to term.[189] Later, she would almost obsessively remind her own daughters and daughters-in-law to avoid riding, dancing, and driving in the first months of a pregnancy; she even tried to forbid them going on long walks.[190] She constantly harbored the gravest concerns for her daughters, found new grounds for reproaching them in every letter, and, in short, subjected them to altogether different standards to those that guided her own conduct.

Maria Theresa refused to let her pregnancies deter or distract her from the business of government, in particular. Physical weakness made her short-tempered and impatient. She continued issuing commands until shortly before her confinement: on June 1, 1754, for example, she spent the morning consulting with her conference ministers on current problems of foreign policy before retiring in the afternoon to give birth to her son Ferdinand—and she returned to her desk only a few days later.[191] She measured others against her own fierce discipline—and found them wanting. "I am back on my feet, but they take long vacations," she complained about her officials ten days after yet another delivery.[192] She likewise did all she could to avoid neglecting her religious duties. Again in 1754, she insisted on genuflecting three times before the cross on Good Friday, despite having just entered the ninth month of her pregnancy.[193] She only exempted herself from fasting rules and therefore dined alone on fasting days.[194] And in the advanced stages of her pregnancy, she no longer took part in long processions and skipped the occasional "apartment," a get-together with her intimate circle at court. But these were the only concessions she allowed herself.

Over the course of time, Maria Theresa found that her pregnancies increasingly affected her freedom of movement, the energy she could devote to her work, and her state of mind. In its impact on her everyday life, her stupendous fertility was a mixed blessing. Given the high childhood mortality rate, dynastic considerations dictated that she produce as many children as possible. It was only too easy for all her male heirs to die prematurely; her own parents' experience of this was still a painful memory. Yet as she grew older her pregnancies became ever more taxing. She suffered from rheumatism; the walks and frequent changes of clothing to which she had been accustomed now grew ever more difficult.[195] Shortly before giving birth to her tenth child, she decided that enough was enough. As she wrote to Antonia of Saxony, to whom she gladly confided such matters at the time, "if the dear Lord will only pre-serve the children I have now, I would be perfectly content to stop at ten; for I feel that it [pregnancy] weakens and ages me and makes me less fit for all mental labor."[196] In June the following year, 1749, she shared her fears that she had once again fallen pregnant.[197] A year later she gave Antonia of Saxony advice for her first pregnancy, sending her pills to counteract her *langueur*—her listlessness and debility—made from a family recipe that for generations had been handed down in her house from mother to daughter. To her regret, she added, she was an expert of many years' standing and now found herself expecting once again.[198] In November 1756, shortly before the birth of her last child Maximilian, she admitted to the electoral princess that war, illness, and the new preg-nancy were weighing down on her.[199] And in 1761 she congratulated An-tonia of Saxony on *not* falling pregnant.[200]

Maria Theresa had eleven daughters and only five sons—an undesir-able ratio. From a dynastic point of view, the birth of sons was of the utmost importance, since it was generally through sons alone that lin-eage, status, title and the scepter of rule were passed on to descendants. Whenever exceptions were made, as in the case of the Pragmatic Sanc-tion, they went against the prevailing social logic and were accepted only with great difficulty, as she herself had so painfully experienced. It was taken for granted that the arrival of a son provided greater cause for cele-bration than that of a daughter. There was no end to the jubilation when the birth of a male heir was announced. And when a second son, Charles, was born in January 1745, Francis Stephen could "barely speak for joy." Maria Theresa herself left the room shortly after the delivery and "in her elation, despite being in so weak a state that she could hardly stand on her feet and had to be supported much of the way, she moved with re-markable haste to the window, opening it and crying out that an arch-duke had been born."[201] By contrast, when Maria Carolina was born in August 1752, Khevenhüller noted that the delivery had been "very smooth, but again resulted in a daughter." A chamberlain had thought-lessly expressed himself in ambiguous terms to those awaiting news in the antechamber—"an ill-conceived pleasantry"—and thereby falsely "occasioned a shout of joy, as if an archduke had been born."[202] It could have been worse; at least there were three sons in reserve by then. At the start of her marriage, when three daughters were born in succession, everyone was keenly anticipating a male heir. It was said that Maria Theresa had taken refuge in St. Joseph, beseeching him for his heavenly intercession. Once her prayers had been granted, she decided to christen her son Joseph in thanks for the saint's support, abandoning her original (and more traditional) plan to name him after her father, Charles.[203]

She did not have to rely on prayer alone to influence the child's sex, however; there were medical solutions as well. The advice to his son offered by Karl Eusebius, prince of Liechtenstein, gives an insight into the practical knowledge on such matters available to the Lower Austrian nobility at the time.[204] His advice was based on age-old medical theories about differences between the sexes and the process of procreation. Eighteenth-century medicine still took women's intellectual and physical inferiority for granted. Since Aristotle and Galen, woman had been considered a defective, more imperfect, less mature version of man.[205] It was therefore assumed that strong and vital semen produced boys, whereas weak semen resulted in either miscarriages or girls. Karl Eusebius therefore cautioned his son not to sleep with his wife too often, since this made for weak and impotent semen. Maria Theresa's father, anxious for a grandson, had for the same reason counseled his son-in-law Francis Stephen to curb his enthusiasm and "take [his] time."[206] The fifth day of the new moon, when the moon is still young, was considered a propitious time for conception, as was the period following the woman's monthly "purification," since then the uterus was particularly clean, not yet having been polluted again by blood; this, too, increased the likelihood of a male child. Finally, the woman was advised to lie on her right side following intercourse with her husband if she wanted a boy; lying on her left would produce a girl. In short, it was always the inferior or less pure procreative method that resulted in female offspring. These rules of conduct were part of the era's fixed repertoire of knowledge, and it may be assumed that Maria Theresa knew and observed them as well.

The birth itself was highly ritualized owing to the associated dangers. A ruler who was "great with child" stood in special need of succor and spiritual support. After the pregnancy was announced, masses were read and devotions held in all the churches of the residence and throughout the land to pray for a smooth pregnancy and successful delivery.[207] To ensure liturgical uniformity, Latin prayer texts, *Pro Praegnante Regina*, For the Pregnant Queen, were printed especially for this purpose and issued to every parish in the lands. Through these collective prayers for the preservation of the All-Highest Archducal House, all subjects could identify themselves as members of a great ritual community and as members of the house. Maria Theresa herself went to one of the lady chapels—Mariazell, Maria Hietzing, or the Augustinian Loreto Chapel—to petition the mother of God for her support as Magna Mater. The spiritual assistance extended to her intensified before delivery, when "the Empress is brought to the birthing chair . . . and endures her final pangs." According to age-old custom, the Most Reverend Sacrament was displayed in a monstrance at the altar of the Hofburg chapel and in other churches.[208] In the residential city, subjects formed an uninterrupted prayer chain that started in the court chapel and was continued in a fixed series for three days at a time in another parish or monastery church in Vienna. At court, too, well-wishers took turns kneeling through the night to pray for the queen.[209]

By tradition, Maria Theresa gave birth in her apartment in the ladies' wing of the Hofburg. Nothing more clearly expresses the character of dynastic rule than the fact that the apartment was the central place where sovereign power was exercised *and* where the children who would one day inherit that power were born. Regardless of social status, childbirth was a social event of the first order. It was everywhere taken for granted that other mothers would be at hand during the delivery to support the expectant mother.[210] This was also a political event in the case of the queen, and her support team traditionally included not just family members in the narrower sense (such as her husband and the empress dowager),[211] but also the most eminent courtiers as her extended household. Whenever Maria Theresa was staying at Schönbrunn and her term was drawing near, the Vienna city gate therefore had to be kept open at all hours so that she could quickly return to the Hofburg at any time. If she opted to give birth at Schönbrunn instead, as she did for Leopold in May 1747, this meant that the top courtiers had to make their way there—a considerable logistical challenge for the grand marshal of the court, who then had to organize coaches, accommodation, and provisions at short notice.[212] The highest male court officials had to keep vigil in the Knights' Chamber until the child had been successfully delivered.[213] Their wives, along with the upper echelon of the female court household, were permitted and indeed expected to attend the delivery.[214] From 1748, however, Khevenhüller repeatedly expressed his concern that this old custom was no longer observed.[215] He blamed these falling standards on the old Countess Fuchs, who had sowed "disorder and irregularity" by interfering in his own, jealously guarded sphere of responsibility. As Maria Theresa's maternal confidante, it was she who controlled access to the birthing room. She paid insufficient heed to court custom and thereby "gave occasion to various confusions and contradictory ordinances with regard to ladies' etiquette," the lord high chamberlain noted with dismay.[216] Attendance at childbirth had always been a coveted privilege. If high-ranking court ladies were now no longer to be allowed in the birthing room, they expected symbolic compensation to avoid humiliation in the eyes of court society. They were at least therefore permitted "to kiss the [queen's] hand a few days before the rest."[217]

By contrast, the services of an experienced and trusted midwife were indispensable. As soon as the term drew near, she took up quarters in the castle so she could spring into action at a moment's notice. Her royal patient came before all other considerations, even her own health. In August 1752 there were grave concerns when the midwife Salerl succumbed to fever and it looked as if she would be unavailable at the decisive moment. "Unbeknownst to the empress, from whom the midwife's illness had been concealed so as not to cause her alarm, the poor woman was fed so much China [quinine] that her fever abated and she was well enough to assist the empress; but she suffered a relapse soon afterwards, and ultimately had to pay for her service with her life."[218]

In the second half of the eighteenth century, attitudes to childbirth underwent a sea change. Learned physicians increasingly appropriated supreme authority over the birthing process for themselves; they asserted their superiority over all other healing professions, discredited unscholarly practices, and gradually banished medical laypersons from the scene.[219] It was not so much Countess Fuchs as the imperial physician, Gerard van Swieten, who was responsible for evicting courtiers from the birthing room. Maria Theresa had summoned him to Vienna in 1745 to look after the health of the imperial family; he was additionally entrusted with the court library, the university, and the censor's office.[220] Van Swieten's appointment signaled a new direction. A number of different medical schools vied for dominance at the time, exposing patients to a muddle of contradictory opinions. The foundations of the various tendencies were all more or less speculative in nature and defied empirical observation. For patients, personal trust therefore played a central role when choosing a doctor.[221] Maria Theresa decided for van Swieten after he had attended the childbed of her sister Marianna in Brussels—albeit ultimately in vain. His reputation as the best-known student of the legendary natural scientist, Herman Boerhaave from Leiden, also spoke in his favor. In what had widely been regarded as a medical miracle, another physician from Boerhaave's circle, Bassand, had already cured Francis Stephen of smallpox in winter 1727–28.

Van Swieten entered the world of religious puerperal ritual like a Trojan horse of rationalism: a good Catholic, to be sure, but one with new, definite ideas about where religion ended and medicine began.[222] Once she had decided for van Swieten, Maria Theresa's faith in his abilities remained unwavering and unconditional. She deferred entirely to his authority in all questions relating to health and sickness. One consequence was that the Medical Faculty of the University of Vienna began to play a leading role in the nascent discipline of obstetrics.[223] Until then, assistance in childbirth had been not so much an object of scholarly erudition as of empirical knowledge. Van Swieten now combined both, practice and science, establishing the first Chair of Obstetrics in 1754 and regulating the medical training of midwives. In 1756, a little too late for Maria Theresa's own deliveries, his student Heinrich Johann Nepomuk Crantz wrote an instruction manual for midwifery that was to become the authoritative textbook for over twenty years and was officially recommended in a court decree from February 11, 1770.[224]

Physicians of the new generation had revolutionary ideas about treating pregnant women. They were more skeptical about prescribing bloodletting as a universal remedy during pregnancy; they criticized the custom of draping windows and withholding food from women in the first few days after childbirth;[225] they disputed that it was dangerous for wet nurses to suckle newborns during menstruation; they devised new and more comfortable methods for swaddling infants; and they even advocated the latest fashion of maternal breastfeeding. They also developed technical instruments, such as forceps and suction caps, aimed at decreasing the risks associated with childbirth, although with initially fatal consequences due to their failure to sterilize the equipment.

Above all, van Swieten and his students wanted to put the entire birthing process into the hands of professional physicians and stamp out competition from healers, feldshers, surgeons, and midwives. Traditional magical practices were subjected to rational scrutiny and found wanting. "Women nowhere exercise greater power than at birth and childbed," van Swieten wrote. "They hurl insults at physicians, as if we had not the faintest inkling of women's business; every old crone attending the delivery has a remedy of her own, which is said to have proven its efficacy over hundreds of years in the first families of the city. Making them see reason is a futile endeavor. That is why I have always arrived more quickly at my goal by letting them apply their harmless and even ridiculous remedies, provided they pose no threat."

Van Swieten was lenient, for example, in allowing a "lynx stone" to be placed around the mother's neck during childbirth.[226] The curative properties of this mysterious *lapis Lyncis*, or lyngurium, supposedly formed of the solidified urine of the lynx, were already attested to in the Old Testament; like many other spiritually potent gemstones of biblical authority, it had been the subject of scholarly speculation since the early Middle Ages.[227]

Such traditions were alive and well at the Viennese court. The wife of the Spanish emissary Mahoni, for example, was given a stone with natural healing properties that had supposedly been worn as an amulet by Maria Theresa herself during her many pregnancies. The emissary's wife wanted to have the stone sent to the court in Madrid to work its magic on the Princess of Asturias. Yet she apparently had her doubts, and in 1771 she made inquiries as to whether the legend was true. Maria Theresa answered in lapidary fashion: "Mahoni can spare the courier. I know this stone, which has certainly been sent me in ten or twelve pregnancies by the woman to whom you refer [Countess Palm], but it has never gotten any further than . . . the caskets of the late [chambermaid] Justel or [lady-in-waiting] Guttenberg, since all my life I have never believed in such trinkets, let alone worn or used them." Tellingly, however, she added: "To please the nun [Countess Palm], I sent it back to her once my confinement was over, knowing that others would be more likely to believe in it if it was associated with my name."[228] Maria Theresa thus took an astonishingly worldly-wise position toward such magical objects—at least in retrospect, for her last pregnancy lay some fifteen years behind her when she wrote these lines. What is remarkable is that, while accepting van Swieten's critique of superstition, she showed no urge to enlighten others. On the contrary, she understood the social magic that radiated from her charismatic authority and was willing to exploit it for her own ends.

So far as the birthing process was concerned, the new science carried the day over religion under van Swieten's aegis—nowhere more conspicuously than in the removal of the relics that had once cluttered the birthing room.[229] In other matters, too, Maria Theresa lent her support to the new methods recommended by her protomedicus. Whereas women had traditionally given birth while sitting in an obstetric chair, they were now encouraged to do so lying down. Maria Theresa had brought her first children into the world in a birthing chair, but she later came increasingly to prefer the new method of recumbent delivery. In 1776, when she sent a traditional birthing stool (*chaise pour accoucher*) that had belonged to Isabella of Parma to her daughter-in-law, Marie Beatrix, in Milan, she added that she would not take it amiss if Beatrix decided not to use it. She herself had given birth six times on a stool and ten times in bed and could thus judge the difference between the two.[230] On the same occasion, incidentally, she also sent Ferdinand another *monument de la famille*, a silver basin that had been used in many births in the house, including his own. This way of founding a tradition by means of symbolically invested objects was ambivalent, however. Not

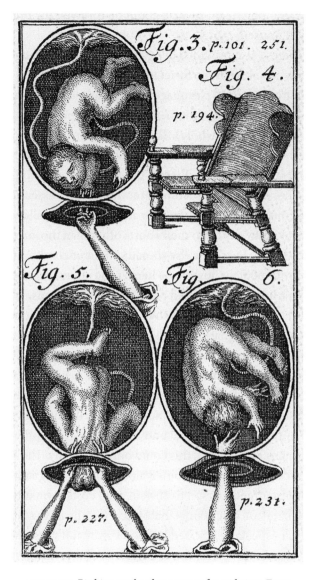

FIGURE 23. Birthing stool and maneuvers for midwives. From
Johann Storch, *Weiber-Krankheiten*, 1747

all objects were associated with happy memories, least of all the birthing
chair used by Isabella, whose deliveries had been extremely difficult.
She had suffered two miscarriages as well as losing another child post
natum; only one daughter survived her. At the time when Maria Theresa
gave her daughter-in-law the birthing stool, both Isabella and her

daughter were long dead. Beatrix could be forgiven for preferring to leave the gift unused.

Maria Theresa also provided her grown-up sons and daughters with personal physicians from van Swieten's coterie of students.[231] There was stiff competition for royal patronage among learned doctors at the time, since princely patients brought them a priceless reputation (along with a modest income, on the whole). This competition could prove fatal for patients if they allowed themselves to be subjected to a variety of diagnoses and treatments. Maria Theresa generally abhorred differences of opinion. In her eyes, clear structures of authority were essential. For this reason she constantly admonished her adult children to allow no physicians (and no midwives) into their courts other than those she had sent them from Vienna. Everyone else should submit unconditionally to her approved protomedicus, just as she herself had always submitted to van Swieten. This injunction applied particularly to surgeons, who ranked well below learned physicians in the hierarchy of professional healers. She reacted with indignation when her son Ferdinand, acting without her consent, dared summon the renowned surgeon Pietro Moscati to Milan as *accoucheur* for his wife.[232] She foresaw inevitable conflict between Moscati, who had made a name for himself through his innovations in obstetrics, and her hand-picked personal physician, Bernhard Faby. Given the temperamental and methodological differences between Germans and Italians, this could only end badly. The Italian surgeon, she ordered, was never to be left alone with her pregnant daughter-in-law. She also urged her son to abstain at all costs from interfering in medical debates or discussing anatomical details in the presence of others. What especially irritated her was Ferdinand's assumption that he, a mere layperson, could form a judgment of his own about the latest scholarly developments and choose between them as he saw fit. As we will see, this also characterized her own attitude to Enlightenment movements in many other respects.

It is hardly surprising that the right to supervise and control the birthing process was so hotly contested. Childbirth was extremely dangerous for both mother and child—albeit significantly less so than in the most up-to-date maternity wards around 1800: the course of medical progress in this area was far from linear. Maria Theresa, too, had experience with death in childbed. In October 1744 her sister Marianna, whom she held in "uncommon affection," went into labor in Brussels. She "spent four whole days in very painful labor and finally, since the child (who was a princess) was already found to have passed away, . . . it was deemed necessary to operate on the mother, Her Highness having previously been given the holy sacraments. . . . The queen did nothing but weep."[233] A woman rarely survived such an operation. The archduchess died on December 16. Maria Theresa's beloved daughter-in-law Isabella, Joseph's first wife, suffered two consecutive miscarriages and died in November 1763 following a third, and her favorite daughter, Maria Christina, lost her first child in May 1767 following a twenty-two-hour labor and difficult delivery; it perished the following day.[234] The first pregnancy of her daughter-in-law Beatrix likewise ended with a miscarriage.[235] And of the eighteen children born to her daughter Maria Carolina, the queen of Naples, only four outlived their mother. How Maria Theresa sought to cope with these losses is shown in the condolence letters she sent her children on such occasions. The Catholic religion was her "sole support amidst adversity." Her only consolation lay in submitting to God's inscrutable will. She even sought to comfort Ferdinand on the death of his one-year-old son with the (false) biblical analogy: "God will show you and your wife how much he appreciates this sacrifice of your beloved child, . . . just as he treasured Abraham's sacrifice of Isaac."[236]

Maria Theresa's condolence letters attest to her keen sense of empathy. She knew what she was talking about, for she herself had lost one of her children, her tenth, during birth. In her biographies and in genealogical tables of the House of Habsburg, this daughter, christened Maria Carolina, goes either unmentioned or unnamed.[237] This accords with a contemporary's remark about miscarriages and stillbirths: "Whenever a monstrous or very frail child enters the world, it is quickly interred so that nobody sees it or hears much about it."[238] When a woman at court once had her baby baptized, Maria Theresa herself observed: "If the child were weak, it would be understandable if the ceremony were held in secret."[239] As for little Maria Carolina, her mother did not let her slip entirely into oblivion. Children from the Archducal House who died in infancy were not entitled to the full ceremonial of a year-long period of court mourning; this was normally reserved for those who passed away after their twelfth birthday.[240] Nonetheless, no newborns departed from this world without rituals of mourning—provided, that is, they had been baptized in good time.

This was the parents' overriding concern in such cases: had the child still been alive when the baptismal ceremony was performed? Little could be done about infant mortality. A timely baptism was therefore all the more important; it alone prevented parents feeling left entirely at the whim of fate. Unborn children had to be wrested from everlasting perdition. Children who died unbaptized had not been redeemed from original sin and were consequently denied a Christian burial. Disqualified from eternal bliss, they languished forever in an intermediate state between heaven and hell, the *limbus puerorum*, where they were spared the torments of the damned but denied the beatific vision of the saved. A widespread belief held that they could come back to earth as revenants, since their unprotected bodies could easily be possessed by demons or misused by witches and sorcerers. Inventive solutions were therefore found to the problem of emergency baptism. Some midwives, for example, squirted baptismal water into the uterus with a syringe. Many parents brought their dead babies to a miracle-working grace chapel, where they could be temporarily revived and quickly baptized before burial. So-called miracle books reported on the countless revivals performed at the Maria Luggau Chapel in Carinthia, for example.[241]

Khevenhüller's account of the unhappy ending to Maria Theresa's tenth pregnancy shows how grave were the concerns that the infant might have perished before baptism.[242] After she unexpectedly went into labor and the altar sacrament had been hastily displayed for worship, he waited with the other courtiers by the chamber chapel, observing with alarm the women rushing to and fro and catching only the whispered remark: "*Nous avons un enfant foible*," we have a weak child. Soon after, the emperor called for the lord high chamberlain, asking him to convey the sad news of the child's death to the empress dowager Elisabeth in Hetzendorf. The emperor confided in him his wife's belief that the child had died unbaptized; she was unable to stifle her sobs. Later, upon returning from Hetzendorf, Khevenhüller learned that the empress had given birth to "an archduchess at around half-past four, yet the child recovered so poorly that—because she was in an awkward position and came out feet first—the midwife baptized her on the spot and she passed away . . . within minutes."[243] Although van Swieten and the midwife insisted that "she had been baptized while still alive," many at court doubted their testimony.

Since the empress herself was not in danger, peace gradually returned to the court. Khevenhüller was instructed to comb the archives for precedents that would help him determine the correct mourning ceremonial. This confronted him with serious difficulties. For one thing, he found that at least one gala day was in order—if not three, as was the case with other deliveries—to celebrate the mother's full recovery, if not the child's. For understandable reasons, Maria Theresa preferred to dispense with such festivities. The mixed messages gave rise to a situation where court ladies did not even know how they were meant to dress. Khevenhüller had renewed occasion to lament that "regular and lawful etiquette" was no longer to be found at court; "everyone wants to play the steward, and nobody can tell the proverbial cook from the cleaner any more." An even more vexing question was what should become of the infant's corpse. It was decided against formally laying out the body in public view, "as is otherwise the custom when young lords are carried off by death," possibly because the child's face had been damaged during delivery ("The poor babe's murderer was written on its brow," Khevenhüller wrote, maliciously alluding to a mistake supposedly committed by the midwife). On the other hand, burying the body in secret was equally undesirable, since it would give rise to speculation of a cover-up: perhaps the child had been a monstrous deformity? Dynastic births were public events, and there could be no deviating from this rule even when the child in question was stillborn. Khevenhüller therefore had the little body secretly brought from Schönbrunn, where the delivery had occurred, to the Hofburg and laid out—though not formally "exposed"—in the summer room. All courtiers were then given a full morning to pay their respects, "to rid these people of any suspicions regarding the child's form and nature."[244] On this occasion, Khevenhüller placed one of his spies with the court physician van Swieten, whom he had vehemently distrusted ever since he had almost completely banished courtiers from the childbed. The empress had been left "at the mercy of the protomedicus van Swieten," he wrote, "where in such cases one can never proceed with too much caution, and the people—if anything amiss were to happen to our lady—would have abundant cause for complaint about the emperor and all of us at court (for having neglected our duty to her)."[245] In other words, as the dynasty's extended family, court society still bore far greater responsibility for the monarch's successful delivery than the learned physician.

A mural by Franz Anton Maulbertsch in the Riesensaal at the Hofburg in Innsbruck documents how Maria Theresa kept alive the memory of her deceased children. Following the death of her husband, who expired there suddenly and unexpectedly in 1765, she had this room painted into a monumental memorial for her family (fig. 24).[246] It shows the four little girls bearing floral wreaths and seated on a cloudy stairway to heaven: in the foreground Johanna Gabriele, who died at the age of twelve; behind her Maria Elisabeth, the firstborn, dead at three; then Maria Carolina, who died shortly after her first birthday; and in the background, discernible in the dark only as a schematic *putto*, the second child, stillborn Maria Carolina. The three girls who passed away at an especially young age lived on symbolically in their homonymous sisters: there was a second Maria Elisabeth and even a third Maria Carolina. In the House of Habsburg, Christian names were always chosen from the same limited reservoir of saints, in ever varying order. The aim was not to stamp children as one-of-a-kind individuals but to mark dynastic identity and continuity.

Dynastic continuity was also ensured by the baptism ceremony, which took the same course for Maria Theresa's children as had her own baptism and a long series of earlier baptisms in the House of Habsburg.[247] She made very few changes to the ceremony over time, but these were significant. Thus, as already mentioned, relics were no longer displayed in the baptismal room under van Swieten's regime. She also decided that salvos would be fired off for daughters as well as

FIGURE 24. Maria Theresa's four early-departed
children. Mural in the Riesensaal in the Hofburg at
Innsbruck, Franz Anton Maulbertsch

sons.[248] In addition, she selected godparents more strategically than in
the past to strengthen relations with other dynasties, pave the way for
new alliances, and settle old disputes. Previously, apart from the pope,
godparents had mostly been drawn from the immediate family; now
they included the royal couple of Poland-Saxony (1741), or Prince-
Elector Clemens August of Cologne, brother to her late rival Charles
VII (1746), Tsarina Elizabeth (1747), George II of England (1750), or
the king and queen of Spain (1752).[249] The sensational rapprochement
with France, which in 1756 turned the entire traditional alliance system

on its head, was likewise preluded by such godparent diplomacy.[250] Needless to say, foreign monarchs did not personally hold the infant over the baptismal font but were represented by an ambassador or princely peer. This ceremonial function was of considerable symbolic value; by no means could it be exercised by every noble courtier, only by a sovereign prince. If the birth came sooner than expected, as in the case of Ferdinand, this could pose serious ceremonial challenges: there was a scramble to find someone suitably qualified to represent the godparents at such short notice.[251]

The festivities celebrating the birth of the long-awaited heir, Joseph, on March 13, 1741 eclipsed anything seen before.[252] This birth was a landmark event, an eleventh-hour vindication of Maria Theresa's disputed legitimacy. In the view of contemporaries, the dynastic interruption of the male line had been bridged just in the nick of time. After all, Maria Theresa had already fallen pregnant when her father was still alive:[253]

Der Enckel lebte schon	The grandson lived already
Bevor der Ahnherr starbe	Before the grandsire died
Obgleich die bange Welt von	Though the fretful world had
seiner Mutter ihn	to wait a while
Erst eine Zeit hernach durch	Ere the precious babe arrived.
die Geburt erwarbe	
Und dauret ja noch jezo immerhin	Now the male line continues
Der Männer-Stamme fort in	In unbroken succession
unzertrennter Reihe	
Wer zweifelt	Who can doubt
Daß der Prinz nicht der Ersezer	The prince's right of accession?
seye?	

No fewer than sixteen ecclesiastical dignitaries celebrated the baptism alongside the nuncio standing in for Pope Benedict XIV. Upon Maria Theresa's solemn emergence six weeks after the birth, the people of Vienna lit up their houses and displayed symbols and epigrammatic poems lavishly celebrating the fruitful union of the houses of Habsburg and Lorraine. Traditionally the city's burghers had demonstrated their

well wishes earlier, at the baptism. On this occasion Maria Theresa deliberately delayed the celebration until the time of her emergence in
order that she might take part herself. In doing so, she subtly shifted the
accent of the festivities: it was less the father (as was otherwise customary) than the mother who was now the object of homage.[254] Thankful
that their prayers had been answered, the parents donated the golden
figure of a child, weighing exactly the same as their newborn son, to
the shrine to the Virgin at Mariazell—just as had been done at Maria
Theresa's own birth and would be repeated for all the sons she bore
thereafter.[255]

When a first son was born to a princely Catholic house, the pope
traditionally sent a gift of consecrated swaddling bands (*fascie*).
Needless to say, these did not serve the same function as common nap-
pies, nor did they resemble them. Richly embroidered sashes made of
gold brocade with pearl trim, they were ceremoniously consecrated by
the pope in Rome in the presence of the imperial envoy and numerous
cardinals. A *nuntius extraordinarius* then personally brought them to
Vienna for a solemn "presentation of swaddling bands." The last time
this had occurred was for Leopold, Maria Theresa's short-lived brother.
After Joseph's birth, when relations with Rome had come under strain
due to the War of the Austrian Succession, the pope skipped the ritual,
not making good the omission for another five years. The *Wienerische
Diarium* reported on the opening of the present in Vienna and pointed
out that the gift, including the golden casket enclosing it, was worth
15,000 scudi.[256] The assessment was clearly necessary, for the papal
swaddling bands had a reputation for not being particularly valuable.
Protestants jeered that "the power of papal benediction substituted for
the preciousness of the gift."[257] The nuncio Serbelloni handed them
over to the empress at Christmas 1746 during a formal audience attended by half the court, at the same time relaying the pope's belated
congratulations on the birth of the now six-year-old heir. All the papal
gifts were spread out below the baldachin in the audience chamber to
be inspected first by the court household, then by the common people.

Just like the consecrated swaddling bands, the queen's bed had traditionally been the object of almost cultic veneration as a symbol of the

dynasty's fertility. At many courts, it was customary for princesses to receive congratulatory visits from foreign diplomats while lying in their bed of state. Maria Theresa was reluctant to continue the practice. So long as her father was alive and she herself had not yet taken power, there had been no need for it. "As queen," she later wrote, "I have only received *en parade* [i.e., lying in bed] on three occasions; all three took place in wartime, and no ambassador or minister was here apart from Robinson; since then I have only let myself be seen on my feet."[258] Following the birth of the heir, however, public access was granted to her bed of state by popular demand.[259]

The royal mother—like mothers from all other echelons of society—had to abstain from appearing in public until her ceremonious "emergence" (*Hervorgang*) from confinement, which took place five to six weeks post-partum. The "blessing forth" (*Hervorsegnung*) was an act of ritual purification that freed the mother from the state of ritual impurity brought about by her confinement. The feast of the Purification of the Blessed Virgin Mary was the day in the ecclesiastical calendar that reflected this act and on which all women who had recently given birth were vicariously celebrated in the Mother of God. At the Viennese court, the "emergence" consisted in mother and child being led in solemn procession to the Loreto chapel in the Augustinian monastery, where the newborn was taken up to the Marian altar. The child's aya had traditionally carried it to the altar in a litter; from 1751 Maria Theresa changed the custom by bearing the infant into the chapel herself.[260] She also dropped the ban on attending divine service during confinement.

In keeping with upper-class tradition, the child was handed over to a wet nurse from the beginning.[261] Great care was given to the choice of wet nurse. The key criterion was that she be in rude good health. The manual for midwifery authorized by the court recommended that wet nurses be between eighteen and twenty years of age and have given birth themselves around six weeks previously. Ideally, they should already have two or three children of their own so that it could be seen how their nurslings had fared under their care. Precise specifications were given on the desired quality of the breasts (neither too full nor too sagging) and the milk (whitish, neither too thin nor too thick).

Sanguine, "blood-rich" candidates with black or chestnut hair were always preferable to "bilious" nurses with flaxen or red hair. They should be sound in limb and not "smell from the mouth, armpits, and feet," since these were all signs of poor health. Naturally, they should also be free of hereditary illnesses such as goiter, the "falling sickness" (i.e., epilepsy), or venereal disease.[262] Maria Theresa insisted that van Swieten personally examine the selected nurses.[263] She also took a keen interest in their diet: "I find it healthy for them to take 6 dishes at midday, 4 in the evening and good soup both day and night."[264] Nonphysical qualities, on the other hand, seem to have played a negligible role.

Newborn "lords and ladies," as they were called, were the objects of the most meticulous attention—albeit of a quite different kind from that which later came into vogue under the influence of a new culture of sentimentality. Whether motherly love is a late eighteenth-century bourgeois invention has been the subject of much debate.[265] There can be no doubt that feelings are subject to historical change, nor that there was a seismic shift in ideas of what makes a good mother and how a mother ought to behave in the years around 1800. Breastfeeding one's own children was an essential aspect of the new ideal of maternal love that Rousseau, in his key work *Emile*, set in sharp opposition to the wet nursing of the "civilized classes." Rousseau's book—with a baby suckling at its mother's breast and children playing under a bust of the author on the frontispiece—appeared in 1762, when Maria Theresa's last child, Max Francis, was already six years old and thus too old to develop a taste for her milk. If Maria Theresa failed to live up to this new ideal, this is not to say that she did not love her children, only that she had an altogether different notion of motherly love.

It is all the more astonishing how the nineteenth-century image of Maria Theresa was radically recast to conform to the new ideal of sentimental maternity. A popular engraving from 1868, based on a painting by the successful Hungarian historical painter Liezen-Mayer, depicts Maria Theresa as a radiantly beautiful young mother dressed in a picturesquely draped blue silk gown. Sitting under trees on a stone step in a secluded park, she is shown giving suck to a child and gazing at it with loving tenderness (fig. 25).[266] The child is not her own—hers is in the

FIGURE 25. Maria Theresa suckling a beggarwoman's child.
Engraving by Albrecht Schultheiss after a painting
by Alexander von Liezen-Mayer, 1868

background, borne on a luxurious lace-trimmed cushion by a lady-in-waiting. Behind the sovereign, a careworn woman in black is sleeping in the shadows: the mother whose hands have just released the cloth that was wrapped around the baby. The image illustrates the popular nineteenth-century legend that Maria Theresa, walking one day in the grounds of Schönbrunn and seeing a beggarwoman overwhelmed by misery and exhaustion, took up her wailing infant and suckled it at her breast: "The empress, who has a child the same age and has more than enough nourishment for its needs, does not hesitate a moment at the heart-rending sight; she takes the poor mite to her own breast and gazes with heartfelt satisfaction at the visibly refreshed little creature."[267] Everyone who saw the image would have been forcibly reminded of the Mother of God, as depicted in the long iconographic tradition of *Maria lactans*, the nursing Madonna. The anecdote was pure fiction; it was completely out of keeping with the eighteenth-century court milieu. Moreover, as a mother, Maria Theresa never allowed herself to be portrayed with her own children resting on her arm. Nor did she ever come into such close contact with her common subjects except on strictly staged ceremonial occasions, as when she washed and kissed the feet of twelve selected common women on Maundy Thursday.[268] The representation of the mother breastfeeding in the park tells us nothing about Maria Theresa but a great deal about the mythology that grew up around her in the nineteenth century.[269] The image combines the feminine ideal of a later age with the ideal of the ruler as a nurturing, loving mother figure who succors her subjects in times of distress. What is here taken literally and depicted in the form of an idyll is Maria Theresa's famous description of herself as the "universal and first mother" of her lands.[270]

7

Distinctions and Refinements

FIGURE 26. Court society in the theater at Schönbrunn on the
occasion of Joseph's marriage to Isabella of Parma, 1769.
Workshop of Martin van Meytens

Audiences

Maria Theresa loved her subjects, who loved or even worshiped her in
return. Such, at any rate, was the claim made by historians and contemporaries. If we ask what exactly this might mean, we come across the
same recurring refrain: she made herself accessible to everyone, even
the lowliest of her subjects. In the words of Alfred von Arneth, "the

allure of her personal appearance, her ability to win the hearts of all she encountered, the ease with which she could be approached, the perceptible sympathy with which she heard the petitions and grievances of her meanest subjects and sought to give them succor and support, the lively expressions of sincere regret with which she sweetened even a negative response . . . : all this made her admired and adored by all who came near her."[1] "She always had the time and inclination . . . to hear the petitions and complaints of her subjects."[2]

Voltaire put it much the same way when discussing Maria Theresa's accession to power in his *Age of Louis XV*:

> She gained possession of all hearts by a popular affability which her predecessors had seldom exercised; she laid aside that formality and haughtiness which can render a throne detestable, without making it more respectable. . . . Maria Theresa admitted to her table all the ladies and officers of distinction; she conversed freely with the Deputies of the States; she never refused to grant an audience, and nobody ever left her discontented.[3]

That Maria Theresa "loved her people" was evidently the reason why her people paid her back in kind. A learned French diplomat who had spent some time in Vienna enthused in retrospect: "It is difficult to know which is more admirable: the utterly winsome and trusting way she treats her subjects, or the precious reciprocation of this love, the popular adoration with which it is returned."[4]

Benevolence, complaisance, and accessibility were not first attributed to the empress in the nineteenth century, when a new ideal of a down-to-earth constitutional 'bourgeois monarchy' became entrenched.[5] Many of her contemporaries already viewed her in this light. Yet what exactly did "loving and beloved by all" mean at the time? First, praise for Maria Theresa had its origins in an age-old topos. Being accessible to everyone and willing to lend them an ear was traditionally considered the sign and symbol of good rule. It corresponded to the classic princely virtue of *clementia* and distinguished the monarch from the tyrant. Traditionally, the good ruler safeguarded peace and justice by responding to complaints, resolving conflicts, and rewarding loyal service. He granted requests and redressed grievances, but he did not outline grand schemes for the future, nor did he seek to transform social relations. Subjects came to him, not the other way around, and he heard them out. This ideal of "responsiveness"[6] accorded with a culture of personal presence and face-to-face communication. Theoretically, at least, anyone could appear before the throne and submit their concerns for the ruler's consideration. During the audience, the ruler was expected to adopt a manner that was at once amiable and grave, for a wise sovereign should inspire both love and fear in his subjects.[7] The extent to which this kind of personal communication actually took place was of course very limited; the monarch ruled from afar and was separated from ordinary subjects by a series of powerful intermediaries. Yet the topos of clemency, moderation, and approachability defined the language used to talk about lordship. It was a language of personal closeness and familiarity—however anonymous the relationship may actually have been for the vast majority of subjects.

For all that the praise heaped on Maria Theresa was rooted in a classical topos, it remains to be asked what the judgment was based on in this particular case. How much truth was there in the legend of Maria Theresa's universal accessibility and natural charm? What was her "secret for attracting the love and admiration of everyone," in the words of Podewils, who took it to be nothing more than a skillfully chosen mask and cynical ploy for exercising power?[8] How are we to imagine direct communication between the queen and her subjects? How and where did they meet, and how did they interact? And who was actually meant by "everyone"?

The classic site for such encounters was the audience chamber, where subjects were literally heard by the ruler. An example of what this looked like to those admitted to her presence is the visit paid to Schönbrunn by Mr and Mrs Gottsched. The Gottscheds were direct subjects of the prince-elector of Saxony, not Maria Theresa, but the land they lived in still belonged to the Holy Roman Empire. In September 1749 Luise Adelgunde Victoria and Johann Christoph Gottsched set out to "visit radiant Vienna and see the monarch who rules over even more hearts than are contained within the borders of her vast empire."[9] In Protestant

German literary circles, the Gottscheds were famous as vigorous campaigners for the purification of German language and literature, an enterprise driven as much by the erudite Luise Gottsched (1713–1762) as by her husband, the renowned Leipzig professor. They had set out for Vienna in search of more than just personal edification and enjoyment. Their chief purpose was to further the cultural and political project of Johann Christoph Gottsched, whose reputation in literary Germany had come under increasing attack from critics. By winning the empress's favor, they hoped to score a victory over his detractors. Gottsched's name was not completely unknown at the Viennese court, where his drama *The Dying Cato* had been staged only the previous year. Nonetheless, the couple could not simply appear unannounced at court. Having arrived in the city, they first needed to be patient. Those seeking admission to court always had to wait an indefinite period of time; they had to "curry favor, bow and scrape," seek out intercessors, and hope for an invitation. During this time, the Gottscheds saw the empress only from afar, when they joined the crowd lining the streets to view the public procession to St. Stephen's Cathedral for the annual thanksgiving service commemorating the lifting of the Turkish siege of Vienna in 1683. Even this glimpse was enough to send Luise Gottsched into raptures. In a letter to Friedrich Heinrich von Seckendorf, an Austrian field marshal,[10] she declared: "The majestic beauty of this monarch, who drew to her all hearts and eyes, . . . moved me to my very soul."[11] In addition, the couple sought out every site in the vicinity of the court recommended by travel guides that could be visited for a fee by travelers of distinction:[12] the magnificent court library, the cabinet of coins, and the picture gallery in the Stallburg,[13] where Luise Gottsched was less impressed by the works of Raphael, Titian, or Rubens than by the empress's portrait.

Further afield, they were also permitted to inspect Klosterneuburg monastery and the royal hunting lodge, Schloss Hetzendorf. Tickets could be bought to the Theater an der Burg, where they once had the pleasure of seeing the empress in her box. They whiled away their time with such outings until their noble connections finally gained them admittance to an audience. Their host in Vienna was Franz Christoph von

Scheyb, a secretary at the Lower Austrian government with poetic ambitions of his own and a staunch advocate of Gottsched's language purification program; indeed, the Gottscheds had hopes of setting up an
Austrian academy with his support. In 1746 he had brought himself to
the court's attention with a panegyric verse epic about Maria Theresa,
and it was through his good offices that the couple came into contact
with Nikolaus Esterházy, who intervened on their behalf to gain them
entry at court.[14]

The lord high steward invited them to present themselves at the entrance room at Schönbrunn on Sunday morning at ten. The former
hunting lodge had only recently been converted, at vast expense, into
an elegant and palatial summer residence. Court architect Nicolaus Pacassi had sought to make it more comfortable than the Hofburg, but he
had also tried to do justice to the House of Habsburg's regained imperial
status, satisfy the latest aesthetic standards, and produce something that
might bear comparison with Versailles. Above all, Schönbrunn offered
more space for large-scale geometrically laid out gardens than the Hofburg, which was restricted by Vienna's old defensive walls to the closely
built, densely populated inner city.[15] As the first version of the summer
palace had met with the emperor's displeasure,[16] work continued until
1750 amid the ongoing business of court. At the time of the Gottscheds'
visit, the complex was thus still partially under construction. In 1749, however, the East Wing with ceremonial apartments had just been completed
(fig. 27). Official visitors entered the castle via the forecourt to the north,
proceeding through the main gate and turning right up the representative
Blue Staircase to the *piano nobile*. If they had been invited to a formal audience with the emperor and empress, they went through an antechamber
and then past Hungarian and German guards along the forty-meter-long
Great Gallery, lined entirely by windows on one side and mirrors on the
other. There they waited until they were admitted to the Small and then
the Large Antechamber, directly adjacent to the Ratstube, the emperor's
audience chamber.[17] The empress's apartments lay on the east side and
were accessible only by a series of other rooms and corridors. There were
more direct ways to get to Maria Theresa's quarters—via the small Chapel
Staircase in the East Wing, for example—but it was a rare sign of favor

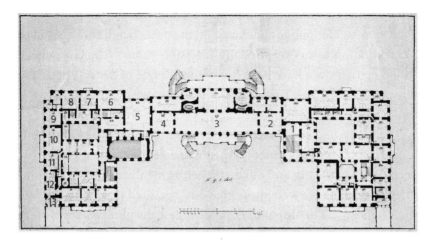

FIGURE 27. *Piano nobile*, Schönbrunn Palace, c. 1750. 1 Blue Staircase,
2 Antechambers, 3 Great Gallery, 4 Antechambers, 5 Hall of Ceremonies,
5–8 Emperor's apartments, 8 Shared bedroom, 8–13 Empress's apartments

and familiarity for visitors to be let up "a special staircase."[18] The usual
path through the Great Gallery into the Large Antechamber followed a
strategy of effective intensification. Each of the high, guard-flanked
double-winged doors through which visitors passed increased their
sense of nervous anticipation. Everything was calculated to generate
ambivalent feelings: with each threshold they crossed, they felt at once
more intimidated and more personally privileged to be there.

Luise Gottsched was careful to avoid mentioning any other visitors in
her description of the event, thereby giving the impression of an intimate
private audience. It is very unlikely, however, that she and her husband
were the only ones received that morning, since the hours following divine service on Sunday were regularly set aside for public audiences.[19] A
public audience differed fundamentally from the strictly formalized,
highly symbolic audiences at which ambassadors of foreign sovereigns
introduced themselves and took their leave,[20] as well as from a private
audience, where guests could enter individually and the doors to the
reception hall were closed again by the doorkeepers. Public audiences,
by contrast, were called such because the doors to the audience chamber
were kept half open.[21] Maria Theresa gave individual audiences only on

rare occasions, much to the annoyance of those who felt entitled to such a distinction. Her public audiences, on the other hand, contributed to her reputation as an exceptionally accessible ruler.[22] The Gottscheds would certainly not have been honored with one of her exceptionally rare private audiences, particularly as their visit went unrecorded in the lord high chamberlain's diary.

The Gottscheds were received by the lord high steward in the entrance room[23] and presented to the three eldest archduchesses, Marianna, Maria Christina, and Elisabeth, "with a highly advantageous commendation. And we were most graciously granted permission to kiss their hands."[24] The imperial couple's eldest daughters were eleven, seven, and six at the time. The hand kiss was an element of the imperial ceremonial first imported from Spain by Charles VI; it was an essential feature distinguishing the imperial court from the other German princely courts. For foreign diplomats, having to perform this gesture not just for the emperor but for the entire imperial family was something of an imposition;[25] for all other visitors as well as members of the court household, it was a favor they could not enjoy often enough. The lord high chamberlain, for example, exploited his privileged access to the empress by kissing her hand at every opportunity, even though he knew how irksome she found it.[26]

After a while, the Gottscheds were called into a room "which adjoined the empress's chamber."[27] There they waited a little longer, making small talk with the chief lady-in-waiting, until the empress appeared. Luise Gottsched describes her emotions in Maria Theresa's presence: "I wanted to drop to my left knee, and pay the empress-queen a Spanish compliment with the most upright German heart," she wrote to Seckendorf, "yet soon I was on both knees, and can be accused of the most Christian sentiments of idolatry."[28] The Saxon Protestant was here alluding to the fact that bending a knee before the emperor had been cause for scandal during times of fierce interconfessional conflict. Among evangelical imperial princes who insisted on their "German liberty," this gesture of submission had been castigated as "Spanish servitude" and papist idolatry. In this moment, Luise intimated to her correspondent, she forgot her sincere German-Protestant loyalties, so overwhelmed was she "by the presence of this great lady, full of the desire to lay my heart at her feet." Falling to their knees was the least that all visitors, regardless of status, had to do in an imperial audience. Spanish court ceremonial actually prescribed three genuflections when approaching the sovereign. This rule was no longer so strictly observed as under Charles VI, much to the lord high chamberlain's chagrin. Yet Maria Theresa was loath to dispense entirely with the genuflection and make do instead with a "French reverence," a deep bow or curtsey. On the contrary: when a stiff-kneed young cavalier failed to perform the gesture to her satisfaction, she was said to have pressed him firmly on the left shoulder and so forced him to his knees.[29] Joseph finally abolished the practice after her death: from now on, he resolved, no man should have to kneel before another.[30]

The heart of the audience was a friendly conversation with Maria Theresa. "The Empress Queen spoke a great deal, partly with me, partly with my husband." Luise does not mention what they talked about, and this played no role anyway. The meaning of an audience rarely lay in what was discussed, but rather in the fact that it took place. The medium was the message. Given the strict economy of attention that prevailed at court, the mere exchange of "compliments" was an asset. Its value could be measured principally by its duration. Yet a further intensification was possible, as Luise Gottsched vividly described in her letter. She had only just heard the empress's words when "someone entered the room whom I would have taken to be the imperial court's first and most gracious minister, if the empress had not said: this is the master. At this we both knelt at the emperor's feet in the previous Spanish position. His Majesty offered his hand to be kissed by my husband and bid us both rise." The amazed visitors felt as if they had been welcomed into Maria Theresa's family circle. Finally, to increase the effect even further, "the empress said full of grace and goodness: Now! You must see my other children too. At which we were led by Princess Trautson to the three other little angels."[31] This was far from unusual. Maria Theresa always introduced visitors to as many of her numerous children as possible, the dynastic capital and living guarantee for the continuity of rule.[32] The Gottscheds misunderstood the presentation as a sign of domestic intimacy. This, together with the empress's friendly conversational tone and the emperor's winning manner, seldom failed to make an impact on visitors. Strangers to the court who had expected stiff formality at its innermost center were taken aback, felt personally honored, and almost inevitably became ardent admirers of the empress. "I had often heard of the scrupulous etiquette at the imperial court," another visitor wrote, "but have found everything directly opposite to that account."[33]

Following the audience, the Gottscheds made sure that an interested public in the Empire would also learn about it.[34] Luise had dedicated one of her translations to the empress, who had sent her a jewel-encrusted hairpin in return.[35] In a Baroque dedicatory poem, the author now informed readers how greatly she, the lowliest of all subjects, had been honored. Anyone could metaphorically throw himself at the empress's feet in florid dedications, but to do so literally was reserved for the fortunate few.[36]

Monarchinn, Darf ich mich zu Deinem Throne schwingen	Allow me, Queen, to rise before thy throne
wo ich voll Ehrfurcht Dich vor kurtzem noch gesehn	Where I beheld thee lately, struck with awe.
So bin ich zwar zu schwach, Dein hohes Lob zu singen:	Too weak to sing thy high renown,
Doch dankbar bin ich noch, Dein Wohlthun zu erhöhn.	Yet will I gratefully extol thy goodness all the more.
Das stralenreiche Pfand, was Du mir zugesendet,	The radiant pledge thou sent'st me,
Das Pfand von Deiner Huld, erhabne Kaiserinn!	The pledge of thy favor, bestowed from on high,
Hat Deiner Großmuth Bild in meiner Brust vollendet	Has rounded out the image of thy magnanimity
Und zeigt, wie groß Du bist, und wie gering ich bin.	And shows how great thou art, how small am I.

Johann Christoph Gottsched likewise promptly published an encomium to Maria Theresa's beauty, mildness, strength of mind, valor, and maternal love, with repeated variations on the same refrain: "One must

see her with one's own eyes! I have seen her!"[37] The effect of these panegyrics was twofold: by commemorating their audience with the empress in poetic form, the couple not only spread her fame; they also (and
above all) burnished their own reputations. The same held true for
everyone who saw her, not just poets: those favored with access to the
imperial family were themselves warmed and illuminated by its after-
glow; those for whom the doors to the audience chamber had once been
opened were more likely to find other doors opening for them in future.

This was an experience the Gottscheds shared with the Mozart
family, among others. In October 1762, Leopold Mozart succeeded in
having his prodigiously talented children Nannerl and Wolferl perform
for three hours straight for the imperial family at Schönbrunn. Once
news of the event spread, the musicians found themselves in demand as
never before. Suddenly the houses of the court nobility stood wide
open to them: Kaunitz, Ulfeld, the Kinskys, everyone wanted to have
the charming piano-playing children play for them as well. Leopold
Mozart put a touching anecdote into circulation: "Wolferl jumped into
the empress's lap, flung his arms around her neck, and kissed her heart-
ily. In short, we were there from three to six, and the emperor himself
came out of the next room and made me go there to hear the infanta
play the violin."[38] Whether this is really what happened cannot be
ascertained—in his otherwise extremely detailed court diary, the lord
high chamberlain made no mention of the performance. Yet the story
of little Wolferl's intimate encounter with the imperial family was too
heartwarming not to find a permanent place in collective memory. In
the nineteenth century it entered the canon of legends that grew up
around the empress, rivaled in popularity only by the mother-child
scene from the 1741 Hungarian diet.[39] The child Wolfgang Amadeus
Mozart was not only placed alongside generals, statesmen, and intellectual luminaries in the great monument on the Ringstrasse, his piano
playing at Schönbrunn was even featured on collector cards of the early
advertising industry.[40] Yet the impression the six-year-old wunderkind
made on Maria Theresa was apparently less lasting. She rewarded him
and his sister with two cast-off gala dresses belonging to her own
children and with a hundred ducats (roughly eight times what Leopold

earned each month in Salzburg); she also invited them to watch the ruling family dine in public.[41] A few years later, however, when her son Ferdinand, having encountered the young Mozart at his wedding festivities, proposed employing him as court kapellmeister in Milan, she urged him to abandon the idea. He should not burden himself with such worthless riffraff, she said. It only damaged the standing of a court when such people and their numerous dependents loitered around like beggars.[42] Musicians, along with poets, scholars, painters, and architects, were, from the ruler's perspective, merely potential servants, no matter how talented they might be; she certainly had no intention of treating them as her equals. How visitors and the broader public perceived the favor of an imperial audience and how the empress herself saw it were clearly two quite different things.

The Gottscheds and the Mozarts belonged to the class of scholars and artists who, under favorable circumstances, could gain entry to court through their exceptional services to the monarch. The same could not be said of "humble subjects." For them to meet the queen in person was the stuff of fairy tales. A case in point was the bizarre audience granted the "court Tyrolean," Peter Prosch.[43] Prosch (1744–1804) was a destitute orphan from Ried in the Zillertal who wandered through Austria and the southern German imperial territories peddling his wares. He happened to fall into the hands of courtiers, endeared himself to them through his antics, and from then on moved from one court to another, tormented and pampered in equal measure. Traversing the boundaries between two worlds, the highest and the lowest, he was regarded as a "human marvel" in both.[44] At Schönbrunn he cut no less exotic a figure than a court Moor or dwarf. With bad luck, Prosch might have been deported to Temesvár as a vagrant;[45] as a favorite of lords and ladies at southern German courts, however, a happier fate awaited him. He made a virtue of necessity by playing the court jester at a time when this was already an anachronism and no longer appealed to enlightened taste. As an old man he recorded his memories in an autobiography published in 1789, the year of revolution. It became something of a bestseller, purchased by the same courtly public described in its pages.[46] Maria Theresa plays a key role in the narrative.

Prosch stylizes himself in his autobiography as a Tyrolean version of Simplicissimus, the hero of Grimmelshausen's famous novel. He writes his life story in the mode of picaresque adventure, enlivening it with motifs drawn from farce and fairytale. Born into a poor peasant family as the youngest of eleven siblings, little Peter loses both parents at the age of eight and is driven from hearth and home. One day the empress, who "is rightly loved by all her subjects as a true mother,"[47] appears to the starving, homeless orphan in a dream and graciously grants him permission to set up a schnapps distillery. He then sets out on a long journey to the imperial castle to make his dream come true. After many mishaps and when all hope seems lost, he finally succeeds in gaining an audience with the empress. His journey reads like a parody of the classic courtier's career with all that pertains to it: influential patrons, recommendations and stuffily worded petitions, repeated attempts to gain admittance, the long wait for a favorable opportunity to present itself, obstacles, reversals, happy coincidences, and, finally, unexpected success.

Prosch depicts his first audience with the empress in late September 1757 from the perspective of the naïve, awkward simpleton who is initially the butt of jokes at court but is eventually taken up and richly rewarded by the benevolent mother figure. After a chance encounter during Mass at the Capuchin church, where Prosch had been serving as an altar boy, Maria Theresa suddenly had the thirteen-year-old summoned to her by a valet. "Filled with joy, trepidation, fear, and trembling, I was led past the guards and up the stairs. . . . I was barefoot and held my hat under my arm. . . . I stared all around me, sang a ditty, and everyone burst out laughing, seeing that I had no idea what I was doing."[48] He wets himself in fear, mistakes a lady-in-waiting for the empress, fails to recognize himself in his multiplied reflection, and trips over his own feet—all traditional motifs of farce employed by the author to entertain his public. It is therefore hard to distinguish a realistic account of the boy's entrée into court society—which did in fact amuse the assembled courtiers—from its subsequent literary elaboration.[49] The same holds true of the artless dialogue that follows, where he soon has the court in stitches by addressing his sovereign lady with the informal second-person singular: "Art thou our Empress Maria Theresl?"

After telling her of his dream, she promises to grant him his wish of a distilling license, yet he still takes the precaution of asking her to confirm the offer in writing.

They then discuss the mutual affection between the sovereign and her subjects:

> "What else do the people of Tyrol say about me, do they love me?" "I've told thee already, ma'am; if I'd heard naught good of thee, I'd ne'er have dreamed aught good of thee, either, and I should not be here today; everyone in our land, from the first to the last, says thou'rt the best of women, and the world will ne'er see thy like again." She laughed heartily and said: "I am pleased to hear it. The Tyroleans are dear to me too, for they are loyal and honest people." She reached with her left hand into her camisole pocket, took out twenty-four Kremnica ducats, and tossed them in my hat. Now my heart skipped a beat, I put the hat down on the ground, ... kissed her hand, took her by the waist, and leapt and capered around her singing "Drall lall la, Drall lall la!" Who was now richer and lordlier than I?[50]

It is obvious why the public was amused by this exchange: the fool drastically highlighted the distance between above and below precisely by ignoring it. In addressing the empress on familiar terms and even physically touching her, Prosch treated her as his equal: "'Aye, Empress,' I said, 'and if e'er thou com'st to Tyrol, I shall be sure to give thee a present too.'"[51] The point lay in the paradox: the little fool could afford to meet the empress eye to eye since, in doing so, he only demonstrated his own foolishness. The reception with the empress was followed, as was customary, by a visit to the young archduke. The ten-year-old Leopold wanted to recruit him as a soldier for his regiment: "He took out his riding whip, I was his steed, and so we turned his room into a riding school." The next day he was presented to court society in the Great Hall; he met the "Spanish Elephanta [sic]" and was allowed "to dance with General Daun's daughter. . . . I performed leaps and somersaults; everyone laughed and made merry."[52]

What Peter Prosch retrospectively told as a fairy tale, as the fulfillment of a prophetic dream following a series of trials and tribulations, with Maria Theresa playing the role of good queen or fairy godmother, actually happened; his account is corroborated in its essentials by other sources.[53] His encounter with the empress catapulted the boy from Tyrol to regional fame: at courts across southern Germany, in Würzburg and Bamberg, Augsburg and Regensburg, Munich and Ansbach, he was now regularly summoned to dispel the boredom of lords and ladies at table. The Bohemian chancellor Count Chotek and his wife put him up for a time in their residence in Josephstadt in Vienna, while in Würzburg he became the favorite of Prince-Bishop Adam Friedrich von Seinsheim. The pranks played on him by the pageboys and cavaliers at the ecclesiastical residences he stayed in were as sadistic as they were inventive: fireworks were sewn into his clothing and then set alight; he was strapped to an electrical apparatus and given electric shocks; he was bound to a wild horse and driven out into the fields; his girlfriend was abducted; he was made godfather to a donkey; he was named "chamberlain of the rear and keeper of the chamber pot"; he and the court Jew were given enemas in the presence of courtiers. The great lords and ladies found such pranks hilarious, delighting in the mortal fear of their "court Tyrolean," but they liked him "very much," he assures the reader, and rewarded him handsomely for their abuses.[54] Time and again he returned to his home village, trying to eke out a living from various business ventures (including the royally licensed distillery), but he always took to the road again when they collapsed.

There were to be other meetings with the empress. When the entire court stayed in Tyrol in 1765 to celebrate Archduke Leopold's marriage to the Infanta of Spain in Innsbruck, she again sought out the now widely-traveled Prosch and entertained her dinner companions with his overly familiar banter. By his own account, Prosch again played the naïve simpleton, addressing their majesties as "Franz" and "Theresl," giving them a dozen gloves as a present, brazenly demanding gifts in return, and dispensing with all ceremonial deference. On the evening of that very day, Francis Stephen unexpectedly suffered a stroke and died.[55] Prosch depicts the emperor's sudden death as if he were a bystander; he even claims to have been personally received by the grieving widow shortly thereafter: "I was called in to the deeply grieving

Empress, who turned to me and said: 'Not so, Peter? What can we mortals do against the will of God? Oh! My dear Francis is no more!' She wept inconsolably, and I was sobbing too much to say anything in reply. I knelt before her, kissed her dress, and left the room in tears."[56] Doubts have been raised about the authenticity of the scene. Yet when Prosch was later imprisoned after a botched suicide attempt, his wife successfully petitioned Maria Theresa to grant him a pardon.[57] According to the autobiography, he was received one last time by the empress, their conversation taking much the same course as at their first encounter: "She talked with me about the Tyrol, asking whether she was loved there and so on," gave him another twelve ducats, and granted him another license.[58]

There can be no doubt that Prosch was indeed received by the imperial family on several occasions, nor that he amused court society with his antics. At the same time, he clearly later tailored his autobiography to suit public taste and embroidered it with conventional farcical elements. What does this tell us about the relationship between Maria Theresa and her ordinary subjects? For the noble audience, the comedy lay precisely in the contrast between the two otherwise separate worlds that came into contact here, located at opposite ends of the social hierarchy: "Thus, the great queen conversed with one of her meanest and poorest subjects."[59] The fool was an exception who made visible the rule. He confirmed the social order by appearing to subvert it: the genre of comedy, the *genus humile*, was reserved for the rabble. The "meanest and poorest subjects" were valued at court primarily as objects of amusement. This was true not just of Prosch but of commoners in general.

Commoners at Court

The legend of the empress's accessibility to everyone, even her humblest subjects, should thus not be taken at its word. "Everyone" did not literally mean everyone.[60] There were invisible barriers keeping ordinary subjects away from court. These borders were so much taken for granted that they were normally not perceived as such and did not need mentioning. The sources only occasionally indicate that "everyone" actually meant "people of distinction."[61] The lord high chamberlain observes in his diary that "everyone" was allowed to watch the king and queen playing cards during a hunting trip to Laxenburg, adding the parenthetical remark: "*gens qualifiés s'entend*," "persons of quality, needless to say." When the records occasionally mention "lesser persons" being admitted to court, these prove on closer inspection to be, at the very least, privy councillors, chamberlains, officers, or cathedral canons.[62] The first formal entry regulation for her court, which Maria Theresa decreed in November 1745, is informative in this regard. In order of rank, it lists a long series of groups enjoying access to the imperial apartments. The term "apartment" encompassed three dimensions: spatial, temporal, and social. In the first place, it designated a suite of rooms in the Hofburg (or at Schönbrunn) used for ceremonial purposes; second, the precisely fixed hours when the emperor or empress consorted there with courtiers; and third, the society itself that gathered in these rooms at these times. The chamber entry regulation described the social hierarchy by assigning specific groups to specific hierarchically arranged spaces. The yardstick of favor was proximity to the center, the secular Holy of Holies: the imperial retirade, the ruling couple's intimate sanctuary. Closest to the retirade was the Ratstube or first antechamber, into which the ambassadors of crowned heads, imperial counts, the highest court officials, and members of chivalric orders were allowed to proceed in hierarchical order. Next came the Large Antechamber, accessible to nonruling counts, barons, knights, senior officers, high officials from the hereditary lands, and so on. Finally came the Knights' Chamber, where "the lesser nobility, doctors and otherwise ennobled persons, archers, and trabants" were permitted to gather. A concluding remark stipulated that "strangers from abroad and initially unknown persons of distinction should apply to the lord high chamberlain for permission to enter the Ratstube or the other antechambers, depending on their rank and title."[63] Anyone who had the "impudence" to enter without authorization was to be thrown out immediately.[64] Commoners had no place in this order. The obvious question of where the borderline ran between *gens de qualité* and everyone else was not answered in regulations such as these. And that is telling: the absence of "commoners" at court was so self-evident that it did not need to be thematized as such. Apart from a fool like Peter Prosch, hardly anyone called the invisible social barrier into question, dispensing with the need to define it with any precision.

Leaving aside court personnel, the opportunities available to people from the lower orders to meet their queen were thus extremely limited. According to the traditional Christian idea of rule, however, everyone should have the opportunity to bring their entreaties or grievances before the throne and be given a hearing, albeit with no guarantee of success. This generally took place in writing, in the form of a petition or supplication (*Supplik*). In principle, this medium stood open to all subjects: in the words of a well-known saying, "anyone may drink water and make a petition."[65] That applied to the imperial court as well, where supplicants were traditionally given generous access conditions that Maria Theresa initially preserved unchanged upon coming to the throne.[66] "Every morning at ten, any private individual may submit . . . his petition. The chamberlain on duty and captain of the guard are instructed to collect submissions at the door to the antechamber and deliver them to the lady-in-waiting, who will then pass them on to the Empress."[67] Yet to petition the ruler in the first place, the supplicant had to know how to write (and to have mastered the necessary formalities), or hire a professional scribe. Even if the petition had been correctly worded, it still might fail to reach its addressee—and whether it was acted on was another matter entirely.

The public audience was actually intended as a forum for requests and complaints. Maria Theresa's fatherly friend Tarouca had advised her at the start of her reign to hold a "public audience" every Sunday and feast day between divine service and her apartment. This was not just convenient for "poor supplicants"; lending an ear to the needy also helped keep these days holy.[68] Yet this was far from easy given the high level of demand. For public audiences, unlike for the apartment, there were no formalized entry regulations. Yet those seeking an audience likewise had to make themselves known to the lord high chamberlain's office, request admittance, and then wait for permission to be granted. When it is stated in a source that access to the empress could be had without effort—"a word to the chamberlain suffices!"[69]—then this presupposes that the supplicant already had the chamberlain's ear. Audacious subjects with particularly urgent requests therefore sometimes resorted to throwing themselves at the empress's feet when she appeared in public. This occurred relatively often in the first decades of her reign. Ordinary subjects could catch a glimpse of their ruler on her way to worship at one of Vienna's churches, during her walks in the area, while strolling in the parks at Schönbrunn, or at public performances in the theater. On these occasions, the borders between court and city became porous.[70] The empress never ventured outside without lifeguards and a personal escort (especially after she had once been warned of an imminent attack[71]), so cunning and daring were needed to draw near her. If the petitioner was desperate enough, a way could nonetheless be found. The Jews of Prague, threatened with expulsion in 1744–45, considered lying in wait for Maria Theresa on her way to church and pleading with her for mercy (in vain, as it turned out), choosing for this purpose a beardless coreligionist in Hussar's uniform who would not immediately be recognized as a Jew.[72] The disgraced Viennese publisher and court printer Johann Thomas Trattner was likewise said to have thrown himself at the empress's feet on her way to chapel after he had done everything he could to secure an audience: "He concealed himself behind the ladies-in-waiting and spared no expense." The gamble allegedly paid off: Trattner struck the right tone and reminded Maria Theresa of her late husband's mercifulness, moving her to tears and clemency.[73] Someone like the court printer Trattner could only get away with this because he already had a personal connection to the court. For a stranger to address the empress in so direct a manner, however, signaled either desperation or madness. Once, during a solemn Mass in the Church of the Trinity, a "madman . . . slipped past the surrounding hartschier guards, suddenly . . . approached Her Majesty, and addressed her with confused words and gestures." The chamberlains immediately seized him and handed him over to the guards. "It later emerged that this poor man had lost his mind only a few hours earlier and had just come from the confessional, where he . . . had repeatedly declared that he had to go and beg the queen for forgiveness, since he would never be saved otherwise."[74]

An even greater sensation was caused by a "catastrophe" that took place on August 6, 1753, and even found its way into foreign newspapers.[75] It concerned a certain Chevalier de Balde, natural son of the last Count Montbéliard and a seamstress. This count had adopted his mistress's children, but his relatives refused to recognize them after his death. The son had since spent years fighting in vain to have his claim to noble status upheld by the Imperial Aulic Council. Then one morning he appeared in the antechamber to the Mirror Room (*Spiegelzimmer*) at Schönbrunn, demanding to be admitted to the empress. When the chamberlain on duty politely and repeatedly explained that she was not holding an audience that morning, "as supplicants could only register and be announced on days set aside for a public audience," the chevalier became violent. Unfortunately, the servant supposed to be guarding the door was answering the call of nature at the time. When the chamberlain himself sought to block the intruder, the chevalier drew his sword and "fell at him in a rage." The chamberlain, who was "very short and frail" anyway, slipped on the smooth parquet floor and just managed to deflect the sword thrust with his hand, injuring it and taking a glancing wound to his side. The empress, who had been working with a secretary in her cabinet, fled to the emperor's apartment, startled by the noise, and summoned the guards. Meanwhile, Archduke Joseph's chamberlain rushed to the scene and restrained the assailant until the trabants and hartschiers finally arrived, disarmed him completely and led him off to the guardroom, "whence he was brought as a madman to the Spanish hospital and finally moved to Rein Abbey in Styria." It was debated at court whether Chevalier de Balde had acted "in delirio or been carried away by his hot temper," that is, whether he should be regarded as insane or simply hot-headed. Maria Theresa decided "from natural clemency" not to pursue the matter in court but to treat the chevalier as a sick man, "in order to avoid the scandal of punishment," as Khevenhüller put it.[76] If a formally correct investigation had been launched and the court found that an attempt had been made on the empress's life, the culprit would have faced the severest punishment for lèse-majesté. A few years later, a mentally unstable domestic servant would be tortured, drawn, and quartered in public for attacking the French king with a knife. Maria Theresa clearly wanted to avoid such a grisly spectacle.

Yet she drew lessons of her own from the assault. Not only were door-keepers to be reinforced by military personnel in future, but rules of access for supplicants were also formalized and tightened. The lord high chamberlain was instructed to restrict "public audiences, to which by age-old custom even unknown persons could be registered and admit-ted," so that nobody could now be placed on the audience list who had not previously established his credentials in writing with the lord high chamberlain. This forced everyone to obtain the signature of the *capo*, or head, of the relevant authority. Foreigners from the Empire had to turn to the imperial vice-chancellor, all other aliens to the court and state chancellor (Kaunitz at the time). Khevenhüller cautioned the em-press that "personal feelings, for example," would cause the highest office-holders at court to block "access to the throne," leading to a situ-ation where "supplicants might well be denied the hearing they need." He therefore advised that she allow supplicants to address her, "where necessary, through me or through alternative channels by means of se-cret memoranda."[77] In any event, the new ruling did a great deal to im-pede access to the empress. In 1755 the Prussian emissary Fürst reported that it had earlier been far easier to procure an audience; now a letter had to be brought to the lord high chamberlain, "signed by the minister of the department to which the matter in question pertains; and the possibility of bringing complaints before the throne is thereby consider-ably reduced."[78]

The empress was thus caught in a structural dilemma. On the one hand, access to her own person had to be channeled somehow. On the other, there was always the danger that those who controlled these channels would abuse their power for their own ends. The inevitable consequence was that many petitioners sought out other, informal ave-nues to come closer to their goals. Emissary Fürst, for example, main-tained that one should first seek to win over one of the ladies-in-waiting who stood in the empress's favor and then entrust her with one's peti-tion. Clergy cultivated good relations with their brethren, the confes-sors of the imperial family.[79] The most promising channel was undoubtedly the privy cabinet secretary, who enjoyed the empress's un-shakable confidence, yet getting through to him could be tricky.[80] Ordi-nary subjects could approach the lesser court personnel who passed in and out of the imperial apartments each day, from servants and waiting maids to stokers. From the imperial perspective, however, it was essential that such informal avenues be closed off. It was therefore strictly forbid-den for chamber personnel to accept and convey petitions, "solicit" the empress, or submit an entreaty on another's behalf,[81] let alone accept payment for their services as intermediaries. Maria Theresa also ordered her children not to fraternize with servants, intercede for others, or grant favors on their own initiative, demanding that they stick to standard ad-ministrative procedure at all times. Whenever one of her daughters mar-ried and left court, her parting advice was that she should never accept petitions as a matter of principle, or at least forward them to the relevant officials.[82] Yet informal channels proved impossible to block; chamber personnel were understandably reluctant to forgo any opportunity to earn additional income. Many boasted of the ease and intimacy with which they conversed with the royal family in their private quarters; some also exploited the expectations of the outside world to play more or less cruel pranks. It was rumored, for example, that one of Archduke Maximilian's chamberlains had confided in a young lady that "his master was desperately in love with her." The lady bragged about her success in society; when the archduke came to hear of it, he brought shame on her by denying everything.[83] The episode shows the extent to which cham-ber personnel could exploit their supposed familiarity with the ruling family to impress—or in this case deceive—the outside world. It was only natural that they should seek to capitalize on it. If this was already true of ordinary man- and maidservants, then it was all the more so of noble members of the court household.

To make it more difficult for the countless courtiers to set themselves up as brokers and parasitical exploiters of imperial power, there was a clearly regulated procedure to be followed by those bidding for posi-tions, promotions, pensions, outstanding payments, and the like.[84] The lord high steward's office, the apex of the entire court organization, bore overall responsibility for the process. Petitions were funneled through his chancellery and then forwarded to the heads of the relevant offices at court, who were expected to provide a written opinion and return it to the chancellery. The lord high steward was thus the eye of the needle through which all the recommendations sent in by the various court departments passed; his task was to collate, consider, and evaluate them on their merits. He then composed a written report or "submission" to the empress and concluded it with a clear finding. The empress had the final say, scribbling her resolution in the margin of the report, then sent it back to the lord high steward for execution.

The files show the kinds of requests that were brought to Maria Theresa's attention from day to day.[85] She had to decide, for example, whether someone was entitled to free medicine from the court apothecary, what would be the future pay scale for kitchen staff, and how much gamekeepers could charge the imperial head chef. The "former court singer Theresia Stinglin" demanded payment of her long overdue "salary of 222 fl 15 kreuzer and a further 120 fl for her role seconda donna as in the opera Zenobia anno 1740," a debt dating back to the reign of Charles VI; the widow of the former *chef de cuisine* in Lorraine symbolically threw herself and her fatherless children at the empress's feet and begged for "maternal mercy." Such mercy was seldom denied: Maria Theresa usually added her *placet* beneath the lord high steward's submission. Sometimes she also wrote marginal comments such as "Granted on this occasion, but not in future." It is striking that the vast majority of petitioners appearing in the lord high steward's files either served at court or had relatives there.[86] This could be because outsiders never gained access to his chancellery in the first place, or because their petitions were rejected without leaving any traces in the archives.[87] Members of the high nobility are also barely represented in the files, suggesting that they found oral communication both more convenient and more in keeping with their social status. One group of supplicants stood too far from the court to benefit from this form of communication, the other stood too close to the queen to have any need of it.

Subjects not only approached the empress with their requests, they also presented her with their complaints of unjust treatment at the hands of their immediate superiors. Traditionally, a good monarch was expected to protect subjects from the depredations of their local over-lords, since only the sovereign was deemed to rise above petty partisan-ship and dedicate himself solely to the common good. Precisely his rela-tive isolation in a far-off residence generally prevented him from being held personally responsible for abuses of power. Authorities closer to home were a more frequent target for criticism, allowing the distant monarch to appear as a fount of justice and mercy.[88]

The case of Maria Theresa was no different. Those languishing under the despotism of their landlords could always look for succor to a far-away, benevolently maternal queen. Her almost magical reputation was safeguarded by the fact that very few people could make their way to the distant capital and potentially be disappointed in their expectations of redress. For subjects from the hereditary lands, securing a personal hearing from court authorities was a difficult, if not impossible under-taking. To dissuade them from even hazarding the attempt, Maria The-resa repeatedly ordered provincial authorities "to warn subjects of the journey to Vienna."[89] To avoid unnecessary expenditure, they were told not to proceed straight to the residence, bypassing the relevant authori-ties. Her father had already forbidden direct appeals to the court on several occasions. Deputies of subjects who ignored him risked arrest. Instead, they were encouraged to take their grievances first to their local authority, then to the regional administration, then to the Representa-tion and Chamber, and only then to the court. Yet redirecting subjects along arduous, costly, and uncertain formal channels was difficult, es-pecially if the officials responding to the complaint were the very ones who had occasioned it in the first place. In the memoranda they submit-ted to the court, appellants repeatedly denounced the "relevant authori-ties" for denying them justice. Clearly, the new agencies created by Haugwitz at the regional and territorial level did not function as planned. Maria Theresa therefore explicitly decreed that local, regional, and territorial authorities always had to respond to complaints in writ-ing. That way, subjects who nonetheless set out for Vienna could at least prove that they had not already been indemnified at any of the lower levels of the administrative hierarchy.[90] But providing such certification was hardly in the interest of officials, who would thereby have offered damning evidence of their own incompetence. In short, it was not easy to set in motion functioning bureaucratic mechanisms that warranted public confidence. Complaints not infrequently got bogged down somewhere along the way. Paradoxically, however, this very unresponsiveness worked to the benefit of the empress's reputation. The more unreliably the authorities went about their work, the more stubbornly subjects came to believe that they would receive a fair hearing only from the gracious sovereign herself. This idea was only rarely tested by reality, given that, for the vast majority of subjects in faraway Bohemia or Hungary, undertaking the journey to Vienna was out of the question. For them, Maria Theresa therefore remained the object of collective fantasy, the fairy-tale queen depicted by Peter Prosch in his narrative.

For her part, Maria Theresa sought as much as possible to avoid direct contact with common petitioners—in stark contrast to her son and later coregent Joseph II. An eyewitness described his novel way of governing in the following terms:

> Whenever he was in Vienna, solicitations or grievances could be submitted to him in writing each day in the comptroller's passage. Providing his health permitted it, he never neglected to come down at the stroke of nine. Here ladies, priests, nobles, merchants, craftsmen, and peasants, all mixed together, formed a line from the imperial staircase to the chancellery. As soon as the emperor descended the staircase, whoever saw him first went down on bended knee (in keeping with Spanish etiquette, which has since been abolished), held his petition between both hands so that it stuck out a little and the emperor could take it immediately, and everyone else did the same. Even though he was a great emperor, he never let anyone wait for a resolution in vain; indeed, by ten o'clock the next morning petitioners would be advised of the Collegium [i.e., council] where they could expect a response.

Yet what the respective departments did with the petitions was another matter: "I was referred with my petition to the Bohemian Court Chancellery but was informed by the same: 'Supplicants cannot be helped for now.'"[91] Joseph's new style of cultivating close contact with commoners while at the same time refusing personal intercession was severely criticized in the imperial family. His brother Leopold, who saw him in action in 1778, remarked with palpable malice:

> He gives no audiences and receives nobody except in the corridor, where his servants bring the lowest, most disreputable, and most infamous individuals. All those who pass by see there every day the most indecent pimps and prostitutes, since he is much drawn to such base and dirty women, whom he pays very handsomely. He readily believes what these humble people tell him, and on the strength of it is prepared to take action against everyone with all kinds of despotic measures. . . . He is excessively rude and harsh with his people, but then very familiar with commoners, servants, etc., who, if they know how to win him over, can get him to do whatever they want.[92]

Such demonstrative contact with commoners, as practiced each day by Joseph in the "comptroller's passage" outside the ceremonial spaces in the Hofburg, was frowned on by court society. It violated the norms of social exclusiveness and class solidarity that nobles expected from their ruler.

This is not what was meant when Maria Theresa's approachability was universally praised—quite the contrary. The access she granted middle-class individuals—people like the Gottscheds and the Mozarts—was valuable precisely because it was and remained an extraordinary honor. Access conditions for subjects were, in fact, markedly more limited under her reign than in her father's day. Indeed, this exclusiveness was arguably what first made it possible for her to adopt so relaxed and familiar a demeanor. The more difficult, prestigious, and desirable it was to secure an audience with the empress, the greater was the effect of her personal charm on the lucky few admitted to her presence—and the greater was their subsequent need to communicate their experience with all the world. In this way, Maria Theresa further entrenched her reputation as a universally approachable, maternally loving monarch, even though it was all but impossible for ordinary subjects to have their concerns heard by her.

There were other forms in which the "people" could participate in life at court. The great rites of transition in the ruling dynasty—coronations, marriages, baptisms, funerals—were jointly celebrated by the ruling elites and the people. These followed the same pattern set by Maria Theresa's baptism in 1717:[93] the event was conveyed to the people through bell ringing and cannon fire and celebrated throughout the land with rogation and thanksgiving services. Mourning and joy were both displayed in ritual form. On joyous occasions, citizens of the residential city were expected to decorate and illuminate their houses at their own expense.[94] Civic worthies erected symbolic triumphal arches and "theatrical scaffolds" or composed poems of praise and homage. Scholars, artists, and craftsmen vied to outdo each other in effort and ingenuity, hoping not least to acquire a good name at court leading to later commissions. Both sides, the imperial house and the populace, evidently had a great deal invested in a common culture of celebration. Every ruler needed an enthusiastic crowd as a lively backdrop to the great festive occasions that punctuated his or her reign. Ritual jubilation was contagious and strengthened allegiance to the ruling house among those who experienced it. On the other hand, nothing was more embarrassing or more detrimental to the legitimacy of rule than having a prince ride in procession down empty streets. Contemporaries were well aware that "what one adores in kings is actually the crowd of their adorers."[95]

Conversely, the lower orders expected that the ruling family would let them share in their celebrations. They did so, for example, in the form of ritualized gestures of munificence: rulers ordered coins to be scattered among the crowds, public fountains to flow with wine, or oxen to be roasted whole.[96] In Italian cities, as when Maria Theresa and Francis Stephen entered Florence in 1739, wealthy citizens donated a so-called *cuccagna*, a triumphal pavilion laden with foodstuffs that was created especially to be demolished and consumed by revelers. Dating back to the Middle Ages, such rituals created a kind of symbolic common table for ruler and ruled. They were not known for their civility. Young men came to blows over the cornucopia, and when the pavilions collapsed, there were regularly injuries and sometimes deaths.[97] In the eighteenth century nobles were both amused and, increasingly, bemused by such antics. In their eyes, the "people" appeared here as a wild, uninhibited, uncivilized, and occasionally threatening mob. Accordingly, precautions were taken and armed troops sent out in force to keep the crowd at bay. Only reluctantly and on rare occasions were commoners allowed to stream into the court unfiltered, in stark contrast to Versailles, where this was a daily occurrence.[98] As a matter of principle, court personnel were instructed to "have the guards restrain common people . . . wanting to intrude . . . at court festivals and functions."[99] Only on very special occasions was an exception made and the residence opened to the general public. Thus, in 1741 the people were permitted to file past the empty bed of state following the birth of the long-awaited heir,[100] while in 1743 they were allowed to view the "ladies' carousel" from the gallery in the winter riding school.[101] It was also customary, as at all great courts, for the masses to watch from behind a barrier as court society served at "open table" on grand gala days. "Whenever they keep open table, everyone is permitted to enter the dining room, provided they appear in clean and neat clothing. . . . Those who look unkempt and unhealthy are also denied access, lest their unpleasant appearance cause the lords at table to lose their appetite."[102] Yet such occasions were a source of unending headaches for the lord high chamberlain, who feared the worst. He noted apropos of Joseph's second marriage in January 1754 that Maria Theresa had admitted far too many spectators "from the goodness of her heart." So many people had entered at once that, had the guards not immediately barricaded the doors to the hall, "such a confusion would have arisen that even the lords themselves could hardly have been saved." He was also unhappy that, on the same occasion, not only qualified persons but also merchants and artisans had been admitted into the ballroom: "there was such a throng, making so scruffy an impression, that it was not at all in keeping with a grand wedding celebration."[103]

An altogether different way of involving commoners in court life consisted in making selected individuals, *pars pro toto*, the recipients of sovereign grace and mercy. Maria Theresa was familiar with this representative clemency from her own childhood, when the number of destitute girls invited to her birthday and showered with gifts always corresponded to her age at the time. She followed the same template when she was made godmother to carefully chosen orphans or when, again on the occasion of Joseph's second marriage, she endowed twenty-five newlywed couples with a dowry of two hundred guilders apiece.[104] The selected beneficiaries of sovereign grace were treated like fictitious family members, giving symbolic truth to the old topos of the queen as mother to her lands, her subjects as her own children. The most prominent such ritual was the washing of the feet on Maundy Thursday. The ceremony was performed not only by the pope and senior clergy but also by several Catholic monarchs, including the imperial couple. It was a set component of Baroque Passion ceremonial for the emperor and empress to wash the feet of twelve poor men and women from the people and serve them at table on the eve of Good Friday.[105] They symbolically abased themselves by performing this lowliest and most unclean of all services on a dozen of their most humble subjects, just as Jesus had abased himself before his disciples the night before his crucifixion. To be sure, the individuals concerned were carefully selected and made presentable before the imperial couple went to work on them with lace-trimmed linen cloths. There was also no real washing involved, nor were any of the dishes served actually consumed.

The ceremony played out in the Knights' Room in the presence of the entire court. Everyone appeared in gala dress, the ladies veiled in black. The emperor and his sons served twelve men at one table, the empress and her daughters twelve women at another. An English visitor conveyed how deeply impressed she was by the scene she witnessed in the overcrowded room in 1771: "I never saw the Empress look so gracefull. . . . She placed all the dishes on the table & took them off, but with a grace that is not to be described; her manner of holding the napkin was so genteel that I cou'd have look'd at her for ever, & if you had heard her talk to those three old Women you w[oul]d have been delighted."[106] Each of the poor guests then laid bare a foot, and the imperial couple knelt down and kissed all the unshod feet one after the other. The washing of the feet was indicated only symbolically, if at all.[107] As she grew older, the arthritic empress could no longer kneel and delegated the task to the eldest of her daughters accompanying her at the time. Finally, each of the visitors was given a pouch full of ducats and bade farewell. Unlike her son, emperor Joseph II, Maria Theresa spoke graciously with the beneficiaries of her charity, some of whom she already knew from previous such occasions. In short, the whole ceremony was an impressive symbolic staging of humility and mercy, the cardinal virtues of a Christian ruler. It was a traditional Catholic ritual of sovereign authority that symbolically upended the social hierarchy for a short time. For all that, the spectacular display of imperial self-abasement did not call into question the great social divide; if anything, it made it visible in the first place.

In spatial terms, courtiers and commoners lived close to each other in Vienna. Nonetheless, it is difficult for us today to get a sense of the vast distance separating their respective lifeworlds. Numerical comparisons fail to do justice to the disparity. It thus says little that two thousand ducats (around five thousand guilders) could change hands over a single evening of faro at court,[108] whereas a chancellery scribe rarely earned more than five hundred guilders in a whole year.[109] The distance between the orders was so great, and so much taken for granted, that at the time—unlike today—hardly anyone would have considered making the comparison. Life at court and life on the streets were literally incommensurable, that is, there were no common standards against which they could be compared. Social order on earth was only imaginable as an order based on inequality; this would change only in the afterlife, or so it was hoped. And such inequality—again in contrast to today's way of thinking—was not seen as illegitimate. Indeed, from a traditional point of view, social harmony all but presupposed inequality. There was a natural hierarchy extending from the lowliest worm all the way up to the heavenly hosts, an all-embracing hierarchy of divine creation into which the hierarchy of human beings was embedded as a small yet integral part. Even if the social order was in constant flux and individual families could rise or fall in status, the whole was nonetheless conceived as a stable harmony in which everyone was assigned his rightful place. In any event, the onus to justify themselves was always on those who disturbed and upset the established order through their vaulting ambition, not on those who held fast to the "praiseworthy old traditions."

The same sense that inequality was an unremarkable, quasi-natural fact of life was reflected in the arts. In rhetoric and poetics, the lower orders had their counterpart in the lower art form, the *genus humile*. In literature peasants figured solely as material for comedy, just as only nobles were deemed worthy subjects of tragedy. In the eyes of the court nobility, the plebs were there for purposes of entertainment and diversion. There were only three different roles available at court to people from the lower orders: as servants, as objects of charity, or as sources of amusement. When the royal couple embarked on pleasure trips to the countryside, their noble hosts got their rustic subjects to put on folkloristic performances for their entertainment: peasant dances, tournaments, a *triomphe rustique de Bachus*, or fake wedding celebrations, including once, as a special attraction, a Jewish wedding.[110] Francis Stephen was particularly fond of such "innocent trifles" and "merriments," but they did not always appeal to the court nobility's more refined tastes.[111] On more than one occasion, Khevenhüller confided to his diary his disdain for the "not very decorous" performances he had been forced to endure in the countryside. Peasants of both sexes would dance "barefoot to bagpipes in their everyday, rain-soaked, and filthy rags," or be "tossed in the air" in clothing that left little to the imagination.[112] More popular were pastoral scenes in which courtiers themselves mimicked rustic pursuits and were rewarded with trophies for their efforts: grapes were harvested and collected in daintily decorated baskets, butter churned in the most delicate porcelain vessels, or gold-plated fish caught from bubbling fountains.[113]

Another event noted by Khevenhüller in his diary was particularly well received. It took place on a pleasure trip that the court undertook to Holíč in Hungary in August 1747.

After dinner, the emperor had a most agreeable surprise for the Empress: she was informed that a number of ladies and knights had arrived from Brno requesting permission to see her and kiss her hand. Once Her Majesty had given her consent, around 10 or 12 couples were seen coming in, all dressed in the latest fashion; but it was immediately obvious that there was something odd and grotesque about their appearance and gestures. It could only be supposed that some riddle must lie behind it all, which was finally solved with much laughter: these masked men and women were peasants from Hanak, who . . . had been taken through their paces by a dancing master a few days earlier so they could at least pay their reverences and conduct themselves with a little more grace. Nothing was more ridiculous than to observe how they danced afterwards in Hanak fashion . . . and carried on over supper, which was set with silver service as if for people of good standing (to carry the farce to its end).[114]

Courtiers delighted in the farce since, by masquerading so ineptly as nobles, the disguised peasants flattered their audience's aristocratic self-image. By reverting to their "natural leaps and gestures," they involuntarily demonstrated that a noble bearing and demeanor was an innate distinction, not something that could be imitated at will. Their bizarre performance was the reverse mirror image of the *Bauernwirtschaften* periodically staged at court, bucolic masquerades where nobles pranced about in expensive imitations of traditional peasant dress.[115] Such role reversals were a much-loved comic motif on stage as well, a stock device in operas such as Pergolesi's *La serva padrona* (*The Servant Turned Mistress*) and comedies such as Molière's *Le Bourgeois gentilhomme* (*The Would-Be Noble*).

The same fancy for passing off low as high and high as low explains another episode in Khevenhüller's diary. One of Maria Theresa's subjects had a young son "born deaf and dumb." Countess Fuchs had taken him under her wing and raised him at court. In the 1753 Carnival season, the empress appeared at a masked ball in a black domino cloak and "entertained herself" by accompanying this child and tacitly presenting him as her son and heir. Since the child was "about the same height as Archduke Joseph," most people were taken in.[116] Khevenhüller provides no further commentary, as if the bizarre jest stood in no need of explanation. All these amusements presupposed a deep, self-evident, and unbridgeable chasm separating courtiers from ordinary subjects; they drew attention to this chasm rather than calling it into question. Masks, too, imperiled the visibility of class borders only at first sight. On closer inspection, peasants betrayed themselves through their uncouth manners, nobles through their fine breeding. Differences between the estates were so deeply engraved in physical appearance that they were impossible to disavow. Even Maria Theresa, the lord high chamberlain wrote, enjoyed disguising herself and passing incognito among her subjects, but she rarely succeeded, as she was "soon recognized by her swift and free gait."[117] In short, the court nobility allowed itself to play little jokes with the social hierarchy because it felt perfectly secure in its preeminence. This only began to change in the last years of Maria Theresa's rule, and then only gradually.

Distinctions and Refinements

Courtly extravagance was not addressed to ordinary subjects. They figured only at the margins. When eighteenth-century bourgeois scholars wrote that splendid displays of sovereign majesty were needed to impress commoners so that they might obey more willingly, this was only half the story.[118] Illiterate subjects in faraway Hungary or Bohemia learned little of what went on in the gilded halls of Vienna and Schönbrunn. The glory of the imperial court was addressed first and foremost to the nobility itself, both those in the hereditary lands and those at other European courts. So long as Vienna and Schönbrunn remained attractive for the high nobility, their appeal to the lower estates was assured.

The court was a highly complex social construct.[119] It was at once the extended household of the ruling dynasty, the center of the hereditary lands, and the heart of the Empire, without these three spheres ever being clearly distinguishable. Sleeping and eating, gambling and dancing, praying and governing, childbearing, marrying, and dying all took place at court; they even happened in the same rooms, albeit not at the same time. Members of the royal family, aristocratic courtiers, guests from the Empire and ambassadors from abroad, scholarly councillors and humble service personnel—an enormous number of people of diverse backgrounds, ranks, and offices met here in a relatively confined space. All of them were competing for the ruler's favor, that most scarce and precious resource. Not least, everyone was out to maintain and defend his or her position in the hierarchy. Life at court must therefore have been extremely demanding. To avoid everything descending into total chaos, all communications—from the menial services performed by the lowest-ranking chamber attendant to a ceremonious audience granted the highest-ranking diplomats—had to be coordinated with the utmost precision. Everyone needed to know when exactly he had to be where exactly, and what exactly he or she was meant to be doing there. What made communication so taxing was that literally every word or action was read as an index of a person's social standing. Courtiers paid close attention to where they could stand or move, the furniture they could sit on, the thresholds they were permitted to cross, how long they had to wait, the clothes they could wear, when and for how long they should doff their hat, whom they could look at and to whom they could offer their hand, the stance—a deep or shallow bow, one, two, or three bends of the knee—they should adopt when approaching others, the order in which they were served at table and the cutlery they were given, whose health was drunk, who was permitted to drive into the inner courtyard and park there and with how many horses, and so on. The social hierarchy was communicated in speech and writing as well, from the correct form of address to the proper wording of a compliment or the size of the signature at the bottom of a document. Almost all of everyday life took ceremonial form and was fraught with symbolism. This entire, highly complex network of symbolic behavioral rules, which both represented the social hierarchy and continually produced it, would have long since broken down had it not been documented in protocol.[120] Unlike simple rules of politeness, which literally went without saying, court ceremonial was fixed in writing down to the minutest details, and in some cases it was even stipulated in contractual form. The hierarchy of persons was set out in instructions given to court personnel, annually published court calendars, general court access rules, and in special ordinances for festive, hunting, and summer seasons. From the seventeenth century onward, all ceremonial occasions were punctiliously set down in writing so that precedent cases could be cited in the event of conflict or uncertainty. It is characteristic of priorities at court that ceremonial was recorded far more scrupulously than, say, the state of treasury finances.[121] At the start of the century, a couple of scholars had sought to codify all this material in a scientific system, but their efforts came to nothing—the rules changed too quickly and proved too obviously unamenable to abstract principles.[122]

Ceremonial framed and defined any given situation; it structured everyday life and provided a modicum of certainty by dictating how participants were to conduct themselves on periodically recurring occasions in accordance with their rank and how, conversely, they were to make sense of the conduct of others. Ceremonial also made it possible to distinguish between different "characters" of one and the same person. Because people at court often combined several functions, courtiers developed an acute sensitivity to changes in social role. Thus, very different ceremonial rules applied depending on whether Maria Theresa was appearing as empress or as queen of Hungary, whether a foreign minister was acting as his master's ambassador or in a private capacity, whether a nuncio was received as the pope's representative or as an archbishop, and whether the lord high chamberlain attended a wedding in his regular official capacity or "took on the lady's role."[123]

Despite all such efforts at precise regulation, ceremonial was rife with conflict; disputes over rank were constantly breaking out. Participants often found it difficult to reach consensus about who should take precedence in any given situation. Not every constellation could be regulated in advance, not every looming conflict averted in good time. While Maria Theresa could adjudicate the hierarchy at her own court, she lacked authority to enforce relations between foreign potentates or decide on the order of precedence within the Holy Roman Empire. Relations between nobles from the hereditary lands and imperial princes staying in Vienna, for example, were particularly tricky, since in this case the competing hierarchies of the Habsburg court and the Holy Roman Empire stood opposed to each other.[124]

Foreign ambassadors caused permanent disruption in court ceremonial. Charged with representing their principal's majesty and dignity in the strict sense of the term, they needed to pay particular heed to every gesture, since the honors shown (or denied) them were received on behalf of the prince they served. Diplomatic ceremonial therefore formed the medium in which potentates came to a public understanding about the state of their relations with each other.[125] Traditionally, the imperial court had claimed precedence over all other monarchies, while these in turn had since the mid-seventeenth century set great store on being treated as equals. In the ceremonial of the ambassadorial audience, two irreconcilable principles were thus at loggerheads: the old principle of a hierarchy of Christendom, on the one hand, and the new equality claimed by sovereigns, on the other. No detail was deemed too trivial to escape scrutiny. In April 1752, for example, there were weeks of argument about how many steps up a new grand staircase—the so-called Ambassadors' Staircase (*Botschafterstiege*), purpose-built for such occasions—the French ambassador would meet the grand marshal of the court on his first official visit to the Hofburg. The ambassador refused to leave his coach until he had been notified that the vice-marshal was already waiting for him at the lower landing.[126]

In light of all this, it is hardly surprising that courtiers were groaning under the increased weight of signs. They therefore marked out ever more times and places of heightened informality, where not every word and gesture immediately betokened rank and status, as was the case *in publico*. Life in the countryside was less formal than life in the city, the rulers' inner apartments less formal than the outer, normal days less formal than gala days, and so on. A zone of informality was also created by going incognito. On such occasions there was an explicit understanding that members of the ruling family would be officially invisible and hence would not need to be paid the customary obeisance. This was a pure fiction: nobody truly went unrecognized. But it was a fiction that provided royals and grandees at court with temporary relief from their obligation to uphold their status at all times, something that was extremely arduous, expensive, time-consuming, and potentially contentious for all involved. These areas of informality were simultaneously privileged enclaves of exclusiveness and familiarity; there was no greater honor than to be admitted to them. Between the maximal intimacy of the royal cabinet, on the one hand, and the maximal formality of the grand public gala, on the other, there were countless fine gradations. They opened up a space for special refinements and distinctions.[127]

The Lord of the Signs

The supreme guardian of this ceremonial semiotic system, and one of the most influential and long-serving officials at court, was Johann Joseph Count—later Prince—Khevenhüller (1706–76).[128] As lord high chamberlain and then lord high steward, he organized and channeled access to the royal couple and enjoyed almost unlimited access himself. He could talk to Maria Theresa at any time, even outside ceremonial occasions and formal procedures, without being observed by others. This was a major advantage, otherwise conferred only on members of the ruling family, ladies-in-waiting, cabinet secretaries, father confessors, or the all-powerful State Chancellor Kaunitz.[129] It is therefore a stroke of good fortune for historians that Khevenhüller saw himself, in line with family tradition, as a chronicler of the imperial court, conscientiously fulfilling his self-imposed duties in this regard over a period of decades.[130] The diary he kept between 1742 and his death in 1776 comprises eight volumes in Hans Schlitter's edition, despite gaps extending over several years.[131] It is among the most detailed and informative sources we have for Maria Theresa's reign.

Khevenhüller came from an old Carinthian baronial family that had served the Habsburgs for decades. Like many nobles from the hereditary lands, several of his ancestors had been implicated in the evangelical opposition to the crown from the estates. Yet the descendants of these rebels had either emigrated or returned to the bosom of the Catholic church. The family tradition of writing up "their own and other histories with peculiar fidelity and diligence" was perhaps a Protestant legacy.[132] One of Johann Joseph's forebears, Franz Christoph Khevenhüller, had written Emperor Ferdinand II's Annals in the Thirty Years' War, while his father, Sigmund Friedrich Khevenhüller, captain of territorial estates in Lower Austria, had kept a detailed journal of life at court. An uncle, Field Marshal Ludwig Andreas Khevenhüller, had been Maria Theresa's greatest pillar of military strength in the War of the Austrian Succession. Elevated to the peerage in 1725, the family was affiliated by marriage with almost all the other influential noble families in the hereditary lands. Johann Joseph himself married a wealthy heiress, the

FIGURE 28. Portrait of the family of Lord High Steward Khevenhüller.
Unknown artist, c. 1760

daughter of Imperial Aulic Council vice president Johann Adolf Metsch, a lady-in-waiting to Maria Theresa's mother. He thereby established the Khevenhüller-Metsch line, made imperial princes in 1763. The young Johann Joseph's career took its expected course. Having studied for a time at the universities of Vienna and Strasbourg and become familiar with the *Ius publicum*, he entered the Lower Austrian government at the age of nineteen. Three years later he gained a seat on the lords' bench of the Imperial Aulic Council, a typical entry-level position for young noblemen from the hereditary lands aspiring to a career in state service. Charles VI sent him as envoy to Holland and Denmark, entrusted him a little later with the Bohemian electoral vote in the Imperial Diet, and rewarded him in 1737 with the title of privy councillor. Maria Theresa inherited her father's loyal servant when she came to the throne and sent him on several expensive diplomatic missions, first to the court in Dresden and then twice, in 1742 and 1745, to Frankfurt for the imperial election. Khevenhüller's service at the head of various court departments began around the same time, first as grand marshal of the court (1742–45), then as lord high chamberlain (1745–65), and finally as lord high steward, a position he held (1765–76) until his death. This last office was the culmination of his career, placing him at the apex of the entire court hierarchy, yet he appreciated it less than the office of lord high chamberlain, which guaranteed him easier everyday access to the ruling couple.[133] Membership of the Court Conference also came with these top posts. Khevenhüller was thus at the same time an old-style adviser—that is, his responsibilities were by no means confined to questions of access, ceremonial, and court personnel. Rather, his counsel was heard in all matters pertaining to internal and external governance.

His activity as a chronicler of life at court extended throughout his decades in office, from 1742 to 1776. The diary that lay before the editor is a partially revised clean copy based on notes jotted down at an earlier stage. It seems that Khevenhüller subsequently brought his rough notes into more polished narrative form. This is evident from occasional additions to the text that anticipate later events and hence cannot have appeared in the original diary entries.[134] On the other hand, his revision was not especially painstaking, as can be seen in the many gaps for names, dates, and so on, which Khevenhüller presumably intended to fill in later. The diary was accompanied by numerous official papers of various kinds, appended and constantly referred to in the text by the author himself. The entire sheaf of papers offered an account of his activity as the loyal servant of his masters, addressed to his descendants, not the general public.[135] For a long time historians treated this source with a degree of disdain and showed remarkably little interest in the author himself. This is because Khevenhüller—like his father before him—reported primarily on everyday court ceremonial, his official area of responsibility, and on his own family affairs. He had relatively little to say about what the nineteenth century took "great politics" to mean: war, diplomacy, constitutional reform. Yet this very fixation on the minutiae of court life is characteristic of the contemporary perspective of the court nobility. For a man like Khevenhüller, it would have made no sense to distinguish between the affairs of the ruling dynasty, those of his own household, his personal office at court, and politics as such. These all belonged inseparably together and were the subject of a single overarching entity, the All-Highest Archducal House and its retinue. And everything Khevenhüller did was done—in his mind, at least—for the good of the dynasty.

Khevenhüller was an old-fashioned aristocrat, completely devoted to the imperial house, the holiness of its traditions, and the dignity of his status. In the diary he appears as a respectful husband and doting, proud father, a dutiful servant and devout, morally upstanding Catholic. His faith in the "pure Christian doctrine, far removed from all political refinement and so-called *esprit philosophique*," was unshakable.[136] Although only thirty-six years old when he began writing his diary, he comes across from the outset as a dignified, somewhat crotchety stickler for tradition. His style is unmistakable, an idiosyncratic late Baroque German interspersed with phrases in French and Latin and a smattering of Austrian dialect. The form of the notes faithfully reflects Khevenhüller's traditionalism: page after page, they breathe a spirit of constancy and unvarying repetition. The author's voice barely changes over thirty-five years. His notes are and remain a more or less comprehensive listing of everyday ceremonial occurrences and entertainments, of seasonal solemnities and elevations in rank, audiences and conferences, marriages and deaths. All this is enlivened with personal commentary and intimate insider information, spiced with anecdotes, malicious remarks, and rumors. One searches in vain, however, for humor, satire, irony, or deeper meaning.

Khevenhüller lacked the esprit and nonchalance required of the consummate aristocrat. He was anxious and plagued by constant worry about his "delicate physical constitution"[137]—not unlike Kaunitz, albeit without his bizarre eccentricities. He admired genuine aristocrats like Harrach and appreciated reliable friends like Tarouca; Haugwitz, by contrast, was a selfish careerist. He looked down on successful upstarts like Bartenstein or van Swieten—all the more so the higher they stood in Maria Theresa's favor. Yet he always sought to provide a fair and balanced judgment. He found this hardest when contemplating "our Lord State Chancellor"; Kaunitz embodied an incomprehensible and

threatening new era, and he therefore bore the full brunt of Khevenhüller's animosity. What irked him most about Kaunitz was his "singularism," that is, the egocentrism and arrogance with which he flouted convention without having to fear any loss of imperial favor. Accordingly,
Khevenhüller recorded Kaunitz's occasional breaches of decorum with
considerable relish.[138]

He himself was convinced of the need for social conformity; every
infringement or modification of the rules posed a threat. He saw his life's
task in maintaining aristocratic exclusiveness and the very highest ceremonial standards. On first taking office, he had found ceremonial protocol in disarray for two reasons: the Hofburg was no longer an imperial
court and the status of the queen's consort was still highly uncertain.
After Francis Stephen was elected emperor, he had anticipated a return
to the good old days. To his great disappointment and even bitterness,
he was forced to ascertain that, "so far as our etiquette is concerned, notwithstanding the imperial honors acquired since then, not much has
changed for the better, a situation which I, along with others who would
gladly see the court restored to its old decorum, endeavor to work
against."[139] Yet he never allowed himself to lose heart, fighting tirelessly
"to save our so badly damaged etiquette—so far as possible, at any rate—
from total ruination."[140] For all his sincere devotion and loyalty, he could
not refrain from criticizing the empress's conduct in his journal entries,
albeit in restrained tones. What he regretted more than anything else was
her lack of resistance to the spirit of novelty confronting her on all sides.
He also lamented the boundless generosity with which she bestowed
largesse on the wrong people and her susceptibility to those who, in his
opinion, were not acting with her best interests at heart. He foresaw an
inflation of imperial patronage, a leveling of differences between the estates, and a loss of prestige for the imperial court, which would naturally
undermine the standing of all who lived and worked there.

The attention Khevenhüller lavished on the correct external forms
strikes us as bizarre today, just as his pomposity now comes across as
faintly ridiculous. Whatever may have been happening in the world at
large, Khevenhüller's eye stayed myopically fixed on the ceremonial details. In November 1755, when the Privy Council was plotting the new

alliance system that would rock all Europe the following year, he wrote: "On the 20th we . . . met in conference regarding the secret negotiations with France. Both Majesties sat on the sofa and the rest of us gathered without rank around the adjacent writing table or secrétaire, as it has become fashionable to call it. Secretary Binder sat to one side at a little table."[141] And that is all. What exactly was discussed at the meeting or what he made of it does not rate a mention.

In short, Khevenhüller embodied the old aristocracy in its obsession with outward forms, its traditionalism, snobbery, and sense of entitlement. He was the embodiment of everything that national-liberal bourgeois historians of the nineteenth century found objectionable about the ancien régime, and that they still deplored in the dual monarchy of their own day. Maria Theresa was the heroine of these historians. The criticisms leveled at her by Khevenhüller were therefore perfectly compatible with the image later historians made of her as a bourgeois queen along modern lines: natural, unstuffy, fundamentally averse to the pomp and ceremony of courtly representation. Yet this is an optical illusion; the lord high steward's exacting standards distort the picture. It goes without saying that Maria Theresa took ceremonial forms very seriously indeed and set great store on representing the status of her house—just not as her lord high steward would like her to have done.

For her part, the empress had an ambivalent relationship with Khevenhüller. It is difficult to assess it with any accuracy, partly because she wrote him very few letters—he was always in her immediate vicinity, after all[142]–partly because she hated gossip and vicious rumor and therefore rarely made negative remarks about trusted servants in her letters to others. Yet given her lively temperament, it seems likely that she would have struggled with Khevenhüller's stiffly formal manner, at least at the start of her reign. She once revealed to Privy Councillor Doblhoff that she wished Khevenhüller were "a little more active," for he could be "very indolent and even negligent" in his duties.[143] On the other hand, she sympathized with his "delicatesse regarding Christianity and morals,"[144] since he was one of the few nobles at court to share her strict views on piety and chastity. In any event, she seems to have increasingly come to appreciate him as a loyal and conscientious servant of her house. She ended up heaping on him the highest offices and distinctions at her disposal, taking a demonstrative interest in his family,[145] drawing him into her circle of intimates, and honoring him—the ultimate sign of royal favor—with personal visits to his house. As her old *ministre de famille*, he also numbered among the very few confidants to whom she could vent her periodic frustrations with Francis Stephen, Joseph, and Kaunitz.[146]

Khevenhüller played a key role as gatekeeper at her court. He oversaw the complicated system of rules governing who was granted access on which occasions and under which conditions to which rooms at court—the crux of all ceremonial order. This order was a kind of complex symbolic grammar that allowed for thousands of different combinations and permutations, and hence offered thousands of degrees of proximity to the empress-queen. With Khevenhüller as her right-hand man, Maria Theresa used this ceremonial grammar in a calculated, increasingly skillful way to distribute "distinctions and refinements."

Court Timetable

The basic elements of ceremonial grammar consisted in the arrangement of space and time; its principle was intensification. Ceremonial rooms were differentiated by status but hardly by function. Indeed, rooms were used with an extraordinary degree of flexibility. Furnishings were moved here and there as needed. Dining tables, for example, were reassembled in the required dimensions for each meal. The same rooms could host solemn audiences or private conferences, but they could equally be used for dining, card games, or even sleeping. In summer, for example, Maria Theresa sometimes had her bed set up in the audience room at Schönbrunn to escape the stifling heat. The function of rooms could remain relatively flexible because an additional element came into play: the order of time. The days and weeks followed a set routine. Whenever the ruling family changed residence for a season, exactly the same times for divine service, audience, apartment, open table, and so on were ordained by decree and communicated to court society.

Maria Theresa had to exercise considerable self-discipline to adhere to this timetable. At the start of her reign, when she found herself assailed by a barrage of demands for her favor and attention, she had turned to Count Tarouca for advice. Tarouca was a perceptive observer of the court patronage system and had the queen's ear; she saw him as one of the few whose judgment was unclouded by ambition. He urged her to establish a fixed routine and drew up a weekly timetable for her.[147] After rising from bed, he allowed her one hour for prayer, coffee (although he considered it unhealthy), and morning Mass, then half an hour for her morning toilette. Since he assumed that she rose at eight, that left time from nine-thirty to eleven-thirty, and again from four to six in the afternoon, for her to receive reports from her various ministers. Each was assigned exactly one hour on alternating weekdays. The fixed schedule was designed to prevent ministers from wasting their time by lingering and chatting needlessly in the antechamber; it would also force them to get to the point and make it easier for Maria Theresa to arrive quickly at a structured overview of the latest developments. At eleven-thirty it was time to give instructions to her cabinet secretary. From then until lunch, at a quarter past twelve, Maria Theresa was to abstain from any serious occupation. For reasons of both enjoyment and health, Tarouca deemed it essential that she sit down punctually for lunch and not let it go cold. After the meal, for which he allocated an hour, she was given time until two-thirty for a second cup of coffee and for resting in her bedroom, perhaps combined with a visit from her then three-year-old daughter Marianna. The hour until three-thirty was set aside for the rest of the family; she could visit her mother and look in on little Maria Carolina and the newborn heir. Tarouca did not insist on this family time—Maria Theresa could always get some more rest instead. At three-thirty, or four at the latest, it was time to get back to work. Now court officials and advisers without regular reporting times could speak to her, unless they were referred to a public audience or apartment. Afterward, the cabinet secretary once again took her instructions. From six until dinner at eight-thirty there was half an hour to say vespers or the rosary, followed by two hours for irregular visitors, games, or other entertainments. One hour after dinner, at the latest, Maria Theresa should retire for the evening and do nothing that might disturb her slumber.

Individual weekdays were specified in turn. On Mondays, Tuesdays, Thursdays, and Fridays she would be briefed by her ministers, while Wednesdays and Saturdays were devoted to correspondence and audiences for foreign emissaries. The Court Conference met at least once a week, on Sunday from nine to eleven, followed by divine service. On Sundays and holidays there was a public audience after vespers and then "apartment," that is, a soirée attended by a small group of insiders; the latter occurred also on Thursdays. Nobody was to be admitted outside the prescribed hours, not even conference ministers, but neither should anybody have grounds for complaining that he had not been heard. The strict schedule that Tarouca devised for the queen was intended, above all, to channel communication. Access to the monarch should be predictable; everyone should be given a hearing in keeping with his office, rank, and standing, but nobody should enjoy after-hours access or exploit informal avenues to the throne. "Grumbling in the antechamber" was also to be minimized; ministers should spend less time gossiping with each other and more time focused on their work.

This advice was informed not just by Tarouca's sensitivity to the logic of patronage at court but also by his experience with the Jesuit education system. He explicitly cites Saint Ignatius as an authority.[148] As a tool for inculcating both physical and spiritual self-discipline, the Ignatian exercises allowed Jesuits to examine their conscience and draw nearer to God. For Maria Theresa, too, there was an unmistakably spiritual dimension to her strict schedule; rather than serving merely pragmatic purposes, it had an additional religious meaning. Time here on earth had to be spent wisely so as not to risk salvation in the hereafter. She made this especially clear in her letters to her son Ferdinand, whom she urged to follow a strictly regimented schedule:

> You will write to tell me how you manage your time; I expect that this is the root of all evils. You have started living in disorder [in Milan], lacking the time to do things properly and punctiliously; you are completely disorganized. You are wasting your most precious time with childish nonsense and dilly-dallying. Seven or eight hours' sleep is more than enough. Even if you don't go to bed until midnight or

one o'clock, you can still get up at seven or eight. Mass should be the first business of the day; you should get dressed promptly, without distraction or chatter.[149]

Appointments for divine service and lunch had to be kept at all costs, "otherwise you will be poorly served, and everyone will fall ill, masters and servants. Once you have grown accustomed to order, you will see just how much pleasure and ease you will take in everything".[150] It was not just a question of preserving his physical well-being and establishing a smooth daily routine, but, as Maria Theresa reminded him time and time again: "The redemption of your soul and your reputation are at stake."[151] In the years leading up to her death, she repeated these warnings incessantly but without success, admonishing him that "there is no real loss in this world but that of time; it is irreparable; with a wasteful, idle life you forfeit your salvation."[152]

She herself stuck to these rules all her life and passed them on to her children. She even kept a considerable tighter schedule than that recommended by Tarouca. In 1770 she described her daily routine to her confidante Countess Enzenberg. In winter she was up at six, in summer often as early as four.[153] Her Sunday audiences commenced at seven in the morning and continued until eleven, while her meetings with individual ministers began at eight, followed a fixed hourly rhythm, and lasted at least until one. The State Council sat from nine to four once a week. "Fridays and Saturdays are for family and other business and for private persons. Afternoons are for reading, sending out orders, and correspondence, and I confess that I have barely a moment to myself."[154] All who saw her praised the unusual discipline she brought to her work and marveled at how much time she devoted to religion, how often she saw her children—up to four times a week, considered very frequent–, how early she retired in the evening, and how little she cared for "spectacles, *plaisirs* and *délassements* (relaxations)," the frivolities "on which so many other princes squander the greatest part of their lives."[155] Compared with most other European courts—with the possible exception of Prussia—her schedule was indeed extraordinary. What others were only too happy to leave to their ministers, she insisted on doing herself.

In her eagerness to know and decide everything, she wrote thousands of letters and pored over thousands of official documents.

Particularly in her later years, we must imagine Maria Theresa spending much of her time reading and writing in her cabinet. As time went on she retreated more and more to her retirade, reduced the number of her public audiences and apartments, gave up her visits to the theater, and attended divine service incognito more frequently.[156] This increasing withdrawal from the public eye cut both ways. Her charisma as a ruler required that she perform a balancing act between accessibility and exclusiveness, maintaining a carefully calibrated mixture of display and concealment, publicity and familiarity. Both extremes were to be avoided. Were Maria Theresa to shut herself off completely in her retirade, universal disappointment would eventually make her court unattractive. If, on the other hand, she made herself available to all and sundry, court service would likewise forfeit its appeal for the high nobility. Once they had withdrawn to their estates, the court would lose its luster and gradually become less attractive for others as well. Maria Theresa was well aware of all this; had she not been, advisers such as Tarouca and Khevenhüller were there to remind her of it.[157]

In weighing up the various demands on her time and attention, Maria Theresa placed her obligations to the high nobility immediately after her duties to God and her family. She tried as much as possible to limit court access to the uppermost echelon of society (even if exceptions confirmed the rule). How seriously she shared her lord high chamberlain's concerns in this regard emerges with all clarity from her letters to her grown-up children. She urged them to recruit their court exclusively from the first families of the realm. She thought it "completely inappropriate to allow anyone and everyone to appear at your court,"[158] sent them detailed lists of persons they should admit, and advised them to receive selected grandees (*primores*)—but nobody else—once or twice a week, "so that they may have an opportunity to do something for their families."[159] She was also prepared to spend the time, money and effort needed to present herself with due majesty. "*Vous devez représenter par tout,*" she continually reminded her children: you must represent at all times and in all places (albeit only when publicly visible, it should be added).[160] The empress loved "occasions where she could show off her majesty in public," attested Khevenhüller, who otherwise never passed up an opportunity to lament the decline in old ceremonial standards.[161] Maria Theresa nonetheless reduced the number of such solemn, representative occasions and tightened the border between public and private over the course of her long reign.

Work on Charisma

In order for Maria Theresa to appear as a resplendent monarch, she needed to be staged as such. "Majesty" was a perceptible, almost palpable quality. Contemporaries were well aware of this. They themselves compared court with a theater—a theater, to be sure, where most actors were at the same time spectators of each other's performances. The monarch's majesty lay not least in the forms that surrounded her "all-highest person" and protected her from symbolic degradation. Her stages were the ceremonial apartments of her residences and Vienna's streets and churches. These stages had to be furnished with appropriately ornate props, marked by thresholds, tiers, barriers, and signals; flanked by guards; and peopled with a cast of the most distinguished pedigree. Not least, the queen herself had to be prepared for her turn on the boards. An impeccable performance on front stage called for a perfectly functioning, inconspicuous backstage. Behind the ceremonial apartments lay a labyrinth of chambers and connecting corridors; the imposing ornamental portals through which visitors passed between armed guards had their counterpart in small concealed doorways; sweeping ceremonial stairways were complemented by hidden spiral staircases; above and below the *piano nobile* lay the attics and basements frequented by the service personnel. An army of invisible helpers operated behind the scenes to ensure that everything functioned smoothly. They were invisible in either the literal or the metaphorical sense: the vast majority were denied access to the ceremonial rooms on solemn occasions; the rest had to remain imperceptible even when physically present.[162]

At the imperial court, the ruling family spent much of their time out of the limelight. This was quite different from Louis XIV's court at

Versailles, where the king's every waking moment—even getting dressed and undressed or visiting the night-stool—was a representative, ceremonial occasion. Maria Theresa's children were unaccustomed to such unrelenting scrutiny. Their father admitted only a single valet to his dressing room, although traditionally at least one chamberlain ought to have been in attendance as well.[163] Marie Antoinette in Versailles and Maria Carolina in Naples were initially struck by the stark contrast between the round-the-clock surveillance they had to endure at the courts of their royal husbands and the relative informality that had always distinguished the court in Vienna, and which had increased still further during their mother's reign.[164] Yet Maria Theresa still devoted the utmost care to preparing herself for her appearances on the public stage.

Generally speaking, we know little about this unseen work on royal charisma. Personal servants were not yet in the habit of penning tell-all memoirs in their anecdotage; there were rarely any doubts about their loyalty to the ruling house, since they had no wish to blight the career prospects of their children and relatives. Yet a few reminiscences shed light on what went on behind the scenes.[165] We are at least indirectly informed about Maria Theresa's morning and evening toilette because Caroline Pichler (1769–1843), the daughter of her chambermaid Charlotte Hieronymus, presided over an important literary salon in Restoration-era Vienna and wrote her memoirs as a seventy-year-old woman. She also revealed some details there about her mother's work in the empress's chamber and cabinet. We are thus dealing with second-hand information, recorded many years after the event and animated, moreover, by a sense of pride and admiration for the empress to whom her parents owed their meteoric rise in society.[166]

Charlotte Hieronymus (1740–1816) was the daughter of a Protestant junior officer in the Duke of Wolfenbüttel's imperial-royal regiment. Her mother died young, forcing her father to bring her along with him wherever his company was posted. His regiment was performing garrison duty in Vienna when he too passed away. Maria Theresa happened to hear of the orphaned child and took her under her wing, even though the Protestant regimental officers sought to conceal her whereabouts from the empress. She provided the girl with a modest pension from her private purse and had her brought up in the Catholic faith by her lady-in-waiting Duplessis, and later by Countess Fuchs. The empress had a habit of financially supporting any Protestant orphans who came her way in order that they might be converted to Catholicism.[167] This had the additional advantage that she could recruit her chamber personnel from a group of especially loyal and discreet young women who had no connections at court and could be relied on not to pester her with pleas on behalf of their relatives.[168] Charlotte Hieronymus proved a gifted and willing pupil, entering court service at the age of thirteen. As a maid, she was required to perform all the tasks that arose in the chamber in the course of the day, from attending to the empress's wardrobe and coiffure to reading her state papers in French, German, Italian, and Latin. Her personal closeness to the empress meant that she was accorded the status of a privy councillor's wife in ceremonial, stood under constant supervision, and could marry only with imperial permission. Her service as maid ended with the kind of court wedding that Maria Theresa loved to orchestrate. Her groom was the imperial privy councillor Franz Sales von Greiner, one of the empress's closest companions.[169]

Historians have tended to portray Maria Theresa as a woman utterly lacking in vanity, claiming that she showed a total disregard for her outward appearance. This was in keeping with the myth of her free and easy, unpretentious nature and emphasized her "honest German," un-French ways: "There has probably been no queen in history who . . . spent less time at her toilette than Maria Theresa."[170] If Caroline Pichler's memoirs are to be believed, the truth was rather different. As her chambermaid recalled, although Maria Theresa was a gracious and considerate mistress, there was no pleasure to be had in serving her at toilette:

> The Empress's toilette was the most tiring and unrewarding of the duties my mother was called on to perform. . . . The arrangement of her hair and headdress were for my mother an all too frequent source of vexation and distress. . . . . Maria Theresa's figure, which was truly of the greatest beauty, and how it might be displayed to its best advantage, preoccupied her far more than would normally be expected of a lady . . . of such esprit, such manly fortitude. . . . My mother

spent her most dismal hours at the Empress's toilette or applying her decoration. . . . Often—very often—a bonnet had to be attached differently four or five times before it met with the mistress's approval. . . . The same could be said of her coiffure. The exalted lady yanked, tugged, and plucked away at her coiffure so vigorously, and for so long, that it came undone and had to be started all over again, which, given the style of coiffure in vogue at the time, usually resulted in its total destruction, so that her hair had to be straightened out and frequently wrapped again in curlpapers and recurled.[171]

This memory cannot have been entirely false, since Khevenhüller also occasionally reports through gritted teeth that the empress stayed away from apartment or open table because her hair could not be curled in time,[172] or because her toilette did not turn out well and she did not wish to appear badly made up in public.[173] Maria Theresa herself warned her children not to spend hours in the dressing room, but she also kept up with the latest fashions and criticized her daughters if she found anything amiss in their clothing or hairstyle. Their wardrobe, she declared, should be neither too eccentric nor too casual, their décolleté not too low, their wigs not too bouffant. In her judgments on her children's appearance, she could be severe to the point of callousness. "Marie has never known how to deport herself well," she once wrote.[174] She reproached Marie Antoinette with piling on the pounds before her time and not cleaning her teeth properly. She never doubted the importance of outward appearances: "Do not allow yourself the slightest negligence in your appearance or in questions of representation."[175]

It would be a mistake to read such remarks as a sign of personal vanity. They reveal instead a simple insight into the need to stage the sovereign body as such. The monarch's public appearance was a state affair.[176] The majestic impression produced by the queen in grand gala, *en grande parure*, was not to be had for nothing; it required time, patient chambermaids, and iron self-discipline. Maria Theresa could not squeeze unassisted into a robe of state such as those worn in her official portraits; she had to be assisted into it piece by piece. Once she had it on, it imposed enormous constraints on her freedom of movement. The *grande parure* produced a majestic deportment all by itself, practically forcing its wearer to adopt an aristocratic bearing. In the mid-eighteenth century, a noblewoman's gown consisted essentially of a laced bodice, *la taille*, and two overhanging skirts, the lower one fully enclosed, the upper, *le manteau*, with a slit at the front, pinned up at the back or sides, and supported by bustles or hoops made of metal, wood, or whalebone, mostly with a train attached. Several underskirts were worn underneath. The bodice, usually tapered at the front, featured a large décolletage; the half-length sleeves ended in frills. Bodices were supported inside by struts and tightened by the maid in several stages.

The viewer's gaze fell not just on a woman's face, neck, and décolletage but also, and above all, on her arms and hands. Courtly fashion dictated that these parts of the body be exposed, framed, and put on display—not the legs, which could be bared by men alone. Short, bunched-up skirts were characteristic of women from the working class. Ladies of distinction could, however, let their feet be seen under their dresses; shod in pointed shoes with high heels, they should be as small and dainty as possible. No limits were set on decoration. The entire gown could be adorned with braids, ribbons, flowers, embroidery, lacework, flounces, and pompoms, not infrequently with precious gems and diamonds as well. The materials decorated in this way were heavy silk brocades worked through with gold and silver thread. In the second half of the century, skirts grew shorter and wigs ever more elaborate.[177] In Paris, hairdressing rose to a high art, both literally and figuratively: hair was piled up to unprecedented heights with frames made from wire, felt, or straw, and decorated with feathers, flowers, or even whole sculptures. Women tottering under such headgear could hardly go out for a stroll, let alone ride in a coach, and even sitting down could be difficult. With their bulging hooped skirts, doorways could be negotiated only by moving sideways. In all, it could take two to three hours to get dressed. The English traveler Lady Mary Coke began her toilette at nine o'clock if she had a midday appointment at court.[178] The ordeal was so laborious and time-consuming that ladies sometimes had no time to go to bed after a ball if they were expected at court the next morning.[179] The everyday alternative to gala dress were various forms of negligee, which despite the

FIGURE 29. *Affectation and Nature.* Copperplate by Daniel Chodewiecki, 1779/80

name were only marginally more casual. Ladies were then said to appear *en sac* rather than *en robe.* The most *popular sac* was the Andrienne or Volante. Here the bodice and skirt were cut from the same piece, with a loose pleat dropping down to the ground at the back. These simpler dresses brought a bourgeois note to court, as indicated by some of the names they were given: a less ornate, more modest variant of the hoop skirt was called Janseniste, after the Catholic reform movement to which many members of the French *noblesse de robe* belonged.[180]

Fashion for men at court resembled that for women in materials, colors, and decoration. Brightly patterned velvet and silk, lace braid, silver, gold, and diamonds were by no means reserved for ladies. Cavaliers sported body-hugging, tight-fitting breeches and silk stockings, heeled shoes, vests, slim jerkins, and lace jabots, as well as wigs and ribbons in their hair; many applied perfume, rouge, and powder and used hand-held fans. The bourgeois culture of the revolutionary period would dictate that men dress completely differently from women, making the noble cavaliers of the ancien régime seem decadent and effeminate in retrospect. The Viennese court was conservative; Charles VI had prescribed the traditional Spanish *Mantelkleid* as obligatory court dress in conscious defiance of French fashion. It consisted of a richly embroidered jerkin with a cloak, breeches, and feather hat.[181] In Vienna any apparent excess or affectation in male or female fashion smacked of French influence. In the 1750s it gave away those who favored an alliance with the French court, or even read dangerous French books. State Chancellor Kaunitz was the leader of this Francophile party. For all his eccentricity, he set the new tone in matters of both taste and politics. His fastidious and idiosyncratic sense of fashion gave his opponents plenty of ammunition. He was said to "disperse twenty pounds of powder into the air in his room and then walk up and down for an hour, so that every hair in his peruke is evenly coated and none has a grain more than any other."[182] The three small brushes he carried with him at all times were the stuff of legend: one for his tobacco containers, one for the diamonds he wore on his clothing, and one for brushing his teeth at table, an operation considered by a dumbfounded English visitor to be the most disgusting he had ever witnessed.[183] "He would probably use rouge and beauty spots if he dared," his enemies scoffed.[184] For her part, the empress associated make-up with erotic indulgence and therefore forbade her daughters from wearing it at her own court, although she made an exception if it was customary in the country they married into, or if their husbands made them wear it.[185] She would have preferred to ban it altogether at home; indeed, she did just that following the death of her husband, although this ban, like so many others, proved unenforceable.[186]

Maria Theresa's rude health and aversion to stuffy, overheated rooms—always a problem given the swarms of people and countless candles lit in the ceremonial apartments—were proverbial.[187] In this she was following, no doubt unwittingly, the Enlightenment discourse on hygiene. Inspired by Rousseau's motto, "Back to nature," fashionable authors of the time turned against powders, pomades, and periwigs and preached the virtues of fresh air and cold water. They reflected a

fundamental paradigm shift in attitudes to cleanliness and personal hygiene.[188] Water had traditionally been viewed as a health hazard. Since
the skin was considered to be porous, hot water could easily cause
harmful agents to enter the body and disturb the balance of humors.
Bathing was therefore best avoided. Only the face and hands were
washed with any regularity, while the rest of the body was rubbed down
with dry towels. The higher estates demonstrated their cleanliness
through frequent changes of undergarments. The finest and whitest
linen, visible to the outside world in protruding cuffs and collars, was a
key sign of social distinction: a steady supply of spotless, snow-white
linen presupposed immense reserves of domestic labor. At the Viennese
court each member of the royal family needed at least one full-time
washerwoman whose responsibilities were confined to whites. The idea
that cleanliness might primarily involve washing the body with water
only emerged in the course of the eighteenth century. Even then, warm
baths continued to be frowned on, associated as they were with oriental
sensuality, dissipation, and idleness.[189]

The entire system of cultural coordinates was going through a fundamental transformation in Maria Theresa's time, with personal hygiene
playing a central role. Hygiene regimes carried different moral connotations. The new frontline ran between masculine-ascetic hardness and
effeminate softness, virtue and vice, enlightened young firebrands and
hidebound traditionalists at court. Calls were already being heard for a
gust of fresh air to blow away the accumulated stuffiness of a thousand
years. In retrospect, Maria Theresa appeared as the pioneer of a new
form of physical discipline that, in reality, would have meant very little
to her. Caroline Pichler wrote in the mid-nineteenth century that the
empress, "despite her high birth and the royal luster that surrounded her
from the cradle, was far from weak with regard to her own body, nor was
she immoderate in her pleasures. She almost never allowed rooms to be
heated, she had no fear of drafts, . . . and even in winter a window often
stood open next to her writing table, through which the wind would
drive snow onto my mother's papers. And just as she was strict towards
herself, detesting every infirmity or debility of the body, so too she
hated all weakness and softness of the soul."[190] In other words, Maria

Theresa's robust constitution was interpreted in hindsight as the external sign of her spiritual virtues, her physical strength equated with moral rectitude. With that, a further mosaic tile was added to the image of the modern, quasi-bourgeois monarch.

In fact, it was precisely courtly fashion that called for the greatest physical self-discipline. This is why the new avant-garde ethos rejected courtly strictures on dress, favoring a plain, unfussy, bourgeois wardrobe in muted colors. Thinkers of the radical Enlightenment regarded sartorial codes as the epitome of social inequality, since nothing showed up differences between the estates as vividly as their clothing. In 1778 the philosopher-prince Voltaire was memorialized in dressing gown and nightcap; he was even painted standing on one leg with his trousers at half-mast, a pose that demonstrated the utmost contempt for social convention.[191] The message was that there were no class distinctions in a nightshirt; nakedness symbolized man in the innocence of the state of nature, transcending all cultural differences.

The courtly cosmos, on the other hand, with its finely graded social distinctions, demanded an extremely precise sartorial code if it was to continue functioning. Clothing varied according to a person's office and standing, but also depending on time and place. Lower court servants wore colorful livery, "half-noble" learned councillors appeared in plain black, officers sported their regimental uniforms.[192] Nobles were permitted and indeed obliged to wear gala attire to "solemnities" at court: Spanish coat dress for the men, ceremonious gowns for the women. Just how precise and sophisticated the symbolic grammar of clothing could be is shown by the court ceremonial prescribed for mourning. The "court lamentation order" issued by Maria Theresa in 1750 distinguished no fewer than nine classes of mourning, depending on how closely the deceased was related to the Archducal House. A bereavement of the fourth class—that is, one marking the loss to the imperial couple of stepchildren and grandchildren, nephews and nieces, sons- and daughters-in-law, uncles and aunts—dictated that "ladies appear in fringed black silk dresses, with black and white fans and shoes, cavaliers in cloth, but with silk buttons and buttonholes and frilled undershirts, black swords, and buckles."[193] This regime lasted only the first three weeks. Other details were prescribed for the next three weeks, and so on for the nine different classes of bereavement. Because this was inordinately expensive for all concerned, courtiers were paid a "mourning allowance." Such nuances may strike us as bizarre today, but they were important in making visible the social differences—here, the degree of proximity to the dynasty— that defined the structure of aristocratic society.

Above all, clothing showed off wealth and magnificence, qualities in which the great courts vied to outdo each other. Gala days were practically defined by the obligation to wear gala clothing, which constituted an essential part of their festive glamor. Written invitations were sent out and "gala announced" for all special occasions. Outside the Hofburg, the rules were relaxed somewhat in the so-called rustic gala. If a lady nonetheless appeared *en sac*, avoiding wearing the tight-fitting bodice "for the sake of comfort"—particularly understandable if she was pregnant—she risked being turned away at the door.[194] This strict dress code was double edged: members of the high nobility belonged by rights to the court but might find gala days too onerous and prefer to stay at home. Those of lesser status, however, placed greater value on admission and were therefore more willing to dress up for the occasion and bear the associated costs. But the imperial court derived its glory and honor from the most eminent grandees; their presence was indispensable. Different standards were therefore upheld for *Zutrittsfrauen*—ladies who had free access to the court and were permitted to dine at the royal table—and *Stundfrauen*, those admitted only at the hours set for apartment. The former, who included the highest female office-holders at court and the wives of their male counterparts, were often allowed to attend the empress in more informal "Andriennes"; the latter were expected to wear full gowns.[195] Outside the court, however, cumbersome hooped skirts increasingly fell out of fashion. Finally, the privilege of appearing *en sac* had to be extended to others as well, "for want of gala clothing or on account of old age," for example.[196] The trend proved irreversible. The winter of 1758–59 saw the introduction of the "small apartment," at which all ladies were now allowed to appear *en sac*.[197]

Courtly fashion was not least a question of economics. Even in her widowhood, Maria Theresa spent at least 30,000 guilders each year on her wardrobe.[198] Yet cash was in notoriously short supply at court; the elaborate gala clothes were beyond the means of many nobles, forcing them to fall heavily into debt. They therefore devised ingenious ways to recycle the valuable raw materials from which the clothes were made. *Parfilage* was a popular pastime among Viennese court ladies in the 1770s: they would sit together at apartment pulling golden threads out of discarded clothes, braids, and fabrics. Some noblewomen always carried around with them a pouch in which they collected such threads for later sale.[199] Courtiers thought nothing of converting the valuable gifts bestowed on them by the empress—typically, diamond-studded tobacco boxes illustrated with her portrait—into cash.[200] This trade was organized by so-called *faiseuses d'affaires* or *revendeuses à la toilette*, women who dealt in all kinds of rare commodities and could provide courtiers with ready money.[201] They performed an important function for those whose high status confronted them with a fundamental contradiction: while their honor demanded that they lead a lavish lifestyle and ostensibly pay no heed to cost, such profligate expenditure could eventually stretch their resources to breaking point and deprive the aristocratic way of life of its material basis. Life at court was extremely expensive, the rewards often uncertain. Nobles from less prosperous families had to weigh up whether they were prepared to risk partaking in the glory and honor of the court, and they could only hope that their investment would pay off in the long run.

Solemnities and Diversions

According to traditional Spanish ceremonial, the imperial family dined alone, under the watchful eyes of court society, foreign emissaries, and selected subjects.[202] The imperial couple sat on cushioned chairs upholstered in gold brocade beneath a golden baldachin, their children to their right and left, and ate from golden dishes while everyone else looked on. Prayers were said before and after the meal. The lord high steward himself oversaw dinner service, pulling out the emperor's chair, replenishing finger bowls, and distributing napkins. The innumerable dishes were brought in by pages, cupbearers, stewards, and carvers, winding their way through half the castle "in orderly fashion and in single file." The cupbearer first tasted the wine before serving it "on bended knee."[203] *Epergnes*—decorative centerpieces for the dining table—featured ornate allegorical motifs befitting the occasion. They were masterpieces of confectionery, an ephemeral and highly elaborate courtly art form.[204] Every detail, every gesture at "open table" had symbolic character and redounded to the greater glory of the monarchy.

Much to Khevenhüller's dismay, however, these majestically solitary ceremonial dinners became ever less frequent. From the winter of 1754, at the latest, they took place only on Sundays following public divine service.[205] Instead, Maria Theresa increasingly dined *en compagnie* with the high nobility in the Knights' Room at the Hofburg, or in the Garden Hall or Great Gallery at Schönbrunn. Over a hundred places might be set and numerous spectators admitted on such occasions. But there was also scope for unlimited degrees of exclusiveness and informality, all the way down to the *table de conspiration* in the queen's cabinet, where an ingeniously constructed table could be winched down so that not even chamber personnel would disturb the intimate gathering.[206] The more select the company, the greater the symbolic value of dining with the ruling family. Maria Theresa used this instrument in a very targeted way to distribute finely graded favors. At the beginning of each season she provided the lord high chamberlain with a handwritten list of people who could be invited to table one or more times a week.[207] The "half-nobility," that is, ennobled learned councillors and their wives, were excluded from this company; even close confidants such as Bartenstein or Koch were not excepted.[208] Anyone who turned up uninvited was discreetly shown the door by a court official.[209]

Maria Theresa had an interest in ensuring that her table retained its allure for the high nobility. This was far from guaranteed. Time and again she registered her disapproval that on gala days "so few ladies were seen at luncheon," even though one or two tables had been set for "more august nobles of both sexes."[210] The invitation lists were deliberately kept secret to conceal who had *not* put in an appearance. Efforts were made to avoid invitees feeling under pressure and "the entertainment thereby . . . degenerating into a ceremonious and hence awkward dinner service."[211] Maria Theresa was prepared to make concessions to the high nobility to make them feel more at ease in her company. Doing away with uncomfortable gala dress was just one example. The advice she gave her children shows the importance she attached to keeping the court nobility on side. "A single mistake can undo a hundred other favors," she warned her son Ferdinand, who had once offended the chief lady-in-waiting by disregarding the seating order at his table.[212]

Away from the table, too, enticing enough high-ranking nobles to take part in court festivities and amusements could be difficult. The same problem affected events held during the winter festive season, when the rules were every bit as strict as at other times of the year. From the beginning of January until the start of the pre-Easter fasting period, a *redoute*, or closed ball, regularly took place in the Hofburg on two evenings a week, alternating on two other evenings with an exclusive children's ball. Special sleigh rides were organized—weather permitting, but with artificially conserved snow, if necessary—where courtiers presented themselves to each other and to the urban public in the greatest possible splendor.[213] Couples were drawn beforehand by lot; the cavalier was expected to foot the bill for a ceremonial sleigh, equipage, and servants (including uniforms), as well as elaborate, purpose-made costumes for himself and his partner, so that costs could easily run to three thousand guilders per person. Neither the sleigh rides nor the balls should be imagined as wild bacchanalian revelries; they were formal, expensive, and often dreary affairs marred by constant disputes over precedence. Even under Charles VI, travelers had observed that such events were "less jolly than at other courts owing to the strict ceremonial"; it proved difficult to "bring together enough couples, and the emperor had to order several chamberlains to make up the numbers."[214] If these festivities had already lost much of their appeal under Charles VI, this was even more so the case during Maria Theresa's reign. Even Khevenhüller found the sleigh rides tedious but "dare[d] not absent" himself.[215] Those who took part in such "delectations" therefore did so primarily to advance their careers. Otherwise they preferred to stay away, forcing the lord high chamberlain to lower admission standards. Because so many high-ranking females excused themselves, in the end even widows of chamberlains and wives of privy councillors were allowed in. Even so, many cavaliers were still unable to find a partner, as Khevenhüller peevishly remarked.[216]

Other problems arose in connection with the great balls at Carnival season. Two balls were held each week at court, alternating with exclusive functions in the Mehlgrube. A perennial source of "indecency, squabbling, and immodesty" was the question of masquerade.[217] During Charles VI's reign there had been no masked balls in Vienna.[218] Francis Stephen knew the custom from his time in Tuscany and now implored his wife to lift the ban. For his sake, in the winter of 1742–43 Maria Theresa solicited written opinions from her ministers and eventually decided to allow masks at grand balls held in the theater, "yet with many restrictions" and solely for the "great nobility." The "half-nobility" was reluctantly given permission to attend these balls as well, but only unmasked.[219] Perhaps Maria Theresa soon came to regret this concession to her husband's thirst for entertainment; at any rate, masked balls were targeted by the chastity campaign she launched in 1748. The organization of balls in the court theater was now entrusted to the officer Rocco de lo Presti, while nobles were no longer allowed to wear masks in the Mehlgrube, where they were more difficult to supervise. To make this bitter pill a little easier for them to swallow, she withdrew permission for the "half-nobility" to be admitted there.[220] The topic reappeared on the agenda every winter; restrictions were periodically reinforced.[221] When it came to festivities outside the Hofburg, too, "the court provided guidance and everything was organized by the Directory, which had to keep the queen informed of all the minutiae and submit to her a daily list of the masked people attending the redoute."[222] As she grew older, the empress increasingly stayed away from masked balls or at least retired early, leaving a chamberlain to make sure that the evening continued "in orderly fashion" and was over by one o'clock.[223] It is not hard to see why private Carnival festivities—with or without the ban on masquerades—were much more popular.

The problem of diminishing appeal least affected the hunting season at Laxenburg, where the inner court regularly spent several weeks early in the year and in the autumn. Interest in this aristocratic pursuit never

FIGURE 30. Maria Theresa playing cards with Batthyány, Nádasdy and Daun.
Anonymous drawing, 1751

seems to have flagged, in part because the circle of participants was especially exclusive, in part because reduced ceremonial standards obtained *en campagne*. Because Maria Theresa, unlike her husband, had no
interest in hunting, she rarely took part herself, which no doubt did
much to make everyone else feel more at ease.

The empress was, however, a keen gambler, even in the years after the
War of Succession, when other pastimes such as dancing and riding had
long ceased to amuse her.[224] Her preference was for card games such as
faro, lansquenet, piquet, tric trac, ombre, or the fashionable new English
game of loo (or lanterloo). Francis Stephen also had a liking for billiards.
Playing cards was not only Maria Theresa's favorite pastime at her evening apartments; it was also an opportunity for the court nobility to
associate with her on a relatively relaxed, informal footing.[225] Gambling
was also in keeping with the casual disregard for money and carefree
spending projected by the aristocracy as an essential part of its self-
image.[226] Yet these regular evenings were not a source of undiluted pleasure for everyone. As early as 1744, Khevenhüller observed that "very

few" courtiers were making an appearance: "apart from the queen, there is sometimes only a single card table."[227] And four years later he grumbled that "when there is an opera in the city, very few ladies appear, and even they generally tend to run away before the Empress has finished her game, which is why [Maria Theresa] recently flew into a rage on that account and publicly expressed her displeasure."[228] There were presumably several reasons for this lack of enthusiasm: for some Maria Theresa's cards evenings were too expensive, for others too boring.

Games of chance of many kinds were played for high stakes by the nobility but repeatedly banned for subjects. When, in the winter of 1743, it was suggested that gambling might be "introduced in public," that is, legalized at least in noble private salons, Maria Theresa made known her opposition to the move and renewed her "strict interdiction," although hardly anyone took it seriously.[229] At court, by contrast, she appeared to delight in driving the sums wagered to dizzying heights, knowing that she could draw at any time from the unlimited supply of funds placed at her disposal by her paymaster. Francis Stephen and his brother Charles were also known to be passionate gamblers and likewise had access to the necessary resources, making games potentially ruinous for other players.[230] This was a subject of frequent complaint for Khevenhüller, who felt obliged to play along *par complaisance*, even though he was appallingly bad at card games and hated risk of any kind. In the winter of 1743–44 several high-ranking courtiers formed an exclusive gambling syndicate with a common bank to which each had "contributed a very substantial sum." Khevenhüller joined in, not "to make a great profit, but rather to amuse the queen and keep her away from disreputable playing companions."[231] The venture was not a success; the bank went bust soon after, not least because Maria Theresa seems to have exploited her high position to her strategic advantage. According to Khevenhüller, she did not like to see the banker end the game until she had recouped her losses, and who would dare refuse her a favor?[232] The unwritten rules of aristocratic fairness stipulated that a player not stand up from the gambling table immediately after a winning streak. Prince Ligne also found that the empress subtly took advantage of her tablemates: "Even if she acted as if she did not care for winning, fortune smiled on her. Once she had amassed mountains of ducats she gathered them in, suddenly remembering that she had an audience to attend or papers to sign. The banker was inconsolable to see his entire kitty disappear. When she became aware of this the next day, she laughed, grew irritated, but quickly assigned to respectable people the proceeds she had perhaps won from a cheat."[233] In a handwritten note to Khevenhüller from July 1744, Maria Theresa herself confessed with an air of contrition to having driven the syndicate to bankruptcy: "I have ruined the banque and now great confusion has arisen as a result, of which I am perhaps the cause."[234]

Gambling at court went on all the same; a new fund was set up and enormous sums of money continued to change hands. Not until the winter of 1757–58 did Maria Theresa allow herself to be convinced of the devastating consequences that would ensue if the court continued to set a bad example for her subjects. "Having frequently and forcefully been told of how excesses were mounting day by day, to the point where in public coffeehouses and taverns, and even among townspeople and craftsmen, faro was played almost all day long, the empress suddenly resolved to renew the old bans on the practice; and, in order to set a good example, the same game (for all that she loved it more than any other) was also abolished at court and lansquenet played instead."[235] The push for gambling to be banned at court, however, seems to have had more to do with fear of financial ruin than with its corrupting influence on subjects. After the second gambling consortium likewise went bankrupt—Khevenhüller alone had invested and lost some ten thousand guilders—not enough courtiers could be found to start a new one.[236] Yet that did not put an end to gambling at court. Far from it: Maria Theresa now discovered that she could generate additional revenue by charging for the privilege. In January 1759 she allowed the nobility to play faro in the court theater under certain conditions, using the proceeds to subsidize commercially unviable theatrical productions.[237]

After Francis Stephen's death, when the atmosphere at court changed fundamentally in every respect—Joseph II never gambled as a matter of principle—all gambling games were once again "strictly forbidden," this time for good.[238] Again, this did not mean that the ban was effective. The English traveler Lady Coke reported in the 1770s that high-stakes gambling was still a fixture of life at court.[239] Maria Theresa herself, however, had become a bitter opponent. Writing to Marie Antoinette in Versailles, she implored her daughter to stop playing cards into the small hours of the morning. It would ruin her health, her looks, and the happiness of her marriage, attract bad company, and only bring her losses in the long run: "You have to free yourself of this passion with a jolt; no one can give you better advice on this than I, who was once in the same situation."[240]

Apart from gambling, hunting, dancing, and visits to the theater, there were not many amusements deemed suitable for the aristocracy. When card games were banished from Maria Theresa's apartments, this made the prospect of an evening spent in her company even less attractive. There were many rival gatherings in nobles' private residences, where both the etiquette and the topics of conversation were considerably less stuffy. If we look, for example, at what the young Karl Count Zinzendorf, a protégé of Kaunitz, had to say about the numerous private soirées he attended in the early 1760s, then it becomes clear why Maria Theresa's apartments were found wanting. In private circles, not only could everyone keep gambling to their heart's content, they could also freely discuss the latest affairs, intrigues, and scandals, as well as the latest writings of Voltaire and Rousseau or the infamous encyclopedia of Diderot and d'Alembert—all of which were officially forbidden.[241] The empress tolerated neither gossip, affairs, and sexual impropriety nor illicit literature in her environs. Over time, this did increasing damage to the relationship of many nobles—not just critical bourgeois outsiders—to Maria Theresa's court and its avenues for sociability. Many found the atmosphere too stifling, too prudish, too rigid, and too pious for their liking.

Music and theater were the exceptions. What entertained and distracted court society above all else were Italian operas, French comedies, *Stegreifstücke* (a burlesque German version of commedia dell'arte), ballet divertimenti, and every conceivable mixed form. Theatrical genres blended into each other, but the borders were also porous between castle and stage, between ball and theater, between the noble public on the one hand and singers and actors on the other. For generations, Maria Theresa's ancestors had devoted themselves to music with considerable talent and connoisseurship, and she herself carried on the family tradition. Court society put itself on stage in artistic form, with courtiers being at once consummate actors and their own public.[242] Baroque musical theater was traditionally a central element of court festive culture and—after architecture—certainly the most expensive. An army of musicians, singers, dancers, painters, and machinists worked to glorify the monarchy. The Theatralstaat, the body of professional theatrical personnel, was included among the liveried court servants; performances took place in the royal residence. Works were commissioned and composed for dynastic festivals—marriages, birthdays, name days, gala days of all kinds. Something of the luster of these performances was subsequently captured in sumptuously illustrated ceremonial descriptions (*Festbeschreibungen*). The paradigmatic courtly genre was the *opera seria*. With plots typically drawn from ancient mythology, these operas showcased tragic entanglements, aristocratic virtues, and heroic, larger-than-life emotions (*affetti generosi*). They usually ended by paying homage to the godlike ruler. Wedding operas, in particular, were pompous, grand affairs that drew the European noble public's attention to the new dynastic union and the blessings it would rain on the houses concerned. To this end, no expense was spared. The last great Baroque opera of this kind was *Ipermestra*, written by the celebrated court poet Metastasio, set to music by the court kapellmeister Johann Adolf Hasse, and performed in the old Leopoldine court theater on January 8, 1744, in the middle of the War of the Austrian Succession, to mark the wedding of Francis Stephen's brother, Charles, to Maria Theresa's sister, Marianna, and to celebrate the dual alliance of the houses of Habsburg and Lorraine with all conceivable pomp and splendor. Maria Theresa had originally planned to have the opera performed by a company of noble ladies and cavaliers. "But this intention was thwarted by the concern that having a reigning queen appear in a spectacle would violate decorum, although we otherwise tend not to be so austere in this regard and could have referred to the example of Louis XIV, who danced in public when comedies were given."[243]

Such grand festive events were only the tip of a much broader culture of performance. Whether sung, danced, or spoken, theater was an integral part of everyday life at court. Noble dilettanti were not yet belittled and disparaged. Just as Maria Theresa had performed in the court theater as a young girl, so too she allowed her own children to appear on stage on dynastic gala days.[244] Members of court society rehearsed alongside paid court musicians and sang, danced, and acted with them at exclusive chamber festivals (*Kammerfeste*), at times with extraordinary virtuosity. The stages on which they performed were not confined to dedicated theater buildings; they could be put up anywhere in the state rooms of the residences, while theaters, conversely, were also used for masked balls, redoutes, and gambling. Nobles behaved at the theater in much the same way they behaved in the royal apartment: they went in and out, played cards, ate and drank, paid each other visits in their boxes, and amused themselves as best they could. Concentrated artistic pleasure and sustained applause for the artists at the end were not the rule. In short, court society had an entirely different, more familiar relationship to music and the theater than that which characterized nineteenth-century bourgeois society. Art was not yet what it would become for the educated middle class: an autonomous, rarefied, quasi-sacral sphere to be approached and aesthetically appreciated in an attitude of reverential contemplation.

From mid-century this late Baroque theatrical culture underwent a fundamental transformation. Like other previously exclusive courtly amusements such as princely hunting grounds and parks, curiosity cabinets, libraries, and picture galleries, the court theater was increasingly opened up to the general public and assumed a different role. Maria Theresa herself contributed significantly to this shift near the beginning of her reign when she ordered an old ballroom at the Michaelerplatz to be converted into a theater. The new house "next to the [Hof]Burg"— today's Burgtheater—was ceremoniously opened on her birthday on May 14, 1748. It contained boxes for the imperial family and was used by the court, but it was also made available to the public on other days. Maria Theresa later acquired the second public theater in Vienna, the "Theater am Kärntnerthor," where commedia dell'arte was traditionally offered in local dialect, whereas Italian and French comedies and operas formed the core repertoire of the Burgtheater. Management of Vienna's theater scene as a whole was leased out to privileged nobles or noble syndicates under the direction of the court. Various financing models were trialed, yet despite admission fees, gambling licenses, and high subsidies from the court, the theaters always ran at a loss, plunging several leaseholders into financial ruin.[245]

Maria Theresa also had new theaters built at Schönbrunn (1747) and Laxenburg (1753), although these were reserved for the aristocracy. Whenever and wherever ladies and cavaliers put on performances, the general public continued to be excluded.[246] The new-fangled, publicly accessible Burgtheater, on the other hand, created new problems of delimitation, order, and control. Whereas members of the ruling family were normally seated in the front row of the parterre at the court theater, in the public theater they needed to be raised above common spectators in boxes of their own. Maria Theresa took this very seriously indeed, as evident from the instructions she wrote for her children's courts. She thus stipulated that they should never go to the theater with fewer than two carriages and a minimum number of retainers, while in the box they should always appear with the captain of the lifeguard, two chamberlains, and two ladies-in-waiting, at the very least. They could invite foreign guests into their box, provided they "were frequently rotated so that it did not become an obligation." Above all, she warned her children never to stray into other boxes, the gallery, or the parterre, "since you should not approach others, they should always approach you."[247] Whenever the ruling family attended a public performance on a festive occasion, the question of who was to be admitted and where they should be seated became pressing. Admission fell in the lord high chamberlain's area of responsibility, so Khevenhüller found himself constantly struggling with thorny issues of access and precedence.[248] In the 1758–59 theatrical season, when the area in the parterre reserved for the paying public was expanded, the problem arose that "the box of the young lords and ladies [Maria Theresa's children] would have looked directly out over the heads of the populace— this was considered unseemly." The empress therefore ordered her children's box to be moved further away from the common people.[249]

During Maria Theresa's reign, the theatrical world—whether opera, theater, or ballet—underwent a series of revolutionary changes that divided the viewing public. Moves to banish the old spirit of the late Baroque from all genres were not to everyone's liking. In the 1750s the new theater director Giacomo, Count Durazzo, supported by Kaunitz, imported the latest innovation of opéra comique from Paris, where it had similarly polarized public opinion. In the 1760s Christoph Willibald Gluck, court composer since 1754, purged opera of all "excessive ornament" and placed music entirely in the service of the libretto; music should "serve the poetry by intensifying the expression of the sentiment, without interrupting the action."[250] The dancing masters Gasparo Angiolini and Jean-Georges Noverre created a new, expressive pantomime ballet as an art form in its own right, intended to provide "a living painting of the passions, mores, and customs of all the nations on earth."[251] At the same time, the imperial-royal counselor, professor of cameralistics, and publicist Joseph von Sonnenfels opened a heated controversy on plays in the vernacular, which were to be cleansed of their "mad buffoonery" and transformed into serious, morally edifying theater along the lines suggested by Gotthold Ephraim Lessing.[252] What all these artistic upheavals, however various their sources and however different their objects may have been, had in common was that they increasingly flattened the traditional opposition between high and low genres, mirroring the chasm between upper and lower classes. Here as there, all extraneous, "unnatural" opulence was to be eliminated, tragic and comical extremes avoided, and "true feeling" brought onto the stage in their stead, in keeping with the taste of a growing public from the educated middle class.[253] Viennese court society was not unaffected by these controversies.[254]

Very few of Maria Theresa's aesthetic judgments have survived; she hardly ever mentioned operatic and theatrical performances in her letters, despite her own musical talent and the interest she took in her children's performances. She occasionally pronounced brief, apodictic verdicts, although these do not give the impression that she was particularly engaged by the artistic controversies of her time. She found a ballet of Angiolini's poor, even impertinent, yet judged Noverre less harshly.[255]

In a letter of recommendation to her daughter-in-law in Milan, she once praised her old music teacher, Johann Adolph Hasse, as her favorite composer; he was "the first to make music lighter and more agreeable."[256] On another occasion, however, she claimed to prefer Italian opera to all Viennese composers, whether Gassmann, Salieri, or Gluck: "They can occasionally write one or two pretty numbers, but in general I always prefer the Italians. In instrumental music there is a certain Haydn who has some peculiar ideas, but he is only just getting started."[257] Beyond dynastic celebrations and noble chamber festivals, she seems to have regarded the theater primarily as a moral problem.[258] On the one hand, it was clear to her that she could not ban "spectacles" outright; they were simply too popular among all of society. On the other, they threatened to open the floodgates to immorality, and forceful measures were needed to stop this from happening. As early as 1748, when Rocco de lo Presti assumed control of Vienna's theaters, she made him promise to uphold high moral standards on the stage. In 1752, when de lo Presti had gone bankrupt and been replaced by Durazzo,[259] she issued a general "edict on holding public spectacles" which massively reduced the number of days when plays could be performed and was intended to stamp out the worst excesses on stage. It was decreed there, inter alia, that no comedies be performed "other than those from the French or Italian or Spanish theater, all local compositions . . . be completely abolished, . . . and no equivocal or foul language be permitted, also, that players caught using the same not go unpunished."[260] The decree was directed against the German-language equivalent of the commedia dell'arte, which, because it was largely improvised, slipped through the cracks of literary censorship and was hard to control. Yet, in her eyes, French theater was hardly less suspect.

Following Francis Stephen's death, all theatrical entertainments were temporarily suspended. In 1767, when Kaunitz sought to engage a French troupe and take on the role of intendant himself with the backing of a shady investor named d'Afflisio, Maria Theresa was aghast. She implored him to engage d'Afflisio as impresario only under the strictest conditions. The contract with him would be declared null and void "if he does not observe decency at all times, both with regard to the performances and the personnel used in them." Her chief concern was thus with immorality both on and off the stage. Kaunitz had to assure the empress that he would "never visit or receive any of these women and girls"; d'Afflisio was also never to appear in public as director or approach her son, the emperor. Only under these conditions was she prepared to sign the contract with the investor, "albeit with trembling hand." On no account should the state chancellor himself or any other senior court official involve himself directly in a production: "Your names are too respectable and precious to be associated with the lowest elements in the monarchy."[261] With the exception of chamber festivals, Maria Theresa increasingly turned her back on the theater. During the Seven Years' War, and particularly after her husband's death, she apparently lost all interest in theater-going and hardly ever put in an appearance.[262] The idea that precisely the public theater, this teeming hotbed of vice, might be transformed into a moral institution for all classes seems no longer to have occurred to her. At any rate, it was Joseph who in 1776 abolished all theater privileges, opened the path for private patronage, and renamed the Burgtheater as Imperial-Royal Court and National Theater.[263]

Knights of the Round Table

Like many other solemnities in Vienna, the grand festive gathering held in the parterre of the Schönbrunn theater to mark the marriage of Joseph, heir to the Habsburg throne, to the Infanta Isabella of Parma, was commemorated by court painter van Meytens in a monumental ceremonial canvas (fig. 26). On closer inspection, we notice that the emperor and the heir to his right, the little Archdukes on the left and right, as well as several cavaliers are wearing a red chain with golden insignia around their necks. Such a ceremonial painting purported to have documentary value: contemporary observers who saw the image at court knew exactly who was depicted there and who was entitled to wear this decoration. The decoration in question was the symbol of the Order of the Golden Fleece, the Noble Ordre de la Toison d'Or.[264] It represented the fleece of the golden ram from the Argonaut saga, which Philip the

Good, Duke of Burgundy, chose as the symbol for the secular order he founded in 1430. He had gathered around him an exclusive community of thirty knights to defend the faith and champion the virtues of chivalry. By the eighteenth century such noble chivalric orders had proliferated. Each court had established its own—the Order of the Garter in London, the Order of the Holy Spirit in Versailles, the Order of the Black Eagle in Berlin, the Order of the Elephant in Copenhagen, and so on. Yet none was so venerable and prestigious as the Order of the Golden Fleece, which had assumed almost mythic stature over the centuries.[265] The Spanish Habsburgs had inherited leadership of the order from the dukes of Burgundy. Following the extinction of the line in 1700, Maria Theresa's father, Charles VI, had claimed the role of head of the order as part of the Spanish inheritance. Although his bid for the inheritance had failed, he succeeded in transplanting the order to Vienna. From 1711 he revived the old Burgundian tradition in all its glory, making induction into that select company the single most coveted distinction among the nobility. The number of knights was capped at fifty. Only members of the high nobility who followed the one true (i.e., Catholic) faith and whose impeccable pedigree could be traced back three generations were eligible for admission. Late-medieval orders were based on the idea of chivalrous virtue and equality; an order's head was considered *primus inter pares*. Charles VI built on this tradition. He met regularly with his knights at order festivals (*Ordensfeste*), above all the festival of the order's patron St. Andreas on November 9 and at the turn of the year. Between December 20 and January 6 a whole series of toison services and toison vespers (from the French *toison*, fleece) took place. Knights appeared in their red velvet, gold-embroidered dress uniforms and order collars to join with the emperor in prayer and at table. On all other festive occasions at the imperial court, too, the toisonists enjoyed extraordinary privileges that visibly marked them out as the emperor's closest familiars. Membership in the order could not be inherited, only bestowed on individuals, and unlike other titles and honors it could not be had for money. For every noble cavalier, whether from the Netherlands or Lombardy, Bohemia, Hungary, or Austria, induction into the order was the ultimate goal and apex of his career;

they all competed with each other for the few places vacated by the death of individual members. In short, the order—or, more precisely, the prospect of membership in the order—was effective in binding grandees in the various Habsburg lands to the Archducal House and focusing their attention on the Viennese court.

The success of Maria Theresa's father in permanently securing the office of grand master for the House of Austria (to this day, incidentally) did not go without saying. With that end in mind, he had made his only son Leopold a knight of the order at his baptism, but the little heir had died a year later.[266] His daughter, on the other hand, could not possibly play the role of a Christian knight and warrior—one of many shortcomings of the female sex. While she could inherit the throne, there was no way she could be admitted into a circle of nominally equal males. Charles VI had instead taken the precaution of inducting Francis Stephen into the order as a young cavalier. After coming to the throne, Maria Theresa had made him grand master of the order as well as coregent, a somewhat dubious act without historical precedent.

To ensure continuity, it was now all the more important that the newborn heir also be made a knight of the order and prospective grand master.[267] At Joseph's baptism on March 13, 1741, the toisonists therefore assembled in full dress uniform, the baptism ceremony doubling up as a chapter meeting. Acting as grand master, Francis Stephen gingerly dubbed the infant knight with "the customary three strokes," spoke the words of investiture, handed over the golden chain, and read to him from the order's Latin statutes. Normally, the ritual demanded that all other members welcome the newcomer in fraternal embrace. Since this was impractical under the circumstances, it was decided instead that they would approach him "one after the other in order of rank on bended knee" and kiss his swaddling bands. It may strike us today as bizarre that the highest statesmen in the realm should line up to kiss the swaddling clothes of a baby, but people took a very different view at the time; ritual gestures of this kind acted as a powerful force for social cohesion. The knights thereby pledged themselves to the principle of dynastic succession. In paying homage to the child as their future sovereign, they implicitly signaled their acceptance that the office of grand master would one day be his. The ritual was a small piece in Maria Theresa's comprehensive, long-term strategy of ensuring that the crisis that had beset her own accession would never be repeated.

The investiture of new toisonists was a grand ceremonious rite that made outsiders painfully aware that they did not belong. Even gravely ill members had themselves carried in by their servants so as not to miss the occasion. When Khevenhüller was inducted in January 1744 and embraced with particular "tenderness and affection," he was so moved that he "burst into tears of joy."[268] Maria Theresa was excluded from this ritual; she could only look on incognito from the oratory of the court chapel. The choice of new candidates was also not hers to make. Francis Stephen evidently refused to let her dominate him for once, jealously protecting one of his few prerogatives in the hereditary lands.[269]

For her part, Maria Theresa was Grand Mistress of the Order of the Starry Cross (Sternkreuzorden), a kind of female counterpart to the Order of the Golden Fleece founded in 1668 by Eleonora of Gonzaga, the widow of Emperor Ferdinand III.[270] The membership criteria matched those for the male order: adherence to the Catholic faith and proof of noble descent for three generations. There was no limit set to the number of members, however. A novice had to be at least sixteen years old and have a husband of equal standing. The ladies' order was conceived as a prayer fellowship, although there were no spiritual oaths or consecration ceremonies. Ladies pledged to worship Christ's cross (a splinter of which was preserved in the Habsburg family treasury) and uphold aristocratic virtues. Four commonly celebrated order festivals each year and a diamond-studded cross as insignia ensured that the Ladies of the Starry Cross were just as conspicuously visible at court as the Knights of the Fleece.

Maria Theresa was well aware of the political value of such symbolic assets. It was a commonplace of contemporary political theory that regents should use this easy means to distinguish nobles for their services and command their loyalty.[271] Early on in the Seven Years' War, shortly after the victory over the Prussians at Kolin, on June 22, 1757, she therefore founded an order with which individual military achievements could be rewarded, calling it the Military Order of Maria

Theresa.[272] This order was something completely new in the House of Habsburg. Unlike the Orders of the Fleece and Starry Cross, it no longer had the character of a blue-blooded prayer and table fellowship. Any officer who had distinguished himself on the field of battle could potentially become a member; he did not even have to be Catholic, let alone a nobleman. The statutes explicitly set out as an "inviolable rule ... that no one, whoever he might be, [should be admitted] on account of his high birth, years of service," or as a mere favor and at the recommendation of others.[273] No limits were set on membership. On the contrary: according to the statutes, the more members there were, the more successfully the order would have met its objective. Instead of having to pay a steep fee for admission, as was otherwise customary, those honored with inclusion would themselves receive a pension. The new order thus pursued a strategy diametrically opposed to that of the Order of the Golden Fleece; it stood for social openness and an ethos of achievement. Even officers who lacked an illustrious family history, inherited wealth, and influential patrons could feel spurred to perform extraordinary feats of valor. In every respect the statutes bore the imprint of Kaunitz, who made himself the order's chancellor.[274] The emperor also figured in this case as protector and grand master, presumably because only a man could be imagined heading a community of war heroes.

All this could not have been to the liking of archconservative aristocrats such as Khevenhüller,[275] particularly given the competition posed to the Golden Fleece. The latter's statutes ruled out membership in any other order. Nonetheless, with Field Marshal Daun and Prince Charles of Lorraine, two Knights of the Fleece were the first to be awarded Grand Crosses of the new military order. This was important to make it sufficiently prestigious and attractive for the high nobility. The lord high chancellor was forced to register another disturbing break with tradition in 1759, when two men of dubious aristocratic pedigree were invested into the Order of the Golden Fleece. When he entreated Maria Theresa, "with the loyalty befitting an old, faithful servant," to block their admission, he was informed that it was too late: Francis Stephen had already made the decision against her advice. It seemed that centuries-old traditions were being swept away by a heedless spirit of innovation.[276] And worse was to come, at least in Khevenhüller's eyes.

Now that he had spurned her advice, Maria Theresa appeared to regret having allowed her husband to head both orders. This, at any rate, is how Khevenhüller explained her decision to found a second new order, this time for civil merit: the Order of St. Stephen. The long-harbored plan finally came to fruition in April 1764, when her son was elected king. She now took on the role of head of the order herself as "king" of Hungary, "since she has inherited the *qualitatem masculinam per fictionem juris virtute pragmaticae sanctionis*"—that is, because she was regarded as a man by virtue of legal fiction.[277] As grand master of the Order of the Golden Fleece, the emperor was vehemently opposed to the idea; according to Khevenhüller, he begged her "with tears in his eyes" to abandon it. Maria Theresa then requested written opinions from her advisers. Khevenhüller sided with the emperor "because, through the multiplication of such orders, all distinctions must necessarily be debased and devalued, not to mention that the toison is so ancient and reputable a house order, hence there is no need to institute a new one to overshadow it."[278] That did not prevent him from seeking membership himself once the order had been established against his advice, nor from taking it amiss when he was passed over for admission three times in a row.[279]

The new order was placed under the patronage of St. Stephen, "the first apostolic king and founder of the Kingdom of Hungary."[280] The order's chancellor was always the Hungarian Court Chancellor. Maria Theresa wanted to show her "particular esteem for this nation,"[281] hoping that it might also make the forthcoming Hungarian diet more amenable to the crown's financial demands. The Order of St. Stephen was much more than a political expedient, however; it was not just addressed to the Hungarian nobility. It represented an ambitious scheme on the part of the monarchy to unite two opposed social goals: it was meant to be a coveted honor that would strengthen the high nobility's loyalty to the Archducal House, while also providing the opportunity for deserving bourgeois officials to scale the social ladder. The honor would take into account not only "birth and dignity" but also "merit."[282] The statutes were therefore a complex mix of the rules of the old Order of the Fleece with those of the new military order. In other words, the Order of St. Stephen aimed to square the circle.

The formalities were modeled down to the smallest details—heraldic symbols, coat of arms, titles, ceremonial—on those of a traditional noble equestrian order. They were even presented as the resurrection of a (completely fictitious) order originally founded by St. Stephen himself.[283] There were to be no more than one hundred members at any time. Their primary duty was to convene once a year at court to pray for departed members and gather with the grand master at table. All knights were given magnificent regalia and insignia, which they were obliged to wear on ceremonious occasions to the exclusion of symbols belonging to any other order. The key privilege membership bestowed on the knights was that they could regard themselves as the sovereign's "familiars." This was manifested chiefly in unimpeded access rights: there was no need for knights to register with the lord high chamberlain in advance if they wished to attend an audience with the queen. They also enjoyed free access to the Privy Councillors' Chamber—"not just at court festivals and ordinary apartments, but also at so-called lesser or games apartments."[284] The order was split up into three classes: there were twenty Grand Crosses, thirty Commanders, and fifty Small Crosses. Priests were also eligible to join. Grand Crosses were reserved for men who could trace their lineage to sixteen noble forebears; Commanders likewise had to be "from the high nobility"; Small Crosses were reserved for "the rest of the deserving aristocracy." What that meant in practice was that a candidate had to be at least a privy councillor. The order was thus exclusively aristocratic—on paper, at least. Yet a back door left the way open for the middle class. The sovereign reserved the right to relieve a worthy candidate of the obligation to prove his noble ancestry and could fast-track the process by providing him with the necessary title as she invested him into the order.[285] At the same time, she waived the fees of several hundred ducats normally charged in such cases and allowed particularly meritorious individuals to be promoted from the lower into the upper classes. When Kaunitz expressed his concerns that this could cause considerable confusion, she sent him a handwritten reply pointing out that "incolation"—that is, the ennoblement of officials in the hereditary lands—was one of the order's main goals.[286]

Maria Theresa took on a traditionally masculine role as the order's grand master and decided which new members were to be admitted. She also presided over the inauguration ceremony and scribbled in the margins of the draft statutes that she would invest new knights *sub throno*, before the throne.[287] She later had herself depicted in this role in a grand ceremonial canvas (see color plate 11).[288] A number of symbolic details indicate that she emphasized the masculine character of her office throughout. For example, she appears to have personally embraced Knights of the Grand Cross upon their investiture. It had originally been proposed that it would be more seemly for her to "lay her hands on their shoulders" instead, but there was no mention of this in the published statutes.[289] She stepped down as grand master only after the death of her husband, when she retired almost completely from court life, transferring the office to her son and new coregent, whom she also appointed head of the two other orders. From now on, she herself looked on incognito.[290]

The fear expressed by aristocratic stalwarts that all this would devalue the Order of the Golden Fleece and lead to an inflation of honors proved prescient. To add to the allure of the Order of St. Stephen and make it "more desirable," in 1765 four high-ranking Knights of the Fleece, including Kaunitz, were exempted from the ban on dual membership and honored with the new Grand Cross.[291] Khevenhüller was aghast to see the singularity and prestige of the old order undermined in this way. His worst fears were confirmed in 1774, when he was forced to note that eleven of the toisonists living in Vienna had excused themselves from attending the order festival—an unprecedented slight.[292] If even the Order of the Golden Fleece had become less attractive for the nobility, the same could be said to an even greater extent of the lower classes of the Order of St. Stephen. In 1765, Maria Theresa confided in him that she would "gladly have found someone of distinction to compete for the Small Cross." In other words, nobody from the old aristocracy had been willing to apply for the honor. Khevenhüller magnanimously helped her out of this "embarrassment" by recommending his younger son, who was then inducted without having to pay the usual fee.[293] A chivalric order that might force them to share a table with freshly ennobled knights held no appeal for cavaliers from the landed aristocracy, and certainly did not justify the high admission cost. They almost had to be coaxed into accepting one of the small crosses. Joseph II was well aware of this: "The court must be grateful if a person from a distinguished family, be he ever so undeserving, accepts or even desires the Small Cross of the Order of St. Stephen, which is meant to be a sign of meritorious service."[294] Maria Theresa's gamble failed to pay off. Using one and the same instrument to honor both the old nobility and deserving newcomers proved unfeasible. The more arrivistes joined their ranks, the less attractive the order became for aristocrats from the hereditary lands.

This dilemma was not confined to the chivalric orders. Other offices that cost their incumbents a great deal of money, but brought them nothing besides honor, were similarly affected by the inflation of honors: they attracted ever fewer noble applicants. Maria Theresa saw herself compelled to appoint chamberlains "whose extraction does not conform exactly to the formal qualification criteria."[295] Steward (*Truchsess*) appointments proved even harder to fill. Seneschals served the royal family at table, a once-coveted honorary position for which applications had almost dried up by the 1750s. It was crucial for the glory of the imperial court, however, that the ruling family be served at open table only by their peers. Maria Theresa therefore resorted to the expedient of forcing everyone of noble origin who applied for a salaried position as privy councillor to apply at the same time for an unsalaried position as steward. Even then, standards relating to noble lineage had to be lowered and a couple of special favors thrown in, such as access to apartment and court balls.[296] In the end, Maria Theresa was even forced to abolish the fee for the office of *Truchsess*.[297]

All these cases were symptomatic of a general structural problem at the imperial court in the second half of the century. The precarious equilibrium in the relationship between the ruling house and the old aristocracy had been increasingly thrown off kilter. Ideally, that relationship was based on mutual advantage. The imperial house relied on the nobility's resources and loyalty to maintain a court befitting its imperial dignity. The nobility was expected to make large-scale investments—in sumptuous clothing, equipages and palaces, embassies, titles, honors, promotions, and so on. Nobles obliged so long as they continued to be attracted to the court, and the court attracted them so long as they could live there—and only there—in a manner befitting their high status without driving themselves ruinously into debt, that is, so long as the ruler rewarded them for their continued presence and service at court with gifts that were more than merely symbolic. For nobles, however, it was essential that this status be inherited, not acquired. They wanted to feel distinguished through their familiar closeness and privileged access to the imperial house. If life at court became too expensive, too arduous, or insufficiently exclusive, they could always retire to their estates.

The aristocratic exclusiveness of court had now come under threat from several quarters. On the one hand, Maria Theresa needed ever more qualified personnel for politics, administration, and the military. In her search for suitable candidates, ancestry mattered less than individual professional expertise. On the other, the renewed outbreak of war was a source of growing financial distress. Now more than ever she needed the hefty fees charged for honorary offices. She had no choice but to lower the entrance barriers for noble appointments at court. In doing so, she set off a downward spiral that increasingly tarnished the court's luster in the eyes of the high nobility and made them ever less willing to spend enormous sums there. Additional factors were in play. Many aristocrats had studied economics and cameralistics and had been won over to the cause of austerity. Plainness, simplicity, unstuffiness, ease of manner, in short "naturalness" in all questions of lifestyle had become increasingly fashionable. A distaste for Baroque ostentation was now a sign of refined taste. All these tendencies came together to make the extravagance of the imperial court seem ever less attractive. This would intensify markedly following Francis Stephen's death—due to Maria Theresa's melancholy no less than to her son's stridently antiaristocratic sentiments.

8

The Seven Years' War

FIGURE 31. Attack on the Prussian camp at Hochkirch on October 17, 1758.
Painting by Hyazinth de La Pegna, c. 1760

Revenge

For Maria Theresa, the Treaty of Aachen that concluded the War of
the Austrian Succession in 1748 had not been the final word on the
matter. She had agreed to it through gritted teeth, but she had never
lost sight of the goal of taking revenge on Frederick II and winning
back her Silesian provinces. Taught from earliest childhood to equate
the interest of the All-Highest Archducal House with the divine will,
she identified her war aims "not merely in the reconquest of Silesia and
Glatz, but in the happiness of the human race and the preservation of
our holy religion."[1]

First, however, the military edge that had helped the upstart from Brandenburg to victory would have to be eliminated. She had learned a great deal from her enemy. After all, the principal objective of her financial and administrative reforms had been to create and supply a great and powerful standing army that could be sent into the field at any time. Further reforms were aimed at placing the military under direct state control, thereby dispensing with the need for mavericks and freebooters like the Pandur commander Trenck.[2] Yet conditions were very different than in Prussia. There the officer corps was drawn from a landed aristocracy that identified to a large extent with the monarchy and the military. In addition, most Prussian soldiers were recruited from the land itself through an elaborate system of conscription. Lords of feudal estates were at the same time officers, the recruits they commanded their subjects. The Prussian system of conscription was aimed entirely at mobilizing the country's resources for the military. This model could not be copied in the Habsburg hereditary lands. On the contrary, in 1759 Maria Theresa was still shuddering at the thought that "a military form of government along Prussian lines would have to be introduced."[3] Instead of forced recruitment, she initially placed her hopes in a volunteer army and the deployment in other regions of regiments from the military frontier. In her core territories, the military was to be kept as clearly separate from the civilian population as possible.

In contrast to Prussia, the military was not especially attractive for the aristocracy in the hereditary lands, with the exception of a few top positions. The officer corps was extremely heterogeneous in its social, linguistic, and confessional makeup. Commanders came from the Netherlands, Italy, the Empire, or Ireland. Many came from a middle-class background, and even Protestants could carve out a career for themselves in the imperial-royal forces. All this considerably reduced their prestige in the eyes of the native nobility: "No one was deemed of lesser consequence than an officer."[4] Maria Theresa had therefore sought from the beginning to demonstrate the high regard in which she held the military, "insofar as they are distinguished and elevated above everyone else at court and elsewhere, as they deserve to be when they are well-run."[5] She not only inspected military maneuvers at every available opportunity, she also decreed that officers down to the rank of major be granted access to the imperial audience chamber, that military uniform could be worn at court, and even that career officers should be included in the order of precedence at court (*Hofrangordnung*)—a daring innovation.[6] Officers now belonged in the circle of imperial "familiars," a spectacular ascent in the social hierarchy for the military class.[7] The granting of regimental commands to the little Archdukes illustrates the same trend. Symbolic measures such as these were not universally welcomed at court.

After the War of Succession, Maria Theresa systematically set about modernizing her forces and professionalizing military service. She instituted reform commissions and appointed an experienced commander, "the uncommonly capable and eminently well-qualified" Leopold Joseph Count Daun (1705–1766), to carry out their recommendations.[8] In 1752 a cadet academy was opened in Vienna Neustadt, where a hundred noble boys and a hundred sons of serving officers—streamed along class lines—were physically and mentally socialized for higher military service. Here they were taught dancing, fencing, horsemanship, geometry, artillery, history, and geography; but they also learned several languages and received religious instruction. All this was offered free of charge to encourage sons of less prosperous nobles to enroll. A parallel military preparatory school in Vienna for boys aged between seven and fourteen acted as a feeder school for the academy. In addition, in 1756 funds for an old orphanage foundation were diverted to establish an imperial-royal engineering school, open to gifted sons from all social backgrounds. "Military engineering," considered a kind of trade, called for greater professional expertise than any other branch of the military and was considered unbecoming by nobles.[9] The task of strengthening the artillery and bringing it up to date with the latest technological developments was placed in the hands of Prince Wenzel Joseph Liechtenstein, who plowed a large part of his fortune into the project. Maria Theresa also introduced a new rule that every officer could be knighted after thirty years of loyal service without having to pay the usual fee.[10]

If the army was to be transformed into a dependable instrument of the empress's will, the physical and mental habits of the soldiery would have to undergo fundamental reform. At the start of her reign, Maria

Theresa had been shocked at the backwardness of the ragtag, ill-disciplined, untrained troops she had inherited from her father. It was imperative, therefore, that "our wartime army be placed on an equal footing in all particulars."[11] Everything was now codified and standardized, from the composition of regiments via weaponry and artillery to uniforms and hairstyles. Above all, new "drill and training regulations" for the infantry were issued immediately after the War of Succession. They set out in minute detail the individual movements each soldier was to perform while saluting, parading, kneeling at prayer, drumming, marching in battle formation, loading and discharging firearms, and standing to attention at the burial of a fallen comrade. A spirit of strict order and geometrical precision was set against the confusion and chaos that constantly threatened to break out on the battlefield. The aim was to make personal bravery dispensable and replace it with the kind of mechanical physical discipline that the Prussian infantry had already modeled to devastating effect. The military was central to all the reform efforts of the interwar period. It was at once the symbol and driving agent of a new, centralized state authority. Modern statehood is practically defined by the sovereign's monopoly on the organized deployment of physical force. In fact, the Habsburg monarchy was and remained far removed from realizing this abstract ideal, and the first reform phase of the late 1740s was followed later, after the Seven Years' War, by a further wave of reforms that partly revoked the earlier initiatives—a similar story to the administrative reforms.

Maria Theresa never saw the Treaty of Aachen as definitive. What could be definitive in a European Great Power system that was in a state of permanent flux? She bided her time, awaiting an opportunity to win back her lost Silesian provinces. In 1749 Kaunitz had already drafted a lengthy memorandum setting out how this goal might be achieved. Prior to the Court Conference on March 7, 1749, Maria Theresa had asked her ministers to put forward their vision of the Archducal House's future foreign policy system in writing. Foreign policy was to be placed on a new, stable, methodically secure foundation. The memorandum that Kaunitz submitted in response was twice as long as those of all other ministers combined, a model of thoroughness, rigor, and political sophistication.[12] Kaunitz demonstrated there what he took statecraft "from a single principle" to mean: he analyzed step by step the motives of the various European powers in their relations with the Archducal House and drew conclusions as to how the great goal of humiliating Prussia might be attained.[13] In doing so, he did not simply proceed from the unchanging "natural state interests" spelled out in political textbooks. He instead took into account the formation of internal factions and influential "particular interests" at individual courts, factoring in the complex interrelations between the motives of all actors. He thereby arrived at completely new, bold political speculations that put traditional friend-foe constellations up for renegotiation.

The only premise that went unquestioned, serving as the basis for all his plans, was that the king of Prussia was the "natural" and by far the most dangerous enemy of the Archducal House. By annexing Silesia, Frederick II had already "excised a large portion of the [monarchy's] body." Now, with a well-drilled army and overflowing coffers, he was in a position to "deal the entire monarchy a deathblow." The hidden premise was that Maria Theresa would never come to terms with the loss of Silesia. The king of Prussia was well aware that the Archducal House would "pass up no favorable opportunity to make good" the loss. The two courts would therefore "continue living in implacable enmity." All Frederick II's policies would therefore be aimed at further weakening the House of Austria if he wanted to hold on to his conquests.[14] Sooner or later, a renewed outbreak of war between the two houses was inevitable. Kaunitz thus counted on a dynamic of mutually reinforcing expectations. For preventive reasons alone, the Prussian king had an interest in continuing his aggressively expansionist policy. For the Archducal House, meanwhile, everything depended on "setting on him as many enemies as possible."[15] The Russian tsarina was already looking out for an opportunity to attack him in anticipation of a Prussian offense. Experience had shown, however, that the house's traditional allies, England and Holland, could not be relied on. Kaunitz's unprecedented, still seemingly "chimerical" plan was therefore aimed at overturning what for centuries had been a constant of the European Great Powers system, the rivalry between the houses of Habsburg and Bourbon, in order to forge a new grand coalition against Prussia. His long-term goal already shimmered before him: "the reduction of the House of Brandenburg to its original state as a minor, thoroughly second-rate power."[16] Yet for various reasons, this goal could not yet be pursued offensively. First, the House of Austria had not yet recovered from the War of Succession and did not command anywhere near enough troops and treasure. And second, Maria Theresa had only just signed a legally binding treaty agreeing to renounce Silesia. The goal would therefore have to be approached by a long and circuitous route. The other powers would have to be imperceptibly yoked to the Habsburg interest by appealing to their "eagerness for expansion." By 1749, Kaunitz already had a specific plan in mind—an adventurous exchange of territories that would see the French crown receive the Duchy of Savoy from Piedmont-Sardinia in return for joining Austria in its fight against Prussia. At the time, the plan still looked like a pipe dream and was not seriously entertained. Yet the basic calculus that Kaunitz had set out in his memorandum guided the Archducal House's diplomacy in the years to come. Ultimately France was won as an ally, albeit under quite different circumstances than originally planned, and a grand coalition was formed to dismember Prussia. Austria even managed to avoid appearing the belligerent party. The only hitch was that the war did not take the course Kaunitz had foreseen.

The Court Conference initially took a skeptical view of Kaunitz's plan. While there was general consensus about the danger posed by Prussia, many cautioned against abandoning the traditional alliance with England and the United Dutch Provinces in favor of a rapprochement with France. The emperor, who had always been less irreconcilably opposed to Frederick II than his wife, advocated breaking through the vicious cycle of mutual distrust and establishing good neighborly relations with Prussia.[17] This was not a strategy favored by Maria Theresa, who evidently shared Kaunitz's premises.[18] It is difficult to know just how bellicose she was at this stage, since few explicit statements on the matter have been handed down. At any rate, she was certainly far more hawkish than her husband. She later retrospectively presented her "system of state" in a confidential memorandum to Field Marshal Daun:

Posterity will hardly believe that, by adopting a cautious approach, I succeeded not only in pacifying the previous sworn enemy of my Archducal House [France], but also in swaying her to take part in the war against Prussia, and moreover in bringing together powers whose essential state interests are completely at odds [Russia, France, Sweden, Saxony, Poland]; consequently in steering everything towards a single final objective on which the welfare, repose, and indeed the very survival of my Archducal House principally depends.[19]

Maria Theresa was utterly convinced of the justice of her cause. Prussia's growing power did not just threaten the Archducal House; it was incompatible with peace in Europe at large, the preservation of the true Catholic religion, and the happiness of the entire human race.[20] In such a worldview, Kaunitz could appear as the heaven-sent agent she needed to launch her mission against the unlawful, ungrateful, and malevolent enemy (who nonetheless owed his house's regal status to her ancestors). Kaunitz confirmed her in her uncompromising stance and strengthened her perception that "justice, and with it the hoped-for divine blessing," was manifestly on the side of the Habsburgs.[21] His personal identification with her dynastic interest (or rather, his interpretation of that interest) was presumably unfeigned—for what could be more flattering to his legendary vanity than to be the one who helped restore the highest-ranking monarchy in all Europe to its ancestral rights?

Maria Theresa was impressed by Kaunitz's diplomatic shrewdness and his commitment to her cause. She probably divined the reasons for his loyalty. At any rate, she decided to place her trust in him and harness his political acumen to her ends. She first sent him for two years as ambassador to Versailles, where he prepared the ground for an alliance between the two courts. As we have seen, from there he skillfully undermined his rivals Ulfeld and Bartenstein, maneuvering to head the new State Chancellery on his return in 1753 and run it as he saw fit.[22] Just as Maria Theresa had defended Haugwitz against his detractors when he set about implementing his administrative reforms, so now she supported Kaunitz in "affairs of state"—not blindly, but trustingly and unswervingly. She had no choice, in a sense, for Kaunitz was not one to take no for an answer. She had to back him to the hilt or not at all, however much he might claim the opposite in his smooth avowals of submission. He showed a cavalier disregard for the ordinary rules of politeness, regularly arrived late at meetings without offering a word of apology, demanded constant consideration of his fragile physical constitution, and later made frequent threats of resignation[23]—in short, he demonstrated that she would have to play by his rules if she wanted to be served by his genius.

European Great Power politics in the 1750s was dominated by rising tension between France and Great Britain.[24] England, now the foremost trading power on the continent, competed with the French crown throughout the world: for bridgeheads in West Africa and India, colonies in North America and the Caribbean, and dominance in the Atlantic maritime trade. The looming colonial conflict between the two powers had direct repercussions for the constellation of powers in Europe, including the antagonism between Prussia and Austria. England was highly vulnerable on the European mainland. On the one hand, it had to protect itself against potential French incursions into the Netherlands, a possible springboard for an invasion of England. On the other, George II relied on continental support for the defense of his electorate of Hanover. Yet from the perspective of the Whig parliamentary majority and the leading state secretary, Duke of Newcastle, the situation on the continent took second place to the furtherance of England's global mercantile interests. His priority was to find continental cover for England in the event of a colonial war against France. At the same time, there was a further potential source of unrest in eastern Europe, where Russia—an ally of Austria and England, but known for being unpredictable—could at any time launch an attack on Sweden or the Ottoman Empire, or prematurely strike out against Prussia. From an Austrian viewpoint, this had to be avoided at all costs. Austria's foreign policy priorities were, first, to gain time for its own military reorganization; second, to prize France away from its alliance with Prussia; third, to unite as many neighboring powers as possible against Frederick while also, fourth, not alienating Britain, an old and powerful ally.

Maria Theresa's strategy, as devised by Kaunitz, was to demonstrate a wish for peace, honor her international treaties, and dispel any suspicion that she was plotting revenge, while at the same time sending out feelers to the French court about a possible alliance. When the maritime powers England and the Netherlands, still her allies, pressed her to extend the so-called Barrier Treaty[25] in support of the fortifications buffering the Dutch Republic from the French, she kept putting them off. Showing all her usual charm, she assured the Dutch emissary Bentinck that she had no intention of regaining Silesia but wished nothing more than never to have to fight Prussia again.[26] She also showed scant interest in the English king's suggestion that she have her nine-year-old son Joseph elected king of the Romans and future emperor, so that France would be denied the chance of destabilizing the Empire again if the imperial throne were to fall vacant in future. In her eyes, the price the prince-electors were demanding for their votes was too high. In a dispatch to London, the British emissary Robert Murray Keith reported that the imperial throne was in such low standing in Vienna as to seem politically unattractive.[27] Meanwhile, the empress concluded a treaty with the king of Spain[28] and negotiated with the king of Sardinia-Piedmont, ensuring that she need fear hostility from neither side in the event of war. In short, her tactics were aimed at keeping her old allies on side and avoiding any new commitments while at the same time preparing the ground for an alliance with France and isolating the king of Prussia as much as possible.

Yet her overtures to Versailles showed few signs of progress, notwithstanding the fact that the French king and queen agreed to stand as godparents for the newborn Archduchess Maria Carolina.[29] Even Kaunitz came to doubt the feasibility of his plan.[30] Meanwhile, outbreaks of violence between English and French settlers in North America became ever more frequent and intense. After English colonists capitulated spectacularly under the young George Washington, the government in London resolved to send troops to North America. Both sides now made preparations for a full-scale colonial war, which as the "French and Indian War" would come to assume a significant role in the prehistory of the United States. In March 1755 London informed the court in Vienna of the threatening consequences for the European continent and requested that the empress send troops to the Netherlands to guard against a possible French invasion. For the Austrians, this was asking too much: they were in no mood to sacrifice themselves for English interests. The reply to the English court was brusque to the point of rudeness. Maria Theresa seemed remarkably uninterested in defending her Dutch provinces; her attention remained squarely fixed on Silesia and Bohemia. The view in Court Conference was that, if it came to war between France and England, the real danger for the Archducal House would come less from France than from Prussia. In that case, self-interest demanded "that as much military force as possible be directed against the king in Prussia at the very beginning of the war, that we attack him relentlessly and stop at nothing to ensure that this dangerous enemy is utterly vanquished and left incapable of causing trouble in future."[31]

On July 9, 1755, the conflict escalated in North America when British troops were defeated by a force of French and American Indians at the Monongahela River near Pittsburgh. It was clear that the colonial war between France and England would soon spill over into Europe, and the government in London began calling on its allies for support. In Vienna, the request was discussed at a momentous meeting of the Court Conference on August 11; Khevenhüller spoke of "one of the prickliest and most delicate matters" that had ever been discussed in his presence.[32] The conference decided against offering any assistance to the maritime powers: "sitting completely still" and leaving the Netherlands to its fate was the lesser evil to "plunging into the danger of total collapse."[33] Soon after, Kaunitz laid out a cunning plan showing how the Archducal House could "draw great advantage from the perilous circumstances."[34] What Kaunitz proposed was nothing short of a coup d'état, drawing grudging admiration even from Khevenhüller, one of his fiercest critics.[35] Kaunitz argued that the time had come to draw France over to the side of the Archducal House. Given the circumstances, an alliance with Austria was now far more valuable to France than persisting with the old, notoriously unreliable Prussians. There were rumors that Frederick II was already working toward a secret understanding with England. Kaunitz therefore recommended putting a strictly confidential offer to the French king: Louis XV's son-in-law, Philip of Bourbon, would receive part of the Austrian Netherlands in exchange for the three duchies of Parma, Piacenza, and Guastella; the Prince de Conti, a member of the French royal family, would be supported in his campaign for the Polish throne; and finally, France would be secretly encouraged to occupy the Dutch ports of Nieuwpoort and Ostende, thereby also furnishing a "respectable pretext" for the mobilization of Austrian forces. In return, all that was required of France was that it withhold its support from Prussia. The real goal was the latter's dismemberment and reduction to the Electorate of Brandenburg's old borders from before the Thirty Years' War. The remaining Prussian territories, cut up into appetizing morsels, were to be used to tempt as many princes as possible to join the anti-Prussian campaign: Russia first and foremost, but also Sweden, the Electorate of Saxony, the Electoral Palatinate, and even the Electorate of Hanover. The Russian tsarina would be the first to be initiated into part of the plan. She would invade Prussia early the following year with an army of eighty thousand men. All this was extremely risky and stood in clear violation of Austria's international treaty obligations. It was therefore essential that absolute secrecy be maintained behind a façade of strict neutrality. Individual steps would have to be coordinated with the utmost care and precision. In short, it all had to be set up in such a way "that the proposal is unleashed as suddenly and instantaneously as a thunderstorm."[36]

Maria Theresa promptly instructed Kaunitz's successor at Versailles, Georg Adam von Starhemberg to establish confidential contact with the French king. Due to the delicate nature of the initiative, the informal path via the royal mistress, who had the king's ear at all times, was the means of choice. Written traces were to be kept to a bare minimum. In the event, Louis XV agreed to the proposal.[37] The secret negotiations were led by Starhemberg and the Abbé de Bernis, a protégé of Marquise de Pompadour. Later, once the treaty had been signed, Maria Theresa showed her gratitude by bestowing valuable gifts on everyone involved in the negotiations. The marquise was given a lacquered writing desk and gold writing instruments valued at around 30,000 guilders. When the Viennese emissary subsequently presented her with the gift along with a letter from Kaunitz, Madame de Pompadour specifically asked for permission to thank the empress in writing. This shows just how tricky this personal contact was considered to be; Maria Theresa's exacting moral standards were a matter of common knowledge, after all. Writing to Antonia of Saxony, Maria Theresa later denied "that we ever had connections with Madame de Pompadour; no letter or business of our minister ever passed through her hands."[38] She never denied sending her the precious gift, though. The fact that the pious and proud monarch's spectacular shift in alliance had been engineered in the boudoir of a mistress, and one of lowly origins at that, practically invited malicious speculation. At the Prussian court, it was rumored that the empress had conducted an intimate personal correspondence with Marquise de Pompadour and addressed her as *cousine*—an "abyss of infamy," fulminated Frederick's sister Wilhelmine.[39] The Prussian king, who was known for using self-authored satires as a propaganda tool, subsequently published a frivolous poem ridiculing Pompadour and Maria Theresa and had it circulated as an anonymous pamphlet.[40] Later historians also felt that the episode required justification and sought to play down the mistress's political role in the negotiations—in stark contrast to Starhemberg, who characterized her intervention as decisive.[41]

Maria Theresa's archenemy had not been idle while secret negotiations were underway in Paris. In early February 1756 news reached Vienna that Frederick II had signed a defensive treaty with the English government on January 16. Neither power had intended to scrap their previous alliances, but they had obviously underestimated the impact of the Westminster Convention. For Vienna the news was a godsend; it gave Louis XV the final push to accept Kaunitz's plan. Outwardly Maria Theresa vented her outrage over perfidious Albion, which she herself had just been secretly plotting to betray. News of the Anglo-Prussian alliance had blindsided her, she claimed; Great Britain had abandoned her, while she herself clung loyally to the old system. Now England should not be surprised if she did the same. She could not concern herself with her faraway provinces but needed to look to the security of her core territories. To Keith's enquiry whether she, the empress and archduchess, would stoop so low as to throw herself into France's arms, she reportedly answered: "I have . . . hitherto signed nothing with France, though I do not know what may yet happen; but whatever does happen, I promise, on my word of honor, to sign nothing contrary to the interest of your royal master, for whom I have a most sincere friendship and regard."[42]

At this point in time, the Versailles defensive treaty, dated May 1, 1756, was long a done deal. However, she did not sign the ratification documents until May 19, a few days after her conversation with the English emissary. Khevenhüller noted that she did so "with uncommon satisfaction, calling it the first treaty she had willingly and cheerfully signed since she came to the throne."[43] One day earlier, on May 18, Great Britain had formally declared war on France. The spectacular overthrow of the old alliance system, the *renversement des alliances*, could no longer be kept secret. The contract—initially only committing the signatories, quite innocuously, to assist each other in the event of attack—was officially announced in the *Wienerische Diarium* a little later.[44]

At the same time, secret talks with France were continuing. Maria Theresa did not want to begin "the great work of wiping out the king in Prussia until she could be sure of France's support."[45] Yet the French king was reluctant to agree to the partition plan, at least not before the Prussian king himself launched an attack. In the summer of 1756 the Austrians, Russians, and Prussians began preparing for war. It was clear to all concerned that war was on the horizon—Prussia had its informants at other courts—but not who would take the first step and when. On several occasions Frederick II had his emissary Joachim Wilhelm von Klinggräff call on Maria Theresa to seek formal assurance that she had no belligerent designs on Prussia, but each time her response was vague and noncommittal. Brushing aside his ministers' concerns, Frederick then quickly mobilized an army of around 65,000 men. On August 29 he marched into the previously uninvolved Electorate of Saxony without making any formal declaration of war. He was almost doing the empress a favor by relieving her of the thankless role of peace-breaker. She herself later remarked that Frederick's attack "suddenly brought the most pleasing hope into a situation of the utmost peril," commenting that "this breach of the peace could not have come at a more opportune moment."[46] The attack forced the French to uphold their contractual obligation to defend Austria. Nonetheless, Maria Theresa acted as if the invasion had taken her completely by surprise: "The Empress took this sad spectacle in Saxony so much to heart that she related the news with tears in her eyes," noted Khevenhüller at the start of September. And the wily tactician Kaunitz, of all people, wrote, in a tone of sincere moral indignation, "Nobody could have imagined that the king in Prussia would have taken such violent measures against Saxony without the slightest provocation."[47]

Generations of historians have examined the background to the Seven Years' War in forensic detail. Needless to say, Prussian-German nationalist historiography justified Frederick's march on Saxony as a necessary defensive measure. Yet even on the Prussian side there were critics of the king's policy who condemned his attack on the innocent bystander Saxony, just as Maria Theresa's admirers could acknowledge her offensive plans and show a degree of sympathy for the preemptive Prussian strike. This latter interpretation was especially popular after the outbreak of the First World War. In his 1917 biography, Eugen Guglia drew an explicit parallel to the German invasion of Belgium in 1914.[48] Yet the priority was always defending the actions of the empress-queen. Today, a hundred years and several more political catastrophes later, a more distanced perspective can be adopted. We can now see that all parties were equally adept at playing the game of political dissimulation. They all shared the same premises, albeit for opposing ends: the good of their own house represented the supreme value and required no further justification. In Maria Theresa's case, it even seemed a God-given duty. The result was a series of unspoken political rules that included mutual hypocrisy. The guiding principle was taken straight from Castiglione's *Book of the Courtier*: in order to dissimulate successfully, any hint of dissimulation had to be sedulously avoided. That is why all parties cultivated a language of moral sincerity, to the extent that many were inclined to believe their own rhetoric. Historians sometimes call the reversal of alliances "the Diplomatic Revolution of 1756," since the cornerstone of the traditional European Great Power system, the longstanding rivalry between Habsburgs and Bourbons, had broken down and almost all actors now entered into new groupings. Yet the concept of revolution is misleading. Even though the constellations had changed, the underlying logic governing people's actions remained the same: with the possible exception of England, all participants were motivated principally by dynastic interests, the power and glory of potentates who ruled over their territories as their heritable property and showed scant concern for their subjects; wars were directed from cabinet rooms; cabals at court influenced the major players' moves.[49]

In the late summer of 1756, all sides anticipated a speedy resolution to the conflict; a decisive campaign was expected for the following year. Yet the war that began with Frederick II's march on Saxony would last seven years. In retrospect, it seemed as if the impending catastrophe had been presaged in the last months of 1755. While Maria Theresa brought her fifteenth child into the world on November 2—Maria Antonia, later known as Marie Antoinette—an unprecedented series of "earthquakes, inundations and celestial phenomena . . . were felt for 61 days from the eastern shores of the ocean to the middle of Germany," including three tremors that flattened Lisbon. All this, Khevenhüller prophesied at the time, would remain "an everlasting reminder of God's punitive wrath."[50]

Seven Years' War

The opening phase of Frederick II's war confirmed his reputation as one of fortune's favorites. Not content with using Saxony as a march-through zone, he effortlessly took Dresden on September 9, 1756, routed the Saxon troops, and confined them to nearby Pirna. Four days later he formally declared war on the queen of Bohemia. The Habsburg army that rushed to assist the beleaguered Saxons was repulsed in early October at Lobositz in Bohemia. Saxon troops were forced to capitulate and their regiments incorporated whole into the Prussian army. Frederick could occupy the land in peace, set up his winter quarters there, and channel its resources into his own war chest.[51] Yet the Electorate of Saxony was part of the Holy Roman Empire. The Prussian invasion represented a breach of the imperial peace and, as such, was subject to sanctions under imperial law. This meant that the emperor could now formally intervene as head of the Empire.[52] Maria Theresa had attempted once before, during the War of the Austrian Succession, to mobilize the imperial confederation for the military objectives of her house. Immediately upon being crowned emperor, Francis Stephen had called on the Empire (in the form of the affected imperial circles) to provide him with military support against Prussia, albeit with minimal success. The appeal was not refused point-blank but became mired in the bog of imperial institutions, and no military assistance was offered. But now the situation was very different.

On September 13, 1756, the emperor wrote to the prince-elector of Brandenburg demanding that he terminate his offensive against the prince-elector of Saxony. At the same time, he issued a decree to the Imperial Diet, formally announced there on September 20, calling on the imperial estates to take up arms against Prussia.[53] In his lengthy legal text, the emperor not only blamed the prince-elector of Brandenburg for breaking the peace, he also released Frederick's officers and subjects from their duty to obey him, called on them to desert, and threatened them with sanctions should they fail to do so. This marked the opening salvo in a series of denunciations and counterdenunciations that unfolded before the eyes of the European reading public. Frederick II had published a brief apologia even before marching into Saxony; now he paid the accusations back in kind. Rather than breaking the imperial peace, he claimed to be waging a war as sovereign king of Prussia against the queen of Hungary and Bohemia. She had been the aggressor; he was merely defending his country's freedom against Habsburg-Catholic domination. He would treat the Saxon lands "like a sacred deposit" and return them to the prince-elector once his mission was accomplished.[54]

Two different templates were thus available for interpreting what had happened. On the one hand, it could be described in the old terminology of the imperial constitution. In that case, it fell to the emperor as supreme judge, in concert with the Imperial Aulic Council and the Imperial Diet, to restore peace to his lands by formally authorizing a *Reichsexekution*, an imperial intervention against a renegade member state. On the other hand, it could also be grasped using the categories of

modern international law, in which case the war was between two independent and equal powers. From this viewpoint, the fact that one of the
combatants happened to occupy the imperial throne was irrelevant. According to natural and international law theory at the time, a state of
nature prevailed in principle between sovereigns, provided they had not
previously concluded any positive contracts with each other. Under
certain conditions they had the right to wage war against each other. It
was thus possible to discuss one and the same process in two different
political languages and oscillate between them.

Yet, even within the discourse of imperial law, the case was far from
unproblematic. It was hard to overlook the fact that the emperor was at
once both judge (as head of the Empire) and litigant (as Maria Theresa's
husband and coregent).[55] The Imperial Diet was largely made up of
Habsburg clients. The Imperial Aulic Council, the supreme court in the
Empire, dispensed justice in the emperor's name, yet it was firmly anchored at the Viennese court, while the Lords' Bench was stacked with
nobles from the hereditary lands. Nobody could seriously believe in the
court's impartiality in this matter. Nonetheless—or perhaps for this very
reason—great pains were taken at the Viennese court to distinguish the
emperor's role as supreme judge from that of the empress-queen as a
party to the conflict. At the beginning of October 1756, Imperial Vice-
Chancellor Colloredo—likewise the incumbent of a high imperial office
and at the same time a member of the Viennese court nobility—advised
the emperor on the correct protocol to follow: Maria Theresa should
write to him, the imperial vice-chancellor, formally notifying him that her
Bohemian lands and the Electorate of Saxony had been invaded and petitioning the emperor "to take immediate action." The emperor should
next formally order the Imperial Aulic Council to issue the same edict for
the Electorate of Saxony as for the Electorate of Bohemia.[56] This should
prevent the possible objection that the empress-queen was not adhering
strictly to the imperial laws that her forebears had sworn sacred oaths to
defend. The court thus placed the greatest emphasis on a constitutionally
correct language, as was characteristic of the highly formalized framework
of the imperial constitution. Yet this rhetoric of strict legality concealed
heterogeneous interests and incompatible political standpoints.

In October 1756 delegates to the Imperial Diet in Regensburg considered the imperial decree. A majority in each of the separate colleges for prince-electors, princes, and estates voted for an imperial "execution" against the breaker of the peace—the Catholic estates belonged to the Habsburg clientele anyway, while some Protestant estates also found that Frederick II had put himself in the wrong by invading Saxony.[57] Despite scouring the plundered Saxon archives for incriminating evidence, Frederick was unable to substantiate his claim that Saxony, together with Austria and France, had long been plotting to attack him. In its official submission from January 17, 1757, the Diet recommended that the emperor declare *Reichskrieg*, imperial war, on Frederick II. The imperial circles were then enjoined by the emperor to field a common army. The king of England warned in vain of a devastating war on imperial soil; last-ditch diplomatic efforts by ecclesiastical electors came to nothing. In the period that followed, then, the armies ranged against each other on the battlefield were drawn on both sides from members of the Empire—not for the first time.

The Imperial Diet's decision meant, among other things, that the crowns of France and Sweden were now not just entitled but even duty-bound to intervene, since in the Westphalian Peace of 1648 they had appointed themselves guardians of the imperial constitution. Kaunitz's plan of a grand coalition against Prussia had succeeded beyond his wildest expectations. As early as January 11, 1757, Tsarina Elisabeth formally joined the anti-Prussian coalition. A little later, Sweden pledged its help against Prussia as a guarantor power of the imperial constitution, notwithstanding the fact that the Swedish king was married to one of Frederick II's sisters. On May 1, 1757, under conditions of strict secrecy, the Franco-Austrian defense pact was expanded into an offensive alliance.[58] The French king promised Maria Theresa over a hundred thousand men, an annual subvention of twelve million guilders, and additional territorial gains at Prussia's expense. Maria Theresa would have to cede the Austrian Netherlands in return, but only once she was again in secure possession of Silesia. Prussia was surrounded on all sides, and its final humiliation seemed only a matter of time.

The 1757 campaign season began badly for the allies, however. Ignoring conventional military wisdom, Frederick launched a large-scale offensive against Bohemia. Nobody in Vienna had seen this coming, leaving no time for the Austrian, French, and Russian troops to join forces. Seeking to precipitate a military decision as quickly as possible, Frederick provoked an open battle near Prague on May 6. It became one of the bloodiest battles of the entire century; within around five hours almost thirty thousand soldiers were dead or wounded. The surviving Austrians under the command of Charles of Lorraine and Field Marshal Maximilian Ulysses Browne fled behind the city walls, where the Prussians cut off their escape routes and proceeded to bombard them.

The court in Vienna was seized by "general consternation, surprise, and perplexity." News from the field was inconclusive and confused. For a time it was unknown what had become of Prince Charles.[59] Once new reports came in detailing the failings of her troops, Maria Theresa was so upset that she could not bring herself "to be seen by her people in such humiliating circumstances."[60] Unlike in the War of Succession, she withdrew entirely from court life; almost all public entertainments were called off. She decided, too, that she could "not possibly publicly celebrate" her upcoming birthday on May 13, spending it incognito with her husband and a skeleton retinue in Laxenburg. There she appeared neither at the hunt nor at supper. Performances of comedies were also canceled, much to the emperor's disappointment. In general, the war loomed far larger in everyday life at court than it had ten years earlier. Even Khevenhüller, hardly the bellicose type, felt a need to chronicle the conflict and chart its course in a series of extended diary entries. Tongues wagged that ladies were now reading military maps instead of prayer books first thing in the morning.[61] Throughout the whole war, court festivals were allowed only "on a very restricted footing."[62] Instead, the empress visited "churches or made pilgrimages, just as everyone had to appear almost every day for a Mass of blessing in the parish church at ten and at four in the afternoon for the rosary, as well as attending liturgy at eight in the evening throughout the octave of St. John of Nepomuk and praying before his columns not far from the castle, where the royal family and everyone else joined with the people in singing German songs."[63] The day of remembrance on May 16 for the Bohemian national saint John Nepomuk was a fixture of the ecclesiastical calendar. Maria Theresa would regularly spend the eight days leading up to it—the so-called octave—undertaking devotional visits to the Augustinian monks. During the siege of Prague, it was therefore only understandable that she would seek heavenly intercession from the martyr who lay buried in St. Vitus Cathedral in Prague.

It was in keeping with traditional practice when faced with emergencies of all kinds that the imperial couple were joined by the entire court personnel and the general public when they made their devotions before a statue of the saint in Laxenburg. In times of war, as during major dynastic events (birth, illnesses, deaths) and natural disasters (earthquakes, storms, floods), common subjects were integrated into religious rituals for coping with the danger. The unity of the dynasty and the people could be experienced only in such a religious community. Collective prayer was an established part of the war effort. Early each year, as was customary at the start of the campaigning season, the eucharist was brought out into the open and prayers were sent up throughout the land *pro felici bello*, for good fortune in war. New rituals were introduced as well: monthly prayer sessions blessing the weapons of war[64] as well as monthly services for the fallen in St. Stephen's Cathedral in Vienna. Maria Theresa always made sure to attend, even if this meant traveling from Schönbrunn especially for the purpose.[65] She herself was virtually unsurpassed in the frequency of her devotions. During the entire war she usually performed benedictions or rites of penance twice a day, and according to Khevenhüller, who was perhaps guilty of exaggeration, she went out almost daily to Maria Hiezing or Mariae Hilf "to pray for God's blessing on her righteous arms."[66] In short, the communication of rulers, court, and people with otherworldly powers was massively intensified during the war. Conspicuous signs that the heavenly powers were taking an interest in terrestrial events were also not lacking. Thus, another patron saint of Bohemia, St. Procopius, depicted in a painting with his eyes shut, miraculously opened his eyes before the battle of Prague "and turned imploringly towards heaven." This, it seems, was something he was known for doing whenever the kingdom was in danger. At any rate, the miracle was "clearly visible" to the fathers of the Benedictine monastery where the picture was hanging and to the "people who flocked" to see it.[67] The queen shared the religious interpretation of the war with her common subjects. Whichever course the conflict took, it could be understood and explained as a divine message to the faithful. When Maria Theresa's own troops were successful, this proved she had God on her side. When her troops were defeated, rather than drawing the opposite conclusion that her cause was unrighteous, she saw in it a divine admonition to repent and reflect on her sins. God was not impartial in this conflict; he necessarily took the side of the Habsburg dynasty, which was fighting for the true Catholic faith. As a just father, he rewarded or chastised the faithful and used their opponents as his instrument, just as he had always used the devil to chastise sinners.

As in the War of Succession, Maria Theresa, unlike Frederick II, was more or less reliant on prayer to influence events on the battlefield. That she could not take to the field herself again proved a serious impediment to the Austrian war effort. She sought to make up for it through her fierce determination to master all the details. She rarely rested content with a mere *placet* to the recommendations put to her by the Court Conference. Her handwritten notes reveal the particulars on which she lavished her attention, from troop formations and glove supplies to rewards for Prussian deserters.[68] The "hunger, misery, and fatigue" suffered by her soldiers were also not unknown to her, although she was unable to form her own impression on the ground.[69] As in the War of Succession, she complained impatiently that "week after week, month after month slips by and nothing happens,"[70] and she demanded to be kept informed by daily courier about "the slightest particulars."[71] From time to time she also sent handwritten letters to the front to inspire her units to greater feats of bravery. In May 1757, for example, she wrote to the commander of the light cavalry, Franz Leopold von Nádasdy, that she would give a hundred ducats for every captured enemy flag or standard and reward with two ducats every soldier who, "saber in hand," brought an enemy battalion into disarray.[72] In some situations she even interfered with the strategy of her generals and urged them to show greater resolve.[73]

After abandoning hope at the start of June 1757—"I am in despair," she confided to Field Marshal Neipperg[74]—events soon began turning in Maria Theresa's favor. In summer the allied troops pulled off a series of spectacular military successes. The Austrian replacement army under Field Marshal Daun was provoked into pitched battle by Frederick II at Kolín near Prague and emerged a clear winner, forcing the Prussian king to break off the siege of Prague and withdraw to Saxony. The French fell in from the west into the Prussian provinces at the lower Rhine, pushed through to Westphalia, and threatened Hanoverian territory. To counter this treat, a so-called army of observation was formed, consisting of Hanoverians and several allied minor imperial estates under the command of the Duke of Cumberland. It was defeated on July 26 at Hastenbeck near Hamelin, withdrew back across the Elbe, and concluded an armistice at Klosterzeven.[75] A little later, the Russians marched into East Prussia and defeated the Prussians on August 30 at the battle of Gross-Jägersdorf, while from September the Swedes marched initially unopposed from Stralsund into Prussian Pomerania. To complete the king's humiliation, Austrian hussars occupied Berlin for a single day in October 1757 in a strategically meaningless yet symbolically important affront. And finally, in the southwest of the Empire an imperial army of around thirty thousand men (rather than a hundred and twenty thousand, as originally planned) had been put together under the command of the Habsburg field marshal Saxe-Hildburghausen. As the autumn of the war's second year drew on, Frederick II saw himself encircled by his enemies: France and the imperial army to the west, Sweden to the north, Russia to the east, and the Habsburg lands to the south. His finances had melted away, and his armies were massively reduced. His bid to secure a quick military victory appeared to be facing catastrophe. The defeat at Kolín was of particular symbolic importance, leaving his reputation as an invincible commander in tatters.

The cause of this victory was "her religious zeal and the good discipline of her troops," Khevenhüller told the empress when she received him, "still in her night clothes" and with "tears in her eyes," to have her hand kissed on the morning of June 20.[76] The "outright victory" was celebrated for days. For two days no tolls were levied at the Vienna city gates and comedies were put on at no cost to the public, and a three-day thanksgiving prayer was held in St. Stephen's Cathedral before the exposed host. Field Marshal Daun was the hero of the hour. His remarkable sangfroid in the heat of battle was universally admired, and he was praised for "possessing, more than any other, the qualities of methodical maneuvering and austere discipline that are so needed against this wily enemy."[77] Maria Theresa's gratitude knew no bounds: she showered him with honors and regarded him for the rest of her life as the heaven-sent savior of her house. Like Khevenhüller, he profited immensely from her legendary munificence.[78] The day of Kolín was celebrated as the second "birthday of the monarchy" and a monthly "eternal devotion" founded in its commemoration. The eighteenth of June was declared the feast day of a specially founded Order of Maria Theresa and Daun made its first knight.[79] Even later, when he had made himself vulnerable to attack through his cautious strategic maneuvering, to the point that some reproached him with deliberately engineering a defeat out of personal resentment, Maria Theresa demonstratively stood by him.[80] Khevenhüller attested the field marshal—not without a tinge of jealousy—"a personal tender attachment to the Empress," who for her part "personally loved him."[81]

Maria Theresa repeatedly voiced her impatience with her generals for showing excessive caution in their eagerness to avoid casualties. In October 1757, for example, she urged them to greater resolution in the Silesian theater to secure lasting strategic advantage from their victory at Kolín.[82] By wresting back control of her lost Silesian provinces, she hoped to create favorable conditions for future peace negotiations, which now appeared to be only a matter of time. Convinced that the positive military situation was not being exploited with sufficient vigor, she interfered with increasing urgency in her generals' strategy. She sent several handwritten letters to her brother-in-law Charles urging him not to refrain from battle for fear of being held responsible for a bad outcome. If the odds of victory or defeat were even, he should try his luck and place his trust in fortune.[83] She would hold to this position in the years to come. In this regard, Maria Theresa evidently stood far closer to her enemy, the hated "monster" Frederick, than to her own generals, who shied away from needless bloodshed. They still followed the conventional maneuvering strategy recommended in military textbooks: pitched battles were to be avoided in favor of wearing down the opposing forces by attrition.[84] The Prussian king pursued the opposite strategy of ambushing his opponents and provoking them into battle, hoping that his troops' superior military discipline would prevail. As a sovereign accountable to nobody for lost positions and fallen soldiers, he could allow himself this "spirit of celerity."[85] This is exactly what Maria Theresa demanded of her generals. Yet however much she might exhort them from afar, in the end she had no choice but to leave decisions on strategy to her commanders on the ground.

In the winter of 1757–58 the tables turned yet again. On November 5, at Rossbach in Saxony, a combined army of French and imperial troops was crushed in short order by a Prussian army only half its size. The Prussian king covered himself in glory. The poorly coordinated troop formations of his opponents had quickly dissolved into chaotic flight; their losses stood around ten times higher than those on the Prussian side.[86] The structural problems facing the hastily thrown together contingents, whose officers were preoccupied with the squabbles over precedence for which the Empire was notorious, were hardly surprising.[87] Kaunitz was under no illusions about their fitness for combat: "One would be gravely mistaken to believe that they can be depended on in the slightest, so far as immediate military operations against Prussia are concerned."[88] And only a few days before the battle, Field Marshal Hildburghausen had complained about problems cooperating with his French colleague Prince de Soubise and the defective chain of command. His fears were to prove prophetic: "I must therefore . . . confess that my hair stands on end when I consider what will become of us when we come face to face with the enemy; for if God does not work a miracle in our favor, it is mathematically inevitable that we will be defeated."[89] The Viennese court took news of the defeat without undue alarm, given that their own army had not disgraced itself. The outlook in Silesia was still bright. For in mid-November, while Frederick II was still held up in Saxony, the Austrians took the important fortress of Schweidnitz as well as the city of Breslau. Yet immediately following his victory at Rossbach, the

Prussian king raced back to Silesia, rallied his remaining troops, and, on December 5, routed the numerically far superior Austrians at Leuthen near Breslau, which capitulated shortly afterwards—a victory that definitively cemented his reputation as a commander of genius among his contemporaries and in the eyes of posterity.[90]

"The Empress wept most of the time and was all but inconsolable."[91] This defeat was a disaster for the Austrian army, which lost over twenty thousand men and almost its entire artillery. Nobody had expected the Prussian king to strike again so quickly.[92] Recriminations now flew back and forth in Vienna. The defeat was mostly blamed on Prince Charles of Lorraine, the supreme commander of the Austrian forces, and on the way the war had been conducted from Vienna—in either case on Maria Theresa, who ultimately bore responsibility for both.

Maria Theresa had already been criticized during the War of Succession for showing undue favor to her brother-in-law and vastly overestimating his abilities as a general.[93] There had been disapproving murmurs at the time about her nepotism toward her brother-in-law; she was said to hold him "in almost as high regard as the duke himself, who loves his brother inordinately." Khevenhüller, whose uncle belonged to the old guard of generals from the glory days of Prince Eugene, repeatedly complained that military discipline had "suffered a great blow" since his death. The discreet advice he had offered Maria Theresa, "particularly regarding the decline in discipline," had fallen on deaf ears.[94] Behind closed doors, it had been put down to Charles's influence whenever botched campaigns, excesses, and the military failures of drunken officers were covered up.[95] Khevenhüller noted how the inexperienced young general had refused to listen to his older colleague Otto Ferdinand von Traun and treated him with disdain, so undermining his "authority with the army." Maria Theresa had reacted by removing Traun, not Charles, to a different theater of war.[96] The catastrophic defeat at Hohenfriedberg in the War of Succession (1745) had been blamed on the inexperience and arrogance of the commanding prince. "Superfine people" had convinced Maria Theresa that Prince Charles would act more responsibly, if only for the sake of his own fame, without an old field marshal looking over his shoulder, but the opposite had proved to be the case. Not least, Charles was a problem for public war reporting. Khevenhüller noted on several occasions that, although attempts had been made to conceal the commander's failures in the official reports published in the *Wienerische Diarium*, public "rumor" had gotten wind of them anyway: "Popular unrest went so far that several arrests . . . were made."[97] After the defeat at Rocoux the following year, everyone again "raged and railed against Prince Charles . . . , despite attempts to make the matter appear in a more positive light."[98]

Now, around ten years later, all this was still in vivid recollection as Maria Theresa once again, ignoring the advice of her councillors, assigned supreme command in the fight against Prussia to her brother-in-law—who was promptly trounced in Prague. "The lady has a good temper, a particular personal affection for her brother-in-law, and makes considerable allowances for her good friends, with the consequence that—although she must be aware of this gentleman's faults—she nonetheless always finds excuses for them and almost shuts her eyes to them," Khevenhüller remarked; even the emperor showed less bias toward his own brother than she did.[99] Charles had also commanded at Leuthen, so "the people . . . unanimously view him and shamelessly denounce him in public as the source of all our woes."[100] Maria Theresa herself was annoyed at how calmly the prince appeared to take the defeat and how "cheerful and light-hearted" he seemed upon returning to court. Yet even then she continued to defend him to others.[101] And when, in December 1757, she finally gave in to pressure from her councillors and transferred supreme command to Daun, she confessed to Ulfeld that the decision had cost her many tears: "Sacrificing this poor prince to the public outcry instead of calling on him to explain himself is an act of weakness that goes against my way of thinking, and surely would have happened at no other time."[102] In defiance of the critics, in March 1758 she made her brother-in-law one of the first two members of the Order of Maria Theresa.

Later historians joined in the chorus of criticism: no other Habsburg general has been so roundly damned by posterity.[103] Contemporaries and historians found their ideas about female character confirmed by Maria Theresa's steadfast loyalty to her manifestly incompetent brother-in-law. It could only be innate feminine weakness that made her cling to him so blindly. This interpretive template could be applied with considerable flexibility. Whether she was reproached for obstinacy, as here, or for inconstancy, as elsewhere, her sex always lay at the root of the problem. Precisely her most ardent admirers resorted to this explanation in seeking to justify their heroine.[104] Yet Maria Theresa's conduct toward her brother-in-law conformed to a dynastic logic that placed loyalty to family above everything else. In the ordinary course of events, no public outcry would have brought her to act against this logic. A further priority was legitimating the contested union of the houses of Habsburg and Lorraine by gaining glory on the battlefield, by far the most valuable symbolic currency in aristocratic society. That neither her husband nor her brother-in-law could ultimately live up to these expectations was presumably too painful an idea for Maria Theresa to contemplate.

Leaving aside the shortcomings of Prince Charles of Lorraine, there were other, structural causes for the defeat at Leuthen. Khevenhüller provided the following summary of critical opinion: "The root of all evil . . . is to be found solely in our domestic constitution. We have two masters: the emperor and the empress; both want to rule." Yet the emperor was

> too easy-going to be able to support so great a burden. The empress for her part is by contrast far too fiery, always in a rush, and hence does not stick to any plan. The capi [i.e. the central office-holders], to whom these frailties on both sides are well known, are adept at profiting from them and delaying or expediting everything at their convenience, particularly as the empress, with the weakness intrinsic to her sex, allows herself to be led astray . . . by everyone and reverses tomorrow what was decided on today.[105]

To nobody's great surprise, confused gender relations were thus the core evil affecting the House of Habsburg. Here too, female weakness was identified as the main problem, this time in the form of excessive fickleness. On the other hand, and somewhat inconsistently, Khevenhüller also criticized the empress for being too perceptive, immediately detecting others' weaknesses, and therefore never placing her complete trust in anyone, much to her own disadvantage. In any event, the Archducal House was hamstrung by its dual government. This "double-headed eagle, so to speak," set everything "in perpetual disorder," with fatal consequences for the military, in particular. This was all the more damaging because the enemy was a master on this terrain: "He oversees and directs everything himself; and whatever he commands is carried out swiftly and to the letter. In our constitution, by contrast, as many instruments must be set in motion as there are capi." This reproach was directed especially against Haugwitz, who, "far too fiery and violent," sought to control everything and gave the empress too simplistic an account of the situation. She relied on him in turn as "a soul dedicated entirely to her cause and a creature of her own hand."[106]

Haugwitz's reform system was one of the many casualties of the Seven Years' War. By the defeat at Prague in 1757, at the latest, the practical problems of this new organization had become glaringly obvious. Three different central authorities with frequently overlapping powers now bore responsible for military affairs: the Court War Council, the General War Commission, and the Court Chamber. This made it especially difficult for troops to be financed smoothly and quickly. Haugwitz reacted by placing the General War Commission, established as an independent institution in 1746, under his own direction in the Directorium in Publicis et Cameralibus. With that, the Directory was more overstretched than ever before.[107] Haugwitz's meddling in military administration had long been a thorn in the side of noble regimental commanders—not just Khevenhüller, whose judgment was occasionally clouded by his animosity toward Haugwitz. As early as May 1757, Maria Theresa had fallen out with Field Marshal Liechtenstein for this very reason. The empress had heard out his criticisms of the new system "with perfect equanimity," but could not be swayed from her conviction that in the hereditary lands, "military service for officers and common soldiers" had now been "set up on the best footing." Liechtenstein dared not show his face in Court Conference for some time after that.[108] It is certainly true that, even after the reforms, the unwieldy Viennese central bureaucracy still did not function as it ought to have done. The empress was keenly aware of its shortcomings In the end, she heeded the advice of Haugwitz's opponents that further changes were necessary, with the result that Kaunitz initiated another wave of reforms in the middle of the war, splitting apart the Directory and largely overhauling Haugwitz's system.[109] When Field Marshal Hildburghausen pointed out to her the many flaws of military organization in a letter from May 1758, she agreed with him wholeheartedly and replied:

> This is also the true cause of my great anxiety and distress, and it is why I shut myself away more and more each day and avoid speaking in company. I sometimes lack the strength to master myself and would not let others see how depressed I am. I have made this confession to nobody other than Koch, from which you can see how greatly I trust in your heart, confiding in you the innermost fears that so confound me, since I myself am guilty of everything and thus cannot be at peace before God and my own conscience. This situation is cruel and you should pity me, though none but God can help me now.[110]

Maria Theresa cannot be charged with lacking insight or moral concern with regard to the military situation.

By the end of 1757, hopes of a quick victory had faded on both sides. Early the next year, the English-Hanoverian army of observation re-formed under the command of Ferdinand of Brunswick, campaigned successfully against the French, and forced them to pull out of the Empire. In April the English parliament agreed to an alliance with the Prussian king, backing up their commitment with both money and troops. Frederick II opened the 1758 campaign by retaking Schweidnitz, marching into Moravia, and laying siege to Olomouc. There were already fears in Vienna that "this monster" would invade Austria.[111] These fears were laid to rest when Frederick had to break off the siege on receiving word that the Russians were nearing his own core territories. In midsummer he moved north in a series of forced marches, fighting one of the war's most brutal battles on August 25 at Zorndorf near Küstrin. By the end of the two-day bloodbath, thirty thousand lay dead and wounded, with neither side emerging victorious. Frederick now marshaled his troops and turned again to Saxony, in hopes of provoking Daun into battle. The

Austrian commander initially evaded him, only to launch a surprise attack on the Prussians in their camp at Hochkirch, east of Dresden, on October 14 (see fig. 31 and color plate 12). The predawn attack literally caught them napping. Under the circumstances, they were lucky to beat a more or less orderly retreat.

The surprise victory at Hochkirch was Daun's gift to Maria Theresa on her name day. He had hurried to write his battle report on the same evening so it would arrive in Vienna in time.[112] The courier reached Schönbrunn late at night on October 15, the Feast of St. Teresa, "when the princes and princesses of the imperial court had retired to their rooms and begun to undress after the court and assemblée with the Empress," as the chambermaid Hieronymus told her daughter. "The glad tidings were quickly sent by the Empress to all the chambers of her children, who hastened back to their illustrious mother's rooms in wonderful disarray—one archduchess still with jewels in her hair but in her nightdress; another in hoop skirt and gala dress with disheveled coiffure; princes half in uniform, half in dressing gown—to add their well wishes on her victory to those on her name-day."[113] While some were celebrating in Vienna, others were removing the dead and wounded from the battlefield at Hochkirch. The numerically far superior Austrian troops had killed or injured nine thousand Prussians and lost seven thousand soldiers themselves. The Habsburg postal service intercepted a letter from Frederick II to his sister Wilhelmine of Bayreuth that soon did the rounds at court. The King confessed there, not just "that he had never suffered so harsh a blow," but that he envied the dead. Death evaded him, though he had long been seeking it.[114] Yet the victory brought Maria Theresa no relief either. She feared that Frederick would exact just as cruel a revenge as after Kolín.[115] In December 1758, as the Prussians occupied Dresden and set fire to the city's outskirts, she wrote to Antonia, Electoral Princess of Saxony and wife of the heir to the throne, with whom she was conducting an increasingly intimate correspondence at this time: "I see myself plunged into an abyss of pain, such as I have never experienced before. . . . You may rest assured that I . . . will expend my last man to free you from this slavery. . . . The dear Lord will take pity on us in the end and save us from the monster."[116] At the same time, she felt constantly compelled to justify herself to Antonia of Saxony, as reports kept emerging of the excesses her troops were committing against ordinary subjects in the Saxon theater of war.[117]

At the start of 1759 the Prussian king was in a disastrous situation. He had lost many of his resources and units and was unable to pursue his usual strategy of aggression. Maria Theresa pressed Daun to exploit the enemy's weakness. Never had there been a more favorable opportunity to take the offensive and end the war on advantageous terms. With Russian assistance, now was the time to go for broke.[118] If one victory could decide everything, then defeat had to be risked. Seeking to allay Daun's concerns, she wrote to him that she regarded it as her duty "to relieve you of anything that disturbs your peace of mind and take the danger solely on myself."[119] Yet Daun did not so easily consent to being relieved of his responsibility. The back and forth between the marshal's cautious objections and demands from both the empress and her Chancellor in Vienna that he show greater initiative would become the leitmotif of the following years.

Despite all the Prussian countermeasures, the Austrian and Russian troops succeeded that summer in assembling a gigantic coalition army of sixty-four thousand men. For once, the sophisticated offensive tactics of the Prussian king failed him; on August 11, 1759, he again suffered a terrible defeat at the battle of Kunersdorf near Frankfurt an der Oder. Nineteen thousand Prussian soldiers were killed, wounded, or taken captive. It was a triumphant victory for the new Austrian field marshal Gideon Ernst Laudon, a Livonian warrior of spartan austerity, tested in the "petty war" under Franz von der Trenck, then rapidly promoted, utterly devoted to the empress and therefore an object of hatred for the established nobility. Laudon was convinced of the need to seize the initiative and take the battle to the enemy, the polar opposite to the risk-averse Daun; he thus seemed just the man Maria Theresa had been waiting for.[120] Frederick II had survived the battle of Kunersdorf by a hair's breadth; he had very few soldiers left and believed the war to be all but lost. Yet the allies were unable to convert their victory into a strategic breakthrough. They dithered, trying and failing to settle on a common course of action. Laudon did not get his way, and the Russians withdrew from the arena. For Frederick it was a sheer miracle—the much-quoted "miracle of the House of Brandenburg"—that he had not been utterly annihilated. When in November the Austrians spectacularly surrounded an entire Prussian army corps that had been on its way to Dresden and forced it to capitulate at Maxen, capturing around fourteen thousand soldiers along with their generals, officers, and artillery, morale was boosted, but to little overall effect. For all their successes in the campaigns of 1758 and 1759, the Austrians were no closer to achieving their war aims and had failed to capitalize on Prussian weakness. Maria Theresa was disconsolate over the outcome of a campaign that had begun so promisingly and now placed all her hopes in what the following year, 1760, would bring.[121]

Yet overall conditions deteriorated considerably over the following months. The French king had long felt compelled to give up the ambitious goals of the secret pact from 1757 and focus his energies on the colonial theater of war. In March 1759 he had concluded a third treaty with the empress, massively reducing his military commitment to the fight against Prussia and reserving the right to take up separate peace negotiations with Britain. Moreover, on August 1, 1759, the French had been defeated by the British in a disastrous encounter at Minden and been forced to retreat from Hanover and Westphalia. Above all, 1759 was an *annus horribilis* for the French global war effort. The British succeeding in blockading the French Atlantic coast, making it impossible to supply the French colonies with troops and materiel. The colonies were now as good as lost. Against the background of British successes at sea, on the one hand, and the deteriorating position of the Prussian king, on the other, England and Prussia made overtures to end the war. In November 1759 their envoys met on neutral ground in Rijswijk with emissaries from Paris, St. Petersburg, and Vienna to propose peace negotiations.[122] France indicated its willingness to take up the offer.

Maria Theresa, however, was incensed. She feared that the French foreign minister, Duc de Choiseul-Stainville, would pull out of the anti-Prussian alliance and conclude a separate peace with Prussia. In December she wrote to Antonia of Saxony: "I would give my life for peace in Europe, but God preserve us from it at the present time, for the remedy would be worse than the disease itself."[123] And in January: "France's impetuous desire for peace and its inadequacy make me fear a separate peace. That would break up the great alliance with a single blow and usher in a general peace, the worst of all possible evils, even worse than another four years of war. The burden weighs more heavily on me than on anyone else, but everything must now be risked to shake off the yoke of slavery, and there will never be a stable peace system so long as the prince of Prussia remains strong."[124] In the Court Conference in Vienna, plans of attack were drafted for the 1760 campaigning season.[125] Once again Maria Theresa urged decisive action, arguing that a lost battle was preferable to an uneventful campaign; once again she declared herself willing to shoulder the responsibility for the consequences of risky decisions. Yet once again, Prussia demonstrated its superiority in large, costly battles.[126] The fighting dragged on inconclusively: Austrian troops plundered Berlin; Prussian troops destroyed Dresden. In September 1760 the French emissary in Vienna, Duc de Choiseul-Praslin, renewed his call for a peace conference. Although France had exhausted its resources, he wrote, his country had made no discernible progress in the fight against Prussia since the start of the war. How could anyone believe that they could suddenly secure the victory that had eluded them these last four years? Maria Theresa thought his words insolent but grudgingly gave her consent to a multilateral peace conference, scheduled to begin in Augsburg in July 1761.[127] The conference never came about, for in early 1761 she was already planning the next campaign in the hope of improving her negotiating position.

But she now lacked some of the essential prerequisites for achieving this aim. Regular sources of finance had long since run dry.[128] The costs of war had soared to over 40 million guilders each year. Not only did her own troops have to be paid and provisioned, money also had to be found for subsidies for the Russians and to cover spiraling interest payments on debt.[129] Since 1758 Maria Theresa had therefore imposed ever more special war levies and extraordinary taxes on her hereditary lands with each passing year: head tax, inheritance tax, horse tax, and so on. Lower Austria and Vienna were squeezed particularly hard. Great ingenuity was shown in raising new forced loans, which were likewise borne by the estates in the hereditary lands, with the result that over 40 percent of regular revenue came to be spent on servicing state debt. By 1760 it had become clear that things could not continue this way for much longer. With a heavy heart, and against the objections of her consort and her heir, Maria Theresa decided to make massive cuts to the number of commissioned officers in the army while halving salaries for those remaining.[130] At the same time, a court committee was created to advise on how state finances could be put on an entirely new footing. To this end a new supervisory body was set up, the Court Audit Office (*Hofrechenkammer*), led by Ludwig von Zinzendorf, one of Kaunitz's protégés.[131] Yet the task of tapping new revenue sources for the war and finding foreign creditors was doomed from the outset. Government bonds were only attractive if potential investors could have some measure of confidence that military actions would prove successful. This looked ever more unlikely, given that financial pressures had already forced troop numbers to be slashed. In October 1761 Maria Theresa wrote to one of her generals: "Credit is at rock bottom, for it can be foreseen that the monarchy will not be getting any bigger, which makes all our plans more difficult, if not impossible."[132] The only escape route from the vicious cycle of military failure, depleted resources, reduced troops, and exhausted credit seemed to be the desperate hope that, in the end, at least some of her war goals could be salvaged. No wonder, then, that Maria Theresa felt increasingly old, cheerless, and downcast.[133] Despite everything, it would take another two years, several lost battles, and thousands of fatalities before she finally accepted that Silesia was lost for good.

King George II of England died on October 25, 1760, and his pro-Prussian prime minister, William Pitt, fell from grace not long after. In British politics, a faction that took a more critical view of Prussia and favored peace was now in the ascendant. The following year, the English parliament cut off Frederick II's subsidy. From 1761, France and Britain negotiated peace separately from Prussia and Austria. In 1762, the last year of the war, the new king of Spain, Charles III, entered the war on the side of his French cousin, albeit to little effect. On February 10, 1763, peace was concluded between France/Spain and Great Britain in

Paris—a treaty that cost France most of its colonial possessions. Fortune turned a final time in Frederick's favor in January 1762, when the Russian tsarina Elizabeth died. Her successor, Frederick's admirer Peter III, moved quickly to make peace with Prussia, a policy continued by his wife, Catherine II, when he was murdered half a year later. Sweden followed suit soon after. Frederick was able to marshal fresh troops and regain control of both Silesia and Saxony in the course of the year. In the end, the Austrians could only hold on to the small Silesian duchy of Glatz. Even Maria Theresa came to realize that her original war aims were beyond her grasp. On May 20, 1762—a Prussia corps had just won another victory at Döbeln in Saxony, and all Austrian troops had to be pulled out of Saxony to protect Bohemia—she wrote with remarkable clear-sightedness on the prospect of peace negotiations: ". . . this is some consolation under the current circumstances; it must be energetically pursued. I fear only our lethargy, and that one keeps pushing on when one should have abandoned illusions long ago."[134] She was now in great haste; with every day that talks were delayed, her position threatened to deteriorate still further. Daun warned that the army could not be kept supplied another winter. In the end she was prepared to settle for very little: "At that time [in the year before] we certainly would have retained Glatz; God grant that we may come out now without loss," she wrote in November 1762, when she finally made a truce with Prussia.[135]

The elector of Saxony offered to broker the peace. On December 30, talks between the Austrian delegate Kollenbach, the Prussian envoy Hertzberg, and the Saxon intermediary Fritsch began without ceremony in the Saxon hunting castle at Hubertusburg. There had previously been a brief symbolic dispute over the location: Frederick II still occupied Saxony, and the Austrians wanted on no account to hold talks in the immediate vicinity of his quarters.[136] Yet even the few objectives set by Kaunitz could not be attained. The Prussian king insisted on restoring the territorial status quo ante bellum. In the end even the fortress of Glatz, still held by Austrian troops, had to be given up. Frederick was also not prepared to compensate Saxony—which he had originally promised to return intact to its ruler—for the widespread devastation it had suffered during the war and the immense contributions he had extracted from it until the last. His only significant concession was a pledge to use his vote in the electoral college to help Joseph get elected king of the Romans and future emperor. If this outcome is compared with the state chancellor's original plans, then it is astonishing that Kaunitz could write a few days after the peace was signed on February 15, 1763: "We can . . . be satisfied with the treaty."[137]

Imperial War, Religious War

Several days before peace was proclaimed, the Empire as a whole had formally declared its neutrality in a resolution of the Imperial Diet. The Treaty of Hubertusburg claimed validity for the entire Empire, although none of the other imperial estates had even been consulted. With the peace agreement, a chapter of imperial history came to an end. The imperial confederation had never been a smoothly functioning political entity. For centuries the complicated federal constitution had been subject to rival interpretations from pro-imperial and pro-princely parties, while the imperial estates had always been internally fractured along various lines. Following the Peace of Westphalia, however, old conflicts were put on ice, giving rise to a kind of strained equilibrium. Imperial institutions hardly ever produced clear and binding decisions, but, paradoxically, this was precisely what made them work: given the complex and conflicting power relations in the Empire, there were no better options. Acute conflicts were not resolved, but they became caught up in the institutional machinery for so long that, in the best-case scenario, the dispute would be abandoned from sheer exasperation. Unfortunately, this approach to conflict management was ill suited to the enmity between two powers of such magnitude as Prussia and Austria. Far from burying the dispute in procedural mechanisms, imperial institutions were starkly polarized in its wake.[138] Instead of a plethora of antagonistic forces, there were now only two camps, each accusing the other of destroying the Empire.

The conflict was also fought as an imperial war against the peace-breaker Frederick II. A formal resolution to that effect had been passed by the Imperial Diet, the Empire's representative assembly, but the imperial estates that cast dissenting votes did not feel bound by it. They either refused to contribute troops to the imperial army or supported the opposing side. Not content with a mere resolution, the emperor launched legal proceedings to have Frederick II declared an outlaw, the same strategy that had been used by Charles V against Martin Luther, without much success, some two and a half centuries earlier.[139] The imperial ban (*Reichsacht*) was a late-medieval sanction that stripped targeted subjects of all their rights, but it was rarely imposed, since it was all but impossible to enforce. In August 1757 the imperial prosecutor at the Aulic Council submitted a formal charge against the elector of Brandenburg. On October 14 the declaration of outlawry was delivered by notary to Plotho, Frederick's delegate to the Imperial Diet, who dismissed it "with the utmost insolence."[140] It was said that Plotho had thrown the imperial messenger down the stairs. Although there was no truth to the rumor, it was a useful one for Plotho, since it represented him showing his utter contempt for the ban on behalf of his master. In December 1757 Prussian troops invaded the Duchy of Mecklenburg, bringing Frederick another indictment before the Imperial Aulic Council. He responded with a note to Regensburg declaring the emperor deposed and encouraging electors to choose a successor. This did not go down well in Vienna, strengthening the resolve there to expedite proceedings against Frederick. In August 1758 the Aulic Council pressed formal charges against Frederick, along with George II (as elector of Hanover) and all the other imperial princes who had thrown in their lot with Prussia.

For all that it may have been legally defensible, this was a politically unfeasible ploy. Prussia and its allies correctly pointed out that all three imperial colleges—electors, princes, and cities—had to be involved in adjudicating the case. With that, at the latest, the process inevitably became stalled by the formal requirement of confessional parity. The religious divide had a long history in the Empire and was embedded in the very structure of the imperial constitution. Ever since Westphalia, imperial institutions had been based on the principle of confessional co-equality. At the Imperial Diet, all matters concerning religion had to be negotiated peacefully between the two parties, such that no side could overrule the other in questions of conscience. Conversely, this meant that any decision that came before the Diet could be blocked as soon as religion came into play. That now appeared likely, since unlike in the War of the Austrian Succession, when Maria Theresa had been allied with the powerful Protestant elector of Hanover, the fronts now ran neatly along confessional fault lines: the Catholic houses of Habsburg and Bourbon stood ranged against the Protestant powers, Prussia and England-Hanover. The Prussian king, although personally indifferent to religion if not openly scornful of it, could turn this to his advantage by successfully presenting himself as the protector of the threatened evangelical faith—never mind that he had overrun Electoral Saxony, the old heartland of the Reformation. The Saxon elector had traditionally chaired the league of Protestant estates at the Imperial Diet, the *Corpus evangelicorum*, notwithstanding the fact that he himself, his family, and his court had long since reverted to Catholicism. That was not the least bizarre feature of the imperial constitution, and it had long been a bone of contention for the Protestant estates.[141] Frederick II had set his sights on leading the Protestant party in the Empire. If he could only have seized control of the *Corpus evangelicorum*, he could have used it as a lever to block the Diet—and ultimately other imperial institutions as well—at any time with recourse to religion. In this case, at least, he succeeded. The Saxon envoy to the Diet bowed to pressure from his Prussian and Hanoverian colleagues; the *Corpus evangelicorum* protested against the process of proscription and declared it unconstitutional. The emperor then admitted defeat, making no further attempts to continue the proceedings. He had done no good service to the Archducal House or the Empire, since the intervention by the *Corpus evangelicorum* was what first cemented the Empire's split into two confessional blocs.[142]

It was to Prussia's advantage that the confessional climate in the Empire had been heating up for some time, for various reasons. Several traditionally evangelical dynasties had returned one by one to the Catholic fold, putting themselves at odds with their mostly Protestant subjects: the Elector Palatine in 1685, the elector of Saxony in 1697, the Duke of Württemberg in 1733. Most recently, in 1749 the heir to the Landgraviate of Hesse-Kassel had converted, fallen out with his family, and turned to Vienna for support.[143] It was generally known that Protestants in the "German" hereditary lands of the House of Habsburg were not at liberty to practice their religion. For evangelical subjects in the Empire, the conflict therefore awakened memories of the Thirty Years War and made them fear that their traditional faith would be suppressed. Religious fanatics fanned these fears by calling on their listeners to take up arms against the beast of the Book of Revelation. In mixed-confession areas, such as the immediate vicinity of the Habsburg territories in Swabia known as Further Austria, there was bloodshed between Catholics and Protestants. Authorities in imperial cities with a confessionally mixed population such as Augsburg, Nuremberg, or Regensburg observed that "the rabble was resolutely for Prussia."[144] Evangelical soldiers proved unwilling to fight for the Catholic Queen against Prussia. Even the Saxon emissary Karl Georg von Flemming complained in May 1757 that Saxon troops had "shown little enthusiasm for being sent to fight against the king in Prussia."[145] In the summer of 1757 sections of the Swabian contingent mutinied, and troops from Württemberg, citing religion, refused to serve under French command. The Duke of Württemberg informed the imperial court that his soldiers, "learning they were destined to fight against the king in Prussia, partly deserted, partly rose in arms against their officers, and simply refused to march." It was deplorable, he wrote, "that simple people could so easily be won over by the word religion."[146] As soon as belief came into play, the fronts hardened and became increasingly polarized.

The God-fearing empress herself tended to stylize the war as a confrontation between true and false religion. Convinced that she was fighting the good fight, she identified one of her war aims in the "preservation of our sacred religion, of which I am now almost the only remaining prop in Germany," and ascribed "hatred of the Catholic religion" to her opponents as a motive for war.[147] This is not to say that she wanted to revise confessional relations in the Empire, as claimed by enemy propaganda. In her secret treaties with France, both sides pledged to keep the Westphalian order intact. Believing she had God on her side was something quite different to using the confessional divide to split the Empire. Maria Theresa was too intelligent to add the fuel of

Catholic propaganda to the fire of imperial politics. Indeed, she was careful to avoid giving her enemies any grounds for accusing her of conducting an anti-Protestant crusade.[148] It was a different story at the papal curia in Rome; there the war was welcomed as a means to drive the "abomination of uncatholic belief" from Christian lands.[149] Thus, Pope Benedict XIV secretly instructed the Catholic clergy in the Empire to give a tenth of their income to the imperial war chest, bringing in around 120,000 guilders. Yet the pope's fundraising exercise served the Archducal House poorly, for his partisanship played directly into Frederick II's hands. Frederick knew very well that the other side was uncomfortable having the pope as an ally and milked the situation for propaganda against his enemy, the "apostolic harpy." Following Daun's victory at Hochkirch, Frederick had his friend, the Marquis d'Argens, circulate a fabricated breve in which Pope Benedict XIV thanked the marshal for his fight against the heretics, gave him a sanctified sword, and urged him to convert "north Germany after the example of the blessed Charlemagne, with the sword, fire, and blood."[150]

Maria Theresa was well aware that the confessional question awakened dangerous memories in Protestant parts of the Empire and breathed new life into old anti-imperial, anti-Catholic resentments. She wrote to her emissary in St. Petersburg in late 1757:

> On the Prussian side, efforts have been underway for some time to use even religion as a pretext for imputing to us the most far-reaching and dangerous intentions, and presenting their king as the sole protector of the Protestant faith. Such deceit can make no impression on judicious and right-thinking minds. But since the least number of people belong to this class, and misguided policy generally seeks to hide under the mantle of religious hatred, it is not difficult to grasp on closer inspection whence comes the deluded and quite extraordinary devotion to the king in Prussia shown, not just by common Protestants, but by rational people as well.[151]

Luise Gottsched was one such rational person. Just how far the climate of opinion had turned against the imperial court since the first year of the war, including in Saxony, is shown by the fact that the feelings of even this once fervent admirer of the empress had cooled appreciably. "How much did my heart feel when I beheld the Empress? How much when she showed me signs of her favor? How I prided myself then on my good fortune in seeing the Empress! . . . Now nothing moves me anymore. . . . The war, this wretched war, has made me indifferent towards all such outward signs," she wrote in February 1758.[152] After the spectacular victories at Rossbach and Leuthen, at the latest, a pro-Frederician mood held sway in the Protestant regions of the Empire. Unlike in the War of the Austrian Succession, this time Frederick was the hero who had carried the day against overwhelming odds. He was the plucky Protestant David to the lumbering Catholic Goliath, the new Gustavus Adolphus fighting to defend religious freedom against Catholic despotism. A burgeoning cult of Frederick entered into the parlors of middle-class homes. His image graced plates and cups, prints and tobacco boxes; hymns to Frederick were composed, songs sung in his honor.[153] Goethe described with mild self-irony how he had adored the Prussian king as an eight-year-old:

> So it was that my sympathies were on the side of Prussia, or more accurately, of Fritz; for what cared we for Prussia? It was the personality of the great king that impressed everyone. I rejoiced with my father in our conquests, willingly copied the songs of victory, and perhaps yet more willingly the lampoons directed against the other side, poor as the rhymes might be. . . . Of the existence of parties, and that he himself belonged to a party, the boy had no conception. His belief in the justness of his position and the superiority of his opinions was strengthened by the fact that he and those of like mind appreciated the beauty and other good qualities of Maria Theresa.[154]

The mood was not just *Fritzisch* and anti-Catholic, it was also anti-French. Particularly in the Empire's west, French troops brought back bad memories. After their defeat at Rossbach, old Francophobic stereotypes enjoyed a renaissance; in songs and pamphlets, ridicule was heaped on the weak, cowardly, effeminate French.[155] The enthusiasm for Frederick also concealed resentment of female rule. For the three states ranged against him had in common that they were more or less openly ruled by women: not just Maria Theresa in the House of Habsburg, but also the Tsarina Elizabeth in Russia and Madame de Pompadour in France, who lent a whiff of the boudoir to "petticoat government." The misogynist Prussian king gleefully played on these prejudices in his satires.[156] In the same spirit, one of the many anonymous authors in the pamphlet war reminded his readers:

> A woman should remain silent in public, saith the apostle. Many nations rule out female descendants from succession and forbid them any share in government. The great mischief often done by females may have prompted this measure. While it cannot be denied that much good has been done by women in some societies, yet are such cases rather the exception than the rule. Those familiar with the names T[heresa] and E[lizabeth] from the war, meanwhile, may secretly judge the matter for themselves. *Intolerabilius nihil est quam femina diues* [nothing is more unbearable than a powerful woman], saith the poet.[157]

Media War, Information War

The Empire-wide popularity of the Prussian king at the empress's expense was due not least to the way the war was fought in the media. The King of the Prussians was also "king of the presses."[158] What was new about this war—except in England, where this had long been everyday practice—was that it was subjected to intense media scrutiny. The Prussian-Protestant side profited from this far more than the Habsburg-Catholic side, given that the printing and publishing industries in the Empire were concentrated in the Protestant regions. The Seven Years' War played out before a significantly broader, more self-conscious, and more critical public than all previous conflicts. This was recognized even at the time. The Hanoverian officer and writer Johann Wilhelm von Archenholz, himself a captain in the Prussian infantry, wrote in his *History of the Seven Years' War*: "One of the most remarkable peculiarities of this extraordinary war was its strange mix of numerous manifestos and scenes of carnage. . . . Great monarchs wished to justify their proceedings before all nations, in order to preserve the respect of even those peoples whose approbation they could easily do without. This was the triumph of enlightenment, which in those times had already begun to spread its beneficent light over Europe."[159] In other words, military engagements were now fought before the court of public opinion. Combatants increasingly acted with one eye to a public that had assumed the role of an independent yet interested observer.

Different readerships were served by different media.[160] On the one hand, there was the old, "intergovernmental" public made up of courts and governments in the Empire and in Europe.[161] The official propaganda manifestos put out by the various warring parties were addressed to them. Whereas princes barely felt the need to justify their conduct to their own subjects, they felt differently when it came to the Empire at large. Because the war was waged as an imperial conflict, undecided imperial estates had to be won over with learned deductions and memoranda. The most important distribution and exchange center for such material was the Imperial Diet in Regensburg. Free copies were handed out to all the delegates, who sent them back to their home courts. Periodicals such as the *Teutsche Kriegs-Cantzley* (*German War Chancellery*) in Regensburg or the *Acta Publica*, published by Trattner in Vienna, printed them in full; they were translated into several languages and distributed on the book market throughout Europe. One bookseller in Regensburg alone was said to have sold in excess of a thousand copies of Frederick II's first *Exposé* in just a few hours.[162] The Viennese court simultaneously published its own memoranda and war reports in the *Wienerische Diarium*, just as it had previously done in the War of Succession. Maria Theresa herself took a keen interest in the media war; in September 1756 she ordered that "an extract on the army's position, and perhaps on the course of events, be compiled by a court war councillor and given to the newspapers here once or twice a week. This is how things were done in the past, and they should be done the same way now."[163]

Meanwhile, there was a much wider reading public in the Empire, far beyond those actively involved in politics, that took an equal interest in the progress of the war. The courts sought to win over this public through targeted propaganda. Literacy rates had climbed over the course of the eighteenth century, albeit with significant regional differences. There was a booming market for books, journals, and newspapers. In 1750 there were around 100 to 120 different newspaper operations, although many of these were short lived. Each copy reached many more than just one or two readers, since newspapers circulated in reading societies, coffee houses, salons, and taverns. The learned mocked the common man's "petty politicking" and joked that these days the "riffraff consisted of nothing but statesmen." Even day laborers could be seen reading newspapers on the street and expressing their "frequently amusing opinions" on the latest developments.[164] This observation could at least be made in Hamburg, the most important press center in the Empire. The literacy rate in the Habsburg lands was not so high, nor was there such widespread demand for printed material. As a consequence, they lacked a printing and publishing industry that could compete beyond the region. For a long time, the European print explosion passed them by.

In the mid-eighteenth century the hereditary lands were still "a wasteland for authors and booksellers."[165] When historians declare that the Enlightenment suddenly dawned on Austria from 1750, this implies that there had been nothing of the sort before.[166] Only a single native newspaper could be read before then, the *Wienerische Diarium*, and it was completely controlled by the court. The annual subscription cost of eight thalers (twelve guilders), equivalent to several months' wages for a day laborer, gives some indication of the size of its readership. By contrast, the two newspapers in Berlin could be had for two thalers apiece.[167] Until mid-century there were also hardly any weeklies or periodicals—the first, the *Teutsche Spectateur* (*German Spectator*), appeared from 1749 onward; there were few printers and publishers, very little in the way of a literary scene, no reading rooms or reading societies. Still, "newspaper singers" publicly declaimed the news of the day, street vendors sold illustrated sheets, and handwritten newspapers circulated in coffee houses. "Backroom scribblers and calumnists" were frowned on by the authorities, however. In 1750 Maria Theresa forbade "coffee makers from distributing any written papers in their coffee houses on pain of losing their business," a decree reissued on several occasions.[168]

Handwritten newspapers escaped censorship, which extended only to printed matter, and even then only imperfectly. They therefore profited from the tightening of print censorship. By 1751, they had become so popular that Maria Theresa felt compelled to ban them completely. Harsh punishments were threatened in an effort to "eradicate this wicked and reprehensible practice," while informants were offered a reward of a hundred gold ducats.[169] Like most rulers at the time, Maria Theresa believed she had both the ability and the obligation to monitor what her subjects were thinking. This called for a jealously guarded monopoly on information. For a long time, the printing industry in the hereditary lands had rested in the hands of one man, Johann Peter von Ghelen, publisher of the *Wienerische Diarium*. Privileged at court since 1721, he enjoyed a monopoly that went unchallenged for decades.[170] His only competitor, the *Mercurius*, had been forced to close in 1724. Ghelen possessed an exclusive right to publish all official communications, regulations, court news, and so on. He drew his information directly from the imperial court and sold it at his own expense. In return, he was obliged to ensure that a number of the *Diarium* appeared on every post day at a fixed price. He also had the right to receive all foreign press publications untaxed and uncensored and mine them for his own newspapers. He skillfully exploited his monopoly for a variety of economic ends; the import of printed material from media centers such as Augsburg, Frankfurt, or Leipzig also lay in his hands. In 1754 he was succeeded as court printer by Johann Thomas Trattner, who from 1757 brought out the *Gazette de Vienne*, the *Wienerische Diarium*'s only rival paper. He used his privileged position to build up a printing and bookselling empire throughout the hereditary lands, drawing hostility through his brazen piracy.[171]

There were important periodicals in the Empire that reached beyond a provincial public: the *Unpartheyische Correspondent* (*Impartial Correspondent*) in Hamburg, the *Historisch-Genealogische Nachrichten* (*Historical-Genealogical News*) from Leipzig, the *Reichs-Post-Reuter* (*Imperial Postal Messenger*) from Altona, or the *Ober-Post-Amts-Zeitung* (*Gazette of the General Post Office*) from Frankfurt, for instance. Just how seriously the courts took the readership of these papers is shown by the policy of active media management conducted in Berlin and Vienna.[172] The courts sent their current war reports to their residents in the various lands in the hope that they could place them in local newspapers. Here the Viennese court was at a distinct disadvantage, since it was considerably further removed—both literally and metaphorically—from the North German press centers than the courts of Berlin, Hanover, or Dresden. In 1757, for example, the Viennese resident at the Lower Saxon imperial circle complained to Kaunitz of the "gall and malice towards our Supreme Court . . . spat out" by the big Hamburg newspapers under the influence of the Prussian resident, and he requested that alternative accounts of the war from the imperial perspective be promptly delivered, since otherwise "such disseminations will only strengthen the already prevalent bias towards Prussia and Hanover."[173] Still, the imperial position provided access to a number of levers denied the Prussian king. The Aulic Council could withdraw the imperial printing privilege from newspaper writers; lampoons could be banned by the imperial censorship commission in Frankfurt, and the Thurn and Taxis postal service could put a stop to the distribution of newspapers. Despite all these advantages, the Viennese court could not entirely prevent pro-Prussian writings circulating in the Empire. Effective censorship was impossible.[174]

All in all, Viennese media policy reacted defensively and with some delay to the aggressive Frederician publicity campaign.[175] Frederick II was a veteran media strategist and personally addressed the public like no other prince before or since (with the exception of Julius Caesar)—as an enlightened wordsmith, as a subtle philosopher, as a razor-sharp satirist, and as the historian of his own life and times.[176] He wrote many of the Prussian battle reports himself as an anonymous "Prussian officer." With that he showed that he enjoyed two advantages over Maria Theresa, who never dreamed of taking up her quill in support of her cause: he was not only his own commander but also his own war reporter and propagandist. There was thus a clear structural asymmetry in Prussia's favor so far as media representations of the war were concerned. This asymmetry was exacerbated by the fact that a majority of prominent writers declared themselves in Frederick's camp. Particularly in Prussia, but also far beyond, a remarkable war euphoria gripped journalism and literature.[177] Enlightened circles in Berlin were by no means as cosmopolitan and peace loving as we like to think. Many authors displayed—at least rhetorically—a "lust for violence and heroism."[178] Not just aristocratic Prussian officers such as Ewald von Kleist, but also sober middle-class lawyers, theologians, and writers such as Ludwig Gleim, Karl Wilhelm Ramler, Thomas Abbt, and Anna Louisa Karsch transfigured war into a moral training ground for the German nation, proclaiming the virtues of heroic courage and disregard for death, Roman masculinity, and republican virtue. Even Lessing was not immune to the mood of patriotic fervor. At last, a worthy theme had been found to spawn a German national literature. For poets no less than for generals, the war presented an opportunity to gain undying fame. Everybody was eager to be the next Horace or the German Voltaire. Archenholz placed Frederick II in the company of Alexander the Great, Augustus, and Louis XIV—all rulers whose glorious wars of conquest were followed by a golden age of arts and sciences. "Now the great cultural epoch of the Germans had begun," and war was its midwife: the "ever-present sight of extraordinary scenes of war had lifted the Germans' spirit."[179] There was nothing on the Austrian side to match this militarized, stirringly patriotic, pro-Prussian literature, no popular success to rival Kleist's heroic poetry, Gleim's *Songs of a Prussian Grenadier*, or Abbt's *Of Death for the Fatherland*. Here and there, Habsburg subjects tried their hand at heroic war poetry. The Jesuit Michael Denis, professor at the Theresianum in Vienna, regaled an educated reading public with leaden alexandrines lauding Maria Theresa's virtues and Daun's victories on the battlefield.[180] Yet the work rarely strayed beyond the confines of conventional occasional poetry and panegyric; no reader was likely to get carried away by it. Pro-Prussian authors, on the other hand, presented a new ideal for a new public: the ideal of a war that would level class distinctions and turn everyone into citizens of a new kind, forging them into one nation. While it remained unclear what exactly the (German? Prussian?) nation consisted of, this image of war was destined for a grand future. In the Napoleonic era and beyond, nationalist propaganda could retrospectively celebrate the Seven Years' War as a German national war. While Maria Theresa had discredited herself through her alliance with the French, Frederick II could appear as a Teutonic hero who had trounced the traditional enemy at Rossbach.

To be sure, the literary effusions of the Prussian bards bore little relation to the reality of armed conflict. Writers, poets, and preachers, most of whom had never been near a battlefield, cultivated a far more bloodthirsty and violent rhetoric than most soldiers. The real armies were anything but the crucible for a new national identity. Ulrich Bräker, who later achieved fame as the "Poor Man of Tockenburg," had been pressed into the Prussian army before deserting, like so many others, at the battle of Lobositz. He described the troops from firsthand observation as a "motley crew of Swiss, Swabians, Saxons, Bavarians, Tiroleans, Italians, French, Poles, and Turks [all of them] sold dogs . . . to be dispensed with in times of peace, and stabbed and shot to death in times of war."[181]

The perspective of those who bore the brunt of the fighting and plundering can be found above all in pamphlets and illustrated broadsheets. Most of these were produced in the urban printing centers in the Empire's southwest, above all in Augsburg and Nuremberg. In both the hereditary lands and Prussia, there was very little in the way of an illustrated press.[182] Caricaturists represented the war as a game of ombre, faro, dice, chess, or billiards. As in a game, war resulted in either victory or defeat; the outcome was uncertain and might depend on sheer luck. Apart from the players, there were spectators who waited until the next round to place their bets. All the actors took part in the same game, since the common rules were known to them all—although this did not rule out the possibility of foul play. Other players' calculations had to be guessed in advance and one's own strategy adapted accordingly to deceive, anticipate, forestall, or exploit them for one's own ends. But the metaphor also had critical overtones of frivolity and cynicism. Unlike other games, the stakes for which the game of war was played consisted of real territories and populations. The same could be said of war as a dance or theatrical spectacle—courtly entertainments by which grandees amused themselves at the expense of their underlings.[183]

Maria Theresa's role in these pamphlets and pasquinades had changed significantly since the War of Succession. She was no longer the persecuted innocent stripped of her clothing by rapacious predators. She was

FIGURE 32. *Depiction of the current political game of ombre in the house of Lady Germania.* Anonymous broadsheet

now one player among others: her sex no longer played a role. In the example depicted here (fig. 32), only men are gathered around the ombre table: the Hungarian magnate, the Prussian officer, the English lord, the French marquis, and so on. For the Prussian player, the game has taken a turn for the worse, and he now lays all his trump cards on the table; the Russian has overestimated his hand; the Hungarian does not want the game to end until he has recouped his losses. This time, too, the innocently suffering victim is a woman, standing plaintively to one side; but she is "Lady Germania" rather than the empress. Germania has given up her house for the card game and wants the players to leave so she may finally enjoy some peace and quiet. Meanwhile, a Turkish night-watchman peers through the window and threatens: "Have done, gentlemen, go home for the night, / If not, I will come in and put out the light." The image called for patriotic unity in "Germany," since otherwise external enemies—a renewed Ottoman invasion seemed a distinct possibility at the time—would exploit the situation to end the game in a manner of their choosing. Such broadsheets appealed to a higher authority than any terrestrial prince: "The king of kings, the lord of creation / Wished peace to descend on the war-torn nation, / And so through concord restore / What had almost been destroyed by war."[184] It is no coincidence that such a viewpoint could flourish in a mixed-confession imperial city such as Augsburg. It was the perspective of the powerless third party, the imperial patriot forced to look on as reckless potentates gambled away the common house.

The war was not just fought over public opinion, it was fought over access to communications between rulers as well. It had long been taken for granted that every potentate had informants at other courts. These were not just official emissaries and residents. Informal patronage relations were cultivated with noble members of other courts; payments were made to secretaries, copyists, and clerks from the opposing side; or information was bought from professional espionage agents.[185] Influential members of the St. Petersburg court, for example, drew pensions from Vienna, which they repaid in the currency of political influence.[186] Both the Saxon chancellery scribe, Menzel, and the secretary of the Austrian emissary in Berlin, Weingarten, were on Frederick's payroll, and they duly sent him copies of correspondence from the courts in Dresden and Vienna.[187]

Maintaining informants was one means of espionage; intercepting the enemy's postal communications was another. To that end, *cabinets noirs*, where letters between courts could be intercepted, cautiously opened, copied, carefully resealed, and sent on, were placed at strategically located posting houses. The French court had pioneered the practice. Maria Theresa repeatedly complained that the Prussians were snooping on her letters. She sent particularly intimate or confidential correspondence by courier or entrusted it to people from her inner circle when they were about to travel abroad.[188] In the winter of 1778–79, when indiscretions involving Archduke Ferdinand's confessor, Wasgottwill von Rollemann, gave rise to considerable ill will between Vienna and Naples, she herself traced the imbroglio back to perlustrated letters and expressed her outrage over the disloyalty—*infidélité*—of the post office.[189] It was the height of insolence that the letters of the court chaplain had evidently been intercepted and unsealed without her permission. For the privacy of correspondence was in her eyes a one-sided affair. Surveillance of letters, she wrote, "is a point allowed and reserved for the sovereign alone; carried out by a private citizen, however, it is a deceitful and infamous act."[190]

Under Maria Theresa, monitoring of the post was expanded and perfected in the 1750s. Her husband's occupancy of the imperial throne conferred a crucial advantage in this regard. As with newspaper censorship, the imperial court enjoyed a special prerogative through its control of the postal system. Under Maria Theresa's ancestors, the Thurn und Taxis imperial post had already set up *cabinets noirs* at key nodal points. Following the War of Succession, Kaunitz advised the empress to expand the postal system as a whole. He explicitly claimed responsibility for everything "concerning secret and state affairs."[191] The key figures in this expansion were Privy Cabinet Secretary Ignaz Koch, one of the empress's most trusted advisers, and Privy Councillor Franz Michael Florence von Lilien, a hyperactive plotter and schemer in the service of the Thurn und Taxis family, who inundated the state chancellor with memoranda on infrastructure projects.[192] He intensified his ties with the imperial house by marrying one of Bartenstein's daughters in 1746, his second marriage.[193] Following the War of Succession, Lilien for the first time established a regular daily postal service in the hereditary lands. It was thanks to him that seventy-seven postal carriages arrived in Vienna each week in the 1750s, far more than in Berlin, and more even than in Hamburg—denser postal networks could be found only in the printing center Nuremberg, the trading metropolis Frankfurt, and in English Hanover.[194] The expansion of the secret surveillance system went hand in hand with that of the postal network.[195]

Before the outbreak of the Seven Years' War, Frederick II had learned of the system from his spy Weingarten and exploited it for his own propagandistic purposes. In a memorandum from December 1756 entitled "Sancta Sanctorum ou secret de tous les secrets," "Secret of all secrets," Lilien reacted to the mishap and described in detail how the secret post boxes could be made more secure. This text sheds light on how the system had developed, how it worked, and the role assigned the empress in all this.[196] According to Lilien, the general of the Imperial Post Office was bound by oath to respect the confidentiality of private communications; the security of the entire postal service depended on it. Only the emperor, as supreme judge, could authorize exceptions to this general rule, and only in defense of the Empire or religion. This was how the system had originally operated under Emperor Joseph I, but over time, "clandestine maneuvers" had gotten out of control and subaltern postal officials in Frankfurt and Augsburg had misused the *cabinets noirs* for their personal gain. For a time, then, the Viennese court had deployed this instrument only with reluctance. The maneuvers had had to be carefully concealed from the Wittelsbach emperor, Charles VII, anyway. Since the Habsburgs had regained the imperial crown, Baron Koch, acting in the best interests of his queen, had expanded the box in Nuremberg and set up new ones in Regensburg, Maastricht, and Duderstadt. They were now distributed at such strategically favorable locations that Vienna was kept informed of what was going on in almost all the cabinets of Europe.

Yet there was obvious potential for controversy here. Fellow imperial princes, as well as foreign powers, were being spied on by an imperial institution and in the emperor's name for the benefit of the Archducal House. It was therefore of the utmost importance, Lilien argued, that the entire surveillance system remained shrouded in secrecy. The structural problem consisted in the fact that many workers had been initiated into the system and could use what they knew to blackmail their superiors and expose the system at any time. To prevent this from happening, it was essential that the postmaster general, the prince of Thurn und Taxis himself, be kept in the dark.[197] This was also in the prince's best interests, Lilien maintained. That way, if anything came to light and an imperial estate lodged a public protest, as the king of Prussia had recently done, he could always proclaim with all sincerity—under oath, if necessary—that he knew nothing of his subordinates' "malpractices." Everyone who worked with the *cabinets noirs* should be "most earnestly entreated" to keep the prince in this state of ignorance; were he ever to find out what they had been up to, they would not go unpunished.[198] In this way, Lilien slyly argued, the number of *cabinets noirs* could be increased without risk. Yet there was still danger involved for the two directors who ran the system, keeping their subalterns in check while at the same time hiding the truth from the postmaster general. These directors took all the risk on themselves and therefore deserved all possible protection as they went about their vitally important business on behalf of the House of Austria. Such protection could only be extended them by the empress herself.[199]

The system of *cabinets noirs* was further expanded in the ensuing war years, when receiving timely information about enemy moves was of vital importance. It may be assumed that the empress herself was aware of this, since everything depended on her providing cover and support. Yet Lilien's cunning scheme failed to work out as planned. There were limits to postal surveillance; the secret of all secrets remained far from watertight. Despite Lilien's arrangements, there were abuses of all kinds; individual workers embezzled money and valuables from the mail. Trust in the imperial postal service dried up as ever more complaints about opened letters were voiced. Finally, the unmasking of a double agent called Ivo Welz brought the surveillance system to light in 1759–60.[200] Lilien had praised the *cabinets noirs* as a means of "preserving imperial authority," but in fact they proved highly ambivalent in this regard.[201] Their discovery once again revealed to the public that the Archducal House was only too willing to exploit the imperial throne for its own ends. It may have seemed self-evident to Maria Theresa that the interest of the Habsburg monarchy was identical with that of the Empire as a whole, but not everyone was equally convinced. The affair accelerated the Archducal House's loss of credibility in the imperial public sphere and gave Frederick II additional material for propaganda.

Disastrous Balance

Unlike other peace agreements, the Peace of Hubertusburg was not publicly heralded in Vienna with spectacular solemnities, cannonades, drums, and trumpets. While triumphal arches were erected for Frederick's return to Berlin, in Vienna there was little cause for celebration. Seven years of war had left behind devastated lands, colossal state debts, and half a million dead in Europe alone—without any change in the territorial status quo in Europe.[202] "But when one thinks of the countless victims this war has claimed, how many provinces have been laid waste, how many families have been ruined, and all this to restore the . . . status quo ante, one wants to scream to the heavens for the insanity of humankind," the Prussian courtier Lehndorff wrote in his diary.[203] Yet the balance of power in Europe had shifted decisively away from France and the Archducal House. Frederick II had established his kingdom as the equal of the old French and Habsburg monarchies. Prussia was now a permanent fixture on the European political stage. Maria Theresa had not only failed to achieve her political goals, she had not only gambled away the modest successes of her administrative, financial, and military reforms, but in many respects she found herself in an even worse position than at the beginning of her reign. State debt had almost doubled since 1740.[204] Kaunitz's brilliant plan had proved a disastrous flop.

Maria Theresa never again sought to make good the loss of Silesia. Her views on war changed fundamentally in the following years, as would be demonstrated in the 1770s. So far as her personal relationship with Frederick II was concerned, however, she remained implacable even after the peace treaty was signed—quite against the unwritten rules of aristocratic courtesy. Questioned on the rumor that the king had written to her "in the most flattering terms and immediately received from her a similar response," she replied: "Not a word of it is true. I am much obliged to the king for writing to me; my quill has never answered him."[205] The numerous representations of the peace on tapestries, copperplates, and coins showing the three monarchs united in amity are to be understood only symbolically, not as documentary truth (see fig. 45).[206] Maria Theresa never met her enemy in person. For his part, Frederick did not share her undying hatred; on the contrary, he spoke of his opponent with respect; paid tribute to her political acumen, strength, and genius; and called her "a woman who could be regarded as a great man."[207]

Maria Theresa and Frederick II were stylized by nineteenth-century historians as the great polar opposites of German history, the incarnation of antagonistic feminine-defensive and masculine-aggressive principles.[208] Yet this says more about nineteenth-century sexual stereotypes than it does about the two monarchs. From today's more distant historical vantage point, they seem to have much in common. Once they had set their sights on a goal, both pursued it with ruthless determination. In their choice of political means, too, they were more similar than they may appear at first glance: both instrumentalized imperial institutions in equal measure. Some historians have nonetheless applied opposing value judgments to their conduct. When the Prussian king was credited with having subordinated reality to his own will and registered only what accorded with his political vision, this was taken as evidence of "masculine" steadfastness.[209] Conversely, when Maria Theresa was said to have felt "eternally" justified in her unwavering enmity toward Frederick, this was regarded as an "authentically female mindset."[210]

In this war, however, the heroic roles were differently cast. The situation was practically the reverse to that in the War of the Austrian Succession. Back then, Maria Theresa had been surrounded by superior enemy forces eager to seize her inheritance and divide the spoils among themselves; now the king of Prussia was faced with a grand coalition of powers who were greedily eyeing his territories. In the War of Succession Maria Theresa had prevailed against all the odds; in the Seven Years' War it was Frederick who triumphed over adversity. Both rulers had their own personal miracle around which a hero cult grew up. Accordingly, it was the War of Succession that played a central role in the Austrian national myth, the Seven Years' War that helped define the Prussian-German myth. In Prussian historiography the war was cast in a morally ennobling light and celebrated as a milestone on the path to the founding of a "lesser German" empire in 1870–71.[211] Austrian historiography saw it much the same way, albeit with considerably less enthusiasm. According to her biographer Eugen Guglia, writing in 1917, Maria Theresa's obstinate struggle to win back Silesia revealed "a divinatory instinct . . . that the House of Austria would one day have to fight against this young state [Prussia] for supremacy in Germany; the Seven Years' War was indeed, as has often been said, a precursor to the war of 1866."[212]

The Holy Roman Empire was also a long-term casualty of the Seven Years' War. From now on, the imperial confederation would be dominated by two great, roughly equal rivals that could cripple, bypass, or even—if ever they saw eye to eye—liquidate imperial institutions.[213] Both antagonists, Maria Theresa and Frederick II, played a part in making their own prophesies come true. Maria Theresa could feel confirmed in her low opinion of the Empire, which she had seen as essentially defunct even before the war broke out: *tout y etait corrompu*.[214] In this opinion she was not far removed from her enemy, who had already foreseen the beginning of the Empire's end when he came to the throne: "The stone has been dislodged which in Nebuchadnezzar's vision fell on the four metals and crushed everything."[215]

9

Dynastic Capital

FIGURE 33. Archduke Leopold as regimental commander.
Workshop of Martin van Meytens, c. 1753

Little Lords and Ladies

By the age of six, Archduke Leopold, Maria Theresa's ninth child, was already commanding a cuirassier regiment of his own. A classical military portrait, produced around 1752 in the workshop of the court painter, Martin van Meytens, shows him in this role. Kitted out in battle gear,

455

the little lord stands on high ground striking a commanding pose. With his left hand he points to his troops marching up a slope behind him. In the background to the right, there is the faint suggestion of a camp; to the left, the space opens out onto a wide landscape over which the archduke asserts his mastery with an imperious gesture.

Leopold's role as regimental commander was not restricted to this painting. He had been assigned his own regiment in 1750, when he was three years old, even if actual command was exercised at first by a lieutenant.[1] Francis Stephen also transferred regimental commands to his other sons when they were still children, something that had not been customary in the imperial house to that point.[2] Khevenhüller describes the formalities observed on such occasions. In July 1756 the emperor was passing through the large antechamber in Schönbrunn when he noticed a child in uniform clutching a petition. Only on second glance did he recognize the child as his own son, Archduke Ferdinand. Sent there by the empress, the child had come to submit a written request for a command that had recently been vacated by the death of a seventy-year-old field marshal. "To observe all the formalities, the little lord had to present himself afterwards to the President of the Court War Council as a newly appointed colonel and pay him an official visit."[3] Archduke Ferdinand was two years old at the time. At his birth he had already received a golden sword from the king of Naples, who hoped that, "following the example of his forefathers," he might wield it "triumphantly against the heathens."[4] The little princes from the House of Habsburg-Lorraine could not be inducted early enough into the glorious military tradition of their ancestors. At the age of seven, at the latest, they presented themselves at court at the head of their own troops. So it was at the consecration of Leopold's regimental flags in 1764, when "the three archdukes, Leopold, Ferdinand, and Maximilian, appeared as colonels and at the head of their regiments, all three parading on horseback and en cuirasse."[5] Maximilian, the youngest, was seven at the time, Ferdinand nine, and Leopold seventeen. On gala days, too, the children appeared in regimental uniform and dined with the generals as their equals.[6]

As befitted their rank, the little Austrian archdukes and archduchesses were treated from birth as "newborn lords and ladies" (*Herren und*

FIGURE 34. Uniforms of Archduke Leopold's regiment.
Illustrated manuscript, Bautzen, c. 1762

Frauen). How they were to be addressed was determined not by their age but by their status as members of the ruling family.[7] As the living guarantee of the continuity of Habsburg rule—a continuity that had been massively called into question upon the death of Charles VI—they represented the dynasty's most valuable capital. With every son born to the ruling couple, the danger that such a catastrophe would be repeated was reduced; with every child, the power of the Supreme Archducal House grew. Each child signified potential capital on the marriage market of the European high nobility. The matchmaking began almost as soon as the infants had left the crib. Accordingly, Maria Theresa devoted as much care and attention as she could to putting her dynastic capital on display—daughters as well as sons. A new style of court portraiture reflected this focus on the next generation. Depictions of the dynasty no longer placed the (male) ancestral line in the foreground, as had been customary in the past. The preferred subject was now the parents surrounded by their ever-increasing brood.[8] The imperial couple's fecundity was celebrated not just in the famous monumental family portraits produced by the Meytens workshop, but also in numerous copperplates and broadsheets. These were cheap enough to be hung even in the homes of commoners (see figs. 35 and 36). The motif of the imperial couple with their children, depicted as a tree consisting of nothing but portrait medallions, can even be found on an altar frontal at the Chapel of Grace at Mariazell. The so-called antependium was a gift for the Mother of God offered by Maria Theresa in thanks for her superabundant progeny.[9] In this way the exemplary fertility of the ruling house was set before the eyes of the faithful when they came to Mariazell to pray for God to bless them in conception, pregnancy, and childbirth.

From early on, the children were put on stage, both literally and figuratively, and exposed to the coolly appraising, occasionally harsh judgment of court society.[10] Along with the children of privileged courtiers, they all regularly rehearsed for roles in opera, ballet, comedy, and occasionally tragedy, just as Maria Theresa had done to great acclaim in her own childhood. No infant was too small to be denied an appearance on stage—on one occasion even Johanna, not yet a year old at the time, was given a cameo role as a cloud-borne cherub. As a special favor, the empress would invite foreign guests or senior officials to the "comedy, where my children dance."[11] Noble parents jealously noted whose children were allowed to take part, how prominently they performed, and how much applause they received. Not least, theater, dance, and song trained them in an unforced and "natural" physical comportment, d'un air aisé et naturel. Children should learn to speak with a mix of honesty and audacity—une honnête hardiesse—and to adopt a noble, assured demeanor, une contenance noble et assurée.[12] Joseph performed in French comedy as a six-year-old, an experience his parents hoped would make him shed his inhibitions.[13] It seems not to have worked, since Khevenhüller criticized his shyness and unclear articulation on more than one occasion.[14] On special dynastic solemnities, the children performed together before a large courtly public. In 1765, for example, when the opera Il parnasso confuso by Metastasio and Gluck and the ballet Il trionfo d'amore by Franz Hilverding were put on for the heir's

FIGURE 35. The imperial couple and their offspring.
Copperplate by Johann Michael Probst, c. 1756

second marriage, the four older sisters sang, Leopold conducted the
orchestra, and the eleven-year-old Ferdinand, the nine-year-old Marie
Antoinette, and the eight-year-old Maximilian danced. The spectacular
performance was a crowd-pleaser, and it was commemorated in turn—
in a performance to the second degree, so to speak—on a grand ceremonial canvas (color plate 15).[15]

Maria Theresa pursued a targeted strategy to present her flourishing offspring to the public, not just on the stage but also in their inherited role as rulers. To this end she introduced a series of remarkable ceremonial innovations following the War of Succession. The bestowal of regiments on her little sons was only one such innovation. Another consisted in celebrating court gala days on the birth- and name days of her children—not from their seventh birthday, as had previously been the case, but from the very beginning, "regardless of age" and for daughters as well as sons.[16] Maria Theresa also paraded her children before visitors at every available opportunity.[17] At the age of seven, at the latest, they were ready to assume their assigned role in the official life of the court: they participated in apartments, public feasts, military parades, church service, and processions, and sat in the front row at the theater. The seven-year-old heir was known to take the opening dance at the court ball, where his six-, seven-, and eleven-year-old sisters were paired with foreign emissaries.[18] Another spectacular innovation was the induction of the little archdukes into the Order of the Golden Fleece. There was nothing new in the heir being made a member of the order upon his baptism; this was a custom already observed by Charles VI.[19] But it was unprecedented for Charles and Leopold—aged ten and eight at the time, respectively—to be formally invested into the order and dressed in its expensive and elaborate uniforms, which first had to be tailor-made to fit their diminutive frames.[20] Another example of such a ceremonial performance concerned dynastic continuity in the kingdom of Hungary. At just three years of age, Joseph appeared at court in Hungarian dress as heir to the throne, and he was depicted as such in state portraiture (see color plate 7).[21] All the sons were demonstratively included in Hungarian rituals of state. At the Pressburg diet of 1751, for example, the ruling couple appeared before the estates together with their three sons, all dressed in local attire. The first, Joseph, was addressed by the representatives in Latin, the second, Charles, in Hungarian. The ten-year-old Joseph replied in Latin, the six-year-old Charles in Hungarian—an extraordinary gesture, given that the Habsburgs could barely speak a word of Hungarian.[22] These symbolic details, attentively noted by onlookers, had a reciprocal effect: not only did they make the Hungarian nobles (from whom the queen had just demanded new taxes) feel particularly valued, they also placed her children at the center of attention.

Maria Theresa also revised the titles by which her children were to be addressed. The changes were more than just cosmetic. Hardly anything was so bitterly fought over as titles; through them, relations between potentates were regulated and legal claims settled. In March 1755, following months of protracted debate in Court Conference and against the advice of her husband and several ministers, Maria Theresa decided that, from now on, each of her children was to be addressed as "Royal Highness" (*Königliche Hoheit*) rather than "Archducal Serenity" (*Erzherzogliche Durchlaucht*). A number of ministers objected to the change, arguing that the venerable title of the Archduchy of Austria was unique and hallowed by tradition. In addition, only "lesser houses" usually felt the need to inflate their titles; the great old families were above all that. Yet the empress held firm, wanting to see the royal rank of her children and their hereditary right to the kingdoms of Bohemia and Hungary ostentatiously displayed at all times and in all places.[23] This occurred through both written titulature and—even more visibly—ambassadorial ceremonial. Most spectacularly, Maria Theresa now required representatives of foreign powers to kiss the hand of each member of the royal family when presenting themselves at their formal introduction and farewell audiences—even the youngest, provided they were no longer confined to the crib.[24] This innovation, introduced shortly after the War of Succession, met with near-universal disapproval and even occasional resistance. In July 1753, for example, the wife of the new Neapolitan emissary threatened to deny the children this ceremonial mark of respect. Yet after her husband had been "made to see the disagreeable consequences she would face in the event of refusal," he thought better of it, persuading his wife to pucker up, "not just for their Imperial Majesties, but for all the young lords and ladies as well."[25] The Duke of Württemberg, who had already refused to kiss the pope's foot in Rome, also initially put up resistance when visiting the Viennese court in 1757. Yet he too eventually relented, even if—and this was the compromise—he would not have to kiss the imperial children's hands in public. He was explicitly warned that, if he refused to back down, "he

FIGURE 36. Glorification of Maria Theresa's fertility, copperplate
by Johann Michael Probst, c. 1756

would no longer be admitted to T[heir] M[ajesties] and would be put
extra commercium by the ministerio"; in other words, he would not
even be received by ministers, let alone by the emperor and empress.[26]
The fiercest resistance came from ambassadors' wives, who preferred to
stay away from the formal audience rather than pay the required obei-
sances. At the start of the Seven Years' War, the matter sparked a more
general crisis, when the wife of the Spanish ambassador, despite protracted negotiations, proved unwilling to kiss even the imperial couple,
let alone their children. More was at stake than a simple gesture of courtesy; the bone of contention was whether or not the king of Spain was
subordinate in rank to the emperor. On the advice of the wily Kaunitz,
the problem was resolved by presenting the kiss as a favor rather than
as an obligation: in future, only those who explicitly sought that favor
would be expected to put a Habsburg hand to their lips.[27] This put an
end to the practice in diplomacy. Yet visiting dignitaries still had to pay

their respects to the children along with their parents, even if the kiss was now voluntary. In autumn 1758 the last ambassador's wife was finally persuaded "to conform perfectly to the etiquette concerning all the young lords and ladies, as recognized by . . . every other court."[28] The youngest archduke was not yet two years old at the time.

Princely Pedagogy

Even in the society of the ancien régime, it was unusual for two-year-old children to receive diplomatic visits or be appointed to regimental commands. It was by no means completely absurd, however. Such practices vividly demonstrate that, in this society, an individual's status was determined by birth, not by talent or achievement. For generations the ruling family had claimed the right and indeed the ability to rule. This is not to say that the individual family members were not dutybound to acquire the necessary skills, emulate the virtues of their forebears, and prove worthy of their inherited privileges—*noblesse oblige*. Education was therefore accorded a central role. It was a key argument justifying the privileges of birth that only those who were *born* to rule could be prepared from the cradle for their heavy responsibilities. This was especially evident to Maria Theresa, who nursed a lifelong grudge against her father for inadequately preparing her for her duties as ruler. She therefore did everything she deemed necessary to qualify her own children for their future roles.

In so doing, she was in many respects adhering to a Europe-wide tradition of princely education. Such an education traditionally followed a hierarchy of norms: in first place stood the fear of God; in second, respect for one's parents and the dynasty; in third, moral purity; and only in fourth place, the knowledge and abilities demanded by one's station. For the future heir, this primarily encompassed both knowledge of state affairs as well as a free, self-assured, sovereign comportment.[29] Since the parents themselves took a hands-off approach, it was crucial that the right teachers be chosen. Like their mother before them, the children were each given their own chamber personnel under the direction of an ayo or aya. Neither they nor the other educators were professionally trained teachers—such training did not yet exist at the time. The children's chamber personnel were therefore not selected for their pedagogic talents; the criteria were quite different. Since the office of ayo or aya was a position of great eminence in the court hierarchy, only members of the high nobility who enjoyed the imperial house's particular favor came into consideration. Most ayos were subsequently made princes, if they were not princes already. Maria Theresa liked to choose former commanders, generals, or other former high-ranking officials for her children. Being called on to educate the ruler's children was considered a signal honor. Maria Theresa used the office, for example, to signal her esteem for the Hungarian nobility by appointing Count Batthyány the heir's ayo, or to compensate for a humiliation, as in the case of Bartenstein, to whom she entrusted Joseph's education.[30] The aya or ayo bore overall responsibility for their charges; they supervised the children's entire household and accompanied them at all public appearances. The chamber personnel, both high and low, looked after the children's everyday needs, ensuring they were kept clean, clothed, and well fed; a confessor tended to their spiritual discipline and a personal physician to their physical health; a series of learned Jesuits fathers equipped them with the necessary knowledge; language, music, dancing, riding, and fencing masters saw to it that they acquired the expected aristocratic accomplishments (see color plate 21: *Exercitia corporis*).

Contrary to the myth of the bourgeois family idyll, Maria Theresa did not spend quality time with her children in an atmosphere of intimacy and familiarity when they were away from the courtly stage. The archduchesses and archdukes were generally left alone with the chamber personnel; the younger children were not even brought along to Schönbrunn except on rare occasions. Maria Theresa seldom paid a visit to the children's room in the Hofburg. At most, she set aside an hour after lunch for her children, a generous amount of time by contemporary standards. Besides, her own crammed timetable left no space for more.[31] Yet when it came to public ceremonies—church services, audiences, apartments, galas, balls, or visits to the theater—the parents always appeared with several children in tow, on special occasions with all of them. Hunting stays in Laxenburg or Holíč were another matter; the older children permitted to come along regarded it as their "inestimable good fortune to see Their Majesties."[32] Maria Theresa's interest in her children's education chiefly took the form of detailed written instructions for those directly responsible. She also composed these for her grandchildren and even for the daughter of her successor, although by that stage Joseph had already been crowned emperor. "The successful arrangements made at my court for the sixteen children God has been pleased to grant me" were to be kept in place for her grandchildren as well.[33] The instructions convey a vivid image of how Maria Theresa organized her children's day-to-day life, the educational goals she set for them, and the values that guided her in the process.[34] But they also betray the ruthlessness with which she diagnosed the weaknesses and character flaws of her children and the means she deemed necessary for combating them.

Infants do not figure in these instructions. As mentioned earlier, they were entrusted after birth to a healthy, physically robust wet nurse who needed no qualification besides her orthodox Catholicism. Until the age of four, the empress wrote, all that was required was for the children to be made "docile and obedient" and acquire the rudiments "of our holy religion," which they should grow to love and respect from earliest infancy.[35] Children could not be taught soon enough to be devout and God-fearing, when they could still be molded through habit and example.[36] Until the age of six, sons and daughters were raised together "in the children's room," where everything had to be done in a spirit of "orderliness, decency, and calm."[37] Maria Theresa placed great emphasis on even her youngest offspring keeping their distance from chamber personnel. They had to be prevented at all costs from developing such close and regular ties to any one individual that they would refuse to be attended by anyone else. They should on no account be cosseted and indulged. As soon as they could sit by themselves, they were no longer to be held in their wet nurse's lap. Nobody was permitted to "prattle" or make jokes in their presence, speak baby talk, play finger games, make faces, sing them to sleep, or tell them stories—all of which the subaltern chamber personnel were inclined to do. The children should learn to walk without leading-strings, if possible, so as not to feel constrained and to become accustomed to a free, upright gait. They were not to be made pliable with sweets or small gifts; it was sufficient reward to praise them and "pay them a compliment."[38] It was also forbidden to scare them with stories of "thunderstorms, fire, ghosts, witches, or other such puerile matters."[39] Their questions should either be answered rationally or not at all; on no account should they be told untruths.[40] In short, the children were to be treated seriously and "rationally" from as early as possible—and thus not treated like children at all.

Every waking hour was accounted for. Hours were precisely allocated for religious duties, meals, lessons, and play, as had been the Archducal House's custom for generations past. The day began and ended with prayers. Devotional exercises were the alpha and omega of a Christian upbringing, since "all other virtues derive from true Christian exercises and obligations." Religion would also later be a source of much-needed consolation for daughters, in particular.[41] Upon awakening, the sign of the cross first had to be made and then a morning prayer offered up. Like their mother, the children had to attend Mass each morning and pray the rosary each afternoon. The end of every day was to be spent reviewing their conscience and contemplating their "creator."

Until the children had grown up, their external devotions were strictly supervised; once they had married and set up a court of their own, however, it was no longer so easy to verify that they were punctiliously observing their religious duties. Overseeing her adult children's spiritual discipline from afar became Maria Theresa's almost obsessive concern.[42]

The closest attention was also paid to the children's bodies; all their bodily functions were subject to careful and unrelenting scrutiny. They were never truly alone; a chambermaid or servant would always pass the night in the room with them. Any unusual physical symptom, whether good or bad, "every minor ailment, pain, or little spot," had to be reported immediately to the physician van Swieten, who visited the imperial family on a daily basis and had to be available for consultation at all hours, day or night. Absolutely nothing concerning their bodies could happen without his authorization.[43] Chambermaids and valets were responsible for cleanliness; it was their job to dress and undress their charges, comb their hair, and see to it that they "washed their mouth and hands each morning and evening and their feet once a week." The dentist visited the heir apparent twice a week early in the morning to clean and look after his teeth.[44] The children's diet was likewise strictly regimented.[45] Only foods previously approved by van Swieten were set before them. Fasting requirements were strictly imposed at the age of five: "In the evenings, fasting soup, eggs, and a cooked dessert, but nothing sweet, no fruit or pastry. Nothing during the daytime except a quarter of a bread roll, if necessary, as a snack, no sugar, sweets, chocolate, or coffee."[46] Partly a question of health, partly one of piety, dietary rules were also a disciplinary tool. When a child expressed an aversion to certain dishes, mealtimes became a battle zone. Maria Theresa decreed that her five- and six-year-old daughters Josepha and Johanna "make no complaints or requests . . . , nor enter into any discourse concerning food," lest they become "fussy" eaters. No child was permitted to refuse the fish dishes served on Fridays, Saturdays, and other fasting days. "Although Johanna has a pronounced aversion to [fish], she should not be allowed to have her way in this matter but should be brought to heel. All my other children showed the same aversion and they all had to overcome it, the seven eldest having fasted with us for two years now, therefore no ground can be given on this point."[47] The fourteen-year-old Marianna, Khevenhüller observed, fell ill on Easter Sunday because the fish she had been made to eat over the preceding fast days had disagreed with her.[48] Diet was one area where the children's wishes counted for nothing; medical treatment was another. Here, too, there was no place for indulgence. Here is Khevenhüller again, this time reporting on the nine-year-old Amalia: "following a recent violent seizure, the poor child had been unwilling to take an enema, which had to be administered by force. As a result, the little lady suffered an injury that then became infected."[49]

Such instances of physical force were exceptional at the Viennese court. Child-rearing methods were relatively moderate compared with what those from other social milieus had to endure. Whereas elsewhere children were beaten without a second thought, here corporal punishment was avoided; children should be brought to obey from insight, not fear, and be instilled with a desire to perfect themselves. They should be guided to the right path "through habit as well as through principles," through rewards and "inducements to propriety," also through rational discussion, but only in the last resort through punishment.[50] Besides, given the social hierarchy, it was tricky for the chamber personnel even to threaten the royal children with violence, let alone act on the threat. The strongest disciplinary tool was public humiliation. It was thus considered a harsh punishment when a child's name day or birthday was either demonstratively passed over in silence rather than celebrated with a court gala, or a gala was announced but the child was forbidden from appearing and accepting the compliments of court society. Archduke Charles, for example, was made to stay in his room on his fourteenth birthday, "officially because he was indisposed, but actually to punish and humiliate him; for this little lord is uncommonly arrogant and sometimes says the most shocking and indelicate things to his chamberlains and servants."[51] His sister Elisabeth was considered inordinately vain and hence in need of humiliation on a massive scale. Her name day was therefore "customarily not celebrated."[52] If punishment was warranted, then it should be merciless and irrevocable; the child's guardian should not be deterred from his purpose by flattery, pleading, protest, or "ignoble scenes. In such a case, when it is no longer deemed necessary to lend an ear to justifications or excuses, these should also not be permitted, and the child should be assured in advance that, by holding his tongue and exercising self-control, he will demonstrate his complete submission and provide his own best defense."[53]

The goal of education was to inculcate in children a manner befitting their high station in life, a certain way of thinking, appearing, and bearing themselves that conveyed an air of sovereign superiority.[54] No distinction was made between moral and physical characteristics. The aim was to internalize an attitude of magnanimity, grace, and reserve. Any suggestion of casual familiarity was to be strictly avoided. Everyone was to be treated with equal courtesy, regardless of rank. "Familiar relations" with subalterns, whether in the positive or negative sense, were frowned on: tomfoolery, flippant remarks, childishness, gossip, teasing, bullying, and anything that suggested intimacy with those of lesser standing.[55]

The greatest danger was posed by sycophants who told the children only what they wanted to hear, fulfilled their every wish, and spoke disparagingly of others in their presence, encouraging selfish, high-handed behavior. Children should instead be taught not to abuse their privileged position, nor "delight in disadvantaging those near them, which is particularly reprehensible in great lords, who find it easy to dismay or embarrass such persons who are not permitted to respond in kind."[56] Only those who treated everyone with respect and exercised self-restraint were respected in return and showed themselves worthy of commanding others. Not least, their physical appearance had to reflect their high estate. This required that they be immaculately dressed, upright in posture, free in movement, with an open countenance, a well-modulated speaking voice, a pleasing expression—all without any hint of artifice or strain. The little "lords" and "ladies" also needed to appropriate the classical princely virtues of magnanimity and benevolence by occasionally giving their personal servants small gifts, dispensing alms, and receiving petitions. In doing so, however, they should take care that they were not acting out of selfishness and calculation or favoring anyone out of "particular affection."[57] Making representations on behalf of others was permissible only within very narrow limits, since court personnel were discouraged from exploiting their access to the children to curry favor with the parents.[58]

At the age of six or seven, children were separated by sex; the heir was kept apart from the rest and given his own court.[59] Sons and daughters were not treated differently in every respect. The strict organization of their daily routine as well as rules concerning cleanliness, diet, and piety were the same for both. The curriculum was similar, too: reading and writing in German as a mother tongue (without dialect), then French and Italian (with the addition of Spanish for the daughters destined for a Bourbon court in Italy), while the sons learned Latin and a little Czech;[60] instruction in religion, history, and geography; also mathematics, geometry, and jurisprudence for the sons; finally music and dance, with riding, fencing, and other military exercises for the boys. The archdukes were tested every three months on what they had learned in the presence of Khevenhüller (in his capacity as president of the

Knights' Academy) and occasionally also the emperor; Maria Theresa never seems to have sat in on these oral examinations.[61]

One difference was crucial: daughters were "born to obey and should get used to this at an early stage"; they had to learn to be compliant and demure, to do their husband's bidding once they were married, and to conform to the customs of the country in every respect.[62] They were therefore instructed not to give orders to even the lowliest footman or gate keeper. Matters were more difficult when it came to the sons. The fundamental dilemma of a princely education presented itself in aggravated form in the case of the heir: training the child to be humble before God, obedient to his parents, and respectful toward his teachers on the one hand, while at the same time preparing him for the throne on the other. The ayo pulled out the prince's chair at public table and passed him his serviette, but he was also supposed to inspire fear and respect and punish him when necessary.[63] For the ayos and chamberlains, the office was therefore a "heavy cross," for all that it brought great honor.[64] As soon as the heir turned six, two noble courtiers took turns serving him each day. The chamberlain on duty accompanied him wherever he went, supervised him as he dressed and undressed, waited on him at mealtimes, and never let him out of his sight, "so that he might be discreetly alerted to the minor slip-ups that are only natural at his age."[65] In the theater or at apartment, the chamberlain always stood directly behind his master—in public, he always had to perform his duty upright–, introduced those who sought to be admitted to his presence, and told him what to say. In a confidential order, the heir's chamberlain was also warned never to interfere in the prince's lessons, to breathe not a word to the outside world about what went on in his study (especially so far as punishment was concerned), and, conversely, to allow no unauthorized persons and no unpleasant news, gossip, or intrigue to infiltrate the court. A chamberlain was supposed to model courtesy, mildness, and moderation in all he did, and to demonstrate abhorrence for sin in general while never speaking ill of anyone in particular, not even enemy nations. Exaggerated praise and flattery were also to be avoided at all costs. The prince was instead always to be treated with openness and honesty, so providing him with a permanent example of how good manners could help him win the affection and gratitude of his subjects. Maria Theresa considered this to be absolutely essential for the six-year-old Joseph: "He should be taught to pay particular attention to people of high standing, told their family names, their connections, their offices, and through a thousand pieces of information, fed him little by little, he will come to shed his tendency to bashfulness, yet always gently and accompanied by brief explanations, without insulting him or making fun of him with ironic reproaches."[66]

All these instructions bespoke a spirit of unobtrusive yet absolute control. The children—and the heir in particular—were to be protected from all unwanted impressions and shielded from all external influences. Every dish they tasted had to be approved by their physicians, every book that crossed their threshold had to receive the blessing of their confessors. Even teachers were not allowed to spend time alone with their pupils, nor were they permitted to speak with them about topics unrelated to their lessons. Joseph's teacher was required to keep a meticulous daily record of his conduct.[67] Maria Theresa was practically obsessed with knowing everything about her children, seeing into their very souls, and regulating their access to the world, even if this meant having to rely on informants. She was tormented by her inability to get her way in this regard. Whether through rebelliousness, reticence, or dissimulation, her children succeeded in escaping her total control.

Hardly any of the children could live up to their mother's high standards. She was unsparing in her criticism of them, their educators, and their companions. She permitted herself no illusions or prejudices in her children's favor, and she required their teachers and confessors to speak candidly with her about their faults.[68] With regard to her daughter Josepha, for example, she wrote that she had an unlovely face, a strange disposition, and was not particularly "able." She was prone to dissimulation and treated her servants poorly. In general, there was something coarse and unbecoming about her conduct.[69] She described the six-year-old Johanna as gifted but willful; she had a strong head and a stubborn streak that would need to be broken.[70] Compliments were also paid at times, as when Johanna gained the approbation of all the world upon making her first journey to Holíč.[71] She praised the seven-year-old

Elisabeth on a journey to Prague for "sitting still like a little statue; she . . . chatted incessantly and quite rationally, without shuffling, slipping, or lapsing from her upright posture, and asked not a single question. One could not have asked for better behavior from a lady of twenty, she has so far surpassed all her elder siblings."[72] She credited her grown-up daughter Amalia with patience, docility, openness, and helpfulness, but found fault with her for having neither taste nor appreciation for the arts and sciences. She therefore had nothing to offer an educated husband. Her French was defective; the less she talked, the better, and she should on no account meddle in government, a business for which she was not clever enough anyway.[73] Carolina was criticized for her irreverence, petulance, and childish curiosity. She had a most unpleasant voice and an ugly way of speaking. She was also even sillier than her little sisters.[74] With Marie Antoinette, by contrast, Maria Theresa was initially very pleased; she praised her grace, amiability, docility, and sweet temper, qualities that were likely to endear the fourteen-year-old to everyone at Versailles. She was concerned, however, by her distaste for reading and any kind of intellectual exertion and, increasingly, by the neglect of her outward appearance reported by informants in Paris.[75] The empress was much less happy with Ferdinand, sent at the age of seventeen to be governor of Milan. She repeatedly wrote to him demanding that he change his ways, castigating him for his indolence, negligence, and effeminacy, his lack of piety and obedience, his arrogance and his narcissism, for which, moreover, he had far less cause than anyone else in the family.[76] Maria Christina was the only one of her offspring spared such criticism.

As it turned out, Maria Theresa would feel most let down by the two sons who would go on to become emperors and remarkable rulers in their own right: Joseph, her successor, and Leopold, who inherited the Grand Duchy of Tuscany from his father in 1765. In her opinion, her firstborn son had been too much cosseted in his earliest childhood and allowed to get his own way, leading him to entertain "certain premature ideas about his highness." She found him incapable of acknowledging his own failings. At the same time, however, he could be perceptive and excessively critical when it came to the internal and external flaws of others.[77] She equally complained about his "bashfulness, so unbecoming to a great lord," the inhibition that, even as a child, he had learned to compensate through ridicule, sarcasm, and contempt.[78] In essence, she denied that he had the capacity for Christian neighborly love. There could be no more serious reproach. She found him entirely lacking in magnanimity, clemency, and general amiability, the very virtues for which she herself was renowned and that made a prince beloved by courtiers and subjects alike. This personal contrast would explode into conflict once Joseph became coregent.

The third son, Leopold, presented Maria Theresa with an even greater pedagogic challenge. No other child, if contemporary reports are to be believed, was so frequently or severely scolded by both parents.[79] Leopold's first ayo, Künigl, was sixty-five years old and in frail health. He was assisted by the brothers Franz and Anton von Thurn, retired generals who had fought in the Seven Years' War and sought to enthuse Leopold for the military. Shortly before the boy's fifteenth birthday, Maria Theresa asked Anton von Thurn to keep a detailed record of his pupil's failings and his success in mending his ways. This he dutifully did.[80] The "faithful list" he compiled covers no fewer than twenty points, bringing the demands placed on the young archduke into sharp and merciless focus. His findings were devastating. The archduke had a gloomy, unpleasant disposition. He was deliberately discourteous, preferred keeping company with commoners, and loved platitudes, gossip, frivolity, and puerile jokes, all of which made him incapable of rational discussion. He had a poor work ethic, and the progress he made in his studies could only be explained by his prodigious intelligence. He had to be forced to keep clean, while his clothing was a matter of indifference to him. He was careless with the truth; when caught lying, he would cry like a little child or fly into fits of rage. He was hot tempered and would try to get his way by deception, if necessary. Generally speaking, he was lacking in openness, trust, and affection. He behaved like someone half his age, loving only those who confirmed him in his childish ways. He had a defective knowledge of human nature and overlooked true merit. Hard-hearted, blunt, and unfeeling toward petitioners as well as his siblings, he picked up malicious prejudices from the ne'er-do-wells with whom he fraternized. The German he spoke was the dialect of low-born, uneducated fellows, which he excused with the spurious reasoning that, as an Austrian prince, he should speak Austrian himself. His deportment was shocking. He could neither walk nor sit respectably, and he had a string of bad habits, such as constantly spitting, chewing his nails, slouching, making a spectacle of himself at table, and avoiding eye contact in conversation. He had no sense of honor and was unwilling to do the right thing for its own sake. Repeatedly threatened with having his privileges withdrawn and his parents notified of his misdemeanors, he had learned to act only from fear of punishment, not from any desire for self-improvement. He tormented himself constantly by hatching vainglorious plans and then plunging into despair when they came to nothing. His piety was solid enough, but he could easily be distracted from his devotions; he was rude to his servants and turned a deaf ear to good advice; he was lazy, unmotivated, and self-pitying. He had no interest (or merely feigned interest) in activities appropriate to his age, and was generous for the wrong reasons, favoring only his own servants. Thurn observed very few signs of improvement in his recalcitrant charge; for all that he was constantly rebuked, the archduke made very little progress. All in all, the direction in which his character was developing was still hard to make out, even if a certain preference for the military could be discerned. This long and (from today's point of view) astonishingly unsystematic litany of complaints, which placed nail-chewing alongside lack of brotherly love, is—*ex negativo*—a detailed mirror of the aristocratic canon of values prevailing at the time. What it makes clear is that external and internal deportment were two sides of the same coin: physical stance reflected moral stature. To be honorable meant to be seen by others, quite literally, as a man of honor. An inner sense of honor had to be outwardly visible.

There were doubtless many other such reports about the children, even if few have survived. Maria Theresa would have destroyed them in the ordinary course of events, just as she burned her children's letters after reading them and ordered them to do the same (although not all of them complied, fortunately). Another source shows how Leopold reacted to the barrage of criticism and how Maria Theresa dealt with her apparently incorrigible son. Three years later, in

May 1765, when Leopold's wedding with the Spanish infanta was imminent and he was on a rare visit to his parents at Laxenburg, Maria Theresa confronted Anton von Thurn with a series of reprimands he was to communicate to his pupil. The next day, she summoned her son to respond to her reproaches in person. She clearly feared that Leopold was unwilling to go ahead with the marriage and had been secretly confirmed in his doubts by his sarcastic brother Joseph. To make matters worse, he had recently embarked on an affair with Countess Erdödy. In short, matters were getting beyond her control. Leopold describes the summit with his mother in a long letter to his ayo, Franz von Thurn, who had stayed behind in Vienna.[81] Point by point, he lists her reproaches along with the justifications he had thought up the previous night. "You can imagine how hard all these points hit me," he wrote. "I answered her with the very answers I had prepared, but in a more succinct form, without embarrassment. . . . She was very gracious with me, it must be said, addressing me more like a good friend than a mother, and I will certainly do all I can to satisfy her in every regard. . . . I am by nature a closed book. For a while I was more open, but since I see that some people are using this against me, I will again become a recluse."[82]

The episode reveals a fundamental dilemma in the relationship between Maria Theresa and her children. Her need to know everything about them was a recurring maternal refrain: "*Ne cachez rien!*—hide nothing!" she wrote time and again. The most frequent reproach she leveled at her children was that they were concealing things from her and going behind her back. Yet the trust she demanded of them was not reciprocated. Wherever they went, the children were monitored by her spies, who were expected to provide her with regular verbal or written reports; even the children's confessors were not exempted from this obligation.[83] Her obsession with knowing everything about her children exacerbated the problem and created a vicious circle of dissimulation. Through her compulsion to absolute openness, she practically forced them to simulate candor or clam up completely.

Needless to say, Maria Theresa's attempts at around-the-clock surveillance proved futile. In fact, the children's personal servants appear to have permitted them substantial liberties whenever they were away from the watchful eye of their ayo or aya. One of Leopold's teachers, for example, was said to have lax disciplinary standards and to lark around with his pupils. Leopold's ayo gave him a book containing passages that offended common decency.[84] In Maria Theresa's eyes, Franz von Thurn was an abject failure.[85] Compared with the standards prevailing in other estates and the tradition of the imperial household, the education received by the little lords and ladies could almost be described as liberal. The eldest daughter, Marianna, remembered her childhood as free and unstuffy, and her education as "masculine and fairly diffuse"; she had plunged herself into all kinds of pleasures, both permitted and forbidden, and devoted day and night to hunting and dancing, card playing and novel reading.[86] And the Duke of Croÿ, who knew his way around both Vienna and Versailles, claimed that the empress had brought up her children "without the earlier rigidity of the House of Austria, and almost encouraged the opposite extreme, viz., allowing her children to grow up in an atmosphere of the utmost levity."[87] The Prussian emissary Podewils believed that she only cultivated the appearance of strictness from time to time. His successor Fürst, by contrast, found her to be "an affectionate and strict mother. . . . There are rewards and also punishments, just as there are among private people."[88]

Even at the time, Maria Theresa's pedagogical methods were thus perceived differently depending on the standard against which they were judged. This applies all the more to later historians. If we are to understand contemporary conditions, however, we need to be wary of anachronism. They should not be judged against a norm that was alien to the period. Maria Theresa's last son left the nursery at exactly the same time that Rousseau was inventing the naturally pure and innocent child, uncorrupted by civilization, and proposing a "natural" education appropriate to its needs—a provocation that flew in the face of everything contemporaries had believed to be self-evident to that point. Later, too, the empress could not bring herself to embrace the "new fashion à la Rousseau." If children were allowed to do whatever they wanted, she warned, they would turn into peasants.[89]

Victims of Politics

As the dynasty's social capital, children could only yield political interest if they were invested wisely—if, that is, they were married off in a strategically calculated way. At its heart, dynastic politics was matrimonial politics; we have already seen ample evidence of this. Indeed, the House of Habsburg was famous for having amassed its sprawling empire through opportune marriages: *Bella gerant alii, tu felix Austria nube*, ran the Latin tag: "Let others wage war: thou, happy Austria, marry." This was somewhat euphemistically phrased, since marriage and warfare were by no means mutually exclusive. On the contrary, marriages sometimes led to competing claims to rule and hence conflict, including armed conflict. Yet ideally, it was assumed that relatives were "friends"— in German, "friendship" (*Freundschaft*) was all but synonymous with in-law relations until the late eighteenth century. More or less all echelons of society used marriage to strengthen social networks, not just the high nobility. Similarly, it was widely assumed that marital arrangements were not just the affair of the individuals concerned but of their families as well. Only those who had no inheritance to bequeath and nothing to lose could afford to let their children wed partners of their choice (assuming anyone was prepared to marry them in the first place). Maria Theresa's marriage schemes were thus nothing out of the ordinary; far more remarkable was her willingness to make a single exception from a standard rule of matchmaking.[90] This rule stipulated that spouses had to be drawn from the same estate or pool of eligible partners: in this case, the pool of sovereign princely dynasties. Boundaries between estates were fluid and were constantly being redrawn. Other Habsburgs were clearly eligible matches for members of the Habsburg dynasty; that way the house would suffer no capital losses, although it would not gain anything, either. The ultimate objective, though, was increasing the dynasty's sovereign territories through an astute choice of bride. Heiresses of other houses were thus a coveted prize for Habsburg princelings. The second goal was using marriage to consolidate political alliances and lay enmities to rest. The hand of an archduke or archduchess was a valuable political commodity that raised justified expectations of services in return. Choosing a member of the same Christian denomination was a desirable but not absolutely necessary criterion. A clear barrier separated Christianity from Islam, however. It was unthinkable on both sides that a Habsburg bride might take an Ottoman groom, or that an archduke might marry a sultan's daughter, even when diplomatic relations between the two powers were at their peak.[91]

These unspoken principles lay behind the marriage policy that Maria Theresa pursued for her children, which eventually issued in the various lines of the House of Bourbon and the ducal House of Modena. Only two marriages—Maria Christina's union with a duke of Saxony and Joseph's second marriage to a duchess of Bavaria—broke the mold. This outcome was the result of many interacting circumstances. Habsburg matrimonial politics needs to be understood as a large-scale, complex game of strategy involving numerous contingent factors. Costs had to be carefully weighed up against benefits, always proceeding with foresight, flexibility, and an eye to other options. Sometimes a plan had to be dropped at an advanced stage of development, calling for face-saving measures on both sides, when a more favorable opportunity presented itself. The early death of preferred candidates always had to be taken into consideration. Under these circumstances, no allowances could be made for children's personal feelings; indeed, they had normally never even met their partners prior to the wedding. Planning generally began long before candidates had reached marriageable age. Leopold's betrothal to Maria Beatrice d'Este, the rich heiress of the Duchy of Modena, was arranged when he was just six years old, for example. The match had to be canceled when Leopold's older brother Charles died, requiring Leopold to wed the king of Spain's daughter, Maria Ludovica, in his place—"You have other princes," the Spanish emissary Mahoni is said to have told a grieving Maria Theresa.[92] The hand of Maria Beatrice now passed to Leopold's younger brother Ferdinand, ensuring that the House of Habsburg still acquired hereditary rule over the Duchy of Modena. Maria Theresa was well aware that such arranged marriages could be a heavy burden, particularly for her daughters, and she showed some sympathy for their plight. She thus wrote about the proposed marriage between Archduchess Josepha and King Ferdinand IV of Naples that, in view of the groom's character flaws, her daughter would have to gird herself for a life that was lonely, self-sufficient, and full of privation: "I view poor Josepha as a victim of politics."[93] This was no less true of poor Carolina, eventually forced to spend fifteen years in wedlock to the king of Naples, or Amalia, who at twenty-three was pledged to the seventeen year old Crown Prince of Parma—not to mention Marie Antoinette, sent to Versailles at fourteen as the dauphin's bride to cement the Franco-Habsburg alliance.[94]

Connections between the Habsburg and Bourbon dynasties were the central threads of the marriage network that Maria Theresa was constantly spinning and respinning. The House of Bourbon had been split along two main lines since the War of the Spanish Succession. One line held the French throne, the other the crown of Spain, the dual kingdom of Naples and Sicily, and (from 1748) the Duchy of Parma. The Italian peninsula had for centuries been the main battleground for the opposed houses of Habsburg and Valois-Bourbon. This finally changed following the War of the Austrian Succession. Charles of Bourbon (1716–1788), eldest son of Philip V of Spain and Elisabeth Farnese, king of Naples from 1735 and king of Spain from 1759, began hatching various marriage plans involving the House of Habsburg. The thirteen children he sired with his wife Maria Amalia of Saxony, seven of whom survived into adulthood, offered ample material for these schemes. Charles himself had once, in 1725, been intended for Maria Theresa until the plan was scuppered by the maritime powers. Now, in 1751, Maria Theresa and Charles envisaged a double wedding between their two houses. The eldest Spanish infanta would marry the Habsburg heir while, conversely, the Spanish heir would wed a Habsburg archduchess. In 1755, when Maria Theresa needed cover from the Spanish Bourbons for her great *renversement des alliances* in the lead-up to the war with Prussia, two additional couplings were contemplated: the future king of Naples, the difficult Ferdinand IV, would be paired off with an archduchess, while the second-born archduke would perhaps marry a Spanish infanta.[95]

Yet Maria Theresa was forced to change tack. In February 1759, in the middle of the war against Prussia and shortly before concluding the second secret treaty in Versailles, Maria Theresa was far more dependent on the French king's goodwill than on that of his Spanish-Neapolitan relative. Louis XV, however, wanted Isabella of Bourbon-Parma to marry the Habsburg heir. Isabella was the eldest daughter of the Duke of Parma and his wife, Louise Elisabeth of Bourbon, a daughter of Louis XV, who for her part had been married at the Spanish court at the age of twelve. Isabella was thus the granddaughter of both the late King Philip V of Spain and Louis XV of France. The French king's proposal put Maria Theresa in a quandary with regard to Charles III, whose daughter had been all but promised to her firstborn son. A plausible, face-saving explanation was required for why the engagement had to be broken off. The ever-inventive Kaunitz recommended shifting the blame to Joseph and his heartfelt devotion to Isabella. It says a great deal about Maria Theresa's views on questions of marriage that she accepted this pretext only with the greatest reluctance. "*Placet,*"she wrote on the margin of Kaunitz's memorandum, "because a better excuse could not be found than blaming it on my son's preference for the Infanta of Parma. But it cannot be laid to his charge, since he is a well brought-up son; and I acquiesce in it as a measure of state, which we and the entire conference agreed to."[96] In other words, she was averse to presenting herself to the Spanish court as an indulgent mother who deferred to the feelings of her son in so central an affair of state as the choice of his bride. For this was far from the case. Joseph had never before set eyes on his betrothed and was understandably anxious about his impending wedding. Yet he was determined to do his parents' bidding, obey divine providence, and conscientiously fulfill his conjugal duties, come what may.[97] Kaunitz, too, thought the heir far too well brought-up to "express a will of his own and . . . put up the least resistance to the All-Highest resolution."[98]

Isabella of Parma may have been the granddaughter of two kings, but her father was merely the head of a ducal offshoot of the House of Bourbon. Strictly speaking, then, she was no suitable match for the heir to the Habsburg throne. Maria Theresa could therefore present the choice of bride to the outside world as proof of her own modest dynastic ambitions. This marriage showed all the world, she wrote to Maria Antonia

of Saxony, that she placed more value on "quality than on great alliances."[99] Besides the reconquest of Silesia, she claimed, she had no ambition for territorial aggrandizement. Her sons would later receive the
Habsburg lands of Milan, Tuscany, and the Netherlands, while her
daughters would be provided for with ecclesiastical endowments in
Styria, Upper Austria, Tyrol, and Prague. All further plans went unmentioned in the letter. Marriage negotiations were an extremely sensitive
matter, one better left undisclosed even to close confidants.

Isabella of Parma

Joseph and Isabella's wedding was held *per procuratorem* in Parma on
September 7, 1760, in the middle of the Seven Years' War. Acting as the
groom's proxy, Prince Liechtenstein escorted the bride with a large retinue to Vienna, where she made her grand entrance a month later.[100] The
public wedding celebrations took place on October 7, 1760. They were
documented by the workshop of the court painter van Meytens in a
series of five large-format ceremonial canvases (see fig. 26 and color
plate 16).[101] No expense was spared: despite the crippling cost of the
conflict, around three million guilders were spent on the wedding. Precisely in a time of war, the unlimited financial power of the Archducal
House had to be demonstrated for it to remain creditworthy. Isabella
thus shared the usual fate of a royal daughter, which she later described
in the following terms: "In the high society in which she is forced to live,
she has neither friends nor acquaintances. It is for this that she has to
leave her family, her home. And why? To belong to a man whose character is unknown to her, to enter into a family where she is received with
jealousy, and to be a victim of the unfortunate policy of a minister who
promises himself an everlasting yet insecure alliance from the match."[102]
Joseph, too, looked forward to the encounter with mixed feelings. In
September 1760 he exchanged a series of letters with his chamberlain,
Salm, who had traveled to Parma to fetch the bride, hoping in the process to stiffen the archduke's resolve and learn what sort of a person the
princess was. Joseph feared he would cut a ridiculous figure at the wedding. He felt himself ill suited to playing the attentive lover, a role that

did not come naturally to him.[103] Although "insusceptible to the charms of love," he did not want to rule out developing affectionate feelings for his bride over time. He was encouraged a little by his informant's assurance that Isabella was a serious person and, like him, interested in a sincere spiritual friendship.[104] Yet the (no longer extant) instructions given him by his father before the wedding day must have added to his fears of married life. As the first encounter drew near, he was gripped by panic.[105]

Isabella of Parma dispelled all his fears. She was in every respect an exceptional woman.[106] The reputation that preceded her—"the most amiable character, combined with an attractive appearance and placid disposition"–understated her virtues.[107] In the three short years she spent in Vienna, from her arrival in October 1760 to her death—shortly before her twenty-second birthday—on November 27, 1763, she seems to have won over the entire court. She was universally described as charming and beautiful. A virtuosic violinist, competent at drawing, and author of philosophical essays and religious reflections, she took an interest in disciplines as diverse as finance, military strategy, and mathematics, and concerned herself with all the themes that were in vogue in enlightened circles at the time.[108] In short, she was exceptionally intelligent, cultivated, and well read. At the same time, she was very much a split personality, by turns captivating and melancholy, enthusiastic and despondent, self-critical to excess and sarcastic in her judgments of others. When Isabella transported the entire family into a state of collective rapture, when she cast a permanent spell over her habitually shy husband and her notoriously hard-to-please mother-in-law, she did so not entirely without guile. The princess was equally proficient in the rules of etiquette and the rhetoric of sentimentality. She was a talented observer of others, and she made it her overriding ambition from early on to win over every member of the imperial family. We know just how assiduously and intelligently she practiced this art from the roughly two hundred letters to Archduchess Maria Christina that have come down to us.

These letters betray an almost obsessive concern with gaining the undivided love and attention of Maria Christina, the same age as Isabella and the object of her consuming passion. She had already started writing to her future sister-in-law before they met, doing all she could to create a climate of friendly intimacy. She called her *ma soeur fidèle*, my faithful sister, and declared her tender admiration for the empress and her love of Germany. Following her arrival in Vienna, the correspondence gradually intensified into ever more effusive expressions of attachment and devotion. The stream of letters did not abate even when the two women were seeing each other almost every day at court. Letters were considered the "mirror of the soul"; they provided an outlet for what could not be said in the strictly ceremonialized everyday life of the court. "My adorable sister," Isabella writes repeatedly, "my goddess! my heart! my angel! Venus! I am mad with love for you; I love you to distraction; I worship you!" She then speaks of her lover's "devilish" character, her cruelty and disloyalty. Much remains incomprehensible to later readers, as when Isabella refers to shared experiences and secrets ("yesterday's adventure"), makes ironic allusions, or uses cover names. Time and again she declares herself deeply wounded, "soaked in tears," because Maria Christina has paid her insufficient attention, and demands proofs of her love; she then begs her to forgive her jealousy. She tries to arrange secret rendezvous for the two of them, refers to their joint "marriage" and a mysterious "wedding present,"[109] calls herself Maria's *amant*, lover, or *mari*, husband, and refers to the two of them— alluding to operas they had attended—as Orpheus and Eurydice, Zerbin and Laurette, or Linon and Lisette.[110] She airs the greatest intimacies without any sense of shame, drastically showing today's readers just how low the threshold of embarrassment was in such matters.[111] At any rate, what is invoked in these letters is far more than Platonic infatuation: "I cover you all over with my kisses," she exclaims, "I kiss everything you let me kiss," or even—in German in the original rather than the usual French—"I kiss your archangelic ass."[112] Maria Christina's reactions have not survived, but they appear to have been more reserved, since Isabella calls her a saint and writes: "Despite your saintliness, I kiss you with all my soul, so that they may be said to be pious kisses, for what comes from the soul is purely spiritual and not of this earth, although I love all that is down-to-earth."[113] On the rare occasions when Isabella mentions her husband, then it is as an unwelcome

FIGURE 37. Joseph, Maria Theresa, Maria Christina, and Isabella.
Workshop of Martin van Meytens, 1763

intrusion, the "rival" of her beloved.[114] Among the essays composed by Isabella there is a short, sarcastic "Treatise on Men": the most useless creatures in all the world, good for nothing other than selfishness, more irrational than animals, elevated by God above women only so that male flaws would cause female virtues to shine all the more brightly. If girls had not been persuaded that they were useless, they would cope very well without their menfolk. The devil had a hand in play when men were created, women had no choice but to make the best of a bad lot.[115]

From today's viewpoint, it seems highly unlikely that the erotic relationship between the two women was confined to the medium of letters. For a long time, however, historians refused to contemplate so scandalous a suggestion. From the nineteenth century onward, they were disconcerted by Isabella's amorous outpourings and had great difficulty reconciling them with the revised moral conceptions of their own time. Nationalist historians felt the need to view members of the imperial household as "intensely sensitive, self-sacrificing natures," and it filled them "with joyful pride to be able to say as much of these serene figures, whose memory is inseparably bound up with the creation of the new Austria."[116] Offensive passages in the correspondence were therefore omitted, and the relationship between the two women was downplayed to one of sentimental, girlish affection. Isabella's relationship with her husband, meanwhile, was transfigured—against all the evidence—into romantic love. Alfred von Arneth saw in the sources "a heartwarming image of peaceful and joyous cohabitation."[117] And according to Adam Wolf, Isabella loved her husband "with all the fire of her soul; she lived in him alone, hungered for his every gaze. She was inconsolable when they were separated even for a day . . ."[118] As late as 1980 it was vaguely asserted that the close friendship between Isabella and Maria Christina had been "frequently misunderstood" but could be "explained quite normally from the special situation of their surroundings."[119] The problem facing historians was that what was understood as "normal" had changed fundamentally since the eighteenth century. The late nineteenth century saw the invention of a new concept, homosexuality, to denote a pathological sexual disposition. Unlike in premodern centuries, when sex between men had been condemned as a mortal sin, same-sex relations were now medically interpreted as a pathological identity affecting the entire human being. This suggested a fixity that had still been foreign to the eighteenth century. Whereas earlier someone may have committed the sin of sodomy, now they were said to *be* homosexual. Same-sex erotic relations between women, by contrast, were not classified under sodomy. For a long time they had been ignored or simply held not to exist.[120] Only in the twentieth century was the concept of homosexuality applied to women as well. Historians now found themselves compelled to defend the relationship between Isabella and Maria Christina against the charge of homosexuality or prevent such a charge from arising in the first place. Yet Isabella's contemporaries, even the eminently strait-laced Maria Theresa, found nothing objectionable in her companionship with Maria Christina.

Isabella's letters need to be read against the background of the eighteenth-century cult of sentimental friendship, which indulged in a rhetoric of passionate emotions and tender embraces, sighs, tears, and kisses, recognizing no clear-cut distinction between spiritual, intellectual, and physical intimacy. The relationship Isabella cultivated with her sister-in-law in their correspondence is unthinkable without the example of the sentimental epistolary novel. This genre offered an emphatic countermodel to everything that sensitive contemporaries found abhorrent in the social norms of the time.[121] True and sincere friendship was celebrated as an absolutely authentic, freely chosen, open, and unselfish communion of souls, the polar opposite of what was taken for granted in society at large: class-bound conventions, conformism, dissimulation, self-interested, strategically minded behavior governed by the rules of quid pro quo. All this was the target of Isabella's impassioned hatred and occasional satire.[122]

In view of this cult of sincerity, it is a striking paradox that Isabella, of all people, should have been so accomplished a master of strategic communication. In her letters to Maria Christina, she not only provides perceptive character sketches of herself, the emperor, the empress, and the heir, she also advises her sister-in-law on how she can secure the affection of her brother Joseph.[123] She counsels her, for example, to show "the archduke" (as she always calls him) how greatly she esteems his wife, Isabella herself, while letting him believe there are no tender feelings in play, only admiration for her character. Maria should also occasionally disagree with her if this seems likely to please him. He hates barefaced flattery, which is why she should speak highly of him in his presence while feigning ignorance that he is within earshot—and so on. Isabella hardly bothers to disguise her disdain for her insensitive husband, who could be so easily manipulated that he failed to perceive her distance and experienced his marriage as the greatest happiness of his life.[124] She gave Maria Christina similar advice on dealing with her father, the emperor: if she wanted to get on his good side, she should avoid making him jealous of the empress and always maintain the appearance of trustworthiness and sincerity.[125] Yet Isabella was skating on thin ice here. For if she was constantly assuring her lover of her unconditional honesty, how could she avoid arousing the suspicion that this, too, was nothing but a manipulative charade? There was no escaping the vicious circle of sincerity and dissimulation, and it is hard to imagine that the astute Isabella was unaware of this.

The most prominent object of her study was the character of the empress. Winning her inclination lay especially close to Isabella's heart.[126] Her strategy could not have been more successful. According to her own pronouncements on the matter, Maria Theresa's enthusiasm for her daughter-in-law exceeded her love for her own children. She never uttered a word of criticism about Isabella. "She is so full of virtues and fine qualities; I cannot thank God enough for her,"[127] the empress wrote, or: "She is the happiness of my life; it is impossible to surpass her";[128] "I love her as I love my own children, if not more so."[129] Isabella was well aware of her high standing with the empress. Before she died, she wrote advice to her sister-in-law, setting out how she could make herself as beloved by her mother as Isabella herself, so as ultimately to steer her in the direction she wanted—for example (it may be assumed), in the choice of her future husband.[130] To this end, Isabella made complex observations about Maria Theresa's character and the network of relations between family members, while still making clear her special fondness for her mother-in-law. "The empress has an exceptionally tender, feeling, and sympathetic heart," open to all who turn to her in distress. And yet: "She mistrusts her own insight, forgetting that few are honest and true friendship is a rarity. That is the source of the mistakes she makes, the root of her frequent indecision, and the reason why she so easily seeks advice from those who, more brazen than others, know how to turn their false zeal to their advantage."[131] Discouraging the empress from drawing outsiders into Maria's own affairs was therefore imperative. She was a good friend and felt a need for friendship herself. Yet it was hard to be friends with a great queen who was also one's own mother, since inequality of rank, obedience, and childish deference were not easily compatible with the frankness characteristic of true friendship. It called for unconditional discretion, honesty, steadfastness, and a thick skin. Foreseeing her own death, Isabella prophesied to Maria Christina: "The Empress will open her heart to you before everyone else. In her initial pain upon my death, she will have nobody dearer to her than you, . . . for she knows that you have been my friend, she knows how I adore you and how you love me." The attendant danger was that the empress, carried away by her "enthusiasm for everything that begins to please her," would prefer her to all her other children and hold her up to them as an example. Maria Christina would have to take care not to arouse their jealousy. If she antagonized them by giving them the impression that she was false and was seeking to dominate the empress, she risked eventually losing the trust of the empress herself. "You know her way of loving her children; it is always mixed with a kind of mistrust and apparent coldness." This held especially true of Joseph, "whom she will either find too unfeeling or too exaggerated in his grief." But that would be dangerous for Maria Christina: "Be careful, for while the archduke may be indebted to you for mourning me, he will be furious with you when he sees that you are the cause of the Empress's reproaches, especially if my death pains him deeply, as is likely."[132] Isabella also warned her beloved sister-in-law of her mother's character flaws: "The Empress is uncommonly spirited, and the decisions she makes on the spur of the moment are often violent." In such cases, she should be appeased and then persuaded to change her mind. That was the way to gain her respect: "uprightness and goodness [la droiture et la bonté] are the fundamental traits of her character." By no means should Maria Christina join in when Maria Theresa criticized her siblings, since later, when the empress reflected on the conversation at her leisure, she would surely take it ill of her. "The Empress loves her children, but she is guided by a false principle of excessive strictness." Maria Christina should therefore encourage her to treat her other children more leniently while at the same time not glossing over their failings, lest the empress discuss them with nonfamily members instead.[133] In short, if Maria Christina heeded her friend's advice and acted on it wisely, she would find herself loved and respected by her mother. In this Maria Christina was wildly successful; she was the only child allowed to choose her own husband and was favored over her siblings in many other respects as well. It cannot be said, however, that she did so without attracting their jealousy.[134]

What is remarkable about Isabella's *Advice for Marie* is not just its psychological acuity but also the fact that she so precisely foresaw her own death and others' reactions to it. Isabella was intimately acquainted with death. Her own mother had died of smallpox in December 1759, at the age of thirty-two. On January 18, 1761, during her time at the court in Vienna, she witnessed her brother-in-law Charles dying—likewise from smallpox—at the age of sixteen. She then observed the protracted death of the twelve-year-old archduchess Johanna, which ended two days before Christmas in 1762.[135] Following the birth of her first child, she herself suffered two miscarriages, in August 1762 and January 1763. Her last child, born three months premature on November 22, 1763, was stillborn; Isabella was already infected with smallpox at the time and passed away a week later. While she had not foretold the date of her death years in advance, as later claimed, she had long suffered from periodic bouts of melancholy and had expressed a death wish in her letters to Maria Christina.[136] The entire court was plunged into mourning. Joseph was as profoundly affected by the loss as Isabella had prophesied: "I have lost everything, my beloved wife, the object of all my affection," he told his father-in-law. "There was never such a princess, never such a wife. And I was in possession of this treasure, and at the age of twenty-two I had to lose it."[137] Maria Theresa lamented to Antonia of Saxony: "The cruel blow inflicted on me by the death of my dear daughter-in-law robs me of all satisfaction and solace,"[138] while to Kaunitz she confided: "All my joy, all my repose perishes with this enchanting and incomparable daughter."[139] She made Joseph's grand chamberlain, Salm, describe her last night in minute detail: "Whether she spoke, whether she suffered, whether she was conscious, whether my son was there the whole time, from what time and in what posture; what he said and did directly thereafter; all this is dear and precious to me. . . ."[140] Immediately after Isabella's death, she ordered the lady-in-waiting Erdödy to cut off a lock of her hair as a keepsake. "And be sure that all her papers are preserved—not a single note should go missing," as her writings would later give solace to the widower and help her daughter emulate her "pious and great mother." In 1764 the empress had the court printer, Trattner, publish Isabella's spiritual observations about life and death under the title *Méditations chrétiennes*.[141] Her first priority, however, was to get her hands on Isabella's papers before Joseph could read them uncensored.[142]

Another Victim

For all that Maria Theresa deeply mourned the passing of her daughter-in-law, she was keen for Joseph to retie the knot as soon as possible.[143] Because Isabella had not produced a male heir to the throne, the continuity of the Archducal House was still in jeopardy. It was also important to seize the opportunity for another useful political alliance. Above all, a prince *had* to be married. It was a fundamental rule of hierarchical society that anyone—whether peasant, townsman, or prince—could only play a political role if he was economically independent and stood at the head of his own household. The married couple were at the heart of the household. Finally, Joseph's needed to remarry because Maria Theresa had been arranging since the summer of 1763 to have him elected king of the Romans (and hence future emperor); as such, he would no longer be a mere archduke. There was thus more than one reason to find a new wife for him as soon as possible. Even before Isabella was dead, there had been speculation about a possible successor.[144] As early as November 1763 the Saxon emissary reported to Dresden that "court and public" alike thought it best for the heir to remarry to help him get over his loss.

Joseph himself saw things differently. The idea of remarrying struck him as intolerably cruel. Yet his father rebuked him with unusual sternness, admonishing him to heed the parental advice offered him for his own good, whatever his own feelings on the matter might be. Francis Stephen was reluctant to force his son's hand, trusting that he would better achieve his goal through love and reason.[145] In other words, Joseph was expected not just to obey, but to obey willingly, a role he would frequently be called on to play later. "To calm him down, we have explained to our son that he will be given time and will not be expected to obey blindly, providing he marries; that we will gladly accede to his wishes when it comes to his choice of bride, and will be happy with anyone, so long as he acts," Maria Theresa revealed to Antonia of Saxony. "This has reassured him. Still, I neglect no opportunity to put in a friendly word on behalf of those who meet with my approval. . . ."[146] Joseph had no option but to relent, hiding his grudging consent behind a façade of free will. "I have to show two different faces," he complained to his father-in-law, the Duke of Parma. He was consenting to a second marriage not for any reasons of state, he said, but purely out of filial obligation.[147] "I will sacrifice myself for you, it is worth the trouble, but I do it only for love of you," he wrote to his mother. "I will defer entirely to your judgment and do your bidding." While he was traveling through the Empire with his father on his coronation trip, his mother, behind the scenes, was sounding out all the possible options.[148] The only candidate who came into consideration for Joseph himself was Isabella's younger sister, Luisa of Parma. Yet she was fourteen years old at the time and had already been promised to the son of Charles III.[149] For her son's sake, Maria Theresa asked the Spanish king if he would give up his son's betrothed to Joseph, but the request was politely declined. A second possibility was the Infanta of Spain, although she had already been pledged to Archduke Leopold. He was magnanimous enough to relinquish his claim, yet Joseph declined the offer, much to his mother's displeasure. Other eligible candidates were dismissed by Maria Theresa from considerations of birth, virtue, or religious orthodoxy. Thus, the daughter of Louis-Philippe, Duke of Orléans, was, as Khevenhüller remarked with barely concealed disapproval:

> not only very young and shapely, but would also come with a dowry of 20 million livres; yet the empress refused to entertain the alliance owing to the *tache de bâtardise* [taint of illegitimacy] she inherited from her paternal grandmother and her late mother's well-known poor conduct. Nor did any of the Lutheran princesses meet her high standards, which is why she also rejected the well-bred and (it is said) uncommonly fair daughter of the Duke of Brunswick-Wolfenbüttel.[150]

Another option was the youngest infanta of Portugal. The fact that she was "very thickset" could be overlooked; what weighed far more heavily against her was her father's hostility to the king of Spain.[151] That left Catholic princesses from the Empire. The Saxon princess Kunigunde and the Bavarian princess Josepha were the front runners owing to their close kinship with the Archducal House. Both had Habsburg mothers and were thus cousins to the groom.[152] The empress ordered discreet inquiries to be made into their external appearance, health, behavior, and moral character.[153] Yet she could do nothing to stop speculation at court, as interested parties moved to present the counter candidate in an unfavorable light. Tongues wagged that there was "nothing remotely pleasant in [Kunigunde's] appearance and demeanor," her "completely red hair" being singled out for particular criticism. She was uncultivated, allowed herself liberties, and was known to go on long rides in the company of stable hands.[154] The pro-Saxon faction sought to dispel such rumors; Countess Salmour even offered to produce an authentic strand of the princess's hair to allay fears about its reddish tint. Both candidates were presented to Joseph in the worst possible light, leading him to express his distaste for the whole business in letters to his mother. After she sharply reprimanded him, he once again made efforts to play the obedient and dutiful son.[155]

To allow Joseph to make up his own mind and choose the lesser of the two evils, his mother came up with the idea of setting up apparently chance encounters with the candidates. He first met with Kunigunde in October 1764 in the spa town of Teplitz during a specially arranged journey to Prague. She had traveled there on the pretext of visiting her brother, who was taking the cure.[156] To be sure, nobody at court believed the encounter to have been sheer coincidence. When Joseph returned, Khevenhüller noted, "From his occasional involuntary grimaces [when the subject was mentioned], people began to suspect that the interview at Teplitz had failed to achieve the desired effect." Critics of the meeting were concerned that it would only result in unpleasantness for the princess, "summoned there to be inspected, as it were," and would "naturally give rise to frosty relations between the two courts."[157] These fears proved justified. Joseph made no secret of his disinclination toward Kunigunde, placing his mother in a very awkward position in relation to the Saxon court. In defiance of tradition, however, she left the choice to Joseph and arranged a little later—again, apparently by chance—for him to meet Josepha of Bavaria in Straubing: a "new inspection," as Khevenhüller indignantly remarked, that was unprecedented "for princes of his high birth, who were only allowed to see a portrait of their intended or proposed bride beforehand."[158] Dynastic matchmaking was an extremely delicate affair. The honor of the interested houses, as well as that of the individual candidates, was always at stake. Maria Theresa permitted her son to conduct a personal review of the two candidates only as a special concession to the grieving widower. The princesses must have found it humiliating to be scrutinized in this way. Yet they were prepared to risk losing face for so glittering a prize. Upon his return, Khevenhüller goes on to report, the newly elected and crowned Joseph was "interrogated by both parents and finally, at his father's repeated insistence, was swayed to choose the Bavarian princess, albeit with a very heavy heart, since her figure could hardly please so young a lord." With "her accustomed alacrity," the empress immediately sent off the marriage proposal to Munich so that the wedding could take place in January.[159] The spurned Kunigunde was to be placated with a sinecure in Prague or in an imperial convent.[160] Joseph himself informed his father-in-law of the fatal choice his parents had confronted him with: he had already found Kunigunde unattractive, but Josepha was "short and fat, her face ordinary, devoid of youthful charm, marred by pimples, red marks, and bad teeth" (although there is no sign of these defects in her official portrait).[161] Unable to decide for himself, he had begged his parents to make the decision for him, and they had chosen Josepha, since "all the public" was in favor of the match. "I have sacrificed myself and accepted my lot," he concluded on a note of resignation: "Pity me!"[162] In retrospect, it is hard to tell which of the two made the greater sacrifice. Even Maria Theresa was unhappy with her decision. "Against my conviction, against my feelings, I had to bring myself to help my poor son make a decision," she wrote to Maria Christina. "You can judge for yourself the state in which this has left me!"[163]

The reason for her choice was obvious. A marriage connection with the House of Wittelsbach seemed to offer the rosiest political prospects, and "not just for the two courts, but for all Germany and especially for the Catholic religion." Imperial Vice-Chancellor Colloredo sketched far-reaching plans for how the Catholic electors could work together harmoniously in imperial institutions in future, uniting in opposition to the recalcitrant Protestant princes. Above all, a possible inheritance beckoned. Were the male line of the Bavarian House of Wittelsbach to die out, as seemed more than likely, the House of Habsburg could lay claim to parts of the Duchy of Bavaria through the marriage. Kaunitz recommended secretly commissioning a diligent young historian to hunt for corresponding documentation and compile a "solid deduction."[164] While it could not be denied that the Elector Palatine had a prior hereditary claim to the Bavarian heartland, the Archducal House could nonetheless reckon with a "significant acquisition of land and people" for Josepha's descendants. As always, however, Kaunitz had the bigger picture in mind: "Certainly, the greatest and most desirable outcome, if it were feasible, would be the union with Austria of the entire complex of Bavarian lands." The idea still sounded chimerical, he wrote, but there was no harm contemplating it. Other interested princes could perhaps be compensated with Further Austria or the Netherlands. Later, when the Bavarian inheritance fell due, Joseph had no need to be told this twice.[165]

The marriage between Joseph and Josepha, then, was no love match. In this respect it was no different from most other royal marriages under the ancien régime. Still, the callousness with which Joseph treated his wife was remarkable even by the standards of the day. He restricted his dealings with her to an unavoidable minimum. The marriage was brief—Josepha fell victim to smallpox in 1767—and childless; that it was also unconsummated is probably a myth, however.[166] "If I were his wife and so mistreated, I would run away and hang myself on a tree in Schönbrunn," his sister Maria Christina reportedly said.[167] The chief lady in waiting supposedly gave up her position because she could no longer bear the sight of this unhappy marriage (*tableau de ce mauvais ménage*).[168]

Maria Theresa also felt pity for her son: Josepha was "neither pretty nor pleasant; I only hope she is good-natured [...]. We will give thanks to God if she at least brings children into the world, provided she bears a prince."[169] While the princess's ugliness surpassed the worst expectations, Khevenhüller claimed, her virtue and devotion, her love and affection for her husband, and her desire to please everyone, deserved the utmost respect.[170] Maria Theresa felt for her daughter-in-law as well, complaining that Joseph was openly snubbing her. With Khevenhüller, she discussed the sorry state of the marriage on more than one occasion.[171] Joseph justified his behavior in a letter to his mother from Silesia, to which he had added a few dutiful lines to his spouse: "I would find writing to the Grand Mughal less unpleasant. She will not rest satisfied with respectful sentiments and has already reproached me on this account. Judge for yourself, dear mother, what I should write to her, or where, by the devil, should I draw other feelings?" Yet outward display was what counted at court, not feelings. By making no attempt to hide his repugnance for his wife, Joseph failed to demonstrate the respect that was her due. With that, he contravened one of the dynasty's supreme values: he showed himself a poor husband. Maria Theresa feared his contempt for married life would prove contagious. As Leopold's wedding drew near, she rejoiced that he would soon be leaving the labyrinth of the family behind him. She also declared her determination to see both his younger brothers follow suit before too long: Joseph was setting a bad example with his withering, sardonic remarks on marriage.[172]

It is remarkable how much attention was paid to Josepha's alleged ugliness when her name was mentioned—notwithstanding all the virtues universally ascribed to her. This was obviously the most convenient excuse for Joseph's shortcomings as a husband and father, which otherwise would have damaged his reputation as father of his country. Three years after Josepha's death, an English admirer of the imperial house who knew her only from hearsay could still write: "How happy it was She died so soon! I never heard of anybody so disgustfull; I mean with no regard to her Person & the disagreeableness of her manner, for everyone agrees She was very good. Her figure exceedingly ugly & so dreadful a humor in her blood that there was no place in her body that was not all broke out. Think of the pretty Emperor being married to such a Woman."[173]

God and van Swieten

Smallpox—or variola, *petites véroles* in French—was continually thwarting not only Maria Theresa's dynastic ambitions but those of other European princely houses as well. William II of Orange, Mary II of England, and Tsar Peter II numbered among its many victims, alongside Maria Theresa's ancestor Emperor Joseph I and three of Francis

Stephen's brothers. Smallpox had a clear lead over the plague as the most devastating fatal illness of the time.[174] In Paris and London, many thousands succumbed to smallpox epidemics in the eighteenth century. Herman Boerhaave, van Swieten's famous teacher, described the initial symptoms: "This contagious matter being mixed with the humors doth immediately produce effects that follow one another pretty near in the following order and method: a standing of the hair, stiffness, acute fever; a great and continual heat; a shining and sparkling of the eyes from a thin and hot liquor fallen therein; a violent pain in the head, neck, limbs; . . . vomiting and nausea; great restlessness, dozing, sleepiness; and in children epileptic fits."[175] The typical red blotches came next, turning into suppurating sores before becoming scabrous. The course taken by the illness was brief and dramatic; the patient either died within a few days or was restored to health. Although survivors enjoyed lifelong immunity to the disease, they sometimes suffered from serious aftereffects, unsightly pockmarks, and potentially even blindness. There were competing theories about the causes, all of them empirically unverifiable; the same uncertainty characterized treatment of the disease. "It seems that here the same general therapy may be applied . . . which has proved its worth in all inflammatory diseases," Boerhaave wrote.

> 1) Blood should be let. . . . 2) The entire skin, mouth, rectum, and bowels should frequently be softened and loosened through enemas and flatulence. 3) The patient should drink copious amounts of thin, mealy, acidic, and cooling water; and take saltpeter from antimony or polychrest salt and thin milky water; and should 4) be fed thin gruel, be given cold air to breathe, and sufficiently covered to promote perspiration.[176]

Such seemingly authoritative measures were not spared criticism, especially at court. Khevenhüller, who lost several children to the illness, claimed to have observed that a certain kind of smallpox was "mainly rife among the nobility. As a consequence, physicians have been much maligned on the not unreasonable suspicion that they resort too much to artifice and go against nature."[177] Van Swieten, who from 1745 held supreme authority as personal physician to the imperial family, was acutely aware of the limits to medical knowledge exposed by the epidemic, having lost his own fourteen-year-old son to the disease in 1750. In the *Commentaries* on Boerhaave, his magnum opus, he wrote that smallpox, "owing to its subtle nature, can be grasped by none of the senses. This is the divine element in such diseases, which so often defies all the pains of art; it is the reason why physicians so often prove powerless to halt their all too rapid progress. All that medicine can do is weaken life itself: for poisons are activated by life."[178] Even trained physicians were unable to offer an effective remedy. Smallpox led very quickly to either death or recovery, meaning that the patient never passed through a chronic phase when medical cures might be applied. That is why demand was equally strong for magical and learned therapies—one seemed to help as much or as little as the other.[179]

For Maria Theresa, religious and medical support were not mutually exclusive. When her daughters Marianna and Josepha fell ill in April 1757, she wrote to their aya: "Since she [my daughter] has shown such faith in St. Blaise, [I am sending you] a little candle, to be hung around the neck or placed under the pillow."[180] Priest and physician were both in attendance in cases of smallpox; sacraments and supplications were as indispensable to the treatment as bleedings and special diets. In life-threatening cases, as at royal deliveries, the Holiest of Holies was displayed on altars and the populace summoned to collective prayer. In addition, orphaned children were chosen for "pox prayer" duty and rewarded with alms in the event of success.[181]

After God, it was her personal physician in whom Maria Theresa placed her greatest trust when illness struck close to home. "Alongside God, I have only your care, toil, and learning to thank for saving the life of my dear son," she wrote to him when Joseph recovered from the pox in 1757.[182] She was known to mention "God and van Swieten" in the same breath.[183] Her relationship with the physician emerges particularly clearly from the instructions she wrote for her son Leopold before his marriage in the summer of 1765.[184] In these instructions, intended to prepare him for heading his own household in Tuscany, she discussed the family's health at some length and implored him to make the same arrangements in Florence that she had made in Vienna. There, she claimed, all divisions and intrigues had ceased following van Swieten's appointment. No one else dared offer a diagnosis or give medical advice; nothing could happen without his express permission, and his instructions had to be followed to the letter.[185] Her first principle was that all sickness came from God, and when the hour of death appointed by God finally arrived, nothing could be done to stop it. Yet this did not justify an attitude of fatalistic resignation. For she was equally convinced that everyone had a moral obligation to look after themselves to the best of their ability. Having found the right physician (who would self-evidently be God-fearing and respectable), it was safe to assume that he too had been sent by God. "If the dear Lord wants to enlighten the physician and come to your aid, He will surely do so through his hands, especially if you blindly carry out his orders."[186] The personal physician she sent off with Leopold, a student of van Swieten's, was instructed to report back to her regularly. He was to play exactly the same role in Florence as his teacher in Vienna. Everyone at court was to submit to his authority, nothing should be hidden from him, and his word should be obeyed without demur. For Maria Theresa, the public differences of opinion she had witnessed at her own court were the work of the devil. "It is a universal principle that whenever anything good . . . is introduced, it meets with dissent and difficulty, while charlatanism triumphs and is never short of advocates."[187] Debate on medical matters only fostered unrest and was therefore forbidden. Even the physician should never attempt to justify his actions. In short, the *protomedicus* was a god among mortals in Maria Theresa's eyes: inscrutable, all knowing, and all powerful. The blind faith she placed in him in all questions of physical health was strictly analogous to the unconditional obedience otherwise owed only to God. Indeed, so far as the body was concerned, van Swieten *was* God; his pronouncements had the weight of a divine oracle. The instructions she composed for her son thus reveal a great deal about her attitude to knowledge, learning, and enlightenment in general.[188]

Smallpox was an ever-present threat at the Viennese court during Maria Theresa's reign. The empress insisted that her children grow accustomed to the idea from early on. Their tutors should "speak with them quite naturally about everything, including the pox and death."[189] In July 1749 Maria Christina survived a mild form of the disease;[190] in January 1757 it was Joseph's turn, as already mentioned.[191] The second-oldest archduke, Charles, was infected at the end of 1761 and passed away on January 18, at the age of sixteen.[192] Less than a year later, on December 23, 1762, his twelve-year-old sister Johanna followed him to the grave; Isabella of Parma observed and described her deathbed agonies.[193] Maria Theresa found solace in the idea that her children had died a beautiful, Christian death. She wrote to Maria Christina: "Your sister did penance for three quarters of an hour, with a scrupulousness, regret, and devotion that brought her confessor to tears; she has been very weak ever since. I cannot thank the dear Lord enough for sending me this consolation. I leave her entirely in His hands and expect that her fate cannot be other than a happy one."[194] Royal deaths, like royal births, were public affairs surrounded by solemn rituals. When death seemed imminent, members of the ruling family received the viaticum, their final eucharist before the journey to the hereafter. Moved by her "familiar most tender religious zeal," Maria Theresa resorted to this measure in 1757, when her eldest daughter Marianna came down with a heavy catarrh. Fortunately, on that occasion the patient recovered.[195] Countess Bentinck was a guest at court when the young Archduke Charles passed away. Her eyewitness account conveys a sense of what this somber ceremony must have looked like. She wrote to a friend as the ritual was about to take place: "He looks to death with calm acceptance and apparently without fear. All of us tremble before the cruel scene awaiting the poor feeling heart of the empress. The dreadful ceremony ordained by religion in these parts"—the countess was Protestant—"where the entire imperial family, the entire court, all the ladies-in-waiting, the entire nobility are required to appear in ceremonial costume and escort the sacrament from the church to the deathbed, this lugubrious procession, the clothes of mourning—it is all so inexpressibly terrifying that even those indifferent [to the archduke] are moved by it. Just imagine how the poor mother must be affected!"[196] As we have seen, the scenario would be repeated a year later when Isabella died. Three and a half years later, on May 22, 1767, her successor,

Josepha, contracted smallpox; she was dead within a week.[197] Ignoring
the danger of infection, Maria Theresa embraced her unloved daughter-
in-law before she was confined to her sickroom. Albert, Maria Christina's husband, subsequently claimed in his memoirs that she had done
so in order to mask her lack of affection. Joseph, the patient's husband,
felt no such need.[198] No one from the imperial family attended Josepha's
burial in the Capuchin Crypt.[199]

As it turned out, the empress's parting embrace almost proved
fatal.[200] The first symptoms appeared on May 23, 1767, just a week after
her favorite daughter, Maria Christina, had endured her first and only
delivery and lost her child. Three days later, Maria Theresa broke out in
pustules. Van Swieten bled her twice in quick succession. The altar sacrament was displayed in all the city's churches, gradually drawing "a vast
multitude, including from nearby parishes and villages."[201] Court servants were ordered by decree to assemble for prayer in the great court
chapel. Along with van Swieten, Joseph had a couch set up in one of the
antechambers and barely left her bedside. On June 1, 1767 the empress
called for the last rites: "the general consternation when the announcement was made . . . can more easily be imagined than described in
words."[202] When the empress successfully overcame the crisis on June 2,
there was jubilation both at court and among the public at large. Selected courtiers such as Khevenhüller, who could hardly speak for tears
of joy, were gradually readmitted to her presence.[203] On June 14 thanksgiving services were held in Vienna's churches to the sounds of drums
and trumpets, even though such festive accompaniment no longer accorded with court taste and had been abolished years earlier.[204] The
good burghers of Vienna outdid each other in their public protestations
of joy; dozens of thanksgiving sermons, speeches, and poems appeared
in print. On July 22, when the empress drove into the city for the first
time since her convalescence, her subjects lined the streets to cheer her
on. She was so moved by their devotion that she personally flung specially minted commemorative coins from her windows on the Burg-
platz.[205] State Chancellor Kaunitz's concern for her health bordered on
the obsessive. By his own admission, the empress's illness had affected
him so deeply that ever since, the mere idea of smallpox made him break

FIGURE 38A. Archduke Charles at the age of sixteen. Drawing by Jean-Étienne Liotard from his portrait series of Maria Theresa's children, 1762

FIGURE 38B. Archduchess Josepha. Drawing by Jean-Étienne Liotard, 1762

into a sweat and tremble convulsively. Those in his surroundings evidently failed to make sufficient allowances for this reaction. Years later he still felt compelled to write a circular to all his servants and colleagues begging them never to mention the illness in his presence, even by allusion, and to skip any passages remotely touching on smallpox in texts that were read aloud to him.[206]

Maria Theresa attributed her recovery from illness—"the prolongation of the days of a useless old woman," as she put it[207]—to God and van Swieten, in that order. Twelve little orphans who had prayed for her were granted an annual pension of thirty guilders,[208] while her personal physician was inducted into the Order of St. Stephen. Yet the epidemic was not over yet. In October of the same year, the fifteen-year-old Archduchess Josepha came down with the virus. She was assumed to have been infected by "poisonous vapors" when she and her mother descended to the Capuchin Crypt to offer prayers of remembrance.

Despite having been dead for some months, her sister-in-law Josepha was still lying in the vault, covered only with a linen sheet, pending delivery of her unfinished sarcophagus. The archduchess received the public viaticum on October 10 and died on October 15—exactly one day after she was meant to have been married *per procuram* in Schönbrunn to King Ferdinand of Naples and have set off for Naples.[209] Contemporaries were unwilling to put this down to sheer coincidence. Khevenhüller spread the rumor that, when visiting the crypt, Josepha had knelt down before the coffin of her late sister Johanna "and entreated her ... (if she found herself before the face of God, as she did not doubt) to pray that, if her impending marriage should imperil the salvation of her soul, the dear Lord might revoke it at the hour appointed for her departure [to Naples]."[210] The next-youngest sister, Maria Carolina, took her place soon after as a victim of politics by having to marry Ferdinand of Naples in her stead, without, however, benefiting from any such act of divine intercession.[211] The last member of the family to be infected was Archduchess Elisabeth, who came down with the pox on October 22. She too was given the public viaticum at her own request, although she recovered from the illness. When she reappeared at court a month later, Khevenhüller noted that she was much changed.[212]

Years before the smallpox epidemic demanded its tribute from the imperial court, Maria Theresa had corresponded with her cousin, Antonia of Saxony, about a new-fangled, still hotly debated treatment: inoculation with smallpox, or variolation. After Antonia's third son had died of the pox in March 1763, she had allowed her six-year-old daughter Amalia to be "in-grafted" with smallpox matter drawn from sick children. Having wrestled long and hard with the decision, the final push was given her by the Prussian king, of all people. "You have given me the courage to take this step," she later wrote to Frederick II. "I have you to thank for saving my children, and for sparing the land of Saxony the many thousands of children whose parents will follow my example."[213] Maria Theresa knew nothing of this source of inspiration when she congratulated Antonia on her "great courage" and expressed her keen

interest in the outcome of this dangerous experiment.[214] Frederick II
had presumably been informed of the method by Voltaire, who for his
part learned of it in the 1750s during a trip to England, where the heir
apparent, George II, had allowed his children to be inoculated as early
as 1722. The method had been publicized in England by Lady Mary
Wortley Montagu, wife of the English ambassador in Constantinople,
who had become familiar with the practice on her journey through the
Ottoman Empire. In 1718 she had successfully tried it on her own son,
and subsequently on her daughter as well.

In the 1760s, then, inoculation with the serum of infected patients
was no longer a novelty in Central Europe, yet it was not without risk
and remained highly controversial. The topic was intensively discussed
among the interrelated dynasties in Vienna, Dresden, and Munich. Antonia's sister Josepha—Joseph's unloved wife, who would herself die of
smallpox two years later—advised against inoculation with the following argument: "If God wants to have me, I am in His hands. One way or
the other, He will do with me as He wills. Neither the Empress nor I
have had smallpox, and I know any number of people who died without
ever having had it, and others who have survived it in old age. We must
place our trust in the Creator; it is for Him to determine how we are to
die; if I am in His grace, all else is indifferent to me."[215] Electress Maria
Anna of Bavaria, Antonia's sister-in-law, was undaunted. She sought to
introduce the new method at court in Munich but foundered on the
resistance of the established court physicians, who, she complained,
never voluntarily adopted a new system, in keeping with their unspoken
motto: "'twas ever thus."[216] She failed to convince her husband, Elector
Max Joseph, who himself succumbed to smallpox in 1777.

In Dresden and Munich the methods of Maria Theresa's all-powerful
personal physician were regarded with equal skepticism.[217] Van Swieten
was no revolutionary. Even at the time, the mechanistic system of the
famous Boerhaave was far from cutting-edge science, yet van Swieten
clung to it throughout his life, seeking to reconcile it with the classical
lore of ancient medicine.[218] Boerhaave had been skeptical about
inoculation—not unjustly, given the high risk of infection. Van Swieten,

too, did not reject it in principle but preferred to reserve his opinion.[219] So long as empirically secured results were not yet available, he cautioned restraint and restricted himself to avoiding harm. There were also determined opponents of inoculation at the Viennese court, including court physician Anton de Haen, a fellow alumnus of Boerhaave's school in Leiden. In short, the issue divided scholars and polarized opinion in ruling families.

As a procedure with an uncertain outcome, inoculation required a willingness to take risks. It was an active decision that might prove fatally misguided. Doing nothing seemed the safer choice—yet once the option of inoculation was on the table, it too was a decision, albeit a negative one. In other words, inoculation transformed the vague danger of death from smallpox into a calculated risk. What had once been in the lap of the gods was now a matter of individual responsibility. One contemporary, the Duke of Croÿ, saw this in a positive light: "It appears that one ought to do it [i.e. inoculate] with good cheer, for if a child were to die, the reproach will remain that the death could have been averted."[220] Through her emissary in London, the empress established contact with the famous Sutton brothers, the English pioneers of inoculation, but they could not be persuaded to make the trip to Vienna. In March 1768 experiments with inoculation got underway in Vienna's orphanage and St. Mark's Hospital. After hesitating initially, van Swieten came around to the view that, given the continuing differences in scholarly opinion, empirical research was needed. He therefore gave permission for the orphanage physicians Rechberger and Locher, supervised by court physician Störck, to inoculate a number of "illegitimate hospital children." The results were meticulously documented. After only two of the newborn infants had died, supposedly from causes other than smallpox, Pater Parhamer, the orphanage director, was asked to immunize older children as well. The abbot was skeptical at first, "fearing as a true father that he might thereby do harm to the abbey's poor orphans," but allowed himself to be persuaded.[221] In total, thirty-four newborns and sixty-seven children between the ages of five and fourteen were successfully inoculated, notwithstanding what

Rechberger called "the shameless lies which slander and prejudice sought to spread."[222] In the face of these overwhelmingly positive results, van Swieten dropped his initial scruples.[223] Not long after, the empress had an "inoculation house" built on the Rennweg in Vienna, where she occasionally inspected inoculations herself.[224]

In September 1768, after "six or nine poor children" had been immunized "for each of my own," Maria Theresa resolved to try the procedure on archdukes Ferdinand and Maximilian and Joseph's daughter, Therese.[225] The task was entrusted to the experienced Dutch physician Jan Ingenhousz, sent from England specially for the occasion. The treatment was successful. The three-year-old boy who supplied variolated matter for little Therese and his parents were each awarded an annual pension of a hundred guilders a year.[226] The following May, Leopold, now Grand Duke of Tuscany, had himself inoculated at his mother's wish, and Joseph traveled especially to Florence to witness the effects of the procedure.[227] He too thought it essential to open the door to truth and shut it to slander.[228] Yet deciding to be inoculated still took a great deal of courage. Maria Theresa's correspondence with her grown-up children in the 1770s continually touched on this theme.[229] In June 1774 she looked on with tense excitement from afar as her son-in-law Louis XVI and his siblings were successfully inoculated after Louis XV had fallen victim to smallpox.[230] Around the same time, four of Leopold's children recovered from the procedure, but the youngest died.[231] Maria Carolina and Ferdinand likewise had their children inoculated, against the advice of those around them. Maria Theresa vacillated according to her experiences at the time. In 1772 she wrote to Ferdinand that she no longer supported inoculation.[232] By 1777 she had changed her tune: "The more I observe this method, the more I am taken with it."[233] The following year she pressed him to have his daughter inoculated as soon as possible,[234] while pointedly leaving the decision in his hands: "You have to want it yourself, . . . no complaisance on this score, your wishes are all that count here."[235]

In comparison to her contemporaries, Maria Theresa thus took a remarkably forward-looking position on the question of inoculation.

Nobody could have known at the time that smallpox immunization (in altered form) would one day become standard medical procedure. Unlike other rulers, she decided for the risky experiment and against an attitude of fatalistic resignation to God's will. She was therefore later celebrated—not without cause—as the "true mother of immunization in this country."[236] If we ask today to what extent she may be regarded as an enlightened monarch, her inoculation policy clearly speaks in her favor. Yet here as elsewhere, light and dark are not so easily separated. The risks of progress were borne primarily by orphaned children. Nobody asked them for their consent.

10

Mother and Son

FIGURE 39. Joseph II and Maria Theresa as porcelain figurines

Death in Innsbruck

The emperor breathed his last on August 18, 1765. His death changed everything. Maria Theresa was transformed overnight into a grieving widow, a part she would faithfully perform for the rest of her life. She never ceased lamenting that fateful day: "I can feel joy no more; even the sun seems dark to me."[1]

The imperial family were staying in Innsbruck at the time. They had come there to celebrate the marriage of Archduke Leopold to Maria Louisa, Infanta of Spain. The capital of Tyrol held important memories for the House of Lorraine. Francis Stephen's grandfather had lived there while Louis XIV occupied his land; his father had been born there; he and Maria Theresa had stopped off there during their marriage journey. Yet Francis Stephen had preferred to celebrate Leopold's wedding in Vienna rather than in Innsbruck; Maria Theresa had overruled him, much to the court's displeasure.[2] The expense involved was prodigious. The old Hofburg in the Tyrolean capital had needed to be renovated in readiness for so momentous a dynastic occasion, and half the court household—including personnel for opera and comedy, and even tapestries, furniture, and cutlery—had had to be carted all the way from Vienna.[3] Nothing seemed to go right. The groom's enjoyment of the wedding ceremony on August 5 was spoiled by a serious intestinal complaint. The opera put on for the occasion (complete with ballet) was a flop with the public; the fireworks fizzled out in the rain. At the end of July news of the death of the Duke of Parma—Joseph's revered first father-in-law—reached Innsbruck, further dampening the mood. In retrospect, participants saw all these mishaps as portents of the coming disaster. The illuminated stone gate of honor looked gloomy and oppressive, more like a funeral monument than a triumphal arch. And during Sunday Mass, the preacher "chose the theme of watchfulness and the uncertainty of the hour of our death, reminding the congregation how no one was safe from an abrupt and precipitous demise."[4] The meaning of these ominous signs was revealed on Sunday, August 18. The emperor had been feeling unwell all day; the night before he had had difficulty breathing and had been unable to sleep.[5] Maria Theresa was worried and advised a good bleeding. He refused, insisting on following his established routine. At noon he amused himself in society. In the evening he visited the theater and saw a play by Goldoni and a ballet by Gluck, as always carrying a spyglass "to get a better view of the galleries frequented by the ladies."[6] After leaving the theater, he suffered a massive heart attack while making his way back to his apartment accompanied by Joseph and a small entourage. He collapsed, Joseph rushed to support him, and he was laid on a lackey's makeshift bed in the antechamber to his apartment. Physicians, surgeons, and his confessor were summoned—all to no avail. He was dead within ten minutes. Joseph rushed to his mother "to prepare her for the fateful blow."[7] Alarmed by the vague report that the emperor was unwell, she set out to visit him in his rooms, passing through the antechamber where he had just expired. Yet because two courtiers were shielding the cot on which he was lying from her gaze, she did not see him. She was compelled "almost by force" to return to her own apartment, where news of her husband's death was brought to her later.[8]

Another source confirms that Maria Theresa was kept away from the scene for as long as possible. Peter Prosch, the Tyrolean peddler and part-time jester, had been at court that day and had amused Francis Stephen at table.[9] He thus had privileged access to events as they unfolded, and he later set down a detailed account of what he saw in his autobiography. If his account is to be believed, Maria Theresa first learned of her husband's death after a courier had already been sent off to Vienna with the news. She had earlier expressed a wish to dine in his company.

> The answer came . . . that he was feeling unwell and therefore did not want to sit at table. She now vehemently demanded to go over and see how the emperor was faring; but she was restrained so far as was possible, and put off with all kinds of earnest speeches, from which she remarked that some misfortune must have come to pass. Once again, she forcefully tried to see for herself how matters stood, but again she was restrained.

Only then did Joseph break the bad news to her.[10]

Maria Theresa was presumably kept away from her husband for as long as possible so that the suddenness of his passing might be concealed from her. A quick, unexpected death was not a good death. The Christian *ars moriendi* consisted in equipping the dying for his journey to the hereafter by making careful preparations, confessing and repenting, and receiving the eucharist and last rites. During the transition to the afterlife, the sinner's soul was in peril and susceptible to diabolical influence. Without penance and absolution in the hours before death, it was uncertain if the sinner would qualify for eternal salvation. The idea that Francis Stephen might have died unshriven was therefore profoundly disturbing. The chronicle kept by the Jesuit college in Innsbruck later reported that the physician and priest had rushed to his side.

Yet although an attempt to bleed the emperor had been unsuccessful, the confessor had still detected signs of life and been able to absolve him of his sins in good time.[11] Maria Theresa later called it her sole consolation that Francis Stephen had taken communion and confession that Sunday morning, as was his habit.[12]

Nothing would ever be the same after Francis Stephen's death. A decade after the event, Maria Theresa could still write to her trusted friend, Countess Enzenberg: "I spend the years, months, weeks, and days in the same simplicity, the same bitterness as on the first day, and I am often glad that bygone days will not return, and that with every moment I am drawing closer to my end."[13] To cite one more example among many, she complained to Tarouca at the start of 1766: "I hardly know myself any more, for I have become like an animal with no true life or reasoning power. I forget everything. I get up at five. I go to bed late, and all day long I seem to do nothing. I do not even think. It is a terrible state to be in."[14] Maria Theresa lived out her widowhood—like so many Habsburg matrons before her—in a state of quasi-monastic asceticism. This emerges with all clarity from a handwritten note she left in her prayer book:

> Widowhood is a penance, a preparation for death. It should comprise 4 main points: 1. frequent taking of the holy sacraments, 2. frequent prayer both spoken and silent, 3. frequent reading of spiritual books, 4. works of mercy mortification and penance. . . . a widow's complete submission to God's will. [After the] loss of her husband, God should be the bridegroom of her soul. If her children displease her, God should be the arbiter. If her relatives displease her, God should be her closest friend. If she is called to judgment, God [should be] her judge. [If she is] despised, God and good conscience [should be] her honor. In poverty her father. In sickness her physician. In crises of conscience God [should be] her comforter, yea her all in all.[15]

On another scrap of paper found in her prayer book, Maria Theresa noted a personal numerical litany: "emperor francis my husband lived 56 years, 8 months, 10 days, died on august 18 1765 at half past 9 in the evening. He thus lived 680 months, 2958 weeks, 20778 days, 496992 hours. My happy marriage lasted 29 years, 6 months, 6 days, at the same hour I gave him my hand, also on a Sunday, he was suddenly taken away from me. That makes 29 years, 335 months, 1540 weeks, 10781 days, 258744 hours."[16] It appears that the ritual repetition of these numbers functioned as a kind of mantra for Maria Theresa, helping her cope with the pain of her loss. From the eighteenth day of each month, she would retreat into a state of quasi-monastic solitude, accompanied only by her confessor, Ignaz Müller, to devote herself to spiritual reflection, tend the memory of her husband, and pray for his salvation.[17]

Yet widowhood was not just a subjective state of bereavement. It was also—and above all—an objective social status made outwardly visible in every conceivable way.[18] "One of her first actions was to order my mother to cut off her hair," the daughter of her chambermaid later recalled. "She got rid of all her colorful decoration and jewelry, distributed her wardrobe among her ladies, had her bedroom draped in gray silk, curtained off her solitary bed with gray hangings, and in this way showed in her outward appearance that life and the world had lost their allure for her."[19] Such behavior was far from abnormal; on the contrary, it was in keeping with the habits of generations of Habsburg widows.[20] From now until the end of her days, Maria Theresa would be defined by her widowhood. Even her new Great Seal announced this status: "By the Grace of God Roman Empress, widow."[21] Strict ritual models dictated how one was to act in her situation, and Maria Theresa followed them to the letter. From now on she would appear exclusively in mourning. She would wear a widow's bonnet and widow's weeds adorned only with the insignia of the Order of the Starry Cross, doing without the flashy jewelry she had worn throughout her married life. She withdrew from the marital bedroom in Schönbrunn to the palace's eastern wing, now redecorated in funereal black. She turned one room, her husband's former private study, into a memorial shrine, the Vieux Laque Room, lining it with life-sized portraits of Francis Stephen and his sons. Similarly, in Vienna's Hofburg she moved into the far more modest second-floor widow's apartment of her mother, Elisabeth, and installed a cabinet of the dead containing portraits of her husband and other deceased family members. She would retreat there for hours passed in silent contemplation.[22]

On the day after his death, Maria Theresa cut off a commemorative lock of her husband's hair and had his likeness taken (see color plate 17).[23] There then began the long sequence of transitional rites practiced in the House of Habsburg since the late Middle Ages.[24] The body was made ready for the waiting period before the resurrection of the dead. Traditionally, different parts of the ruler's body were interred in different places: the heart in the Herzgrüftl of the Loreto Chapel in the Augustinian Church, the intestines in the Church of St. Stephen, and the rest of the embalmed corpse in the Capuchin Crypt.[25] The dispersal of the late sovereign's mortal remains was important for two reasons: it meant he could be near several saints at the Last Judgment, but in the meantime he could also be honored in several locations at once. This practice of interment was closely linked to the cult of saints' relics, a centerpiece of Christian ritual since late antiquity. Saints led a dual existence in heaven and on earth; their power (*virtus*) was communicated to the faithful through their bodies, which were incorruptible right down to the tiniest splinter of bone or droplet of blood. Altars were built on top of them, the Christian liturgy conducted around them. Relics made saints physically present in this world as advocates for the living. Their salvific influence made the faithful want to draw as close to them as possible. From the tenth century onward, the bodies of dead rulers were treated like those of saints—indeed, they were not infrequently venerated as saints themselves. The magic of the place where the body (or part of the body) was interred lived on in the Habsburg ritual of royal burial, even and especially after the Reformation had rejected all relic worship as idolatrous. Catholic burial practice now became an essential marker of confessional difference. The corpse's closeness to the mother of God was of particular importance, since anyone in her vicinity at the hour of the resurrection of all flesh was promised privileged access to eternal salvation. Yet none of her relics was to be found on earth; according to Catholic dogma, Mary had been assumed body and soul into heavenly glory upon her death. Instead, the faithful worshiped her in wonder-working Madonnas or in replicas of the Casa Sancta, her birth house, which angels had miraculously translated from Nazareth to Loreto. Beginning with Ferdinand IV, the Habsburgs thus had their hearts interred in the Loreto Chapel in the Augustinian Church to benefit from the Virgin's redeeming proximity. In the background stood the idea that physical objects not only abstractly symbolize spiritual power but bring it to palpable, real presence—an idea now spurned by Protestants, who assumed a fundamental division between the material and the spiritual world. For Protestants, faith related solely to the inner self, not the outer.

The sovereign body continued to be ritually eviscerated in keeping with the Habsburg cult of the ruler, although the heart and intestines were not always separately interred. Francis Stephen's corpse was treated no differently. On August 20, Khevenhüller, acting in his capacity as lord high chamberlain, was obliged to "attend the cruel office of the opening of the body. This continuing for a very long time, I became wretchedly ill, in part from the heat and the stench, in part (and probably mainly) owing to the oppressive atmosphere"; he later spent several hours passed out in his quarters.[26] Meanwhile, the emperor's body was cut open to remove the heart and intestines. The former was placed in a silver chalice, the latter in a copper vessel. Not until ten o'clock at night could the embalmed corpse be laid out in the Riesensaal of the Hofburg in Innsbruck. Khevenhüller had to give up his own Spanish coat and collar specially for the occasion. The emperor's face, still frozen in a rictus of pain, was covered by a cloth, while his body was surrounded on the bier by insignia of rule and dozens of candles, lit for one day only owing to the stifling August heat. The body was then placed in the coffin.

Having lain in repose for three days in Innsbruck, the corpse was transported to Vienna. There it was again solemnly laid out in a closed coffin for three days in the Knights' Room at the Hofburg before being interred in the imperial crypt at the Capuchin Church. Here it was housed in the spectacular sarcophagus that Maria Theresa had commissioned from court sculptor Balthasar Ferdinand Moll over a decade earlier. Even contemporaries thought that it more closely represented a love nest than a coffin (fig. 40).[27] The young royal couple recline gracefully on the tomb plate as on a bed, Francis Stephen shown as an ancient Roman emperor, Maria Theresa as queen of Hungary. They turn to face each other at the hour of resurrection at the Last Judgment, a scene

FIGURE 40. The imperial couple on the stately sarcophagus in the Capuchin Crypt.
Balthasar Ferdinand Moll, 1758

reflected in the fresco on the vault above. They are both grasping the Hungarian scepter, while Maria Theresa additionally clasps the coronation sword in her left hand—an entirely unconventional artistic representation of joint rule and conjugal love. "Every August 18th, the anniversary of her husband's death, she visited his tomb, then shut herself in her room, confessed her sins, fasted, and spent the day in sorrowful remembrance and devout prayer."[28] This was not just an annual commemorative ritual. She also descended to the Capuchin Crypt (or later, had herself lowered in a lift) whenever she wanted to commune with the deceased before making an important decision, to the point that their coregency seemed to have been prolonged beyond the grave.

The weeks-long ceremonies of mourning united the court, the royal capital, the hereditary lands, and the entire Holy Roman Empire in a single sacral community. Memorial services were held not just in Innsbruck and Vienna, but in all the great cities of the realm: in Brussels, Florence, Prague, Pressburg (Bratislava), and Frankfurt, to name a few. In all its symbolic gradations, society turned out to mourn the emperor. In Vienna church bells rang out for an hour, calling the city to the requiem Mass. A funereal structure, or *castrum doloris*, thirty-three meters high, was set up in the Augustinian court church. Illuminated by around eight thousand wax candles, it glorified the deceased ruler in strict accordance with the rules of art and learning. The burghers of Vienna erected an only slightly less sumptuous *castrum doloris* in the Church of St. Stephen.[29] In eulogies and pamphlets, all the conventions of panegyric were duly observed. For the hereditary lands, the highest degree of public mourning was announced.[30] The entire court appeared in exactly prescribed mourning attire. Ladies were no longer permitted to wear makeup.[31] All amusements were banned for months; operas, ballets, balls, and card games were prohibited. In her grief, the widow shared a ritual connection with even her lowliest subjects. Yet Maria Theresa herself remained hidden from view. She abstained from the vigils for the dead that began on September 1. She withdrew almost completely from public life at court and in the city, shut herself in her apartment for days on end, and followed divine service from the oratory in the chamber chapel, where no prying eyes could see her. Audiences were canceled and only her intimates admitted to her presence. Not until October did she did she resume her evening card games, and then only with a select few table companions. When officials came to her with urgent business, she directed them "to the young lord [i.e. Joseph], frequently repeating that she no longer wanted to be seen by the world."[32]

Far more of her time and attention was taken up with organizing memorials for the deceased. She ordered commemorative medallions to be struck and donated a large sum for requiem Masses. The residence at Innsbruck stood at the center of her plans. She discussed refurbishing it in her correspondence with the governor, Count Enzenberg, and the governor's wife. She had the room where Francis Stephen died transformed into a chapel. A tunicle made—partly by her own hand—from one of his dressing gowns was sent to Innsbruck, where it was worn for the first time on her wedding anniversary.[33] In Innsbruck she also established a noble chapter of canonesses (*Damenstift*) charged with praying in perpetuity for Francis Stephen's soul.[34] In February 1766 she wrote to Countess Enzenberg: "More than ever I think back to my beloved Innsbruck; it seems to me that I can only recover my peace of mind where I lost it."[35] And when, in February 1766, she dispatched court building director Pacassi to Innsbruck to carry out extensive rebuilding works, she explained herself to Countess Enzenberg: "Poor Innsbruck can probably no longer hope to make a brilliant court, but it can still become one of retirement." She called Innsbruck "the place where I always long to be."[36] This sounds as if she intended to relinquish power and make the remote palace behind the mountains her widow's seat. In fact, she never returned to the scene of Francis Stephen's death. Instead, she had the residence at Innsbruck transformed by the painter Franz Anton Maulbertsch into a monumental memorial to the House of Habsburg-Lorraine. The former "Riesensaal" was refashioned in accordance with her instructions into a "Familiensaal," dominated even today by a large-scale dynastic portrait series depicting the entire imperial family, including the children who died before their maturity.[37]

Life at court was fundamentally transformed by the emperor's death—in part because Maria Theresa became a recluse, in part because Joseph had now become emperor, formally occupied the highest rank at court, and could put his own stamp on court life. No theatrical performances or balls were held throughout the entire winter of 1765–66. Up to New Year's Day of 1766, the empress maintained the strictest incognito and allowed no one to kiss her hand in public. Not until May 1, 1766, was full court mourning relaxed somewhat.[38] Yet if courtiers thought that everything would now gradually return to normal, they were sorely mistaken. During the period of mourning, numerous court traditions were gradually dropped, never to return. The change in court costume caused the biggest stir. When Joseph, now become grand master of the Order of the Golden Fleece, appeared at the order's festival, he no longer wore the order's collar over Spanish court dress but over a plain regimental uniform—a slap in the face for knights of the order. Not long after, he abolished Spanish dress as the formal court uniform, a move that threw the entire semantic order at court into disarray. Wearing Spanish dress had been a valuable symbolic privilege; when it was taken away, a key marker of social distinction at court went with it. The abolition of Spanish dress was therefore rightly understood as a programmatic message addressed to the nobility, which feared further attacks on its social preeminence.[39] In December 1765 the children's birthday and name day receptions were allowed to lapse, initially "on account of the all too fresh sorrowful memory," yet gala days were permanently canceled soon after, replaced by a single congratulatory reception on New Year's Day along French lines.[40] One by one, the imperial family's public visits to the churches and convents of the city fell victim to the new spirit of austerity: the procession to the Jesuits at the Feast of St. Francis Xavier, to the Augustinian Loreto Chapel on the day of the Annunciation of Our Lady, to the Capuchins on Palm Sunday, to St. Michael's and the Jesuits on Corpus Christi, to St. Paul's for the Feast of Guardian Angels, to the 6000 Guilders Service (named after a seventeenth-century imperial donation) in November. Joseph even canceled the annual visit to the public thanksgiving service for liberation from plague, held since 1680 at the Plague Column in Vienna, a decision "the people did not take well."[41] At court, special services for the Order of the Fleece were massively reduced, and there was general consternation when even the washing of the feet on Maundy Thursday and the visit to saints' graves on Good Friday, fixed paraliturgical elements of Holy Week, were suddenly called off.[42] Khevenhüller, deeply disturbed by these developments, was ultimately forced to register "that the so-called Court Calendar, in which all court devotions and church services are noted, has been reformed *ex mandato superiori* [by higher command] by around a half, and in the copies printed for next year most such church visits have been left out."[43]

All these changes reflected a broader policy of financial retrenchment that Joseph introduced just after his father died, much to the displeasure of the court nobility.[44] His austerity measures went even further. He cut the number of court officials by combining his own staff with his mother's.[45] He transferred management of the court theater into private hands[46] and offered paying guests admission to court balls.[47] He exterminated the wild boar previously kept for the hunt in Vienna's environs and opened the court hunting grounds, the Prater, to the public as a recreational precinct, complete with coffee houses and fairground amusements.[48] He permitted ladies at court to be driven only by two-horse carriages rather than six as before, with the result that their coaches could no longer compete with those of "city ladies,"[49] and he banned runners from joining the court sleigh ride.[50] He transferred his father's considerable private fortune to the state treasury,[51] reduced the interest paid on capital deposits held in the city bank,[52] and collected outstanding payments for chamberlains' keys.[53] He picked a fight with imperial aulic councillors by publicly criticizing their sluggish ways and imposing on them a fifth sitting day each week. In doing so, he violated the fundamental principle that face always had to be preserved when dealing with people of high rank.[54] Taken together, the countless greater and lesser reforms introduced by Joseph resulted in a situation where the court lost much of its allure and came to seem "petty" in the eyes of many.[55]

A new spirit of frugality was in the air, combined with a strict performance ethic and an unprecedented disdain for pomp and ceremony. Joseph cited the catastrophic state debt of around 300 million guilders as the rationale for his cost-cutting measures. No inroads had been made into the debt since the war ended, while the taxation burden, which had been increasing ever since, could not possibly be raised any further. As recently as 1764, Maria Theresa had tried in vain to exact more tax revenue from the Hungarian diet.[56] Khevenhüller did not understand why the empress did nothing to stop her son's "bizarre innovations, . . . given she still has enough power to rectify him on this score, and the termination of such age-old customs is said to bode ill for the future."[57] He accounted for her lack of resistance by concluding either that she sympathized with some measures or that they were unable to rouse her from her state of profound despondency. Yet whereas Maria Theresa may have been prepared to accept some innovations and greeted others with indifference, Joseph pursued them enthusiastically and on principle. His various reforms at court were not driven purely by a spirit of economy; they were informed by a new system of political values, a new model of good government. By breaking with the old customs and ceremonial formalities, Joseph fatally undermined the late Baroque culture of rule—even if few saw this at the time. For on such (supposedly) immutable rituals rested the (supposedly) inviolable facticity of the traditional system of rule. Once these rituals were abolished, the entire political and social hierarchy no longer appeared as something incontestable, self-evident, and divinely ordained, but rather as the vain and arbitrary contrivance of mere mortals.

An Emperor without a Country

The death of Francis Stephen had given rise to a peculiar situation.[58] According to Habsburg house laws, Joseph, the firstborn son, stood to inherit the throne in the hereditary lands. Primogeniture was the cornerstone of dynastic logic, elevating Joseph above his siblings. In family portraits he was depicted as the sun around whom all the other children orbited like so many planets.[59] In addition, Francis Stephen had named him the sole heir of his considerable private fortune.[60] Joseph only had to agree in writing to renounce the Grand Duchy of Tuscany in favor of his brother Leopold, making this territory henceforth an independent secundogeniture of the House of Habsburg-Lorraine.[61]

Through his father's death, Joseph thus became at once the male head of the dynasty and the supreme overlord of the Holy Roman Empire of the German Nation. His parents had seen to this in the nick of time by having him crowned king of the Romans in 1764. His election and coronation *vivente imperatore* (during the emperor's lifetime) guaranteed the house its continuing hold over the imperial throne and was an important force for political stability in Europe. Joseph had already been pledged Brandenburg's electoral vote in the Peace of Hubertusburg. Maria Theresa skillfully moved to secure the votes of the other electors prior to the election, knowing that there was no legal requirement that a successor be chosen during the emperor's lifetime and wishing to avoid an open majority vote. In early 1763 she had already begun making confidential arrangements with the house's "closest relatives and best friends."[62] She promised her cousin, Maria Antonia of Saxony, that she would support her husband's bid to be elected king of Poland, even though the chances of this happening were slim and the plan was taken no further after Joseph's election.[63] The elector of Bavaria was won over with the prospect of a marriage between the two houses. The other electors voted for Joseph partly because they were loyal Habsburg clients anyway, like the archbishop of Mainz, and partly because they were unwilling to risk new military conflicts and interventions from abroad.[64] Maria Theresa thus succeeded on this occasion—unlike in 1745—in having the Habsburg candidate unanimously elected king of the Romans and future holy Roman emperor.

Accompanied by his father, Joseph made the obligatory coronation trip to Frankfurt in March 1764, just a few months after Isabella's death. He found it sheer torture, but he slipped back into his old role of dutiful son and did as he was told.[65] During the election, he waited with his father outside the Frankfurt city walls. Once it was over, they were both invited to ride into the city in triumph. The event was immortalized in collective memory by Goethe, who witnessed the spectacle of Joseph's coronation as a fourteen-year-old. Looking back from after the end of the Holy Roman Empire, Goethe depicted the ritual sequence as a majestic and bizarre piece of "world theater," one whose anachronistic features already presaged the demise of the political construct still presenting itself that day in all its medieval splendor.[66] Yet onlookers were impressed at the time. Even Francis Stephen, who normally had little patience for royal pageantry, could not help but feel moved when he again received the crowd's cries of acclamation, as he had twenty years earlier, and rode with his son from the Cathedral of St. Bartholomew to the city hall, the Römer, where the coronation feast was held in accordance with the Golden Bull of 1356—albeit before mostly empty place settings, since the secular princes had long since stopped participating in the spectacle. And Maria Theresa was also not there to accompany her son. She had resented making the trip to Frankfurt when her husband had been crowned emperor, and she was hardly going to agree to make the journey a second time. From a Viennese perspective, Frankfurt was far away, the Empire a kind of foreign country, and the imperial throne now "really only a shadow" of its former self.[67] Responsibility for organizing the whole lay not with the imperial court but with the elector of Mainz as imperial arch chancellor. To be sure, Maria Theresa later had the grand ritual event immortalized in a representative cycle of paintings she commissioned from the court painter's workshop.[68] The House of Habsburg was happy to profit from the symbolic capital that the emperorship still brought with it.

Through his election *vivente imperatore*, Joseph automatically became emperor upon his father's death. The Habsburg hereditary lands were a different matter. There his mother was still very much in charge. This resulted in an even more acute asymmetry than in his father's lifetime: whereas Francis Stephen had still ruled independently over Tuscany, Joseph was now an emperor without a country of his own.[69] Needless to say, this hardly seemed compatible with his constitutional preeminence. "For as long as there has been a German Empire, it has never before been the case that an elected Roman emperor has assumed the burden of rule without having a country and people under his dominion that might enable him to exercise the primary duty of his imperial office, namely, the active protection of the Empire's estates," read a memorandum submitted to the imperial widow. It was therefore imperative that the emperor "be given increased prestige and power, in keeping with the dignity of his office."[70] Some were expecting Maria Theresa to hand over the reins of power to the heir. Transferring rule over the hereditary lands to her son would not only have enhanced the authority of the imperial throne, it would also have accorded with contemporary ideas about proper relations between the sexes. It was not unusual for a royal widow to lay down her regency once her son came of age. Many statements made by Maria Theresa immediately after Francis Stephen's death, and later as well, convey the impression that the scepter of rule had become an intolerable burden to her.[71] In November 1765, for example, she wrote to Tarouca: "I am so overwhelmed that I am losing my last remaining vestige of sanity, so that I would have been forced to retire even if my heart had not been set on it [anyway]."[72] Or in March 1766 to Count Thurn: "If only

I followed my inclination, I would go into complete retirement, if I did not see that my unhappy person could still be of some use."[73] And so on, until December 1778, two years before her death: "I could at any time withdraw gladly from it all and have no regrets."[74]

Yet she never did abdicate. Not for her the role of dowager-widow played by so many others who ruled as guardians until their sons had attained their majority. She was a great sovereign in her own right by virtue of the Pragmatic Sanction and her two coronations. She was convinced that this was a responsibility entrusted her by God, one that should therefore not simply be surrendered to her son, however much she might sometimes long to be rid of it. In all likelihood, she never seriously contemplated stepping down from the throne. Instead, the obvious solution was to make her son coregent in the hereditary lands, like her husband before him. The question was solely whether she could do so on her own authority or had to seek the assent of the estates. Nobody had any concerns about the Austrian, Bohemian, and Dutch estates. Only the Hungarians were considered strong and stubborn enough to raise their voices in protest—they were notorious, after all, for their *principia republicana*.[75] Maria Theresa solicited advice on the question from various quarters, including from Bartenstein, who had once been instrumental in arranging Francis Stephen's coregency. They all found it neither advisable nor necessary to consult the estates. Nor was a new oath of allegiance required. As sovereign overlord, Maria Theresa was perfectly entitled to have Joseph declared coregent *in consortium regiminis* and merely communicate the decision to her people by edict.[76] Acting on this advice, on September 17, 1765, Maria Theresa entrusted her future heir with "the joint care and government of all Our inherited kingdoms and lands," albeit with the telling proviso: "without, however, renouncing wholly or in part the particular government of Our states, which are to remain indivisibly united."[77] With that, she explicitly maintained her grip on power. Although Joseph was assigned responsibility for several functions of government, such as military affairs, these could be taken out of his hands at any time. He owed his position as coregent solely to her grace and favor. So long as his involvement in politics was confined to symbolic acts and he proved willing to defer to Maria

Theresa, the indeterminacy of his status was not a problem. That had always been his father's strategy. If, however, the new coregent was no longer prepared to do his mother's bidding and conflict broke out, the outcome was anyone's guess.[78] There were no precedents or guidelines for such a situation. The dilemma was not lost on foreign observers. Sources close to the French embassy reported: "She [the empress] jealously guards her authority, which she has never had to share with anyone. When her husband died, she spoke of retiring and handing over the affairs of government to her son, but her natural taste for dominance soon gained the upper hand and brought her to abandon the plan she had hatched in her initial grief."[79] The English traveler Henry Swinburne put it more succinctly: "The Emperor is allowed no power."[80] And Prince Ligne, ever a perceptive observer, drastically compared Joseph's regency with a "permanent priapism," or less scurrilously, with "itches he can never satisfy."[81]

How Enlightenment Came to the Court

Enormous care had been lavished on Joseph's education: given the "natural lottery" of dynastic inheritance, the future happiness of the entire state rested on his character. All the more unfortunate, then, was the evident mismatch between the enormity of the task awaiting him and his parents' poor opinion of him. When he was ten years old, his mother complained that he had been seduced by the flattery of his hangers-on "into taking pleasure in seeing himself obeyed and honored while finding criticism unpleasant and indeed almost intolerable. He indulges all his whims but behaves discourteously, even rudely, towards others."[82] Deficient self-knowledge, poor judgment, hardness of heart, not least diffidence, expressed in an insecure and shy demeanor—in Maria Theresa's eyes, all this boded ill for the future.[83] Whenever she compared her eldest son with her husband, the comparison was always to Joseph's disadvantage.[84] She would then cheer herself up by telling herself that Joseph was basically of sound character and would surely improve with time. Far from keeping her misgivings to herself, she discussed them openly with family members and courtiers.

His parents spared no pains in preparing the heir for what awaited him and training him in the art of rule. When he was thirteen, high-level meetings were held and a flurry of memoranda produced on the subject of his curriculum. Maria Theresa commissioned no less senior a figure than Bartenstein to devise an educational program for the archduke (prompting him to toss off a couple of textbooks in short order). Christian August Beck, professor for public law at the Theresianum and a former Protestant who had studied in the Enlightenment strongholds of Leipzig and Jena, was appointed tutor in the most important subjects, law and modern history.[85] Jesuit fathers had traditionally been responsible for education in Catholic dynasties, but they initially played a negligible role in Joseph's upbringing. Instead, modern rational law infiltrated the House of Habsburg.

Beck, like his colleague at the Theresianum, the previously mentioned cameralist Johann Heinrich Gottlob Justi, had graduated from the school of Protestant German natural and international law associated with such distinguished names as Samuel Pufendorf, Christian Thomasius, Justus Henning Boehmer, and Christian Wolff.[86] This relatively young academic discipline played a crucial role in the emergence of a bureaucratic elite that was shaped less by noble birth than by a shared mentality and political discourse. Over time, the impact of the new doctrine of natural law spread far beyond the Protestant world. Even Catholic nobles sent their sons to Jena, Halle, or Leipzig, while, conversely, Protestant scholars were appointed to posts in Catholic lands (although most converted beforehand). Natural and international law increasingly found their way into Catholic university curricula. Maria Theresa herself was convinced of the importance of *ius publicum universale et gentium* in training candidates for state service.[87] Paul Joseph Riegger was the first to teach natural and international law in the hereditary lands, from 1733 in Innsbruck and then from 1753 in Vienna. He was succeeded by his student Karl Anton von Martini, who also tutored Archduke Leopold. Martini's students, such as Joseph von Sonnenfels and Franz von Zeiller, in turn went on to become some of the key figures in Habsburg judicial policy.[88] As a core curricular component at universities, natural law doctrine was especially influential, since not only later jurists but also economists, cameralists, political scientists (*Policeywissenschaftler*), and experts in statecraft had generally completed preliminary studies in natural law. This created a common intellectual outlook that went some way to bridging differences of social background and confession by facilitating the formation of a bureaucratic esprit de corps. The precondition was that higher learning had been increasingly aristocratized from the late seventeenth century onward. By gradually abandoning its scruples about university study, the nobility had clawed back top positions in justice and administration from middle-class functionaries. In the eighteenth century jurisprudence was the discipline of choice for aristocratic students, and Halle, Leipzig, Jena, and Göttingen were their preferred universities. Kaunitz was a product of this academic socialization, as were (for example) the Hungarian reformer Pál Festetics, Tobias Philipp von Gebler, and the brothers Ludwig and Karl von Zinzendorf, whom Kaunitz installed in key positions in Vienna.[89]

All these men spoke the language of natural and international law. Borrowing their methodological toolkit from the natural sciences, they saw themselves cutting through the tangle of competing opinions to lay bare the immutable, supposedly incontestable laws of social life. To arrive at absolute certainty in the field of practical philosophy, too, proponents of natural law emulated—superficially, at least—the rigor and precision of geometry. Starting from certain incontrovertible premises, they purported to arrive through a series of logically compelling arguments at a system of normatively binding propositions. Of decisive importance for this school of thought was the so-called demonstrative style of teaching, a method for deriving even the most specific rights and duties from antecedent principles of human nature. Such claims made an easy target for ridicule. One wag quipped that if the preeminent natural law theorist, Christian Wolff, had lived any longer, he would have demonstrated the tailor's duty to make his trousers neither too tight nor too baggy. One of the central categories from which everything else was derived was the legal concept of a free contract. Starting out from the fiction of a state of nature in which all men were free and equal, the evolution of society was conceived as a step-by-step sequence of voluntary contractual agreements. With that, almost anything could be rationally justified. Every kind of social and political order had been created by design and was thus open to revision, at least in theory. According to natural law doctrine, individuals gave up their natural freedom, either in part or in full, when they established a community and submitted to a sovereign power that acted in the common interest and selected the best means for pursuing that interest. The supreme goal was general happiness—however that might be imagined in its particulars. With this formula, natural law opened the floodgates to the reforming and restructuring agendas of bureaucratic elites. Natural law offered a criterion that could be applied in cases of doubt against existing common and statutory law. Above all, it was a method, and this method could be harnessed to political intentions of all stripes: it could be used to confirm class privilege or contest it, to expand monarchical rule or limit it. Natural law doctrine contained a latent revolutionary potential. For in submitting all elements of law to its tribunal, it also potentially called them into question.

At the Viennese court, several high officials shared this mentality from the 1750s onward—in opposition to the empress herself. Christian August Beck, an academic grandchild of the Enlightenment luminary Christian Thomasius, brought the heir into contact with the doctrine.[90] Beck's lectures on natural law were anything but revolutionary in content, smoothly adapted to conditions in the Empire and hereditary lands. Yet they communicated principles from which more radical conclusions could also be drawn. The heir learned, among other things, that "majesty is singular and supreme in every state," and that its incumbent "can be neither judged nor punished by anyone in the world."[91] He also learned that "our duties towards others [are based] on the natural equality of humankind and the philanthropy which flows from it," and that "all religious compulsion runs counter to natural law."[92] Joseph was a diligent student whose examination results received the highest praise. "The tuition given His Royal Majesty by Privy Councilor von Beck proved so effective that he showed marked progress in natural and international law, for which he demonstrated . . . a particular liking."[93] With the doctrine of natural law, Joseph acquired not only a fixed repertoire of ideas and mental categories but also a sense of belonging to an enlightened intellectual elite that felt itself superior to the older generation. This gave him the self-assurance he needed to hold his own against anyone at court—including his mother. His teacher also strengthened him in the conviction that a monarch's power was limited by nothing other than his duty to work for the happiness of the state. He was therefore beholden to no one when it came to the question of how such happiness was best attained. The only point on which clarification was lacking, fatally, was who exactly wielded sovereign power at the Viennese court. Natural and international law provided no answers for the special case of a coregency between mother and son.[94]

Following his marriage, Joseph's parents had initiated him little by little into the practicalities of statecraft. He was made to attend meetings of the various central authorities and grasped nothing of the thousand trivialities discussed there, as he later admitted. From 1761 on he had also been invited to attend sessions of the newly established State Council, where he represented the imperial couple in their absence.[95] Over the years he sent his mother a steady stream of memoranda setting out political principles of extraordinary radicalism.[96] This was especially true of a memorandum—cautiously labeled "Rêveries," or "Dreams"— that he wrote in 1763, while his father was still alive. It shows that he had drawn rather different lessons from his natural law classes than his teacher had intended and his mother would have condoned. He had probably also read some of the "dangerous books" that Maria Theresa had tried in vain to banish from her realm: Montesquieu, Rousseau, Diderot, and similarly subversive fare. At any rate, the positions he defended in his "Rêveries" were deemed so outrageous, and so indefensible, that even a nineteenth-century national-liberal historian such as Alfred von Arneth refused to publish them and quoted from them, at best, in heavily abridged form.[97] In the "Rêveries," Joseph grappled with the problem of how a sovereign could put himself in a position to do all that was necessary for the good of the state. His solution was simple yet radical: by "reducing the standing and wealth of the grandees," *abaisser et apauvrir les grands.* The sovereign found himself hindered at every turn, however, by all the "regulations, statutes, and oaths" held up as the sacred repository of ancient freedoms by the many "petty kings" who sought to evade his authority. "A single head" was needed to make the decisions that would guarantee the happiness of the state. Joseph therefore recommended a kind of fixed-term dictatorship or "limited despotism," *despotisme lié*: a mandate from the provinces, set at ten years, "to do everything for their benefit without seeking their consent."[98] Even the State Council, the highest consultative body in the monarchy, would be sidelined. It was obvious that the institutional representatives of the provinces, the estates, would never see eye to eye with Joseph on this, especially in Hungary. For Joseph's radical proposals included doubling taxation on noble estates, cutting salaries for aristocratic idlers in high office, taking an ax to wasteful court expenditure in general, but also simplifying and merging central authorities, establishing more streamlined chains of command with clearly defined responsibilities, and abolishing all special favors, exceptions, and backdoor dealings. Some would suffer, he conceded, but chronic illnesses called for drastic remedies.[99]

Maria Theresa wisely kept this explosive document to herself. Yet a couple of months after being named coregent, Joseph composed a new memorandum on the state of the monarchy that could no longer simply be ignored.[100] This too was a fairly haphazard wish list of reforms propped up by general propositions taken from textbooks on natural law. On this occasion, to be sure, Joseph eschewed antiaristocratic rhetoric and adopted a more pragmatic approach. Yet his views were essentially unchanged, as his mother recognized when she remarked that the new memorandum showed "the ever-recurring way of thinking."[101] Joseph was still proclaiming that he "could never regard it as just to flay two hundred good peasants in order to overpay an idle lord." He castigated the sluggishness and incompetence of the authorities, demanded that appointments be based solely on performance rather than on pedigree, punishment be carried out without regard to the culprit, and penalties for marriages between those of unequal standing be abolished. For "at birth we inherit only bare life from our parents. Whether king, count, citizen, or peasant, it makes not the slightest difference."[102]

Maria Theresa quietly filed away Joseph's memoranda and did nothing to promote their cause—although it was in some respects not so far removed from what she herself had advocated upon coming to the throne. Indeed, the overall situation bore more than a passing resemblance to that which had confronted her in 1740: a war-devastated economy and skyrocketing state debt; an army of incompetent and indolent officials; jurisdictional overlaps and mountains of meaningless paperwork; parasitic aristocrats leeching off impoverished subjects. Joseph's proposals also sounded not dissimilar to her own. She too had cut expenditure at court when she came to power, ordered wild game to be shot, and thrown overboard the worthless ballast of tradition; she too had stood up to her father's long-serving grandees, criticized the selfishness of the estates, and put systematic reforms on the agenda. Despite all these initiatives, the problems facing the realm had if anything grown more acute in the twenty-five years since. Yet Joseph spoke a different, far more radical and uncompromising language than his mother. Much in the 1765 memorandum could only be read as a barely concealed attack on her most deeply held convictions—for example, that "neither age nor ancestry, neither alliances nor friendships, and neither chastity not bigotry" should play a role in ministerial appointments. Mother and son were poles apart, above all, in matters of religion and censorship: the sovereign was not obliged to police the individual's conscience, only the state as a whole; "the freedom innate to human beings must be given as much latitude as possible."[103] Such a sentence was characteristic of the new mentality that came to prevail among European educated elites in the last third of the eighteenth century, but it was utterly foreign to Maria Theresa. For her, there was no such thing as a "freedom innate to human beings" from which universal human rights could be derived. On the contrary, she felt deeply threatened by the critical spirit that characterized the new, "enlightened" habitus of the "self-styled philosophers." She refrained from taking part in the debates animated by this new spirit, nor did she read the relevant "dangerous books." She constantly warned her children of the *philosophie à la mode*, which she believed to be nothing other than a sophisticated form of *amour propre*.[104] The generational conflict that convulsed the House of Habsburg during the years of Joseph's coregency was also an epochal one.

Trials of Strength

Joseph found himself in an extremely awkward, historically unprecedented situation. Ever since the death of his father, he had been playing three roles involving three distinct responsibilities that were not at all easy to reconcile. First, as elected head of the Holy Roman Empire he owed his mother nothing; indeed, he clearly outranked her in the imperial hierarchy. Second, he exercised joint sovereignty over the hereditary lands with his mother, but what exactly that meant was anyone's guess. Third, he was his mother's son and hence duty-bound to obey her. Given their contrasting temperaments and philosophical views, a clash of roles was only a matter of time.

It began with Joseph's actions as emperor. He took his new title very seriously and immediately set about making long overdue reforms to the highest imperial courts.[105] Maria Theresa was alarmed and turned to Johann Anton, Count Pergen, who had long been her emissary in Electoral Mainz and knew the ins and outs of imperial politics as well as anyone. As she wrote to inform him, she had never before interfered in imperial affairs and had no wish to do so in future. Nonetheless, she wanted to be useful to her son in his reform endeavors. She disagreed with Joseph's intention to entrust them to Imperial Vice-Chancellor Colloredo, who, after all, was officially responsible for such matters. Instead, Pergen was to influence the emperor and insinuate to him how he should rule over the Empire to his own glory and the general good— an instruction that Pergen failed to carry out to her satisfaction.[106] In a similar vein, she had earlier urged Kaunitz to show an interest in her son: "He is flattered and pleased when he talks to you, but he . . . prefers others to seek out his company."[107] Yet Joseph was not so easily manipulated, particularly in his capacity as imperial overlord.

The first affront arose from a long-simmering dispute over the imperial fief of San Remo. The Republic of Genoa, a traditional enemy of the Habsburgs that enjoyed the protection of the French and Spanish courts, had long claimed sovereignty over the city.[108] The citizens of San Remo had appealed to the Imperial Aulic Council in 1753 for protection against the Genoese. Under Francis Stephen, the matter had been allowed to lapse, since intervention from the imperial court would have meant open conflict with Genoa and hence also with France. This was incompatible with Kaunitz's foreign policy objectives. Yet in 1766, when San Remo again petitioned the Imperial Aulic Council for support, Joseph, unlike his father, was not prepared to sacrifice his authority as emperor to Kaunitz's alliance policy.

Keeping the all-powerful state chancellor on side was especially important to Maria Theresa at this point in time. Not long before, in June 1766, she had refused to accept his offer of resignation. Kaunitz had recognized that he was threatened by serious competition—not just from the emperor and coregent, but also from the ambitious Prince Starhemberg, whom Maria Theresa planned to invite to Vienna as successor to the late Count Haugwitz. In April 1766 the death of two of his closest colleagues had therefore prompted Kaunitz to request that she relieve him of all his titles and offices. In an emotionally charged appeal, Maria Theresa reproached him for abandoning her in her hour of need. She claimed—probably correctly—that he was jealous of the heir and flatly turned down his request. Kaunitz professed outrage over the slur on his good character but was prepared to put off his resignation for another two years (and did not renew the request later). Both Maria Theresa and Joseph then assured him in the warmest possible terms of their everlasting gratitude. If this had been Kaunitz's strategy all along, then it was a successful one—at least so far as Maria Theresa was concerned. By agreeing to stay at his post, he tied the empress to him all the more securely.[109] Joseph, however, refused to give in to emotional blackmail. In this situation, the San Remo question, although fairly insignificant in itself, became the spark that ignited the powder keg of unspoken tensions between Maria Theresa, Joseph, and Kaunitz.

Kaunitz had drafted a document to be sent to the French court pledging that the matter would be taken no further in the Imperial Aulic Council—it was normal for such cases to spend years in limbo, anyway. Yet Joseph took this as an infringement on his imperial prerogatives. He composed (in German, for a change) an unusually strongly worded reply to Kaunitz and sent it to his mother along with an accompanying letter (in French) in which he declared his readiness to submit blindly to her will. In the German text, he presented himself as the champion of "justice towards the weak and the oppressed" in the San Remo question. "Empty fears and fanciful political schemes cannot deter me from my decision, which I have arrived at by good sense and mature deliberation. . . . I shall allow my council to speak and I shall approve its conclusion. . . . Should I abandon duty, honor, and reputation . . . with a brazen and childishly mocking excuse, sacrificing all this . . . to a particular friendship?" Finally, he accused Kaunitz of seeking "to set Her Majesty the Empress on a collision course with me, giving her sacred word in a matter that she cannot promise and I cannot deliver." In short, he could only reject Kaunitz's proposal or, better yet, forget all about it.[110] Yet Joseph appended to this German document two different versions of a letter addressed to the French court, leaving his mother to choose between the two. He thus left the decision in her hands while at the same time making clear just how reprehensible he found one of the two options. This was a double-edged strategy, combining devoted submission to his mother with vehement criticism aimed at Kaunitz—criticism that necessarily deflected on her. With these two letters in two different languages, he indirectly showed her the incompatibility of his two roles: here the compliant son proclaiming his deference in the courtliest French, there the emperor barking his commands in the bluntest German.

Maria Theresa did not appreciate this subtle strategy. On the contrary, it expressed everything she found unbearable about her son in particular and the intellectual airs of the "fashionable philosophers" in general. She promptly replied with a long, searching, unusually direct letter that, following an innocuous sounding introduction, gradually built up to a damning indictment of Joseph's character.[111] The style of his German missive had pained her, she wrote: "that you could think this way, and take satisfaction in mortifying others and publicly humiliating them." She had always tried to do the exact opposite: "I have preferred to get people to do what I wanted by kind words, to persuade them rather than force them. This has served me well; and I hope that you will find as much support in your states and from your servants as I have." Giving her the final say in the San Remo decision was nothing more than sarcasm. That was his affair, and she found it a just one. But his behavior toward her most important adviser had been hurtful and malicious. "Decent people" would be repelled by such ill-treatment, leaving him surrounded by "rogues, toadies, and flatterers." In ever new turns of phrase, she varied the same reproach: his letter revealed his true character, with all its currishness, irony, malice, and want of fellow feeling. He delighted in making others look ridiculous just to show off his intelligence. Much as his sister Elisabeth coquetted with her beauty, so he flaunted his wit: every bon mot, every turn of phrase he had read or picked up somewhere he would apply "at the first opportunity," solely to impress others, "without considering whether it is seemly." If he continued to act in this way, he would never find the true friends he so urgently needed as regent. It was clear whose image stood before her mind's eye throughout this tirade, even if, as usual, she never called him by name: "this hero who has made so much talk about himself, this conqueror, has he a single friend? Has he not reason to distrust the whole world? What sort of a life is that from which humanity is banished?"[112]

Maria Theresa's rancor had a specific background. Nobody could ignore the fact that her own son resembled her worst enemy both physically and intellectually.[113] In his memoranda, he also proposed that the military recruitment system be reorganized entirely along Prussian lines.[114] His discourtesy toward long-serving ministers, his sarcasm, his newfangled philosophy, his military uniform, his spartan habits, his disdain for forms regarded as sacrosanct by others: these were all sure signs that "this young lord *absolument* wants to imitate the king in Prussia and deal with everything *militairement*." Worse still: "He had even surreptitiously set up an interview with the said monarch," as Khevenhüller noted with dismay.[115] During the summer of 1766, as the San Remo affair was coming to a head, Joseph traveled through Bohemia and Saxony to the border of the "promised land" Silesia, visiting battlefields of the Seven Years' War along the way. This too could be regarded as an act of tacit homage to his hero.[116] He had originally intended to meet the Prussian king in person, thereby placing Maria Theresa in a serious quandary.[117] Behind her back, Joseph had signaled his interest in a meeting. An invitation was extended by the Prussian emissary for what would be made to look like a chance encounter. When Maria Theresa got wind of the plan, she sent an express courier after Joseph and made him cancel the rendezvous at the last moment. In the seventeenth and eighteenth century, it was extremely rare for two rulers to meet in person. Entering another sovereign's territory could easily be interpreted as a hostile act. Many therefore followed the emperor's travels with consternation: "A king of France had never set foot on foreign soil, unless he was at the head of his armies," the Duke of Croÿ noted on the occasion of Joseph's trip to Versailles in 1777.[118] If they met at all, rulers did so at the exact border between their lands. Yet such summits were typically beset by intractable problems of status and ceremonial. Wary of losing face, each side was reluctant to make the first move. It was thus easier to communicate via emissaries. Here too both parties placed great emphasis on keeping their intentions secret for as long as possible and then staging the meeting as a spontaneous initiative from the other side. While the emperor was still on the road, Frederick dispatched one of his cavaliers to lure him with skillful compliments to Berlin and impress him there with elaborate "military displays," as Khevenhüller suspected. But Joseph was so "startled and chastened by his mother's message" that he turned down the proposal, and the face-to-face meeting never came about.[119] Maria Theresa must have directly accused her son of imitating her enemy, for Joseph protested in reply that he would never take the king of Prussia "as a model," this being completely incompatible with the stance of an *honnête homme*.[120] Here as always, Joseph reacted to his mother's scolding with the utmost submissiveness, rhetorically kissed her hands a thousand times and clasped her knees, praised her incomparable maternal heart, and abjectly declaimed his own guilt, worthlessness, despondency, and inexpressible filial devotion. After being taken to task for his part in the San Remo affair, too, he wept "tears of gratitude" for her all too justified criticism.[121] Such excessive rhetoric struck an even more obsequious tone than ordinary subjects were expected to adopt when addressing the empress. When the coregent resorted to such phrases, he drew attention to the structural dilemma in which both mother and son were trapped and from which each of them suffered in different ways. This rhetoric of submission did nothing to prevent a series of increasingly dramatic showdowns over the following years.

FIGURE 41. Joseph plowing a field. Anonymous broadsheet, 1769

The second major crisis in the mother-son relationship broke out over an apparently minor formality. The issue in question was the joint signature attached to decisions reached by the State Council, an issue that nonetheless went to the heart of the problems plaguing the coregency. In January 1769 Joseph wrote to his mother—as always in a tone of deep devotion, but at the same time with fixed resolve—that he could not bring himself to countersign the council's decisions unless he added the distancing qualifier *ex consilio* or *qua corregens*. His peace of mind, his happiness, and his reputation all depended on it, since the joint signature went against the essence of monarchy, which could have but a "single" head.[122] The problem had arisen because the State Council, Kaunitz's domestic policy creation, was about to resume regular sessions in the presence of the two monarchs.[123] Maria Theresa replied both promptly and emotionally, likewise in writing. She regarded his request as a gross impertinence. The joint signature had been practiced for the last twenty-eight years; it was dear to her as an expression of her heartfelt love for her husband and now her son, who as coregent would surely wish to prove himself worthy of his father. Yet Joseph refused to budge. In his wordy reply, he claimed that precisely his filial love, his gratitude, and his respect for her forced him to insist on this favor, a trifle for her but a matter of the utmost importance to him. "Do you think I have so black and ungrateful a soul that I would pester you without a compelling reason?"[124] His mother responded with mounting irritation to these rhetorical ploys: "I know you can speak and write well." But he was mistaken if he believed that she would change a simple, tried-and-tested custom on a mere whim, without giving her a valid reason. "God only knows how much I suffer," she added. A little later, having had her standpoint confirmed by State Councillor Starhemberg, she wrote again, this time adopting a more conciliatory tone: "You know just how willing I am to accommodate everyone, and especially you. For this there are a thousand proofs. I devote myself to the affairs of state solely for love of you. I can no longer hope to reap the fruits of my labor myself. I thus do it all for your sake, yet you of all people stand in my way and carefully hide the reason for the sudden and unpredictable decisions on which you so stubbornly insist."[125] On this matter she refused to give an inch. But so too did Joseph. He launched a renewed assault: was she not aware of his deepest feelings for her, his obedience, his sincerity, his sense of duty? The petition he most humbly dared to submit was meant to prevent any false ideas arising about who really held power at court. For sooner or later, this would bring the monarchy a thousand disadvantages, cause intrigue to flourish, and ultimately undermine the happy understanding between the two of them. This was what compelled him to risk losing her affection. He had already lost his peace of mind, so painful did he find the idea that she might be dissatisfied with him. In the past he had been prepared a hundred times to yield to her, for all that his reason had pleaded the opposite. He begged her to put an end to his torment and spare him the signature, and he would forevermore be her first subject and most obedient servant. Here the letter comes to an end. It is remarkable that the whole conflict played out in epistolary form, even though they could just as easily have discussed the matter face to face. It was Maria Theresa who shied away from a personal meeting. Instead, she continued pulling out all the emotional stops in the medium of writing. She herself, she replied, was suffering doubly from the unfortunate situation. "I was already at the point of coming to you and enfolding you in my arms to end this cruel situation, but what holds me back is that you so repeatedly and willfully dig in your heels." She was prepared, she added, to work with him to find a solution, but she was too upset for now and needed time to regain the spiritual composure that alone made her sorrowful days tolerable. And finally: "What I expect from you, as the certain proof of your affection and love, is that you will in future sign everything just as before until new arrangements have been made. You know my delicacy; it is not my wish to force anyone to do anything."[126] At this Joseph finally admitted defeat, announcing with studied deference: "I have the honor of laying at your feet the most objective document [*I'acte le plus réel*] of my most complete submission. I have signed all the papers you were good enough to send me."[127]

I have cited the correspondence at some length because it so clearly indicates the full extent of the dilemma in the relationship between mother and son. Joseph's intention was clear: he was no longer willing to play along with the charade of what was a coregency in name only. By adding a Latin disclaimer to his signature, he sought to demonstrate his distance and thereby make clear to himself, his mother, and the world at large where real power lay. He had good political and procedural reasons for doing so. Years of experience with a pliant consort had accustomed Maria Theresa to presenting her own sovereign will in the plural. Joseph, by contrast, was not prepared to maintain this façade of consensus, which potentially meant accepting responsibility for decisions he had never made and that went against his most deeply held convictions. He was all too often at loggerheads with his mother, and there was no prospect that things would be any different in future. Finally, Maria Theresa had only just rebuffed his most pressing reform proposals—for example, in the question of deportation convoys to Temesvár.[128] What really doomed any possibility of compromise, however, was Maria Theresa's insistence on personalizing the political question of the coregency, turning it into the ultimate touchstone of filial loyalty and devotion. She refused, in other words, to draw a line between "private" feelings and political acts. In the end, only her opinion counted. It is a moot point whether she was genuinely unable to understand her son's problem, as she claimed, or whether she wanted to force a showdown for strategic reasons. At any rate, she was the winner in this battle of wills—Joseph demonstratively surrendered. The price she paid for her victory, however, was the loss of the very sincerity that lay so close to her heart and which she so obsessively required of others.

In the period that followed, Joseph increasingly went out of his mother's way at court and left Vienna for a months-long tour of Italy. In the letters he sent her from abroad, he always demonstrated the most complete submission, accepting without demur her command that he not visit the hostile republic of Genoa, for example.[129] In August 1769 he finally met with Frederick II in Neisse, Saxony. Although the spectacular encounter had been arranged this time by Kaunitz, not without Maria Theresa's agreement, she still regarded it with deep suspicion.[130] In January 1770 Joseph was again struck by personal tragedy when his only child, Theresa, died at the age of seven. His letters from this period reveal an intensity of anguish that far surpassed what was considered normal at the time for those in his situation.[131] Maria Theresa later blamed this emotionally devastating blow for the breakdown in their relationship, thereby ignoring Joseph's real, genuinely political intention.

The relationship between mother and son took another turn for the worse in January 1771. The question of the coregent's responsibility was still unresolved. This was especially unfortunate given the serious political problems that needed to be addressed. On the eastern border of the Habsburg empire, Russia and Turkey had been at war since 1768; what position should Austria adopt? There was terrible famine in Bohemia; how could it be allayed? Joseph pushed for active intervention, and he confided in his brother that he experienced his mother's indecisiveness as sheer martyrdom. Maria Theresa was feeling particularly unwell that winter, despite putting on a brave face: "I won't be finished off so easily."[132] For months she suffered from facial erysipelas; she was increasingly immobilized by her obesity, experienced shortness of breath, had pains in her right arm, and could write only with difficulty. She was listless, depressed, tired of life: "Why did the pox not take me away? What a blessing that would have been!"[133] Yet the discord with her son pained her even more than her physical ailments. Once again, the signature question was the bone of contention. The traditional *promotion militaire*, the ceremonious announcement of military promotions at the start of the new year, had long been fertile ground for jealousy and disappointment. On this occasion, the nephew of Prince Liechtenstein, a loyal servant of many years' standing, had been passed over. Joseph complained to his brother that he had submitted alternative proposals but had been forced to cosign the unchanged promotions list at his mother's behest. Nonetheless, she was now publicly making him responsible for it.[134] From her perspective, the situation was exactly the opposite. In her eyes, the previous round of promotions had been an example of important decisions being taken behind her back. She only learned about them later, when it was too late for her to do anything but still had to take the blame.[135] This was precisely the consequence of the unclear division of powers that Joseph had predicted.

Paradoxically, the empress never felt herself more powerless than after she had won the battle of wills with her son, who now prostrated himself before her in professions of unconditional obedience. She complained about this to many in her circle, including her trusted old servants Khevenhüller and Colloredo. But she was particularly outspoken when confiding in Marquise d'Herzelles, the former aya of her granddaughter Theresa, with whom she felt connected in their common grief for the child. In the early 1770s, it was to her that she regularly confided her complaints about *l'empereur*, as she always called him. Each time she implored the Marquise to burn the letter immediately—a request that was obviously ignored—and share its contents with nobody, least of all with Joseph.[136] He was deliberately avoiding all contact with her, she claimed, for he knew himself to be in the wrong. He was treating her just like he used to treat poor Josepha: "Judge for yourself how greatly my heart is suffering, which lives for this son alone and deifies him. It is even more bitter than death."[137] Following his capitulation in the procedural dispute, his resistance had now shifted to other areas. The major new battlefields were his dissolute lifestyle and his devotional practice. When his confessor died, he had brusquely refused to allow his mother to nominate a successor. He went infrequently to confession, neglected

his prayers, seldom attended Mass, and avoided reading spiritually edifying books. He also failed to observe fasting rules, despite not having
obtained the obligatory dispensation from the papal nuncio or his personal physician. She explained his conduct by claiming that he deliberately wanted to strike her where it would hurt her most. Confession was
a highly contentious matter. On the one hand, the confessing priest was
for Catholic sovereigns the sole earthly authority—apart from their
own conscience—that could curb unbridled despotism and moral law-
lessness. On the other, the practice of confession stood at the center of
decades-long religious debates in France, Italy, and the Habsburg Netherlands, debates that also increasingly polarized the Viennese court. The
Jesuits' traditional dominance as court confessors had been under attack since the 1760s, with penitential theology forming a key point of
difference between the opposing sides in the ecclesiastical dispute.[138]
When Joseph now refused to accept a Jesuit father as his confessor, instead opting for a low-ranking court chaplain—a mere *curé*, in Maria
Theresa's disapproving eyes—he could be seen as taking a stand against
the Jesuits in this dispute. But Maria Theresa took his decision, in the
first instance, as a calculated affront to her own maternal authority.

His sexual libertinism—the numerous indecencies, *choses indécentes*,
that came to her attention—was at least as bad.[139] Her preference had
been for Joseph to remarry after the death of his second wife, but this time
she had not forced her will on him.[140] When Leopold's first son (and later
emperor) Francis was born in 1768, the male succession was assured and
Joseph relieved of the pressure to find a new bride.[141] Maria Theresa was
all the more alarmed by his moral failings. On the one hand, she thought
him a "great misogynist" and called him "the most unjust man, so far as
women are concerned."[142] On the other, he could "not get by without
women" and surrounded himself with them "until midnight and later,"
consorting with them "on walks, in gardens, outside my apartment, in the
theater, in their houses. There is a constant toing and froing."[143] Others,
including his brother Leopold, later claimed he had a penchant for "sordid
women and prostitutes."[144] Joseph himself openly discussed his relationship to the various ladies at court with his brother, calling himself—
perhaps ironically—a "libertine" and "free as a bird in the woods."[145]

Maria Theresa tended to attribute Joseph's behavior to the influence of the sinister figures around him, people like his cabinet secretary, Augustin Thomas von Wöber. She was horrified by the appointment. In her eyes, Wöber was a dreadful misanthrope who had no time for churchgoing and the sacraments, scoffed at the law, read Machiavelli, got by on eight kreuzers a week, and always wore the same coat. All this clearly made him just the man to serve her son![146] Khevenhüller, to whom she likewise regularly complained about the "domestic cross" she had to bear, confirmed her in such suspicions, claiming that some were "assiduously seeking to . . . wrest the scepter from her hands and, by making her abdicate prematurely or otherwise renounce her principal duties (too many of which she had already surrendered), depose her entirely." But Khevenhüller also offered words of comfort: God would not have miraculously saved her from the pox without good reason; so too he would lighten the burden of government "through His divine succor." As a woman of piety, she had a duty not to relinquish that heavy burden: "for love of her lands and so that religion, assailed more and more each day by freethinking precepts and indifferentism, might not perish altogether."[147]

The situation was equally painful for Joseph, albeit for different reasons. Given the war on the eastern border and the famine in Bohemia, his priority was to overcome both the crippling bureaucratic blockade in Vienna and his mother's political irresolution. He longed to tackle the fundamental social wrongs in his own land through a renewed burst of reforms while also playing a more offensive role in the intractably complicated eastern theater of war. Writing to his brother Leopold, he heaped such withering scorn on his mother that Alfred von Arneth thought it wise to cut numerous passages from his edition of their correspondence.[148] In the winter of 1770–71 he found her indecisiveness "worse than ever" and saw himself condemned to sit on his hands, to the glory of obedience.[149] His extended journey through the Kingdom of Bohemia in autumn 1771, during which he formed his own idea of the unimaginable misery prevailing there, only exacerbated the dilemma. There was no concerted plan at home or abroad, he lamented to his brother while on his tour of inspection, only inaction, paralysis, and confusion. The new administrative system had been introduced in Bohemia but not implemented in its entirety. No one knew what was happening on the ground, intrigues and cabals confronted him on all sides— in short: there was total stagnation. He was now thirty years old, in the prime of his life, thirsting for action and fired with love for his country; yet not only was he forced to look on passively at the unfolding calamity, he himself was blamed for it, despite having done no wrong.[150] All that remained for him was to reveal in writing his shocking insights into the "abhorrent web" of deception, exploitation, malfeasance, and corruption, and offer an updated list of radical reform proposals on that basis.[151]

That the emperor himself had deigned to visit his subjects in the poorest provincial backwaters and inspect their dire conditions with his own eyes, without regard for rank, ceremony, health, and comfort, was perceived at the time as revolutionary. Only the Prussian king was known for taking such a personal interest in his meanest subjects. This behavior, which stood in stark contrast to the traditional habits of rule, made the emperor enormously popular in enlightened circles.[152] Even his mother was impressed by the extent of his engagement and the results of his fact-finding missions. To his shocking memorandum from Prague, denouncing a myriad of ills and abuses, she replied in November 1771 with a long, highly emotional letter that wrestled with the problem of why they were always clashing so painfully when they were both driven by the same good intentions. In a spirited appeal for mutual understanding, she made a remarkable effort to attain a measure of critical self-distance:

> Does the problem lie in ourselves, since we are both too blinded by our convictions? After all, we want others to think and act like us, while we ourselves have different opinions about the cause and the route to be followed. . . . My experience may be useful to you by way of advice, but not in order to stop you carrying out what, after careful consideration, you consider desirable. . . . Tell me honestly, in writing or by word of mouth, as I have always begged you to do, my defects, my weaknesses. I shall do the same, but let no one apart from us believe or suspect that we have different views. . . . Let us prescribe for ourselves

PLATE 17. Francis Stephen on his deathbed, 1765. Anonymous drawing made for Maria
Theresa's "Cabinet of the Dead" (*Totenkabinett*), based on a sketch commissioned by Maria
Theresa immediately after his death.

PLATE 18. The fall of heresy, Gurk Cathedral, Carinthia, based on a design by the Vienna theater architects Giuseppe and Antonio Bibiena (1740–41). A golden aureole high above the pulpit represents the Holy Spirit. Below, the allegory of the church is flanked by two cherubs. The cherub on the left bears the papal tiara, the one on the right is spearing the snake of heresy with the Holy Lance. The allegory of faith with cross, chalice, and veiled face is seated lower down on the left. A Protestant preacher dressed in black plunges dramatically to everlasting perdition, preceded by his heretical book.

PLATE 19. Altar painting in the Church of St. Teresa in the Nadelburg, artist unknown. On the left St. Teresa of Avila, on the right Joseph II and two factory workers

PLATE 20. Schönbrunn Palace, Ehrenhof. Bernardo Bellotto, known as Canaletto, 1759–60

PLATE 21. Exercitia corporis. From Philipp von Rottenberg/Carl von Roettiers, *Institutio archiducalis.* Visual training aid from the textbook for Archduke Ferdinand, 1769

PLATE 22. Portrait of Maria Theresa in Turkish costume. Undated copy, presumably of an original by Jean-Étienne Liotard, attributed to Martin van Meytens

PLATE 23. Maria Theresa as field commander in Hungarian coronation dress. From the commemorative album of the Eucharistic Brotherhood of the Cathedral Basilica of Eger (1757). Watercolor on parchment

maxims and rules; take the trouble to write them down; then we will discuss them together to decide on a set of fixed guidelines.[153]

The letter makes clear just how much Maria Theresa suffered from her progressive estrangement from her son and how determined she was to recognize and rectify her own part in it. This was no isolated case. Since coming to power, she had repeatedly urged other trusted advisers, such as Tarouca or Kaunitz, to provide her with a candid account of her defects.[154] She had clearly learned an important lesson from the classic "mirror for princes," which typically warned that the greatest danger for rulers was to surround themselves with lackeys and lickspittles who would never tell them the truth.

The Regency Dilemma

Maria Theresa's self-criticism may have come too late; at any rate, Joseph did not stop complaining about his mother to Leopold. She drove him mad with her petty secretiveness, her refusal to take a stand, her reliance on the shifting suggestions of opposing parties.[155] At the same time, however, he used the impetus provided by her new peace overture to push for a reorganization and restaffing of key offices.[156] The experience of his travels had led him to take a more sober view of the administrative reforms: these had so far proved "fruitless and exorbitant"; precious little had filtered down to the local level, and every new system produced its own, novel problems. In Joseph's opinion, any effective measures against the bureaucratic malpractice that was exploiting subjects and draining state coffers would have to proceed along quite different lines: from below rather than from above, through regular inspections and monitoring of "what was happening on the ground."[157] Yet this presupposed—paradoxically—another *renversement* at the level of the central authorities. In the Bohemian memorandum, he had already called for "an honest, unselfish, and at the same time judicious, hardworking person" to head the whole. He would be tasked with "lead[ing] the State Council, the chiefs and ministers, positions at court, and the lands in all their particulars."[158] This posed a direct challenge to Kaunitz and his system of domestic state administration, which he had brought under his control through the creation of the State Council.[159] Joseph had in mind the office of a prime minister, invested with whatever powers were needed to break up a patronage network that, in his eyes, was responsible for the evils afflicting the land. A fresh wave of reforms was needed, only this time starting at the roots. When, a year on from his Bohemian journey, nothing had yet been done, he again implored his mother "to place her blind trust in one man alone and let him act in a well-nigh despotic manner"; this he saw "as the sole means . . . by which the knot of our present constitution may gradually be untied through dicasterial [i.e., formal administrative] deeds."[160] The sweeping powers granted this man would amount to a kind of temporary dictatorship, but they would eventually be made superfluous by the establishment of formal processes, not unlike the authority wielded by the omnipotent wise legislator in Rousseau's *Contrat social.* Joseph's plan was thoroughly radical in intent: the powers of the queen herself were to be checked through formal procedural rules.

In Joseph's view, this was impossible so long as Kaunitz and his cronies were at the helm. His plan would have reduced Kaunitz's role to that of a pure foreign minister acting under the prime minister's direction. Given the relationship of close confidence between Maria Theresa and Kaunitz, Joseph was clearly once again steering toward outright conflict with his mother. It began when Kaunitz composed a 240-page memorandum on the reorganization of internal affairs and gave it to Joseph to read. Joseph reacted on April 27 with copious notes in a last-ditch effort to break the prevailing paralysis.[161] In this remarkable document, Joseph criticized his mother's government more openly and more fundamentally than ever before.[162] At stake was nothing less than the idea that the queen should unreservedly and irrevocably bind herself to certain procedural rules. Put more pointedly, Joseph was suggesting that self-imposed limits be placed on absolute rule—to be sure, a voluntary self-limitation without external oversight. Joseph was aware of how great an imposition this major change entailed. He therefore remarked by way of introduction that he hardly dared propose such a change, and that sticking with old, ingrained habits was by far the more natural course. Solely his "conviction of what was truly for the best, which must override all other considerations or concerns," gave him the courage to bring so audacious a proposal to his mother's attention. Yet he stressed that his reform plan would only succeed if it was followed to the letter and not subjected to the slightest subsequent revision. It was essential for the flourishing of the whole that the "strictest order," once introduced, "should be punctiliously observed without exception [by everyone], up to and including Your Majesty."[163] What he had in mind, in other words, was a formal order for arranging government affairs that would possess a higher authority than the monarch herself. Up to now, "the singular midpoint where everything from the monarchy has converged is Your Majesty's supreme person, which, in a manner inconceivable to me and everyone else, has without assistance, . . . without the least order in the chancellery, through constant and arduous labor, and through your own most happy memory, so tirelessly and gloriously steered the ship of state through so many years." But then—"Your Majesty will forgive me for speaking so bluntly"—he unsparingly described the adverse effects of one-woman rule: "lacking the faintest knowledge" of where matters stood, she had been forced either to make uninformed decisions or to place her faith in third parties who might not always be guided by the purest of motives. Everything would run more smoothly if the queen "would only once bind herself and all her affairs to a somewhat dicasterial order."[164]

Tellingly, this "dicasterial order" was in Joseph's eyes a "masculine" order, as opposed to the "feminine" patronage network presided over by his mother. All courtesy was now thrown out the window. What was needed were

the indispensable services of trusted and capable men, who out of duty and in their way of thinking would be far removed from all feminine meddling and partisanship, in whom tittle-tattle, patronage-peddling, [and] poor judgment need not be feared, and for whom discretion would be an accustomed duty, not a burden. . . . If Your Majesty would only experiment with allowing business which Nature has made masculine in character to be transacted by men, Your

> Majesty would notice the same difference as I would if girls and women had been supplied to me as soldiers, foresters, hunters etc.

How difficult it must be for her, he went on to write, having either to read everything herself or "through others' reading often missing precisely the most important and crucial point, for only a man versed in affairs can get at the essence of the thing and single out those points on which judgment is most vital in coming to decisions."[165] What is remarkable in this argument (which neither Joseph nor his mother ever referred to again) is that the influence-peddling and patronage-hunting that had, for centuries, been standard social practice at court—and not just there—were now suddenly presented as specifically feminine traits. Promoting the interests of family members, relatives, and friends was now regarded as the preserve of women, whereas only men appeared to be capable of conducting themselves "professionally," that is, in the service of an abstract idea. This line of argument heralded an epochal shift. In the nineteenth century, the idea that professionalism and objectivity were reserved for men would become commonplace. Private and public spheres grew further and further apart; women were increasingly excluded from the rough-and-tumble of public life, professional work, and the state and were confined instead to the "private" sphere of house and home. And the more this was the case, the more it seemed to confirm innate sexual characteristics.[166]

Joseph's key recommendation was "the provision of greater powers" to two "cabinets" responsible for internal and external affairs, respectively. Every single item of business, including petitions and appeals, every "last note," was to be initially submitted "in writing" to the relevant cabinet and registered there before being sent to the sovereign for a decision or forwarded to other departments for further processing. All decisions, without exception, would be redirected from these cabinets to the departments for the various lands. In this way, the influence of Maria Theresa's confidants, ladies-in-waiting, and chamberlains would be neutralized. The latter—specifically, Pichler and Neny—would likewise be included in the new cabinet office, no longer enjoying privileged access to the ruler. On closer inspection, then, the model represented by the new cabinets was the polar opposite to the previously "private" royal cabinet; they were formalized central authorities run along precisely defined bureaucratic guidelines.[167] The ruler would still have the final say, but solely on the basis of procedures that eliminated all informal avenues to the throne and personal favors.

Joseph knew just how hard all this would be for his mother to accept. He therefore took the precaution of appending a somewhat more moderate proposal in case she balked at undertaking so radical a reorganization of the center: an "alternative outline" for restructuring the State Council alone.[168] He was unsparing in his criticism of that institution, too. Twelve years after it had been established, the State Council still lacked procedural statutes or "regulations governing its operations," as initially foreseen. The recommendations made by Joseph were likewise aimed at increased standardization, central oversight, and relief from time-wasting trivialities. As in the Bohemian memorandum, he also foresaw the need for *one* person, situated directly beneath the ruler, to triage all incoming items of business. He declared himself willing to take on this role himself.

On May 1, 1773, when Kaunitz presented the empress with his own memorandum on reforming the State Council, he told her that the emperor's ideas had already been incorporated into the document. Maria Theresa reacted with every sign of gratitude. She called the reform project that had now been set in motion her "testament," a last hope in her desolate situation. Should it fail, she scrawled in the margin of Kaunitz's submission, she would "no longer be able to bear this burden, having dedicated myself to the world for 56 years, [and] will devote my last moments wholly to the repose and retirement I need."[169] It was in Kaunitz's hands that the empress thus placed the entire package of reforms, effectively appointing him judge in his own case, since Joseph's plans were ultimately aimed at unseating Kaunitz. With that, she sent a clear signal that she had greater confidence in her longstanding adviser than in her own son.[170]

At the same time, in the early summer of 1773 Joseph planned a new tour of inspection—this time to Galicia, to the territories newly acquired (to Maria Theresa's displeasure) from Poland.[171] She sought in vain to deter him from this "terrible journey" and assailed him with a fresh volley of reproaches. She needed him at her side, she said; he was filling her last years with bitterness and exploiting her complaisance. He obeyed only his own will and always got his way in the end with his sophistry.[172] Joseph set out nonetheless for the new territory of Galicia, which stood under the direct administration of the State Chancellery (and hence Kaunitz), and found conditions there to be catastrophic. His criticism could only be taken by Kaunitz as a personal affront. In November 1773, returned from his trip, Joseph arranged for the state chancellor to stop administering the province.[173] This led the following month to the final and perhaps most violent crisis in the relationship between mother and son. The catalyst was Kaunitz once again tendering his resignation on December 7. The empress turned him down: she was not surprised by his request, she wrote, but she was neither willing nor able to accept it and would thus ignore it. If the state was beyond salvation then she would rather join him in retirement.[174]

Two days later, a completely demoralized Joseph—"I am killing myself for nothing!"[175]—wrote a long, unusually open, almost imploring letter to his mother in which he again tried to explain the dilemma of his situation. He did not even know who he was anymore, he lamented, since she had done everything in her power to leave people in the dark about his position.

> As your Majesty and God are my witnesses, I foresaw this ever since you declared that you had no wish for the position of coregent to be an empty title. All my bitterness, my repeated appeals, my entire conduct, everything has its root in this cause. . . . I could not play the role of my late illustrious father. So what did I do? I tried to travel, to avoid . . . close contact with Your Majesty; I always maintained a distinction in the matter of the signatures, sought out distractions, and sent you meticulous reports of each new plan . . . , well aware that two wills can never remain in complete agreement without wavering, by which they must necessarily open the way for cabals, intrigues, and factions. On every occasion, I acted in accordance with these principles, but I faced, if I may say so, no opponent other than Your Majesty yourself.[176]

She was deluded if she believed him to be "ambitious or anxious to command"; on the contrary, he was incapable of directing the affairs of state: by nature lazy, lacking in application, superficial, frivolous. "I must say, to my shame, that . . . except for my zeal and my firmness when the good of the state and its service are involved, there is nothing very solid about me. But in these two points I believe I may withstand any trial." Like all her other loyal servants, he would willingly express his opinion when she asked him for it. She was free to reject his advice, but she had to let him give it based solely on his convictions and insights. In the end, though, the power of decision was reserved for her alone: "Just as we [her servants] have only opinions and no will, so Your Majesty has only will and no opinions." Joseph had evidently absorbed the lesson from his classes in natural law that there could only be one will in the state, that of the sovereign. In this sense, he demanded that his mother clarify how things stood between them, specifically, that she make an unambiguous distinction between the roles of adviser and ruler. If this proved unacceptable to her, if he became a thorn in her side or got in the way of other, more useful advisers, "then permit me, for God's and your reputation's sake, . . . to withdraw from everything, as I long to do."[177]

The fact that there were now three resignation offers on the table made the dilemma apparent. The empress reacted in conciliatory fashion. She was feeling a little more confident, she wrote. If she would not retire into seclusion after all, then only because Joseph did not wish it and because the state was in so parlous a condition. "Your and Kaunitz's abandoning me, the death of all my intimate advisers, irreligion, the depravity of morals, the jargon people talk nowadays, which I have such difficulty understanding—all these sufficiently explain why I should feel overwhelmed." She therefore now entrusted her son with setting up the new State Council; he could call on whomever he pleased for advice. Everything would be done according to his instructions.[178]

In the end, none of the three withdrew from government. Maria Theresa retained her royal prerogative, Kaunitz remained state chancellor, and Joseph became head of the renovated State Council. In the months that followed, the reform was essentially realized along the lines envisaged in Joseph's second, more moderate proposal.[179] On May 12, 1774, the new procedural statute came into effect.[180] All the threads for internal affairs came together in Joseph's hands; he alone submitted the important questions to the empress for her decision. It thus appeared as if the mother-son hierarchy had been formally regulated, just as Joseph had wished. In fact, the State Council was spared further reforms in the period that followed, although this did not put an end to the conflict between Maria Theresa and Joseph.

Seen from a distance, their relationship was a disaster. Those in their immediate surrounds who had to bear the brunt of the conflict saw this more clearly than the antagonists themselves, who had become trapped in a communicative dead end. Khevenhüller for example, to whom they frequently complained about each other, found the "afflictions of the dual government" hard to bear.[181] Striving to be loyal to both his masters, he counterfactually resolved to abide by the firm principle of never disturbing the much-needed accord between mother and son, but rather consolidating it. While not denying the confusion breaking out everywhere, he tried nonetheless to encourage the young man to have complete confidence in his mother. To make sense of the dilemma, he resorted to the courtier's classical explanation for such behavior: he blamed the adverse interference and insinuations of bad people on both sides.[182] Khevenhüller evidently believed that the quasi-natural consensus between mother and son would be automatically restored once the pernicious influence of outsiders had been eliminated. He showed no awareness of the deeper structural dilemma. Philipp Count Cobenzl, from 1779 vice-president of the State Chancellery under Kaunitz, was more perceptive. Looking back in his memoirs, he wrote:

> Royal authority was not really shared, the empress kept it all for herself. Yet she would not do anything without the consent of her successor and coregent. For his part, he never agreed with his mother from pure complaisance if she opposed his own way of seeing things. While not lacking in due deference, he drove her to despair by refusing to relent in their discussions. On several occasions, I found her in tears after such disputations. She then sent me to the emperor to

hear his decision on a matter, and the emperor, who wished to decree nothing on his own, sent me back to her.[183]

Joseph was right: by name and nature, the power of decision in a monarchy ultimately lies with one person alone. The show of unity put on for the outside world could only be a fiction. Maria Theresa's ideas reflected a traditional culture of consensus anchored in religion. In her eyes, concord was a sign of divine presence, discord the work of the devil.[184] The truth could only be singular; all that was needed was to find it. That the politically correct decision might result from compromise, that conflicting interests are not fundamentally illegitimate, and that openly expressed dissent is not necessarily an evil, but rather a precondition for reconciling opposed interests—such ideas were alien to the political culture of absolutist rule into which Maria Theresa had been socialized. Equally foreign to her, however, was the political culture of "enlightened despotism" represented by Joseph. For all their differences, mother and son were united in their expectation that political salvation would come from *one* head—the only question was whose head that might be. So long as he was prevented from having his way, Joseph saw no other option than to play the obedient son in ostentatious fashion while denying personal responsibility for his mother's decisions.

There were no winners in the trials of strength between mother and son; both saw themselves as the loser. In her own perception and that of her supporters, Maria Theresa was the one who always exercised restraint and gave ground, who never pressured her son or forced him to act against his will. "So far as I am concerned, I am neither inquisitive nor demanding," she said of herself; "my children would have to do me this justice!"[185] If her statements are to be believed, she suffered enormously from her falling out with Joseph, whom she believed to be good at heart but easily misled.[186] She wrote once to her favorite daughter, Maria Christina, that the emperor "has my pity; that is nothing but old ladies' talk, but that's the way it is. I love him dearly; I always admit he is in the right when we argue; after a couple of hours I regret vexing him so."[187] Despite genuine attempts at reconciliation, however, she was clearly incapable of recognizing the structural quandary in which the creation of the coregency had placed them. An essential difference, and perhaps the most fundamental reason for their dramatic failure to communicate, was that Maria Theresa always took conflict with her son personally. For her it indicated a want of love, trust, and sincerity, whereas Joseph demonstratively distinguished between his obedience as a son and his impersonal dissent—a distinction she, in turn, dismissed as mere sophistry. The more violently he disagreed with her, the more deferentially he couched his dissent. In this way, he tried to force her to separate the issue at hand from his person and take his ideas seriously as concerns that were politically motivated. By always viewing Joseph's actions through the prism of the mother-son relationship, Maria Theresa blinded herself to such objective concerns. These were not limited to reorganizing the top tiers of government. They related to a range of basic topics that polarized public opinion at the time: the question of religious toleration, for example, or freedom of the press, or a ban on torture. Their stance on such matters divided the enlightened avant-garde from the traditionalists—even if the proponents of Enlightenment did not agree on everything. Mother and son stood on opposite sides on these questions. For Maria Theresa, the discourse of Enlightenment was nothing but godless, self-infatuated, fashionable jargon. In the House of Habsburg, the front line of the debate ran simultaneously between the two regents and between two generations. But Joseph's concerns also related to questions of war and peace, not least his personal ambition to intervene in the territorial chess game played by European potentates. For in eastern Europe, a highly complex military conflict was unfolding against the background of the trials of strength between mother and son. The question confronting the House of Habsburg was what role it would have to play to uphold its great power status. On this point, as on so much else, Joseph and Maria Theresa were at loggerheads.

Cutting Up the "Polish Cake"

At the end of the Seven Years' War, the situation in eastern Europe was unclear and marked by general distrust.[188] In 1764 Frederick II had entered into an alliance with the new tsarina Catherine II, potentially his most dangerous enemy, to guard against possible Habsburg revisionist intentions. His fears were not unfounded, for Kaunitz was still busily hatching plans to compensate for the loss of Silesia—even, if necessary, in alliance with the Prussian king. But Frederick II himself was also on the lookout for opportunities to augment his territorial holdings. Finally, Russia had established itself as a new European great power and was pursuing the strategy of a stable northern alliance system that would give it a free hand along its southeastern frontier. The relative peace that descended following the long war was due to universal exhaustion, not to a stable equilibrium of forces, let alone political satiety on the part of the main actors. The goal of the game was still to acquire more territory without incurring aggression from everyone else. The potential spoils lay in the regions between the great powers' territories and at their periphery. Whoever showed signs of structural weakness— Poland or the Ottoman Empire, for instance—was a potential victim. The only question was how the interests of Europe's potentates, who rightly viewed each other with keen suspicion, might be coordinated in such a way that they all received an equal share in the booty rather than frustrating each other's designs. Contemporaries called this *Konvenienzpolitik*, "balance-of-power politics" or "politics of convenience." It required the flexibility to seize the right moment and exploit it to one's advantage. Such a moment presented itself in Poland following the death of King August III in 1763.

The elective monarchy of Poland-Lithuania was dominated by a sizeable lesser nobility that was fiercely proud of its ancestral political freedom. In the Polish diet, nothing could be decided without a unanimous vote. This freedom made the country particularly susceptible to internal divisions and foreign influence. In this case, it was Catherine II who, allied with Frederick II, blocked the Saxon candidate for the throne and saw to it that her protégé, Stanisław Poniatowski, was elected king of Poland in his stead. This development was unwelcome in Vienna but nothing was done about it. Yet the newly crowned Polish king proved increasingly reluctant to do the Tsarina's bidding. At the same time, a powerful faction of Polish nobles pursued political reforms aimed at regaining national autonomy and shaking off Russian "protection."

Unamused, the Tsarina launched a military intervention to put a stop to the reform process, prompting the Polish rebels to band together in the so-called Confederation of Bar. The rebels appealed for help from Russia's enemies, the French king and the Turkish sultan. Russian troops battling the confederates then crossed the border to the Ottoman Empire and committed depredations against the local populace, leading the sultan to declare war on Russia in October 1768. Two originally distinct conflict zones—Poland and the Balkans—were now suddenly and explosively connected.

How should the Habsburg empire respond? The old ally, Russia, had become a threat; conversely, the Turks had been transformed from enemies into reliable, peaceful neighbors since the last war had ended in 1739. Poland-Lithuania was an important buffer against the tsarist empire, and Maria Theresa had no intention of jeopardizing the stability it provided. Kaunitz, on the other hand, saw grand possibilities in the offing. In 1768 he sketched one of his notoriously ambitious plans for exchanging and partitioning territory: Frederick II would give back Habsburg Silesia and be compensated with Polish lands. Nothing came of the plan—it still seemed too chimerical at this stage. But the idea of coming to an arrangement with the old Prussian foe and carving up a weakened Poland was in the air. For now, Kaunitz urged a rapprochement with Prussia to counter Russian expansionism and capitalize on the war against the Ottoman Empire. He therefore set up a meeting between the two monarchs, eventually held in August 1769 in the Prussian border town of Neisse.[189] The following year, Frederick paid a return visit in Moravian Neustadt, also attended by Kaunitz. The first encounter, in particular, attracted enormous Europe-wide attention and would be commemorated in Borussian nationalist mythology.

The two monarchs celebrated each other as men of the Enlightenment who preferred rational conversation to the trappings of ceremony and as military commanders proudly showing off their well-drilled troops. Even if Frederick received Joseph—traveling incognito, as always—with an austere lack of formality, they took pains to treat each other with exquisite courtesy and respect. In the detailed account he wrote for his mother, Joseph made no secret of his admiration for

Frederick's "genius." Frederick, in turn, found Joseph ambitious, eager to learn, friendly, mild-mannered toward others, and hard on himself.[190] On both sides, the value of the summit was primarily symbolic: the Prussian upstart, newly admitted to the circle of great powers, could plume himself before the eyes of the world on the emperor's visit and impress him with lengthy discourses on ancient military authors; Joseph could converse with the philosopher-king as his intellectual equal on such topics as judicial reform and population policy, be regaled with anecdotes about such luminaries as Voltaire and Maupertuis, and be made to feel a citizen of the enlightened republic of letters.[191] Much taken with each other's company, they nonetheless parted ways without having reached agreement on any issues of substance. The Prusso-Russian alliance was not called into question.

Catherine II, meanwhile, successfully continued her war against the Ottoman Empire. As a countermeasure, Austrian troops established a military cordon on the eastern border of the Habsburg empire. Its official purpose was to keep both foreign troops and the plague at bay, but it also sent a warning to Russia. The Austrian military took the opportunity to occupy Szepes (Zips) county, a collection of towns pawned to Poland since the fifteenth century, and subsequently pushed the cordon further into southern Poland. Although not convinced of its legality, Maria Theresa gave her consent to the operation. In the summer of 1770 the Ottomans suffered a series of catastrophic setbacks on land and at sea. The Russians annexed the northern Black Sea coast and the semi-autonomous principalities of Moldavia and Wallachia; the Tsarina turned down a peace overture made through Vienna and Berlin. Austria was now forced to confront the question of how it would react to Russian territorial gains: should it join in the fight against Russia, or should it seek compensation to restore "equilibrium"? After all, according to the logic of *Konvenienzpolitik*, now that one power had enriched itself unpunished, the others were entitled to a piece of the pie themselves.

To halt Russian expansion, in late 1770 Kaunitz argued for entering the war on the Ottoman side and letting the Turks foot the bill. Earlier still, there had been discussion at the Viennese court on whether certain regions of the Ottoman Empire between Russia and Austria could be

FIGURE 42. The cutting of the "royal cake" from the
perspective of a French caricature: Catherine II (left)
and Frederick II (right) point imperiously to a map
of Poland; Stanisław Poniatowski clasps his crown to
his head to prevent it slipping off; Joseph II averts his
face in shame but still lays claim to his piece on the
map. Maria Theresa is nowhere to be seen. *Le gâteau
des rois* by Nicolas Noël Le Mire, copperplate based
on a design by Jean-Michel Moreau, 1772

partitioned. Such plans were far from unusual. In 1770 even the normally irenic Khevenhüller submitted a memorandum to the empress,
written on his own initiative, advising her that it was only right and fair
for Austria to take a province or two from the Ottoman Empire, preferably Bosnia, Serbia, and Wallachia, considering that it was on its last legs
anyway. The sultan would almost be grateful, he claimed. To keep the
king of Prussia out of the game, he could be placated with tracts of Poland.[192] Frederick II had already entertained this idea himself. Since

October 1770, his brother Henry had been engaged in confidential negotiations in Saint Petersburg about possibilities "for sharing the cake"
(*de partager le gâteau*), as it was called.[193] In February 1771 the king made
his brother's partition plan his own, disguised as a peace initiative.

Joseph thought direct intervention in the war against the Tsarina,
the option advocated by Kaunitz, too risky. Yet as 1770 made way for
1771, he shot off one memorandum after another setting out how the
present situation could be exploited to best advantage. To cover all contingencies, he demanded of his mother that an army of fifty to sixty
thousand men from the Dutch and Italian territories be amassed in
Hungary.[194] Maria Theresa alone explicitly opposed any involvement in
the war as well as any partition of territories, whether at the expense of
the Ottoman Empire or of Poland. In October 1768, when she had first
gotten wind of such plans, she had written to Antonia of Saxony: "No
partitions, my dear friend!"[195] She never wavered from this stance. She
was equally opposed to intervening on the Turkish side. In January 1771
she proclaimed, "I have never made a more difficult decision in my entire sorrowful career. It must be so. Hence: the emperor and I have
agreed not to wage war against the Russians." They were Christians, after
all, and the Turks had been the aggressors. But she also could not bring
herself to take up arms against the Turks. And she was adamantly opposed to making common cause with the Prussian king.

> People will find this decision weak and timorous; I admit it, but I
> cannot bring myself to decide on a war I believe to be unjust and
> against my conscience. At my age, one has riper judgment. After the
> dreadful wars which I have had to conduct, I know what is to be ex-
> pected, above all in this land [Russia], given the plague and hunger
> prevailing there. I would have to expose my army to all that, the elite
> of my generals, even my own son. . . . Nothing that may come can
> deter me from my purpose.[196]

This was the situation in the winter of 1770–71, when Joseph de-
spaired of his mother's supposed irresolution. In fact, she had already
made her decision, even if it was not to his and Kaunitz's liking. He
bitterly reproached her for blocking all his plans,[197] declaring to his

brother: "If we . . . show such weakness, I will find myself compelled to make a public demonstration and explain to the public that I, at least, have no part in it."[198] In July 1771 the Viennese emissary Thugut in Constantinople negotiated a vaguely defined defensive alliance with the sultan. Throughout the summer, the Austrian policy toward the war was ambiguous and difficult for outsiders to understand, not least owing to disagreement among the three main actors in Vienna.[199] Meanwhile, plans for dismembering Poland developed apace in Prussia and Russia, yet both powers were aware that this could not be done without involving Austria, whose troops were now threateningly stationed in Polish territory. In early 1771 Frederick II invited the Viennese court to join in the partition plan.[200] Joseph took advantage of the favorable situation and subsequently struck a deal to have a large piece of the cake incorporated into the Habsburg empire.

Throughout all this, the empress obstinately resisted any kind of partage at the cost of third parties. Her priority was to extricate herself "from the entanglement with fairness" and without gaining anything for herself. Any further advances her troops made into Poland would, she feared, end up antagonizing Prussia, Russia, *and* Turkey. She aimed instead to bring all three parties to agree to a peace treaty involving no major territorial concessions. What she was not prepared to accept, however, was Russia and Prussia securing themselves advantages in Poland: "In this case I could not be the only one to go away empty-handed." Yet enriching herself at Poland's or Turkey's expense was out of the question; indeed, she had only just concluded a treaty in good faith with the Turks. The only party who came into consideration for compensation claims was the king of Prussia, who might be induced to cede the county of Glatz, for example, or one of his western dominions. "Through this clear and sincere conduct, I believe . . . that we can extract ourselves from the situation to some advantage, perhaps, or at least with less disturbance to the equilibrium."[201] Her letters to Joseph were nothing if not forthright. In January 1772 she characterized the entire policy on the Russo-Turkish question as misguided: the deployment of Italian and Dutch troops in Hungary, the unfortunate convention with the Turks, the threatening tone toward the Russians, the mysterious stance toward friends and enemies alike, the whole tendency to profit from the war between Russians and Turks by expanding the Habsburg empire's own borders while preserving the semblance of respectability, *honnête*. "Policy *à la prussienne*," she called this. Even if Kaunitz succeeded in acquiring Wallachia or Belgrade through his diplomacy, the moral cost would be too great:

> Throughout my entire unhappy reign we have tried, at least, to maintain a sincere and fair position of honesty, moderation, and reliability in our engagements, earning the admiration of Europe and the respect of our enemies. Since last year, all this is at an end. . . . Nothing in the world pains me more than the loss of our good reputation. Sadly, however, I must admit that we deserve it, and this is what I want to change by repudiating the bad and ruinous principle of profiting from others' conflicts.[202]

In a long, searching memorandum from February 5, 1772, she again set out her views with all desirable forcefulness. Prussia, not Russia, was and remained their most dangerous enemy and its expansion the greatest evil. Instead of offering their services as an honest broker between Russia and Turkey, earning the gratitude of both powers, and preventing the dismemberment of Poland, they had recklessly played into the Prussian king's hands. By occupying Polish territory, they had given him the pretext he needed to do the same. With "false, miscalculated, inconsistent, and dangerous steps," they had maneuvered themselves into the awkward situation of "themselves contributing to the aggrandizement of two powers, our rivals and enemies, and receiving from them in return as a gift, so to speak, something that they had as little right to bestow as we had to acquire. . . . By what right can we steal from an innocent whom we have always prided ourselves on defending and supporting?" She dismissed the argument suggested by balance-of-power politics that they ought not to stand idly by while others enriched themselves. Among private people, such behavior would be considered a shameful crime—should rulers be exempted from the laws of natural justice?[203] Soon after, when Prussia and Russia had formally agreed to annex Polish territories, she wrote to Kaunitz: "All partition is fundamentally unjust and to our detriment. I cannot sufficiently regret this proposition and must confess that I am ashamed to show my face."[204] It can hardly be denied that her view of things was not only morally superior but also politically rational.

Meanwhile, the Austrian emissary in Berlin increased the Viennese compensation demands. In the end, the empress grudgingly accepted the policy pushed by her son and state chancellor. For all her scruples and objections, she did not prevent the formal partition treaty from taking place in Saint Petersburg on August 5, 1772. In the end, it was her signature that appeared on the document.[205] Shortly before, she had written to Kaunitz, "I find that nothing else can be done for now, but I cannot view with equanimity the enlargement of these two powers, still less the fact that we will be sharing in it."[206] It was left to her and her daughter Marie Antoinette, now wife to the French heir, to appease her grandfather-in-law Louis XV, a traditional friend of Poland.[207] France, like England, had come out of the affair with nothing.

The partition affected roughly a third of Polish territory. The slice apportioned to Austria was the largest, encompassing around 80,000 square kilometers with a population of 2.6 million Poles, Ruthenians, and Jews, and Joseph had tried to the last to carve out even more. The borderline remained disputed until 1776, when Ottoman Bukovina was signed over to Austria as well. The new province had no history as a self-contained entity, nor was it defined by any natural or cultural borders; it was purely and simply the product of political deal-making. It was named Galicia and Lodomeria in reference to supposedly ancient Hungarian claims to the principalities of Halych and Vladimir, claims that the court librarian Franz Adam Kollár had reconstructed from archival evidence to give the annexation a veneer of historical tradition and legality.[208] The new territory was of dubious value to the Archducal House: it was connected to the Habsburg core territories only by a narrow land bridge; the populace was poor, the economy underdeveloped; no loyalty could be expected from the native nobility. Even Kaunitz, who had achieved his objectives and "exulted not a little" in his success in Vienna, could not help admitting later that it had all been a mistake.[209] The deal was undoubtedly of greatest value to Frederick II, who by acquiring Polish West Prussia gained a link between his heartland and

East Prussia. The coup was celebrated in Borussian historiography as a "masterpiece of Frederician diplomacy," while the king himself praised it as "the first example which history furnishes of a partition so regulated, and peaceably terminated, between three great powers."[210] In fact, it was the first time a country had been partitioned by third parties without prior military conquest or dynastic extinction. The great powers learned from the experience that they could prey on lesser powers by working together. It would not be the last time Poland was partitioned, nor was Poland to remain the only object of such politics; the ecclesiastical imperial principalities and the Ottoman Empire would later fall victim to such calculations as well.[211]

At the Viennese court, the question of who was responsible for the ill-fated partition remained painful for all concerned. It went to the very heart of the regency dilemma. Maria Theresa had given her assent to Joseph's policy. While she did not approve of it, she had not formally transferred rule into his hands, as she had announced time and again she would. She was therefore obliged to take responsibility for the decision before God and the world. Fully aware of this, she was tormented by pangs of conscience. In July 1772, shortly before signing the partition treaty, she had written to her confidante d'Herzelles: "You could say: 'Why do you not provide a remedy? You are the sovereign, after all.' That is precisely the point that is killing me."[212] And later, to her son Ferdinand: "This dreadful partition of Poland is costing me ten years of my life. You will see how unhappily this whole affair will unfold. How many times have I refused to agree to it! . . . God grant that I not be held responsible for it in the next world. I confess that I cannot stop talking about this topic. I have taken it so to heart that it poisons and embitters all my days, which are sad enough as it is."[213]

Even Joseph, who had so enthusiastically supported Kaunitz's partition plan—for all that they disagreed on points of detail—showed scruples after the event. Khevenhüller reported that the emperor had wanted to make last-minute changes to the treaty but had been held back by Kaunitz. The Lord High Steward, for his part, made a point of never having been a party to the negotiations and was forthright in voicing his moral and political reservations about the deal.[214] Khevenhüller defended the emperor and placed the blame largely on Kaunitz, who was giving himself most of the credit anyway. Joseph had attempted to justify the treaty in conversation with him. "Yet although this lord has an innate *droiture* . . . he does not fail to see the invalidity of the purported right of convenience and right of the strongest."[215] Joseph felt he had good reason to disclaim responsibility, given his mother's continued refusal to cede power to him. The English emissary Lord Stormont reported that Joseph, for all his misgivings, had defended the necessity of the partition but had also downplayed his own part in the affair: "for he was not an Actor but a Counsellor."[216] This was the very distinction that Joseph had always advanced against his mother in the regency question: it was not for him to decide, only to give advice. Prince Ligne later recalled a salon conversation in which a lady of the court asked the emperor how he could condemn a thief when he had just robbed Poland. "He replied: my mother, who enjoys your perfect confidence and attends Mass as often as you do, played a pretty part in it. I am merely her first subject."[217]

The conflict over the first partition of Poland would not be the last of its kind between mother and son. The pattern would repeat itself again and again, whether the bone of contention was religious tolerance, the War of the Bavarian Succession, or serfdom.[218] Consensus proved elusive, but mother and son were equally unable to agree on a clear division of responsibilities. They would spend the entire coregency trapped in a communicative blind alley.

11

The Religion of Rule

FIGURE 43. Vienna, Freyung from the northwest with the Schottenkirche
and procession. Painting by Bernardo Bellotto, known as Canaletto, 1759/60

On Earth as It Is in Heaven

The *vedute* of Bernardo Bellotto, better known as Canaletto (1722–1780),
convey a good impression of everyday street life in Vienna in the age of
Maria Theresa. The native of Venice, previously court painter in Dresden and later in Warsaw, lived in Vienna between 1759 and 1761, where
he painted not only Schönbrunn Palace and Schloss Hof (presumably
commissioned by Maria Theresa) but also a series of cityscapes, all

observed with apparently documentary precision and teeming with detail: Mehlmarkt, Lobkowitzplatz, the Dominikanerkirche, Universitätsplatz. Two of these *vedute* show the public square known as the Freyung, one from the southeast (color plate 25), the other from the northwest (fig. 43).[1] In this second picture, the scenery is bordered by the Schottenhof on the left and the Palais Harrach to the right; in between, the view opens onto an ensemble of partly medieval, partly Baroque dwellings. The painting is dominated by the imposing western façade of the Schottenkirche. In the shadow of the adjacent building to the left, we glimpse a procession emerging into the square from the church. Liveried servants bearing wax candles march at its head; behind them, a throng of worshipers can be seen spilling out through the church portal. A gleaming red baldachin and two flags direct the viewer's attention to the priest with the *venerabile*, the "Supreme Sacrament of the Altar." Only on second glance do we notice that all the figures in the picture's fore- and middle ground are facing the sacral event. Scattered individuals and small groups of men, women, and children, marked by their clothing as belonging to different social strata, turn left, fall to their knees, or bow down before the blessed sacrament. A grand coach is prominently displayed in the sunlight in the middle of the square. It is empty apart from the coachman, who is standing in his seat: it seems that the cavalier kneeling to the left has just hastened from the coach to pay reverence to the *venerabile*, along with everyone else.

The painting shows what happened not only here, at Corpus Christi processions, but whenever the consecrated host, the physically present body of the Lord, appeared in public. The same scene would recur, for example, during the so-called *Versehgang*, when the priest would bear the sacrament through the streets on his way to call on a dying parishioner. Anyone who crossed the priest's path had to pay public homage to the body of Christ. Members of the royal family set an example for everyone else by climbing out of their carriage, kneeling down, and escorting the sacrament, sometimes all the way to the house of the dying. Protestants frequently gave cause for conflict by neglecting to drop to their knees, as required.[2] Jews were forbidden even to glimpse the *venerabile* lest they cause offense; they had to stay in their houses and were not even allowed to appear at their windows when it was carried past.[3] The specific veneration of the host was a cornerstone of Catholic piety that had emerged in polarizing opposition to Protestantism. This piety was essentially based on theatrical demonstration. The blessed sacrament was publicly presented and staged in several ways. It was borne through the fields in supplicatory processions to ensure fertility, or it was exposed on altars and prayed to for forty hours to ward off acute dangers. Just setting eyes on it was supposed to have a beneficial effect and could, under certain circumstances, bring about remission from sin. Corpus Christi was the epitome of this kind of pious eucharistic display. Street processions were always also spectacular triumphal marches of Catholicism.

Paradoxically, the sacred was always and everywhere visibly present amidst the profane environment; it structured time and space.[4] The profane quotidian realm took its rhythm from the festive calendar of the Catholic ecclesiastical year, while profane space was articulated by a plenitude of sacral sites. Vienna alone "has almost as many places of grace and miracle-working images as churches," we read in one of the historical-topographical handbooks that catalogued all these numinous sites.[5] The Catholic religiosity of the Habsburg lands could be experienced at every turn: it was there to be seen, heard, touched, and smelled. This did not preclude regional differences. Individual lands, cities, guilds, and corporations each boasted their own patron saints with accompanying rituals, centered on miracle-working pictures, relics, chapels, columns, and statues. The Catholic religion could draw on an inexhaustible supply of potent symbols and practices to establish a collective identity for both individual parishes and the monarchy as a whole. Nothing was better suited than shared religious rituals for bringing together the subjects of all the hereditary lands and estates.

Catholic religion was a religion of rule. This was especially true of Habsburg religiosity. On the one hand, heads of the house regarded themselves as having been specially chosen, equipped, and charged to rule by God on the basis of their religious zeal. On the other, like many princes in the confessional age, they used the Catholic religion to discipline subjects from the pulpit and secure their allegiance to the dynasty.

Only devoutly Catholic subjects, it was believed, could be obedient subjects. The hereditary lands had not always and everywhere been Catholic: Bohemia had not, nor had the Archduchy of Austria. Indeed, not even all members of the Archducal House had always stood above suspicion when it came to their Catholic orthodoxy. The rebellion of the Protestant estates in Bohemia and Austria had been bloodily put down by Ferdinand II, marking the beginning of the Thirty Years' War. Since then, Protestant heresy had been equated with punishable political disobedience and a re-Catholicization strategy had been pursued with renewed vigor—including after the Peace of Westphalia. Put negatively, this meant the conversion, suppression, or deportation of so-called Acatholics;[6] expressed in positive terms, it entailed the promotion of Catholic piety—given an unmistakably Habsburg twist in *pietas austriaca*—at every available opportunity.

Pietas austriaca involved the conviction that the Archducal House of Austria had long ago been entrusted by the Almighty with the mission of guiding the true and only-soul-redeeming Catholic religion to victory. Not least with the sword: in times of religious schism, the church had to be a militant one, an *ecclesia militans*. The relationship between God and the dynasty was based on reciprocity: the House of Austria worked to increase the glory and honor of God and his church in the world; in return, God bestowed his blessing on the dynasty and ensured that its fame grew steadily along with its temporal power. Maria Theresa's "Political Testament" shows just how seriously she took this sacred duty.[7] In more practical terms, *pietas austriaca* also meant that the Habsburgs promoted existing supraregional cults, and occasionally instituted new ones, to unite subjects in the various lands under their rule. The most prominent of these, apart from the ritual veneration of the eucharist, were the cult of the True Cross—a nail from which adorned the house's treasury of relics[8]—and the cult of the sainted Babenberg patriarch Leopold, whose bones in Klosterneuburg were paid annual pilgrimage by the court.[9] By far the most popular form of state-sponsored popular worship, however, was the adoration of the Virgin Mary. The Habsburgs' Maria was a warrior-protectress, the "commander-in-chief," the *generalissima* of the imperial armies. Her name had been emblazoned on battle flags when her troops fought against Turks and Protestants; it was to her they owed all their great victories from Lepanto to White Mountain. In perpetual remembrance and thanksgiving for such triumphs over unbelievers, columns to the Mother of God had been erected everywhere, including on the Platz am Hof in Vienna, where a triumphant Mary was shown crushing the serpent of heresy underfoot. It was through her, so the motto read, that the Habsburgs reigned, ruled, won victory, and kept the peace: *Per Mariam Austrici regnant, imperant, vincunt, pacem stabiliunt.*[10]

The significance of Baroque forms of Catholic piety was that they provided a stable scaffold of rituals that joined the ruling dynasty and their subjects in shared religious devotions, on the one hand, while preserving the distance between them, on the other. God's dominion in the hereafter reflected the rule of monarchs in the here and now.[11] It was not by chance that princes were called "terrestrial gods" by their panegyrists. Catholic liturgy and royal ceremonial were closely connected. The forms for honoring and worshiping God and the king were practically indistinguishable, and the same language was used to speak of both. Rulers in heaven and on earth were addressed with the same abject deference and by means of numerous intercessors. The liturgical procession was a copy of its royal equivalent; the same resplendent baldachin canopied the sacrament and the ruler; the golden liturgical instruments at the Lord's table resembled the golden tableware laid out at festive court meals; the chasuble had its counterpart in the coronation regalia—in short, heavenly and earthly rule mirrored and reinforced each other.

What Catholic religiosity and political-social order had in common may be summed up in three keywords: theatricality, graduality, and reciprocity. Theatricality means that both other-worldly and this-worldly rule were literally set before subjects' eyes in ritual displays of overwhelming material splendor. The term "graduality" indicates that the relationship between individual believers and their God, as well as that between individual subjects and their ruler, was characterized by a long hierarchical chain of intermediaries and intercessors. Individuals did not enjoy direct access to God—God was as awesomely remote from them as their sovereign. In between stood the lesser and greater, the more or less powerful guardian angels and saints, led by Mary, the Mother of God, who stood nearest the divine throne and was the mightiest advocate of them all. Finally, reciprocity means that people's dealings with the powers beyond, like their relations among themselves, were governed by the law of quid pro quo. Celestial and terrestrial grace were not to be had for nothing; material and immaterial sacrifices had to be made in expectation of return favors. For all that it was reciprocal, however, the relationship was anything but symmetrical. Faithful Christians or loyal subjects could never be completely certain that their petition would be granted, compelling them to abase themselves before their lord in a pose of grateful anticipation. Social logic thus followed the same rules and expectations in heaven as it did on earth.

Maria Theresa had been brought up in the tradition of *pietas austriaca*, identified with it, and practiced it at all times. A large part of her everyday life was taken up with public religious engagements. In the ritual rhythm dictated by the liturgical calendar, she and her court visited sacred sites in Vienna and its vicinity, just as her ancestors had done before her.[12] At the start of her reign, she took part in no fewer than four different Corpus Christi processions and seven to the golden column dedicated to the Virgin Mary in the Platz am Hof. In addition, there was the pilgrimage to St. Leopold in Klosterneuburg and, in Holy Week, the pilgrimage on foot to the calvary hill of Hernals, as well as visits to up to twenty replicas of the "holy sepulcher." On feast days of the various order saints, she visited the Viennese churches of the Jesuits, Augustinians, Scots, Franciscans, Capuchins, Dominicans, Minims, Theatines, Black Spanish, White Spanish, Salesians, and Carmelites—a far from exhaustive list. Maria Theresa made a point of devoting equal attention to all religious orders "to please all the clergy."[13] The degree of care put into staging such events reveals that not just God's honor was at stake here, but that of the faithful as well. The Jesuits, for example, refused to march as a group in the Corpus Christi procession lest they be placed behind the other orders.[14] Heaven's luster and glory were reflected in God's flock on earth. In a book of instructions for court, it was explicitly stated that courtiers should attend public church visits and processions so that the throng would be "all the more multitudinous and impressive."[15] The court's sacral activities were announced in the annual court calendars, placed on record, lavishly commemorated in copperplate engravings, and made known to the general public in the *Wienerische Diarium*—no differently than would have been the case for secular solemnities.[16]

The otherwise separate worlds of the dynasty and common subjects came together whenever such occasions for public worship arose. *Pars pro toto*, rulers celebrated the festivals of the church year both in front of their subjects and on behalf of their subjects, since they felt a responsibility before God for the Catholic orthodoxy and welfare of the entire body politic, in this world and in the world to come. The cult of saints and the tradition of pilgrimage gave religious backing to the monarchy as a whole. Perhaps the best illustration of this is the Chapel of Grace at Mariazell in Styria. The site where the first Marian miracle was reported in 1157 had by the seventeenth century become the center of a cult encompassing all the hereditary lands.[17] Pope Paul V had brought the site to particular prominence by granting the chapel a plenary indulgence; since then, whoever went on pilgrimage to Mariazell and did penance on the Marian feast days of August 15 or September 8 could have their sins completely remitted. In 1724 Pope Benedict VIII extended the indulgence to all eternity. Donors from Upper and Lower Austria, Bohemia, Moravia, and Hungary dedicated their own altars in Mariazell to the Mother of God; pilgrims from all these countries came to pray to her in their distress, to testify to her miraculous support, and to present offerings of thanksgiving.

Rational Religion

While traditional Catholic piety, as shown in exemplary fashion in Mariazell, was not confined to the "common rabble," over the course of the eighteenth century it came under increasing criticism from the educated classes, including in the hereditary lands. This criticism came from various quarters and had mutually reinforcing theological, aesthetic, moral, economic, and political grounds.

A new "rational" Catholic theology demanded, firstly, a return to the fundamentals of faith: Christ and the gospels, penance, and grace. It called for greater immediacy of the individual believer to God, at the expense of the countless intermediaries who had pushed their way between them, and also at the expense of all paraliturgical rituals, belief in miracles, and image worship. Faith was to be purged of its magical quid pro quo logic, the idea that laypeople could purchase redemption on earth or in heaven by making all kinds of dubious deals with the powers above. In short, it called for spiritualization, internalization, and a moral deepening of Catholic religiosity, a clear division between this world and the world to come. This was the message conveyed by the Italian polymath Lodovico Antonio Muratori (1672–1750), whose work *Della regolata divozione dei cristiani* (*The Science of Rational Devotion*) first appeared in German translation in 1759 at the instigation of Archbishop Migazzi of Vienna. Published by Trattner's in Vienna, it was enormously influential in the hereditary lands.[18] Muratori's project was by no means directed against the papal curia, and it would later meet with approval from the "enlightened" French pope, Clement XIV (r. 1769–74). The religious reform movement of Jansenism, by contrast, steered toward open confrontation with the papacy. From the beginning of the century, it had spread out from France, the Netherlands, and Italy into the Habsburg heartlands, gaining ever more adherents among the educated class.[19] Drawing on Augustine's doctrine of grace, Jansenists maintained that human beings were tainted by original sin. They could do nothing to rid themselves of it and could only hope for the completely unmerited gift of divine grace. At the same time, the Jansenists espoused a rigid, ascetic morality and a piety centered on confession and penance. This was directed primarily against the Jesuits, who stood *pars pro toto* for the worldly power of the clergy and the papal curia's influence on Catholic states. In all these ways, Jansenist doctrine came fairly close to Protestant theology. In 1713 the writings of the prominent Jansenist Quesnel were therefore condemned as heresy in the papal bull *Unigenitus*. In France, this led to a schism in society: the French royal family despised Jansenism as a stronghold of bourgeois and aristocratic opposition to the crown. The fact that many Jansenist writings stood on the papal index did not prevent them from being read and sold in the hereditary lands, however.[20]

The theological critique of traditional piety went hand in hand with a transformed aesthetic. The noise, pomp, and excessive physicality of traditional religious practice, the bloody street theater of self-flagellators and cross-bearers, the naïvely worshiped images of the Virgin and trophies of war displayed in churches,[21] the miracle stories and votive offerings, the bombast of Baroque rhetoric—all these now offended the refined tastes of the educated elite as barbaric relics of a distant past.[22] It was a question, not least, of social distinction: those who thought highly of themselves distanced themselves from the antiquated, overwrought piety now increasingly associated with the "common rabble." Religious sensibility was communicated in all areas of life, even down to a person's taste in clothing; a certain type of plain white robe was called a "janseniste." A new aesthetic of simplicity, modesty, and moderation was advancing to cultural hegemony—in speech, in thought, in dress, in devotional practice, in every aspect of physical and spiritual comportment.

Such criticism of popular religion on aesthetic grounds was bound up with a claim to moral superiority over the common people, perceived as lazy, sinful, ignorant, and superstitious. The authorities had often found themselves powerless to control the religiosity of layfolk and their fraternities. Traditional devotional practices, especially collective pilgrimages lasting days on end, were thought to encourage idleness, dissipation, wastefulness, and disrespect toward those in authority; they could easily degenerate into outright rebellion. This concern is forthrightly voiced in a pastoral letter from the archbishop of Vienna, Johann Josef von Trautson, one of the *neoterici*, or religious innovators.[23] In an episcopal circular written in 1752, Trautson denounced priests who, instead of proclaiming the plain gospel truth, offered "nothing but vain and empty-headed sophistries" or, even worse, "incite the fickle lowliest rabble to laugh . . . at the highest authorities" and "subject the most sacred truths to ridicule." Some priests stirred up the people against their betters and became the standard bearers of rebellion, whereas their rightful task was to encourage them "to endure the most onerous discomforts in humility and obedience, and to accept that all the tribulations of our time are imposed on us in punishment of sin and can only be averted through repentance."[24]

Another focus of enlightened Christianity was economics. Measured against the yardstick of economic utility, traditional religion could only be condemned as an extravagant waste of resources. Yet Catholic religion—rightly understood—could not possibly be incompatible with economical rationality. It now appeared as a "foolish delusion" that God "could take pleasure in intermission from labor," to quote the influential teacher of natural law, Paul Joseph Riegger, in a memorandum written for the empress.[25] The cameralists had made the unsettling observation that the Catholic economies were lagging far behind their Protestant rivals: Protestants worked harder and squandered less of what they earned on frolics and festivities. Above all, less capital lay dormant. Yet the economic critique was concerned with more than just reducing the number of work-free holidays; it also targeted the mass of assets in clerical hands, the enormous wealth and tax privileges enjoyed by monasteries and convents, and the masses of monks and nuns who sponged off the "producing class" without even increasing the population through procreation. Over the centuries the church had acquired up to 40 percent of land in the hereditary lands, been granted rights of usufruct, and been ceded regalian rights—royal income from the salt mines in Bohemia, for example.[26] Maria Theresa herself remarked with disapproval in her "Political Testament" that her ancestors, fired by zeal for the true religion, had been all too generous in their endowments to the church. Measured against the new criteria of efficient national economy, and given the catastrophic financial situation following the War of Succession (and even more so after the Seven Years' War), this situation now seemed untenable. If the already hard-pressed commoners were to be made to shoulder an even heavier tax burden, then the wealthy religious orders and monasteries could no longer be allowed to get away with modest voluntary contributions.

Economic rationality and fiscal responsibility were not the only areas of concern—the salvation of people's souls was also at stake. Fact-finding missions reported that parishes were too large and there were not enough priests to go around, pastoral care was woefully inadequate, and few if any measures were in place to ensure that parishioners never strayed from the narrow path of orthodoxy. Subjects could not be adequately supplied with sacraments and children were denied instruction in the catechism, opening the floodgates to "heretical false beliefs." What most disturbed Maria Theresa was the discovery that in some hereditary lands the number of "Acatholics" was far greater than had previously been believed.[27] The mass deportation to Transylvania of the most recalcitrant heretics under Charles VI had not sufficed; structural changes were needed to root out the problem. But priests, schools, and seminaries all cost money. Given the state of the royal treasury, funds to reform the church could only come from the church itself. This would steer the crown toward conflict with the clergy in the hereditary lands and with the pope himself.

The religious debates in the second half of the century involved a complex mix of theological, aesthetic, moral, economical, fiscal, ecclesio-political, and constitutional considerations. Taken together, all these arguments gave rise to the overwhelming conviction that something had to change. The only point of dispute was what exactly that was, how it was to be effected, and by whom. Who had the authority to carry out the necessary reforms: the queen, the bishops (some of whom were independent princes residing outside the hereditary lands), or the pope? At issue, in other words, was the fundamental question of the relationship between secular and spiritual power. Natural law doctrine had a clear answer to that question: the church was responsible solely for spiritual welfare; in all other matters it was subordinate to the sovereign state; the religious were subjects like everyone else. Taken with due seriousness, this amounted to a revolutionary innovation.

How Maria Theresa navigated this complicated situation has long been the subject of controversy among historians.[28] Even contemporaries struggled to reconcile her religiosity with her position on ecclesiastical affairs. All observers, Catholics and Protestants alike, were struck by her immoderate piety, yet it was unclear how this related to her policy toward the clergy. In 1756, for example, the Swedish emissary Nils von Bark reported back to his court that a fiery zeal for her religion defined the empress's conduct, sometimes even at the cost of what was politically prudent. On the one hand, she was a stickler for traditional religious observances and rigorously persecuted Protestants— something that, in the eyes of enlightened contemporaries, ran counter to all principles of rational politics. On the other, no one could claim that she was bigoted or blindly did the church's bidding. Indeed, she had targeted the monasteries' wealth with such steely determination that the grumbling of priests had already abated somewhat. Was her ostentatious personal piety perhaps just a strategy to provide cover for her ecclesiastical policy?[29] "She sang vespers with the Capuchin monks in church, while in her cabinet she wounded the Roman court so deeply that sooner or later it would have bled to death," was the posthumous verdict of one enlightened critic.[30] And her archenemy Frederick II remarked sardonically: "The empress is not so pious as to confuse politics with religion and deceive herself about her true interests."[31] In other words, did private piety and public *raison d'état* oppose each other and was the empress a hypocrite, as Protestant critics and ultramontane church historians claimed with rare unanimity?[32]

Maria Theresa's religious and ecclesio-political position defies simple categorization and was not free of internal contradiction. This distinguished it from the stance of her son and coregent, who took such a clear, radical, and consequential position toward the church that in the nineteenth century, he gave his name to an entire political movement, "Josephinism." The term denotes secularization of church property, the transformation of priests into state officials, radical hostility toward icons and rituals, massive suppression of all Baroque ornament and opulence, rigorous sobriety and thrift, social leveling, and the elevation of economic cost-benefit analysis above all other considerations. Religion still had a place under the new regime, but it was seen as an indispensable means to the end of an obedient, law-abiding populace.[33] The goal of Josephinian religious policy was ultimately political, not religious: the "happiness of the state," not the salvation of its subjects. Maria Theresa did not think in such terms and her stance was far more ambiguous. On the one hand, she initiated many of the policies that her son went on to pursue with unswerving conviction following her death.

On the other, an unbridgeable gulf separated her from her son on the fundamental question of religious toleration. In church historiography, however, Maria Theresa continues to be overshadowed by her son. She has been called "the mother of Josephinism" and her personal religiosity has even been dubbed "Josephinian."[34] Others, sensing the inadequacy of this label, identified a specific form of "Theresianism."[35] Yet neither term is satisfactory, since such "-isms" suggest a coherence and homogeneity that are downright misleading in Maria Theresa's case. "Josephinism" is a political battle cry from the postrevolutionary nineteenth century; it dates from an era of ideological partisanship unknown to prerevolutionary times.[36] For some, Josephinism entailed the "brutal violation" of the church; for others, it signified the triumph of the sovereign nation-state.[37] No such simple antithesis existed during Maria Theresa's reign. The old ways had been stirred up and had yet to settle into a new status quo. Maria Theresa's position can be explained from this situation of increased turbidity. She belonged to no camp and pursued no consistent agenda in her actions. Generalizing labels thus do not take us very far. We can only register the simultaneity of the nonsimultaneous: ritualized public piety *and* devout spirituality, sovereignty in relation to the Holy See *and* the imposition of confessional conformity on subjects, campaigns against superstition *and* against freethinking. Those who were personally close to her also formed anything but a homogeneous bloc: she had Jesuits *and* Jansenists as confessors, Khevenhüller *and* Kaunitz, Tarouca *and* van Swieten as trusted advisers. From today's point of view, all this is hard to reduce to a common denominator. The question is: for all her inconsistency, was there a certain logic behind Maria Theresa's religious policy?

Public and Private Religion

At the start of her reign, there were already subtle hints of a change in style, barely perceptible gestures distancing her from the religiosity of her forebears. Immediately after taking power, she had reduced the number of public church visits at court.[38] From 1742 she no longer had relics put on display in her birthing room. She showed no interest in

sacralizing her person, as had her predecessors on the throne—
especially Leopold I but also her own father. In Göttweig Abbey in
Lower Austria, for example, Charles VI had allowed himself to be depicted aureoled in a heavenly chariot in a kind of classical apotheosis,[39]
and it was common practice for artists to lend saints the facial features
of members of the ruling family. This intermingling of the sacred and
the profane was not to Maria Theresa's liking. A "ghastly altarpiece" by
Paul Troger in the Hofkirche in Innsbruck, showing herself as St. Helena and Francis as the emperor Constantine, was removed at her
behest.[40] She clearly had no wish to be associated—as seemed only
natural—with the iconography of Mary and the Christ child, either.[41]
Tellingly, none of her numerous state portraits shows her dandling the
heir on her arm. When appearing in church, she took care not to present
herself as an object of quasi-religious veneration. In contrast to her forebears, she refused a baldachin over her prayer stool, which would have
invited comparison with the baldachin over the Holy of Holies.[42] In 1758
she also got rid of the traditional panegyric to the ruler in public church
services.[43] Maria Theresa abhorred flattery on principle, even more so
in the context of divine worship. As she grew older, she increasingly
went to church incognito, either hidden to others in the oratory or "with
a patch or visor in front of her face," a half-veil that produced a "symbolic
division between ruler and churchgoer."[44] All these measures indicate
that Maria Theresa placed ever more value on differentiating between
roles: she clearly wished to attend divine service as a simple Christian
worshipper rather than as the adored monarch.[45] Among the faithful,
however, she still took pride of place. She thus ensured that prayers for
the imperial couple were offered at Mass, even though the requirement
to call the rulers by name had long been dropped from the Canon of the
Mass. In 1761 she even had Pope Clement XIII grant the entire hereditary lands a privilege to that effect.[46]

For Maria Theresa religion was a public affair, and the ruler had a
public role to play in upholding it. She considered defending the Catholic faith her supreme duty as a ruler, feeling herself personally accountable before God for the orthodoxy of her subjects. The first principle of
her religious policy was to "care for the temporal as well as spiritual

salvation of her subjects as a true mother to her country."[47] Before anything else, this meant setting a good example herself. When her daughter
Maria Carolina became queen of Naples in 1768, Maria Theresa urged
her to perform her religious duties punctiliously,

> in private as well as in public. Since the dear Lord has predestined you
> to rule, you must lead by example, especially in this perverse age, when
> our holy religion is practiced and loved so little. It seems that the great
> are ashamed to profess their faith, while the people are mostly mired
> in superstition, which ought not to be confronted directly with the
> truth. Their minds should rather be guided home step by step through
> the appointment of dedicated priests and good schoolmasters. . . . Un-
> ceasing attention to such matters is a central duty of any sovereign. The
> example set by the sovereign is all important.[48]

Maria Theresa thus saw herself fighting on two fronts at once: against
the enemies of religion in the upper classes and against superstition
among the common folk. She was implacably opposed to freethinking
tendencies—anyone who scoffed at religion was silenced with sharp
words and glares.[49] When it came to ordinary subjects, on the other
hand, a certain adjustment to their habits was needed to steer them
imperceptibly in the right direction. In this respect, her stance resembled that of the Jesuits, who followed the principle of strategic adapta-
tion or "accommodation" when bringing Christ's word to the heathen.
Maria Theresa also preached conformity in outward behavior to those
of her daughters who were married off to foreign courts.[50] "Conform
entirely to what is the custom at your court," she advised Marie Antoinette. "All eyes will be fixed on you, so avoid giving offense. . . . Stay on
your knees for as long as possible, that is the seemliest position for setting a good example." Yet she should also not push her conformity to
the point where it could appear hypocritical: "Do not allow yourself an
exaggerated bearing that might seem sanctimonious."[51] Such advice
suggests that Maria Theresa may likewise have persisted in some strict
forms of devotion solely from prudential considerations and therefore
did not protest when Joseph began to do away with them at court following Francis Stephen's death.[52]

Yet it is idle to speculate on whether Maria Theresa's demonstrative public piety represented a form of strategic accommodation or expressed her own innermost convictions. The alternative is not mutually exclusive; sincerely held beliefs could prove politically expedient as well. At any rate, she drew on the traditional cult of relics, images, and miracles in many ways. She donated a handmade robe to the Infant Jesus of Prague, a miracle-working wax-coated wooden statue,[53] and to commemorate the miracle of the cross that had taken place during the siege of Prague in 1742, she had a chapel built there twelve years later.[54] When visiting Prague Cathedral in 1754, she had several particles removed from the skeleton of St. Vitus; Khevenhüller and his wife were among those favored with fragments of bone.[55] In 1748 she ordered relics of the cross held in the imperial treasury to be embedded in the court chapel tabernacle, while as late as 1771, she had the arm of St. Stephen translated with great ceremony to Buda.[56] In 1769 she undertook a final pilgrimage to Mariazell.[57] The ceremonial repertoire of life at court required that she gain periodic dispensation from punishment for sin by visiting the icon of Maria Candia in St. Michael's Church in Vienna, as she did in 1773 for the icon's jubilee.[58] On such occasions she was accompanied by her family and all the court.

Maria Theresa encouraged her children to pray to several of the more prominent saints, at least. Apart from the Virgin Mary, this minimal list consisted of St. Joseph and the child's respective patron saint, as well as the holy angels.[59] The children were also made to recite the entire litany of saints, since "through this litany we beseech the dear Lord's help by the merits of his saints."[60] Behind this stood the traditional idea that the saints in heaven had amassed a vast store of merits, a *thesaurus meritorum*, some of which they could release to mortal supplicants to secure them the blessing of divine grace. This material, earthly conception of merit and grace could no longer be reconciled with enlightened religiosity. Her son Ferdinand appears to have resisted Maria Theresa on this point. When he passed through Mariazell and Innsbruck on his way to Milan in 1771, she wrote to him asking that he pray for her at both chapels of grace. At the same time, she implored him to refrain from making fun of the explanations he would surely be given of the miracles worked there.[61] And in a letter she sent him in 1778, she explicitly defended the imperial family's participation in the public cult of saints. Even Joseph, she added, had just made a good impression by attending the Feast of St. John of Nepomuk in Prague. She concluded: "We must . . . set a good example, including in matters that are edifying though they may not be necessary." She went on to make a revealing comparison:

> How many kindnesses have we not shown undeserving subjects sim-
> ply to attain our political objectives? Why should the saints, of all
> people, be left out and put us to shame? A Potemkin, Orlov, Brühl,
> and others [foreign ministers on whom the emperor had bestowed
> favors for political reasons] were and are feted by the greatest rulers.
> Not to mention subalterns; even these we reward handsomely with
> gifts and honors for the sake of a treaty or concession. . . . You rightly
> point out that God almighty cannot be compared with us poor crea-
> tures. This is undoubtedly true. But God allows us to worship His
> own [saints] and approach Him through their merits and interces-
> sion, and He looks down on us with loving kindness when we confess
> our own wretchedness in a spirit of sincere self-abasement, and He
> will give us credit if we do so with humility and resignation.[62]

What Maria Theresa here for once directly thematized and defended with a somewhat convoluted argument was the pious quid pro quo logic connecting heaven and earth. For her, the saints were God's courtiers, as it were. As sovereign she showered them with strategic favors as she would the first ministers of the Russian or Saxon court. Just as she ex-pected return services from foreign courtiers, so too she expected them from the saints in the form of advocacy before the Almighty. God would smile on his supplicants and reward them if they paid obeisance to the heavenly court—provided such obeisance was genuine rather than feigned.

Despite appearances, this declaration of allegiance to the cult of saints did not contradict Maria Theresa's policy of culling religious holi-days and thinning the crowded firmament of Austrian saints. In 1768, for example, she indicated that she would no longer support candidates for canonization in the papal curia,[63] while in 1772 she named Joseph the sole patron saint for Inner Austria.[64] These cuts were not aimed at doing away with the cult of saints but at concentrating and homogenizing it throughout the hereditary lands. Subjects were enjoined "to observe . . . the remaining obligatory feast days and holidays (among which the day of St. Leopold, owed reverence as patron of Austria, St. John of Nepomuk and Wenceslaus in Bohemia, St. Joseph in Styria etc., are to be particularly understood and included) with all the more ardent zeal and increased devotion." Less would now be more.[65]

Maria Theresa's statements on her faith cannot be said to satisfy the criterion of strict theological consistency. She was no scholar and never aspired to be one. She drew on the tradition of Habsburg *pietàs* and adapted it to suit her purposes. She never called into question the principles of public religion. On the contrary, she saw nothing but sophistry in religious disputes, which she hated and feared for their propensity to ensnare the faithful. She admonished her children to avoid the company of the unorthodox as much as possible, to hold fast to the faith of their forefathers, and to obey their confessors "blindly." The spirit of systematic doubt that stalked the land precisely in questions of religion, the critique of all tradition and authority, the central Enlightenment precept of using "one's own reason without guidance from others" (Kant)—all this was an intolerable affront, insolence, and threat. This emerges most clearly from her admonitions to her son Maximilian, whom she had sent off on a grand tour of Europe. She emphatically warned him not to be taken in by the dazzling brilliance of those who cast scorn on religion, but to profess openly his allegiance to Christianity. This was now more important than ever, given that "people want to conceal religion in their hearts, for fear of exposing themselves to ridicule or being considered sanctimonious and unenlightened. This tone now prevails everywhere."[66] In part, at least, Maria Theresa seems to have adhered almost defiantly to the traditions of public piety because they had fallen out of fashion. In her two-front war against freethinking and superstition, the former danger no doubt struck her as far more threatening than the latter.

Maria Theresa attended to her private devotions with the same conscientiousness she devoted to the duties of demonstrative public *pietàs*.

Over time, however, her devotions in the seclusion of the retirade or the court chapel oratory took up ever more of her time, even as she reduced her involvement in public solemnities, due not least to her steadily deteriorating health and physical immobility. Her most detailed and insistent instructions to her children concerned their private religious practice as well. She prescribed them silent prayer and frank examination of their conscience several times a day, a daily Mass or two, as well as regular devotions, monthly confession, and penance.[67] The imperial family's confessors, a Jesuit monopoly for centuries, played a key role as spiritual leaders. Devotional reading was no less important. Yet the diet of edifying literature consumed by Maria Theresa, which she also prescribed her daughters, reveals that she herself did not follow her Jesuit confessors with the same blind obedience she demanded of her children. Her favorite books were all classics of Jansenist piety, writings associated with the famed Cistercian nunnery of Port-Royal, destroyed in 1710 on Louis XIV's orders as a hotbed of Jansenist heresy: *L'essai de morale* by Pierre Nicole, a nephew of the abbess of Port-Royal and, together with Blaise Pascal and Antoine Arnauld, one of the most influential Jansenists; *L'Année Chrétienne* by Nicolas Letourneux, one of the Cistercian nuns' confessors; the *Catéchisme de Montpellier*—this and the prior work had been placed on the Index of Forbidden Books by papal censors—and finally *L'Abrégé de l'Écriture Sainte* by François-Philippe Mésenguy and the *Heures* of the Cardinal de Noialles—all in all, a small Jansenist reference library that Maria Theresa apparently kept hidden from her Jesuit confessors behind a curtain.[68]

Jansenist theology had a long-lasting influence in the church of the hereditary lands and at court in Vienna. Maria Theresa's grandmother and aunt, the empresses Eleonore and Amalia, and her mother, the Guelphic convert Elisabeth Christine, had also owned Jansenist writings. Not least, Francis Stephen had brought with him from Lorraine a Jansenist-tinged, stoical, and intellectual piety disdainful of outward forms. He passed it on to his children, and Maria Theresa transfigured his religious stance following his death into a shining example.[69] The Jansenist movement gained momentum throughout the 1760s.[70] The hereditary lands "were inundated by a wave of German-language

Jansenist literature,"[71] and the emperor herself promoted translations of these works. The Viennese archbishop, Christoph Anton Migazzi, belonged to the network (albeit only until his elevation to the rank of cardinal led to a change of heart), as did several influential members of the Viennese diocesan chapter, bishops, theology professors, and high-ranking court officials: people such as the auxiliary bishop Ambros Simon Stock; the learned Benedictine abbot Franz Stephan Rautenstrauch; the bishop of Laibach (Ljubljana), Karl Johann von Herberstein; the head of the Italian department in the State Chancellery, Joseph von Sperges; the privy cabinet secretary, Corneille de Neny; or the court physician Anton de Haen. Jesuit influence was eclipsed as Jansenists and other religious innovators were appointed to key positions in bishoprics, cathedral chapters, university professorships, and reform commissions. As the common enemy against whom Jansenists, Catholic enlighteners, and freethinkers could unite despite all their other differences in opinion, Jesuits were the losers in this overall development.

Maria Theresa herself was far from ill disposed toward the Society of Jesus, yet she too increasingly replaced the Jesuits in her inner circle with Jansenists. A conflict over the archduchesses' curriculum proved the catalyst for a break with the centuries-old Habsburg tradition of having only Jesuits as confessors. The padres had taken issue with the emperor's choice of Muratori's *Rational Devotion* as reading material for her daughters. In 1760 she therefore replaced their two confessors with a confessed Jansenist, a simple priest who worked as a correspondent on the famed Jansenist periodical *Nouvelles ecclesiastiques*. In the period that followed, most other court confessors were gradually relieved by Jansenists—above all, the "spiritual leader" of the empress herself, the Jesuit father Ignaz Kampmüller. He forfeited her trust when he allegedly relayed confidential information about the impending expulsion of the Jesuits from Spain to the curia. While she never dismissed him from office, in 1767 she replaced him de facto with the provost of the Augustinian Convent of St. Dorothea, Ignaz Müller (1713–1782), a key figure in Viennese Jansenism. Khevenhüller, whose hidebound traditionalism made him a natural ally of the Jesuits, observed this development with stern disapproval, writing of Ignaz Müller in 1773: "In recent years, and especially since her [the empress's] latest episode of smallpox, he has so mastered her admittedly tender conscience that, although she still confesses to P. Kampmüller (her confessor since childhood), she otherwise undertakes nothing in any matter of importance without first consulting the provost [Müller], and she meets with him privately on the eighteenth of every month, as her *jour de retraite*, to discuss matters of conscience." Following the dissolution of the Society of Jesus and Kampmüller's resignation, Maria Theresa immediately had the provost appointed "her spiritual adviser with an annual salary of 1,000 guilders." The only explanation Khevenhüller could offer for Müller's theological stance was personal animosity and partisanship: "This spiritual man was always a declared enemy of the Jesuits because, as it is said, they refused him admittance to their order; and since he attacks . . . their doctrine at every opportunity, he was even suspected of being a secret Jansenist."[72] Others, however, described Provost Müller as a harmless, morally upright, pious, yet also somewhat dimwitted man, who steered clear of politics and was unfairly blamed for all the empress's unpopular decisions.[73]

In fact, Maria Theresa treated her spiritual counsellors with great self-assurance and was by no means as susceptible to their influence as the lord high steward supposed. In 1768 she advised her daughter Carolina that she should find a new confessor if she had lost trust in her current one. She clearly saw the paradoxical situation in which the ruling family's spiritual directors found themselves: "As sovereign, you are in a more delicate situation than anyone else," she wrote to Carolina. On the one hand, confessors were supposed to have absolute authority over the conscience of their royal penitents; on the other, as domestic servants belonging to the court personnel, they could be dismissed at a moment's notice. This did not make it easy for them to be as strict and severe in the confessional as their vocation demanded. "Encourage him [the confessor] to tell you the truth in a clear and seemly manner," she advised her daughter, "so that he does not spare you and treats you like everyone else. . . . At the same time, you should take his instructions and advice with respect, meekness, and docility, so that he will not think that the truth displeases or upsets you."[74] The tone she herself adopted when speaking with her confessors was respectful, albeit not without a hint of playful irony. For example, she once asked Kampmüller in writing for permission to bring forward her devotions by a day owing to a court festival, adding: "if you do not perhaps forbid me [to attend] it on account of my so tepid and dissolute life. As usual at six o'clock."[75] Yet she also insisted that court confessors not exert the slightest influence on matters unrelated to their pastoral duties. As she wrote to Carolina: "You will not draw your confessor into any of your affairs, whether they be general or private in nature. . . . One should heed their advice and speak with them sincerely, yet without involving them in one's private life or mixing with them on a familiar footing. . . ."[76] In other words, Maria Theresa was clearly capable of making the necessary distinction between her roles as a believer and a ruler. So far as her own salvation was concerned, she wanted to be treated like any other sinner and was prepared to do as her confessor told her. In all other matters she remained his sovereign overlord, and he was a subject just like everyone else. This was a crucial distinction.

Maria Theresa's religiosity strikes us today as contradictory. Yet there are no indications that she herself sensed any contradiction between her public and private religious practice, even though the former cleaved to Jesuit tradition and the latter bore distinctly Jansenist traits. In a certain sense, she had learned from both: the Jesuits had taught her that she could only achieve her objectives by adapting to her surroundings, while the Jansenists had taught her that the believer stands directly before God and can draw solace from His grace.[77] From the 1760s onward she increasingly favored Jansenist counsellors, and after Francis Stephen's death the more dourly ascetic, inward-looking characteristics of her personal religiosity came to the fore. Yet she was too much the sovereign to allow herself to be drawn into the factional strife between Jansenists and Jesuits, or to side openly with one side over the other. Regarding herself as the royal protector or patroness of any one party was incompatible with her conception of rule. On the contrary, she saw herself as elevated above all the particularisms, factions, and interests in which her courtiers and subjects were embroiled. This applied not just to her personal piety but to her church policy as well.

Church Policy

Throughout the eighteenth century, relations between the Catholic monarchies and the papacy were tense. As mentioned earlier, there were structural reasons for this. The general tendency for power to be centralized in a unitary state conflicted with the prerogatives and privileges traditionally claimed by the church. The priesthood enjoyed numerous exemptions and was in many respects free from state interference; ecclesiastical jurisdiction, including over the laity, competed with secular courts; care for the poor as well as hospitals, schools, universities, and book censorship had traditionally been in the hands of the clergy; the tithe for the church never flowed into state coffers. The underlying problem was very old. The Reformation had resolved it in favor of the evangelical princes in the sixteenth century. In Catholic lands, by contrast, the rivalry between secular authority and the Roman church continued, providing ever new material for conflict. The more energetically monarchs sought to gain economic, juridical, and political control over all their subjects in equal measure—not least because ruinous wars had made this ever more necessary—the more intolerable the church's special rights and exclusive possessions came to seem.

The assertion of state control over the church played out on two fronts, one external, the other internal. The external front involved diplomatic relations with the Holy See. Just how much the relationship between the Habsburgs and the curia had cooled was revealed in the sensitive medium of ceremonial. The difficulties associated with papal representatives in Vienna were notorious. At Maria Theresa's baptism, at her marriage, at her children's baptisms and weddings, at Joseph's coronation in Frankfurt—time and again, the nuncio's presence brought up problems of rank.[78] The papal legate was adamant that he would not tolerate being seated at the same table as the Duke of Lorraine, standing behind the archbishop of Vienna, or crossing paths with the Venetian ambassador. His fear of losing his ceremonial precedence reflected the Holy See's precarious status in a shifting system of international law. The pope found it hard to reconcile his claim to supremacy over all worldly potentates with the reality that he had long been merely one ruler among many, and not an especially powerful one at that. The principle of equality among sovereign nations and independence in both external and internal affairs came at the papacy's expense. In the nuncio's rearguard actions to defend papal primacy at table, at the altar, and at the font, it became clear that the Habsburgs had their own ideas about the duties of a Catholic ruler and were unwilling to take orders from the pope. This was particularly true of Maria Theresa. From the beginning of her reign, her relationship with the curia had been extremely distanced, especially since Pope Benedict XIV (r. 1740–58) had taken a pro-Bavarian stance in the War of Succession. So long as the two great Catholic dynasties, the Habsburgs and the Bourbons, were still enemies, the pope could exploit their rivalry to his ends and play them off against each other. This was no longer possible after the "Diplomatic Revolution" of 1756. The Habsburg-Bourbon alliance, gradually consolidated through marriage connections between the courts in Vienna, Versailles, Madrid, Naples, and Parma, allowed the Catholic monarchies to present a broad united front to the curia. Provided this front held firm, the pope could do little to block their efforts at establishing and consolidating national churches.

Initial measures to reform the church had already been undertaken under Haugwitz's aegis following the War of the Austrian Succession.[79] At the time, Maria Theresa had done all she could to secure the pope's assent while simultaneously making clear that she would not put up with direct papal interference in her lands.[80] Benedict XIV, for his part, was fundamentally moderate and accommodating. In 1753 she negotiated with him a massive reduction in holidays by around two-thirds, a key economic initiative aimed at creating a more industrious workforce. Twenty-four saints' days were declared "half holidays," with subjects expected to attend Mass while spending the rest of the day at work, although this did not quite function as planned.[81] Likewise with papal consent, the clergy in the hereditary lands were subjected to an extraordinary levy for a period of fifteen years, nominally to fund the defense against the unfaithful (Turks and Protestant Prussians).[82] At the same time, between 1752 and 1755 a first great wave of anti-Protestant persecution and deportations swept over the hereditary lands.[83] The existence of so many previously overlooked "mangy sheep" in the Catholic flock was attributed to significant deficiencies in pastoral care, leading to plans for fundamental parish reform financed by a tax on wealthy abbeys and monasteries.[84] In addition, the minimum age requirement for taking monastic vows was to be raised and the financial threshold for establishing a religious order lowered. All these plans had to be shelved at first, however, since Kaunitz, who was placed in charge of church policy in 1753, did not want to risk confrontation with the pope.[85]

This did not initially change when the state's church policy came back on the agenda following the Seven Years' War. The total financial exhaustion of the Habsburg lands gave discussions a sense of urgency: the rich resources of the church, which had for so long lain fallow, were finally to be exploited for the state, the clergy transformed into useful cogs in the machinery of state, the people educated to enlightened piety, morally upright conduct, and economic rationality. As newly crowned coregent, Joseph supported the push for reform with conviction and energy, albeit without the State Chancellor's diplomatic pragmatism.[86] Conflict with the curia seemed inevitable. As early as 1762, Maria Theresa had taken the precaution of having the house archives scoured for documents attesting to the Habsburgs' age-old right to tax the clergy in their lands without papal permission.[87] The Habsburg duchy of Milan, where Kaunitz and the Austrian governor Karl Joseph Firmian became embroiled in the 1760s in a protracted dispute with the curia over various contentious issues of church policy, turned into a test case for future conflicts.[88] Since agreement in all these matters could not be reached while Clement XIII (r. 1758–69) was still on the apostolic throne, a crucial change in Viennese policy was decided on in 1768: if reforms were impossible with the pope's consent, then they would have to be made without it. With that, the relationship between the Catholic state and the church took on an entirely new complexion.[89]

The crisis broke out over the problem of how the clergy was to pay its dues to the state. Put simply, it boiled down to this: should the taxes imposed on the faithful continue to go to the church, which would then voluntarily reassign some of its revenue to the state under exceptional circumstances, or should these taxes flow directly and permanently into state coffers? And who would decide on the rate at which they were set, what they would be spent on, and who exactly would pay how much? More fundamentally still: would the state be allowed to exercise authority over the outward form, the property, and the rights of ecclesiastical corporations? In short, the idea was to subordinate the church to the state. The necessary arguments lay to hand and dominated the public discourse in Catholic Europe. In 1763 the auxiliary bishop of Trier, Nikolaus von Hontheim, writing under the pseudonym Febronius, had caused a sensation with a treatise declaring the imperial church's independence from Rome.[90] Not long after, the Viennese professor of natural law Paul Joseph Riegger made a similar claim in the first volume of his standard work on church law.[91] At court in Vienna, such arguments had the backing of Franz Joseph Heinke, a Jansenist-minded scholar and court councillor who had trained at Halle, the Prussian stronghold of natural law doctrine, and been appointed to the Court Chancellery in 1767 on van Swieten's recommendation.[92] In January 1768, Kaunitz advised the empress to call for a new policy on the church, cannily appealing to her "vigilance and care" for religion, "which is intricately tied to the welfare of the state. Virtuous, Christian subjects perfectly carry out their duties towards their princes and consensus in religion unites the forces of the state, just as religious difference tends to be the mother of discord, enmity, persecution, rebellion, etc."[93]

The appeal fell on fertile soil, coinciding as it did with Maria Theresa's own ideas about rule. Supported by Kaunitz and frustrated in particular by the lagging negotiations with the curia on the question of taxation, in 1768 she adopted a new position toward the pope: "In the event that the papal court should refuse its consent, no further dealings will be entered into with it; rather, I am determined to make use of my due rights and proceed in this matter *propria autoritate*."[94] *Propria autoritate*—by her own sovereign authority—was the watchword of this shift, which made all previous negotiations with the pope appear as a voluntary concession on her part. General developments in Europe were a key contributing factor. One by one, the kings of Portugal, France, and Spain had expelled the Jesuits from their realms and had long been steering on an anticlerical course. Public opinion had been stirred up by theories of Jesuit conspiracy. The breaking point came on January 30, 1768, when the pope excommunicated Duke Philip of Parma for his policy in support of a state church.[95] This was an unprecedented affront that no Catholic monarch could afford to ignore; it was viewed as an anachronistic relapse into medieval fantasies of papal temporal suprem- acy. The Duke of Parma's Bourbon kin, the kings of France and Naples, promptly occupied the papal territories of Avignon and Benevento. Maria Theresa had previously kept out of the growing hostility between the other Catholic monarchs and the Holy See, but the Duke of Parma was the father of her daughter-in-law and her future son-in-law. When the pope asked her to mediate, she declined the request,[96] and she had the bull of excommunication banned from her lands.[97] Together with the Bourbon monarchs, Kaunitz seized the opportunity "to convince [the pontiff] once and for all . . . that the days of his presuming to dictate to secular princes on matters not relating to faith . . . were over."[98]

In doing so, Kaunitz drew on the arsenal of arguments placed at his disposal by natural law. The legal situation that had previously defined discussions with the curia resembled a thicket of miscellaneous sources—papal statutes and edicts, bilateral treaties, privileges, old customs—from which any number of competing legal claims could be derived. Natural law doctrine provided an ax for clearing a path through this thicket. It offered a stringent basis for arguing that the church's spe- cial rights should be revoked by making a clear, simple, and very Prot- estant distinction. It distinguished between "temporal" rule over people's bodies, on the one hand, and "spiritual" rule over their souls, on the other, limiting the church to the latter. Accordingly, the church's jurisdiction extended exclusively to "the preaching of the gospel, Chris- tian dogma, divine service, the conferring of the sacraments, [and] cleri- cal discipline, so far as the latter falls within the realm of conscience."[99] All matters relating to the church's external form in a given territory were to be determined by the state that exercised power over that terri- tory; in this respect, priests were as much subjects as everyone else. Canon law had validity only at the sovereign's concession; the church's rights of autonomy were privileges that had been granted by the sover- eign at a particular point in time, and they could be withdrawn if the public good required it. The argument was theologically reinforced with reference to the founding of the first church: anything that could not be traced back to the mission entrusted by Christ to his apostles pertained to the sphere of worldly authority. In other words, the church was to be restricted to its core business of regulating relations with the hereafter.[100] Court Councillor Heinke spent much of 1768 putting these ideas to paper with all the clarity and force he could muster.[101] At the same time, the theory began to be put into practice. On June 15, 1768, Maria Theresa gave her seal of approval to a secret instruction, based on these same principles, for the newly formed religious bureau in Milan. The ultramontane church historian Ferdinand Maass dubbed it the "Magna Carta of state religion."[102] The comparison is forced, given that the document in question was a secret government instruction rather than a contractually binding constitutional act. Nonetheless, the paper concisely formulated the "new system" and declared it the basis of future policy. Those involved were aware of just how radical a change this was. The new system was to be publicized in print, although it would not appear officially under the monarch's name but rather as the private learned opinion of Court Councillor Heinke. In light of "the prevailing . . . way of thinking," this would protect her from "spiteful" reactions.[103]

Open confrontation with the pope eventually broke out over the proposal to transfer book censorship in Lombardy from the church to the state. This was no trifling matter, given the church's traditional claim to monitor and control access to information: vigilant shepherds had to keep the "sheep" under their care "from grazing in poisoned pastures."[104] Pope Clement XIII personally directed an urgent appeal to the empress's conscience in a bid to block the initiative, but his appeal fell on deaf ears. She referred the papal missive to Kaunitz, who recommended that she ignore it—which is exactly what she did. When a nuncio subsequently requested an audience, she informed him with telegraphic brevity: ". . . have no time and give no audiences he can apply to the lord high chamberlain."[105]

In the period that followed, the template provided by the Milanese instruction was applied to other hereditary lands as well; in Vienna a committee for church matters was set up within the court chancellery and staffed with Heinke and other Jansenist-minded officials. In the 1770s this committee rapidly issued one reform decree after another, now implemented without papal agreement solely on the basis of royal authority.[106] Ecclesiastical orders were regulated by the state in line with its requirements: the age of profession—the permanently binding vow to live by the order's rules—was raised to twenty-four, the upper limit of the dowry paid upon entering a nunnery was lowered, a long series of monastic privileges was eliminated. Religious orders were no longer permitted to send money to Rome, take on debt and engage in commercial enterprise, sell wine or beer, impose punishments of imprisonment, elect foreigners to lead the community, and so on. In Lombardy ever more rigorous measures were taken: there, the first monasteries for mendicant orders were dissolved and their assets confiscated by the state. The monasteries' loss was to be the parishes' gain. Seminaries were established, priestly training regulated by the state, and instruction in the catechism made compulsory for children. The church's right to offer sanctuary to debtors and criminals and launch inquisitorial proceedings was also challenged. Finally, the campaign against ostentatious forms of Baroque piety was taken up with renewed vigor, the "half" holidays now entirely abolished, processions lasting several days prohibited (with the exception of the pilgrimage to Mariazell)—and so on and so forth. Despite all this, there was no escalation in the conflict with the curia. The intransigent Clement XIII died in February 1769, and under the influence of the Bourbon monarchs the Franciscan Lorenzo Ganganelli was elected pope in May 1769, taking the name Clement XIV. Joseph, who had personally visited the conclave, described him to his mother as an *homme d'esprit*, a man of humble origins, and a sworn enemy of the Jesuits. The fact that the entire Roman aristocracy was against him only made him more sympathetic in Joseph's eyes.[107] As it turned out, the new pope placed far fewer obstacles in the path of Habsburg church policy than his predecessor.

The extent to which Maria Theresa identified with the national church system initiated by Kaunitz is disputed. She wrote no treatises on canon law or theological memoranda. Isolated statements by Kaunitz suggest that he felt obliged to appease the empress's tender conscience in order to steer her carefully and cautiously in his preferred direction.[108] Some historians have therefore described Maria Theresa as an unwitting tool, a weak woman of limited intellect who let herself be manipulated by her wily chancellor. This explanation was meant to excuse her; blame for her religious policy was attributed to her female sex, notorious for its lack of willpower, capacity for abstract thought, and analytic acumen.[109] Yet Maria Theresa's marginalia to the new principles on church-related matters show that she knew very well what she was demanding of the curia, the clergy, and her subjects.[110] Whenever she encountered resistance, she referred explicitly and emphatically to the new system. For example, when the Court Chancellery again characterized tax payments by the clergy as *donum gratuitum*, a freely given donation, she wrote: "I must find it disconcerting that the chancellery now wants to deviate once more from my previously announced intention and from the accepted principle of applying incontestable sovereign rights over the clergy."[111] To recalcitrant churchmen such as the archbishop of Vienna, Cardinal Migazzi, who had protested the tax, she responded sharply: the archbishop was "to be given no answer to his all too importunate statement"; if the sums owed by his diocese were not paid in due time, this would be regarded as an "irresponsible default" and legal action would be taken against the negligent taxpayers.[112] Maria Theresa thus resolutely supported her chancellor's new system in so far as it allowed her to assert her sovereign rights over the church. She was not Kaunitz's pliant, submissive instrument, for all that she still preferred to seek consensus whenever possible.[113]

This was also true of Maria Theresa's position on the Jesuits, another bone of contention among historians: a hypocrite to some, for others she was a victim of her advisers.[114] The scandal engulfing the Society of Jesus—accused of fraud, high treason, and no end of other evil machinations and finally dissolved in 1773 by Pope Clement XIV—was one of the great topics dominating the media and polarizing public opinion in late-eighteenth century Europe.[115] With its global network, its shady financial dealings, its lenient moral teaching, and its opaque political influence, the powerful order acted as a lightning rod for animosity toward the Roman church. The front line no longer ran between Protestants and Catholics but between modernizing forces and their opponents; it cut across the Catholic clergy, the courts, and the entire public sphere. How people viewed the Society of Jesus became almost a test for their enlightened or traditionalist credentials.

The empress could not be assigned unambiguously to either party.[116] On the one hand, she regularly paid public visits to the Professhaus, the Jesuits' headquarters in Vienna, remained loyal to her Jesuit confessor Kampmüller to the end, offered asylum at her court to fathers expelled from Spain,[117] and steadfastly kept out of the Bourbon monarchies' quarrel with the curia. On the other, she always maintained that Jesuits had no business meddling in politics.[118] Not only—as already mentioned— did she replace her court confessors one by one with Jansenist candidates; she also gave free rein to van Swieten, a declared enemy of the Jesuits, who from the 1750s onward had them removed from key positions at the University of Vienna and the censorship board and gradually deprived them of their monopoly on the control of information.[119] While she long refused to join the Bourbon crowns in petitioning the pope to have the order disbanded, she dropped her opposition once Marie Antoinette's marriage to the French dauphin was on the cards. "Despite the high regard in which I have always held this community [the Society of Jesus], and which they have earned through their zeal and their meritorious conduct in my lands, we will do nothing to block their dissolution if the pope regards it as appropriate and useful," she informed the Spanish king in April 1773. At the same time, she made clear "that I cannot acknowledge that the pope has any right to dispose of the goods and persons belonging to the order."[120] In line with the principles of her new ecclesiastical policy, this was a right she reserved for herself alone. Accordingly, when the Society of Jesus was officially suppressed on July 21, 1773, through the papal bull *Dominus ac Redemptor*, Maria Theresa immediately moved to set up a commission advising her on how to manage the confiscated assets.

In September 1773, she commented to her cabinet secretary, Neny, that "the fate of the Jesuits has now been decided. I sorely regret it, but there is nothing to be done about it; we will have to make the best of it for our holy religion and state. . . . I cannot express how greatly this unhappy dissolution troubles and upsets me. I have never felt so abandoned. Kaunitz, Blümegen, Kressl, Kolowrat are not here."[121] And to Countess Enzenberg: "so far as the Jesuits are concerned, I am deeply saddened and in despair. I have loved them all my life and found them to be nothing other than pious. Yet now I have allowed control to slip from my grasp and transferred it to a commission." To be sure, she added, the Jesuits had squirreled away millions in Protestant countries. "I would be glad if I could cover all this up, but I fear there is still much more to come to light."[122] She sounded disconsolate, and as so often in her twilight years, seemed weighed down by her cares, yet she felt deceived by the Jesuits and was determined to turn the situation to her political advantage.

Contemporaries drew their own conclusions from the behavior of an empress who had always presented herself as a friend to the Jesuit order. Depending on their sympathies, she was regarded as either a duplicitous harridan or a woman betrayed, a victim of Jansenist conspiracy or an Enlightenment heroine. The English traveler Henry Swinburne remarked in his memoirs that no one should underestimate the empress: "for if every drop of blood of the Jesuits were demanded, and necessary for the marriage of her daughters, she would without hesitation spill it."[123] Khevenhüller, by contrast, saw her as someone "who easily allows herself to be misled." Observing the papal bull's speedy implementation in the hereditary lands, he noted that "the good woman was most to be regretted for having been induced to take such a step against her own inclination and, as I am certain, against her innermost conviction, a step she will repent on her deathbed and no longer be capable of undoing."[124] Other rumors suggested that the empress had only agreed to the order's dissolution because her Jesuit confessor had betrayed her confidence by providing his superiors with a transcript of her Easter confession.[125] Yet another witness, believing that the Jesuit "worm" needed to be "trodden underfoot," offered the following words of praise: "It pleases the empress to heed all good advice. . . . It even seems that the older she gets, the more she disdains the false principles of bigoted persons devoted to the prejudices and errors of the old barbarism."[126]

In fact, the order's suppression served Habsburg church policy extraordinarily well; indeed, it would later act as a model for the dissolution of monasteries under Joseph. The commission responsible for implementing the papal bull proceeded with the utmost discretion at first, hoping to prevent the Jesuits from quickly transferring their wealth to a safe haven abroad.[127] Not until September 10 did Migazzi, the archbishop of Vienna, announce the order's suppression in the hereditary lands. The Court Chamber immediately moved to seize its liquid assets. Members of the order who had not yet taken a binding vow were dismissed; the remainder were assigned to the regional bishoprics and later redeployed in pastoral ministry. They were also forced to vacate their colleges and received a monthly stipend of a mere sixteen guilders from their confiscated wealth, later increased to twenty-five—barely more than the salary paid a heater of rooms at court. Jesuits were removed from all chairs in theology, ethics, metaphysics, and history, and in a handbillet, the empress even personally ordered that their pedagogic writings (*de moribus, disciplina et correctione*) be banned.[128] The rest of the order's fortune was earmarked for the state school system. It was smaller than expected. The commission charged with suppressing the order was convinced that most of it had been smuggled abroad—including to Prussia, ironically—and pressed Maria Theresa to impose tough sanctions. For her, this was a step too far: there was no incriminating evidence, and the missing funds could no longer be recovered like this, anyway.[129] When the commission reproached her for her gullibility, she defended herself:

> For many years, I have not been so partial to the Society [of Jesus]; I and my children have taken both education and the confessional out of their hands. Nobody sought as forcefully as I to strip the Society of all theology professorships as soon as it was suppressed.... After all this, I cannot be considered too biased in its favor, nor too gullible, but I do trust myself never to do anything, or allow anything to be done, against my conviction.[130]

Vampires, Faith Healers, and Calendar Makers

So far as religious matters were concerned, Maria Theresa found herself
fighting on several fronts at once: against the papal curia's claim to authority, against the common people's "superstition," and against the
"freethinking" of the educated class. In her battle against superstition,
she deferred to van Swieten, following his lead no less unquestioningly
than she did in matters of health. He was the one who determined the
difference between magic, quackery, and medicine. The borderlines between these fields were anything but self-evident; on the contrary, they
were intensively debated and redrawn in eighteenth-century public discourse. In this respect, society was riven by deep fissures that cut across
class boundaries. For the Enlightenment vanguard, critique of superstition was *the* public battleground on which they self-consciously deployed the weapons of empirical observation and critical reasoning. Yet
what some branded superstition, others saw as good Catholic piety,
hallowed by time and tradition. Maria Theresa's bans on traditional
practices therefore met with blank incomprehension and passive resistance among commoners, from the clergy, and at court.

For example, when the new calendar for 1772 was published and the
faithful became aware that more holidays had been canceled than ever
before, such that even St. Joseph, patron saint of the land and Archducal
House of Austria, would no longer have a holiday of his own, many at
court were aghast "that so God-fearing a lady . . . should have agreed to
this and, rather than correcting the wretched vogue for overturning
everything, should have succumbed to it instead."[131] Since the 1750s, the
primary carrier from whom she had contracted this modish infection
had been her personal physician. In general, van Swieten was a thorn in
the side of court society: a Dutchman of soberly ascetic, middle-class
manners, a proud empirical scientist who endeared himself to the empress on account of his fierce work ethic and personal loyalty but refused to adapt to courtly ways. He therefore struck many as "very uncouth and insolent" and was "uncommonly loathed by the public."[132]
When he died in June 1772, Khevenhüller complained that Maria Theresa had "not only consulted him and blindly followed his advice and

recommendations in his sphere, . . . but extended her trust in him so far that she frequently let herself be guided by him *in internis,* particularly in matters of religion—not always for the best, alas."[133] Yet where van Swieten's own sphere began and where it ended, in other words, where the border between natural science and theology ran, is precisely what stood in question. Empirical science was increasingly making inroads into areas previously reserved for theology, contesting its traditional claims to explain the world. Theology, for its part, found itself on the defensive and was forced to delimit itself more clearly from magical practices. At the same time, both learned disciplines, theology as well as medicine, had a vested interest in eliminating unprofessional competition from the laity. In this situation, the right to decide what counted as truth and what could be dismissed as superstition was hotly contested. As someone who enjoyed the confidence of the empress, van Swieten had a significant head start in this competitive struggle.

He used that head start to launch an ambitious campaign against any traditional cultic practices that smacked of superstition. These included customs such as New Year's singing, Three Kings Day, St. John's Fire, and ringing church bells to ward off thunderstorms; Good Friday processions with scenic images, cross-bearers, and flagellants; the priestly trade in sanctified objects, amulets, candles, and rosaries; the hanging of consecrated palm branches, roots, and herbs on people's doors; and especially witchcraft, treasure hunting, necromancy, and unauthorized exorcism.[134] The campaign was occasioned by a renewed outbreak of vampirism in Moravia, Silesia, and Hungary in 1754.[135] The practice of digging up the bodies of the dead in the belief that their unredeemed souls would go on haunting the living until they had been posthumously made harmless by priests had already caused a stir in the 1720s. In the winter of 1724–25, a mysterious epidemic had broken out among the Orthodox Greek population in the province of Gradisca near the Turkish border, even drawing attention from the *Wienerische Diarium.*[136] Disturbingly, those who fell victim to the epidemic did not decompose in their graves but retained their fresh complexion and were even seen to bleed from the nose and mouth. A recently deceased man was identified as the cause of all these fatalities; he was said to have drained his victims of their vital powers. "Vampyr" had established itself as the common term for this phenomenon. The postmortem rituals applied by priests to unredeemed souls were known as *magia posthuma*.[137] A second wave had taken place in Serbia in 1730–31, prompting the Austrian military administration to get involved. There were fears that the frightened population might migrate en masse from the affected border regions. Two regimental physicians had been charged with investigating the phenomenon. After exhuming a number of corpses, they ascertained that most exhibited the now-familiar symptoms of vampirism.[138] In the period that followed, scholars of both theology and medicine had studied the phenomenon intensively and devoted dozens of books and articles to it. Vampires became the subject of lively debate in academies and salons and attracted interest even at the Viennese court. Natural historians were skeptical, asserting that the reported cases had to be attributable to natural causes. Theologians were eager to have their say as well: only Christ had the ability to rise from the grave after death; mere mortals could do so neither of themselves nor with the help of the devil. Yet it was in God's power to work supernatural miracles and bring the dead back to life, as both the Bible and recent history amply attested. In this instance the Catholic clergy were divided. Pope Benedict XIV himself had nothing but derision for vampirism.[139] In this ambivalent situation, the crucial question was: who had the final say on such matters?

Now, between 1745 and 1755 a new series of unexplained deaths occurred in Moravia, Silesia, and Hungary that the people blamed on vampires and sought to combat with posthumous magic. Van Swieten grasped the opportunity for a general campaign against superstition and prejudice, ignorance and false religion. Two experienced military physicians and anatomists were tasked with investigating the series of mysterious illnesses. "Following mature deliberation and close examination," they arrived at the conclusion that the outbreak could be put down to unhealthy Greek Orthodox fasting rules, combined with excessive consumption of spirits and chronic malnutrition. The undecayed condition of the corpses they dug up could be explained by the winter cold and by chemical processes arising from the specific composition of the soil. The whole "commotion" derived from nothing more "than a vain fear,

a superstitious credulity, a dark and vivid fantasy, simplicity, and ignorance on the part of that people," that is, adherents of the Greek Orthodox faith on the military frontier of the Ottoman Empire.[140] Priestly
fraud was suspected, since Orthodox presbyters were said to earn good
money by ritually condemning and executing exhumed vampires, this
"barbaric trial against the poor deceased."[141]

The findings of the learned commission not only prompted van Swieten to publish an enlightened screed against vampirism, they also
flowed into an edict aimed at killing off superstition of all kinds—belief
in ghosts, witchcraft, treasure hunting, soothsaying, spirit summoning,
and so on. All "such sinful malpractices" would no longer be left to the
clergy. They would now be brought immediately to the attention of "the
political authorities," who would investigate them "with the assistance
of a rational physician." If fraud was involved, the guilty parties were to
be punished with the utmost severity.[142] The ban on exhuming suspected vampires and putting them on trial was directed not just at the
Greek Orthodox priests but at the Catholic clergy as well. It had since
come to light that the episcopal consistory in Olomouc, the capital of
Moravia, had played a role in the posthumous burning of such undead,
including seven children.[143] The boundary line between reason and superstition thus did not coincide with that between devout Catholics, on
the one hand, and Greek Orthodox Serbs and Romanians "at the furthest end of Christendom," on the other.[144] Bishops were now sternly
admonished to "provide their subordinate consistories and clergy with
the necessary pastoral instructions on this matter, and thereby rid them
of the prejudices with which some of them may be encumbered."[145] The
decree referred to Maria Theresa's "mild, serene, and equitable temperament," which had moved her to issue the strictest commands to "eradicate such outdated superstition." In future, whenever some chance
event arose "whose natural cause is not yet sufficiently understood,
nobody should have the temerity to meddle in this affair without previously notifying Her Majesty."[146]

According to the decree, only professional doctors, *physici*, were
competent to tell the difference between truth and superstition, not
priests and certainly not the unlettered masses. The campaign against

priestly fraud, prejudice, and ignorance was only superficially directed against the proverbial backwoodsmen in regions such as faraway Transylvania. The Greek Orthodox priests with their rituals of executing the dead were representative of the unenlightened clergy as a whole, and the crusade against belief in vampires was thus also a proxy war.[147] To all appearances a civilizing mission against benighted and heterodox peasants on the fringes of the Habsburg realm, van Swieten's campaign was ultimately far more: a campaign to assert the predominance of empirical science over religion.

Vampire hunters were not the only targets of van Swieten's campaign; he also went after books of dreams, oracular literature, and "calendars with occult interpretations concerning impending eclipses, bloodletting, cupping, purging, and bathing . . . etc."[148] Treasuries of arcane astrological and alchemical knowledge, such calendars informed readers of the days on which certain procedures could be carried out to best effect. They were published by none other than van Swieten's own protégé, court book printer Trattner. An extremely wily businessman, Trattner feared the ban would prove a massive drain on his revenue and therefore produced the calendar in two different versions: one for the common people, still replete "with horoscopes, prophesies, bloodletting tables, and the like," and an expurgated version for the court. His subterfuge was found out, provoking so violent a quarrel between Trattner and van Swieten that the normally unflappable court physician, pushed beyond the limits of his endurance, apparently "spat in [his opponent's] face," leading Trattner to seize "his Excellency," throw him to the sofa, and give him a "drubbing." Van Swieten complained to the empress, Trattner was banished from the city, and he was only restored to her good graces after he had begged for her forgiveness and a placated van Swieten had intervened on his behalf.[149] Even if the anecdote is wholly or partly invented, it is still informative for what it suggests about widespread opposition to the campaign against superstition.[150]

Most bans were ignored or circumvented; some even drew public protest. This is what happened when so-called "figured" Good Friday processions were abolished in the Tyrol in 1752. These were theatrical processions featuring elaborate scenic representations of the Passion narrative, in the tradition of late medieval Passion plays. As a well-known regional specialty, they had a not insignificant economic dimension for the community, much like the calendar for the court book printer. In the opinion of the authorities, however, they were more entertaining than edifying, encouraged ruinously competitive overspending, gave rise to all manner of excesses, and ill became the seriousness of the sacred mystery celebrated at Eastertide. The Tyrolean townships protested against the ban and defended the religious value of the spectacle, although they failed to sway the regional Representation and Chamber in Innsbruck. The populace stuck to its views and refused to relent; the dispute dragged on for three years. In Easter 1755 authorities in Innsbruck feared an insurrection and contemplated sending in the military. The Court Chancellery in Vienna advised that the ban on processions be reissued under threat of severe punishment, but "should the hoped-for obedience still not be forthcoming, you should then resort to force of arms."[151] Disturbances broke out nonetheless, resulting in harsh punishments for the ringleaders. The conflict surrounding the Good Friday processions was not yet over. Processions continued to be held in the Prince-Bishopric of Brixen, and elsewhere Passion plays were simply performed without a parade. Parishes were not willing to have their pious attraction taken off their hands.

There were many reasons why the reforms encountered such tenacious resistance. All these measures not only interfered with the necessary exchange of gifts between heaven and earth and the habitual rhythms of work and leisure, everyday scarcity, and feast-day abundance, they also—and above all—deprived people of their religious agency. In a highly uncertain and unpredictable world, traditional religious practices gave the faithful a sense of control, making them feel less helplessly exposed to the dangers lying permanently in wait for them. Risks and dangers that could be addressed through active means seemed less menacing. Through magical apotropaic gestures, blessings, supplicatory processions, and pilgrimages, simple believers gave themselves a power over their own destiny they were largely denied by the official church liturgy. Laypeople were assigned a passive role in divine worship. They had no idea what the priest in front of them was murmuring in

Latin—they quite literally thought that *hoc est corpus meum* was "hocus-pocus." Being suddenly required to give up their customary religious practices made people feel anxious and insecure. Faced with their non-compliance, parish priests had two options: they could either tow the official line, in which case the outlawed practices would simply continue to be performed behind their backs, or they could side with their parishioners and spearhead the resistance, in which case they would keep their standing with the faithful—for most, no doubt, the more likely option. This led, however, to a rift opening up within the Catholic clergy.

This is also shown in the way the state dealt with diabolical possession and witchcraft. Van Swieten's edict on superstition from 1755 stipulated that the "political authorities" should be immediately notified in such cases as well, since simple countryfolk all too easily took "what they had dreamt, or seen only in their imagination, or been fed by people intent on deceiving them," as evidence of sorcery and were "frequently confirmed in their credulity by prejudiced priests."[152] This created an environment where fraud could flourish. In 1758 priests were expressly banned from performing exorcisms, at least without prior approval from the secular authorities, owing to the "deception and abuse that has often occurred hitherto."[153] Yet it was unclear where deception and abuse began. Nobody who did not wish to be taken for a dangerous freethinker openly disputed the idea that the devil walked abroad, or that people could perform acts of magic with his assistance. At Mariazell, numerous votive images bore witness to salvation from diabolical temptation and liberation from demonic possession. One such example was the impressive triptych by the journeyman painter Johann Christoph Haitzmann, who had twice sold his soul to the devil only to be saved by the Mother of Grace in Mariazell (fig. 44).[154] *Crimen magiae*, the crime of sorcery on the basis of a pact with the devil, was still listed in the new Theresian Criminal Code of 1769.[155] Yet the jurists who wrote the code were clearly ill at ease with the classification, insisting that each individual case be examined to determine whether it involved fraud, madness, the mere frustrated intent to perform magic, or in fact "true magical mischief said to require diabolical support." The authors made known their doubts about this last possibility. They referred

FIGURE 44. The journeyman painter Johann Christoph Haitzmann's pact with the devil.
Oil sketches, Mariazell, 1725–29

repeatedly to "so-called witchcraft," drew attention to the serious blun-
ders committed by earlier prosecutors, and so increased the burden of
proof as to make a conviction for *true* sorcery all but impossible. In
principle, they argued, one of the other three causes was always to be
suspected, and if the case was investigated with the proper care and

caution, it would duly be discovered in the end. The possibility of diabolical influence should only be entertained if the damage inflicted could not be traced back to imagination, madness, or deception—and this should be left for the highest court in the land to decide.

The problem was by no means purely academic. In the late 1760s and early 1770s, a number of different faith healers and exorcists had attracted public attention. The most celebrated was Johann Joseph Gassner, a parish priest who attracted the sick and needy in the Empire's southwest and successfully drove out swarms of demons.[156] In Hungary the Franciscan monk Rochus Szmendrovich likewise scored spectacular successes with his exorcisms.[157] He and his fellow exorcists could point to the gospel when they interpreted illnesses as a consequence of demonic possession and cast out demons with spiritual means. Church authorities were far from unanimous in how they viewed such phenomena—who could distinguish with any certainty between the "natural" and the "diabolical" causes of a disease? The question of exorcism polarized society in much the same way as the Jesuit question. Around 150 publications appeared on Gassner alone, arguments for and against alternating with bewildering rapidity. A theological report submitted by the University of Ingolstadt came out on Gassner's side, and he found a prominent supporter in no less a personage than the prince-bishop of Regensburg.

Maria Theresa's view on the matter was clear. In 1755 she had already defended a position that came astonishingly close to Enlightenment theology: "Our religion no longer requires such convincing proofs as it had need of at the beginning; since God died for us sinners and redeemed us no more has been heard of possessed persons [and] I believe that no more exist," she noted in the margin of a submission from Court Chancellor Chotek.[158] And in 1772, when a miracle-working healer turned up in the Duchy of Milan, she wrote to her son Ferdinand: "I am glad that this priest who heals or cures through faith is not with me here. I recommend that you incarcerate him. But what annoys me is that there is still a belief in the possessed; at the very least, they should not be allowed to appear in public or be exorcized; they should be kept in a hospital like lunatics or impostors."[159] This shows the self-assurance with which Maria Theresa took it upon herself to adjudicate such questions. For if theologians, jurists, and physicians were unable to reach consensus on whether they were dealing with charlatanry, delusion, or the devil's work, then the crucial question was who had the final say on such matters and how they were defined. Van Swieten and Maria Theresa saw eye to eye on this point:[160] the campaign against superstition established the interpretive monopoly of the state, which sought advice from professional experts and shunned their nonprofessional rivals: the monk who earned extra income with consecrated holy water, the midwife who applied a magical lynx stone, or the priest who healed the sick by driving out their demons.[161]

The state consolidated its authority by arrogating to itself the power to make decisions on questions that bitterly divided public opinion. Yet Maria Theresa herself never got involved in these debates. She disliked theological or philosophical disputation in principle and refused to tolerate public discussion of the justness of her reforms. She reacted mercilessly to sermons that incurred her displeasure,[162] and she eventually had all political criticism from the clergy declared illegal.[163] If she resolutely opposed such phenomena as soothsaying and faith healing, then this was not because she had weighed up the rational arguments for and against but because she followed her chief physician with unwavering confidence on these questions. Paradoxically, her critique of superstition was more the consequence of her faith in his authority than the result of a process of critical reflection.

Freethinkers and Fashionable Philosophers

Maria Theresa fundamentally and vehemently rejected the spirit of criticism and systematic doubt that characterized her age: "That's how our enlighteners are, *ni foi ni loi ni honneté*—neither faith, nor law, nor honor."[164] What she abhorred in these self-appointed spokesmen of Enlightenment, these *philosophes à la mode*, was their presumptuousness, the optimism with which, blithely ignoring the centuries-old wisdom of tradition, they based all their judgments solely on their individual reason. She feared this attitude and felt obliged to suppress it through prohibitions and punishments. As she herself stated: "Nothing is more comfortable, nothing better suited to flatter our self-love, than freedom without restraint. This word has taken the place of religion in our enlightened century, when everyone wants to think and act from conviction or calculation. The past is condemned in its entirety for its ignorance and prejudice, despite a total lack of information about past and present. These cliffs are all the more perilous for having everything that flatters our pride and our passions."[165] The greatest danger arose from books and conversations about books: "All these new books, and especially the discussions [arising from them], incite mischief, undermine all virtue and morality, foster lassitude, license, ease, and indifference towards religion and natural ties to parents, sovereigns, and authorities, so that it is hardly surprising to see our young people so muddle-headed."[166]

Maria Theresa therefore attacked "freethinking" even more vociferously than superstition. The two campaigns were not mutually exclusive; on the contrary, both were concerned with monitoring people's knowledge, thoughts, and beliefs. Everywhere she looked, Maria Theresa detected indifference and a lack of respect for true religion, not least at court and among her officials. In April 1767, hoping "to put a stop to the widespread, extremely vexatious sin of freethinking and sacrilege so reprehensibly committed by those audacious enough to hold forth too freely, or even contemptuously, about sacred religion and its mysteries," she therefore issued a handwritten edict to Lord High Chamberlain Ulfeld. He was to see to it that top-ranking officials at court, the presidents of provincial administrations, and commanders in the military "actively prosecuted" the sin of unbelief in their respective spheres of influence, ensuring that "due reverence" was paid to God and his holy church. Everyone "whose own conscience reproached them . . . on this score" should be "earnestly exhorted and admonished to repent and change their ways." Should they prove recalcitrant, they were "to be subjected without mercy to the harshest possible punishment in view of the seriousness of the offense." Anyone who heard "blasphemous speeches" without immediately reporting them to the authorities would suffer the same punishment as the blasphemer himself. Any books that incited freethinking and mockery of religion should be burned by their owners within eight days; whoever remained in possession of such books, or even knew of their whereabouts, would likewise be threatened with severe punishment. Military officers were ordered to purge their regiments of "those who blasphemously mock God and religion"; failure to comply would see them stripped of their command.[167] Lord High Chamberlain Ulfeld, meanwhile, was unsure if he had understood the edict correctly. He inquired whether it should literally be proclaimed to all subordinates, since he feared the problem might be far more widespread among high officials than in the lower ranks. The master of the hunt had warned him that the simple gamekeepers beneath him "would have no idea what the resolution meant." And Lady-in-Waiting Goëss, mistaking the ban on freethinking (*Freigeisterei*) for a warning about free-roaming ghosts (*freie Geister*), had asked what the lord high chamberlain's order "concerning spirits" was all about. Maria Theresa reacted with irritation: "This business has not gone as intended," bringing criticism and ridicule instead of respect.[168] At any rate, the strict decree appears to have been taken no further, otherwise some of her closest companions would hardly have escaped punishment themselves.

Nonetheless, the empress still insisted that everyone at court and in the civil service scrupulously observe the religious formalities. All officials at court and in the hereditary lands had to attend Sunday worship as well as annual confession and communion. In 1764 Maria Theresa had urged her son Leopold to introduce this requirement to his own court, too.[169] By 1774, at the latest, everyone was legally obliged to demonstrate that they had performed their duty of confession and communion on Maundy Thursday. Absentees had to produce a written apology. Even Kaunitz formally begged the empress for forgiveness when he had been unable to take part in the Maundy Thursday service at court, duly presenting her with his certificate of confession.[170] In January 1772 one observer noted just how strictly the commandment to keep the Sabbath was policed at court: during times of divine worship, nobody risked getting caught out in the streets. Only recently, a servant of Prince Auersperg who had been bringing his master his gala dress on a Sunday had been arrested on the spot and thrown into prison.[171] The price

Maria Theresa paid for such vigilance was hypocrisy in her presence and derision behind her back. Aristocratic libertines such as the Hungarian magnate Count Nitzky or Prince Ligne openly made fun of her; they prayed the rosary when necessary while at the same time scoffing "at the Empress's superstition."[172] In Protestant Germany, needless to say, such enforced piety occasioned either outrage or amusement (depending on temperament). For the Prussian traveler Friedrich Nicolai, Vienna epitomized everything those in the Protestant North wrongly believed to have died out already: "We, nurtured on our sweet dreams of Enlightenment, will scarce credit that in our purportedly so enlightened eighteenth century all this priestcraft really still exists."[173]

The most important weapon in the fight against freethinking and superstition was book censorship, that is, the inspection of all written matter, whether printed or unpublished, for dangers to religion, good morals, and political order.[174] The censorship system Maria Theresa had inherited in 1740 was unsatisfactory. Various institutions were entitled to a say in it: professors at the University of Vienna, bishops, provincial governors, the Court Chancellery. Manuscripts were vetted for publication by Jesuits in the faculty of theology and philosophy, while border officials searched travelers' belongings for contraband literature from abroad. All this occurred in haphazard fashion. There was no central coordinating body, nor were there any generally acknowledged criteria for issuing a ban. Charles VI had already tried to change this but had only added to the confusion. In the course of Haugwitz's ambitious reform program, Maria Theresa therefore once again put book censorship on the agenda, not least to put a stop to public criticism of the reforms. Given his role in reorganizing the university and directing the court library, van Swieten seemed the right man for the job. The court physician set about bringing order to the chaos and depriving the Jesuits of their interpretive monopoly over written matter. Evaluation of domestic and foreign literature would now be entrusted to a board of carefully selected secular and ecclesiastical experts. In 1753, at the end of a long and occasionally heated process, a central state censorship commission was set up under van Swieten's direction. It reached its decisions by majority vote and published the results each year in a *Catalogus librorum prohibitorum*.

Van Swieten and his allies understood censorship as a tool of Enlightenment, which needed help from the state if it was to vanquish the combined forces of superstition, sin, and "irreligion." Nobody gave a thought to freedom of the press; reason could not be expected to triumph without external support. It is telling that the same person could be both censor and censored: the prominent Enlightenment thinker, journalist, and state official Joseph von Sonnenfels, whose weekly magazine *Der Vertraute* had been banned in 1765, was himself appointed to the censorship commission in 1770.[175] As in most other European states, censors in Vienna had to perform a continuous balancing act: the light of reason should not be extinguished, but it was even more important that it not be allowed to flare up into an all-consuming blaze. A long series of old and new classics therefore ended up on the list of forbidden books: not just a provocateur such as Machiavelli or an atheist such as La Mettrie, but also works by Montaigne and Bayle, Voltaire and Rousseau, even the literary productions of Grimmelshausen, Fielding, Lessing, and Wieland.[176] Yet the list had an ambivalent effect: conceived as a guide for state officials, it also offered the interested public a welcome overview of new and noteworthy books from abroad. The list was therefore itself forbidden in 1777. Most of the books on the index were still accessible anyway. Works of the French Enlightenment did not even need to be smuggled across the border; they circulated in pirated editions brought out by Viennese printers, which even advertised their illicit wares.[177] In the hereditary lands, too, the book market expanded rapidly in the second half of the century. Political, moral, and economic treatises, polemics, and novels poured from the presses, along with periodicals such as the *Wienerische Gelehrte Nachrichten, Der österreichische Patriot,* or *Der Mann ohne Vorurteil.* Everyone knew that the censorship commission was hopelessly deluged by the ever-rising tide of publications.[178] A rumor even went around that one of the most scandalous books of the century, *Les trois imposteurs* (*The Treatise of the Three Impostors*)—Moses, Jesus Christ, and Mohammed—had been spotted in the imperial court library.[179]

This was presumably a dig at the library's director, van Swieten. He had powerful enemies both inside and outside the censorship commission who had the empress's ear: initially the Jesuits, then, following their dismissal from the commission, Archbishop Migazzi, but also court confessor Ignaz Müller. Maria Theresa reserved for herself the final say in questions of censorship, and she followed her esteemed personal physician by no means so blindly in questions of religious oversight as in other matters. Her position was unpredictable. Sometimes she took his side, as in 1752, when she agreed with him that Montesquieu's celebrated work *On the Spirit of the Laws* could be removed from the catalogue of forbidden books.[180] On other occasions, however, she acted against the advice of her own censorship board, pushing van Swieten to the brink of resignation. An especially spectacular case of this kind was her personal intervention against the antipapal work by "Febronius," which had been unanimously approved by the commission shortly before. She refused to back down even when van Swieten personally appealed her veto, preferring to side with his archenemy Migazzi. She also remained silent when the pseudonymous author was subsequently forced to retract, despite Kaunitz explaining to her that his principles were publicly taught at all universities in her own lands. Yet what might be suitable for discussion among scholars was not necessarily fit for common use; in Maria Theresa's eyes, dogmatic disputes had no place in the public sphere.[181] In 1768 she decreed that in important cases concerning religion she would now decide herself rather than leaving the commission to make a majority ruling. With that, she undermined her own board and opened the way for informal interventions.[182] When van Swieten, pleading poor health, resigned from the commission, she wrote: "I pledge the censorship commission my complete protection, so long as it continues in accordance with the principles of the worthy van Swieten. . . . Nobody can and should give better testimony than I to his tireless zeal and labor, his truth and clarity, free of reserve or passion. . . . His zeal and example in religion were as pure as his loyalty to my person and my family."[183]

But her actions belied her words: following van Swieten's departure, the censorship commission steered an ever more rigid anti-Enlightenment course. After van Swieten's death in 1772, Maria Theresa no longer had a reliable compass in her battle against superstition and freethinking.

Haugwitz, Daun, and Tarouca were also dead; only Kaunitz, himself a freethinker, remained. The older Maria Theresa became, the more isolated she felt amid all the Enlightenment sympathizers and libertines at court and in the educated public, the more doggedly she sought to impose the true Catholic religion on her children, her court, and her realm; and the more hopeless an undertaking that came to seem, the more she retreated into a mood of embittered resignation.

If there was one constant among all the contradictions that characterized the empress's attitude toward religion and the church, one conviction from which she never wavered, then it was surely her assurance that God had given her a direct mandate to rule on the basis of dynastic succession. It followed from this, first, that the defense of the true Catholic faith, the honor of the dynasty, and the welfare of the hereditary lands were inseparably interlinked; and, second, that she was responsible before God for the orthodoxy of her subjects. Papal mediation was not needed for this. Jansenist teaching strengthened her in the conviction that she had a personal connection to God—a Protestant principle, properly speaking. Inherited, divinely bestowed sovereignty allowed for the greatest freedom of action and made it possible for her to adopt a stance of radical independence in the event of conflict. Nobody else, not even the pope, could know what her divine mandate required of her. The problem, however, was that maximal freedom of action simultaneously entailed maximal uncertainty. What if her assurance that she was always acting in accordance with the divine will were to disappear and the ritual patterns of behavior bequeathed by tradition were to forfeit their rock-solid security? This problem would grow ever more acute over the course of her reign, particularly as her eldest son, who likewise had the law of dynastic succession on his side, came to advocate principles incompatible with her own.

12

Strangers Within

FIGURE 45. Wall hanging on the Peace of Hubertusburg with Turkish, Moorish, and Indian motifs (detail), 1776–78

Unity and Diversity

Following the Peace of Hubertusburg, a team of skilled artisans sewed an unusual tapestry, around two meters high and one and a half meters wide, consisting of over thirteen by thirteen painstakingly embroidered cloth patches (fig. 45). Unfortunately, nothing is known about who made this enigmatic textile or to what end.[1] What we do know is that the patchwork rug celebrates the peace concluded at Hubertusburg in 1763. The large oval at its center contains the armorial crests of Austria, Saxony, and Prussia, while Maria Theresa, Frederick II, and Frederick August II are shown joining hands above. Closer inspection reveals a wealth of extraordinary motifs. United here in new-found amity are not just the three monarchs and soldiers from various lands and armed services but also mythological figures, characters from the Bible, and people from all backgrounds and every region of the world: Amor and Bacchus, Adam and Eve, Pandurs and Hussars, peasants and peasant women, post riders and chimney sweeps, Christ with the cross—and, scattered among them, Turks, and Moors, an uncommonly wide-ranging picture puzzle spanning all conceivable times and places. What the hanging shows is that strangers from far away clearly figured in the popular imagination and were integrated somehow into people's view of the world. Yet the universe presented in this tapestry is also remarkably disordered and unsystematic, in stark contrast to the strictly hierarchical universe that presented itself to the upper echelons.

What is perceived as foreign and what as familiar is a question of perspective. For Maria Theresa and her forebears, foreignness was primarily defined in religious terms. A foreigner was anyone who did not bear allegiance to the one, true, holy Catholic religion, in a word, "Acatholics." For Maria Theresa, the age of confessionalism was not yet over. In the tradition in which she had been brought up, the ruler self-evidently had to ensure that religious unity and uniformity prevailed throughout the realm. There were various reasons for this. On the one hand—as already mentioned—rulers saw themselves as responsible before God for their subjects' spiritual salvation. On the other, only pious and orthodox subjects were considered trustworthy and obedient; religious deviance could be understood as a form of political rebellion. In fact, subjects in the hereditary lands were anything but homogeneous, including in their religious beliefs and practices, and they never had been. In Hungary, for example, Catholics made up only around half the population, in Transylvania they were in the minority, and in Prague around a quarter of the population were Jewish. Even the residential capital, Vienna, reflected the religious diversity that characterized the extremely heterogeneous conglomerate of lands ruled by the Archducal House—a "mishmash of all nations":[2] there were Jews, Muslims, Calvinists, Lutherans, Greek, Uniate, and Armenian Christians, Anti-Trinitarians, indifferentists, and presumably also (covert) atheists. Many nonconformists enjoyed individual privileges, some benefited from corporative privileges, while others lacked all safeguards.[3] The accepted presence of so many different faith communities in Vienna and elsewhere in the hereditary lands had nothing to do with a policy of toleration in the Enlightenment sense, however. Here, as in Old Europe in general, it was a matter of liberties (in the plural)—contractually guaranteed exceptions from the rule—rather than of universal religious liberty (in the singular). Individuals did not enjoy an in-principle right to freedom of worship. Specific people, corporations, families, or communities enjoyed precisely defined concessions at particular places. In Vienna, for example, such exceptional rights were possessed by foreign ambassadors, merchants, military personnel, and Protestant members of the Imperial Aulic Council and their families. While they could not be completely forbidden from holding religious services, these were only tolerated behind closed doors. As little as possible of what went on should be visible and audible to the outside world for fear of contagion.[4] In outward appearance, "Acatholics" were expected to assimilate to their surroundings as best they could by observing fasting rules, kneeling down before the Holy of Holies when it was carried through the streets, keeping Catholic holidays, and so on.[5] A perpetual bone of contention were the Protestant private chapels of the Danish, Swedish, and Netherlandish embassies, whose services attracted many outsiders, including even members of the native nobility. Such renegade behavior met with great disfavor from on high; Maria Theresa ordered "that a stop be put to the matter, albeit with a minimum of fuss."[6] Yet although the imperial house frowned on any kind of religious deviance, not all dissenters were socially isolated. Their sweeping negative characterization as "Acatholics" brushes over their significant differences. How the Catholic majority treated the many strangers in their midst did not just depend on their religious affiliation but above all on the position they occupied in the social hierarchy and the social, economic, and symbolic capital they had at their disposal.[7]

Nonetheless, the social pressure placed on "Acatholics" to return to the bosom of the Roman church remained enormous, especially in the case of individuals who lived far from their homeland and lacked support from family or community in their Catholic environment—widows, orphans, merchants, military officers, and the like. Conversion in the opposite direction was regarded as "perversion" and was strictly prohibited. Various religious orders made it their ambition to proselytize Protestants, Jews, and Muslims; the Jesuits in Vienna alone prided themselves on roughly one hundred successful conversions each year. While converts were lured with numerous benefits and privileges, those who stubbornly persisted in their false beliefs were disadvantaged in many ways. To be sure, there were Protestants at court: chamberlains, for example, who were permitted to bear the chamberlain's key but prevented from serving.[8] Anyone serious about seeking advancement, however, had no choice but to convert. Maria Theresa's own mother had been forced to renounce her faith before her marriage, while generals like Laudon or Hildburghausen, scholars like Justi or Beck, and high officials like Wurmbrand, Ulfeld, Bartenstein, Haugwitz, Binder, or the Zinzendorfs had joined the Catholic church at the start of their careers.[9] The social pressure and dramatic moral dilemmas such a move could entail are exemplified by Karl von Zinzendorf, a great-nephew of the famous founder of the Brethren's Congregation at Herrnhut, who for years resisted selling his faith for worldly gain before eventually relenting, becoming a Teutonic knight and rising to the highest ranks in financial administration.[10] From a ruler's perspective, converts had the advantage that they were not generally embedded in a social network of friends and relatives. They could therefore be expected to demonstrate less interest and greater loyalty. Maria Theresa's chambermaid and reader Charlotte Hieronymus, for example, was the orphaned daughter of a soldier and had been baptized into the Protestant faith before being selected for service by the empress and brought up Catholic.[11] Maria Theresa herself was keen to see "Acatholics" in her surroundings return to the fold.[12] From the "convert chest" established by her grandmother, but also from her own private purse, she promoted the cause of conversion and supported needy ex-Protestants, especially nobles fallen on hard times.[13] When so obdurate a heretic as General of the Artillery Count Schulenburg, "who was uncommonly fanatical in his Lutheran faith," was persuaded to take the Catholic sacraments shortly before his death—when he could "no longer resist . . . the continuous stirrings of divine grace"—his "beautiful and almost miraculous conversion" was celebrated as a great public event in the presence of the imperial family, the archbishop, and the entire court, and his heirs could look forward to generous support from the empress.[14]

Many of the converts regarded their own conversion with a pinch of cynicism. One example was Friedrich von der Trenck, the Prussian nephew of the infamous Austrian warlord. Hoping to get his hands on his late uncle's fortune, he "put on the mantle of Romish faith" and declared himself "heir to the last Trenck: I received fresh credit . . . and the queen was moved to grace by the sight of the newly converted heretic, so that I found myself winning one trial after another and being favored in every conceivable way."[15] The frivolous freethinker Trenck wrote these lines in Prussian captivity, having long since forfeited both his uncle's fortune and the empress's favor. For converts who stayed in Vienna and made a career there, the matter appeared in a different light. Regardless of how strenuously they had previously resisted, as soon as they embraced Catholicism, the arrangement seemed in retrospect to have been divinely ordained. Bartenstein, son of a pious Lutheran from Strasbourg, complained for years to an old friend in Hamburg about how greatly his religion impeded his progress at court but expressed his confidence that the obstacle could be overcome through competence and sheer hard work. When his Lutheranism nonetheless threatened to stymie his career, he allowed himself to be converted by two

Benedictines with Jansenist sympathies, although he concealed the news from his father. Nonetheless, he was convinced in hindsight that his conversion had been the will of God. He later thanked the learned father who had dispelled his doubts for helping him overcome his internal resistance to accepting God's grace.[16] Cases such as this one show that it is misleading to ask whether the conversion was "authentic" or strategic. The alternative rarely presented itself to those affected. How the conversion was interpreted depended on the time and the observer. In hindsight, spiritual conversion and its advantageous worldly consequences for the convert formed a harmonious whole, particularly when the entire Catholic environment confirmed the convert in this interpretation.

"Fear and Loathing": The Jews

Not all Acatholics were the same. Jews found themselves in a fundamentally different situation to members of Christian denominations, for there was no land whose ruler shared their religion and was prepared to offer them right of residence, asylum, or diplomatic support. In their Christian environs, they were viewed purely and simply as aliens. Maria Theresa was particularly ill-disposed toward them. A frequently cited handwritten resolution on her policy toward the Jews reads: "I do not know of a worse public plague than this nation; with their fraud, usury, and money dealing, they reduce people to beggary [and] engage in all sorts of evil transactions that an honest man abhors; therefore, they are to be kept away from here and [their numbers] reduced as far as possible."[17] She had little personal experience with Jews. In Vienna, unlike in Prague, there were very few Jewish families, and she preferred Protestants as bankers. On the rare occasions when she came into contact with Jews, she made no attempt to conceal her revulsion. In 1750, for example, she wrote to her friend Trautson from Brno that the many Jews affected her "so badly that I never want to stay here."[18] And she was shocked by the number of Jewish residents in Bohemia: "Forty-four thousand Jews, I confess, inspire fear and loathing" (*horreur et dégout*).[19] Yet for all that, she had reason to be grateful. In 1741 the Munich court

Jew Wolf Wertheimer and his son Samuel in Vienna had been almost alone in trying to mediate between her and the prince-elector of Bavaria to prevent the attack on her inheritance. As creditors of both courts, they had a vital interest in not getting caught between the two sides in the event of war.[20] And the Portuguese banker Diego d'Aguilar, holder of the Austrian tobacco monopoly, placed 300,000 guilders at her disposal for developing Schönbrunn after her finances had been completely ruined by the War of Succession.[21]

Even Maria Theresa's devoted admirer, Alfred von Arneth, was forced to acknowledge "the spirited aversion" his heroine "always showed towards the Jews," even against the advice of her ministers and the opposition of the territorial estates: "Only gradually and with difficulty could they bring her to adopt more moderate measures, if not more moderate views."[22] Whereas the nineteenth-century national-liberal Arneth still criticized her on this account, her pronounced Judeophobia found favor with later writers who cited her in support of their own anti-Semitism. In 1942, for example, Heinrich Ritter von Srbik, one of the leading National Socialist historians in Austria, noted with approval that Maria Theresa had been "an instinctive enemy of Jewry"— "instinctive" meaning innate, natural, and hence infallible.[23] Friedrich Walter, the éminence grise of Austrian administrative history, decorated in 1964 with the Cross of Honor for the Arts and Sciences (First Class), included Maria Theresa's previously cited resolution in a short treasury of quotations from the empress he compiled for domestic use in 1942.[24] After 1945 this aspect of her politics tended to be passed over in silence. By 1968, when Friedrich Walter came to edit a far larger selection of letters and official documents on Maria Theresa's reign, her Jewish policy was no longer found worth mentioning. The same could be said of the deluxe volumes released to mark the two-hundredth anniversary of her death in 1980.[25]

The status of Jews was precarious in all European countries; nowhere did they enjoy unrestricted, automatic right of residence. Only the privileged few were permitted to remain in the country. Writs of protection offered only temporary respite and could be revoked without notice.[26] Princes charged a premium for them while at the same time profiting from the services of court Jews. They constantly imposed new levies, forced Jews to buy up the overpriced products of state manufacturers, delegated tax-collecting duties to community leaders, and made the well-off pay for their less fortunate coreligionists. Nonprivileged Jews formed a broad underclass that lived in poverty and eked out a living in niche livelihoods. Yet even privileged Jews were subject to harsh restrictions. Jews were barred access to guilds and public offices and were prevented from owning land, serving in the military, or marrying Christians. On the other hand, they enjoyed considerable corporative autonomy, as was generally the norm in premodern Europe, and were free to regulate their own community affairs.

Even by the standards of the time, however, Habsburg Jewish policy was particularly harsh, and it became ever more so during Maria Theresa's reign. Maria Theresa was behind the last great mass expulsion of Jews in premodern Europe. The pretext, as so often, was a malicious rumor. When Prague was temporarily occupied by Prussian troops in the winter of 1744, it was claimed that the Jews had collaborated with the enemy, as was only to be expected of such notorious traitors and liars.[27] According to the *Wienerische Diarium*, the Jews, who "shrink from no iniquity and always stand on good terms with the enemy," had given material support to the occupying forces; two hundred of the Jewish rabble had secretly removed cannons from the city and armed themselves to protect enemy property.[28] When the Prussians pulled out in late November, Austrian hussars entered Prague, plundered the Jewish quarter, and razed it to the ground. Further atrocities were committed against the Jewish population elsewhere in Bohemia.[29] Some were tortured and murdered, including one man who was nailed to a gate by his hands; prayer houses and cemeteries were desecrated; Torah scrolls were ripped up and trampled underfoot. In Prague there was "no house without someone who had been killed, wounded, or beaten to a pulp."[30] Contemporaries linked this persecution to the destruction of Jerusalem and described it in biblical images: "The dead bodies fell as dung upon the open field."[31]

Yet the worst was still to come. In December 1744 Maria Theresa decreed that all Prague's Jews were to leave the city by year's end, that is, immediately.[32] There had been a Jewish community in Prague since the Middle Ages; at well over ten thousand people, it made up around a quarter of the city's total population and was by far the largest Ashkenazi community in Europe. According to legend, it had already been established at the time of the Temple's destruction, "to the honor and glory of Israel and the entire exile, only daughter of her mother [Jerusalem]." It was considered the capital city and chief ornament of European Judaism: "Who will depict the magnificence of our synagogues, our houses of learning, our great palaces, built to an incomparable height from marble, our town hall with the Tower of David, a building that turns every head?" For centuries, the Jewish quarter's denizens had been the pride of their people: "thousands of active men, men of piety and asceticism, powerful rabbis, celebrated Gaonim [textual scholars] without number."[33]

When the writ of expulsion was announced, leaders of the Jewish community attributed the disaster to the notorious "Jew-haters" in Maria Theresa's entourage. Above all, they suspected the Bohemian court chancellor, Kinsky, of having turned her against them. The queen herself, it was repeatedly claimed with a confidence as great as it was unfounded, was all-gracious and all-merciful and must therefore have been misled.[34] She had to be persuaded to put off the decree until an investigation had been carried out to find and punish the real culprits, the "misbegotten sons of our people,"[35] rather than making the innocent majority pay for the sins of a few.

Several influential court Jews had access to European potentates as sources of ready cash and exotic goods. In Vienna, too, there was a fairly small community of Jewish merchants and purveyors to the court. They resided in the Judenstadt quarter, later known as Leopoldstadt, where they enjoyed similar privileges and exemptions to other courtiers. They were subject to the jurisdiction of the grand marshal of the court and were allowed to trade exclusively in cash, jewelry, tobacco, and delicacies.[36] The activities of these influential merchants reached all the way to Prince Charles of Lorraine, the imperial widow, the elector of Mainz, the kings of England and Denmark, and even the pope. With not a moment to lose, the Jews of Vienna and Prague now set about activating their commercial and kinship networks throughout the Empire and far beyond, in Dresden and Hannover, Hamburg, Frankfurt and Mainz, Augsburg, Bamberg and Würzburg, Holland and England, Venice, Mantua, Turin, and Rome.[37] Everywhere they urged their influential coreligionists to use their contacts with the powerful to intervene with the queen on their behalf. Given the need for haste, Jewish couriers bearing the call for help throughout Europe were specifically exempted from the Sabbath rest.[38] After all, it was only a matter of days before the decree took effect. Directly appealing to the queen for clemency was out of the question, given her refusal to accept petitions from Jews. And no one at court was willing to incur her displeasure by speaking up for the Jewish community. Among her ministers, "not one dared utter so much as a word, still less submit a memorandum." Wolf Wertheimer, court Jew in Augsburg, was informed from Vienna that the queen had been "so enraged" by the rumors from Prague "that some good fellows, upon mentioning something in the Jews' favor, had been reprimanded with a scathing torrent of abuse. Unfortunately, nothing can be done to soothe her temper." There had even been an order to deny Jews entry at court and arrest anyone who dared defy it.[39] In their desperation, the Jews contemplated openly addressing Maria Theresa on the street on her way to church. Yet this also proved impossible: the queen was nine months' pregnant at the time and rarely left her private chambers.[40]

Those Jews who regarded Maria Theresa as a benevolent sovereign and the Bohemian chancellor Kinsky as their sworn enemy were sorely mistaken. It was Kinsky who strongly advised the queen against implementing the decree, even as he took pains not to appear as a friend to the Jews (as indeed he was not). In a written opinion he conceded that the Jews, where they appeared in greater numbers, made themselves an "object of revulsion to bourgeois society". Only a handful made an honest living, while the rest seemed intent on fleecing Christians of their worldly goods. Nonetheless, he gave sound reasons against the expulsion, citing both Christian neighborly love and economic considerations. The Jews of Prague would be unable to obey the queen's command as quickly as she wanted, since the many children, elderly, and infirm among them could not possibly be expected to trudge through the rain and snow in the depths of winter. There were not enough carriages to transport so many thousands of people with all their belongings; many would perish en route or "considerably add to the number of vagrants wandering the land."[41] Above all, Kinsky warned against the economic consequences of expulsion. At least the rich Jews should be spared, since commercial activity in Bohemia would grind to a halt without them and many private people, not to mention state finances, depended on their loans and taxes.

Both arguments fell on deaf ears. While Maria Theresa grudgingly agreed to put off implementing the order until the end of January, she was not prepared to abandon it. The matter clearly lay close to her heart. She registered her mounting impatience in a series of handwritten notes: "All the Jews must go and [I have] made this clear often enough."[42] A commission led by the Bohemian council president, Leopold von Kolowrat, was tasked with implementing the order, but the matter was handled in dilatory fashion and postponed twice again, until March 1745. Then the royal command was finally carried out, albeit still with some hesitation on the part of the authorities. With that, the largest Jewish community in the Habsburg empire was dissolved; over ten thousand people were forced out of their homes. Many reportedly died on the road.[43] It was to be the last great expulsion of Jews in Old Europe before the era of the Holocaust.

The Jews resettled just outside Prague and attempted to go about their normal business in the city by day. In June 1746 Maria Theresa responded by extending the ban to a radius of two hours' journey from Prague. Anyone caught sheltering a Jew in the no-go areas would have to pay a stiff penalty. When officials inquired if the new edict applied to the Jews who had already been living near Prague before the decree, the queen replied by hand: "They too must go," and set August 1746 as a deadline.[44] The task was removed from the all-too-irresolute Bohemian commission and transferred to the military instead. By the late summer of 1746 there were no more Jews in Prague and its environs; only a few bedridden invalids, elderly, infants, and heavily pregnant women were still staying in a Jewish lazaretto near the city. In informing Maria Theresa of the successful execution of her decree, the Bohemian governor's office also drew attention to the negative effects that were already making themselves felt. Yet far from heeding their concerns, Maria Theresa now widened the decree to encompass all Jews living in Bohemia and Moravia. In addition, she strictly prohibited expelled Jews from taking refuge in any of her other domains, including Hungary. This order encountered even fiercer resistance. The estates repeatedly raised their objections with the queen, calculating the expected economic cost down to the last penny. Trade in Bohemia had mainly been in the hands of the Jews. Bohemian nobles relied on Jewish merchants to market the product of their estates, while Jews supplied artisans with the raw materials for their trade. Now that Jewish commerce had largely shut down, commodities became scarce and expensive as the few non-Jewish merchants seized the opportunity to drive up prices. Even the craftsmen of Prague, otherwise not known for their sympathy to the Jews, complained about the damage to their livelihoods.

The various efforts of Jews themselves to gain high-profile advocates for their cause met with considerable success.[45] The elector of Mainz intervened with a personal letter to Maria Theresa, while even the pope and the Ottoman sultan campaigned on their behalf. When her husband, Francis Stephen, passed through the Bohemian town of Prossnitz in mid-January, the entire Jewish community, young and old, came out to meet him with Torah scroll and canopy in a grand supplicatory procession. The head of the community prostrated himself before the coach and begged for mercy, prompting Francis Stephen to open the carriage window and promise help.[46] Yet all these intercessions could do nothing to make Maria Theresa change her mind. From Prague came the disillusioned report that the queen, while acknowledging that Jews might be honorable people, simply did not want them in her lands—an attitude that rational argument was powerless to shift.[47] Nonetheless, the command was eventually rescinded, mainly because Maria Theresa could no longer ignore the repeated petitions of the Bohemian estates. It was the time of Haugwitz's great financial reforms, and she desperately needed the estates' cooperation. In the end, she reluctantly yielded to the objections of the Bohemian deportation commission, which had the support of Haugwitz, and put off implementing the order for the next ten years. In the meantime, she ordered an investigation into how the Jews could be expelled within six years without detriment to the country. The price they had to pay for their reprieve was a so-called tolerance contribution to the sum of 300,000 guilders. In September 1748 the Jews of Prague were allowed to return to their utterly devastated and plundered ghetto. Plans to expel them from all Bohemia and Moravia were quietly shelved.

Maria Theresa's undisguised hostility stands in stark contrast to the paeans of praise the Jews showered on her on every occasion—even in Prague. In the Jewish chronicle *Igereth Machalath*, which also recounts the horrors of the mass expulsion, she is extolled for her "wisdom, beauty, and good works," while her accession to the throne is seen as divinely ordained.[48] At special events it was taken for granted that Jewish communities would compete with other civic corporations to present the monarch with the most lavish symbolic and material offerings. In 1751, for example, the Jews of Prague dedicated a public "cry of thanks" to the empress following the victory at Kolín, and in 1780 the chief rabbi of Prague, Landau, delivered a eulogy for her upon her death.[49] Even in confidential letters, her name was always mentioned respectfully and with the formulaic addition, "exalted be her honor." And although the community leaders were otherwise entirely realistic in assessing their own situation, they held fast with astonishing tenacity to the belief that Maria Theresa, their gracious sovereign, was well disposed toward them and had been deceived by her advisers. To understand this attitude, it must be borne in mind that there was simply no other recourse open to them at the time. Jews depended for their very existence on imperial or royal protection. Ever since the thirteenth century, when the Staufer emperor, Frederick II, had offered them his imperial patronage as *servi camerae* or *Kammerknechte* (servants of the chamber), they had owed their most important privileges, and even their right to remain in the Empire, to the Roman-German emperors.[50] Responsibility for protecting the Jews lay primarily with the emperor, not with territorial lords, and Maria Theresa did as little as her predecessors to interfere with this formal arrangement.[51] Indeed, it lay in her own best interests, since her sovereign authority would suffer damage if she could not effectively defend the Jews against mob violence. All experience to the contrary, the Jews therefore desperately held fast to this sanctuary for want of any alternative.

Jewish loyalty to the Archducal House was invoked in a widely circulated pamphlet that appeared in 1745, during the War of Succession, under the name of *Löwle Kemmel*. A "heroic lay" in the style of Old Testament chronicles, it celebrates Maria Theresa as a victorious queen who had defeated her enemies with God's help, a new Judith, Susanna, and desirable lover in the manner of the *Song of Songs*: "Her arm is strong and mighty in battle. Her enemies cannot prevail against her, the LORD protects her with his shield, and she performs wonders matched by no man." The chronicler castigates his fellow Jews for their treason and praises Maria Theresa for driving them out of Bohemia. Taking a leaf from the Old Testament books of prophecy, he interprets the sufferings of the people of Israel as a just punishment sent them by God: "But we have sinned against the LORD by consorting with the queen's enemy and selling him the city of Prague."[52] The children of Abraham "have been condemned in the sight of the queen, and our race is become an abomination, and has grown foul-smelling in Bohemia. . . . Behold, they have brought this disaster upon themselves; for the queen will not have acted without cause."[53] Over hundreds of verses, the writer extols the virtues of the queen, who has shown mercy on the Jews despite their shameful treachery: "A song has been made in remembrance that we have been allowed back into this land and can eat garlic, and onions and shallots"—and so on and so forth in ever new grotesque variations.[54] Needless to say, this panegyric was not really written by a Jew; the author's name was fictitious. The bizarre epic flowed from the quill of the Nuremberg lawyer and prolific scribbler Christoph Gottlieb Richter, later known as the author of the *Lebens- und Staats-Geschichte der Frauen Maria Theresia* (*Life and State History of Lady Maria Theresa*), who had permitted himself a literary jest with this pseudo-Jewish text.[55] Yet the work evidently appealed to a Christian readership—so much so, in fact, that Richter followed it with a string of similar publications under various Jewish-sounding pseudonyms, including one on the Seven Years' War. The Jews of Prague, not Maria Theresa, were the victims of his satire. Her conduct toward the Jewish community clearly did her great credit in the eyes of the Christian public.

Alfred von Arneth asked in his biography how the untold misery of the banished could have failed to touch Maria Theresa's heart and why economic arguments also failed to persuade her. He saw the reason in her fixed conviction that she was doing God's work in banishing the Jews—those notorious traitors, swindlers, and unregenerate Christ-killers—from her realm. According to Christian doctrine, their refusal to recognize Jesus Christ as the Messiah and their role in delivering him to be crucified accounted for their ongoing bondage until the Last Judgment. Finally, Maria Theresa knew herself to be acting in line with the tradition of her forebears[56]—even if this tradition now appeared economically irrational and anachronistic in the eyes of her enlightened officials. In 1670 Leopold I had thrown the Jews out of Vienna at the request of the town's non-Jewish merchants after his Spanish wife had blamed them for her miscarriage. Maria Theresa's father had taken an even harsher approach. The so-called *Familiantengesetz* of 1726 had set precise upper limits on the number of Jewish families domiciled in Habsburg lands: 8,451 in Bohemia, 5,106 in Moravia, and 119 in Silesia. To ensure that this number would not be exceeded in future, only the eldest son from each family was entitled to marry—a regulation, incidentally, likewise enforced by Frederick II of Prussia, otherwise vaunted for his religious tolerance. Wealthy Jews could still buy themselves exemption, however. In 1738 Charles VI had ordered the Jews out of Silesia and expelled all nonprivileged Jews from Bohemia, although the provincial estates had protested the measure at the time. When Maria Theresa came to the throne, she took up where her father had left off and reissued his order of expulsion, although not all noble estate owners chose to obey it. The order affected over nine hundred people in Breslau alone.[57] Still, the actual implementation of the decree proved as ineffectual as the 1745 expulsion from Bohemia and Moravia. Fortunately for those concerned, the estates continued to block such measures.[58] Following the failure of her expulsion policy, Maria Theresa was forced to return to the customary strategy of restricted toleration and financial exactions. Only those who were useful to the state and could afford to pay the steep tolerance levies were allowed to remain. In 1753 and 1764 she released new statutes that synthesized, consolidated, and partially tightened the earlier restrictions on Jews.[59] These were accompanied by repeated payments and controls; a quarterly reporting requirement was even introduced in 1764. All this was intended to ensure that the prescribed upper limits for Jewish subjects were not surpassed.[60] Unlike in other monarchies, Maria Theresa's Jewish policy was not motivated primarily by economic concerns. Until her death, it was her innermost desire "to reduce the numbers of Jews here, and by no means, on any pretext, increase them further."[61]

"Incurable Mangy Sheep": Crypto-Protestants

Protestants were Acatholics too, and their Habsburg rulers likewise felt compelled to "stamp out" their "false creed." Yet their legal situation was different from that of the Jews. In the Holy Roman Empire, Protestant princes and cities had enjoyed legal equality with their Catholic counterparts since the Peace of Westphalia, at the latest; confessional parity prevailed in imperial institutions. Yet Protestants, like Catholics, were not free to worship as they pleased. The peace treaty concerned corporative legal entitlements and had nothing to say about individual beliefs. Sovereign rulers still determined their subjects' denomination, even if they could no longer change this at will. Nonconforming minorities were protected in the public profession of their faith only where and to the extent it had demonstrably already been practiced in 1624. For the rest, rulers were expected only "to tolerate" subjects practicing their anomalous faith in the privacy of their own homes and attending divine worship in neighboring Protestant territories. Those who wished to emigrate should be allowed to do so on fair terms. All this meant that religious freedom was a historically established, contractually secured concession, not an abstract, individual basic right. This concession could be fiercely contested in individual cases. Local confessional conflicts were therefore still common in the eighteenth century. In such cases, Protestant subjects found political support in the *Corpus evangelicorum*, the organization of Protestant estates in the Imperial Diet.[62]

FIGURE 46A-D. Four angels at the base of the Marian column in
Vienna slaying four monsters: heresy, hunger, pestilence, and war

Even the limited protections afforded minorities of different faiths in
the Holy Roman Empire under the Treaty of Westphalia were denied
Protestants in the Austrian hereditary lands. The Habsburgs had seen
to it that the toleration provisions did not apply to them (with a few
exceptions such as in Silesia).[63] Indeed, they believed themselves both

obliged and perfectly entitled "to eradicate creeping doctrinal errors through well-ordered statutes": the sovereign had "a free hand to regulate religious affairs in the German hereditary lands entirely as he pleases," and this meant, in extreme cases, separating the "mangy incurable sheep from the healthy flock."[64] In this respect, too, Maria Theresa was acting firmly in the tradition of her forebears, something that increasingly scandalized enlightened public opinion outside her lands. "Those professing the evangelical faith have always suffered terribly in the hereditary lands of the Most Serene House of Austria. But in recent times, when people have been priding themselves on their reasonableness, fairness, and humanity, new heights of oppression have been reached," one Protestant commentator wrote.[65]

After the rigid re-Catholicization policy of the seventeenth century, the Habsburgs thought they had successfully driven heresy out of their "German" lands, if not from Hungary and Bohemia. By the 1730s, however, it had become apparent that they were mistaken. Protestants had proved adept at hiding their "false beliefs" behind a façade of conformity. In the alpine valleys in the region between Upper Austria, Styria, Carinthia, the Salzkammergut, and the Prince-Bishopric of Salzburg (the last not under Habsburg dominion), there were still numerous peasant households which for generations had secretly held fast to their Protestant faith under the most adverse conditions. In this they were aided by a close-knit network of fellow believers, the generally isolated setting of their farms, support from neighboring Protestant territories and wandering preachers, and, above all, their well-guarded treasury of Protestant literature: Luther bibles, evangelical devotional works, prayer books, and hymnals, carefully hidden and sometimes even disguised with fake covers. As would be seen, many of these peasants and farm hands (both male and female) could read to a high standard, had a remarkably thorough grasp of theology, and strongly identified as Protestant—although or perhaps because they had to conceal this from their Catholic environment. This was no easy matter and gave rise to considerable soul-searching. Just how far could they pretend to be good Catholics? To what extent could they participate in "mangled popish" ceremonies without risking their spiritual salvation? There was disagreement among Protestant theologians over how a Christian could and should live by the gospel under conditions of persecution. In the hereditary lands, a catalogue was circulated containing "guidelines for how Protestants hiding in the Land above the Enns are to conduct themselves." It did much to salve the troubled conscience of crypto-Protestants, instructing them to greet Catholic priests "with courtesy and friendliness and diligently appear at their parish services." They were allowed to go to confession but need only declare as many sins as they saw fit. They should keep images of the saints, rosaries, and holy water in their houses but not make use of them. Otherwise, they should avoid broaching theological topics in taverns and trust nobody, not even their own domestic servants. The biggest problem was the Eucharist, which the Papists did not receive in both forms, as Christ had commanded. If they were unable to take part in a nearby Protestant communion at least once a year, then the faithful should drink the wine given them after Mass while "secretly reciting the words of institution." They should put off extreme unction for as long as possible, but if it could no longer be avoided "then take it, for it cannot damn you." Only the Tridentine creed was a step too far: "you must not affirm it but abhor it in your hearts."[66] Not all Protestants were so accommodating, however. In his widely circulated *Evangelischer Sendbrief* (*Evangelical Open Letter*), Joseph Schaitberger, a Protestant exiled from Salzburg on account of his beliefs, rejected the "hypocritical faith of the mouth" in favor of open confession. One should not "pull the foreign yoke with the unbelievers" but stand up for God's word, even if this meant having to emigrate.[67]

Catholic authorities, meanwhile, were ever less prepared to put up with outward conformity and mere lip service; they wanted to reach people's hearts and souls as well. Increased pressure through missionary work, especially on the part of the Jesuits, revealed the extent to which apparently observant parishioners had strayed from the path of orthodoxy: "Precisely the official investigation prompted Protestants to become more self-assertive."[68] More and more underground Protestants now publicly declared their faith and demanded permission to worship in private. In 1731 a petition calling for Protestant preachers to be admitted was signed by nineteen thousand subjects of the Prince-Bishop of

Salzburg and submitted to the *Corpus evangelicorum*. The archbishop reacted by summarily expelling all the "misbelievers" from his territory. The forced departure of almost thirty thousand Salzburg Protestants in 1731–32 was perceived throughout the Empire as an unprecedented scandal, one that Frederick William I of Prussia, who resettled a large number of them in his country, was able to exploit to his considerable economic and political advantage. In the neighboring Austrian hereditary lands, events in Salzburg also caused disquiet. It was evident there, too, that the "ash-covered embers" had not yet been extinguished and had now "blazed up in bright flames."[69] Emissaries of the *Corpus evangelicorum* offered the Protestants their support and promoted mass emigration. Charles VI set up reformation commissions and ramped up the pressure on the nonconformists, whom he now declared to be rebels. Yet he did not wish to make the same mistake as the prince-archbishop of Salzburg and lose thousands of valuable skilled workers to emigration. Instead, he resorted to the means of transmigration, ordering the most intransigent heretics to be deported to the southeastern periphery of his lands, to Hungary and Transylvania. These were thinly populated regions where Protestants had to be tolerated anyway on the basis of longstanding privileges. Between 1734 and 1737, around eight hundred people who had proved stubbornly resistant to conversion were transmigrated from Carinthia and the Salzkammergut or forcibly drafted into the military (see color plate 18).

With the change of throne and the War of Succession, the problem of underground Protestantism receded temporarily into the background. At the beginning of 1752, however, Maria Theresa placed the topic at the top of her agenda after isolated local conflicts broke out in Upper Austria and Carinthia and subjects collectively professed the evangelical faith. On March 17 she convened a Court Conference to discuss the newly virulent "errors in religion," calling in the imperial confessors, Ignaz Bittermann and Ignaz Kampmüller, as well.[70] It was agreed that a commission on religion, chaired by Court Councillor Doblhoff, would be launched with the task of systematically investigating the situation on the ground. The inquiries it made in regions notoriously prone to heresy not only revealed the shocking extent of "infection" with the "plague," "bane," or "tare" of Protestantism, but also the root causes: the clergy's irresponsible "forbearance and indifference" and grave deficiencies in pastoral care. To rectify the situation, an edict on religion was promulgated building on the strategy pursued by Charles VI. Many more such edicts were to follow.[71]

The basic principles underlying this law were set out in a comprehensive nineteen-point paper.[72] It stated that the empress-queen, in her commitment to "the temporal as well as spiritual welfare of her subjects," could not permit "emigration that caused both the soul and the subject to be lost." The "weeds" that had proliferated unchecked for so long could not be allowed to "continue growing." All the spiritual and temporal remedies at her disposal had to be applied immediately to guide the already "infected flock" back onto "the road to salvation" and "gradually make clean the land sullied with false doctrine." Maria Theresa blamed the apostasy primarily on ignorance and misconceptions about Catholicism; she was clearly unable to comprehend that the theologically well-versed crypto-Protestants might have a firmer grasp of the opposing doctrine than many of the obedient, mostly illiterate Catholic sheep. It was imperative that "this source of ignorance be stopped through the apostolic zeal of pious missionaries." She acknowledged that this would take time and money. Success would not come quickly, "especially among hardened spirits and those in whom heresy has struck deep roots." They were to be "given time and space, that they might be enlightened by the missionaries and brought to see the error of their ways." Yet the "Principia" betray a certain skepticism regarding the abilities of these missionaries. They should not interfere with the normal work of parish priests. Instead, they would be given precise instructions "that they might temper their zeal, exercise great patience and meekness, talk to people at their level, and win hearts through their upright conduct and loving kindness." Particular attention was to be paid to ensuring an adequate supply of spiritual directors, orthodox schoolmasters, and good Catholic books. Some of Maria Theresa's advisers saw peasant literacy as the root of the problem, pointing to the staunch Catholicism of the illiterate Carinthians and Slovenes, and advised her to shut down schools in the infected areas. She chose not to accept their recommendations.[73]

Drastic measures were announced against the foreign agents, book-sellers, and organizers of conventicles who spread the poison. They would be arrested, their guilt ascertained "in accordance with the law," and the documents forwarded to the relevant "religious consessus," or church council, to decide their punishment. The court—that is, the Court Chancellery and ultimately the monarch herself—reserved the right to determine which of the most dangerous troublemakers and rabble-rousers would be deported. Heretical widows would have their children taken away from them and placed in good Catholic homes. There was also a novel plan to establish "conversion houses" in the in-fected areas, where those deemed highly unlikely to convert "without such total separation and continuous strenuous application" would re-ceive compulsory religious instruction. The church itself was supposed to finance all these measures. To this end, Maria Theresa established a religious fund to channel payments from richly endowed clergy, al-though the contributions ended up falling well short of expectations.[74] In addition, no one could buy a house until the priest had attested to the orthodoxy of their beliefs or own books without the priest's signa-ture and seal of approval. Finally, Protestants would now be denied pub-lic burial in a cemetery, having to make do with secret interment in a "remote location" instead. Over time, it was hoped, this suite of mea-sures would do away with the plague of heresy.

In the infected regions, work on systematically eradicating the evil immediately got underway. The regions were split up into districts and over seventy missionary stations established over a wide area, each con-sisting of a "spiritual" and a "secular" arm. The secular commissioners of religion were expressly given authority over local landowners; they interrogated suspects, confiscated Protestant literature, examined newly arrived settlers and officials, monitored conversations about religion in taverns, checked to see whether children were regularly attending cat-echism classes, and imposed a variety of sanctions on offenses against the edict on religion, ranging from fines to the pillory and imprison-ment. They were aided in their task of sniffing out heresy by a legally mandated obligation to report suspicious behavior. Anyone who de-nounced family members or neighbors would be handsomely rewarded;

conversely, those withholding such information risked severe punishment.[75] At the same time, clergymen set out on the arduous work of conversion. Besides missionaries stationed at a fixed location, there were also itinerant preachers who roamed the countryside, talking to everyone they encountered and instructing them in the true Catholic faith. They all had to report back twice a month to their superiors, who would relay news of their success to the religious authorities in Graz, Linz, or Klagenfurt, which in turn were accountable to their respective territory's central administrative body, the Representation and Chamber.[76] Ideally, all information would be gathered in the Bohemian-Austrian Court Chancellery in Vienna, which reported directly to the empress. Maria Theresa devoted considerable attention to the matter and took a keen personal interest in the missionary reports.[77]

The referral of particularly recalcitrant heretics to conversion houses was decided on by the religious authorities. Managed by civilians and guarded by soldiers, the houses were situated at strategic locations such as Klagenfurt, Kremsmünster, Rottenmann, or Judenburg. They were modestly furnished buildings, on the whole, with just a few rooms where up to ten heretics could be confined and reeducated by a missionary or parish priest. The funds needed to maintain these houses were always in short supply. Hiring, furnishing, and heating the premises proved extraordinarily difficult, as did guarding the inmates and providing for their needs. There were escape attempts, harsh punishments, and occasional deaths due to hunger or cold.[78] Above all, the houses served to isolate particularly prominent, influential, and stubborn heretics from their social surroundings, so making them more susceptible to conversion. Some were confined for only a month, others for several months, some for up to a year. But such lengthy spells were exceptional; in the end, peasant households were to be spared excessive economic hardship. Sometimes the farmer and his wife were incarcerated in turn so that their livelihoods might not be ruined.[79] The aim was to get people to solemnly recant their heresy by taking a sacred oath on the Tridentine creed, preferably in full public view on Maundy Thursday in their home parishes. Should they then relapse into their old ways—should Lutheran books be found in their possession, for example—they would no longer be heretics requiring conversion but perjurers deserving exemplary punishment.

Those who could not bring themselves to take the oath on the Tridentine creed became candidates for the next wave of transmigration. The empress herself had the final say on the matter. Within the next four years, around three thousand souls were deported from the hereditary lands to Hungary and Transylvania.[80] Deportees were forbidden from setting their domestic affairs in order and bidding farewell to their families. Parents were separated from their underage children: those older than seven were placed in an orphanage, those younger were given to Catholic families to be brought up in the true faith. Only unweaned infants were allowed to stay with their mothers. Maria Theresa gave these arrangements her explicit approval.[81] Deportees were made to foot the bill for their own transportation; paupers received some money from the religious fund to defray their expenses. The marches to the extreme southeast of the Habsburg empire lasted many weeks; more than a few perished on the difficult journey. Having arrived at their destination, deportees generally had no means of making a living. While the authorities were required to convert their property—assuming they had any—into cash and send it on to them, this occurred sluggishly or not at all. Many people tried to return to their homes; more than half died or disappeared from the sight of the authorities soon after their arrival. Only a very few succeeded in making a new life for themselves abroad. The transplantation was not just a humanitarian disaster; it was also an abject failure as a project of population policy.

From 1753 onward the *Corpus evangelicorum* repeatedly made formal intercessions at the Imperial Diet protesting against these tribulations and persecutions involving "prison terms and corporal punishments, restraints, beatings, confiscation of property."[82] The empress responded by claiming that the issue was not really religion but rather rebellion and subversion, "masquerading under the guise of religion." Nobody had been clapped in irons, only benign means had been used against the heretics, transmigrations were not rushed, everyone was given ample time to reconsider, everything was proceeding lawfully—in short, nobody was suffering the slightest hardship.[83] Still, Maria Theresa felt the need to publish a detailed refutation of these charges, with all the necessary documents attached, in a bid to demonstrate imperial impartiality toward the different confessions in the Empire and respect for the Westphalian order.

Anti-Protestant persecution eased somewhat during the Seven Years' War, perhaps in part because Maria Theresa did not want to provide the Prussian king with fodder for propaganda in his ostensibly religious war.[84] Missionary activity intensified when peace returned, yet no further transmigrations took place for many years.[85] A final major phase of persecution, claiming 178 victims, broke out in 1773–74 in Stadl, a parish in the Mur valley in Upper Styria.[86] The area had already been identified twenty years earlier as a hotbed of heresy. There had been numerous conversions at the time; the ringleaders and recalcitrants had been sent to the conversion house and subsequently deported. The catalyst for the new wave of persecution was the pronounced missionary zeal of an ambitious chaplain named Matthias Cajetan Michelitsch who had requested and received support for his harsh inquisitorial methods from the bishop of Seckau, Johann Philipp, Count Spaur. Backed by the bishop's guidelines, but also by the denunciation order in the 1752 edict on religion, the chaplain used the confessional to force the people of Stadl to denounce the heretics in their midst. Before, during, and after confession, parishioners were asked to nominate anyone who, to their knowledge, had betrayed any hint of false doctrine. Telltale signs included being able to read well, debating articles of faith, avoiding holy water, and never publicly praying the rosary.[87] If penitents were suspected of holding back information, they could be denied absolution from sin, refused communion, and hence be faced with the dreadful prospect of eternal hellfire. Those suspected of heresy themselves had to denounce their coreligionists in order to prove that they were genuinely willing to be converted, and thereby escape the conversion house, compulsory recruitment, or transmigration. The fact that denunciations were extorted from "father against son, son against father, wife against husband, and servant against master" seemed outrageous, since it called into question the very foundations of social order, loyalty, and hierarchy.[88]

The fruit of this ambitious new tactic was resistance—not just from Protestants, but also from many good Catholic parishioners appalled to see the sacrament of confession so misused. In early 1772 they dispatched a farmhand called Adam Reiter to Vienna to plead their case at court. Once arrived, Reiter somehow got in touch with the elderly imperial-royal court and war agent, Joseph Mathola de Zolnay, who offered his assistance. Mathola, himself a Protestant, purported to be more influential than he was. He interceded with the responsible official in Stadl on behalf of his coreligionists, pointing out "that Her Imperial Royal Apostolic Majesty persecutes nobody on grounds of wrongful religion.[89] In doing so, however, he himself came under suspicion of fomenting unrest. Nonetheless, in April 1772 a new delegation of peasants set out on the long journey to Vienna, again using Mathola de Zolnay to seek permission at the highest level for the free exercise of religion or, failing that, emigration.[90] The Court Chancellery referred the matter back to the Inner Austrian territorial government, which in turn assigned it to the steward of the manor. This steward, a certain Rauch, now made a fatal mistake: under intense interrogation, he had his peasants write down the names of everyone who had instigated the delegation to Vienna, falsely promising that the more names they revealed, the less they need fear transmigration. This resulted in a mass outing of crypto-Protestants. Almost four hundred names appeared on the list, including those of dozens of children.

This "Evangelical List" was the cause of great consternation in Vienna. After all the time and effort that had been spent on missionary work, how could so many subjects still openly profess Protestantism and brazenly demand the *liberum exercitium religionis*? A new committee of inquiry was appointed; its chair, Wolfgang Count Stubenberg, submitted his detailed report to the Court Chancellery on March 24, 1773.[91] The unwonted missionary fervor the investigation brought to light was too much even for the empress.[92] Two imperatives conflicted here: on the one hand, it was vitally important that every last heretic be tracked down and converted; on the other, it was undesirable that the full extent of the contagion be revealed for all to see, since this would only encourage the heretics and further increase the risk of infection. The commission therefore criticized the excessive ambition of the chaplain and bishop, accusing them of overstepping their pastoral authority. The criticism was not motivated by any empathy for the persecuted Protestants, however. What stood behind it was, rather, the new approach to ecclesiastical policy pursued at court since 1768.[93] The Court Chancellery responded to the Stubenberg report by assigning the clergy primary responsibility for the "public outbreak" of heresy. It would be best if the whole debacle could be hushed up. This was impossible, however, since too much was now at stake: "the restoration of the disturbed public peace, the sovereign right of superintendence in church affairs, the avoidance of future schisms, the temporal and eternal salvation of so many subjects and their descendants, [and] also putting the clergy back in their place, that they might no longer do harm through their innovations."[94] The refusal of confession, absolution, and communion was tantamount to excommunication. In the Court Chancellery's view, such ecclesiastical penalties did not just concern the *forum internum*, the church's power over the conscience, they also had consequences for public order. They therefore fell under secular jurisdiction and could only be imposed with the sovereign's consent.

Maria Theresa lent her full support to the Court Chancellery's criticism and sent a sharply worded letter to the bishop of Seckau, accusing him of misusing the confessional and breaking the seal of confession.[95] The overly enthusiastic inquisitors Matthias Michelitsch and Philipp Karl Rauch were relieved of their posts, and four additional priests and a new mission head were appointed. Maria Theresa personally stipulated that in future, "force, harsh punishments, and other measures likely to cause so great a furor, are to be avoided as far as possible. Heretics should be guided to lasting conversion through . . . careful instruction." Yet if the seduced got off lightly, no such mercy should be shown their seducers; here the "most severe corporal punishments" were in order. With regard to the "transplantation of all too hardened sectarians," Maria Theresa decreed that "if such [transplantation] cannot entirely be avoided," each individual case should first be brought to the court's attention.[96]

The new mission head, an unusually meticulous and conscientious priest by the name of Gletler, now oversaw the office systematically yet in a spirit of "love and gentleness." It is to him that we owe the pains-taking documentation of the mission's operations. His approach to missionary work went down in history as the paradigmatic "Stadl method." He never tired of quizzing subjects about each other, inter-rogating suspects—albeit no longer during confession—and finally either converting them to the true faith or having them deported.[97] Some were the same people who had already come to the authorities' attention some twenty years earlier, taken an oath to the Catholic creed, and had now perjured themselves; others were the children left behind by those deported at the time. Gletler was painfully aware of the mission's dilemma: he used all the psychological and physical tools at his disposal to achieve his goal of leading wayward sheep back to the church, only to be confronted with the shattering awareness that most of the confessions he had extracted under duress had been false, insin-cere, and hypocritical. There was no sure way of telling whether some-one's faith was genuine or feigned; what went on inside people's minds and souls was hidden from view. Forced denunciations produced noth-ing but distrust and unrest, forced conformity nothing but misery and dissimulation.

The extant Stadl interrogation files provide haunting testimony to this dilemma, even if they are filtered through the inquisitor's perspec-tive.[98] Subjects displayed a wide range of reactions and strategies when interrogated. Some wept, babbled, trembled, and cowered, while others held staunchly to their beliefs. Some identified themselves as good Catholics, others admitted to being Protestant, some even said they saw no difference between the two. Some denounced their neighbors with-out hesitation, others stubbornly refused to play the role of Judas. Some grew flustered and contradicted themselves, others maintained an air of unflappable calm. An illiterate farmer called Joseph Oberreuter said that "the clergy were only out to seduce people, they had lost the gift of true faith, and simple peasants [had] received [this gift] instead, for it was written: *revelasti ea parvulis* [thou hast revealed these things unto babes]."[99] Like Martin Luther when summoned before Charles V at the Diet of Worms, he vowed to change his ways if "convicted by the clear testimony of holy scripture."[100]

One example may serve to give faces and names to the fates of many: the Rieberer family. Urban Rieberer, born in 1719 and thus about the same age as Maria Theresa, was a serf in the seignory of Schwarzenberg in Einach, that is, he was personally subject to the manorial lord and owed him feudal dues. He was literate and owned a collection of Protestant books. Under interrogation, he stated that he had been raised Catholic but had spent the last thirty years as a Protestant "and wanted to remain and die so." He had no wish to be "better instructed," he would "rather move away. He says, Christ was not asked whether he was Lutheran or Catholic but how he lived, he thinks the same way." In December 1773 Rieberer was delivered to the conversion house in Judenburg, where he declared himself willing to convert. Returned to his home village, he recanted and confessed that he had never seriously intended to abandon his Protestant beliefs. He was then deported and died on August 2, 1774, shortly after arriving in Transylvania. His wife, Helena Riebererin, née Hasenbacherin, whom he had married in January 1752, likewise came under suspicion. She swore by the Tridentine creed, fell into apostasy, and so made herself guilty of perjury. This brought her a spell in jail, where she was still languishing when her husband and two of her children were deported in early 1774. After a year's imprisonment, she was transferred to the poorhouse, where she died "of emaciation" on March 13, 1776. Her eldest son, Sebastian, born shortly before his parents' marriage on January 9, 1752, had been brought up Protestant and lived in the same village as a bachelor farmhand. He likewise owned several forbidden books and "shows an impudent liberty in confessing his faith, otherwise a skillful, handsome man." His sister Maria was a single maidservant, raised in the Protestant faith like her brother, and was also found in possession of illicit literature; she too openly professed her faith. Both were deported to Transylvania along with their father. Only the youngest daughter, Anna, stayed behind; barely fifteen at the time, she was sent to the orphanage in Graz in January 1774. Maria did not long survive transportation; she died in 1775 at the age of nineteen. Only Sebastian succeeded in establishing a new life in Transylvania. He married a widow from Upper Austria, a fellow deportee, and earned a living as a "very hardworking carpenter." They had four children together. Unlike his wife, who died while giving birth to their last child, Sebastian Rieberer survived the downfall of the old order. He passed away in 1820, at the age of sixty-nine, "from a cold."[101]

Urban Rieberer was among the peasants who set out for Vienna to seek justice or at least mercy from the sovereign. All these attempts achieved nothing or made matters worse for the Protestants. The first two delegations to Vienna from Stadl, as well as Mathola de Zolnay's attempts at mediation, proved counterproductive: they not only resulted in the fatal "Evangelical List," they also placed the intermediary in serious legal difficulties. Mathola de Zolnay was arrested as an "agitator", only escaping harsh punishment due to his advanced age and his written promise never again to side with the Protestant cause.[102] Urban Rieberer and a companion never even made it to Vienna; they were forced to turn back after being swindled out of their travel money. The journey further incriminated Rieberer in the eyes of the authorities and led to his internment in the conversion house. In September 1772 the peasants Hans Reiter and Hans Waiger made their way to Vienna to find out what had become of Mathola de Zolnay's promised intercession. The agent took them to see a "lord, where the memoranda submitted to the empress tend to end up," but the peasants understood not a word of what he told them. Following his return from Vienna, Reiter was committed to the conversion house. A further attempt to petition the sovereign for mercy had even more dire consequences. After Hans Reiter and another peasant called Simon Schalk had been able to break out of the conversion house, they again set out for Vienna in the summer of 1773. Having arrived there, they appealed to the pastor at the Danish embassy and asked him and a Protestant Aulic councillor to petition the empress on their behalf. To no avail—the two men were apprehended and summarily deported.[103] A journeyman weaver who traveled to Vienna to find out what had become of Schalk and Reiter was admitted neither to the Danish emissary nor to Mathola de Zolnay's house; instead, he was threatened with "irons and shackles" and chased out of town.[104] All these failed supplicants fell victim to the myth of the empress-queen as a merciful and maternal ruler who was willing to lend an ear to even the lowliest of her subjects.

How to deal with heretics was one of many topics of disagreement between Maria Theresa and her eldest son. While she had always regarded deportation as a last resort and could not entirely suppress her growing skepticism toward the practice, this did not prevent her from using it repeatedly as an instrument of policy. Joseph, by contrast, was opposed to it on principle. He took the now orthodox Enlightenment view that conscience should not be made to suffer any kind of constraint and that the state should content itself with demanding outward obedience of its subjects.[105] He had also seen for himself what conditions were like in the colonized areas. He happened to be touring Transylvania in early to mid-1773, as events were unfolding in Stadl. Among the thousands of petitions he received there, many were from transmigrated Protestants. Upon his return, he made no attempt to conceal his criticism of forced resettlement.[106] One of the many crises that punctuated the coregency came to a head in December 1773. Once again, Joseph pleaded with his mother to relieve him of his responsibilities or give him real power; once again, she ignored him.[107] In April 1774 she had one hundred and sixty-two people deported from Styria in two waves.[108]

On November 7, 1774, Joseph ordered the Court Chancellery to put a stop to the "transplantations," unless the heretics themselves expressed a wish to migrate.[109] He is unlikely to have done so with his mother's knowledge and consent. In any event, the Court Chancellery vehemently advised her against the change in policy: "the baneful consequences of such tolerance would be impossible to ignore." The inevitable result of such largesse would be "new pride, excesses, and seduction." Nobody could account before God for the certain outcome: "that the share of heretics, which has been steadily decreasing since Luther's times, should ensnare and eventually consume the greater Catholic portion."[110] Only the threat of deportation had prevented this from happening before. In 1772 and 1773, too, the heretics had "taken fresh heart, since they believe they will be allowed to stay in the land and even establish a chapel." The Court Chancellery reminded the empress of the arguments she herself had put forward in the 1750s as well as the policy of her "glorious forefathers," who had not shirked from corporal and even capital punishment in their fight against heresy. Should the

"former constitution" now be overturned? In this situation, Maria Theresa surprisingly backed her coregent with the curt announcement: "My
previous resolution is clear." Heretics were no longer to be deported
against their will. In all cases concerning emigration, "I reserve the final
decision for myself."[111] Nonetheless, on October 11, 1776, another seventeen Styrian Protestants were forcibly resettled. In total, at least four
times as many people were deported for heresy during Maria Theresa's
reign than under her father—not to mention the transmigrations ordained for other reasons.[112] Even then the matter was not yet at an end.

Her willingness on this occasion to condone her son's order does not
mean that she had come to share his views about tolerating noncon-
formist beliefs. On the contrary, in the final years of her reign the question of toleration gave rise to another, even fiercer battle of wills between mother and son.[113] The conflict was occasioned by religious
disturbances in Moravia in early to mid-1777.[114] Underground Protestantism was stronger there than anywhere else. The province's proximity
to Prussia made it seem especially dangerous; petitions had already
been submitted to Frederick II calling on him to intervene. In 1774 hundreds of Moravians had been deported to Transylvania. In early 1777 a
number of ex-Jesuits sought to commend themselves by spreading the
false report that Maria Theresa had decided to guarantee the free exercise of religion. The tactic succeeded in luring Protestants from cover.
Gradually, inhabitants of over sixty villages professed their Lutheranism
and held public worship. When it emerged that they had fallen into a
trap, there was widespread unrest. Catholic churches were blockaded;
the situation escalated and individual demonstrators were shot in the
tumult. Maria Theresa complained to her son Ferdinand about the impossible dilemma with which she was faced. On the one hand, she could
not accede to the peasants' demands. As Queen of Bohemia, she had
sworn a solemn coronation oath to give no succor to "non-Catholics."
On the other, "deporting thousands of people, even to Hungary, would
be a great loss. It is a difficult decision to make, particularly at the present time. This greatly preoccupies and saddens me."[115]

Joseph was traveling through France when he learned of events in
Moravia. Alarmed by the news, he wrote to his mother, urging her not

to launch a frontal assault on the Lutherans: "religious diversity in a state is an evil only when associated with fanaticism, disunity, and partisanship. It disappears automatically when one treats members of all sects with perfect equality and leaves the rest to Him who alone rules all hearts."[116] Wanting to save people's souls against their will was an overreach of state power; this was something better left to the Holy Spirit. Besides, no souls could ever be won over by force; on the contrary, "one will lose far more useful and necessary bodies. . . . These are my views, as Your Majesty knows; and I fear that my complete conviction will make it impossible for me to change them so long as I live."[117]

Maria Theresa was aghast. This attitude shook her worldview to its foundations. What Joseph was to call "general toleration" was for her a term of abuse, synonymous with "indifferentism, the greatest misfortune which has ever befallen the monarchy." She answered him with letters of almost despairing forcefulness, firing back with all the arguments at her disposal. He would ruin the state with his toleration and lead countless souls into perdition. True religion clearly meant nothing to him, he had no love for it if he cared so little to protect and propagate it. He should look to the Protestants, who never allowed such indifference in their own countries. "One needs good faith, immutable rules—where will you find them and keep them?"[118] Joseph reacted promptly with an attempt to meet her halfway. She had misunderstood him completely; toleration was not to be confused with indifference to religion. Protestants would soon enough be convinced of the truth of the Catholic religion if they were allowed to live unmolested in their Catholic surrounds. Whoever banned alien religions showed only that he was afraid of competition, whereas true belief had nothing to fear.[119]

These arguments left his mother unmoved. In her view, leaving their spiritual salvation to the discretion of individuals was absolutely incompatible with the religious and political duty of a devout ruler. She took a new, even more emphatic approach: "I speak politically, not as a Christian: nothing is so necessary and salutary as religion" (as always, she used the word in the singular, since for her there was only one religion, everything else being irreligion, plague, poison, and heresy). Religion alone, she insisted, could impose constraints on human vice. "Will you allow everyone to fashion his own belief as he pleases? No fixed cult, no submission to the church—what will then become of us? The result will not be quiet and contentment, but rather the rule of force and other disasters such as those we have already seen." She again reproached Joseph for his spirit of contradiction and his mania for novelty, which imperiled both the happiness of the state and his own salvation. And to banish the specter of individualism, she again invoked what, after God, was the source of supreme authority for her: the tradition of her forebears:

> You would ruin yourself and drag the monarchy down with you into the abyss, [mocking] all the heavy cares of your forefathers, who labored mightily to bequeath these lands to us and improve their condition by introducing our holy religion to them, not, like our enemies, with violence and cruelty, but with sorrow, toil, and at great cost. No spirit of persecution, but still less any spirit of indifference or toleration, will guide me all the days of my life; and I wish to live only so long as I can hope to descend to my ancestors with the consolation that my son is no less great or God-fearing than them, and has turned his back on false reasoning, wicked books, and those who flaunt their cleverness at the expense of all that is most holy and venerable, wanting to introduce an imaginary freedom which can never exist and which would degenerate into license and outright revolution.[120]

She wrote those words in July. In Vienna, meanwhile, debates were underway about how to proceed in Moravia. A majority in Kaunitz's State Council recommended clemency, while the Court Chancellery and the Bohemian authorities—dominated by the great landholders—pushed for severe collective punishment: jail, forced labor, or deportation. Maria Theresa heeded the latter's advice and decided on September 12, 1777, to have the leaders deported. Joseph, now returned from France, journeyed on to Moravia to get his own view of the situation. When he learned of the punishments, he found extraordinarily harsh words— supposedly directed against those who had issued the commands, but actually addressed to his mother. These orders were so diametrically opposed to what have been recognized at all times as the principles of our religion and good government, and indeed of sound reason, that I have no doubt at all that Your Majesty, in your perceptiveness, will find a remedy as necessary as it is speedy. Can anything more absurd be imagined than these decrees? Converting people by turning them into soldiers or sending them down the mines, to forced labor? . . . Whoever thought up this rescript is the unworthiest of your servants, a man who merits my contempt for being as stupid as he is villainous.[121]

In short: he implored his mother either to rescind the order, which he could not reconcile with conscience, duty, and reputation, or to relieve him of his responsibilities as coregent—the same old refrain.[122] As always, his mother refused to budge, replying tetchily: "I cannot conceal how greatly it saddens me that you always make this shameful proposal whenever the slightest difference of opinion comes between us." Such an attitude would be permissible in a private person, but not in a ruler ordained by God.[123] Joseph made a further futile attempt to explain his dilemma: should he hold his tongue when she gave a command he knew to be unjust? So long as he bore joint responsibility, he felt obliged to register his protest, otherwise his silence would work like a poison that would eventually kill him. Nothing would please him better than to be her obedient son, which is why he entreated her to take state affairs out of his hands.[124] Maria Theresa sidestepped the issue as usual, replying in a spirit of resignation: "It is cruel to love each other and torment one another so."[125] At the same time, she demonstrated her ongoing dominance: when the Moravian peasants sent a delegate to the emperor pleading with him to intercede with the empress on their behalf, she had the man arrested.[126]

In fact, Maria Theresa was by no means as deaf to her son's remonstrations as she made out. She herself was not entirely convinced that punitive measures were for the best. Kaunitz was also advising her to let her subjects worship freely in the privacy of their own homes. Compulsion only bred animosity, he argued, and was incompatible with the commandment to "love thy neighbor"; emigration was detrimental to the economy, while experience had shown that forced resettlement simply did not work. She thus had every reason to allow Protestants the *exercitium religionis privatissimum*.[127] Kaunitz took an even bolder stance than Joseph: he proposed that such toleration be extended to all subjects, not just the intransigent Moravian communities, and that the public be notified of this change in policy. Joseph was not prepared to go so far, fearing a general edict of toleration would provoke other communities into insubordination and rebellion. In this, at least, he got his way. On November 14, 1777, the Moravian authorities were confidentially informed that Protestants were to be tolerated so long as they did not draw attention to themselves. Those incarcerated beforehand would nonetheless still be deported to Hungary. They would have to leave behind their children but would be accompanied by their wives, regardless of whether or not the latter were declared Lutherans.[128] Even then the matter was not yet put to rest. In February 1780 a number of Moravian Protestants again professed their faith in public. Joseph now demanded that general toleration be openly introduced in all lands and be made binding for territorial governments in future. Until her dying day, Maria Theresa could not bring herself to agree to this. On May 13, 1780, when around four thousand Moravian Protestants assembled on her birthday to hold an open-air service, she had their leaders arrested and deported to Hungary.[129]

Maria Theresa's position on the question of punishments was more indecisive, more vacillating, and less resolute than her letters to Joseph indicate. She openly admitted her scruples to others, including Ferdinand. She did not think of herself as a persecutor but as a mild and merciful mother to her country. In September 1778 Court Councillor Johann Adam von Posch asked her whether it was true, as had been reported in the Empire, that she had drawn up a list of all the Protestants in the German hereditary lands so that she might "do away with them completely." Posch had responded to the rumor, he wrote, by saying that the empress was "far too reasonable, too fair, and too humane to contemplate anything of the kind." She confirmed: "Your answer could not be bettered. I can assure you that no such idea has ever entered my head. But you can see from this how maliciously I am slandered."[130]

Immediately after Maria Theresa's death, Joseph made himself the toast of Enlightenment Europe by issuing his famous edict of toleration granting limited freedom of worship to all non-Catholic subjects.[131] For Jews, the edict opened the path to full assimilation.[132] Yet it came too late for many underground communities in Upper Austria, Carinthia, and Styria. The last major forced deportation had taken place there in 1774, while the last conversion houses had been closed in 1775 on economic grounds. By the time the edict of toleration appeared, the problem of crypto-Protestantism had been all but eradicated, at least in the Austrian hereditary lands.[133] In many areas, the "soft" approach had borne fruit. Many underground communities that had been around since the Reformation, surviving through centuries of persecution, had disappeared for good.

Our Good Turks

The Marian column that Leopold I had had erected at the Platz am Hof in Vienna in 1667 in thanks to the Mother of God, and which remained a central focus of Habsburg piety under Maria Theresa, shows four monsters at its base—a dragon, basilisk, lion, and snake—succumbing to four armored angels (fig. 46). The monsters represent the four plagues of the Habsburg monarchy: pestilence, hunger, Turks, and heresy. These plagues were condensed at the region bordering the Ottoman Empire—"the outermost fringe of Christendom."[134] Everything terrible seemed to come from there: not just the Turks and other ravaging hordes, but also epidemics, locusts, vampires, gypsies, and sectarians of all kinds. These marchlands were noted for their enormous religious diversity, especially Transylvania, where the estates had been formally guaranteed special religious privileges since 1691. Catholics formed a minority in the province; they lived alongside Calvinists, Lutherans, Jews, Armenians, even Antitrinitarians, Baptists, and adherents of the messianic sect of Sabbatai Zevi. The majority of subjects in the southeastern borderlands, the "Rascians" (Serbs) and "Wallachians" (Romanians), followed the Greek Orthodox rite.[135] It was therefore no coincidence that whatever and whoever was feared, shunned, or excluded at the center of the monarchy was banished here, to the Empire's periphery: Protestant heretics as well as agitators, women of ill repute, and "riffraff" of all kinds.[136]

The border with the Ottoman Empire was not a line but rather a broad frontier zone which—as we have seen—was governed by military administration. This swathe of territory was home to armed free peasants whose regiments formed the backbone of the Habsburg army. In Maria Theresa's day, the "military frontier" described a great arc extending over nineteen hundred kilometers from the Adriatic coast in the west, passing through Croatia, Slavonia, and the Banat along the Sava and Danube rivers, before curving northeast to the Carpathians and Bukovina in the northeast.[137] The Transylvanian border zone was the last to be integrated into the military organization. The border had shifted repeatedly over the centuries through the Turkish wars. Regions were thinly populated and power relations remained murky in some parts; not infrequently, people's loyalties oscillated between Habsburg and Ottoman overlords. In the eighteenth century, there were individual villages that were officially Habsburg yet still paid tribute to the Ottomans,[138] and there were people who claimed to be both Muslim *and* Christian, purporting not to recognize the difference between the two or considering it to be irrelevant.[139] Especially after the last great Turkish war (1736–39), Habsburg policy was aimed at creating greater clarity in the region. It was no longer just a question of protecting the core territories against potential Turkish invasion. The goal was also to extend Habsburg hegemony, settle colonists, and increase the Catholic share of the population.[140]

The military frontier served as a bulwark, not just against the Ottomans but against contagion as well, both literal and metaphorical; it was intended to safeguard the "health of the body politic."[141] Plague, in particular, was thought to seep from the Ottoman Empire into Habsburg lands. There had been a devastating epidemic in 1713; in 1738 plague had again broken out in the southeastern corner of the Habsburg empire. In 1728 Charles VI had laid the foundations for a gigantic *cordon sanitaire* stretching all the way from the Adriatic to the Carpathians. Under Maria Theresa, who assigned responsibility for it to the Court Sanitary

Commission (*Sanitätshofkommission*) in Vienna, the gaps were closed one by one until the last was sealed in 1770.[142] The movement of people, livestock, and goods was supervised all along the military frontier. To this end, an unbroken chain of guardhouses (*Tschartaken*) was set up. Located around a quarter of an hour's journey from each other, within hearing of cannon fire, they were manned by squads of armed peasants. On important trade routes, the guardhouses were interspersed by quarantine stations (*Kontumazstationen*) where people, animals, and goods could cross the border at fixed times, but only after strict purification rituals and a waiting period of twenty-one days—twice as long if fears of an epidemic were running high. Medical officials at the quarantine stations were required to report any unusual findings to local authorities.

Johann Caspar Steube—cobbler, interpreter, and traveler to the Orient—was stationed in the 1770s in a frontier regiment at the quarantine station of Schuppanek in the Banat. He provided a vivid account of how the control mechanisms established by Maria Theresa worked in practice. Two rows of thorn-studded palisades separated Habsburg from Ottoman territory and surrounded a square area with two gates. Anyone entering from the Turkish side was inspected and escorted to the quarantine station. This was a large, many-roomed facility where the "exposed" were quarantined in strict isolation. Anyone who had come from the Turkish side, or been in contact with them in any way, had to undergo confinement. No one who worked there—"the quarantine surgeon, the goods inspector, and all the cleaning assistants"—was allowed to leave the station grounds. Contact between the exposed and everyone else was strictly prohibited: "Not just everyone entering from Turkey, regardless of status, must obey the strict quarantine laws, but also anyone who has set foot on Turkish soil, however briefly. Indeed, all it takes is for someone to touch the fence . . . for him to have to go straight into quarantine (provided this comes to the attention of a cleaning assistant), and the same occurs if someone so much as brushes the coattails of an exposed person."[143] If someone whose period in quarantine was about to end made contact with a new arrival, their confinement would begin all over again. Inmates' meals were delivered to them from a nearby tavern via a mobile table conveyed on rails between the outer and inner palisade. Payment was left in a bowl filled with vinegar before the table was pushed back. Once their quarantine was over, inmates were given a pass and allowed to continue their journey. Most Turkish trade goods were likewise quarantined. These had to be stored in a shed for twenty-one days before they could be freighted onward. If there was no free space left in the storeroom, cross-border trade ground to a halt. Various foodstuffs were exempted from quarantine; to clean them, Steube reports, assistants "take a basin full of vinegar and splash some of it on top,"[144] with payment being made simply by throwing money over to the merchants on the other side of the palisade. Letters from the Ottoman Empire were either quarantined or attached to a stick, inserted through a gap in the fence, and then "fumigated with coltsfoot" before being sent on.

In their archaic ritualism, the purification measures directed at anything and anyone of Turkish origin resembled the taboos still commonly placed on hangmen and knackers. The enlightened Steube made no attempt to conceal how ridiculous he found all this. But the strict taboo on contact had an important symbolic effect. It created a high symbolic barrier between "us" and "them," between what was known, safe, and familiar and the alien, impure menace lurking beyond the palisades. Maria Theresa wanted to limit the flow of traffic between the two sides and ensure "that the Turks and Turkish subjects . . . are kept out of the hereditary lands and held at the border so far as is feasible."[145] Yet the problem grew with rising demand for Turkish merchandise such as coffee, tobacco, silk, fruits, and carpets. If trade with the Levant could not be taken out of the hands of Ottoman merchants—mostly Jews, Armenians, and Greeks—and brought directly under Habsburg control, then these merchants should at least be placed under permanent supervision whenever they entered the hereditary lands. This was made possible by the border quarantine stations, where they could be registered and assigned residential permits. Merchants from the Ottoman Empire were the guinea pigs for a novel method of monitoring individuals that later provided a model for registering and controlling native subjects as well.[146] Needless to say, the quarantine system severely handicapped Levantine trade. When Joseph returned from his journey to Trieste and the military frontier in 1775, he passed a devastating judgment on the border regime as a whole: it was "unfair, vicious, useless, flawed, costly, and indeed delusional, highly disadvantageous to both Your Majesty and the common man. . . . Vexation, misery, emigration, impoverishment, famine, and death" would be the inevitable result, and the "unfortunate sanitary system" made "the misery all the greater." He consequently demanded massive cuts to the regiments at the military frontier, generally free trade, and "abolition of the ridiculous sanitary stations."[147] Although he did not get his way on all these points, the relevant authorities were dissolved the following year, trade barriers lowered, and quarantine rules relaxed.

In fact, relations with the "Turks"—the customary term for Muslims as well as all Ottoman subjects[148]—had already changed fundamentally under Maria Theresa's reign.[149] As early as 1717, the English ambassador's wife, Lady Montagu, had denounced the plague reports put about in travel books as so many fairy tales: "Those dreadful stories you have heard of the plague have very little foundation in Truth."[150] When Montagu's English travel letters appeared in print between 1763 and 1767, and then in French translation shortly after, they entered a changed atmosphere, while they themselves helped further shift informed public opinion on the Turks. In popular almanacs and moral weeklies, "Muselmen" appeared in an ever more positive light.[151] Other travelers also played a part in eliminating traditional prejudices, including the aforementioned Johann Caspar Steube: "Many people are convinced that the Turks differ greatly from us in their manner of dress and physical form, that they are half-monsters knowing neither loyalty nor faith, and wonder why God does not wipe them from the face of the earth." He himself had consorted with them for years and could personally vouch for the fact that they were "formed just like us, that most of them are very good people, . . . and that their clothing is far longer-lasting and better fitting than our own, but also that they often put Christians to shame in their loyalty and faith, . . . and I cannot avoid paying the Turks a compliment at Christian expense in saying that I have often been better treated by them than by my coreligionists."[152]

Over the course of the century, the Turks became an object of fascination for many Europeans in a new way: wise and enlightened despite their "despotic" form of government, tolerant and respectful despite their false creed, they appeared as reliable merchants, kind-hearted companions, and peaceful neighbors, in short: a bright contrast to the stultifying darkness of Christian Europe. To gauge just how drastically the image of the Turk had been transformed, we need only recall how the Turkish wars were still commemorated throughout the hereditary lands.[153] The repudiation of the Turkish threat had shaped the political and religious identity of the Habsburg empire and paved the way for a Habsburg resurgence in the Empire and in Europe. Triumphal representations of vanquished, captured, killed, or downtrodden Ottomans could be encountered the length and breadth of the hereditary lands. Habsburg generals glorified their victories in heroic equestrian statues, ceiling frescos, and copperplate engravings. Turkish loot—magnificently worked weapons, tents, robes, harnesses, and the like—was proudly showed off in treasure rooms. Even the skull of the Ottoman supreme commander, Kara Mustafa, and the iron chain with which the besieging forces had closed off the Danube in 1683, could be inspected in the imperial armory.[154] The spoils included Turkish men and women who had been carried off as prisoners of war and subsequently baptized.[155] The memory of the wars was kept alive at all levels of society, not just by an aristocratic elite intent on preserving their heroic exploits in the medium of art. Wooden *Türkentrutz* (Turk protection) figures were placed on house roofs and wells to ward off evil, while votive panels recalling miraculous escapes from captivity were donated to churches. In Passion paintings, the enemies of Christ were portrayed as Ottoman soldiers; fearsome Turkish warriors adorned every possible utensil, from drinking vessels to cake molds; wooden Turks' heads served as targets at tournaments, from the "ladies' carousel" at court to country fairs.[156] Songs were sung and tales were told of Turkish atrocities and legendary escapes, commemorated in the Turkish linden trees, Turkish wells, and Turkish rocks that dotted the landscape. Pamphlets and copperplates from the period of the Turkish wars were still being reprinted in the mid-eighteenth century, and anniversaries of the great victories in battle were celebrated each year with thanksgiving processions.

FIGURE 47. Portrait of Maria Theresa and her daughter Marianna
in Turkish costume. Drawing by Jean-Étienne Liotard, 1745

At the beginning of the century, the "Turk or Greek"—the terms
were used more or less interchangeably for inhabitants of the Ottoman
Empire—still appeared on the Styrian *Völkertafel* (*Table of Nations*) as
a "lying devil." His clothing was feminine, his politics duplicitous, his
ruler tyrannical.[157] This changed significantly, if not entirely, over the
course of Maria Theresa's reign. The new fashion *à la turque* originated
in France and reached the Habsburg lands with a certain delay. In the
theater and in the opera, Turkish themes were all the rage. Lessing's
Sultan Saladin was not the only one of his kind; plays such as Rameau's
Le Turc généreux, Voltaire's *Zaïre,* or Favart's *Soliman II* were performed

at court in Vienna.[158] The commercial deals transacted through the harbor of Trieste stimulated the processing of Turkish fabrics, the enjoyment of Turkish coffee and tobacco, the consumption of Turkish fruit, the use of Turkish rugs and divans, and the introduction of Turkish motifs to female fashion.[159] And when Maria Theresa and her daughter Marianna had themselves depicted in Turkish dress, being painted in "oriental" costume became the dernier cri in court circles (fig. 47).[160] Nobles who had served on the military frontier or traveled to Constantinople brought back decorative Oriental lackeys from abroad. Elegant living à la turque could be brought to a pitch of perfection by having a little Moorish boy to serve coffee, as seen in the Khevenhüller family portrait (see fig. 28 and color plate 22).[161]

Understandably, the fact that the Ottoman Empire no longer posed a serious military threat following the peace of 1739 played a key role in the turcophilic atmosphere at court. Word gradually got around that "the Turks are no longer the fearful people who once made their neighbors tremble. To a certain extent, therefore, this vital outer wall [the military frontier] has become unnecessary. It should be shifted northwards, where a far more dreadful power has shot up overnight like a toadstool."[162] Whereas Charles VI had still waged war against the Turks at the side of the Russians, an expansive tsarist empire now appeared to be the far more pressing danger. When she came to the throne, Maria Theresa had desperately relied on Ottoman neutrality and had therefore hurriedly sorted out the last questions on the border left unresolved after the exorbitant peace of 1739.[163] In the War of Succession, her enemies failed in their attempts to draw the Sultan over to their side. Indeed, thanks to the clever tactics of the Habsburg resident in Constantinople, the Sultan condemned Frederick II's attack on Silesia, even offering his services as peace broker.[164] Maria Theresa was appreciative of the offer but turned it down: distrust was still too high. Frederick II met with just as little success in the Seven Years' War, notwithstanding his assiduous and expensive courtship of the Ottomans as allies against Maria Theresa. "Our good Turks" could be depended on, she wrote to Antonia of Saxony in 1763.[165] During the Russo-Turkish war of 1768–74, she refused to capitalize on Ottoman weakness, ignoring Kaunitz's expansionist schemes and Joseph's pleas. Her reasons were not entirely philanthropic: aggrandizement at Turkish expense would not only endanger peace, it was also not worth the effort. These "insalubrious provinces devoid of all culture, depopulated or settled by devious Greeks," would weaken the monarchy rather than strengthen it.[166] Instead, she created a sensation by engineering an admittedly short-lived and half-hearted Habsburg-Ottoman alliance.[167] There were no wars between the Habsburg and Ottoman empires throughout Maria Theresa's long reign; this only changed under Joseph II in 1788.

The Habsburgs had long shown a level of interest in their enemies' culture that was unusual for the time. In contrast to the Ottomans, they not only sent envoys to the other court from time to time but maintained permanent embassies in Constantinople. They had also traditionally sponsored and trained local Christian youths in Turkey as apprentice dragomans (*giovani di lingua* or *Sprachknaben*). Maria Theresa now placed diplomatic relations with the Ottoman Empire on a new footing. On the one hand, she transferred responsibility for Turkish affairs from the Court War Council to the State Chancellery under Kaunitz, thereby bringing it into line with the Christian monarchies. On the other, at Kaunitz's instigation she set up what was called the Oriental Academy in a country house near Klosterneuburg, modeled on a similar academy in Paris.[168] This remarkable institution was a kind of college where, at any given time, around ten gifted students were trained to become interpreters, translators, and other diplomatic personnel destined for service in the Middle East. There they learned Turkish, Persian, Greek, French, and Latin while at the same time acquiring the manners of pious and virtuous Christian gentlemen. Over time, the curriculum became ever more ambitious. Besides mastering foreign languages, students were expected to familiarize themselves with the literature and religion, history and government of the Ottoman Empire; they were exposed to Arabic fables and poems, medieval Arab philosophy, and "the most beautiful passages" in the Quran—in short, the budding scholars were trained to become cultural mediators in the fullest sense of the term.[169] Maria Theresa took a lively personal interest in her "Oriental language boys," visited them in their academy on several occasions, and looked on with benevolent condescension as they performed half Turkish, half French plays at court under the direction of their teacher, the Jesuit father Joseph Frantz.[170] The academy was a success, and it pointed the way to the future. For Habsburg diplomacy, it drove forward the process of professionalization while fostering the learned study of Oriental languages. Its alumni demonstrated significantly greater cultural competence than their counterparts from rival European powers.

During Maria Theresa's reign, several Ottoman envoys extraordinary visited the Viennese court—in 1741 to ratify the Peace of Belgrade; in 1748 to extend the treaty; in 1755 and 1758, after there had been a change of throne in the Ottoman Empire and the new sultan wished to emphasize continuing good relations; and finally in 1774, following the conclusion of the Russo-Turkish war.[171] The envoys were always received with the full ceremonial honors ordinarily accorded representatives of sovereign potentates.[172] This meant that the first and farewell audiences were grand, spectacular occasions, particularly as everything had to be done twice over: the envoy first paid a call on the emperor, then visited the empress several days later as Queen of Hungary. The entire court assembled each time to see the many exotic gifts brought by the envoy put on public display. Between the two audiences, the envoy and his retinue were lavishly entertained and at the end they all received precious farewell gifts in return. The complex ceremonial rules governing such audiences were largely routinized. People generally spoke the same symbolic language and knew how to behave in a manner befitting the occasion, even if the Turkish envoy might sometimes not bow deeply enough or might commit some other minor breach of protocol.[173] Still, an envoy of the sultan was subject to special rules otherwise unknown among Christian potentates. These included having to kiss the hem of the emperor's robe, a gesture of submission needed to prevent doubts arising about the equal status of emperor and sultan. The fact that Maria Theresa was a female ruler caused considerable embarrassment all around. From an Ottoman point of view, it was inconceivable that a woman should exercise power and grant audiences in her own right. In addition, when the envoy Mustafa Hatti Effendi had his first audience with her in May 1748, she was pregnant with her tenth child.[174] The conventions of diplomatic ceremonial clashed—yet again—with the rules governing relations between the sexes, and only makeshift solutions to the problem could be devised. As Khevenhüller noted in his diary,

> although he [the envoy] had great difficulty kissing the robe and did not perform it properly in his audience with the emperor, today [with the empress] he improved in this point; and since decorum prohibited him from touching and kissing the hem of the Empress's robe (as that of a lady and woman), . . . Her Majesty gathered in her hand the hem of the jacket she normally wears in her apartment and offered it to the ambassador instead (so as to signify the robe kiss). He kissed it with great deference while deeply inclining his head; although even this act of submission—truth be told—is not altogether decent; and in fact for a man (let alone a Turk) to draw so near to the chest or bodice of a lady (let alone so great a woman) seemed overly familiar; yet such could hardly be avoided given the need to adhere to the old etiquette.

For all his modesty, Khevenhüller approved of the arrangement.[175] Kissing the imperial "apartment jacket" became established as a rule, although on a later occasion another Turkish envoy "grasped the hand concealed beneath the proffered jacket and kissed it instead, an impropriety which could quite easily be prevented by lengthening the said jacket and its tip or tail."[176] Where the envoy planted his lips was not so trivial a matter as it may appear to us today, since diplomatic protocol was always about not "foregoing ancient rights." Even the most minute gestures could be read as an abandonment of traditional claims to status and could bring fatal consequences in their wake.[177]

This insistence on ceremonial standards was offset, however, by the imperial couple's willingness to show the Turkish envoy their particular esteem through all manner of symbolic refinements. Thus, as the envoy later noted with satisfaction in his written report on the mission, the emperor and empress both wore gifts he had given them earlier when they appeared at his farewell audience: a Turkish sword and a dress made of Turkish fabric, respectively.[178] Ottoman envoys were generally impressed by Maria Theresa, albeit not always correctly informed. Mustafa Hatti Effendi noted of his 1748 mission that the empress was "highly intelligent and well-versed in the affairs of government"; even her advanced pregnancy did not get in the way of her handling all petitions herself.[179] Ahmed Resmi Effendi, who came to Vienna during the Seven Years' War, likewise showed considerably greater interest in the empress than in her husband. He found her hard-working, thrifty, and naturally peace-loving—perhaps on account of her sex. This was not meant as a compliment: the state coffers were empty, the power of the house was dwindling, the prince-electors were refractory, and the Holy Roman Empire was presumably close to collapse. Following the death of her father, he reported, Maria Theresa had inherited the imperial crown and then passed it on to her husband. Frederick of Prussia had once sought her hand in marriage, but the emperor had rejected the suit owing to Frederick's Lutheran faith.[180] This was not altogether accurate. In general, however, the Ottoman envoys acted no differently than European diplomats did on Turkish soil: they translated foreign conditions into the concepts and categories with which they were already familiar.[181]

In June 1774, when another Ottoman envoy, Suleiman Effendi, came to Vienna after the end of the Russo-Turkish war to settle outstanding border questions, his visit provoked a frenzy of enthusiasm. The craze for all things Turkish was at its height. His visit was the talk of the town; everyone sang the envoy's praises and wanted to see him with their own eyes. Joseph wrote to his brother that ladies were unashamed to have their cheeks fondled by his lackeys and kitchen boys.[182] Maria Theresa herself was greatly impressed by his piety. As she reported to her son Ferdinand in Milan, all conversations and activities in Vienna now revolved around the Turkish envoy, an earnest man of seventy-two. He was almost besieged by young ladies and gentlemen of the nobility; they pestered him so much with their company that he barely found time for his prayers and meditations on the hereafter. "He says very wise things and abhors painted faces," Maria Theresa noted approvingly. "When some of our ladies appeared in décolleté, he remarked to the interpreter than they must be very poor, since they did not have a veil to cover themselves, and our young people clearly lack any occupation, as they can be seen on the streets all the time."[183] This impressed the moralistic empress, who found "the good Muselmen"[184] in many respects more congenial than the frivolous ladies and young libertines of her own court. The old Turkish aristocrat perfectly matched the ideal of the Muslim sage who, in moral-exemplary tales, held up a mirror to dissolute Europeans. In short, mutual admiration here bridged the gulf of religious difference. Habsburg-Ottoman contacts under Maria Theresa confirm the image that recent historians have made of early modern Christian-Muslim relations. In ancien régime diplomacy, European and Ottoman aristocrats generally met face to face and shared the same norms of courtly behavior.[185] A far wider chasm yawned between nobles and commoners. While Maria Theresa treated fellow sovereigns— regardless of their faith—with every sign of respect, she ruthlessly subjected her own people to religious constraints that were already anachronistic in the Age of Enlightenment.

13

Subjects

FIGURE 48. Rent-master and peasant. Unknown artist, castle at
Kirchberg am Walde, Lower Austria, eighteenth century

Our Loyal Subjects

Maria Theresa's love for her subjects stands at the heart of her myth. She
always saw "her subjects' true welfare as the sole object of her endeavors";[1] her policy stood "in the service of her subjects' happiness"; she
was "committed to the general good of the people."[2] But what exactly is
meant by "the people," who were "her subjects," how is their "true welfare" to be envisaged? Such phrases are as suggestive as they are

imprecise. Yet the very manner in which collective subjects such as "the people" (*das Volk*) are talked about creates social facts. The question is therefore how such terms were understood by contemporaries themselves and how they shaped social perceptions. How did Maria Theresa herself speak about the people over whom she ruled, and what ideas did she associate with them?

The monarch spoke in the plural of "my subjects," "my lands," or "my provinces"—in French *mes peuples, mes pays,* or *mes provinces*—when emphasizing her emotional connection to them, always adding the possessive pronoun "my" or "our." She famously called herself the "general and first mother of the said dominions" in her first great memorandum of 1750–51.[3] And in the second (1755–56), she complained of the pain it caused her that "the affection of my subjects, whom I have always loved as a mother," had diminished perceptibly.[4] In letters to her children, she repeatedly drew their attention to her "tenderness" toward her "peoples," for example, when instructing her son Ferdinand about his duties as regent: "Solely my long experience and the tender love I bear my peoples, in whom I have always found support and solace in my greatest vicissitudes and losses, have sustained me and constituted my happiness. Great and small, all of them deserve my justice and gratitude."[5] Or, in 1778, when she was seeking to persuade Joseph to end the war against Prussia: "God preserve you for your loyal subjects, . . . you owe it to them to care for them as a father."[6] His "lands and subjects," she said elsewhere, were all the more deserving of his love because they displayed such "great zeal and so little dissent."[7] In her view, subjects merited tender love, maternal concern, and compassion, but they were not owed any explanations: "A sovereign need never account for his conduct to anyone."[8] Nonetheless, she sometimes expanded her idea of "my subjects" to include privileged estates, at least when wishing to stress their loyalty and goodwill[9]—quite in contrast to the estates themselves, which always referred to themselves as lords, not subjects.

On the other hand, Maria Theresa used the collective singular *das Volk, le peuple*—now without the possessive pronoun—whenever she was faced with popular "grumbling," whenever discontent, rebellion, or unrest was in the air, whenever the windows of officials were being smashed in or dues and services refused.[10] In her 1755–56 memorandum, for example, "the people in the capital" are said to have been "as unrestrained as they were contumacious" when she first came to the throne.[11] Or she communicated to her daughter Marie Antoinette her concern that "the people" in Vienna were excessively agitated over the French emissary Rohan.[12] She avoided referring to "my subjects" when they presented themselves to her as a hostile mass—the phrase was evidently too strongly associated in her mind with loyalty, love, and obedience.[13] In other words, "my subjects" or "my lands" were normatively charged turns of phrase implying a paternalistic (or "maternalistic") outlook. They encompassed everything that God had bequeathed the monarch and her dynasty as their quasi-natural inheritance. Subjects owed God and the monarch unquestioning, "childlike" obedience. The phrase "my subjects" entailed a complete, self-contained, and internally consistent normative system: the relationship between subjects and their monarch mirrored that between human beings and their creator or children and their parents.

What the term "subjects" did not signify was an organized political whole capable of articulating its own interests. The independent political unit confronting the monarch was "the land"—roughly, territory or province. A land could only take collective action, however, through its estates. These estates—the institutionalized sum of the landed aristocracy, civic notables, and ecclesiastical corporations, which convened periodically at territorial diets (*Landtage*), were listed on a register of estates (*Landtafel*), and presided over their own archive and treasury (*Landesarchiv, Landeskasse*)—designated themselves collectively as "the land," since they alone spoke and acted on behalf of the whole and in its name. If they occasionally also called themselves the "representatives" or "guardians" of the entire land, then this simply meant that whatever arrangements they reached with the sovereign were binding for all who dwelled in the land.[14] Maria Theresa, too, sometimes used the term "land" in this sense, as a synonym for territorial estates (*Landstände*), particularly when negotiating with the estates on questions of taxation.[15] A word that was completely absent from Maria Theresa's vocabulary was *Bürger* in the sense of "citizens," *cives, citoyens*: the key concept in natural law doctrine for the fictive totality of all those who freely come together to form a community, submit to a government, and enjoy equal political rights. Maria Theresa used the term only in the old-fashioned sense to mean burghers possessed of special communal privileges.[16]

The word "subject" (*Untertan*) had another, narrower meaning for Maria Theresa. She commonly used it as a collective singular—"the subject," often synonymous with "the peasant"—to designate the unfree rural populace attached to manorial estates, and this is the sense in which it will be used in this chapter. The word "population" or "populace" (*Bevölkerung*) did not yet figure in her vocabulary. At the time, this was still a new-fangled term encompassing everyone who lived in a territory, regardless of social status or lordship rights, a quantifiable entity. There will be more to say about this later.

The overwhelming majority of people in the Habsburg hereditary lands—an estimated 80 percent of the population—lived from and on the land as subjects of a landlord.[17] These subjects, in the narrow sense of the term, were denied a voice at territorial diets and had no political representation at the provincial level (which is not to say that they could not organize themselves politically in their village communities). Their relationship to the faraway monarch in Vienna and her central authorities was highly indirect. A simple farmhand or maid was confronted by a long series of higher-ups: first came the head of household or paterfamilias, then the local steward of the landlord, the village judge, and the parish priest, then the lord himself, then the Circle Office (*Kreisamt*), then the territorial administration (the *gubernium*, the Representation and Chamber, or whatever other names it was given), and only then, finally, the central authorities in Vienna with the supreme matriarch at their head. The inevitable consequence was that "the subject is as ignorant of his superiors as they are of him."[18]

Landlords directly appropriated a large part of the economic yield generated by peasant farmsteads—so-called "rustical land"—in the form of money or payments in kind, as well as requiring peasants to cultivate the landlords' own "dominical land."[19] They also collected, administered, and passed on their subject's "contributions," that is, taxes earmarked for the sovereign. While their own estates had no longer been entirely tax-free since Haugwitz's reforms, their tax burden was still significantly lighter than that of their peasants. Furthermore, lords raked in all kinds of charges, perquisites, and levies and were additionally entitled to fees payable upon deaths, marriages, and other property transfers. At the same time, they dispensed justice to their subjects and could impose a wide range of punishments at their discretion, including imprisonment and corporal punishment. Peasants were not at liberty to make the most important decisions in their lives. They were not allowed to marry, move away from their farm, or seek a new livelihood without their lord's permission. Lords could exploit their position of superiority in many ways. They claimed the right to incorporate peasant land that had fallen vacant into their own demesne; they could buy the harvest from peasants as a standing crop and then sell it at market for a profit; they could coopt peasants' children to work for them as farmhands, increase dues and services, impose stiff financial penalties, and so on. The murkiness of property relations also made it easy for lords to minimize their own contributions to the sovereign while siphoning off peasant payments intended for the territorial treasury.

Some peasants were better off than others. The legal status of the rural populace varied greatly so far as flexibility of dues and services, personal freedoms, and market access were concerned. Some peasant families enjoyed relatively favorable property rights; they could not be turned out of their homes at will and could hand down assets to their next of kin. Others occupied their farmsteads only temporarily and could be "relocated" without notice. In some areas, peasants performed compulsory labor services (*robot*) for their lord for an unspecified period of time; in others, these were limited to a fixed number of days; in still others, services were compounded for cash payments. In the east, lords tended to run larger feudal estates and were more reliant on *robot*, while in the west they mostly charged ground rents, giving peasants considerably greater scope to manage their own economic affairs. In the Tyrol—a striking exception—peasants had freehold tenure of their land and were even entitled to participate in territorial diets. Most of these differences were anchored in regional common law, but some could be traced back to individual privileges or had simply been usurped at some point in time—it was often hard to tell exactly how. This diversity in legal conditions from land to land, and not infrequently from one farm to the next, was far from unusual. Inequality of rights was the rule, not the exception, under the ancien régime. Hardly anyone objected in principle to legal inequality and personal unfreedom. On the contrary, inequality before the law was seen by most people as an immutable, necessary condition for social stability and harmony, a view that came under increasing pressure in the second half of the eighteenth century.

Traditionally, central authorities far away in Vienna had no oversight over local conditions in the territories and adopted a hands-off policy. Yet unchecked exploitation of peasants by local grandees did significant harm to state finances. Impoverished and oppressed subjects were a meager source of contributions, nor did they make for healthy and strong soldiers. Joseph trenchantly summed up the situation: "Who suffers? The subjects and Your Majesty."[20] Since Haugwitz's day, reforming officials had therefore sought to bypass local lords and exert direct influence on the situation of subjects.[21] This could not be done to the same extent everywhere. At one end of the spectrum stood territories such as Hungary, where the estates had retained their privileges and were exempt from almost all central reform initiatives. At the other end stood the Banat, where there were no estates' rights to be respected. Since it had been taken back from the Ottomans, the Banat had been ruled from Vienna like a colony. The other territories were all situated somewhere between these two extremes; here local lords could appeal to their time-honored rights and liberties. Abolishing or limiting manorialism was prohibited by both class solidarity and legal tradition. Maria Theresa scotched the idea upon her accession to the throne: "Completely doing away with subservience can never be deemed feasible, since there is no country where the distinction between lords and subjects is unknown; it would deprive some of all restraint and leave others dissatisfied, but everywhere it would fly in the face of justice."[22] Joseph's *Rêveries*, written in youthful enthusiasm in 1763, recommended "reduc[ing] the standing and wealth of the grandees," but they were dismissed by his mother in pained embarrassment and remained confined to the realm of fantasy.[23] She instead endeavored, in however modest a fashion, to integrate landlords into the taxation system while monitoring their rule over subjects. The aim was to ensure that landlords could no longer enrich themselves without impediment at their peasants'—and the state's—expense. This was the central concern of Haugwitz's financial and administrative reforms, and to that end a suite of measures was introduced: "tax rectification," the establishment of circle offices, and a series of individual peasant protection laws. "Rectification" meant that the central government drew up a complete register of all fixed assets, along with their yields and encumbrances, using written tax declarations made by the lords themselves (sworn declarations or *Fassionen*, from the Latin *fateri*, to confess). On this basis, Vienna then mandated that the tax burden be equitably shared in accordance with uniform rules. In addition, exact accounts were to be kept in "dues booklets" to prevent peculation and other irregularities.[24] With that, both sides were to be provided with legal security: peasant taxes could no longer be summarily increased by landlords, but neither could they be reduced or even abolished by the central authorities.

Circle offices (*Kreisämter*) were Haugwitz's organs for implementing the new system. One of his most revolutionary innovations had been to organize all territories into circles and introduce state administrative functions at the lowest level, which had previously been left untouched by central power. This was an unprecedented affront to local grandees. So far as possible, circle offices were supposed to be staffed by officials unaffiliated by ties of friendship, blood relation, or marriage to the local nobles they monitored. Circle officials were charged with undertaking regular local inspections and interrogating peasants and stewards about each other. They were to oversee the raising, collection, and transfer of contributions; broadcast sovereign decrees; keep a watchful eye on village judges; sniff out malfeasance, embezzlement, and corruption among local stewards; and generally defend subjects against the depredations of their lords.[25] Conversely, they were also there to keep unruly subjects in check and could, where necessary, call for military support against troublemakers. These and other detailed stipulations were supplemented over the years by numerous further decrees issued in response to particular abuses of power, often based on initiatives from below, from circle officials themselves. Yet they failed to form a coherent, systematic whole, nor did they apply in equal measure in all the monarchy's provinces.

There were nonetheless appreciably fewer peasant uprisings and revolts during Maria Theresa's reign than in the period before and after. The reforms of 1748–49 entailed a structural shift in the peasants' favor, albeit not in all territories. Maria Theresa was therefore not entirely wrong in characterizing herself as a loving mother to all her subjects. According to cameralist orthodoxy, the happiness of the state consisted in a numerous, industrious, disciplined, obedient, and hence also prosperous population. Subjects were valuable capital who needed—at least in theory—to be nurtured and protected in order to preserve, or better yet increase, their capacity to pay taxes. Writing in 1769, Maria Theresa proposed the following general maxim:

> The first consideration must be to sustain the peasantry, as the most numerous class of subjects and the foundation and greatest strength of the state, in . . . such a condition that they can feed themselves and their families and afford to pay general taxes in times of peace and war. Hence, it follows that neither an urbarium nor an agreement, and still less a custom, however old it may be, can be allowed to stand if it proves irreconcilable with the aforementioned maintenance of the subject population.[26]

These were fighting words addressed to the landlords. Yet whenever the financial needs of the central government conflicted with peasant protection, state revenues took undisputed priority. For all the lip service paid to providing subjects with relief from exactions, political reality "dictated that a maximum in contributions be raised."[27] Once a sum had been decided on, central authorities showed only moderate interest in how justly and equitably it was raised on the ground. It was one thing to bridge the gulf between the monarch and her subjects with lofty rhetoric and abstract principles; it was quite another to contravene aristocratic solidarity in social practice and shift the brute weight of tradition. The great Austrian, Bohemian, and Hungarian landlords were at the same time the key pillars of Maria Theresa's rule. It was to them she entrusted most diplomatic missions, military regiments, and high offices at court. They were her companions at cards at her evening apartments. If necessary, she had to be prepared to make herself extremely unpopular with them and risk her reputation as a benevolent sovereign. Her courtiers were literally and metaphorically closer to her than her subjects, whose everyday reality she had never witnessed with her own eyes. At different times in her life, Maria Theresa was prepared to varying degrees to take up the cudgels against the high nobility on behalf of the peasantry, and in this she was supported to varying degrees by her own top officials. She did not always show the same pugnacity and persistence toward the aristocracy that she demonstrated in the first phase of reform following the War of Succession. And her relations with her subjects also underwent considerable fluctuations.

Information Overload

Maria Theresa had clearly recognized that one of the core problems confronting her government was an information deficit in Vienna. The strategy of local grandees, she wrote as early as 1750–51, consists in "concealing conditions in their territories from the sovereign, hence in taking care that the latter is not too precisely informed of such conditions."[28] Yet this was not solely a moral problem—the falseness and "viciousness" of landlords; it was also structural in nature: it was simply too much to expect that the absolute monarch could gain an overview of all her lands from a single vantage point. The metaphor of the machine of state derived a considerable part of its allure from the suggestion that the princely machine builder could take in and direct all its operations with a single glance from outside. This optimistic belief in the possibility of control generated an insatiable demand for information, which in turn spawned ever greater quantities of data that ultimately threatened to overwhelm central command.

The idea that the monarch would want to know everything about her lands, that she would systematically seek out information and not just react to concerns brought before the throne, was far from self-evident.

The early modern period saw a gradual yet fundamental shift from a time-honored, passive-responsive style of rule to a new, active-investigative mode.[29] Joseph's attention-grabbing tours of the hereditary lands were a perfect enactment of this investigative style of rule and at the same time the opposite of a traditional court progress: he traveled incognito under the name of Count Falkenstein, with a minimal retinue, on horseback, and under extremely spartan conditions, in order to see rather than be seen.[30] Through these journeys, Joseph not only escaped his mother's direct influence, he also formed his own ideas about conditions on the ground and thereby live up to the Enlightenment ideal of unprejudiced empirical research. Only through personal observation—so the optimistic expectation—could one avoid succumbing to the illusions of tradition and partiality. "Upon my honor," he wrote of his journey through Transylvania, "I had no prejudices. But I saw, I heard, I combined...."[31] Joseph not only set down his experiences in compendious reports for his mother, he also confronted territorial authorities with long catalogs of questions to which he demanded written responses. These journeys struck a tremendous chord with subjects. They practically deluged the traveling coregent with their petitions, which he collected in the tens of thousands. For Maria Theresa, meanwhile, these "terrible voyages" were an annoyance.[32] She disputed that they could really provide him with deeper insights into conditions in the land,[33] repeatedly sought to dissuade him from undertaking them, and bemoaned her failure to change his mind to anyone who would listen. She was nonetheless forced to concede: "The people are crazy about him; they have never seen an emperor, and one so friendly and down-to-earth."[34] The addressees of Joseph's journeys were not just common subjects and the educated middle-class public, whose ideal of empirical knowledge he was demonstratively upholding, but also the State Council, which he charged with working the information he had gathered into a concrete program of reforms, and especially his mother, to whom he reflected a kind of negative mirror image of her own style of rule. "This is the true state of affairs," he once wrote to her. "Anyone who thinks otherwise should not read the minutes, nor the reports of a councilor of commerce, but examine the situation on the ground for himself and talk to the people, as I have done."[35]

For Maria Theresa, this was out of the question. Such personal tours of inspection were incompatible with her idea of sovereign majesty, which demanded that she "represent always and everywhere."[36] The few journeys she undertook were either lavishly ceremonial stately progresses or courtly pleasure trips; she also occasionally inspected her troops if they happened to be stationed nearby. She therefore relied on her loyal officials to gather the necessary information and forward it to the central authorities. For Maria Theresa was no less obsessed than her son by the need to keep herself as closely informed as possible. Her handwritten marginalia to innumerable official documents show just how much she insisted on knowing firsthand. She perused countless memoranda and projects, submissions from the State Council and State Chancellery, judgments of the Supreme Judiciary, balance sheets from the Court Chamber, tables from bureaus of commerce, reports from her foreign emissaries, territorial governors, and court commissions—and even these made up only a part of what crossed her desk each day, supplemented by her weekly correspondence with her grown-up children and their overseers.[37] She read these documents with such attention to detail that not even minor errors escaped her notice. "Ad no. 66. A transcription or computational error seems to have occurred," she scribbled in the margin of a table provided by the central bureau of commerce, or: "I find it not a little perplexing that the table for 1762 has been submitted only at the end of 1764"; the central authorities should inform the negligent bureau "of the table's incorrectness" and order it not only "to submit a more reliable table for the year 1763 forthwith," but also "to communicate my dissatisfaction concerning such negligence."[38]

Yet the more information flooded in, the more difficult it became to gain an overview. Reflections had long been made on how the central authorities could keep pace with the expansion of knowledge.[39] None other than Gottfried Wilhelm Leibniz had already given thought to how the growing volume of paperwork, *chartarum moles*, could be cut back and the knowledge contained therein presented in a more accessible format.[40] His answer had pointed the way to the future: information that might prove of use to the state was to be extracted from the mass of empirical data about the land and its people and converted into numerical tables. Yet this presupposed that information had already been collected in standardized form, through uniform questionnaires. Questionnaires were to be turned into lists, lists into tables, and tables—later—into statistics.[41] In much the same vein, Maria Theresa stipulated in her instructions for Court Chancellor Chotek:

> Given especially . . . that thorough knowledge of how things really stand is needed for any improvements [to be made], it is uncommonly useful for a state balance to be drawn up each year encompassing all the residents of each province, all internal *producta naturae et artis, importationen* and *exportationen* [natural and manufactured goods, imports and exports], from which everything can be captured at a glance as if in a mirror; I am therefore enclosing . . . a draft . . . to that end.[42]

Through such standardized charts, information was to be detached from the concrete, personal, local context—"abstracted," in the literal sense of the term—and made visible, comparable, and accessible as a compact set of data for purposes of central planning and administration. This had far-reaching instrumental and symbolic effects on the process of state formation. Anyone and anything quantified by the central government—peasant farmers and their chattels, for example—it thereby used for its own ends, treating them as homogeneous, countable, measurable units. With that, a homogeneous entity was anticipated, conceptualized, and fabricated that did not yet exist outside the tables and charts in which it was statistically captured: a territorial state with a "population."

Yet establishing such a novel, centralized technology of rule was no easy matter. From the seventeenth century, new methods for gathering and processing data had been devised throughout Europe, yet such plans rarely went beyond the experimental stage and were realized only piecemeal. So too in the hereditary lands. Isolated trials had been made in the past, but it took the existential crisis of the Seven Years' War for systematic, standardized, transterritorial information-gathering measures to be implemented on a grand scale for the first time. The initiative came from the military. In order to be better prepared for a future war and optimally utilize all the land's resources, reliable information was needed about the land itself.

On the one hand, the land had to be exactly surveyed and described.[43] There was already no shortage of maps, including some commissioned by the ruler. But these were maps of individual territories or of the Holy Roman Empire as a whole. It is telling that Maria Theresa showed no interest in the latter; for her, the Empire was a foreign country. The political unit she wanted to see represented in cartographic form was *her* state, the Habsburg lands in their entirety. The project was first suggested by Franz Moritz von Lacy and Daun, who had personally experienced the fatal consequences of deficient topographical data in many situations in the last war. In 1764 Maria Theresa commissioned a comprehensive survey of all her lands, beginning with the particularly vulnerable regions of Bohemia and Moravia. The "Josephinian Land Survey," as it came to be called, was not completed until 1787, long after Maria Theresa's death. Its implementation was entrusted to the military and shrouded in secrecy. This monumental work of cartography, consisting of around 3,500 individual maps at a scale of 1:28000, was circulated in only a few hand-drawn copies, and never appeared in print, with the exception of the parts representing the Habsburg Netherlands. There was a written supplement to each map offering a wealth of additional information. It was clear from the outset that the entire undertaking would be valuable for more than just military purposes. Indeed, the project was expanded several years later with an eye to its fiscal usefulness, in particular. A second series of even larger-scale maps was commissioned, this time containing detailed information on property rights, taxation revenues, and land use; on the inhabitants of each territory, their language, religion, and legal customs; and on the potential for demographic, agrarian, and commercial growth. In short, the cartographic project grew into a vast database that could be mined for every conceivable political end.

The mapping of the territories was closely connected with the introduction of a new recruitment system.[44] Joseph, to whom Maria Theresa had transferred oversight of the military following his father's death, and Court War Council President Lacy strongly advocated a canton system along Prussian lines. Troops had previously been drawn mainly from the military frontier region or recruited from the Empire and abroad. Subjects from the Habsburg heartlands had traditionally only served as auxiliaries. Joseph's idea was to conscript soldiers from the entire non-privileged subject population, make them serve for only part of the year, and thereby secure the military a central position in society. By 1768 he had overridden his mother's objections as well as resistance from Kaunitz.[45] Territories were now to be divided into military recruitment zones, and "the entire male sex" registered in advance. In this way, authorities could gain an overview of the manpower at their disposal and evaluate which men could be drafted into the military without seriously damaging the land's economy. On March 10, 1770, Maria Theresa decreed a "general description of the souls and draft animals" in the Austrian and Bohemian hereditary lands; Hungary and the Dutch and Italian territories were exempt, as usual. Jointly directed by the Court War Council and the Court Chancellery, the enormous project was concluded within just two years. For all the inevitable difficulties and shortcomings, the central government had succeeded in establishing an unprecedented, "sensationally fine-mesh network of state control."[46]

There had been precursors to this "conscription of souls." Since the Council of Trent, parish priests had kept a register of baptisms, marriages, and deaths. Maria Theresa had already built on this in 1753–54, when censuses of the entire population were carried out in several hereditary lands by means of standardized questionnaires. In the following years, the process was repeatedly tinkered with: at first, priests were charged with collecting the information, then landlords and city magistrates; on one occasion individuals had been counted, on another households; the census was initially meant to be conducted at three-year intervals, then annually; and the categories used to classify individuals were also modified. The fact that the censuses would serve as a basis for recruitment had been hushed up, since it was feared that, otherwise, hardly anyone would volunteer accurate information. Yet the results still did not inspire much confidence. When new censuses were carried out in 1763 prior to the introduction of a new head tax, this time according to income classes, the total population was found to have declined sharply. The sources of error were legion, the opportunities for manipulation obvious. Even Court Chancellor Chotek, in whose area of responsibility the census fell, was accused of having underreported the number of people on his estates by some one thousand souls.[47]

The 1770–71 "conscription of souls" (*Seelenkonskription*) differed fundamentally from its precursors—not just on account of its inordinate expense. One key difference was that its implementation was not left in the hands of local authorities. Instead, mixed military-civilian special commissions were appointed at all levels of the hierarchy. Another difference was that all dwellings in every town and borough—from the pauper's hovel to the Hofburg in Vienna—were now included in the tally. This unprecedented equality in treatment outraged many grandees, but no exceptions were tolerated. Maria Theresa personally dictated how the count was to proceed.[48] Commissioners traveled systematically from place to place and from house to house, numbering front doorways in black. "German" numerals were used for Christians and Roman numerals for Jews—this distinction was still thought necessary. Commissioners inspected each dwelling in the presence of the entire household; separately counted the men, draft animals, women, and Jews; questioned the head of household; and filled out forms: name, age, marital status, qualifications, height, disabilities, and so on. Individuals were categorized to determine their fitness for military service. Since women and Jews were disqualified in advance, less information was required of them. For the first time personal names became fixed: henceforth, family names provided to officials were binding and could no longer be changed. New "path signs" were also erected to allow officials to find their way in sparsely populated regions. The completed forms were collected, copied, analyzed, and forwarded in separate copies to military and civilian authorities at the next level of the hierarchy. In some cases, extra rooms had to be hired to accommodate all the paperwork that came pouring into circle offices and provincial governors' offices. Some 2,300 reams of paper were allocated for Moravia alone (although this proved excessive). Court printer Trattner made a fortune printing all the forms. The census arrived at a grand total of 1,100,399 dwellings, with six copies of several sheets having to be made for each dwelling.

The "conscription of souls" provided central authorities in Vienna not just with highly aggregated numerical data on the sovereign's subjects but also with graphic descriptions of their abject living conditions. The roving census-takers had been ordered to sum up their findings by means of a detailed list of questions and supplement it with their own observations. The "Political Notes" they dispatched to Vienna present a harrowing picture of poverty, disease, exploitation, and injustice.[49] Hunger stalked the land in 1770–71, and subjects bewailed their plight to officials in the most heartrending terms. Commissioners now spoke up for the weary and oppressed. They unanimously praised the cooperative attitude of their informants, hardly doubting the credibility of the grievances aired before them. Unimaginable abuses were brought to light: the precarious rights of peasant ownership, oppressive *robot* services and feudal dues, the damage caused by game, extortion at the hands of lords and mistreatment at the hands of stewards, the puffed-up priests and inadequate pastoral care, wretched or completely nonexistent schools, the cripplingly hard labor carried out by small children, the diseases afflicting man and beast, the sheer filth, desolation, and despair. Vivid details were not lacking:

> Poultry is kept and fed in the rooms throughout the winter, providing a breeding ground for untold vermin. The rooms themselves have tiny windows which can only be opened a crack by means of a small bolt, and hence never let in enough air. People sleep on the bench by the stove or behind the stove. They rarely remove their clothes, and damp clothing is generally left to dry on their bodies, conditions which are unconducive to human health even in years of plenty.[50]

At the same time, the commissioners almost unanimously emphasized that subjects bore no personal responsibility for their misery: "The people are sober, take great pains to provide for themselves, and are not the least prone to indulgence," it was said, or: "The hardworking farmer knows how to put even the smallest plot of land to good use."[51] If subjects failed to obey sovereign decrees, then this was "not from malice, but out of ignorance," because commands had not been properly communicated to them. In some regions, village judges displayed laws only in writing, or officials published "mostly obscure excerpts . . . which the peasant fails to grasp," assuming he was capable of reading them in the first place. The consequence of all this was that subjects "break the laws not from disobedience, but for want of a clear understanding."[52]

The nobles of the land, Court Chancellor Heinrich von Blümegen at the fore, were far from pleased with these findings. The commissioners, they fumed, were in cahoots with the malcontents. Did they even have the right and authority to hear complaints? After all, there were already well-functioning formal mechanisms in place for registering grievances. Subjects were accused of treason, spite, and deliberate misrepresentation.[53] In fact, the conscription of souls entailed a significant increase in central power that threatened to come at the cost of local grandees. Merely the symbolic effect of leveling the differences between estates was palpable: by taking the unprecedented step of subjecting everyone in the hereditary lands to one and the same administrative procedure, the central government was treating nobles as if they were subjects. There was a reason why nobles were unwilling to have their castles and palaces enumerated. The state now knew all its subjects by name, place of domicile, and personal information, and only by this means did they become *its* subjects in the strict sense of the term.[54] As would be seen, many peasants saw conscription as a first, promising step to emancipation from their feudal overlords.[55]

There can be no doubt that Maria Theresa was personally committed to the whole conscription project and followed its progress with the keenest interest. It may also be safely assumed that she kept herself informed of the findings, which began trickling into Vienna in the autumn of 1771. The "Political Notes" submitted by the territorial commissioners appear to have made a deep impression on her, perhaps deeper than that left behind by all her son's earlier memoranda. At any rate, her attitude toward the "poor subjects" changed significantly over the following years. The findings of the conscription of souls threw into massive doubt the economic and political agenda she had pursued hitherto. Until then she had subscribed to the cameralist doctrine that all that was needed to promote the general good was to awaken the reserves of industry that lay dormant within her subjects. The "Political Notes" now suggested that the problem did not lie with any lack of effort.

Diligence and Discipline

Maria Theresa had always seen her subjects as "for the most part idle and sluggish."[56] Her cameralist advisers had taught her that they needed to be roused from their lethargy. In the eighteenth century, industry still retained the original meaning of the Latin *industria*, diligence; industrialization literally meant increased industriousness. During this period, industrialization in the Habsburg lands did not take the form of technical innovations resulting in an increase in labor productivity. It meant more people doing more work. According to cameralist doctrine, economic stimulus was to be achieved by identifying and tapping unused labor reserves in the population.[57] The traditional subsistence economy offered an easy target for this policy, since it was geared, crudely speaking, to meeting the immediate requirements of the household, to providing it with "sustenance befitting its estate." From the point of view of a subsistence economy, it made little sense to risk producing for a specific market sector—with all the exposure to price fluctuations and competitive pressures this entailed—in the hope of maximizing profit. Production surpluses, in so far as they even existed, were traditionally consumed collectively rather than saved or reinvested. There was good reason for this, since communal feasting strengthened the sense of neighborly solidarity that people relied on in times of dearth. From the perspective of cameralist officials, however, all this had to be combated as idleness and wasteful expenditure. Creating more industrious subjects was at once an economic, political, and moral imperative. Among other things, it involved abolishing holidays, fighting the tradition of absenteeism on a Monday ("Saint Monday"), reducing the number of mendicant orders, and establishing spinning houses, workhouses, and prisons for "idle hands." In short, cameralist economic policy was aimed at disciplining subjects.

"Peopling" (*Peuplierung*) was another key concern of the dominant economic doctrine—with fatal consequences, as would be seen in the 1770s. The hereditary lands, like almost everywhere else in Europe, had seen a sharp increase in population in the eighteenth century anyway, leading to a situation where many farms could no longer even support their own tenants. This boost in population was given further political impetus when traditional restrictions on marriage were relaxed and landlords were explicitly requested to grant their subjects permission to marry.[58] Various strategies for employing and feeding the growing population were put in place. On the one hand, crop yields were increased by all available means: forests were cleared and marshlands drained, village commons enclosed and placed in private hands, fields where cereals were grown were no longer allowed to lie fallow every third year but were planted with potatoes, clover, or madder instead, and so on. On the other hand, large-scale (re)settlement projects were set in train, partly through incentive, partly through force.[59] The regions earmarked for transmigration, primarily the Banat and Transylvania, had traditionally been home to seminomadic pastoralists and were thus hardly virgin territory. Now they were to be settled with peasants and intensively cultivated, since farming offered a sounder basis for taxation than transhumant pastoralism. To populate the Banat, Maria Theresa authorized extensive advertising campaigns in the Empire, setting off two waves of colonization. The population there exploded from around 25,000 in 1711 to almost 300,000 in 1780.[60] The new arrivals were not made to feel especially welcome, however, and many initiatives delivered far less than had been promised. Officials vastly overestimated the effectiveness of their interventions in the field of agrarian policy.

The same held true of the novel approach to dealing with the Hungarian "gypsies," as they called themselves at the time—a special case of Theresian population policy.[61] Gypsies were no longer to be exterminated—that is, forcibly removed from Habsburg territory—as had previously been customary.[62] The old policy of expulsion was now superseded by a new policy of domestication (*Domicilierung*), that is, settlement and assimilation. Maria Theresa issued a series of decrees over the course of her reign (1758, 1761, 1767, and 1773) intended to transform the gypsies into loyal tax-paying peasants. To ensure that they actually settled down, they were not only provided with farmland and seed, they were also forbidden from keeping horses, owning carriages, and leaving the land without official authorization. Such measures were designed to make it impossible for them to return to their traditional ways of horse breeding, tinkering, and peddling. Consequentially, they were deprived of their corporate autonomy and placed instead under regular Hungarian county administration. They were also registered for recruitment and their households subjected to regular inspections by the authorities. Since a group's social identity is bound up with its (self-)designation, their collective names were changed as well for administrative purposes: the former gypsies (*Zigani*) were now referred to nonspecifically as "new settlers" (*Neusiedler*) or "new residents" (*Neubürger*). Finally, they were banned from marrying among themselves. Mixed marriages were promoted instead, provided couples could demonstrate a "respectable" way of life and knowledge of the Catholic faith. Since the project of reeducation could not begin early enough, children were to be taken away from their parents at the age of five and placed in the care of good Catholic peasant families. While nobody seriously contemplated physically exterminating a whole ethnic group—such dreams were reserved for a later century— the goal was still to wipe out the gypsies as a "nation" with a distinct cultural identity and incorporate them without trace into the Catholic rural population. Here, too, authorities vastly overestimated their ability to bring about demographic change.

The growth in population, which, from a cameralist viewpoint, was pleasingly rapid, made the creation of new employment opportunities beyond the agricultural sector both possible and urgently necessary. Industrial policy was a preferred topic among economic theorists. With Silesia, the monarchy had lost by far its most industrially advanced and prosperous province; this loss was now to be compensated with all the means at its disposal. Maria Theresa's economic policy was based on the still-prevalent mercantilist ideal of an active balance of trade: imports of manufactured goods were to be reduced to a bare minimum, while as many goods as possible were to be produced domestically (and preferably exported as well). In pursuit of this aim, generous subsidies were extended to producers of manufactured goods, especially luxuries, consumption of which otherwise caused money to flow abroad. Landlords who established a manufactory on their lands were relieved of the usual restrictions—taxes, dues, guild regulations, billeting and recruitment obligations—and supported with state credit, albeit often with only modest success, since they lacked the necessary technical skills and knowledge. The rural textile industry, run on the basis of cottage labor and distribution, was considerably more important. Unlike guild workers, cottage laborers were not permitted to market their wares on their own account, receiving raw goods from a distributor and delivering him the finished goods at a fixed price. These could then be sold at a profit on the supraregional market. From the perspective of economic theorists, manufacturing and cottage labor in the countryside had the great advantage that the strict rules governing skilled labor within the city walls did not apply to them. Domestic secondary industries, especially textile production, created urgently needed employment opportunities for the rapidly growing rural underclasses: for the landless poor, for peasant smallholders, and for farmers who could no longer live off their own produce. Piecework was shared out among the whole family, including and especially women, children, the elderly, and the infirm.

It was the heyday of grand economic schemes. The innovation-friendly monarch was practically swamped with proposals for reinvigorating the moribund industrial and agricultural economy.[63] A copy of her "Supreme Resolutions for Reviving Industry, Trade, Factories, and Manufactures in the Imperial Royal Hereditary States" was made between 1764 and 1766 by a diligent official from the Court Office of Commerce (*Kommerzienhofstelle*), a kind of economic ministry under the direction of Karl Count Zinzendorf. They give an idea of the kind of studious consideration Maria Theresa devoted to such questions. From the extermination of thieving sparrows to the planting of fruit trees on country roads, from sericulture and apiculture to improvements in the quality of domestic hair powder, no object was deemed too trivial not to merit a personal response in the form of a handbillet or resolution.[64]

Maria Theresa was particularly interested in promoting cottage industries. The spinning of flax, hemp, wool, or cotton seemed especially well-suited to mobilizing the dormant labor reserves of her subjects. Spinning could be done by anyone at any time and anywhere, including in prison and in the barracks; even small children could help out, and it provided gainful employment during the winter months, when there was not much other work to be done. Spinning not only stimulated domestic textile production, it also had a disciplinary effect by keeping otherwise idle hands busy. On March 17, 1753, Maria Theresa issued a court decree encouraging landlords to revive the old custom of "spinning duty" (*Gespunstschuldigkeit*), "by which means the subject is roused from his accustomed idleness and torpor, induced to cultivate and spin flax, principally with regard to those of his children not yet fit for more onerous labor, linen weaving is promoted ever more vigorously, and, in consequence of all this, a sounder industrial basis is furnished . . . for adequately sustaining the . . . growing population."[65] The names of landlords who excelled in this regard were to be communicated to the monarch by local and provincial authorities so that she might convey her personal goodwill. Spinning duty was also explicitly excluded from the *robot* services from which peasants could purchase exemption. In 1765 the monarch ordered that every child aged between seven and fifteen in all cities and market towns should learn to spin in winter: not just the children of the poor, who otherwise lacked means of support, but children of artisans as well. Maria Theresa's own daughters led by example (see color plate 28). Many parents, needing their children for domestic and farm work, were reluctant to comply. A more sharply worded command was then issued and recalcitrant parents threatened with punishment.[66] Yet children were not the only ones marched off to the spinning wheel. Wherever Maria Theresa suspected idleness, in poorhouses, prisons, and orphanages, spinning was prescribed as a remedy, "it being my earnest will that these people be spurred to constant labor."[67] Even the military was not spared. In 1768 a directive went out to all the territories requiring soldiers in their barracks, together with their wives and children, to spin flax, wool, or cotton.[68] An earlier resolution from October 26, 1763, made clear that subjects could be made to work against their will: "Along with other useful intentions, the establishment of factories in a state has as its object that the idle be given an opportunity to work and earn a living for themselves. Those unwilling to take up this opportunity . . . are to be confined to workhouses to that end."[69] According to the teaching of the Viennese cameralist Sonnenfels, the chief objective of industrial policy, to which all other ends were subordinate, was "to multiply employment."[70] In short, the promotion of domestic industry and the creation of industrious, morally disciplined subjects were two sides of the same coin.

The Nadelburg at Lichtenwörth, not far from Wiener Neustadt, offers a paradigmatic example of Maria Theresa's industrial policy (in this twofold sense of the word "industry").[71] Under state management from 1751, the Nadelburg was a combination of hammer mill, workers' settlement, manufactory, parish, and orphanage. Much as in a large premodern household, no distinction was made between life and livelihood. The whole was a self-contained social cosmos made up of masters, journeymen, apprentices, laborers, and a state administrator. Around half of all workers were children, many of them orphans from Vienna's charity hospital, the Bürgerspital. The complex of buildings, which can still be visited today, consisted of several rows of uniform small houses with kitchen gardens, a factory, a mansion, a park, and not least a church, dedicated to St. Teresa and personally designed by the court architect, Pacassi (see color plate 19).[72] The settlement was segregated as completely as possible from the neighboring village. The fine gate through which the complex was entered, crowned with the imperial double-headed eagle, was kept closed at night. This precaution was deemed necessary not least because, among the workers hired from the Empire, there were many Protestants who had to be kept under close watch so long as they declined to convert to Catholicism. The enterprise enjoyed numerous privileges. It could buy materials and tools almost duty-free, and it was licensed to sell its products—needles, buttons, and small ironware of various kinds—throughout the hereditary lands. It was subject neither to urban guild regulations nor to other customary charges. Unlike in a modern factory, production was not centralized and organized around a strict division of labor. Workers eked out a precarious existence, forced to apply for individual commissions from salaried masters and compete with each other for piece rates. They were forbidden from leaving the manufactory and seeking work elsewhere without the administrator's permission.[73] The inmates of this protoindustrial institution were thus doubly disadvantaged: like serfs, they were personally unfree, and like wage earners, they were exposed to ruinous competitive pressures. Meanwhile, different rules applied to orphans. They worked without pay; the hospital paid the manufactory four kreutzers a day per head for their maintenance. Despite all this, the Nadelburg—like most privileged enterprises of this kind—turned only a meager profit.[74]

For Maria Theresa, such institutions were works of Christian *caritas*. She ordered her officials to undertake regular inspections and personally pored over their reports. She was particularly keen for child laborers to receive basic instruction in reading, writing, arithmetic, and, above all, the one true Christian religion (i.e., Catholicism). She took a keen interest in the management of other workhouses and orphanages as well, intervening in even the most minor operational details, just as she did in her own children's upbringing. For the orphanage in Graz, for example, she specified that the children should go to confession and take communion on the first Sunday of each month, regularly pray for members of the Archducal House, devote two days in Holy Week to spiritual exercises, and be examined on the catechism. She demanded that "serious attention be paid to the eradication of vermin" and a maid appointed for this purpose. Children were to be regularly bathed, and "each orphan, regardless of sex, is to be given two pairs of winter socks." They should no longer be sent out twice a week to gather alms, as had previously been the case, but only once every three months, since takings were slim anyway. Instead, they should take a walk in the fresh air twice a week, albeit only during "recreation hours," so as to have an "opportunity to stretch their legs."[75] Her own children did not enjoy much more leisure time than this.

It would be anachronistic to apply modern standards of child protection to Maria Theresa's industrial policy. In the eighteenth century, putting children to work in the family home or on the farm was both commonplace and unobjectionable. All that was new was involving them to so great an extent in industrial labor. This practice was not unique to the Habsburg lands—indeed, it had long been trialed in other countries. There were also prominent antecedents for commercially exploiting child labor, notably the famous orphanage established in Halle by the Pietist divine August Hermann Francke. So far as the disciplining of her subjects was concerned, Maria Theresa was acting no differently from most of her pious and enlightened contemporaries.

New Schools

The keystone to the economic, moral, and religious disciplining of her subjects was Maria Theresa's celebrated elementary school reform of 1774.[76] Until then, she had mainly focused on improving aristocratic education and Latin schools, as *the ratio studiorum* of the Jesuits, who had practically monopolized higher education in the hereditary lands, appeared to have lost step with the times. In 1746 she had founded the Collegium Theresianum, a combination of knights' academy and Jesuit college, where young nobles from the hereditary lands were to be transformed into the kind of public servants demanded by the new system: loyal, professional, urbane, and articulate. Her commitment to the institution is shown by the fact that she allowed it to be housed in her old summer palace, the Favorita, where the Theresianum still exists today as an elite high school. She herself reviewed the curriculum and entrusted oversight over the school to the lord high chamberlain, who personally supervised every examination.[77] Although the education system continued to be controlled by the Jesuit order, it was now subject to state superintendence, in line with the oft-cited dictum "The school system is and always will be a matter of state."[78] Curriculum and teaching methods were adapted to meet the changed requirements: Latin was sidelined in favor of German, useful subjects such as arithmetic and geography were promoted, and rote learning fell out of favor.[79]

Maria Theresa turned her attention to "German" schools—that is, elementary schools in contrast to "Latin" higher schools—only much later, although the dire state of rural education had been a cause for

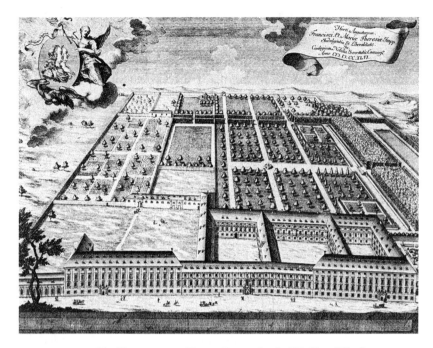

FIGURE 49. The Theresianum in Vienna. Copperplate by J. E. Mansfeld, after 1755

concern in Vienna ever since the campaign against crypto-Protestantism in the 1750s. The findings of the conscription of souls from 1770–71 exposed the extent of illiteracy more drastically than ever before. There was at least one school in every town, and one in most rural parishes as well, yet the majority of children never went to school because their parents needed them at home. Schoolmasters were untrained, relied on odd jobs to supplement their meager wages, and were held in low regard. The problem was discussed in the State Council from 1770 onward, leading to the establishment of territorial school commissions. A vigorous and heated debate about school reform ensued. Numerous memoranda were submitted to the monarch; some even advised calling for help from Protestant scholars in the Empire, since the Catholic education system was woefully inferior to its Lutheran counterpart. When the higher education system in the hereditary lands collapsed following the dissolution of the Jesuit order in 1773, the school question suddenly shot to the top of the political agenda. At the same time, new opportunities opened up as the order's property, including its school buildings, passed into state hands. Against this background, Maria Theresa put an end to the debates at court by personally writing to Frederick II—with whom peaceful relations had been temporarily restored following the Polish partition—asking him to send the celebrated pedagogue Johann Ignaz Felbiger to Vienna for a time. Felbiger, abbot of the Augustinian monastery in Silesian Sagan, had made a name for himself through his innovative teaching methods, which had already been sporadically introduced in Habsburg territories. He had also written a modern catechism and reformed the Catholic school system in Silesia. Frederick II duly dispatched the abbot to Vienna, where he formed his own impressions of the situation in the hereditary lands and subsequently drafted a comprehensive, systematic "General school ordinance for German normal, major, and minor schools in all imperial and royal hereditary lands." This was proclaimed as law in December 1774.[80]

The preamble stated programmatically that "the education of youth of both sexes, being the most important foundation for the true happiness of nations," merited the monarch's particular attention, given the formative influence of early education on a person's entire way of living and thinking. That is why "the darkness of ignorance" had to be dispelled "and everyone instructed in keeping with their estate"—not in keeping with their academic ability, to be sure, since allowing the impecunious children of peasants to flood colleges and universities would only prove a drain on the public purse. In other respects, the school ordinance was nothing short of revolutionary. It introduced compulsory schooling in both city and countryside for all boys and girls aged between six and twelve. "Without exception," every child who was not home-schooled by a qualified tutor had to attend a German school, where they would not only receive instruction in religion, morals, and the three Rs but also be led in paths of "righteousness" and rational "economy." Even labor service for the landlord would no longer be accepted as an excuse for skipping class (at least in the winter months). A hierarchical system of inspections was imposed on all German schools, "normal schools" for teacher training were set up, subjects and methods of instruction were mandated, and uniform textbooks prescribed.

Instructional groups were to be determined by performance rather than by age or gender; the effort and progress of each pupil was to be recorded in a "diligence catalogue," with prizes awarded to the most diligent and best behaved. Not least, Felbiger sought to raise the social standing of schoolmasters by according them a certain ceremonial status and strictly forbidding them from moonlighting as tavern keepers or musicians.

Felbiger was an indefatigable popularizer of Enlightenment ideals— committed not only to diffusing religion and good morals throughout the land, but also to teaching subjects progressive new knowledge and skills that could lighten their arduous everyday lives. In the spirit of Enlightenment pedagogy, and with an obvious dig at the Jesuits, he demanded that young people "have their minds enlightened, not tormented unnecessarily with rote learning. Everything should be made clear to them, and they should be taught to express themselves correctly and comprehensively on what they have learned."[81] The *Methodology for Teachers* accompanying the school ordinance declared that "children should not obey despotically; they should be made to realize that it is reasonable and in their best interests to act in accordance with the teacher's wishes."[82] Maria Theresa applied these principles to her own children's education. Indeed, she was so taken with Felbiger's "beautiful" and "useful" ideas that she had the *Methodology* translated into all the official languages of the monarchy and introduced in all the German-Bohemian hereditary lands, and even in Hungary.[83]

The school reform was a powerful tool for political centralization and cultural homogenization, not least through its impact on the spread of German. In the Bohemian lands, German and Czech had coexisted for centuries, with most subjects understanding enough of the other language to meet their everyday needs. Both languages were spoken at institutes of higher learning and universities, although German became increasingly dominant as the language of rule, especially in the upper echelons of society. Officials in Vienna regarded a lack of proficiency in German as an impediment to their civilizing mission. The report on the conscription of souls in Moravia, for example, found that Bohemian peasants were worse off than their German counterparts because "their inability to speak a language other than their own prevents them from mingling with more refined and rational company, and therefore condemns them to languish in their native stupidity."[84] Following the Seven Years' War, Maria Theresa had already prioritized the promotion of German, decreeing that only schoolmasters who spoke both languages could be employed in the Bohemian lands. The school reform embraced the goal of bilingualism, stipulating that all children be instructed first in their mother tongue and then in German. This aspect of the reform did not meet with universal enthusiasm.[85]

The General School Ordinance met with resistance for many reasons—at court and in the territorial school commissions, from landlords and from subjects themselves. There were three main objections aimed at Felbiger's reform. First: "If country folk could read, they may well read bad books, and so get muddle-headed ideas about religion." Maria Theresa never accepted the validity of this argument. For all her concerns about godless books, she was convinced that literacy ultimately helped people arrive at a better understanding of the true Catholic religion. Second: "Bringing enlightenment to country folk may awaken in them the desire for a better and easier position in society, and consequently decrease the number of people so urgently needed to till the fields." Here, too, Felbiger could placate his critics. After all, his plans were intended to improve the peasants' lot and reduce their grounds for discontent. And finally: "Educating the young takes a lot of time," time they did not have owing to their obligation to work for their parents and landlords.[86] This was the thorniest problem, and Felbiger was prepared to make concessions on this point. Yet many subjects did not see why they should have to forgo their children's labor, at least for part of the year, while at the same time incurring additional expenses for school fees and clothing. Conversely, many schoolmasters and priests were unhappy that they would now be put through extensive training, examinations, and inspections without any increase in pay. The entire reform project was chronically underfunded, despite the fact that the expropriation of the Jesuits had freed up more money for schooling than ever before. The territorial estates were also supposed to contribute to a newly established school fund. Yet the estates paid far less than promised, while the Jesuit honey pot drew attention from rival claimants. The fund was administered by an education committee chaired by Court Councillor Franz Karl von Kressel, a confidant of Maria Theresa appointed in 1774 to replace Archbishop Migazzi.[87] Much of the conflict generated by the school reform concerned how these resources were to be allocated. Felbiger, who enjoyed the ruler's absolute confidence, was competing with several other parties at court for access to the Jesuit kitty. This made him extremely unpopular; even Archduke Leopold considered him a fraud and schemer.[88] To make matters worse, he also wanted to reform the military school system in line with his methodology. To both the Court War Council and Joseph II, this smacked of improper interference.

The correspondence between Maria Theresa and Court Councillor Greiner, a key figure in the last years of her reign, conveys a vivid impression of Felbiger's position at court under these conditions.[89] Franz Sales Greiner had entered the Directorium in Publicis et Cameralibus under Haugwitz and soon proved himself a hardworking, loyal, and ambitious young man. In 1766 he had married Maria Theresa's former maid and reader, Charlotte Hieronymus, and proceeded to embark on a stellar career. Five years later he became the youngest court secretary in the Bohemian-Austrian Court Chancellery. Not long after, the empress elevated him to the knighthood and promoted him ahead of all his colleagues to the rank of privy councillor at the Court Chancellery. Nobody was more keenly aware than Greiner himself that his rapid rise exposed him to resentment and slander. But the empress was so fond of him that he felt emboldened to ask her for one favor after another (although she was not always obliging). Greiner also knew how to make himself indispensable to the empress, remaining steadfastly loyal to her through all the bitter political conflicts of those years while at the same time subtly stoking her mistrust in whichever "contrary party" she was facing at the time, including her own son.[90] She allowed him to draft her decrees for her—"have him make me a resolution, but sweetly"[91]—and clearly believed his repeated protestations of humility and selflessness, offered not without a certain self-righteous insistence. Her ease in his company is perhaps best shown in the tone of playful irony the otherwise humorless old monarch occasionally allowed herself with him.

When Greiner fell ill after pushing through an unpopular new beverage tax in Vienna, she wrote to him: "drink lots of warm beer before the beverage tax is imposed."[92] Seeing themselves surrounded by opponents, the ruler and her secretary struck an almost conspiratorial tone. This also applied to the education committee, which came into Greiner's sphere of responsibility as Court Chancellery secretary. He complained, for example, about the "enmity" of the lawyer Martini, moved to have Martini's powers in the committee curtailed, and suggested doing away with the committee altogether. At the same time, he made recommendations to the empress about how the Jesuit funds should be spent and who should receive which pension.[93] In short, he enjoyed the monarch's ear and inclination in an area where financial disputes mixed with conflicts over policy.

Greiner was vital to the success of the school reform; he made himself Felbiger's mouthpiece and protected him from the machinations of his enemies. He thus briefed the empress on who was agitating in the background against the reform, who was causing "difficulties," and who was ignoring her orders. He also informed her of a rumor, spread by Felbiger's enemies with the intention of forcing his return to Prussia, that the abbot had fallen from grace—"for his adversaries well know that if the abbot stays here, the normal institute [i.e. the new Normal School in Vienna] will not be so easy to destroy, which is what they still wish for."[94] The gravest threat to Felbiger was the claim that he was secretly a heretic. An anonymous member of the high clergy had written a line-by-line commentary on Felbiger's collection of church songs and denounced them as un-Catholic. Greiner made himself the abbot's advocate. "Of this I am certain: no one in the world will see these songs as Lutheran hymns, . . . and if I may say so," he added with extraordinary temerity, "there is no need to furnish each line with an ultra-Catholic opinion."[95] But Maria Theresa was not one to take questions of Catholic orthodoxy lightly, and she demanded that Felbiger respond to the accusations "point by point." She revealed to Greiner how wearisome she now found the reform project: "from this correspondence you will see how this whole normal matter [i.e. the school reform] has come to disgust me."[96]

In view of all these hurdles and obstacles, it seems all the more remarkable that the General School Ordinance did not remain confined to the realm of bureaucratic fancy. Indeed, "with regard to its practical effects on schooling, it overshadowed anything being done in the Protestant territorial states at the same time," not excepting the legendary Prussian General School Regulation (*Generallandschulreglement*).[97] In the decades that followed, the hundreds of teachers who graduated from the newly established Normal School in Vienna took the new system with them wherever they went. Rural schools proliferated, while those that already existed were brought step by step into conformity with the new order. The professionalization and social standing of teachers gradually increased, as community concerns about compulsory schooling waned. This success is reflected in school attendance figures, above all in the Archdiocese of Vienna, where the percentage of children attending school shot up from 40 percent in 1780 to a sensational 94 percent in 1807.[98] However, the reform of the German schools was not matched by an equally successful reform of the higher education system, which took a long time to recover from the dissolution of the Jesuit order. Although some former Jesuit schools were carried on by Benedictines, Piarists, or ex-Jesuits, there was a fall in the total number of colleges (*Gymnasien*). The period of schooling was shortened by a year as a cost-cutting measure, and since attendance was no longer free of charge, colleges became more socially exclusive than the Jesuit schools had ever been.[99]

The elementary school reform, by contrast, was undoubtedly the most lastingly successful achievement of Maria Theresa's later reign. It was also one of only a few items on her agenda that did not lead to open conflict with her son, even if Joseph wrote disparagingly to Leopold that the empress allowed herself to be influenced by "little people," had no idea of what she was doing, and was driving the education system to rack and ruin.[100] Yet the reform was a success not least because the empress had entrusted its implementation to Felbiger himself and given him clear authority over all the territorial school commissions. In some respects, this recalls the first great wave of reforms following the War of Succession. As with Haugwitz back then, so now with Felbiger she called in a man from Prussian Silesia and showed herself prepared to learn lessons from the Prussian model. As then, she placed her unconditional trust in this one reformer, invested him with wide-ranging powers, and held fast to him in the face of fierce resistance—a resolve she had lost in almost all other policy matters. In Leopold's opinion, church and school affairs were all that still claimed her personal attention.[101] Finally, the school reform had a genuinely religious dimension for Maria Theresa. Contrary to how it may have appeared in hindsight, she had no interest in providing her subjects with "an exit from their self-incurred tutelage," in line with Kant's celebrated definition of Enlightenment. Her foremost concern was to inoculate them against the pox of heresy. The school reform was meant to produce pious, hardworking, and obedient subjects, not an independent-minded citizenry.

Iustitia et Clementia

Iustitia et clementia was the motto Maria Theresa had adopted for her reign—two classical, corresponding princely virtues. *Iustitia* stood for the severity and impartiality of the law, *clementia* for the grace that tempers such severity and makes exceptions to the law. Both were virtues traditionally ascribed to a ruler as supreme judge and lawgiver, as the fountainhead of justice and the law. To be sure, the monarch had always been considered bound to the estates for advice and consensus in exercising these central sovereign prerogatives. In the aftermath of Haugwitz's reforms, however, Maria Theresa was dismissive of these traditional corporative participation rights (apart from in Hungary): "nothing is to be done with the estates; they lack both mind and will; we must proceed by decree."[102]

She took her own role as supreme judge and lawgiver all the more seriously. Until 1753, she had every decision taken by higher courts in the individual hereditary lands brought before her for personal review. The Supreme Judiciary, established in 1749 as the highest court in all the Austrian hereditary lands, had to provide her with a copy of every document it released; she signed off on all its judgments herself.[103] It went without saying that the monarch could intervene in judicial procedures as she saw fit.[104] Court President Christian August von Seilern's idea that the Supreme Judiciary's judgments should command respect even from the ruler struck her as both impudent and incompatible with the notion of royal sovereignty. It would mean, as an outraged Court Councillor Greiner explained to her, that "the sovereign would cease to be sovereign, and pronouncements made by the judiciary would be more infallible than papal judgments *in dogmaticis!*"[105] By implication, only the judgments of the sovereign herself were infallible. Even though judicial institutions became increasingly professionalized, the monarch still remained—along with God—the ultimate source from which all justice flowed.

There was no division of powers in the modern sense. *Politica* and *judicialia*, the administrative and judicial branches of government, kept at least notionally separate under Haugwitz's reform, were later reunited.[106] The judiciary's lack of independence had its counterpart in the low formalization of procedures and the tangle of competing judicial powers. While the monarch was traditionally considered the highest judge in the realm, this did not mean that she actually stood at the apex of an orderly judicial hierarchy. Lords, civic magistrates, the clergy, universities, guilds, and corporations of all kinds traditionally possessed judicial powers of their own, by no means all of them exercised by men trained in the law.[107] Bohemian magnates even claimed the right to impose severe corporal punishments for crimes committed on their estates. The sources of law in the hereditary lands were no less various than the judicial institutions. Each territory had its own, unwritten common law, its "praiseworthy customs" (*Löbliches Herkommen*): privileges, statutes, political contracts, and so on. In addition, there was a vast body of more or less generally valid law ordained by the ruler, as set out in ordinances: court decrees, patents, rescripts, resolutions, police regulations, and whatever else they might be called. Then there was the independent Canon Law of the church as well as the scholarly systems of Roman and natural law. All this gave rise to endless dispute about which source of law took precedence under which circumstances. Against this complicated background, the ruler's power of legislation, the core of all sovereign rights, grew both quantitatively and qualitatively in importance. The volume of positive law—that is, law fixed in writing by the ruler—had been expanding exponentially for some time, becoming ever more impenetrable in the process. Maria Theresa's most pressing priority was therefore to gain a clear overview of the monarchy's own legislative record. At the start of her reign, the most recent collection of laws available to her was the *Codex Austriacus* from 1704. She then called several times for the collection to be brought up to date—an extremely daunting and unappealing task for any jurist.[108] A continuation covering the period up to the death of Charles VI was printed in 1752, yet it was not until 1777 that a supplement finally appeared, taking the *Codex Austriacus* from 1740 to 1770.[109]

Getting a clear picture of her own legislation was the lesser problem. The codification of the law in a comprehensive sense—that is, the task of collating, writing down, and systematizing existing territorial laws, of which the laws decreed by the sovereign made up only a small part— proved far more difficult. Codification did not simply mean sifting through, classifying, and transcribing the various regional legal traditions; it also meant constraining the plurality of the law and subordinating it to state authority. One God, one monarch, one state, one law: such was the motto. In the words of an anonymous memorandum, nothing could be more conducive to the general good than "for all subjects to come together . . . under one God, one territorial prince, and one law."[110] In future, the law should not only be one and the same throughout all the lands (to the extent that this was feasible); it should also be clear, easily accessible, and understandable to all. This presupposed that it had been set down in its entirety in writing. Once written down, the law was to be as unambiguous as possible. It could only be changed by sovereign fiat, not through custom, judicial practice, or scholarly interpretation. Such, at any rate, was the rationalist pipe dream. Yet the prevailing laws of the lands could not be swept aside so easily and replaced by a new, rigorously systematic law of the land. Even bold reformers did not go so far, since not even the sovereign herself could simply do away with existing territorial law. She had, after all, sworn oaths to uphold it when receiving homage from the estates. Two incompatible ideas of the law stood opposed here: law as a project, to be created by the legislator in accordance with rational, abstract principles, and law as a repository of tradition that had grown up organically over time and needed to be safeguarded in its diversity. In each individual case, a pragmatic compromise had to be struck between these two opposing poles.[111]

To a certain extent, Haugwitz's reform package entailed a standardization of the law. The establishment of a Supreme Judiciary for all the "German" hereditary lands necessitated common legal norms on which jurists could base their judgments. Following the War of Succession, Maria Theresa made this goal her own. She appointed two legislative committees, one for civil law, the other for criminal law. After initial discussions, the committee for civil law agreed in June 1753 to retain only those existing territorial laws which, "correctly deduced from sound first principles, accord with both true jurisprudence and the practice of the most civilized nations." Anything not ultimately derived from "these infallible sources" should "be ameliorated, where necessary, by means of new sovereign legislation, and a uniform and universally binding law thus introduced and established."[112] At the same time, however, it became clear that a survey would need to be carried out in each territory before the project of standardization could get underway. Maria Theresa resolved this in a handwritten instruction: "Everyone is to be reminded that the intention is not just to provide uniformity to the laws, but to do so with the utmost haste."[113] She set a time frame of just three months for the task; the digest of territorial law was to be submitted on October 1. As a spur to industry, she further stipulated that committee members should have their stipends halved over that period, receiving the remainder only upon successful completion of their labors. In her eyes, the main problem was the sluggish inefficiency of the court system and the godless trickery of lawyers, a "plague on the state" that obstructed the course of justice and cried out for punishment. But the enterprise's greatest source of legal and political controversy lay elsewhere.

The task was fiendishly complicated. It was certainly not for lack of effort that the jurists failed to meet their assigned deadline. At least committee members managed to reach consensus on how they would organize their vast material and the method they would adopt. By

June 1755 they had submitted—not without a certain justifiable pride—
the first three compendious folio volumes. Yet these dealt only with the
first section of civil law, personal law. Maria Theresa was unimpressed.
It was all too slow and wordy for her liking. She demonstrated her mistrust in her usual way by appointing a second committee to watch over
and correct the work of the first. There were now two committees working side by side, the original compilation committee in Brno and the
revision committee in Vienna. This did nothing to expedite proceedings. Concerns voiced by harried and humiliated workers went un-
heeded. Meanwhile, opponents to the codification, rightly fearing that
it posed a threat to their time-honored particular law, marshaled their
forces. That the previously published sections had clearly done nothing
to simplify or clarify private law offered them a welcome argument to
call into question the meaning and purpose of the entire undertaking.

Given all the difficulties, it is remarkable that the final draft of the
Codex Theresianus for all the German-Bohemian hereditary lands could
finally be submitted for royal approval in 1766: Hungary, the Netherlands, and the Italian territories were explicitly treated as foreign countries. The code represented a precarious balancing act between preservation and rational transformation. It involved a series of compromises
between the compilation committee, which tended to privilege the
plurality of territorial law, and the revision committee, which insisted
on standardization according to natural law principles. Needless to say,
pillars of the traditional property regime such as serfdom went unchallenged; anything else would have been tantamount to social revolution.
This codification was nonetheless something fundamentally new. Although material law itself remained essentially unchanged, its basis of
validity was radically unified. Through its incorporation into a code
authorized by the sovereign, all law, regardless of origin and content,
was transformed into statutory law, binding only by sovereign decree.
The *Codex Theresianus* therefore represented a significant break with
premodern legal culture.

As would soon become apparent, however, it was doomed from the
outset. For the aristocratic old guard it went too far; for the rationalist-
minded reformers it went nowhere near far enough.[114] Even as

discussions were held about which of the monarchy's languages the code would be translated into, objections were being raised and changes demanded from all quarters. In 1769 the entire matter was brought before the State Council, an official report commissioned, and yet another revision begun. Finally, Kaunitz himself took the matter in hand in October 1770 and subjected the code to a devastating critique.[115] In his view, all the labors of the previous years had resulted, at best, in a useful compendium of materials. With the strict rationalist's optimism, he demanded that the learned subtleties of Roman law be done away with, replaced by a clear, simple legal code that accorded with the dictates of reason and natural justice. In Kaunitz's spirit, Maria Theresa ordered a complete revision in August 1772: "It should all be done as quickly as possible, provided there is no loss of clarity, without going into . . . excessive detail."[116] Around twenty years after the codification project had gotten underway, it thus recommenced more or less from scratch. Yet the window of opportunity for a compromise akin to the 1766 version had since closed. The work dragged on as resistance to rational law increased. In 1780, when Maria Theresa called for yet another report from the State Council, Secretary Franz Georg von Keeß came to the finding that laws should always be in keeping with the spirit, mores, and mentality of a nation. A uniform body of laws for all territories was therefore not even desirable.[117] The codification of civil law was eventually completed in 1811 as the ABGB (*Allgemeines Bürgerliches Gesetzbuch*, General Civil Code), long after Maria Theresa's death and under completely different circumstances.

The codification of criminal law fared little better, although the responsible committee had ended its work in 1769, albeit with dubious success.[118] So far as practices, crimes, and punishments were concerned, the *Constitutio criminalis Theresiana* differed only in degree from the famous criminal code (*Halsgerichtsordnung*) brought out by her ancestor Charles V in 1532. It still offered the same spectrum of gruesome premodern punishments: the blasphemer's tongue was to be ripped out and the perjurer's hand hacked off, whoever entered into a pact with the devil would pay for it by being burned alive, while those found guilty of *lèse-majesté* would be nipped with red-hot pincers before being drawn

FIGURE 50. Torture instructions. *Constitutio
Criminalis Theresiana*, 1769

and quartered. The enlightened public greeted such measures with
scorn. A reviewer in the *Göttingische Gelehrte Anzeigen* drew attention to
the "particularly curious" supplements in which "the methods of torture
customary in Prague and Vienna are very clearly depicted in thirty-four
copperplates." He concluded sarcastically: "A vignette in which the Most
Serene Empress is shown surrounded by instruments of torture was rejected by this great monarch's refined taste and most beneficent way of
thinking."[119] If anything, the meticulous technical instructions for executioners in the form of accurately drawn charts caused even greater offense than the retention of torture as a method in criminal procedures
(fig. 50). Kaunitz, too, expressed his acute embarrassment that Maria
Theresa's name had been associated with such barbaric practices, which
"other civilized nations" such as England, Saxony, and Prussia had

already abolished.[120] The effectiveness of torture as a method of criminal investigation had long stood in doubt, and now the utility of cruel physical punishments was likewise called into question.

The theater of terror was characteristic of premodern criminal justice. Such grisly spectacles were still being put on in the eighteenth century, particularly when supreme authority came under visible threat. The best-known case is the 1757 execution in Paris of the failed regicide Damiens, quartered for attacking the king with a knife, but even the enlightened minister Marquês de Pombal in Portugal had a man he suspected of planning an attempt on his life torn apart by horses in 1775.[121] For all that, the death penalty was imposed relatively rarely in early modern times, and carried out even less. The cruelty of this exemplary punishment, it might be said, stood in inverse relation to its frequency. This accorded with the structural weakness of premodern rule, which simply lacked the executive means necessary to pursue and punish crime whenever and wherever it occurred, opting instead for isolated, yet all the more spectacular, performances to restore order and move the awed populace to "reflective horror." This was equally true of Maria Theresa's approach to criminal justice. A number of pamphleteers reported during her reign on "well-merited punishments" for serial thieves, counterfeiters, swindlers, and murderers of both sexes in Vienna who faced public execution with the sword or at the gallows. In some cases, the offending hand was first chopped off, the head mounted on a spike and exhibited, or the body burned and the ashes scattered.[122] In the public eye, however, Maria Theresa was renowned for her leniency. The empress hated imposing the death penalty, it was said, and did so far less frequently than other monarchs.[123] For example, the Bohemian circle captain (*Kreishauptmann*) Karl David, sentenced to death for high treason in Prague in 1743, was pardoned at the last minute, just as the executioner was preparing to sever his oath-taking hand, behead him, quarter him, and display his dismembered limbs in all four cardinal directions.[124] In 1780, with the reported remark "A great stone has fallen from my heart," she pardoned the cashier of the Office of the Great Seal in Vienna, facing execution for having forged the seals of office.[125] She pardoned Franz Anton Count Nostitz, who in 1752 had killed a fellow peer in a duel, although she otherwise always insisted that no mercy be shown to duelists.[126] She even found it in her heart to pardon Franz von der Trenck, renowned and reviled for his wartime atrocities. Nobles with powerful intercessors doubtless stood a better chance of benefiting from her clemency. The practice of pardoning convicted criminals was by no means considered a check on sovereign omnipotence. On the contrary, by premodern standards a distinguishing feature of the monarch's plenitude of power was precisely the ability to make exceptions to the rule. Enlightened judicial reformers took offense at these many exceptions. They wanted to make the criminal justice system not only more useful for the state but also more reliable, more uniform, and more predictable; then theatrical cruelty could be dispensed with as well. The enlightened monarch—like the just God, in whose image he was formed—should have no need to make exceptions; he would demonstrate his wisdom far better by strictly upholding the laws he himself had put in place.

Criminal justice was a polarizing theme in the second half of the century; indeed, it was one of the touchstones of Enlightenment thinking. The treatise by the Milanese jurist Cesare Beccaria, *Dei delitti e delle pene* (*On Crimes and Punishments*), had provoked debate upon its publication in 1764. In Vienna the Freemason Joseph von Sonnenfels (1733–1817), son of a baptized Jew from Nikolsburg in Moravia, blazed a trail against torture and the death sentence. Sonnenfels, an eloquent and spirited defender of Enlightenment ideals who campaigned for the purification of the German tongue and the moral improvement of the theater, had gained the protection of aristocratic patrons thanks to his many talents. In 1763 he was made professor of police and cameral sciences at the University of Vienna and in 1769 he was appointed to the Lower Austrian State Council.[127] As Vienna's "director of illuminations," his job was to enlighten the city in both senses of the word. In 1777 he oversaw the installation of around 3,500 hand-lit oil lanterns on the streets of Vienna—the first city in Europe to boast all-night street lighting. He spread even more light as a critical essayist and editor of the Viennese journal *The Man without Prejudice*. Of all his services in the cause of Enlightenment, his judicial and political campaign against torture earned him the most lasting fame in enlightened public opinion.[128] Yet he had his sights set on more than just the abolition of torture. This was merely the empirical pretext for calling fundamentally into question the relationship between state force and the critical public sphere.

By 1769, when the *Constitutio Criminalis Theresiana* came into force, Sonnenfels was already no stranger to conflict with the censors.[129] In his treatise on government, published four years earlier, he had taken a stand against torture and capital punishment, both of which he believed to be counterproductive.[130] Conservative forces such as Archbishop Migazzi, long opposed to everything he stood for, had sought to muzzle him at the time. In this instance, Maria Theresa had allowed Sonnenfels to exercise his academic freedom, despite siding against him in another.[131] Joseph II held him in high regard and appointed him to the education committee in 1769, thereby making a victim of censorship a censor himself. This did nothing to stop his enemies at court from launching a fresh attack on his teachings, which openly contradicted the law now that the Theresian criminal code had come into effect. They succeeded in convincing Maria Theresa. On August 22, 1772, she issued a decree prohibiting professors from speaking out on torture and the death penalty. Sonnenfels reacted by vigorously defending his role as a state official in public discourse: the empress had every right to demand that the law be obeyed, but she had no right to forbid that it be criticized. On the contrary, he felt duty bound to profess in public what he believed to be true, since he could not hope otherwise to use his influence to improve existing conditions.[132] Meanwhile, however, he renewed his appeal for her to do away with torture.

Around the same time, a report by the Faculty of Medicine at the University of Vienna came to the same result; Court Chancellor Heinrich von Blümegen also sympathized with Sonnenfels. Maria Theresa felt unsettled and irresolute. She took the issue seriously, she said, declaring that "the many objections still raised with regard to torture necessitate that this subject, of such importance for the state, be further investigated in order that I might set my mind at rest." All territorial governments, the Supreme Judiciary, and the State Council were asked to give their opinion on "whether torture should be abolished entirely, or whether it should be restricted to certain kinds of criminal offenses";[133] leaving the current system unchanged was thus not even mentioned as an option at this stage. Opinions were predictably divided. A majority of territorial governors recommended sticking with the status quo. Sonnenfels himself was outvoted in the Lower Austrian government and wrote a dissenting opinion. Scandalously, this opinion appeared in print and made it to Vienna, allegedly without Sonnenfels's involvement, although no one believed him even at the time.[134] Throwing such a question before "the judicial bench of the public" (to quote contemporary parlance) was a typical Enlightenment gesture. In doing so, he formally put himself in the wrong by betraying the confidentiality of his office. But this was precisely his message: so weighty a topic ought not to be discussed behind closed doors. It should be thrashed out in public in order that the truth might emerge victorious from the free conflict of opinions.

A formal reprimand from the empress was the only price he had to pay for his temerity. When both a majority in State Council and Joseph declared themselves for Sonnenfels's position, Maria Theresa decided not to make a decision, delegating the task to her son: "I entreat the emperor, who has studied the law, trusting in his fairness, perspicacity, and philanthropy, to decide this work without my counsel, since I do not understand it myself."[135] Joseph, who had previously made his position emphatically clear, now suddenly shrank before the responsibility. He put together a new advisory committee that ended in a stalemate of four votes to four. Maria Theresa finally asked Chancellor Blümegen for his advice, which tipped the balance. On January 2, 1776, the empress issued a handbillet abolishing torture in judicial proceedings, albeit only in the German hereditary lands, Galicia, and the Banat. Enlightened public opinion roundly applauded the decision. This victory was attributed to the "vivid impression" that Sonnenfels's tract had made on "the mind of our land's best mother, its gracious and philanthropic monarch."[136] But she herself remained far from convinced that she had done the right thing. Immediately after making the decree, she wrote to Archduke Ferdinand: "There are many reasons for and against; I was for the latter, since I am no lover of innovation."[137]

The capital offenses set out in the *Constitutio Criminalis Theresiana* were a separate matter requiring further discussion. At any rate, a more lenient approach to punishment was never seriously entertained. Even if the death penalty were to be meted out more sparingly in future, this was not from any humanitarian considerations but because it was believed that delinquents could best serve the state as a source of free labor. Both Joseph and Sonnenfels preferred the workhouse and forced labor as a punishment for serious crimes. In this point, at least, Maria Theresa and the reformers saw eye to eye. As we have seen, however, her instrument of choice was compulsory resettlement in the Banat.[138]

Rebellion in Bohemia

The years 1771–72 visited especially severe hardship on Maria Theresa's subjects. Almost all Central Europe shivered through two unusually cold and wet summers resulting in poor harvests, inflation, famine, and outbreaks of disease.[139] In the Habsburg monarchy the Bohemian lands were by far the worst affected. Between 1770 and 1773 around 600,000 of roughly 4.3 million people fell victim to hunger and the epidemic illnesses that came in its wake.[140] Bohemia was especially vulnerable, for two reasons. For one, it had been the central theater of two recent wars and had not yet had a chance to recover from the devastation. Second, of all the lands in the monarchy, Bohemia was the one where subjects were most severely disadvantaged by property relations, *robot* obligations were highest, and serfdom was most pronounced—even more so than in Hungary, which had seen widespread unrest in 1766.[141] Montesquieu cited the country in his *Esprit des lois* to illustrate the continuance of ancient slavery in modern Europe, and contemporaries found the unfreedom and oppression of the Bohemian peasantry beyond all imagining.[142] Maria Theresa had a limited view of the situation. She had occasionally undertaken royal progresses through Bohemia and Moravia and been hosted by local grandees such as the Choteks, Kolowrats, Czernins, Buquoys, and Gallases; she had also been the guest of the Kaunitz family in Moravian Austerlitz.[143] During such trips, she had asked to be taken on "excursions to become better acquainted with the districts of the city of Prague,"[144] but these were hardly fact-finding missions. The excursions consisted of prearranged inspections, banquets, hunts, trips to the theater, and various entertainments at which peasants provided a dash of local color, at best.[145]

Yet even in Vienna, the catastrophic situation faced by subjects in Bohemia had become glaringly obvious. In the first years of Maria Theresa's reign, isolated uprisings had already broken out after Maria Theresa had failed to redeem the promise to do away with serfdom that Charles VII had made to peasants during the Bavarian occupation. Haugwitz's reforms had, if anything, increased the burden on serfs rather than lightening it. Since local lords now had to pay contributions themselves, they made up for it by forcing more peasants to work longer hours on their seigneurial lands. When, following the Seven Years' War, a committee was sent to Habsburg rump Silesia to register encumbrances on estates in a legally binding urbarium (supposedly with the mutual agreement of lords and subjects), it became clear just how many obstacles would have to be overcome.[146] In Bohemia and Moravia, unlike in Silesia, such an urbarium had already been compiled under Charles VI in a Robot Patent from 1738, but it no longer matched the situation on the ground, since many landlords had since imposed extra duties or confiscated peasant lands. This was now to be revised and standardized. Landlords, who had no interest in changing the status quo, defended themselves by arguing that, even in 1738, a decree intended to improve the peasants' lot had only provoked them into rebellion. But they could not prevent Maria Theresa from commissioning an investigation into individual lords, at least. Among the evidence of blatantly oppressive malpractice the investigation brought to light, abuses on the estates of Prince Mansfeld were so horrendous that the prince was fined two thousand ducats and ordered to pay his subjects compensation; the responsible circle officials, who had turned a blind eye to his misconduct, were stood down from their posts.[147] In July 1770 Maria Theresa ordered that all circles be investigated for similar abuses.[148]

From early 1771 the news from Bohemia was ever more alarming. The snow had not yet melted by Easter, "and given that crops in the hereditary lands and the Empire have suffered from stunted growth ever since the previous harvest, and various places are consequently afflicted by famine, the fear is all the greater," Khevenhüller noted.[149] The commissioners' reports composed in 1770–71 on the occasion of the conscription of souls, which arrived in Vienna from July 1771, painted a harrowing picture of a land racked by hunger and disease.[150] The poor were resorting to eating "bread produced with flour made of oats mixed with grass or flour dust," giving rise to "convulsions and epilepsy."[151] Many landlords held back their reserves of grain to sell them to their own subjects at extortionate prices. "The poverty of the people living in these parts is almost indescribable. It is so dire that they cannot even clothe themselves, but mostly walk around half-naked."[152] The commissioners left readers in no doubt that structural causes, not the recent poor harvests, were to blame for the misery: "*Robot* will be the complete ruin of the farmer, since in most places it is imposed with such harshness that peasants lack the time to till their fields by day."[153] *Robot* terms of seven (!) days a week were not unheard of, forcing peasants to tend to their own lands by night or risk starvation. Lacking the money to purchase exemption, their productivity was affected by their inability to enjoy the fruits of their own labor. Many were therefore threatening to migrate to Prussia. Peasants who "support themselves in keeping with their class", on the other hand, would be of far greater benefit to the state "than those who eke out a pitiful existence, cannot be induced by any means to think of their offspring, and are more the instruments for sustaining a small class of human beings than they are human beings themselves".[154] The officials who wrote these words were anything but revolutionaries. They never called into question "the subject's duty to perform compulsory labor [*robothen*] for his superiors—only every duty must be moderate, purposeful, and fairly assigned," and this was demonstrably not the case in the Bohemian lands.[155] All the commissioners therefore never tired of warning that "current conditions [must] be reformed, otherwise the most dreadful consequences will inevitably ensue."[156]

The most dreadful consequences had long since come to pass; the "extreme misery" of the Bohemian lands was plain for Maria Theresa to see.[157] In early 1771 she dispatched Court Councillor Kressel to Bohemia as her plenipotentiary, authorizing him to take immediate action against the famine; if necessary, the military was to be called on for support. She also freed up state funds to purchase grain from Hungary and have it transported to Bohemia and Moravia.[158] Yet all this was still woefully inadequate. 1771 brought a second failed harvest. Prayers of supplication were held over several days in St. Stephen's Cathedral "to placate our dear Lord, whose wrath continues to visit hunger and sickness on poor Bohemia, such that . . . 70,000 souls have already perished through these two rods [i.e. divine instruments of punishment], despite everything humanly possible having been done" through the provision of foodstuffs, medicines, and "no less than a million in hard cash," noted Khevenhüller.[159] On June 1 Maria Theresa ordered that "a general urbarial regulation, as in Silesia, be carried out in Bohemia as soon as possible."[160] In October and November 1771 Joseph personally toured the areas hardest hit by famine. From Prague he launched a scathing attack on the "vicious constitution" of the Bohemian lands and ventured his opinion on what should be done to fix it.[161] At the same time, on October 6, 1771, following protracted and heated preliminary talks, his mother finally appointed the urbarial commission for Bohemia.[162] She entrusted its direction to the son of her old lord high chamberlain. Franz Khevenhüller was deeply unhappy about this mission, which could only bring him grief from his peers and which he tackled with a noticeable lack of enthusiasm.[163] Others took to the task with greater verve and conviction, however: middle-class officials, unrelated by blood or marriage to the old families, who had a different view of conditions in Bohemia—"loyal rebels," as they have aptly been called.[164]

The most radical member of the commission was Franz Anton von Blanc (1737–1806), a bailiff's son from Waldkirch in Further Austria. Blanc had initially embarked on a military career before being discharged from service due to injury and made royal adviser in Prague. Maria Theresa had subsequently appointed him to the urbarial commission for Silesia, where he had distinguished himself through his intelligence, diligence, and perseverance. Unlike his colleagues with a legal background, he dared to question the "good old tradition" constantly invoked by landlords as an incontestable legal entitlement, replacing it with the criteria of the common good and what the peasants could reasonably be expected to endure. Maria Theresa took his side on the matter. In 1769 she had already resolved for Silesia that "the old custom should no longer be applied or cited in any instance." This represented an unprecedented affront to how the law had traditionally been understood.[165] Blanc now also defended this position as secretary in the Bohemian-Austrian Court Chancellery and as member of the new urbarial commission for Bohemia.[166] He received cover chiefly from Tobias Philipp von Gebler (1722–86), the quintessential enlightened bureaucrat. Gebler hailed from Thuringia and had studied at the most renowned Protestant universities before converting and entering Habsburg service in 1754, where he made a name for himself as an economic policy expert in the intendancy of Trieste. A freemason and playwright, he corresponded with Lessing and Nicolai, who considered him a mediocre dramatist but a worthy torchbearer of Enlightenment at the otherwise benighted Viennese court.[167] From 1762 he sat in the Court Chancellery, from 1768 in the State Council. Concerning the reports arriving in Vienna from Bohemia, he commented: "We regard with astonishment, indeed with unfeigned horror and the most painful consternation, the extreme misery in which poor subjects are languishing through the oppressiveness of their lords."[168] Along with Gebler, Franz Anton von Raab (1722–83), a jurist from Carinthia, had also carved out a career in imperial administration in Trieste. In 1773 Maria Theresa summoned him to Vienna as court councillor in the Commerce Committee and entrusted him with the exemplary task of transforming labor services into monetary contributions on her own lands in Bohemia, splitting up the great demesnes, and allocating them to small farmers in hereditary tenure. For all the obstacles he encountered, Raab acquitted himself so successfully that his name came to be identified with the program: people spoke henceforth of "Raabization." Maria Theresa later applied the Raab system to the former Jesuit estates and her demesnes in the other hereditary lands as well.[169]

In the urbarial commission, committed reformers like Blanc now had to work side by side with dyed-in-the-wool aristocrats such as Kolowrat, son-in-law of Khevenhüller senior and simultaneously president of the Court Chamber, City Bank, and Commerce Committee. The task required from all parties a significant willingness to compromise. So long as the old laws were upheld as sacrosanct and untouchable, progress was impossible. The common objective—providing relief to the peasants without excessively disadvantaging their lords—gave rise to endless difficulty and debate. The very foundations of the commission's work were called into dispute. For example, should "intolerable" burdens on subjects be lifted immediately even if lords could demonstrate they had the law on their side? And even if it was decided that they should, at what point did peasant obligations first become intolerable?[170] The devil was in the detail; the various types of service peasants owed their lords had to be considered in relation to differences in peasant wealth. Following lengthy deliberations, a majority finally settled on guidelines for regulating peasant dues. Among other things, *robot* should in future no longer exceed three days a week. The landlords then sat on their hands when asked to draft the corresponding urbariums. By mid-1773, two years after the urbarial commission had first convened, only a single Bohemian magnate, Ferdinand, Count Trautmannsdorff, had produced a new register of dues for his estates. Maria Theresa began to lose patience and demanded that peasants should at least be offered temporary relief. The State Council urgently advised her against this, since this would only cause further confusion. Negotiations in Vienna got underway once more.

Since January 1771, Joseph had constantly complained to his brother Leopold about the lack of concerted action on Bohemia shown by officials and his mother's "lethargy and apoplectic languor." All his writing and speaking had failed to sway her; now she was harvesting the fruits of her inaction.[171] To Khevenhüller, too, he complained in November 1772 that his mother, "having asked for so many expert opinions from all quarters, is nonetheless still unable to reach a final decision and supply the necessary remedies."[172] He thought of himself—and is remembered to this day—as an advocate for the poor oppressed peasants. In his memoranda he repeatedly called for the abolition of aristocratic prerogatives and presented even the most controversial reforms as feasible, provided they were pursued with the necessary political will. Symbolically, too, he acquired the reputation of a friend of the people.[173] In

1769, on his journey to meet Frederick II in Neisse, he had personally plowed a field to demonstrate his deep respect for agricultural labor (see fig. 41). The impact of this symbolic gesture was tremendous, both in the enlightened public sphere—especially among avant-garde physiocrats, who preached the superiority of the "producing" to the "sterile" classes—and in the peasant population itself.[174] Within a short period of time, the plowshare he had wielded was being touched as a precious relic, a monument to the farming emperor had been erected, and news of his public relations coup was being spread in illustrated pamphlets. The peasants of Bohemia, it was said, "love the emperor to distraction, and confidently expect him to release them from their fetters."[175]

The roles thus appeared—and still appear today—to be clearly divided: here the Enlightenment radical and peasant emancipator Joseph, who promised to clear away the "mass of medieval rubble beneath which Austria still lay buried"; there the vacillating and conservative Maria Theresa, more concerned with maintaining good relations with the aristocracy than with alleviating her peasants' plight.[176] Yet closer inspection reveals a different picture. The transformation of serfs into independent, productive, tax-paying smallholders was one of the empress's key priorities in the last years of her reign. In November 1772 she wrote to Blanc that the "abolition of serfdom . . . is the only thing that would keep me at the helm of state."[177] At the same time, she commissioned Raab to implement this plan on her own domain lands, pushed ahead with it in the face of fierce resistance, and was supported by her trusted adviser Greiner, who constantly urged her to ignore the "blackest calumnies" of the "opposition party."[178] She showed herself determined to use her sovereign power to reform the untenable Bohemian situation in the peasants' favor. If she assumed that she would finally be acting in concert with her son, however, she was sorely mistaken.

In early 1774 Khevenhüller found "the lady in a far better mood than before on account of Bohemian matters, and seemingly in excellent health"—notwithstanding the fact that "the proposals pertaining to the new urbarium were still in a state of constant confusion."[179] At this point in time, Maria Theresa had decided to grant her son's request to take the

Bohemian urbarial business into his own hands. Yet for reasons that are not entirely clear, Joseph now backed away from his earlier, ostentatiously pro-peasant position. He found it difficult to steer a middle path between the legitimate interests of both sides. A uniform regulation for all Bohemia, he feared, would fail to do justice to the diversity of conditions in the land. Instead, he ordered the lords to "come to an agreement with their subjects themselves . . . and draw up the urbaria." Only if they failed to reach agreement within six months would the directive worked out by the commission be introduced.[180] The Bohemian estates raised their voices in massive protest against this directive, even though it left most of their privileges intact. They took the view that they were the original owners of all the land, which they had ceded to the peasantry only under certain conditions. The state had no legal right to interfere in this domain. They defined *robot* as "the labor intrinsic to [the subject's] status and befitting his place in creation."[181] The increased contributions demanded by central government, as well as peasants' tendency to intemperance, extravagance, and idleness, were to blame for their poverty, not the labor duties imposed on them by their landlords. It was up to the parties directly concerned—that is, each individual landlord and his subjects—to come to a contractual agreement about the appropriate level of peasant dues. Both the State Council and Kaunitz immediately rejected this position. Yet Joseph now sided with the lords, a volte-face his foremost biographer has rightly described as "puzzling."[182] Maria Theresa signed the resolution on February 8, 1774, and the patent was published on April 21. Court Councillor Gebler had demanded, at least, that upper limits be set which agreements made by landlords with their peasants should not be allowed to surpass. But the estates were unhappy about this, too, and Joseph, who had recently shown great confidence in their goodwill, relented once more. In light of the nobles' superior bargaining position, there was now even a possibility that peasant obligations might be increased in individual cases.

The impact of this patent on subjects was nothing short of disastrous. Many parishes refused to sign anything, awaiting a further decree from the empress. There were rumors of a mysterious "golden imperial patent" which would free them from serfdom and had been withheld from them by their lords. The six-month deadline for individual agreements came and went without a result. Early the following year, 1775, subjects gave vent to their disappointed expectations. In March they refused to pay their feudal dues, left fields untended, attacked stewards, and stormed and laid waste to a number of stately homes. Many previously concealed Protestants—Hussites—were said to have been among the rebels: looting churches, destroying images of the saints, and desecrating the bread of the eucharist.[183] A distraught Maria Theresa wrote to her son Ferdinand: "The excesses go far, they are plundering castles and even shooting at the troops, who are responding in kind; this will quickly put an end to the matter, I hope, but it give me no hope for the future."[184] And to Kaunitz: "What has happened dramatically changes both the situation and the measures that will have to be taken. I am dispirited and depressed."[185] The Venetian emissary Contarini reported home that around fifteen thousand subjects had revolted against their masters, but they had been spread out over several districts and had failed to join forces. The forty thousand soldiers had no difficulty crushing the poorly organized rebellion.[186] Commanders were explicitly instructed to show leniency toward the rebels. There were nonetheless some fatalities, and individual ringleaders were executed.[187] Khevenhüller noted that the empress did not yet want to see the Bohemian unrests "from the proper angle, alas," yet his son-in-law Kolowrat was able to persuade her to proceed "at last with greater severity" against the delinquents.[188]

All observers at court were agreed that the peasants' disappointed hopes were responsible for the outbreak of violence. But who had awakened these false expectations and how? Leopold later judged it to have been the emperor, who had made all sorts of well-meaning promises on his travels but then done nothing to act on them and shifted "the odium onto the empress" instead.[189] Khevenhüller suspected that "the real cause of this sorry affair may well have been the excessive blandishments and promises made during the conscription [of souls]. For the sake of popularity, the emperor personally indicated at times that he was inclined to make highly favorable changes in due course with regard to the total abolition of serfdom." Khevenhüller, who generally frowned on "the young lord" for being so eager to "win over the public," added that all this could have been avoided if the Jesuits had still been around.[190] But the empress, too, had "embraced quite erroneous principles on account of the wretched urbarium" and "believed all Bohemia, great and small, to be suspect and partisan *in corpore et membris.*"[191] He was not mistaken in this; Maria Theresa was now more distrustful than ever before.

The empress lacked a reliable compass to guide her out of her quandary. All her well-meaning measures had backfired. She herself had put the abolition of serfdom on the agenda—and this very policy now seemed to be plunging her lands into chaos. She had delegated the urbarial question to Joseph at his insistence—and he had arrived at a completely different decision than all his previous statements on the matter had led her to expect. Writing in May 1775 to her daughter Marie Antoinette in Paris, where famine had likewise struck, she drew parallels between their situations: "Our people in Bohemia used just the same language as that you report to me, except that yours used it about the high price of bread, and ours about their feudal dues. They too claimed there was an abolition order. This spirit of rebellion is becoming commonplace: this is the consequence of our enlightened century. I have often lamented it."[192] Maria Theresa shared with her confidant Mercy-Argenteau in Paris her view that disappointed expectations had fueled the revolt: "The emperor, who takes the pursuit of popularity too far, has not given these people any formal promises on his various journeys, but he has said far too much about their freedom in religious matters and towards their landlords. The conscription also played its part, when the officers likewise talked and promised too much and gave people hope."[193]

The rebellion prompted Maria Theresa to remorseless, embittered reflection on her own situation. In the same letter to Mercy-Argenteau, she wrote that she was so tired, so cheerless, that she was doing more harm than good. Her presence alone, she said, had a dispiriting effect on others. Everywhere, including in Moravia, Styria, Austria, and even before the gates of Vienna, subjects were growing more and more impudent.

> You will judge me for not keeping order. Much could be said about this. My age, my illness, my depression since the death of my adorable husband left me in complete apathy for two years; and after

almost all my trusted ministers and friends had left me, I could no longer regain the necessary equilibrium I had lost through my private misfortunes. The tenderness and weakness of an old woman and mother have done the rest. The state has suffered enough, I can no longer allow things to go on the way they are.[194]

And she said of Joseph: "When he comes to bear the burden on his own, he will understand the difficulties as well and no longer be able to hide behind me." He was intelligent enough, his judgment was sound and his heart not yet corrupted.[195] To both Mercy and Court Councillor Greiner, she intimated her wish to retire and leave the business of government entirely to her son. As was only to be expected, both correspondents were aghast at the idea and begged her to spare the state such a catastrophe. If he could prevent her abdication with his own blood, Greiner swore dramatically, he would do so, to which she bluntly replied: "I cannot go on like this, neither for my salvation nor the good of the state, and there is nothing so irksome as my present situation."[196] As always, she failed to act on her threat. She had too little faith in her son's ability to rule and saw him—as he saw her—as both indecisive and unpredictable.[197]

Joseph, for his part, shared his mother's diagnosis, albeit with a different inflection and without the same degree of self-criticism. In his letters to Leopold, he returned repeatedly to her weakness and irresolution. He wrote in July:

The minor disturbances still breaking out here and there are but the natural results of the government's indecision. For five years it has been deluding the subject with the prospect of alleviations without ever letting him experience them, and threatening the lord with reductions without daring to make him suffer them. Impatience gets the better of some, while others resort to intrigue. The former agitate, the latter obstruct, and there is a constant toing and froing. The Empress is driven mad, people grumble about her in really quite unseemly language. As soon as anything is decided and even published, it is rescinded or changed. It is appalling, and since I myself remain steadfast, they show no mercy in ripping me to shreds.[198]

In conversations with Khevenhüller, too, he denied all responsibility for giving subjects false hope and shifted the blame onto his mother, who never let him do anything.[199] And again to Leopold on August 9, 1775:

Do you really think it possible for the empress to decide anything in this accursed urbarial business? She has made the effort more than ten times to order that matters be settled; it has never lasted longer than the time it takes to write out or print the orders and patents. Other people have always intervened to amend, delay, or even revoke them. . . . I would long since have put an end to all that and offered to arrange everything myself, but this is impossible; I doubt too much that they will really let me have my way and not countermand the orders she has given me.[200]

An impartial man, someone who neither feared the crowd nor took any notice of the nobility's objections, would have to be sent to Bohemia with full plenary powers. But there were few such men in the monarchy. If subjects were now in open revolt, then the government itself had incited them with its many unredeemed promises and idle threats.

In August 1775, when Joseph was writing these words about his mother, renewed discussions about the Bohemian urbarial regulation had been underway in Vienna for more than six months. The patent from April 1774 had clearly been a failure. There were now two competing proposals: a more landlord-friendly one from Court Councillor Egid von Borié and a more peasant-friendly one from the radical official Blanc. At this juncture, Joseph reverted to his earlier course and sided with Blanc's proposal. This classified subjects into six different classes, prescribing distinct obligations for each. The upper limit of three days *robot* each week was on no account to be exceeded.[201] Following heated debate in the State Council, Maria Theresa finally opted—"not without considerable apprehension"—for Blanc's solution. But now Kaunitz was opposed: he thought it wrong to issue a new patent, since this would appear to reward the peasants for their insubordination. Maria Theresa pushed ahead regardless. The new Robot Patent, dated August 13, 1775, was promptly proclaimed in all Bohemian circle offices in the presence of two representatives of every village commune. This time, there would be no room for doubting that the patent bore the stamp of imperial authority.[202]

Although Joseph himself had argued for Blanc's proposal, he continued to voice his dissatisfaction to Leopold; the law had been "jumbled up in an . . . almost unintelligible manner" and would fail to have the desired effect.[203] At the same time, he complained about his mother's lack of courage and resolve as the sole cause of the catastrophe. She could be the happiest woman in the world, he claimed, if only she could bring herself to make a decision. Instead, her weakness and irresolution were placing the entire monarchy in jeopardy. The unspoken implication was that she should formally transfer the scepter of rule into his hands and retire for good.[204] But she had no intention of doing so. In December Joseph asked once again—and with just as little success as before—to be relieved of his coregency, and in March 1776 it was Kaunitz's turn to retender his resignation. Everything remained as it had been. The three could find no way out of their communicative labyrinth.

The Bohemian question continued to weigh on Maria Theresa. A committee of investigation reported renewed uprisings and many subjects secretly emigrated to Prussia. "Bohemian affairs preoccupy me once again and in the most unpleasant manner, not because there are disturbances, but because they have to be prevented," she wrote to Maria Christina. "What the landlords and officials get up to is unbelievable, such despicable malignancy!"[205] In Vienna, yet another revision of the Robot Patent was on the cards. It was now Maria Theresa who wanted to adopt a more hardline approach toward the landlords—and was opposed by her son. In January 1777 Joseph wrote to Leopold that the empress was in the process of repealing the solemnly decreed urbarium of August 1775, completely abolishing serfdom, and arbitrarily overturning centuries-old property relations. Landlords' concerns were no longer being heeded, and they were now threatened with the loss of over half their income; this would drive many indebted nobles into bankruptcy.[206] After Johann Joseph Khevenhüller, the last of the old confidants from the high aristocracy, passed away on April 18, 1776, the reformers around Greiner, Gebler, Blanc, and Raab gained the ascendancy over Maria Theresa, incurring all the more hatred from others.

Greiner's correspondence with Maria Theresa makes clear just how polarized the court had become. A small, radical reform party that had won over the empress and sought to retain her confidence stood implacably opposed to Joseph and the rest.[207] The reformers pursued the goal of introducing the Raab system universally, not just on the royal demesnes. "Freedom and property can surely do nobody any harm," as could be seen "throughout the civilized world," Greiner wrote to the empress, rising to a pitch of Enlightenment pathos: "Should then the poor Bohemians not be allowed to become free, and Your Majesty always be prevented from carrying out Your laudable work, the production of universal liberty!" In reality, things were not so simple. Maria Theresa noted with resignation: "Raab's system always seemed too nice to the lords."[208]

The reform party had a precarious status at court. The air was thick with distrust, intrigue, and recrimination. The total silence between mother and son only made things worse. Joseph went out of his way to avoid her. When he was not traveling abroad, he stayed in the Hofburg while she resided at Schönbrunn. Other than on ceremonial occasions, they communicated only in writing. Instead of talking face to face, they spoke about each other to third parties. The atmosphere was toxic. Maria Theresa warned Greiner not to be overly trusting, since "malice and interest are rife."[209] Greiner himself was targeted in a smear campaign, although he was able to mount a successful defense.[210] Blanc, however, was sidelined. He had gone too far in his partisan zeal by trying to turn Kaunitz against Joseph. When Joseph got wind of it, he forced his mother to post the chancellery secretary back to his homeland in faraway Further Austria, albeit with no reduction in salary.[211] With that, the most important proponent of radical reform was removed from the scene and a renewed revision of the Robot Patent thwarted. In early 1777 Maria Theresa had still been relatively optimistic, writing to Ferdinand: "I think that if the emperor can at least remain neutral, if not support me, I may succeed in abolishing serfdom and feudal dues. . . . Unhappily, though, the lords, seeing they could no longer impress me, have thrown their weight behind the emperor."[212] Not long after, her hopes had been shattered: "I was just about [to advance

the cause of justice against tyranny in Bohemia] when the landlords—
who, by the by, are all ministers—suddenly raised doubts in the emperor's mind and destroyed the work of two years in a single instant."[213]
She poured out her woes in a letter to her old confidante, Rosalie Countess Edling: "Dearest, best, oldest good friend. . . . What a state I am in!
It defies description. Inconsolable and full of cares in body and soul for
my most precious, faithful lands, for my sons. Poor Bohemia! I can say
no more than: Thy will be done! The cup is heavy and bitter."[214]

Gradually and almost imperceptibly, Maria Theresa and Joseph had
swapped sides in the debate on serfdom: Joseph now voiced his doubts
even as his mother stood up for the oppressed subjects against the magnates' "tyranny." In the confrontation with her son, Maria Theresa appropriated an enlightened rhetoric of freedom she otherwise abhorred,
while Joseph, conversely, suddenly seemed to have forgotten all his radical rhetoric and presented himself as a moderate mediator. It is hard to
say how this switch in roles came about, and harder still to find objective
reasons for it—particularly as Joseph performed another spectacular
volte-face after his mother's death by summarily abolishing serfdom in
the Bohemian lands.[215] To make sense of these contradictions, it should
be remembered that the coregents were embroiled at the time in a
whole series of further disputes that periodically erupted in violent epistolary exchanges: first their position on the Russo-Turkish war, then the
Polish partition, and finally the controversy concerning religious tolerance. There was discord on other policy issues as well. In questions of
trade liberalization, for example, Maria Theresa was far more inclined
than her son to back reformers such as Count Cobenzl.[216] Simmering
constantly in the background was the permanent, unresolved conflict
over the shared responsibilities of rule—what Khevenhüller called the
"affliction of the dual reign," the fundamentally "contradictory way of
thinking" of the two monarchs.[217] The mother-son conflict clearly developed its own polarizing dynamic independently of whichever topic
was under discussion at the time, dooming the prospect of lasting collaboration. Their respective advisers only confirmed them in their hostility and mutual distrust. The details of the reforms to land policy were
far too complex to be captured in such simplistic slogans as "freedom

versus tyranny." No one knew exactly what the consequences and side effects of various measures might be. It was therefore seductively easy to blame fatal developments on the other person.[218]

A further mass uprising in Bohemia never eventuated, even though the Robot Patent of August 1755 was not revised, only supplemented with a series of individual peasant protection laws. Indeed, most subjects on Bohemian noble estates experienced tangible relief; the landlords frequently had to replace *robot* with wage labor, driving many estates into economic ruin. Some landlords sold their enterprises to investors with sufficient capital, while others voluntarily introduced the Raab system. Yet the system did not deliver everything it had promised. The farmsteads given to peasants in hereditary leasehold often proved too small to provide them with a sustainable livelihood. In the longer term, the reforms signified a liberalization of the agrarian economy, with consequences that were not always to the benefit of all subjects.[219]

In the final years of her reign, Maria Theresa had her mind fixed firmly on the hereafter. Guided by the traditional princely virtues of clemency and mercy, she felt accountable chiefly before God and the dynasty. By contrast, Joseph craved fame and honor from the European public. Modeling himself on Frederick II, he addressed the new public sphere created by the print media and aspired to go down in history as a friend to the people and enlightened monarch.[220] Just as mother and son addressed distinct audiences, so too their relations with ordinary subjects differed considerably. Joseph made himself out to be one of them. He cultivated an air of egalitarian philanthropy that was registered with pained embarrassment at the Viennese court. His grandfather, Charles VI, had likewise been criticized for consorting with "little people," but the difference was that there had been no enlightened media public at the time that might have applauded him for it. Maria Theresa, on the other hand, never even contemplated bridging the gulf that separated her from commoners. Representing her own majesty always and everywhere—and hence never lowering herself to their level—was one of her cast-iron principles. Mother and son did have one thing in common, though: neither was willing to concede ordinary subjects any right to political participation. Yet her "love of her subjects" was something altogether different to his "popularity." In this respect, the generational conflict in the House of Habsburg was equally an epochal one.

The Last War

In 1778 conflict over the Bavarian succession opened the last agonizing act in the drama between mother and son.[221] Prince-Elector Max Joseph of Bavaria was without a male heir, and the European courts were breathlessly awaiting his demise. With his cousin Prince-Elector Charles Theodore of the Palatine, who likewise lacked a legitimate successor, he had made a secret pact naming each other heirs of their respective territories. No one in Vienna had yet gotten wind of the deal. In anticipation of the prince's death, Kaunitz had been digging in the archives for legal titles and plotting to acquire as much of the Bavarian inheritance as possible for the House of Habsburg. On the one hand, Joseph could make certain claims on his own behalf; he had, after all, been married to a Wittelsbach in Josepha.[222] On the other, the emperor—in cahoots with Imperial Vice-Chancellor Colloredo—had an even more ambitious plan in mind. In his capacity as the Empire's supreme feudatory, he hoped to reclaim the lapsed imperial fiefs of Upper and Lower Bavaria in the astonishingly optimistic expectation that none of the other imperial princes would object. In 1776 Charles Theodore of the Palatine had already authorized his emissary in Vienna to explore how the situation might best be exploited to his and Joseph's mutual advantage. He dreamed of ruling over a kingdom of his own on the Lower Rhine, and he now saw a chance to make this dream come true by offering the emperor the Electorate of Bavaria in exchange for the Habsburg Netherlands.

On December 30, 1777, the Bavarian elector unexpectedly died of smallpox (he had distrusted the new-fangled method of inoculation).[223] Charles Theodore promptly declared himself his successor, thereby calling forth rival inheritance claims from branch lines of the Wittelsbach dynasty.[224] The emperor immediately pressured him to draw up a contract confirming Habsburg claims to parts of Lower Bavaria and the Upper Palatine. This Charles Theodore duly did on January 3, 1778.[225]

Three days later, imperial troops of fifteen thousand men marched into Lower Bavaria and temporarily occupied the administrative seat of Straubing—with the aim of reducing Bavaria's exchange value for the prince-elector. At the same time, Kaunitz offered the Palatine emissary a range of possible territories in exchange for Bavaria: Further Austria, Galicia, and so on, but not the coveted Habsburg Netherlands. A spirit of sober commercial calculation guided these negotiations: Kaunitz set out figures before the Palatine envoy demonstrating that the Netherlands brought in substantially more annual taxation revenue than Bavaria. At this point in time, Joseph was still blithely convinced that the coup would bring the House of Habsburg significant territorial gains without costing much, still less provoking a war.[226] In this he was deceived. When, in April 1778, he proposed to the king of Prussia that they amicably negotiate an exchange of territories, Frederick seized the opportunity to present himself as the selfless defender of the German princes and the entire imperial constitution, which the emperor could not simply trample underfoot in the manner of a Turkish sultan.[227] Frederick II had his own interests in southern Germany, where the small Hohenzollern princedoms of Ansbach and Bayreuth were likewise about to fall vacant. A third war between Austria and Prussia thus seemed imminent, and it soon became apparent that Austria was completely isolated. Charles Theodore declared his wish to steer clear of military entanglements. The king of France, Maria Theresa's son-in-law and putative ally, showed an almost humiliating lack of interest. The Russian tsarina threatened to side with Prussia. Most imperial princes— Saxony, Hannover, even many Catholic princes—likewise took Frederick's side. In the Empire, a barrage of pamphlets targeted Joseph's abuse of the imperial office. Attempts to engage the Imperial Diet to arbitrate the dispute, and thus avoid calling on foreign intermediaries such as France or Russia, came to nothing. Joseph mobilized some one hundred and eighty thousand men to protect the borders to Prussia and Saxony and took to the field, together with his brother Maximilian and brother-in-law Albert von Teschen, to await the Prussian attack.

Following fruitless last-ditch attempts at diplomacy, Frederick II formally declared war on July 3. Three days later, two Prussian armies advanced into Bohemia, one from Saxony, the other, commanded by Frederick himself, from Silesia. Yet the great open battle expected by both sides never materialized. Prussian troops suffered enormous supply problems in impoverished Bohemia; Frederick II lost around a quarter of his soldiers through hunger, disease, and desertion. While imperial troops did succeed in maneuvering the Prussians out of Bohemia by the end of winter, neither side was keen to launch a new campaign the following year, and in March 1779 peace talks began in Silesian Teschen. France and Russia brokered the deal, securing future influence in the Empire as guarantor powers. The contract, signed on May 13, 1779, gained the House of Habsburg nothing but a small strip of land east of the Inn River with the towns of Braunau and Schärding, the so-called Innviertel. Prince-Elector Charles Theodore could take the throne in Bavaria; the competing claimants to the inheritance were paid off. Frederick II, by contrast, secured the margraviates of Ansbach and Bayreuth and emerged yet again as the real winner from the whole affair.

Maria Theresa had been fiercely opposed to this war from the outset. Even her foreign policy oracle, Kaunitz, was powerless to change her mind. She had clearly learned from the bitter experience of two previous wars. Even as news of the Bavarian prince's death reached Vienna, she emphatically warned her son not to enter into a political adventure that she predicted would only end in disaster, jeopardize the welfare of her lands, and incur universal hostility. Even if Habsburg claims to Bavaria had been less dubious than they actually were, this did not justify starting a Europe-wide conflagration for the sake of so slender an advantage. Subjects were oppressed badly enough as it was; a new war would bleed them dry. It would also destroy the arduously restored trust of the other powers, with even more devastating consequences than in the two previous wars. Maria Theresa took the same position as during the haggling over Poland. It was fatal to pursue a policy of Prussian-style aggrandizement and throw all legal obligations to the winds. In the long term, nothing could be gained from such a policy, everything lost.[228] Joseph brushed aside her dire warnings. He wrote breezily to Leopold: "Her Majesty is, as you can well imagine, a little unnerved, but she is friendly enough to agree with the good reasons put before her."[229] This was far from the case. Indeed, his mother painted an even grimmer picture of the consequences of going to war. At stake was the welfare of untold thousands of people, as well as the very existence of the monarchy and the Archducal House. "I cannot bring myself to act against my conscience and conviction. . . . If war breaks out, count on me no more. I will retire to Tyrol to spend my last days there in absolute seclusion and do nothing but weep for the unhappy fate of my house and my people."[230] As always, she neglected to carry out the threat when the dreaded event came to pass.

Yet during the diplomatic tug-of-war of the following months, she initially held back and left Kaunitz and Joseph in charge. So long as there was still hope of forestalling open conflict, she refrained from intervening in official negotiations. She instead exchanged countless letters with Joseph, sometimes several in the course of a single day, but she modified her rhetorical strategy. She adopted a more conciliatory tone, flattered his vanity,[231] showered him with praise, appealed to his filial duty and his paternal responsibility for his subjects, and implored him to keep the peace at any price. At the same time, she ordered Field Marshal Lacy to keep her up to date about Joseph and tirelessly applied for support from Marie Antoinette and Mercy-Argenteau at the court in Versailles, thereby putting her daughter in an extremely difficult position.[232] She also inundated her relatives and familiars with letters expressing her despair and anxiety over her son's belligerence.[233] As always, Joseph cultivated a tone of obsequious respect in his communications with her, kept her regularly informed about the course of events, begged her for permission with regard to trivialities, and seconded her scornful remarks about "Fritz," the "monster," and his "perfidious insinuations." In short, he played the perfect son even as he disregarded his mother's reservations in brash expectation of victory.

In late June Maria Theresa was still assuring Joseph that she had not the least intention of interfering with his plans but urged him to abandon his destructive ideas all the same.[234] Following the outbreak of war at the beginning of July, she seized the initiative rather than withdrawing from the fray, as announced. She was strengthened in her resolve by a note from July 7 in which Joseph, clearly panicked by the first Prussian cannonades, called on the monarchy to rally all its forces. To stand up to the vastly superior enemy forces without allies in this "ruinous and highly dangerous war," it was vital that "every conceivable means be found to increase revenue" and as many regiments as possible be fielded from all the lands. Everyone, "from the throne to the last peasant," would have to play their part in preserving the monarchy, "immediately and without delay, . . . without the slightest consideration . . . for whatever ills may ensue."[235] This was an overreaction, no doubt, but it corresponded exactly to what Maria Theresa had feared and had repeatedly forewarned him about. On July 12, 1778, in agreement with Kaunitz but behind her son's back, she sent her envoy Franz von Thugut to Frederick II to broach a settlement. She and Kaunitz had discussed the wording of her peace overture in some detail. "*Monsieur mon frère et cousin,*" she addressed Frederick II, maternal solicitude moving her to resume negotiations without the knowledge of her son, the emperor, in order to bring them to a peaceful conclusion.[236] The letter was deliberately couched in a tone of concerned motherly love. Kaunitz had previously worked out a sober exchange offer bristling with facts and figures. She ordered him to rewrite this text as "unbecoming a careworn lady."[237] There was thus a conscious strategy behind Maria Theresa's rhetoric of a loving mother filled with worry for her children. By adopting the role of a frail and fretful old woman, she could at least partially disguise the fact that she was engaging in an unprecedented act of political sabotage against her own son, the emperor.

When Joseph, still ignorant of all this, had written to his mother explaining just how desperate the situation had become and expressing his hopes for an honorable peace, she felt emboldened to reveal all.[238] The news had a disastrous effect on Joseph. He felt profoundly humiliated and ashamed. In a society in which honor was everything, he, the emperor and commander, had been treated like a child by his mother before the enemy and in the eyes of the world. His initial reaction was to throw a tantrum. Through this unparalleled action, he wrote, she had irreparably damaged everything she held dear, including her reputation and the honor of the monarchy as a whole, and she had completely compromised his policy, destroyed his public credit, and strengthened the hand of the Prussian despot to boot. He was considering abandoning everything and going to Italy.[239] Yet the tone of his letters changed from day to day, from extreme outrage to feigned submissiveness to embittered recrimination. He felt so humiliated that he even concealed the affair from his closest confidant, Leopold.[240] Maria Theresa dismissed his reproaches: what she had done had been difficult but she would do the same again. It was worth sacrificing personal honor to save the hereditary lands: "We were once a great power; now we are one no more."[241] Writing to her daughter in Versailles, however, she acknowledged the risk she had taken: "If I make peace now, I not only stand open to the charge of great trepidation, but also make the king [of Prussia] even more powerful." She nonetheless now openly took matters in hand and continued negotiating with Frederick II with the goal of restoring peace at almost any cost.[242] She demanded cooperation and a show of consensus from her son: "On questions of principle we must be in unconditional agreement. . . . When it comes to the formalities, I am entirely amenable to your wishes."[243] Joseph refused at first to have anything to do with the shameful proceedings. She had started these unbelievable negotiations without him; the least she could do now was to spare him any further involvement in the matter, which he never wanted to hear of again.[244] Yet, even in this point his stance wavered several times over the course of the war between docile subservience and a pugnacious determination to go on fighting.[245] Until the end, Frederick II doubted whether Joseph would be prepared to support any peace deal brokered by his mother. Indeed, the emperor never lost sight of his original plan for Bavaria. He revived it in the 1780s, following his mother's death, giving Frederick II renewed opportunity to present himself as the defender of the Holy Roman Empire against the attacks of its own supreme head. Maria Theresa regarded the Peace of Teschen as the last political success of her life. On the day the treaty was signed, she wrote to Kaunitz: "Today I have ended my career in glory with a Te Deum; . . . the rest will not amount to much."[246]

The shift in Maria Theresa's position since the two earlier wars of her reign was striking. Whereas she had previously always insisted on keeping up the fight at any price, stubbornly turning down any unfavorable offer of peace, now she fought just as insistently to preserve (and, later, restore) the peace at all costs. Whereas she had previously always urged her generals to take the offensive, now she implored them to avoid open battle. Whereas religion had previously always strengthened her in her resolve to go on fighting, now it moved her to bring the war to an end. What made this war different from its two predecessors? For one thing, Maria Theresa had waged her first two wars as sovereign warlord. Now she had Joseph to deal with as both emperor and coregent. In this latter role she herself had invested him with military supreme command and many other duties. In the first two wars she had felt herself—albeit with less and less justification—to be in possession of certain unimpeachable, hallowed rights that had to be defended or wrested back from the enemy. Now she was forced to witness her own son pursuing the "Prussian model" of barely disguised expansionist policy.

As in many similar earlier cases, the dilemma arose from a lack of clarity about who was in charge. The empress always yielded her sovereignty only half-heartedly to her coregent, which is to say that she did not yield it at all, since sovereignty was by definition indivisible. She made do with diffuse responsibilities and held fast to the fiction of a quasi-natural consensus between mother and son. Joseph, meanwhile, resisted his mother's suffocating embrace. He refused to humor her by putting on a show of unanimity, insisting instead on a clear-cut alternative: only one of the two could be regent, only one of them could bear responsibility. That this was his mother, not him, he demonstrated in his letters through a rhetoric of abject subservience. In fact, he acted independently in line with his own ideas. The unclear situation allowed him to launch a number of risky and contentious political projects—the Polish partition, the Bavarian invasion—while at the same time denying all blame for their unintended consequences: after all, his mother, as sovereign, bore ultimate responsibility. That Kaunitz, too, was pursuing his own agenda, on some occasions supporting the mother and on others the son, did nothing to simplify the situation. All three were engaged in an elaborate game of concealment: Maria Theresa kept the writings of one hidden from the other; Kaunitz denied Joseph access to his memoranda; Joseph avoided communicating with Kaunitz for weeks on end.[247] Following the war, the chancellor once again asked to be relieved of his office and was once again refused. The unstable three-way relationship was as disastrous in its effects on the Archducal House's foreign policy as it was on its domestic policy. The real winner was the Prussian king: in effect, the constellation allowed Frederick II to adjudicate internal disputes in the House of Habsburg.[248]

Joseph's brother Leopold watched the unfolding dilemma with deep dismay. In 1778 both Maria Theresa and Joseph had asked him to come to Vienna in the hope of securing his support for their positions. During his stay, Leopold kept a secret journal in which he clearly outlined how both parties had contributed to the predicament. "He [Joseph] cleverly manages to place the blame for everything he does or proposes either on the Empress or on others." But it was Maria Theresa who had first made this possible: "If I were in her shoes, . . . I would have transferred all my business to the emperor at once and abdicated forthwith and . . . retired to Innsbruck. . . . The empress would then have had her peace, her conscience would have been at rest, and, by leaving the emperor to his own devices, . . . she would have forced him to work."[249] In failing to do so, she had relieved him of all responsibility.

One of the casualties of this unhappy constellation was the very legitimacy of the dynastic principle. For loyal servants of the Archducal House, the unedifying spectacle presented by mother and son was therefore hard to bear. In a memorandum submitted to the emperor, the elderly Field Marshal Laudon "most humbly" remarked that, in such a sorry dispute, everyone would have to take the mother's side against the son, "even if he happened to be in the right." The devotion of subjects, Laudon suggested, was part of the inheritance Joseph would receive from his mother. A wise ruler could "not possibly present subjects with the example of a son living in discord with his exalted mother and then expect them to perform the filial duties that he himself had neglected."[250] Laudon had touched on the central point. Dynastic rule ultimately derived its stability from obedience as a self-evident, unquestioned duty requiring no further justification: children's obedience to their parents, subjects' obedience to their ruler, everyone's obedience to God. These three keystones were mutually reinforcing, and removing just one stone threatened to bring the whole edifice crashing down.

14

The Autumn of the Matriarch

FIGURE 51. The widow Maria Theresa at her
escritoire with Athena, a plan of Schönbrunn,
and books. Anton von Maron, 1773

Fallen into the Sere

Maria Theresa described the last decade of her life in countless private letters as an impatient waiting for death: "I have lived long enough."[1] She felt lonely and abandoned, sick in body, heart, and head, oppressed by the weight of her responsibilities, and resigned—for all her unstinting efforts—to the impossibility of alleviating the misery afflicting her lands, or even achieving concord within her own family. "My age and my infirmities, which mount from day to day, no longer grant me a moment's respite, and my cares and losses drive me to utter ruination."[2] She had become increasingly isolated; life at court had been reduced to a bare minimum. Almost all her old confidants had died: Countess Fuchs in 1754, Haugwitz in 1765, Daun in 1766, Bartenstein in 1767, Ulfeld in 1770, Tarouca in 1771, van Swieten in 1772, her private secretary Neny in 1776; the elderly Khevenhüller passed away on April 18, 1776. One child after the other had married and left the Viennese court: Leopold in 1764, Maria Christina in 1766, Maria Carolina in 1768, Maria Amalia in 1769, Marie Antoinette in 1770, Ferdinand in 1771. Only Marianna, the eldest, Maximilian, the youngest, and Elisabeth were still with her in Vienna—apart from the emperor, of course, to whom she was bound in a mutually tormenting love-hate relationship. Besides her confessor Ignaz Müller, Kaunitz was the only one of the older generation of advisers to survive the empress. He retained his unrivaled authority in political matters to the end—"I would be completely lost without him"[3]— although she did not always follow his advice, having no wish to antagonize her son unnecessarily. While she complained about Kaunitz's "daily increasing debilities and extravagances," she did so "always with the proviso that he was irreplaceable in this sphere." When he once again tendered his resignation in early 1779, she once again refused him.[4] Relations with her trusted correspondents, Maria Antonia of Saxony and Marquise d'Herzelles, cooled appreciably at the start of the 1770s.[5] In short, she could now count her close friends on the fingers of one hand. Khevenhüller noted how the empress bemoaned her "incapacity to continue shouldering the burden of government and that we no longer cared for her."[6]

Maria Theresa had long felt ugly, old, tired, weak, and careworn. She was only fifty-two when she wrote:

> Outwardly I may appear to be in good health; I am very fat, more than my dear departed mother, and also ruddy in complexion, particularly since the pox, but my feet, chest, and eyes are ruined; the first are very swollen; I expect them to rupture any day. My eyes are quite worn out; the worst is that neither monocle nor spectacles are any use to me. There is some dampness in the lungs, I believe, since I have difficulty breathing, including when standing still and even when lying down. I have no cause for complaint; every life must come to an end. For fifty years I enjoyed the best of health.[7]

She suffered from chronic respiratory problems and complained incessantly about "fluxes"—swelling or inflammation of her teeth, eyes, face, head, feet—diffuse ailments of various kinds for which van Swieten's successor, Anton von Störck, invariably prescribed a course of bloodletting. Warm weather and overheated rooms caused her more discomfort than ever. At night she suffered from insomnia, prompting the ingenious court councillor, Wolfgang von Kempelen, to construct a mechanically adjustable bed for her use.[8] She now found walking so difficult that she had to be carried or driven over even very short distances. She had hand-operated lifts installed everywhere so that lackeys would not always have to bear her up or down the stairs on a litter: in the Hofburg, at Schönbrunn, Laxenburg, and not least in the Capuchin Crypt, where the steps were too narrow and steep for a sedan chair.[9] In the early 1770s she relocated once again, ordering her apartments in the Hofburg and at Schönbrunn to be moved one floor lower to the *piano nobile* and the parterre, respectively.[10] In the Hofburg, a confessional box was custom built for her in a kind of wall cabinet behind the chapel oratory. "Nothing is worse and more unpleasant for oneself and others than growing old, above all for women," she wrote her daughter-in-law Beatrix.[11] To her favorite daughter, Maria Christina, she put it more succinctly: "I cannot go on."[12]

But these letters to her closest companions tell only half the story. In fact, the empress was far from resigned to her fate, either in a psychological or a political sense. She continued to put her views robustly to officials such as Field Marshal Lacy: "I will not be done away with so easily."[13] She concealed her depression from foreign visitors; her personal charisma still worked its charm. "She is . . . tho' very fat not at all incumber'd with it, a genteel slope," wrote her English admirer, Lady Coke. She "holds herself extremely well, & her air the most Noble I ever saw: 'tis still visible her features have been extremely fine and regular, tho' the swelling from the small pox never quite got down & a little degree of redness remaining: more spirit & sense in her eyes then [sic] I think ever saw, & the most pleasing tone of voice in speaking."[14] She also kept up her formidable workload; her daily routine was as packed as ever; only her public appearances became ever more infrequent.[15] She invested all the more care and money into beautifying her immediate surrounds. Not by chance, her widow's portrait from 1773 shows her seated at her escritoire holding a plan of Schönbrunn in her hand (fig. 56).[16] Her building activity gained renewed momentum. The "dismal nook" in which she felt herself to be languishing was actually the most bright and airy summer palace imaginable. Schönbrunn, her pet architectural project over many years, was sumptuously redesigned in the 1770s despite empty coffers and her own professed ennui. Hohenberg, the court architect, brought the gardens up to date with statues, fountains, and an ancient ruin, crowning the knoll in the Great Parterre's sight line with an early classicist colonnaded belvedere, the Gloriette.[17] The Bohemian painter Johann Wenzel Bergl decorated the apartments on the palace's garden side—used by Maria Theresa in summer as her salon, writing room, and bedroom—with illusionistic rococo landscape paintings. They can still be admired there today. Parrots and flamingos move through exotic scenery; garlands of flowers and fruit climb up walls and doors to the ceiling; the bedroom resembled a light-saturated Baroque garden pavilion (color plate 27).[18]

Maria Theresa's letters to her children reveal no hint of this cheerful mood. Her sole remaining consolation on earth, she repeatedly asseverated, was the well-being of her children and her grandchildren. She lamented the emptiness and loneliness of her life in Vienna and was pained to think that she might never again see those of her children who had married abroad.[19] Yet what stood in the way of family visits was not just her own physical immobility but also the unwritten ceremonial barrier of high rank, which made it seem inappropriate for a ruler to leave her own territory.[20] A monarch admitted others to her presence, she did not pay calls on them herself.[21] This rule applied not just to the empress, but also to those of her daughters who had become queens in other lands, Marie Antionette in France and Carolina in Naples-Sicily. Their courts likewise expected them not to set foot outside their domains.[22] For the children who functioned as representatives or regents in Habsburg lands—Maria Christina in Hungary, Ferdinand in Milan, or Leopold in Tuscany, for example—a visit to their mother in Vienna posed fewer difficulties, at least from a ceremonial point of view. Yet every journey of state brought with it an immense outlay in time, money, personnel, and logistics, all of which were relatively minor considerations compared with the obstacles arising from the sometimes fraught personal relations between family members. For all these difficulties, however, planning visits from her children was one of the elderly empress's preferred pastimes.

For example, Ferdinand and Beatrix traveled from Milan to Vienna in the summer of 1775 and were lavished with such extraordinary distinctions—it was estimated "that the Milanese court's sojourn cost the empress over a million on account of all the gifts and festivities"[23]—that reports on the visit positively seethed with envy and resentment.[24] Yet once her guests had packed their bags and gone home, Maria Theresa was left feeling lonelier than ever in her palace. So acute was her anguish and so great the void in her life, she confided in her daughter-in-law Beatrix that it made her *grantig* (grumpy)—an "Austrian expression," she added.[25] The visit paid by Ferdinand and his entourage had so cheered and revived her, in fact, that Maria Theresa began toying with the idea of seeing her other faraway children at least once more before she died. With Marie Antoinette, she contemplated a rendezvous at the border between France and the Habsburg Netherlands, but in the face of the insurmountable difficulties so long and arduous a journey would pose, she soon dropped this bold plan.[26] Around the same time, in November 1775, the even more daring idea occurred to her that she and Joseph might meet with all her children and grandchildren from

Florence, Milan, and Naples in Görz (Gorizia), in the extreme south of
the hereditary lands and on the border to the Venetian republic. Maria
Christina and her husband, Albert, who were traveling through Italy
anyway, should join them as well, with a stopover in Trieste on the return journey to pay a visit to Amalia of Parma. There had never been
such a reunion of almost the entire family. The topic dominated their
correspondence for months, and it sheds light on the highly complicated relations between family members. The question was not just who
should come where, when, and how, but also whose idea it had been in
the first place and who would give whom greater pleasure.

Joseph claimed authorship of the plan to Leopold and showed himself determined to overcome all difficulties, even though he was fully
aware of his mother's irresolution; he had deliberately kept the idea to
himself at first and then waited for his mother's desire to see her
daughters to grow before springing it on her.[27] Maria Theresa, on the
other hand, praised Beatrix and Marianna as the *dépositaires*, custodians,
of this secret pet project of hers.[28] In March Joseph jubilantly informed
his brother that the journey was confirmed and the departure date set
for April 23, 1776. It had cost him a great deal to talk his mother out of
her fears, which unfortunately had been stoked by third parties. The
rendezvous had been arranged at short notice, he admitted, but Leopold
had no need to be concerned—any problems could be overcome. His
top priority, he wrote, was to make his brother and mother happy and
see everyone satisfied, "enjoy the journey to my own satisfaction, and
be able to call myself the initiator of the same."[29]

Yet Maria Theresa's letters now sounded a different note. To Maria
Christina, who was already in Italy, she spelled out the troubles and
dangers she would have to endure: "I have accepted the invitation to
this journey against my own conviction. . . . I make this sacrifice, which
is no trivial matter, for the emperor, for Leopold, and for you."[30] A little
later she wrote that Leopold and his wife were now causing difficulties,
the whole trip was in jeopardy; she had known this from the outset but
would submit unprotestingly to the emperor's will. Kaunitz had again
threatened to resign from office because he was continually confronted
by handicaps and humiliations (tacitly: through Joseph); if she were to

lose him, travel would be out of the question. In general, it puzzled her that the emperor was so keen for the trip to go ahead. On the other hand, she confessed to behaving like a child: "Once the matter has been decided on, I can hardly await the moment." Everyone was supposedly suffering from this decision: Marianna had made herself sick with excitement; Elisabeth spent the whole time weeping and praying. Confidentially, the empress also shared with Maria Christina her suspicion that the families from Florence and Naples did not get along with each other and distrusted each other. Finally, the encounter with Amalia of Parma was very disagreeable to her, while the father-in-law of Carolina of Naples had refused her permission to undertake the trip. She, the empress, would be accused of not having done more to secure the Spanish king's consent.[31] The entire business was proving so irksome that she wondered whether they were traveling not to Görz but to America.[32] All this did not exactly convey the thrill of anticipation. Not long afterward, however, she declared, "I confess that the idea of the journey fills me with joy, I am only a little anxious on account of my age and failing strength."[33] She was coughing heavily and beset by fever but had no wish to postpone the journey. On the contrary, she longed to be on her way.[34]

On April 1, 1776, the long baggage train with servants and kitchen and cellar supplies was sent on ahead: in the end, things could not be done as simply and *bourgeoisement* as Joseph had originally had in mind. In mid-April Maria Theresa complained of splitting headaches; the emperor was also unwell, so the trip would have to be postponed by ten days.[35] Joseph reassured his brother that she was not so unwell after all: this idea had only been put into her head. She was afraid of dying but wanted to set out nonetheless; all this was utterly inexplicable.[36] On April 18 she warned Maria Christina that if the journey suffered further delay, it would have to be called off on account of the expected summer heat. She put on a brave face and claimed: "I am doing everything in my power to avoid delay, which was not my idea in the first place. I have enough friends to provide me with a pretext, but I am incapable of acting this way. I would see through this impossibility [*la gageure*], cost what it may. . . . Enough! These three months will pass like all the rest."[37]

On April 22 she declared herself restored to health, but she was still very weak and was reserving her energies for the upcoming journey.[38] Two days later, Joseph had clearly grown exasperated by the stream of ambiguous messages. He demanded—in writing, as always, even though they were both in Vienna—that his mother decide whether or not she would travel to Görz; he would understand if she called off the journey, and would respect her decision whichever way it fell.[39] She summoned him to her presence. There followed a heated tête-à-tête, during which the decision was made to cancel the whole trip.[40] The empress thereupon informed her children in Italy that Joseph had been the one to back out of the trip, owing to his concern for her health and to general public protest.[41] To Maria Christina, she abandoned herself to a mood of profound desolation and self-recrimination. Only now had it become clear to her just how attached she had always been to this wonderful plan: "I am inconsolable, and although I long fought against it, at the bottom of my heart I had always felt an ardent desire to realize this project."[42] The prospect of never seeing her children again made her despair, and it was all her fault: "I no longer belong in my position; I am the one who spoils everything."[43] She sought to give her other children the impression, however, that she was not to blame for the fiasco; instead, she had been the victim of Joseph and the public. This interpretation of events apparently prevailed. Leopold, at any rate, was of the opinion that Joseph had thwarted the encounter.[44] At the same time, Maria Theresa devised a new scheme. She broached to Maria Christina her wish that Leopold and his wife come to see her in Vienna, stressing that this should not be presented as her idea. On the one hand, Leopold should visit his mother on his own initiative; on the other, she made clear that she would brook no opposition: she would not be able to rest until she saw him again.[45] As was only to be expected, Leopold and his wife acceded to her wish, however reluctantly, but pretended to do so of their own free will.[46]

The Görz episode brings relations between Maria Theresa and her grown-up children into sharp focus. Not all the roles played by participants in the drama can be reconstructed, since not all the correspondences have survived. Yet a comparison between Maria Theresa's letters to Maria Christina and the Milanese couple, on the one hand, and Joseph's letters to Leopold, on the other, reveals the same pattern that had such fatal consequences when it came to more important political questions. The empress and her coregent distrusted each other's intentions. She refused to be pinned down, evaded difficult decisions, and made a fine art of giving equivocal answers. She always saw herself as the one who sacrificed herself for others—first on account of the journey, then on account of its cancellation—even though she was pulling the strings and seeking to manipulate her children all the time. Maria Christina, in particular, served her as a tool for imposing her maternal will, thereby souring relations with her siblings.[47] Joseph emerged as the loser from this psychodrama. He had not only failed to achieve his objective, he was also blamed by everyone else for this failure. In the end, it seems, no one was happy.

Alter Ego Maria Christina

Over the course of her life, Maria Theresa's physical movements were confined to an ever-narrowing circle. If she left the Hofburg, it was then only to stay at Laxenburg for the New Year's season and from there to summer in Schönbrunn, no more than an hour's coach ride away. Were it not for Joseph she would not go to Laxenburg at all, she confided in others, while Joseph himself found the place terminally dull.[48] The lavish royal progresses she had made in earlier years to have her own or her husband's rule celebrated and to receive homage from the estates, as in Florence, Prague, Innsbruck, or even Frankfurt, were long behind her. At most she occasionally inspected troops stationed in the vicinity, yet even the few miles to Mödling were too much for her.[49] She only willingly took on the rigors of travel for trips to see Maria Christina and Albert in Schlosshof or Pressburg (Bratislava). Even in the last year of her life she made several short trips to see them.[50]

Maria Christina (la Marie, Mimi, or Mimerl), the fifth child, played a completely different role than all her siblings (color plate 28). Born on May 13, 1742, her mother's twenty-fifth birthday, she was treated by Maria Theresa in many respects as the empress's own alter ego.[51] Maria was the only one of her children about whom she never ventured a word of criticism or complaint in her letters. Among the children, Maria stood out for her vivacity, dominance, and willfulness. She was also smart and both musically and linguistically highly gifted, all qualities she shared with her mother. Her sister-in-law Isabella was not the only one in whom she inspired amorous feelings; she was also said to have had an affair with that notorious libertine, Prince Louis Eugene of Württemberg. Whatever truth there may have been in the rumor, the empress thought it advisable to refuse the prince admission to her court.[52]

Maria Theresa seems to have recognized herself in this daughter. Their life circumstances were strikingly similar in several key points. Maria Christina's marriage was also a love match to a man who stood well below her in the aristocratic hierarchy: Albert Casimir (1738–1822), sixth son of Frederick August II, elector of Saxony and king of Poland, an almost penniless prince with no prospect of inheriting his father's electorate, let alone the Polish crown—hardly a worthy match for a Habsburg. Together with his brother Clemens, he had first turned up at the Viennese court in 1760. He had then served as an imperial field marshal-lieutenant in the Seven Years' War, winning Maria Christina's heart upon his return. From then on, Maria Theresa worked for the match in a way that was completely out of character, supporting it behind her husband's back and against his stated intentions. Much to the dismay of those concerned, Francis Stephen was planning to marry Maria Christina to Benedetto of Chablais, the son of his sister, the queen of Sardinia. He had already once invited the young man to Innsbruck for Leopold's wedding so that the prospective bride and groom might get to know each other. In this situation, Maria Theresa showed an empathy in supporting her daughter's wishes that was beyond her other children's wildest imaginings. She acted as a trusted friend and secret accomplice against the "conspiracy of the opposing party," giving her daughter written assurance of her ongoing support. Yet open resistance to Francis Stephen was out of the question. She therefore advised her daughter to place her confidence in her alone, who was suffering just as much from the emperor's chatter, the rest of the family's envy, and town gossip but would let nothing and nobody shake her attachment to

Prince Albert, her protégé. But they should proceed with the·utmost caution, she warned Maria Christina; she should keep the matter to herself while getting in her father's good graces through a thousand compliments and courtesies.[53] Meanwhile, the empress sought to gain time by prolonging the rival party's formal marriage negotiations, which Kaunitz was conducting in the emperor's name.

Yet Maria Theresa's clandestine support proved unnecessary when Francis Stephen died in Innsbruck in 1765. With that, the path was cleared for a *mariage par inclination,* a romantic love match. On this occasion, Maria Theresa treated social norms and the objections of her ministers with sovereign disregard. Khevenhüller confided to his journal that she had decided for Prince Albert

> solely from her own initiative and due to her personal liking for this young man, without the prior knowledge of the Conference, indeed, as she herself confessed, against her ministers' stated opinion on the matter, to which of course her own extraordinary fondness for her daughter, and the inclination for the prince professed by the latter (in all decency and modesty, to be sure), played a large part. As she herself acknowledged and openly admitted to me and the other ministers, this alliance would not be the most seemly according to the principles of statecraft, and . . . might be seen as a beggars' wedding.[54]

A woman who married beneath her social standing normally paid for it with the loss of her inherited status. Yet in this case measures were taken to ensure that Maria Christina—like Maria Theresa herself— brought the privileges of her birth and the title of Archduchess of Austria with her into the marriage, against the prevailing marital law, which stipulated that the wife take on her husband's status. In the marriage contract from April 5, 1765, the bride's high birth was explicitly deemed more important than her inferior sex. The contract not only saw her retain her rank, name, title, and coat of arms, it also guaranteed her a very large fortune. The size of the endowment Maria Christina received from her mother was concealed from her siblings for good reason. It was exceptionally generous: besides jewelry, silver cutlery, clothing, the usual dowry of 100,000 guilders, and annual "hand or play money," it included the estates of Mannersdorf and Altenburg as well as bonds and cash worth over 666,821 guilders—all in all, a fortune of more than four million guilders. This amounted to half the sum total set aside for all the other children combined.[55] Albert, for his part, was inducted into the orders of St. Stephen and the Golden Fleece, received gifts of precious jewelry, and was made field marshal. In defiance of tradition, the couple moved to the royal residence in Pressburg rather than the court of the bridegroom's parents in Dresden. Also placed at their disposal was the former Palais Tarouca in Vienna, where the important collection of graphic arts they established is housed to this day.[56] Right down to the smallest details, then, Maria Theresa arranged everything according to the template provided by her own marriage. So that Albert would not be without a title and territory, she enfeoffed the couple with the Duchy of Teschen, a small province of Bohemia that had previously belonged to Francis Stephen.[57] Albert was appointed governor of Hungary, the same office that Francis Stephen had been granted by Charles VI in the land that lay closest to her heart. Maria Christina and Albert sent each other love letters in the period leading up to the wedding, as had her parents during their engagement a generation earlier. Maria Theresa even went so far as to offer them her former conjugal apartments in the Hofburg after she had vacated them.[58] She advised her daughter never to make her husband feel conscious of her own superior position, advice she claimed to have followed at all times herself,[59] and she described Albert as "your dear old fellow," just as she herself had playfully addressed Francis Stephen as "my dear old fellow."[60] As she wrote to Countess Enzenberg: "It gladdens my heart to see the married couple together, if anything at all can still give me pleasure; they often remind me of my former joys."[61] Nothing, she claimed on her deathbed, had been a purer source of delight to her than this marriage brought about at her instigation—or so Albert reported later.[62] In short, Maria Christina's marriage was in many respects a nostalgic reprise of her mother's. Needless to say, such favoritism was not lost on the other children: "Towards Maria and Prince Albert, she has the utmost tenderness and trust. They twist the empress around their little finger; she continually singles them out for special treatment, and the Empress cannot live without them."[63] A foreign observer put it more bluntly: "They drain her prodigiously."[64]

Yet not everything went their way. Following the difficult birth of a daughter who died within hours of being delivered, Maria Christina never again bore a child, while Carolina, Ferdinand's wife Beatrix, and above all Leopold's wife Ludovica presented the empress with new grandchildren year after year. And however lovingly the marriage of Maria and Albert may have been celebrated in their letters to each other, however devoutly he may have cultivated its memory in his memoirs,[65] the favorite daughter was bitterly resented by almost all her siblings. Leopold offered countless variations on the same theme in his secret diary of 1778–79: Maria understood how to gain absolute power over her mother; the empress completely depended on her and gave her everything she wanted so as not to risk upsetting her. Maria exploited her grip on her mother to the full: "She makes a great show of it in public, condescends to everyone, threatens to put in a word with the empress, meddles in everyone's affairs, gives herself airs, offers her protection, promises and secures positions, pensions, and benefactions." She was nonetheless "universally feared and reviled," as much in her own family as in the country at large, especially in Hungary: "everyone speaks ill of her." She was greedy for money despite being lavishly provided for, sponging off the empress and letting her shower her with gifts; she paid for nothing herself and piled up ever more savings. Finally, and above all, she sowed hatred, discord, and envy, constantly seeking to turn the empress against her son, the emperor.[66] These were all standard elements traditionally found in criticism of court favoritism. For Maria occupied an important structural position. She was the one who had the ear of the aged monarch, having been able to monopolize all her trust and channel all her patronage in support of her own ends. With that, she almost inevitably drew upon herself the hatred, flattery, and obsequiousness of everyone else. She presumably owed this privileged position not just to the fact that the old empress saw in Maria the reflection of her own lost happiness, but also to her personal skill in empathizing with her mother and perfectly matching her expectations. In all this, she proved a successful student of the late Isabella, who in her

"Advice for Maria" had spelled out exactly what she needed to do to attain this very position of favoritism.[67] That Leopold was not entirely inaccurate in his diagnosis, for all its malicious distortion, is shown by Maria Theresa's letters to Maria Christina, in which she used her darling daughter as a conduit for communicating with her other children without apparently realizing that Maria Christina was pursuing her own agenda.[68]

Maria Theresa had not only made Maria Christina her representative in Hungary (alongside Albert), she also had her in mind as a future governor of the Netherlands—in this case in her own right, with Albert acting merely as prince consort. When Charles of Lorraine died in August 1780, Maria Christina took his place.[69] Here, too, she conformed to an old pattern. The Habsburgs exercised their rule over faraway territories by appointing a minister plenipotentiary to oversee the everyday tasks of government, on the one hand, while, on the other, using close family members to represent their own person and the dynasty as a whole. The All-Highest Archducal House was all that held the motley array of Habsburg lands together—they had no shared bureaucracy, no uniform laws, no common supreme court, no joint crown, not even a common name. Maria Theresa had never visited many of her lands: Transylvania, for example, or the Banat, Istria, Milan, and Galicia. The "Spanish Netherlands," along with Lombardy the last remnant of the Habsburgs' vast Spanish inheritance, were also unknown to her, and she was unable to speak the language. In 1744, when she was solemnly inaugurated Countess of Flanders and had sworn *per procuratorem* to protect the old rights and liberties of the estates, she had never set foot in the land.[70] While there were several Flemish nobles in imperial service— the Ligne or Arenberg families, for instance, or individual confidantes such as the Marquise d'Herzelles[71]—the Netherlands were otherwise more or less terra incognita on Maria Theresa's mental map; only a few brief remarks on the subject have been recorded.[72] She entrusted the government to the Netherlandish department in Vienna, which had superseded the old 'Supreme Council' in 1757 and was subordinate to Kaunitz's State Chancellery, as well as the plenipotentiary in Brussels. From 1753 this was Karl Philipp Count Cobenzl, a protégé of Kaunitz.

They ruled together in close mutual consultation, bypassing the governor, Charles of Lorraine, who for his part was happy to lavish his attention and resources on courtly representation. In connection with the shift in alliances of 1756, the Habsburg Netherlands were bargaining chips in Kaunitz's grand strategy, and even if Maria Theresa was not prepared in the end to swap them for Bavaria, the fact that this was even seriously contemplated shows how much the territory was treated as the mere object in a dispassionate cost-benefit exercise, a financial resource and disposable asset. So long as this prosperous land continued to generate substantial revenue and supply troops in sufficient numbers, Vienna was prepared to respect its old rights and liberties. In this sense, the empress warned her son shortly before her death not to infringe on the constitution and government of the Netherlands: "This is our only happy land, and it provides us with so many resources. You know how greatly these people cling to their old, somewhat ridiculous prejudices, but they are obedient and loyal and contribute far more in taxes than our so extensive and discontented German territories! Who could ask for more?"[73] Joseph chose not to follow his mother's advice. Only a few years after her death, the privileged estates in Brabant revolted, and under the radicalizing influence of French Revolution, brought a sudden end to the old order—including Maria Christina's governorship.[74]

Model Sons, Model States

For centuries, the Italian peninsula had been caught up in the dynastic tug-of-war between the houses of Habsburg and Bourbon. In the Peace of Rastatt (1714), Charles VI had managed to hold onto the wealthy Duchy of Milan for the House of Austria as part of the Spanish inheritance. Tuscany had been added in 1738 in exchange for Lorraine. On the other hand, in 1735 Charles VI had been forced to surrender the Kingdom of Naples-Sicily, comprising the entire southern half of the Italian boot below the papal states, to the Bourbons in the aftermath of the War of the Polish Succession, albeit on condition that the land would not be united with the Kingdom of Spain. And under the terms of the Peace of Aachen (1748), Maria Theresa had likewise been forced to hand over the small northern Italian Duchy of Parma to a branch line of the House of Bourbon.[75] Conditions had always been highly unstable; the Italian territories had traditionally been treated in times of war as expendable dynastic property. Yet all this changed in 1756, when the so-called Diplomatic Revolution brought about an alliance between the Spanish and French Bourbons and the Habsburgs, who hoped thereby to challenge their more dangerous enemies, England and Prussia. Stabilizing relations through a dense network of intermarriages now lay in the interest of all three houses. Maria Theresa could thus marry off two of her daughters in Italy: in 1768 Carolina became the wife of King Ferdinand IV of Naples, and in 1769 Amalia wed the Duke of Parma.[76] Finally, the crowning glory of her entire marital policy and the cornerstone of the alliance system was the marriage of her youngest daughter, Maria Antonia, to the future king of France in 1770. With that, Vienna could draw on a finely graduated kinship network to exert political influence across all Europe. But capitalizing on this influence required frictionless communication and unconditional deference to the matriarch in Vienna. In Maria Theresa's view, the dynastic system would only work if her sons and daughters, like her faraway ministers, proved willing and reliable instruments of her will. But this was the case only to a very limited extent, if at all.

Maria Theresa had significant reservations about Italians. She had sent her sons and daughters into a land with which she felt little sympathy. She had seen Tuscany with her own eyes in 1738, on her grand tour to receive homage in Florence, but this was the last time she would cross the Alps. At least she could speak fluent Italian, or more accurately, Tuscan; Italian aristocratic families were connected with the court in Vienna and occupied several high offices there. Maria Theresa's ideas about Italy were nonetheless shaped to an astonishing degree by national stereotypes. Beyond the Alps, Italians were frivolous pleasure seekers, either hypocritical or godless. A contemporary German Enlightenment polemic could declare that "over the last two centuries, Italy has sent us atheists, Machiavellians, foreign vices, and Jesuits. Apart from that, we have received from there, for good or ill: lemons, oranges, macaroni, relics, the Genoese lotto, castrati, and papal nuncios."[77] The empress was convinced that Italians were notoriously untrustworthy and garrulous, inclined to falsehood and sycophancy, and more susceptible than others to nepotism, jealousy, and intrigue.[78] Yet the sons and daughters she sent to Italy encountered very different conditions upon their arrival, found themselves faced by different challenges, and dealt with them in very different ways. What they all had in common was their mother's determination to control them from afar.

Leopold, who had inherited the Grand Duchy of Tuscany from his father in 1765 at the age of eighteen, enjoyed the greatest formal autonomy.[79] The land had the status of an independent secundogeniture of the House of Habsburg-Lorraine, meaning it could not be amalgamated with the other hereditary lands. Leopold was therefore a sovereign in his own right; he resided with his wife Ludovica (or Louise) in the Palazzo Pitti in Florence as grand duke, not as a mere governor.[80] Still, as the younger son he owed obedience to both his mother and his elder brother, leading to a bitter dispute over his father's will at the very start of his reign. Joseph had settled the dispute unilaterally by transferring the substantial cash reserves Francis Stephen had extracted from his Tuscan subjects to Vienna's state coffers.[81] While the empress had pledged not to interfere with internal affairs in Tuscany, she also expected to be kept fully informed so that she might be of use to her son. In other words, Leopold should always seek advice from Vienna, and while formally presenting such tutelage as voluntary consultation, decide nothing for himself.[82] Furthermore, Count Botta Adorno, who had already managed affairs for Francis Stephen, was to stay on as chief minister. Maria Theresa also dispatched her son's former ayo, Franz von Thurn, to keep a close eye on him, having previously arranged for Thurn to marry one of her ladies-in-waiting so that she could monitor Archduchess Ludovica as well. Yet Thurn failed to report back as promptly or as comprehensively as she would have liked, provoking her to rebuke him severely. When he died not long after, it was said that the shock caused by the harsh imperial reprimand had killed him. Whatever the truth in the rumor, it speaks volumes for the power ascribed to Maria Theresa.[83] From 1766 Leopold's successor as maternal overseer and lord high steward was Franz Count Rosenberg, who enjoyed the empress's complete confidence and whom she therefore used as a go-between in difficult family missions. Although Rosenberg reported punctiliously back to her in the following years and never tired of praising Leopold's intelligence, prudence, and sagacity, it took years for her opinion of her son to improve and her mistrust to abate.

Better than all his siblings, Leopold was eventually able to wrest free of his mother's long-range control, ruling alone from 1771, without a chief minister appointed by Vienna. Ironically, the withdrawn Leopold, about whose character Maria Theresa held such grave doubts,[84] turned out to be the most successful of all her children—not just in the judgment of later historians, but in the eyes of contemporaries and even, eventually, Maria Theresa herself. From her point of view, his and his wife Ludovica's ability to present her with a new grandchild year after year was especially commendable. The couple had sixteen children in all, twelve of whom were born in their grandmother's lifetime. Fourteen survived infancy and—"particularly gratifying"—only four were girls. This increasingly relieved Maria Theresa of her anxiety about the continuance of her line. Leopold's first son, Francis (born 1768), became holy Roman emperor in 1792, styled himself emperor of Austria in 1804, and relinquished the imperial crown under pressure from Napoleon in 1806, thereby dissolving the Holy Roman Empire. In the competition to bear the most children, Ludovica was always held up to the other daughters(-in-law) as a shining example: "The archduchess leaves nothing to be desired with respect to fertility and successful pregnancy."[85] She did everything by the book, got plenty of bed rest, and refrained from dangerous physical activity, while the other daughters came in for repeated criticism on these points.

Leopold was exceptional not just on account of his prodigious offspring, however. He showed himself to be a model ruler as well as a model husband.[86] Earnest and orderly, systematic and logical, self-disciplined and strict toward others, he belonged to a generation of rulers who brought to the throne a new, unusually serious sense of their duties. Leopold had been taught by the natural law theorist Karl Anton von Martini, whose contractualist notion of the state he had made his own. Seeking to govern in the interest of civil society, not just that of the dynasty, he saw himself as a progressive ruler rather than one beholden to tradition. Tuscany, which in 1765 had just escaped the grip of terrible famine, became the flourishing model of modern physiocratic economic policy. Here, in this relatively compact territory, Leopold realized what Joseph, hemmed in on all sides as emperor and coregent, was unable to achieve in the Empire and the hereditary lands. The country had already brought his father enormous wealth. Leopold now set about enacting a comprehensive program of physiocratically inspired reforms, supported above all by native Enlightenment advisers such as the brothers Pompeo and Filippo Neri.[87] When Maria Christina and Albert were making their extended tour of Italy, they could not praise the land's prosperity highly enough—quite in contrast to the territories under papal or Bourbon rule. There, wherever they went they registered derelict roads, untilled fields and impoverished peasants, corrupt officials and undisciplined troops, parasitical clergy and indolent nobles.[88] Leopold, on the other hand, had liberalized the grain trade, abolished tax farming, improved peasant property rights, and reduced the church's wealth. In doing so, he had even managed to win over local bigwigs for his reforms by systematically consulting them, taking their concerns seriously, and modifying the reform process accordingly. In other words, Leopold cultivated a style of government that was geared toward consensus. This was by no means confined to economic policy. The Grand Duchy of Tuscany was the first country in all Europe to repeal the death penalty, and it nearly became the first constitutional monarchy as well, that is, a monarchy whose sovereign would be bound to a written constitution in the new style. Yet Leopold's pathbreaking constitutional project for Tuscany was never implemented; the consequences of the French Revolution doomed it to obsolescence.[89]

Habsburg Lombardy, the Duchy of Milan, was another laboratory for enlightened reform. Yet unlike Tuscany, the territory was effectively governed from Vienna through a chief minister, acting in regular consultation with the corresponding department in central administration. A member of the dynasty was entrusted with the task of symbolically representing rule by the Archducal House.[90] After 1771 this was the then seventeen-year-old Archduke Ferdinand, along with his wife, Beatrice d'Este, the wealthy heiress of the Duke of Modena. From 1759 to 1790 the business of government lay in the hands of minister plenipotentiary Karl Joseph Count Firmian, working in close collaboration with Kaunitz and the Italian department of the State Chancellery in Vienna.[91] Senior Habsburg officials posted to Milan discovered there a local Enlightenment in full swing. In Milan, significantly earlier than in Vienna, Prague, or Pressburg, the latest French books were discussed, letters exchanged with the leading *philosophes* in Paris, and political questions publicly debated in the legendary journal *Il Caffè*. Renowned Enlightenment figures such as Pietro Verri, Cesare Beccaria, or Pompeo Neri were consulted by the government on matters of reform and appointed to public office. On the whole, the experiment proved extremely successful, although conflict could not always be avoided. For example, the new church policy was first given a trial run in Milan before being rolled out in the hereditary lands.[92] State revenue shot up dramatically over the decades, from around 6.6 million lira in 1761 to almost 15 million lira in 1794. This was achieved primarily by doing away with privileges and optimizing economic productivity, not by increasing taxes for ordinary subjects. Regalian rights that had been forfeited over the centuries were bought back, administrative reforms were introduced, the country was mapped, and the tax burden was spread more evenly. Later on, private tax farming was abolished, ecclesiastical property was partially secularized, and first steps were taken to liberalize trade.[93]

Ferdinand, the governor general, played no part in these initiatives. He eventually became his mother's favorite son precisely because he refrained from interfering in government, making no claim to such "fashionable titles" as "hero," "scholar," "philosopher." He contented himself instead with his representative role and concentrated on being "a good Christian, a good husband, father, and friend to his friends."[94] In September 1771 Maria Theresa sent the seventeen-year-old Ferdinand, accompanied by a large retinue, to act as her representative in Milan. On October 14 he met there for the first time his bride, Beatrix (or Marie Beatrice), four years his senior. The sumptuous wedding took place the next day, still remembered not least because the then fifteen-year-old Mozart composed an opera, *Ascanio in Alba*, for the occasion.

The bride, an excellent match, had been chosen for him by God, Maria Theresa told her son. She might not be pretty, but she had "much to commend her" and was "pleasant," virtuous, amiable, and reasonable.[95] A nuptial contract between the houses of Habsburg and Modena had already been concluded in 1761 without specifying which archduke the heiress would marry. In April 1766 Beatrix was then engaged to Ferdinand in absentia, and she had been ardently loved at the Viennese court—*passionnément*, as Maria Theresa put it—ever since, despite no one in the family having set eyes on her.[96] Following the engagement, the empress regularly exchanged letters with her son's fiancée and filled her in on the groom's progress. As became clear soon after the marriage, her merits consisted chiefly in bearing children and exerting a disciplining influence on her young husband.[97] One and a half years after the wedding, Maria Theresa wrote with evident satisfaction to the Marquise d'Herzelles: "She and Ferdinand are quite in love with each other. She is somewhat haughty towards him [*elle prend le haut ton*]. Provided it remains this way, everything in moderation and for the good, I have nothing against it. As for the rest, he is managing better than I would ever have believed."[98] The couple were exemplary in how intensively they shared details of their married life with her. From the moment they first met, they had to report exactly how their feelings for each other were developing.[99] She herself usually wrote to them each Thursday, sometimes even more frequently, and she demanded of them at least one letter a week in return. If she was kept waiting, she heaped reproaches on them: "I burned with longing for letters from you!"[100] For her, one of her children's marriages was "only perfect if they let me know all about it."[101] It particularly pleased her when the archduke took his "incomparable father" for his model in even the tiniest details of domestic life.[102] Maria Theresa's letters veered between emotional extremes: one minute she was praising Ferdinand for his good heart, his empathy, his sterling qualities as a father, the next she was castigating him for his profligacy, his disorderly affairs, his apathy, his lukewarm and intermittent devotions. Yet there could be no doubt that he was one of her favorites, incurring him the enmity of his siblings. Leopold considered him a "very weak man of mean intelligence and little talent, despite the

high opinion he has of himself, . . . absentminded, indecisive, and scat-
terbrained," devious, proud, and avaricious, dominated by his wife and
resented by the populace.[103]

The insistence with which Maria Theresa pried into her children's
affairs, together with her never-ending, almost ritualized litany of admonitions, is especially easy to reconstruct in the case of Ferdinand and
Beatrix. Unlike almost all her other children, they never complied with
her demand that they destroy her letters to them (just as she, in turn,
destroyed the letters she received from her children)—a sign of mute
insubordination suggesting that the Milanese pair were not, perhaps, as
docile as they seemed. Yet in this case, too, Maria Theresa did not rest
content with weekly letters, demanding regular updates from the
couple's confessor, personal physician, chamberlains, ladies-in-waiting,
and other informants as well. Even though almost their entire retinue
came from Vienna and had been handpicked by her, the flow of information still never met with her satisfaction. Ferdinand's confessor wrote
regularly but in insufficient detail. Above all, Khevenhüller junior, Ferdinand's lord high steward, left much to be desired. In early 1772 she felt
compelled to send Count Rosenberg to Milan to check on her son's
progress. Rosenberg could provide her with reassurance. He had made
his own careful observations and conducted interviews with Firmian,
Khevenhüller, and Hardegg. None had cause for complaint. The archduke was "honest, good-natured, quick to learn, and approachable,
much taken with his wife and wise in his behavior in every respect." He
read the papers diligently but had no interest in books, unfortunately.
"Relations between husband and wife could not be more intimate." Beatrix had wit and esprit; she was more mature than her husband and
therefore had the upper hand in the marriage. She was prone to fits of
jealousy, although he had done nothing to justify them. There was also
no truth to the rumor that the archduke was personally unpopular; he
was a touch shy, that was all. His wife shielded him too much from other
people at court. A little more popularity could do him no harm.

These reports, like the couple's correspondence with the mother,
make clear just how much was expected of them and how little room for
maneuver they were allowed. Their duty was to fear God, to procreate,

and above all to represent Her Imperial Majesty wherever they went, *représenter par tout*. Government affairs and the archduke's subjects are conspicuous in their absence from the correspondence. Ferdinand's lack of religious discipline was a perennial topic,[104] as was the daughter-in-law's latest pregnancy and the health of family members. The exchange of family portraits and their likeness to the sitter was also frequently discussed.[105] So far as grandchildren were concerned, Maria Theresa initially sent messages of encouragement when yet another girl was born—"what matters is that she is healthy!" When the number of granddaughters grew out of hand, however, she no longer hid her disappointment: she could have done without the "fifth little Theresa," she wrote.[106] On the other hand, she praised the "charming children" and encouraged competition to produce the prettiest grandchildren.[107] It was she who decided on their names,[108] selected the personnel for the "children's room,"[109] and gave instructions on their upbringing.[110] If she suspected the couple of concealing something from her, she immediately adopted an icy, distanced tone. Beatrix and Ferdinand upset her, for example, by initially failing to inform her of a new pregnancy. When she learned of it through her informants, she wrote frostily: "To regain my trust, I hope that, in future, you will prove better able to convince me of your tender feelings for me and your obedience to my commands and wishes."[111]

The court and nobility were another recurring theme in the correspondence. On the one hand, care needed to be taken not to stretch the land's resources; on the other, there should be no false economies, since the couple had to represent the glory of their house in appropriate fashion. They should bind the native nobility to their court by holding regular apartments, dispensing calculated favors, adequately rewarding loyal service, but also upholding strict and exclusive rules of access. In this respect, the young court needed a "system for the future," and this was the task Maria Theresa assigned to Count Firmian. She had in mind a methodical arrangement "with which I do not wish you to interfere, since this is detestable and does not belong in your sphere." Ferdinand should tell anyone who petitioned him that the matter was entirely out of his hands and that he would not even seek to put in a good word with the empress, since, as she asserted, "I have reserved all decisions for myself alone, according to the principles of the court [in Vienna] and our family."[112] Granting or denying access was the most unpleasant duty of any ruler, she said, and she wished to relieve him of this burden. All Ferdinand needed to do was give his *placet* to papers placed before him by her minister plenipotentiaries. His mother would decide who had access to court; who received which offices, perquisites, pensions, and gifts; how many horses, carriages, and lackeys the coupled needed when they went out for a drive; which livery the bodyguard should wear; and even such trivialities as Beatrix's court dress and Ferdinand's coiffure (not just one, but several rows of locks).[113] Ferdinand was not even allowed to appoint his own equerry.[114] If he did anything on his own initiative—commenting on the list of prisoners to be pardoned at the beginning of his rule, for example—he could expect an instant dressing-down from his mother.[115] She really only asked him for his opinion when choosing the design and trim of the new state coach she was having made for him in Brussels. Otherwise, her watchword was always: "*C'est de moi, que cela doit venir*! I am the one who must decide!"[116]

Recalcitrant Daughters

If Maria Theresa was unprepared to concede any political influence to a male governor like Archduke Ferdinand, then it might be thought she would be even less likely to tolerate signs of independence from those of her daughters she had married off to foreign courts. Yet such was not the case. Maria Theresa had other roles in mind for her three daughters in Naples, Parma, and Versailles: they had been deployed as tools in her well-calculated system of dynastic alliances. At times this might have required them to play an active political role by informally taking the business of government out of the hands of their uninterested or incompetent husbands. Admittedly, the instructions Maria Theresa gave her daughters upon setting out on their new lives give a very different first impression. She exhorted them never to agree to intercede for others, to cultivate no protégés and favorites, to pay no heed to flatterers, to avoid getting caught up in intrigues, to obey their husbands, and never to interfere in affairs of state. This was imperative if they wished to acquire a spotless reputation as princess consorts. Adolescent girls lacking all experience and personal connections were well advised to steer clear of such entanglements at first. Only by avoiding being used as instruments of particular factions at court, and by maintaining a show of marital concord, could they eventually hope to gain a position of political influence—in line with their mother's intentions, to be sure. Since the daughters owed their formal status at court solely to their marriage, they needed to display unconditional loyalty to their husband in public; only through him could they shape policy without drawing undue attention to themselves. Hence Maria Theresa's sage advice: "The world must believe that you are thinking and acting only according to the king's taste."[117] Yet once the monarch's wife was seen—both by her husband and by the court—to stand above all private interest and partisan strife, significant avenues for political influence opened up for her. Maria Theresa was far from discouraging her daughters to pursue such opportunities: after all, if they were to be a reliable instrument of her maternal will, they could not be a tool for others.

Nineteenth-century historians saw such conjugal influence on princes as the epitome of illegitimate "petticoat government," a symptom of widespread European decadence under the ancien régime. Maria Theresa's two daughters in Italy, Carolina of Naples and Amalia of Parma, appeared, in addition, to historians of the Italian nation-state as symbolic figures of foreign rule and national fragmentation. Much the same could be said of Antonia (better known as Marie Antoinette), whose story has always been told as a prehistory to the French Revolution: a lurid portrayal of social mores that captured *pars pro toto* the moribund, dissolute state of the old social order. This was a social order characterized not least by its eminent compatibility with gynocracy, which the virtuous revolutionaries planned to do away with once and for all. Antonia's drama has been told often and well: the painful separation from her home court; difficulties with her indolent husband; idleness, naïveté, and profligacy; court intrigues and pornographic pamphlets; the diamond necklace affair; the tragic finale under the guillotine. While the story of the other two sisters took a less dramatic and bloody course, all three had much in common. This was due not least to the fact that their life stories conformed to a general structural template provided by the European dynastic order.

All three were pawns in a game of political strategy. Their own wishes, whatever these may have been, were never taken into account.[118] They were all either married off as children—Carolina at the age of fifteen, Antonia at fourteen—or assigned a husband who was himself a child, like the twenty-three year-old Amalia, wed to the seventeen year-old Infante of Parma. They were all more or less closely related to their husbands. All were engaged *per procuratorem* at their own court, without ever having met their groom, and they were then conveyed in a spectacular bridal procession to the border of their future country of residence, drawn to their fate by countless six-horse carriages. On crossing the border, they all went through a solemn handover ritual that separated them both physically and symbolically from their old family in preparation for their new social existence. In the case of Antonia, who literally had to remove every last thread of her Habsburg past from her person, this transformation was especially extreme.[119] They were all charged with bringing strapping sons into the world, which is why all Europe's attention was fixed on their body, their health, and their fertility. All had the misfortune of being unable to produce the expected sons for several years, a failure that saw them subjected to humiliating inspections, admonitions, and public ridicule. All three discharged their childbearing responsibilities with dubious success: although Carolina had eighteen children, the first, a daughter, did not appear until 1772, while the first son was not born until 1775, some seven years into the marriage; only four children survived their mother.[120] After months of unconsummated wedlock, Amalia eventually bore her husband seven children; the first, a girl, appeared in 1770. Poor Antonia had to wait until 1778 to be delivered of her first child, likewise a daughter, following long years of torturous sexual inactivity on the part of her husband. Two of her five subsequent pregnancies ended in miscarriage. All three daughters were watched over by Austrian envoys and other overseers of their mother; all three had to put up with intrusive systems of reporting and surveillance. Moreover, they all had the bad luck to be married to laughable caricatures of what characterized a model prince in the eyes of the world: a hyperactive, semi-literate buffoon in Naples; a religious fanatic with distinctly plebeian tastes in Parma; a sexually inhibited and indecisive melancholic in France. All three husbands were ill qualified for their roles, all three were no match for their strong-willed wives, and all three were not taken seriously by them: Carolina called the king of Naples a "good-natured fool";[121] Antonia pityingly described the king of France as "the poor man";[122] Amalia regarded her spouse, five years her junior, as incapable, feeble, and lazy.[123] Maria Theresa, who believed that a wife should uphold the rightful order of things to the outside world and unconditionally support her husband in his illusion of superiority, however weak he might be, took them to task for treating their masters so condescendingly. The three daughters also had in common that they immediately became caught up in factional politics at their new courts, as opponents of their husbands' unpopular prime ministers rallied around them and invested in them their hopes for change. And finally, all three refused to do their mother's bidding as compliant instruments of her will. There the similarities ended. Carolina, Amalia, and Antonia interpreted their roles very differently, depending on their temperament, that of their husbands, and conditions at court. Their relationship with their mother in Vienna varied accordingly. The fact that their marriages followed the same basic pattern, requiring highborn daughters to sacrifice their personal happiness for the good of the dynasty, did not preclude them from each experiencing her tale of woe in her own individual way.

Carolina of Naples

Maria Theresa regarded her second-youngest daughter Carolina (or Marie Charlotte), born in 1752, as the one who most closely resembled her.[124] The mother was well aware of just how challenging it would be for her fifteen-year-old daughter to marry the adolescent Bourbon, King Ferdinand IV of Naples: "I tremble for her," she confided in Countess Enzenberg.[125] In her unusually detailed instructions, she gently prepared her daughter for the trial that awaited her: "Every beginning [of a marriage] is hard, and your situation is harder than anyone else's."[126] At the age of eight, Ferdinand had formally inherited rule of Naples and Sicily from his father, who had moved to Madrid to take the Spanish throne as Charles III. In reality, Ferdinand, like his brother-in-law of the same name in Milan, played a purely symbolic, representative role as dynastic placeholder, while his father's minister plenipotentiary, the elderly Bernardo Tanucci (1698–1783), saw to the business of government. This arrangement continued unchanged after Ferdinand attained his majority. Nonetheless, he played the role of king in a manner that stood in bizarre contrast to the strict Spanish ceremonial and monumental new royal palace in Caserta. The groom's behavior was astonishing even by the standards of the day. The young Mozart, anything but a hidebound courtier, showed his irritation: "It's better to tell you in private what sort of a person the king is, rather than describing it in writing."

Leopold and Beatrix, who had escorted the bride to Naples, could not conceal their dismay in recounting Carolina's dramatic farewell from her retinue, and they had nothing good to report of their meeting with the groom. Count Rosenberg, who had been sent on ahead, had prepared them for the king's eccentricities and urged them "to give the queen every encouragement to perform her conjugal duties without any sign of revulsion."[127] "It will be hard for the queen," wrote Leopold the night before the wedding.[128] That this was no exaggeration emerges clearly from Carolina's letters to her former teacher, Walburga von Lerchenfeld, to whom she poured out her misery and homesickness. On the occasion of the wedding of her favorite sister, Marie Antoinette, whose company she obviously longed for, she wrote to their former aya and close friend:

> When I imagine that her fate will perhaps be the same as mine, I want to write volumes to her on the subject, and I very much hope that she has someone like me [to advise her] at the beginning. If not, to be frank, she may succumb to despair. One suffers real martyrdom, which is all the greater because one must pretend outwardly to be happy. I know what it is like, and I pity those who have yet to face it. . . . I would rather die than endure again what I went through at the beginning.

In the meantime, though, she had evidently made the best of a bad situation: "Now all is well, which is why I can say—and this is no exaggeration—that if my faith had not told me, 'Set your mind on God,' I would have killed myself."[129]

Joseph visited his sister in Naples a year after her marriage and related to his mother in pitiless detail what he had seen there.[130] He depicted the child king as hideously ugly: his face repulsive, his body lacking all proportion, awkward in gait, shrill in tone, ludicrously dressed, his behavior boorish and grotesque. It was impossible to hold a rational conversation with him and he had no interest in books. His sole pleasure was in infantile pranks and tasteless jokes. He surrounded himself with idle lickspittles. Brawling in his high-pitched voice, he drove his courtiers at a gallop through the vast rooms of the palace; kicked and punched them at will; pinched, frightened, and tickled the ladies; and rolled around with them on the floor. Opulent marble halls provided the backdrop for games of forfeit, sack races, and guard battalion exercises. In several rooms the king kept a menagerie of birds, rabbits, rats, mice, and other small animals; his hunting dogs lolled around on exquisite armchairs. He particularly relished practical jokes, Joseph reported, as when he smeared jam on a cavalier's hat or threw a live mouse in a woman's face. For all that, Ferdinand was anxious to the point of absurdity and lived in fear of his own subjects. He devoted most of his time to a bizarre form of hunt, driving game animals into a walled enclosure and then clubbing them to death like a peasant or shooting at them wildly without regard for his retinue. Joseph spared his mother no details in his report. She had to read, for example, about how her royal son-in-law sat on his close stool in full view of his courtiers, his trousers bunched around his ankles, and what he then did with his excreta. His entire conduct was of an obtrusively repellent physicality. He showered his imperial brother-in-law with embraces and even made him witness his sexual advances, which Carolina tolerated with visible reluctance. And so it went on over many pages, one grotesque detail after another. Ferdinand trampled on everything that distinguished an aristocrat from the common people: courtesy, self-discipline, good taste, the art of conversation. To be sure, this was not entirely uncommon; the Tyrolean Peter Prosch experienced something similar firsthand at ecclesiastical courts throughout the Empire.[131] The difference was only that Ferdinand, rather than confining his jokes to individual victims drawn from the common people, acted no differently with grandees, foreign envoys, and even his imperial brother-in-law. Yet his conspicuously childish behavior was not the worst of it; Joseph also registered a complete absence of religion and morality. Ferdinand was ignorant of the Ten Commandments and believed instead in ghosts and revenants. He had no fear of hell and thought nothing of adultery, lying, theft, even murder. Joseph blamed all this on his lack of education. He nonetheless found some redeeming features in his brother-in-law, who clearly loved his wife very much. In short, he was an "indefinable being." By contrast, Joseph provided his sister with a glowing testimonial: she lived virtuously, simply, and modestly; was truthful, good-natured, and intelligent; paid no heed to false counsel; loved her mother; and sought to honor her in every respect. While she saw through her husband's flaws and could not bring herself to love him, she regarded him with more compassion than abhorrence. Yet he dared not predict what might become of the couple in future.[132] The aim was clearly to provide Maria Theresa with as graphic an illustration as possible of what she had inflicted on her daughter through her choice of husband.

The observations from the Neapolitan court sent to Vienna by other visitors—Leopold, Rosenberg, Kaunitz junior, later Albert of Saxony—were less blunt in tone but otherwise confirmed Joseph's bleak account of the marriage.[133] They concurred in blaming conditions on Tanucci, who had an interest in keeping Ferdinand under his thumb so as not to jeopardize his own, all-powerful position in the kingdom. He succeeded in banishing all men of good sense from the king's society and surrounded him instead with his own craven toadies so that he remained the sole intermediary between the son and his father in faraway Spain. Ferdinand was afraid of Tanucci, the embodiment of paternal wrath; Charles III relied on him for want of any plausible alternative. The minister was able to conceal the growing misery in the land from both father and son, skillfully manipulating both monarchs to increase his own unrivaled authority. He had countless enemies at court and was hated by the people.[134]

Tanucci's unpopularity was also due to the fact that, under Charles III, he had played the role of radical reformer in the kingdom of Naples-Sicily. Like Haugwitz under Maria Theresa, he had proceeded systematically against aristocratic and clerical privilege to strengthen central authority and increase state revenue. A generation ago, Naples had been *the* center of enlightened political economy in Europe. Great expectations had attached to the young King Charles at the start of Bourbon rule in 1735. A generation of young scholars around Antonio Genovesi had set out to transform the kingdom's moribund economic and political structures in line with the latest scientific knowledge. Political economy had been established here as a university discipline in 1754, earlier than anywhere else, and had fostered a discourse that had politically energized the educated public in a new way.[135] In Naples, scholarly expertise and practical politics seemed to have entered into an alliance for the common good. Charles's minister Tanucci was celebrated in Enlightenment circles as the initiator of programmatic administrative, economic, and legal reforms. The kingdom's rigorously anticlerical, anti-Jesuit, and antipapal course was also associated with his name. Yet this stance had made him many enemies. To make matters worse, the devastating famine of 1764–66 had discredited mercantilist economic policy and polarized the general public. When Carolina arrived in Naples, the reform euphoria was as spent as the elderly Tanucci himself. The minister now found himself attacked on two sides: by the intrigues of the opposing faction at court, the clergy, and local families, on the one hand, and, on the other, by the fundamental criticism of physiocratic economists and radical enlighteners.

Maria Theresa's position toward the chief minister was ambivalent. While seeing in him a kind of Neapolitan Haugwitz, who needed to be supported against the vocal aristocratic-clerical reaction, he was also her rival when it came to influencing the young King. Her instructions to Carolina reflect this ambivalence. On the one hand, she advised her not to take against Tanucci from the outset: "It is the fate of all zealous ministers to serve as a target for the rivalrous and envious." However, "by this I do no mean that you should rely wholly on Tanucci's guidance." Breaking his hold on the king would not be easy: "One must therefore proceed with great caution before deciding to oppose a man like Tanucci, who . . . has the confidence of both kings."[136] Her path must always proceed via the husband and above all remain invisible: "Even if the king permits you to take part in his government, lets you in on his affairs, discusses them with you, and even asks for your advice, you should never show any outward sign of it; give him all the honor in the eyes of the world and be satisfied with his heart and his confidence."[137] To prepare the archduchess for her task, Kaunitz gave her a detailed briefing on the political situation in Naples prior to her departure. He was pleasantly surprised by her interest, her quick understanding, and her sound judgment. He also advised her to "take after the example of the previous queen . . . by always personally attending sessions of the privy council and other important meetings."[138] Joseph recommended that she familiarize herself thoroughly with her new environment before "stepping in," and Leopold was convinced that she "will reign there soon enough."[139] In other words, key figures in Vienna undoubtedly expected to be able to exercise influence in Naples through Carolina. Yet she would need to use all her tact to keep the local nobility and the Spanish court on her side. Carolina should therefore adapt to local ways, "indeed become a Neapolitan," and make every effort to win over her father-in-law.

Maria Theresa was keen on maintaining good relations with Charles III and dispelling any suspicion that she might be seeking to exert political influence through her daughter. When rumors reached her ears of the adolescent couple's indecent escapades in Naples—consorting with the wrong class of people, coach rides at night, public rowdiness— she demonstratively distanced herself from her wayward daughter (and from her other daughter in Parma as well), conveyed her dismay to Charles III through her Spanish envoy, Mahoni, and urged him to use his paternal authority, supported by his able servant Tanucci, to restore order. In doing so, she took the opportunity to stress how she had forbidden her daughters any kind of political influence.[140] But the initiative backfired badly when Charles III confronted the pair with the empress's reproaches and forwarded them the envoy's report. With that, he frustrated Maria Theresa's usual strategy of keeping her various correspondents in the dark about each other's communications with her. Carolina was indignant and outraged. The letter she immediately shot off to Maria Theresa bespeaks an extraordinary self-assurance. She berated her mother in no uncertain terms for going behind her and her husband's back, and she drastically depicted the physical and psychological shock the news of her betrayal had had on them. Rumors of their misconduct were nothing but lies and calumnies; she had always adhered to her mother's precepts in everything she did. "Why did Your Majesty not inform me of this yourself and wait to see whether I obeyed forthwith? She could then still have conveyed it to the king of Spain." Her mother had so discredited them in the eyes of Charles III that he was now not even permitting them to explain themselves. And their standing with Tanucci had also been undermined. "My dear husband and I do not want anyone to interfere in our marriage, which thank God is a very good one. We have now been married a year and a half and have never had an argument lasting longer than half an hour, never! . . . Without scenes of this kind, our happiness would be complete."[141] None of her children dared adopt such a tone toward Maria Theresa, not even Joseph. But she was indisputably in the wrong on this occasion. Deeply distraught, she appealed to Leopold to intervene through his wife, Charles III's daughter. She had not said everything she was purported to have said, the envoy had crudely falsified her warnings—but she could not deny having written to the Spanish king. She had lost all her credibility, not least with Joseph: "He will greatly disapprove of my conduct and find it disconcerting that I have sacrificed my daughter. Yet if I have done so, then only for reasons of state." She had only wanted to win over the king and stop her daughter from plunging into an abyss![142] Yet since her secret strategy had now been exposed and thereby frustrated, Maria Theresa felt compelled to back down and send her daughter a conciliatory response.[143] She was forced to admit that Carolina, who had obviously come to terms with her fate and learned to put up with her husband, had wisely done exactly what her mother had urged her to do: she had remained steadfastly loyal to him because her own position depended on it. By complaining about them to third parties as if they were naughty children, the empress had done them lasting damage in the eyes of their own court and made it impossible for them to emancipate themselves from the almighty Tanucci. Yet this was precisely what Maria Theresa surreptitiously expected the royal couple to do, and she admitted as much to her confidant, Mercy: she had no objection to Carolina having a hand in running the affairs of state. In the period that followed, she assiduously pulled strings and gave her backing to Tanucci's opponents in a bid to put an end to his "despotism."[144]

This was also what Carolina had been working toward and finally achieved in 1776.[145] Once she had subdued her husband and massively improved her own standing by producing a son, she had Ferdinand dismiss the old minister, against Charles III's opposition, and replace him as state secretary with the former Sicilian emissary in Vienna. And in 1778 she began regularly attending meetings of the State Council as the heir's mother, just as Kaunitz had initially advised her to do.[146] In short, she showed herself to be a true daughter to her mother: not just externally but above all temperamentally. Sanguine, spirited, intelligent, and accommodating, yet also strong-willed and confrontational when necessary, she proved a masterful manipulator of her husband—albeit for her own ends, not those of her mother. She had always successfully resisted having a lady-in-waiting sent from Vienna to spy on her, and she was similarly adept at evading supervision by the imperial emissary, Wilczek. She was too much like her mother to tolerate being used as her instrument.

Maria Theresa could not begrudge her daughter her respect. In 1772 she reported to Marquise d'Herzelles: "The Queen is conducting herself very well . . . and I am assured that the king has already mended his boorish and filthy ways."[147] "I love this daughter very much, and she deserves it too," she wrote to Countess Enzenberg, meaning: in contrast to Amalia in Parma and Antonia in Versailles.[148] She subsequently held up Carolina to the other children as a paragon of candor and obedience,[149] and even King Ferdinand, about whose character defects she was under no illusions, eventually rose in her estimation to become (temporarily) her second-favorite son-in-law, *gendre bien aimé*.[150] She expressed herself more frankly to Maria Christina, who in 1775 was to travel to Naples to ascertain that all was in order: "You know how dear your sister is to me; justice compels me to say that she is, after you, the one who has shown me the most true inclination, asked for my advice, and heeded it too. But young and spirited as she is, partnered with so heated and ill-mannered a husband, surrounded by all possible ills, what hope can there be for her? It is a miracle that things are still running as they are, and," she added in canny self-awareness, "more harm than good is to be expected from advice offered from abroad."

Even Carolina had not always been open and trusting with her, she complained.[151] That she was not quite so satisfied with her independent and strong-willed daughter in Naples as she claimed is also confirmed by Leopold, who in 1778 noted in his diary that the empress hardly bothered any more with "Neapolitan affairs as she is somewhat irritated with the queen, who does not appreciate others mixing in her business."[152] Toward the end of her life, pity for Carolina regained the upper hand: "The poor Queen deserves ... sympathy," she wrote in April 1780.[153]

Amalia of Parma

Amalia, six years older than Carolina, presented problems of an altogether different kind. After other, more favorable marriage plans had fallen through, she had been married against her will to the Infante Ferdinand of Parma from the House of Bourbon (1751–1802), a grandchild of the French king, nephew to the Spanish king, and brother to the late lamented Isabella.[154] Ferdinand had been made Duke of Parma at the tender age of fourteen, his mother Elisabeth Louise having died in 1759 and his father Philipp in 1765.[155] When he married Archduchess Amalia in 1769, he had formally attained his majority; in reality, however, he depended entirely on the two Bourbon courts, which supported him financially and had arranged the marriage on his behalf. Government of the petty principality lay in the hands of the French minister, Guillaume Du Tillot, who continued on the radical, anticlerical course he had already charted under the late duke. As a child, Ferdinand had been regarded in philosophical circles as something of a wunderkind. He was considered an exceptional product of a philosophical education in the

new French fashion, which taught the child to think for himself—
through severe punishment, if needs be. His father had engaged as tutors
the officer and mathematician Auguste de Keralio and the renowned
philosopher Etienne Bonnot de Condillac, a first-rate scholar who consorted with Voltaire and the *Encyclopédistes* and thus represented everything that Maria Theresa instinctively abhorred. The precocious Infante
was said to be fluent in six languages and prodigiously knowledgeable in
all the arts and sciences, from history to experimental physics. Already
known as a gifted speaker in State Council, the lad was witty and intelligent, virtuous and clear-headed. In short, he promised to become the
perfect ruler.[156] Maria Theresa was likewise impressed by his reputation;
she advised her daughter to keep her mouth shut at the court in Parma,
since she could not possibly converse at the same level with "so intelligent and learned a prince."[157] The empress clearly had little confidence
in Amalia's abilities: "I cannot repeat often enough that you are insufficiently educated and otherwise ill fit to rule." She would be better off
sticking to her domestic duties and not attempting to dominate her husband, even though he was some five years her junior.[158]

Yet Ferdinand failed to fulfill the expectations associated with the
enlightened pedagogical experiment. On the contrary: rebelling against
the rigid control of his tutors, he fled into the ritualistic, Baroque, old-
style piety imparted to him by his Dominican confessors. By dismissing
his faith as superstitious "old wives' piety," his tutors only succeeded in
teaching him the art of dissembling. The little Infante clandestinely
wove rosaries out of corn kernels, painted his own images of the saints,
and secretly vowed to live as a Dominican. After he had become duke
and shaken off his tutors, he openly cultivated this pious way of life and
ignored all the efforts of his Bourbon relatives to take him in hand. He
cared little for etiquette and shocked Parmesan court society by surrounding himself with Dominicans, Capuchins, and commoners, constantly praying, fasting, and going on pilgrimages, ringing bells by hand,
but also carousing late into the night and self-flagellating.[159] Such conduct was not just unbecoming of a prince and detrimental to princely
authority. It also suggested that it was only a matter of time before the
sharply anticlerical policy of minister Du Tillot would be reversed.

The marriage with Amalia was a catastrophe from the beginning. While Maria Theresa still clung to the illusion that the "grace of the marriage sacrament" had completely transformed her previously passive daughter, the marriage actually remained unconsummated for months due to a physical defect of her husband.[160] Amalia also did the exact opposite of what her mother had told her to do. This, at any rate, was what the Spanish minister Grimaldi reported back from Parma to Madrid: she took after her mother by dominating her husband and placing her own name beneath ducal decrees; she was too liberal in bestowing favors, accepted recommendations from everyone, and let the Italian party at court stir her up against Du Tillot.[161] By contrast, Franz Philipp von Knebel, whom Maria Theresa had sent to Parma as Amalia's minder, leaped to her defense, pointing out that the Infante himself wished to put an end to his prime minister's harsh regime. Kaunitz, too, felt that the young archduchesses in Parma and Naples ought not to be treated like "little she-devils"—*petites diablesses*—on account of minor infractions; after all, both their husbands were sovereigns and bore ultimate responsibility for what went on at their courts.[162] Yet Maria Theresa, who saw good relations with the Bourbon monarchies threatened by parallel accusations against Carolina and Amalia, was alarmed. As already mentioned, she asked Charles III to intervene against her unruly children in Parma and Naples. This did nothing to improve their relations with their mother when news of her meddling came to their notice.[163] At the same time, she sent Count Rosenberg to Parma to find out whether the marriage had been consummated, how the pair were behaving, and what Amalia might be up to.[164] She even contemplated having the marriage annulled in the extreme event that the Infante should prove incapable of performing his conjugal duty. Rosenberg was instructed to seek a clear diagnosis from the duke's personal physician on this point. So far as the other accusations were concerned, she learned that they had more to do with the Infante's unbecoming conduct toward others, particularly his preference for commoners and priests, than with her daughter. But a change could not be achieved through force, she warned, only with meekness and respect. If all this proved to no avail, she now concluded, her daughter would sooner or later have to take over the regency for her husband: "I myself believe that my daughter will eventually have to govern, but this will happen only with the consent of the kings [of France and Spain], if they ask it of her."[165]

A stream of special envoys from the three great courts stopped off at Parma over the next three years.[166] The empress was in a state of constant anxiety and feared that letters would be intercepted and details of the dispute brought to public attention. When this inevitably occurred, Parma became the "laughing stock of all Europe."[167] The envoys' reports varied in tone: depending on their home court and factional loyalties, they criticized either Amalia's lust for power or Ferdinand's bigotry, defended the couple against the Prime Minister or vice versa. What was considered truly scandalous was that Amalia and Ferdinand had abolished court hierarchy and made no distinction between high and low, young and old. They lavishly and indiscriminately scattered material signs of their favor—always on the wrong people, in Maria Theresa's view—and drove the court ever deeper into debt. There were conflicting reports about the state of their marriage; it seemed to vacillate between conflict and reconciliation. At any rate, Amalia fell pregnant and bore her first child, a daughter, in late 1770.

The Infante and Infanta were united in their bitter struggle against the "worthless blackguard" Du Tillot[168] and Chief Lady-in-Waiting Malaspina. For the anti-French, pro-Roman party at court, this was a godsend. In an effort to bend the couple to their will, the two Bourbon kings made them sign a contract agreeing to give the Prime Minister sole regency for the next four years.[169] They signally failed to honor this pledge, causing the continual break-out of conflict. In August 1771 the Infante formally asked his grandfather and uncle to dismiss the minister; Amalia approached her mother for support. The three courts were forced to acknowledge that the hated Du Tillot's position had become untenable. Charles III discharged him in October 1771, with a demonstratively generous pension, and replaced him with a Spaniard, José Agostino de Llano. This did little to change the situation. The couple were soon once again rebelling against the restraints placed on them by the new minister. The self-assertive Amalia let him know as much in writing:

I am enough of a physiognomist to have seen through you at our first audience. So I am happy to assure you that I will not interfere in affairs of state, but also that I am in charge of my affairs and in my house. The Infante and I are so united that we have one and the same will. I have enough power here to command obedience, I am loved and feared. . . . I am a German: I know what I am owed, never forget that. I have the gift to make myself feared and loved, so obey![170]

Such an open show of dominance was unprecedented. Amalia not only presumed to speak in her husband's name, she also arrogated to herself the authority of the All-Highest Archducal House. By insisting so stridently on her power, she also gravely erred in tone. For rulers in general, and for Maria Theresa in particular, the cardinal rule was the more power, the greater the need for mercy; the harsher the substance, the softer the form. Amalia clearly vastly overestimated her room for action.

Yet Amalia, misjudging the avenues available to her, refused to take orders from her mother. Rosenberg informed the empress that his mission had failed. Maria Theresa then broke off all contact with her daughter and ordered her other children to do the same. Nobody was to write to her, let alone meet her. The others were to avoid the Duchy of Parma when traveling abroad and make a detour via Venetian territory. She even required Ferdinand to refuse contact if Amalia should have the temerity to surprise him with a visit to Milan.[171] Yet she clearly felt the need to justify her severity. "Things have come to a point where your sister forces me to betray her," she wrote to Archduke Ferdinand. "You can imagine how I suffer to see her running to her doom, without being able to prevent it."[172] And to Mercy she sent a handwritten note: "I have found it necessary to act in this way, for I know my daughter's obstinacy. But despite all the trouble she makes me, she is still my child. I would not like her to be driven to the utmost, but I also have no wish for her to be sent back to me."[173] If she harbored the unspoken hope that Amalia would now relent, it was to prove mistaken. The daughter was every bit as inflexible as her mother and cut off all communication with her, only adding to Maria Theresa's concerns.[174]

PLATE 24. Maria Theresa as a widow surrounded by her grown-up children. From left: Maria Christina, Albert von Sachsen-Teschen, Maximilian, Marianna, Elisabeth, Joseph. Tempera by Heinrich Friedrich Füger, 1776

PLATE 25. Street scene in Vienna. Freyung from the southeast. Bernado Bellotto, known as
Canaletto, 1759–60

PLATE 26. Joseph II and Leopold in Rome, 1769. Double portrait by
Pompeo Batoni

PLATE 27. Schönbrunn Palace, Bergl Rooms

PLATE 28. Self-portrait of Archduchess Maria Christina at the spinning wheel, mid-eighteenth century

PLATE 29. Marie Antoinette. Elisabeth-Louise Vigée-Lebrun, 1779

PLATE 30. Maria Theresa and her children in Laxenburg. Unknown artist,
eighteenth century

The unwritten code of dynastic conduct dictated that grown-up children should freely and uncomplainingly obey the family head, out of inclination and conviction. Forcing them to obey contravened the dynastic rulebook, for compulsion was something reserved for subjects, that is, for those subjected to rule. Submitting to external force was incompatible with the aristocratic ethos of freedom, pride, and honor. While it was sometimes necessary to discipline family members for dynastic rule to function internally, this could not be shown to the outside world. Admonitions had to be made as gently, *doucement*, as possible; subordination to the dynastic interest had to come joyfully and voluntarily, since whoever wanted to rule over others first had to rule over himself. Domestic self-discipline was fundamental to the way ruling families maintained their legitimacy. An openly threatening tone was reserved solely for emergencies.[175] But this had to be kept strictly confidential and should never come to the attention of the outside world. Perhaps the worst aspect of Amalia's unprecedented recalcitrance was that it was impossible to keep under wraps. It made the All-Highest Archducal House the laughingstock of Europe.

These years saw a flurry of letters between the courts in Vienna, Versailles, and Madrid concerning how the unruly children could be brought into line. At the French court, there was talk of separating the couple, sending the Infante abroad, and banishing Amalia to Vienna, much to Maria Theresa's horror. Even the deployment of Spanish troops was contemplated for a time. Despite the intransigence she showed toward Amalia, Maria Theresa sought to persuade other courts to impose milder sanctions, to exonerate her own daughter, and to shift the blame onto the Infante. The couple could not be compelled to virtue and obedience, she argued. Instead, financial pressure should be applied so that sheer economic necessity would drive them back into the family bosom.[176] And this is what happened. In late 1772, when the Infante added fuel to the fire by summarily dismissing Minister Llano, pension payments were terminated, all Bourbon and Habsburg personnel were withdrawn from Parma, and the weekly courier service between the courts was abolished. Maria Theresa gave these measures her explicit approval. The two would have to be treated like outcasts—*interdits*;

even if the other courts managed to patch things up, she herself would never resume the correspondence with her daughter, she wrote.[177] "They have been left high and dry; now they will perhaps have a year to rejoice in their freedom and independence from all foreigners. The break with both families is a high price to pay for this freedom."[178] For once, Joseph shared his mother's opinion. If anything, his verdict was even harsher: "imbecilic and filled with the blackest malice," he called the ducal pair.[179]

Even when the Infante formally announced that the Infanta had been delivered of a child on July 5, 1773, Vienna refused to budge. No gala was put on to celebrate the event, no apartment given; the empress sent only a short, coolly worded message of congratulation.[180] She commented on the grandson's birth to Kaunitz: "Those who have the most luck generally deserve it the least."[181] Yet the existence of an heir strengthened the duke and duchess's position. The king of Spain, invited to stand godfather to the boy, conferred on him the Golden Fleece at his baptism.[182] Both kings signaled to the Infante their willingness to reconcile on condition that he recalled Minister Llano, and they asked Maria Theresa to communicate the same offer to the Infanta. Yet although Maria Theresa had likewise long hoped for a reconciliation (or at least stated as much in her letters to others), she refused to write to her daughter. After all that had happened, she would not be the one to make the first move.[183] The Bourbon kings had no such scruples and engineered the rapprochement without Maria Theresa's involvement. After putting up a brief show of resistance, the ducal couple made the required gesture of submission and recalled the detested Minister Llano back to their court. In the autumn of 1773, Maria Theresa breathed a sigh of relief that the "reconciliation with Parma is now complete. . . . I hope it lasts. Spain and France have acted magnanimously."[184]

Amalia subsequently retreated to a manor in Sala and went her own way. From 1774 the couple lived separate lives, paying each other only isolated visits, although this did not prevent them having four more children. In the period that followed, the Infante pursued his own political agenda—especially after Llano had understandably left the land a second time, this time of his own volition—and revoked Du Tillot's ecclesiastical reforms one by one. The pious Duke was not unpopular among the people, it was said, while in Enlightenment circles there was considerable bitterness over the obvious failure of his philosophical education.[185] Until her death, Maria Theresa found herself unable to stick to a single course toward her most wayward daughter, veering between kindness and coldness, pity and implacability. From time to time she sympathized with "the unhappy one" (la malheureuse), yet she complained at the same time about her continued "intrigues and subterfuges"; Amalia also continued to rack up debt.[186] At least Maria Theresa allowed the other children to meet with her, and she always hungered for news from Parma. In connection with the abortive plan for a family reunion in Görz, she even considered meeting Amalia. In 1775 she wrote to Maria Christina: "The situation of your sister, which in truth she has brought entirely upon herself, is unpleasant, but also not completely unbearable. I feel very sorry for her."[187] She had also come to see the Infante in a more favorable light, particularly as excessive saying of the rosary and zealous devotion to the saints could hardly count as serious offenses.

> I often doubt what I hear said about him. . . . Others keep mistresses, hunt, gamble, have horses, etc. etc., and since he has no means of his own, he must have something. Who is entirely without flaws? One has to be satisfied so long as he has no vices. Your sister has sometimes suspected him of drinking a little too much with the monks, which could be true; that would be a sin. You will tell me everything you find out about this poor prince.[188]

Albert later gave a bleak account of his stay in Parma: Amalia had changed a great deal, her looks had faded, she was distant to her children and led her own life far removed from her husband, who for his part came across as self-conscious and unfeeling. Her oldest daughter was already a great beauty, but so sad that it made one melancholy.[189]

Maria Theresa never sought to bring about a personal reconciliation, even when a fresh opportunity presented itself at the end of 1780. "You must know," she confided in Archduke Ferdinand, "that your sister has always tormented me to come here, and not to roast her slowly over a low fire, but to say whether or not there is hope for her." The couple had asked her for money to endow the oldest granddaughter with a sinecure, but Maria Theresa had brusquely turned down the request. Amalia had since fallen ill, and the Infante begged that she be allowed to travel to Vienna for specialist treatment. Yet Maria Theresa decided that the illness was feigned and refused permission: "I could never agree for her to come here. . . . The emperor has said he would not stay a day longer if she were to come."[190] She nonetheless subsequently fretted over her daughter's health. Amalia had been feverish for sixty days, was emaciated and depressed, albeit not so weak as had initially been thought, she informed Ferdinand in October. And in November she wrote to Beatrix: she had heard that Amalia was still unwell, but she was refusing to do as she was told.[191] Amalia eventually recovered, but her mother died the same month without ever seeing her again.

In the eyes of her family, Amalia's crime was that she had misunderstood her role as member and representative of the dynasty. She had wrongly considered herself free to disregard whatever she was told and live exactly as she pleased, at least in her private life—perhaps an unintended consequence of the Enlightenment philosophy to which Ferdinand had been exposed and which had infected Amalia instead. Her crime consisted in her unabashed yearning for freedom and her stubborn, openly avowed disobedience toward parental authority. For Maria Theresa, this was unforgivable. The verdicts of later historians were even harsher than those of contemporaries. In hindsight, one wonders what excesses the Infanta could have committed to justify being branded the "Messalina of the eighteenth century," the "most grievous wrongdoer against her mother."[192] Extravagance, indiscriminate bestowal of favors, hunting trips accompanied only by a groom, physical separation from her husband: all these were faults shared with many other princesses of the time. And her defiance of courtly conventions, her popularity among the common people, her unrestricted accessibility, her generous almsgiving—these were the same qualities for which Maria Theresa had always been universally admired. Yet for all Amalia's similarities with her mother, she lacked the status that allowed her to assert herself effectively. For nineteenth-century historians, Amalia's biggest fault was her female dominance, her inversion of gender roles in the House of Parma. A ruler of Maria Theresa's stature could get away with it; she enjoyed the status of a towering exception. But what was found admirable in her was enough to cast a minor princess like Amalia into disrepute.

Marie Antoinette

The matriarch faced a further massive problem in steering her youngest daughter, Antonia, who following protracted negotiations had married the French heir Louis (XVI) in 1770.[193] In this case, asserting control from faraway Vienna was especially important—but also especially difficult—due to the importance of France and the relevance of the anti-Prussian alliance. As future queen of France, Maria Antonia would assume the highest rank of all Maria Theresa's children after Joseph. At the same time, she was the one who married youngest and was the most isolated at her new court. When she left the Holy Roman Empire and was transformed from Archduchess Maria Antonia into Marie Antoinette, *madame la dauphine*, going through a handover ritual on a small island in the Rhine near Strasbourg, she had to leave behind everything that constituted her identity. Apart from special envoy Starhemberg, no one from her retinue was permitted to accompany her to Versailles.[194]

As with all her other daughters, Maria Theresa provided her with detailed instructions that she was to read once a month and thereby internalize. Alongside the usual religious exercises, reminders to obey her husband, and warnings against playing favorites, Marie Antoinette was also enjoined to nurture the alliance as its living pledge. She should speak as often and as warmly as possible with her husband's grandfather, Louis XV, about the connection between the courts, which had now become a particularly close one: "You can never say too much about the feelings I have for him."[195] Yet regular meditation on the maternal instructions was not enough; remote control had to be continuous, flexible, and unbroken. Maria Theresa had as few illusions about the fifteen-year-old's maturity and character as she did about her other children. This time, however, she had to go to work as cautiously and strategically as possible, "taking extra precautions for secrecy."[196] Just how elaborate the mother's surveillance system was can be precisely ascertained from the surviving correspondence between her, her daughter, and the Viennese ambassador in Versailles, Florimond Claude Comte de Mercy-Argenteau.[197]

Mercy (1727–94), member of a Flemish family that had served the Habsburgs for generations, had long acted as emissary for the Archducal House, having previously negotiated the Franco-Habsburg marriage project with Choiseul. As imperial ambassador in Versailles, he was now the sole formal intermediary between mother and daughter. His possibilities were limited, however, since at court he was confined to official contacts with the Dauphine and could rarely speak to her unobserved. It was easier in the countryside, in Fontainebleau, Marly, or Trianon, assuming that Marie Antoinette invited him along on these outings. Mercy therefore relied on a second confidant: her reader Abbé de Vermond, who was with her each day, managed her correspondence, and kept him minutely informed about everything that happened in her rooms.[198] In addition, Mercy used a number of other paid informants and claimed "that there is no hour for which I could not account for what the Archduchess said, did, and heard."[199] At her mother's behest, letters were sent back and forth between Vienna and Versailles once a month: on the one hand between Maria Theresa and her daughter, on the other between Maria Theresa and Mercy. A minority of these letters were sent with the regular weekly post and were intended to be visible to all; indeed, it was almost expected that they would be intercepted and transcribed, offering an opportunity to communicate indirect messages to those who were surreptitiously reading along. By far the majority, however, were entrusted to a secret courier service that ran directly from Mercy to Maria Theresa's cabinet secretary, Pichler, passing through no other hands. These letters bore the inscription *tibi soli*, for you alone, and were passed unopened to the empress by the secretary.[200] The couriers always received the letters just before their departure and had to keep to a tight schedule, so that the recipient would immediately be alerted to any irregularity suggesting interception. The empress even kept the exchange hidden from Joseph; when he once asked to be shown the letters, she gave him only a select few.[201] While Marie Antoinette apparently followed her mother's instructions by burning the letters after reading them, Maria Theresa had them copied by Pichler—against her stated intentions—and filed in her private library.[202]

The crux of the matter was that communication between Vienna and Versailles ran along two separate channels but only one side was aware of this. Marie Antoinette was under the impression that her correspondence with her mother was strictly confidential. In fact, Mercy knew all about it, whereas Marie Antoinette was kept in the dark about her mother's correspondence with Mercy. The ambassador not only kept the empress closely informed about day-to-day affairs in Versailles, he also cunningly manipulated her unsuspecting daughter. He not infrequently gave Maria Theresa advice on what she should write in her letters, even proposing particular turns of phrase. He also informed her about how Marie Antoinette reacted to the letters, what she said in response, and how she followed—or failed to follow—their stipulations.[203] Conversely, Mercy instructed Marie Antoinette on how she should communicate with her mother and praised, criticized, or corrected what she wrote.[204] In her naïveté, Marie Antoinette never cottoned on to how her mother came to have such detailed knowledge of her activities, putting it down to public chatter. She clearly believed her mother when she assured her: "Do not believe that Mercy has sent me word of this!"[205] Another aspect of the maternal control system was that Marie Antoinette was not allowed to exchange letters with everyone in the family, only with the emperor—albeit only under certain circumstances determined by the emperor himself—her brother-in-law Albert, and her sister Carolina, whom she was encouraged to emulate in all respects.[206] Maria Theresa expected that her relatives and servants would divulge to her whatever Marie Antoinette told them. She thus learned from Rosenberg that the Dauphine had placed her trust in him, and she reacted with a sharply worded rebuke.[207]

Such highly asymmetrical communication was far from unusual for Maria Theresa, even if she practiced it less systematically with her other children. Around each child she spun a web of partly overt, partly covert surveillance. Not even Joseph escaped it. Whenever he set off on his travels, she put informants on his tail without his knowledge. She thus demanded of Count Rosenberg that he "give as good an account as you can [of the emperor's trip to Italy]: I am relying on you. You will let me know of the least incident—heaven forbid—without passing over anything in silence. You will reveal nothing about this letter." And: "I betray nothing of all this to my children. I must tell you that the emperor has not read me your letters to him, but he knows that I write to you occasionally. You will make no use of this letter."[208] It especially pained her that Joseph never showed her the letters he sent and received. She knew nothing of his intensive correspondence with Leopold and was incensed to learn that he took other siblings into his confidence. She complained to Ferdinand, for example: "I would never have believed that the emperor writes to you, as he has told me. I took that for a jest meant to annoy me, but I must admit, I am impressed to see the lengths to which he carries things."[209] In accordance with the principle "divide and conquer," she did all she could to prevent her children communicating with each other behind her back. Instead, she played them off against each other and forged hidden alliances, sharing with one confidential information about another and making them all feel singled out by her trust. She thus assured Ferdinand: "You should know that no one ever sees your letters, even the trivial ones; so you should never cite them to the emperor, since he also never shows me his. I will also not do it, or if I do, I will tell you beforehand; you may therefore express yourself quite freely."[210] In theory, at least, the family placed great value on the privacy of correspondence. When a letter that Marie Antoinette had written to the emperor during the War of the Bavarian Succession was opened by Maria Theresa, she excused it as an accident. She had, she claimed, immediately closed it without so much as glancing at its contents.[211]

Maria Theresa thus sat spiderlike in the web of communications connecting the family—or, at least, she sought to occupy the point where all the threads converged. What she did not know was that there was someone who monitored and manipulated her correspondence in turn: Kaunitz. If she thought that the strictly confidential parts of her correspondence with Mercy and other foreign emissaries escaped her State Chancellor's attention, then she was mistaken. In 1768, well before Marie Antoinette's marriage, he had personally ordered Mercy to set up a covert back channel with the empress via Cabinet Secretary Neny "and make it look as if he [Neny] alone was the depositary of secrets." He expressly instructed Mercy "to exercise caution in not enclosing her let- ter to me, but giving it directly . . . to the couriers, also not sending me a transcript so that I can state in all truthfulness that I had not received one." Instead, he asked Mercy to provide him with "the contents of her correspondence in only a few words and extracts on a specially sealed sheet." Kaunitz would return these summaries to Mercy's hands and em- ploy the same procedure with Kaunitz's secret replies, "so that no trace of our private correspondence—all perfectly innocent, to be sure— remains in the diplomatic archives."[212] So it came to pass; in the period that followed, Mercy sent Kaunitz regular reports on his correspondence with the empress, who, as he put it, relished long, florid descriptions, whereas he could restrict himself to the two or three key points with the State Chancellor.[213] In Kaunitz, the empress had thus met her match in covert communications. The state chancellor's idea of politics was differ- ent from her own, however. In his eyes, emotionally charged mother- daughter relations were irrelevant. For him, foreign policy was the pro- fessional concern of a ministry, not a matriarch's family affair. He nonetheless could not dispense with the young archduchesses as instruments—albeit extremely unreliable ones—of foreign policy.[214]

The manner in which Maria Theresa organized her epistolary com- munication stood in stark contrast to the standard of unreserved truth- fulness and candor she imposed on her children. She appears to have been unaware of any self-contradiction. "I am honest myself," she wrote to Marie Antoinette, "and demand [exiger] the strictest honesty from others, and since I am by no means demanding [exigeante], but very obliging, I can demand this [exiger]."[215] The family letters were highly ambivalent. They were always two things at once: a medium of intimate dialogue and a strategic instrument of control. In the eighteenth century, private letters had evolved under the influence of sentimental epistolary novels to become *the* medium for authentically sharing feelings and ex- pressing individuality.[216] Maria Theresa, too, demanded that her children allow "the heart itself to speak" in their letters to her.[217] This was a far from easy or self-evident task: it presupposed mastery of a vocabulary of emotions and a register of varying degrees of formality and informality. There was nothing spontaneous or "natural" about this highly differentiated culture of letter-writing; it was something that had to be learned. The archducal children were trained in it from an early age; Maria Theresa read their letters as documents of their progress and corrected them for style and orthography.[218] The fine art of correct address could not be neglected even in the family setting. Only when the empress gave them explicit permission could the children dispense with the prescribed compliments and honorifics and call her simply "Madame" and "*Votre Majesté*," "VM" for short.[219] She, in turn, addressed her children as "*ma chère fille*," "*monsieur mon cher fils*."[220] Yet even the relaxation of strict ceremonial forms was for its part a consciously cultivated form. Maria Theresa was an expert at drawing different registers of proximity and distance in her letters. She wrote to the children in a discourse of sentimental devotion to convey her feelings of tender love, sympathy, and concern: she spoke of *attachement, amitié, tendresse, passion, consolation*. This by no means ruled out various levels of indignation all the way up to severe reproach. Precisely this language of emotional closeness imposed a moral obligation on the respondent to be completely open and honest in return and conceal nothing. Strategic dissimulation was considered shameful and *malhonnêt*, dishonorable. The opposite of "truthful" was "political": "Your word, your conduct must always be the same: truthful, without any hint of politics [*sans aucune politique*], this word is unknown to us."[221] In this view, "political" behavior was synonymous with calculating, self-interested, hypocritical scheming. The sphere of family relations should be free of all that; here, "only the heart should speak." Yet this was precisely what made letters a suitable medium for maternal control and supervision—the flip side of sentimental epistolary culture. There is a certain irony in the fact that Maria Theresa trusted her children the least and continually violated her own stipulation of honesty in her dealings with them, whereas she was most consummately deceived (albeit without malicious intent) by those in whom she placed her unreserved confidence, such as Mercy and Kaunitz.

The question of how Maria Theresa influenced French policy via her daughter has not only exercised generations of historians, it was also the subject of lively debate at the time. The Habsburg alliance had always been opposed by many at Versailles. Their belief that it was injurious to the French monarchy appeared to have been confirmed by the catastrophic events of the Seven Years' War.[222] From the beginning, the alliance had been tainted by its association with the king's mistress, whose feminine wiles had supposedly brought it about. Habsburg enemies, mostly grouped around the *parti des dévots* at court, saw in Marie Antoinette a dangerous foreigner and referred to her by the derogatory nickname *l'Autrichienne*, "the Austrian woman" (or "the Austrian bitch"). In late 1770 this "party" could celebrate the fall of the pro-Habsburg foreign minister Choiseul, banished from court after losing favor with the king. Ever since, his opponents worried that Choiseul would be restored to grace as soon as Marie Antoinette became queen. Her brother Joseph's ruthless policy toward Poland also did considerable damage to the standing of the House of Habsburg in France. Many saw in the emperor a dangerous Machiavellian; some even feared that he might seek to revive old claims to Lorraine. A ball held to celebrate the wedding in Versailles was even boycotted because Louis XV had granted a position of unprecedented priority at the festivities to members of the House of Lorraine.[223] Upon her arrival, the Dauphine found herself confronted by numerous enemies at court, although the enthusiasm she inspired among the "people" (of Paris, that is) was generally acknowledged.[224] There were several reasons for this: she was young, beautiful, innocent, and virtuous, in shining contrast to the mistresses of the king, who had a reputation as an aging libertine and was himself smitten with her looks. In addition, she profited from the popularity of Choiseul, who stood for parliamentary opposition to royal "despotism." Whether her grace and beauty would make her a suitable instrument of Viennese policy—as Maria Theresa hoped, Kaunitz doubted, and her enemies feared—would be shown in due course.

Her mother had let her know from the beginning that, while she might possess considerable charm, she was lacking in intelligence, discipline, and strength of will.[225] Conversely, Marie Antoinette's relationship with her mother was marked by awed distance and submissiveness. She spoke of her "always with deep respect," her lady-in-waiting

Campan wrote later, "but she always wished that there would never arise so great a distance between her and her own children as reigned in the imperial family."[226] Mercy reported to Maria Theresa what the Dauphine had revealed to him: "I love the Empress, but I am afraid of her even from afar, and even when I write to her, I never feel at ease towards her."[227] This is obvious from the brief letters she wrote each month in flawed orthography and a clumsy child's handwriting. Sentence for sentence, they betray her efforts to ingratiate herself with her mother and present herself in the best possible light. Even after a severe ticking off, Marie Antoinette expressed her fulsome gratitude for her mother's "tenderness in making me see the error of my ways."[228] On more than one occasion, Mercy recounted to the empress her daughter's distress and dejection following a maternal dressing-down. This is not to say that she changed her ways in light of her mother's admonitions, as Maria Theresa regularly learned from Mercy's parallel letters.

The greatest impediment to Marie Antoinette's standing at court, however, was the fact that her marriage remained unconsummated for some seven years. Only half a year older than her, her husband was phlegmatic, anxious, and inhibited. He was also hapless in bed; a narrowing of the foreskin, not diagnosed until later, apparently made sex a torment for him. What went on behind the bedcurtains was no private matter—it was an openly discussed affair of state, and a source of unending humiliation for all concerned. Far more was at stake than a failure to fall pregnant or produce an heir: until sexual intercourse had taken place, the marriage was not yet considered valid. According to church matrimonial law, a marriage consisted not just in the mutual taking of vows, nor in the public blessing of the newlywed couple and the ensuing festivities. What first completed the sacrament was *consummatio carnalis*, consummation in the flesh. Until this had occurred, Marie Antoinette was neither wife nor dauphine, and the connection could be revoked at a moment's notice. There was no way to hide the shameful fact that the couple were unwilling or unable to perform what was expected of them. On the one hand, they were under the constant indirect surveillance of the chamber personnel; on the other, Louis had to keep his royal grandfather regularly informed of how things stood, just as Marie Antoinette had to report back to her mother. Consummation was the main topic of countless letters—between Maria Theresa and her daughter, Maria Theresa and Mercy, Mercy and Kaunitz, Maria Theresa and Joseph, Joseph and Leopold. While these letters were confidential, the problem itself was as widely known and discussed as any other political matter.[229]

Almost every month, Marie Antoinette reported on the latest "visit of Générale Krottendorf," the family codeword for menstruation, and her mother grew impatient if she had been silent on this topic for some time.[230] When she missed her period in the first months after the wedding, Marie Antoinette regretted to inform her that there no obvious reason for this. Her mother consoled her at first and urged patience: they were both still very young, the Dauphin was shy and inexperienced; excessive zeal only caused harm in such cases.[231] But with each passing month she grew ever more irritated and her daughter ever more despondent. She was compared unfavorably with her sister Carolina, who had become "the wife of her husband" on the very first night.[232] Even a miscarriage struck her as less unfortunate than no pregnancy at all.[233] Although her husband treated her gently and slept with her regularly, Marie Antoinette wrote in self-justification, he suffered from terrible inhibitions. The fault was not hers alone—she was trying her best.[234] When the situation was still unchanged after three years, Louis XV sent in his personal physician to have a serious discussion with the couple. A little later, the rumor circulated that the Dauphin had now become "a real husband," but the unhappy daughter had to inform the empress that there was "no truth in it," although they "had gone a little further" than usual. Two months later, in summer 1773, she herself considered "the marriage to have been consummated . . . , albeit not to the point of falling pregnant."[235]

Still, the mere rumor of consummation was enough that on June 8, 1773, the couple finally celebrated their ceremonial entrance to the city of Paris and were cheered by an enthusiastic crowd, a ritual that had deliberately been held off until then. Maria Theresa likewise assumed—wrongly, as it turned out—that her daughter had now "become a woman." This did nothing to make Marie Antoinette's situation any easier. For as more time passed without news of pregnancy, she found herself subjected to increased maternal pressure—especially once she had become queen following the death of Louis XV on May 10, 1774. Now her mother regarded her apparent barrenness as a moral failing on her part. Her daughter was keeping dubious company away from the king, frittering away whole nights on excursions to Paris, operas, masked balls, gambling, horse racing. She was not even sleeping in the same bed as her husband, as Mercy pointed out in his regular dispatches to the empress. She should "make better use of her nights" in future, her mother growled.[236] Gradually, the first satirical songs about the impotent king and his lascivious wife began doing the rounds in the streets and salons of Paris—a serious cause for concern, given that sexual incapacity had always been code for political impotence.[237] Marie Antoinette's justification was that the king himself had no objection to her innocent pleasures. Besides, he had no interests other than hunting and amateur blacksmithing. He was also continually delaying the minor operation that his doctors had recommended he undergo. She was not sleeping *lit à part*, separately from the king, she assured her mother time and again; there were plenty of witnesses in Versailles who could vouch for this.[238] The matter was discussed in salons and ambassadorial reports. When her sister-in-law, the Countess of Artois, gave birth to a son and the danger arose that the throne could fall to a branch line, Marie Antoinette's position at court became even more difficult, and she was plunged into depression.[239]

Finally, her brother Joseph set out for Versailles in early 1777 to put things to rights. He had been planning the trip for years, which he combined with his usual high-profile research expeditions throughout the land. His sister anticipated the visit with mixed feelings. But his conversation with the king finally untied the knot. On August 30, 1777, seven years into her marriage, Marie Antoinette announced to her mother with palpable relief that the deed had been done: "It has been eight days since our marriage was consummated. The act was repeated and yesterday it was more complete than the first time."[240] Maria Theresa reacted less enthusiastically than might have been supposed. She now had her daughter's personal physician report directly to her each month on the onset of menstruation.[241] When there was still no word of her having conceived, Marie Antoinette came in for another tongue-lashing: she was clearly not devoting her full attention to this vitally important matter, preferring to squander her energies on vain amusements. Marie Antoinette dismissed this as so much baseless gossip peddled by pamphleteers and ill-disposed courtiers, but her denials were futile: Mercy was keeping the empress well-informed about her nightly dissipations. Yet although she generally only went to bed around the time her husband was getting out of it, he clearly did his conjugal duty from time to time. At any rate, Marie Antoinette finally fell pregnant the following year, much to Maria Theresa's relief: "I cannot thank God enough that He has granted me the grace to see, you, my dear daughter, more solidly set up for the future."[242] The alliance, sorely tested around this time by the War of the Bavarian Succession—many at the French court took Prussia's side in the conflict—now seemed to have been "happily consolidated by blood."[243] Yet the child, born on December 19, 1778, turned out to be a daughter, causing Maria Theresa to lose patience yet again.[244] A male heir eventually arrived on October 22, 1781, but the empress was no longer alive to hear the good news—and there would soon no longer be a throne for him to inherit.

Childlessness greatly weakened the role that Maria Theresa had planned for her daughter at Versailles. It was the same role that Carolina and Amalia—each in her own way—fulfilled unsatisfactorily or not at all: that of functioning as the matriarch's long arm at a foreign court. The instructions Marie Antoinette received from Vienna were contradictory from the outset. On the one hand, she was exhorted not to accept letters of introduction and to steer clear of palace intrigue.[245] On the other, her mother also demanded that the dauphine give preferential treatment to her German compatriots and exert her influence against such unwelcome figures as emissary Rohan—just as Maria Theresa had once done as heiress at her father's court.[246] But this presupposed that Marie Antoinette had already found favor with the old King. "In everything you do," her mother wrote, "I ask that you convince him of your reverence and affection by seizing every opportunity to please him. . . . You have but a single task: to please the king and do his will."[247] What stood in her way was her relationship with the Comtesse Du Barry, Louis XV's official mistress. Raised in an atmosphere of moral rectitude, Marie Antoinette found conversing with the lowborn courtesan Du Barry, "this most stupid and impertinent creature," incompatible with her notions of status and honor.[248] She railed against this imposition, strengthened in her stance by her husband's pious aunts. Increasingly irritated, Maria Theresa demanded that she subordinate such scruples to political opportunism and her maternal will. But it soon became apparent that the dauphine could not resist getting drawn into the cabals at court and would not be controlled so easily from afar.

When the old king died of smallpox in May 1774, the key players in Vienna redoubled their efforts and increased the frequency of their correspondence. The good times for her daughter were now at an end, Maria Theresa prophesied.[249] Kaunitz gave Mercy precise instructions on how the queen should influence her husband, above all in his choice of ministers—she should do so in such a way that her influence never appeared as such, either to her husband or to others.[250] The attempt at dissimulation backfired. When Louis XVI called Choiseul back from exile for her sake and swapped Aiguillon, a minister she particularly despised, for the pro-Habsburg Vergennes, Khevenhüller commented with his usual sensitivity to public opinion: "The young Queen is said to have played the greatest part in this last incident and, in general, to hold much sway with the king, a circumstance that is already making other courts gravely concerned that ours may be gaining . . . too great an influence in France."[251] This was the plan, at least. Maria Theresa explicitly revoked her original instructions and wrote to her daughter: "If I have so often advised you not to meddle with recommendations, this was due to the danger I saw on account of your soft heart. . . . Yet now that the choice has been made and the king has a new council, I am no longer worried, and you would act quite wrongly and against my intentions if you steered clear of all that."[252] Yet when Marie Antoinette actually began acting on her own behalf, received Duc de Choiseul without the king's permission, and boasted in a letter to Rosenberg about how easily she could manipulate her husband, the "poor man," Maria Theresa was incensed.[253] She vented her indignation to Mercy:

"What style! What a way of thinking! It confirms my worries all too well. She is advancing in great strides towards her own downfall."[254] And to Marie Antoinette herself: "I see only intrigue, vulgar spite, delight in mockery and persecution; an intrigue which would do very well for a Pompadour or a Du Barry."[255] Joseph, disinclined anyway to deploy his sister as an instrument of foreign policy, was even more forthright: "Have you ever asked yourself what right you have to meddle in the affairs of the government and the French monarchy? . . . What knowledge have you acquired that you believe your judgment or your opinion to be of any value?"[256] Marie Antoinette reacted coolly to her brother's scolding while making more of an effort to make amends with her mother. Later, during the War of the Bavarian Succession, when the Prussian king wanted to extract his French *cher cousin* from the Habsburg alliance, she sought to do her bit to keep the alliance together, although she could not prevent her husband from negotiating with Frederick II behind her back.[257]

Over time, Marie Antoinette's conduct became ever more controversial, public criticism of her increasingly polemical.[258] She was accused of using her position to promote her closest confidants at court and dispose of unwanted ministers such as the irksome reformers Turgot and Malesherbes.[259] She was vulnerable to attack from the court and the European public on three main fronts: first, unprecedented profligacy despite extremely precarious state finances; second, illegitimate favoritism; third, exercising political influence in favor of a foreign power and at France's expense. So far as her heedless way with money and other extravagances were concerned—bizarre coiffures, luxurious wardrobes, nocturnal excursions to Paris, intimate horse rides with male favorites, games of chance with exorbitant losses, and so on—her mother never tired of preaching against them, albeit without success. When it came to playing favorites and exercising political influence, the problem from the Viennese perspective was not so much that Marie Antoinette patronized particular people and showered them with pensions and offices—after all, this was a structural principle of court society. The problem was rather that she favored the wrong people, acted on her own initiative, ignored the directives coming from Vienna, and used her opportunities unwisely. She drew particular criticism for increasingly retreating from the stage at Versailles to her small pleasure palace of Trianon, thereby severely limiting the circle of potential favorites and disappointing everyone else. The fine art of distributing patronage, as mastered by Maria Theresa, consisted in keeping as many courtiers as happy as possible with small symbolic gestures of attention, so strengthening them in the expectation that they might one day benefit from even greater largesse. If a significant majority of courtiers saw themselves permanently left out in the cold, the inevitable consequence would be widespread dissatisfaction, envy, and resentment.

Maria Theresa knew these mechanisms and saw a catastrophe approaching, although certainly not the one that eventuated. Having foretold her daughter a radiant future when she became queen,[260] her forecasts became increasingly gloomy, her warnings ever more resigned. Following Maria Theresa's death, public criticism of the queen spiraled into bizarre conspiracy theories: from allegations that she had embezzled French state funds and stashed them away in Vienna and authorized contract killings to scurrilously pornographic accusations of incest. The more rapidly the monarchy's fortunes sank, the more perverse became the pamphleteers' defamations against their once adored queen. Maria Theresa was spared having to see her direst prophecies surpassed by reality.

Maximilian

In the end, according to her son Leopold, Maria Theresa was unhappy with all three daughters.[261] All three slipped free of the maternal leash, all three fell short of her lofty standards, and all three failed the task she had assigned them, albeit in different ways and to varying degrees. When her youngest son Maximilian was being prepared for his future responsibilities to the dynasty, she wrote with disillusionment: "My children's education has always been my chief and dearest concern. If not everything has turned out in accordance with my instructions, my commands, and the care I showed, then this is not my fault, but a consequence of the thousand circumstances which ensure we can never attain perfection in anything in this world."[262] Despite this insight, she kept trying to control her children until the day she died.

Maximilian Franz, born in 1756, was his "mother's darling" in the opinion of many historians.[263] Nonetheless, the matriarch did not hesitate to use him as a pawn to further the dynastic interest. She initially had him in mind for the governorship of the Netherlands until Maria Christina and Prince Albert took over that office. She then contemplated making him Viceregent of Hungary, awarding the ten-year-old the Grand Cross of the Order of St. Stephen in preparation for the appointment. In addition, he was earmarked to succeed his uncle, Charles of Lorraine, as grand master of the Teutonic Order, that is, to take on the traditional role of the supreme Christian knight—although, in the absence of any crusades to the Holy Land, the office had for centuries served only as a source of distinction and preferment for the high nobility. For this reason, Maximilian had received special permission from the pope to be inducted into the Teutonic Order at just fourteen years of age. His mother had thus foreseen a military career for him, sending him on grand tours through the Empire, the Netherlands, France, and Italy to acquire the necessary aristocratic polish.[264] He apparently needed it; observers described him as "somewhat brusque, difficult to approach in society, and not very communicative."[265] According to Khevenhüller, the unorthodox decision to send off an emperor's son "to foreign lands" was made because his "education had not turned out for the best, at least so far as his bearing and external gestures are concerned." Maria Theresa's go-to man for difficult missions, Rosenberg, was appointed his escort, but he "had to be dragged by the hair, as it were, to this onerous assignment."[266] As always, Rosenberg was required to report directly by courier to Cabinet Secretary Pichler, and he was instructed not to let the eighteen-year-old Maximilian out of his sight: "My son will decide nothing on his own . . . ; he will not take a step without your knowledge," the empress decreed.[267] She was filled with concern that her son might be infected by the dangerous ideas that seemed to be running rampant at foreign courts. She therefore urged him to turn a deaf ear to conversations against religion and good morals and take his leave of any gathering where such godless discourse was tolerated.[268] She received detailed reports of his behavior from Leopold and Ferdinand, who played host to Maximilian during his travels. What she read gave her little cause for hope. In a lengthy character study, Leopold described his brother as intelligent and judicious, modest and resilient, but also impassive and indifferent, without any drive to intellectual and physical exertion. He preferred the company of domestics and commoners, made fun of others, lacked empathy, distrusted everyone, shut himself off, and revealed no emotion, whether genuine or feigned.[269] Ironically, these were the very charges that had been leveled against Leopold himself by his tutors when he was the same age; nonetheless, his report was hardly marked by understanding and leniency. His mother shared his harsh judgment. To Ferdinand, she complained time and again how greatly Maximilian displeased her. She found him to be "ice cold," callous and unfeeling, "incapable of making a woman happy"—in stark contrast to Ferdinand himself, the devoted son and loving husband, whose letters always moved her to tears.[270]

Maximilian was wrenched from his listlessness, however, when the War of the Bavarian Succession broke out and he was summoned to accompany his brother Joseph to campaign in Bohemia, there to learn the art of command. He contracted a serious infection in the field and had to return to Vienna, where his recovery dragged out for months. The problem was an open lesion on his right leg, which constant interference from his doctors only exacerbated and prevented from healing properly. His indifference now proved a virtue, and his mother's opinion of him underwent a reversal; from now on she never tired of praising his stoicism and fortitude.[271]

Now that a military career was out of the question, a different role had to be found for him. As luck would have it, the elderly archbishop-elector of Cologne and prince-bishop of Münster, Max Friedrich von Königsegg, was not expected to live much longer.[272] His leading minister, Caspar Anton von Belderbusch, had signaled to the empress on several occasions that when the time came, a member of the imperial family would stand a good chance of being elected his successor. The ambitious minister offered his services to the House of Habsburg in the (justified) hope of having his family promoted to a higher position within the aristocracy. The two important ecclesiastical principalities of the Electorate of Cologne and Münster, which had long before been united in Wittelsbach hands, formed a strong counterweight to the dominant Prussian influence in the northwest of the Empire. Maria Theresa initially shrank from the significant outlay this would entail—nothing could be arranged without applying copious grease to the electors' palms. Maximilian himself was less than overjoyed at the prospect of entering the clergy, and Joseph was also opposed.[273] Yet, in the end, the empress took the advice of Kaunitz and Imperial Vice-Chancellor Colloredo to deal a blow to Prussian influence in the Empire, doing all she could to win the prince-elector and the cathedral canons for her son's candidacy. The political coup succeeded. The necessary papal dispensations were quickly granted, and on July 9 Maximilian was ordained into minor orders and took the tonsure; he donned clerical garb soon after. On her own account, Maria Theresa found it hard to get used to the sight, whereas he himself apparently came to terms with his fate.[274] In August 1780, against massive Prussian resistance, he was elected coadjutor by both cathedral chapters with the right of succession. A veritable "minor canonical war" had been needed to bring this about, since succession to the two ecclesiastical principalities was considered a matter of European import.[275] Aided by her daughter, Maria Theresa had received diplomatic cover from the French king, while Frederick II had even sought support from St. Petersburg and been rebuffed. By Kaunitz's reckoning, the gifts for members of the two cathedral chapters cost the Archducal House a grand total of 948,315 guilders and 48 kreuzers, not including the subsidy of 50,000 guilders paid annually to the old Prince-Elector Max Friedrich until his death.[276]

His mother now expected Maximilian to let her direct him as she pleased. When he set out for the Electorate of Cologne to be inaugurated as the new coadjutor at the residence in Bonn, she gave him the usual parting instructions about how to behave: be generous, but not too generous; be affectionate, but not overly familiar; be content with his representative role and leave everything else to his escort, Johann Franz von Hardegg. Maria Theresa was keen to influence her son while he was still coadjutor, knowing that as soon as he became prince-elector he would, as ruler of a politically important imperial territory, enjoy greater formal independence than any of her other sons. Yet even as he was making his way to Bonn, the apparently docile, submissive Maximilian showed that he was quite capable of taking the initiative. He had given the imperial archchancellor and elector of Mainz an expensive gift without first asking his mother for permission. To add insult to injury, she had first read about it in the newspaper. "That you concealed the gift of diamonds from me hurt me greatly," she admonished him. "I wished you would see me not just as a mother, but also as your friend and best counsellor. Yet this cannot be forced: it is up to the heart to decide. This secrecy reveals a lack of trust, whether from calculation or a false sense of shame, and it must be stamped out."[277] This would prove to be Maria Theresa's final attempt to assert her maternal will over her children from afar. By the time Maximilian became archbishop-elector of Cologne on April 21, 1784, his mother had already been dead three and a half years. That he was ordained into major orders—quite unusually for a prince-bishop—and regularly celebrated Mass himself; that he took the government of the prince-archbishopric into his own hands—again unusually— and introduced a series of enlightened reforms; that, in short, he belied his reputation by taking his ecclesiastical and secular responsibilities very seriously, all this she did not live to see for herself.

Stay-at-Homes

The unequal treatment of children from the high nobility reflected dynastic logic and was nothing out of the ordinary, although this was cold comfort for those who felt jealous of their more privileged siblings. Individuals were expected to submit uncomplainingly to whatever was best for the family. This could mean that some daughters remained single, mostly because a marriage in keeping with their status would have been too costly. In addition, it was customary in all echelons of society for one daughter—often the eldest or youngest—to stay at home to look after her parents in their old age. The low status of lifelong spinsters was considered humiliating by many of those affected. Francis Stephen's unwed sister, Princess Charlotte of Lorraine, suffered acutely on this account.

She felt she cut a "ridiculous" figure "when, with her imposing stature and forty years of age, she had to trot along behind so many young and beautiful archduchesses . . . like an old virgin with the air of a duenna." She heaped reproaches on her brother, the emperor, for having blocked her marriage.[278] Among Maria Theresa's daughters, there were two who shared this fate and coped with it in very different ways: Marianna, born in 1738, and Elisabeth, born in 1743 (color plate 24).

Elisabeth had always been considered the fairest of the daughters but was also deemed capricious, coquettish, flighty.[279] Because she never left her home court, she never corresponded with her mother, and little is known of her. There had been various candidates for marriage—first Stanisław Poniatowski, king of Poland, then the duke of Chablais (whom her father had also intended for Maria Christina), but for various reasons the matches never came about.[280] She survived the small-pox epidemic that ravaged the Archducal House in 1767 disfigured by scars, massively reducing her chances of finding a husband. "Elisabeth is still the same, you know her better than I do, she has become dreadfully ugly and old," Marie Theresa bluntly informed Marquise d'Herzelles.[281] Elisabeth nonetheless came under renewed maternal consideration as a piece on the dynastic chessboard in 1768, when the daughters of King Louis XV, desperate to break the power of his mistresses, sought to persuade him to remarry. But Louis, some thirty-three years her senior, showed little interest. He fended off his daughters with the argument that he was prepared to marry the archduchess if only he could convince himself of her attractiveness with his own eyes.[282] A personal meeting, no matter how skillfully disguised, was out of the question—such an "inspection" would have been simply too humiliating.[283] Maria Theresa would have gladly seen the alliance strengthened through so eminent a match, and she was prepared, if necessary, to turn a blind eye to the king's notorious philandering. But it was incompatible with the honor of the Archducal House for her daughter to be appraised in so degrading a fashion. She let it be known in Versailles that she could easily afford to maintain her daughters in a style befitting their high status and had no need to economize by "sacrificing a princess, as it were."[284] This put a stop to any marriage plans.[285]

In fact, Elisabeth was the only one of her children whom Maria Theresa did not provide with a suitable marriage, benefice, or special capital
fund.[286] Elisabeth never ceased lamenting the injustice of her fate. Upon
hearing of Maximilian's expensive election, "she began sobbing that
everyone else was established and she alone had been left in the lurch
and condemned to stay with the emperor, which she would never accept. We all had trouble calming her down," Maria Theresa reported in
a letter to Maria Christina, adding unsympathetically: "It is sad to see
such poor reasoning [*raisonnement*]."[287] Even in company, Elisabeth
could be witheringly sarcastic and critical when referring to her mother.
In 1777, as she was recovering from a badly abscessed molar, the English
ambassador came to express his sympathies. On his account, she told
him that she did not deserve his pity:

> "Believe me," said she, "for an unmarried archduchess of forty years,
> a hole in the cheek is a pleasure; for," added she, "no event which
> breaks through the sameness and tediousness of my life ought to be
> considered as a misfortune." She told him it was a blot on the reign
> of Marie Therese to have kept her old daughters under restraint like
> children and denied them the pleasure of mixing in society.[288]

It seems to have occasionally dawned on Maria Theresa that her two
unmarried daughters might have grounds for complaint. She once
noted self-critically that they would have to be given "a couple of amusements, since they face nothing but boredom all year round in my retirade and must constantly put up with my bad mood."[289]

Her unwillingness to accept her fate made Elisabeth unpopular
among her siblings; they found her irritable, resentful, gossipy, and devious. Family members treated her with disdain or at best pity. She was
"shunned and feared by everyone on account of her terrible tongue, her
extravagant and unwise discourse," noted her brother Leopold. But he
also mentioned that she spent much of her time bringing up an orphaned girl left at her doorstep.[290] The French emissary gave a very
different description of her in 1770: generous, vivacious, and witty,
sometimes caustic, but of a cheerful and pleasant disposition.[291] Following her mother's death, Joseph saw to it that she was made abbess of

the Damenstift in Innsbruck, a convent for noble ladies that Maria Theresa had founded in 1765 to keep Francis Stephen in perpetual prayer.

The eldest daughter, Marianna, likewise lived out her days as a spinster at the Viennese court. But she coped differently with her unhappiness, turning inward in masochistic piety rather than against the outside world in sarcastic despair.[292] When she was nine, she had briefly come under consideration as a potential bride for the duke of Savoy.[293] There had been no more talk of marriage after that; her mother had selected her to keep her company until the end of her life. A serious illness at the age of eighteen—according to Khevenhüller, a "catarrh" of such severity that she had already been given the last rites[294]—had left her with a deformed spine. Since then, she had been almost constantly unwell and generally stayed away from public life at court, except when having to represent her mother on ceremonial occasions such as baptisms or the washing of the feet service on Maundy Thursday. After her father's death, at the age of twenty-eight she was made abbess of the Damenstift in Prague, a benefice that brought in 80,000 guilders a year without her having to reside there.[295] Observers described her as a generous, sensitive, and intelligent soul; she was praised for her witty conversation and her many talents.[296] Her scholarly interests were far more than an aristocratic pastime. She shared her father's enthusiasm for natural history, attended lectures in mathematics and physics, corresponded with fellow scholars, and collected minerals, plants, and insects, which she paid handsomely to have sent to her from all around the world. She prepared a catalog of commemorative medallions for her mother, illustrating them with copperplates engraved by her own hand. The Imperial Engraving Academy in Vienna and the Academy of Arts in Florence made her an honorary member. Following the death of her mother, she eschewed the Damenstift in Prague for the far more modest Elisabethan convent in Klagenfurt, where she surrounded herself with a circle of scholars and freemasons.[297] This convent houses two documents from the 1770s that attest to her relentless self-examination.[298] Neither was meant to be seen by others; they both stage a spiritual self-dialogue intended to strengthen herself in her own faith: "I have written this so that God's extraordinary mercy and my overwhelming errors and weaknesses might be set more often before my eyes."[299]

One text was a confession in the Augustinian mold. Marianna depicts herself there as "born with fiery and violent passions, which a purely masculine and fairly haphazard education increased still further."[300] As a young girl, she had plunged into whichever pleasures took her fancy, both permitted and forbidden; she had frittered away her days and nights hunting and dancing, gambling and reading novels. Her near-fatal illness at the age of eighteen had been a first divine warning, but she had failed to heed it at the time. The second providential test was the sudden death of her beloved father, which finally brought her to mend her ways: "through this most terrible and devastating blow, God at last called me to Himself." This dramatic caesura put an end to her carefree days and ushered in a period of profound and ongoing self-reproach. For if her father's death was God's punishment for her sins, then she was to blame for it. She withdrew entirely from society, disavowed all amusements, and whipped herself into a penitential frenzy. In hindsight, she now repented with the same "exaggerated zeal," the same "fiery and immoderate temperament," with which she had formerly pursued a life of dissipation. With God's help, however, she had gradually come to know herself and found the sole means to tame her otherwise "ungovernable spirit," one "diametrically opposed" to her natural tendency: voluntary submission to a completely unvarying routine: "I became aware that I would have to treat myself like a child."[301]

Marianna's God was mercilessly strict and cruel. The most difficult trial he imposed on her was a decades-long, secretly nurtured, passionate, and unconsummated love for an unnamed "friend." God had given her "a very tender and constant heart." Her status and

> a certain haughty manner towards others have long preserved me from the danger of hearing myself loved. I have never been vain and considered myself incapable of pleasing others. . . . I never wanted to play a comedy like so many I have seen, once I loved I thought of no one else, and loved constantly through 21 years, the last just the same as the first.[302]

The friendship evidently remained platonic. In her personal testaments, she never broaches the topic of why she did not marry this or any other man. She may have so fully internalized her deference to her mother's wishes that she never allowed herself even to contemplate a missed chance at happiness. Her renunciation consisted not in refusing to marry her friend—this was never an option—but in freely and resolutely breaking off all contact with him: "I cannot deny that this battle [with myself] was the greatest [I have ever fought], that it still is. Of my own free will, I had to tear myself away from a passion that I have never disputed." God had demanded this sacrifice of her, but she expected him in return to give her the "supernatural strength needed to pronounce judgment against my friend and my own heart. I have abandoned everything, and I know that it would be far more complete if I could wipe him from my heart as well. But this I know not how to do."[303]

A second testament provides insight into Marianna's lonely and joyless everyday life at court, a diary in which she accounted for the minor triumphs and failures of her daily inner struggle during the Lenten season of 1773. Her quotidian life was marked by physical illness and spiritual despondency, "sadness and depression."[304] Her greatest joy was on the rare occasions when, attending early morning Mass, she was able to follow the service "with attentiveness and zeal" and then wait on her mother to kiss her hand. Yet she usually tormented herself over her incapacity for "collected, undistracted" prayer, and her chief daily concern was succumbing to ever-present temptation and speaking ill of her "neighbor." She detested her unavoidable appearances in the "great world," when she had to present herself "in keeping with her station"; the danger of sin lurked at every corner. To make matters worse, such scruples earned her only contempt from her siblings.

In their eyes, her behavior smacked of arrogance and bigotry. At court she was "disdained and reviled," her brother Leopold remarked.[305] Her reclusiveness struck many as secretive and scheming, her piety as hypocritical and smug, her charitable giving as presumptuous and ruinous.[306] Her sister-in-law Isabella of Parma saw in her the epitome of a "false friend" and made her the subject of a malicious pen portrait.[307]

The sensitive Marianna was well aware of all this animosity piled up against her. On the occasion of a grand gala, she noted that she had to "put up with being ridiculed and shunned, which enraged me on the inside and constantly added to my feelings of disdain and bitterness."[308] Her only friends were her ladies-in-waiting and her sister Amalia in Parma, the outcast. Yet she was more upset about her own failings than about being slighted by others. Even her charitable works were poisoned by self-doubt. Whenever she put in a good word for someone, bought prisoners their freedom, stood godmother to a child, or gave alms, she worried that there was nothing meritorious about what she had done, since it had been done out of personal inclination or mere habit. Even spiritual conversations brought on pangs of conscience: she feared seeking in them "more vainglory than usefulness" and found it "reprehensible" when she wanted to make a good impression on the priest. All the good she did was transformed by her self-tormenting conscience into self-love and vanity. In short, her acutely developed sense of her own sinfulness was a trap from which there was no escaping. Almost all her journal entries conclude with the consolation "that this day has again reduced the number of my days and brought me closer to the hour of my redemption."[309]

The only point on which her conscience was clear was her "childish respect and love" for her mother.[310] She suffered alongside her when she was unwell, and stayed by her side through her dying days. Yet she never spoke of her with the same affection she showed toward her father. For her part, Maria Theresa was sparing in her signs of maternal love. Since the empress always had her close at hand, there was no need for them to correspond. In letters to her children and confidants, she briefly and dutifully mentioned Marianna's poor health: "Marianna . . . is never well three days in a row."[311] Once she reported on her quarrels with a lady-in-waiting.[312] If Leopold's notes are to be believed, she saw her daughter infrequently, treated her badly, and made no attempt to conceal her low regard for her in public: "Maria Anna is without influence, she lives entirely on her own . . . and is treated with outright contempt and disrespect by both the empress and the emperor, who never look her in the face and humiliate her appallingly."[313] Yet it was Marianna who spent days attending to her mother during her final illness, which she later set down in a warmhearted and moving account.[314]

Marianna was not the only one who kept her inner life carefully hidden from view. Comparison of the various sources, combined with historical distance, reveals that much in this family was not as it seemed. More than one of the children was gravely mistaken about who was a friend and who a foe, who could be trusted and who not. Joseph described the atmosphere without illusion: "No trace of fellowship, no rational, agreeable, or shared viewpoint. . . . The small talk, the pleasantries that pass from lady to lady, from archduchess to archduchess, shut everyone off, and the question 'What should one say on the matter?' stifles all companionship."[315] While a discourse of sincerity and affection was assiduously cultivated, suspicion and duplicity were rife. The gap between external and internal perspectives was perhaps at its widest in Leopold, the brother held in the highest esteem by the rest. Joseph was devoted to Leopold, placed his trust in him alone, and confided in him regularly[316]—little suspecting that Leopold secretly harbored deep feelings of resentment toward all his siblings. We know this from the encrypted diary he kept during his stay in Vienna in 1778–79, a pitiless analysis of the "state of the family" and the entire monarchy.[317] Having been roundly chastised by his mother as a child for his lack of sincerity, Leopold had clearly learned the courtier's art of dissimulation.[318] A closed book to the outside world, he opened up—like Marianna—in dialogue with himself on paper. He had an almost obsessive, pedantic compulsion to write everything down, a tic already perceived by his contemporaries as graphomania.[319] Consumed by bitterness at having to defer to the despotic and unloved Joseph, he poured out his resentment in a torrent of barely punctuated, endlessly repetitive prose. Protected by a secret code of his own devising, he dissected the family's sustaining lies and tensions with an unusually perceptive eye. What he revealed behind the façade of domestic harmony was nothing short of a vipers' nest.

His mother emerges from the diary as a hopelessly overwhelmed, crusty, and slightly dotty old woman. Weakened in mind and body, she no longer remembered her own decrees, trusted only a few subaltern officials, and either sowed confusion in government business or simply resigned herself to inaction. She had "lost her courage and valor," deeply disappointed at having achieved none of her objectives and being blamed for this by the outside world. Leopold trenchantly analyzed the relationship between Maria Theresa and Joseph in all its ambivalence: disappointed that "he does not appear so great a man as she would like," the empress was nonetheless jealous "of the considerable renown he enjoys with the public."[320] "They argue continuously whenever they are together."[321] To the detriment of state affairs, the antagonism between them was widely known, since each openly disparaged the other in public. Joseph comes off even worse in Leopold's account than his mother:

> A hard, violent man, full of ambition, who says and does anything to be praised and talked about by others. He does not know what he wants, . . . disdains all industry and hard work. . . . He cannot abide opposition and is animated by arbitrary, violent principles and by the strongest, most brutal, harshest despotism. He loves no one. . . . He especially delights in making the Empress feel that she needs him and that she would be lost without him.[322]

Joseph ridiculed his mother in the presence of others and persecuted her favorites, hated and feared Christina and Albert, despised Marianna and Elisabeth. Yet "towards us"—Leopold himself—"he shows sincere solicitude, confidence, and friendship,"[323] which were clearly not returned in kind. Ironically, the much-loved Leopold was the one who best understood how to conceal his boundless resentment. Joseph, however—the prickly, riven, hated despot—genuinely loved his brother and believed this love to be reciprocal, much as he had been deceived about the love of his first wife. In short, nothing was as it seemed in this family. Leopold's grim panorama of the "state of the family" reveals the pitfalls into which the emotional pressure to be absolutely honest can lead. By always demanding complete openness of her children, Maria Theresa spawned only hypocrisy, intrigue, and deception.

Bad Weather for a Great Journey

Maria Theresa felt increasingly embittered and isolated in her twilight years. In August 1778 she stipulated in her will that her children should stay away from her burial—out of consideration for their feelings, as she put it. "If a mother and wife can still hope to have any influence after her death, then I beg this last sign of obedience from my family."[324] When her leg was injured in a fall in September 1779 and she was bedridden for a time, she wrote to Ferdinand: "My first thought was that the dear Lord does not want under any circumstances to restore me to Him, and this made me sad."[325] To the old reasons for her bitterness, new ones were added: an awareness of a general loss of control, compounded by her unhappiness about the war and her uneasy conscience on account of her subjects' suffering;[326] her unfulfilled hopes for the birth of an heir in France; her ruined relationship with Amalia; the latent tensions with Joseph and his provocatively lengthy absences, most recently his journey through Russia;[327] finally, in July 1780, her grief at the death of her brother-in-law Charles and her outrage when Joseph simply sold off his uncle's entire estate.[328]

In the cold, wet November of 1780 Vienna was ravaged by disease. Elisabeth had a bad cough; Marianna was unable to keep down her food for days; Kaunitz was holed up at home.[329] Everyone was sick, Maria Theresa wrote to Milan on November 20; she worried for her two daughters. She herself—now aged sixty-three—suffered, as always in winter, from shortness of breath and a heavy cough, but she assured her children: "Do not imagine that I am ill!"[330] Yet just a month before, on October 15, she had made a new will, and on November 3 she had written to Mercy: "Things cannot go on like this much longer, I think; my cares are too great and mount from day to day, and I am without all support and assistance."[331]

On All Souls' Day she had descended to the cold and musty Capuchin Crypt and prayed in the court chapel with the Augustinians; then, on November 8, in the rain, she had inspected the pheasant hunt at Schönbrunn.[332] On November 20 she took a turn for the worse, withdrew to her apartments, and skipped daily Mass, but she went back to working at her escritoire in the days that followed. She had a light fever, a weak pulse, and breathing difficulties that deteriorated into choking fits as the evenings wore on. She hardly went to bed at night any more. Despite her protestations that there was nothing wrong with her besides the usual cough, Christina and Albert came from Pressburg to Vienna on November 24. They found her much changed. Störck, her personal physician, advised her to take the last rites. "Solely Her Majesty's strong will and courage allowed her . . . to get up again and speak with us as before."[333] Joseph assumed his mother had been talked into imagining herself at death's door. He even accused Störck of exaggerating her illness so that he might later play the role of savior.[334] On November 25, unbeknownst to her children, Maria Theresa summoned the provost Ignaz Müller to hear her confession. Her nights now became more restless, her choking fits more frequent, although she still ate with a hearty appetite and chatted at length with her children "but often dozed off, then the rattling in her chest was dreadful and her breath very short; she spoke in her sleep as well."[335] On November 26, a Sunday—she had just attended a dinner with some two hundred guests[336]—she insisted on receiving the viaticum from the papal nuncio, the final sacramental meal before the journey to the afterlife. This gave rise to one last conflict between mother and son. Joseph, who had not witnessed her choking fits firsthand, failed to recognize the gravity of the situation and talked her out of Extreme Unction, at least, while she insisted on taking the eucharist. Yet, after spending the night of November 26 in her antechamber, he "began to lose all hope." On this night, Maria Theresa wrote her last letter to Leopold to confer her blessings on him and his family.[337] On the morning of November 27, news that the empress was dying was made public. The lord high steward announced that, given the seriousness of her illness, "grave consequences were to be expected."[338] Courtiers assembled for prayer in the court chapel with Capuchins, Augustinians, and Minorites, and in all the lands of the monarchy, the Holy of Holies was displayed in churches personally selected by the empress so that subjects might pray for her soul. All theatrical events and entertainments were banned. There began instead a pious, godly

FIGURE 52. *Theresa's Last Day.* Hieronymus Löschenkohl, washed pen and ink drawing, preliminary study to a copperplate engraving, 1780–81

spectacle acted out in accordance with the rules of the Christian *ars moriendi*, the art of dying.

Death deferred its arrival for three more days.[339] Maria Theresa spent most of that time sitting upright in her armchair in her bonnet and the brown men's dressing gown she liked to wear. On November 28, at Störck's recommendation and in the presence of her children, she received Extreme Unction. "She joined in all the prayers with great devotion," Marianna wrote. Then,

> when the ceremony was over, we all stood up and left her with her confessor; after a quarter hour she bid us all enter; the emperor, Maximilian, Maria, her husband, Elisabeth, and I, we sat in a circle around her chair, she addressed us for more than a quarter hour

without any change to her voice, she commended us to the emperor, she thanked us for our love of her, she said the most touching things, saw us all dissolve into tears and retained her composure, . . . the emperor wanted to answer her but could not, he sobbed and knelt down before her. She gave him her blessing, he kissed her hand, she kissed him . . . finally she looked at us and said: away with you, it costs me too much to see you like this.[340]

After this she settled her affairs, finalized her funeral arrangements, wrote a great deal, talked with Joseph and the other children for long spells, thanked her ladies-in-waiting and servants, "publicly begged their pardon" and "commended them to the emperor."[341] Marianna repeatedly emphasized in her report that the empress remained calm and fully conscious until the end, without the least sign of fear, impatience, or a troubled conscience. If she wished that her suffering might come to an end, then not for her own sake, but to spare her children and familiars the distressing sight. At five o'clock in the morning on November 29, she drank two cups of milky coffee in Joseph's company. She then asked all the children to come and speak with her in turn. What followed is described in the official ceremonial protocol as a handover of power:

> This was now the time when Her Majesty the Empress-Mother gave her son the letters, and with trenchant, sensible words she again commended the other children to him, the welfare of his subjects, and help for the poor. . . . She turned to Joseph, the heir to the throne, and appointed him father over them. Finally she sent away the daughters, as she did not want us to see her die.[342]

Only Joseph, Maximilian, Albert, and Störck stayed with her.[343] She turned down a last offer of a medicinal draft as well as the advice that she catch a little sleep: "How could I wish to sleep when I may be called before my judge at any moment. I fear sleep as I do not wish to be taken by surprise. I want to see death coming."[344] She asked her doctor to "hold the candle for me for a while and close my eyes, as this would be asking too much of the emperor." Shortly before nine o'clock on the evening of November 29, "she got up suddenly from her chair and took a few steps towards the chaise longue before collapsing. She was helped up as well as possible, the emperor said to Her Majesty you are in an uncomfortable position; yes she said, but good enough for dying in. She took three more breaths and passed away."[345]

That was Marianna's account. Others varied the details and put different words in the dying empress's mouth. Princess Liechtenstein, who likewise wrote a long letter about her death, had her remarking to Joseph on looking out the window at the November rain: *"Voilà un bien mauvais temps pour le grand voyage*—what bad weather for the great journey!"[346] Death was nothing more than the passage from one room to the next, she also supposedly said, and to her servants: "Saint Andreas," whose feast was celebrated on November 30, "will surely come looking for me." Others reported the conventionally pious last words, "My God, receive my soul."[347] All reports concurred that Maria Theresa had died a fine death and proved herself "a true Christian heroine:"[348] "There is no example of a more heroic death, such strength, such courage, such presence of mind. Only the Christian religion is capable of producing such effects."[349] All reports also emphasized the harmony that prevailed between mother and son in her final hours. The emperor spent days at her side, watched over her at night, and performed "all temporal and spiritual obligations with a perfection that could serve as a model for any son."[350] No doubts could be allowed to arise about their mutual reconciliation. For the hour of death was also the final trial and the moment of truth. While agonizing death throes betrayed a contest between good and evil spirits for the soul of the deceased, a calm, composed, self-aware death revealed strength of faith and divine grace. It was an infallible sign that this was a soul predestined for eternal salvation. Maria Theresa was an expert in the art of dying. She had made careful preparations for her end and was relieved at having pulled it off: "During her lifetime, she had often resolved to die like this and she frequently told me so," wrote Marianna. "She now said: I have always endeavored to die such a death and I feared I might not, now I see that with God's grace, anything is possible."[351]

There was less harmony outside the imperial quarters. Subjects' reactions were more mixed than expected. In his memoirs, Prince Albert later described the shock felt by all those at court and in town who had known the empress personally. But the common people, *le populace*, had been so angered by the recently introduced beverage tax that many greeted the funeral procession "with scandalous indifference."[352] Published opinions, on the other hand, glorified the departed: "Everyone sang her praises, and there has probably never been a great princess who was mourned everywhere with such good reason."[353] Anecdotes circulated about how news of her death had been received. Marie Antoinette was said to have burst into tears in the presence of the entire Versailles court while dining at the royal table.[354] Kaunitz had taken the precaution of staying away from the imperial antechamber, presumably owing to "his notorious fear" of infection, and had sent his deputy Cobenzl in his stead, but he shed two heavy tears when told the news in company.[355] Many people, men as well as women, wept openly and without embarrassment. Prince Ligne, for example, told of a hardened Hungarian grenadier who had shed tears over the death of "his King—*Rex*."[356] Frederick II, like every other European prince, sent his formal condolences and wrote his friend d'Alembert the oft-cited lines that the empress had "honored the throne and her sex"; for all their wars, he had never been her enemy.[357] The Jansenists, it was said, exulted in the fact that the empress had summoned neither the hated Archbishop Migazzi nor one of the ex-Jesuits to her deathbed.[358] Everyone could find what he wanted in the deceased: the pious Christian sovereign and protectress against modish philosophy as well as a beacon of reason and justice. Above all, she was remembered as a lovingly devoted mother to her children and subjects. The fame of the near-divine empress was invoked in countless, often tiresomely conventional variations, in poetry and prose, funeral decorations and copperplates.[359] Even luminaries from Protestant Germany such as Wieland, Klopstock, and Matthias Claudius published odes and eulogies.[360] In the visual medium, an intimate portrait of the death scene proved far more popular than the traditional allegorical tableaux celebrating her rule: the Viennese silhouette cutter Hieronymus Löschenkohl laid the foundation for his future publishing success with his bestselling copperplate, *Theresa's Last Day* (fig. 52).[361]

A period of official court mourning was prescribed not just in Vienna but also in Versailles, Florence, Milan, Naples, and Brussels. The imperial body was embalmed, as was the custom in the Archducal House; the heart and entrails were removed and stored in silver vessels. When they opened the corpse, the doctors found that both lungs were "as hard as stone." This explained why the catarrh had proved fatal: "Her Majesty was unable to expel the catarrhous matter, which then settled on the few remaining mobile parts of the lungs and the inflammation put an end to the last 24 hours."[362] Face veiled in black, the corpse was laid out for three days on a relatively plain catafalque in the Augustinian court chapel—and not, as was usually the case, in a room of the castle.[363] The laying out of the body, the burial in the crypt, and the Masses for the soul of the departed all proceeded in strict accordance with the empress's instructions. As befitted the more modest Theresian court mourning order, there was no sumptuously Baroque *castrum doloris*, and the usual funeral oration was skipped at her behest.

Yet her "earnest wish that none from the family should appear at my public exposition, burial, or exequies" was ignored by Joseph.[364] In other respects, too, the emperor went against his mother's last will in his new role as head of the dynasty and sole ruler. As a sign of her legendary munificence and Christian mercy, she had not only provided generous lifelong pensions and bequests to her ladies-in-waiting and servants, all the way down to the last two chamber heaters, but she had also ordered that 500 guilders be distributed as alms for the poor in each of thirty-one towns in her lands where masses were read for her soul; that every single member of her armed forces, including all guards, pensioners, and invalids, having "performed such meritorious service during my tumultuous reign, and endured so much on my account," receive a whole month's extra salary; and finally, that all alms and pensions currently paid out by her Privy Payments Office "and other particular privy coffers" be continued.[365] In her last handwritten note, she directed Paymaster Mayer to transfer 100,000 guilders from her private reserves to the normal school fund and entrusted the distribution of the moneys to Felbiger and Blümegen, foreseeing that Joseph would act against her testamentary wishes and discontinue the payment of pensions from her various private purses.[366] This is exactly what happened. He financed the army bequest, for which Maria Theresa's "meager remaining funds" were far from adequate, from his own, "private" fortune, not from state coffers—in contrast to his mother, he placed value on this distinction.[367] The empress had left her affairs in unimaginable confusion, he wrote to Leopold; she should never have made such exorbitant financial provisions without consulting him, the sole heir. He was determined to order things rationally, paying no heed to the expected howls of protest.[368]

All previous efforts at reform suddenly looked like insipid compromises. Within an astonishingly short period of time, Joseph initiated a series of measures he had stymied only shortly before, while he was still coregent. A lonely regime of consequential rationality, sobriety, and utility was now put in place. The emperor nailed shut the doors of Schönbrunn Palace, banned courtiers from kissing his hand on bended knee, made drastic cuts to his siblings' apanages, did away with benefactions for countless individuals, and introduced instead a pension and survivors' benefits scheme for government officials. He reorganized the health and poor relief systems, extended freedom of the press and abolished serfdom, dissolved monasteries and transformed order churches into pawnshops and barracks; in short, he set in motion a revolution from above. If November 29, 1780, was for some the end of an epoch, for others it was a fresh start. The beginning of Joseph's sole rule was hailed by many as the "universal victory of reason and humanity," the dawning of a new era. The journalist Johann Pezzl declared the year of Maria Theresa's death to be "the year of salvation, the boundary marker of the enlightened philosophical century."[369]

15

Epilogue

Princely Virtues

All contemporary observers—whether or not they had ever personally met Maria Theresa, from the poor "court Tyrolean" Peter Prosch to the aristocratic bon vivant Charles-Joseph de Ligne, from the sentimental English traveler Lady Coke to emissaries from Prussia, Sweden, England, France, or Venice—were remarkably consistent in their appraisal of her key character traits:

> Her perseverance in the face of adversity, the genius and vigor with which she overcame it, the wisdom of her government, her sensible choice of ministers, her moderation, her love for her subjects, all this is known throughout the world. . . . Her love for her children, the particular care she personally devotes to their education, her piety, her generosity to all who approach her, the unfailing friendship she extends to all who prove worthy of it, and her manner with them—all this redounds to her praise.[1]

Piety, steadfastness and vigor, wisdom and moderation, benevolence and munificence—these were the traditional princely virtues, although they were by no means ascribed to every monarch in equal measure. In essence, they accorded with the catalogue of virtues in the *Princeps in Compendio*, the abbreviated mirror for princes that had served in the House of Habsburg as a textbook for the archdukes since the early seventeenth century (and had still been required reading for Joseph II).

While such assessments do not directly reflect Maria Theresa's "authentic" character, "how she actually was," they do reveal how she was perceived in her day and the standards against which she was judged. Appraisals of her rule reflect norms and values specific to their time, to which she clearly oriented herself with great success. Her dilemma was that these standards changed fundamentally over the course of her reign.

Piety and trust in God were the fountainhead of all princely virtues. Maria Theresa had been raised in the conviction of the House of Habsburg's God-given destiny, and in this conviction she never wavered. From it she derived both the right and the duty to rule. The Archducal House had not been given an unqualified divine mandate, however; in return, it had an obligation to promote God's honor and defend the true Christian religion from its enemies. Each individual ruler was merely a link in a dynastic chain spanning many generations. Piety toward God and devotion to ancestral traditions coincided in *Pietas Austriaca*, and the continuity of the dynasty had a sacral dimension. A rich repertoire of solemn rituals constantly revitalized it and invested it with an aura of immutability and inviolability. The conviction that, along with the rule bestowed on her through the Pragmatic Sanction, she had been given a special part to play in upholding the divine order, lay at the basis of Maria Theresa's confidence that God had endowed her with the qualities she needed to shoulder this heavy burden. Her belief in the Archducal House's sacred inheritance, and her own role in it, gave her an overriding sense of duty, responsibility, and endurance. In short, it equipped her with the "steadfastness and cordiality" that the mirror for princes required of a good ruler.[2] The fact that this inheritance had been attacked from all sides upon her accession to the throne only strengthened her in the belief that she had received a divine mandate to defend it. This explains the extraordinary confidence and determination with which she approached the highly complex, bewildering, and uncontrollable situation that confronted her at the beginning of her reign. Her sure knowledge of her own historical role, her unwavering conviction that she had religion, tradition, and the law on her side, allowed her to navigate these perilous waters with assurance rather than throwing up her hands in despair or delegating responsibility to an ever-changing cast of ministers. Her faith in divine providence and her self-belief were thus two sides of the same coin.[3] Depending on perspective, historians have seen her behavior as either admirably resolute or willfully stubborn. For all her charm, observers at court remarked—not without a critical undertone—on her "natural taste for rule, which she never shared with anyone else";[4] she was "dominated by a sense of her high position and inordinately jealous of her power."[5] Belief in her God-given duty not only gave her the strength to fight a long and unrelenting war in defense of her inheritance, or to push through urgently needed reforms in the face of opposition from her traditional allies in the nobility, it also gave her the determination to win back Silesia at all costs, to persist against all advice in brutally expelling the Jews from Bohemia, and to show no mercy in eradicating crypto-Protestantism from her lands. The flip side of her sense of duty toward her paternal inheritance was her pitilessness toward all who had to suffer the consequences—in many cases fatal—of her unwillingness to compromise. Her divine mission justified such sacrifices and helped banish scruples from her mind. Finally, the conviction of having received a mandate directly from God allowed her to act against his servants on Earth, sacrificing ecclesiastical privileges to the dynastic interest. Belief in the sanctity of tradition as the basis of her sovereignty licensed her to do whatever she deemed necessary. Paradoxically, it even made it possible for her to break with tradition at times.

Maria Theresa's sex was both a blessing and a curse for her government. On the one hand, it gave her opponents a welcome pretext to question her legitimacy as sovereign when her father died, and it provided ample material for propaganda in the War of Succession. In addition, as a woman she was unable to take command on the battlefield. Despite her robust physical constitution, her many pregnancies wore her down and restricted her mobility. On the other hand, her sex became an ever more valuable asset over the course of her reign, since it made her pluck and tenacity seem all the more remarkable. Her public image as a valiant heroine, beautiful woman, and loving mother were central to her myth and helped establish her legendary reputation even in her lifetime. Yet she herself avoided drawing attention to her sex in her public appearances. On the contrary, she carefully separated her physical sex from her role as ruler, wearing two "masculine" crowns and appearing on horseback on ceremonial occasions as *Rex*, not *Regina*. She did nothing to challenge the traditional gender hierarchy in marriage. Indeed, she instructed all her daughters to submit to their husbands, at least outwardly. As the female heir to masculine crowns, she was a singular exception. In her case, the gender hierarchy was partially suspended; her inherited rule canceled out her sex, so to speak. It is telling, for example, that she never exploited the obvious opportunity to have herself portrayed in the Christian iconographic tradition of the Madonna with the Christ Child, to profit thereby from her association with the heavenly queen—it remained for posterity to make good the omission. If she characterized herself as the "general and first mother of her lands," it was in the same sense that male princes presented themselves as father figures. It was not her femininity that was emphasized, as the nineteenth and twentieth century mistakenly assumed, but instead her paternalist conception of rule as a form of parenting that demanded childlike obedience from her subjects.

Her phlegmatic and amiable husband did nothing to stand in her way. If anything, he strengthened her position by generally deferring to her wishes, avoiding open conflict, and seeking fields of activity outside the court. Having grown accustomed to his inferior standing at the Habsburg court from an early age, he could more easily accept his wife's institutional and personal dominance and renounce the role of the naturally superior male—half by necessity, half of his own free will. For this he was punished by contemporaries with disdain and by historians with oblivion. His wife repaid him with deep affection far beyond the grave. Yet her relationship with him was ambivalent: she occasionally belittled him before others yet took offense if they treated him with disrespect.[6] Her temperament was directly complementary to his own. According to the categories of the time, she was considered sanguine, "blood-rich," meaning that her superabundant vitality had to be offset with regular bloodletting. People in her surrounds feared her "vivacity", her impatience, her fiery temper, her outbursts and fits of rage, for which she then felt ashamed and begged forgiveness, sometimes in writing: "I am sorry to have flared up."[7] She demonstrated her sovereignty precisely in confessing and apologizing for her lack of self-control, including to subalterns. Many regarded her impulsiveness as the sign of a fickle mind and complained that her "excessive liveliness can lead astray and overturn even the happiest ideas and most salutary counsel."[8] Her faith that she had divine right on her side by no means precluded feeling uncertain about how the righteous end was to be attained. The devil was literally in the detail, and she frequently corrected herself. The problem remained latent so long as her sole sovereignty went unchallenged. It came out into the open once her son Joseph had been made coregent.

A basic structural problem of every monarchy was choosing the right advisers, since it was a truism that "a prince cannot bear so heavy a burden on his own."[9] Mirrors for princes were therefore also mirrors for their counselors. A good adviser should be disinterested, discreet, and incorruptible. Although he should offer his opinion freely and frankly, he should not insist on it if his prince took a different view. Every monarch was confronted by the fundamental dilemma that advisers "without ambition and interest" could be distinguished only with difficulty from the craven toadies who flourished at court; these should be "avoid[ed] like the plague."[10] Given that the monarch represented the source of all possible symbolic and material goods, no one in his orbit was completely disinterested. At the same time, everyone competing for his favor cultivated a rhetoric of complete selflessness, sincerity, and incorruptibility. With its logic of personal patronage, the court was thus inevitably marked by structural hypocrisy.[11] "Little people" were particularly suspected by the established aristocracy of seeking preferment through flattery. This view was shared by Maria Theresa, who never tired of warning her children against vanity and self-love lest they fall prey to sycophants and lickspittles. She herself was known for disdaining "empty words of praise" and flowery compliments.[12] Instead, she encouraged her closest advisers to speak openly with her about her mistakes, and she herself sometimes proved capable of self-criticism.[13] Yet this offered no solution to the structural dilemma of the court patronage system. If there were no disinterested advisers at court, since everyone was competing for central favor, then it was crucial that the ruler appoint advisers whose interests coincided with her own and who could therefore be relied on to give her their undivided loyalty. This was the case for Bartenstein, Haugwitz, van Swieten, Ignaz Koch, Greiner, and Pichler, all of whom came to the Viennese court from elsewhere and therefore had no preexisting clientele to provide for; but it was also true to a certain extent of Kaunitz.[14] Needless to say, these confidants were viewed with envy by others—Khevenhüller's diaries give ample testimony of this. Whoever enjoyed the ruler's particular confidence automatically became the target of malicious rumor and intrigue from rivals. Maria Theresa sought to get around the problem by never entertaining any doubts about her advisers once they had gained her trust, and she urged her children to do the same.[15] A lack of trust in one's friends and relatives was a cardinal social sin, the secular equivalent to religious doubt. The advice given by her closest confidants was no more to be called into question than Catholic dogma; indeed, so far as possible, dissenting voices were to be blocked out. This accorded with Maria Theresa's temperamental aversion to protracted debate and differences of opinion. Her trust had the character of a final and irreversible decision, just as doubt was forbidden in questions of belief. This self-imposed restriction made it easier for her to cope with a highly complex situation in the first decades of her reign. All this changed with Joseph's coregency: the strategy failed her when it came to her own son.

Maria Theresa's reputation as a wise ruler required that she credibly embody a stance of sovereign impartiality. The ideal monarch was supposed to tower above the fray of petty politics. She constantly reminded her children to treat everyone outside the family with the same distanced courtesy and to avoid demeaning themselves by exchanging intimacies, gossiping, or hatching plots. She disliked making others appear ridiculous,[16] and she detested any form of mockery, irony, or sarcasm in her children, just as she hated seeing them engage on terms of easy familiarity with their social inferiors. As sovereign, she once wrote to Marie Antoinette, one should stand so far above cabals that one simply could not be insulted: "How could such a measly Broglie [a French nobleman] possibly injure you? I do not understand. No one has ever done me or any of your ten brothers and sisters the least injury. . . . You should pay no heed to such matters."[17] When foreign observers gushed about Maria Theresa's familiarity, this was therefore a misunderstanding. The person of the ruler was protected against intrusiveness and degradation not just by a multitude of symbolic barriers, but also—and not least—through her own distanced bearing.

The regal stance of absolute superiority also required Maria Theresa to overlook any minor instances of fraud, deceit, or nepotism she observed at court. Mistakes made in her environment should be tactically forgiven to save the face of those affected and spare them humiliation. If one of her dependents lost face, the reputation of the entire group would suffer.[18] In cases of doubt, Maria Theresa therefore preferred to risk being duped rather than doubt the good intentions of others.[19] A number of anecdotes attest to her deliberate clemency. Count Nitzky, Royal Commissar in the Banat, had knowingly been paid five times the amount owed him by the Court Chamber. She let him go unpunished, it was said, because she had failed to notice the Court Chamber's mistake and therefore took the blame herself.[20] The Prince de Ligne likewise boasted in his memoirs of never having lost the empress's favor, despite having given her many reasons to withdraw it—"frivolities which drew her maternal ire for a moment but which, being a great sovereign, she soon forgave me."[21] The calculated decision not to impose public sanctions served in aristocratic society as a subtle means for maintaining social norms. By signaling that she had noted the offense but would not pursue it, the empress appealed to the culprit's honor as a member of the aristocracy. The sole exception confirms the rule: her relentless chastity campaign, including against nobles and their paramours, not only proved ineffective, it also damaged her own standing.[22] Their code of honor demanded that aristocrats *voluntarily* submit to the unwritten rules of their class (from which chastity was conspicuously absent)—physical force was something reserved for subjects. That this expectation was largely a fiction was irrelevant: when it came to preserving honor, appearances were all that mattered.[23] Those guilty of more serious normative infractions were simply banished from court—packed off to a remote monastery or sent abroad, like the

imposter Fräulein Schönbaden, or committed to a hospital, like Chevalier de Balde.[24] The education of princes in the House of Habsburg
rested on the same principle of voluntary submission to a class-specific
code of conduct; corporal punishment was thus unbecoming for the
children of an empress. For Maria Theresa, demonstrative leniency was
a means to bind beneficiaries more closely to her in future; clemency
was a magnanimous gift calling for gratitude and loyalty in return. Maria
Theresa drew on the same logic when dealing with the Bohemian magnates who had paid homage to her enemy, Karl Albrecht of Bavaria, in
the War of Succession. By forgiving them, she placed them even more
deeply in her debt.[25] Yet leniency stood in latent tension to justice—
clementia and *iustitia* were binary opposites.[26] Justice required that
everyone be punished for their crimes without regard for their person.
In cases of normative conflict, however, Maria Theresa tended to favor
clemency over justice, mercy over the law, particularly when deciding
on nobles with a history of meritorious service to the All-Highest Archducal House, as in the case of Franz von der Trenck, spared the death
penalty for his atrocities thanks to her intervention.[27]

Like clemency, bounty, *liberalitas*, was a form of generosity, and generosity, *magnanimitas*, was one of the cardinal princely virtues for which
Maria Theresa was universally praised. Generosity referred to the patronage dispensed by a ruler, whether material or symbolic, gauged in
offices and pensions or in access and attention. Maria Theresa, like all
her fellow sovereigns, had to tread a fine line here, since there were always far more expectations than could be satisfied.[28] She therefore impressed on her children the need to strike a careful balance between
economy and magnanimity, a lesson familiar from mirrors for princes.[29]
On the one hand, as a good ruler she was expected to reward service
appropriately; on the other, she had only limited means at her disposal
to do so. This was true of the symbolic resource of personal attention,
which she could only lavish on a small number of people, and it was
especially true of material resources, which had shrunk dramatically
over the course of two ruinously expensive wars. Yet it was in the nature
of royal patronage that it was *not* distributed equally. This is what distinguished a favor, which left the beneficiary in the giver's debt, from

the satisfaction of a legal entitlement, for which a justified claim could be made. The system of court patronage was based on a logic of gift rather than one of contractual obligation.[30] While a loyal servant may have had a moral claim to acknowledgement from the ruler, it was up to the ruler to decide when and how this would be offered. Reciprocal expectations were based solely on the fact that lord and servant shared the same code of aristocratic honor; they were strictly unenforceable. Maria Theresa thus presented herself as *amie de mes amis*, "a friend to my friends, appreciative of the good services they render me,"[31] but she frequently left them waiting for signs of her appreciation. When the expected reward finally came, it appeared as a voluntary favor which obliged the recipient to gratitude. In this way, both sides were connected through a never-ending chain of gifts and countergifts, services and rewards, which could never—and this was the crux of the matter—be fully balanced out. From the ruler's perspective, it was enough to bestow occasional acts of largesse on select individuals to keep everyone else's hopes alive.[32] But she could do so only by seeming equally accessible, approachable, and benevolent to all people (of rank, that is).

Maria Theresa pursued this strategy with remarkable success, gaining a legendary reputation as a munificent ruler despite the fact that she had implemented a rigid austerity policy at the start of her reign.[33] Later, too, she did not reward everyone at court in equal measure. While she doled out lucrative material favors—in the last year of her life alone, they amounted to some 650,000 guilders—they were distributed extremely unequally. Daun and Khevenhüller, for example, drew extraordinarily high pensions, while Ulfeld, Bartenstein, Esterházy, and Chotek were richly compensated for their loss of office.[34] Maria Theresa had taken to heart the advice given her, at the start of her reign, by Tarouca. He had shown her a way out of the structural dilemma posed by life at court. Everyone was besieging her incessantly with petitions and claims, some justified, others not, and it was impossible for her to satisfy them all. According to Tarouca, this would be a constant source of resentment and rivalry, an evil that could not be completely remedied but could nonetheless be minimized. He recommended two strategies: first, she should distract the court's attention through amusements of various kinds; second, she should appear regularly before courtiers and grant generous access to her person.[35] What worked for Maria Theresa would work for her children, too: she always encouraged them to appear affectionate, sympathetic, forgiving, and generous rather than harsh, brusque, or temperamental.[36]

This did not mean doing away with ceremonial, however. The image of an unstuffy and affectionate middle-class family household is a myth. While Maria Theresa was free of personal vanity, she was acutely aware of the need to put her majesty on show and demonstrate who she was at every step—*il faut représenter par tout*, she taught her children, one must represent everywhere.[37] Her charismatic presence rested not just on the majesty of the All-Highest Archducal House and the inherited authority of her office, as professionally staged by a small army of architects and sculptors, portrait painters and copperplate engravers, musicians, actors, and writers, tailors and milliners, but also on her personal charm. Maria Theresa was a virtuoso in the art of communication, both face to face and in writing. As everyone who met her willingly attested, she made people feel as though she took an individual interest in them. She herself saw her concern for others, in good times and in bad, as her most valuable talent.[38] When people close to her fell ill, she visited them at their sickbed; when death struck, she wrote condolence letters of touching empathy.[39] She drew on a variety of rhetorical registers, understood how to adjust her tone to suit the occasion and interlocutor, and could subtly regulate the social temperature. In her handbillets and marginalia, she cultivated a matter-of-fact style stripped of Baroque ornament; in her correspondence with her husband and children, she preferred a language of tender sentimentality that could shift at any moment into harsh criticism. Communicating with close confidants, she was quite capable of irony and self-distance, yet she detested sarcasm, frivolity, and urbane sophistication. It would be idle to speculate on whether her legendary warmth was genuine or feigned. Opinions among her contemporaries were divided. The Swedish emissary Bark thought the empress incapable of dissimulation: "Her face betrays what is going on inside her, and it is easy to see whether something gives rise to pleasant or unpleasant sensations in her."[40] Around the same time, the Prussian emissary offered the exact opposite opinion: "She can disguise and control herself so well that it is hard to tell from her face and posture what is going on inside her."[41]

Not everyone basked in the warmth of her friendliness and sympathy; the radius of personal communication was strictly limited. Maria Theresa's accessibility to "even her lowliest subjects" is a historiographical fairytale. In fact, court access rules were tightened under her reign, common supplicants were referred to formal bureaucratic channels, and particularly insistent petitioners were thrown into prison.[42] Commoners were kept at arm's length; favors were only granted through personal advocacy.[43] Access to her person was no less unequally distributed than all other gifts. What Maria Theresa called "my subjects" was an abstract entity largely divorced from personal experience. Her beneficence was confined to traditional symbolic acts of Christian neighborly love, which she extended *pars pro toto* to individual paupers: throwing armfuls of coins from her coach window, washing feet on Maundy Thursday, or paying pensions to converted orphans. Real subjects came into consideration primarily as taxpayers and were the object of a remarkably merciless policy aimed at enforcing political and religious discipline. In this respect, however, Maria Theresa's perspective changed significantly in the last years of her reign.

In all her virtues, Maria Theresa was bound by a centuries-old tradition of rulership ethics—an ethics of close interpersonal relations that was appropriate at court or in town but was ill-suited to ruling modern states. The traditional rules of premodern society were not impersonal, formal, and abstract norms that applied equally to all. They were tacit, unwritten, and ambiguous. Differing according to estate and rank, they called for moderation, cool-headed calculation, and tact. Mastering these rules meant striking a fine balance between leniency and strictness, clemency and justice, thrift and generosity. Measured against these standards of premodern virtue ethics, Maria Theresa could appear as an exemplary ruler, but she was less well equipped to meet the demands of modern statecraft. The old princely virtues proved incapable of solving new problems.

Control Fantasies

During her travels through Europe in the 1770s, the English aristocrat Lady Mary Coke spent two long periods in Vienna. Through the good offices of the English emissary, she was admitted to court and granted a private audience, where she gained firsthand experience of the empress's legendary charm. She gushed about her virtues and the harmony in the imperial family, delighted in her closeness to the emperor, and assiduously documented every sign of esteem or favor in her letters home. Yet when her impression of having been made an honorary family member in Schönbrunn proved to be an illusion, her love curdled into hatred.[44] The empress, she wrote home, had inexplicably taken a grudge against her and sought to do her harm, Joseph II was studiously avoiding her company, and even the dauphine in Versailles had been forbidden by her mother from having any contact with her. As if all this were not enough, Lady Mary gradually began to suspect that the empress was plotting her complete social, if not physical, destruction. Wherever she went as she traveled through Italy and France, she saw herself trailed by imperial spies and henchmen who secretly read her correspondence and watched over her every move. Whatever trials and tribulations befell her en route—theft, substandard lodgings, delayed mail, a coach accident—she attributed to the machinations of the almighty empress in Vienna.[45]

It is telling that Maria Theresa became the object of such persecution mania in the 1770s. For what Lady Mary fantasized was nothing less than a pathologically intensified version of the very system of surveillance and control that Maria Theresa was seeking to implement at the time. She was said to maintain an extensive spy network and lend an ear to even her humblest subjects—not to hear their complaints but to keep up to date on the latest rumors. "She even allows them to whisper in her ear," wrote one English observer.[46] Maria Theresa's reputation was that of an all-knowing, all-powerful spider presiding over a web of communications that stretched halfway across Europe. This reputation reflected reality less than it did her own, ever growing need for control. For Maria Theresa, ruling from a distance was a lifelong theme. From the center of her court to the most far-flung corners of her lands, she was practically obsessed by the need to know everything, direct everything, control everything, and subject everyone—family, court, troops, and subjects— to the same iron discipline she imposed on herself.

Maria Theresa was a woman of practically inexhaustible stamina. She insisted on being kept personally informed about everything in writing:[47] judgments of the Supreme Judiciary, deliberations of the Court Conference and State Council, emissaries' reports and dispatches from commanders in the field, regular letters from her married children and their chaperones—and this was just the tip of the iceberg. She read and wrote indefatigably, always sifting, registering, or destroying what she read. Her attempts to exert control extended not least to her own place in history. She sought—not always with success, thankfully—to preserve only what she wished to preserve. She destroyed most of her husband's papers, attempted to get rid of her daughter-in-law Isabella's correspondence, forced her children and confidants to burn her letters, and set aside specially chosen papers for the archives. By consolidating the holdings of the various hereditary lands in the newly established House, Court, and State Archive, she retroactively established a homogeneous tradition for the entire monarchy where none had existed before. She wanted nothing less than to dictate to posterity how her reign would be judged.[48]

Yet this was only one element in a far grander, all-encompassing system of control. Other elements included surveying the land and counting the populace; reviewing and systematizing laws and customs; forcing subjects to take the high road of true religion, diligence, and righteousness;[49] closing the borders "at the furthest end of Christendom" and allowing no one to enter without permission;[50] systematically censoring all printed matter to suppress criticism, superstition, and freethinking;[51] exhaustively monitoring foreign correspondence;[52] and, not least, imperceptibly steering allied European powers in the direction dictated by Kaunitz's political system through family members placed at foreign courts—an immensely ambitious agenda that was far beyond the reach of any eighteenth-century monarch, no matter how "absolute." Yet Maria Theresa's advisers, above all the brilliantly egotistical State Chancellor and State Council President, adhered to the seductive image of the "machine of state," which suggested that all this could be achieved through rational planning and central organization. In doing so, they succumbed to an optimism typical of the time they lived in. The numerous reforms that two financially and demographically disastrous wars had made inevitable undoubtedly brought about considerable structural change. They weakened the intermediate levels of authority in the core lands, allowed more resources to flow directly into state coffers, and made it possible to maintain an army of unprecedented size. Yet the wars subsequently fought with this enormous army undid many of the achievements of reform, taking subjects back to square one. The "new system" catalyzed a reform dynamic that then became self-perpetuating. Much changed, but not always as planned. Unintended consequences required ever new waves of reform, leading to increased bureaucracy, ballooning costs, and a more complex state apparatus. The planners' confidence that the machine of state would be simpler, clearer, and easier to manipulate proved misplaced.[53] To celebrate Maria Theresa as the founder of the modern state is to confuse the reformers' rationalist fantasies with reality. The idea of the unmoved mover at the center, the still point where all the threads come together and all the plans originate, vastly overestimates the ruler's agency. This autocratic style of politics was unable to cope with the new political challenges; more complex, participative procedures were needed. Constant tinkering with central administrative bodies was not enough; the reforms had to start at the local level. All the same, Maria Theresa learned how matters really stood in the furthest backwaters of her lands from the commissioners she sent out on the conscription of souls, and what she learned clearly made an impact on her.[54]

Maria Theresa also sought to create channels of influence by strategically placing her children at foreign courts. While this expanded her field of action, it further intensified her demand for control. Her need for information was insatiable. The voluminous correspondence she conducted with the ministers, chamberlains, confessors, and physicians who informed her from afar about her children never delivered what she had promised. Her strategy of total control had fatal consequences:

the greater her expectations, the more profoundly they were disappointed. The dynastic system here revealed its structural weakness. The children could only function as her representatives if they were completely passive, like Ferdinand, the good son. If they were strong-willed and assertive, they went their own political way and distanced themselves from their mother, like Leopold and Carolina. Or they slipped the maternal leash and were drawn instead into partisan conflicts at their own court, like Marie Antoinette. Even as children, they had been insufficiently disciplined for her liking and had never been able to live up to her high standards—least of all Joseph and Leopold, in whom she placed the greatest hopes. Her letters and instructions were filled with reproachful concern. Maria Theresa distrusted her own children far more than her closest advisers even as she demanded they be completely open and trusting with her. She herself spoke with a forked tongue, held her cards close to her chest, and played one correspondent against another. Through her obsessive demand for sincerity, she achieved the exact opposite result: nothing was as it seemed. The family was riven by resentment and jealousy, factionalism and partisanship, hypocrisy and dissimulation.[55]

Out of Step

In the last years of her life, Maria Theresa came to feel like a relic from a bygone era. She observed with abhorrence what she called "enlightened philosophy à la mode," the brazen idea that people can and should have the courage to use their own reason. Some of her eulogists could therefore celebrate her as a bulwark against the new age.[56] There is an irony in the fact that she herself was an independent thinker of keen intelligence, considerable critical acumen, and great strength of will. Kant's reservations about the fair sex, in particular, did not apply to her; she had no need to free herself from self-incurred tutelage.[57] Yet she was unwilling to concede to others the same self-confidence in their own powers of reasoning. After all, *she* was the sovereign by divine right, and God had therefore given *her* the necessary temperamental and intellectual gifts.

She was deeply skeptical of philosophical concepts and suspected them of sophistry. The political discourse of rational law, with its abstract axioms, geometrical deductions, and universal rights, was alien to her. Instead, she spoke of her rule in an emotionally charged language of personal closeness, drawing heavily on ideas of love, sympathy, concern, and loyalty. She felt accountable solely to God and her descendants. At best, she was prepared to consider the opinions of her fellow crowned heads of Europe; she refused to plead her case before the self-appointed tribunal of a critically informed public—this she left to her more media-savvy archenemy, Frederick II. She placed her trust in people, not principles. Yet this made it possible for Enlightenment ideas to find their way into her court in the form of several Trojan horses: first van Swieten, then Kaunitz and his protégés, and later men like Martini and Heinke, Gebler and Raab. In retrospect, her position appears contradictory in many respects. On the one hand, she condemned the spirit of tolerantism and had non-Catholics deported, on the other, she rigorously subordinated the Roman church to state authority.[58] On the one hand, she promoted the old aristocratic families at court and quashed her son's egalitarian ideas, on the other, she ended up vehemently— more vehemently than her son!—advocating the emancipation of Bohemian peasants from the "tyranny of the lords."[59] Her position was never underpinned by any coherent theoretical program, whether Enlightenment or anti-Enlightenment. Her contempt for *philosophie à la mode* was more a vague resentment toward a certain style of thinking and living than a fully thought-out political conviction. Even the latest children's hairstyle could appear to her as a rotten byproduct of the spirit of Enlightenment: "The girls now wear their hair cut short on their forehead, like boys. This displeases me no end. . . . Next thing we will see children with no clothes at all, running around like negroes. Everything is carried to extremes nowadays. . . . You see where this enlightened age is taking us."[60]

It was the death of Francis Stephen, and her halfhearted transfer of the coregency to Joseph, that brought Maria Theresa's reign out of kilter. The generational conflict was at the same time an epochal one; mother and son spoke a different language. Maria Theresa considered her eldest son incapable of ruling independently and could not bring herself to abdicate, despite frequently threatening to do so. She tacitly expected Joseph to submit to her will and hide any differences of opinion behind a façade of consensus while outwardly taking joint responsibility for her decisions. But Joseph turned out to be less docile than his father. He insisted on voicing his often fierce disagreement, giving way only when forced to do so by his mother. He stubbornly refused her the show of concord she wanted, despite her repeated attempts at emotional blackmail. There was no room in her religious worldview for open dissent between mother and son; disunity was not in keeping with the dynasty's divine mandate. The fatal consequence was that the latent tension between the two could explode into open conflict at any moment. Senior officials had no idea whose orders they should follow, and responsibility for political decisions passed backward and forward at excruciating length, as in the case of the Russo-Turkish war, the Polish partition, the War of the Bavarian Succession, and peasant policy. The split at the top inevitably fostered factionalism and court intrigue. Ambitious advisers had an interest in exacerbating divisions between mother and son and exploiting the situation to their own advantage.[61] The dilemma was not lost on the empress. She admitted that all her good intentions somehow went awry but avoided taking the obvious way out of the dilemma. She felt too weak to bear the regency on her own but too strong to relinquish it.

The system of court patronage also lost its equilibrium. Maria Theresa now made herself guilty of what she had always strongly criticized in her children. She increasingly withdrew to her retirade, making attendance at court less and less attractive for the nobility. She distrusted almost everyone and consulted only a select few—"little people," as Joseph disdainfully called them. She lent an ear to gossip and allowed herself to be caught up in intrigue.[62] Her altered view of herself increasingly came to be reflected in the way she was viewed by others, and her charisma and authority suffered from the fact that she no longer abided by her own rules.

The standards by which she was judged had changed as well. Imperceptibly yet irrevocably, the old princely virtues lost their basis in reality. Abstract legal principles increasingly replaced royal patronage. Officials preferred a secure, regular income and were no longer content to wait, cap in hand, for exceptional gifts of grace. Policies aimed at improving subjects' general welfare discredited selective, symbolic almsgiving. Patronage was criticized on account of its arbitrary character, munificence appeared as redistribution from above to below: "What is called generosity in kings, very often consists in bestowing that money on the idle part of their subjects which they have squeezed from the industrious."[63] Personal favor, patronage, and protection, the time-honored structural principles of court society, were now seen as typically feminine traits. Joseph von Sonnenfels, both a renowned force for Enlightenment and a fervent admirer of the empress, defended her after her death from the charge that not all subjects had benefited equally from her largesse: Maria Theresa's excessive bounty toward individuals was due to "the estimable, but often too delicate sentimentality of her sex."[64] This anticipated the gender hierarchy of the nineteenth century: the system of court patronage was identified with effete, decadent gynocracy, while strictly formalized, bureaucratic administrative procedures were seen as inherently masculine.[65]

Toward the end of her life, little was left of the world into which Maria Theresa had been born in 1717. The relics had been packed away, rituals were no longer taken seriously, her educators, the Jesuits, had been destroyed, the religion of rule had lost its luster, the great Habsburg empire had been bested by a third-rate upstart, and her own son and heir was no longer convinced by beliefs that had once been taken for granted. The extraordinary confidence she had displayed at the start of her reign now seemed misplaced. She felt out of step with the times. The world in which her rules were the right ones no longer existed. She knew it and she suffered because of it, but it did not prompt her to call those rules into question. Her tragedy was to insist on norms that hardly anyone else still shared and to look on as they sank into obsolescence. Having lost her self-assurance and her sovereign self-regard, her perseverance was transformed into peevishness, her decisiveness into indecision. She changed—in the parlance of the day—from a sanguine personality into a melancholic one. At the start of her reign she had known with absolute certainty, for all the external challenges she faced, "that everyone recognizes what I am owed and who I am."[66] By the end she regarded herself as *un naturel d'un autre siècle,* a being from another century, and focused all her remarkable willpower and discipline on dying a beautiful death.[67]

ACKNOWLEDGMENTS

FOR A LONG TIME, I seriously doubted whether this biography would appear in time for the 300th anniversary of Maria Theresa's birth on May 13, 2017. I would never have met the deadline without the many people who supported me through their interest, advice, criticism, practical assistance, and encouragement. The basis of everything else was the productive collegial atmosphere at the Historical Seminar of the University of Münster, the Cluster of Excellence "Religion and Politics," and the collaborative research project, "Cultures of Decision-Making." In particular, I owe Gerd Althoff, André Krischer, Matthias Pohlig, Michael Sikora, Tilman Haug, Philip Hoffmann-Rehnitz, Ulrich Pfister, Iris Flessenkämper, and Detlef Pollack more than they probably realize. My special thanks go to Anne Roerkohl who was my critical first reader. It would be impossible to name everyone who provided me with helpful tips; I mention only Manja Quakatz for introducing me to scholarship on the Ottomans and Vít Kortus for making accessible a number of texts in Czech. The ever-obliging team headed by Thomas Just, director of the Haus-, Hof- und Staatsarchiv in Vienna, made my work at the archive a real pleasure.

I had the great good fortune to spend a year at the Institute for Advanced Study in Berlin. Without the paradisiacal working conditions there, a perfect mix of intellectual stimulation and concentration, this book could not have been written. I thank Luca Giuliani, Thorsten Wilhelmy, Daniel Schönpflug, Katharina Wiedemann, and above all the highly competent service staff, especially the library team—Sonja Grund, Anja Brockmann, Stephan Gellner, and Thomas Reimer, who made literally all my bibliographical dreams come true. I owe my colleagues from the 2015–16 cohort an enormous debt of gratitude—above all Ina Hartwig, who shared with me the challenges of biographical writing, but also Jane Burbank, Karol Berger, Anna Maria Busse Berger, El Hadj Ibrahima Diop, Michael Gordin, Anselm Haverkamp, Daniel Jütte, Gertrude Lübbe-Wolff, Naoko Matsumoto, Jonathan Sheehan, Felicita Tramontana, Ralph Ubl, Barbara Vinken, and Constanta Vintila-Ghitulescu.

My friends and colleagues in Berlin also provided me with many valuable suggestions: Etienne François, Daniela Hacke, Johannes Helmrath, Leonhard Horowski, Klaus Krüger, Wilfried Nippel, Alexander Schunka, Xenia von Tippelskirch, Claudia Ulbrich, and Aloys Winterling.. Matthias Schnettger and Thomas Winkelbauer made me aware of several mistakes that could be corrected in the second edition, for which I am especially grateful. I thank Stefan von der Lahr and Andrea Morgan at C.H. Beck publishers for the great professionalism they showed in editing and producing the book, as well as for their forbearance in accommodating my wishes under tight time constraints. Several generations of eager student assistants have been pushed beyond reasonable limits. For their patience and care I thank Theresa Bellermann, Hannah Frie, Jan Philipp Engelmann, Laura-Marie Krampe, Ole Meiners, Sven Solterbeck, Miklas Böhmer (for instant IT assistance), and above all Hendrik Holzmüller, who bore the main burden with great composure at the end. As always, Brigitte König's and Sabine Ubags's practical and emotional support was invaluable.

My special thanks go to Yair Mintzker; without his recommendation the English translation would not have been possible. I thank Brigitta van Rheinberg at Princeton University Press for supervising the English version with such professionalism and Margery Tippie for copyediting. Finally, I cannot thank Robert Savage enough for his translation, which attests not only to his attention to detail, expertise, and perfectionism, but also to his acute sensitivity. Collaborating with him has been an enriching experience and has helped me better understand my own text.

Barbara Stollberg-Rilinger
Berlin, December 2020

ABBREVIATIONS

ADB   *Allgemeine Deutsche Biographie*, ed. Historical Commission
of the Royal Academy of Science, 56 vols. Munich 1875–1912.

ÄZA   Ältere Zeremonialakten (older ceremonial papers)

BAA   Walter, Friedrich (ed.), *Maria Theresia. Briefe und Aktenstücke
in Auswahl* (Freiherr-vom-Stein-Gedächtnisausgabe.
Ausgewählte Quellen zur Deutschen Geschichte der
Neuzeit, 12). Darmstadt 1968s

BKF   Arneth, Alfred von (ed.), *Briefe der Kaiserin Maria Theresia
an ihre Kinder und Freunde*, 4 vols. Vienna 1881

BLKÖ   Wurzbach-Tannenberg, Constant von (ed.), *Biographisches
Lexikon des Kaiserthums Österreich*, 60 vols. Vienna 1856–91

FA   Familienakten (family papers)

fol.   Folio page

HHStA   Haus-, Hof- und Staatsarchiv Vienna

HKA   Hofkriegsarchiv Vienna

IPO   Instrumentum Pacis Osnabrugense (Treaty of Osnabrück)

KHM   Kunsthistorisches Museum Vienna

KMT   Schlitter, Hans/Khevenhüller-Metsch, Rudolf (ed.), *Aus der
Zeit Maria Theresias. Tagebuch des Fürsten Johann Josef
Khevenhüller-Metsch, Kaiserlichen Obersthofmeisters, 1742–1776*,
vols. 1–7. Vienna/Leipzig 1908–1925; vol. 8, ed. Maria
Breunlich-Pawlik and Hans Wagner, Vienna 1972

LHA   Lothringian House Archive

MACS Arneth, Alfred/Auguste Mathieu Geffroy (ed.), *Correspondance secrète entre Marie Thérèse et le comte de Mercy-Argenteau avec les lettres de Marie Thérèse et Marie Antoinette*, 3 vols. Paris 1874

MJC Arneth, Alfred von (ed.), *Maria Theresia und Joseph II. Ihre Correspondenz sammt Briefen Joseph's an seinen Bruder Leopold*, 3 vols. Vienna 1867

MIÖG Mitteilungen des Instituts für Österreichische Geschichtsforschung

MÖStA Mitteilungen des Österreichischen Staatsarchivs

NDB *Neue Deutsche Biographie*, ed. Historical Commission of the Bavarian Academy of Sciences, 26 vols. [to date]. Berlin 1953–2016

OMaA Obersthofmarschallamt

OMeA Obersthofmeisteramt

ÖNA Österreichisches Nationalarchiv

ÖNB Österreichische Nationalbibliothek

ÖZV II Kretschmayr, Heinrich/Joseph Kallbrunner/Friedrich Walter/Melitta Winkler (ed.), *Die österreichische Zentralverwaltung 1491–1918, 2. Abteilung: Von der Vereinigung der österreichischen und böhmischen Hofkanzlei bis zur Einrichtung der Ministerialverfassung (1749–1848)*. Vienna 1925–38

r recto (front side)

StPKB Staatsbibliothek Preußischer Kulturbesitz

v verso (back side)

ZP Zeremonialprotokolle (ceremonial protocols)

NOTES

1. Prologue

1. Arneth, *Geschichte Maria Theresia's* I, v–vi.

2. Arneth, *Geschichte Maria Theresia's* I, 2.

3. Collectors' pictures produced by the firm Herba Druck, *Deutsche Geschichte*, vol. 2: "Vom Ende des 30jährigen Krieges bis zur Gegenwart." I wish to thank Bernhard Jussen for drawing my attention to this material.

4. See Wandruszka, *Maria Theresia*, 82; brief overviews in Wandruszka, "Die Historiographie"; Wandruszka, "Im Urteil der Nachwelt" (where the period of National Socialism is omitted); Hochedlinger, "Political History."

5. In the words of the civil servant Heinrich Gottfried von Bretschneider, Linger, *Denkwürdigkeiten*, 225.

6. Thus—as one example among many—Trapp, "Maria Theresia und Tirol," 131.

7. See Telesko, *Maria Theresia*, 147 ff.

8. Adolph W. Künast, *Kaiserin Maria Theresia, die Stammmutter des Hauses Habsburg-Lothringen in ihren Leben und Wirken: Gedenkbuch zur Enthüllung ihres Monumentes und zum 40-jährigen Regierungsjubiläum Seiner Majestät Kaiser Franz Josef I*, Vienna 1888, preface.

9. Specifically, these are the four generals Daun, Khevenhüller, Laudon, and Abensperg-Traun on horseback; on the pedestal reliefs, the generals Liechtenstein, Lacy, Hadik, and Nádasdy; then the advisers and ministers Kaunitz, Bartenstein, Starhemberg, and Mercy-Argenteau; Haugwitz, Grassalkovich, Bruckenthal, Riegger, Sonnenfels, and Martini; the physician van Swieten, the numismatist Joseph Hilarius Eckhel, the historiographer György Pray, as well as Gluck, Haydn, and the infant Mozart. *The Men around Maria Theresa* and *The Empress's Paladins* are also titles of popular books from the 1950s by Friedrich Walter.

10. See Alexander Novotny, "Arneth, Alfred Ritter von," in NDB I, 1953, 364–65. Arneth's colleagues and successors carried on his tradition: historians such as Adam Wolf, Adam Beer, Hans Schlitter, Theodor von Karajan, Eugen Guglia, Josef Kallbrunner, Heinrich Kretschmayr, and Friedrich Walter.

11. In the preface to Arneth, "Maria Theresia und der Hofrath von Greiner," (1859), 5–6.

12. Friedrich Nietzsche, *Untimely Meditations*, 68.

13. See Wandruszka, "Die Historiographie"; Wandruszka, "Im Urteil der Nachwelt"; Stourzh, "Vom Umfang der österreichischen Geschichte"; Suppanz, "Maria Theresia"; Gehler, *Ungleiche Partner?*; Heindl, "Mythos Nation"; Plaschka, *Was heißt Österreich?*; Telesko, *Maria Theresia*;

Fillafer, "Rivalisierende Aufklärungen"; Fillafer, "Die Aufklärung"; Wallnig/Frimmel/Telesko, *18th Century Studies*.

14. E.g., Raponi, "Il mito"; Cerman, "Tereziánská legenda" (I thank Vit Kortus for drawing my attention to this essay); Drabek/Plaschka/Wandruszka, *Ungarn und Österreich*.

15. I borrow the phrase from Christian Meier, "Von der Faszination des Biographischen," in *Interesse an der Geschichte*, ed. Frank Niess, Frankfurt am Main and New York, 1989, 100–11, here 101.

16. Sonnenfels, *Rede auf Marien Theresien* (unpaginated).

17. This is the subtitle given to the German edition of Crankshaw's biography.

18. This is the view taken by Hofmannsthal, "Maria Theresien," 11 ff.; for a comparison with Catherine the Great, see Meehan-Waters, "Catherine the Great and the Problem of Female Rule," *The Russian Review* 34: 293–307..

19. Anon., "Der Adel." *Eine Wochenschrift*, Prague, no. 9, December 27, 1775, 144. On what follows see Barta, "Maria Theresia," 354; Suppanz, "Maria Theresia"; Kaduk, *Maria Theresia und ihre Bruder*; Mauser, "Maria Theresia"; Heindl, "Mythos Nation"; Heindl, "Maria Thérèse." The literature on female rule in the Early Modern period has become legion; see Wunder, *"Er ist die Sonn"*; Wunder, "Herrschaft"; Hausen, "Die Polarisierung"; Honegger, *Die Ordnung der Geschlechter*; Schulte, *Der Körper*; Puppel, "Gynäkokratie"; Sluga/James, Women; Consandey, La Reine de France; Keller, Gynäkokratie; Bastian et al., Geschlecht der Diplomatie; Braun/Keller/Schnettger, *Nur die Frau des Kaisers?*.

20. The Venetian emissary Foscarini already described the young archduchess as possessing *una certa virilità d'animo*, cited in Arneth, *Geschichte Maria Theresia's* I, 356.

21. See the examples in Michaud, "Laudatio," 676–77.

22. *Sammlung merkwürdiger Aufsätze*, 8.

23. E.g., Wolf, *Marie Christine* I, 53; Guglia, *Maria Theresia* II, 114–15, calls her a "masculine woman."

24. Similar observations were made about Catherine II, Elizabeth I, or Queen Victoria. Even on a 2015 campaign poster for the German Liberal Party (FDP), the female candidate was advertised as "our man for Hamburg."

25. Frederick II, cited in Barta, *Maria Theresia*, 341.

26. "Patriotisches Schreiben des Teutschen Friedens, . . ." Vienna 1743, 9, cited in Küster, *Vier Monarchien*, 100.

27. On the gender discourse of rationalism, see Honegger, *Die Ordnung der Geschlechter*.

28. Anon., *Betrachtung über die Etiquette mit Anwendung auf die Präcedenz der Gesandten und Monarchen durch Beyspiele aus der Geschichte erläutert*, n.d., n.pl.

29. Heinrich Finke, *Die Frau im Mittelalter*, Munich 1913; see Stollberg-Rilinger, "Väter der Frauengeschichte."

30. On the figure of the exceptional woman, see Isabelle Graw, "Aneignung und Ausnahme. Zeitgenössische Künstlerinnen: Ihre asthetischen Verfahren und ihr Status im Kunstsystem." PhD diss. Frankfurt/Oder 2003; see also Pohlig, *Vom Besonderen zum Allgemeinen*; Puppel, *Virilibus curis*.

31. Andreas, *Das theresianische Österreich*, 9.

32. Srbik, *Gestalten und Ereignisse*, 37–38.

33. Andreas, *Das theresianische Österreich*, 9.

34. Wandruszka, *Maria Theresia*, 64; Crankshaw, *Maria Theresia*, 18; Haussherr, *Verwaltungseinheit*, 97, among many others.

35. Otto Krack, *Geleitwort zur Neuausgabe von Arneth*, BKF I, 1909, 11–12. Numerous further examples in Telesko, *Maria Theresia*; Suppanz, "Maria Theresia"; Barta, *Maria Theresia*; Kaduk, *Maria Theresia und ihre Brüder*; Heindl, "Marie-Thérèse"; Mauser, *Mütterlichkeit*.

36. Hofmannsthal, "Maria Theresia," 12.

37. Sacher-Masoch, *Maria Theresia als Sultanin*.

38. For more detail, see Kaduk, *Maria Theresia und ihre Brüder*; Telesko, *Maria Theresia*, 177 ff. Kaduk's thesis is that it was not so much her biological sex that made Maria Theresa the female antithesis of Frederick II as her place in a dichotomous historical narrative. Men could also occasionally occupy the "female" position.

39. Kretschmayr, *Maria Theresia* (first edition 1925, further editions in 1938, 1939, 1943), 142.

40. Kralik, "Die deutsche Arbeit der Habsburger," in Adam Müller-Guttenbrunn (ed.), *Ruhmeshalle deutscher Arbeit in der österreichisch-ungarischen Monarchie*. Stuttgart/Berlin, 54.

41. Andreas, *Das theresianische Österreich*, 9–10.

42. Srbik, *Gestalten und Ereignisse*, 13, 35–42.

43. Srbik, *Gestalten und Ereignisse*, 37 ff.

44. Heer, *Humanitas Austriaca*, 18 ff., 34–35, 77.

45. Hausenstein, *Europäische Hauptstädte*, 95 ff. The author (1882–1957) was for some time head of the literature section at the *Frankfurter Zeitung* and published a great many popular works on cultural history.

46. Exceptions are the short biographical sketch by Wandruszka, *Maria Theresia*, and the more popular biography by Herre, *Maria Theresia*.

47. Hochedlinger, "Political History," 18.

48. Barbara Sichtermann, *Herscherinnen*, Folge 5: Maria Theresia, in *EMMA* 3 (2010), online, http://www.emma.de/hefte/ausgaben-2010/sommer-2010/herrscherinnen-maria-theresia. Accessed 14/08/2013. An important exception is Barta, *Maria Theresia*. In the overview volume *18th Century Studies in Austria 1945–2010*, ed. Wallnig, Frimmel, and Telesko, Maria Theresa does not appear in the context of the history of women and gender. As Saurer, *Frauengeschichte in Österreich*, 43–44, has pointed out, not only were "general historians" long uninterested in gender history; the opposite was also true.

49. They include the works on the imperial court by Andreas Pečar, Mark Hengerer, Eric Hassler, and Paula Sutter Fichtner. By contrast, Maria Theresa's era is considered in Duindam, *Vienna and Versailles*; Kubiska-Scharl/Pölzl, *Hofpersonal*; Wührer/Scheutz, *Zu Diensten*; Pangerl/Scheutz/Winkelbauer, *Der Wiener Hof*.

50. See, for example, the works by Grete Klingenstein, Christine Lebeau, Franz Szábo, Renate Zedinger, Ivo Cerman, William Godsey, Sandra Hertel, Michael Hochedlinger, Simon Karstens, and others.

51. See the works by David Do Paço, Márta Fata, Andreas Helmedach, Waltraud Heindl, Hans Christian Maner, Stefan Steiner, Anton Tantner, and others; see chapter 13, this volume.

52. See the works by Ilsebill Barta, Michael Yonan, Werner Telesko, and others.

53. A brief overview is offered in Wandruszka, *Maria Theresia*. On the occasion of Maria Theresa's three hundredth anniversary, several biographies and collected volumes appeared, too

late to be consulted for this book: Elisabeth Badinter, *Le pouvoir au féminin* (New York 2016); Bettina Braun, *Eine Kaiserin und zwei Kaiser* (Bielefeld 2018*)*; Thomas Lau, *Die Kaiserin* (Vienna 2016); Braun/Kusber/Schnettger, *Weibliche Herrschaft*; (Berlin, 2020) Iby, et al., *Maria Theresia* (Vienna 2017); Telesko, et al., *Die Repräsentation Maria Theresias* (Wenen 2020).

54. Crankshaw, *Maria Theresia*; Tapié, *Maria Theresia*; Vallotton, *Maria Theresia*; Bled, *Marie-Thérèse*.

55. Etzlstorfer, *Maria Theresia*; while more serious, Franz Herre's biography *Maria Theresia* is unsupported by original archival research and lacks references to the sources. The children's book by Brigitte Hamann, *Ein Herz und viele Kronen. Das Leben der Kaiserin Maria Theresia*, Vienna 1985, is *sui generis*.

56. The classic account is Arneth, *Geschichte Maria Theresia's*, X, 737 ff.; or Walter, *Kaiserin Maria Theresia*.

57. See most recently Simon Karstens, "Die Summe aller Wahrheiten und Lügen: Ein Erfahrungsbericht zur geschichtswissenschaftlichen Biographie," *BIOS* 24 (2011): 78–97; Andreas Bähr, "Die Waffen des Athanasius Kircher SJ (1602–1680): Prolegomena zu einer biographischen Enzyklopädie." *Saeculum* 65 (2015): 135–76.

58. Meier, *Die Faszination des Biographischen*, 109.

59. According to Edoardo Grendi. See also Carlo Ginzburg, "Mikro-Historie," p. 000; Giovanni Levi, "On Microhistory," in Peter Burke, ed., *New Perspectives on Historical Writing*, Cambridge 1991, 93–113; Pohlig, *Vom Besonderen zum Allgemeinen*.

60. This is the criticism made by Bourdieu, *The Biographical Illusion*. He means that every biographer tends to reproduce the meaning that the hero himself imposes on his life story.

61. See Stephan Jaeger, "Multiperspektivisches Erzählen in der Geschichtsschreibung des ausgehenden 20. Jahrhunderts," in Vera and Ansgar Nünning, eds., *Multiperspektivisches Erzählen*, Trier 2000, 323–46.

62. I allude to the formulation of Meier, *Von der Faszination des Biographischen*, 101.

2. The Heiress Presumptive

1. Ceremonial for the birth and baptism of Archduchess Maria Theresa, HHStA OMeA ÄZA 27–12.

2. *Kayserlicher Hof- und Ehrenkalender 1717.*

3. Stöckelle, "Über Geburten," 18, 21.

4. HHStA OMeA ÄZA 27–11.

5. E.g., Marquard Herrgott, . . . ; see Lhotsky, "Apis Colonna."

6. On what follows, see HHStA OMeA ÄZA 27–12; HHStA ZP 1717; *Wienerisches Diarium* 1717; cf. Stöckelle, "Über Geburten"; Stöckelle, "Taufzeremoniell."

7. See Montequieu, *Voyage*, 535; Keyßler, *Neueste Reisen*, 213.

8. Matthaeus Merian, cited in Csendes/Opll, *Wien* II, 25; similarly, Keyßler, *Neueste Reisen*, 1232; Loen, *Gesammelte Kleine Schriften* I, 5; cf. Lorenz, *The Imperial Hofburg*; Lorenz/Mader-Kratky, *Die Wiener Hofburg*.

9. See Rohr, *Einleitung*; Hofmann, *Das Spanisches Hofzeremoniell*; Hengerer, *Kaiserhof und Adel*; Pečar, *Die Ökonomie der Ehre*; on the comparison between the courts, see Duindam, *Vienna and Versailles*.

10. Stöckelle, "Taufzeremoniell," 317.

11. Stollberg-Rilinger, *Rituale*, 55 ff.

12. Ceremonial at the birth and baptism of the Archduchess Maria Theresa, HHStA OMeA ÄZA 27–12.

13. Ibid. Color plate 1: Reliquary with a nail from Christ's cross, cf. Fillitz, Katalog Schatz-kammer, no. 101.

14. Ceremonial at the birth and baptism of the Archduchess Maria Theresa, HHStA OMeA ÄZA 27–12.

15. Stöckelle, "Taufzeremoniell," 283–84; Küchelbecker, *Allerneueste Nachricht*, 8672 ff.

16. Körper, *Studien zur Biographie*; Pölzl, "Die Kaiserinnen"; see also Peper, *Konversionen*, 113 ff.; Römer, "Der Kaiser," 49–50; Schunka, "Irenicism."

17. Keyßler, *Neueste Reisen*, 1229; similarly Loen, *Gesammelte Kleine Schriften* I, 18–19.

18. See, e.g., the anecdote in Seckendorff, "Journal secret," 221–22.

19. Rohr, *Einleitung*, 171.

20. Stöckelle, "Taufzeremoniell," 293.

21. Berger, *Wiennerisches Diarium*; Reisner/Schiemer, "Das Wien(n)erische Diarium"; Lang, "Die Zeitschriften"; Duchkowitsch, "Österreichs Tagespresse"; Weber, *Avisen*; Fischer/Haefs/Mix, *Von Almanach*; Bauer, "Nachrichtenmedien." See chapter 8, this volume.

22. Ceremonial at the birth and baptism of the archduchess Maria Theresa, HHStA OMeA ÄZA 27–12.

23. Rohr, *Ceremoniel-Wissenschaften*, 176. "Image" here means a cast figurine.

24. Coreth, *Pietas Austriaca*, 65, interprets the sacrifice as an analogy to Jesus: the parents sacrifice the child in the same way that Mary and Joseph sacrificed their child in the temple; the child's sacrifice brings salvation to the nations.

25. HStA ZP 10, 1717, fol. 39 ff.

26. Ibid: *Votum et quem caelis impetratum, caelis restitutum, vivum sistere non possunt Leopoldum filium, fecunditatis primitias in auro aequilibri reddunt CaroLUs et eLIsabetha aeternUM DeVotI.*

27. See Krischer, "Souveränität als sozialer Status."

28. Schnettgger, *Der Spanischer Erbfolgekrieg*; overview in Schelling, *Höfe und Allianzen: Deutschland 1648–1763*, Berlin 1998, 257 ff.

29. Lembke, *Als die Royals*.

30. Schulze, "Hausgesetzgebung."

31. Montagu, *Complete Letters* I, 305.

32. HHStA Hausarchiv FA, 2; see Redlich, *Die Tagebücher*.

33. An anonymous and undated half-figure portrait shows her as a child with a doll, herself with doll-like features and with the proportions of a small child, yet in a fashionably tailored, lace-trimmed dress. Only the bonnet tied under her chin, which completely covers her hair, distinguishes her clothing from that of a grown-up. See Koschatzky, *Maria Theresia* (catalog), 26–27, no. 01,09; see also ibid., 29, no. 01,13.

34. Kretschmayr, *Maria Theresia*, 16.

35. Guglia, *Maria Theresia* I, 16; then Herre, *Maria Theresia*, 21.

36. Crankshaw, *Maria Theresia*, 31: "Mix of pomp and coziness."

37. See the literature on Spanish ceremonial cited above, note 9.

38. KMT III, 170–73. In Francis Stephen's will from 1751, Countess Fuchs was remembered as the couple's closest confidante, KMT VI, 401. See also Maria Theresa's correspondence with her lady-in-waiting Trautson née Hager, in van Rhyn, "Unveröffentliche Briefe."

39. KMT III, 173.

40. ZP 14, fol. 69v, April 1728.

41. ZP 14, fol. 290v-291r, 12 May 1729.

42. ZP 14, fol. 388r, 13 May 1730.

43. ZP 14, fol. 446v-447r, 12 May 1731.

44. Sources in Arneth, *Geschichte Maria Theresia's* I, 355.

45. See for example Keyßler, *Neueste Reisen*, 1231; further examples in Mourey, "Tanz- und Ballettkultur," 172–73; Sommer-Mathis, *Tänzer*; Grasberger, "Ein Goldenes Zeitalter," 379–80; Hadamowsky, "'Spectacle mussen sein,'" 387–88; Daniel, *Hoftheater*, 69 ff. See also chapter 7, this volume.

46. Cited in Mraz/Mraz, *Maria Theresia*, 25 (source citation missing).

47. Daniel, *Hoftheater*, 34 ff.

48. Keyßler, *Neueste Reisen*, 1229.

49. See Arneth, *Geschichte Maria Theresia's* I, 13–14.

50. Born in 1676 in Udine, Marinoni taught engineering and mathematics at the Lower Austrian Landschaftsakademie and at the Institute for Nobles. He later taught at the Engineering Academy, penned works on astronomy, and set up an observatory in Vienna. At the start of the century he had designed the new defensive trenches around Vienna. See Bressan/Grassi, *Maria Teresa*, 135 ff.

51. Serenissimarum Archiducum Mariae Theresiae et Mariae Annae Institutiones Historiae, Chronologiae, et Geographiae, pars I-II, ÖNB Wiener Hofbibliothek, Manuscripts no. 7731–7732.

52. Serenissimarum Archiducum Mariae Theresiae et Mariae Annae Institutiones Historiae, Chronologiae, et Geographiae, pars I, ÖNB Wiener Hofbibliothek, Manuscripts no. 7731, fol. 14v.

53. Ibid., fol. 303–316: *Umgekehrte und aus der Natürlichen Ordnung gestellte Historische Fragen Ad memoriam exercendam vexandamve institutae quaestiones.* This appears to have been a written examination. The answers have been entered on the first pages in a clumsy child's handwriting (fol. 303–309), but nothing more follows.

54. Political Testament of 1750/51, BAA 64.

55. James Sheehan, *Der Ausgang des alten Reiches*, Berlin 1994, 42.

56. Crankshaw, *Maria Theresia*, 34.

57. See the letters written between 1724 and 1728 by the tutor Langer about Prince Francis's education at the Viennese court, HHStA LHA 25.

58. See Cerman, *Habsburgischer Adel und Aufklären.*

59. Pichler, *Denkwürdigkeiten*, 14 ff.

60. See Becker, *Sprachvollzug im Amt.*

61. Handwritten note, July 24, 1720, *in Die Briefe König Friedrich Wilhelm I. von Preußen an den Fürsten Leopold zu Anhalt-Dessau, 1704–1740,* ed. Otto Krauske, Berlin 1905, 171.

62. Zedinger, *Franz Stephan*, 31 ff.; Zedinger, *Hochzeit*; Zedinger, *Erziehung*; Arneth, *Geschichte Maria Theresia's* I, 15–16; Guglia, *Maria Theresia* I, 32 ff.; appraisals of the Venetian envoys in Arneth, *Die Relationen* (1725) 45, 62–63; (1732) 75–76; (1736) 80 ff., 129 ff.

63. On what follows, see Zedinger, *Hochzeit*; Zedinger, *Erziehung*.

64. Negotiations of emissary Baron de Jacquemin with the Viennese court concerning the marriage project: HHStA LHA 43–3, fol. 142–43.

65. HHStA LHA 43–3, fol. 104–105: . . . *se conformer au génie de leurs Majestés*.

66. ZP 12, 1723, fol. 201.

67. Letter from Charles VI to Duke Leopold of Lorraine, 2. 9. 1723, HHStA LHA 111, no. 435, fol. 21–22, printed in Arneth, *Geschichte Maria Theresia's* I, 354.

68. In the Schweizerhof building; see Benedik, "Die herrschaftlichen Appartements," 568.

69. See KMT II, 10, 50; Garms-Cornides, "'On n'a qu'a vouloir,'" 106.

70. Letters of the confessor Pater Assel 1724–1726, HHStA LHA 25, fol. 36–73.

71. BKF I, 295, see ibid., 71. [BKF I]

72. Letters of the confessor Pater Assel 1724–1726, HHStA LHA 25, fol. 56–58.

73. See Arneth, *Geschichte Maria Theresia's* I, 15–16.

74. Cited in Zedinger, *Hochzeit*, 81.

75. Francis was enfeoffed with the Duchy of Lorraine by an imperial commissioner without much pomp and ceremony, but in Paris he was all the more spectacularly invested with his other fief, Bar-le-Duc. The French regent placed value on this demonstration of a bond of personal allegiance. Although the new duke had been assured that the enfeoffment ceremony would take place behind closed doors, the doors were kept open in Versailles so that everyone could see how the emperor's close protégé kneeled down three times before the French king. See Zedinger, *Hochzeit*, 72.

76. For more detail, see Zedinger, *Hochzeit*, 94–115.

77. HHStA OMeA ÄZA 37 (1735–1744).

78. Protocols of the Court Council from December 9, 1735, December 17, 1735, and January 6, 1736. HHStA OMeA ÄZA 37–3, here fol. 3r–6r.

79. Report on the engagement and marriage of the Archduchess Maria Theresa to Duke Francis of Lorraine, HHStA OMeA ÄZA 37–10.

80. *Wiener Diarium* 10, 1736. On the sequence of rooms, see Lorenz/Mader-Kratky, *Die Wiener Hofburg*, 320 ff.

81. Report on the engagement and marriage of the Archduchess Maria Theresa to Duke Francis of Lorraine, HHStA OMeA ÄZA 37–10, fol. 3r–v.

82. On February 1, 1736. Report on the engagement and marriage of the Archduchess Maria Theresa to Duke Francis of Lorraine, HHStA OMeA ÄZA 37–10, fol. 5r7r. See Zedinger, *Hochzeit*, 116 ff.

83. HHStA LHA 35, no. 51, fol. 38–49.

84. To Francis Stephen, February 8, 9, and 10, 1736, Arneth, *Geschichte Maria Theresia's* I, 356–57; BAA, 23. See the statements of emissaries Robinson and Foscarini, in Arneth, *Geschichte Maria Theresia's* I, 356.

85. HHStA OMeA ÄZA 37–10, fol. 7r–20v; *Wiener Diarium*, 12.2.1736. See in general Zedinger, *Franz Stephan*, 104 ff.; Zedinger, *Hochzeit*, 116 ff.

86. HHStA OMeA ÄZA 37–10, fol. 16r.

87. HHStA OMeA ÄZA 37–10, fol. 7r ff. See also the description of the lord high steward, Siegmund Friedrich Khevenhüller, ÖNB Codex 14085, 475 ff.; *Wiener Diarium*, 12.2.1736.

88. Report on the engagement and marriage of the Archduchess Maria Theresa to Duke Francis of Lorraine, HHStA OMeA ÄZA 37–10, fol. 14r.

89. The depiction is not to be understood in documentary fashion; according to the ceremonial protocols (HHStA OMeA ÄZA 37, fol. 74) and an illustrated broadsheet (Koschatzky, *Maria Theresia* [catalog], 42, no. 03,11), the nuptial couple sat to the emperor's right; see also Telesko, *Maria Theresia*, 237.

90. See also the marriage of Joseph II with Josepha of Bavaria, 1765, KMT VI, 77.

91. Sommer-Mathis, "*Tu felix*," 68 ff.

92. Court conference from January 6, 1736, HHStA LHA 35–51, fol. 68–77. On problems of precedence, see also HHStA OMeA ÄZA 37–10 and 37–22; Moser, *Teutsches Hof-Recht* I, 534 ff.—see Zedinger, *Franz Stephan*, 116–17; Garms-Cornides, "Liturgie und Diplomatie," 141 ff.

93. Stollberg-Rilinger, *Emperor's Old Clothes*, 130 ff.

94. KMT I, 156, 184, 191–92, 200, 205, likewise the emissaries: KMT I, 234, 241, 256; conflicts after 1745, when Francis became emperor: KMT II, 164; V, 34; VI, 79. See Garms-Cornides, "Liturgie und Diplomatie," 141 ff.; see also chapter 5, this volume.

95. Francis Stephan of Lorraine still insisted on being addressed as "Altesse Royale," continued for a time to bestow Lothringian titles of nobility, and elevated peers—that is, he still acted as head of the "sovereign house of Lorraine," even though he had been forced to renounce his lands in May 1736. Officially, he did not relinquish the lands of Lorraine and Bar until September 1736 and February 1737, respectively.

96. List of court positions: HHStA OMeA ÄZA 37, no. 4.

97. Pečar, *Die Ökonomie der Ehre*; Hengerer, *Kaiserhof und Adel*; Duindam, *Vienna and Versailles*; Duindam, "The Courts"; Ehalt, *Ausdrucksformen*; Hassler, *La cour de Vienne*; Kubiska-Scharl/Pölzl, *Die Karrieren*; Pangerl/Scheutz/Winkelbauer, *Der Wiener Hof*; Mikoletzky, "Der Haushalt"; Žolger, *Der Hofstaat*.

98. Küchelbecker, *Allerneueste Nachricht*, 157 ff.; Keyßler, *Neueste Reisen*, 81st and 82nd letters; Neueste, Voyage en Autriche, 535 ff.; Loen, *Gesammelte Kleine Schriften* I.

99. All court positions, together with the corresponding office-holders and their periods in office, are listed in the court calendars in Kubiska-Scharl/Pölzl, *Die Karrieren*.

100. Hengerer, *Kaiserhof und Adel*, 631.

101. Kubiska-Scharl/Pölzl, *Die Karrieren*, 367.

102. Kubiska-Scharl/Pölzl, *Die Karrieren*, 411–12.

103. Montesquieu (ed.) (1949): *Voyages en Autriche*. Vol. 1 of *Oeuvres complètes*, edited and annotated by Roger Caillois. Paris 1949, 39.

104. Loen, *Gesammelte Kleine Schriften* I, 5 ff.

105. For more detail, see chapter 5, this volume.

106. See chapter 5, this volume.

107. Küchelbecker, *Allerneueste Nachrichten*, 159–60.

108. Loen, *Gesammelte Kleine Schriften* I, 5 ff.

109. See Keller, *Hofdamen*.

110. See Schlögl, *Anwesende*.

111. Pečar, *Die Ökonomie de Ehre*, 118 ff. A diamond-studded imperial portrait given to Prince Adam Franz von Schwarzenberg had an estimated value of 15,000 fl, while the regular salaries

of top court officials amounted to around 2,000 guilders a year. Charles VI rejected the court conference's recommendation that emoluments be considerably increased on the grounds that he preferred "to dispense individual benefits at my pleasure."

112. ÖZV II, 2, Aktenstücke, 394–95, no. 74.

113. *Aularum beneficia sunt lenta, praecipies injuriae,* Moser, *Teutsches Hof-Recht* II, 779.

114. Schmitt, *Gespräch über die Macht,* speaks of the "paradox of power": the more power a ruler is ascribed, the more that is expected from him on all sides, the greater is his reliance on intermediaries: "The more power is concentrated in one place and in the hands of one person, the more the question of access to that place and that individual is intensified. The more fierce, grim, and mute also becomes the struggle among those who occupy the antechamber. . . . Every increase in direct power also thickens the atmosphere of indirect influences. . . . The potentate himself becomes all the more isolated the more direct power is concentrated in his individual person."

115. Kubiska/Scharl/Pölzl, *Die Karrieren*; Bauer, *Repertorium.*

116. An impressive idea of this is conveyed by the instructions of the Duke of Lorraine to his son's chaperone, Craon, intended "to give an idea" of people at the court in Vienna, *comme on les doit regarder a notre egard* (1723), HHStA LHA 43, no. 2, fol. 191–96; as well as the advice given by Friedrich August von Harrach to his younger brother, edited by Garms-Cornides, "'*On n'a qu'a vouloir.*'"

117. On this concept, borrowing from Bourdieu, see Pečar, *Die Ökonomie der Ehre.*

118. Arneth, *Geschichte Maria Theresia's* I, 46 ff.; in more detail Zedinger, *Franz Stephan,* 128 ff.; Garms-Cornides, "Verspätete Hochzeitsreise?"; Bressan/Grassi, *Maria Teresa,* with copperplate series on the journey of homage, 170–71.

119. See Stollberg-Rilinger, *Rituale,* 107 ff.

120. *Beneficar le persone di credito e ben afette fù sempre una delle grand'arti de' Monarchi,* cited in Arneth, *Geschichte Maria Theresia's* I, 371.

121. Arneth, *Geschichte Maria Theresia's* I, 86.

122. Guglia, *Maria Theresia* I, 38, 40.

123. Kretschmayr, *Maria Theresia,* 20.

124. Crankshaw, *Maria Theresia,* 42.

125. To Ulfeld, March 31, 1762, BKF IV, 199.

126. HHStA Family Correspondence A 34–A35 (Correspondence of Maria Theresa 1737–40).

127. HHStA Family Correspondence A 35–1, fol. 72–75.

128. HHStA Family Correspondence A 35–1, fol. 105–106.

129. HHStA Family Correspondence A 34–2 Repertorium Maria Theresa. 1738, fol. 114–17.

130. See the overview of patronage studies in Emich et al., "Stand und Perspektiven."

131. See the pathbreaking work by Wolfgang Reinhard, *Paul V. Borghese (1605–21). Mikropolitische Papstgeschichte,* Stuttgart 2009; on the process for electing the pope, Günther Wassilowsky, *Die Konklavereform Gregors XV. (1621–22): Wertekonflikte, symbolische Inszenierung und Verfahrenswandel im posttridentischen Papsttum,* Stuttgart 2010. Later, for example, Joseph II reported having visited the conclave that elected Clement XIV on his journey to Rome in 1769.

132. Pastor, *Geschichte der Päpste,* XVI, 3–17.

133. HHStA Familienkorrespondenz A 35–2, fol. 51, 68–92.

134. The term is used by Wolfgang Reinhard.

135. On Sinzendorf: Instructions of the Duke of Lorraine, HHStA LHA 43, no. 2, fol. 191r; Charles of Lorraine had no illusions: Urbanski, "Unveröffentlichte Aufzeichungen," 94; see also Arneth, *Geschichte Maria Theresia's* I, 62 ff.

136. HHStA Family Correspondence A 34–2, fol. 30, A 34–2, fol. 2: Repertorium of Maria Theresa's correspondence 1736, compiled by her secretary Wolfscron.

137. Ibid.

138. Seckendorff, "Journal secret," 225.

139. Urbanski, "Unveröffentlichte Aufzeichnungen," 94; likewise Seckendorff, "Journal secret," 208: "hated and despised by the people"; Seckendorff, "Journal secret," 220–21: "wicked heart," etc.

140. Seckendorff, "Journal secret," 201. Christoph Ludwig von Seckendorff (1709–1781) was initially at the Berlin court as legation secretary, then in Vienna, where he was a member of the Imperial Aulic Council from 1735; see Gerhard Rechter, "Christoph Ludwig von Seckendorff-Aberdar," in NDB 24 (2010), 120–21.

141. Braubach, "Ein Satire," 40.

142. Seckendorff, "Journal secret," 208. On the desolate mood in Vienna in these years, see also in the same work, 192, 202, etc.

143. The second-born daughter died on June 6, 1740. See chapter 9, this volume.

144. Quotes from Charles VI in Barta, *Familienporträts*, 68–69, 156; Hennings, *Und sitzet zur Linke Hand*, 197, 201 (without source reference); Redlich, *Die Tagebücher*; Seckendorff, "Journal secret," 270: The Duke of Lorraine was to be pitied—no reasonable man took his side; the birth of a princess dashed all hopes.

145. Seckendorff, "Journal secret," 201.

146. This is Braubach's surmise, "Ein Satire," 75–76.

147. Braubach, "Ein Satire," 22 ff.

3. The War of Succession

1. On the deathbed scene, depicted in his own hand by Francis Stephen, see Arneth, *Geschichte Maria Theresia's* I, 53–54.

2. The terms Upper and Lower Austria are ambiguous. On the one hand, Upper and Lower Austria were the names given to the archduchies above and below the Enns, respectively; this is the sense in which I will be using them in what follows. On the other, in the sixteenth and seventeenth centuries, *both* these duchies were called Lower Austria, while Tyrol, Vorarlberg, and the Habsburg possessions in Alsace, Switzerland, and Swabia went by the name of Upper Austria. This older usage will not be employed here.

3. Schilling, *Hofe und Allianzen*, 306.

4. In the early modern period, once the prince-electors had asserted their voting rights and the pope had lost his right to crown the emperor, the elections of the Roman-German king and the emperor coincided de facto. If the emperor's successor was elected and crowned during his lifetime, he was called "Roman king" until the ruling emperor died, when he assumed the imperial title.

5. For an overview, see Stollberg-Rilinger, *Das Heilige Römische Reich deutscher Nation*.

6. Moser, *Teutsches Staats-Recht* II, 327–28; Ludewig, *Vollständige Erläuterungen* II/1, 639–46.

7. Zedler, *Großes Vollständiges Universal-Lexicon* XV, 342–48 ("Kayserin"); ibid., LIV, 106–7 ("Weiber-Regiment"); see Puppel, "Gynäcocratie"; in general, Braun/Keller/Schnettger, *Nur die Frau des Kaisers?*; Keller, "Frauen und dynastische Herrschaft"; Wunder, *"Er ist die Sonn"*; Wunder, "Herrschaft und öffentliches Handeln."

8. Zedler, *Großes Vollständiges Universal-Lexicon* LIV, 106–7 ("Weiber-Regiment").

9. Where female rulers did not need to be feared by their male relatives as rivals for the throne, having been explicitly and irrevocably excluded by the law of succession, as in France, this paradoxically made it easier for them to rule on behalf of their underage sons; see Cosandey, *La Reine*.

10. See Braun, "Maria Theresia."

11. On the status problems faced by the Lorraine contingent when dealing with foreign diplomats, above all the nuncio, who refused Francis Stephen the respect due a crowned head, see KMT I, 156, 184, 187–88, 191–92, 200, 205, 234, 241, 256; see also chapter 2, this volume; Garms-Cornides, "Liturgie und Diplomatie," 141 ff.

12. On the general significance of this spatial arrangement, see Elias, *Court Society*.

13. Graf, "Das kaiserliche Zeremoniell"; Benedik, "Die herrschaftlichen Appartements"; Benedik, "Zeremoniell"; Mader-Kratky, "Modifizieren."

14. *La principale ed unica sua passione era di non vedersi eguale il marito*, according to the *relazione* of the Venetian emissary, Marco Contarini, written in 1746. Arneth, *Die Relationen*, 290–309, here 304–5.

15. According to Apostolo Zeno, October 20, 1740, cited in Arneth, *Geschichte Maria Theresia's*, I, 370.

16. Heigel, *Das Tagebuch*, 4; on his wife, Maria Amalia of Austria, and her relationship with Maria Theresa, see Kägler, "'so lang diese Frau'"; further information is provided in the reports of the diplomats posted to Vienna by the court in Munich: Grypa/Schmid, *Die Bericht*.

17. See in general Hawlik–van de Water, *Der schöne Tod*; Pangerl/Scheutz/Winkelbauer, *Der Wiener Hof*, 539–43.

18. See Arneth, *Geschichte Maria Theresia's* I, 89: "Particularly in the lower classes, it was increasingly believed that the government had been dissolved with the emperor's death and the prince-elector of Bavaria would be coming to seize possession of the Austrian lands" (source not cited).

19. See Rauscher/Scheutz, *Die Stimme*, 43, 93–94.

20. Arneth, *Geschichte Maria Theresia's* I, 89.

21. On the homage given by the territorial estates, see Godsey, "Herrschaft und politische Kultur," here 151.

22. The archducal hat used here dated from 1616 and was thus not the same one worn by Rudolf IV. Yet by conserving this very specimen in Klosterneuburg and bringing it out each time an act of hereditary homage was performed, an individual history was created that made it uniquely distinctive—a sacralization strategy similar to those common to all the great European monarchies.

23. Kriegl, *Erbhuldigung*; Bressan, *Maria Teresa*, 37 ff.; see Koschatzky, *Maria Theresia* (catalog), 61, no. 66,01; on homage in the land, ibid.,70, no. 07,05; Arneth, *Die Relationen*, 221–89

(Capelo, 1744); see Benedik, "Zeremoniell"; Godsey, "Herrschaft und politische Kultur"; Arneth, *Geschichte Maria Theresia's* I, 89–90.

24. According to Apostolo Zeno, cited in Arneth, *Geschichte Maria Theresia's* I, 99.

25. Arneth, *Geschichte Maria Theresia's* I, 99.

26. Heigel, *Das Tagebuch*, 2–3. On the overall background, see Heigel, *Der Österreichischer Erbfolgekrieg*; Arneth, *Geschichte Maria Theresia's* I, 171–93; further Gotthardt, *Die Kaiserwahl Karls VII.*; Press, "Das wittelsbachisches Kaisertum"; Aretin, *Das Alte Reich* II, 413–70; Koch/Stahl, "Wahl und Krönung"; brief overviews in Schilling, *Höfe und Allianzen*, 287–97; Duchhardt, *Balance of Power*, 303–12.

27. Arneth, *Geschichte Maria Theresia's* I, 171.

28. See Arneth, *Geschichte Maria Theresia's* I, 172 ff.; Beales, "Love and the Empire"; Reinöhl, "Die Übertragung."

29. Tarouca to Harrach, 17. 12. 1740, Karajan, *Maria Theresia und Graf Sylva-Tarouca*, 16–17. According to Khevenhüller, the ministers had no confidence in Francis Stephen; even when he took over the chair of the Court Conference, they withheld their reports from him and waited until Maria Theresa had returned; KMT II, 25–26.

30. Aretin, *Das Altes Reich* II, 418–19, 543–44.

31. Aretin, *Das Altes Reich* II, 419. Johann Jakob Moser discusses this at length in *Teutsches Staats-Recht*, part 32, 393–94. In 1741, several disquisitions appeared on this question addressed to a broad imperial public.

32. Seckendorff, "Journal secret," 207.

33. Kunisch, *Friedrich der Große*, 159 ff.; Blanning, *Frederick the Great*, 80 ff.

34. Kunisch, *Staatsverfassung und Mächtepolitik*, 71.

35. Frederick II to Maria Theresa and Francis Stephen, December 6, 1740 (handwritten), in Arneth, *Geschichte Maria Theresia's* I, 374–78; Droysen, et al. *Die politische Correspondenz* I, 123–24, no. 184.

36. Rescript from Maria Theresa to emissary Botta, December 8, 1740, in Arneth, *Geschichte Maria Theresia's* I, 377.

37. Explanation from January 5, 1741, in Arneth, *Geschichte Maria Theresia's* I, 131 ff.

38. On the course of the war, see Arneth, *Geschichte Maria Theresia's* I, 136 ff.; Anderson, *War of the Austrian Succession*, 59 ff.; Kunisch, *Friedrich der Große*, 185 ff.; Blanning, *Frederick the Great*, 97 ff.

39. According to the Abbot of Niederaltaich in his diary; Schuegraf, "Das französische Lager," 31.

40. A detailed account from the perspective of diplomatic history may be found in Arneth, *Geschichte Maria Theresia's* I, 171–252.

41. See Aretin, *Das Altes Reich* II, 420 ff.

42. To Kinsky, in Arneth, *Geschichte Maria Theresia's* I, 394–95.

43. For example, Arneth, *Geschichte Maria Theresia's* I, 236; Press, "Das wittelsbachisches Kaisertum," 213, speaks of her "iron determination."

44. Aretin, *Das Altes Reich* II, 419.

45. In Arneth, *Geschichte Maria Theresia's* I, 245.

46. In Arneth, *Geschichte Maria Theresia's* I, 396.

47. Treaty of Nymphenburg, September 19, 1741.

48. Secret convention of Kleinschnellendorf, October 9, 1741.

49. Arneth, *Geschichte Maria Theresia's* I, 334.

50. The events are recounted in Arneth, *Geschichte Maria Theresia's* I, 247 ff., 318 ff.; Anderson, *War of the Austrian Succession*.

51. Arneth, *Geschichte Maria Theresia's* I, 238.

52. Arneth, *Geschichte Maria Theresia's* I, 257 ff.

53. On Hungary in the seventeenth and eighteenth century, see Evans, *Das Werder der Habsburgermonarchie*; more briefly, Evans, "Maria Theresa and Hungary"; on the nobility, territorial diet, and system of rule, Barcsay, *Herrschaftsantritt*; Fazekas, "Der Verwaltungsgeschichte"; Brakensiek, "Communication"; most recently, the regional study by Brakensiek/Vári/Pál, *Herrschaft an der Grenze*.

54. Barcsay, *Herrschaftsantritt*; Szíjartó, Diet; Szíjartó, Der Ungarische Landtag.

55. For example, Arneth, *Geschichte Maria Theresia's* I, 258.

56. Bahlcke, "Hungaria elibrarata?," 306.

57. Kolinovics/Kolichich, *Nova Ungariae Periodus*; Schwandtner, *Scriptores rerum hungaricarum*, part 7; Arneth, *Geschichte Maria Theresia's* I, 257 ff.; Barcsay, *Herrschaftsantritt*, 43 ff., 65 ff., 131 ff., 181 ff., 205 ff.

58. The form in which a city received its overlord was highly significant. By solemnly handing over the key to the city, the civic worthies showed that rule was being offered of their own free will; by giving it back, the new ruler showed respect for their traditional autonomy. In this case, too, no detail was left to chance, from the regent's Hungarian attire to the ritual expressions of welcome and the ceremonial place accorded her husband. See Barcsay, *Herrschaftsantritt*, 65 ff., 131 ff.

59. Schwandtner, *Scriptores rerum hungaricarum* II, 539.

60. The wording is cited in full in Schwandtner, *Scriptores rerum hungaricarum* II, 592–93.

61. Official depictions of the coronation in the *Wiener Diarium*, supplement to no. 51, June 28, 1741; Schwandtner, *Scriptores rerum hungaricarum* II, 571 ff.; Richter, *Lebens- und Staats-Beschreibung*, 210 ff.; see Meynert, *Das königliche Krönungsceremoniel*; Barcsay, *Herrschaftsantritt*, 205 ff.; Holcik, *Krönungsfeierlichkeiten*, 38 ff.; images in Bressan/Grassi, *Maria Teresa*, 44 ff.; Polleroß, "Austriacus Hungariae Rex."

62. Barcsay, *Herrschaftsantritt*, 210–11.

63. HHStA ZP 18, 1741; on the conference of June 17, 1741, see Barcsay, *Herrschaftsantritt*, 206.

64. Richter, *Lebens- und Staats-Beschreibung*, 216.

65. Barcsay, *Herrschaftsantritt*, 43–44, 206. In Richter, *Lebens- und Staats-Beschreibung*, 214, however, we read: "Long live Maria Theresa our queen!"

66. Holcik, *Krönungsfeierlichkeiten*, 44.

67. Richter, *Lebens- und Staats-Beschreibung*, 216.

68. Conference of June 17, 1741; see Barcsay, *Herrschaftsantritt*, 206; Polleroß, "Austriacus Hungariae Rex."

69. KMT I, 192. The papal nuncio had refused to take his cardinal's biretta from a woman until the Lord High Chamberlain changed his mind with this justification.

70. Meynert, *Das königliche Krönungsceremonie*, 6 ff.

71. Arneth, *Geschichte Maria Theresia's* I, 265, 279. Citation of emissary Capello, ibid., 403; so too at the Bohemian coronation, see KMT I, 144, 146.

72. Richter, *Lebens- und Staats-Beschreibung,* 217–18.

73. Arneth, *Geschichte Maria Theresia's* I, 287–88.

74. Kolinovics/Kolichich, *Nova Ungariae Periodus,* 302: *soluta in lachrymas.*

75. Arneth, *Geschichte Maria Theresia's* I, 291 ff.

76. Kolinovics/Kolichich, *Nova Ungariae Periodus,* 488 ff.

77. Kolinovics/Kolichich, *Nova Ungariae Periodus,* 492, likewise Capello, cited in Arneth, *Geschichte Maria Theresia's* I, 405.

78. Kolinovics/Kolichich, *Nova Ungariae Periodus,* 493–94.

79. Pichler, *Denkwürdigkeiten,* 17.

80. Wraxall, *Historical and the Posthumous Memoirs* II, 299 ff.; Coxe, *History* III, 268 ff.; Swinburne, *Courts* I, 349–50.

81. Ribeiro, *Dress,* 264.

82. Voltaire, "Late Empress Queen's Appeal"; translation modified. The story is varied around a generation later in Dutens, *Mémoires,* 362–63, where the heir on her arm is already two or three years old. The legend is still being recycled in the catalog of the Austrian national exhibition, *Österreich zur Zeit Josephs II.,* 324, no. 14. On the formation of legends in general, see Mraz, "Anekdoten"; Telesko, *Maria Theresia,* 160 ff.; Heindl, "Marie-Thérèse," 23–24; Koschatzky, *Maria Theresia und ihre Zeit,* 463 ff.; Barcsay, *Herrschaftsantritt,* 263 ff.

83. Koschatzky, *Maria Theresia und ihre Zeit,* 99, 102, 463 ff.; Papp, "Reflexionen zur Ikonografie," 102 ff.

84. Wraxall, *Historical and the Posthumous Memoirs* II, 302–3, cites a purported eyewitness; likewise Swinburne, *Courts* I, 349–350; Coke, *Letters* IV, 49.

85. Mraz, "Anekdoten," 203.

86. Anonymous, "Völkertafel," in Koschatzky, *Maria Theresia und ihre Zeit,* 446.

87. Wandruszka, "Die Historiographie," 24.

88. Arneth, *Geschichte Maria Theresia's* I, 405; Heindl, "Marie-Thérèse," 23–24.

89. Arneth, *Geschichte Maria Theresia's* I, 298–300.

90. Wandruszka, "Die Historiographie," 24; Niederhauser, "Maria Theresia," 31 ff.

91. E.g., in the collectors' albums *Magarinewerke Fritz Homann AG., 1000 Jahre Deutscher Geschichte,* no. 118; *Magarinewerke Fritz Homann AG., Geschichte unserer Welt,* no. 93; *Gartmann Kakao Sammel-Album,* no. 609/5; *Verlag der A.-G. für Automatischen Verkauf Berlin,* Album 7, no. 269/2 (I thank Bernhard Jussen, Frankfurt am Main, for this information).

92. Arneth, *Geschichte Maria Theresia's* I, 302–303; 309 ff.

93. Arneth, *Geschichte Maria Theresia's* I, 305–306; on general developments after 1741, see the overview in Evans, "Maria Theresa and Hungary"; Mraz, *Maria Theresia als Königin von Ungarn.*

94. Memorandum from Bartenstein, in KMT II, Appendix 544 ff.

95. Evans, "Maria Theresa and Hungary."

96. KMT VI, 57.

97. BKF IV, 381. The relic had previously been brought to Vienna in a grand ceremony; see Kervyn de Lettenhove (Konstantin), *Lettres inédites,* 30.

98. The 1741 agreement to incorporate the Banat, wrested back from the Ottomans in 1739, also only began to be implemented in 1778, see Mraz, *Maria Theresia als Königin von Ungarn*, 16; Evans, "Maria Theresa and Hungary," 204–205.

99. Color Plate 4. Coronation series of seven oil paintings by Franz Messner and Wenzel Pohl, 1769–1770; see Galavics, "Barockkunst." In the same setting, court painter Franz Anton Maulbertsch executed the ceiling fresco on the foundation of the Order of St Stephen. It depicted the scene in which Maria Theresa bestows the order's insignia on Count Batthyány.

100. Aretin, *Das Alte Reich* II, 430 ff.; Hartmann, *Karl Albrecht*; citation in Heigel, *Das Tagebuch*, 51.

101. The witness in question was the Duke of Croÿ, who stood in French service: Pleschinski, *Emmanuel de Croy*, 41–42.

102. Zedinger, *Franz Stephan*, 202 ff.

103. See Anderson, *War of the Austrian Succession*, 154 ff.

104. Details on the course of the war in Arneth, *Geschichte Maria Theresia's* II–III; K.u.K. Kriegsarchiv, Österreichischer Erbfolgekrieg; Guglia, *Maria Theresia* I, 137–313; a brief account in Hochedlinger, *Austria's Wars*.

105. See Barta, *Familienporträts*, 68 f.; Koschatzky, *Maria Theresia* (catalog), 96 ff.

106. Anonymous broadsheet, c. 1742, see Koschatzky, *Maria Theresia* (catalog), no. 13,05; Barta, *Familienporträts*, 69–70. Compare with Anthony van Dyck, *Susanna and the Elders* (1626), or Artemisia Gentileschi, *Susanna and the Elders* (1610), among many others.

107. Anonymous broadsheet, c. 1742, see Koschatzky, *Maria Theresia* (catalog), no. 13,06; Mraz/Mraz, *Maria Theresia*, 58.

108. *Een Vrouw van eedel Bloet wird hier beroooft van Lant en Goet.* Anonymous broadsheet, c. 1742, Rijksmuseum Amsterdam.

109. *The consultation of the Physicians, on the Case of the Queen of Hungary.* Anonymous broadsheet. Vienna, Albertina, Hist. Bl. Maria Theresia 624, see Koschatzky, *Maria Theresia* (catalog), no. 13,02.

110. *Eröffnung des Balles, den die europäischen Mächte im großen Saale Deutschland abgehalten haben.* Anonymous etching, 1742, see Mraz/Mraz, *Maria Theresia*, 65.

111. *Politisches Billardspiel.* Copperplate by Johann Martin Will, Augsburg; Budapest, Magyar Nemzeti Museum, Inv. no. 58.1153; see Koschatzky, *Maria Theresia* (catalog), no. 13,03.

112. Frankfurt coronation medallion, 317, no. 291.

113. Arneth, *Geschichte Maria Theresia's* II, 244 ff.; for an opposing view, see Berning, "Nach alltem löblichen Gebrauch," 179 ff.

114. To Kinsky from Prague, May 1743, in Arneth, *Geschichte Maria Theresia's* II, 514; BAA, 33.

115. Berning, "Nach alltem löblichen Gebrauch," 170 ff.

116. Schmidt, *Wandel durch Vernunft*, 148.

117. Ramhoffsky, *Drey Beschreibungen*, KMT I, 144 ff.; Koschatzky, *Maria Theresia* (catalog), 90 ff.; Bressan/Grassi, *Maria Teresa*, 50 ff.

118. KMT I, 145.

119. Arneth, *Geschichte Maria Theresia's* III, 429; on the female title, see Berning, "Nach alltem löblichen Gebrauch," 182. On the imperial coronation, see chapter 4, this volume.

120. Richter, *Lebens- und Staatsgeschichte*, 1747, part 4, 1–2; see Telesko, "Herrschaftssicherung," 42–43.

121. Arneth, *Geschichte Maria Theresia's* II, 515; Hassenpflug-Elzholz, *Böhmen*, 429 ff.; Berning, *"Nach alltem löblichen Gebrauch,"* 183 ff. On the "terrible ceremonies" later in Prague (1750), see Maria Theresa to Countess Trautson, in van Rhyn, "Unveröffentlichte Briefe," 268.

122. Berning, *"Nach alltem löblichen Gebrauch,"* 185. On Linz, see Arneth, *Geschichte Maria Theresia's* II, 515.

123. KMT I, 147; see in general Cerman, "Opposition."

124. Guglia, *Maria Theresia* I, 190 ff; Arneth, *Geschichte Maria Theresia's* II, 283 ff.

125. See Maria Theresa to Ulfeld, BKF IV, 184.

126. Treaty of Worms, September 13, 1743 (cession of Piacenza and parts of Lombardy to Sardinia); see Guglia, *Maria Theresia* II, 279 ff.

127. Guglia, *Maria Theresia* I, 196–97.

128. Mazura, *Die preußische und österreichische Kriegspropaganda*.

129. Report of the Venetian emissary Erizzo, November 27, 1746, in Arneth, *Geschichte Maria Theresia's* III, 436–37.

130. According to the English emissary Robinson, August 4, 1745, cited in Coxe, *History* III, 163; see Arneth, *Geschichte Maria Theresia's* III, 87 ff., 425; Guglia, *Maria Theresia* I, 261.

131. On the imperial election, see Zedinger, *Franz Stephan*, 179 ff.; Aretin, *Das Alte Reich* III, 25–26.

132. See Zedinger, *Franz Stephan*, 190. On the pro-Austrian writings of the election debate, see Vajnágy, "The Habsburgs."

133. Arneth, *Geschichte Maria Theresia's* III, 104 ff.; Aretin, *Das Alte Reich* III, 19 ff.; see below.

134. KMT II, 192–93.

135. KMT II, 193; Khevenhüller's opinion, KMT II, 467 ff.

136. Arneth, *Geschichte Maria Theresia's* III, 372; Guglia, *Maria Theresia* I, 302 ff.

137. Anderson, *War of the Austrian Succession*, 193 ff.

138. Ulfeld to Kaunitz, June 30, 1748 and July 17, 1748, in Arneth, *Geschichte Maria Theresia's* III, 486.

139. To Kaunitz, October 5, 1748, cited in Arneth, *Geschichte Maria Theresia's* III, 488.

140. Arneth, *Geschichte Maria Theresia's* III, 384.

141. Guglia, *Maria Theresia* I, 296.

142. Hochedlinger, "Rekrutierung," 329–330.

143. Schuegraf, "Das österreichische Lager," 71.

144. To Kinsky, December 1741, BAA, 27–28; Arneth, *Geschichte Maria Theresia's* I, 414–15.

145. Cited in Arneth, *Geschichte Maria Theresia's* II, 549.

146. Rohr, *Einleitung*, 493.

147. The heroine bemoans the *misera servitù del nostro sesso*, cited in Guglia, *Maria Theresia* I, 27–28.

148. From the "Political Testament,'" her apologia from 1751, BAA, 81.

149. Hinrichs, *Friedrich der Große*, 48.

150. In an oft-cited letter to her commander Khevenhüller, she sent a portrait of herself with the successor to the throne, describing it as the "queen abandoned by the whole world with her

male heir." To Khevenhüller, BAA, 29. Contemporary historians already remarked on this: Richter, *Lebens- und Staatsgeschichte* I, 266; Anonymous, *Geschichte und Taten* I, 661; see Barta, *Familienporträts*, 72–73.

151. Telesko, *Maria Theresia*, 11 ff., 23, 65 ff., 123 ff.

152. See chapter 6, this volume.

153. Urbanski, "Unveröffentlichte Aufzeichnungen," 91: "Certainly, from the first day of her reign, her admirable natural realism was tied to her womanhood in almost organic fashion, and currents of affection spilled over unconsciously and imperceptibly from the main pole, her husband, to her charming brother-in-law." See Hinrichs, *Friedrich der Große* 74 ff. See chapter 8, this volume.

154. To Francis Stephen, August 24, 1742, BAA, 32.

155. To Ulfeld, July 31, 1743, BAA, 33.

156. To Field Marshal Traun, Arneth, *Geschichte Maria Theresia's* II, 547.

157. Cited in Guglia, *Maria Theresia* I, 154, and see 152.

158. To Francis Stephen, August 24, 1742, BAA, 32.

159. Ibid., BAA, 33; Arneth, *Geschichte Maria Theresia's*, II, 490–491. See too her later self-assessment: "Up to the Peace of Dresden I acted boldly, shrank from no risk, and spared no effort. . . ." Political Testament of 1750–51, BAA, 80.

160. To Dietrichstein, February 14, 1746, BAA, 50. See also the letters to Field Marshal Neipperg, BKF IV, 139 ff.

161. To Dietrichstein, undated (1745?), BKF IV, 164.

162. To Doblhoff, December 1, 1741, BAA, 26–27.

163. To Doblhoff, January 12, 1742, BAA, 30.

164. To Bartenstein, May 5, 1743, in Guglia, *Maria Theresia* I, 192; see also Hinrichs, *Friedrich der Große*, 133 ff.

165. To Ulfeld, early 1744, BAA, 38.

166. To Dietrichstein, mid-1745, BAA, 45.

167. To Dietrichstein, undated, BAA, 46.

168. To Dietrichstein, August 18, 1748, BAA, 58; see also the letter from January 24, 1746, BAA, 48.

169. KMT II, 178–79.

170. Tarouca to Maria Theresia, Autumn 1754, Karajan, *Maria Theresia und Graf Sylva-Tarouca*, 27.

171. See chapter 7, this volume.

172. August 27, 1744, KMT I, 241; by contrast, scuffles broke out during the solemn consecration of the Kolowrat regiment's flag when an officer took offense. May 15, 1748, KMT II, 224–25.

173. Luh, *Kriegskunst*, 177 ff.

174. Luh, *Kriegskunst*, 200, 208.

175. E.g., KMT I, 249; II, 146, 217, 283, 349; to Archduke Ferdinand, BKF I, 299, 325; to Countess Trautson, van Rhyn, "Unveröffentlichte Briefe," 271–72.

176. So, for instance, at the maneuvers of Moltke's and Harrach's regiments, September 10, 1749, KMT II, 349.

177. To Trautson, August 1754, van Rhyn, "Unveröffentlichte Briefe," 271.

178. KMT I, 144–45, 153, 164; II, 41–42, 46–47, 96, 98, 107–108 etc. See Küster, *Vier Monarchien*, on the relatively modestly celebrated victory at Dettingen, at which only a few Austrian troops had been involved.

179. On Maria Theresa's policy toward the press, see chapter 8, this volume.

180. KMT I, 235.

181. KMT II, 63 ff. on the defeat at Fontenoy on June 4, 1745. See also the special edition of the *Wiener Diarium* printed to accompany no. 52, 1745. On the defeat at Maastricht in July 1747, which shows how unpleasant truths were "made known to the public," see KMT II, 166, 437.

182. To Ferdinand, September 8, 1774, BKF I, 299.

183. To Franz Count Thurn, Leopold's Aya, 1761, BKF IV, 17, 21. All sons were given their own regiments as children; see chapter 9, this volume.

184. E.g., Hinrichs, *Friedrich der Große*, 48.

185. KMT I, 196: thanks to Maria Theresa's example, riding had become the latest fashion among the ladies of Vienna; on the risks to pregnancy, KMT II, 108–109; KMT I, 117–18: the tendency of some women to ride "in the male position" gave rise to "remarks."

186. Guibert, *Journal* I, 293.

187. See Seitschek, "Karussell," with an exact reconstruction of the rules; Iby/Koller, *Schönbrunn*, 83; for a general overview, Béhar/O'Kelly, *Spectaculum*, 593 ff.; for France, Wrede, *Ohne Furcht*, 322 ff.

188. Beschreibung des . . . Frauen-Carrousels, Vienna 1743, cited in Küster, *Vier Monarchien*, 111; see *Wienerisches Diarium* from January 9, 1743.

189. Description in the ceremonial protocols, in Seitschek, "Karussell," 412 ff.

190. *Gazette de France* from February 9, 1743, quoted in Küster, *Vier Monarchien*, 113.

191. KMT I, 111, 113, 117–18; quote from Francis Stephen in Arneth, *Geschichte Maria Theresia's* II, 506.

192. Arneth, *Geschichte Maria Theresia's* II, 193–94.

193. On van Meytens' coronation cycle, see Macek, "Der Krönungszyklus"; Telesko, *Maria Theresia*, 83 ff. Images of the 1743 carousel are also found outside the hereditary lands, for example, in the Dresden copperplate cabinet (image reproduced in Seitschek, "Karussell," 367).

194. Fleming, *Der vollkommene teutsche Soldat.*

195. Fleming, *Der vollkommene teutsche Soldat.*

196. Crankshaw, *Maria Theresia*, 113.

197. Luh, *Kriegskunst*, 27 ff., 34 ff.

198. Luh, *Kriegskunst*, 42 ff.

199. For a general overview, see Luh, *Kriegskunst*, 13 ff.

200. Marian Fussel and Michael Sikora, eds., *Kulturgeschichte der Schlacht*, Paderborn 2014.

201. KMT I, 127.

202. Schuegraf, "Das französische Lager," 31.

203. KMT I, 239; much the same could be said of the later battles of Lobositz (October 1, 1756) and Zorndorf (August 25, 1758).

204. See Spies/Winter, *Die Schlacht bei Dettingen*; Küster, *Vier Monarchien.*

205. Spies/Winter, *Die Schlacht bei Dettingen*, 78.

206. Cited in Spies/Winter, *Die Schlacht bei Dettingen*, 62.

207. "The battle of Dettingen," in *Genealogisch-historische Nachrichten von den allerneuesten Begebenheiten*, part 54, Leipzig 1744, 491 ff., here 509–10; Spies/Winter, *Die Schlacht bei Dettingen*, 63. See the description of the field hospital set up in the Saint Afra school in Meissen following the battle of Kesselsdorf on December 15, 1745, written by one of the pupils at the school, the young Gotthold Ephraim Lessing: Lessing to J. G. Lessing, February 1, 1746.

208. Hochedlinger, "Rekrutierung," 339.

209. Hochedlinger, "Rekrutierung"; Duffy, *Army*.

210. Rothenberg, *Die österreichische Militärgrenze*, 98; for a general overview, see Kaser, *Freier Bauer*.

211. Kunisch, *Der Kleine Krieg*; Rink, *Partheygänger*.

212. Arneth, *Geschichte Maria Theresias* I, 260, citation on 401.

213. Arneth, *Geschichte Maria Theresias* I, 267; on the copperplates of Martin Engelbrecht, see Popelka, "Martin Engelbrecht"; Bleckwenn, "Der Kaiserin Hayducken."

214. Mraz/Mraz, *Maria Theresia*, 87.

215. Krajasich, "Die österreichische Militrgrenze"; Schwicker, *Geschichte*; Rothenberg, *Die österreichische Militärgrenze*; Göllner, *Die Siebenbürgische Militärgrenze*; Kaser, *Freier Bauer*.

216. M. Engelbrecht, *Théatre*, quoted in Popelka, "Martin Engelbrecht," 45. See also Anonymous, *Merckwürdige Historische Nachrichten von den bey den jetzigen Kriegen von neuem bekannt gewordenen Völckern*, Jena 1743.

217. See Kosean-Makrau, "Die gefälschten Memoiren," who unabashedly takes the side of his hero and downplays the charge of *raptus*—rape by Trenck and his officers—to a "private pastoral idyll" with a "clearly willing girl" (ibid.,17). On the burning, see KMT II, 218–19.

218. Von der Trenck, *Die "Blutbibel"*, 42.

219. Von der Trenck, *Die "Blutbibel"*, 42 ff.; see Julian Pallua-Gall, "Trenck, Franz Freiherr von der," ADB 38 (1894), 566–68; Arneth, *Geschichte Maria Theresias* IV, 103 ff.; also Franz von der Trenck's autobiography (*Merckwürdiges Leben*), where he dismisses the atrocities he was alleged to have committed as malicious rumors while claiming that others acted no better, anyway. The unusually partisan biography by Preradovich, *Das seltsame wilde Leben*, 1980, follows the memoirs entirely and transfigures Trenck into a dashing adventurer.

220. Von der Trenck, *Die "Blutbibel"*, 23; likewise Hinrichs, *Friedrich der Große*, 111.

221. Hinrichs, *Friedrich der Große*, 110–11.

222. From the Bavarian perspective, Heigel, *Das Tagebuch*, 53, 78.

223. Hinrichs, *Friedrich der Große*, 110.

224. Schuegraf, "Das französische Lager"; ibid.

225. Schuegraf, "Das französische Lager," 37, 39, 42; Schuegraf, "Das österreichische Lager," 37, 42, 46.

226. Schuegraf, "Das französische Lager," 18, 37.

227. Schuegraf, "Das französische Lager," 24, 31–32, 34.

228. Schuegraf, "Das österreichische Lager," 37.

229. Schuegraf, "Das österreichische Lager," 47, 59–60.

230. Schuegraf, "Das französische Lager," 24, 47.

231. Schuegraf, "Das französische Lager," 44; Schuegraf, "Das österreichische Lager," 14–15.

232. Schuegraf, "Das österreichische Lager," 18.

233. Hinrichs, *Friedrich der Große*, 110.

234. Hinrichs, *Friedrich der Große*, 110.

235. Hinrichs, *Friedrich der Große*, 111.

236. Franz von der Trenck, *Merckwürdiges Leben*, quoted in Kurt Sonntag, *Trenck der Pandur und die Brandschatzung Bayerns*, Munich 1976, 41–42; on the source's unreliability, see Kosean-Mokrau, "Die Gefälschte Memoiren."

237. Kosean-Mokrau, "Die Gefälschte Memoiren," 17.

238. Preradovich, *Das seltsam wilde Leben*, 263. There is a legend, still being told to tourists in Croatia today, that Maria Theresa and Trenck subsequently met in Kutjevo, a former Cistercian monastery. There they shut themselves off in the wine cellar and spent a week in each other's arms, making love a grand total of seventy times, as indicated by the seventy notches still visible in the wall today. An indentation in a nearby stone table supposedly shows that the empress's passion was strong enough to melt stone. (I thank Maria Pakucz, Bucharest, for this information.)

239. According to the investigating committee's final report; see Preradovich, *Das seltsam wilde Leben*, 263.

240. Ulfeld to Maria Theresa, December 19, 1746, in Arneth, *Geschichte Maria Theresia's* IV, 106.

241. Khevenhüller, KMT II, 258; von der Trenck, *Die "Blutbible"*, 44, writes that the protector in question was the Prince of Lorraine; see also Hinrichs, *Friedrich der Große*, 111, according to whom Trenck bribed one of the empress's chambermaids to save himself.

242. The characterization of Königsegg as a nobleman of "boundless selflessness" in Hinrichs, *Friedrich der Große*, 78 ff.

243. KMT I, 258, 518.

244. Arneth, *Geschichte Maria Theresia's* IV, 104 ff.; Ulfeld to Maria Theresa, March 3, 1747.

245. To Doblhoff, July 30, 1748, BKF IV, 219–20.

246. Handwritten resolution, in Arneth, *Geschichte Maria Theresia's* IV, 104.

247. Allegedly, Trenck personally promised her to be the first to cross the Rhine and drive back the French. Arneth, *Geschichte Maria Theresia's* II, 394–95, 548–49.

248. To Doblhoff, July 30, 1748, BKF IV, 220. See Maria Theresa's later efforts to punish excesses, e.g., BAA, 82 etc.

249. Montagu, *Complete Letters* I, 338.

250. To Charles of Lorraine, January 27, 1742, in Arneth, *Geschichte Maria Theresia's* II, 465.

251. Cited in Arneth, *Geschichte Maria Theresia's* II, 465.

252. Arneth, *Geschichte Maria Theresia's* II, 110 ff., 489.

253. Stollberg-Rilinger, *Rituale*, 172–73.

254. To Francis Stephen, in Arneth, *Geschichte Maria Theresia's* II, 489.

255. Report of the Venetian emissary Capello, July 28, 1742, in Arneth, *Geschichte Maria Theresia's* II, 111–12, 489 (he uses the verb *saccheggiarono*).

256. Francis Stephen to Maria Theresa, July 29, 1742: HHStA Familienkorr. A 36–1, fol. 539.

257. Guglia, *Maria Theresia* I, 151.

258. Moser, *Kleine Schriften* I, 47–48.

259. Francis Stephen to Frederick II, in Arneth, *Geschichte Maria Theresia's* I, 397; see also the view of Hinrichs, *Friedrich der Große*, 60, on good relations between Francis Stephen and Frederick II.

260. Rohr, *Einleitung*, 493–94.

261. Luh, *Kriegskunst*, 214.

262. Schuegraf, "Das österreichische Lager," 10.

263. Rohr, *Einleitung*, 496–97.

264. KMT V, 16 ff.

265. Schuegraf, "Das französische Lager," 18.

266. Schuegraf, "Das französische Lager," 21.

267. Schuegraf, "Das österreichische Lager," 60.

268. Schuegraf, "Das österreichische Lager," 31.

269. See chapter 8, this volume.

4. Empress, Emperor, Empire

1. Goethe, *Autobiography*, 167.

2. Goethe gives a psychological explanation for this. *Autobiography*, 167–8.

3. Goethe, *Autobiography*, 151; translation modified.

4. To date, there has been no study of how empresses were crowned; for a brief account, see Stollberg-Rilinger, *Emperor's Old Clothes*, 161 ff., as well as scattered remarks in Braun/Keller/ Schnettger, *Nur die Frau des Kaisers?*

5. Arneth, *Geschichte Maria Theresia's* III, 104 ff., 429–30; further Aretin, *Das Alte Reich* III, 28 ff.; Zedinger, *Franz Stephan*, 188 ff.

6. Francis Stephen to Maria Theresa, August 5, 1745; to Ulfeld, August 18, 1745, in Arneth, *Geschichte Maria Theresia's* III, 430.

7. Cited in Arneth, *Geschichte Maria Theresia's* III, 106, 430. Maria Theresa's letters to her chambermaid Hager show how she viewed the coronation journey: van Rhyn, "Unveröffentlichte Briefe," 175 ff.; she says nothing there about the coronation ritual.

8. Ulfeld to Francis Stephen, August 22, 1745, in Arneth, *Geschichte Maria Theresia's* III, 429.

9. See also Arneth, *Geschichte Maria Theresia's* III, 105–6; Aretin, *Das Alte Reich* III, 28; Schmid, "Franz I.," 236; Yonan, *Empress*, 30; Rohrschneider, *Österreich*, 39. Zedinger, *Franz Stephan*, 189 ff., believes that Maria Theresa felt betrayed by the empire and therefore turned down the coronation.

10. Zedler, *Großes Vollständiges Universal-Lexicon* XV, s. v. Kayserin; see Braun/Keller/ Schnettger, *Nur die Frau des Kaisers?*; on Maria Theresa, Braun, "Maria Theresan, Herrscherin."

11. Zedinger, *Franz Stephan*, 192.

12. KMT VI, 31, 41, 206 etc.

13. KMT III, 41. So too in oaths of office, KMT III, 229. For an overview, see Benedik, "Zeremoniell"; Graf, "Das kaiserlich Zeremoniell"; Pangerl/Scheutz/Winkelbauer, *Der Wiener Hof*, 268 ff.

14. KMT II, 316; KMT III, 41, 51, 168 (Venice); Maria Theresa often also dispensed with the dual audience, however, and received only once, but then always *as queen*; KMT III, 24, 27–29, 68, 186, 199.

15. The lord high chamberlain once noted that the French emissary had committed the faux pas of presenting his accreditation to Maria Theresa instead of the emperor: KMT III, 24; see also Moser, *Kleine Schriften* I, 30: Maria Theresa did not accept a compliment because the emperor had been ignored.

16. Quoted by the English emissary Robinson, August 4, 1745, in Coxe, *History* III, 318; see Arneth, *Geschichte Maria Theresia* III, 87 ff., 425; she expressed similar sentiments to her Imperial Diet delegate Palm in 1745, cited in Rohrschneider, *Österreich*, 42. Maria Theresa immediately sought to capitalize on the regained imperial dignity for the War of Succession by attempting (albeit unsuccessfully) to muster imperial troops.

17. See Matsche, "Maria Theresias Bild," 203; Telesko, "Herrschaftssicherung," on further depictions of Maria Theresa as empress with the imperial crown. She is still listed as "Empress of Austria" in the indexes of specialist historical works. Even Alfred von Arneth, who ought to have known better, called her "Austria's greatest Empress"; Arneth, "Maria Theresia und der Hofrath von Greiner," 6.

18. On Francis Stephen as emperor: a brief account in Arneth, *Geschichte Maria Theresia's* IV, 145 ff.; thoroughly explored in Aretin, *Das Alte Reich* III, 19 ff.; Schmid, "Franz I . . . der unbekannter Kaiser"; Schmid, "Franz I. und Maria Theresia"; Schmidt, *Wandel durch Vernunft*, 153 ff.; Zedinger, *Franz Stephan*, 179 ff.; a cursory overview in Gnant, "Franz Stephan"; for more detail, see recently Rohrschneider, *Österreich*.

19. See KMT VI, 136–37; Francis Stephen's will, ibid., 401.

20. See chapter 2, this volume. On the nuncio, see KMT I, 156, 184, 191–92, 200, 205, likewise the diplomats: KMT I, 234, 241, 256; KMT II, 44–45, 49; Sorel, *Recueil des instructions*, 257–58 (instruction for Mirepoix, 1737) for many others. One example: note on the nonappearance of the nuncio and the Venetians emissary at the court table (HHStA OMeA ÄZA 37–22). See Garms-Cornides, "Liturgie und Diplomatie."

21. Hinrichs, *Friedrich der Große*, 54 ff., 153–54; Ranke, "Maria Theresa und ihr Hof," 676 ff.; Arnheim, "Das Urtheil," 291–92 ("complete submission to the Empress's views"); KMT II, 10, 50, 94, 158; VI, 136–37; Ligne, *Fragments* I, 111; Zinzendorf, *Aus den Jugendtagebücher*, 200.

22. Hinrichs, *Friedrich der Große*, 55.

23. KMT VI, 15.

24. Instruction De Feu de Majesté l'Empereur François I pour son fils Leopold donnée 1765, ÖNB Wiener Hofbibliothek, Codex Series N. 1713; see Wandruzska, *Die Religiosität*.

25. See KMT I, 131–2; on the many noble members of Viennese lodges, see Krivanec, "Die Anfänge."

26. *une amitié sincère et une confiance entire entre Mari et Femme*; Instruction De Feu de Majesté l'Empereur François I pour son fils Leopold donnée 1765, ÖNB Wiener Hofbibliothek, Codex Series N. 1713, fol. 3r-7r.

27. Instruction De Feu de Majesté l'Empereur François I pour son fils Leopold donnée 1765, ÖNB Wiener Hofbibliothek, Codex Series N. 17131 8r-v.

28. See chapter 6, this volume.

29. Hinrichs, *Friedrich der Große*, 49.

30. KMT II, 111.

31. Quoted on the occasion of Francis Stephen's death in 1765: KMT VI, 136.

32. This, at any rate, was the claim made by Podewils himself: Hinrichs, *Friedrich der Große*, 153–54.

33. KMT II, 270, 314.

34. Hinrich, *Friedrich der Große*, 62.

35. KMT II, 49–50, 381–82.

36. Cited in Arneth, *Geschichte Maria Theresias* VII, 153. An impression of his idiosyncratic prose is conveyed in his handwritten testament, printed in KMT VI, 396 ff. He barely spoke German and almost never wrote it, not to mention Latin; see KMT VI, 122.

37. See chapter 6, this volume.

38. Instruction De Feu de Majesté l'Empereur François I pour son fils Leopold donnée 1765, ÖNB Wiener Hofbibliothek, Codex Series N. 1713, fol. 24v.

39. KMT II, 94. June 15, 1746. Negotiations with the Spanish ambassador concerned which ceremonial concessions could be demanded of the king of Sardinia-Piedmont, Francis Stephen's in-law.

40. This was observed, for example, by the English emissary Williams, cited in Arneth, *Geschichte Maria Theresias* IV, 149–50.

41. Zedinger, *Franz Stephan*, 241 ff.; see also Benedik, "Zeremoniell."

42. *le purgatoire dans ce monde*, according to Instruction De Feu de Majesté l'Empereur François I pour son fils Leopold donnée 1765, ÖNB Wiener Hofbibliothek, Codex Series N. 1713, fol. 7r.

43. Cited in Arneth, *Geschichte Maria Theresias* IV, 145.

44. E.g., KMT VI, 113.

45. Mikoletzky, *Kaiser Franz I*; Mikoletzky, "Die privaten 'geheimen Kassen'"; Zedinger, *Franz Stephan*, 224 ff.

46. On the Privy Court Conference and the State Chancellery, see chapter 5, this volume.

47. Hinrichs, *Friedrich der Große*, 55 ff., 63; similarly Ranke, "Maria Theresia und ihr Hof," 683.

48. Schmid, "Franz I . . . der unbekannter Kaiser." Podewils, who otherwise gave him little credit, saw him as the brains behind Haugwitz's financial reforms. Hinrichs, *Friedrich der Große*, 141.

49. On Kaunitz and Bartenstein, see chapter 5, this volume.

50. Hinrichs, *Friedrich der Große*, 55–56: "This princess [Maria Theresa] and her ministers steer him, above all in imperial affairs, which he knows precious little about"; see ibid., 86–87, 92 ff., 103.

51. See HHStA Staatskanzlei, Vorträge Kartons 51 ff.

52. Note on the foreign system from March 18, 1749, HHStA Staatskanzlei Vorträge 62 (Konferenzvota 1749), quotation on fol. 25r. Maria Theresa called for opinions on March 7, 1749. According to Schmid, "Franz I . . . Der unbekannter Kaiser," 9, the first memorandum in the series was in all likelihood offered by the emperor himself.

53. Hinrichs, *Friedrich der Große*, 64; ibid., 154 on the question of revising the secession of Silesia in 1747; see Schmid, "Franz I . . . Der unbekannter Kaiser," 10.

54. KMT IV, 141, December 31, 1757.

55. According to Schmid, "Franz I . . . Der unbekannter Kaiser," 7–8; see Zedinger, *Franz Stephan*, 17.

56. See Schnettger, *Imperium Romanum*. On the Austrian historiography regarding the old empire, Brauneder/Höbelt, *Sacrum Imperium*. Arneth, *Geschichte Maria Theresia's* IV, 149–50, speaks of the weight of the imperial crown but barely discusses Francis in his role as emperor.

57. Cited in Seckendorff, "Journal secret," 126.

58. Exceptions: Schmid, "Franz I . . . Der Unbekannter Kaiser"; Schmid, Franz I Zedinger, and Zedinger/Schmale et al. have revised the image of Francis I but almost entirely neglected imperial policy. That is no less true of Schmid, *Wandel durch Vernunft*, 153 ff. The most important source is still Aretin, *Das Alte Reich* III, 19–112; see now Rohrschneider, *Österreich*, as well as the works by Haug-Moritz.

59. See Haug-Moritz, *Die Krise*.

60. See Guglia, *Maria Theresia* I, 224; in more detail Mazura, *Die preußische und österreichische Kriegspropaganda*; Küster, *Vier Monarchien*.

61. Gerhard Dilcher, "Vom ständischen Herrschaftsvertrag zum Verfassungsgesetz," *Der Staat* 27 (1988): 161–93.

62. Stollberg-Rilinger, *Emperor's Old Clothes*, 239 ff., 269 ff.

63. E.g., Maria Theresa to Khevenhüller, 1758, in Wolf, *Aus dem Hofleben*, Appendix, 331.

64. See Stollberg-Rilinger, *Emperor's Old Clothes*, 145–46; Klueting, *Das Reich*; on the question of tolerance see chapter 12, this volume.

65. On the basic features of the imperial constitution, see Stollberg-Rilinger, *Das Heilige Römische Reich deutscher Nation*; on the relationship between the Empire and the hereditary lands, see Brauneder/Höbelt, *Sacrum Imperium*.

66. Guglia, *Maria Theresia* I, 226.

67. Anonymous memorandum submitted by Colloredo in 1746, HHStA Reichskanzlei Vorträge 6d; minutes of the conference ministers from March 1749 (Königsegg, Ulfeld, Harrach, Colloredo, Khevenhüller, Bartenstein, and Kaunitz): HHStA Reichskanzlei Vorträge 62.—For a general overview, see Aretin, *Das Alte Reich* III, 33–34; Schmidt, *Wandel durch Vernunft*, 153 ff.; Rohrschneider, *Österreich*, 42 ff.

68. Votum Colloredos (1746), HHStA Reichskanzlei Vorträge 6d, fol. 111–12.

69. See in general Stollberg-Rilinger, *Das Heilige Römische Reich deutscher Nation*, 10 ff.

70. On the rank order of European potentates, see Lünig, *Theatrum ceremoniale*.

71. Press, "Patronat," 36; Rohrschneider, *Österreich*.

72. She had claimed as much in two written protests and had them officially published by the prince-elector of Mainz in Regensburg. On the Empire during the Wittelsbach intermezzo, see Aretin, *Das Alte Reich* II, 413 ff.; Duchhardt, "Philipp Karl von Eltz"; Solf, *Die Reichspolitik*; Meisenburg, *Der deutsche Reichstag*.

73. KMT I, 147.

74. HHStA OMeA ÄZA 45–10 (submission with Maria Theresa's handwritten resolution on establishing a new chamber order); HHStA OMeA ÄZA 45–11 (Conference opinions and imperial resolutions on establishing a new chamber order); see Benedik, Zeremoniell; Graf, Zeremoniell.

75. Lord High Chamberlain Khevenhüller still found the ceremonial insufficiently imperial for his liking.

76. On the emperor's dispute with the prince-electors and princes over the rite of investiture, a crisis symptom of the imperial confederation, see Stollberg-Rilinger, *Emperor's Old Clothes*, 256 ff.; Begert, *Die böhmische Kur*, 547 ff.; Braun, "Maria Theresia," 217.

77. See in general Stollberg-Rilinger, *Emperor's Old Clothes*.

78. The imperial history specialists see eye to eye on this: e.g., Aretin, *Das Alte Reich* III, 30, 81; Haug-Moritz, *Die Krise*.

79. Schmidt, *Wandel durch Vernunft*, 153.

80. On Ostein, see Solf, *Die Reichspolitik*.

81. Hinrichs, *Friedrich der Große*, 86–87; Wertheimer, "Zwei Schilderungen," 206, 216, 223.

82. Hinrichs, *Friedrich der Große*, 86–87; Wertheimer, "Zwei Schilderungen," 206, 216, 223.

83. KMT II, 53. On Colloredo's career, see Johann Christoph Allmayer-Beck, "Colloredo-Waldsee, Rudolph Joseph Fürst von," NDB 3 (1957): 329.

84. Hinrichs, *Friedrich der Große*, 86–87.

85. In 1742 the State Chancellery had been separated from the Austrian Court Chancellery as the center of foreign policy; see, chapter 5, this volume.

86. On Kaunitz, see chapter 5, this volume.

87. Rohrschneider, *Österreich*, 64 ff.; Groß, "Der Kampf." Through Francis Stephen's passivity and his own weak power base, the balance of power shifted from the Imperial Chancellery to the State Chancellery, from Colloredo to Ulfeld and Bartenstein and later to Kaunitz.

88. See Haug-Moritz, *"Des Kaysers rechter Arm"*; Eisenhardt, "Der Reichshofrat"; Rasche, "Urteil."

89. On the crisis that beset the Imperial Chamber Court in the 1740s, see Aretin, *Das Alte Reich* III, 63 ff.

90. Ortieb/Polster, "Die Prozessfrequenz."

91. This was the opinion ventured by Colloredo in 1749: HHStA Staatskanzlei Vorträge 62 (Konferenzvota 1749), fol. 88.v.

92. Haug-Moritz, *Die Krise*; Aretin, *Das Alte Reich* III, 59 ff.; on the failed attempt to settle the interconfessional conflict in Hohenlohe, ibid., 71 ff.

93. Ortlieb/Polster, *Prozessfrequenz*; Rasche, "Urteil," with extensive references.

94. Ranke, "Maria Theresia und ihr Hof," 680 ff.; on criticism in general, see Haug-Moritz, *"Des Kaysers rechter Arm,"* 23.

95. See in general Dorfner, *Mittler zwischen Haupt*.

96. Ortlieb/Polster, "Die Prozessfrequenz," 201 ff.; Haug-Moritz, *"Des Kaysers rechter Arm."* Under Joseph II, the number of cases brought before the court increased again considerably.

97. See Friedrich, *Drehscheibe Regensburg*; Stollberg-Rilinger, *Emperor's Old Clothes*, 218 ff.; Rohrschneider, *Österreich*.

98. Rohrschneider, *Österreich*, 44 ff.

99. Montesquieu, *Oeuvres* II, 1284. See also Aretin, *Heiliges Römisches Reich* II, 107 ff.; Moser, *Teutsches Staats-Recht* VI/1, 196; Keyssler, *Neueste Reisen*, 1438.

100. Trauttmannsdorff to Kaunitz, May 20, 1785, in Aretin, *Heiliges Römisches Reich* II, 108–109.

101. This was Colloredo's view, HHStA Staatskanzlei Vorträge 62 (Konferenzvota 1749), fol. 75–90, here 89v.

102. See Braun, *Princeps et episcopus*.

103. KMT IV, 79, 321 ff.

104. KMT IV, 150.

105. KMT III, 219.

106. KMT III, 128, 378 ff.

107. KMT VII, 18, 238 ff.

108. KMT II, 177, 445–46, 459; KMT III, 94, 356 ff.

109. KMT III, 182.

110. HHStA Reichskanzlei, Vorträge 6d, fol. 111 ff., here 116v.

111. This is how Colloredo summarized the imperial strategy in a lengthy memorandum submitted to Joseph following his coronation, KMT VI, 495.

112. See the missive from Count Seinsheim, the candidate's brother, to Colloredo, July 24, 1753, KMT III, 379–80.

113. See Braun, *Princeps et episcopus.*

114. See Braun, *Princeps et episcopus.*

115. See Braun, *Princeps et episcopus.*

116. To Antonia of Saxony, April 4, 1763, Lippert, *Briefwechsel*, 162 ff.; 274–75.

117. To Antonia of Saxony, November 6, 1771, Lippert, *Briefwechsel*, 274 ff.

118. See Braun, *Princeps et episcopus*, 66–67; details in Arneth, *Geschichte Maria Theresia's* X, 692 ff.; see chapter 14, this volume.

119. See Grillmeyer, *Habsburgs Diener*, 67–212; and most recently Rohrschneider, *Österreich*, 72 ff., 245 ff.; the obsequious partisan account found in Freytag, "Das Prinzipalkommissariat," is outdated.

120. For the specifics see Grillmeyer, Streng geheim; on Thurn und Taxis, see Grillmeyer, *Habsburgs Diener*; on the secret service, see chapter 8, this volume.

121. Moser, *Teutsches Staatsrecht* XXXXIV, 362, 364.

122. Freytag, "Das Prinzipalkommissariat," 255 ff.; Grillmeyer, *Habsburgs Diener*, 49; Rohrschneider, *Österreich*, 72 ff.

123. On the Order of the Golden Fleece, see chapter 7, this volume.

124. This was the verdict of the French emissary Du Buat, Sorel, *Recueil des instructions* XVIII, 335; the British emissary described him as weak and lethargic, cited in Rohrschneider, *Österreich*, 79; see also the judgment of the Bohemian emissary Trautmannsdorff in Aretin, *Heiliges Römisches Reich* II, 109.

125. Kollmer, *Die Familie Palm*, 79 ff.

126. "Do not plume yourself on your deeds, but consider them a trifle, and, if circumstances allow it, ascribe them to others," Zedler, *Großes Vollständiges Universal-Lexicon* XIII, 405–12, s.v. Hof, here 410.

127. Colloredo, KMT III, 465–66; similarly Khevenhüller, KMT III, 203.

128. Kollmer, *Die Familie Palm*, 83 ff.; Grillmeyer, *Habsburgs Diener*, 111 ff.; Rohrschneider, *Österreich*, 81 ff., 93 ff.

129. Franz Michael Florence von Lilien; for more detail, see Grillmeyer, *Habsburgs Diener*, esp. 90 ff., 117 ff. See also chapter 8, this volume.

130. Rohrschneider, *Österreich*, 95.

131. KMT III, 203; Colloredo, in KMT III, 465–66.

132. The envoys of the old princes formally protested whenever the Prince of Thurn and Taxis was called on to give his opinion during council deliberations; see Stollberg-Rilinger, *Emperor's Old Clothes*, 225–26.

133. For more detail, see Rohrschneider, *Österreich*, 245–71, whose sources show that Maria Theresa (and Kaunitz) were always the first addressees of the relevant correspondences; see for example the missives the Prince of Thurn and Taxis sent to Maria Theresa on March 16, 1753 (HHStA RK Kleinere Reichsstände 519, fol. 229–30), then to Francis three days later (HHStA RK RP Berichte 89b). In the end, however, the emperor was formally thanked for the introduction; Rohrschneider *Österreich*, 268. See also the memoranda on improving the imperial postal system: these were always directed at Maria Theresa, never the emperor, HHStA Reichsakten in specie 21–24; see chapter 8, this volume.

5. Reforms

1. For more detail, see Pons, *Die Kunst*, 88 ff.; Bertele-Grenadenberg, "Uhren," 438; Koschatzky, *Maria Theresia* (catalog), 340, no. 69, 6. See also the website of the Office of the Austrian President: http://www.bundespraesident.at/aufgaben/praesidentschaftskanzlei/virtueller -rundgang/rosenzimmer (20.09.2015).

2. Pons, *Die Kunst*, 100 ff.

3. The clock is described, for example, by Count Karl Zinzendorf in June 1761. Zinzendorf, *Aus den Jugendtagebücher*, 206.

4. Picture in Bertele-Grenadenberg, "Uhren," 440.

5. Bertele-Grenadenberg, "Uhren," 441 ff.

6. Examples in Bertele-Grenadenberg, "Uhren," 441 ff.

7. KMT II, 65, 67; a similar spectacle was offered in 1754 by a machine-maker from Bern: KMT III, 181, 456. Maria Theresa was interested in a *Museum mathematicum* set up by the Jesuits, KMT III, 194; see also KMT II, 164; III, 5.

8. Maria Theresa mentions the mechanical bed (*lit*) in a letter to her son Ferdinand, BKF I, 286, see BKF I, 157. See in general Alice Reininger, *Wolfgang von Kempelen: Eine Biographie*, Vienna 2007.

9. See Stollberg-Rilinger, *Der Staat*; on natural law doctrine, see chapter 10, this volume.

10. Hobbes, *Leviathan*, Introduction; Hobbes, *On the Citizen*, Introduction.

11. During his time as a professor in Vienna, he had also been active as a financial and mining adviser in Hungary but had been forced to quit Habsburg service in 1754, probably for speculating in silver mining. He then earned his living partly in the service of various masters, partly as a freelance author of voluminous economic and political works. He ended his adventurous life in the Brandenburg fortress of Küstrin, where Frederick II had imprisoned him for embezzling state funds. See Erhard Dittrich, "Justi, Johann Heinrich Gottlob," in NDB 10 (1974), 707–709; Ulrich Adam, *The Political Economy of Johann Gottlob Justi*, Oxford 2006.

12. Sommer, *Der österreichischen Kameralisten dogmengeschtlischer Darstellung*, 2 vols., Wien 1920–25; see also Keith Tribe, *Governing Economy: The Reformation of German Economic Discourse, 1750–1840*, New York/Cambridge 1988; Guillaume Garner, *État, économie, territoire en Allemagne: L'espace dans le caméralisme et l'économie politique, 1740–1820*, Paris 2006.

13. Justi began his professorship in Vienna with an inaugural lecture, "On the relation between a flourishing state of the sciences with the means which make a state powerful and happy," published in Leipzig in 1754.

14. Dickson, *Finance* I, 24 ff.; Guglia, *Maria Theresia* II, 14.

15. Johann Heinrich Gottlob Justi, *Gutachten von den vernünftigen Zusammenhange und practischen Vortrage aller Oeconomischen und Cameralwissenschaften . . . benebst einer Antrittsrede von dem Zusammenhange eines blühenden Zustandes der Wissenschaften mit denjenigen Mitteln, welche einen Staat mächtig und glücklich machen*, ed. D.E.v.K., Lepizig 1754, 77.

16. Johann Heinrich Gottlob Justi, *Die Chimäre des Gleichgewichts von Europa*, Altona 1758, 42 ff.; *Der Grundriß*, 94, 231, 320 ff., 329, 333, 393; many further examples in Stollberg-Rilinger, *Der Staat*, 105 ff.

17. Justi, *Der Grundriß*, 319 ff., here 333.

18. Justi, *Der Grundriß*, 329.

19. Justi, *Der Grundriß*, 324.

20. Overview in Sikora, *Der Adel*.

21. See the example of Hungary discussed in chapter 3, this volume.

22. On the changed symbolic self-representation of the estates in the hereditary lands from the sixteenth to the eighteenth century, see Polleroß, "Pro Deo Caesarae et Patria."

23. See chapter 4, this volume.

24. On Bohemia, see the overview in Hanke, *Handbuch der Geschichte* II: *Die böhmischen Länder*; Cerman, "Opposition," is critical of the older historiography. On Hungary see chapter 3, this volume.

25. See Lorenz/Weigl, *Das barocke Wien*.

26. On the Court Chamber, see Dickson, *Finance* I, 219 ff.; Walter, *Die Geschichte* (ÖZV II,1,1), 91–92; sources: ÖZV II,2,40–63.

27. "Like an elderly mastodon," in Dickson's memorable phrase, *Finance* II, 1; on the reform of the Court Chamber ibid., I, 219 ff.—Maria Theresa herself later called it a "lifeless body," Political Testament of 1750–51, BAA, 79.

28. ÖZV II,2, 45 ff.

29. ÖZV II,2, 46 ff.; on the general contempt in which the Court Chamber was held, see also the Political Testament of 1750–51, BAA, 79.

30. ÖZV II,2, 50.

31. ÖZV II,2, 51 ff.

32. ÖZV II,2, 54–55.

33. ÖZV II,2, 56 ff.

34. Dickson, *Finance* I, 219.

35. On the military reform, see Walter, *Kaiserin Maria Theresia* (ÖZV II,1,1), 18 ff. On criticism of it, KMT II, 142; KMT II, 192–93, 457; KMT II, 344 speaks of "exercises introduced according to the Prussian example."

36. Ruzicka, *Friedrich Graf von Haugwitz*.

37. ÖZV II,2, 130–52.

38. See, for example, the principles set out in a 1747 memorandum, ÖZV II,2, 181–88.

39. Ranke, "Maria Theresia und ihr Hof," 691.

40. Political Testament of 1750–51, BAA, 83.

41. Quoted from a 1749 conference opinion, in all likelihood written by the emperor himself: HHStA Staatskanzlei Vorträge 62 (Konferenzvota 1749), fol. 26r. (see chapter 4, this volume).

42. A representative example is Kretschmayr, *Maria Theresia*, 96: Haugwitz wanted a "bureaucracy standing above parties and nations."

43. Godsey, "Herrschaft," 175.

44. KMT VI, 133 ff.

45. KMT VI, 135–136; see the disparaging remarks in KMT IV, 142 etc. Ranke, "Maria Theresia und ihr Hof," 691, states that Haugwitz received valuable gifts from Maria Theresa and even drew a salary of 75,000 guilders. Ranke also attests to his lavish spending.

46. Ranke, "Maria Theresia und ihr Hof," 691; see Hinrichs, *Friedrich der Große*, 121, 124, 131–32 etc.

47. Memorandum (late 1747), ÖZV II,2, 181–86.

48. See Walter, *Die Geschichte*; Walter, *Österreichische Verfassungs- und Verwaltungsgeschichte*; brief summary: Walter, *Die theresianische Staatsreform*; further Arneth, *Geschichte Maria Theresia's* IV; an indispensable, more recent study: Dickson, *Finance*; further Ruzicka, *Friedrich Graf von Haugwitz*, chapters 3–4.

49. Ruzicka, *Friedrich Graf von Haugwitz*, 134 ff., quote on 142.

50. ÖZV II,2, 158–69; Ruzicka, *Friedrich Graf von Haugwitz*, 168 ff.; Dickson, *Finance* I, 265 ff.

51. Rescript from August 1747, ÖZV II,2, 162.

52. ÖZV II,2, 175.

53. KMT II, 207. Protocol of the conference and ministers' written opinions: ÖZV II,2, 195–206; see also KMT II. 467–76.

54. Harrach also held the office of Lower Austrian land marshal, standing in for his brother; see Hans Wagner, "Narrach, Friedrich August Gervas Graf von, in NDB 7 (1966), 700. See also above, chapter 2.

55. Conference Protocol from January 29, 1748, ÖZV II,2, 202.

56. Conference Protocol from January 29, 1748, ÖZV II,2, 203–204.

57. Conference Protocol from January 29, 1748, ÖZV II,2, 205.

58. Conference Protocol from January 29, 1748, ÖZV II,2, 205–206.

59. Conference Protocol from January 29, 1748, ÖZV II,2, 206; see the later account in the Political Testament of 1755–56, BAA 119.

60. Hinrichs, *Friedrich der Große*, 131.

61. To Ulfeld, May 1748, in Arneth, *Geschichte Maria Theresia's* IV, 22–23. The handbillet in question was written in reply to a text by Harrach that is no longer extant.

62. KMT II, 243, 249.

63. KMT II, 249; Khevenhüller speculated that Harrach did not wish to risk his handsomely remunerated offices.

64. Cited in Arneth, *Geschichte Maria Theresia's* IV, 18.

65. Arneth, *Geschichte Maria Theresia's* IV, 19. For example, the chancellor of the royal court in Brno, Blümegen, was named the territory's lord high chamberlain. See, however, the Political Testament of 1755–56, BAA, 120, where Maria Theresa claims that Blümegen pledged his support without any prospect of reward, since nothing had been promised him in advance.

66. Cited in Arneth, *Geschichte Maria Theresia's* IV, 19.

67. Hinrichs, *Friedrich der Große*, 134.

68. Cited in KMT, II, 560.

69. KMT, II, 350–51.

70. ÖZV II,2, 230–33.

71. Instruction from July 14, 1748 on the institution of deputations, ÖZV II,2, 211–20 (footnote).

72. See Braun, *Princeps et episcopus*.

73. Memorandum from early 1749, ÖZV II,2, 255.

74. Memorandum from early 1749, ÖZV II,2, 255.

75. ÖZV II,2, 255.

76. Dickson, *Finance* I, 224 ff., speaks of a coup d'état; handbillets in ÖZV II,2, no. 67, 269–94; BBA, 60–61.

77. KMT III, 264; IV, 6; see Lorenz/Weigl, *Das barocke Wien*, 76 ff.; Dickson, *Finance* I, 232.

78. See handwritten note to Seilern, May 2, 1749, ÖZV II,2, 274 ff.; see also Maasburg, *Geschichte der obersten Justizstelle*.

79. KMT II, 318.

80. KMT II, 322.

81. Beck, *Versuch*, 46 ff.—On the form of the princely handbillet, see also Meisner, *Urkunden- und Aktenlehre*, 35, who remarks of Prussia that something "remarkable" happened in the eighteenth century: "these 'private' pieces of writing suddenly assumed the character of an official decree" and mutated into cabinet orders.

82. *Wiener Diarium*, Sonderblatt from May 14, 1749; Bartenstein composed the text; see Maasburg, *Geschichte der obersten Justizstelle*, 369 ff.; KMT II, 319–20.

83. See in general Vismann, *Akten*, 205 ff.; Friedrich, *Die Geburt des Archives*; Auer, "Zur Rolle der Archive." In the nineteenth and twentieth centuries, documents were imagined as living organisms (the root word for "organization"). For example, in Meisner, *Urkunden- und Aktenlehre*, 81 ff., 90, documents are said to "grow" first in the register and then in the archive. The archive is the "house where documents live." Documents should be classified by their provenance and not by their objective context, due to "respect for the life" of the documents and their organic interdependence.

84. Hochedlinger, *Österreichische Archivgeschichte*, 36 ff.

85. KMT III, 106.

86. Bartenstein, "Allerunterthänigster Nota," November 18, 1753, cited in Arneth, *Geschichte Maria Theresia's* IV, 132, 518.

87. Hochedlinger, *Österreichische Archivgeschichte*, 40.

88. Dickson, *Finance* I, 225.

89. KMT II, 321.

90. KMT II, 321.

91. KMT II, 320.

92. According to the Venetian emissary Diedo, cited in Arneth, *Geschichte Maria Theresia's* IV, 508–509; see ibid., 25–26. Maria Theresa's condolence letter to Harrach's brother; see KMT II, 328 ff., 544.

93. Philipp Kinsky, the former Bohemian court chancellor, had already passed away on January 12, 1749; Harrach died on June 4, 1749. On the possible reasons for the feebleness of the resistance, see also Dickson, *Finance* I, 228–29.

94. "Authority" here in the sense given it by Heinrich Popitz, *Phänomene der Macht*.

95. Haugwitz, undated memorandum, ÖZV II,2, 207.

96. KMT II, 252–53.

97. "Philipp Joseph von Rosenberg-Orsini (1691–1765)," see Wurzbach, *Biographisches Lexikon*, XXVII, 18–19. It is unclear from Khevenhüller's account why Rosenberg's career had taken a backward step under Charles VI.

98. Rosenberg's letter in KMT II, 516–57.

99. KMT II, 252–53.

100. KMT II, 340.

101. KMT II, 318.

102. A detailed account in Dickson, *Finance* I, 229 ff.

103. KMT II, 303–304 on Kaunitz's first appearance in the Court Conference on February 25, 1749.

104. Hinrichs, *Friedrich der Große*, 39 ff. (January 18, 1747).

105. Hinrichs, *Friedrich der Große*, 131. Podewils welcomed the Haugwitz system as an imitation of the Prussian one.

106. Dickson, *Finance* II, 35, from KMT II, 252 (thunderstorm); II, 276–77, 556 (locust plagues, in the summer of 1749 also in Vienna: ibid., 348); KMT II, 331–32 (earthquake).

107. The words are those of Philipp von Rosenberg, KMT II, 516.

108. For more detail, see chapter 6, this volume.

109. In the Political Testament, BAA, 81, 126.

110. Don Manoel Tellez de Menezes e Castro, Conte (from 1735 Duca) de Silva Tarouca; see Karajan, *Maria Theresia und Graf Sylva-Tarouca*, Introduction; Arneth, *Geschichte Maria Theresia's* II, 194. Arneth, ibid., IV, 68, notes that Maria Theresa gave him 100,000 guilders in 1755.

111. On Tarouca's central role in the expansion of Schönbrunn, see Yonan, *Empress*, 78 ff.

112. KMT III, 105.

113. Ulfeld on July 13, 1750, in Arneth, *Geschichte Maria Theresia's* IV, 532; likewise later, see Arneth, *Geschichte Maria Theresia's* IV, 244–45. In 1757 Kaunitz moved Maria Theresa to dissolve the Italian and Dutch council and incorporate their responsibilities into the State Chancellery—his own department. Tarouca was deeply insulted that the empress was clearly no longer satisfied with his performance in office. He therefore retained his title but voluntarily turned down a part of the pension he was offered. See Arneth, *Geschichte Maria Theresia's* IV, 532.

114. Undated letter, between 1751 and 1754, Karajan, *Maria Theresia und Graf Sylva-Tarouca*, Appendix, 17.

115. Undated handwritten letter, autumn 1754, Karajan, *Maria Theresia und Graf Sylva-Tarouca*, Anhang, 28: "*Je ne suis plus la meme chose, et pour moi plus aucun divertissements. Il ne faut plus y penser. Tachons a vivoter, et au moins de ne pas faire sentir aux autres.*"

116. Kallbrunner edition, reprinted in BAA, 63–97, no. 72, and 108–130, no. 88; this is the edition cited here.

117. BAA 96–97, 108.

118. BAA, 130.

119. Kalbrunner, *Kaiserin Maria Theresias Politisches Testament*, 21.

120. BAA, 82–83, 86. In the first testament, Bartenstein, Tarouca, and her private secretary Ignaz Koch are named along with Haugwitz as her sole supports and commended to her successors; in the second, only Haugwitz and Bartenstein are left.

121. BAA, 129.

122. So, for example, Arneth, *Geschichte Maria Theresia's* IV, 1 ff.; Walter, *Die theresianische Staatsreform*; Kretschmayr, *Maria Theresia*; Kallbrunner, *Kaiserin Maria Theresias Politisches Testament*, Introduction; Dickson, *Finance* II, 3–4, is more critical.

123. BAA 71.

124. BAA 65, similarly 80, 115.

125. BAA, 65.

126. BAA, 111 ff.

127. BAA, 111, 126, 129. On the comparison between Charles VI's and Maria Theresa's finances in the Political Testament, see the careful assessment by Dickson, *Finance* II, 3 ff.

128. A famous and oft-cited formulation, BAA 66, similarly 81.

129. BAA, 89, similarly 69, 70, 74, 76.

130. BAA, 93, similarly 124.

131. BAA, 76.

132. BAA, 96.

133. BAA, 95.

134. BAA, 95, similarly 122–23, 129.

135. BAA, 122.

136. BAA, 95, 96.

137. BAA, 129.

138. To Ulfeld, February 2, 1746, BKF IV, 171; see also to Ulfeld, October 31, 1746, BKF IV, 175.

139. BAA, 65, 81–82, 125.

140. See Braubach, *Versailles und Wien*; Arneth, "Johann Christoph Bartenstein"; Klingenstein, "Kaunitz kontra Bartenstein"; Klingenstein, "Institutionelle Aspekte"; Dickson, "Baron Bartenstein"; Peper/Wallnig, "Ex nihilo nihil fit"; on Bartenstein and his career, see KMT VI, 253–54.

141. On his conversion and on Protestantism at the Viennese court more generally, see chapter 12, this volume.

142. Seckendorff, "Journal secret," 151, 202, 221–2, 224, 270; Karajan, *Maria Theresia und Graf Sylva-Tarouca*, introduction, 16 ff. In allusion to the title of a French comedy, he was called *maître et valet*, master and servant in one, see Braubach, "Ein Satire"; KMT II, 52.

143. Hinrichs, *Friedrich der Große*, 92 ff.

144. KMT III, 10; many similar statements could be cited.

145. Klingenstein, "Institutionelle Aspekte"; Klingenstein, "Kaunitz kontra Bartenstein."

146. Hinrichs, *Friedrich der Große*, 80 ff.; Wertheimer, "Zwei Schilderungen," 226.

147. KMT III, 10, 73; VI, 253–54.

148. HHStA, Staatskanzlei, Vorträge, Konferenzprotokolle und Referate der Jahre 1740 ff.

149. KMT II, 200–201.

150. See Bartenstein's own memorandum from 1762, in Arneth, "Johann Christoph Bartenstein," 176. For a concise account of the Vienna Court Conference and the role played in it by Bartenstein, see Klingenstein, "Institutionelle Aspekte", 79–80; Klingenstein, "Kaunitz kontra Bartenstein," 248; see also Bartenstein's own depiction in Arneth, "Johann Christoph

Bartenstein," 176 ff. These administrative procedures have rarely been the subject of detailed investigation; historians generally show a greater interest in outcomes than in the decision-making process. Archival science has devoted more attention to the topic; see (on Prussia) Meisner, *Urkunden- und Aktenlehre*, 56 ff.; Vismann, *Akten*, 217; from the perspective of communications history, Schlögl, *Anwesende*, 178; see also Dickson, *Finance* I, 297 ff.

151. Arneth, "Johann Christoph Bartenstein," 177.

152. Arneth, "Johann Christoph Bartenstein," 177.

153. E.g., ÖZV II,2, No 63, on the Court Chamber reform. See also the advice in the Habsburg "mirror for princes" *Princeps in compendio*, 14 ff.

154. The quotes are taken from an anonymous conference opinion, most probably written by Francis Stephen: Note on the Foreign System from March 18, 1749, HHStA Staatskanzlei Vorträge 62 (Konferenzvota 1749), fol. 27r. The emperor was presumably writing under the influence of the dramatic Court Conference in January of the same year, when conflict about the reforms had broken out. See also Kaunitz to Koch, May 19, 1750, Schlitter, *Correspondance secrète*, 9.

155. Arneth, "Johann Christoph Bartenstein," 178.

156. The categories of early twentieth-century administrative studies, which opposed autocratic and collegial decision-making (Meisner, *Urkunden- und Aktenlehre*, 56 ff.), are therefore anachronistic; both were still indistinguishable in the old councils. See also the administrative procedure of the new Directorium in Publicis et Cameralibus in Ranke, "Maria Theresia und ihr Hof," 693.

157. See Hahn, "Geheim"; Simmel, "Das Geheimnis."

158. Note on the Foreign System from March 18, 1749, HHStA Staatskanzlei Vorträge 62 (Konferenzvota 1749), fol. 28r.

159. Klingenstein, "Kaunitz kontra Bartenstein," 248; Schlitter, *Correspondance secrète*, September 20, 1750, 13–14; see April 21, 1750, ibid., 5; May 12, 1750, ibid., 7, and May 19, 1750, ibid., 9.

160. Bartenstein wrote this in reference to the Directory, which functioned in the same way as the Court Conference. Remarks of the Directorial Vice-Chancellor Freiherr von Bartenstein on the New Finance System introduced in 1748, January 31, 1756, Nachlass Zinzendorf MS 2 b, 29–129, here 63, 66, 75, 84, see Dickson, "Baron Bartenstein," 14.

161. Arneth, "Johann Christoph Bartenstein," 178.

162. Schlitter, *Corresponance secrète*, 9; see the aforementioned Note on the Foreign System from March 18, 1749, HHStA Staatskanzlei Vorträge 62 (Konferenzvota 1749), fol. 27r.

163. Kaunitz to Koch, 21. 4. 1750, Schlitter, *Correspondance secrète*, 5.

164. KMT II, 151 (April 1747), 163 (June 1747).

165. KMT II, 151.

166. Max Braubach, "Koch, Ignaz Freiherr von", in NDB 12 (1979), 265–6. On the influence of the later cabinet secretary Neny, see Arneth, "Graf Philipp Cobenzl," 107.

167. KMT I, 146.

168. Hinrichs, *Friedrich der Große*, 97 ff. The lord high steward's Chancellery bore official responsibility, however, for petitions regarding court positions and the like; see chapter 7, this volume.

169. KMT II, 139, 422; see ibid., 168.

170. The words are Maria Theresa's, BAA 81–82; likewise Hinrichs, *Friedrich der Große*, 97; even Khevenhüller esteemed him despite his low "extraction."

171. See chapter 8, this volume.

172. On Kaunitz, see Klingenstein, *Der Aufstieg*; Klingenstein, "Kaunitz kontra Bartenstein"; Szábo, *Kaunitz*; Szábo, "Favorit"; Szábo, *Between Privilege and Professionalism*; Klingenstein/ Szábo, *Staatskanzler*; Schilling, *Kaunitz*; Lebeau, *Aristocrates et grands commis*; Beales, "Joseph II's Rêveries," I, 141 ff.; further Novotny, *Staatskanzler Kaunitz*; Walter, *Männer*, 66 ff.; Lettner, *Das Spannungsfeld*.

173. Arneth, *Geschichte Maria Theresia's* IV, 318 ff.; on the 1749 memorandum: Pommerin/ Schilling, *Denkschrift*; Schilling, *Kaunitz*; Szábo, *Kaunitz*; Klingenstein, "Kaunitz kontra Bartenstein"; see chapter 8, this volume.

174. KMT II, 303–4; see Wraxall, *Historical and the Posthumous Memoirs* III, 346 ff.

175. Cited in Arneth, *Geschichte Maria Theresia's* IV, 542, and see 320 ff.

176. Details in Szábo, *Kaunitz*, 20 ff.

177. This was the verdict given by the Prussian emissary Christoph Heinrich von Ammon in 1756, quoted in Hinrichs, *Friedrich der Große*, 142 ff.; similar remarks were still being made in the 1770s: Swinburne, *Courts*, I, 336–37: "cold and insensible," Keith, *Memoirs* II, 197.

178. Ligne, *Fragments* I, 114.

179. KMT III, 70–71; III, 241. Frederick II called him frivolous in his taste and meticulous in his affairs (cited in Alexander Novotny, *Staatskanzler Kaunitz*, 206). See the opinion voiced by the member of a French embassy: Kaunitz should not be judged by his manners; Wertheimer, "Zwei Schilderungen," 224.

180. Ulfeld to Maria Theresa, cited in Arneth, *Geschichte Maria Theresia's* IV, 321.

181. Primarily because the Archducal House no longer controlled the Imperial Vice-Chancellery at the time (due to the election of a Wittelsbach as emperor) and needed another central court office for foreign relations.

182. Gracián, *Hand-Orakel*.

183. Hinrichs, *Friedrich der Große*, 82; KMT III, 71, 109.

184. Letter from Kaunitz to Koch, December 1751, in Schlitter, *Correspondance secrète*, 155–62.

185. For more detail, see Klingenstein, "Kaunitz kontra Bartenstein," 256 ff.

186. Gracián, *Hand-Orakel*, maxim 219, 97.

187. KMT III, 69 ff., 108 ff. See Klingenstein, "Kaunitz kontra Bartenstein," 261.

188. KMT III, 69.

189. Schlitter, *Correspondance secrète*, Appendix, 359 ff.

190. Printed in KMT III, 371 ff.

191. KMT III, 112.

192. Arneth, *Geschichte Maria Theresia's* IV, 346.

193. KMT III, 70.

194. See Arneth, *Geschichte Maria Theresia's* IV, 321.

195. KMT III, 69 ff.

196. KMT III, 109–10.

197. See Lebeau, *Aristocrats et grands commis*.

198. KMT III, 242–43.

199. Criticism of Kaunitz in KMT III, 114–15, 119, 123; IV, 138, 143–44; V, 9, 14, 103. See Klingenstein, "Institutionelle Aspekte," 87 ff.; Szábo, "Favorit," 352.

200. To Ulfeld, undated (December 1757), BKF IV, 196; see also the ensuing letter to Ulfeld, ibid., 196–97.

201. Proposal regarding the improvement and speedier conduct of internal and external state business, May 10, 1740, HHStA Landesarchiv ÖA Österreich—Staat Karton 1, Facs. 2 (1679–1749), fol. 292–295, citation fol. 295v.

202. HHStA Nachlass Zinzendorf MS 2b fol. 10–29, fol. 29–129; see Dickson, "Baron Bartenstein."

203. On the problems of reform, see the detailed account in Ranke, "Maria Theresia und ihr Hof," 697, 700 ff.; KMT V, 99, 103. When a devastating fire broke out in Vienna and destroyed many houses, the populace blamed the new administrative system, KMT V, 110.

204. Source in ÖZV II,3. See Arneth, Geschichte Maria Theresia's VII, 1 ff.; Walter, Die Geschichte (ÖZV II,1,1), 254 ff.; Walter, "Kaunitz' Eintritt"; Szábo, Kaunitz, 83 ff.; Dickson, Finance I, 233 ff.

205. Memorandum from December 14, 1760, ÖZV II,3, no. 77, 11, see the memorandum from December 9, 1760, ibid., 7.

206. Marginalia to Kaunitz's memorandum from December 14, 1760, ÖZV II,3, 12.

207. Kaunitz, Haugwitz, Daun, Stupan, Blümegen, and Borié as well as the secretary Anton König.

208. State council agenda, ÖZV II,3, 25–26.

209. Kaunitz to Maria Theresa, January 13, 1762, ÖZV II,3, 31.

210. State council agenda, ÖZV II,3, 15 ff.

211. This was soon compromised, however: in January 1762 Daun was named president of the Court War Council while keeping his seat in the State Council. Kaunitz protested vehemently but without success.

212. ÖZV II,3, 21–22.

213. ÖZV II,3, 18.

214. ÖZV II,3, 33ff.

215. Criticism in KMT VI, 96–97; see Walter, "Kaunitz' Eintritt," 50 ff.

216. See Dickson, Finance I, 237 ff.

217. ÖZF II,3, 95 ff.; see Walter, "Kaunitz' Eintritt," 53 ff.

218. Walter, Die Geschichte (ÖZV II,1,1), 281 ff.; Dickson, Finance I, 238 ff.

219. On Ludwig von Zinzendorf's social background and career trajectory, see Lebeau, Aristocrates et grands commis, 107 ff.; on his new model for financial administration, see ibid., 163 ff.

220. On the reforms of 1764–65, Walter, Die Geschichte (ÖZV II,1,1), 366 ff.; Dickson, Finance I, 244 ff.; KMT VI, 196–97, 446 ff.

221. Walter, Die theresianische Staatsreform, 60; Walter, "Introduction," BAA, 63. Conversely, the state reform of 1749 was regarded from a Czech perspective as a "break with [Bohemia's national] autonomy."

222. Kallbrunner, Kaiserin Maria Theresias Politisches Testament, Introduction, 20.

223. Kallbrunner, Kaiserin Maria Theresias Politisches Testament, Introduction, 11–12.

224. Walter, Verwaltungsreform, 59; Walter, Die Geschichte, 191 ff.

225. See Kretschmayr, Maria Theresia, 104–105.

226. Leopold von Ranke, Die großen Mächte: Politisches Gespräch, ed. Theodor Schieder, Göttingen 1963, 61.

227. See Kühl, Organisationen.

228. Dickson, Finance I, 264 ff; Obersteiner, Theresianische Verwaltungsreformen; von Bredow, "Die niederösterreichischen Kreisämter"; for the Tyrol, Stauber, Der Zentralstaat, 225 ff. See chapter 8, this volume.

229. Attempts at calculation in Dickson, Finance I, 305 ff.

230. Dickson, Finance I, 305 ff.

231. Schmitt, Gespräch über die Macht.

6. Body Politics

1. Kantorowicz, The King's Two Bodies; further, Schulte, Der Körper; Cosandey, La Reine, etc.

2. Hobbes, On the Citizen I, 17.

3. Barta, "Maria Theresia," 347 ff.

4. Psalm 45, 3 ff.

5. Hobbes, Leviathan, I, 10.

6. Instruction from Prince Karl Eusebius von Liechtenstein (before 1681). Eighteenth-century transcription, Fürstlich Liechtensteinisches Domänenarchiv, VA 5-2-2, 130. (I thank Michael Sikora for providing me with the transcription.) See Maria Theresa to Franz, Count of Thurn: "A great prince must be formed in such a way that he wins everyone's hearts through his pleasant physiognomy."

7. Arneth, Geschichte Maria Theresia's I, 87; IV, 136–37. See the remarks of her brother-in-law, Charles of Lorraine, in Urbanski, "Unveröffentlichte Aufzeichnungen," 96–97: "very fine and beautiful"; Ranke, "Maria Theresia und ihr Hof," 672; the Venetian emissary Foscarini in Arneth, Geschichte Maria Theresia's I, 356; on the loss of her once legendary beauty in her old age, see below, n. 15.

8. E.g., Wraxall, Historical and the Posthumous Memoirs, 304 ff.; Anon., Über die Frage; Pichler, Denkwürdigkeiten, 28; see chapter 3, this volume.

9. Under the Jewish pseudonym Löwle Kemmel, Helden-Lied, 4.

10. Cited in Arneth, Geschichte Maria Theresia's IV, 519.

11. Ranke, "Maria Theresia und ihr Hof," 672.

12. To Tarouca (undated), Karajan, Maria Theresia und Graf Sylva-Tarouca, 83; she described herself even more bluntly to Countess Edling in 1769, BAA 248–49, 250.

13. Lippert, Briefwechsel, 9; see ibid., 86 (1760); 103 (1761).

14. To Countess Trautson, née Freifrau Hager, 1754, van Rhyn, "Unveröffentlichte Briefe," 271; see also to Countess Trautson 1750, ibid., 268: "I am losing weight without falling ill, this pleases me a great deal."

15. Coke, Letters III, 312; Moore, A View, 265–56; Swinburne, Courts I, 355: her face was still beautiful, but she was "enormously fat and unwieldy."

16. Barta, Familienporträts; Yonan, Empress; Yonan, "Portable Dynasties"; Matsche, "Maria Theresias Bild"; Telesko, Maria Theresia, 62 ff.; Telesko, "Herrschaftssicherung."

17. The banker Johann Fries, who had a monopoly on the "thaler business" between 1752 and 1776, exported over 20 million Maria Theresa thalers to the eastern Mediterranean. The coin continued to be minted after 1780 and spread throughout the Middle East and Africa. It continued to be produced by several European colonial powers during the Second World War.

18. Marin, *Das Porträt.*

19. Roethlisberger/Loche, *Liotard*; Royal Academy London, exhibition catalog *Liotard*; Koschatzky, "Jean-Etienne Liotard." See, e.g., Maria Theresa to Marie Antoinette, November/December 1770, Christoph, *Maria Theresia: Geheimer Briefwechsel*, 30, 32.

20. Yonan, "Portable Dynasties"; Steppan, "Kaiserliche Gesandte."

21. Barta, *Familienporträts*, 6, 56, 154 (antependium), 25 (faiences).

22. Anon., *Beantwortung der Frage* (unpaginated, 18), albeit here referring to Sweden.

23. Anon., *Königin in Ungarn*; see Barta, *Familienporträts*, 19–20.

24. KMT VIII, 65. See also the copperplate, fig. 17 in chapter 4, this volume.

25. Hinrichs, *Friedrich der Große*, 39. See, for example, the Venetian emissary Foscarini on Maria Theresa as heiress, cited in Arneth, *Geschichte Maria Theresia's* I, 356: "*Non manca di bellezza, ed essendo piuttosto gracile di corporatura e di poco vivo colore.—Sta il comportamento compost e la guardatura inclinante al grave, ma non però scompagnata di grazia.*"

26. Zedler, *Großes Vollständiges Universal-Lexikon*, XXXV, Col. 822–30, s.v. Schönheit des Frauenzimmers, here 823. On clothing at court, see also chapter 7, this volume.

27. KMT I, 118; II, 172–73.

28. Zedler, *Großes Vollständiges Universal-Lexikon*, XXXV, Col. 822–30, s.v. Schönheit des Frauenzimmers.

29. E.g., KMT II, 357.

30. Instruction of Prince Karl Eusebius von Liechstenstein (before 1681), Fürstlich Liechstensteinisches Domänenarchiv, VA 5-2-2, 131.

31. See Barta, "Maria Theresia," 341 ff.

32. Anon., *Über die Frage* (unpaginated).

33. The words appear on a copperplate reproduced in Barta, "Maria Theresia", 347–48; numerous further examples in Barta, *Familienporträts*, 62 ff.

34. See also the adages occasioned by the birth of the heir in 1741, in Ghelen, *Wiennerische Beleuchtungen*, as well as those produced for dynastic marriages. Even Enlightenment figures such as Wilhelm Ludwig Wekhrlin, *Denkwürdigkeiten von Wien*, 60, took a similar view.

35. Léon Bloy, cited in Vinken, "Marie Antoinette," 89.

36. The instructions that Prince Eusebius von Liechtenstein composed for his son around 1680 give a vivid idea of sexual norms in the Viennese high nobility; Fürstlich Liechtensteinsches Domänenarchiv, VA 5-2-2, here 122.

37. See the strict rules that Empress Elisabeth Christine gave to the superintendent of her ladies-in-waiting on January 11, 1740, in Pangerl/Scheutz/Winkelbauer, *Der Wiener Hof*, 225–28.

38. The fifteen-year-old Maria Theresa performed in the *Singspiel Il cisibeo consolato*; Hadamowsky, "'Spectacle mussen sein,'" 387.

39. See, e.g., KMT IV, 73, 92; V, 98; reflections on marriage KMT II, 272 ff.

40. Luhmann, *Liebe als Passion*, esp. 89, 95–96, 114, 150, 163, on the relationship between *amour propre* and marriage.

41. This is the thesis advanced by Luhmann, *Liebe als Passion*.

42. Luhmann, *Liebe als Passion*, 60, with numerous quotations.

43. On the correspondence with Marie Antionette, see Christoph, *Maria Theresia: Geheimer Briefwechsel*, Introduction; on the correspondence with Joseph, see Beales, "Joseph II's Rêveries," 87, 151; on Isabella of Parma's correspondence, see Isabella de Bourbon-Parme, "*Je meurs d'amour pour toi . . . ,*" Introduction; see chapters 9 and 10, this volume.

44. Eduard Fuchs, *Illustrierte Sittengeschichte vom Mittelalter bis zur Gegenwart*, 6 vols, Munich 1909–12; see Ulrich Weitz, "Unser Zeitalter lechzt nach dem Bilde, . . ." in *Eduard Fuchs und die Bildsprache der deutschen Arbeiterbewegung vom Sozialistengesetz bis zur Novemberrevolution*, Stuttgart 1990, 296 ff. The genre still exists today, though happily no longer banned for women: Anna Ehrlich, *Auf den Spuren der Josefine Mutzenbacher: Eine Sittengeschichte von den Römern bis ins 20. Jahrhundert*, Munich 2005.

45. E.g., Fuchs, *Illustrierte Sittengeschichte* III, 81.

46. Loen, *Gesammalte Kleine Schriften* I, 20–21; see also Keyßler, *Neueste Reisen*, 1213 ff.; later Wekhrlin, *Denkwürdigkeiten von Wien*, 69: "her entire life is devoted to pleasure"; Pilati, *Reisen* I, 28–29; see the copious additional material in Kauffmann, "'Es ist nur ein Wien.'"

47. Montagu, *Complete letters* I, 270.

48. As illustrated in the following anecdote: the imperial commander Prince Sachsen-Hildburghausen, a conqueror in every respect, had suffered a defeat in the Turkish war and had married shortly thereafter. He summed up his experiences in the lewd ditty: "Though Banjaluka refused me the wreath [Kranz], / I stormed it with my . . ." [Here the reader infers the missing phallic rhyme word, "sheath" (*Schwanz*).—Translator's note.] Imperial Aulic Councilor Seckendorff reported: "The prince gave these verses to the emperor to read. He laughed out loud and wanted to show them to the empress, who had just come in. But the prince tore them out of the emperor's hands, saying, 'For God's sake no, Y. M.! Her Imperial Majesty cannot be allowed to see this: she would never forgive me.'" Seckendorff, "Journal secret," 222–23; see also 123–24, 147, 213–14. Charles VI mentions his mistresses in his diary, see Redlich, *Die Tagebuch*, 148.

49. Garms-Cornides, "'On n'a qu'a vouloir,'" 110.

50. On Countess Josepha von Althann, KMT III, 187.

51. Husslein-Arco/Lechner, Meytens, 110 ff. The painting was in the private collection of Count Carl Gustav von Tessin; it allegedly hung in his bedroom. Van Meytens was appointed imperial court painter in 1732.

52. KMT VI, 110; see Wandruszka, *Leopold II.*, I, 113.

53. E.g., Rothe, *Die Mutter und die Kaiserin*, introduction, 10.

54. See the engagement letters in chapter 2, this volume.

55. Charles-Joseph de Ligne is referring here to his own father; Ligne, *Fragments* I, 72. Ligne, later well-known as a rake, had already been made Maria Theresa's chamberlain as a young man.

56. Ranke, "Maria Theresia und ihr Hof," 677; Arnheim, "Das Urtheil," 291–92; the English emissary Robinson in Arneth, *Geschichte Maria Theresia's* I, 25; Guibert, *Journal* I, 297 ff.; Coxe, *History* III, 154, 162.

57. Karajan, *Maria Theresia und Graf Sylva-Tarouca*, 17. Similarly Charles of Lorraine, Urbansky, *Aufzeichnungen*, 91–92; Pichler, *Denkwürdigkeiten*, 11–12.

58. Ottillinger, Paradebett; Benedik, "Die herrschaftlichen Appartements"; Yonan, *Empress*. The "Rich Bedroom" (*Reiches Schlafzimmer*) in the Hofburg, dominated by Maria Theresa's bed

of state, was no longer used as such in the nineteenth century and was preserved unchanged. It was thus turned into a museum, a place dedicated to the memory of Maria Theresa.

59. Iby, Schönbrunn; Yonan, *Empress*, 83 ff.; see the plan of Schönbrunn (chapter 7, fig. 27), room no. 8 (today the Napoleon Room).

60. Seckendorff, "Journal secret," 148: *"faire comme des paysans, qui couchant regulièrement et des nuits entières avec leurs femmes."* Other gibes about marriage in ibid., 123–24, 147.

61. See Telesko, *Maria Theresa*, 107; Telesko, "Die Maria-Theresien-Krypta"; Telesko, "'Hier wird einmal gutt ruhen seyn.'"

62. To Marie Antoinette, October 3, 1777, Christoph, *Maria Theresia: Geheimer Briefwechsel*, 225 (omitted in MACS III, 118).

63. To Marie Antoinette, November 3, 1780, Christoph, *Maria Theresia: Geheimer Briefwechsel*, 342 (omitted in MACS III, 482). Louis XVI generally did not sleep with Marie Antoinette, in either the broader or the narrower sense.

64. Hinrichs, Podewils, 49; see also Yonan, *Empress*, 84–85.

65. Arneth, *Geschichte Maria Theresia's* IV, 147.

66. To Maria Christina, 1766 (undated), Wolf, *Marie Christine* I, 66–73; BAA, 208 ff.

67. To Maria Christina 1766 (undated), Rothe, *Die Mutter und die Kaiserin*, 124–5; Wolf, *Marie Christine* I, 68–69. See chapter 13, this volume.

68. To her sister Marianna, October 21, 1744, BAA, 39–40.

69. To Marianna, October 3, 1744, BAA, 39; Arneth, *Geschichte Maria Theresia's* II, 453.

70. E.g., KMT II, 44–45; see KMT IV, 13.

71. KMT III, 205–206.

72. To Maria Christina, April 1766, Rothe, *Die Mutter und die Kaiserin*, 122; Wolf, *Marie Christine* I, 66.

73. See chapter 10, this volume.

74. To Ferdinand, 1. 10. 1771, BKF I, 70–71.

75. Wolf, *Marie Christine* I, 9; see Hinrichs, *Friedrich der Große*, 50: "She would like to lead a bourgeois marriage with the emperor."

76. This was the line already taken by the daughter of her maid, Caroline Hieronymus, Pichler, *Denkwürdigkeiten*, 11–12; Guglia, *Maria Theresia* II, 213 ("housewife and mother"); Herre, *Maria Theresia* I, 161–62 ("family home"); Wandruszka, *Leopold II* I, 35–36 ("ménage bourgeois"); Vocelka/Heller, Private Welt, 25; Lever, Marie Antoinette, 10. An exception is Crankshaw, *Maria Theresa*, 128: "the conception of Maria Theresa as a good bourgeois is no less silly than the belief she took lovers."

77. Barta, *Familienporträts*, 133 ff.; Yonan, "Nobility and Domestic Conviviality."

78. Maria Theresa was deeply touched that her son Ferdinand imitated this in his own marriage: BKF I, 161.

79. Goethe, *Aus meinem Leben* IX, 195.

80. See chapters 9 and 10, this volume.

81. A great many examples of such matches, and the career strategies associated with them, can be found in Khevenhüller, E.g., KMT II, 32, 71, 85, 90, 106, 124–5, 138, 139, 144, 179, 186, 211, 214, 247, 253, 268, 271 ff., 277–78, 364.

82. KMT II, 73 ff.; see also KMT VIII, 112–13.—See Maria Theresa's letters to her from the years 1745–55; van Rhyn, "Unveröffentlichte Briefe."

83. KMT II, 74.

84. KMT I, 119.

85. KMT II, 329. See also the remarks on widely known affairs of the high nobility in KMT I, 125–26; 211–12; KMT II, 245–46. Joseph II made fun of Khevenhüller's bashfulness.

86. Hinrichs, Podewils, 71–72, 74–75, 86–87, 106 ff.

87. E.g., Count Schulenberg with Countess Esterhazy, KMT VIII, 36, 74–75.

88. See, for example, KMT III, 101, 106, 113, 114, 115, 117, 168, 146–47, 174–75, 176, 193, 194, 195–96, 226–27, 236, 240, 245, 272.

89. KMT II, 144; KMT V, 103, 105–106; for a general overview, see Hadamowsky, Wien— Theatergeschichte, 199–254.

90. Tarouca to Maria Theresa, Autumn 1754, Karajan, Maria Theresia und Graf Sylva-Tarouca, 27–28; see above, chapter 3.

91. KMT III, 45. In May 1759, the dancer Santini was expelled at Maria Theresa's behest and escorted to Venice by a security commissar—a great loss for the Vienna ballet; KMT V, 102.

92. Casanova, Geschichte I, 152; see III, 37.

93. KMT II, 145.

94. KMT II, 145.

95. KMT II, 200 ff., 467.

96. Hadamowsky, Wien—Theatergeschichte, 205 ff.

97. See chapter 7, this volume.

98. KMT II, 202.

99. Arneth, Geschichte Maria Theresia's IX, 399 ff; Steiner, Rückkehr, 301 ff.; Schnitzer, Höfische Maskeraden; Scheutz, Karneval. None other than Leopold von Sacher-Masoch wrote a novella on the topic, entitled The Chastity Commission.

100. KMT II, 202.

101. Hinrichs, Friedrich der Große, 112 ff.; only foreign ministers were to be spared.

102. See Reinhardt, De Sade.

103. Herre, Maria Theresia, 146 ff.; Großegger, Theater, 71; Schnitzer, Höfische Maskeraden, 255; Barta, "Maria Theresia," 349 ff.

104. ÖZV II,2, 405–406; ÖZV II,1,1, 247; Kallbrunner, Zur Geschichte, 142 ff.; Arneth, Geschichte Maria Theresia's IX, 399–400, 603 cites the relazione of the Viennese emissary Corer from the beginning of 1753, according to which a "security and chastity commission" had been amalgamated with the Lower Austrian Representation and Chamber.

105. [Lamberg], Mémorial I, 157 ff.

106. Wekhrlin, Denkwürdigkeiten von Wien, 100 ff.

107. Hinrichs, Friedrich der Große, 115.

108. E.g., Bark in Arnheim, "Das Urtheil," 290; Guibert, Journal, 297 ff.; Ligne, Fragments I, 119, 132, 144; Ranke, "Maria Theresia und ihr Hof," 676–77; Wraxall, Historical and the Posthumous Memoirs III, 482–83; Trenck, Die "Blutbibel", 77; Casanova, Geschichte III, 260–63, VIII, 248–52; the story of his expulsion ibid., X, 257–64.

109. According to a French observer writing two decades later: Weretheimer, "Zwei Schilderungen," 214.

110. Trenck, Die "Blutbibel", 77.

111. Casanova, Geschichte III, 260–61.

112. Arnheim, "Das Urtheil," 290.

113. Arneth, *Geschichte Maria Theresia's* IX, 399 ff. (citation on p. 400) reports on a number of cases where Maria Theresa intervened when a nobleman wanted to make another's wife his mistress with the husband's consent, or when a young couple from the nobility eloped abroad. Another case in Koschatzky, *Maria Theresia* (catalog), 316–17, no. 62,08.

114. Hinrichs, *Friedrich der Große*, 50.

115. KMT V, 74; see V, 92, 115.

116. Szábo, *Kaunitz*, 22.

117. Memoire de morale et de Gouvenement d'Etat pour l'usage de S.A. Royale Renante (1723), HHStA LHA, 43–1, fol. 22–28.

118. Ibid., fol. 28.

119. On Charles of Lorraine, see Hinrichs, *Friedrich der Große*, 72: "He is dissolute, not very gallant, and prone to gross indulgence."

120. "Listes des Galanteries de Bruxelles," "Chiffres pour le parler par geste," Brussels, Archives Générales du Royaume, Secretarie van State en Oorlog/Sécrétairerie d'État et de Guerre, Tome 100, no. 2605, fol. 102–107.

121. Pichler, *Denkwürdigkeiten*, 11.

122. Pichler, *Denkwürdigkeiten*, 28.

123. Zedinger, *Franz Stephan*, 268 ff.; Guglia, *Maria Theresia* II, 190–91, thinks that everything possibly played out "within the bounds of harmless gallantry." Arneth, *Geschichte Maria Theresia's* IV, 149, names Countess Auersperg as well as Countess Johanna Tarouca, née the Duchess of Holstein-Beck and Countess Canal, née Pálffy.

124. Ranke, "Maria Theresia und ihr Hof," 676–77; see the remarks in Hinrichs, *Friedrich der Große*, 60.

125. Hinrichs, *Friedrich der Große*, 58.

126. Frederick II to Wilhelmine of Bayreuth, Droysen, et al., *Die Politische Correspondenz* X, 429, also cited in KMT III, 193, 463.

127. Arneth, *Geschichte Maria Theresia's* IV, 149. She is generally referred to without commentary as Francis Stephen's mistress; e.g., Guibert, *Journal* I, 297–98; Wraxall, *Historical and the Posthumous Memoirs* II, 353, etc. That this is more than idle rumor is expressly confirmed by Coke, *Letters* III, 333, 360. Zedinger, *Franz Stephan*, 270–71, calls this "stubborn gossip." The emperor had made her husband an imperial prince in 1746. On her death at the age of thirty-eight on October 21, 1775, see KMT VIII, 110.

128. KMT IV, 17.

129. KMT IV, 18, 23, 49, 78; V, 92, 115; VI, 30, 85, 115, 121, 124.

130. KMT IV, 16, 18. When Maria Theresa refused to accompany her husband on a hunting trip to Laxenburg, she was said to be annoyed about the presence of Princess Auersperg. Conversely, when she personally invited the hunting party, including Auersperg, to join her at Schloss Hof, this gave rise to "considerable speculation." KMT V, 101, 106, 107, 110, 111.

131. To Maria Christina (undated, 1761?), BKF II, 356: *Votre rêve est faux.*

132. See KMT VI, 30, 115, 121 (August 1765); see also the criticism of his daughter-in-law Isabella of Parma: the emperor was too much under the influence of Princess Auersperg; Badinter, *Isabella*, 239; Arneth, *Geschichte Maria Theresia's* VII, 49.

133. Ligne, *Fragments* I, 68; I, 110; I, 143–44 n. 7; see II, 114.

134. Ligne, *Fragments* I, 203; see his story "Cleon et Roxelane," Contes immoraux, in Ligne, Œuvres romanesques I, 102–107.

135. Ligne, *Fragments* I, 110. See ibid., I, 68: "I had a number of generals and even ministers in Vienna in my antechamber at the time when I stood in the favorite's favor" (*dans le temps de ma faveur auprès de la favorite*).

136. The comedy "Crispin rival de son maître" (1707) was the first literary success of the young Alain-René LeSage, who later became famous with the novel *Gil Blas*. (The play's performance at the Viennese court in May 1756 is attested in KMT IV, 19; it had previously been staged in April 1753: KMT III, 101.) In a memorandum from March 1767 in which the rector of the Theresianum, Pater Kerens, classified comedies by their seemliness, the play was placed in the third and last, most offensive, category; the priest found it "shocking." The memorandum is edited in KMT VI, 529–36, here 534.

137. Zedinger, *Franz Stephan*, 269–70.

138. Seven letters from Francis Stephen and one from Béatrice de Ligneville are extant; see Zedinger, *Franz Stephan*, 272 ff.

139. . . . *malgré mon âge je suis encore en passion.* Quoted in Zedinger, *Franz Stephan*, 274–75, 346–47. Maria Theresa evidently had no inkling of the affair; after Francis Stephen's death she was happy to receive Béatrice de Ligneville: BKF IV, 472.

140. For more detail, on the basis of Neny's correspondence with his brother in Vienna: Bernard, "Patrice-François de Neny"; a brief account in Zedinger, *Franz Stephan*, 269.

141. See Joseph II to Maria Theresa, May 16, 1769 (MJC I, 268): he speaks there of the stir caused by the adventuress (*aventurière*) Mademoiselle Juliana Maria von Schönbaden.

142. Bernard, "Patrice-François de Neny."

143. E.g., to Ferdinand, October 3, 1771, BKF I, 73; to Amalia, June 1769, BKF III, 3 ff., Rothe, *Die Mutter und die Kaiserin*, 144 ff.; to Carolina, April 1768, BKF III, 32 ff., Rothe, ibid., 220 ff.; to Marie Antoinette, May 4, 1770, MACS I, 6 ff., Rothe, ibid., 367.

144. To Ferdinand, July 21, 1774, BKF I, 288–89.

145. See chapters 9, 13, and 14, this volume.

146. Maria Theresa to Maria Christina, 1766 (undated), Wolf, *Marie Christine* I, 66 ff. See letters to Maria Carolina, April 1768, BKF III, 32 ff.; to Amalia, June 1769, BKF III, 3 ff.; to Marie Antoinette, November 4, 1770, MACS I, 15 ff.

147. To Mercy-Argenteau, July 31, 1779, MACS III, 333 ff.

148. Justi, *Allerunterthänigstes Gutachten*, 17–18.

149. Walter, *Österreichische Verfassungs- und Verwaltungsgeschichte*, ÖZV II,1, 242 ff.; ÖZV II, 2, Documents, no. 74, 391–406.

150. ÖZV II,2, Documents, no. 74, 405.

151. Directorial decree, February 12, 1752, ÖZV II,2, Documents, no. 74, 405.

152. Obersteiner, *Theresianische Verwaltungsreformen*, 175.

153. The effect of these policing initiatives in Styria is investigated in Obersteiner, *Theresianische Verwaltungsreformen*, esp. 173 ff.

154. Obersteiner, *Theresianische Verwaltungsreformen*, 175.

155. This Auersperg, born in 1723, was (or rather her husband was) a distant relative of Francis Stephen's lover.

156. See the decree from June 1754, Kropatschek, *Sammlung* II, 357–60.

157. Obersteiner, *Theresianische Verwaltungsreformen*, 177.

158. Cited in Obersteiner, *Theresianische Verwaltungsreformen*, 177.

159. Ammerer/Weiß, *Strafe*.

160. Steiner, *Rückkehr*, 299n ff.; also Steiner, *Schnepfenjagd*.

161. Steiner, *Rückkehr*, 308.

162. *Wienerisches Diarium* 1753, no. 86; see Steiner, *Rückkehr*, 319.

163. Steiner, *Rückkehr*, 314; with a precise reconstruction of the composition of individual deportations and developments between 1744 and 1768.

164. Steiner, *Rückkehr*, 317 ff.

165. Steiner, *Rückkehr*, 329 ff.

166. Steiner, *Rückkehr*, 348–49.

167. Steiner, *Rückkehr*, 330.

168. Source edited in Steiner, *Rückkehr*, 548 ff. See ibid., 361 ff.; Beales, "Joseph II's Rêveries," I, 246 ff.

169. Cited in Steiner, *Rückkehr*, 367.

170. Kropatschek, *Sammlung* III, 248 ff., 254 ff.; also in Klueting, *Der Josephinismus*, 44 ff.

171. Kropatschek, *Sammlung* III, 249–50.

172. Otto Ulbricht, *Kindsmord und Aufklärung in Deutschland*, Munich 1990; Michalik, *Kindsmord*.

173. See genealogical table, p. 1024.

174. Rohr, *Einleitung*, 168–69.

175. KMT I, 117.

176. J. Frank, *System* II, 62; Johann Storch, *Weiberkrankheiten*, Vienna 1747; see Duden, "Ein falsch Gewächs."

177. To Ferdinand, July 1, 1773, BKF I, 214.

178. Maria Theresa to Tarouca, September 1766, Karajan, *Maria Theresia und Graf Sylva-Tarouca*, 62: "I will have my daughter bled so she will fall pregnant."

179. Stolberg, *Homo patiens*, 123–24.

180. KMT II, 357.

181. KMT II, 262, 357; III, 18, 147.

182. E.g., KMT II, 328, 357.

183. Arneth, *Geschichte Maria Theresia's* I, 54.

184. A similar court decree was proclaimed in June 11, 1611; see Deuticke, *Geschichte der Geburtshilfe*, 113.

185. Steidele, *Hebammenkunst*, following Deuticke, *Geschichte der Geburtshilfe*, 101–102; the same view is still held by J. Frank, *System* (1779), see Martus, *Aufklärung*, 812 ff.

186. Arneth, *Geschichte Maria Theresia's* I, 400.

187. Arneth, *Geschichte Maria Theresia's* I, 400.

188. KMT II, 262 ff.; also long kneeling in the Easter liturgy: KMT III, 21; see Stöckele, *Über Geburten*, 38 ff.; Arneth, *Geschichte Maria Theresia's* IV, 169.

189. To her sister Marianna, October 21, 1744, in Arneth, *Geschichte Maria Theresia's* II, 452–53, BAA, 39–40.

190. BKF I, 128, 139 on her own stillbirth; to Ferdinand, BKF I, 95, 127, 135 ff., 160, 180 ff., 185, 197, 206, 212, 217–18, 219–20, 312–13, 316 ff.; to Marie Antoinette: Christoph, *Maria Theresia: Geheimer Briefwechsel*, 31, 78–79, 109; to Beatrix, BKF III, passim.

191. E.g., KMT II, 26; KMT III, 178.

192. To Dietrichstein, February 11, 1745, BAA, 42; see also to Dietrichstein, February 24, 1746, BKF IV, 171.

193. KMT III, 169; likewise in 1755: KMT III, 232.

194. KMT II, 19.

195. E.g., KMT III, 16, 20, 51.

196. To Antonia of Saxony, Lippert, *Briefwechsel*, 5–6.

197. To Antonia of Saxony, Lippert, *Briefwechsel*, 7–8.

198. To Antonia of Saxony, Lippert, *Briefwechsel*, 10–11, 13.

199. To Antonia of Saxony, Lippert, *Briefwechsel*, 23.

200. To Antonia of Saxony, Lippert, *Briefwechsel*, 113.

201. KMT II, 22.

202. KMT III, 55.—On a bet between Maria Theresa and Prince Dietrichstein on the sex of her next child, see Pichler, *Denkwürdigkeiten*, 16; and Koschatzky, *Maria Theresia* (catalog), 224. See to Marie Beatrix, September 12, 1774, BKF III, 183.

203. This was reported by the Venetian emissary Capello, cited in Arneth, *Geschichte Maria Theresia's* I, 400, see ibid., 255–56.

204. Instruction of Prince Euseubius von Liechtenstein, Fürstlich Liechtensteinsches Domänenarchiv, VA 5-2-2, 139–47.

205. See Laqueur, *Auf dem Leib*. Together with Aristotle and Hippocrates, the learned physician, Galen of Pergamon (2nd century CE), was *the* authority for premodern European medicine.

206. Charles VI to Francis Stephen, cited in Hennings, *Und sitzet zur linken Hand*, 197.

207. Not just in Vienna: Moser, *Teutsches Hof-Recht*, 636.

208. KMT II, 21, 153; III, 266. See Stöckelle, "Über Geburten."

209. KMT IV, 55.

210. See Labouvie, *Andere Umstände*.

211. In 1748, however, she wrote to Antonia of Saxony that she would rather spare her husband this scene: Lippert, *Briefwechsel*, 5–6.

212. KMT II, 152–53.

213. KMT II, 21–22, 148–49, 151 ff. In 1755, while still a minor, Joseph had been kept away from the birth of his youngest sister, Maria Antonia, in order that he "might not see or hear anything unseemly and indecent for his age"; KMT III, 266.

214. KMT II, 79: the chief ladies-in-waiting and the women of the lord high steward had to appear at the delivery; this was still the case at Maria Amalia's birth in 1746 and Leopold's in 1747, KMT II, 152–53. On birth and baptismal ceremonial, see Irene Kubiska's contribution in Pangerl/Scheutz/Winkelbauer, *Der Wiener Hof*, 493–59.

215. Only three court ladies were in attendance when the empress suffered a stillbirth in 1748; a fourth arrived too late, KMT II, 266.

216. KMT III, 56, 266.

217. KMT III, 266–67.

218. KMT III, 59.

219. See Horn, "Wiener Hebammen."

220. Brechka, *Gerard Van Swieten*, 111 ff.; Broman, *Transformation*; Lesky/Wandruszka, *Gerard Van Swieten*; on Maria Theresa's relationship to van Swieten, see BKF I, 14 ff.; see chapter 9, this volume.

221. See Stolberg, *Homo patiens*.

222. See also chapter 9, this volume, also her letter to Beatrix, BKF III, 161: despite her sixteen children, she knew nothing about medicine and wanted to know nothing, too, so that she might better obey her physician.

223. Important contemporary books on midwifery were written by the Viennese doctors Crantz (1756), Steidele (1774), and Plenk (1768). On the medicalization of midwifery from the late eighteenth-century onward, see Seidel, *Eine neue "Kultur des Gebärens."*

224. Heinrich Johann Cranz, *Einleitung in eine wahre und gegründete Hebammenkunst*, Vienna 1756.

225. Franz Deuticke, *Geschichte der Geburtshilfe*, 85.

226. Franz Deuticke, *Geschichte der Geburtshilfe*, 83.

227. See Christel Meier-Staubach, *Gemma spiritalis: Methode und Gebrauch der Edelsteinallegorese vom frühen Christentum bis ins 18. Jahrhundert*, Munich 1977, 325 ff.

228. To Hofrat Posch, July 17, 1771, BKF IV, 329.

229. Stöckelle, "Taufzeremoniell," 293.

230. To Ferdinand, August 12, 1773, BKF I, 220; December 16, 1776, BKF II, 58–59; see KMT III, 266: "now mostly in bed."

231. To Ferdinand, July 16, 1777, BKF II, 92: only German physicians from van Swieten's school.

232. To Ferdinand, March-April 1773, BKF I, 188 ff.

233. KMT I, 251, 266–67. See Maria Theresa's letters to her sister Marianna, BAA, 38–39, 40.

234. See to Antonia of Saxony, July 21, 1767, Lippert, *Briefwechsel*, 256–57.

235. See to Ferdinand, July 9, 1772, BKF I, 135–36.

236. To Ferdinand, July 9, 1772, BKF I, 135–36.

237. The children who died in infancy all go unmentioned in Hamann, *Die Habsburger*, 442. Maria Carolina, who died on the day of her birth, is completely left out of Koschatzky, *Maria Theresia* (catalog), 15; she is mentioned but not named in Crankshaw, *Maria Theresia*, 8–9, as in a meticulous genealogical table from 1837 in Pangels, *Die Kinder*.

238. Rohr, *Einleitung*, 171.

239. To Countess Trautson (1750), van Rhyn, "Unveröffentlichte Briefe," 268.

240. Pečar, *Die Ökonomie der Ehre*, 90.

241. On Maria Luggau, see Lobenwein, "'Je gresser die lieb'" 149.

242. KMT II, 262 ff.; see Stöckelle, "Geburten," 38 ff., 84 ff.

243. Max Francis also received an emergency baptism in 1756 after an unusually difficult birth. Khevenhüller reports that the act of baptism had almost been repeated the following day during the official ceremony, although this was inadmissible under church law; KMT IV, 55–56.

244. According to the Venetian emissary Diedo, see Arneth, *Geschichte Maria Theresia's* IV, 519–20.

245. KMT II, 266.

246. The architectural expansion of the palace under Pacassi and the painting of the interior by Franz Anton Maulbertsch, among others, lasted from 1765 to 1776. Maria Theresa had a portrait of Joseph with his two late wives and his deceased daughter displayed in another hall of the castle at Innsbruck. See Barta, *Familienporträts*, 43 ff.; Telesko, "Maria Theresias 'Familia Augusta.'"

247. See chapter 2, this volume.

248. Stöckelle, "Taufzeremoniell," 293.

249. See the overview in Stöckelle, "Taufzeremoniell," 319 ff.

250. In 1759–50, Kaunitz had already been looking for French godparents for Maria Theresa's next child in the event it was a boy (which was not the case); see Arneth, *Geschichte Maria Theresia's* IV, 319.

251. KMT III, 178–79.

252. See Arneth, *Geschichte Maria Theresia's* I, 254 ff.; Barta, *Familienporträts*, 37–38, 70–71, 157–58; Küster, *Vier Monarchien*, 102 ff.; Telesko, *Maria Theresia*, 124; Telesko/Hertel/Linsboth, "Zwischen Panegyrik."

253. Ghelen, *Wienerische Beleuchtungen*, 96; cited in Barta, *Familienporträts*, 38; see Telesko/Hertel/Linsboth, "Zwischen Panegyrik," with additional examples.

254. Telesko/Hertel/Linsboth, "Zwischen Panegyrik."

255. The same practice was observed for Maria Theresa's sons Charles (in 1745) and Maximilian Francis (in 1757), just as her own parents had observed it for her late brother Leopold; see Stöckelle, "Geburten," 27.

256. *Wienerisches Diarium*, August 27, 1746, no. 69, see Stöckelle, "Tauzeremoniell," 298. A scudo was a silver coin weighing around 23 grams.

257. Rohr, *Einleitung*, 174. See Richard Blaas, "Das Fest der geweihten Windeln," *Wiener Monatsheft* 36 (1962): 26–27; Stöckelle, *Taufzeremoniell*, 297–98.

258. To Ulfeld, March 31, 1762, BKF IV, 199.

259. HHStA ZP 18, fol. 75r. The child was later presented to the people of Vienna at the Hofburg window before being sent on the journey to Hungary; see Arneth, *Geschichte Maria Theresia's* I, 267.

260. Stöckelle, "Über Geburten," 94; Stöckelle, *Taufzeremoniell*, 307 ff.

261. In 1776 Khevenhüller described it as "against the current custom" when the daughter of the French emissary, Comtesse de Matignon, breastfed her child; KMT VIII, 82; see to Marie Antoinette, 25.11.1778, MACS III, 270.

262. Crantz, *Einleitung*, 177 ff.

263. To van Swieten (undated, May 1754?), BKF IV, 235.

264. Cited in Haslinger, "Franz Stephan," 103–104.

265. Badinter, *Die Mutterliebe*; see Opitz, "Pflicht-Gefühl."

266. Engraving by Albrecht Schultheiß after Alexander (von) Liezen-Mayer, published as a woodcut in "Daheim" 1868, 237, and frequently photographically reproduced, E.g., Telesko, *Maria Theresia*, 164–65; illustration in Koschatzky, *Maria Theresia*, 466; see Prologue, this volume.

267. Hyacinth Holland, "Liezen-Mayer, Alexander von," *ADB* 51 (1906): 709–15 [online version] URL: http://www.deutsche-biographie.de/pnd117004375.html?anchor=abd

268. See chapter 7, this volume.

269. A similar legend can be found in Meiji-era Japan in a kabuki play by Mokuami Kawatake (1885). I thank Naoko Matsumoto, Tokyo, for this reference.

270. Political Testament of 1750–51, BAA, 66.

7. Distinctions and Refinements

1. Arneth, *Geschichte Maria Theresia's* I, 253, based on Podewils's report; Hinrichs, *Friedrich der Große*, 39 ff.

2. Arneth, *Geschichte Maria Theresia's* II, 192–93; X, 743–44.

3. Voltaire, *Age of Louis XIV* III, 33; translation modified.

4. Dutens, *Mémoires*, 343–44. Further evidence that she was worshiped by all: Ligne, *Fragments* I, 119; Arnheim, "Das Urtheil," 289; Weretheimer, "Zwei Schilderungen," 213–14; Coke, *Letters* III, 320, 464; IV, 67; see also Michaud, "Laudatio," 686–87; an example of later historians' judgments is Andreas, *Das theresianische Österreich*, 8: she sought "her sole reward and happiness in the love of her subjects."

5. See Frevert, *Gefühlspolitik*, on Frederick II as "lord over hearts"; Martus, *Aufklärung*, 586 ff.

6. See Brendecke, *Imperium und Empirie*.

7. According to the Habsburg mirror for princes, *Princeps in compendio*, 23 ("be friendly"), 61 ff. ("give everyone a hearing").

8. Hinrichs, *Friedrich der Große*, 40; see chapter 3, this volume.

9. Luise Gottsched to Friedrich Heinrich von Seckendorf, October 1749, in Gottsched, "Mit der Feder," 147 ff.; see Martus, *Aufklärung*, 594 ff.; on Frau Gottsched, Susanne Kord, *Little Detours: The Letters and Plays of Luise Gottsched (1713–1762)*, Rochester NY 2000.

10. Charles VI had blamed Seckendorf for defeat in the last Turkish war and confined him in a fortress; Maria Theresa had him released as soon as she came to the throne.

11. Luise Gottsched to Friedrich Heinrich von Seckendorf, October 1749, in Gottsched, "Mit der Feder," 148.

12. Küchelbecker, *Allerneueste Nachricht*; Keyßler, *Neueste Reisen*, 1213 ff.; Guibert, *Journal* I, 290 ff.; Pilati, *Reisen* I, 21 ff. See Gudrun Swoboda (ed.), *Die kaiserliche Gemäldegalerie in Wien und die Anfänge des öffentlichen Kunstmuseums, I: Die kaiserliche Galerie im Belvedere (1776–1837)* (Vienna/Cologne/Weimar 2013).

13. Today Old Court Pharmacy and parts of the Spanish Riding School.

14. Franz Christoph von Scheyb, *Theresiade: Ein Ehren-Gedicht*, Vienna 1746; Martus, *Aufklärung*, 595; Telesko, *Maria Theresia*, 112–13.

15. Iby, "Das Schönbrunn," 13–14; Yonan, *Empress*, 86 ff.; Iby/Koller, *Schönbrunn*, 90 ff., with numerous illustrations of the rooms in their present state; Telesko, "Die Erbinn," on the decorations of the two galleries. Official diplomatic audiences were held in Schönbrunn from 1746 onward, KMT II, 91.

16. KMT II, 119–20.

17. No. 1–4 on the plan shown in fig. 27; see Iby, "Schönbrunn," 13–14; Yonan, *Empress*, 83 ff. Where exactly the Gottscheds were received cannot be reconstructed with any certainty.

18. KMT VI, 249.

19. E.g., KMT I, 220, 237.

20. Krischer, "Das Gesandtschaftswesen"; Stollberg-Rilinger, *Emperor's Old Clothes*, 138 ff.; Yonan, *Empress*, 86 ff.; Benedik, "Zeremoniell"; Graf, "Das kaiserliche Zeremoniell."

21. See Graf, "Das kaiserliche Zeremoniell," 576; Benedik, "Zeremoniell." Moser, *Teutsches Hof-recht*, 299: "Ordinarily, only one wing is opened up; both, however, are open to the sovereign and her family."

22. Hinrichs, *Friedrich der Große*, 45; Ranke, "Maria Theresia und ihr Hof," 672–73.

23. Presumably antechamber number 4.

24. Luise Gottsched to Friedrich Heinrich von Seckendorf, October 1749, Gottsched, "Mit der Feder," 148–49.

25. KMT IV, 4–5; see Ranke, "Maria Theresia und ihr Hof."

26. KMT II, 34; II, 156; see Moser, *Teutsches Hof-recht* II, 681–82.

27. Presumably the second or great antechamber (no. 5). It is not entirely clear what is meant by "the Empress's room"; her apartments did not directly border on the second antechamber but were reached via several connecting rooms; see Iby, "Schönbrunn," III. 5.

28. Luise Gottsched to Friedrich Heinrich von Seckendorf, October 1749, Gottsched, "Mit der Feder," 149.

29. Linger, *Denkwürdigkeiten*, 225.

30. In January 1787; on the context, see Stollberg-Rilinger, *Emperor's Old Clothes*, 257.

31. Luise Gottsched to Friedrich Heinrich von Seckendorf, October 1749, Gottsched, "Mit der Feder," 149.

32. Later, the little archdukes and archduchesses were even integrated into official diplomatic ceremonial, and the diplomats were required to kiss the hands of all the imperial children; see chapter 9, this volume.

33. Moore, *A View* II, 266.

34. Johann Christoph Gottsched, "*Zwei Gedichte, womit gegen . . . ,*" Kassel 1750, 42–49; see Telesko, *Maria Theresia*, 113–14. Lessing, too, received an audience with Maria Theresia in 1775; unlike the Gottscheds, he made no great fuss about it. Gotthold Ephraim Lessing to Karl Lessing, May 7, 1755, in *Sämtliche Schriften*, ed. Karl Lachmann, Leipzig 1907, XVIII, 138; see the statements on Lessing's visit to Vienna in Richard Daunicht (ed.), *Lessing im Gespräch*, Munich 1971, 358 ff.

35. Luise Gottsched mentions this later in a letter to Dorothee von Runkel dated February 4, 1758. The letter was written during the war, at a time when she took a different view of things; see Gottsched, "Mit der Feder," 289.

36. Gottsched, "Mit der Feder," 48: "I saw you, this is my undying fame!"

37. Gottsched, "Mit der Feder," 14 ff.

38. Deutsch, *Mozart: Die Dokumente*, 17 ff.; see Gruber, *Wolfgang Amadeus Mozart*, 14; Solomon, *Mozart*, 40–41; Beales, *Mozart and the Habsburgs*.

39. See chapter 3, this volume.

40. E.g., Cigaretten-Bilderdienst Hamburg-Bahrenfeld (Reemtsma), *Bilder deutscher Geschichte*, no. 97; Eckstein-Halpaus Zigarettenfabrik, *Ruhmesblätter deutscher Geschichte*, no. 123; Homann Margarinewerke, *Geschichte unserer Welt*, no. 126 (Sammlung Bernhard Jussen, Frankfurt am Main).

41. An opera that Mozart wrote for the imperial household in May 1768 remained unperformed owing to intrigues. The performance of his works for the consecration of the orphanage church on the Rennweg, however, was known to have been attended by Maria Theresa.

42. BKF I, 92; also in Deutsch, *Mozart: Die Dokumente*, 124. On August 5, 1773, Mozart had another audience with Maria Theresa but without any subsequent commissions: see Solomon, *Mozart*, 75 ff.; Baur, *Mozart*, 235. Arneth, *Geschichte Maria Theresia's* IX, 291, fails to mention the letter to Ferdinand and claims instead that the empress "probably" took "first place" among Mozart's admirers.

43. *Prosch, Leben*; the autobiography was first published in his lifetime, in 1789, but fell largely into oblivion in the nineteenth century and was not reissued until the twentieth. See Petrat, *Die letzten Narren*.

44. Prosch, *Leben*, 57.

45. See chapter 7, this volume.

46. This is revealed by the lists of subscribers, which contain numerous names from the south and southwest German nobility.

47. Prosch, *Leben*, 35.

48. Prosch, *Leben*, 50 ff.

49. In letters to Countess Enzenberg, the wife of the governor of Tyrol, Maria Theresa wrote of the *naiveté du Tirolien*; see the quote in Trapp, "Maria Theresia und Tirol," 135; on Tyrol's unique status in the hereditary lands, see Stauber, *Der Zentralstaat*.

50. See Braun, *Princeps et episcopus*.

51. Prosch, *Leben*, 54.

52. Prosch, *Leben*, 55–56.

53. See KMT VI, 124.

54. Prosch, *Leben*, 110 etc.

55. Prosch, *Leben*, 100–109; see KMT VI, 124: Francis Stephen amused himself at table in Innsbruck "with a Tyrolean merchant he knew from Vienna, who entertained him in the manner of his country. He is known for relishing the company of such people."

56. Prosch, *Leben*, 108–109.

57. Prosch, *Leben*, 152.

58. Prosch, *Leben*, 166–67.

59. Prosch, *Leben*, 103.

60. See Arnheim, "Das Urtheil," 291, according to which Maria Theresa (seen in 1756 from the perspective of the Swedish emissary Bark) granted an audience to anyone who requested it (*à tous ceux qui Lui en demandent*). Hinrichs, *Friedrich der Große*, 45, wrote in 1747 that it had become more difficult to gain an audience; at the beginning of Maria Theresa's reign, "everyone" had been freely admitted, whereas now one had to apply through a lady-in-waiting. So too already *Princeps in compendio*, 61 ff.

61. This is made explicit in *Princeps in compendio*, 61 ff.; see also the above-cited passage in Voltaire, *Siècle de Louis XV*.

62. The example is cited in Arneth, *Geschichte Maria Theresia's* IV, 143. See too Maria Theresa to Maria Christina, April 1766, in Wolf, *Marie Christine* I, 63–65.

63. Chamber entry regulation, 20.11.1745, HHStA ZA SR 11 (instruction book 2), 205–211, ed., in Pangerl/Scheutz/Winkelbauer, *Der Wiener Hof*, 283–285, here 282; see Benedik, "Zeremoniell"; Graf, "Das kaiserliche Zeremoniell."

64. KMT II, 37.

65. See Neuhaus, "Wassertrinken"; Schennach, "Supplikationen"; Nubola, *Bittschriften*; Haug-Moritz/Ullmann, *Supplikationspraxis*.

66. Loen, *Kleine Schriften* I, 21–22: "The emperor's anterooms, especially on court and feast days, are full of great lords and diplomats by noon. The high are here low, and princes, counts, and lords mingle here with the lowliest nobles, officers, scribes, and all kinds of people. This place alone, the estates in the world all appear to be equal; for as soon as the emperor appears, everyone bows with equal submissiveness before His Majesty." Similarly, Küchelbecker, *Allerneueste Nachricht*, 382 ff.; Keyßler, *Reisen*, 1230; see Pečar, *Die Ökonomie der Ehre*, 151 ff.; Pangerl/Scheutz/Winkelbauer, *Der Wiener Hof*, 263 ff.

67. Ranke, "Maria Theresia und ihr Hof," 672–73.

68. Tarouca to Maria Theresa (undated, 1741–1742): "*C'est aussi sanctifier les Fêtes, que d'écoutter benignement les pauvres pretendants.*" Karajan, *Maria Theresia und Graf Sylva-Tarouca*, 6.

69. Guibert, *Journal* I, 283–84: "*un mot au Chambellan suffit presque toujours pour y être admis.*"

70. See Dutens, *Mémoires*, 343–44, who praises her free walks in the park (although these were supervised by the lord high steward).

71. It turned out to be a false warning, however; KMT I, 150–151 (May 1743).

72. Lieben, "Briefe," 396–97. See chapter 12, this volume.

73. Linger, *Denkwürdigkeiten*, 226 ff.

74. KMT I, 156.

75. KMT III, 132–33.

76. KMT III, 133.

77. KMT III, 133; the formulation is not entirely clear; which "alternative channels" were meant is left unsaid.

78. Ranke, "Maria Theresia und ihr Hof," 673.

79. See the futile attempts by the Abbot of Niederaltaich to prevent the ruinous sequestration of his monastery by pleading with the confessor Kampmüller and the cabinet councillor Königsegg to intercede on the monastery's behalf; Schuegraf, "Das österreichische Lager," 65, 68.

80. See Hinrichs, *Friedrich der Große*, 97 ff.; an example in Arneth, "Graf Philipp Cobenzl," 107; see chapter 6, this volume.

81. Examples in Wührer/Scheutz, *Zu Diensten*, 662, 634, 701; see Kubiska-Scharl/Pölzl, *Die Karrieren*, 73.

82. To Marie Antoinette, April 21, 1770, MACS I, 4; to Maria Christina, April 1766, BKF II, 361 ff.; to Amalia, June 1769, BKF III, 13.

83. Linger, *Denkwürdigkeiten*, 229.

84. Kubiska-Scharl/Pölzl, *Die Karrieren*, 61 ff.; Kubiska-Scharl, "Formalisierte Gnade"; B. Wunder, "Die Institutionialisierung."

85. Examples from HHStA OMeA Alte Akten (Ältere Reihe), 37 (1746).

86. "Outsiders who had nothing to do with the court clearly took this path . . . only rarely or were rebuffed without leaving behind any traces in the records," according to Kubiska-Scharl/Pölzl, *Die Karrieren*, 70.

87. See Hengerer, *Kaiserhof und Adel*, 625 ff.

88. Luebke speaks of "naïve monarchism"; see also Rauscher, "Krieg—Steuern—Religion—Recht," 271–72; see chapters 11 and 13, this volume.

89. Kropatschek, *Sammlung* VII, 72, 498, 536 ff. See the examples of failed peasant deputations to Vienna in chapters 11 and 13, this volume.

90. Kropatschek, *Sammlung* VII, 498. Individual studies for the eighteenth century are very rare; see Grüll, *Bauer*; Schennach, "Supplikationen"; Bredow, "Die niederösterreichischen Kreisämter"; Rauscher, "Krieg—Steuern—Religion—Recht."

91. Leopold, "Stato della famiglia." 344.

92. Leopold, "Stato della famiglia." 344.

93. See chapter 2, this volume.

94. Whether the urban population really "wanted and demanded nothing more" than to put on grand illuminations is doubtful (KMT II, 35 ff.). See KMT III, 192: the people of Prague grumbled about the illuminations at the empress's visit in 1754, owing to the associated costs and the fire risk. See also the sardonic criticism in Moser, Hofrecht I, 293.

95. Montaigne, *Essais*, 3 vols., France 1580, III, 8.

96. This was the case in many coronation rituals, not just in the Holy Roman Empire; see Stollberg-Rilinger, *Rituale*. Lottery, *cuccagna* and wine fountain for the peasants: e.g., KMT IV, 28; coins were thrown after Maria Theresa's recovery from smallpox, for example: KMT VI, 252.

97. So too in Milan at the entry of Archduke Ferdinand in 1771, when a young girl was killed; see BKF I, 85. The custom was criticized as barbaric and cruel by the Marquis de Sade, of all people; see Reinhardt, *De Sade*, 145.

98. See Rohr, *Einleitung*, 76–77; Duindam, *Vienna and Versailles*.

99. So in the instruction for the Master of the Staff (*Oberstabelmeister*) from December 14, 1769, in Pangerl/Scheutz/Winkelbauer, *Der Wiener Hof*, 116 ff.

100. HHStA ZP 18, fol. 75r; see chapter 6, this volume.

101. Seltschek, "Karussell," 413. Similarly, a grand ball was held following Maria Theresa's recovery from smallpox in 1767; KMT VI, 268.

102. Rohr, *Einleitung*, 75.

103. KMT VI, 79–80. There was a similar ruckus on the occasion of the marriage of Archduke Leopold in Innsbruck in July 1765: KMT VI, 111–2. Disapproval of the "mob" being allowed in at gala dinners is also expressed in Coke, *Letters* III, 327, 329, 347.

104. KMT VI, 80–81.

105. See Scheutz, "Der vermenschte Heiland"; see also Jörg Sonntag, "Eine verkehrte Ordnung als Ordnungsfundament? Analytische Refelxionen zur mittelalterlichen Gründonnerstagsfußwaschung als Inversionsritual," in Dominik Fugger, ed., *Verkehrte Welten*? (HZ, supplementary volume 50), Munich 2013, 102–26.

106. Coke, *Letters* III, 384 ff.; IV, 58. Joseph II initially abolished the washing of the feet after the death of his father, KMT VI, 231–32, although the ritual was subsequently reinstated; see KMT VII, 13.

107. This, at any rate, was how Karl von Zinzendorf depicted the ceremony on April 8, 1762, Breunlich/Mader, *Karl Graf von Zinzendorf*, 278–79. He was also far less impressed than Lady Coke, finding that the emperor and archdukes had performed the ritual "quite negligently."

108. E.g., KMT III, 13 (2000 ducats), 236 (3000 ducats).

109. The pay records of the lord high steward's office from 1763 indicate that the four chancery clerks received between 200 and 600 guilders each, in Scheutz and Wührer, *Zu Diensten*, 947.

110. The *triomphe rustique* took place in the course of the festivities organized by Khevenhüller's wife: KMT IV, 28–29. It was therefore far more positively appraised by Khevenhüller than the peasant dances staged by Kaunitz.

111. KMT IV, 28.

112. KMT III, 253–54; KMT I, 161, 179; KMT VI, 119.

113. KMT II, 346; III, 254 (butter churning); KMT II, 105; VI, 57; *Wiener Diarium*, September 1, 1751 (fishing); KMT I, 182; II, 180; V, 69 (grape harvesting).

114. KMT II, 172–73.

115. See Schnitzer, *Höfische Maskeraden*.

116. KMT III, 87.

117. KMT I, 118.

118. See Gestrich, "Höfisches Zeremoniell."

119. See chapter 2, this volume.

120. The standard work on ceremonial in general, despite all the necessary modifications, is still Elias, *Court Society*; further Berns/Rahn, *Zeremoniell*; Hahn/Schütte, *Zeichen und Raum*; Stollberg-Rilinger, "Höfische Öffentlichkeit"; Stollberg-Rilinger, *Emperor's Old Clothes*; on the imperial court, Pečar, *Die Ökonomie der Ehre*; Duindam, *Vienna and Versailles*; Hengerer, *Kaiserhof und Adel*; Pangerl/Scheutz/Winkelbauer, *Der Wiener Hof*.

121. Hengerer, "Die Zeremonialprotokolle"; Hengerer, "Die Abrechnungsbücher."

122. The most important were Lünig, *Theatrum ceremoniale*, and Rohr, *Einleitung*.

123. KMT I, 209.

124. See, e.g., the resulting problems in the relation between the rank of imperial prince and the office of chamberlain in KMT II, 42–43, 44–45, 116, 154, 198, 360; see Pečar, "Gab es eine höfische Gesellschaft"; Duindam, "Habsburg Court."

125. This was especially tricky at the Viennese court because the status of the House of Lorraine was so ambiguous and contentious. See chapter 2, this volume.

126. Benedik, "Die herrschaftlichen Appartements," following HHStA OMeA ZP 23, 1751–52, fol. 446 ff.—See also the dispute concerning the ambassadorial hand kiss, chapter 10, this volume.

127. E.g., Maria Theresa to Khevenhüller, March 19, 1754, Wolf, *Aus dem Hofleben*, 328: access *par finesse et distinction* for his daughter-in-law; or KMT IV, 128: access to the chamber as a particular refinement for the Prince of Zweibrücken.

128. On the family, see the brief accounts in Adam Wolf, "Khevenhüller," in ADB 15 (1882), 705–706; Kurt Peball, "Khevenhüller," NDB 11 (1977): 569 (no personal entries, only entries for the family); Wurzbach, BLKÖ XI, 211–12 is also brief and riddled with errors; see also Wolf, *Aus den Hofleben*; Schlitter, "Einleitung," in KMT I, 1–98; Breunlich-Pawlik, "Die Aufzeichnungen"; on the Khevenhüllers in the context of grandees from the hereditary lands, see also Lebeau, *Aristocrates et grands commis*, 26 ff. Surprisingly, there is no more recent biographical study of Khevenhüller.

129. Hengerer, *Kaiserhof und Adel*, 625 ff. The sphere of influence of the grand marshal of the court was further removed than that of the Lord High Chamberlain. There is an example of the influence attributed to the lady-in-waiting Guttenberg and cabinet secretary Neny in Arneth, "Graf Philipp Cobenzl," 107.

130. On his father's diaries, see Breunlich-Pawlick, "Die Aufzeichnungen."

131. Vol. 1: *1742–44*, vol. 2: *1745–49*; [lacuna 1750–51]; vol. 3: *1752–55*; vol. 4: *1756–57*; vol. 5: *1758–59*; [lacuna 1760–63]; vol. 6: *1764–67*; [lacuna 1768–69]; vol. 7: *1770–73*; vol. 8: *1774–76*, with addenda by the son to 1780. Hans Schlitter's edition contains a great deal of additional source material in the notes.

132. Testament of Count Bartholomäus Khevenhüller from 1610, cited in Breunlich-Pawlik, "Die Aufzeichnungen," 235.

133. 1765 second lord high steward, 1770 first. See Kubiska-Schorl/Pölzl, *Die Karrieren*, index. On his unloved reassignment to the office of Lord High Steward, see KMT VI, 140–41.

134. For example, he foreshadows Francis Stephen's death, KMT VI, 122, 158.

135. Schlitter's edition contains the additional papers, insofar as they were still extant at the time. The value of the edition therefore goes far beyond the actual diary. There is no modern historical-critical edition. Großegger, *Theater*, offers only a small selection. Hugo von Hofmannsthal consulted the diary when writing his libretto for *Der Rosenkavalier*.

136. KMT V, 87.

137. E.g., KMT III, 125 and passim.

138. "Singularism": KMT IV, 87, further criticism E.g., KMT III, 114–5, 119, 123, 252 ff.; IV, 11, 46, 76, 123, 138, 143–44; KMT V, 9, 14; KMT VIII, 12, 41 ff.; 68, 106.

139. KMT II, 103; see KMT I, 187–88; KMT II, 86, 140–41, 156, 163–64; KMT IV, 2; KMT V, 101.

140. KMT II, 37.

141. KMT III, 268. For the traditional view, see Walter, *Männer um Maria Theresia*.

142. Edited in Wolf, *Aus dem Hofleben*, 326–36.

143. To Hofrat Doblhoff, October 22, 1743, BAA, 36.

144. The quote is taken from one of Maria Theresa's few letters to Khevenhüller (1754), in Wolf, *Aus dem Hofleben*, 328.

145. "*Toute la famille a des merites envers notre Maison,*" she wrote to Marie Beatrix on March 24, 1771, BKF III, 116.

146. She did so at the beginning, when she appointed Kaunitz, KMT III, 70–71; but also on many subsequent occasions, e.g., KMT VII, 49, 62, 76; VIII, 12.

147. Karajan, *Maria Theresia und Graf Sylva-Tarouca*, 3–9. On Tarouca, see chapter 6, this volume.

148. Tarouca explicitly refers to Ignatius of Loyala's exercises, Karajan, *Maria Theresia und Graf Sylva-Tarouca*, 8.

149. To Ferdinand, March 5, 1772, BKF I, 105–106, repeated almost verbatim 162–3, likewise 125, 128, 133–34, 156–57, 176, 185, 207, 218, 248, 254, 266, 270, 272.

150. To Ferdinand, October 28, 1772, BKF I, 163.

151. To Ferdinand, June 9, 1774, BKF I, 281.

152. To Ferdinand, May 2, 1774, BKF I, 276; see ibid., 248, 254, 266, 270, 272, 278, 281, 284, 315, 322, 346; BKF II, 13, 98–99, 109, 123, 184, 190 ff., 226–27, 230–31.

153. E.g., to Ferdinand, September 2, 1772, BKF I, 148.

154. Maria Theresa to Countess Enzenberg, October 6, 1770, BKF IV, 500.

155. Bark (1756), cited in Arnheim, "Das Urtheil," 391, and Fürst (1755) in Ranke, "Maria Theresia und ihr Hof," 670–74; similarly Hinrichs, *Friedrich der Große*, 53 (1747); Pichler,

Denkwürdigkeiten, 10–11. See KMT III, 174, 226; from the early 1750s, she then mostly retired for the evening before supper at nine o'clock. See also the note in her prayer book recording her daily routine in her widowhood: Wolf, *Marie Christine* I, 81–82.

156. See, e.g., to Ferdinand, November 4, 1779, BKF II, 222. See chapter 11, this volume.

157. E.g., Karajan, *Maria Theresia und Graf Sylva-Tarouca*, 18, 22.

158. To Ferdinand, March 12, 1772, BKF I, 110.

159. To Ferdinand, April 9, 1772, BKF I, 117; see her regulations for admittance BKF I, 95–96, 161–62, 187, 231; for Leopold: Instruction de S. M. L'Impeatrice pour le Ceremoniel aux Cours de ses Enfans 1765. ÖNB Wiener Hofbibliothek, Codex Series N. 1713, fol. 47–52.

160. To Ferdinand, May 14, 1772, BKF I, 123.

161. KMT VI, 30.

162. See Elias, *Court Society*; Goffman, *Presentation of Self*; further Krajewski, *Der Diener*.

163. See Khevenhüller's disapproving commentary, KMT I, 258–59.

164. E.g., Marie Antoinette to Maria Theresa, July 12, 1770, MACS 18 ff.; see Pichler, *Denkwürdigkeiten*, 22; Graf, "Das kaiserliche Zeremoniell," 575–76.

165. In France, for example, the memoirs of Madame de Pompadour's maid: Du Hausset, *Memoires*.

166. Pichler, *Denkwürdigkeiten* I, 7 ff.; written down between 1837 and 1844. See Stefan Jordan, Pichler, Caroline, geb. von Greiner, in NDB 20 (2001), 411–12; Pichler, *Denkwürdigkeiten*; Heindl, "Caroline Pichler."

167. See Wagner, "Royal Graces"; Wagner, "Fürstengnade"; Wagner, "Das Geheime Kammerzahlamt."

168. Pichler was one of them: *Denkwürdigkeiten* I, 10.

169. See Arenth, Greiner.

170. Crankshaw, *Maria Theresia*, 34; Wraxall, *Historical and the Posthumous Memoirs* II, 307–308.

171. Pichler, *Denkwürdigkeiten*, 12–13.

172. In the 1740s, close-fitting curls and a slender silhouette were all the fashion. Maria Theresa had her hair cut short and put in curls for her coronation in Prague in 1743; see Ribeiro, *Dress*, 155 ff.

173. KMT III, 22; see also KMT III, 101, 103, 177.

174. "*Marie n'a jamais eu le ton de se bien mettre*," to Ferdinand, February 1, 1776, BKF II, 8. See to Maria Carolina, August 9, 1767; Rothe, *Die Mutter*, 217–18; April 1768, ibid., 228, 231; see to Ferdinand, July 23, 1772, BKF I, 139, on hairstyles and baths.

175. To Marie Antoinette, November 1, 1770, MACS, 83 ff.; Rothe, *Die Mutter*, 368 ff.

176. For a general overview, see Roche, Culture of Clothing; Mansel, *Dressed to Rule*; Ribeiro, *Dress*; for the details: Biedermann, Deutschland im 18. Jahrhundert.

177. Maria Theresa did not go along with the fashion for ever more elaborate wigs featuring feathers, flowers, and even whole sculptures, as promoted in 1765 by the fashionable Parisian hairdresser Legros. After Francis Stephen's death, she wore a widow's cap with her hair cut short underneath.

178. On the constant "trouble of dressing," Coke, *Letters* III, 312, 314, 328, 342 ff., 457, 461, 472; Coke, *Letters* IV, 1.

179. KMT VIII, 11.

180. *"Janseniste, s. m. (Mode.) c'est un petit panier à l'usage des femmes modestes, & c'est la raison pour laquelle on l'a appellee janséniste,"* according to Diderot/d'Alembert, Encyclopédie VIII, 1766, 450. *Panier* refers to the hoop cage worn under the skirt.

181. See Keyßler, *Neueste Reisen*, 1229: "In their dress, they [their majesties] do not make a great to-do and are an enemy of all affected French fashions."

182. Swinburne, *Courts* I, 352–53; Ammon, in Hinrichs, *Friedrich der Große*, 144.

183. Swinburne, *Courts* I, 352–53; Ammon, in Hinrichs, *Friedrich der Große*, 144.

184. Ammon, in Hinrichs, *Friedrich der Große*, 143–44. In Vienna, it was considered eccentric for men to wear rouge other than at masked balls, see Ligne, *Fragments* I, 148. Rouge was not worn by all ladies, but a lady who went completely without powder was a source of bemusement; see Coke, *Letters* III, 337–38, 375.

185. To Amalia, June 1769: "Adapt to the customs of the land, even if you have to wear make-up," BKF III, 5, 10–11.

186. See chapter 10, this volume.

187. Pichler, *Denkwürdigkeiten*, 18 ff. Coke, *Letters* III, 331, 361–62. To mark the engagement of Maria Theresa's sister Marianna to Charles of Lorraine, 10,000 wax candles were said to have been lit in the winter riding school; Koschatzky, *Maria Theresia* (catalog), 352, no. 71,08.

188. Vigarello, *Wasser und Seife*; for Germany Frey, *Der reinliche Bürger*.

189. To Ferdinand, BKF I, 139: she advised him to bathe regularly, given the Italian heat, but only with his physician's permission. See Burschel, *Die Ehrfindung*.

190. Pichler, *Denkwürdigkeiten*, 18 ff. On Maria Theresa's love of fresh air, even at freezing temperatures, see Coke, *Letters* III, 331, 361–62.

191. Jean Huber, *Voltaires Morgentoilette*, n.p. 1784; statue of Voltaire by Jean-François Houdon, 1778.

192. Although only from 1751; until then, officers were not allowed to appear in uniform at solemnities since court hierarchy, not military hierarchy, was observed at court.

193. Regulation for court mourning, Vienna 1750, in Pangerl/Scheutz/Winkelbauer, *Der Wiener Hof*, 561 ff.

194. KMT II, 180; KMT III, 57–58, 217.

195. E.g., KMT I, 234, 247–48, 251, 263; KMT II, 130; KMT III, 180; KMT V, 25.

196. In December 1754, KMT III, 217; see also the instructions to Ferdinand for the court in Milan: BKF II, 153, 171.

197. KMT V, 97.

198. This was the amount she drew each year for her wardrobe from the Privy Payments Office.

199. Coke, *Letters* III, 316, 335.

200. The notoriously hard-up Prince de Ligne thus sold Maria Theresa a diamond-studded tobacco box featuring the portrait of Louis XV, albeit not before removing the royal portrait. The box was a personal gift from the king himself.

201. See Laurence Fontaine, "Protektion und Ökonomie," in Tilman Haug, Nadir Weber, and Christian Windler (eds.), *Protegierte und Protektoren: Asymmetrische politische Beziehungen zwischen Partnerschaft und Dominanz*, Cologne/Weimar/Vienna 2016, 261–78.

202. See in general Ottomeyer/Völkel, *Die Öffentliche Tafel*; Stollberg-Rilinger, *Ordnungsleistung*; Völkel, "Der Tisch des Herrn"; Löwenstein "Voraussetzungen"; Haslinger, *Franz Stephan*; Cachée, *Die Hofküche*.

203. Instruction for the master of the staff, December 14, 1769, in Pangerl/Scheutz/Winkelbauer, *Der Wiener Hof*, 116 ff. See the eyewitness report from February 22, 1761: Breunlich/Mader, *Karl Graf von Zinzendorf*, 195–96.

204. Haslinger, Franz Stephan, 110 ff.

205. Open table and public church visits originally took place on Fridays and Sundays; from November 1754 they were restricted to Sundays, KMT III, 214; see KMT III, 17; KMT I, 187, 259.

206. KMT I, 170 on the new *table de conspiration* in the Hofburg (1743). On the fine gradations in access for the nobility, e.g., KMT I, 185, 237, 241, 251. Over a hundred places, e.g., KMT IV, 36. See also Breunlich/Mader, *Karl Graf von Zinzendorf*, 248; Krajewski, *Der Diener*, 123.

207. One such list for Laxenburg in Wolf, *Aus dem Hofleben*, 331–32; see, e.g., KMT VI, 38, 172.

208. KMT I, 146; only the *Primores*: KMT III, 252.

209. A cavalier who had publicly complained about this was barred access to court and only readmitted some time later out of Christian mercy, KMT I, 250.

210. KMT II, 102.

211. KMT III, 214.

212. To Ferdinand, February 10 and 17, 1774, BKF I, 258 ff.

213. Description of a sleigh ride from 1771 from an outsider's perspective: Coke, *Letters* III, 366–67.

214. Keyßler, *Neueste Reisen*, 1231–32; see Pečar, *Die Ökonomie der Ehre*, 181; Scheutz, "Fasching."

215. KMT III, 225.

216. KMT II, 203–204; KMT III, 225; on the unpopularity of balls, also KMT II, 56, 145; KMT VII, 2.

217. KMT I, 118; KMT II, 202, 467.

218. Küchelbecker, *Allerneueste Nachricht*, 251–52.

219. KMT I, 118.

220. January 1748: KMT II, 202–203; January 1749: KMT II, 295; January 1752: KMT III, 1 ff., 8–9, 11–12.

221. See the ball order in the *Wiener Diarium* 1752, no. 2; see Scheutz, "Fasching," 148–49. An alleged breach of the ban on masquerades by the composer and kapellmeister Dittersdorf cost him his position as bishop of Großwardein after he was denounced to Maria Theresa; see Dittersdorf, *Lebensbeschreibung*, 153 ff.

222. KMT III, 2.

223. KMT III, 2, 13, 158.

224. KMT IV, 81; see Koschatzky, *Maria Theresia* (catalog), 112; Zollinger, *Geschichte des Glücksspiels*; Zollinger, "Das Glücksspiel in Wien."

225. When she was not playing cards, Maria Theresa occasionally busied herself with needlework, as was customary for highborn ladies.

226. See the evidence in Zollinger, *Geschichte des Glücksspiels*, 51 ff.; von der Trenck, *Die "Blutbibel"*, 217 ff.

227. KMT I, 260.

228. KMT II, 245; court balls were inferior to the nobility's balls: KMT V, 85.

229. KMT I, 190; see his criticism of gambling at court in KMT II, 38, 130; KMT III, 236; gambling had been tolerated mainly on Francis Stephen's account: KMT IV, 71. Despite the ban, noble gamblers got off lightly. When a certain Freiherr von Spleny embezzled over 180,000 guilders to cover his faro debts and later confessed all to the emperor, he was relieved of his office but not otherwise punished; KMT VIII, 109.

230. See Wagner, "Das geheime Kammerzahlamt."

231. KMT I, 203.

232. KMT I, 237; see KMT I, 210–11, 262, 306.

233. Ligne, *Fragments* I, 185–86.

234. Printed in KMT I, 306. Regular rounds and the rules of admission observed for the occasion, high wins and losses: KMT II, 130, 191; KMT II, 213, 282, 360, 369, 373; KMT III, 13, 30, 236; KMT IV, 4, 10, 16, 25, 31, 71, 81, 125–26, 128; KMT V, 127.

235. KMT V, 8–9.

236. KMT V, 60.

237. Zollinger, *Geschichte des Glücksspiels*, 72–73. See KMT III, 268; KMT V, 73–74, 85, 92; KMT VI, 30, 172. On August 13, 1764, Maria Theresa saw herself compelled to play faro because the round table used in this game allowed conflicts of rank to be more easily avoided: KMT VI, 50–51.

238. KMT VI, 149, 209; ban: KMT VI, 172, 219; see Beales, "Joseph II's Rêveries" I, 66, and chapter 10, this volume.

239. E.g., Coke, *Letters* III, 323, 325, 348, 354, 461; IV, 9 speaks of Loo and Ombre.

240. To Marie Antoinette, November 5, 1777, and December 5, 1777, MACS III, 127–28, 143–44; Christoph, *Maria Theresia: Geheimer Briefwechsel*, 210, 212–13; see Zollinger, "Das Glücksspiel," 68–69.

241. Breunlich/Mader, *Karl Graf von Zinzendorf*, passim; see Lebeau, *Aristocrates et grands commis*, 141 ff.; see in general Cerman, *Habsburgischer Adel und Aufklärung*.

242. See in general Daniel, *Hoftheater*, 66 ff.; Blanning, *Culture of Power*, 53 ff.; Abbate/ Parker, *A History of Opera*, 91 ff.; Béhar/Mourey/Schneider, *Maria Theresias Kulturwelt*; Zech- meister, *Die Wiener Theater*; Hadamowsky, *Wien—Theatergeschichte*; Szábo, "Cultural Transfor- mation"; ", *Im Dienste*. Brief overviews in Koschatzky, *Maria Theresia*; Grasberger, "Ein Goldenes Zeitalter"; Hadamowsky, "'Spectacle mussen sein,'"; Dietrich, "Theater"; Campianu, "Terpsichore."

243. KMT I, 202.

244. See chapters 2 and 9, this volume.

245. Details in Hadamowsky, *Wien—Theatergeschichte*, 199 ff.; Zechmeister, *Die Wiener Theater*.

246. KMT III, 32: the public always excluded from noble performances; see, e.g., KMT II, 160–61, 208–209; in KMT III, 8–9, Khevenhüller remarks, however, that noble amateurs could no longer hold their own against professional actors.

247. Instruction de S. M. L'Impeatrice pour le Ceremoniel aux Cours de ses Enfans (1765), ÖNB Wiener Hofbibliothek, Codex Series N. 1713, fol. 47–52, here 49r–v.

248. KMT I, 146, 252; II, 351–52, 355–56; KMT III, 8, 32; see also chapter 9 on children's comedies.

249. KMT V, 83.

250. Christoph Willibald Gluck, *Alceste*, Preface, Vienna 1767. See Haas, *Gluck und Durazzo*; Brown, *Gluck*; Abbate/Parker, *A History of Opera*, 143 ff.

251. Jean-Georges Noverre, *Lettres sur la danse et sur les ballets*, Lyon 1760; see also Mourey, "Tanz- und Ballettkultur."

252. Joseph von Sonnenfels, *Briefe über die Wienerische Schaubühne*, Vienna 1768; see his pro memoria from 1770 in Zechmeister, *Die Wiener Theater*, 57 ff.; in general Karstens, *Lehrer*, 281 ff.

253. This was Sonnenfels's demand; see Zechmeister, *Die Wiener Theater*, 51 ff. for a detailed account of the various French and German reform movements.

254. Aesthetic judgments, e.g., KMT II, 70, 161–61, 300, 315–16, 337, 352; on Gluck "without special applause" IV, 55; on the dispute over German theater, see KMT VI, 227, 529 ff.; KMT VII, 157; KMT VIII, 15; on the new ballet, KMT VIII, 72–73, 81, 98–99.

255. Campianu, "Terpsichore," 412. According to KMT IV, 102, Maria Theresa banned a new impromptu on account of the poor composition.

256. To Marie Beatrix, August 17, 1771, BKF III, 119.

257. To Marie Beatrix, November 12, 1772, BKF III, 149.

258. Zechmeister, *Die Wiener Theater*, 49 ff.

259. Durazzo had originally come to Vienna as Genoese emissary. From 1752 to 1764 he was placed in charge of Vienna's theaters—first with Prince Esterhazy, then, from 1753, on his own. See Schneider, "Durazzo," on the purification of French comedy from improprieties.

260. Edict from February 17, 1752, in Otto Teuber, *Das Theater Wiens*, II/1, Vienna 1896, 63.

261. To Kaunitz, May 1767, cited in Hadamowsky, *Wien—Theatergeschichte*, 223; see Arneth, *Geschichte Maria Theresias* IX, 272; Zechmeister, *Die Wiener Theater*, 79–80.

262. E.g., to Antonia of Saxony 1761, Lippert, *Briefwechsel*, 86, 103, 117. She only made an exception when her grandson Francis, the later heir to the throne, was born on March 16, 1768; see Hadamowsky, "'Spectacle mussen sein.'"

263. Hadamoswky, *Wien—Theatergeschichte*, 227 ff.

264. Müller, *Der Orden*; on early modern chivalric orders, see Dikowitsch, *Baroque*; on the Order of the Fleece in Austria, see Weber, "Der österreichische Orden"; Pečar, *Die Ökonomie der Ehre*, 173 ff.; Wrede, *Ohne Furcht*, 248 ff.; excerpts from the sources in Pangerl/Scheutz/Winkelbauer, *Der Wiener Hof*, 287 ff.

265. Wrede, *Ohne Furcht*, 252.

266. It was unusual even at the time to induct a newborn infant into an order; the emperor therefore furnished a report intended to banish all possible scruples: HHStA OMeA ÄZA 27-6-1a.

267. Pangerl/Scheutz/Winkelbauer, *Der Wiener Hof*, 525–26. The 1716 baptism of Maria Theresa's brother Leopold was exemplary in all regards: HHStA OMe ZA ZP 9, fol. 86–111; see Rohr, *Einleitung*, 173–74; Stöckelle, "Taufzeremoniell," 294–95.

268. KMT I, 201; see KMT IV, 70–71; VI, 30–31, 132.

269. KMT IV, 53; V, 138–39.

270. Dikowitsch, *Barock*, 53 ff.; on Eleonora of Gonzaga the Younger, see Schnettger, "Die Kaiserinnen aus dem Haus Gonzaga," in Braun/Keller/Schnettger, *Nur die Frau des Kaisers?*, 117–40.

271. E.g., Justi, *Allerunterthänigstes Gutachten*, 30 ff.

272. See Georg Ludwigstorff, "Der österreichische 'Militär-Ehren Orden,'" in Dikowitsch, *Barock*, 27–33; Hochedlinger, "Mars Ennobled," 169 ff. See the depiction of the first public bestowal of the Maria Theresa Order by Francis Stephen to Field Marshall Daun on March 7, 1758, Iby/Koller, *Schönbrunn*, 85; see also the ceiling fresco by Gregorio Gugliemi in the Small Gallery at Schönbrunn (1761), ibid., 100.

273. Dikowtisch, *Barock*, 29.

274. To Khevenhüller's intense displeasure, Kaunitz also delivered the festive address at the first promotions ceremony on March 7 the following year—a somewhat tricky task, given that the fortunes of war had since turned against the Habsburgs, KMT V, 13–14.

275. KMT V, 13–14.

276. KMT V, 138–39.

277. KMT VI, 31; see the Statutes of the Praiseworthy Chivalric Order of the First Apostolic King Stephen (January 30, 1764), printed in KMT VI, 307–16; ibid., 310, point 12: "We as king of Hungary."

278. KMT VI, 31; see Christian Steeb, "Kaiser Franz I. and seine ablehnende Haltung gegenüber der Stiftung des königlich ungarischen St.-Stephans-Ordens," in Dikowitsch, *Barock*, 35–40.

279. KMT VI, 32, 151, 252. Khevenhüller eventually received the Order of St. Stephen (First Class) in 1770, KMT VII, 16–17.

280. Statutes, KMT VI, 307–16. On later developments in the nineteenth century, see Rudolf Kucera, *Staat, Adel und Elitenwandel: Die Adelsverleihungen in Schlesien und Böhmen 1806–71 im Vergleich*. Göttingen 2012. The order was revived by Victor Orbán in 2011 as a Hungarian national order of merit.

281. Handwritten note from Maria Theresa to Prince Esterházy, February 20, 1764, in KMT VI, 322.

282. Statutes, Point 23, KMT VI, 312.

283. Statutes, KMT VI, 307; see Kaunitz's comment in KMT VI, 319.

284. Statues, Points 15 and 16, KMT VI, 311.

285. Statutes, Points 3, 6, 17, and 23, KMT VI, 308 ff.

286. Maria Theresa's handwritten marginal note on Kaunitz's opinion, KMT VI, 317, 318.

287. Handwritten marginal note on the statues, KMT VI, 312.

288. Submission from Esterházy, March 10, 1764, KMT VI, 322–23. The first Knight Grand Cross was Count Hatzfeld. The first conferment of the Grand Cross to an eminent ecclesiastical dignitary from the Empire, the bishop of Passau, was no less lavishly staged in February 1765; KMT VI, 86.

289. See the papers relating to Count Chotek's draft from May 12, 1760, in KMT VI, 294 ff., here 305; draft statutes from January 30, 1764: KMT VI, 307 ff., here 313.

290. KMT VI, 140, 185.

291. KMT VI, 151; Esterházy's submission from March 26, 1764. KMT VI, 324 ff. on the selection of the first knights of the order.

292. KMT VIII, 53.

293. KMT VI, 81.

294. Memorandum from November 17, 1771, KMT VII, 373–98, here 386. Nonetheless, in 1771 Maria Theresa contemplated increasing the number of members. Predictably, Khevenhüller advised her against it, at least for the first class, "since by multiplying the same, the current eagerness to partake of this distinction would naturally be diminished," KMT VII, 101.

295. KMT V, 9–10.

296. KMT IV, 58–59.

297. See the instruction for the Master of the Staff (1774) in Pangerl/Scheutz/Winkelbauer, *Der Wiener Hof*, 122.

8. The Seven Years' War

1. Maria Theresa to Daun, July 24, 1759, in Kunisch, "Der Ausgang," 216–22, here 222.

2. On military reforms, see Allmayer-Beck, "Die Armee"; Duffy, *Sieben Jahre Krieg*; Hochedlinger, "Mars Ennobled"; Hochedlinger, "Rekrutierung."

3. Maria Theresa to Daun, July 24, 1759, in Kunisch, "Der Ausgang," 216–22, here 220.

4. So the commander Franz Moritz Lacy, in a memorandum recalling the army under Charles VI, cited in Duffy, *Sieben Jahre Krieg*, 145.

5. Handbillet to the Court War Council, June 1753, BAA, 105.

6. Decree from February 25, 1751; Hochedlinger, "Mars Ennobled," 151–52.

7. Chamber admission regulation from 1745: HHStA OMeA ÄZA 45–10; edited in Pangerl/Scheutz/Winkelbauer, *Der Wiener Hof*, 283; see chapter 7, this volume.

8. Cited in KMT III, 208–209. On Daun, see Heinrich Benedikt, "Daun, Leopold Joseph Maria, Graf von, Fürst von Thiano, in NDB 3 (1957): 528–29; the only biography is the older work by F. L. von Thadden, *Feldmarschall Daun: Maria Theresias größter Feldherr*, Vienna 1967.

9. For more detail on the social composition, see Hochedlinger, "Mars Ennobled."

10. Hochedlinger, "Mars Ennobled," 162 ff.

11. Daun, *Regulament und Ordnung*, Preface.

12. Pommerin/Schilling, *Denkschrift*; see Schilling, *Kaunitz*; Szábo, *Kaunitz*, 258 ff.; Arneth, *Geschichte Maria Theresia's* IV, 266 ff.; Braubach, *Versailles und Wien*, 404 ff.

13. Pommerin/Schilling, *Denkschrift*, 193.

14. Pommerin/Schilling, *Denkschrift*, 205.

15. Pommerin/Schilling, *Denkschrift*, 225.

16. Kaunitz, memorandum from September 7, 1778, printed in Aretin, *Heiliges Römisches Reich* II, 2 ff.—Kaunitz's most important memoranda and presentations relating to the war are edited in Küntzel, "Österreichische Acten"; further Pommerin/Schilling, *Denkschrift*; Beer, "Denkschriften"; also scattered in KMT III and IV, Appendices.

17. Arneth, *Geschichte Maria Theresia's* IV, 267–68; see also Excerpt from Conference Opinions Regarding the Foreign System, April 19, 1749, Beer, *Aufzeichnungen des Grafen Bentinck*, 129–42.

18. On this long-disputed question, see Guglia, *Maria Theresia* II, 96–97; Arneth, *Geschichte Maria Theresia's* IV, 282; Braubach, *Versailles und Wien*, 405–406.

19. Maria Theresa, "Memorandum to Daun, July 24, 1759," in Kunisch, "Der Ausgang," 216–22, here 219.

20. Kunisch, "Der Ausgang," 220. See Kaunitz's dictum from August 6, 1757, according to which Prussia's continued existence was incompatible with the happiness of the human race, cited in Arneth, *Geschichte Maria Theresia's* V, 219, 508.

21. E.g., in a submission from April 1755, printed in KMT III, 502 ff., here 504.

22. See chapter 5, this volume.

23. On his offers of resignation in 1766 and 1773, see BAA, 220 ff., BAA, 251; see also chapters 10 and 13, this volume; "Joseph II's Rêveries," 142–43.

24. See the brief overviews in Füssel, *Der Siebenjährige Krieg*; Duchhardt, *Balance of Power*, 319 ff.; Schilling, *Höfe und Allianzen*, 450 ff.; from the mass of literature from the Austrian perspective, see Arneth, *Geschichte Maria Theresia's* IV, chapters 10–16; Guglia, *Maria Theresia* II, 93 ff.; Szábo, *Seven Years' War*; Hochedlinger, *Austria's Wars*, 330 ff.; on the French perspective, Externbrink, *Friedrich der Große*; on the Prussian perspective, Kunisch, *Friedrich der Große*, 329 ff.; Blanning, *Frederick the Great*, 224 ff.; on the global perspective, Danley/Speelman, *Seven Years' War*; Baugh, *The Global Seven Years War*.

25. Treaty from November 15, 1715, in which Emperor Charles VI had given the Dutch Republic a series of fortresses on the territory of the Habsburg Netherlands as a defensive barrier against France.

26. Beer, *Aufzeichnungen des Grafen Bentick*, 24–25 (October 22, 1749).

27. Report of Keith from July 19, 1751; cited in Klingenstein, "Institutionelle Aspekte," 78; on the negotiations, see KMT III, 316–30.

28. Treaty of Aranjuez, April 14, 1752; see Guglia, *Maria Theresia* II, 108–109; Arneth, *Geschichte Maria Theresia's* IV, 336 ff.

29. August 13, 1752; see KMT III, 55.

30. Maria Theresa held fast to it: Schlitter, *Correspondence secrète*, 147; see Arneth, *Geschichte Maria Theresia's* IV, 330 ff.; Guglia, *Maria Theresia* II, 107.

31. Conference from March 31, 1755, submissions in KMT III, 501–13, here 508.

32. KMT III, 256.

33. Report on the Court Conference session, August 10, 1755, cited in Arneth, *Geschichte Maria Theresia's* IV, 549.

34. Presentation by Kaunitz to the Court Conference, August 21, 1755 (protocol from August 28, 1755); edited, in "Österreichen Acten," 145–60; see Arneth, *Geschichte Maria Theresia's* IV, 388 ff.; Guglia, *Maria Theresia* II, 130 ff.; Schilling, *Kaunitz*, 189 ff.

35. KMT III, 552: "*a coup d'état où il s'agit d'un remède prompt, violent, mais necessaire.*"

36. Presentation by Kaunitz, August 28, 1755; Küntzel, "Österreichen Acten," 158.

37. Arneth *Geschichte Maria Theresia's* IV, 432 ff.; 457–58; Braubach, *Versailles und Wien*, 428 ff.; Schilling, *Kaunitz*, 189 ff.; Dade, *Madame de Pompadour*, 154 ff.

38. Maria Theresa to Antonia of Saxony, October 10, 1763, Lippert, *Briefwechsel*, 185; see also KMT V, 84.

39. Dade, *Madame de Pompadour*, 176 ff.—See, e.g., Kunisch, *Aufklärung*, 39, 803.

40. "Lettre de la Marquise de Pompadour à la Reine de Hongrie (1759)," in *Œuvres posthumes de Frédéric II, Roi de Prusse*, suppl. 3, Berlin 1789, 241–50; see Pečar, *Die Masken*, 97ff; Kunisch,

Aufklärung und Kriegserfahrung, 805–806, on the Marquis d'Argens's praise of Frederick's satire.

41. Dade, *Madame de Pompadour*, 183–84; see Guglia, *Maria Theresia* II, 161; Arneth, *Geschichte Maria Theresia's* IV, 153–54. On the role of women in diplomacy at the time in general, see Windler/von Thiessen, Geschlecht der Diplomatie.

42. Report of the English emissary Keith, cited in Coxe, *History* III, 363 ff.

43. KMT IV, 22.

44. Anzeige einer Neutralitäts-acte und Defensiv-tractats mit dem französischen königlichen Hof: *Wienerisches Diarium*, no. 48, June 16, 1756.

45. See Conference opinions on the question from May 23, 1756, in KMT IV, 158–76, here Khevenhüller's opinion, 160; Kaunitz's opinion in Küntzel, "Österreichen Acten," 384–92; see Arneth, *Geschichte Maria Theresia's* IV, 450 ff.; Guglia, *Maria Theresia* II, 136 ff.

46. Maria Theresa to Daun, in Kunisch, "Der Ausgang," 219.

47. KMT IV, 42, 206.

48. Guglia, *Maria Theresia* II, 149 n. 1; see Arneth, *Geschichte Maria Theresia's* IV, 487 ff.

49. Schilling, "Formung und Gestalt"; Gräf, "Funktionsweisen"; Thiessen, "Diplomatie."

50. KMT III, 274–75. Aftershocks were still being felt in February 1756, see KMT IV, 9; Campan, *Mémoires* I, 36–37.

51. Brief overviews of the main events: Füssel, *Der Siebenjähriger Krieg*, 32 ff.; Schilling, *Höfe und Allianzen*, 450 ff.; Duchhardt, *Balance of Power*, 363 ff.; Guglia, *Maria Theresia* II, 148 ff.; Hochedlinger, *Austria's Wars*, 337 ff.; more detail in Arneth, *Geschichte Maria Theresia's*, V and VI; a recent account is Szábo, *Seven Years' War*.

52. Aretin, *Das Alte Reich* III, 87 ff.

53. On the war from the imperial perspective, see Aretin, *Das Alte Reich* III, 86 ff.

54. For a detailed account of the pamphlet war, see Schort, *Politik*, 41 ff., here 43.

55. This point was made by the legal scholar Friedrich Karl von Moser, cited in Schort, *Politik*, 65, 90.

56. Submission from Imperial Vice-Chancellor Colloredo, October 2, 1756, in KMT IV, 228–33.

57. Aretin, *Das Alte Reich* III, 91 ff.; Rohrschneider, *Österreich*, 52 ff.; from a French perspective Externbrink, *Friedrich der Große*, 120 ff. Brunswick-Wolfenbüttel, Hessen-Kassel, Saxony-Gotha, and Schaumburg-Lippe voted against the imperial execution. Austrian diplomacy had at first unsuccessfully tried to persuade the king of England to remain neutral as elector of Hanover.

58. KMT IV, Appendix, 367–76, Maria Theresa's instructions to Starhemberg, ibid., 371–72.

59. See KMT IV, 83 ff., 94 ff.

60. KMT IV, 86 ff.

61. General Tiller to Daun, cited in Arneth, *Geschichte Maria Theresia's* VI, 432.

62. KMT V, 4.

63. KMT IV, 88, 93.

64. KMT IV, 79, 88, 118. See Hollerweger, *Die Reform*, 63 ff.

65. KMT IV, 50, 93; KMT V, 16, 21–22, 42, 48, 97.

66. KMT IV, 47.

67. KMT IV, 113–14.

68. KMT IV, 222–23, 227, 233–34, 230–40, 243–44; further examples in letters to Field Marshal Neipperg, BKF IV, 142 ff.

69. E.g., to Ulfeld, November 17, 1757, BKF IV, 195.

70. KMT IV, 250.

71. To Neipperg, October 1757, BKF IV, 149.

72. Arneth, *Geschichte Maria Theresia's* V, 191–92.

73. Above all with Prince Charles in autumn 1757; see below.

74. To Neipperg, early June, 1757, BKF IV, 148.

75. Overview of events in Füssel, *Der Siebenjähriger Krieg*, 37 ff.; Hochedlinger, *Austria's Wars*, 338 ff.; Szábo, *Seven Years' War*, 61 ff.

76. KMT IV, 98–99.

77. KMT IV, 123.

78. See Wagner, "Das geheime Kammerzahlamt"; Wagner, "Fürstengnade."

79. On the order, see chapter 7, this volume; eternal devotion: KMT IV, 108; on the "birthday of the monarchy," Arneth, *Geschichte Maria Theresia's* V, 200; Maria Theresa to Joseph II, June 17, 1778, MJC II, 292.

80. See, e.g., Ligne, *Mon journal*, 486–87; on malicious gossip about Daun following the battle of Liegnitz on August 15, 1760, see Arneth, *Geschichte Maria Theresia's* VI, 142 ff.

81. KMT VI, 165–6; Khevenhüller criticized Daun's "irresolution, derived from an exaggerated spirit of circumspection," which led him to err on the side of "hesitancy and dilatoriness."

82. Arneth, *Geschichte Maria Theresia's* V, 231 ff.

83. Arneth, *Geschichte Maria Theresia's* V, 234.

84. Kunisch, *Friedrich der Große*, 344–45; Kunisch, *Das Mirakel*, 77 ff.

85. KMT VI, 165–66.

86. Arneth, *Geschichte Maria Theresia's* V, 250 ff.

87. On conflicts of precedence, KMT IV, 115; see also Luh, *Kriegskunst*, 210–11, 215–16.

88. Submission from Kaunitz, July 31, 1757, in KMT IV, 380 ff., here 382.

89. Hildburghausen to the emperor, November 2, 1757, in KMT IV, Appendix, 400–401; see KMT V, 112, 132–33.

90. The myth of Leuthen confirmed in Kunisch, *Friedrich der Große*, 380 ff.

91. KMT IV, 137.

92. See KMT IV, 140 ff.

93. See above, chapter 3.

94. KMT II, 29, 62 ff., 68–69; see also Hinrichs, *Friedrich der Große*, 74 ff.

95. E.g., KMT I, 175; the special consideration shown to Franz von der Trenck was also ascribed to Francis Stephen and Charles's protection, see chapter 3, this volume.

96. KMT II, 28–29.

97. KMT II, 62 ff., 68–69 after the battle of Hohenfriedberg in June 1745; see BKF IV, 191; similarly after the battle of Lüttich in October 1746, KMT II, 120.

98. KMT II, 120 (October 18, 1746); see *Wiener Diarium*, October 26, 1746; Arneth, *Geschichte Maria Theresia's* II, 225 ff.

99. KMT IV, 100. After Daun had clinched victory at Kolín and liberated the prince's troops from Prague, the empress prematurely and mistakenly credited this to her brother-in-law.

100. KMT V, 1–2.

101. KMT V, 3–4; see to Ulfeld, August 10, 1757 and November 17, 1757, BKF IV, 193, 195. Replacing incompetent commanders could be a problem due to loss of face; consider the example of Esterházy, KMT V, 34–35.

102. To Ulfeld, December 1757, BKF IV, 198. Antonia of Saxony was sympathetic and spoke of a sacrifice that God would reward: to Maria Theresa, June 23, 1758, Lippert, Briefwechsel, 32.

103. Arneth, Geschichte Maria Theresia's V, 165–66; Szábo, Seven Years' War, 106 ff., 127–28. But see Ligne, Mon Journal, 143, on the battle of Hochkirch. Regardless of the factual objectivity of the criticism, it must be asked whether nationalist undertones were not in play against the "Frenchman" from Lorraine.

104. Eugen Guglia thus calls it an "authentically female line of reasoning" that she felt "eternally" justified in relation to Frederick II on account of the injury he had once done her. Guglia, Maria Theresia II, 144.

105. KMT IV, 141.

106. " . . . son âme donnée et une créature de sa main," KMT IV, 142.

107. For an overview of the changes to military administration, see Hochedlinger, Austria's Wars, 303 ff.; Hochedlinger, "Rekrutierung"; Walter, ÖZV II,1,1, 224–30, 254–61.

108. KMT IV, 93.

109. Reform law from January 1, 1762, see chapter 6, this volume; on historians' criticism of the cumbersome system of Habsburg military administration, see Kunisch, Friedrich der Große, 346; on the structural defects of Habsburg warfare, see Kunisch, Das Mirakel, 83 ff.

110. Cited in Arneth, Geschichte Maria Theresia's V, 362.

111. Pichler, Denkwürdigkeiten, 22.

112. Ligne, Mon Journal, 145, 317, 483.

113. Pichler, Denkwürdigkeiten, 22.

114. KMT V, 71; Khevenhüller's quote does not capture the exact wording of the letter; see Droysen, et al., Politische Correspondenz XVII, 311–12.

115. To Antonia of Saxony, December 21, 1758, Lippert, Briefwechsel, 33: "La bataille . . . n'at put me relever."

116. To Antonia of Saxony, December 21, 1758, Lippert, Briefwechsel, 33–34.

117. Lippert, Briefwechsel, 37, 53–54, 78, 80–81, 99. See, e.g., Arneth, Geschichte Maria Theresia's V, 111.

118. Arneth, Geschichte Maria Theresia's VI, 429.

119. State letter to Daun, June 21, 1759, Arneth, Geschichte Maria Theresia's V, 429; on the debate about the correct strategy, see Kunisch, Das Mirakel.

120. Johannes Kunisch, "Laudon, Ernst Gideon Freiherr von," in NDB 13 (1982), 700–701. See Wertheimer, "Zwei Schilderungen," 232; Laudon was "excessively modest, reserved, taciturn," but the empress never held him in great affection.

121. To Antonia of Saxony, November 12, 1759, Lippert, Briefwechsel, 56; see Arneth, Geschichte Maria Theresia's VI, 38 ff.

122. See Arneth, Geschichte Maria Theresia's VI, 69 ff. On discussion of the proposal in Vienna, KMT V, 266 ff.

123. To Antonia of Saxony, December 9, 1759, Lippert, *Briefwechsel*, 64.

124. To Antonia of Saxony, January 28, 1760, Lippert, *Briefwechsel*, 70.

125. Arneth *Geschichte Maria Theresia's*, VI, 95 ff.

126. The battles of Liegnitz, August 15, 1760, and Torgau, November 3, 1759. See Arneth, *Geschichte Maria Theresia's* VI, 147 ff., 156–57, 161–62.

127. Arneth, *Geschichte Maria Theresia's* VI, 188 ff.

128. See Arneth, *Geschichte Maria Theresia's* VI, 254 ff.; an essential and detailed account in Dickson, *Finance* II.

129. Dickson, *Finance* II, 36 ff.

130. Arneth, *Geschichte Maria Theresia's* VI, 259 ff.

131. Lebeau, *Aristocrates et grands commis*, 159 ff.

132. To Count d'Ayasasa, October 1761, BKF IV, 430.

133. E.g., Lippert, *Briefwechsel*, 86, 103, 124.

134. To Ulfeld, May 20, 1762, BKF IV, 201–202.

135. To Ulfeld, November 13, 1762, BKF IV, 206.

136. Arneth, *Geschichte Maria Theresia's* VI, 394–95.

137. To Starhemberg, Feburary 18, 1763, cited in Guglia, *Maria Theresia* II, 169.

138. See Stollberg-Rilinger, *Emperor's New Clothes*, chapter 5; see chapter 4, this volume.

139. Aretin, *Das Alte Reich* III, 98 ff.; in more detail Schort, *Politik*, 142 ff.

140. KMT IV, 135–36.

141. See Kalipke, *Verfahren*; Haug-Moritz, *Corpus evangelicorum*; Aretin, *Das Alte Reich* III, 101 ff.; on the religious dimension, see Burkhardt, "Religious War"; Fuchs, "Der Siebenjährige Krieg"; Schmidt, *Wandel durch Vernunft*, 161 ff.; Schort, *Politik*, 99 ff.; Pörtner, "Propaganda," 474 ff.

142. Schort, *Politik*, 168; on subsequent debates on procedural questions prompted by plans for a peace conference in Augsburg, see ibid., 186 ff.

143. KMT IV, 6, 15, 148.

144. Schort, *Politik*, 110 ff., citation on 114, with abundant further evidence of pro-Prussian opinion in the Empire and abroad. On Protestant polemical pamphleteering, ibid., 243 ff.; on further confessional conflicts in the Empire at this time, see Kalipke, *Verfahren*.

145. Cited in KMT IV, 354–55 n. 108.

146. KMT IV, 103, 379–80.

147. Memorandum to Daun, in Kunisch, "Der Ausgang," 217, 220.

148. E.g., to Ulfeld, July 5, 1757, BKF IV, 193. See also Schort, *Politik*, 163 ff. on an unwelcome partisan anti-Protestant text penned by the abbot of St. Emmeram. Maria Theresa took a very different approach to Protestants in the hereditary lands, subjecting them to a relentless campaign of persecution; see chapter 12, this volume.

149. Burkhardt, *Abschied*, 165–66; Burkhardt, "Religious War"; Aretin, *Das Alte Reich* III, 103–104.

150. "Frederick II to d'Argens, May 13, 1758," in *Friederich der Große, Mein lieber Marquis*, Zurich 1985, 129–30, 179–80; Bref De S. S. Le Pape A M. Le Maréchal Daun, in Preuß, *Œuvres* XIX, 71–83; Volz, *Die Werke Friedrichs des Großen* V, 219 ff. See Schort, *Politik*, 268 ff.; Pečar, *Die Masken*, 97 ff. "Apostolic harpy" referred to Maria Theresa's title "Apostolic Majesty," bestowed on her by Pope Clement XIII; see Arneth, *Geschichte Maria Theresia's* IX, 8–9.

151. Maria Theresa to Esterházy, December 23, 1757, Arneth, *Geschichte Maria Theresia's* V, 280–81.

152. Luise Gottsched to Frau von R., February 4, 1758, "Mit dem Feder," 289.

153. Abundant evidence in Schort, *Politik*; Blitz, *Aus Liebe*; Adam/Dainat, "*Krieg ist mein Lied*"; sources in Ditfurth, *Die historischen Volkslieder*; Brüggemann, *Der Siebenjährige Krieg*.

154. Goethe, *Autobiography*, 35.

155. The concept is taken from Burgdorf, *Reichskonstitution*.

156. The concept is taken from Burgdorf, *Reichskonstitution*.

157. *Irenophili zufällige Gedanken*, 6—see also "Das große Hahnengeschrey, Oder: Vorstellung der jetzigen Kriegszeiten," in Ditfurth, *Die historisches Volkslieder*, 78–79. The entire land was sighing "under the yoke of an Austrian woman," wrote the influential journalist Friedrich Karl von Moser, cited in Schort, *Politik*, 90.

158. Cited in Füssel, *Der Siebenjährige Krieg*, 92.

159. Archenholz, "Geschichte des siebenjährigen Krieges," in Kunisch, *Aufklärung und Kriegserfahrung*, 96–97.

160. See in general Schort, *Politik*; Arndt/Körber, *Das Mediensystem*; Friedrich, *Drehscheibe Regensburg*; Martus, *Aufklärung*, 632 ff.; Anklam, *Wissen*, 189 ff.; on the hereditary lands, Duchkowitsch, "Österreichs Tagespresse"; Seidler/Seidler, *Das Zeitschriftenwesen*; W. Seidler, *Buchmarkt*; Karmasin/Oggolder, *Österreichische Mediengeschichte*; Welke, ". . . zu Österreichs Gloria"; on the War of Succession, Mazura, *Die preußische und österreichische Kriegspropaganda*; Küster, *Vier Monarchien*; see chapter 3, this volume.

161. The concept is taken from Burgdorf, *Reichskonstitution*.

162. Schort, *Politik*, 45–46.

163. To Neipperg, September 1756, BKF IV, 144. On war reporting, see Anklam, *Wissen*.

164. Quotes in Schort, *Politik*, 121, here relating to Hamburg.

165. Küster, *Vier Monarchien*, 71; see Fournier, *Gerhard van Swieten*, 403–4, on the result of a 1749 survey in the hereditary lands; Frank, "Buchhandel," is more optimistic, but for the second half of the century; see also Lavandier, *Le Livre*. On the Viennese press, Berger, *Wiennerisches Diarium*; Duchkowitsch, "Österreichs Tagespresse"; Lang, "Zeitschriften"; Tautscher-Gerstmayer, *Die geschriebenen Zeitungen*; Welke, ". . . zu Österreichs Gloria"; esp. Schort, *Politik*, with copious additional examples; recently Karmasin/Oggolder, *Österreichische Mediengeschichte*.

166. Wandruszka, *Leopold II.*, I, 30. Names of learned monks in the hereditary lands, such as Placidus Fixlmillner, Kosmas Schmalfuss, or Magnauld Ziegelbauer, therefore did not appear on the horizon of German enlightened public opinion.

167. Prices in Schort, *Politik*, 37.

168. Decree from February 7, 1750, *Supplementum Codicis Austriaci*, 479, cited in Küster, *Vier Monarchien*, 77.

169. Handbillet from October 19, 1751, *Wiener Diarium* 84, 1751; see Berger, *Wiennerisches Diarium*, 114–15. The handbillet warned of newspapers and their "false, unfounded, and deliberately invented" content.

170. Berger, *Wiennerisches Diarium*, 116 ff.; Reisner/Schiemer, "Das Wien(n)erische Diarium."

171. Schort, *Politik*, 62–63.

172. Welke, "... zu Österreichs Gloria"; Schort, *Politik*, 203 ff.

173. Cited in Welke, "... zu Österreichs Gloria," 180–81.

174. See the summary in Schort, *Politik*, 242–43, 285.

175. On the "newspaper war" in Hamburg and Altona between the imperial and Prussian residents (1756–60), see Welke, "... zu Österreichs Gloria."

176. Pečar, *Die Masken*.

177. For more detail, see Blitz, *Aus Liebe*, 198 ff., here 216; see also Martus, *Aufklärung*, 648 ff.; Adam/Dainat, "*Krieg ist mein Lied*"; Stockhorst, *Krieg und Frieden* (with contributions only on the Prussian perspective); on contemporary historiography, Schort, *Politik*, 373 ff.

178. Martus, *Aufklärung*, 649.

179. Archenholz, "Geschichte," in Kunisch, *Aufklärung und Kriegserfahrung*, 498.

180. Denis, *Poetische Bilder*; see Johannes Birgfeld, "Kriegspoesie für Zeitungsleser oder Der Siebenjährige Krieg aus österreichischer Sicht," in Adam/Dainat, "*Krieg ist mein Lied*," 214–39. On the Austrian side, Josef von Sonnenfels took up the discourse of patriotism with his treatise "On Love for the Fatherland" without, however, adopting Abbt's belligerent tone.

181. Bräker, *Lebensgeschichte*, 135, 118. See also Bleckwenn, "Soldatenbriefe; Holger Böning, Krieg und der 'gemeine Mann' im 18. Jahrhundert," in Stockhorst, *Krieg und Frieden*, 71 ff. Even folk songs from the war tended to be less bloodthirsty in their rhetoric than, say, Gleim's "Songs of a Prussian Grenadier" or his "Zorndorf Ode."

182. See the list in Drugulin, *Hustorische Bilderatlas*, 389 ff.; Coupe, *German Political Satires*, I, 225–30; Schort, *Politik*, 285 ff. The stronghold of political caricature was England; the German papers appeared stuffy by comparison.

183. Dance: Johann David Nessenthaler, *Der Neu eröffnete Politische Masqirte Ball der kriegenden Pouissancen in Germania*, Augsburg 1758 (StPKB MS Dept. Sign. YB 7634 m; Coupe, *German Political Satires*, I,226); see also Ditfurth, *Die historisches Volkslieder*, 24.—Card games: Anon., *Das Spiel des Kriegs zwischen den kriegenden Pouissancen*, Hist. Museum of the City of Vienna, Inv. no. 74 568 (Drugulin, *Historische Bilderatlas*, no. 4559).—Faro: J. P. Haid, *Pharao Spiel der im Krieg begriffenen Herren Officier*, Augsburg, n.d. (StPKB: YB 6696 kl; Coupe, *German Political Satires* I, 229).—Chess: Johann Martin Will, *Man kan mit gutem Grund den Krieg zum Spiel vergleichen* ... (Hung. Nemzeti Museum Budapest Inv. no. 2102; Mraz/Mraz, *Maria Theresia*, 109; Drugulin, *Historischer Bilderatlas*, no. 4556).—Dice: Politischer Discours der Kriegenden Nationen bey einem Glas Wein (Drugulin, *Historischer Bilderatlas*, no. 4557).—Billiards: Johann Martin Will, *A la Guerre oder Historisch Politisch Kriegerisches Billard Spiel der streitenden Mächten in Teutschland*, Augsburg 1758 (Coupe, *German Political Satires*, No. I, 128).—Tournament: Johann David Nessenthaler, *Politisches Ritter Tournier*, Augsburg, n.d. (StPKB YB 6713 m).—Cricket: Matthew Darly, *The Cricket Players of Europe*, London c. 1757 (British Museum Collection No. 1868,0808.4059).

184. Adam Michael Probst, *Theater Kriegender Potentaten*, Augsburg 1757, see Schilling, *Höfe und Allianzen*, 462.

185. On England as a case study, see now Pohlig, *Marlboroughs Geheimnis*.

186. Arneth, *Geschichte Maria Theresia's* V, 40 ff.

187. Arneth, *Geschichte Maria Theresia's* IV, 489, 560; so too Frederick II himself in his history of the Seven Years' War: Volz, *Die Werke Friedrichs des Großen* III.1, 22, 36–37.

188. E.g., to Antonia of Saxony, Lippert, *Briefwechsel*, 26; to Ferdinand, BKF II, 149 ff., 162 ff., 174, 188.

189. To Ferdinand, 1778, BKF II, 149 ff., 162 ff., 165, 174, 188 on the scandal concerning a leak from a source close to Ferdinand's confessor Dr Wasgottwill von Rollemann; briefly discussed in Arneth, *Geschichte Maria Theresia's* X, 182–83.

190. " . . . c'est un point reserve et permis seul au souverain; à un particulier c'est une malhonnête et infame action." To Ferdinand, October 7, 1778, BKF II, 151. She excused herself when she accidentally opened a family letter not addressed to her: to Marie Beatrix, 1775, BKF III, 194.

191. Submission from Kaunitz concerning the reorganization of the postal service, December 31, 1749, HHStA Reichsakten in specie 21–22, fol. 54–55.

192. On Lilien (1696–1776), who later became director-general (*Generalintendant*) of the imperial and Netherlandish Post, see Grillmeyer, *Habsburgs Diener*, 90 ff., 117 ff.; Grillmeyer, *Habsburgs langer Arm*; Behringer, *Im Zeichen des Merkur*, 587 ff.; Rohrschneider, *Österreich*, 261 ff.; see chapter 6, this volume, on the intrigue against Palm. On Maria Theresa's involvement with the Lilien family, see also her letter to Posch, November 24, 1779, BKF IV, 339. What follows is based on HHStA Reichsakten in specie, 21–25. See also examples of the Prussian post being intercepted in KMT III, 354, 364.

193. Behringer, *Im Zeichen des Merkur*, 588. The exact date of the marriage is unknown but must postdate the death of his first wife in 1746. Theresia Lilien née Bartenstein died in 1754.

194. See the list in Behringer, *Im Zeichen des Merkur*, 612, based on a source from the year 1756.

195. See, e.g., HHStA Reichsakten in specie 12–3, fol. 50r-53v: anonymous and undated (demonstrably in Lilien's handwriting) "*Projet: Autant que l'ordre des surveillants sert pour procurer des eclaircissements et pour conduire à la justesse des conseils et des mesures, qu'il y a prendre autant ce meme ordre doit etre soigneur, adroit, vigilant, et a besoin de la protection*"; HHStA Reichsakten in specie 23–1, fol. 51r-60r: "Sancta Sanctorum ou secret de tous les secrets," Vienna, December 29, 1756.

196. HHStA Reichsakten in specie 23–1, fol. 51r-60r: "Sancta Sanctorum ou secret de tous les secrets," Vienna, December 29, 1756. The title alludes to a medieval text attributed to Aristotle, "Secretum secretorum"; Kaunitz was the addressee.

197. These procedures are therefore undocumented in the central archive of the Thurn and Taxis family; see Behringer, *Im Zeichen des Merkur*, 678.

198. Sancta sanctorum, HHStA Reichsakten in specie 23–1, fol. 55r.

199. Sancta sanctorum, HHStA Reichsakten in specie 23–1, fol. 59v.

200. Grillmeyer, *Habsburgs Diener*, 120 ff.; HHStA Reichsakten in specie, 24, 25, 26.

201. "*des moyens pour soutenir l'autorité Imperiale, les Interets de la Réligion, aussi bien que ceux de la Maison d'Autriche*," February 8, 1757, HHStA Reichsakten in specie 23–1, fol. 66 ff.

202. Summaries in Schilling, *Höfe und Allianzen*, 472; Schmidt, *Wandel durch Vernunft*, 173 ff.; Duchhardt, *Balance of Power*, 368 ff.; Szábo, *Seven Years' War*, 424 ff.

203. Quoted in Schilling, *Höfe und Allianzen*, 472.

204. According to Dickson, *Finance* II, 1–2, the state had racked up debts of 280 million guilders.

205. To Ulfeld, late February 1763, BKF IV, 209.

206. See Drugulin, *Historische Bilderatlas*, 405–406, no. 4792–4802; Koschatzky, *Maria Theresia* (catalog), 182–83, no. 28,2–28,4; on festivities in Berlin, see Kunisch, *Friedrich der Große*, 444–45.

207. Frederick II, "Political Testament of 1768," in Dietrich, *Politische Testamente*, 670–71, 628–29; similarly the "Political Testament of 1752," ibid., 380–81, 450–51.

208. See chapter 1, this volume.

209. Kunisch, *Friedrich der Große*, 408, based on Theodor Schieder and the English emissary Mitchell.

210. Guglia, *Maria Theresia* II, 144.

211. See Johannes Burkhardt, "Wie ein verlorener Krieg zum Sieg umgeschrieben wurde: Friedrich der Große, der Siebenjährige Krieg und der Friede von Hubertusburg," in Johannes Burkhardt (ed.), *Sprache, Macht, Frieden. Augsburger Beiträge zur Historischen Friedens- und Konfliktforschung*, Augsburg 2014, 265–308. However, one can only share Burckhardt's finding that the Empire emerged from the war as the true victor if one ignores signs of disintegration in the imperial confederation in the last decades of its existence.

212. Guglia, *Maria Theresia* II, 170: Silesia "was worth a further armed conflict, a renewed exertion of all the energies residing in her people." Ibid., 150: the war "consolidated" the empress's reputation "in the world."

213. See the findings in Arneth, *Reich* III, 107 ff.

214. Addressing the Dutch emissary Bentick, Beer, *Aufzeichnungen des Grafen Bentick*, 23.

215. Frederick II to Voltaire, October 26, 1740, Preuß, *Œuvres* XXII, 48–49, no. 153.

9. Dynastic Capital

1. KMT IV, 33; on Leopold's training for Maria Theresa's beloved military see BKF IV, 17, 21.

2. Joseph had been assigned command at the age of seven, KMT II, 199, 291. See Allmayer-Beck, "Die Armee," 76; Thümmler, *Die Österreichische Armee*, 62, plate 70; Kugler, "Die Entwicklung." Illustration in Husslein-Arco/Lechner *Martin van Meytens*, 70–71 (with partly false information), see too the portrait of Joseph and Charles Joseph as children studying fortifications, ibid., 68–69. In 1774, Maria Theresa entrusted command of a carbine regiment to her first grandson. He was just six years old at the time.

3. KMT IV, 32 on July 7, 1756.

4. KMT III, 217.

5. KMT VI, 53; Joseph at seven years of age, KMT II, 291, but not before, KMT II, 199.

6. KMT VI, 45, 212.

7. On the children see Wachter, "Die Erziehung"; Pangels, *Die Kinder*; Kovács, "Die ideale Erzherzogin"; Barta, *Familienporträts*.

8. This is the richly illustrated thesis of Barta, *Familienporträts*; see also Koschatzky, *Maria Theresia* (catalog), 206 ff.

9. "Familia Augusta," illustration in Barta, *Familienporträts*, 6, ill. 37; see Koschatzky, *Maria Theresia* (catalog), 207; Telesko, "Maria Theresias 'Familia Augusta.'"

10. E.g., KMT I, 208; KMT II, 29–30, 46, 119, 160–161, 180, 194–95, 209, 357–58, 375; KMT III, 8–9, 33; KMT IV, 8–9; KMT V, 60–61, 77; KMT VI, 77–78. See Dietrich, "Theater"; Hadamowsky, Wien—Theatergeschichte, 204 ff.; Daniel, Hoftheater, 37.

11. To Court Councillor Doblhoff, April 5, 1746, BKF IV, 218–9; Beer, Aufzeichnungen des Grafen Bentick, 10.

12. Report on Joseph's education, 1759, in Conrad, Recht und Verfassung, 101.

13. KMT II, 142 (January 1747).

14. E.g., KMT II, 194–95, 357–58, 375; III, 8–9, Khevenhüller was particularly critical when his own children were not performing alongside the archduke.

15. E.g., KMT VI, 77–78; see Zechmeister, Die Wiener Theater, 266; Jahn et al., Verbündet, 35 Ill. 3 and 4; Koschatzky, Maria Theresia (catalog), 357–58; Sommer-Mathis, "Tu felix," plate III.

16. KMT II, 34, 530 ff. (old custom); but see KMT III, 44: on June 24, 1752, "in line with the most recent ordinance," a gala was announced for the name day of Archduchess Johanna, who was two years old at the time.

17. See the example of the Gottscheds, chapter 8, this volume; see also Campan, Mémoires I, 36 ff.

18. KMT II, 223, 359; KMT III, 63–64.

19. Joseph first attended the order's festival in 1754, sporting the collar of the order for the occasion. KMT III, 260 ff., 267.

20. See chapter 7, this volume. Pangerl/Scheutz/Winkelbauer, Der Wiener Hof, 291–92. In 1754–55 the Court Conference deliberated the corresponding ceremonial at festivals of the Golden Fleece, see KMT III, 466, 475.

21. KMT I, 194; Agnes Husslein-Arco and Georg Lechner, Martin van Meytens der Jüngere (catalog), Vienna 2014, 66–67. The portrait of the heir in Hungarian costume was also featured in a medallion above one of his mother's state portraits; illustrated in Barta, Familienporträts, 8, Ill. 53. The same image of Joseph was also integrated into a 1749 group portrait of all the children, reproduced in Mraz/Mraz, Maria Theresia, 178.

22. Arneth, Geschichte Maria Theresia's IV, 184–5. At the age of seven, for example, Joseph also attended the annual change of office in the Lower Austrian government, KMT II, 213.

23. KMT III, 203, 232–33. Submissions to the Court Conference, ibid., 467–75. The topic occupied the Court Conference from as early as December 1748, see KMT II, 288, 530. It recommended that the heir no longer bear the titles Infant of Spain, Prince of the Two Sicilies, and Prince of Jerusalem, and that he should receive exactly the same ceremonial treatment as the Bourbon princes. In 1748 there was as yet no word of including the other children in audience ceremonial.

24. KMT II, 364–65 (October 1749: no further distinction between the Princess of Lorraine and the archduchesses); KMT III, 21 (Easter 1752); KMT III, 89 (February 1753, diplomatic audiences with Archduchess Johanna for her third birthday); KMT III, 95 (March 1753, introductory visit of the Venetian emissary to all the young lords and ladies); likewise in the following year, KMT III, 168. Only the two-year-old Marie Antoinette was still too young to receive compliments: KMT IV, 127.

25. KMT III, 125–26.

26. KMT IV, 89.

27. KMT IV, 4–5; KMT VIII, 33; Ranke, "Maria Theresia und ihr Hof," 730.

28. KMT V, 64–65.

29. See *Princeps in compendio*, 78 ff.; the pedagogic maxims of Francis Stephen's father: *"Memoire de morale et de Gouvernement d'Etat pour l'usage de S. A. Royale Regnante,"* HHStA LHA 43, fol. 37–126; on the Habsburg tradition see also Kovács, "Die ideale Erzherzogin."

30. See his remarks on Joseph's education, KMT III, 402–11. Archduke Francis, Maria Theresa's grandson, was also given an officer as a tutor, MJC II, 105.

31. See chapter 7, this volume; according to Ranke, "Maria Theresia und ihr Hof," 674, she saw the children three to four times a week in the Hofburg; see Campan, *Mémoires* I, 36 ff.

32. So the eighteen-year-old Leopold to Count Thurn, May 1765, in Wandruszka, *Leopold II.* I, 99.

33. Instructions for Countess Almesloë, the aya of Ferdinand's children in Milan (1773), BKF IV, 127 ff. On the education of Joseph's daughter see the correspondence between Maria Theresa and d'Herzelles in Lettenhouve, *Lettres inedités*; Beales, "Joseph II's Rêveries" I, 155–56.

34. Kovács, "Die ideale Erzherzogin," 53 ff. Instructions for Archduke Joseph's chamberlains (October 1747): KMT II, 448 ff.—Rules of Instruction for Archduke Joseph: Arneth, *Geschichte Maria Theresia's* IV, 522–53.—Instruction for Archduke Joseph's ayo, Count Batthyány (1751): BKF IV, 5 ff. Instruction for Archduke Leopold's second ayo, Count von Thurn (1761): BKF IV, 17 ff.; directive to Thurn (May 1762), BKF I, 21 ff. Instructions for Archduchesses Johanna and Josepha's aya, Countess Lerchenfeld (November 1756): BKF IV, 101 ff.; (October/November 1763): BKF IV, 116 ff. Daily timetable for Joseph: van Rhyn, "Unveröffentlichte Briefe," 276–7; report on his education: Conrad, *Recht und Verfassung*, 85 ff. On educational instructions see in general Arneth, BKF I, Introduction.

35. To Almesloë, BKF IV, 127.

36. To Beatrix, May 13, 1779, BKF III, 359–60.

37. To Almesloë, BKF IV, 128: *"avec ordre, décence et tranquilité."*

38. See Kovács, "Die ideale Erzherzogin," 54–55. Against mollycoddling the children through soft kisses: to Ferdinand, September 12, 1776, BKF II, 47.

39. To Lerchenfeld, BKF IV, 103.

40. Instruction for Joseph's chamberlains, KMT II, 450.

41. E.g., to Batthyány, BKF IV, 9; to Lerchenfeld, BKF IV, 102.

42. See chapter 13, this volume.

43. To Joseph's chamberlains, KMT II, 450; to Lerchenfeld, BKF IV, 101; to Thurn, BKF IV, 19; to Almesloë, BKF IV, 127. On van Swieten's daily routine see Brechka, *Gerard Van Swieten*, 113–14.

44. To Joseph's chamberlains, KMT II, 450; see to Lerchenfeld, BKF IV, 102.

45. To Lerchenfeld, BKF IV, 101–2, 105, 119.

46. To Lerchenfeld, BKF IV, 105; see to Rosenberg, BKF IV, 102.

47. To Lerchenfeld, BKF IV, 101.

48. KMT III, 22.

49. KMT III, 255.

50. To Thurn, BKF IV, 20–21; to Batthyány, BKF IV, 6; Bartenstein on Joseph's education, Conrad, *Recht und Verfassung*, 30–31; see Hinrichs, *Friedrich der Große*, 50.

51. KMT V, 86–87.

52. KMT IV, 52; III, 75; similarly V, 74.

53. To Batthyány, BKF IV, 7–8.

54. "*Sa façon de penser, d'annoncer et de se produire,*" to Thurn, BKF IV, 18.

55. E.g., to Batthyány, BKF IV, 7; to Thurn, BKF IV, 20; to Lerchenfeld, BKF IV, 103; to Joseph's chamberlains, KMT II, 449–50.

56. To Batthyány, BKF IV, 9.

57. To Batthyány, BKF IV, 9; see also BKF I, 55.

58. Maria Theresa thus rejected the fifteen-year-old Leopold's application on behalf of a court office-holder for deferred payment of a debt; to Leopold, BKF I, 13–14.

59. See KMT II, 181 ff. Joseph should be gradually removed from female company following his sixth birthday. See also Conrad, *Recht und Verfassung,* 85 ff.

60. Spanish and Italian for Josepha: to Lerchenfeld, BKF IV, 120. A little Czech for Leopold, but no Austrian dialect: to Thurn, BKF IV, 24. The Italian grandchildren should also learn to speak German first: to Almesloë, BKF IV, 127.

61. E.g., KMT II, 56; III, 4, 20, 30, 53, 79, 177, 200, 207, 230, 242, 257. Discussion of the proposed curriculum for Joseph under Bartenstein's direction (January 1754): KMT III, 402 ff.

62. To Lerchenfeld, BKF IV, 103.

63. To Batthyány, BKF IV, 10–11.

64. KMT II, 182.

65. KMT II, 448.

66. KMT II, 450.

67. Conrad, *Recht und Verfassung,* 94–95.

68. E.g., to Thurn, BKF IV, 36; to Rosenberg, BKF IV, 80 ff.

69. To Lerchenfeld, BKF IV, 103, 117–88, 120.

70. To Lerchenfeld, BKF IV, 103.

71. To Lerchenfeld, BKF IV, 111, 113.

72. To Countess Trautson, 1750, van Rhyn, Briefe, 181.

73. To Amalia, June 1769, BKF III, 3 ff.

74. To Carolina, April 1768, BKF III, 44 ff.

75. To Marie Antoinette, May 4, 1770, MACS I, 6 ff.; November 1, 1770, MACS I, 15 ff.; to her chaperone, the Viennese emissary in Paris, Mercy-Argenteau, September 1, 1770, MACS I, 46 ff.

76. To Ferdinand, March 10, 1769, BKF II, 61–62; April 13, 1771, BKF I, 64–65.

77. To Batthyány, BKF IV, 8–9.

78. Others shared this criticism of the heir: his "unclear, slow speech" (KMT II, 194); he was "unsociable," and should "grow more accustomed to the commerce du monde" (KMT II, 301–2), etc. See Beales, "Joseph II's Rêveries," I, 29 ff.

79. Maria Theresa to Count Franz Thurn, 1761, BKF IV, 17 ff.; to Count Franz Thurn, May 1762, BKF IV, 21 ff.; to Leopold, 1765, BKF I, 11 ff.; to Count Anton Thurn, 1766, BKF IV, 33 ff.; Instruction de feu de Majesté l'Empereur François I pour son fils Leopold donnée 1765, ÖNB Wiener Hofbibliothek, Codex Series N. 1713, fol. 1–36; Instructions De l'Imperatrice Reine, ibid., fol. 37–52. See Wandruszka, *Leopold II.,* I, 45 ff., 81 ff., 110 ff.

80. Fidèle tableau de S. A. R. l'archiduc Léopold, May 15, 1762, BKF IV, 22 ff.

81. Leopold to Count Franz Thurn, May 20, 1765, in Wandruszka, *Leopold II.,* I, 101 ff.

82. Leopold to Count Franz Thurn, May 20, 1765, in Wandruszka, *Leopold II.*, I, 103–104.

83. E.g., BKF I, 68, 70; BKF IV, 84 ff.

84. Wandruszka, *Leopold II.*, I, 41, 48.

85. Maria Theresa's sharp criticism of Franz von Thurn: January 12, 1766, MJC I, 170 ff. Thurn died immediately after, giving rise to rumor that the letter had killed him.

86. Innerkofler, *Eine große Tochter* 53–54.

87. Pleschinski, *Emmanuel de Croÿ*, 332.

88. Ranke, "Maria Theresia und ihr Hof," 674; Hinrichs, *Friedrich der Große*, 50. By contrast, Swinburne, *Courts* I, 341, thought the children's education extremely harsh, as did Marie Antoinette's lady-in-waiting: Campan, *Mémoires* I, 36 ff.—On the daughter-in-law Isabella's opinion, see below.

89. To Mercy, January 13, 1779, MACS III, 283. See, in general, Barta, "Maria Theresia," 345.

90. On Maria Christina and Albert of Saxony, see chapter 13, this volume.

91. It was not unheard of, however, for baptized ex-Muslims to become the mistresses of princes.

92. To Kaunitz, May 1762, BKF IV, 249 ff. On marriage negotiations regarding Modena in April 1752: KMT III, 289 ff.; June 1752: KMT III, 301 ff.; contract with the Duke of Modena, May 11, 1753, see Arneth, *Geschichte Maria Theresia's* IV, 239 ff., 337 ff.; Kleinmann, *Politik*.

93. To Lerchenfeld, October 13, 1763, BKF IV, 116.

94. See chapter 13, this volume.

95. See KMT III, 347 ff. (January 1753); Arneth, *Geschichte Maria Theresia's* IV, 336 ff., ibid V, 451 ff.

96. March 25, 1759, Arneth, *Geschichte Maria Theresia's* V, 456.

97. Joseph to his chamberlain Count Anton Salm, September 10, 1760, Zweybrück, "Briefe," 114–15; see "Joseph II's Rêveries," I, 69 ff.

98. Kaunitz to Starhemberg, March 30, 1759, Arneth, *Geschichte Maria Theresia's* V, 538.

99. To Maria Antonia of Saxony, January 28, 1760, Lippert, Briefwechsel, 69–79: "*plûtot aux qualitez qu'aux grandes alliances.*"

100. Maria Theresa regretted the enormous expense that fell on Liechtenstein: to Liechtenstein, January 1760, BKF IV, 406 ff.

101. Entrance, wedding, open table, dinner, and serenade, see color plate 16 and ill. 26 above.

102. Badinter, *Isabella*, 100–101 (February 1761?).

103. Joseph to Salm, September 10, 1760, Zweybrück, "Briefe," 115: "*pour l'amour, vous savez, que je ne fais pas l'agreable et l'amant, et que c'est meme contre ma nature.*"

104. Joseph to Salm, September 17, 1760, Zweybrück, "Briefe," 116–17.

105. Joseph to Salm, September 20 and 28, 1760, Zweybrück, "Briefe," 117–18.

106. Badinter, *Isabella*, first published the letters unabridged, in sharp contrast to the edition of Hrazky, "Die Persönlichkeit"; see also Sanger, *Isabelle*; Arneth, *Geschichte Maria Theresia's* VII, 33 ff.; Beales, "Joseph II's Rêveries" I, 69 ff.; Wolf, *Marie Christine* I, 13 ff.

107. To Antonia of Saxony, June 9, 1760, Lippert, "Kaiserin Maria Theresa," 83–84; see Liechtenstein's report to Maria Theresa, September 4, 1760, Zweybrück, "Briefe," 115 n1; the judgment of her brother-in-law Albert of Saxony in Arneth, *Geschichte Maria Theresia's* VI, 500; KMT VI, 103: "such universal and unqualified approbation."

108. The essays edited in Hrazky, "Die Persönlichkeit," 191 ff.

109. Badinter, *Isabella*, 123–24.

110. Badinter, *Isabella*, 157, 123 ff. *Orphée et Eurydice* by Gluck and Calzabigi had just (1762) created a stir at court; Laurette and Zerbin are characters from the comic opera *Le peintre amoureux de son modèle* by Louis Anseaume and Egidio Duni (1757). On the title roles in *Lisette and Lino* (1762) see Henri Bédarida, *Parme et la France de 1748 à 1789*, Paris 1928, 454–55.

111. See letters 83, 85, 87, 111, and 119 in Badinter's edition, which Hrazky tacity omitted from his edition of the correspondence. Arneth had removed the letters and recommended they be destroyed, see Tamussino, *Isabella*, 196 ff., 299 n1.

112. Badinter, *Isabella*, 146–47, 151; see Tamussino, *Isabella*, 204–205.

113. Badinter, *Isabella*, 145, see 130.

114. Badinter, *Isabelle*, 188.

115. Traité sur les Hommes, ed. in Hrazky, "Die Persönlichkeit," 194–95.

116. Zweybrück, "Briefe," 114.

117. Arneth, *Geschichte Maria Theresia's* VII, 60.

118. Wolf, *Marie Christine* I, 23.

119. Karl Gutkas, *Kaiser Joseph II.*, "Maria Theresia ältester Sohn und Nachfolger," in Koschatzky, Maria Theresia, 176–85, here 178; likewise Gutkas, *Kaiser Joseph II.*, 45 ff.; also Pangels, *Die Kinder*, 168–69; for a very different view see Tamussino, *Isabella*, 201 ff.; Badinter, *Isabella*, 60 ff.

120. See Steidele, *"Als wenn Du mein Geliebter wärest,"* 52.

121. The classic of the genre, Rousseau's *Julie ou la Nouvelle Héloïse*, appeared in 1761 and was known to them both; Tamussino, *Isabella*, 210.

122. See her parody of a court letter of recommendation, Badinter, *Isabella*, 96–97, 100–101. Isabella herself wrote extensive reflections on the nature of true friendship and the extent to which friendship was possible with a monarch, or even with one's own mother: ibid., 242 ff.

123. *Quelques questions à définir au sujet de gagner le cœur de l'Archiduc*, Badinter, *Isabella*, 107 ff.

124. See Albert of Saxony's judgment in his memoirs, in Arneth, *Geschichte Maria Theresia's* VII, 503.

125. Conseil à Marie, Badinter, *Isabella*, 237 ff.

126. Badinter, *Isabelle*, 237–52.

127. To Countess Edling, July 9, 1761, BKF IV, 517.

128. To Maria Louisa of Parma, Isabella's sister, September 14, 1763, in Arneth, *Geschichte Maria Theresia's* VI, 499; see, e.g., BKF IV, 310.

129. To Antonia of Saxony, February 4, 1763, Lippert, *Briefwechsel*, 153; to Maria Christina, 1763?/1764?, BKF II, 357–58; to Maria Christina, October 4, 1771, BKF II, 371–72.

130. Conseil à Marie, Badinter, *Isabelle*, 237–52.

131. Badinter, *Isabelle*, 240–41.

132. Badinter, *Isabelle*, 244 ff.

133. Badinter, *Isabelle*, 251–52.

134. On Maria Christina's marriage to Albert of Saxony see this volume, chapter 14.

135. Badinter, *Isabella*, 98 (Charles); ibid., 166, 168, 172 ff. (Johanna).

136. Breunlich/Mader, *Karl Graf von Zinzendorf*, 378; see Arneth, *Geschichte Maria Theresia's* VII, 61 ff., with further sources 502 ff.; Tamussino, *Isabella*, 215 ff., 258 ff.

137. Joseph to the Duke of Parma, November 29, December 11, December 30, 1763, Bicchieri, "Lettere," 111 ff.; Maria Theresa on Joseph's conduct at Isabella's sickbed: Zweybrück, "Briefe," 121 ff.

138. To Antonia of Saxony, December 23, 1763, Lippert, Briefwechsel, 201–202; to Antonia of Saxony, December 29, 1763, Lippert, Briefwechsel, 206.

139. To Kaunitz, November 26, 1763, in Arneth, *Geschichte Maria Theresia's* VII, 62.

140. To Salm/Zweybrück, "Briefe," 123.

141. Arneth *Geschichte Maria Theresia's* VII, 40, 500.

142. Handwritten note, Zweybrück, "Briefe," 122–23; see Tamussino, *Isabella*, 269–70.

143. See Beales, "Joseph II's Rêveries" I, 82 ff.; Arneth, *Geschichte Maria Theresia's* VII, 87 ff.

144. Pezold to Count Flemming, November 26, 1764, Lippert, Briefwechsel, 209 n4.

145. Points donées par S. M. L'Empereur François, . . . January 28, 1764, HHStA Hausarchiv, Familienkorrespondenz A 26, 13 ff.; see Beales, "Joseph II's Rêveries" I, 82–83. The letter from Joseph to which Francis Stephen replied has not survived.

146. To Antonia of Saxony, February 9, 1764, Lippert, Briefwechsel, 211 ff.

147. "*Je ne puis me presenter qu'en deux faces differentes,*" Joseph wrote to the Duke of Parma, August 23, 1764, Bicchieri, "Lettere," 117–18; see Joseph to Maria Theresa, March 1764, MJC I, 25, 32, 37, 84–85.

148. Joseph to Maria Theresa, April 12 and 14, 1764, MJC I, 97–98, 101.

149. See Joseph to Maria Theresa, April 1774, MJC IO, 97–98, 101, 106 ff., 111 ff., 123 ff., handwritten memorandum from Maria Theresa, MJC I, 111 ff.

150. Elisabeth Christine, later queen of Prussia.

151. KMT VI, 64; see Kaunitz's submission, September 20, 1764, KMT VI, 333 ff.

152. Kunigunde (1740–1826) was the youngest daughter of Augustus III of Saxony-Poland and the Habsburg Maria Josepha, a daughter of Emperor Joseph I. Josepha of Bavaria (1739–67) was the sister of Maximilian, elector of Bavaria, and Maria Antonia of Saxony. Like her, she was a daughter of Emperor Charles VII and the Habsburg Maria Amalia.

153. To Antonia of Saxony, January 16 and Feburary 9, 1764, Lippert, Briefwechsel, 209 ff.; to Pergen, February 24, 1764, BKF IV, 282 ff. Joseph's distaste for both the Bavarian and Saxon candidates: Joseph to Maria Theresa, March/April 1764, 26–27, 30, 84–85, 94, 106 ff.

154. Pezold to Count Flemming, December 31, 1764, Lippert, Briefwechsel, 209 ff., n4.

155. Joseph to Maria Theresa, April 1764, MJC I, 94, 108 ff.

156. KMT VI, 63 ff.; Maria Theresa to Antonia of Saxony, September/October 1764, Lippert, Briefwechsel, 233 ff., 447 ff.

157. KMT VI, 65.

158. KMT VI, 67; see Arneth, *Geschichte Maria Theresia's* VII, 99 ff.

159. KMT VII, 68, the formal documents (November 13, 1764), ibid., 339 ff.

160. Materials in Lippert, Briefwechsel, 236 ff., from the perspective of Kunigunde and the Saxon court, ibid., 447 ff. Antonia of Saxony, who was closely related to both candidates— Josepha was her sister, Kunigunde her sister-in-law—had fallen out with them for Maria Theresa's sake.

161. Illustration, e.g., in Koschatzky, *Maria Theresia* (catalog), 239, no. 40, 19.

162. Joseph to the Duke of Parma, November 13, 1764, Bicchieri, "Lettere," 120–21.

163. To Maria Christina, in Arneth, *Geschichte Maria Theresia's* VII, 103, 510–11.

164. Submissions from Colloredo and Kaunitz, KMT VI, 340 ff., citation on p. 341. The historian commissioned with the task was Franz Ferdinand von Schröter, who in 1764 had taken part in a competition of the Bavarian Academy of Sciences. He had set out to demonstrate that Austria had never been subject to the Duchy of Bavaria. Unsurprisingly, he failed to win the Bavarian prize but received a hundred ducats from the empress instead. See ibid., 345 ff.

165. Submission from Kaunitz, KMT VI, 344. On the War of the Bavarian Succession see chapter 13, this volume.

166. Joseph to Leopold, October 4 and November 14, 1765, HHStA FA Sbd. 7, cited in Beales, "Joseph II's Rêveries" I, 87.

167. Wolf, *Marie Christine* I, 37, source unattributed.

168. KMT VI, 206.

169. To Countess Enzenberg, March 6, 1765, BKF IV, 457. See to Ferdinand, BKF I, 84, 92.

170. KMT VI, 75.

171. KMT VI, 164, 177, 237 ff.

172. Leopold to Franz von Thurn, Wandruszka, *Leopold II.,* I, 103.

173. Coke, *Letters,* III, 325.

174. Stollberg, *Homo patiens*; Dinges, "Medizinische Policey"; Barthel, *Medizinische Policey*; exhibition catalog *Gottes verhengnis*; on smallpox see Tamussino, *Isabella,* 258 ff.; Flamm/Vutuc, "Geschichte"; Wimmer, *Gesundheit*; Rechberger, *Vollständige Geschichte*; on van Sweiten, see Lesky/Wandruszka, *Gerard Van Swieten*; Brechka, *Gerard Van Swieten*; Erna Lesky, "Heilkunde und Gesundheitswesen," in: Koschatzky, *Maria Theresia,* 192 ff.

175. Hermann Boerhaave, *Boerhaave's Aphorisms,* London, 1715, 376; translation slightly modified.

176. Ibid.

177. KMT II, 77. See KMT II, 72; KMT IV, 32, 63–64, 85, 122; KMT V, 5, 33.

178. Van Swieten, *Erläuterungen,* I/1, 306.

179. See Dinges, "Medizinische Policey."

180. To Countess Lerchenfeld, April 1757, BKF IV, 106–107 (it is unclear which of the daughters is intended). The St. Blaise blessing by means of crossed candles was (and is) a sacramental of the Catholic church and served to ward off or heal illnesses of the throat.

181. According to Wagner, "Das geheime Kammerzahlamt," twelve orphaned children received a lifelong pension because they had successfully prayed for Maria Theresa during her smallpox infection.

182. To van Swieten, February 1757?, BKF IV, 237.

183. To Countess Lerchenfeld, April 1757, BKF IV, 107. On the great esteem in which she held the personal physician, see also her letters to van Swieten, BKF IV, 233 ff. (*"mon meilleur ami, confident et bienfaiteur"*); BKF IV, 505 ff. Similar remarks on the occasion of her sister Marianna's death: BKF I, 127–8, 130 ff. See Brechka, *Gerard Van Swieten,* 143 ff.; Arneth, *Geschichte Maria Theresia's* II, 454 ff., VII, 319 ff.

184. To Leopold, August 1765, BKF I, 14 ff. (sanitary rules); there was also a general instruction that is not edited in BKF; see Wandruszka, *Leopold II.,* I, 110 ff.

185. See, e.g., her admonition to Countess Trautson (ca. 1754), van Rhyn, "Unveröffentlichte Briefe," 273: "I am incensed that you do not summon van Swieten and dismiss the other

[physician]. . . . I do not jest in such matters." See to Beatrix, August 23, 1773, BKF III, 161: "So far as medicine is concerned, I wanted to remain ignorant so as to be more obedient"; see also MACS III, 192–3.

186. To Leopold, BKF IV, 16.

187. To Leopold, BKF IV, 19.

188. See chapter 11, this volume.

189. To Countess Lerchenfeld, November 1756, BKF IV, 103.

190. KMT II, 335–36.

191. KMT IV, 63 ff. Marianna's serious illness in 1757 was not a case of smallpox.

192. Maria Theresa to Countess Edling, January 1761, BKF IV, 515–56, 519; KMT V, 136–37; Pangels, *Die Kinder*, 281 ff.

193. Isabella describes her death: Badinter, *Isabelle*, 166–67, 172 ff.

194. To Maria Christina, December 1762, BKF II, 357; to Countess Lerchenfeld, December 1762, BKF IV, 115.

195. KMT IV, 77; see Stangl, "Tod," 79 ff.

196. Comtesse Bentick to Princess von Aldenburg, January 13, 1761, Soprani/Magnan, *Une femme*, 108–109.

197. KMT VI, 237 ff.

198. Albert of Saxony, "Mémoires de ma vie" II, fol. 8, cited in Arneth *Geschichte Maria Theresia's* VII, 525, and Lippert, Briefwechsel, 257; see also KMT VI, 237.

199. KMT VI, 242.

200. Arneth, *Geschichte Maria Theresia's* VII, 319 ff.; KMT VI, 239 ff.; Joseph to Kaunitz, May 31, June 1 and 3, 1767, Beer, Briefwechsel, 445 ff.; Albert of Saxony, *Mémoires de ma vie* II, fol. 8, Lippert, Briefwechsel, 257–58 n2; Prince Albert to Maria Antonia of Saxony, May 27, 1767, Lippert, Briefwechsel, 481 ff. Albert was also infected but recovered from the illness.

201. KMT VI, 240.

202. KMT VI, 242.

203. KMT VI, 244–45; see Telesko/Hertel/Linsboth, "Zwischen Panegyrik."

204. KMT VI, 246 ff.

205. KMT VI, 252.

206. Handwritten note from Kaunitz, in Arneth, *Geschichte Maria Theresia's* VII, 547–48.

207. To Antonia of Saxony, July 21, 1767, Lippert, Briefwechsel, 257–58; see also Arneth, *Geschichte Maria Theresia's* VII, 327 ff., 546 ff.

208. Wagner, "Das Geheime Kammerzahlamt."

209. KMT VI, 272 ff.; Maria Theresa to Maria Christina, October 4, 1771, BKF II, 373; Arneth, *Geschichte Maria Theresia's* VII, 331 ff.; see Hausmann, *Herrscherin*, 15 ff.

210. KMT VI, 274; Campan, *Mémoires* I, 37–38.

211. KMT VI, 279, 552; on Maria Carolina, see this volume, chapter 14.

212. KMT VI, 278.

213. Antonia of Saxony to Maria Theresa, July 7, 1763, Lippert, Briefwechsel, 167 ff.; see Antonia to Fredrick II of Prussia, ibid., 168 n4.

214. To Antonia of Saxony, June 10, 1763, Lippert, Briefwechsel, 167. Antonia's uninoculated husband Frederick Christian, elector of Saxony, likewise died of smallpox not long after, just two months after coming to the throne.

215. Queen Josepha to Antonia, April 17, 1765, Lippert, Briefwechsel, 457 ff. In September 1766 Maria Antonia wanted to have herself inoculated, but her doctors advised her against it. She fell ill but recovered, see Lippert, Briefwechsel, 263.

216. Maria Anna of Bavaria to Maria Antonia of Saxony, June 27, 1767, Lippert, Briefwechsel, 487–88 with n1.

217. Maria Anna of Bavaria to Antonia of Saxony, June 28, 1767, Lippert, Briefwechsel, 488–89.

218. Probst, "Van Swieten als Arzt," 91.

219. Brechka, *Gerard Van Swieten*, 115 ff.

220. Pleschinski, *Emmanuel de Croÿ*, 250.

221. Rechberger, *Vollständige Geschichte*, 14–15.

222. Rechberger was presumably referring particularly to the slander of de Haen, the personal rival of the inoculation advocate, Störck.

223. See Brechka, *Gerard Van Swieten*, 118.

224. KMT VII, 21; to Marquise d'Herzelles, Kervyn de Lettenhove, *Lettres inédites*, 17. See Flamm/Vutuc, "Pocken-Bekämpfung."

225. "... *six ou neuf par les miens*," BKF IV, 289.

226. Wagner, "Das Geheime Kammerzahlamt."

227. To Antonia of Saxony, May 1769, Lippert, Briefwechsel, 266; see to Lacy, May 1769, BKF IV, 369; Joseph to Maria Theresa, May 24, 1769, MJC I, 278 ff.

228. Joseph to Maria Theresa, May 24, 1769, MJC I, 279.

229. E.g., to Ferdinand, BKF I, 61, 123, 158, 273, 275, 285–86, 287, 290, 292; BKF II, 10, 109, 136, 147, 149; Marie Antoinette to Maria Theresa, June/July 1774, MACS II, 182; on Naples, see Hausmann, *Herrscherin*, 89, 96.

230. To Ferdinand, July 1774, BKF I, 285–86; KMT VIII, 23, 32; Marie Antoinette and Mercy to Maria Theresa, June 1774, MACS II, 175, 182–83; see also Pleschinski, *Emmanuel de Croÿ*, 249–50.

231. To Ferdinand, July 21 and 28, 1774, BKF I, 290.

232. To Ferdinand, October 8, 1772, BKF I, 158; see to d'Herzelles, October 2, 1772, Kervyn de Lettenhove, *Lettres inédites*, 40.

233. To Beatrix, May 26, 1777, BKF III, 279.

234. To Ferdinand, October 8, 1772, BKF I, 158; August 26, 1778, BKF II, 136; to Beatrix, BKF III, 310, 320, 324–25.

235. To Ferdinand, May 4, 1774, BKF I, 275; similarly to Marie Beatrix, May 26, 1777, BKF III, 279.

236. Rechberger, *Vollständige Geschichte*, 7.

10. Mother and Son

1. To Countess Enzenberg, November 9, 1765, BKF IV, 464–65.

2. According to Khevenhüller: KMT VI, 103.

3. KMT VI, 110 ff.; Bernard/Zedinger, "Schicksalstage"; see Arneth, *Geschichte Maria Theresia's* VII, 138 ff.; Zedinger, *Franz Stephan*, 279 ff.; Zedinger, *Innsbruck 1765*; Trapp, "Maria Theresia und Tirol"; exhibition catalog, *Maria Theresa and Tyrol*; Beales, "Joseph II's Rêveries" I, 134 ff.; Wandruszka, *Leopold II.*, I. 106 ff.

4. KMT VI, 122, see 115, 120, 124.

5. Descriptions of the circumstances of his death in KMT VI, 125 ff., as well as in the travel diary of Privy Cabinet Secretary Neny: Bernard/Zedinger, "Schicksalstage," 145–46; further Albert of Saxony to Antonia of Saxony, August 21, 1765, Lippert, Briefwechsel, 464 ff.; Pichler, *Denkwürdigkeiten*, 26 ff. The letters all offers slightly different details. See also Brauneis, "Franz Stephan von Lothringen."

6. KMT VI, 124.

7. Neny, in Bernard/Zedinger, "Schicksalstage," 145.

8. See the eyewitness report by Neny, Bernard/Zedinger, "Schicksalstage," 145–46; and KMT VI, 126.

9. Prosch, *Leben*, 100 ff. The report has been previously disregarded by historians, although it is entirely credible on account of its consistency with Neny and Khevenhüller. That Prosch entertained the emperor at table on that day is confirmed by KMT VI, 124. On Prosch see chapter 7, this volume.

10. Prosch, *Leben*, 107.

11. "*Per aliquot minuta signa vitae deprehenderit, proin etiam absolverit.*" Historia Collegii Societatis Jesu Omnipotenti ab A. 1747 ad A. 1773 (Innsbruck, Bibliothek Ferdinandeum, Dip. 596), III, 80, quoted in Brauneis, "Franz Stephan von Lothringen," 272.

12. Arneth, *Geschichte Maria Theresia's* VII, 517.

13. To Countess Enzenberg, February 20, 1775, BKF IV, 510–11; see further letters in Lavandier, *Le Livre*. See also to Archduchess Josepha, August 1765, BKF III, 25–26; to Ferdinand, August 1765, BKF I, 59; to Kaunitz, August 28, 1765, Beer, Briefwechsel, 432–33.

14. To Tarouca, January 30, 1766, Karajan, Sylva-Tarouca, 60. See also, e.g,. KMT VI, 417.

15. Handwritten notes from Maria Theresa, in Wolf, *Marie Christine*, 79–82.

16. Wolf, *Marie Christine*, 79–80.

17. KMT VII, 24.

18. On early modern widowhood in general, see Schattkowsky, *Witwenschaft*; Ingendahl, *Witwen*. On Maria Theresa, Yonan, "Conceptualizing the Kaiserinwitwe"; Yonan, *Empress*, 45 ff.

19. Pichler, *Denkwürdigkeiten*, I, 27.

20. Compare the practice of other empresses such as Eleonore of Palatine or Maria of Spain, who lived considerably more strictly as widows: Braun/Keller/Schnettger, *Nur die Frau des Kaisers?*

21. Matsche, "Maria Theresias Bild," 203. It is remarkable that she characterized the position of Empress as divinely ordained.

22. To Countess Enzenberg, December 1765, BKF IV, 467; KMT VII, 206; see Brauneis, "Franz Stephan von Lothringen," 296 ff.; Barta, *Familienporträts*, 43 ff.; Yonan, *Empress*, 97 ff. Legend has it that she had one of Francis Stephen's coats made into a dressing gown, which she then wore until the day of her death: Koschatzky, *Maria Theresa* (catalog), source unnamed; likewise Brauneis, "Franz Stephan von Lothringen," 298. The story is probably based on Maria Theresa's letter to Countess Enzenberg, February 12, 1766, BKF IV, 468 69.

23. KMT VI, 126–27.

24. Brauneis, "Franz Stephan von Lothringen"; Stangl, "Tod"; Hawlik-van de Water, *Der schöne Tod*; Hawlik-van de Water, *Die Kapuzinergruft*; Hertel, "Kontinuität"; exhibition catalog, *Maria Theresa and Tyrol*; in general, Hersche, *Muße* I, 573 ff.

25. Bynum, *The Resurrection of the Body*, 200 ff., 318 ff.; Mitterauer, "Bedeutsame Orte." From a Protestant viewpoint, see, e.g., Rohr, *Ceremoniel-Wissenschafft*, 279 ff.

26. KMT VI, 129–30.

27. KMT VI, 136; on the sarcophagus, see Telesko, *Maria Theresia*, 90–109; Telesko, "'Die Maria-Theresien-Krypta'"; Telesko, "'Hier wird einmal gutt ruhen seyn.'"

28. Pichler, *Denkwürdigkeiten*, 27.

29. On the funeral solemnities in various cities, see Brauneis, "Franz Stephan von Lothringen," 283 ff.; Telesko, *Maria Theresia*, 102 ff.

30. See Pangerl/Scheutz/Winkelbauer, *Der Wiener Hof*, 557–72.

31. The ban on makeup, even for the wives of foreign diplomats, was unusual and was met with fierce resistance, see Joseph to Leopold, October 4, 1765, MJC I, 140; report of the Saxon emissary Pezold in Lippert, *Briefwechsel*, 294–95 n4.

32. KMT VI, 137, 139.

33. To Countess Enzenberg, February 12, 1766, BKF IV, 468–9, see exhibition catalog, *Maria Theresa and Tyrol*, Innsbruck 1958, 79–80, no. 142–144; Koschatzky, *Maria Theresia* (catalog), 322, no. 64,04. It was not unusual for worldly parade clothes to be transformed into ecclesiastical robes. The Spanish coat dress that Francis Stephen had worn at his wedding was likewise reworked into a priestly vestment and can be seen today in the treasury in Vienna, see Fillitz, *Katalog*, 79, no. 118; Koschatzky, *Maria Theresia* (catalog), 320.

34. KMT VII, 156–7.

35. To Countess Enzenberg, February 12, 1766, BKF IV, 468 ff.

36. To Count Enzenberg, May 1, 1766, in exhibition catalog, *Maria Theresa and Tyrol*, 84, No. 154.

37. To Countess Enzenberg, August 9, 1766, BKF IV, 480. See the contributions of Hanzl-Wachter, Telesko, and Zedinger in Zedinger, *Innsbruck 1765*; Barta, *Familienporträts*, 43 ff.

38. KMT VI, 172, 179.

39. Joseph to Leopold, October 31, 1765, MJC I, 150; KMT VI, 149–50, 156, 159, 207, 518 ff., on the consequences, e.g., KMT VII, 233 ff.; see Stollberg-Rilinger, *Emperor's Old Clothes*, 248 ff.

40. KMT VI, 156, 209–10, 215 (January 1767). Maria Theresa defended this to Khevenhüller by claiming that gala days had been exorbitantly expensive for the nobility. On the congratulatory reception with excessive hand kissing on New Year's Day, see MJC II, 104.

41. KMT VI, 205; ibid., 149–50, 155, 156, 170–71, 185, 186, 213–14, 227, 229; KMT VII, 40, 52. See Kovács, "Kirchliches Zeremoniell"; see chapter 11, this volume.

42. KMT VI, 232; but later resumed, KMT VII, 13.

43. KMT VI, 161 (in relation to 1767); see Garms-Cornides, "Liturgie und Diplomatie," 146.

44. On these measures, see Arneth, *Geschichte Maria Theresia's* VII, 200 ff.; Beales, "Joseph II's Rêveries" I, 139 ff.; financial reforms were being mooted from 1764; relevant memoranda in KMT VI, 353 ff.

45. KMT VI, 169; on the new mourning order of 1767: Pangels/Scheutz/Winkelbauer, *Der Wiener Hof*, 564 ff.

46. KMT VI, 172; see Zechmeister, *Die Wiener Theater*.

47. Scheutz, "Fasching," 147.

48. KMT VI, 175–76; VII, 44.

49. KMT VI, 179.

50. KMT VI, 216.

51. This led to a conflict with his brother Leopold, who claimed the fortune for Tuscany, see Arneth, *Geschichte Maria Theresia's* VII, 171 ff.

52. KMT VI, 179; see Arneth, *Geschichte Maria Theresia's* VII, 206 ff.; Dickson, *Finance* I, 248 ff.

53. KMT VI, 101.

54. Joseph to Leopold, September 12, 1765, MJC I, 131 ("they will cry a little"); KMT VI, 174–75, 432 ff.

55. KMT VI, 179, 160–61, 219.

56. On the Hungarian diet of 1764, see Arneth, *Geschichte Maria Theresia's* VII, 105–37.

57. KMT VI, 159, 208, 210.

58. Biographies: Beales, "Joseph II's Rêveries"; Bérenger, *Joseph II*; Gutkas, *Kaiser Joseph II*.

59. Barta, *Familienporträts*, 60–61 (see color plate 14); the Joseph narrative of the Old Testament also served as a visual template, according to which the brothers' sheaves bowed down before Joseph's sheaf.

60. KMT VI, 396 ff.; to Countess Enzenberg, September 12, 1765, BKF IV, 462.

61. Secundogeniture means that the territory was always inherited by the second-born son of the ruling family.

62. To Antonia of Saxony, April 4, 1763, Lippert, Briefwechsel, 164, see ibid., 172, 177 ff., 189 ff. To Pergen, December 26, 1763, February 24, 1763, BKF IV, 281 ff. To Liechtenstein, February 26, 1764, BKF IV, 309–310. See Beales "Joseph II's Rêveries" I, 110 ff.; Arneth, *Geschichte Maria Theresia's* VII, 70 ff.

63. Instead of the underage Saxon elector, whose mother ruled on his behalf following the death of her husband in December 1763, Stanisław II Poniatowski was elected king of Poland in September 1764 with Russian and French support. See Lippert, Briefwechsel, 185 ff., 214–15, 221.

64. There had been plans for Joseph's coronation as king when he was just nine years old, although Maria Theresa had been unwilling to cover the cost at the time. On Joseph's election and coronation, see Stollberg-Rilinger, *Emperor's Old Clothes*, 203 ff.; Beales, "Joseph II's Rêveries" I, 110 ff.; Arneth, *Geschichte Maria Theresia's* II, 64 ff.; on the context, Aretin, *Das Alte Reich* III, 113 ff.

65. E.g., Joseph to the Duke of Parma, April 25, 1764, Bicchieri, "Lettere," 116. Joseph's letters to his mother from the coronation journey: MJC I, 24–127.

66. Goethe, *Aus meinem Leben* IX, 180 ff.; see Stollberg-Rilinger, *Emperor's Old Clothes*, 205 ff. with further testimonies; retold in Macek, *Die Krönung*; contemporary descriptions: KMT VI, 2 ff., 282 ff.; on Archduke Leopold's travel diary, see Wandruszka, *Leopold II.*, I, 61 ff.

67. To Pergen, early 1763, quoted in Pangels, *Die Kinder*, 104.

68. See Macek, "Die Krönungszyklus."

69. See Stollberg-Rilinger, *Emperor's Old Clothes*, 246 ff. After discussing the matter with the order chapters, Maria Theresa transferred the office of grand master in all three orders—Golden Fleece, Maria Theresa Order, Order of St Stephen—to her son in the immediate aftermath of Francis Stephen's death; KMT VI, 140.

70. Opinion of Bartenstein (junior), September 5, 1765, KMT VI, Appendix, 385.

71. KMT VI, 139; see to Khevenhüller, KMT VI, Appendix, 430.

72. To Tarouca, November 1765, Karajan, *Maria Theresia und Graf Sylva-Tarouca*, 57. In February 1766, ibid., 69–70, she wrote: "I will transfer the entire military into my son's hands. . . . This branch of the monarchy was the only one that lay close to my heart. I have given it up; all the rest will cost me nothing more." Rumors on her intention to abdicate following the emperor's death: e.g., Swinburne, *Courts* I, 350.

73. To Thurn, March 1766, BKF IV, 37–38.

74. To Ferdinand, December 3, 1778, BKF II, 163–64; see to Joseph, December 1773, MJC II, 27 ff.; on her intention to abdicate in 1773, see below.

75. Opinion of Court Councillor Koller, KMT VI, 393, KMT VI, 141, 381 ff.

76. KMT VI, 141, 381 ff.; see Beales, "Love and the Empire"; Reinöhl, "Die Übertragung"; Karajan, *Maria Theresia und Joseph II.*

77. Explanation from September 17, 1765, KMT VI, 394–95.

78. Only Imperial Aulic Councillor Bartenstein (junior), who like his father had been asked for his opinion, reflected on the problem: in the unlikely event of a difference of opinion between mother and son, a majority of ministers in the State Council could decide the matter. KMT VI, Appendix, 387.

79. Anonymous report from the Viennese court (early 1770), Wertheimer, "Zwei Schilderungen," 214; similarly anon., *Portrait de Joseph II*, 7, or the Venetian emissary Renier, February 1, 1766: the sovereign was "jealous of her authority" and had taken back all the concessions she had made to her son in her anguish; quoted in Arneth, *Geschichte Maria Theresia's* VII, 526.

80. Swinburne, *Courts* I, 39.

81. Ligne, *Fragments* I, 133, 266: "*priapisme continuel; les irritations, sans pouvoir les satisfaire.*" See Mansel, *Prince of Europe*, 73 ff., 97.

82. To Batthyány, 1751, BKF IV, 5; see chapter 9, this volume.

83. To Batthyány, BKF IV, 8–9; KMT II, 301–302, 194; report from 1759, Conrad, *Recht und Verfassung*, 101. See chapter 9, this volume.

84. Badinter, *Isabella*, 251–252: Joseph's *ennui*, his tendency to jealousy, etc.

85. See Conrad, *Recht und Verfassung.*

86. See chapter 5, this volume; see Brauneder, "Vom Nutzen"; Stollberg-Rilinger, "Vom Volk."

87. Resolution on Chotek's submission, April 1, 1769, in Arneth, *Geschichte Maria Theresia's* IX, 189.

88. See Karstens, *Lehrer*; see also chapter 13, this volume.

89. See Lebeau, *Aristocrates et grands commis*, 84 ff.; for Prussi, Hellmuth, *Naturrechtstheorie*; for Festetics, Evans, "Maria Theresa and Hungary."

90. Completely edited in Conrad, *Recht und Verfassung.*

91. Conrad, *Recht und Verfassung*, 221.

92. Conrad, *Recht und Verfassung*, 276 ff.

93. Bartenstein, May 18, 1759, Conrad, *Recht und Verfassung*, 80; likewise Khevenhüller, who regularly attended the examinations, e.g.,KMT IV, 107; KMT V, 2.

94. The case is dealt with in a single sentence in Beck: Conrad, *Recht und Verfassung*, 231.

95. ÖZV II,3, no. 77, 20; see Beales, "Joseph II's Rêveries" I, 90 ff. Criticism of the discussions: MJC III, 336.

96. Editions: opinion on the military from April 3, 1761: MJC I, 1–12. "Rêveries" of 1763: Beales, "Joseph II's Rêveries." Memorandum on the state of the monarchy from December 1765: MJC III, 335–361. Memorandum "Si vis pacem para bellum," December 28, 1766: KMT VI, 458–67. Memorandum after the Bohemian trip, November 17, 1771: KMT VII, 373–98. "Note" from April 27, 1773: ÖZV II,3, 48–73. Memorandum from May 17, 1775 from Trieste: KMT VIII, 258–66. On a further, unpublished memorandum from early 1768, see Beales, "Joseph II's Rêveries" I, 177 ff. On the memoranda in general, Beales, "Joseph II's Rêveries" I, 164 ff.; overview in Dickson, *Finance* I, 447–48.

97. See the more decorous paraphrase in Arneth, *Geschichte Maria Theresia's* VII, 65 ff. The most offensive passages were omitted from later citations, too. Arneth tacitly purged his edition of the correspondence between Joseph and Leopold of any phrases that might seem excessively radical. On his editorial procedures see Beales, "Joseph II's Rêveries," 142 ff.

98. Beales, "Joseph II's Rêveries," 155–56.

99. "*Aux grands maux, il faut de l'éméthique*," Beales, "Joseph II's Rêveries," 159.

100. Memorandum on the state of the monarchy from December 1765: MJC III, 335–61. See Arneth, *Geschichte Maria Theresia's* VII, 188 ff.; Beales, "Joseph II's Rêveries" I, 164 ff.

101. Quoted in Arneth, *Geschichte Maria Theresia's* VII, 199.

102. MJC III, 354.

103. MJC III, 342, 352.

104. E.g., to Ferdinand, June 11, 1772, BKF I, 130; to Maximilian, April 1774, BKF II, 322–23; to Marie Antoinette, June 2, 1775, MACS II, 341–42; to Ferdinand, August 14, 1779, BKF II, 203.

105. Joseph to Leopold, September 12, 1765, MJC I, 128 ff.; see Aretin, *Das Alte Reich* II, 124 ff.; Stollberg-Rilinger, *Emperor's Old Clothes*, 245 ff.; see the memoranda on the imperial constitution that Joseph received in November 1766: KMT VI, 479–518; Conrad, *Recht und Verfassung*.

106. To Pergen, October 3 and November 13, 1765, BKF IV, 286 ff.; to Kaunitz (1767?), BKF IV, 256: Joseph refused to take advice in imperial matters; this was Pergen's fault. See the biographical sketch in Bernard, *From the Enlightenment*.

107. To Kaunitz, August 28, 1765, Beer, Briefwechsel, 432–33; to Kauntiz (undated), BKF IV, 259.

108. Beales, "Joseph II's Rêveries" I, 123 ff., 147 ff.; Bérenger, *Joseph II*, 161–62; Szábo, *Kaunitz*, 61 ff.; on San Remo, see Schnettger, *"Principe sovrano*," 363 ff.; on Joseph's intervention, ibid., 391 ff.

109. Beer, Briefwechsel, 489 ff.; KMT VI, 446 ff.; see Arneth, *Geschichte Maria Theresia's* VII, 296 ff.; Beales, "Joseph II's Rêveries" I, 143–44; Szábo, *Kaunitz*, 61 ff.

110. Joseph (without addressee), September 11, 1766, MJC I, 194 ff.

111. To Joseph II, September 14, 1766, MJC I, 199 ff.

112. To Joseph II, September 14, 1766, MJC I, 199 ff.

113. E.g., Wertheimer, "Zwei Schilderungen," 212–13.

114. KMT VI, 458 ff.; see Beales, "Joseph II's Rêveries," 183 ff.

115. KMT VI, 187.

116. Joseph to Maria Theresa, July 8, 1766, MJC I, 185.

117. KMT VI, 187–88; Joseph to Maria Theresa, June/July 1766, MJC I, 180 ff.; see Küntzel, "Über den Plan"; Beer, "Die Zusammenkünfte"; Arneth, *Geschichte Maria Theresia's* VIII, 93 ff.

118. Pleschinski, *Emmanuel de Croÿ*, 338.

119. KMT VI, 189.

120. Joseph to Maria Theresa, July 10, 1766, MJC I, 186–87.

121. Joseph to Maria Theresa, September 15, 1766, MJC I, 205–206.

122. Joseph to Maria Theresa, January 19, 1769, MJC I, 233–34; see Beales, "Joseph II's Rêveries" I, 198 ff.; Arneth, *Geschichte Maria Theresia's* VII, 236 ff., who calls Maria Theresa's behavior "typically feminine."

123. On the State Council, see chapter 5, this volume; ÖZV II,3, no. 77; Hock/Bidermann, *Der österreichiste Staatsrath*, 23 ff.; Beales, "Joseph II's Rêveries" I, 198 ff.

124. The exchange of letters from January 1769 in MJC I, 233–42.

125. To Joseph, January 28, 1769, MJC I, 237–38.

126. To Joseph, January 1769, MJC I, 240–41.

127. Joseph to Maria Theresa, January 29, 1769, MJC I, 242.

128. Following his tour of Hungary and the Banat in summer 1768, see chapter 7, this volume.

129. Joseph to Maria Theresa, early 1769, MJC I, 243 ff.; see Arneth, *Geschichte Maria Theresia's* VII, 469 ff.

130. E.g., to Lacy, August 1769, BKF IV, 370; Arneth, *Geschichte Maria Theresia's* VIII, 155 ff.; Beer, "Die Zusammenkünfte"; see below.

131. Joseph to his daughter's lady-in-waiting, Marquise d'Herzelles, January 1770, Kervyn de Lettenhove (Constantin), *Lettres inédites*, 17 ff. The marquise left the court a little later; Joseph may have offered her his hand in marriage; see Beales, "Joseph II's Rêveries" I, 201 ff.

132. To Lacy, January 27, 1771, BKF IV, 379.

133. To Countess Enzenberg, February 7, 1771, BKF IV, 503; to d'Herzelles, March 1, 1771, Kervyn de Lettenhove (Constantin), *Lettres inédites*, 23.

134. Joseph to Leopold, January 10, 1771, MJC I, 322. KMT VII, 55–56: the list provoked "considerable, not unjustified disgust"; Khevenhüller also held Joseph responsible for it.

135. To d'Herzelles, March 1, 1771, Kervyn de Lettenhove (Constantin), *Lettres inédites*, 25; see January 10, 1771, ibid., 21–22; and a year and a half later she spoke of "this terrible promotion," July 2, 1772, ibid., 32–33.

136. To d'Herzelles, January 10, 1771, Kervyn de Lettenhove (Constantin), *Lettres inédites*, 22. She also vented her spleen about Joseph to her emissary in Versailles, Mercy-Argenteau, Court War Councilor Lacy, and her daughter-in-law Beatrix in Milan.

137. To d'Herzelles, January 10, 1771, Kervyn de Lettenhove (Constantin), *Lettres inédites*, 21–22; March 1, 1771, ibid., 23 ff.

138. Hersche, *Der Spätjansenismus*; see chapter 11, this volume.

139. To d'Herzelles, March 1, 1771, Kervyn de Lettenhove (Constantin), *Lettres inédites*, 24.

140. Arneth, *Geschichte Maria Theresia's* VII, 467–68.

141. E.g., to Rosenberg, February 1769, BKF IV, 66.

142. To Marie Beatrix, late 1770?, BKF III, 114.

143. To d'Herzelles, July 2, 1772, Kervyn de Lettenhove (Constantin), *Lettres inédites*, 33; September 27, 1772, ibid., 36–37.

144. Wandruszka, *Leopold II.* II, 344; also Ligne, *Fragments* I, 190; see Mansel, *Prince of Europe*, 73–74.

145. To Leopold, February 24, March 26, and November 17, 1772, MJC I, 365–66, 3868–7; see ibid., I, 2242–245, 228, 230, 374; MJC II, 55–56, 58, 74–75; a contrasting account in his letter

to Maria Theresa, MJC I, 256; on Joseph's relations with women at this time, see Beales, "Joseph II's Rêveries" I, 330 ff.

146. To d'Herzelles, July 31, 1772, Kervyn de Lettenhove (Constantin), *Lettres inédites*, 33–34; Joseph himself on the appointment: MJC I, 373.

147. KMT VII, 62–63, 49, 76; KMT VIII, 89–90.

148. This was demonstrated by Beales, "Joseph II's Rêveries" I, 208 ff. The passages omitted in MJC I, 321 ff. can be found in HHStA Hausarchiv FA, Sbd. 7. In Friedrich Walter's wide-ranging selection of letters and documents, only one letter was included from the altercations of 1770–1773 (MJC I, 350 ff. = BAA, 299 ff.).

149. Joseph to Leopold, March 21, 1771, MJC I, 324. Even Khevenhüller took a similar view: KMT VII, 60.

150. Joseph to Leopold, September 19, 1771, HHStA Hausarchiv FA, Sbd. 7, Alt 15/2, fol. 214; see Beales, "Joseph II's Rêveries" I, 208; Joseph to Maria Theresa, September 25, 1771, MJC I, 344–45; October 27, 1771, MJC I, 247 ff.

151. KMT VII, 373 ff. On the famine in Bohemia, see chapter 13.

152. See, for example, the pamphlets showing the emperor personally plowing the soil in Bohemia in 1769. These were disseminated in several variants until the late nineteenth century: exhibition catalog *Austria in the Age of Emperor Joseph*, 352 ff., on the nineteenth century, ibid., 696 ff. (Ill. 41).

153. To Joseph, November 1771, BAA, 299 ff.

154. E.g., Political Testament, BAA, 83; Tarouca to Maria Theresa, April 27, 1754, Karajan, *Maria Theresia und Graf Sylva-Tarouca*, 21–22; Maria Theresa to Kaunitz, June 7, 1766, in Arneth, *Geschichte Maria Theresia's* VII, 300 ff., BAA, 220 ff.; Maria Theresa to Joseph, December 9, 1773, MJC II, 27 ff.; see also her self-criticism when writing to Countess Trautson, van Rhyn, "Unveröffentlichte Briefe," 268.

155. Joseph to Leopold, December 19, 1771, HHStA Hausarchiv FA, Sbd. 7 Alt 15/2; similarly January 16, 11 May, 25 May, 11 June, 1772; see Beales, "Joseph II's Rêveries" I, 215.

156. Joseph to Maria Theresa, November 27, 1771, MJC I, 352 ff.; similarly in April, MJC I, 335 ff. See Beales, "Joseph II's Rêveries" I, 207 ff.

157. Memorandum from Bohemia, KMT VII, Appendix, 377.

158. Memorandum from Bohemia, KMT VII, Appendix, 376.

159. Joseph to Leopold, October 29, 1772, MJC I, 383: what went on in the State Council was like consulting a heathen on "whether it is more useful to pray to Jupiter, Juno, or Fitzliputzli." On the State Council, see chapter 5, this volume.

160. So already in a memorandum from June 13, 1772, in Schünemann, "Die Wirtschaftspolitik," 216 ff.

161. See his letters to Leopold from early 1773, MJC II, 5 ff.; Beales, "Joseph II's Rêveries" I, 216 ff.

162. ÖZV II,3, no. 77, 48–73; see MJC II, 6–7; see also Arneth, *Geschichte Maria Theresia's* IX, 293 ff. (Arneth, who usually cites from the sources at length, has only a few words to say about this particular memorandum, ibid., 309); Beales, "Joseph II's Rêveries" I, 218 ff.; Hock/Bidermann, *Der österreichische Staatsrath*, 29 ff.; Szábo, *Kaunitz*, 99 ff. Similar suggestions also in the memorandum from June 13, 1772: Schünemann, "Die Wirtschaftspolitik," 41 ff.

163. ÖZV II,3, no. 77, 50.

164. ÖZV II,3, no. 77, 51–52.

165. ÖZV II,3, no. 77, 52.

166. See Hausen, "Die Polarisierung."

167. On the concept of formalization, see Stollberg-Rilinger, "Die Frühe Neuzeit."

168. ÖZV II,3, no. 77, 60 ff.

169. Handwritten resolution by Maria Theresa, ÖZV II,3, no. 77, 73.

170. On the opaque processes surrounding the various reform memoranda and who knew about them when, see ÖZV II,3, no. 77, 73 ff.; Beales Joseph II, I, 218 ff.; Hock, Der österreichische Staatsrath, 31 ff.; Bérenger, Joseph II, 162 ff.

171. On the Polish partition see below.

172. To Joseph, June 20, 1773, MJC II, 9 ff.; to Maria Christina, May 4, 1773, BKF II, 375; to Marie Beatrix, BKF III, 160; to Lacy, April 25, 1773, BKF IV, 394; to Ferdinand, July 1, 1773, BKF I, 214.

173. Karajan, Maria Theresia und Joseph II, 10–11; for more detail see Glassl, Das österreichische Einrichtungswerk.

174. Correspondence between Joseph, Maria Theresa, and Kaunitz, December 1773: MJC II, 21 ff.

175. Joseph to Leopold, December 9, 1773, MJC II, 21–22.

176. Joseph to Maria Theresa, December 9, 1773, MJC II, 23 ff.

177. Joseph to Maria Theresa, December 9, 1773, MJC II, 23 ff.

178. To Joseph, December 9, 1773, MJC II, 27 ff.

179. ÖZV II,3, no. 77, 76 ff.

180. ÖZV II,3, no. 77, 80 ff.

181. KMT VIII, 85, similarly 78, 89–90, 73, 83, 119.

182. KMT VIII, 89–90.

183. Arneth, "Graf Philipp Cobenzl," 130–31.

184. "In scissura mentium Deus non est," God does not exist in the splitting of minds, according to Pope Gregory the Great.

185. "Ni curieuse, ni exigeant," to Marie Beatrix, April 6, 1772, BKF III, 134.

186. E.g., to Lacy, BKF IV, 370, 377, 383; to Marie Beatrix, late 1770?, BKF III, 134.

187. To Maria Christina, October 4, 1771, BKF II, 374.

188. Brief overviews: Duchhardt, Balance of Power, 370 ff.; Müller, Die Teilungen Polens (with a review of the long and controversial history of scholarship); from an Austrian perspective Hochedlinger, Austria's Wars, 350 ff.; Guglia, Maria Theresia II, 298 ff.; Beales, "Joseph II's Rêveries" I, 272 ff. (ibid., 279–80 on previous research); more detail in Arneth, Geschichte Maria Theresia's VIII; Beer, Die Erste Theilung; Lukowski, Partitions; Roider, Austria's Eastern Question, 111 ff.

189. On the two meetings, see Arneth, Geschichte Maria Theresia's VIII, 154 ff., 192 ff.; Beer, "Die Zusammenkünfte"; Kunisch, Friedrich der Große, 493 ff.

190. Frederick II to d'Alembert, August 28, 1769, Preuß, Œuvres XXIV, 510–11.

191. Joseph to Maria Theresa, August 1769, MJC I, 300–15; see Maria Theresa to Lacy, August 1769, BKF IV, 370; Albert of Saxony's report in Arneth, Geschichte Maria Theresia's VIII, 566–67; Count Mercy's report and further sources in Beer, "Die Zusammenkünfte," 489 ff.

192. KMT VII, 300 ff.; Beer, Die Erste Theilung III.

193. E.g., Joseph to Leopold, January 31, 1771, MJC I, 331; KMT VII, 141; see the caricature "Le gateau des rois" (ill. 42).

194. Joseph to Leopold, December 1770—February 1771, MJC I, 316 ff.

195. To Antonia of Saxony, October 1768, Lippert, Briefwechsel, 185–86.

196. Resolution of Maria Theresa, MJC I, 325–26 n1.

197. Joseph to Maria Theresa, January 19, 1771, MJC I, 325 ff.

198. Joseph to Leopold, January 24, 1771, MJC I, 328 ff.; see January 31, 1771, MJC I, 331; March 1771, MJC I, 333–34.

199. Joseph to Leopold, September 25, 1771, MJC I, 344–45.

200. Joseph to Leopold, May 1771, MJC I, 341–42.

201. Memorandum from Maria Theresa, January 22, 1772, Beer, *Die Erste Theilung* III, 340–41.

202. MJC I, 362–63, designated there as a letter to Joseph. According to Beales, "Joseph II's Rêveries" I, 297, it is actually a letter to Kaunitz from January 22, 1772.

203. Opinion de S. M. l'Impératrice-Reine sur le parti à prendre en consequence de la note du baron van Swieten, February 5, 1772, MACS I, xxviii ff.; Arneth, *Geschichte Maria Theresia's* VIII, 375 ff., 601–602.

204. To Kaunitz, February 17, 1772, BAA, 309.

205. Arneth, *Geschichte Maria Theresia's* VIII, 389 ff.; Beer, *Die Erste Theilung* II, 191 ff.

206. To Kaunitz, August 3, 1772, BAA, 321; see to Lacy, August 23, 1772, BAA, 321–22.

207. To Mercy, the emissary in Paris, June 1, 1772, MACS I, 307–308, BAA, 317–18; July 2, 1772, MACS I, 320–21, BAA, 319 ff.

208. Hochedlinger, *Austria's Wars*, 354. Lemberg became the administrative center. The new province was initially subordinate to the state chancellery. In 1774 it was assigned its own Galician court chancellery before being transferred in 1776 to the Austrian-Bohemian court chancellery. On the historical justification for the claim: Franz Adam Kollár, *Vorläufige Ausführung der Rechte des Königreichs Ungarn auf . . . Reußen und Podolien*, Vienna 1772.

209. KMT VII, 140; see Hochedlinger, *Austria's Wars*, 355.

210. Preuß *Œuvres* VI, 52; this and the quote from Otto Hintze in Bömelburg et al., *Die Teilung*, 16.

211. On the parallels between Poland and the imperial confederation, see Bömelburg et al., *Die Teilung*.

212. To d'Herzelles, July 2, 1772, Kervyn de Lettenhove (Constantin), *Lettres inédites*, 32–33.

213. To Ferdinand, September 17, 1771, BKF I, 151, BAA, 322. Galicia consumed only money and troops: to Ferdinand, September 29, 1774, BKF I, 302; to Ferdinand of Brunswick, 1776, BKF IV, 532.

214. KMT VII, 140.

215. KMT VII, 141. Khevenhüller therefore advised him to advance old claims to the County of Zips to justify the treaty.

216. Quoted in Beales, "Joseph II's Rêveries" I, 298.

217. Ligne, *Fragments* I, 251.

218. See chapters 11, 12, and 13, this volume.

11. The Religion of Rule

1. See Andreas Schumacher (ed.), *Canaletto, Bernardo Bellotto malt Europa*, exhibition catalog, Alte Pinakothek, Munich 2014, 246, Ill. 142; Knofler, *Das Theresianische Wien*, 41 ff. On its counterpart (color plate 25) we see Freyung from the opposite perspective, from the southeast; the square is abuzz with market stalls and shoppers. The two paintings combined give a complete picture of this urban square, and indeed of eighteenth-century life in general, juxtaposing the secular and the spiritual, everyday reality and holiday.

2. See, e.g., Keyßler, *Neueste Reisen*, 1214. On the ruling family's worship of the Holy of Holies, see catalog *Prinz Eugen*, 261, no. 10, 7.

3. Judenordnung from September 23, 1753, Pribram, *Geschichte* I, 161.

4. Coreth, *Pietas Austriaca*; Kovács, "Kirchliches Zeremoniell"; Hersche, *Muße*; Pammer, *Glaubensabfall*; overview in Tropper, "Von der katholischen Erneuerung"; further Leeb/Pils/Winkelbauer, *Staatsmacht*; Samerski, "Hausheilige"; Seitschek, Religiöse Praxis; Schmal, *Die Pietas*; on Hungary, Bárth, *Katholische Aufklärung und Volksfrömmigkeit*. On the sacral topography of Vienna and surrounds, see also Guglia, *Maria Theresia* I, 14 ff.

5. Fuhrmann, *Alt- und neues Österreich* I, 345.

6. See chapter 12, this volume.

7. See chapter 5, this volume, n116 ff.

8. See color plate 1.

9. See Samerski, "Hausheilige"; Holubar/Huber, *Die Krone des Landes*.

10. Coreth, *Pietas austriaca*.

11. Schütte, "Höfisches Zeremoniell"; Völkel, *Der Tisch des Herrn*; Pammer, *Glaubensabfall*, 103 ff.

12. This is documented day by day by Khevenhüller, KMT, as well as in court calendars and ceremonial protocols. See Kovács, "Kirchliches Zeremoniell"; Schmal, *Die Pietas*.

13. To Maria Christina, April 1766, Wolf, *Marie Christine* I, 63; BAA 217.

14. Karl von Zinzendorf on May 21, 1761, Zinzendorf, *Aus den Jugendtagebüchern*, 201–202.

15. Instruction for the Crown Equerry (*Oberststabelmeister*), 1769, Wührer/Scheutz, *Zu Diensten*, 990.

16. E.g., the copperplate series of Viennese churches with representations of procession by Kleiner, Vera et accurate delineation; or the historical-topographical handbook by Fuhrmann, *Alt- und neues Österreich*; see Seitschek, "Religiöse Praxis."

17. Hüttl, *Marianische Wallfahrten*, 154 ff.; Stadelmann, "Mariazell"; Eberhart/Fell, *Mariazell*; exhibition catalog *Prinz Eugen*, no. 17.3 (exorcism). The name Mariazell alludes to the Casa sancta, the house of Mary supposedly transported by angels to Loreto, which was reproduced in numerous Loreto chapels beyond the Alps.

18. Lodovico Antonio Muratori, *Della regola divozione cristiani*, Venice 1747. On the reception in Austria, see Pammer, *Glaubensabfall*.

19. Named after the Dutch theologian Cornelius Jansen, Bishop of Ypres (1585–1638); Lorenz, *Der Jansenismus*.

20. The papal bull *Unigenitus* had been officially recognized by Charles VI in 1715. In the Habsburg Netherlands, however, Charles of Lorraine banned all theological debate on the subject in his capacity as governor, prompting the papal nuncio to lodge a protest with Maria Theresia; see Winter, *Der Josephinismus*, 36–37.

21. See, e.g., the scorn heaped on such practices by the Protestant writer Wekhrlin, *Denkwürdigkeiten von Wien*, 28 ff.

22. Hersche, *Muße*.

23. The term is Khevenhüller's, with critical undertones, KMT IV, 71.

24. Pastoral letter from the Archbishop of Vienna, 1752, in Hersche, *Der aufgeklärte Reformkatholizismus*, 12 ff.

25. Paul Joseph Riegger, in Arneth, *Geschichte Maria Theresia's* IX, 57 ff., here 69.

26. This was a bone of contention, see Arneth, *Geschichte Maria Theresia's* IX, 79 ff.

27. See chapter 12, this volume.

28. Walter, "Die Religiöse Stellung"; Maaß, "Maria Theresia"; Klingenstein, *Staatsverwaltung und kirchliche Autorität*, 76 ff.; Hersche, "War Maria Theresia eine Jansenistin?"; Schindling, "Theresianismus"; Hollerweger, *Die Reform*, 49 ff.

29. Arnheim, "Das Urtheil," 290, speaks of *"esprit de zèle et prétendue conviction; . . . pour cause ou sous prétexte de religion."* See also Ranke, "Maria Theresia und ihr Hof," 674.

30. Franz Rudolf von Großing, *Allgemeines Toleranz- und Religionssystem für all Staaten und Völker der Welt*, Leipzig 1784, 98, quoted in Maaß, "Maria Theresia," 201.

31. Volz, *Politische Correspondenz*, vol. 26, 128.

32. E.g., Maaß, "Maria Theresia," 205 ff.

33. The literature on Josephinism as an intellectual movement and its practical implications for church policy is legion, particularly as it overlaps in many respects with research on late Jansenism, Catholic Enlightenment, and enlightened despotism in the Habsburg lands. See only the collections of source material by Maaß, *Der Josephinismus*; Maaß, "Vorbereitung"; Klueting, *Der Josephenismus*; as well as the studies by Winter, *Der Josephinismus*; Maaß, *Der Frühjosephinismus*; Reinhardt, *Zur Kirchenreform*; O'Brian, "Jansenists"; Hersche, *Der Spätjansenismus*; Hersche, "War Maria Theresia eine Jansenistin?"; Klingenstein, *Staatsverwaltung*; Beales "Joseph II's Rêveries,"; brief overviews in Wangermann, "Matte Morgenröte"; Wangermann, "Reform Catholicism"; Aretin, "Der Josephinismus"; Beales, "Josephinismus"; Lehner, "What is 'Catholic Enlightenment'?"; also the volumes edited by Kovács, *Katholische Aufklärung*; Klueting, *Katholische Aufklärung*; Schmale/Zedinger/Mondot, *Josephinismus*; Bendel/Spannenberger, *Katholische Aufklärung*; Robertson/Timms, *Austrian Enlightenment*; Cerman/Krueger/Reynolds, *Enlightenment*; Burson/Lehner, *Enlightenment*; Lehner/Printy, *A Companion*; H. "Wolf, Katholische Aufklärung?"; on the historiography, see Fillafer/Wallnig, *Josephinismus*.

34. "Maria Theresa was the mother and Kaunitz the father of Josephinism": Maaß, "Vorbereitung," 297; Hersche, *Muße* II, 982–83; Hollerweger, *Die Reform*, 51, speaks of Maria Theresa's "Josephine" piety.

35. Schindling, "Theresianismus."

36. See Beales, Josephinism; Fillafer, Introduction to Fillafer/Wallnig, *Josephinismus*.

37. Church historians such as the Jesuit father Ferdinand Maaß represent one side, national historians such as Arneth or, later, Friedrich Walter the other.

38. KMT II, 77; III, 74: 1753 saw the discontinuation of the court pilgrimage to Klosterneuburg to worship the patron saint, Leopold.

39. Ceiling fresco by Paul Troger above the imperial staircase in Göttweig Abbey (1739); see Matsche, "Die Kunst."

40. To Countess Enzenberg, December 26, 1765; see Trapp, "Maria Theresia und Tirol"; Koschatzky, *Maria Theresia* (catalog), 135. Nonetheless, such "sacral identification portraits" exist for Maria Theresa as well, depicting her as St. Barbara or as Teresa of Ávila, for example; see Telesko, *Maria Theresia*, 66 ff.; Reitböck, "Das Altarbild."

41. Only a single, almost unknown exception is mentioned by Telesko, *Maria Theresia*, 68.

42. On the occasion of the journey to Pressburg in 1744; KMT I, 237–38.

43. KMT V, 64. The occasion, Khevenhüller noted, was the Feast of St. Roch, when the Augustinian prior "bellowed out almost an entire sermon instead of the brief compliment that would have been seemly."

44. Eybl, "Die katholische Hofprediger," 438.

45. Klingenstein, *Staatsverwaltung*, 78, claims that Maria Theresa's religiosity was already a "purely personal, individual" piety, a private matter anticipating the Enlightenment separation of religion and politics.

46. Hollerweger, *Die Reform*, 54; Schmal, *Die Pietas*, 148.

47. *Principia generalia* (c. 1752), in Tropper, *Staatliche Kirchenpolitik*, 222 ff.

48. To Carolina, April 1768, BKF III, 32 ff., here 33; similarly to Leopold, August 1765, BKF I, 22 ff.; to Maximilian, April 1774, BKF III, 322 ff.; to Marie Antoinette, April 21, 1770, MACS I, 1 ff.; to Amalia, June 1769, BKF III, 9–10; to Beatrix, May 1, 1779, BKF III, 359–60; to Ferdinand, April 4, 1776, BKF II, 16.

49. To Carolina, April 1768, BKF III, 35–36; to Maximilian, April 1774, BKF III, 336–37.

50. To Carolina, April 1768, BKF III, 43–44.

51. To Marie Antoinette, April 21, 1770, MACS I, 2; likewise to Carolina, April 1768, BKF III, 43–44.

52. See chapter 10, this volume; see also Maria Theresa's attitude to the apotropaic amulet of Countess Mahoni, discussed in chapter 6.

53. Koschatzky, *Maria Theresia* (catalog), 319–20, no. 63,06.

54. KMT III, 193.

55. KMT III, 196–97.

56. Coreth, *Pietas austriaca*, 41–42; Schmal, *Die Pietas*, 207. On the arm of St. Stephen, see chapter 3, this volume.

57. Hersche, *Muße* II, 1008.

58. KMT V, 95 (1759); VII, 176 (1773).

59. To Carolina, April 1768, BKF III, 46.

60. To Maximilian, April 1774, BKF III, 330.

61. To Ferdinand, September 23, 1771, BKF I, 66–67.

62. To Ferdinand, May 21, 1778, BKF II, 118–19.

63. Maaß, *Der Josephinismus* I, 291.

64. Tropper, *Staatliche Kirchenpolitik*, 28–29; Pammer, *Glaubensabfall*, 112 ff.

65. Decree on the reduction of holidays from October 6, 1771, Klueting, *Der Josephinismus*, 160–61; on the futility of the law, see Hersche, *Muße* II, 1016 ff.

66. To Maximilian, April 1774, BKF III, 318 ff.

67. See, in this volume, chapter 7 on her daily routine, chapter 10 on her widowhood.

68. To Carolina, April 1768, BKF III, 45–46; to Marie Antoinette, November 1770, MACS I, 8; to Mercy, MACS I, 84; see Hersche, "War Maria Theresia eine Jansenistin?"

69. See the text written by Francis Stephen, "Lermite dans le monde," HHStA Familien-Urkunden 2011/2012; see Wandruszka, "Die Religiosität"; Zedinger, *Franz Stephan*, 267, 346; see chapter 4, this volume.

70. Hersche, "War Maria Theresa eine Jansenistin?"; Hersche, *Der Spätjansenismus*, esp. 148 ff.; Winter, *Der Josephinismus*; further Kovács, "Einflüsse"; overview in Harm Klueting, "The Catholic Enlightenment in Austria or the Habsburg Lands," in Lehner/Printy, *A Companion*, 127–46.

71. Hersche, "War Maria Theresia eine Jansenistin?", 16.

72. KMT VII, 181–82. On Maria Theresa's attitude to the Societas Jesu, see further below.

73. This was the view of Court Councillor Bretschneider: Linger, *Denkwürdigkeiten*, 231–32.

74. To Carolina, April 1768, BKF III, 34.

75. To Kampmüller, c. 1766, BKF II, 373 n2.

76. To Carolina, April 1768, BKF III, 34–35.

77. For example, she repeatedly wrote to her children and confidantes that she submitted completely to God's grace, trusting entirely in his divine will, e.g., to Carolina, April 1768, BKF III, 55.

78. See chapter 2, this volume; Garms-Cornides, "Liturgie und Diplomatie"; on Joseph's 1764 election as king of the Romans, see Maaß, *Der Josephinismus* I, 196 ff.; Arneth, *Geschichte Maria Theresia's* IX, 13.

79. See Maria Theresa's remarks in the Political Testament of 1751, Kallbrunner, *Kaiserin Maria Theresias Politisches Testament*, 38; Maaß, *Der Frühjosephinismus*, 13–14.

80. She had thus decreed in 1748 that ecclesiastical ordinances were not to be published without her prior authorization: decree from March 18, 1748, in Klueting, *Der Josephinismus*, 20.

81. Arneth, *Geschichte Maria Theresia's* IV, 56 ff.; IX, 57 ff.; Hersche, *Muße* II, 999–1000, 1016–17.

82. See Maaß, *Der Frühjosephinismus*, 88 ff.; Szábo, *Kaunitz*, 209 ff.; Benedikt, "Der Josephinismus"; Klueting, *Der Josepinismus*, 83 (handwritten note of Maria Theresa from August 10, 1763).

83. See chapter 12, this volume.

84. Reinhardt, *Zur Kirchenreform*; Maaß, *Der Frühjosephinismus*, 36 ff.; KMT IV, 184 ff.— "Mangy sheep": Principia generalia (1752), quoted in Tropper, *Staatliche Kirchenpolitik*, 224.

85. Maaß, *Der Frühjosephinismus*, 13 ff.; Szábo, *Kaunitz*, 209 ff.; Benedikt, *Der Josephinismus*.

86. See above all the 1765 memorandum on the state of the monarchy, MJC III, 335 ff.

87. See Maaß, *Der Frühjosephinismus*, 62 ff.

88. In the 1760s conflict erupted over questions of diocesan boundaries and appointments to bishoprics, relations between the curia and the canton of Graubünden (which lay within the Habsburg sphere of influence), ecclesiastical control of income from the Bohemian saltworks, and taxation of the clergy in the hereditary lands. See Maaß, "Vorbereitung"; Maaß, *Der Frühjosephinismus*, 88 ff.; Arneth, *Geschichte Maria Theresia's* IX, 1 ff.

89. Szábo, *Kaunitz*, 223 ff.; Maaß, *Der Josephinismus* I, 56 ff; Arneth, *Geschichte Maria Theresia's* IX, 14 ff.

90. Justinus Febronius, *De statu ecclesiae et legitima potestate Romani pontifices liber singularis*, Frankfurt am Main 1763.

91. Paul Joseph Riegger, *Institutiones iurisprudentiae ecclesiasticae*, vols. I–IV, Vienna 1765–72, 2nd ed. 1770–80; Joseph Riegger, *Corpus iuris publici et ecclesiastici Germaniae academicum*, Vienna 1764.

92. Maaß, *Der Josephinismus* III.

93. Maaß, *Der Josephinismus* I, 256 ff.

94. Resolution on Kaunitz's submission from February 26, 1768, Maaß, *Das Josephinismus* I, 266; see Maaß, "Vorbereitung," 314.

95. Szábo, *Kaunitz*, 223 ff.; Arneth, *Geschichte Maria Theresia's* IX, 17 ff.; Maaß, *Der Josephinismus* I, 267 ff.

96. *Placet* to Kaunitz's submission from July 28, 1768, Maaß, *Der Josephinismus* I, 317–18.

97. Maaß, *Der Josephinismus* I, 325–26.

98. Submission from Kaunitz, March 20, 1768, Maaß, *Der Josephinismus* I, 267 ff.; see ibid., 282 ff. See also Joseph to Leopold, March 1768, Arneth, *Geschichte Maria Theresia's* IX, 550–51. Maria Theresa later revealed to Court Councillor Greiner how "inestimably important" it was to her that papal claims to authority and infallibility be rejected; Arneth, "Maria Theresia und der Hofrath von Greiner," 41.

99. Kaunitz's instruction for the religious authority (Giunta Economale) in Milan, June 2, 1768, Maaß, *Der Josephinismus* I, 288 ff.; Klueting, *Der Josephinismus*, 118–19; see previously Kaunitz to Maria Theresa, March 20, 1768, Maaß, *Der Josephinismus* I, 267 ff.

100. Kaunitz's historically argued memorandum from 1769 in Maaß, *Der Josephinismus* I, 368 ff.

101. Heinke's memoranda in Maaß, *Der Josephinismus* III.

102. Maaß, *Der Josephinismus* I, 79; Kaunitz's instruction for the religious authority (Giunta Economale) in Milan, June 2, 1768, Maaß, *Josephinismus* I, 288 ff.; Klueting, *Der Josephinismus*, 118–19; Kaunitz's submission from June 15, 1768, Maaß, *Der Josephinismus* I, 292 ff.

103. Opinions of conference ministers on the publication of Heinke's "new doctrine," in Maaß, *Der Josephinismus* I, 310 ff.

104. Papal missive to Maria Theresa, August 20, 1768, Maaß, *Der Josephinismus* I, 319 ff.

105. Resolution on the nuncio's enquiry from September 15, 1768, Maaß, *Der Josephinismus* I, 325.

106. Edited in Maaß, *Der Josephinismus* II; excerpts in Klueting, *Der Josephinismus*, 176 ff.

107. Joseph to Maria Theresa, May 1769, MJC I, 273.

108. Kaunitz to Sperges, June 6, 1768, Maaß, *Der Josephinismus* I, 291–92 (*tranquillare l'animo di Sua Maesàt*).

109. This point is made emphatically in Maaß, *Der Josephinismus* I, 83.

110. E.g., Maaß, *Der Josephinismus* I, 318.

111. State Council records 1769 no. 803, March 15, 1769, quoted in Maaß, *Der Frühjosephinismus*, 118.

112. 1769, quoted in Maaß, *Der Frühjosephinismus*, 118; see instruction for the emissary at the Holy See, BAA, 512–13.

113. She thus continued to seek consensus with the pope, even if this was strictly unnecessary according to the new principles of church policy; see Maaß, *Der Josephinismus* I, 100.

114. Hersche, *Der Spätjansenismus*, 156, speaks of a "goodly portion of hypocrisy."

115. On the public discourse see Vogel, *Der Untergang*.

116. See Arneth, *Geschichte Maria Theresia's* IX, 90 ff., 172–73; Hersche, *Der Spätjansenismus,* 154 ff.; Szábo, *Kaunitz,* 241 ff.; Beales, "Maria Theresa"; sources in Maaß, *Der Josephinismus* II.

117. KMT V, 69, 87.

118. In 1757, for example, she had taken offense at a critical sermon given by the Jesuit father and court preacher Tausch. The priest was reprimanded at her behest: to Ulfeld, June 5, 1757, BKF IV, 193. Fathers from other orders who criticized her policies were treated no differently: KMT VI, 209. She also did not appreciate Pater Kampmüller making himself the pope's mouthpiece in urging the hereditary lands to follow the *Unigenitus* bull; see Winter, *Der Josephinismus,* 36.

119. Arneth, *Geschichte Maria Theresia's* IX, 159 ff.; Klingenstein, *Staatsverwaltung;* Klingenstein, "Van Swieten"; further Plachta, "Zensur"; Wagner, "Die Zenzur."

120. To Charles III of Spain, April 4, 1773, Arneth, *Geschichte Maria Theresia's* IX, 93–94. See the instructions to Marie Antoinette that she strictly refrain from speaking about the Jesuits at Versailles, April 21, 1770: MACS I, 1 ff.

121. To Corneille de Neny, September 1773, Arneth, *Geschichte Maria Theresia's* IX, 568.

122. To Enzenberg, October 16, 1773, Arneth, *Geschichte Maria Theresia's* IX, 77–78.

123. Swinburne, *Courts* I, 229.

124. KMT VII, 182; KMT VIII, 12; see VIII, 13–14, 69, 80–81, 89–90.

125. According to Court Councillor Bretschneider: Linger, *Denkwürdigkeiten,* 231–32.

126. The witness in question was the Tridentine territorial captain (*Landeshauptmann*) and lawyer Carlo Antonio Pilati di Tassulo, *Reisen* I, 9–10.

127. Arneth, *Geschichte Maria Theresia's* IX, 99 ff.; Szábo, *Kaunitz,* 241 ff.; documents in Maaß, *Der Josephinismus* II, 171 ff., 183 ff.

128. Arneth, *Geschichte Maria Theresia's* IX, 108.

129. Arneth, *Geschichte Maria Theresia's* IX, 109 ff.

130. Resolution on the protocol of the dissolution commission, January 14, 1774, in Arneth, *Geschichte Maria Theresia's* IX, 118–19.

131. KMT VII, 110–11.

132. KMT III, 77, similarly III, 186, but see 270; see chapter 6, this volume.

133. KMT VII, 132.

134. Wolf/Zwiedeneck, *Österreich,* 142; see Arneth, *Geschichte Maria Theresia's* IX, 395–96; Hersche, *Muße* II, 1013 ff.; Kovács, "Spätmittelalterliche Traditionen"; Kovács, "Kirchliches Zeremoniell"; Hollerweger, *Die Reform;* Pammer, *Glaubensabfall;* Dimt, *Volksfrömmigkeit.*

135. Court rescript from March 1, 1755, Kropatschek, *Sammlung* III, 172–73.

136. Sources on belief in vampires in Hamberger, *Mortuus non mordet;* see Arlaud, "Vampire"; Bräunlein, "Frightening borderlands"; Augustynowicz/Reber, *Vampirglaube;* Schroeder, *Vampirismus;* Kreuter, *Der Vampirglaube;* Bohn, *Der Vampir,* 18–19, calls vampirismus "a liminal phenomenon situated at the margins of multiethnic empires or in the twilight zones of the western hemisphere."

137. Ioannis Zelepos, "Vampirglaube und orthodoxe Kirche im osmanischen Südosteuropa: Ein Fallbeispiel für die Ambivalenzen vorsäkularer Rationalisierungsprozesse," in Helmedach et al., *Das osmanische Europa,* explains vampirism as a regional popular belief that Greek Orthodox theologians brought under their control through post mortem excommunication rituals.

138. Reports of the feldsher Flückinger, January 26, 1732, in Hamberger, *Mortuus non mordet*, 49 ff.

139. Hamberger, *Mortuus non mordet*, 254.

140. Van Swieten, *Abhandlung*, Augsburg 1768, in Hamberger, *Moruus non mordet*, 84.

141. Schroeder, *Vampirismus*, 51.

142. Decree from March 1, 1755, in Kropatschek, *Sammlung* III, 172–73, Hamberger, *Mortuus non mordet*, 85–86.

143. Hamberger, *Mortuus non mordet*, 83; Arlaud, "Vampire," 134.

144. Quote from Court Councillor Bretschneider, who served in Transylvania: Linger, *Denkwürdigkeiten*, 311 ff.

145. Decree from March 1, 1755, Kropatschek, *Sammlung* III, 172–73, Hamberger, *Mortuus non mordet*, 86.

146. Preface to van Swieten, *Abhandlung*, in Hamberger, *Mortuus non mordet*, 86.

147. The fight against vampirism was connected with the government's campaign against the Greek Orthodox church in Serbia and Croatia. In 1754 monks were driven out of the Greek Orthodox center, the monastery of Marča, where the privileges of peasant soldiers settled in the borderlands (*Wehrbauern*) were stored. The monastery was transferred to the Uniate church, which likewise followed the orthodox rite but was in communion with the Roman Catholic church. The government's campaign, combined with the reorganization of the military frontier, led to a rebellion of the Warasdiner border regiment. See Kaser, *Freier Bauer*, 353 ff., 602–603.

148. Calendars: court rescript from December 16, 1755, Kropatschek, *Sammlung* III, 267; dream books: court rescript from March 1, 1755, ibid., III, 173.

149. Linger, *Denkwürdigkeiten*, 226 ff.

150. Hersche, *Muße* II, 1013 ff.; on the specific case in Tyrol see A. Dörrer, *Tiroler Umgangsspiele*, 446 ff.; Hollerweger, *Die Reform*, 56 ff. Pammer, *Glaubensabfall*, 255 ff., takes an optimistic view of the reception of reform Catholicism by subjects in Upper Austria, but he makes no reference to the abolition of pilgrimages and holidays.

151. Dörrer, *Tiroler Umgangsspiele*, 474–75; Hollerwege, *Die Reform*, 56–57.

152. Court rescript from March 1, 1755, Kropatschek, *Sammlung* III, 172–73.

153. Court rescript from June 7, 1758, Kropatschek, *Sammlung* III, 416–17.

154. Haitzmann's notes are known today primarily due to Sigmund Freud's interest in them. See catalog *Prinz Eugen*, 348 ff.

155. Constitutio Criminalis Theresiana, Art. 58: on magic, witchcraft, soothsaying, and suchlike, 167 ff.; see court rescript from November 5, 1766, Kropatschek, *Sammlung* V, 138–57. On individual witch trials see Pörtner, "De crimine magiae."

156. Midelfort, *Exorcism*; Hanauer, "Der Teufelsbanner"; Johann Joseph, in: NDB 6 (1964), 84–85. Joseph II finally directed the prince-bishop to expel Gaßner from Regensburg in 1777 after Pope Pius VI had rejected his teaching and forbidden him from performing exorcisms on the sick.

157. See Bárth, *Katholische Aufklärung*; further examples in Pörtner, "'De crimine magiae.'"

158. Koschatzky, *Maria Theresia* (catalog), 476.

159. To Ferdinand, July 30, 1772, BKF I, 141. See also the affair concerning a Franciscan priest called Terentianus: "he should be locked up and made to pay for what he has done; he is a rascal [*coquin*]," to Ferdinand, February 23, 1775, BKF I, 319.

160. Court decree from March 1, 1755, Kropatschek, *Sammlung* III, 172–73, no. 385.

161. BKF IV, 242; on midwifery, see chapter 6, this volume.

162. The empress banished from the city a priest who had criticized grandees from the pulpit without noticing that the empress was listening incognito, KMT VI, 208–209. Similar cases in Koschatzky, *Maria Theresia* (catalog), 316 (March 13, 1754, HHStA old cabinet documents, Carton 2, fol. 412v-422r); letter to Ulfeld, June 5, 1757, BKF IV, 193.

163. Court decree from October 5, 1776, Kropatschek, *Sammlung* II, 168–69, no. 37.

164. To Court Councilor Greiner, 1777: Arneth, "Maria Theresia und der Hofrath von Greiner," 60.

165. To Maximilian, April 1774, BKF II, 321 ff. Enlightenment thinkers were also fond of accusing each other of self-love, vanity, or "conceit"; see Pečar/Tricoire, *Falsche Freunde*, 175 ff.; Martus, *Aufklärung*, 290.

166. To Ferdinand, August 14, 1779, BKF II, 203; see to Ferdinand, June 11, 1772, BKF I, 130; to Marie Antoinette, June 2, 1775, MACS II, 341; to Marquise d'Herzelles, 1771, Kervyn de Lettenhove (Constantin), *Lettres inédites*, passim.

167. KMT VI, 538 ff.

168. KMT VI, 540.

169. To Leopold, August 1765, BKF I, 23: he should do everything the same as at home and brook no excuses.

170. Arneth, *Geschichte Maria Theresia's* IX, 138; see Arneth, "Graf Philipp Cobenzl," 120–21.

171. Coke, *Letters* IV,1 2.

172. Linger, *Denkwürdigkeiten*, 213–14.

173. Friedrich Nicolai, *Beschreibung einer Reise durch Deutschland und die Schweiz im Jahre 1781*, Stettin 1784, V, 15.

174. Fournier, *Gerhard van Swieten*; Klingenstein, *Staatsverwaltung*; Klingenstein, "Van Swieten"; further, Arneth, *Geschichte Maria Theresia's* II, 454 ff.; VII, 196 ff.; IX, 148 ff.; Brechka, *Gerard Van Swieten*; Plachta, "Zensur"; Haug, "'In Frankreich verboten'"; Walter, "Die zensurierten Klassiker."

175. Karsten, Sonnenfels, 216 ff.; Fournier, *Gerhard van Swieten*, 428.

176. Fournier, *Gerhard van Swieten*, 424–25.

177. Haug, "'In Frankreich verboten.'"

178. The book market in the hereditary lands expanded by leaps and bounds from the 1750s; see Bachleitner/Eybl/Fischer, *Geschichte*; P. Frank, "Buchhandel"; Lavandier, *Le Livre*; W. Seidler, *Buchmarkt*.

179. Guibert, *Journal* I, 292, writes that one of the most erudite men had assured him of this, but adds: "*chose à verifier*," a matter requiring verification.—The inadequacies of the censorship system were almost proverbial, see, e.g., Riesbeck, *Briefe*, 124–25. Karl von Zinzendorf's diary also reveals an intimate familiarity with French literature.

180. Fournier, *Gerhard van Swieten*, 412 ff.

181. Arneth, *Geschichte Maria Theresia's* IX, 148 ff.; Maaß, *Der Josephinismus* II, 232; Fournier, *Gerhard van Swieten*, 432 ff. See Maria Theresa to Seilern, March 18, 1774, BKF IV, 350: "I do not wish to introduce here the English freedom in writing, our nation lacks the fire." She acted similarly in the case of the purified new edition of Riegger's textbook on canon law, where she

likewise moved to expurgate criticism of belief in papal infallibility despite sharing this criticism herself; see her remarks to Court Councillor Greiner, in Arneth, "Maria Theresia und der Hofrath von Greiner," 45–46 versus 41.

182. Klingenstein, "Van Swieten," 103.

183. Quoted in Arneth, *Geschichte Maria Theresia's* IX, 168; Fournier, "Gerhard van Swieten," 443–44.

12. Strangers Within

1. Falkenberg, *Wandbehang*. The meaning of the date sewn into the center, "anno 1776," is unclear; it could be the date when the hanging was completed, but perhaps its makers took it for the year when peace was concluded.

2. The words are taken from a popular poem in Keyßler, *Neueste Reisen*, 1213; Montagu, *Complete Letters*, I, 291 ff., writing in 1771, calls Vienna "inhabited by all nations."

3. Overview of religious diversity in Klingenstein, "Modes"; on Transylvania, Fata, "Die Religiöse Vielfalt."

4. See Klingenstein, "Modes"; Leeb/Pils/Winkelbauer, *Staatsmacht*; on Protestants in Vienna: Scheutz, "Legalität"; Schnettger, "Ist Wien eine Messe wert?"; on Muslims, Greeks, and Jews: Do Paço, *L'Orient à Vienne*.

5. Evidence of conflict on this score in Keyßler, *Neueste Reisen*, 1214 ff.; KMT I, 166–67; VI, 38.

6. Handwritten note from Maria Theresa complaining about Hungarian nobles who attended the Lutheran church "and not our own": ÖNB Autographen 9/49–27, quoted in Koschatzky, *Maria Theresia* (catalog), 316, no. 62,06.—See from a Protestant perspective: Chemnitz, *Vollständige Nachrichten*.

7. For imperial court councillors: Schnettger, "Ist Wien eine Messe wert?", 616; for Muslims: Do Paço, *L'Orient à Vienne*.

8. Examples in KMT I, 166–67, III, 187, 230–31, 262.

9. Peper, *Konversionen*, 85 ff.; Scheutz, "Legalität"; Schnettger, "Ist Wien eine Messe wert?"

10. Breunlich/Mader, *Karl Graf von Zinzendorf*, 563, to his brother Ludwig: "*personne ne me persuadera jamais d'acheter ces riens au dépens de ma conscience*." Even the choice of language in the diaries expresses his inner conflict: dialogues with God are written in German, notes on everyday social life in French: ibid., e.g., 197, 204, 209, 227, 230, 235–36, 241, 249, 252, 257–58, 264 ff. He was converted on March 14, 1764, by Maria Theresa's confidant, the provost Ignaz Müller.

11. Pichler *Denkwürdigkeiten* I, 10.

12. Consider, e.g., her grave concerns about a Catholic orphan raised in Protestant Dresden. Maria Theresa to Antonia of Saxony, January 1760, Lippert, *Briefwechsel*, 65, 67, 72.

13. Peper, *Konversionen*, 68 ff.; Wagner, "Fürstengnade."

14. KMT III, 93, 163.

15. Von der Trenck, *Die "Blutbibel"*, 74 ff.

16. Bartenstein to Montfaucon, December 16, 1719, quoted in Braubach, *Versailles*, 374.

17. Resolution from June 14, 1777, Pribram, *Urkunden und Akden* I, 425–26.

18. Maria Theresa to Countess Trautson, 1750, van Rhyn, "Unveröffentlichte Briefe," 179. Another example from Pressburg in Arneth, *Geschichte Maria Theresia's* IV, 50–51 (source not identified).

19. To Ferdinand, August 26, 1773, BKF I, 226: "*quarante-quatre mille juifs, j'avoue, cela fait horreur et dégout.*"

20. Mevorach, "The Imperial Court-Jew Wolf Wertheimer."

21. Brugger et al., *Geschichte der Juden*, 352.

22. Arneth, *Geschichte Maria Theresia's* IV, 41.

23. Srbik, *Gestalten*, 40.

24. Walter, *Maria Theresia: Briefe und Aktenstücke*, 39. Walter (1896–1968) worked in the Vienna State Archive until 1945, qualified as a professor at the University of Vienna in the same year, and was adjunct professor there from 1959.

25. Walter, *Maria Theresia: Briefe und Aktenstücke*; Koschatzky, *Maria Theresia* (catalog); Koschatzky, *Maria Theresia*; Mraz/Mraz, *Maria Theresia*.

26. Battenberg, "Des Kaisers Kammerknechte"; Breuer/Graetz, *Tradition und Aufklärung* I; Brugger et al., *Geschichte der Juden*; Lohrmann, *Zwischen Finanz und Toleranz*; Drabek, "Die Juden"; Karniel, *Die Toleranzpolitik*, 103 ff.

27. With this argument, for example, van Swieten ensured in 1753 that Jewish physicians, apothecaries, and midwives would continue to be forbidden from practicing these professions in the hereditary lands: "*Cette nation, toujours alerte à duper tout le monde, trouveroit par là une occasion à faire des fraudes infinies et très difficile à deterrer*"; Pribram, *Geschichte* I, 347–48.

28. *Wiener Diarium*, November 18, 1744; see Lieben, "Briefe," 363 ff.

29. In December 1744 in Bohemian Lipa, for example; see Bergl, "Der Judenmord" (the man nailed to a gate). In 1745 the Jews were driven from Sulz in the Vorarlberg by the local militia, the *Landsturm*, which was meant to have been deployed against the French.

30. Description in a contemporary Jewish chronicle: Lieben, "Igereth Machalath," 335 ff., here 337.

31. Benjamin Wolf from Prague, December 2, 1744, Lieben, "Briefe," 365; see Lieben, "Igereth Machalath," 335 ff.

32. Arneth, *Geschichte Maria Theresia's* IV, 41 ff.; a detailed account in Bergl, "Das Exil"; Plaggenborg, "Maria Theresia"; Drabek, "Die Juden."

33. Lieben, "Igereth Machalath," 341–42.

34. Lieben, "Briefe," 393, 416, 418.

35. Lieben, "Briefe," 388; see also Lieben, "Igereth Machalath," 341 ff.

36. See Brugger et al., *Geschichte der Juden*, 382 ff.; Breuer/Graetz, *Tradition und Aufklärung* I, 106 ff.; Lohrmann, *Zwischen Finanz und Toleranz*; Drabek, "Die Juden"; on Jewish bankers in Vienna see Dickson, *Finance* I, 140 ff. Sephardic Jews enjoyed generally better rights in areas under Habsburg rule than Ashkenazim, and they had greater privileges in the Italian territories than in the other hereditary lands. Among the Jews in Italy, the community in the harbor city of Trieste were granted exceptional status.

37. Lieben, "Briefe," 410.

38. Lieben, "Briefe," 411.

39. Lieben, "Briefe," 371.

40. Lieben, "Briefe," 371, 378, 396.

41. Arneth, *Geschichte Maria Theresia's* IV, 43; from a Jewish perspective Lieben, "Igereth Machalath," 345 ff.

42. Arneth, *Geschichte Maria Theresia's* IV, 44–45; there too the commentary of the Venetian emissary Erizzo from June 5, 1745: for all her charm, she was much taken with "the feeling of her supreme position and uncommonly jealous of her sovereign authority."

43. Lieben, "Briefe," 458; Lieben, "Igereth Machalath," 345 ff.

44. Arneth, *Geschichte Maria Theresia's* IV, 46.

45. Mevorach, "The Imperial Court-Jew Wolf Wertheimer."

46. Lieben, "Briefe," 428.

47. Lieben, "Briefe," 423.

48. Lieben, "Igereth Machalath," 297. When Maria Theresa and Francis Stephen were welcomed in Florence in 1739 as Tuscany's new rulers, the Jewish community there erected a *cuccagna*, an ornamental pyramid made out of food. See Brugger et al., *Geschichte der Juden*, 382–3.

49. Brugger et al., *Geschichte der Juden*, 348, 616.

50. See Lieben, "Briefe," 419: the spokespeople for the Jewish community argued that Maria Theresa's forefathers had tolerated the Jews for over a thousand years; they should not stop doing so now, in the middle of a war. See Battenberg, "Des Kaisers Kammerknechte."

51. See, e.g., Kropatschek, *Sammlung* V, 458 on protections for the Jews.

52. Kemmel [i.e., Richter], *Helden-Lied*, 4; see Cerman, "Maria Theresia."

53. Kemmel [i.e., Richter], *Helden-Lied*, 40–41.

54. Kemmel [i.e., Richter], *Helden-Lied*, 22.

55. Richter (1717–74) had studied law in Altdorf and Marburg and practiced as a solicitor. In 1754 he was imprisoned in Nuremberg for falsifying documents. (See Johann Georg Meusel, *Lexikon der vom Jahr 1750 bis 1800 verstorbenen teutschen Schriftsteller*, XI, Leipzig 1811, 280–81.) Richter took as his literary model Robert Dodsley's chronicle of the battle of Dettingen in 1744, a poem in praise of George II of England that imitated the Old Testament Book of Kings and purported to be the work of a fictitious Jewish author. Richter translated this immensely successful work into German and followed it with several self-authored works of a similar ilk; see Cerman, "Maria Theresia."

56. Brugger et al., *Geschichte der Juden*, 382 ff.; Breuer/Graetz, *Tradition und Aufklärung* I, 100 ff.; Lohrmann, *Zwischen Finanz und Toleranz*; Drabek, "Die Juden"; Plaggenborg, "Maria Theresia"; Burger, *Heimatrecht*, 19 ff.

57. Brugger et al., *Geschichte der Juden*, 376.

58. Plaggenborg, "Maria Theresia," 6.

59. Order concerning the Jews (*Judenordnung*) from 1753: Pribram, *Geschichte* I, 341–46; from 1765: ibid., I, 374–83. In connection with administrative reforms in the Banat, taxation of Jews was tripled there in 1773; see Mraz, *Maria Theresia als Königin von Ungarn*, 209, no. 298.

60. Tantner, *Ordnung der Häuser*.

61. Handwritten note on a submission from the Court Chancellery, September 1778, Pribram, *Geschichte* I, 428.

62. On the political instrumentalization of the Corpus evangelicorum by Prussia, see chapter 8, this volume; Reissenberger, "Das Corpus evangelicorum"; Pörtner, "Propaganda"; Haug-Moritz, *Corpus evangelicorum*; Kalipke, *Verfahren*.

63. On exceptions codified in the Treaty of Westphalia (IPO AA. V. §§38–41) see Klueting, *Das Reich*, 22 ff.

64. Principia generalia (1752), printed in Tropper, *Staatliche Kirchenpolitik*, 222–26, here 222 and 224. The campaign against crypto-Protestantism is now very well researched, after Arneth, *Geschichte Maria Theresia's* IV, 51–52, dismissed it in two pages. The first detailed study was Zwiedineck-Südenhorst, *Geschichte*; for Maria Theresa's reign above all Loesche, "Aus der Endzeit"; Loesche, "Maria Theresias letzte Maßnahmen"; Buchinger, "Die 'Landler'"; on Styria, Knall, *Aus der Heimat*; on Carinthia, Tropper, *Staatliche Kirchenpolitik*; further Scheutz, "Die Fünfte Kolonne"; Steiner, *Rückkehr*, 266 ff.; Pörtner, "Die Kunst des Lügens"; a comprehensive recent overview of the various phases and individual hereditary lands in Leeb/Scheutz/Weikl, *Geheimprotestantismus*.

65. Anon., *Vollständige Geschichte*, Preface.

66. List from the neighboring Protestant County of Ortenburg from March 23, 1756, printed in Knall, *Aus der Heimat*, 13–14.

67. According to 2 Cor 6:14; Joseph Schaidtberger, *Neu vermehrter evangelischer Sendbrief, darinnen 24 nützliche Bücher enthalten*, Nuremberg 1732.

68. Scheutz, "Die Fünfte Kolonne," 341.

69. Comprehensive collection of source material: Tropper, *Glut unter der Asche*.

70. See KMT III, 17, Appendix 288–89; overviews in Steiner, *Rückkehr*, 266 ff.; Scheutz, "Die Fünfte Kolonne," 342 ff.; Buchinger, Landler, 148 ff. (Upper Austria), 272 ff. (Carinthia).

71. See Report of the Doblhoff Commission in Zwiedineck-Südenhorst, *Geschichte*, Appendix, 521–26; on the 1752 edict Tropper, *Staatliche Kirchenpolitik*, 74 ff.; Buchinger, "Die 'Landler,'" 151 ff. An edict from 1778 summarized the edicts issued between 1752 and 1778: printed in Knall, *Aus der Heimat*, 318–20.

72. What follows is from Principia generalia, printed in Tropper, *Staatliche Kirchenpolitik*, 222–26.

73. Peper, *Konversionen*, 65; Knall, *Aus der Heimat*, 45.

74. Reinhardt, *Zur Kirchenreform*; see above, chapter 11. On problems setting up the religious fund, see KMT IV, Appendix, 185–200.

75. Edict in Knall, *Aus der Heimat*, 319.

76. Scheutz, "Die Fünfte Kolonne."

77. See Court Chancellor Blümegen to the Bishop of Seckau, August 31, 1773, in Knall, *Aus der Heimat*, 307, see ibid., 17 n23; as well as the extensive resolutions and handwritten comments in Zwiedineck-Südenhorst, "Geschichte der religiösen Bewegung," 538–39, 542 ff., 546.

78. Scheutz, "Die Fünfte Kolonne," 371.

79. Scheutz, "Die Fünfte Kolonne," 354 ff.

80. The figure of 2992 for the 1750s alone is given by Knall, *Aus der Heimat*, 9. See Buchinger, "Die 'Landler,'"; on the context of the deportations of other minorities see Steiner, *Rückkehr*.

81. Resolution in Zwiedineck-Südenhorst, "Geschichte der religiösen Bewegung," 538–39.

82. Intercession from February 28, 1753, from November 6 and December 20, 1754; see Anon., *Anhang oder weitere Nachricht*; Anon., *Vollständige Geschichte*; see Reissenberger, "Das Corpus evangelicorum"; Steiner, *Rückkehr*, 274 ff.; Pörtner, "Propaganda," 473–74; Scheutz, "Die Fünfte Kolonne," 353.

83. Rescript from September 17, 1753, in Anon., *Vollständige Geschichte*, 51 ff.; see Steiner, *Rückkehr*, 277–8.

84. See above, chapter 8; e.g., Maria Theresa to Ulfeld, July 5, 1757, BKF IV, 193, BAA, 140–41. Criticism of her religious policy from Protestant emissaries in Ranke, "Maria Theresia und ihr Hof," 674; Arnheim, "Das Urtheil," 290; Wraxall, *Historical and the Posthumous Memoirs* III, 482–3; Arneth, *Geschichte Maria Theresia's* IV, 51–52. During the war, Francis Stephen insisted that Protestant subjects in contested Silesian territories not be deprived of any of their religious privileges; see Arneth, *Geschichte Maria Theresia's* V, 230, 509–10. On Prussia see Pörtner, "Propaganda."

85. See the visitations of mission stations in 1763–64, Tropper, *Staatliche Kirchenpolitik*, 98 ff.; individual transmigrations in Buchinger, "Die 'Landler,'" 221, 309.

86. Buchinger, "Die 'Landler,'" 319 ff.; Knall, *Aus der Heimat*.

87. Further examples in Knall, *Aus der Heimat*, 96–97.

88. Presentation of the Bohemian-Austrian Court Chancellery, in Zwiedineck-Südenhorst, *Geschichte*, 530.

89. Mathola de Zolnay to the steward, Rauch, April 4, 1772, in Knall, *Aus der Heimat*, 32. (Mathola de Zolnay's name appears in a number of variations, e.g., Matolay, Mattala, de/von Zolna, etc.)

90. Presentation of the Bohemian-Austrian Court Chancellery, in Zwiedineck-Südenhorst, *Geschichte*, 529 ff.; Knall, *Aus der Heimat*, 21 ff.

91. Knall, *Aus der Heimat*, 17 ff.

92. Presentation of the Bohemian-Austrian Court Chancellery with Maria Theresa's handwritten commentary, in Zwiedineck-Südenhorst, *Geschichte*, 526 ff.

93. See chapter 12, this volume.

94. Opinion of the Court Chancellery, in Zwiedineck-Südenhorst, *Geschichte*, 535.

95. Court Chancellor Blümegen to the Bishop of Seckau, August 31, 1773, in Knall, *Aus der Heimat*, 307–10.

96. Resolution of Maria Theresa [July 3, 1773], in Zwiedineck-Südenhorst, *Geschichte*, 538–39.

97. The new guidelines for the Stadl mission in Knall, *Aus der Heimat*, 329–31.

98. Extensively documented in Knall, *Aus der Heimat*.

99. Matt 11:25, Luke 10:21 ("I thank thee, O Father, Lord of heaven and earth, because thou hast hid these things from the wise and the prudent, and hast revealed them unto babes"). Knall, *Aus der Heimat*, 90.

100. Knall, *Aus der Heimat*, 42.

101. Knall, *Aus der Heimat*, 38, 47, 110, 112, 125, 210–11 (Urban Riederer), ibid., 125 (Helene Riebererin), ibid., 171–72 (Maria Riebererin and Sebastian Rieberer), ibid., 211 (Anna Rieberer).

102. Knall, *Aus der Heimat*, 28–29, 32, 50, 53 n116.

103. Scheutz, "Die Fünfte Kolonne," 362, 369–70; Knall, *Aus der Heimat*, 28–29, 32, 50, 53, 133–34.

104. Thomas Petzner's interrogation record in Knall, *Aus der Heimat*, 142–43.

105. Barton, *Im Zeichen der Toleranz*; Karniel, *Die Toleranzpolitik*.

106. Beales, "Joseph II's Rêveries" I, 359 ff.; Fata, "Die Religiöse Vielfalt."

107. MJC II, 21 ff.; see chapter 10, this volume.

108. Lists in Buchinger, "Die 'Landler,'" 324 ff.

109. Joseph to the Court Chancellery, November 7, 1774, Zwiedineck-Südenhorst, *Geschichte*, 544; see Knall, *Aus der Heimat*, 258–59. In November 1773 Maria Theresa had decreed that no one should be conscripted to the military solely on account of heresy: to Blümegen, November 26 and 27, 1773, Zwiedineck-Südenhorst, *Geschichte*, 542 ff.

110. Decree from November 7, 1774; counterproposal of the Court Chancellery, November 18, 1774, Zwiedineck-Südenhorst, *Geschichte*, 544 ff.

111. Resolution to the counterproposal of the Court Chancellery from November 18, 1774, Zwiedineck-Südenhorst, *Geschichte*, 546.

112. Buchinger, "Die 'Landler,'" 151; the list from 1776 ibid., 333–34; on the other transmigrations Steiner, *Rückkehr*.

113. See the correspondence from June–September 1777, MJC II, 141 ff; see also Arneth, *Geschichte Maria Theresia's* IX, 139 ff.; X, 61 ff.; Maaß, *Der Josephinismus* II, 46 ff.; sources ibid., 240–53, no. 66–73; Beales, "Joseph II's Rêveries" I, 465 ff.; Karniel, *Die Toleranzpolitik*, 189 ff.

114. On Moravia Loesche, "Maria Theresias letzte Maßnahmen"; brief overview in Stefan Steiner, "Transmigration," 331–60, here 345 ff.; further, Macek, "Geheimprotestanten," 252–53.

115. To Ferdinand, May 29, 1777, BKF II, 86–87. "*Le parti ... est délicat à prendre, et cela m'occupe beaucoup et m'attriste*"; June 5, 1777, ibid., 87–88: at fault were the unbelievably negligent priests, but also the landlords, who had not the foggiest idea what was going on.

116. Joseph to Maria Theresa, June 19, 1777, MJC II, 140–41.

117. Joseph to Maria Theresa, undated, June 1777, MJC II, 141–42.

118. To Joseph, July 5, 1777, MJC II, 146–47.

119. Joseph to Maria Theresa, July 20, 1777, MJC II, 151–52.

120. To Joseph, undated, July 1777, MJC II, 157–58.

121. Joseph to Maria Theresa, September 23, 1777, MJC II, 160–61; see chapter 10, this volume.

122. Joseph to Maria Theresa, September 23, 1777, MJC II, 160–61; see chapter 10, this volume.

123. To Joseph, September 25, 1777, MJC II, 162.

124. Joseph to Maria Theresa, September 26, 1777, MJC II, 163–64.

125. To Joseph, September 27, 1777, MJC II, 165.

126. Arneth, *Geschichte Maria Theresia's* X, 70; Beales, "Joseph II's Rêveries" I, 470.

127. Maaß, "Maria Theresia" II, 240 ff.; Beer, "Denkschriften," 158 ff.

128. Loesche, "Maria Theresia letzte Maßnahmen"; Steiner, "Transmigration," 348–49; see Joseph to Leopold, October 5, 1777, MJC II, 166.

129. Arneth, *Geschichte Maria Theresia's* X, 74–75; Beales, "Joseph II's Rêveries" I, 472; Maaß, *Der Josephinismus* II, 251–52.

130. To Court Councillor Posch, September 28, 1778, BKF IV, 336; see also to Court Councillor Greiner, who advised against using force and compulsion on the Moravian Protestants: "with force, I am agreed, nothing is to be done, but with seriousness matters may be prevented"; Arneth, "Maria Theresia und der Hofrath von Greiner," 40.

131. See Barton, *Im Zeichen der Toleranz*; Karniel, *Die Toleranzpolitik*.

132. Pribram, *Geschichte* I, 440 ff.

133. This is the conclusion drawn by Knall, *Aus der Heimat*, 100–101, on the success of the "Stadl method"; but see Buchinger, "Die 'Landler,'" 151, for a different opinion in relation to the transmigrations.

134. Linger, *Denkwürdigkeiten*, 211 ff. See chapter 13, this volume.

135. Fata, "Die Religiöse Vielfalt."

136. Steiner, "Wien—Temesvar"; Steiner, *Rückkehr*; Spannenberger/Varga, *Ein Raum im Wandel*; see also chapter 6, this volume.

137. Volkmer, *Siebenbürgen*; Maner, *Grenzregionen*; Roth, *Die planmäßig angelegten Siedlungen*; Fata, "Migration"; on the military frontier: Schwicker, *Geschichte*; Rothenberg, *Die österreichische Militärgrenze*; Göllner, *Die Siebenbürgische Militärgrenze*; Kaser, *Freier Bauer*; Jesner, "Habsburgische Grenzraumpolitik"; brief overviews: Krajasich, "Die österreichische Militägrenze"; Heppner, "Die österreichishe Militärgrenze." See also chapter 3, this volume.

138. See, e.g., KMT III, 416.

139. Montagu, *Complete Letters*, 319.

140. See Koller, "Grenzwahrnehmung"; Maner, *Grenzregionen*; Jesner, "Habsburgische Grenzraumpolitik"; Komlosy, *Grenze*; Heindl/Sauer, *Grenze und Staat*; on colonization policy in the Banat see Roth, *Die planmäßig angelegten Siedlungen*.

141. Lesky, "Die österreiche Pestfront," 88.

142. See the groundbreaking studies by Lesky, "Die österreiche Pestfront"; Lesky, "Österreichisches Gesundheitswesen"; from a more recent cultural studies perspective see Bräunlein, "Frightening borderlands."

143. Steube, *Von Amsterdam*, 112 ff.; Sanitäts-General-Normativ, January 2, 1770, Kropatschek, *Sammlung* VI, 3 ff.

144. Steube, *Von Amsterdam*, 117.

145. Maria Theresa's resolution from June 12, 1767, Hofkammerarchiv, Allerhöchste Entschliessungen, quoted in Otruba, *Die Wirtschaftspolitik*, 133–34.

146. See Heppner/Posch, *Encounters*; Jesner, "Habsburgische Grenzraumpolitik"; Heindl/Sauer, *Grenze und Staat*.

147. Joseph's report from Trieste, May 17, 1775, KMT VIII, 258–266, here 258–9; see Dickson, *Finance* I, 448.

148. On the terminology see Andreozzi/Panariti, "Trieste," 225.

149. On Habsburg-Ottoman relations and cultural exchanges, see Do Paço, "Ottoman Empire"; Kühnel, "Westeuropa"; Do Paço, *L'Orient à Vienne*; Heiss/Klingenstein, *Das Osmanische Reich*; Tietze, *Habsburgisch-osmanische Beziehungen*; Sutter Fichtner, *Terror und Toleration*; Schmidt-Haberkamp, *Europa und die Türkei*; Helmedach, et al., *Das osmanische Europa*; Heppner/Posch, *Encounters*; Heindl/Saurer, *Grenze und Staat*; on diplomatic history: Sicker, *From the Treaty of Karlowitz*; Roider, *Austria's Eastern Question*; Strohmeyer/Spannenberger, *Friedens- und Konfliktmanagement*; Treml/Crailsheim, *Audienzen und Allianzen*; Fischer, *Österreich*.

150. Montagu, *Complete Letters* I, 338.

151. Greilich, "Alles."

152. Steube, *Von Amsterdam*, 117–18; see Greilich, "Alles"; Sutter Fichtner, *Terror und Toleration*, 73 ff.; Do Paço, *L'Orient à Vienne*.

153. See the exhibition catalogs Prinz Eugen; *Was von den Türken blieb*; *Die Türken*; Grothaus, *Erbfeind*; Grothaus, *Zum Türkenbild*; Tomendahl, *Das türkische Gesicht*.

154. Swinburne, *Courts* I, 355.

155. Quakatz, "'Conversio Turci.'"

156. *Türkenstechen*—tilting at Turkish targets—was a popular entertainment at such fairs. On Maria Theresa's 1743 ladies' carousel, see above, chapter 3; see Pangerl/Scheutz/Winkelbauer, *Der Wiener Hof*, 359; Koschatzky, *Maria Theresia* (catalog), 219, 222; see also the visual training guide accompanying the *Exercitia corporis* for Archduke Ferdinand, color plate 21.

157. Depiction of the Styrian *Völkertafel* on Wikipedia, s.v. Völkertafel: https://de.wikipedia .org/wiki/V%C3%B6lkertafel_(Steiermark) (02.01.2019).

158. Zechmeister, *Die Wiener Theater*; Grothaus, Zum Türkenbild, 84 ff.

159. Overview in Bevilacqua/Turquerie, "Culture"; Ribeiro, *Dress*; on trade see Andreozzi/Panariti, "Trieste."

160. Maria Theresa and Maria Anna in Turkish costume, etching by Liotard, 1744, see Koos, *Haut*, 113–14, 352; Yonan, *Empress*, 149; Koschatzky, *Maria Theresia*, 316; Koschatzky, *Maria Theresia* (catalog), 108 ff., 117, no. 15,05. Better known is the 1745 portrait in Oriental dress with a mask; Koschatzky, *Maria Theresia* (catalog), 109–10, no. 15,4; see Koos, *Haut*, 113–14. Turkish costume books: *Was von den Türken übrig blieb*, 61.

161. Portrait of Johann Josef Khevenhüller's family, c. 1760, reproduced in Koschatzky, *Maria Theresia*, 417. See also the portrait of Joseph with a Moor as page, copperplate by Andreas Pfeffel after Gabriel Matthaei (privately owned, reproduced in Etzlstorfer, *Maria Theresia*, 629), or the portrait of Count Adolph von Wagensperg (1724–73), who served as frontier colonel in Croatia, with a Moor (ÖNB, Porträtsammlung, reproduced in Obersteiner, *Theresianische Verwaltungsreformen*, 262). There was also the famous court moor Soliman, who attended Isabella of Parma's entry and whose corpse was later preserved by Francis II for his natural history collection; see Sauer, "Angelo Soliman." Kubiska-Scharl/Pölzl, *Die Karrieren*, record a Martin Johann Soliman (1715–20), ibid., 398, and a "Gabril Solimano," Pastin Bereiter (1712–25), ibid., 703.

162. Taube, *Historische und geographische Beschreibung*, 80.

163. Roider, *Austria's Eastern Question*, 91 ff.; Sicker, *From the Treaty of Karlowitz*; brief overview in Parvev, "Du, Glückliches Österreich"; Parvev, "'Enemy Mine'?"; research survey in Kühnel, "Westeuropa."

164. KMT II, 384 ff.; on the sultan's stance in the Seven Years' War, see KMT III, 457 ff., 477 ff.; Roider, *Austria's Eastern Question*, 95 ff.

165. To Antonia of Saxony, July 1763, Lippert, Briefwechsel, 172.

166. See KMT VIII, 40; to Mercy-Argenteau, July 31, 1777, MACS III, 229 ff.: "*Je suis bien élognée de me preter jamais au partage de l'empire turc.... provinces malsaines sans culture, dépeuplées ou habitées par les Grecs perfidies.*"

167. See chapter 10, this volume; on the 1771 alliance with the Ottomans see Roider, *Austria's Eastern Question*, 112 ff.

168. Joseph to Maria Theresa, September 23, 1777, MJC II, 160–61; see chapter 10, this volume.

169. Rathkolb, *250 Jahre*; Starkenfels, *Die kaiserlich-königliche Orientalische Akademie*; Petritsch, "Erziehung"; Sutter Fichtner, *Terror und Toleration*, 117 ff., quote ibid., 128.

170. KMT IV, 139.

171. First and farewell audiences: Hagi Halil Effendi, April 17 to July 8, 1741, and Mustafa Hatti Effendi, May to October 1748, see KMT II, 225, 229–30, 261–62, 268; *Wienerisches Diarium* 1748, no. 49 and 83; Maria Theresa to Antonia of Saxony, August 1748, Lippert, Briefwechsel, 4–5. Hagi Halil Effendi, April 12 to August 30, 1755, see KMT III, 240 ff., 244, 257. Hammer-Purgstall, *Des türkishen Gesandten*, March 13 to July 12, 1758, see KMT V, 26, 41, 171–72; see Wienerische Diarium from April 22, 1758, no. 32; his diplomatic report published in translation by Hammer-Purgstall, *Des türkishen Gesandten*, April 16 to July 26, 1774; see KMT VIII, 31 ff., 37–38. On the audiences see, too, Graf, "Das kaiserliche Zeremoniell"; Do Paço, *L'Orient à Vienne*, 199 ff.

172. See the emissary's report: Hammer-Purgstall, *Des türkishen Gesandten*, 18 ff. (with different dates provided than those in the Viennese sources); on the genre of the diplomatic report, see Hitzel, "*Sefâretnâme.*"

173. KMT II, 229–30. The emissary sent from Algiers to Vienna in 1758 made a far more exotic impression; scandalously, he brought along a Christian slave as a gift; KMT V, 66, 198 ff.

174. KMT II, 225, 229–30, 259, 261–62, 268; from a Turkish perspective we have the reports of Mustafa Hatti (1748) and Ahmed Resmi (1758), see Hammer-Purgstall, *Des türkishen Gesandten*; Faroqhi, "Was man in Wien," 206 ff.

175. KMT II, 230.

176. KMT VIII, 33.

177. This point was made by Khevenhüller against Kaunitz, who wanted to do away with ambassadorial kisses to the jacket and hand, KMT VIII, 33.

178. Faroqhi, "Was man in Wien," 206.

179. Faroqhi, "Was man in Wien," 205 ff.

180. Faroqhi, "Was man in Wien," 207 ff.

181. Faroqhi, "Was man in Wien," 210.

182. Joseph to Leopold, June 9, 1774, MJC II, 36–37; see Werkhlin, Denkwürdigkeiten, 44–45.

183. Maria Theresa to Ferdinand, June 23, 1774, BKS I, 283–84, 291–92; to Ferdinand, September 8, 1774, BKF I, 299; Joseph to Leopold, June 9, 1774, MHC II, 36–37.

184. To Mercy-Argenteau, September 1, 1770, MACS I (*les bons musulmans*).

185. Jürgen Osterhammel speaks of "inclusive Eurocentrism." Osterhammel, *Unfabling the East*, Princeton 2018.

13. Subjects

1. Arneth, "Maria Theresia und der Hofrath von Greiner," 5.

2. Otruba, *Die Wirtschaftspolitik*, 29; as recently as 2016, "concern for the welfare of her subjects" was said to have been "Maria Theresa's guiding idea," Anita Winkler, Wer überwacht wen?—Josephs II. Beamtenstaat, http://www.habsburger.net/de/kapitel/wer-ueberwacht -wen-josephs-ii-beamtenstaat? (05.01.2019)

3. BAA, 66.

4. Political Testament from 1755–56, BAA, 126.

5. To Ferdinand, April 13, 1771, BKF I, 65.

6. To Joseph, August 9, 1778, MJC III, 32; see to Joseph, August 6 (*mes bons pays*), August 8 (*mes pauvres sujets saccagés*), August 20 and 22 (*nos pauvres pays saccagés*), MJC III, 20, 23, 57, 60.

7. To Joseph, June 17, 1778, MJC II, 293.

8. To Joseph, August 20, 1778, MJC III, 57; to Joseph, August 10, 1778, MJC III, 37.

9. E.g., to Joseph, August 13, 1778, MJC III, 43: *fidèles sujets* for Hungarian nobles.

10. Khevenhüller, too, generally spoke of "the people" (*das Volck*) whenever there was popular unrest, for example, when a fire had burned out of control owing to incompetence on the part of the authorities, KMT III, 79.

11. Political Testament of 1755–1756, BAA, 109.

12. "*Irrité à l'excès*," she wrote to Marie Antoinette, October 3, 1773, MACS II, 52.

13. When reporting to her son-in-law Albert about a popular revolt in Madrid in 1766, for example, she had no word for the rebels and only ever spoke of *ils*, them; Wolf, *Aus dem Hofleben*, 348.

14. See Stollberg-Rilinger, *Vormünder des Volkes?*

15. E.g., in the Political Testament of 1755–56, BAA, 122, 129.

16. On the history of the term, see Heindl, "Bildung und Recht"; on the concept of subjects (*Untertanen*) in the Codex Theresianus, see Friedrich, "Gleichförmigkeit"; see also chapter 10 ("How Enlightenment came to the Court").

17. Estimate given by Feigl, *Die niederösterreichische Grundherrschaft*, 52. Maria Theresa designated them as subjects in the narrower sense of the term, e.g., Political Testament of 1750–51, BAA, 95: "the poor and especially the subjects."

18. Report of the Court War Council from August 7, 1771, in Hochedlinger/Tantner, *Der größte Teil der Untertanen*, 93. See further below.

19. On the condition of subjects and their relations with landlords, see the older works of Grünberg, Leibeigenschaft; Mell, *Die Anfänge*; Feigl, *Die niederösterreichische Grundherrschaft*; Grüll, *Bauer*; Link, *Emancipation*; further, Rauscher/Scheutz, *Die Stimme*. On economic and agrarian policy, see the edited volumes Plaschka/Klingenstein, *Österreich* I; Matis, *Von der Glückseligkeit*; Cerman/Luft, Untertanen (on Bohemia); Berindei et al., Der Bauer, there esp. the overview by Vilfan, Agrarsozialpolitik; Sandgruber, *Ökonomie*.

20. Note from November 17, 1771, KMT VII, 377.

21. On the reforms see chapter 5, this volume.

22. Statement from 1742, quoted in Otruba, *Die Wirtschaftspolitik*, 107.

23. Beales, "Rêveries," see chapter 10, this volume.

24. The extremely complicated details in Hackl, *Die Dominikal- und Rustikalfassion*; Hackl, *Die Theresianische Steuerrektifikation*.

25. See Kropatschek, *Sammlung* I, 118 ff., as well as a long series of further individual decrees. On the strategy of "triangulation," i.e., the establishment of a triangular relationship between central administration, local lords, and subjects, see the works by Stefan Brakensiek, most recently Brakensiek/von Bredow/Näther, *Herrschaft und Verwaltung*; on the demand from below for stronger central intervention and on the dynamic of state formation, see Blockmans/Holenstein/Mathieu, *Empowering Interactions*.

26. Quoted in Hock, *Der österreichische Staatsrat*, 68–69 (source not provided).

27. This is the conclusion drawn by Hackl, *Die Theresianische Steuerrektifikation*, 583–84. Examples of Maria Theresa supporting landlords against circle offices are provided in Obersteiner, *Theresianische Verwaltungsreformen*.

28. Memorandum from 1750–51, BAA, 77.

29. On Maria Theresa's fundamentally negative understanding of rule, see chapter 7, this volume.

30. Joseph's travels: Banat and the Slavonic military frontier in 1768; Italy in 1769; Silesia in 1769 (meeting with Frederick II in Neiße); Hungary in 1770; Moravia in 1770 (meeting with Frederick II in Neutstadt); Bohemia and Upper Austria in 1771; Galicia and Transylvania in 1773; Croatia, Istria, and Upper Italy in 1775; France in 1777; Russia in 1780. See Beales, "Joseph II's Rêveries" I, 242 ff., esp. 251 ff.

31. Joseph to Court Councillor Keller, July 10, 1773, quoted in Hock, *Der österreichische Staatsrath*, 28; on his tours see also Pauser/Scheutz/Winkelbauer, *Quellenkunde*, 108–19.

32. E.g., to Lacy, July 21, 1775, BKF IV, 411; to Marie Antoinette, Christoph, *Maria Theresia: Geheimer Briefwechsel*, 63–64; to Ferdinand, BKF I, 142, 199, 220; BKF II, 38, 43, 50, 64, 70, 71 ff., 77–78; to Beatrix, BKF III, 160, 266, 279.

33. "For all your perspicacity and zeal, it is impossible that you could observe everything and draw the right conclusions on these journeys of two or three months," to Joseph, June 20, 1773, MJC II, 9 ff.

34. To Ferdinand, June 10, 1773, BKF I, 211.

35. Report on the journey to the military frontier and the Trieste littoral, May 17, 1775, KMT VIII, 263.

36. E.g., to Ferdinand, May 14, 1772, BKF I, 123; to Mercy, January 13, 1779, BAA, 498; see chapter 7 ("Court Timetable").

37. See chapter 7 ("Court Timetable").

38. OeStA Hofkammerarchiv, Allerhöchste Entschließungen, October 15, 1770, and October 11, 1764, quoted in Otruba, *Die Wirtschaftspolitik*, 19.

39. Schmitt, *Gespräch über die Macht*; Vismann, *Akten*, 205 ff.; the field of statistics studies is immense: for a start, see Behrisch, *Berechnung*; Bendecke/Friedrich/Friedrich, *Information*, above all the contribution by Behrisch, "Zu viele Informationen!"; on the hereditary lands, Becker, "Beschreiben"; further, Becker/Krosigk, Figures of Authority; Dickson, *Finance* I, 297 ff.; Lebeau, *Finanzwissenschaft*; on the symbolic function of information, see Feldman/March, *Information*.

40. Gottfried Wilhelm Leibniz, Staats-Tafeln, 1680.

41. Behrisch, "Zu viele Informationen!" 469.

42. Handwritten note to Rudolph Chotek, January 26, 1762, ÖZV II,3, 126–27.

43. See Dörflinger/Kretschmer/Wawrik, *Österreichische Kartographie*, 75–97; overviews in Vann, "Mapping"; Pauser/Scheutz/Winkelbauer, *Quellenkunde*, 1060–94.

44. Hochedlinger, Doppeladler; Hochedlinger, "Rekrutierung."

45. See Joseph's memorandum on the military from 1766 and Kaunitz's response in KMT VI, 458–75; Maria Theresa's opinion from February 1767 in KMT VI, 475–77.

46. Hochedlinger, "Die gewaffnete Doppeladler," 248–49; see the pathbreaking study by Tantner, *Ordnung der Häuser*, as well as the source edition of Hochedlinger/Tantner, . . . *der gröste Teil*; see also Gürtler, Volkszählungen; the findings in Dickson, *Finance* I, 438 ff.

47. Hochedlinger/Tantner, . . . *der gröste Teil*, xxxii.

48. Hochedlinger/Tantner, . . . *der gröste Teil*, xliv; many other vivid details in Tantner, *Ordnung der Häuser*; on criticism of landlords ibid., 156 ff.

49. Edited in Hochedlinger/Tantner, . . . *der gröste Teil*.

50. This example—one of many that could be cited—comes from the Circle of Prachin in Bohemia, Hochedlinger/Tantner, . . . *der gröste Teil*, 43.

51. Hochedlinger/Tantner, . . . *der gröste Teil*, 92–93 (on Upper Austria).

52. Hochedlinger/Tantner, . . . *der gröste Teil*, 93, 104, 145; see also Dickson, *Finance* I, 322 ff.

53. Tantner, *Ordnung der Häuser*, 156 ff.

54. Hochedlinger/Tantner, . . . *der gröste Teil*, lxiii.

55. See on the Bohemian uprising, this volume.

56. Kropatschek, *Sammlung* II, 31–32.

57. On industrial policy see Pribram, Gewerbepolitik I; Matis, *Der Glückseligkeit*; Otruba, *Die Wirtschaftspolitik*; see also Pfeisinger, *Arbeitsdisziplinierung*; on the domestic market see Komlosy, *Grenze*; Sandgruber, *Ökonomie*.

58. E.g., court decree from March 17, 1753, Kropatschek, *Sammlung* II, 31–32.

59. See the extensive overview in Helmedach, "Bevölkerungspolitik."

60. Figures in Otruba, *Die Wirtschaftspolitik*, 170; a detailed account in Roth, *Die planmässig angelegten Siedlungen*.

61. See Mayerhofer, *Dorfzigeuner*. The term *Zigeuner*, gypsy, was used at the time as both an endonym and a (mostly derogatory) exonym. It referred both to a "nation"—that is, a distinct ethnic group—and to wayfarers, vagabonds, and in general. It would be anachronistic to speak of Sinti and Roma for this period; see Lucassen, *Zigeuner*.

62. "Extermination" is a frequently used term; see Kropatschek, *Sammlung* III, 340; V, 407; VII, 212; VIII, 235.

63. For examples see Bressan/Grassi, *Maria Teresa*, 131–53.

64. HHStA Hofkriegsarchiv Hs. 290–94; a selection in Otruba, *Die Wirtschaftspolitik*. On the highly instructive campaign against sparrows, see Wacha, *Spatzenvertilgung*.

65. Kropatschek, *Sammlung* II, 31–32.

66. Decree from November 7, 1765, see Pribram, *Geschichte* I, 156 ff.; Otruba, *Die Wirtschaftspolitik*, 190.

67. Handbillet from March 4, 1766 referring to the Viennese prison, the Stockhaus.

68. Circular ordinance to all territorial governments apart from Lower Austria from March 28, 1768; decree for Lower Austria from May 7, 1768, Pribram, *Geschichte* I, 158; see also Otruba, *Die Wirtschaftspolitik*, 38–39, for a command to this effect personally issued by Maria Theresa.

69. Resolution on a submission of the Council of Commerce, October 26, 1768, quoted in Pribram, *Geschichte* I, 158.

70. Sonnenfels, Grundsätze II, 194.

71. Müller, "Die k. k. Nadelburger Fabrik"; Knofler, Nadelburgh; Pfeisinger, *Arbeitsdisziplinierung*, 232 ff.

72. The picture above the high altar shows Christ crucified and St. Teresa of Avila, as well as Joseph II and two workers kneeling down before them; see Reitböck, "Das Altarbild." I thank Anne Roerkohl for this reference.

73. Knofler, Nadelburgh, 159–60.

74. The Nadelburg was therefore sold in 1769 to Count Batthyány, although he was unable to make it any more profitable.

75. Hofkammerarchiv, "Allerhöchste Entschließungen, July 22, 1768," quoted in Otruba, *Die Wirtschaftspolitik*, 195–96.

76. Description and sources in H. Engelbrecht, *Geschichte* III; Hammerstein/Herrmann, *Handbuch* II.

77. Khevenhüller took his duties in this regard very seriously; see, e.g., KMT III, 52, 60, 202, 210–11, 212. On aristocratic education see Cerman, "Habsburgischer Adel und das Theresianum"; Cerman, *Habsburgische Adel und Aufklärung*.

78. This celebrated axiom is taken from a court decree from October 13, 1770, Kropatschek, *Sammlung* VI, 293–94.

79. See the regulations for studies from 1752, in H. Engelbrecht, *Geschichte* III,461 ff.; the Court Education Commission (Hofstudienkommission) was set up in 1760; on colleges (*Gymnasien*) see Grimm, *Die Schulreform*; Riedel, *Bildungsreform*; on van Swieten and the Jesuits see chapter 11, this volume.

80. General school ordinance for German normal, major, and minor schools in all imperial and royal hereditary lands, December 6, 1774, Kropatschek, *Sammlung* VII, 116–37, also in H. Engelbrecht, *Geschichte* III, 491–501. See ibid., part 3, 89 ff.; Neugebauer, "Niedere Schulen"; further Krömer, *Johann Ignaz von Felbiger*.

81. General school ordinance, Article 8, in Engelbrecht, *Geschichte* III, 495.

82. Methodology for teacher at German school in the imperial-royal hereditary lands, . . . Vienna 1775, in Engelbrecht, *Geschichte* III, 501–502.

83. To Ferdinand, July 7, 1774, BKF I, 286. The school ordinance was introduced in Hungary in 1774 as *Ratio educationis*.

84. Hochedlinger/Tantner, . . . *der größte Teil*, 129.

85. See Eder, *Auf der mehrere Ausbreitung*, esp. 74 ff.; H. Engelbrecht, *Geschichte*, 130–31. The reform met with resistance among Slovenes in Styria and Carinthia, due to the compulsory use of German as the language of instruction.

86. Anon., *Was sind Trivialschulen?*, Vienna 1776, 2nd ed. 1782, quoted in H. Engelbrecht, *Geschichte*, 337.

87. Sources in KMT VII, 453 ff.

88. Leopold, "Stato della famiglia," in Wandruszka, *Leopold II*, I, 337.

89. Greiner's submissions, with mostly handwritten responses from Maria Theresa, in Arneth, "Maria Theresia und der Hofrath von Greiner"; on the biography of Franz Salesius von Greiner (1730–98), better known as Caroline Pichler's father, see ibid., 6–10.

90. E.g., Arneth, "Maria Theresia und der Hofrath von Greiner," 43–44, 50, 52, 58–59, 69, 71 ff. In her correspondence with Greiner, Maria Theresa always called her son K. See Leopold's opinion, "Stato della famiglia," in Wandruszka, *Leopold II.*, I, 337–38.

91. E.g., Arneth, "Maria Theresia und der Hofrath von Greiner," 58 ff., quote on 55.

92. Arneth, "Maria Theresia und der Hofrath von Greiner," 17.

93. Arneth, "Maria Theresia und der Hofrath von Greiner,"43–44, 45–46, 49, 50, 51.

94. Arneth, "Maria Theresia und der Hofrath von Greiner," 42, 51, 52–53, 58–58, quote on 53.

95. Arneth, "Maria Theresia und der Hofrath von Greiner," 56.

96. Arneth, "Maria Theresia und der Hofrath von Greiner," 53.

97. This point is made by a specialist in Brandenburg-Prussian history, Neugebauer, "Niedere Schulen," 237; a less positive assessment of the reform in Sandgruber, *Ökonomie*, 150–51.

98. These and further figures in Neugebauer, "Niedere Schulen," 240.

99. Grimm, *Die Schulreform*; on Hungary and the Piarists see Riedel, *Bildungsreform*.

100. Joseph to Leopold, November 14, 1779, MJC III, 235–36.

101. Leopold, "Stato della famiglia," in Wandruszka, *Leopold II.*, I, 336.

102. To Court Councillor Greiner in relation to the Bohemian estates, Arneth, "Maria Theresia und der Hofrath von Greiner," 37.

103. Maasburg, *Geschichte der obersten Justizstelle*; Kocher, *Höchstgerichtsbarkeit*.

104. See Kocher, "Rechtsverständnis"; Heindl, "Bildung und Recht." She even exerted occasional (albeit informal) influence on trials at the two highest courts despite having nothing to do with them as empress, strictly speaking. An example is the case of the Sickingen family, KMT VIII, 52, 69, 218, 227–8. See also the references in Maria von Loewenich, "Amt und Prestige: Die Kammerrichter in der ständischen Gesellschaft" (1711–1806). Diss. Münster 2011.

105. Arneth, "Maria Theresia und der Hofrath von Greiner," 39–40.

106. See chapter 5, this volume.

107. On jurisdictional disputes see, e.g., KMT II, 83, 394.

108. Overview in Dickson, *Finance* I, 316 ff., with figures on increased legislative activity.

109. Thomas Ignaz Freiherr von Pöck, *Supplementum Codicis Austriaci oder Chronologische Sammlung, . . .*], Vienna 1777; Kropatschek, *Sammlung*, appeared after Maria Theresa's death. Both excluded Hungary, the Netherlands, and the Italian territories.

110. Quoted in Harrassowsky, *Der Codex Theresianus* I, Supplement I, 14.

111. Harrassowsky, *Geschichte der Codification*; Strakosch, *Absolutism*; Brauneder, "Das Allgemeine Bürgerliche Gesetzbuch"; Margret Friedrich, "Gleichförmigkeit"; Kocher, *Höchstgerichtbarkeit*; Kocher, "Rechtsverständnis"; Heindl, "Bildung und Recht"; Mertens, *Gesetzgebungskunst*; see also Arneth, *Geschichte Maria Theresia's* IX, 193 ff.; Guglia, *Maria Theresia* II, 59 ff.; Hock/Bidermann, *Der österreichische Staatsrath*, 41 ff.; Dickson, *Finance* I, 315 ff.

112. Quoted in Harrassowsky, *Geschichte der Codification*, 50. The principles of the committee's work were integrated into the Codex: Harrassowsky, *Codex Theresianus* I, Supplement II, 16 ff. See Strakosch, *Absolutism*, 50 ff.; Margret Friedrich, "Gleichförmigkeit," 113 ff. The committee was presided over by the vice-president of the Supreme Judiciary, Blümegen, and met in Brno, as Blümegen was based there at the time.

113. Quoted in Harrassowsky, *Geschichte der Codification*, 48–49.

114. See Harrassowsky, *Geschichte der Codification*, 122 ff.; Strakosch, 78 ff.

115. In a memorandum from October 1770; see Strakosch, *Absolutism*, 90 ff.; Szábo, *Kaunitz*, 181 ff.

116. Quoted in Mertens, *Gesetzgebungskunst*, 291.

117. Opinion of Secretary Kees, shared by the president of the Supreme Judiciary, Seilern; see Harassowsky, *Geschichte der Codification*, 141–42.

118. See Kwiatkowsky, *Die Constitutio*; Maasburg, *Zur Entstehungsgeschichte*; Beales, "Joseph II's Rêveries" I, 236 ff.; Ammerer, "Aufgeklärtes Recht."

119. Review of [P. H. Seyberth], in *Göttingische Anzeigen von gelehrten Sachen* 59 (Göttingen 1769): 537–41.

120. Hock/Bidermann, *Der österreichische Staatsrath*, 42–43.

121. See the echo in KMT VIII, 115–16.

122. See the digital collection: http://www.digital.wienbibliothek.at/wbrobv (accessed 06.01.2018).

123. Coke, *Letters* IV, 52; see Kwiatkowsky, *Die Constitutio*, 44 ff.: in 1778, for example, ten out of fifty death sentences were carried out in Bohemia, Moravia, and Silesia. So far as I am aware, more precise statistics are unavailable.

124. See Johann Gottfried Haymann, *Neueröffnetes Kriegs- und Friedens-Archiv*, vol. 1, Leipzig 1744, 186 ff.

125. In August 1780, following the petition for mercy by the writer Johann Rautenstrauch. When Rautenstrauch was unmasked by Deputy Governor Heberstein as the author of the petition, he was sentenced by court decree to three days' imprisonment; see BLKÖ XXV, 1873, 61 ff.

126. In 1752, the imperial chamberlain Count Franz Anton Nostitz had killed Count Werschowitz in a duel in Prague. Nostitz was condemned to "lose his head," but, after a long spell of confinement in a tower, he was eventually pardoned through the intercession of his uncle, the elector of Trier; KMT III, 20–21; see to Antonia of Saxony, Lippert, Briefwechsel, 170 ("*la-dessus point de grace*").

127. See Reinalter, *Joseph von Sonnenfels*; Osterloh, *Joseph von Sonnenfels*; Cattaneo, "Beccaria und Sonnenfels"; Karstens, *Lehrer*; see also chapter 7, this volume.

128. E.g., KMT VIII, 126–27; *Ephemeriden der Menschheit* (Basel/Mannheim/Leipzig 1776), no. 2: 96–97.

129. See Arneth, *Geschichte Maria Theresia's* IX, 198 ff.; Beales, "Joseph II's Rêveries" I, 236 ff.; Karstens, *Lehrer*, 332 ff.; Osterloh, *Joseph von Sonnenfels*, 167 ff.

130. Joseph von Sonnenfels, *Sätze aus der Polizey, Handlungs- und Finanzwissenschaft*, Vienna 1765, 305 ff.

131. Arneth, *Geschichte Maria Theresia's* IX, 204–205.

132. Arneth, *Geschichte Maria Theresia's* IX, 208.

133. Decree from November 19, 1773, in Arneth, *Geschichte Maria Theresia's* IX, 579.

134. Joseph von Sonnenfels, *Über die Abschaffung der Tortur*, Zurich 1775; see Karstens, *Lehrer*, 324 ff.

135. Arneth, *Geschichte Maria Theresia's* IX, 213.

136. Anon., "Abschaffung der peinlichen Frage in den österreichischen Erblanden," in *Ephemeriden der Menschheit* (Basel/Mannheim/Leipzig 1776), no. 2: 96–97.

137. To Ferdinand, January 4, 1776, BKF II, 2.

138. Steiner, *Rückkehr*; see chapters 6 and 1, this volume, as well as below in this chapter.

139. See Vasold, "Die Hunger- und Sterblichkeitskrise," on the medium-term revolutionary consequences for the ancien régime.

140. Figures in Hanke, "Das Zeitalter," 478; Beales, "Joseph II's Rêveries" I, 342. On the excesses of the famine see, e.g., Guibert, *Journal* I, 249 ff., 309 ff.

141. On serfdom in Bohemia and the reforms beginning in the 1760s: Arneth, *Geschichte Maria Theresia's* IX, 335 ff.; X, 41 ff.; Grünberg, *Die Bauernbefreiung*, 67 ff.; Link, *Emancipation*; Beales, "Joseph II's Rêveries" I, 338 ff.; Dickson, *Finance* I, 118 ff.; Liebel-Weckowicz/Szábo, "Modernization Forces"; overviews in Hanke, "Das Zeitalter," 475 ff.; Čechura, "Zu spät"; Cerman/Luft, *Untertanen*, here especially the case study by Alena Pazderová, Gutsherrschaft und Untertanen in der Herrschaft Reichenau an der Knežna, 177–201. An instructive case study is the refusal of Robot services by peasants in the Waldviertel in Lower Austria in

1769–1778, see Grüll, *Bauer*, 423 ff.; Rauscher, "Die Bauernrevolte"; Winkelbauer, *Robot und Steuer*, 110 ff.

142. Montesquieu, *Esprit des lois* VI, 1; Guibert, *Journal* I, 300–301; Riesbeck, *Briefe*, 115, 413 ff.; see also the description of conditions from the perspective of the Bohemian village judge František J. Vavák, in Helmut Klocke, "Zur Publizistik über die Lage der böhmischen Bauern im 18. Jahrhundert und im Vormärz," in Berindei et al., *Der Bauer*, 253–73. See also the description given by the English emissary Lord Stormont in 1765, in Dickson, *Finance* I, 389 ff.

143. E.g., in summer 1754, at the laying of the foundation stone for the noble chapter of nuns in Prague, KMT III, 194 ff.

144. KMT III, 194.

145. See chapter 7, this volume.

146. Details in Grünberg, *Die Bauernbefreiung* II, 67 ff.

147. Grünberg, *Die Bauernbefreiung* II, 172 ff.; Arneth, *Geschichte Maria Theresia's* IX, 342 ff.

148. Grünberg, *Die Bauernbefreiung* II, 192 ff.; Arneth, *Geschichte Maria Theresia's* IX, 347; Beales, "Joseph II's Rêveries" I, 346 ff.

149. KMT VII, 69.

150. Hochedlinger/Tantner, *. . . der gröste Teil*, 42 ff. (on Bohemia), 122 ff. (on Moravia). Other memoranda submitted to Vienna around the same time painted a similar picture; see Beales, "Joseph II's Rêveries" I, 348.

151. On Bohemia, Beales, "Joseph II's Rêveries," 63, 67.

152. Beales, "Joseph II's Rêveries," 54.

153. From Moravia, Beales, "Joseph II's Rêveries," 148.

154. Beales, "Joseph II's Rêveries," 149.

155. Beales, "Joseph II's Rêveries," 82.

156. Beales, "Joseph II's Rêveries," 151.

157. To Countess Enzenberg, October 23, 1771, BKF IV, 504; similarly to Ferdinand, October 10, 1771, BKF I, 78; October 17, 1771, BKF I, 80; February 13, 1772, BKF I, 102.

158. Sources in KMT VII, 369 ff.; see Blaich, "Die wirtschaftspolitische Tätigkeit."

159. KMT VII, 114–15.

160. Quoted in Grünberg, *Die Bauernbefreiung* II, 195.

161. Joseph, memorandum from Bohemia, November 17, 1771, KMT VII, 373–98; Joseph to Maria Theresa, October 17 and 27, 1771, MJC I, 346 ff.; see chapter 10, this volume.

162. Grünberg, *Die Bauernbefreiung* II, 196 ff.

163. See KMT VII, 109, and Franz Khevenhüller, who continued his father's diary, himself, on the thanklessness of the mission (KMT VIII, 124).

164. Waltraud Heindl, *Gehorsame Rebellen: Bürokratie und Beamte in Österreich*, Vienna/Cologne/Graz 1991.

165. Resolution on Chotek's submission, August 4, 1769, quoted in Arneth, *Geschichte Maria Theresia's* IX, 342; Blanc's memorandum in Grünberg, *Die Bauernbefreiung* II, 102 ff.

166. See Erich Angermann, Blanc, Franz Anton von, in NDB 2 (1955), 283–84; Karl Grünberg, "Franz Anton von Blanc: ein Sozialpolitiker der theresianisch-josefinischen Zeit," in *Schmollers Jahrbuch* 35 (1911): 1155–1238.

167. See Hans Schläger, "Tobias Philipp Freiherr von Gebler: Sein Leben und Wirken in Österreich," PhD Vienna 1971; Gustav Gugitz, "Gebler, Tobias Freiherr von," in NDB 6 (1964),

122; Hock/Bidermann, *Der österreichische Staatsrath*. Gebler belonged to the same masonic lodge in Vienna as Mozart, whose *Magic Flute* refers back to Gebler's play *Thamos, King of Egypt*. See Richard Maria Werner (ed.), *Aus dem josephinischen Wien: Geblers und Nicolais Briefwechsel*, Berlin 1888.

168. Quoted in Hock/Bidermann, *Der österreichische Staatsrath*, 68.

169. See BLKÖ 24 (1872), 155–57.

170. The extremely complicated details in Grünberg, *Die Bauernbefreiung* II, 196 ff.; Arneth, *Geschichte Maria Theresia's* IX, 342 ff.

171. Joseph to Leopold, September 25, 1771, MJC I, 344; similar complaints on January 24, 1771, MJC I, 329; February 21, 1771, MJC I, 332–33.

172. November 1, 1772, KMT VII, 149.

173. Characteristically, when Joseph opened the Prater, the former court hunting grounds, to the public, he ordered that the following inscription be placed there: "A place of recreation dedicated to all the people by their admirer."

174. See exhibition catalog *Österreich zur Zeit Kaiser Josephs*, 352 ff., on the nineteenth century, ibid., 696 ff.; Koschatzky, *Maria Theresia* (catalog), 237; Beales, "Joseph II's Rêveries" I, 338 ff. The educated would have known from Jesuit missionary reports that the plowing of the soil was an age-old ritual performed by the emperor of China, the epitome of political wisdom and stability.

175. Riesbeck, *Briefe*, 417.

176. See Wolf, *Marie Christine*, 10, or Hanke, "Das Zeitalter," 491.

177. Quoted in Arneth, *Geschichte Maria Theresia's* IX, 349.

178. Arneth, "Maria Theresia und der Hofrath von Greiner," 33 ff., 49–50; see, e.g., to Albert of Teschen, Wolf, *Aus dem Hofleben*, 360.

179. KMT VIII, 9, 199–200.

180. Resolution on the presentation of the Bohemian-Austrian Court Chancellery, February 28, 1774, KMT VIII, 200; see Grünberg, *Die Bauernbefreiung* II, 226 ff.; Arneth, *Geschichte Maria Theresia's* IX, 353 ff.

181. Grünberg, *Die Bauernbefreiung* II, 221–22.

182. Beales, "Joseph II's Rêveries" I, 346; in a similar sense, also Wangermann, "Matte Morgenröte"; Liebel-Weckowicz/Szábo, "Modernization Forces."

183. Cabinet Secretary Pichler, quoted in Arneth, *Geschichte Maria Theresia's* IX, 594. On the rebellion see Grünberg, *Die Bauernbefreiung* II, 243 ff.

184. To Ferdinand, March 29, 1775, BKF I, 323.

185. Arneth, *Geschichte Maria Theresia's* IX, 593.

186. Contarini's extensive reports in Arneth, *Geschichte Maria Theresia's* IX, 594 ff.

187. Arneth, *Geschichte Maria Theresia's* IX, 359–60.

188. KMT VIII, 69, 67.

189. Leopold, "Stato della famiglia," in Wandruszka, *Leopold II.*, I, 344–45.

190. KMT VIII, 66–67, 68–69, 76.

191. KMT VIII, 66–67.

192. To Marie Antoinette, June 2, 1775, MACS II, 341.

193. To Mercy-Argenteau, May 4, 1775, MACS II, 329–30. The peasants had actually invoked the conscription of 1770–71; see Grünberg, *Die Bauernbefreiung* II, 245.

194. To Mercy-Argenteau, May 4, 1775, MACS II, 329–30.

195. To Mercy-Argenteau, May 4, 1775, MACS II, 329–30.

196. Arneth, "Maria Theresia und der Hofrath von Greiner," 34.

197. E.g., to Countess Enzenberg, February 20, 1775, BKF IV, 511: with the emperor, one could never be sure whether he would change his decisions at the next moment, since he always liked to surprise others.

198. Joseph to Leopold, July 20, 1775, MJC II, 71. Numerous further examples—some of them omitted by Arneth in his edition of the correspondence—in Beales, "Joseph II's Rêveries" I, 351 ff.

199. July 1775, KMT VIII, 89.

200. Joseph to Leopold, August 9, 1775, 81–82. Court Councillor Kressel, who had been sent to Prague, arrived at a similar judgment, Hock/Bidermann, *Der österreichische Staatsrath*, 77. On the complicated state of ongoing discussions about the rebellion see Grünberg, *Die Bauernbefreiung* II, 249 ff.

201. Arneth, *Geschichte Maria Theresia's* IX, 365 ff.; Grünberg, *Die Bauernbefreiung* II, 257 ff.; on September 7, 1775, the validity of the regulation was extended to Moravia; see ibid., 267 ff.

202. Kropatschek, *Sammlung* VII, 265–348; on Maria Theresa's doubts see KMT VIII, 73, 93, 96, 243–44; see Grünberg, *Die Bauernbefreiung* II, 252.

203. Joseph to Leopold, October 6, 1775, MJC II, 87–88.

204. Joseph to Leopold, September 14, 1775, MJC II, 84; Joseph to Maria Theresa, December 1775, MJC II, 94 ff.; Joseph to Leopold, February 8, 1776, HHStA Hausarchiv FA Sbd. 7 (not included in Arneth's edition), see Beales, "Joseph II's Rêveries" I, 354; see also chapter 12, this volume.

205. To Christina, February 15, 1776, BKF II, 400, "*malice noir*"; February 29 and March 18, 1776, BKF II, 404, 407. On the subsequent course of the patent's implementation, see Grünberg, *Die Bauernbefreiung* II, 271 ff.

206. Joseph to Leopold, January 16, 1777, HHStA FA Sbd. 7 (not included in Arneth's edition); see Beales, "Joseph II's Rêveries" I, 355; Blanc's new, radical proposal in Grünberg, *Die Bauernbefreiung* II, 294–95.

207. Only the empress and some subalterns took a different view to him, Joseph wrote to Leopold, HHStA FA Sbd. 7 (not included in Arneth's edition); see Beales, "Joseph II's Rêveries" I, 356.

208. Arneth, "Maria Theresia und der Hofrath von Greiner," 19–20, 33 ff., 49–50; see Arneth, *Geschichte Maria Theresia's* IX, 376 ff.

209. To Greiner, Arneth, "Maria Theresia und der Hofrath von Greiner," 32. See also the depictions of Cobenzl (Arneth, "Graf Philipp Cobenzl," 26, 114 ff.) or of Khevenhüller, e.g., KMT VII, 105 ff. Whoever in Joseph's eyes was "too relenting to mother," such as Blümegen, needed to be sidelined as far as possible.

210. Arneth, "Maria Theresia und der Hofrath von Greiner," 23 ff., 73–74.

211. Joseph to Leopold, February 6 and 13, 1777, HHStA FA Sbd. 7 (not included in Arneth's edition); Maria Theresa to Ferdinand, February 13, 1777, BKF II, 69–70; see Beales, "Joseph II's Rêveries" I, 356.

212. To Ferdinand, beginning of 1777, BKF II, 66.

213. To Ferdinand, February 13, 1777, BKF II, 69–70.

214. To Countess Edling, Summer 1778, BKF IV, 525.

215. Patent from November 1, 1781, see Beales, "Joseph II's Rêveries" I, 356 ff.

216. See Arneth, "Graf Philipp Cobenzl," 20 ff. In 1775 Maria Theresa introduced a more liberal customs scheme and partially abolished internal tolls within the monarchy. On the other conflicts, see chapters 10 and 12, this volume.

217. KMT VIII, 78, 85; see ibid., 89–90, 73, 83, 119; see also the notes of Count Cobenzl: Arneth, "Graf Philipp Cobenzl," 130–31.

218. See Leopold's opinion, "Stato della famiglia," in Wandruszka, Leopold II.: I, 342 ff.

219. See Hanke, "Das Zeitalter," 489 ff.; Liebel-Werkowicz/Szábo, "Modernization Forces"; Vilfan, "Die Agrarsozialpolitik," 30 ff.; Čechura, "Zu spät," 131 ff.

220. In 1778 Leopold also noted that Joseph paid attention to coffee house talk and that Maria Theresa was jealous of her son's popularity; see Wandruszka, Leopold II I, 326, 336, 342 ff.

221. On the conflict over the Bavarian succession, see Arneth, Geschichte Maria Theresia's X, chapters 9–16; Hochedlinger, Austria's Wars, 364 ff.; Beales, "Joseph II's Rêveries" I, 386 ff.; from the imperial perspective, Aretin, Das Alte Reich III, 183–212; from a Bavarian perspective, Press, "Bayern am Scheideweg"; from a Prussian perspective, Kunisch, Friedrich der Große, 503 ff.; Blanning, Frederick the Great, 325 ff.; from a French perspective, Buddruss, Die französische Deutschlandpolitik; Lever, Marie Antoinette, 178 ff.

222. On Kaunitz's exchange plans from 1764 on the occasion of Joseph's marriage to Joseph, see above, chapter 9; see Press, "Bayern am Scheideweg," 294; Hochedlinger, Austria's Wars, 364. At the start of the century, Prince Max Emanuel of Bavaria himself had once planned swapping his ancestral lands for the Netherlands.

223. See chapter 9 this volume.

224. Inheritance claims were made by Max Joseph's sister, Princess Maria Antonia of Saxony, as well as Duke Karl August of Pfalz-Zweibrücken, supported by Karl Theodor's sister-in-law, Duchess Maria Anna von Pfalz-Sulzbach.

225. Contract from January 3, 1778. Karl Theodor feared Frederick II's old claims to Jülich-Berg and wanted to secure imperial support against them.

226. Joseph to Leopold, January 12 and 15, 1778, MJC II, 174 ff.

227. Handwritten letter from Frederick II to Joseph II, April 14, 1778, Politische Correspondenz Friedrich des Großen XV, 394–96; see Kunisch, Friedrich der Große, 506–507.

228. To Joseph, January 2, 1778, MJC II, 170 ff.; Leopold and Maria Christina took a similar view: Wandruszka, Leopold II. I, 327–28; Wolf, Marie Christine I, 156–57.

229. Joseph to Leopold, January 12, 1778, MJC II, 175.

230. To Joseph, March 14, 1778, MJC II, 186 ff.

231. E.g., MJC II, 195–96, 203, 208 ff., 213–14, 221, 227–28, 233, 243, 248, 265, 287.

232. See her correspondence with Marie Antoinette and Mercy, MACS III, 150 ff.; Lever, Marie Antoinette, 178 ff., see below, chapter 14.

233. E.g., to Albert of Teschen, Wolf, Aus dem Hofleben, 362 ff.; to Ferdinand, BKF II, 113 ff.; to his wife Beatrix, BKF III, 300 ff.; to her nephew Prince Ferdinand of Brunswick, who stood on the opposing side, BKF IV, 536 ff.

234. To Joseph, June 21, 1778, MJC II, 302.

235. German-language note written by Joseph, July 7, 1778, MJC II, 325–26.

236. To Fredrick II of Prussia, July 12, 1778, Œuvres de Frédéric le Grand VI, 198.

237. Details in Arneth, *Geschichte Maria Theresias* X, 449 ff., quote ibid., 451–52; see BAA, 452–53. She was otherwise herself known to argue by comparing taxation revenue, e.g., to Joseph, June 19, 1778, MJC II, 296–97.

238. Joseph to Maria Theresa, July 11, 1778, MJC II, 333–34; Maria Theresa to Joseph, July 13, 1778, MJC II, 336 ff.

239. Joseph to Maria Theresa, July 15, 1778, MJC II, 341 ff., July 16, 1778, MJC II, 344–45.

240. Joseph to Leopold, July 18, 1778, MJC II, 351 ff.

241. To Joseph, July 25, 1778, MJC II, 366 ff.

242. To Marie Antoinette, August 6, 1778, MACS III, 233–34; negotiations: to Frederick II of Prussia, July 22, August 1, and August 6, 1778, Preuß *Œuvres* VI, 201, 205, 206. See Maria Theresa to Albert of Teschen, Wolf, *Aus dem Hofleben*, 366 ff., 373; to Mercy, July 31, 1778, MACS III, 229 ff.; to Joseph, August-September 1778, esp. MJC III, 23–24, 31–32, 36–37, 57–58.

243. To Joseph, July 25, 1778, MJC II, 366 ff.; July 31, 1778, MJC II, 378 ff.

244. Joseph to Maria Theresa, July 24, 1778, MJC II, 366; see August 1778, MJC III, 13–14, 26–27, 28 ff., 48–49, 73 ff., 77–78.

245. For more detail on these inconsistencies see Beales, Beales, "Joseph II's Rêveries" I, 408 ff.

246. Handwritten letter to Kaunitz, May 23, 1779, in Arneth, *Geschichte Maria Theresias* X, 633.

247. For details see Beales, "Joseph II's Rêveries" I, 419 ff.

248. Press, "Bayern am Scheideweg," 318; see also chapter 10, this volume.

249. Wandruszka, *Leopold II.* I, 363–64, see 330–31, 344. Like his mother, Leopold was against the war but his visit did not fulfill her high expectations. Joseph was jealous and felt that Leopold had pushed him to one side. In the end, both mother and son disclaimed responsibility for having brought Leopold to Vienna.

250. Quoted in Wilhelm von Janko, *Laudon's Leben*, Vienna 1869, 397.

14. The Autumn of the Matriarch

1. To Albert of Saxony, April 23, 1778, Wolf, *Aus dem Hofleben*, 368.

2. To Ferdinand, May 18, 1772, BKF I, 124.

3. She admitted as much not just to Kaunitz himself but to others as well, e.g., to Maria Christina, June 10, 1776, BKF II, 446; to Ferdinand, October 17, 1780, BKF II, 302–303.

4. KMT VII, 128–29.

5. To Antonia of Saxony, May 1771, Lippert, Briefwechsel, 273, 276: the intimacy of old was lacking. The correspondence with Herzelles broke off suddenly in mid-1773. The few letters exchanged thereafter are cool and formal; Kervyn de Lettenhove (Constantin), *Lettres inédites*, 44 ff.

6. He wrote this in May 1772 following her conflict with Joseph over the Polish partition, KMT VII, 129–30.

7. To Countess Edling, August 7, 1769, BKF IV, 521–22; see to Countess Enzenberg, BKF IV, 488, 510, 517 ff.; to Herzelles, Kervyn de Lettenhove (Constantin), *Lettres inédites*, 40 ff.; to Ferdinand, BKF I, 99, 100, 110, 114, 118, 124, 126, 152, 158, 169, 171–72, 184, 192, 206, 295–96, 304, 309; BKF II, 210, 213–14; to her daughter-in-law Beatrix: BKF III, 133, 150, 153, 182, 211, 274,

275–76; to Maria Christina, BKF II, 399, 445, 450–51, 463. See the opinions expressed by outsiders about her physical condition: Wraxall, *Historical and the Posthumous Memoirs* II, 305 ff.; Coke, *Letters* III, 312; Swinburne, *Courts* I, 355; Giubert, *Journal* I, 283–84.

8. To Ferdinand, July 7, 1774, BKF I, 286.

9. See Lorenz/Mader-Kratky, *Die Wiener Hofburg*, 278; Wolf, *Marie Christine* I, 174.

10. Lorenz/Mrader-Kratky, *Die Wiener Hofburg*, 277 ff.; Iby/Koller, *Schönbrunn*, 140 ff., see also further below.

11. To Beatrix, October 6, 1777, BKF III, 297.

12. To Maria Christina, June 29, 1776, BKF II, 451.

13. To Lacy, January 27, 1771, BKF IV, 379.

14. Coke, *Letters* III, 317.

15. On her daily routine as widow: Wolf, *Marie Christine* I, 81–82; to Ferdinand, September 2, 1772, BKF I, 148; to Countess Enzenberg, October 6, 1770, BKF IV, 500; Leopold, "Stato della famiglia," in Wandruszka, *Leopold II*. I, 338; see chapter 7, this volume.

16. See Yonan, "Conceptualizing the Kaiserinwitwe"; Yonan, *Empress*, 51.

17. Iby/Koller, *Schönbrunn*, 190 ff. Lord Swinburne found the Gloriette "as ugly as possible," Swinburne, *Courts* I, 341.

18. Today "Goëss apartment"; Iby/Koller, *Schönbrunn*, 140 ff.

19. E.g., to Ferdinand, January 27, 1774, BKF I, 225.

20. See chapter 10 ("Trials of Strength"), this volume.

21. See, e.g., Instruction de S. M. L'Imperatrice pour le Ceremoniel aux Cours de ses Enfans 1765, ÖNB, Wiener Hofbibliothek, Codex Series N. 1713, fol. 49v.

22. Marie Antoinette to Maria Theresa, February 27, 1776, MACS II, 425; the king of Spain forbade his daughter-in-law Carolina from traveling to Görz; see to Maria Christina, March 28, 1776, BKF II, 411.

23. KMT VIII, 103. She visited Vienna a second time in wnter 1777–78.

24. Maria Theresa to Beatrix, BKF II, 194–95, 197–98, 200, 292 ff., 298–99. On the 1775 visit see KMT VIII, 89 ff.; Joseph to Leopold, July–August 1775, MJC II, 66 ff., 76 ff.

25. To Beatrix, January 1, 1776, BKF III, 210, see 217, 274.

26. Marie Antoinette to Maria Theresa, January 14, 1776, MACS II, 414; Maria Theresa to Mercy, February 12, 1776, MACS II, 422–23.

27. Joseph to Leopold, November 1775 to May 1776, MJC II, 89–90, 93–94, 103 ff.; Maria Theresa to Maria Christina, late December, 1775, BKF II, 376, 378.

28. To Beatrix, April 8, 1776, BKF III, 226–27.

29. Joseph to Leopold, March 27, 1776, MJC II, 106–107.

30. To Maria Christina, March 28, 1776, BKF II, 410–11.

31. To Maria Christina, March 30, 1776, BKF II, 411 ff.; the positive sentiment without the critical passages verbatim to Beatrix, March 30, 1776, BKF III, 226; see to Ferdinand, March 28–May 9, 1776, BKF II, 14 ff.

32. To Ferdinand, March 28, 1776, BKF II, 14–15.

33. To Maria Christina, April 1, 1776, BKF II, 417.

34. To Maria Christina, April 4, 8, and 11, 1776, BKF II, 417 ff.

35. To Maria Christina, April 15, 1776, BKF II, 422–23; to Ferdinand, April 11 and 18, 1776, BKF II, 18–19.

36. Joseph to Leopold, April 16, 1776, MJC II, 111.

37. To Maria Christina, April 18, 1776, BKF II, 423.

38. To Beatrix, April 22, 1776, BKF III, 228–29; to Maria Christina, BKF II, 425–26.

39. Joseph to Maria Theresa, April 24, 1776, BKF I, 9–10; see KMT VIII, 133, 270–71.

40. Joseph to Leopold, April 24, 1776, MJC II, 112–13.

41. To Maria Christina, April 24, 1776, BKF II, 426, with a copy of Joseph's letter; to Ferdinand, April 25, May 2 and 9, 1776, BKF II, 20–21; to Beatrix, April 29, 1776, BKF III, 229–30.

42. To Maria Christina, April 29, 1776, BKF II, 428–29; to Ferdinand, May 2 and 9, 1776, BKF II, 20–21.

43. To Maria Christina, April 25, 1776, BKF II, 427–28.

44. Wandruszka, *Leopold* II. I, 307; but see Joseph's opposing view, ibid., 327; Maria Theresa to Ferdinand, May 9, 1776, BKF II, 21; to Maria Christina, May 6, 1776, BKF II, 433: Leopold would probably blame her.

45. To Maria Christina, May 6 and 9, 1776, BKF II, 433–44.

46. See Wandruszka, *Leopold II.* I, 307.

47. E.g., Joseph to Leopold, May 23, 1776, MJC II, 115.

48. To Maria Christina, May 6, 1776, BKF II, 433; KMT VII, 91; Joseph to Leopold, July 7, 1775, MJC II, 65.

49. Mödling was around twenty-five kilometers from Vienna and was often visited by the court "owing to the beautiful prospect," KMT VII, 146; by 1774 the trip had become too arduous for her.

50. In 1766 Maria Theresa had arrangements put in place that would allow her to lodge in Pressburg at any time; see to Maria Christina, April 29, 1766, BKF II, 367. Stays in Schlosshof: KMT VIII, 29, 34, 95, 104, 161, 184, 193; in Pressburg: KMT VII, 10, 86, 151, 165, 190; KMT VIII, 15, 74, 117, 190, 194. She paid her last visit to Pressburg in September 1780.

51. See Wolf, *Marie Christine*; Benedik/Schröder, *Die Gründung*, esp. the contribution by Sandra Hertel, "Erzherzogin Marie Christine"; further Arneth *Geschichte Maria Theresia's* VII, 244 ff.; Pangels, *Die Kinder*, 162 ff.

52. Charles-Joseph de Ligne, a friend of the Prince of Württemberg, reports that Maria Theresa banned him from the Viennese court, along with everyone else who had played a part in the affair between Maria Christina and Prince Ludwig of Württemberg; Ligne, *Fragments* II, 262.

53. To Maria Christina, before August 1765, BKF II, 358 ff.; Arneth, *Geschichte Maria Theresia's* VII, 253–54.

54. KMT VI, 158; Joseph, on the other hand, had no objections; see Joseph to Leopold, November 14, 1765, MJC I, 152 ff.; Maria Theresa to Kaunitz, November 1765, BKF IV, 254.

55. Hertel, Erzherzogin Marie Christine, 40; Wolf, *Marie Christine* I, 39 ff.; Arneth, *Geschichte Maria Theresia's* VII, 257.

56. On the collection see Benedik/Schröder, *Die Gründung*.

57. Only Maria Christina and her children had an inheritance claim on the duchy, not Albert.

58. Wolf, *Marie Christine* I, 37.

59. Wolf, *Marie Christine* II, 215 ff.

60. To Maria Christina, April 29, 1766, BKF II, 366.

61. To Countess Enzenberg, May 1, 1766, BKF IV, 474; see to Countess Enzenberg, December 26, 1765, BKF IV, 467.

62. Albert von Sachsen-Teschen, "Mémoires de ma vie," quoted in Arneth, *Geschichte Maria Theresia's* X, 730.

63. Leopold, "Stato della famiglia," in Wandruszka, *Leopold II.* I, 341.

64. Swinburne, *Courts* I, 341.

65. Albert von Sachsen-Teschen, "Mémoires de ma vie," Hungarian National Archive, P 298, N2. A. II 12/1–4.

66. Leopold, "Stato della famiglia," in Wandruszka, *Leopold II.* I, 350 ff. See also Zinzendorf, *Aus den Jugendtagebüchern*, 10.12.1763.

67. See chapter 9, this volume.

68. E.g., to Maria Christina, December 1775, BKF II, 376 ff., as well as the Görz correspondence, see above.

69. On the Habsburg Netherlands see Hertel, *Maria Elisabeth*; Zedinger, *Die Verwaltung* (further information there on regional studies); Arneth, *Geschichte Maria Theresia's* X, 198 ff.; Gérard, *Impératrice*.

70. See Bressan/Grassi, *Maria Teresa*, 60 ff.

71. See the brief sketch by Georges Engelbert, "Maria Theresia als Landesmutter der Niederlande," in Koschatzky, *Maria Theresia*, 113–16.

72. According to Arneth, who ought to have known, *Geschichte Maria Theresia's* X, 228.

73. To Joseph, July 22, 1780, BKF I, 3.

74. When Joseph came to rule in his own name, there were heated disputes with the governor. On Maria Christina's role in the Brabant Revolution, see Wolf, *Marie Christine*, 177 ff.; Hertel, *Erzherzogin Marie Christine*, 46 ff.

75. In 1735 Charles VI transferred Naples-Sicily to the House of Bourbon, albeit on the proviso that it had to be ruled as a secundogeniture and could not be united with the Kingdom of Spain. Maria Theresa lost the Duchy of Parma to Philip of Bourbon in the Treaty of Aachen (1748).

76. On the politics of matrimony see chapter 9, this volume.

77. [Friedrich Carl von Moser], *Geschichte der Päbstlichen Nuntien in Deutschland*, vol. 1, Frankfurt/Leipzig 1788, Preface.

78. E.g., to Carolina, BKF III, 41–42. See also Stauber, *Der Zentralstaat*, 49 ff., on Austrian perceptions of the border to Italy.

79. Instruction De Feu Sa Majésté l'Empereur François I pour son fils Leopold donée 1765. ÖNB, Wiener Hofbibliothek, Codex Series N. 1713, esp. fol. 19 ff. on the Italians.

80. Wandruszka, *Leopold II.*; Wandruszka, *Österreich und Italien*; overview in Capra, "Habsburg Italy."

81. Zedinger, *Franz Stephan*, 147 ff. On the inheritance conflict MJC I, 155 ff.

82. To Count Anton Thurn, March 10, 1766, BKF IV, 33 ff.; see Wandruszka, *Leopold II.* I, 156 ff.

83. Maria Theresa to Count Franz Thurn, January 12, 1766, MJC I, 170 ff.; January 23, 1766, MJC I, 175–76; Leopold to Joseph, February 1, 1766, MJC I, 174–75.

84. See chapter 9, this volume.

85. To Beatrix, BKF III, 381, see III, 375; to Ferdinand, BKF I, 146, 204, 288–89.

86. Wandruszka, *Leopold II.* I, 355.

87. Venturi, *Italy and the Enlightenment*; Wandruszka, *Leopold II.* I, 171 ff.

88. Wolf, *Marie Christine* I, 91 ff., esp. 99–100. On the myth of the Theresian age in Italy see Raponi, "Il mito."

89. On Leopold's constitutional project for Tuscany see Wandruszka, *Leopold II.* I, 368 ff.

90. The governorship was set up on the Netherlandish model; see, e.g., to Ferdinand, November 15, 1779, BKF II, 223.

91. Venturi, *Italy and the Enlightenment*; Wandruszka, *Österreich und Italien*; De Maddalena et al., Economia, Istituzioni; overviews in Capra, "Habsburg Italy"; Dipper, Die Mailänder Aufklärung.

92. See chapter 11, this volume.

93. Capra, "Habsburg Italy," 228–29.

94. E.g., to Ferdinand, BKF I, 146, 188–9, 204: good rulers are "*bons chrétiens, bons maris, bons pères, amis de leurs amis.*"

95. To Ferdinand, 1771, BKF I, 67, 77, 83.

96. To Beatrix, 1766, BKF III, 79. Maria Theresa's letters to Beatrix are edited by Arneth in BKF III.

97. Ferdinand and Beatrix had four children in Maria Theresa's lifetime, in 1773, 1775, 1776, 1779. They later had another five. Two were boys, one of whom died at the age of one.

98. To Herzelles, November 30, 1772, Kervyn de Lettenhove (Constantin), *Lettres inédites*, 41–42.

99. To Ferdinand, April to September 1771, BKF I, 65, 67, 68.

100. "*Je brûlais d'envie de recevoir des lettres,*" to Ferdinand, April 16, 1772, BKF I, 118.

101. To Ferdinand, May 26, 1773, BKF I, 206.

102. For example, by wearing a dressing gown. To Ferdinand, BKF I, 50, 126, 161, 165.

103. Leopold, "Stato della famiglia," 353.

104. To Ferdinand, BKF I, 104 ff., 113, 125, 128, 133–4, 141, 157, 162–3, 171, 176, 185, 207, 218, 234, 248, 254, 266, 270, 272, 276, 278, 281, 284, 315, 322, 346; see chapter 9, this volume.

105. E.g., to Beatrix, BKF III, 87, 88, 91, 92, 94, 95, 96, 97, 99, 104, 117.

106. The "fifth little Theresa" referred to the daughter of Marie Antoinette. On the sex of her grandchildren, see to Ferdinand, BKF I, 241–42, 276, 278, 281, 287, 300, 313, 321, 325–26, 345; to Beatrix, BKF III, 338–39, 383.

107. E.g., to Ferdinand, October 12, 1780, BKF II, 298–99.

108. E.g., to Ferdinand, BKF I, 232.

109. To Ferdinand, BKF I, 208–209, 226–27, 231, 310. She sent her grandchildren educators from Vienna so that they could learn German.

110. To the aya Countess Almesloë (1773), BKF IV, 127 ff.; to Ferdinand, October 5, 1773, BKF I, 231.

111. To Ferdinand, April 8, 1779, BKF II, 187; see to Beatrix, BKF III, 352, 355.

112. To Ferdinand, October 8, 1771, BKF I, 75–76.

113. To Ferdinand, BKF I, 75–76, 79, 89, 93 ff., 107, 110, 112, 117–8, 122–23, 130, 145, 153, 162, 171, 187, 231.

114. To Ferdinand, October 13, 1771, BKF I, 79 on the appointment of a man as equerry: she agreed with the choice but his religion and morals would need to be investigated: *"sur ces deux points aucune grâce."*

115. E.g., to Ferdinand, BKF I, 72–73, 76, 89, 169.

116. To Ferdinand, November 15, 1779, BKF II, 223, see 228.

117. To Carolina, early April 1768, BKF III, 32 ff., here 40, BAA, 233 ff.; see to Amalia, late June, 1769, BKF III, 1 ff., BAA, 242 ff.

118. For example, Carolina was not only the third child of this name but also the third choice as marriage candidate for the king of Naples; see chapter 9, this volume.

119. See Fraser, *Marie Antoinette*; Vinken, "Marie Antoinette."

120. In the literature, it is sometimes stated that Carolina had seventeen children because her stillbirth is not included.

121. Joseph II, Relation, ed. in Corti, *Ich, eine Tochter*, 725.

122. Marie Antoinette to Rosenberg, July 13, 1775, MACS II, 362.

123. Amalia to Rosenberg, Arneth, *Geschichte Maria Theresia's* VII, 394–95; but see Maria Theresa to Rosenberg, March 1772, BKF IV, 73–74.

124. To Enzenberg, March 23, 1768, BKF IV, 488. On Carolina see Corti, *Ich, eine Tochter*; Tamussino, *Des Teufels Großmutter*; Hausmann, *Herrscherin*; Arneth, *Geschichte Maria Theresia's* VII, 344 ff.; Wandruszka, *Leopold II.*, I, 204 ff.; on Naples see Imbruglia, *Naples in the Eighteenth Century*. Her marriage contract with the king of Naples, originally drawn up for Josepha, in KMT V, 237, 252.

125. To Enzenberg, March 23, 1768, BKF IV, 488. Neipperg had investigated the situation at court in Naples in 1763 and shared his impressions with Maria Theresa,; see Corti, *Ich, eine Tochter*, 19 ff. The Viennese emissary in Naples, Kaunitz junior, and his wife were further sources of information, see Wolf, Eleonore von Liechtenstein, 87.

126. To Carolina, early April, 1768, BKF III, 36.

127. Rosenberg to Leopold, in Corti, *Ich, eine Tochter*, 52.

128. Corti, *Ich, eine Tochter*, 52 ff.

129. Carolina to Countess Lerchenfeld, June 19, 1768, in Arneth, *Geschichte Maria Theresia's* VII, 553–54, see ibid., 366 ff.; Corti, *Ich, eine Tochter*, 62 ff.

130. Joseph II, Relation de Naples, April 21, 1769, ed. in Corti, *Ich, eine Tochter*, 721–46.

131. Prosch, *Leben*, see above, chapter 7.

132. Joseph II, Relation de Naples, in Corti, *Ich, eine Tochter*, 725 ff., 746.

133. Albert's accounts in Wolf, *Marie Christine* I, 102 ff.; Leopold and Rosenberg in Corti, *Ich, eine Tochter*, 52 ff. A sympathetic Leopold later noted in his secret diary that Carolina was "a good woman, but lacking in knowledge of the world, experience, patience, caution, and someone to advise her. She is very upset about the bad habits of the king, an excessive womanizer and badly brought up to boot. He makes her look after the business of government and the children's education all on her own." Leopold, "Stato della famiglia," in Wandruszka, *Leopold II.* I, 353.

134. Joseph to Leopold, MKC I, 216 ff.; Relation de Naples, in Corti, *Ich, eine Tochter*, 735 ff.

135. See Venturi, *Italy and the Enlightenment*, 198 ff.; Imbruglia, *Naples in the Eighteenth Century*; John Robertson, *The Case for Enlightenment. Scotland and Naples, 1680–1760*, Cambridge 2005.

136. Maria Theresa's instruction for Carolina, quoted in Corti, *Ich, eine Tochter*, 34–35; abbreviated in BKF III, 32 ff.

137. To Carolina, April 1768, BKF III, 37.

138. Corti, *Ich, eine Tochter*, 38–39.

139. Joseph to Leopold, April 16, 1768, MJC I, 216; Leopold to Maria Theresa, May 7, 1768, quoted in Corti, *Ich, eine Tochter*, 49.

140. Avis que donne l'impératrice, BKF III, 56 ff.; on the "epistolary war" between Spain, Naples, Parma, and Vienna see Hausmann, *Herrscherin*, 84–85.

141. Carolina to Maria Theresa, October 6, 1769, BKF III, 56 ff.

142. To Leopold, October 19, 1769, BKF I, 25 ff.; Leopold to Maria Theresa, October 30, 1769, BKF I, 30.

143. To Carolina, October 22, 1769, BKF III, 62 ff.; see to Court Councillor Posch, October 20, 1769, BKF IV, 326–27.

144. See the correspondence between Maria Theresa and Mercy, MACS I, 283–84, 288, 290–91, 296 ff., 308, 457–58; II, 482.

145. Corti, *Ich, eine Tochter*, 102 ff.

146. See KMT VIII, 171.

147. To Herzelles, November 30, 1772, Kervyn de Lettenhove (Constantin), *Lettres inédites*, 42.

148. To Countess Enzenberg, April 25, 1772, BKF IV, 505.

149. E.g., to Ferdinand, October 31, 1771, BKF I, 84; December 1, 1779, MACS III, 376–77; to Mercy, September 30, 1779, MACS III, 357.

150. To Maria Christina, March 22, 1780, BKF II, 467.

151. To Maria Christina, December 1775, BKF II, 378–79; to Ferdinand, February 24, 1780, BKF II, 253; but see to Marie Antoinette, October 3, 1773, MACS II, 52: Carolina had sacrificed far more.

152. Wandruszka, *Leopold II.*, I, 338.

153. To Beatrix, April 20, 1780, BKF III, 412.

154. On Amalia (or Marie-Amélie) see Arneth, *Geschichte Maria Theresia's* VII, 370 ff.; Pangels, *Die Kinder*, 286 ff.; Badinter, *Der Infant von Parma*.

155. On his conflict with the pope, which had led to excommunication, see above, chapter 11.

156. Badinter, *Der Infant von Parma*, 23 ff., 51 ff.; see the enthusiastic report of the Venetian emissary Renier in Arneth, *Geschichte Maria Theresia's* VII, 555.

157. To Amalia, late June, 1769, BKF III, 1 ff.

158. To Amalia, late June, 1769, BKF III, 13.

159. Badinter, *Der Infant von Parma*, 40 ff.

160. Badinter, *Der Infant von Parma*, 71 ff.; the quote is in Arneth, *Geschichte Maria Theresia's* 7, 556.

161. Arneth, *Geschichte Maria Theresia's* VII, 385–86.

162. Kaunitz to Mercy, October 30, 1769, Arnth/Flammermont, Correspondance secrète de Mercy-Argenteau II, 360–61.

163. See above.

164. Points pour Parme, to Rosenberg, October 1769, BKF IV, 67 ff.

165. To Rosenberg, October 1769, BKF IV, 68–69.

166. See Arneth, *Geschichte Maria Theresia's* VII, 396 ff.

167. To Rosenberg, March 1772, BKF IV, 20. See to Pergen, November 1796, BKF IV, 290: "Stop the German newspaper writer from touching on anything related to Chavelin's mission in his paper. . . . I am greatly embarrassed, Knebel and Rosenberg tell me nothing, Kaunitz also says he knows nothing." Perhaps her letters had been intercepted. "I confess I am greatly agitated."

168. The infante called him "*vile canaille*," see Mercy to Maria Theresa, October 15, 1771, MACS I, 231–32.

169. To Mercy, June 6, 1771, MACS I, 169–70.

170. Quoted in Arneth, *Geschichte Maria Theresia's* VII, 557.

171. To Ferdinand, October 15, 1772, BKF I, 159.

172. To Ferdinand, May 1772, BKF I, 121–22, see I, 123–4; to Maria Christina, May 2, 1772, BKF II, 374.

173. To Mercy, June 1, 1772, BKF I, 308.

174. Parma was an abiding theme in Maria Theresa's correspondence: e.g., to Ferdinand, BKF I, 25 ff., 69, 76 (October 1776: Amalia had become "the talk of all Europe"), 95, 98, 100, 140 (July 1772: no word from Parma), 170 (December 1772: she did not even know if Amalia was pregnant). To Court Councillor Posch, August 16, 1771, BKF IV, 329–330 ("I know nothing of Parma other than that my daughter is said to have a fever"). To Herzelles, November 30, 1772, Kervyn de Lettenhove (Constantin), *Lettres inédites*, 42.

175. As when Joseph was resisting her plans for him to remarry; see chapter 9, this volume.

176. To Leopold, December 19, 1772, BKF I, 32 ff.; see the correspondence between Maria Theresa and Mercy, 1771–72, MACS I, 169, 181, 273, 287, 300, 316, 319, 331, 332–33, 342–43, 351–52.

177. To Mercy, handwritten letter, November 30, 1772, MACS I, 379–80.

178. To Ferdinand, December 3, 1772, BKF I, 167; to Mercy, November 30, 1772, MACS I, 379–80.

179. Joseph to Leopold, December 1772, MJC I, 388–89.

180. To Ferdinand, July 15, 1773, BKF I, 217–18, see I, 225.

181. To Kaunitz, July 10, 1773, in Arneth, *Geschichte Maria Theresia's* VII, 558–59.

182. To Ferdinand, August 12, 1773, BKF I, 221–22.

183. To Mercy, July 17, 1773, MACS II, 10 ff.; August 2, 1773, MACS II, 16; but see the earlier letters to Mercy, February 1, 1773, MACS I, 408; May 4, 1773, MACS I, 448.

184. To Countess Enzenberg, October 16, 1773, BKF IV, 508; to Marie Antoinette, August 29, 1773, MACS II, 34; to Mercy, September 14, 1773, MACS II, 37; see KMT VIII, 53, 116.

185. Badinter, *Der Infant von Parma*, 115 ff.

186. To Ferdinand, BKF I, 270–71, 280, 285, 311–12, BKF II, 35, 105, 131, 142, 251; to Beatrix, August 5, 1776, BKF III, 241. See Leopold's diary entry from 1778: "She [the empress] is extremely upset about Parma and wishes to hear nothing more about it," Wandruszka, *Leopold II.* I, 338.

187. To Maria Christina, December 1775, BKF II, 380–81.

188. To Maria Christina, December 1775, BKF II, 380–81; see to Leopold, December 19, 1772, BKF I, 33–34: the couple were more ridiculous than sinful.

189. Wolf, *Marie Christine* I, 123 ff. Leopold later called Amalia "very unhappy due to her weakness and that of her husband, her own extravagances, debts, and poor conduct," Wandruszka, *Leopold II.* I, 352–53.

190. To Ferdinand, October 19, 1780, BKF II, 304 ff.; see Joseph's harsh reaction to the idea of Amalia returning to Vienna: to Maria Theresa, October 20, 1780, MJC III, 317–8. See also Maria Theresa to Maximilian, October 18, 1780, Reinöhl, Briefe, 43: "*elle* [Amalia] *fut tout au monde pour venir ici*"; October 28, 1780, ibid., 47: "*votre soeur n'est pas bien ni de corp ni d'esprit....*"

191. To Beatrix, October 30, 1780, BKF III, 439; to Ferdinand, November 3, 1780, BKF II, 308.

192. Arneth, *Geschichte Maria Theresia's* VII, 416; Pangels, *Die Kinder*, 320. Just as with Marie Antoinette, rumors of the couple's supposed sexual excesses also played a role; see Badinter, *Der Infant von Parma*, 114 ff.

193. See Lever, *Marie Antoinette*; Fraser, *Marie Antoinette*; Félix, *Louis XVI et Marie-Antoinette*; Duprat, *Marie-Antoinette*; Kaiser, *Who's Afraid*. Unlike Maria Theresa, Antonia has attracted considerable interest from women's and gender studies, e.g., Maza, *Private Lives*; Hunt, *Family Romance*; Cosandey, *La Reine*; Baeque, *Body Politic*; Goodman, *Marie Antoinette*; Wolff, *Hapsburg Letters*; Schulte, "Madame ma Chère Fille"; Vinken, "Marie Antoinette"; Gruder, "The Question."

194. Landes, *Marie Antoinette's Remise*; on her marriage and marriage contract see KMT VII, 4 ff., 14 ff., 200 ff., 225 ff., 235 ff. See the portrait by Elisabeth Vigée-Lebrun, color plate 29.

195. To Marie Antoinette, April 21, 1770, MACS I, 1 ff.; May 4, 1770, MACS I, 6 ff.

196. To Mercy, May 24, 1770, MACS I, 8.

197. Arneth/Geffroy, Introduction, MACS I, 1 ff.; further Gossi, Mercy-Argenteau als Vermittler; Helmut Neuhaus, Mercy-Argenteau, Florimund Claudius Graf von, in NDB 17 (1994), 127–8. After Mercy was recalled from Paris when Leopold came to the throne in 1790, he was one of the few who sought until the last to save the queen.

198. Mathieu Jacques Abbé de Vermond (1735–1806) had been sent to Vienna by Choiseul, the architect of the marriage pact, to prepare Marie Antoinette for her task. He clearly enjoyed the confidence of all three parties.

199. Quoted in Gossi, Mercy-Argenteau als Vermittler, 20.

200. Maria Theresa's instructions to Mercy, May 24, 1770, MACS I, 8 ff.; end of July 1773, MACS II, 13–14.

201. To Mercy, June 16, 1774, MACS II, 176.

202. Mercy, too, preserved the correspondence intact. From his posthumous papers, it eventually ended up in the imperial private library. Remarkably, the correspondence remained a secret until 1864, when it was transferred by Emperor Franz Joseph to the House, Court, and State Archive and—surreptitiously purged of all "offensive" passages—published by Arneth. On the publication history see Arneth/Geffroy, Introduction, MACS I; Christoph, *Maria Theresia: Geheimer Briefwechsel*, Einleitung. Most of the passages on the consummation of the marriage omitted by Arneth and Geffroy are restored in Girard, Correspondance; Christoph, *Maria Theresia: Geheimer Briefwechsel*, reinstates them all. Stefan Zweig used the complete material for

his Freud-inspired, novelistic account of Marie Antoinette's life story (*Marie Antoinette: The Portrait of an Average Woman*, Leipzig 1932).

203. Strategic discussions on letters to Marie Antoinette, e.g., MACS I, 28, 220, 230, 243, 280, 341, 379. Maria Theresa quoted some of Mercy's phrases verbatim in her letters to Marie Antoinette, e.g., September 1, 1779, MACS III, 348 ff.

204. E.g., Mercy to Maria Theresa, August 16, 1775, MACS II, 372.

205. To Marie Antoinette, May 8, 1771, MACS I, 160.

206. To Marie Antoinette, April 21, 1770, MACS I, 4–5.

207. Marie Antoinette to Rosenberg, July 13, 1775, MACS II, 362 ff., unexpurgated in Christoph, *Maria Theresia: Geheimer Briefwechsel*, 154 ff.; Mercy to Maria Theresa, August 16, 1775, MACS II, 370 ff., Maria Theresa to Mercy, August 31, 1775, MACS II, 373; see further below.

208. To Count Rosenberg, late February 1769, BKF IV, 63 ff.

209. To Ferdinand, September 14, 1779, BKF II, 212; see also BKF I, 129; II, 306.

210. To Ferdinand, December 5, 1776, BKF II, 56.

211. To Joseph, June 26, 1778, MJC II, 305.

212. Kaunitz to Mercy, November 11, 1768 in Arneth, *Geschichte Maria Theresia's* VII, 563–64, see Arneth/Flammermont, *Correspondance secrète* II, 343–44; Mercy to Kaunitz, ibid., II, 375.

213. Mercy to Kaunitz, December 17, 1770, Arneth/Flammermont, *Correspondance secrète* II, 381–82.

214. E.g., Kaunitz to Mercy, February 10, 1772, Arneth/Flammermont, *Correspondance secrète* II, 404; ibid., 360–61, 394; see also Kaunitz's memorandum on the role that Marie Antoinette—now Queen of France—would play in foreign policy, June 1774, ibid. II, 453 ff.

215. To Marie Antoinette, January 13, 1773, MACS I, 407. It does not seem to have occurred to her that her formulation was self-contradictory.

216. See, e.g., Robert Vellusig, Schriftliche Gespräche. Briefkultur im 18. Jahrhundert, Vienna/Cologne/Weimar 2000; Weber, Zwischen Arkanum und Öffentlichkeit; Schulte, "'Madame ma Chère Fille'"; Wolff, Hapsburg Letters; see also chapter 11, this volume, on Isabella of Parma's correspondence with Maria Christina.

217. To Albert von Sachsen-Teschen, Wolf, *Aus dem Hofleben*, 347.

218. To Ferdinand (c. 1762), BKF I, 55–56; March 6, 1767, BKF I, 60; to Beatrix, January 4, 1779, BKF II, 340; to her grandson (and eventual emperor) Franz, October 17, 1779, BKF I, 49 ff.; to Marie Antoinette, February 10, 1771, MACS I, 129–30.

219. To Ferdinand, March 6, 1767, BKF I, 55–56, 59–60; to Albert von Sachsen-Teschen, Wolf, *Aus dem Hofleben*, 347; to Maximilian, May 4, 1775, Reinöhl, Briefe, 26; to Marie Antoinette (with reference to Louis XVI), June 16, 1774, MACS II, 180.

220. *Monsieur, Herr* and *Madame, Frau* were aristocratic forms of address; these terms were used within the family to communicate highborn status.

221. To Ferdinand, October 8, 1771, BKF I, 75–76. This reflects an understanding of the term "political" that had been widespread since the seventeenth century; see Otto Brunner, Werner Conze, Reinhart Koselleck, eds., *Geschichtliche Grundbegriffe*, vol. 4, Stuttgart 1978, s. v. Politik III: Das Politikverständnis der Neuzeit, 807–74, esp. 826 ff.

222. Kaiser, Who's Afraid.—Buddruss, *Die französische Deutschlandpolitik*, 134 ff., barely mentions Marie Antoinette's influence.

223. Kaiser, *Ambiguous Identities*. The nine-day public festivities, put on at a cost of over five million livres, was ill-fated from the outset. Mass panic broke out in Paris with well over a hundred dead and injured; see KMT VII, 26, 242. Cröy, *Tagebuch*, 241–42, mentions only that there were not enough windows for spectators.

224. E.g., Campan, *Mémoires* I, 73–74; see Cröy, *Tagebuch*, 236 ff.; KMT VIII, 51, 61, 207–208.

225. To Marie Antoinette, April 21, 1770, MACS I, 1 ff.

226. Campan, *Mémoires* I, 37.

227. Mercy to Maria Theresa, January 16, 1773, MACS I, 404.

228. E.g., Marie Antoinette to Maria Theresa, November 12, 1775, MACS II, 393.

229. The topic has been much discussed, see, e.g., Lever, *Marie Antoinette*, 50–51, 74 ff., 164 ff.; Duprat, *Marie Antoinette*, 89 ff.

230. E.g., Christoph, *Maria Theresia: Geheimer Briefwechsel*, 23–24, 36, 62, 107, 239, 244, 250, 311. The codeword's origin is unclear. There was a Bavarian General Krottendorf, commander of Ingolstadt from 1742, who fought on the opposing side in the War of Succession (see Wurzbach, *Neues allgemeines Adelslexikon* V, 303). Maria Theresa was presumably also referring to a missing period when Maria Theresa sent her daughter-in-law Beatrix—one year into her marriage and still not pregnant—the enigmatic salutation: *"un heureux Alleluja*, but no red Easter egg"; to Ferdinand, April 16, 1772, BKF I, 119.

231. To Marie Antoinette, February 10, 1771, Christoph, *Maria Theresia: Geheimer Briefwechsel*, 35; May 8, 1771, ibid., 40; July 9, 1771, ibid., 49; August 17, 1771, ibid., 52–53; see the correspondence with Mercy, MACS I, 44, 81, 137, 167–68, 238, 247–48, 328, 388.

232. To Marie Antoinette, October 31, 1771, Christoph, *Maria Theresia: Geheimer Briefwechsel*, 65–66. See also Arneth/Flammermont, *Correspondance secrète*, 366, 384–85; further sources cited in Lever, *Marie Antoinette*, 50–51, 57.

233. Marie Antoinette to Maria Theresa, October 13, 1771, Christoph, *Maria Theresia: Geheimer Briefwechsel*, 60.

234. Marie Antoinette to Maria Theresa, November 15, 1771, Christoph, *Maria Theresia: Geheimer Briefwechsel*, 64; December 18, 1771, ibid., 66–67; July 17, 1772, ibid., 73; January 13, 1773, ibid., 81; April 18, 1773, ibid., 91–92.

235. Marie Antoinette to Maria Theresa, March 15, 1775, Christoph, *Maria Theresia: Geheimer Briefwechsel*, 90; May 17, 1773, ibid., 95–96; July 17, 1773, ibid., 100.

236. To Marie Antoinette, November 30, 1774, Christoph, *Maria Theresia: Geheimer Briefwechsel*, 140; see also 146 ff.

237. Marie Antoinette reported this to her own mother: December 15, 1775, Christoph, *Maria Theresia: Geheimer Briefwechsel*, 172. See Lever, *Marie Antoinette*, 146–47; see Gruder, "The Question," for further examples.

238. Marie Antoinette to Maria Theresa, June 22, 1775, Christoph, *Maria Theresia: Geheimer Briefwechsel*, 149; see ibid., 165, 170, 172, 176, 186, 209. She had a concealed passageway built between the apartments so that the king's nocturnal visits to her chamber (or an absence thereof) were not a matter of public knowledge.

239. Marie Antoinette to Maria Theresa, December 17, 1774, Christoph, *Maria Theresia: Geheimer Briefwechsel*, 141; July 13, 1776, ibid., 186; see Mercy to Maria Theresa, December 18, 1774, MACS II, 274.

240. Marie Antoinette to Maria Theresa, August 30, 1777, Christoph, *Maria Theresia: Geheimer Briefwechsel*, 221; Mercy to Maria Theresa, September 12, 1777, MACS III, 113; Louis XVI personally thanked Joseph, December 22, 1777, Christoph, *Maria Theresia: Geheimer Briefwechsel*, 234; see Joseph to Leopold, October 4, 1777, HHStA Hausarchiv FA, Sbd. 7, quoted in Beales, "Joseph II's Rêveries" I, 374–75; Lever, Marie Antoinette, 169. On Joseph's journey to France see Mercy to Maria Theresa, MACS III, 49–83; Joseph to Leopold, MJC II, 34–35, 123 ff., 130 ff., 133 ff.; Joseph's instructions for his sister, May 29, 1777, in Arneth, Marie Antoinette, Joseph II. und Leopold II., 4–18.

241. To Marie Antoinette, October 3, 1777, Christoph, *Maria Theresia: Geheimer Briefwechsel*, 226 (omitted in MAS III, 118).

242. In reaction to the king's official handwritten announcement of the pregnancy, to Marie Antoinette, May 17, 1778, MACS III, 201.

243. To Marie Antoinette, August 23, 1778, MACS III, 245.

244. To Marie Antoinette, May 1, 1779, Christoph, *Maria Theresia: Geheimer Briefwechsel*, 292, see ibid., 293, 306, 308, 309; MACS III, 502, 510, 512, 518.

245. To Marie Antoinette, April 21, 1770, MACS I, 4; to Mercy, August 1, 1770, MACS I, 28.

246. E.g., Mercy to Maria Theresa, February 25, 1771, MACS I, 134 (confident that she would sway the dauphin); Maria Theresa to Marie Antoinette, February 10, 1771, MACS I, 128–29 (a good word for the former French emissary in Vienna, Durfort); May 8, 1771, MACS I, 159–60 (greater engagement for the Germans at court); to Mercy, July 2, 1772, MACS I, 320–21 (concern for good relations in view of the tricky Polish policy); correspondence between Mercy and Maria Theresa, August—October 1773, MACS II, 31–32, 35–36, 46 (too little influence, particularly with Rohan); later, during the War of the Bavarian Succession, the influence became especially virulent, see, e.g., MACS III, 181 ff. Other examples could be cited. Mercy's relative confidence that Maria Theresa could be steered in the direction desired by Vienna was not entirely selfless, given his obvious interest in improving his own standing in Vienna.

247. To Marie Antoinette, September 30, 1771, MACS I, 217 ff.

248. Marie Antoinette to Maria Theresa, July 9, 1770, MACS I, 17.

249. To Mercy, May 18, 1774, MACS II, 149; to Ferdinand, BKF I, 276–77.

250. Memorandum from Kaunitz, ed., in Correspondance secretè de Mercy-Argenteau II, 453 ff. Mercy had explicitly requested such instruction: to Maria Theresa, May 7, 1774, MACS II, 137–38.

251. KMT VIII, 28. Kaiser, Who's Afraid, 254 ff., argues that Marie Antoinette's actual influence on the king was slight.

252. To Marie Antoinette, June 16, 1774, MACS II, 179 ff.

253. Marie Antoinette to Rosenberg, July 13, 1775, MACS II, 362 ff.

254. Handwritten letter to Mercy, July 31, 1775, MACS II, 360.

255. To Marie Antoinette, July 30, 1775, Christoph, *Maria Theresia: Geheimer Briefwechsel*, 160 (not in MACS); see Mercy to Maria Theresa, August 16, 1775, MACS II, 370 ff.; Maria Theresa to Mercy, August 31, 1775, MACS II, 373.

256. Joseph to Marie Antoinette, July 30, 1775, Arneth, *Marie Antoinette, Joseph II. und Leopold II.*, 1 ff., here 2.

257. Kaiser, "Who's Afraid"; Buddruss, *Die französische Deutschlandpolitik*, 211 ff.; Lever, *Marie Antoinette*, 178 ff.

258. Summary in "The Question."

259. Mercy to Maria Theresa, May 16, 1776, MASC II, 446 ff.; to Marie Antoinette, May 1776, MACS II, 449 ff.

260. To Marie Antoinette, July 16, 1774, MACS II, 204 ff.

261. Leopold, "Stato della famiglia," 338.

262. To Maximilian, April 1774, BKF II, 317.

263. Arneth, *Geschichte Maria Theresia's* VII, 477 ff., X, 692 ff.; Braubach, *Maria Theresias jüngster Sohn*, 24.

264. On the plan for Maximilian's education, see Joseph to Maria Theresa, July 22, 1775, MJC II, 72 ff.; instructions for Maximilian, 1774, BKF II, 317 ff.

265. Wertheimer, "Zwei Schilderungen," 215.

266. KMT VIII, 16–17.

267. To Rosenberg, April 1774, BKF IV, 80 ff., with instructions for the confessor and personal physician; on traveling incognito see KMT VIII, 202–303.

268. To Maximilian, 1774, BKF II, 317 ff., esp. 322, 337; October 7, 1775, Reinöhl, *Briefe*, 33.

269. Leopold's report on Maximilian, 1775, ed. in Varrentrapp, "Bericht," 1 ff.

270. To Ferdinand, BKF I, 282–83, similarly ibid., 271, 274, 278, 280, 284, 294, 297.

271. To Ferdinand, August 1779, BKF II, 201, 206–207, 209, 268; to Beatrix, April 1779, BKF III, 354.

272. Braubach, Max Franz, 39 ff.

273. Joseph to Leopold, November 14, 1779, MJC III, 236; December 14, 1779, MJC III, 239.

274. To Beatrix, June 26, 1780, BKF III, 425; August 28, 1780, BKF III, 434.

275. Braubach, Max Franz, 55 ff., quote on 63; on Maria Theresa's strategy towards ecclesiastical principalities in the Empire, see chapter 4, this volume.

276. Braubach, Max Franz, 64.

277. To Maximilian, September 22, 1780, Reinöhl, *Briefe*, 34 ff.

278. KMT III, 190–91.

279. See Pangels, *Die Kinder*, 238; Maria Theresa occasionally found words of praise for Elisabeth as a child: to Countess Trautson, van Rhyn, "Unveröffentlichte Briefe," 181.

280. Arneth, *Geschichte Maria Theresia's* VII, 269 ff.; Pangels, *Die Kinder*, 223 ff.

281. To Herzelles, November 30, 1772, Kervyn de Lettenhove (Constantin), *Lettres inédites*, 43.

282. Mercy to Kaunitz, December 29, 1768, Arneth/Flammermont, *Correspondance secrète* II, 347 ff.

283. See Kaunitz to Mercy, February 24, 1769, quoted in Arneth, *Geschichte Maria Theresia's* VII, 540. See also chapter 9, this volume, on Joseph II's second choice of bride.

284. Mercy to Kaunitz, February 4, 1769, quoted in Arneth, *Geschichte Maria Theresia's* VII, 540.

285. In 1780 there was an unfounded rumor that Elisabeth would marry Duke Charles Eugene of Württemberg. Maria Theresa assumed that Frederick II had launched it from sheer malice; see BKF II, 300.

286. See Leopold's criticism, "Stato della famiglia," Wandruszka, *Leopold II.*, I, 341, 349. In the 1764 testament a prebend had been earmarked for her, while the 1767 testament considered her as a bride for the Duke of Chablais, see Arneth, *Geschichte Maria Theresia's* X, 732–33.

287. To Maria Christina, May 29, 1780, BKF II, 461–62.

288. Swinburne, *Courts* I, 342–43.

289. To Maria Christina, February 1, 1776, BKF II, 396, see BKF II, 392.

290. Leopold, "Stato della famiglia," Wandruszka, *Leopold II.*, I, 349. Joseph called her practically insane in a letter to Leopold, Beales, "Joseph II's Rêveries" II, 54.

291. Wertheimer, "Zwei Schilderungen," 215–16.

292. On Marianna see Innerkofler, *Eine große Tochter*; Pangels, *Die Kinder*, 23 ff.; only brief references in Arneth, *Geschichte Maria Theresia's* IV, 153–54, VII, 245–45; further Kernbauer/Zahradnik, *Höfische Porträtkultur*, on Marianna's posthumous papers in Klagenfurt.

293. KMT II, 197 (December 1747).

294. KMT IV, 77–78.

295. On the ceremonial inauguration see KMT VI, 164–65.

296. Swinburne, *Courts* I, 344; Wertheimer, "Zwei Schilderungen," 215; KMT VI, 204.

297. No one could understand Marianna's wish to retreat to the desolate convent in Klagenfurt—see Maria Theresa to Ferdinand, October 3, 1771, BKF I, 73; Joseph to Leopold, July 3, 1775, MJC II, 61. On the convent see Innerkoßler, *Eine große Tochter*, 12 ff.; Pangels, *Die Kinder*, 31 ff.; Arneth, *Geschichte Maria Theresia's* IV, 153–54. She is remembered in Klagenfurt to this day; even a wax figurine of Marianna in the cloak her mother was wearing at her death can be seen there; see Koschatzky, *Maria Theresia* (catalog), 341.

298. "Selbstbekenntnis," printed in Innerkofler, *Eine große Tochter*, 53–58; "Tagebuch," ibid., 61–72.

299. "Selbstbekenntnis," Innerkofler, *Eine große Tochter*, 58.

300. "Selbstbekenntnis," Innerkofler, *Eine große Tochter*, 53–54.

301. "Selbstbekenntnis," Innerkofler, *Eine große Tochter*, 54–55, 57.

302. "Selbstbekenntnis," Innerkofler, *Eine große Tochter*, 57.

303. "Selbstbekenntnis," Innerkofler, *Eine große Tochter*, 57–58.

304. "Tagebuch," Innerkofler, *Eine große Tochter*, 61 ff., here 64.

305. Wandruszka, *Leopold II.*, I, 341, 348; Joseph called her a harpy in a letter to Leopold, Beales, "Joseph II's Rêveries" II, 54.

306. Wandruszka, *Leopold II.*, I, 348.

307. Les charmes de la fausse amitié, ed. in Hrazky, "Die Personlichkeit," 195–96.

308. "Tagebuch," Innerkofler, *Eine große Tochter*, 66.

309. "Tagebuch," Innerkofler, *Eine große Tochter*, 74.

310. "Tagebuch," Innerkofler, *Eine große Tochter*, 69.

311. E.g., to Herzelles, November 30, 1772, Kervyn de Lettenhove (Constantin), *Lettres inédites*, 43.

312. To Ferdinand, January 28, 1773, BKF I, 178, one of very few more extensive statements about Marianna.

313. Leopold, "Stato della famiglia," in Wandruszka, *Leopold II.*, I, 341, 348.

314. Report of Archduchess Marianna on the death of her mother, ed. in Innerkoßler, *Eine große Tochter*, 76–85; Vehse, *Maria Theresia*, 205–15; see also Arneth, *Geschichte Maria Theresia's* X, 719 ff.; Pangels, *Die Kinder*, 54 ff., see also further below.

315. Joseph to the aya Marquise d'Herzelles in an instruction on the education of his daughter Therese, 1766, quoted in Pangels, *Die Kinder*, 45–46.

316. This is evident throughout in Joseph's letters to Leopold, e.g., MJC II, 44–45, 60, 117 ff.

317. In German translation in Wandruszka, *Leopold II.* I, 334–54.

318. See chapter 9, this volume.

319. Wandruszka, *Leopold II.* I, 354 ff.

320. Leopold, "Stato della famiglia," in Wandruszka, *Leopold II.* I, 334 ff.

321. Leopold, "Stato della famiglia," in Wandruszka, *Leopold II.* I, 335, 339–40.

322. Leopold, "Stato della famiglia," in Wandruszka, in *Leopold II.* I, 342–43, similarly 345.

323. Leopold, "Stato della famiglia," in Wandruszka, *Leopold II.* I, 347.

324. Codicil to her will, August 1, 1778, Schlitter, *Das Testament*, 154–55; BAA, 466. Arneth, *Geschichte Maria Theresia's* X, 731 ff., does not mention this stipulation when discussing her will and interment.

325. To Ferdinand, September 30, 1779, BKF II, 213. On her increasing isolation and bitterness see, e.g., ibid., 210, 212; to Maximilian, October 1, 1780, Reinöhl, *Briefe*, 38; to Beatrix, November 2, 1778, BKF III, 331–32.

326. To Ferdinand, April 14, 1779, BKF II, 187 ff.

327. E.g., to Joseph, August 9, 1778, MJC III, 32 ("*ne me haïssez pas*"). On the Russian trip, e.g., to Ferdinand, BKF II, 257, 262, 267; to Marie Antoinette, November 3, 1780, MACS III, 482. A planned journey to England never came about, much to Maria Theresa's relief.

328. To Maximilian, October 14, 1780, Reinöhl, *Briefe*, 42; to Ferdinand, October 17, 1780, BKF II, 301–302; to Mercy, November 3, 1780, MACS III, 484–85.

329. To Marie Antoinette, November 3, 1780, MACS III, 482; to Ferdinand, November 15, 1780, BKF II, 310 ff.; see already October 5, 1780, BKF II, 297–98, and August 8, 1780, BKF II, 288: she was suffering from the heat and had submitted to a bleeding but assured her son that all was well.

330. To Beatrix, November 20, BKF III, 443, see 441–42; likewise to Maria Christina, November 20, 1780, Wolf, *Marie Christine* I, 166–67.

331. To Mercy, November 3, 1780, MACS III, 484–85. This was her last letter to Versailles.

332. Report of Archduchess Marianna on the death of her mother, ed. in Innerkoßler, *Eine große Tochter*, 76–85, as well as in Vehse, *Maria Theresia*, 205–15 (quoted in what follows); see the last letters to Maria Christina in Wolf, *Maria Christina* I, 165 ff.; Albert von Sachsen-Teschen, "Mémoires de ma vie," quoted in Arneth, *Geschichte Maria Theresia's* X, 837–38; HHStA OMeA, Zeremonialprotokolle 35, fol. 366 ff. Further reports on the empress's death from second hand: Lettre de la Princesse Leopoldine Liechtenstein sur les derniers jours de l'Imperatrice Marie-Thérèse, ed. in Wolf, *Marie Christine* II, 221–28; anonymous report to Count Balassa, ed. in Killay, *Geheimbericht*, 343–44; Cobenzl's memoirs, Arneth, "Graf Philipp Cobenzl," 131; Pichler, *Denkwürdigkeiten*, 60 ff.; Sonnenfels' first lecture after the death of Maria Theresa, in *Sammlung merkwürdiger Aufsätze* I, 24–46; Coxe, *History* III, 480–81. See Arneth, *Geschichte*

Maria Theresia's X, 719 ff.; Hawlik–van de Water, *Der schöne Tod*; Pangels, *Die Kinder*, 54 ff.; Hertel, "Kontinuität."

333. Marianna's report in Vehse, *Maria Theresia*, 208.

334. Albert von Sachsen-Teschen, "Mémoires de ma vie," quoted in Arneth, *Geschichte Maria Theresia's* X, 837; see Joseph to Leopold, 23–27 November, 1780, MJC III, 322 ff.; Joseph to Kaunitz, November 28, 1780, Beer, *Joseph II*, 20.

335. Marianna's report in Vehse, *Maria Theresia*, 209.

336. Hertel, "Kontinuität," 256.

337. To Leopold, November 27, 1780, BAA, 520; see Joseph to Leopold, November 27, 1780, MJC III, 324.

338. HHStA OMeA, Zeremonialprotokolle 35, fol. 366v.

339. Marianna's report in Vehse, *Maria Theresia*, 210.

340. Marianna's report in Vehse, *Maria Theresia*, 211.

341. Marianna's report in Vehse, *Maria Theresia*, 212.

342. HHStA OMeA, Zeremonialprotokolle 35, fol. 371r.

343. In 1774 she had already written to Maximilian: "I have chosen you to be the one to close my eyes," BKF II, 317.

344. Marianna's report in Vehse, *Maria Theresia*, 213.

345. Marianna's report in Vehse, *Maria Theresia*, 214.

346. Liechtenstein, "Lettre," in Wolf, *Marie Christine II*, 226; similarly Kállay, "Ein Geheimbericht," 343; Sonnenfels, Erste Vorlesung, in *Sammlung merkwürdiger Aufsätze* I, 35.

347. Liechtenstein, Lettre, in Wolf, *Marie Christine* II, 222, 224. Other last words in the *Sammlung merkwürdiger Aufsätze.*

348. Marianna's report in Vehse, *Maria Theresia und ihr Hof*, 215.

349. Liechtenstein, Lettre, in Wolf, *Marie Christine* II, 224. A man of Enlightenment like Cobenzl pointed out that she had died piously but not in an "excess of devotion," Arneth, "Graf Philipp Cobenzl," 131. For Wraxall, *Historical and Posthumous Memoirs* I, 274–75, her death raised her above Frederick II and Roman emperors such as Augustus, Hadrian, and Vespasian.

350. Ibid II, 222–23; see, e.g., Albert, "Mémoires de ma vie," quoted in Arneth, *Geschichte Maria Theresia's* X, 838.

351. Marianna's report in Vehse, *Maria Theresia und ihr Hof*, 211–12; Cobenzl furnished a similar report: Arneth, "Graf Philipp Cobenzl," 131: "*Voilà quinze années que je me préparais à mourir; je n'ais jamais imagine qu'on mourrait si facilement.*"

352. Albert von Sachsen-Teschen, "Mémoires de ma vie," quoted in Arneth *Geschichte Maria Theresia's* X, 838.

353. E.g., Croÿ's *Geheimes Tagebuch*, 382–83.

354. Ligne, *Fragments* II, 25, 164.

355. Arneth, "Graf Philipp Cobenzl," 131.

356. Ligne, *Fragments* I, 244; see Mansel, *Prince of Europe*, 92.

357. Frederick II to d'Alembert, January 6, 1781, Preuß, *Oeuvres de Frédéric de Grand XXV*, 191–92: "*J'ai cependant donné des regrets à la mort de l'Impératrice-Reine; elle a fait honneur au trône et à son sexe; je lui ai fait la guerre, et je n'ai jamais été son ennemi.*"

358. Hersche, *Der Spätjansenismus*, 158.

359. German-language speeches and poems of mourning in *Sammlung merkwürdiger Aufsätze*; on French eulogies and their in part opposed interpretations, see Michaud, "Laudatio" (there even on p. 685: *image de Dieu*); Loupès, *Telle mère, tel fils.*

360. Christoph Martin Wieland, *Teutscher Merkur*, 1781; eulogies by Klopstock, Claudius, and others in *Deutsches Museum*, Leipzig 1781, pt. 2, 97–98, 178 ff.; Georg Christoph Lichtenberg, "Frankreichs Trauer über Maria Theresia," in *Göttinger Taschen-Calender 1782*, 88–97.

361. Sommer, *Hieronymus Löschenkohl*, 17, 21 ff. An allegorical engraving on Maria Theresa's death, e.g., in Michaud, "Laudatio," 689.

362. Marianna's report in Vehse, *Maria Theresia*, 205.

363. Together with her insignia of rule: the archducal hat, the crowns of Hungary and Bohemia, and—astonishingly—the imperial house crown, which strictly speaking was reserved for Joseph alone. The imperial crown did not come into question; it was safeguarded in Nuremberg and only taken out for coronations. On the mourning ceremonial see Wolf, *Marie Christine* I, 172 ff.; Hertel, "Kontinuität"; Pangerl/Scheutz/Winkelbauer, *Der Wiener Hof*, 529–30; Liselotte Popelka, "Freuden- und Trauerzurüstungen," 355–62.

364. Schlitter, *Das Testament*, 154; Liechtenstein, "Lettre," in Wolf, *Marie Christine* II, 225; on the different versions of the will made between 1754 and 1780 see Arneth, *Geschichte Maria Theresia's* X, 727; Beales, "Joseph II's Rêveries" II, 53 ff.

365. Schlitter, *Das Testament*, 152 ff.

366. Additional notice for Paymaster Mayer, missing in Schlitter's edition of the will, in Arneth, *Geschichte Maria Theresia's* X, 727.

367. Wagner, "Royal Graces," 22 ff.; Wagner, "Das geheime Kammerzahlamt," 174–75.

368. Joseph to Leopold, January 3, 1781, Arneth, *Joseph II und Leopold*, 1; January 31, Feburary 8 and 12, 1781, ibid., I, 5 ff.; on his first measures in general see Beales, "Joseph II's Rêveries" II, 68 ff.

369. Johann Pezzl, *Faustino oder das philosophische Jahrhundert*, [Zurich] 1783, 331–32.

15. Epilogue

1. Dutens, *Mémoires*, 343 ff.; see the characterizations of Maria Theresa, e.g., in Arneth, *Die Relationen* I, 280–81, 304–305; Hinrichs, *Friedrich der Große*; Ranke, "Maria Theresia und ihr Hof"; Arnheim, "Das Urtheil"; Sorel, *Recueil des instructions*, 347; Wraxall, *Historical and the Posthumous Memoirs* II, 297 ff., 342 ff.; Coxe, *History* III, 482–83; Swinburne, *Courts* I, 341–42; Wertheimer, "Zwei Schilderungen," 213–14; Moore, *A View* II, 265–66; Guibert, *Journal* I, 283–84 (despite a comparatively critical view); Coke, *Letters* III and IV, passim; not to mention the eulogists and biographers: Sonnenfels, *Rede*; Anon., *Untersuchung der Frage*; Richter, *Lebens- und Staats-Geschichte*; Fromageot, *Histoire*; Jumel, *Éloge.*

2. Anon., *Princeps in compendio*, Latin first edition 1632, a German translation appeared in 1713. A new bilingual edition with commentary in Notker Hammerstein, ed., *Staatslehre der Frühen Neuzeit*, Frankfurt am Main, 1991, 483–40, 1170–71. Earlier authorial attributions to Emperor Ferdinand II or Ferdinand III are no longer accepted today. On fear of God and steadfastness see Points I, II, and IX.

3. See chapter 5, this volume ("I am no longer what I was").

4. Wertheimer, "Zwei Schilderungen," 214.

5. The judgment was made by a French observer in 1770, quoted in Wertheimer, "Zwei Schilderungen," 214. The Venetian emissary Erizzo used almost exactly the same words in 1745 when commenting on the expulsion of the Bohemian Jews, in Arneth, *Geschichte Maria Theresia's* III, 45.

6. See chapter 4, this volume ("Francis I").

7. E.g., to Court Councillor Greiner, Arneth, "Maria Theresia und der Hofrath von Greiner," 31; see to Countess Trautson: "I am quick to anger," van Rhyn, "Unveröffentliche Briefe," 268; on her regret over rows with Francis Stephen and Joseph, see chapter 4 ("Francis I") and chapter 10, both in this volume ("Trials of Strength," "The Regency Dilemma").

8. KMT II, 330; see KMT II, 51, 65, 100, 170–71, 178–79, 182, 184, 200–201, 213, 249; KMT IV, 90, 92, 98, 100, 123, 141 ff.; so too the judgment of Isabella, Badinter, *Lettres*; Wolf, *Marie Christine* II, 21–22; impulsive scenes are described in Hinrichs, *Friedrich der Große*, 63, 83; KMT I, 198 ff.; KMT II, 178; KMT III, 53.

9. *Princeps in compendio*, Point III.

10. *Princeps in compendio*, Point XIV.

11. See chapter 2, this volume; Winterling, "Hof."

12. See Beer, *Aufzeichnungen des Grafen Bentick*, 5. Examples include her refusal of a baldachin in church and a funeral sermon.

13. Political Testament of 1750–51, BAAA, 83; to Kaunitz, June 1766, Rothe, *Die Mutter*, 210; to Joseph, November 1771, MJC I, 350–51; Arneth, "Maria Theresia und der Hofrath von Greiner," 316; Karajan, *Maria Theresia und Graf Sylva-Tarouca*, 11.

14. See chapter 5 ("A New System," "Change of Favorites"), chapter 13 ("New Schools").

15. This is clearest in her relationship with van Swieten, but also with Haugwitz. See also Tarouca's advice: Karajan, *Maria Theresia und Graf Sylva-Tarouca*, 14–15.

16. According to the Swedish emissary Bark, 1756, Arnheim, "Das Urtheil," 291.

17. E.g., to Marie Antoinette, September 30, 1771, MACS II, 218–19; see also KMT III, 412. All the children were given similar advice on their departure, see Rothe, *Briefe*, 144, 156, 178, 220, 225.

18. See Goffman, *The Presentation of Self in Everyday Life*. New York, 1959.

19. E.g., to Ferdinand, BKF I, 72, 288–89; to Albert von Teschen, in Wolf, *Aus dem Hofleben*, 251: she would rather appear weak than unjust.

20. Linger, *Denkwürdigkeiten*, 216 ff., 230 ff.

21. Ligne, *Fragments* I, 76, 115, 144–45.

22. See chapter 6 ("Chastity Campaign").

23. The estates also placed great value on such fictions of voluntary compliance when it came to tax demands or reforms, see chapter 2 ("The Wedding") and chapter 5 ("A New System").

24. See chapter 6 ("Rumors") and chapter 7 ("Commoners at Court").

25. See chapter 3 ("The Queen is Naked").

26. *Princeps in compendio*, Point IV.

27. See chapter 2 ("Pandurentheresl").

28. See Tarouca's description of the dilemma in the early 1750s, Karajan, *Maria Theresia und Graf Sylva-Tarouca*, 13 ff.

29. *Princeps in compendio*, Point V; see, e.g., to Ferdinand, BKF I, 117–18, 236.

30. See chapter 2 ("The Logic of Favor").

31. E.g., to van Swieten, BKF IV, 243; to Joseph, MJC I, 160–61; to Ferdinand, BKF I, 156.

32. E.g., chapter 13 ("Marie Antoinette"); see Stollberg-Rilinger, "Zur moralischen Ökonomie des Schenkens."

33. At the start of her reign she ordered a freeze on salaries and allowed many privileges to die out. KMT I, 103, 274–75, 285–76; see Political Testament of 1750–51, BAA, 72–73.

34. Wagner, "Fürstengnade"; see chapter 5 ("Change of Favorites"). See the judgments in KMT IV, 27, 56–77, 103; V, 15, 34–35, 78–79, 229 ff.

35. See chapter 7 ("Court Timetable," "Work on Charisma").

36. " . . . *pas dure, rude, et avoir de l'humeur, mais* [. . .] *gracieuse, compatissante, indulgente, charitable*," to Carolina, April 1768, BKF III, 51.

37. To Ferdinand, BKF I, 117; see chapter 7 ("Distinctions and Refinements").

38. To Ferdinand, November 8, 1779, BKF II, 223: "*qu'on sente le bien et le mal des autres.*"

39. E.g., to van Swieten, BKF IV, 233; to Leopold, BKF I, 25; to Beatrix, BKF III, 243 ff.

40. Arnheim, "Das Urtheil," 291.

41. Hinrichs, *Friedrich der Große*, 44.

42. See chapter 7 ("Commoners at Court"); chapter 12 ("Incurable Mangy Sheep"); chapter 13 ("Our Loyal Subjects," "Diligence and Discipline").

43. E.g., to Ferdinand, BKF II, 312–13: nobody is to be admitted without a letter of recommendation.

44. Coke, *Letters* III, 468, 476, 479.

45. Coke, *Letters* IV, 275–76, 284–85, 298–99, 301, 359.

46. Wraxall, *Historical and the Posthumous Memoirs* II, 325–26; Coxe, *History* III, 482. In 1770 Maria Theresa had turned to Antoine-Gabriel de Sartine, the Paris Lieutenant-Général, requesting information on his new police organization. Sartine had Police Commissioner Le Maire write an account of the Paris institution. The author dedicated it to Maria Theresa: [Jean-Baptiste-Charles Le Maire], *La police de Paris en 1770. Mémoire inédit compose par ordre de G. de Sartine sur la demande de Marie-Thérèse, avec une introduction et des notes par A. Gazier*, Paris 1879.

47. E.g., KMT III, 37; see chapter 5 ("Reforms"), Chapter 7 ("Court Timetable").

48. See chapter 5 ("I Am No Longer What I Was").

49. See chapter 12 ("Incurable Mangy Sheep"), chapter 13 ("Information Overload," "Diligence and Discipline," "Iustitia et clementia'").

50. See chapter 12 ("Our Good Turks").

51. See chapter 11 ("The Religion of Rule").

52. See chapter 8 ("Media War, Information War").

53. See chapter 5 ("Reforms").

54. See chapter 13 ("Information Overload").

55. See chapter 14 ("The Autumn of the Matriarch").

56. Jumel, *Éloge*; a different opinion is offered by Joseph von Sonnenfels, in *Sammlung merkwürdiger Aufsätze* I, 42–43; see Michaud, "Laudatio"; Wandruszka, "Im Urteil der Nachwelt."

57. Immanuel Kant, "Beantwortung der Frage: Was ist Aufklärung?," in Berlinische Monatsschrift, December 1784.

58. See chapter 11 ("The Religion of Rule"), chapter 12 ("Incurable Mangy Sheep").

59. See chapter 10 ("How Enlightenment came to the Court"), chapter 12 ("Rebellion in Bohemia").

60. To Beatrix, May 26, 1777, BKF III, 280.

61. See chapter 10 ("The Regency Dilemma," "Cutting Up the "Polish Cake"); chapter 131 ("New Schools," "Rebellion in Bohemia," "The Last War").

62. See Leopold, "Stato della famiglia"; Arneth, "Graf Philipp Cobenzl," 107 ff.; Wertheimer, "Zwei Schilderungen," 213–14: her addiction to gossip tarnished her good name.

63. Moore, *A View* II, 336; see Moser, *Teutsches Hof-Recht*, 779; see also the remarks on Joseph in KMT VIII, 118; see Stollberg-Rilinger, Zur moralischen Ökonomie des Hofes.

64. Sonnenfels, in *Sammlung merkwürdiger Aufsätze* I, 41–42.

65. Joseph, ÖZV II,3, no. 77, 52, see chapter 9 ("The Regency Dilemma").

66. The context was that foreign diplomats were threatening to stay away from her coronation. HHStA OMeA, Zeremonialprotokolle 18, 1741 (Court Conference from April 8, 1741).

67. To Ferdinand, December 2, 1779, BKF II, 231.

REFERENCES

Unprinted Sources

Österreichisches Staatsarchiv, Abt. Haus- Hof- und Staatsarchiv

Reichskanzlei, Ministerialkorrespondenz, Karton 11
Reichskanzlei, Vorträge des Reichsvizekanzlers, 6d, 6e
Reichskanzlei, Kleinere Reichsstände, Karton 519
Reichskanzlei, Reichsakten in specie, Kartons 21, 22, 23, 24, 25
Staatskanzlei, Vorträge, 52, 53, 54, 58, 59, 62, 75, 114
Hausarchiv, Familienakten, Sammelbände 2, 3, 4, 5, 6, 7, 10
Hausarchiv, Familienakten, Kartons 18, 41, 42, 43, 44, 45, 46, 47, 48, 49, 50, 51, 54, 55, 96
Hausarchiv, Familienkorrespondenz A, Kartons 25, 26, 35, 36, 37
Hausarchiv, Familienkorrespondenz B, Kartons 18, 25, 28
Obersthofmarschallamt, Akten 3, 4, 5, 6
Obersthofmeisteramt, Obersthofmeisteramtsakten, Ältere Reihe, Kartons 34, 35, 36, 37
Obersthofmeisteramt, Zeremonielldepartement, Ältere Zeremonialakten, Kartons 27, 37, 45
Obersthofmeisteramt, Hofzeremonielldepartement, Zeremonialprotokolle 10, 11, 16, 17, 18, 19, 35
Länderabteilungen, Österreichische Akten, Österreich—Staat 1
Kabinettsarchiv, Kabinettskanzlei, Nachlass Zinzendorff, Handschriften 2, 127
Sonderbestände R, Nachlass Fritz Reinöhl

Österreichische Nationalbibliothek

Manuskripte, Codex Nr. 14084–14085
Wiener Hofbibliothek Nr. 7731–7732

Fürstlich Liechtensteinsches Domänenarchiv: VA 5-2-2

Printed Sources

"Abschaffung der peinlichen Frage in den österreichischen Erblanden," in *Ephemeriden der Menschheit* (1776): 97–98.

Acta publica, oder Sammlung aller Staatsschriften, welche seit denen im Jahr 1756 zu London und Versailles geschlossenen Allianz-Tractaten an das Licht gekommen sind und noch kommen werden. 4 vols. Vienna / Prague 1756–58.

Anon. *Anhang oder weitere Nachricht von den Bedrängnissen der Evangelischen Glaubensgenossen in den Landen des Erzherzogthums Oesterreich dem Lande ob der Ens, Steiermark und Kärnthen zur Vertheidigung ihrer Unschuld gegen die Verunglimpfungen ihrer Verfolger.* Leipzig 1754.

——. "Portrait de Joseph II attribué à un Ambassadeur à la Cour de Vienne, et tracé en 1773." Vienna 1773.

——. *Untersuchung der Frage: Warum die Königin in Ungarn so ausserordendlich geliebet werde?* N.p., 1745.

——. *Vollständige Geschichte der neuesten Bedruckungen.* n.d. Preface.

Arneth, Alfred von. *Briefe der Kaiserin Maria Theresia an ihre Kinder und Freunde.* 4 vols. Vienna 1881.

——. *Die Relationen der Botschafter Venedigs über Österreich im achtzehnten Jahrhundert nach den Originalen* (Fontes rerum Austriacarum, 22–23). Vienna 1863.

——. "Graf Philipp Cobenzl und seine Memoiren." *Archiv für österreichische Geschichte* 67 (1885): 1–177.

——. "Johann Christoph Bartenstein und seine Zeit." *Archiv für österreichische Geschichte* 46 (1871): 1–214.

——. *Joseph II. und Leopold von Toscana: Ihr Briefwechsel von 1781 bis 1790.* Vienna 1872.

——. *Marie Antoinette, Joseph II. und Leopold II: Ihr Briefwechsel.* Leipzig 1866.

——(ed.). "Maria Theresia und der Hofrath von Greiner," in *Sitzungsberichte der Phil.-hist. Classe der Österr. Akademie der Wissenschaften* 30 (1859): 307–78.

——. *Maria Theresia und Joseph II: Ihre Correspondenz sammt Briefen Joseph's an seinen Bruder Leopold.* 3 vols. Vienna 1867.

——. *Maria Theresia und Marie Antoinette: Ihr Briefwechsel während der Jahre 1770–1780.* Paris 1865.

——. "Zwei Denkschriften der Kaiserin Maria Theresia." *Archiv für österreichische Geschichte* 47 (1871): 267–354.

Arneth, Alfred von, and Jules Flammermont (eds.). *Correspondance secrète du Comte de Mercy-Argenteau avec l'empereur Joseph II. et le prince de Kaunitz.* Paris 1889–91.

Arneth, Alfred von, and Auguste Mathieu Geffroy (eds.). *Correspondance secrète entre Marie Thérèse et le comte de Mercy-Argenteau avec les lettres de Marie Thérèse et Marie Antoinette.* 3 vols. Paris 1874.

Arneth, Alfred Ritter von. *Geschichte Maria Theresia's.* 10 vols. Vienna 1863–79.

Arnheim, Fritz (ed.). "Das Urtheil eines schwedischen Diplomaten über den Wiener Hof im Jahre 1756." *MIÖG* 10 (1889): 287–94.

Articulen des algemeined Land-Tag-Schlusses . . . aufdem Koniglichen Prager Schloss. Prague 1683–1794.

Bauer, Wilhelm, Otto Erich Deutsch, and Joseph Heinz Eibl (eds.). *Mozart: Briefe und Aufzeichnungen.* Expanded edition, ed. Ulrich Konrad. Kassel 2005.

Beales, Derek. "Joseph II's Rêveries." *MÖStA* 33 (1980): 142–60.

Beck, Christian August. *Versuch einer Staatspraxis, oder Canzeley-Übung, aus der Politik, dem Staats- und Völkerrechte.* Vienna 1754.

Beer, Adolf (ed.). *Aufzeichnungen des Grafen Bentinck über Maria Theresia.* Vienna 1871.

——(ed.). "Denkschriften des Fürsten Wenzel Kaunitz-Reitberg." *Archiv für österreichische Geschichte* 48 (1872): 3–162.

———(ed.). *Die erste Theilung Polens*, vol. 3: *Documente*. Vienna 1873.

———(ed.). *Joseph II., Leopold II. und Kaunitz: Ihr Briefwechsel*. Vienna 1873.

Bergl, Josef. "Der Judenmord in Böhmisch-Leipa am 9. Dezember 1744." *Jahrbuch der Gesellschaft für Geschichte der Juden in der Cechoslovakischen Republik* 2 (1930): 241–84.

Bicchieri, Emilio (ed.). "Lettere famigliari dell'Imperator Giuseppe II a Don Filippo e Don Ferdiando Duchi di Parma (1760–1767) con note e documenti," in *Atti e memorie delle RR. deputazioni di storia patria per le provincie modenesi e parmensi* IV (1868): 105–24.

Borié, Ägyd Valentin von. "Staats-Betrachtungen über gegenwärtigen preußischen Krieg in Teutschland [. . .], Wien 1761," in *Aufklärung und Kriegserfahrung. Klassische Zeitzeugen zum Siebenjährigen Krieg*, ed. Johannes Kunisch. Frankfurt am Main 1996, 651–734.

Isabella de Bourbon-Parme, *"Je meurs d'amour pour toi": Lettres à l'Archiduchesse Marie-Christine, 1760–1763*, ed. Elisabeth Badinter. Paris 2008.

Bräker, Ulrich. *Lebensgeschichte und natürliche Ebentheuer des Armen Mannes im Tockenburg* (1789), ed. Werner Günther. Stuttgart 1965.

Braubach, Max. "Eine Satire auf den Wiener Hof aus den letzten Jahren Kaiser Karls VI." *MIÖG* 53 (1939): 21–78.

Breunlich, Maria, and Marieluise Mader (eds.). *Karl Graf von Zinzendorf: Aus den Jugendtagebüchern 1747, 1752 bis 1763*. Vienna / Cologne / Weimar 1997.

Briefe Preußischer Soldaten aus den Feldzügen 1756 und 1757 und über die Schlachten bei Lobositz und Prag. Berlin 1901.

Brüggemann, Fritz (ed.). *Der Siebenjährige Krieg im Spiegel der zeitgenössischen Literatur*. Leipzig 1935.

Burgenländische Landesregierung (eds). *Maria Theresia als Königin von Ungarn. Ausstellungskatalog im Schloss Halbthurn*, edited by Gerda Mraz and Gerald Schlag. Eisenstadt 1980.

Campan, Jeanne Louise Henriette. *Mémoires sur la vie privée de Marie-Antoinette, reine de France et de Navarre, suivis de souvenirs et anecdotes historiques sur les règnes de Louis XIV et de Louis XV*, 2nd ed. 2 vols. Paris 1823.

Carrach, Johann Philipp. *Reichs-Grund-Gesetz- und Observanz-mäßiger Bericht von der Reichs-Acht*. Halle 1758.

Casanova, Giacomo (ed.). *Geschichte meines Lebens*. Berlin 1985.

Chemnitz, Johann Hieronymus. *Vollständige Nachrichten von dem Zustande der Evangelischen und insonderheit von ihrem Gottesdienste bey der Königlich Dänischen Gesandtschafts Capelle in der Kayserlichen Haupt und Residenzstadt Wien*. N.p. 1761.

Christoph, Paul (ed.). *Maria Theresia: Geheimer Briefwechsel mit Marie Antoinette*. Vienna 1980.

Cogniazo, Jacob de. *Geständnisse eines österreichischen Veterans in politisch-militärischer Hinsicht auf der interressantesten Verhältnisse zwschen Östreich und Preußen wärend der Regierung Friedrich d. II*. With historical annotations. Breslau 1788–91.

Coke, Mary. *Letters and Journals of Lady Mary Coke*, ed. James Archibald Home. 4 vols. Edinburgh 1889.

Conrad, Hermann (ed.). *Recht und Verfassung in der Zeit Maria Theresias: Die Vorträge zum Unterricht des Erzherzogs Joseph in Natur- und Völkerrecht, sowie im Deutschen Staats- und Lehensrecht*. Cologne / Opladen 1964.

———. "Verfassung und politische Lage des Reiches in einer Denkschrift Josephs II. von 1767/68," in *Festschrift Nikolaus Grass*, ed. Louis Carlen, et al. Innsbruck 1974, 161–85.

Constitutio Criminalis Theresiana oder der Römisch-Kayserl. zu Hungarn und Böheim ... Majestät Mariae Theresiae ... peinliche Gerichtsordnung. Vienna 1769.

Coxe, William. *History of the House of Austria, from the foundation of the Monarchy by Rudolph of Hapsburg, to the death of Leopold the Second, 1218 to 1792,* vol. 2. London 1847.

Crantz, Heinrich Johann Nepomuk. *Einleitung in eine wahre und gegründete Hebammenkunst.* Vienna 1756.

[Daun, Leopold Joseph Maria Graf von]. *Regulament und Ordnung des gesammten Kaierlich-Königlichen Fuß-Volcks von 1749.* Facsimile of original edition. Vienna 1749, introduction by Georg Ortenburg. Osnabrück 1969.

Dengler, Fritz (ed.). "Bayerischer Wald und Donaugefilde in schwerer Kriegszeit: Ein Bericht über das Kriegsgeschehen des Jahres 1742 in Teilen Niederbayerns mit der Oberpfalz mit Tagebuchaufzeichnungen des Abtes Marian Pusch von Niederaltaich im Mittelpunkt." *Der Bayerwald* 53 (1961).

Denis, Michael. *Poetische Bilder der meisten kriegerischen Vorgänge in Europa, seit dem Jahr 1756.* Vienna 1760–61.

Des Heiligen Römischen Reichs vollständiger Genealogisch- und Schematischer Calender. Frankfurt am Main 1743–46.

Deutsch, Otto Erich (ed.). *Mozart: Die Dokumente seines Lebens.* Kassel, et al. 1961.

Die Unbekannte. Eine wahre Geschichte. Vienna 1785.

Ditfurth, Franz Wilhelm Freiherr von (ed.). *Die Historischen Volkslieder des Oestreichischen Heeres von 1638–1849. Aus fliegenden Blättern, handschriftlichen Quellen und dem Volksmunde.* Vienna 1874.

———(ed.). *Die historischen Volkslieder des siebenjährigen Krieges.* Berlin 1871.

Dittersdorf, Karl von. *Lebensbeschreibung. Seinem Sohne in die Feder diktirt* Leipzig 1801.

Droysen, Johann Gustav, et al. (eds.). *Die politische Correspondenz Friedrichs des Großen.* 46 vols and one supplementary volume. Berlin 1879–1939.

Dutens, Louis. *Mémoires d'un voyageur qui se repose, contenant des anecdotes historiques, politiques et littéraires, relatives a plusieurs des principaux personnages du siècle.* Paris 1806.

Engelbrecht, Martin. *Théatre de la milice étrangère: Schaubühne verschiedener in Teutschland bishero unbekannt gewester Soldaten von ausländischen Nationen.* Augsburg 1742–44.

Engl, Franz and Theodor Wührer (eds.). *Innviertel 1779. Reisejournal Kaiser Joseph II. Generalstabsbericht Oberst von Seeger.* Schärding 1979.

Fleming, Hanns Friedrich von. *Der vollkommene teutsche Soldat.* Leipzig 1726, reprinted Osnabrück 1967.

Fournier, August. *Gerhard van Swieten als Censor* (Sitzungsberichte der Kaiserlichen Akademie der Wissenschaften, Phil.-hist. Klasse, 84). Vienna 1876.

Fromageot, Pierre. *Histoire du règne de Marie-Thérèse.* Paris 1781.

Fuhrmann, Mathias. *Alt- und Neues Oesterreich, Oder Compendieuse Universal-Historie, Von dem alt- und neuen, geist- und weltlichen Zustand dieses Landes. . . .* Vienna 1734.

———. *Historische Beschreibung und kurz gefaßte Nachricht von der Römisch Kaiserl. und königlichen Residenz-Stadt Wien und ihren Vorstädten.* Vienna 1767.

Galanterien Wiens. Auf einer Reise gesammelt und in Briefen geschildert von einem Berliner. [Vienna] 1784.

Garms-Cornides, Elisabeth. "'On n'a qu'a vouloir, et tout est possible' oder 'i bin halt wer i bin': "Eine Gebrauchsanweisung für den Wiener Hof, geschrieben von Friedrich August Harrach für seinen Bruder Ferdinand Bonaventura," in *Adel im "langen" 18. Jahrhundert*, ed. Gabriele Haug-Moritz. Vienna 2009, 89–111.

Genealogisch-historische Nachrichten von den allerneuesten Begebenheiten: Welche sich an den europäischen Höfen zutragen. . . . Leipzig 1743–44.

Ghelen, Johann Peter von (ed.). *Wiennerische Beleuchtungen / Oder Beschreibung Aller deren Triumph und Ehren-Gerüsten / Sinn-Bildern / Und anderen . . . Auszierungen . . . zu Ehren der . . . Geburt . . . Josephi.* . . . Vienna 1741.

Girard, Georges (ed.). *Correspondance entre Marie-Thérèse et Marie-Antoinette.* Paris 1933.

Goethe, Johann Wolfgang von. *Aus meinem Leben: Dichtung und Wahrheit*, vol. 9. Works; Hamburg ed. 9th ed. Munich 1981.

———. *Autobiography*, translated by George Bell. London 1897.

Goodman, Katherine (ed.). "Adieu Divine Comtesse," in *Luise Gottsched, Charlotte Sophie Gräfin Bentinck und Johann Christoph Gottsched in ihren Briefen*. Würzburg 2009.

Gottsched, Johann Christoph [and Gottsched, Luise Adelgunde Victorie] (ed.). *Zwey Gedichte, womit gegen das Ende des 1749sten Jahrs Beyderseits Römisch-Kaiserliche auch zu Hungarn und Böheim Königliche Majestäten allerunterthänigst verehret worden.* Cassel 1750.

Gottsched, Luise. "Mit der Feder in der Hand," in *Briefe aus den Jahren 1730–1762*, ed. Inka Kording. Darmstadt 1999.

Gracián, Balthasar. *Hand-Orakel und Kunst der Weltklugheit. Deutsch von Arthur Schopenhauer*, ed. Arthur Hübscher. Munich 1985.

Griselini, Franz. *Versuch einer politischen und natürlichen Geschichte des Temeswarer Banats in Briefen an Standespersonen und Gelehrte.* Vienna 1780.

Grotehenn, Johann Heinrich Ludwig. *Briefe aus dem Siebenjährigen Krieg, Lebensbeschreibung und Tagebuch*, ed. Marian Füssel and Sven Petersen. Potsdam 2012.

Grouchy, Vicomte de, and Paul Cottin (eds.). *Journal inédit du duc de Croÿ, publié d'après le manuscrit autographe.* Paris 1906–07.

Grün, Anastasius [Anton Alexander von Auersberg]. *Spaziergänge eines Wiener Poeten.* Hildesheim / Zürich / New York 2011.

Grypa, Dietmar and Aloys Schmid (eds.). *Die Berichte der diplomatischen Vertreter des Kaiserhofs aus München an die Staatskanzlei zu Wien während der Regierungszeit des Kurfürsten Max III: Joseph 1745–1749.* Munich 2000.

Guibert, François-Apolline Comte de. *Journal d'un voyage en Allemagne fait en 1773.* 2 vols. Paris 1803.

Hamberger, Klaus (ed.). *Mortuus non mordet: Dokumente zum Vampirismus, 1689–1791.* Vienna 1992.

Hammer-Purgstall, Joseph. *Des türkischen Gesandten Resmi Ahmet Efendi Gesandtschaftliche Berichte von seinen Gesandtschaften in Wien im Jahre 1757 und in Berlin im Jahre 1763.* Berlin / Stettin 1809.

Handelmann, Heinrich. "Vom Wiener Hof aus der Zeit der Kaiserin Maria Theresia und Kaiser Joseph's II., aus ungedruckten Depeschen des Grafen Johann Friedrich Bachoff von Echt, königlich dänischen Gesandten (von 1751 bis 1781)." *Archiv für österreichische Geschichte* 38 (1867): 457–67.

Harrasowsky, Philipp Harras Ritter von (ed.). *Der Codex Theresianus und seine Umarbeitungen.* Vienna 1883.

Heigel, Karl Theodor (ed.). *Das Tagebuch Kaiser Karls VII. aus der Zeit des österreichischen Erbfolgekriegs.* Munich 1883.

Herrgott, Marquard. *Genealogia Diplomatica Augustae Gentis Habsburgicae.* . . . 3 vols. Vienna 1737.

Hersche, Peter (ed.). *Der aufgeklärte Reformkatholizismus in Österreich.* Bern / Frankfurt am Main 1976.

Hinrichs, Carl (ed.). *Friedrich der Große und Maria Theresia: Diplomatische Berichte von Otto Christoph Graf von Podewils, Königlich preussischer Gesandter am österreichischen Hofe in Wien.* Berlin 1937.

Hochedlinger, Michael, and Anton Tantner (eds.). *. . . der größte Teil der Untertanen lebt elend und mühselig": Die Berichte des Hofkriegsrates zur sozialen und wirtschaftlichen Lage der Habsburgermonarchie 1770–1771.* Vienna 2005.

Homann, Johann Christoph. *Tabula Geographica Europae Austriacae.* N.p., n.d. (ca. 1724–30).

Hrazky, Josef. "Die Persönlichkeit der Infantin Isabella von Parma." *MÖStA* 12 (1959): 174–239.

Hübner, Eberhard Friedrich (ed.). *Franz von der Trenk, Pandurenobrist: Dargestellt von einem Unpartheiischen. Mit einer Geniegeschichte.* N.p., n.d. (1790).

Innerkoßler, Adolf Pater. *Eine große Tochter Maria Theresias, Erzherzogin Marianna: Jubelgabe zur Feier des 200jährigen Bestehens vom Elisabethinen-Konvent.* Innsbruck 1910.

Irenophili zufällige Gedanken über einige politische Paradoxa bey jetzigem Kriege. N.p. 1758.

John, Johann Dionis. *Lexikon der k. k. Medizinalgesetze.* Introduction by E. G. Baldinger. Prague 1790–1791.

Jumel, Jean-Charles. *Éloge de Marie-Thérèse, impératrice-reine d'Hongrie et de Bohème.* . . . Paris 1781.

Justi, Johann Heinrich Gottlob von. *Allerunterthänigstes Gutachten von dem vernünftigen Zusammenhange der und practischen Vortrage aller Oeconomischen und Cameralwissenschaften . . . benebst einer Antrittsrede von dem Zusammenhange eines blühenden Zustandes der Wissenschaften mit denjenigen Mitteln, welche einen Staat mächtig und glücklich machen,* ed. D.E.v.K. Leipzig 1754.

———. *Der Grundriß einer guten Regierung in fünf Büchern.* Frankfurt am Main / Leipzig 1759.

Kállay, István (ed.). "Ein Geheimbericht über den Tod Maria Theresias." *MÖStA* 34 (1981): 342–44.

Kallbrunner, Josef (ed.). *Maria Theresia als Herrscherin: Aus den deutschen Denkschriften, Briefen und Resolutionen (1740–1756).* Leipzig 1917.

———(ed.). *Kaiserin Maria Theresias Politisches Testament.* Munich 1952.

Karajan, Theodor Georg von (ed.). *Maria Theresia und Graf Sylva-Tarouca: Feierliche Sitzungsberichte der Kaiserlichen Akademie der Wissenschaften,* Appendix. Vienna 1859.

Kayserlich- und Königlicher Wie auch Ertzherzoglicher dann dero Haupt- und Residenz-Stadt Wien Staats- und Standeskalender auf das Gnadenreiche Jahr Jesu Christi. . . . Vienna 1738–75.

Keith, Robert Murray. *Memoirs and correspondence (official and familiar) of Sir Robert Murray Keith, K.B., envoy extraordinary ad minister plenipotentiary at the courts of Dresden, Copenhagen, and Vienna, from 1769–1792, . . .* ed. Mrs. Gillespie Smyth. London 1849.

Kemmel, Löwle [Richter, Christoph Gottlieb]. *Helden-Lied über die Königin in Ungarn und ihre Gnade gegen die Juden.* N.p. 1745.

Kervyn de Lettenhove (Joseph Marie Bruno Constantin) (ed.). *Lettres inédites de Marie-Thérèse et de Joseph II.* Brussels 1868.

Keyßler, Johann Georg. *Neueste Reisen durch Deutschland, Böhmen, Ungarn, die Schweiz, Italien und Lothringen....* Hannover 1751.

Kleemann, Nikolaus Ernst. *Reisen von Wien über Belgrad bis Kilianova... in den Jahren 1768, 1769 und 1770.* Vienna 1771.

Kleiner, Salomon (ed.). *Vera et accurata delineatio omnium templorum et coenobiorum... oder Wahrhaffte und genaue Abbildung aller Kirchen und Klöster... der Residenz-Statt Wien.* Augsburg 1724–37.

Klingenstein, Grete, Eva Faber, and Antonio Trampus (eds.). *Europäische Aufklärung zwischen Wien und Triest: Die Tagebücher des Gouverneurs Karl Graf von Zinzendorf 1776–1782.* Vienna 2009.

Klueting, Harm (ed.). *Der Josephinismus: Ausgewählte Quellen zur Geschichte der theresianisch-josephinischen Reformen.* Darmstadt 1995.

———. *Das Reich und Österreich 1648–1740.* Münster 1999.

Kolinovics, Gábor, and Márton György Kolichich. *Nova Ungariae Periodus.* Buda 1790.

Kollár, Adam Franz. *Vorläufige Ausführung der Rechte des Königreichs Hungarn auf... Reußen und Podolien.* Vienna 1772.

Kretschmayr, Heinrich, et al. (eds.). *Die österreichische Zentralverwaltung 1491–1918,* part 2: *Von der Vereinigung der österreichischen und böhmischen Hofkanzlei bis zur Einrichtung der Ministerialverfassung (1749–1848).* Vienna 1925–38.

Kriegl, Georg Christoph. *Erbhuldigung, welche der Allerdurchleuchtigst Grossmächtigsten Frauen Frauen Mariae Theresiae, zu Hungarn und Boheim Königin, als Ertzherzogin zu Österreich von denen gesamten Nieder-Österreichischen Ständen... allerunterthänigst abgelegt den 22. November anno 1740 und auf Verordnung wohl ermelten loblichen Herren Ständen mit allen Umständen ausführlich beschrieben worden.* Vienna 1740.

[Kropatschek, Joseph] (ed.). *Sammlung aller k.k. Verordnungen und Gesetze vom Jahre 1740 bis 1780....* 9 vols. Vienna 1787.

Küchelbecker, Johann Basilius. *Allerneueste Nachricht vom Römisch-Kayserlichen Hofe nebst einer ausführlichen Beschreibung der Kayserlichen Residenz-Stadt Wien und der umliegenden Örter....* Hannover 1730.

Kunisch, Johannes (ed.). *Aufklärung und Kriegserfahrun. Der "Siebenjährige Weltkrieg" 1756–1763 in klassischen Texten der Zeitzeugen: t, Friedrich der Große, Borié, Abbt.* Frankfurt am Main 1996.

Küntzel, Georg (ed.). "Österreichische Acten zur Vorgeschichte des siebenjährigen Krieges," in *Preußische und österreichische Akten zur Vorgeschichte des Siebenjährigen Krieges,* ed. Gustav Berthold Volz and Georg Küntzel. Stuttgart 1899, 143–746.

[Lamberg, Maximilien Joseph]. *Mémorial d'un mondain, Volume 1,* 2nd ed. London 1776.

Lehmann, Johann. *Reise von Preßburg nach Hermanstadt in Siebenbürgen.* Leipzig 1785.

Lehndorff, Ernst Ahasverus Heinrich von. *Dreissig Jahre am Hofe Friedrichs des Großen: Aus den Tagebüchern Ernst Ahasver Heinrich von Lehndorffs, Kammerherrn der Königin Elisabeth Christine von Preußen,* ed. Karl Eduard Schmidt-Lötzen. Gotha 1907.

Lieben, Samuel Hugo (ed.). "Igereth Machalath, eine hebräische Chronik des 18. Jahrhunderts," in *Jahrbuch der Gesellschaft für Geschichte der Juden in der Cechoslovakischen Republik* 2 (1930): 293–402.

——. "Briefe von 1744–1748 über die Austreibung der Juden aus Prag," in *Jahrbuch der Gesellschaft für Geschichte der Juden in der Cechoslovakischen Republik* 4 (1932): 353–479.

Ligne, Charles-Joseph Prince de. *Fragments de l'histoire de ma vie*, ed. Jeroom Vercruysse. Paris 2000.

——. *Mon Journal de la guerre de Sept Ans*, ed. Jeroom Vercruysse and Bruno Colson. Paris 2008.

Linger, Karl Friedrich (ed.). *Denkwürdigkeiten aus dem Leben des k.k. Hofrathes Heinrich Gottfried von Bretschneider, 1739 bis 1810*. Vienna 1892.

Lippert, Woldemar (ed.). *Kaiserin Maria Theresia und Kurfürstin Maria Antonia von Sachsen. Briefwechsel 1747–1772: Mit einem Anhang ergänzender Briefe*. Leipzig 1908.

Loen, Johann Michael von. *Gesammelte Kleine Schrifften*, vol. 1. Frankfurt/Leipzig 1750.

Ludewig, Johann Peter von. *Vollständige Erläuterung der Güldenen Bulle*. Frankfurt 1719.

Lünig, Johann Christian (ed.). *Theatrum ceremoniale historico-politicum, Oder Historisch-und Politischer Schau-Platz Aller Ceremonien. . . .* Leipzig 1719.

Maaß, Ferdinand (ed.). *Der Josephinismus: Quellen zu seiner Geschichte in Österreich 1760–1850*. Amtliche Dokumente aus dem Wiener Haus-, Hof- und Staatsarchiv. 5 vols. Vienna 1951–61.

——. "Vorbereitung und Anfänge des Josephinismus." *MÖStA* 1 (1948): 289–444.

Marie-Caroline, Reine de Naples et de Sicile. *Correspondance inédite avec le marquis de Gallo*. Paris 1911.

Mikoletzky, Hanns Leo (ed.). "Ein Sammelband mit Briefen Franz Stephans." *MÖStA* 23 (1970): 105–27.

Montagu, Lady Mary Wortley. *The Complete Letters*, ed. Robert Halsband. Vol. I: *1708–1720*. Oxford 1965.

Montesquieu, Charles-Louis de Secondat, Baron de la Brède. *Meine Reisen in Deutschland 1728–1729*. Selected, edited, and with comments and introduction by Jürgen Overhoff. Translated by Hans W. Schumacher. Stuttgart 2014.

——. *Oe de Fré*, ed. Roger Caillois. 2 vols. Paris 1949.

Moore, John. *A View of Society and Manners in France, Switzerland, and Germany*. 2 vols. Paris 1803.

Moser, Friedrich Carl von. "Abhandlung von der Staats-Galanterie," in Friedrich Carl von Moser, *Kleine Schriften zur Erläuterung des Staats- und Völker-Rechts*. Frankfurt am Main 1751, 1–181.

——. *Patriotisches Archiv für Deutschland*. Frankfurt am Main / Leipzig 1786.

——. *Kleine Schriften zur Erläuterung des Staats- und Völker-Rechts*. Frankfurt am Main 1751.

——. *Teutsches Hof-Recht*. 2 vols. Frankfurt am Main 1754.

——. *Versuch einer Staats-Grammatik*. Frankfurt am Main 1749.

[Moser, Friedrich Carl von]. *Was ist: gut Kayserlich, und: nicht gut Kayserlich?* [Leipzig] 1766.

Moser, Johann Jakob von. *Teutsches Staats-Recht*. 50 parts. Nuremberg 1737–54.

Muratori, Lodovico Antonio. *Die wahre Andacht des Christen: Untersuchet und von Ludewig Anton Muratori . . . in italiän. Sprache beschrieben, nunmehr aber ins reine Deutsch übers*. Vienna 1762.

Neues Genealogisch-Schematisches Reichs- und Staats-Handbuch. Frankfurt am Main 1748–65.

[Pezzl, Johann]. *Skizze von Wien.* Vienna / Leipzig 1785.

Pichler, Karoline. *Denkwürdigkeiten aus meinem Leben: Mit einer Einleitung und zahlreichen Anmerkungen nach dem Erstdruck und der Urschrift neu herausgegeben von Emil Karl Blümml.* Munich 1914.

[Pilati di Tassulo, Carlo Antonio]. *Reisen in verschiedene Länder von Europa, in den Jahren 1774, 1775 und 1776; oder Briefe, die aus Deutschland, der Schweiz, Italien, Sicilien und Paris geschrieben worden,* vol. 1. Leipzig 1778.

Plenk, Joseph Jakob. *Anfangsgründe der Geburtshilfe.* Vienna 1768.

Pleschinsky, Hans (ed.). *Emmanuel de Croy, Nie war es herrlicher zu leben: Das geheime Tagebuch des Herzogs von Croy 1718–1784,* 2nd ed. Munich 2011.

———. *"Nie war es herrlicher zu leben": Das geheime Tagebuch des Herzogs von Croy 1718–1784,* 2nd ed. Munich, 2011.

Pommerin, Rainer / Lothar Schilling (ed.). *Denkschrift des Grafen Kaunitz zur mächtepolitischen Konstellation nach dem Aachener Frieden von 1748, in Expansion und Gleichgewicht. Studien zur europäischen Mächtepolitik des Ancien régime,* ed. Johannes Kunisch. Berlin 1986, 165–239.

Preuß, Johann David Erdmann (ed.). *Oeuvres de Frédéric le Grand.* 30 vols. Berlin 1846–56.

Pribram, Alfred Francis (ed.). *Urkunden und Akten zur Geschichte der Juden in Wien,* vol. 1: *1526–1847.* Vienna / leipzig 1918.

Princeps in compendio, Das ist: Etliche Kurtze zusammengefaste Puncte oder Regeln, Welche ein Regent bey seiner Regierung zu beobachten nöthig hat (1632). N.p. 1701.

Prosch, Peter. *Leben und Ereignisse des Peter Prosch eines Tyrolers von Ried im Zillerthal oder das wunderbare Schicksal: Geschrieben in Zeiten der Aufklärung.* 1st edition 1789. Munich 1964.

Ramhoffsky, Johann Heinrich. *Drey Beschreibungen, Erstens: Des Königlichen Einzugs, welchen . . . Maria Theresia in . . . Dero Königliche drey Prager Städte gehalten, Andertens: Der Erb-Huldigung . . . ; Drittens: . . . Königlich-Böhmischen Crönung.* Prague 1743.

Ranke, Leopold von (ed.). "Maria Theresia und ihr Hof im Jahr 1755: Aus den Papieren des Großkanzler von Fürst." *Historisch-politische Zeitschrift* 2 (1835): 667–740.

Rautenstrauch, Johann. *Biographie Marien Theresiens.* Vienna 1779.

Rechberger, Anton Johann. *Vollständige Geschichte der Einimpfung der Blattern in Wien nebst der besten Art selbe vorzunehmen.* Vienna 1788.

Reinöhl, Franz (ed.). *Briefe der Kaiserin Maria Theresia an Erzherzog Maximilian Franz.* Historische Blätter, vol. 6. Vienna 1934.

Relation de l'inauguration solemnelle de Sa Sacrée Majesté Marie Therese Reine de Hongrie et de Boheme; Archiduchesse d'Autriche &c. comme Comtesse de Flandres, célébrée à Gand, Ville Capitale de la Province, le XXVII. Avril 1744. Ghent 1744.

Richter, Christoph Gottlieb. *Lebens- und Staats-Geschichte der Allerdurchlauchtigsten Großmächtigsten Fürstin und Frauen, Frauen Maria Theresia. . . .* Nuremberg 1743–47.

Riesbeck, Johann Kaspar. *Briefe eines reisenden Franzosen über Deutschland an seinen Bruder in Paris. hg. und bearb. von Wolfgang Gerlach nach der Originalausg.* Zürich 1783, Stuttgart 1967.

Rohr, Julius Bernhard von. *Einleitung zur Ceremoniel-Wissenschafft der Grossen Herren. . . .* Berlin 1733; repr. Weinheim 1990.

Rothe, Carl (ed.). *Die Mutter und die Kaiserin: Briefe der Maria Theresia an ihre Kinder und Vertrauten.* Vienna 1968.

Sammlung merkwürdiger Aufsätze und Nachrichten über den Tod der großen Kaiserinn Maria There-sia. Linz 1781.

Scheyb, Franz Christoph von. *Theresiade: Ein Ehren-Gedicht.* Vienna 1746.

Schlitter, Hans (ed.). *Correspondance secrète entre le Comte Anton Wenzel Kaunitz-Rietberg, Am-bassadeur impérial à Paris, et le Baron Ignaz de Koch, Secrétaire de l'Impératrice Marie-Thérèse, 1750–1752.* Paris 1899.

———(ed.). "Das Testament Maria Theresias, in Österreich." *Zeitschrift für Geschichte* 1 (1918): 143–55.

Schlitter, Hans, and Rudolf Khevenhüller-Metsch, (eds.). *Aus der Zeit Maria Theresias: Tagebuch des Fürsten Johann Josef Khevenhüller-Metsch, Kaiserlichen Obersthofmeisters, 1742–1776,* vols 1–7. Vienna / Leipzig 1908–25; vol. 8, ed. Maria Breunlich-Pawlik and Hans Wagner, Vienna 1972.

Schuegraf, Joseph Rudolph (ed.). "Das französische Lager bei Hengersberg 1742, aus dem Tage-buche des Herrn Abtes Marian Pusch von Niederaltaich gezogen und neu bearbeitet." *Ver-handlungen des Historischen Vereins für Niederbayern* 5 (1856).

———(ed.), "Das österreichische Lager bei Hengersberg 1742, aus dem Tagebuche des Herrn Abtes Marian Pusch von Niederaltaich gezogen und neu bearbeitet." *Verhandlungen des Historischen Vereins für Niederbayern* 7 (1861).

Schwandtner, Johann Georg (ed.). *Scriptores rerum hungaricarum veteres. . . .* Vienna 1746.

Schwerdtfeger, Josef (ed.). "Eine Denkschrift des Großherzogs (nachmaligen Kaisers) Franz Stephan von Lothringen-Toscana aus dem Jahre 1742." *Archiv für österreichische Geschichte* 85 (1898): 361–78.

Seckendorff, Baron Christophe Louis de. "Journal secret," in *Denkwürdigkeiten aus dem Leben der Königl. Preußischen Prinzessin Friederike Sophie Wilhelmine Markgräfin von Bayreuth vom Jahr 1709 bis 1733.* Tübingen 1811, 1–290.

Sluga, Glenda, and Carolyn James (eds). *Women, Diplomacy and International Politics Since 1500.* New York 2015.

Sommer-Mathis, Andrea. *Die Tänzer am Wiener Hofe im Spiegel der Obersthofmeisteramtsakten und Hofparteienprotokolle bis 1740.* Vienna 1992.

Sonnenfels, Joseph von. *Gesammelte Schriften.* Vienna 1783–87.

———. *Grundsätze der Polizey-, Handlungs- und Finanzwissenschaft.* Vienna 1777.

———. *Rede auf Marien Theresien, Kaiserinn, Königinn von Hungarn und Böheim: An ihrem Ge-burtstage in der feierlichen Versammlung der Deutschen Gesellschaft in Wien gehalten.* Vienna 1762.

Soprani, Anne, and André Magnan (eds.). *Une femme des lumières: Écrits et lettres de la comtesse de Bentinck 1715–1800.* Paris 1997.

Sorel, Albert (ed.). *Recueil des instructions données aux ambassadeurs et ministres de France depuis les traités de Westphalie jusqu'à la Révolution française: Publié sous les auspices de la Commission des archives diplomatiques au Ministère des affaires étrangères,* vol. 1: *Autriche.* Paris 1884.

Steube, Johann Caspar. *Wanderschaften und Schicksale von Johann Caspar Steube, Schuhmacher-und italiänischer Sprachmeister in Gotha.* Gotha 1791.

Storch, Johann. *Unterricht vor Heb-Ammen. . . .* Gotha 1747.

Swinburne, Henry. *The Courts of Europe at the Close of the Last Century,* ed. Charles White. 2 vols. London 1841.

Taube, Friedrich Wilhelm von. *Historische und geographische Beschreibung des Königreiches Slavonien und des Herzogthumes Syrmien, sowohl nach ihrer natürlichen Beschaffenheit, als auch nach ihrer itzigen Verfassung und neuen Einrichtung in kirchlichen, bürgerlichen und militärischen Dingen.* Leipzig 1777–78.

Teutsche Kriegs-Canzley. Frankfurt am Main / Leipzig 1757–63.

Thümmler, Lars-Holger (ed.). *Die Österreichische Armee im Siebenjährigen Krieg: Die Bautzener Bilderhandschrift aus dem Jahre 1762.* Berlin 1993.

Anon. *Untersuchung der Frage: Warum die Königin in Ungarn so ausserordendlich geliebet werde?* N.p., 1745.

van Rhyn, René (ed.). "Unveröffentlichte Briefe der Kaiserin Maria Theresia." *Österreichische Rundschau* 33 (1912): 171–81, 268–77.

van Swieten, Gerhard. *Abhandlung des Daseyns der Gespenster, nebst einem Anhang Vom Vampyrismus.* Augsburg 1768.

———. *Erläuterungen der Boerhaavischen Lehrsäze von Erkenntniß und Heilung der Krankheiten,* 2nd ed. Vienna 1778.

Varrentrapp, Conrad (ed.). "Bericht Leopolds von Toskana an Joseph II. über Maximilian," in *Beiträge zur Geschichte der Kurkölnischen Universität Bonn.* Bonn 1868.

Vollständige Geschichte der neuesten Bedruckungen der Evangelischen in den Erblanden des Hauses Oesterreich mit den dazu gehörigen Urkunden und Beweisschriften. N.p., 1763–64.

Vollständiges Diarium von der höchst-begückten Erwehlung des . . . Herrn Franciscus . . . zum Römischen König und Kayser. . . . Beigegeben: Vollständiges Diarium von der höchst-erfreulichen Crönung des . . . Herrn Franciscus Erwehlten Römischen Kaysers. . . . Frankfurt am Main 1746.

Voltaire [François-Marie Arouet]. *The Age of Louis XIV,* translated by R. Griffith. London 1781.

———. "Late Empress Queen's Appeal to the Hungarians." *Gentlemen's Magazine* 58/2 (1788): 780.

———. "Précis du siècle de Louis XV." *Oeuvres complètes,* vol. 19. Paris 1820.

Voltelini, Hans von (ed.). *Eine Denkschrift des Grafen Johann Anton Pergen über die Bedeutung der römischen Kaiserkrone für das Haus Österreich,* in *Gesamtdeutsche Vergangenheit. Festgabe für Heinrich Ritter von Srbik zum 60. Geburtstag.* Munich 1938, 152–68.

von der Trenck, Friedrich. *Die "Blutbibel" des Friedrich Freiherrn von der Trenck (1727–1794).* Cologne / Weimar / Vienna 2014.

———. *Merckwürdiges Leben und Thaten Des Weltberühmten Herrn Francisci Frey-Herrns von der Trenck, Ihro Römisch-Kayserl. und Königl. Majestät in Ungarn und Böhmen etc. etc. würcklichen Obristen und Inhaber eines Sclavonischen Banduren-Regiments. . . . Von Ihm selbst bis zu Ende des Jahrs 1747 fortgesetzt.* Frankfurt / Leipzig 1748.

Volz, Gustav Berthold (ed.). *Die Werke Friedrichs des Großen.* 10 vols. Berlin 1913–14.

Walter, Friedrich (ed.). *Maria Theresia: Briefe und Aktenstücke in Auswahl (Freiherr-vom-Stein-Gedächtnis-Ausgabe),* vol. 12: *Ausgewählte Quellen zur Deutschen Geschichte der Neuzeit.* Darmstadt 1968.

[Wekhrlin, Wilhelm Ludwig]. *Denkwürdigkeiten von Wien: Aus dem Französischen übersetzt.* Vienna 1777.

Wertheimer, Eduard (ed.). "Zwei Schilderungen des Wiener Hofes im XVIII. Jahrhundert." *Archiv für österreichische Geschichte* 62 (1881): 199–237.

Wolf, Adam. *Aus dem Hofleben Maria Theresia's. Nach den Memoiren des Fürsten Joseph Khevenhüller.* 2nd ed. Vienna 1859.

Wraxall, Nathaniel William. *Historical Memoirs of his Own Time.* London 1815.

———. *The Historical and the Posthumous Memoirs of Sir Nathaniel William Wraxall, 1772–1784.* London 1884.

Wührer, Jakob, and Martin Scheutz (eds.). *Zu Diensten Ihrer Majestät: Hofordnungen und Instruktionsbücher am frühneuzeitlichen Wiener Hof.* Vienna / Munich 2011.

Zedler, Johann Heinrich (ed.). *Großes Vollständiges Universal-Lexicon aller Wissenschafften und Künste.* . . . 64 vols, 4 suppl. vols. Halle / Leipzig 1731–54.

Zinzendorf, Karl Graf von. *Aus den Jugendtagebüchern 1747, 1752 bis 1763: Nach Vorarbeiten von Hans Wagner,* ed. Maria Breunlich and Marieluise Mader. Cologne / Weimar / Vienna 1997.

Zweybrück, Franz (ed.). "Briefe der Kaiserin Maria Theresia und Josefs II. und Berichte des Oberssthofmeisters Grafen Anton Salm, 17. März 1760 bis 16. Jänner 1765." *Archiv für österreichische Geschichte* 76 (1890): 111–25.

Literature (from 1800)

Abbate, Carolyn, and Roger Parker. *A History of Opera: The Last 400 Years.* London 2012.

Adam, Wolfgang, and Holger Dainat (eds.). *"Krieg ist mein Lied": Der Siebenjährige Krieg in zeitgenössischen Medien.* Göttingen 2007.

Adamson, John (ed.). *The Princely Courts of Europe: Ritual, Politics, and Culture under the Ancien Régime 1550–1750.* London 1999.

Allmayer-Beck, Johann Christoph. "Die Armee Maria Theresias und Josephs II.," in *Österreich im Zeitalter des aufgeklärten Absolutismus,* ed. Erich Zöllner. Vienna 1983, 71–83.

———."Wandlungen im Heerwesen zur Zeit Maria Theresias," in *Maria Theresia. Beiträge zur Geschichte des Heerwesens ihrer Zeit,* ed. Museum of Military History, Vienna. Graz / Vienna / Munich 1997, 101–38.

Ammerer, Gerhard. "Aufgeklärtes Recht, Rechtspraxis und Rechtsbrecher," in *Ambivalenzen der Aufklärung: Festschrift für Ernst Wangermann,* ed. Gerhard Ammerer and Hanns Haas. Munich 1997,

Ammerer, Gerhard, and Alfred Stefan Weiss (eds.). *Strafe, Disziplin und Besserung: Österreichische Zucht- und Arbeitshäuser 1750–1850.* Frankfurt am Main 2006.

Ammerer, Gerhard, et al. (ed.). *Bündnispartner und Konkurrenten der Landesfürsten? Die Stände in der Habsburgermonarchie.* Vienna and Munich 2007.

Anderson, Matthew Smith. *The War of the Austrian Succession, 1740–1748.* Harlow and New York 1998.

Andreas, Willy. *Das Theresianische Österreich und das achtzehnte Jahrhundert.* Munich and Berlin 1930.

Andreozzi, Daniele and Loredana Panariti. "Trieste and the Ottoman Empire in the Eighteenth Century," in *Europa und die Türkei im 18. Jahrhundert / Europe and Turkey in the 18th Century,* ed. Barbara Schmidt-Haberkamp. Bonn 2011, 219–30.

Anklam, Ewa. *Wissen nach Augenmaß: Militärische Beobachtung und Berichterstattung im Siebenjährigen Krieg.* Berlin, et al. 2007.

Aretin, Karl Otmar Freiherr von. "Der Josephinismus und das Problem des katholischen aufgeklärten Absolutismus," in *Österreich im Europa der Aufklärung. Kontinuität und Zäsur zur*

Zeit Maria Theresias und Josephs II., ed. Richard Georg Plaschka and Grete Klingenstein. Vienna 1985, 509–24.

Aretin, Karl Otmar von. *Das Alte Reich 1648–1806.* 3 vols. Stuttgart 1997.

———. "Das Problem der Kriegführung im Heiligen Römischen Reich," in *Politischer Wandel, organisierte Gewalt und nationale Sicherheit,* ed. Ernst Willi Hansen, et al. Munich 1995, 1–10.

———. *Heiliges Römisches Reich 1776–1806: Reichsverfassung und Staatssouveränität.* 2 vols. Wiesbaden 1967.

Arlaud, Daniel. "Vampire, Aufklärung und Staat: Eine militärmedizinische Mission in Ungarn, 1755–1756," in *Gespenster und Politik, 16. bis 21. Jahrhundert,* ed. Claire Gantet and F. d'Almeida. Munich 2007, 127–44.

Arndt, Johannes / Esther-Beate Körber (eds.). *Das Mediensystem im Alten Reich der Frühen Neuzeit (1600–1750).* Göttingen 2010.

Asch, Ronald W. (ed.). *Hannover, Großbritannien und Europa: Erfahrungsraum Personalunion 1714–1837.* Göttingen 2014.

Auer, Leopold. "Zur Rolle der Archive bei der Vernichtung und (Re-)Konstruktion von Vergangenheit," in *Speicher des Gedächtnisses: Bibliotheken, Museen, Archive,* ed. Moritz Csáky, et al. Vienna 2001, 57–66.

Augustynowicz, Christoph and Ursula Reber (eds.). *Vampirglaube und Magia posthuma im Diskurs der Habsburgermonarchie.* Münster 2011.

Bachleitner, Norbert, Franz M. Eybl, and Ernst Fischer (eds.). *Geschichte des Buchhandels in Österreich.* Wiesbaden 2000.

Bachtrögl, Robert. *Die Nadelburg: Ein Denkmal vom Beginn des Industriezeitalters.* Lichtenwörth 2009.

Badinter, Elisabeth. *Die Mutterliebe: Die Geschichte eines Gefühls vom 17. Jahrhundert bis heute.* Munich 1981.

———. *Der Infant von Parma oder Die Ohnmacht der Erziehung* (1st ed.: *L'Infant de Parme,* Paris 2008). Munich 2010.

Baecque, Antoine de. *The Body Politic: Corporeal Metaphor in Revolutionary France, 1770–1800.* Stanford 1997.

Bahlcke, Joachim. "Hungaria eliberata? Zum Zusammenstoß von altständischer Libertät und monarchischer Autorität in Ungarn an der Wende vom 17. zum 18. Jahrhundert," in *Die Habsburgermonarchie 1620–1740: Leistungen und Grenzen des Absolutismusparadigmas,* ed. Petr Mat'a and Thomas Winkelbauer. Stuttgart 2006, 301–15.

Bahlcke, Joachim, Karen Lambrecht, and Hans-Christian Maner (eds.). *Konfessionelle Pluralität als Herausforderung. Koexistenz und Konflikt in Spätmittelalter und früher Neuzeit.* Leipzig 2006.

Baier, Karl. "Mesmer versus Gaßner: Eine Kontroverse der 1770er Jahre und ihre Interpretationen," in *Von der Dämonologie zum Unbewussten: Die Transformation der Anthropologie um 1800,* ed. Maren Sziede and Helmut Zander. Berlin 2015.

Bak, János, and Géza Pálffy (eds.). *Crown and Coronation in Hungary 1000–1916 A.D.* Budapest 2020.

Balász, Eva, and Ludwig Hammermayer, et al. (eds.). *Beförderer der Aufklärung in Mittel- und Osteuropa. Freimaurer, Gesellschaften, Clubs.* Essen 1987.

Ball, Gabriele (ed.). *Diskurse der Aufklärung: Luise Adelgunde Victorie und Johann Christoph Gottsched.* Wiesbaden 2006.

Barcsay, Ákos. *Herrschaftsantritt im Ungarn des 18. Jahrhunderts: Studien zum Verhältnis zwischen Krongewalt und Ständetum im Zeitalter des Absolutismus,* Sankt Katharinin 2002.

Barta, Heinz, and Günther Pallaver (eds.). *Karl Anton von Martini: Ein österreichischer Jurist, Rechtslehrer, Justiz- und Bildungsreformer im Dienste des Naturrechts.* Vienna and Berlin 2007.

Barta, Ilsebill. *Familienporträts der Habsburger: Dynastische Repräsentation im Zeitalter der Aufklärung.* Vienna / Cologne / Weimar 2001.

———. "Maria Theresia: Kritik einer Rezeption," in *Die ungeschriebene Geschichte: Historische Frauenforschung,* ed. Wiener Historikerinnen. Vienna 1984, 337–57.

Bárth, Dániel. *Katholische Aufklärung und Volksfrömmigkeit im Ungarn des 18. Jahrhunderts,* in *Katholische Aufklärung und Josephinismus: Rezeptionsformen in Ostmittel- und Südosteuropa,* ed. Rainer Bendel and Norbert Spannenberger. Cologne / Weimar / Vienna 2015, 79–101.

Barthel, Christian. *Medizinische Policey und medizinische Aufklärung: Aspekte des öffentlichen Gesundheitsdiskurses im 18. Jahrhundert.* Frankfurt am Main 1989.

Barton, Peter F. (ed.). *Im Zeichen der Toleranz: Aufsätze zur Toleranzgesetzgebung des 18. Jahrhunderts in den Reichen Josephs II., ihren Voraussetzungen und ihren Folgen.* Vienna 1981.

Bastian, Corina, et al. (eds.). *Das Geschlecht der Diplomatie: Geschlechterrollen in den Außenbeziehungen vom Spätmittelalter bis zur Gegenwart.* Cologne / Weimar / Vienna 2014.

Battenberg, Friedrich. "Des Kaisers Kammerknechte: Gedanken zur rechtlich-sozialen Situation der Juden in Spätmittelalter und Früher Neuzeit," in *Historische Zeitschrift* 245 (1987): 545–99.

Bauer, Volker. "Nachrichtenmedien und höfische Gesellschaft. Zum Verhältnis von Mediensystem und höfischer Öffentlichkeit im Alten Reich," in *Das Mediensystem im Alten Reich der Frühen Neuzeit (1600–1750),* ed. Johannes Arndt and Esther-Beate Körber, Göttingen 2010, 173–94.

———(ed.). *Repertorium territorialer Amtskalender und Amtshandbücher im Alten Reich: Adreß-, Hof-, Staatskalender und Staatshandbücher des 18. Jahrhunderts.* Frankfurt am Main 1997–2005.

Baugh, Daniel A. *The Global Seven Years War, 1754–1763: Britain and France in a Great Power Contest.* Harlow 2011.

Baumgart, Peter. "Joseph II und Maria Theresia 1765–1790," in *Die Kaiser der Neuzeit. 1519–1918. Heiliges römisches Reich, Österreich, Deutschland,* ed. Anton Schindling and Walter Ziegler. Munich 1990, 249–76.

Baur, Eva Gesine. *Mozart: Genius und Eros: Eine Biographie.* Munich 2014.

Beales, Derek (ed.). *Enlightenment and Reform in Eighteenth-Century Europe.* London and New York 2005.

———. "How Did Joseph II Govern?," in *Anzeiger der Österreichischen Akademie der Wissenschaften, Philosophisch-historische Klasse* 144 (2009): 49–59.

———. "Josephinismus," in *Der Aufgeklärte Absolutismus im europäischen Vergleich,* ed. Helmut Reinalter and Harm Klueting. Vienna / Cologne / Weimar 2002.

———. *Joseph II,* vol. 1: *In the Shadow of Maria Theresia 1741–1780.* Cambridge 1987.

———. *Joseph II,* vol. 2: *Against the World, 1780–1790.* Cambridge 2009.

———. "Love and the Empire: Maria Theresa and her Co-regents," in *Royal and Republican Sovereignty in Early Modern Europe,* ed. Robert Oresko, et al., Cambridge and New York 1997, 479–99.

————(ed). "Maria Theresia, Joseph II and Suppression of the Jesuits," in *Enlightenment and Reform in Eighteenth-Century Europe*, ed. Derek Beales. London and New York 2005, 207–26.

————. "Mozart and the Habsburgs," in *Enlightenment and Reform in Eighteenth-Century Europe*, ed. Derek Beales. London and New York 2005, 90–116.

————. "Writing a Life of Joseph II: The Problem of his Education," in *Biographie und Geschichtswissenschaft*, ed. Grete Klingenstein, et al., Vienna 1979, 183–207.

Becker, Peter. "Beschreiben, Klassifizieren, Verarbeiten: Zur Bevölkerungsbeschreibung aus kulturwissenschaftlicher Sicht," in *Information in der Frühen Neuzeit: Status, Strategien, Bestände*, ed. Arndt Brendecke, Markus Friedrich, and Susanne Friedrich. Berlin 2008, 393–419.

————(ed.). *Sprachvollzug im Amt. Kommunikation und Verwaltung im Europa des 19. und 20. Jahrhunderts.* Bielefeld 2011.

Beer, Adolf. *Die erste Theilung Polens.* 3 vols. Vienna 1873.

————. "Die Zusammenkünfte Josephs II. und Friedrichs II. in Neiße und Neustadt." *Archiv für österreichische Geschichte* 47 (1871): 383–527.

Begert, Alexander. *Böhmen, die böhmische Kur und das Reich vom Hochmittelalter bis zum Ende des Alten Reiches: Studien zur Kurwürde und staatsrechtlichen Stellung Böhmens.* Husum 2003.

Béhar, Pierre, Mare-Thérèse Mourey, and Herbert Schneider (eds.). *Maria Theresias Kulturwelt.* Hildesheim / Zürich / New York 2011.

Béhar, Pierre, and Helen Watanabe O'Kelly (eds.). *Spectaculum Europaeum: Theater and Spectacle in Europe (1580–1750).* Wiesbaden 1999.

Behringer, Wolfgang. *Im Zeichen des Merkur: Reichspost und Kommunikationsrevolution in der Frühen Neuzeit.* Göttingen 2002.

Behrisch, Lars. *Die Berechnung der Glückseligkeit: Statistik und Politik in Deutschland und Frankreich im späten Ancien Régime.* Ostfildern 2016.

————. "Zu viele Informationen! Die Aggregierung des Wissens in der Frühen Neuzeit," in *Information in der Frühen Neuzeit: Status, Strategien, Bestände*, ed. Arndt Brendecke, Markus Friedrich, and Susanne Friedrich. Berlin 2008, 455–73.

Brendecke, Arndt, Markus Friedrich, and Susanne Friedrich (eds.). *Information in der Frühen Neuzreit: Status, Strategien, Bestände.* Berlin 2008.

Beidtel, Ignaz, and Alfons Huber. *Geschichte der österreichischen Staatsverwaltung, 1740–1848.* Innsbruck 1896.

Bély, Lucien. "La politique extérieure de la France au milieu du XVIIIe siècle," in *Der Siebenjährige Krieg (1756–1764): Ein europäischer Weltkrieg im Zeitalter der Aufklärung*, ed. Sven Externbrink. Berlin 2011, 75–98.

Bendel, Rainer, and Norbert Spannenberger (eds.). *Katholische Aufklärung und Josephinismus. Rezeptionsformen in Ostmittel- und Südosteuropa.* Cologne / Weimar / Vienna 2015.

Benedik, Christian. "Die herrschaftlichen Appartements: Funktion und Lage während der Regierungen von Kaiser Leopold I. bis Kaiser Franz Joseph I., in Wiener Hofburg." *Österr. Zeitschrift für Kunst und Denkmalpflege* 51 (1997): 552–70.

————. "Zeremoniell und Repräsentation am Wiener Hof unter Franz Stephan von Lothringen," in *Franz Stephan von Lothringen und sein Kreis / L'empereur François Ier et le réseau lorrain / L'imperatore Francesco I e il circolo lorenese*, ed. Renate Zedinger and Wolfgang Schmale. Bochum 2009, 79–93.

Benedik, Christian, and Klaus Albrecht Schröder (eds.). *Die Gründung der Albertina: Herzog Albert und seine Zeit*. Exhibition catalog, Albertina Vienna. Ostfildern 2014.

Benedikt, Heinrich. "Der Josephinismus vor Joseph II.," in *Österreich und Europa: Festgabe für Hugo Hantsch*, Graz, et al. 1965, 183–201.

Berindei, Dan, et al. (eds.) *Der Bauer Mittel- und Osteuropas im sozio-ökonomischen Wandel des 18. und 19. Jahrhunderts*. Cologne and Vienna 1973,

Bérenger, Jean. *Joseph II: Serviteur de l'État*. Paris 2007.

———. *La Hongrie des Habsburgs*, vol 1: *De 1526 à 1790*. Rennes 2010.

Berger, Martha. *Wiennerisches Diarium 1703–1780: Ein Beitrag zur Entwicklung des Verhältnisses zwischen Staat und Presse*. Vienna 1955.

Bergl, Josef. "Das Exil der Prager Judenschaft von 1745 bis 1748," in *Jahrbuch der Gesellschaft für Geschichte der Cechoslovakischen Republik* 1 (1929): 263–331.

Berglar, Peter. *Maria Theresia: Mit Selbstzeugnissen und Bilddokumenten* (Rowohlts Monographien, 286). Reinbek bei Hamburg 1988.

Bernard, Bruno. "Patrice-François de Neny, Charles de Cobenzl et la prisonnière du Fort Monterey (1769–1770)," *Cahiers Bruxellois* 29 (1988): 79–105.

Bernard, Bruno, and Renate Zedinger. "Schicksalstage in Innsbruck: Corneille de Neny, Sekretär Maria Theresias, berichtet von den Ereignissen im Sommer 1765," in *Festung und Innovation: Jahrbuch der Österreichischen Gesellschaft zur Erforschung des achtzehnten Jahrhunderts*, ed. Harald Heppner and Wolfgang Schmale. Bochum 2005, 127–46.

Bernard, Paul P. *From the Enlightenment to the Police State. The Public Life of Johann Anton Pergen*. Chicago 1991.

Bernath, Mathias. *Habsburg und die Anfänge der rumänischen Nationsbildung*. Leiden 1972.

Berning, Bettina. *"Nach alltem löblichen Gebrauch": Die böhmischen Königskrönungen der Frühen Neuzeit (1526–1743)*. Cologne / Weimar / Vienna 2008.

Berns, Jörg Jochen, and Thomas Rahn, eds. *Zeremoniell als höfische Ästhetik in Spätmittelalter und Früher Neuzeit*. Tübingen 1995.

Bertele-Grenadenberg, Hans. "Uhren und Automaten," in *Maria Theresia und ihre Zeit*, ed. Walter Koschatzky. Salzburg and Vienna 1979, 437–45.

Beutelspacher, Martin. *Kultivierung bei lebendigem Leib: Alltägliche Körpererfahrung in der Aufklärung*. Weingart 1986.

Bevilacqua, Alexander, and Helen Pfeifer Turquerie. "Culture in Motion, 1650–1750." *Past & Present* 211 (2013): 75–118.

Bibl, Victor. *Die Wiener Polizei*. Leipzig / Vienna / New York 1927.

Bidermann, Hermann Ignaz. *Geschichte der österreichischen Gesammt-Staats-Idee*, vol. 2. Innsbruck 1889.

Biedermann, Karl. *Deutschland im 18. Jahrhundert*. Leipzig 1854.

Biró, Vencel. "Die katholische Restauration. Karl VI., Maria Theresia, Joseph II.," in *Kirche—Staat—Nation: Eine Geschichte der katholischen Kirche Siebenbürgens vom Mittelalter bis zum frühen 20. Jahrhundert*, ed. Joachim Bahlcke and Krista Zach. Munich 2007, 157–75.

Blaich, Fritz. "Die wirtschaftspolitische Tätigkeit der Kommission zur Bekämpfung der Hungersnot in Böhmen und Mähren (1771–1772)." *Vierteljahrschrift für Sozial- und Wirtschaftsgeschichte* 56 (1969): 310–36.

Blanning, Tim. *The Culture of Power and the Power of Culture. Old Regime Europe 1660–1789.* Oxford 2002.

———. *Frederick the Great, King of Prussia.* New York 2015.

———. *Joseph II and Enlightened Despotism.* London 1970.

Bleckwenn, Hans. "Der Kaiserin Hayducken, Husaren und Grenzer: Bild und Wesen 1740–1769," in *Maria Theresia als Königin von Ungarn,* ed. Provincial Government of Burgenland. Eisenstadt 1984, 113–24.

Bled, Jean-Paul. *Marie-Thérèse d'Autriche.* Paris 2001.

Blitz, Hans-Martin. *Aus Liebe zum Vaterland: Die deutsche Nation im 18. Jahrhundert.* Hamburg 2000.

Blockmans, Wim, André Holenstein, and Jon Mathieu (eds.). *Empowering Interactions: Political Cultures and the Emergence of the State in Europe, 1300–1900.* Farnham 2009.

Bogner, Ralf (ed.). *Documenta Austriaca: Literatur und Kultur in den Ländern der ehemaligen Donaumonarchie.* Hildesheim / Zürich / New York 2011.

Bohn, Thomas. *Der Vampir: Ein europäischer Mythos.* Cologne / Weimar / Vienna 2016.

Bömelburg, Hans-Jürgen, Andreas Gestrich, and Helga Schnabel-Schüle (eds.). *Die Teilungen Polen-Litauens: Inklusions- und Exklusionsmechanismen—Traditionsbildung— Vergleichsebenen.* Osnabrück 2013.

Born, Robert. "Bollwerk und merkantilistisches Laboratorium. Das Temeswarer Banat in den Planungen der Wiener Zentralstellen (1716–1778)," in *Grenzregionen der Habsburgermonarchie im 18. und 19. Jahrhundert: Ihre Bedeutung und Funktion aus der Perspektive Wiens,* ed. Hans-Christian Maner. Münster 2005, 37–49.

Bosl, Karl (ed.). *Handbuch der Geschichte der böhmischen Länder,* vol. 2. Stuttgart 1974.

Bourdieu, Pierre. "The Biographical Illusion," in *Identity: A Reader,* ed. Paul du Gay, Jessica Evans, and Peter Redman. London 2000, 297–303.

Bradley, David C. *Judith, Maria Theresa, and Metastasio: A Cultural Study Based on Two Oratorios.* Tallahassee 1985.

Brakensiek, Stefan. "Communication between Authorities and Subjects in Bohemia, Hungary and the Holy German Empire, 1650–1800: A Comparison," in *Empowering Interactions. Political Cultures and the Emergence of the State in Europe, 1300–1900,* ed. Wim Blockmans, André Holenstein, and Jon Mathieu. Farnham. 2009, 149–62.

Brakensiek, Stefan, Corinna von Bredow, and Birgit Näther (eds.). *Herrschaft und Verwaltung in der Frühen Neuzeit.* Berlin 2014.

Brakensiek, Stefan, András Vári, and Judit Pál. *Herrschaft an der Grenze: Mikrogeschichte der Macht im östlichen Ungarn im 18. Jahrhundert.* Cologne / Weimar / Vienna 2014.

Braubach, Max. *Maria Theresias jüngster Sohn Maximilian Franz: Letzter Kurfürst von Köln und Fürstbischof von Münster.* Vienna 1961.

———. *Versailles und Wien von Ludwig XIV. bis Kaunitz: Die Vorstadien der diplomatischen Revolution im 18. Jahrhundert.* Bonn 1952.

Braun, Bettina. *Eine Kaiserin und zwei Kaiser: Maria Theresia und ihre Mitregenten Franz Stephan und Joseph II.* Bielefeld 2018.

———. "Maria Theresia, Herrscherin aus eigenem Recht und Kaiserin," in *Nur die Frau des Kaisers? Kaiserinnen in der Frühen Neuzeit,* ed. Bettina Braun, Katrin Keller, and Matthias Schnettger. Cologne /Weimar / Vienna 2016, 211–28.

————. *Princeps et episcopus: Studien zur Funktion und zum Selbstverständnis der nordwestdeutschen Fürstbischöfe nach dem Westfälischen Frieden.* Göttingen 2013.

Braun, Bettina, Frank Göttmann, and Michael Ströhmer (eds.). *Geistliche Staaten im Nordwesten des Alten Reiches: Forschungen zum Problem frühmoderner Staatlichkeit.* Cologne 2003.

Braun, Bettina, Katrin Keller, and Matthias Schnettger (eds.). *Nur die Frau des Kaisers? Kaiserinnen in der Frühen Neuzeit.* Cologne / Weimar / Vienna 2016.

Braun, Bettina, Jan Kusber, and Matthias Schnettger (eds.). *Weibliche Herrschaft im 18. Jahrhundert: Maria Theresia und Katharina die Große.* Bielefeld 2020.

Brauneder, Wilhelm. "Das Allgemeine Bürgerliche Gesetzbuch für die gesamten Deutschen Erbländer der österreichischen Monarchie von 1811," in *Gutenberg Jahrbuch* 62 (1987): 205–54.

————. "Die Pragmatische Sanktion als Grundgesetz der Monarchia Austriaca von 1713 bis 1918," in Wilhelm Brauneder, *Studien I: Entwicklung des Öffentlichen Rechts.* Frankfurt am Main 1994, 85–115.

————. "Vom Nutzen des Naturrechts für die Habsburgermonarchie," in *Naturrecht und Staat: Politische Funktionen des europäischen Naturrechts (17.—19. Jahrhundert),* ed. Diethelm Klippel. Munich 2006, 145–70.

Brauneder, Wilhelm, and Lothar Höbelt (eds.). *Sacrum Imperium: Das Reich und Österreich 996–1806.* Vienna 1996.

Brauneis, Walther. "Franz Stephan von Lothringen—am Ende des Weges," in *Innsbruck 1765: Prunkvolle Hochzeit, fröhliche Feste, tragischer Ausklang* (Das Achtzehnte Jahrhundert und Österreich, vol. 29), ed. Renate Zedinger. Bochum 2015, 273–98.

Bräunlein, Peter J. "The Frightening Borderlands of Enlightenment: The Vampire Problem," in *Studies in History and Philosophy of Biological and Biomedical Sciences* 43 (2012): 710–719.

Brechka, F. T. *Gerard Van Swieten and His World 1700–1772.* The Hague 1970.

Bredow, Corinna von. "Die niederösterreichischen Kreisämter als Scharnier zwischen Landesregierung und Untertanen—Kommunikationsprozesse und Herrschaftspraxis," in *Herrschaft und Verwaltung in der Frühen Neuzeit,* ed. Stefan Brakensiek, Corinna von Bredow, and Birgit Näther. Berlin 2014, 25–36.

Brendecke, Arndt. *Imperium und Empirie: Funktionen des Wissens in der spanischen Kolonialherrschaft.* Cologne / Weimar / Vienna 2009.

Brendecke, Arndt, Markus Friedrich, and Susanne Friedrich (eds.), *Information in der Frühen Neuzeit: Status, Bestände, Strategien.* Berlin 2008.

Brendle, Franz, and Anton Schindling (eds.). *Religionskriege im Alten Reich und in Alteuropa.* Münster 2006.

Bressan, Marina, and Marino de Grassi (eds.). *Maria Teresa: Maestà di una sovrana Europea.* Monfalcone 2000.

Breuer, Mordechai and Michael Graetz (eds.). *Tradition und Aufklärung 1600–1780,* vol. 1: *Deutsch-jüdische Geschichte in der Neuzeit.* Munich 1996.

Breunlich-Pawlik, Maria. "Die Aufzeichnungen des Sigmund Friedrich Graf Khevenhüller 1690–1738." *MÖStA* 26 (1973): 235–53.

Brix, Emil, Ernst Bruckmüller, and Hannes Stekl (eds.). *Memoria Austriae I: Menschen, Mythen, Zeiten.* Vienna 2004.

———. *Memoria Austriae II: Bauten, Orte Regionen*. Vienna 2005.

Brockhoff, Evelyn, and Michael Mathäus (eds.). *Die Kaisermacher: Frankfurt am Main und die Goldene Bulle 1356–1806*. Exhibition catalog. Frankfurt am Main 2006.

Broman, Thomas H. *The Transformation of German Academic Medicine, 1750–1820*. Cambridge 1996.

Broucek, Peter. *Der Geburtstag der Monarchie: Die Schlacht bei Kolin 1757*. Vienna 1982.

Browning, Reed. "The Duke of Newcastle and the Imperial Election Plan 1749–1754," in *Journal of British Studies* 7 (1967): 28–47.

Brückner, Wolfgang. *Bildnis und Brauch: Studien zur Bildfunktion der Effigies*. Berlin 1966.

———. "Zum Wandel der religiösen Kultur im 18. Jahrhundert: Einkreisungsversuche des Barockfrommen zwischen Mittelalter und Massenmissionierung," in *Sozialer und kultureller Wandel in der ländlichen Welt des 18. Jahrhunderts*, ed. Ernst Hinrichs and Günther Wiegelmann. Wolfenbüttel 1982, 65–83.

Brugger, Eveline, et al. (eds.). *Geschichte der Juden in Österreich*. Vienna 2006.

Buchinger, Erich. "Die 'Landler,'" in *Siebenbürgen: Vorgeschichte, Durchführung und Ergebnis einer Zwangsumsiedlung im 18. Jahrhundert*. Munich 1980.

Buddruss, Eckhardt. *Die französische Deutschlandpolitik 1756—1789*. Mainz 1995.

Buisseret, David (ed.). *Monarchs, Ministers, and Maps: The Emergence of Cartography as a Tool of Government in Early Modern Europe*. Chicago 1992.

Bundesministerium für Wissenschaft und Forschung / Österreichische Akademie der Wissenschaften (ed.). *Österreich im Europa der Aufklärung. Kontinuität und Zäsur in Europa zur Zeit Maria Theresias und Josephs II*. Vienna 1985.

Burckhardt, Carl. *Maria Theresia*. Lübeck 1932.

Burgenländische Landesregierung (ed.). *Maria Theresia als Königin von Ungarn*. Exhibition catalog, Schloss Halbthurn. Eisenstadt 1980.

Burger, Hannelore. *Heimatrecht und Staatsbürgerschaft österreichischer Juden: Vom Ende des 18. Jahrhunderts bis in die Gegenwart*. Vienna / Cologne / Graz 2014.

Burkhardt, Johannes. *Abschied vom Religionskrieg: Der Siebenjährige Krieg und die päpstliche Diplomatie*. Tübingen 1985.

———. "Religious War or Imperial War? Views of the Seven Years' War from Germany and Rome," in *The Seven Years' War. Global Views*, ed. Mark H. Danley and Patrick J. Speelman. Leiden / Boston 2012, 107–34.

Burschel, Peter. *Die Erfindung der Reinheit: Eine andere Geschichte der frühen Neuzeit*. Göttingen 2014.

Burson, Jeffrey D. and Ulrich L. Lehner (ed.). *Enlightenment and Catholicism in Europe: A Transnational History*. Notre Dame 2014.

Bužek, Vaclav and Peter Mat'a. "Wandlungen des Adels in Böhmen und Mähren im Zeitalter des 'Absolutismus,'" in *Der europäische Adel im Ancien Régime*, ed. Ronald Asch. Cologne 2001, 287–322.

Bynum, Caroline. *The Resurrection of the Body in Western Civilisation, 200–1336*. New York 1994.

Cachée, Josef. *Die Hofküche des Kaisers: Die k.u.k. Hofküche, die Hofzuckerbäckerei und der Hofkeller in der Wiener Hofburg*. Vienna 1985.

Campbell Orr, Clarissa (ed.). *Queenship in Europe 1660–181: The Role of the Consort*. Cambridge 2004.

Campianu, Eva. "Terpsichore im Wien der Kaiserin," in *Maria Theresia und ihre Zeit*, ed. Walter Koschatzky. Salzburg / Vienna 1979, 405–12.

Capra, Carlo. "Habsburg Italy in the Age of Reform." *Journal of Modern Italian Studies* 10 (2005): 218–33.

Cattaneo, Mario A. "Beccaria und Sonnenfels: Die Abschaffung der Folter im theresianischen Zeitalter," in *Cattaneo, Aufklärung und Strafrecht*. Baden-Baden 1998, 49–62.

Čechura, Jaroslav. "Zu spät und zu friedlich? Die Bauernrevolten in Böhmen und Mähren 1500–1800," in *Die Stimme der ewigen Verlierer? Aufstände, Revolten und Revolutionen in den österreichischen Ländern (ca. 1740–1815)*, ed. Peter Rauscher and Martin Scheutz. Munich 2013, 119–33.

Cerman, Ivo. *Habsburgischer Adel und Aufklärung. Bildungsverhalten des Wiener Hofadels im 18. Jahrhundert*. Stuttgart 2010.

———. "Habsburgischer Adel und das Theresianum in Wien 1746–1784: Wissensvermittlung, Sozialisation und Berufswege," in *Adelige Ausbildung: Die Herausforderung der Aufklärung und die Folgen*, ed. Ivo Cerman and Lubos Velek. Munich 2006, 143–68.

———. "Maria Theresia in the Mirror of Contemporary Mock Jewish Chronicles," in *Judaica Bohemiae* (2002): 5–47.

———. "Opposition oder Kooperation? Der Staat und die Stände in Böhmen 1749–1789," in *Bündnispartner und Konkurrenten der Landesfürsten? Die Stände in der Habsburgermonarchie*, ed. Gerhard Ammerer, et al. Vienna and Munich 2007, 342–61.

———. "Tereziánská legenda. Vývoj obrazu Marie Terezie v historických životopisech [Die theresianische Legende. Die Entwicklung des Bildes Maria Theresias in den historischen Biographien]," in *Společnost v zemích habsburské monarchie a její obraz v pramenech (1526–1740) [Die Gesellschaft in den Länder der Habsburgermonarchie und ihr Bild in den Quellen (1526–1740)]*, ed. Václav Bužek and Pavel Král. Budweis 2006, 149–65.

Cerman, Ivo, Rita Krueger, and Susan Reynolds (ed.). *The Enlightenment in Bohemia. Religion, Morality and Multiculturalism*. Oxford 2011.

Cerman, Ivo, and Robert Luft (ed.). *Untertanen, Herrschaft und Staat in Böhmen und im "Alten Reich."* Sozialgeschichtliche Studien zur Frühen Neuzeit. Munich 2005.

Christ, Günter. *Praesentia Regis: Kaiserliche Diplomatie und Reichskirchenpolitik vornehmlich am Beispiel der Entwicklung des Zeremoniells für die kaiserlichen Wahlgesandten in Würzburg und Bamberg*. Wiesbaden 1975.

Clark, Samuel. *State and Status: The Rise of the State and Aristocratic Power in Western Europe*. Cardiff 1995.

Coreth, Anna. *Pietas Austriaca: Österreichische Frömmigkeit im Barock*, 2nd ed. Vienna 1982.

Corti, Egon Caesar Conte. *Ich, eine Tochter Maria Theresias: Ein Lebensbild der Königin Marie Karoline von Neapel*. Munich 1950.

Cosandey, Fanny. *La Reine de France: Symbole et pouvoir, XVe–XVIIIe siècle*. Paris 2000.

Coupe, W. A. *German Political Satires from the Reformation to the Second World War*. Part I: *1500–1848 Plates, Commentary*. New York 1993.

Crankshaw, Edward. *Maria Theresia: Die mütterliche Majestät*. Munich 1975.

Csendes, Peter, and Ferdinand Opll (eds.). *Wien: Geschichte einer Stadt*. 3 vols. Vienna 2000–2003.

Dade, Eva Kathrin. *Madame de Pompadour: Die Mätresse und die Diplomatie.* Cologne / Weimar / Vienna 2010.

Daniel, Ute. "Höfe und Aufklärung in Deutschland: Plädoyer für eine Begegnung der dritten Art," in *Hofkultur und aufklärerische Reformen in Thüringen. Die Bedeutung des Hofes im späten 18. Jahrhundert,* ed. Markus Ventzke. Cologne / Weimar / Vienna 2002.

———. *Hoftheater: Zur Geschichte des Theaters und der Höfe im 18. und 19. Jahrhundert.* Stuttgart 1995.

Danley, Mark H., and Patrick J. Speelman (eds.). *The Seven Years' War: Global Views.* Leiden / Boston 2012.

Denzler, Alexander. *Über den Schriftalltag im 18. Jahrhundert: Die Visitationen des Reichskammergerichts von 1767 bis 1776.* Cologne / Weimar / Vienna 2016.

Des Kaisers Rock: Uniform und Mode am österreichischen Kaiserhof, 1800 bis 1918. Exhibition catalog. Halbturn and Eisenstadt 1989.

Deuticke, Franz. *Geschichte der Geburtshilfe in Wien,* ed. Dr. J. Fischer. Vienna 1909.

Dickens, Arthur Geoffrey (ed.). *Europas Fürstenhöfe. Herrscher, Politiker und Mäzene 1400–1800.* Graz 1978.

Dickson, Peter George Muir. "Baron Bartenstein on Count Haugwitz' 'New System' of Government," in *History and Biography. Essays in Honour of Derek Beales,* ed. Timothy C. W. Blanning and David Cannadine. Cambridge 1996, 5–18.

———. *Finance and Government under Maria Theresia 1740–1780.* 2 vols. Oxford 1987.

———. "Monarchy and Bureaucracy in Late Eighteenth-Century Austria." *English Historical Review* 10 (1995): 323–67.

Die Türken—und was von ihnen blieb. Exhibition catalog. Vienna 1978.

Dietrich, Margret. "Theater am Hofe—Zwischen Tradition und Wandel," in *Maria Theresia und ihre Zeit,* ed. Walter Koschatzky. Salzburg and Vienna 1979, 393–403.

Dikowitsch, Hermann (ed.). *Barock—Blütezeit der europäischen Ritterorden.* Exhibition catalog. Schallaburg, Sankt Pölten 2000.

Dimt, Gunter (ed.). *Volksfrömmigkeit in Oberösterreich.* Exhibition catalog. Linz 1985.

Dinges, Martin. "Medicinische Policey zwischen Heilkundigen und "Patienten" (1750–1830)," in *Policey und frühneuzeitliche Gesellschaft,* ed. Karl Härter. Frankfurt am Main 2000, 263–95.

Direktion des Heeresgeschichtlichen Museums in Wien (ed.). *Maria Theresia: Beiträge zur Geschichte des Heerwesens ihrer Zeit.* Graz / Vienna / Cologne 1967.

Direktion des k.u.k.-Kriegsarchivs (ed.). *Österreichischer Erbfolgekrieg 1740–1748.* Vienna 1896–1905.

Do Paço. David. "'Durch die Türkey': A Way to an Urban History of 18th Century Vienna," in *Forschungswerkstatt: Die Habsburgermonarchie im 18. Jahrhundert,* ed. Gunda Barth-Scalman, et al. Bochum 2012, 241–52.

———. "Les amertumes de la Pomme d'or. Ambassades orientales, cultures et raisons utilitaires à Vienne, 1740–1792," in *Multiple kulturelle Referenzen in der Habsburgermonarchie des 18. Jahrhunderts,* ed. Wolfgang Schmale (Das achtzehnte Jahrhundert und Österreich, 24). Bochum 2010, 47–74.

———. *L'Orient à Vienne: Cosmopolitisme et intégration dans l'Europe des Lumières.* Oxford 2015.

―――. "The Ottoman Empire in Early Modern Austrian History: Assessment and Perspectives." *EU Working Paper* 7 (2014). URL: http://cadmus.eui.eu/bitstream/handle/1814/31652/MWP_WP_DoPaco_2014_07.pdf (01.05.2016).

Dörflinger, Wolfgang. "Vom Aufstieg der Militärkartographie bis zum Wiener Kongress (1684–1815)," in *Österreichische Kartographie: Von den Anfängen im 15. Jahrhundert bis zum 21. Jahrhundert*, ed. Wolfgang Dörflinger, Ingrid Kretschmer, and Franz Wawrik. Vienna 2004, 75–97.

Dörflinger, Wolfgang, Ingred Kretschmer, and Franz Wawrik (eds). *Österreichische Kartographie: Von den Anfängen im 15. Jahrhundert bis zum 21. Jahrhundert*. Vienna 2004.

Dorfner, Thomas. *Mittler zwischen Haupt und Gliedern: Die Reichshofratsagenten und ihre Rolle im Verfahren (1658–1740)*. Münster 2015.

Dörrer, Anton. *Tiroler Umgangsspiele*. Innsbruck 1957.

Dörrer, Fridolin. "Zeremoniell, alte Praxis und 'neuer Geist. Zum Verhalten der Herrscher und Regierungen in Wien und Florenz zu den Nuntien. Beispiele aus den Jahren um 1760," in *Römische Historische Mitteilungen* 43 (2001): 587–630.

Drabek, Anna M. "Die Juden in den böhmischen Ländern zur Zeit des landesfürstlichen Absolutismus," in *Die Juden in den böhmischen Ländern*, ed. Ferdinand Seibt. Munich / Vienna 1983, 123–43.

Drabek, Anna M., Richard G. Plaschka, and Adam Wandruszka (eds.). *Ungarn und Österreich unter Maria Theresia und Joseph II: Neue Aspekte im Verhältnis der beiden Länder*. Vienna 1982.

Drugulin, Wilhelm Eduard. *Historischer Bilderatlas: Verzeichnis einer Sammlung von Einzelblättern zur Cultur- und Staatengeschichte vom 15. bis in das 19. Jahrhundert*. Leipzig 1863.

Duchhardt, Heinz. *Handbuch der Geschichte der Internationalen Beziehungen*, vol. 4: *Balance of Power und Pentarchie: Internationale Beziehungen 1700–1785*. Paderborn 1997.

―――. "Philipp Karl von Eltz, Kurfürst von Mainz: Erzkanzler des Reiches (1732–1743)." *Studie zur kurmainzischen Reichs- und Innenpolitik*. Mainz 1969.

Duchkowitsch, Wolfgang. *Absolutismus und Zeitung: Die Strategie der absolutistischen Kommunikationspolitik und ihre Wirkung auf die Wiener Zeitungen 1621–1757*. Vienna 1978.

―――(ed.). *Mediengeschichte. Forschung und Praxis*. Vienna / Cologne / Graz 1985.

―――. "Österreichs Tagespresse im Banne der Obrigkeit. Kommunikationskontrolle vor 1848." *Journalistik* 5 (1983): 16–29.

Duden, Barbara. "'Ein falsch Gewächs, ein unzeitig Wesen, gestocktes Blut': Zur Geschichte der Wahrnehmung und Sichtweise der Leibesfrucht," in *Unter anderen Umständen: Zur Geschichte der Abtreibung*. Berlin 1993, 27–35.

Duffy, Christopher. *The Army of Maria Theresia*. London / Vancouver 1977.

―――. *Sieben Jahre Krieg. 1756–1763: Die Armee Maria Theresias*. Vienna 2003.

Duindam, Jeroen. "The Courts of the Austrian Habsburgs 1500–1750. The Archduchy of Austria and the Kingdoms of Bohemia and Hungary," in *The Princely Courts of Europe: Ritual, Politics, and Culture under the Ancien Régime 1550–1750*, ed. John Adamson. London 1999, 165–87.

―――. "The Habsburg Court in Vienna: Kaiserhof or Reichshof?," in *The Holy Roman Empire: A European Perspective*, ed. Peter H. Wilson, et al. Oxford 2012, 91–120.

―――. *Vienna and Versailles: The Courts of Europe's Dynastic Rivals, 1550–1780*. Cambridge 2003.

Duprat, Annie. *Marie Antoinette: Une reine brisée*. Paris 2006.

Duchhardt, Heinz. *Balance of Power und Pentarchie: Internationale Beziehungen 1700–1785*. Paderborn 1997.

Eberhart, Helmut, and Heidelined Fell (eds.). *Mariazell—Schatz und Schicksal: Katalog der Steirischen Landesausstellung*. Graz 1996.

Eder, Ulrike. "Auf die mehrere Ausbreitung der teutschen Sprache soll fürgedacht werden," in *Deutsch als Fremd- und Zweitsprache im Unterrichtssystem der Donaumonarchie*. Innsbruck 2006.

Ehalt, Hubert Christian. *Ausdrucksformen absolutistischer Herrschaft: Der Wiener Hof im 17. und 18. Jahrhundert*. Vienna and Munich 1980.

Eisenhardt, Ulrich. "Der Reichshofrat als kombiniertes Rechtsprechungs- und Regierungsorgan," in *"Zur Erhaltung guter Ordnung": Beiträge zur Geschichte von Recht und Justiz. Festschrift für Wolfgang Sellert zum 65. Geburtstag*, ed. Jost Hausmann and Thomas Krause. Cologne / Weimar / Vienna 2000, 245–67.

Elias, Norbert. *The Court Society*, translated by Edmund Jephcott. Oxford 1983.

Emich, Birgit, et al. "Stand und Perspektiven der Patronageforschung," in *Zeitschrift für historische Forschung* 32 (2005): 233–65.

Engelbrecht, Helmut. *Geschichte des österreichischen Bildungswesens: Erziehung und Unterricht auf dem Boden Österreichs*. 2 vols. Vienna 1983.

Etzlstorfer, Hannes. *Maria Theresia. Kinder, Kirche & Korsett: Die privaten Seiten einer Herrscherin*. Vienna 2008.

Evans, Robert J. W. "The Austrian Habsburgs: The Dynasty as a Political Institution," in *The Courts of Europe, Politics, Patronage and Royalty, 1400–1800*, ed. Arthur Geoffrey Dickens. London 1977, 121–45.

———. *Das Werden der Habsburgermonarchie 1550–1700*. Vienna 1986.

———. "Maria Theresa and Hungary," in *Enlightened Absolutism. Reform and Reformers in Later Eighteenth Century Europe*, ed. Hamish M. Scott. London and Ann Arbor 1990, 189.

Externbrink, Sven (ed.). *Der Siebenjährige Krieg (1756–1764): Ein europäischer Weltkrieg im Zeitalter der Aufklärung*. Berlin 2011.

———. "Frankreich und die Reichsexekution gegen Friedrich II: Zur Wahrnehmung der Reichsverfassung durch die französische Diplomatie während des Siebenjährigen Krieges," in *Altes Reich, Frankreich und Europa. Politische, philosophische und historische Aspekte des französischen Deutschlandbildes im 17. und 18. Jahrhundert*, ed. Olaf Asbach, Klaus Malettke, and Sven Externbrink. Berlin 2001, 221–53.

———. *Friedrich der Große, Maria Theresia und das Alte Reich: Deutschlandbild und Diplomatie Frankreichs im Siebenjährigen Krieg*. Berlin 2006.

Eybl, Franz M. (ed.). *Das Achtzehnte Jahrhundert und Österreich*, vol. 17: *Strukturwandel kultureller Praxis: Beiträge zu einer kulturwissenschaftlichen Sicht des theresianischen Zeitalters*. Vienna 2002.

———. "Die katholischen Hofprediger," in *Religion Macht Politik. Hofgeistlichkeit im Europa der Frühen Neuzeit*, ed. Matthias Meinhardt, et al. Wiesbaden 2014, 429–46.

Falkenberg, Regine. "Wandbehang zum Frieden von Hubertusburg 1763," in *Tuchintarsien in Europa von 1500 bis heute*, ed. Dagmar Neuland-Kitzerow, et al. Berlin 2009, 176.

Faroqhi, Suraiya. "Was man in Wien erfahren konnte," in *Europa und die Moderne im langen 18. Jahrhundert*, ed. Olaf Asbach. Hannover 2014.

Fata, Marta. "Die religiöse Vielfalt aus Sicht des Wiener Hofes: Beobachtungs- und Bewertungskriterien des Mitregenten Joseph II. während seiner Reise nach Siebenbürgen 1773," in *Historisches Jahrbuch* 133 (2013): 255–76.

———. "Migration im kameralistischen Staat Josephs II: Theorie und Praxis der Ansiedlungspolitik in Ungarn, Siebenbürgen, Galizien und der Bukowina von 1768 bis 1790." Münster 2014.

Fazekas, István. "Die Verwaltungsgeschichte des Königreichs Ungarn und seiner Nebenländer (1526–1848)" in *Herrschaftsverdichtung, Staatsbildung, Bürokratisierung. Verfassungs-, Verwaltungs- und Behördengeschichte der Frühen Neuzeit,* ed. Thomas Winkelbauer and Michael Hochedlinger. Vienna 2010, 479–502.

Fazekas, István, et al. (eds.). *Frühneuzeitforschung in der Habsburgermonarchie. Adel und Wiener Hof—Konfessionalisierung—Siebenbürgen.* Vienna 2013.

Feigl, Helmuth. *Die niederösterreichische Grundherrschaft: Vom ausgehenden Mittelalter bis zu den theresianisch-josephinischen Reformen,* 2nd ed. St. Pölten 1998.

Feldman, Martha S. / James G. March. "Information in Organizations as Signal and Symbol," *Administrative Science Quarterly* 26 (1981): 171–86.

Félix, Joël. *Louis XVI et Marie-Antoinette: Un couple en politique.* Paris 2006.

Fieseler, Christian. *Der vermessene Staat: Kartographie und die Kartierung nordwestdeutscher Territorien im 18. Jahrhundert.* Hannover 2013.

Fillafer, Franz Leander. "Die Aufklärung in der Habsburgermonarchie und ihr Erbe," in *Zeitschrift für Historische Forschung* 40 (2013): 35–97.

———. "Rivalisierende Aufklärungen: Die Kontinuität und Historisierung des josephinischen Reformabsolutismus in der Habsburgermonarchie," in *Die Aufklärung und ihre Weltwirkung,* ed. Wolfgang Hardtwig. Göttingen 2010, 123–68.

Fillafer, Franz Leander, and Thomas Wallnig (eds.). *Josephinismus zwischen den Regimen: Eduard Winter, Fritz Valjavec und die zentraleuropäischen Historiographien im 20. Jahrhundert.* Vienna / Cologne / Weimar 2016.

Fillitz, Hermann. *Katalog der weltlichen und geistlichen Schatzkammer, neue Auflage, besorgt von E. Neumann.* Vienna 1977.

Fischer, Ernst, Wilhelm Haefs, and York-Gothart Mix (eds.). *Von Almanach bis Zeitung: Ein Handbuch der Medien in Deutrschland, 1700–1800.* Munich 1999.

Fischer, Nora. "Kunst nach Ordnung, Auswahl und System: Transformationen der kaiserlichen Gemäldegalerie in Wien im späten 18. Jahrhundert," in *Die kaiserliche Gemäldegalerie in Wien und die Anfänge des öffentlichen Kunstmuseums,* vol. 1: *Die kaiserliche Galerie im Belvedere (1776–1837),* ed. Gudrun Swoboda. Vienna / Cologne / Weimar 2013, 22–89.

Fischer, Robert-Tarek. *Österreich im Nahen Osten: Die Großmachtpolitik der Habsburgermonarchie im Arabischen Orient 1633–1918.* Vienna / Cologne / Weimar 2006.

Flamm, Heinz, and Christian Vutuc. "Geschichte der Pocken-Bekämpfung in Österreich," in *Wiener Klinische Wochenschrift* 122 (2010): 265–75.

Fleckner, Uwe, Martin Warnke, and Hendrik Ziegler (eds.). *Handbuch der politischen Ikonographie.* 2 vols. Munich 2011.

Förschner, Gisela. *Frankfurter Krönungsmedaillen.* Frankfurt am Main 1992.

Fournier, August. "Gerhard van Swieten als Censor," in *Sitzungsberichte der phil.-hist. Classe der kaiserlichen Akademie der Wissenschaften* 84 (1876): 387–466.

Frank, Johann Peter. *System einer vollständigen medicinischen Polizey.* 15 vols. Frankenthal 1779–1819.

Frank, Peter R. "Buchhandel in maria-theresianischer Zeit," in *Das Achtzehnte Jahrhundert und Österreich,* vol. 17: *Strukturwandel kultureller Praxis. Beiträge zu einer kulturwissenschaftlichen Sicht des theresianischen Zeitalters,* ed. Franz M. Eybl. Vienna 2002, 141–52.

Franz Xaver Messerschmidt 1736–1783. Exhibition catalog, Österreichische Galerie Belvedere. Ostfildern 2002.

Fraser, Antonia. *Marie Antoinette: The Journey.* New York 2011.

Frevert, Ute. *Gefühlspolitik: Friedrich II. als Herr über die Herzen?* Göttingen 2012.

Frey, Manuel. *Der reinliche Bürger: Entstehung und Verbreitung bürgerlicher Tugenden in Deutschland 1760–1860.* Göttingen 1997.

Freytag, Rudolf. "Das Prinzipalkommissariat des Fürsten Alexander Ferdinand von Thurn und Taxis." *Jahrbuch des Historischen Vereins Dillingen* 25 (1912): 247–74.

Friedrich, Margret. "Gleichförmigkeit und Glückseligkeit: Zum mentalen Wandel im Rechtsdenken des theresianischen Zeitalters," in *Das Achtzehnte Jahrhundert und Österreich,* vol. 17: *Strukturwandel kultureller Praxis Beiträge zu einer kulturwissenschaftlichen Sicht des theresianischen Zeitalters,* ed. Franz M. Eybl. Vienna 2002, 111–30.

Friedrich, Markus. *Die Geburt des Archivs: Eine Wissensgeschichte.* Munich 2014.

Friedrich, Susanne. *Drehscheibe Regensburg: Das Informations- und Kommunikationssystem des Immerwährenden Reichstags um 1700.* Berlin 2011.

Frimmel, Johannes, and Michael Wögerbauer (eds.). *Kommunikation und Information im 18. Jahrhundert: Das Beispiel der Habsburgermonarchie.* Wiesbaden 2009.

Fritz-Hilscher, Elisabeth (ed.). *Im Dienste einer Staatsidee: Künste und Künstler am Wiener Hof um 1740.* Vienna / Cologne / Weimar 2013.

Fuchs, Antje. "Der Siebenjährige Krieg als virtueller Religionskrieg an Beispielen aus Preußen, Österreich, Kurhannover und Großbritannien," in *Religionskriege im Alten Reich und in Alteuropa,* ed. Franz Brendle and Anton Schindling. Münster 2006, 313–43.

Füssel, Marian. *Der Siebenjährige Krieg: Ein Weltkrieg im 18. Jahrhundert.* Munich 2010.

———. "Ungesehenes Leiden? Tod und Verwundung auf den Schlachtfeldern des 18. Jahrhunderts." *Historische Anthropologie* 23 (2015): 30–53.

Füssel, Marian, and Michael Sikora (eds.). *Kulturgeschichte der Schlacht.* Paderborn 2014.

Füssel, Marian, and Thomas Weller (eds.). *Ordnung und Distinktion: Praktiken sozialer Repräsentation in der ständischen Gesellschaft.* Münster 2005.

Galand, Michèle. "Le journal secret de Charles de Lorraine, gouverneur général des Pays Bas autrichiens." *Revue belge de philologie et d'histoire* 62 (1984): 289–301.

Galavics, Géza. "Barockkunst, höfische Repräsentation und Ungarn," in *Maria Theresia als Königin von Ungarn,* ed. der Burgenländischen Landesregierung. Eisenstadt 1984, 57–70.

Garms-Cornides, Elisabeth. "Liturgie und Diplomatie Zum Zeremoniell des Nuntius am Wiener Kaiserhof im 17. und 18. Jahrhundert," in *Kaiserhof—Papsthof (16.-18. Jahrhundert),* ed. Richard Bösel, Grete Klingenstein, and Alexander Koller. Vienna 2006, 125–46.

———. "Verspätete Hochzeitsreise? Politik und Zeremoniell auf der Italienreise Franz Stephans und Maria Theresias (1738/39)," in *Franz Stephan von Lothringen und sein Kreis,* ed. Renate Zedinger and Wolfgang Schmale. Bochum 2009, 149–69.

Gehler, Michael, et al. (eds.). *Ungleiche Partner? Österreich und Deutschland in ihrer gegenseitigen Wahrnehmung.* Stuttgart 1996.

Gérard, Jo, Marie-Thérèse. *Impératrice des Belges.* Brussels 1987.

Gerhard, Ute (ed.). *Frauen in der Geschichte des Rechts: Von der Frühen Neuzeit bis zur Gegenwart.* Munich 1997.

Gestrich, Andreas. "Höfisches Zeremoniell und sinnliches Volk: Die Rechtfertigung des Hofzeremoniells im 17. und frühen 18. Jahrhundert," in *Zeremoniell als höfische Ästhetik in Spätmittelalter und Früher Neuzeit,* ed. Jörg Jochen Berns and Thomas Rahn. Tübingen 1995, 57–73.

Ginzburg, Carlo. "Mikro-Historie. Zwei oder drei Dinge, die ich von ihr weiß." *Historische Anthropologie* 1 (1993): 169–92.

Glassl, Horst. *Das österreichische Einrichtungswerk in Galizien 1772–1790.* Wiesbaden 1975.

Gnant, Christoph. "Franz Stephan von Lothringen als Kaiser," in *Franz Stephan von Lothringen und sein Kreis,* ed. Renate Zedinger and Wolfgang Schmale. Bochum 2009, 115–29.

Godsey, William. "Adelsautonomie, Konfession und Nation im österreichischen Absolutismus, ca. 1620–1848. *Zeitschrift für Historische Forschung* 33 (2006): 197–239.

———. "Herrschaft und politische Kultur im Habsburgerreich: Die niederösterreichische Erbhuldigung (ca. 1648–1848)," in *Aufbrüche in die Moderne. Frühparlamentarismus zwischen altständischer Ordnung und modernem Konstitutionalismus 1750—1850, Schlesien—Deutschland—Mitteleuropa,* ed. Roland Gehrke, et al. Cologne / Weimar / Vienna 2005, 141–77.

Goffman, Erving. *The Presentation of Self in Everyday Life.* New York 1959.

Goldenbaum, Ursula (ed.). *Der Appell an das Publikum: Die öffentliche Debatte in der deutschen Aufklärung 1687–1796.* Berlin 2004.

Göllner, Carl. *Die Siebenbürgische Militärgrenze: Ein Beitrag zur Sozial- und Wirtschaftsgeschichte, 1762–1851.* Munich 1974.

Gooch, George P. *Maria Theresia and Other Studies.* London 1951.

Goodman, Dena (ed.). *Marie Antoinette: Writings on the Body of a Queen.* New York / London 2003.

Gossi, Herbert. "Der Graf F. C. Mercy-Argenteau als Vermittler zwischen Maria Theresia und Marie Antoinette." PhD diss. Vienna 2000.

Gotthardt, Elmar. *Die Kaiserwahl Karls VII.: Ein Beitrag zur Reichsgeschichte während des Interregnums 1740–1742.* Frankfurt am Main 1986.

"Gotts verhengnis und seine straffe": Zur Geschichte der Seuchen in der Frühen Neuzeit. Exhibition catalog. Wolfenbüttel 2005.

Graf, Henriette. "Das kaiserliche Zeremoniell und das Repräsentationsappartement im Leopoldinischen Trakt der Wiener Hofburg um 1740." *Österreichische Zeitschrift für Kunst und Denkmalpflege* 51 (1997): 571–87.

Gräf, Holger Th. "Funktionsweisen und Träger internationaler Politik in der Frühen Neuzeit," in *Strukturwandel internationaler Beziehungen: Zum Verhältnis von Staat und internationalem System seit dem Westfälischen Frieden,* ed. Jens Siegelberg abd Klaus Schlichte. Wiesbaden 2000, 105–23.

Grasberger, Franz. "Ein Goldenes Zeitalter der Musik," in *Maria Theresia und ihre Zeit,* ed. Walter Koschatzky. Salzburg / Vienna 1979, 379–86.

Greilich, Susanne. "'Alles, was sich bei den Türken ereignet, ist immer bedeutend': Turkophilie und Turkophobie in der populären Presse," in *Europa und die Türkei im 18. Jahrhundert*, ed. Barbara Schmidt-Haberkamp. Bonn 2011, 177–90.

Grillmeyer, Siegfried. *Habsburgs Diener in Post und Politik: Das "Haus" Thurn und Taxis zwischen 1745 und 1867*. Mainz 2005.

———. "Habsburgs langer Arm ins Reich. Briefspionage in der Frühen Neuzeit," in *Geschichte der Briefspionage*, ed. Klaus Beyrer. Frankfurt am Main 1999, 55–66.

Grimm, Gerald. *Die Schulreform Maria Theresias 1747–1775: Das österreichische Gymnasium zwischen Standesschule und allgemeinbildender Lehranstalt im Spannungsfeld von Ordensschulen, theresianischem Reformabsolutismus und Aufklärungspädagogik*. Frankfurt am Main 1987.

Groß, Lothar. "Der Kampf zwischen Reichskanzlei und österreichischer Hofkanzlei um die Führung der auswärtigen Geschäfte." *Historische Vierteljahrschrift* 22 (1924/25): 279–312.

Großegger, Elisabeth. *Theater, Feste und Feiern zur Zeit Maria Theresias, 1742–1776: Nach den Tagebucheintragungen des Fürsten Johann Joseph Khevenhüller-Metsch, Obersthofmeister der Kaiserin*. Vienna 1987.

Grothaus, Maximilian. *Der "Erbfeind christlichen Namens": Studien zum Türkenfeindbild in der Kultur der Habsburgermonarchie zwischen 16. und 18. Jahrhundert*. Graz 1986.

———. "Zum Türkenbild in der Adels- und Volkskultur der Habsburgermonarchie von 1650 bis 1800," in *Das Osmanische Reich und Europa 1683–1789: Konflikt, Entspannung und Austausch*, ed. Gernot Heiss and Grete Klingenstein. Munich 1983, 63–88.

Gruber, Gernot. *Wolfgang Amadeus Mozart*, 2nd ed. Munich 2006.

Gruder, Vivian. "The Question of Marie-Antoinette." *French History* 16 (2002): 269–98.

Grüll, Georg. *Bauer, Herr und Landesfürst: Sozialrevolutionäre Bestrebungen der oberösterreichischen Bauern von 1650 bis 1848*. Linz 1963.

Grünberg, Karl. *Die Bauernbefreiung und die Auflösung der gutsherrlich-bäuerlichen Verhältnisse in Böhmen, Mähren und Schlesien*. 2 vols. Leipzig 1893–1894.

———. "Franz Anton von Blanc, ein Sozialpolitiker der theresianisch-josefinischen Zeit," in *Schmollers Jahrbuch* 35 (1911): 1155–1238.

Guglia, Eugen. *Maria Theresia: Ihr Leben und ihre Regierung*. 2 vols. Munich 1917.

Gürtler, Alfred. *Die Volkszählungen Maria Theresias und Josefs II. 1753–90*. Innsbruck 1909.

Gutkas, Karl. *Kaiser Joseph II*. Vienna 1989.

Haag, Sabine, and Alfred Wieczorek (eds.). *Sammeln! Die Kunstkammer des Kaisers in Wien*. Exhibition catalog. Vienna 2012.

Haas, Robert. *Gluck und Durazzo im Burgtheater: Die Opéra comique in Wien*. Zürich / Vienna / Leipzig 1925.

Hackl, Bernhard. Die Theresianische Dominikal- und Rustikalfassion in Niederösterreich 1748–1756: Ein fiskalischer Reformprozeß im Spannungsfeld zwischen Landständen und Zentralstaat, Frankfurt am Main 1997.

———. *Die Theresianische Steuerrektifikation in Ober- und Innerösterreich 1747–1763: Die Neuordnung des ständischen Finanzwesens auf dem Sektor der direkten Steuern als ein fiskalischer Modernisierungsprozeß zwischen Reform und Stagnation*. Frankfurt am Main 1999.

Hadamowsky, Franz. "'Spectacle müssen sein'; Maria Theresia und das Theater," in *Maria Theresia und ihre Zeit*, ed. Walter Koschatzky. Salzburg and Vienna 1979, 387–92.

————. *Wien—Theatergeschichte: Von den Anfängen bis zum Ende des ersten Weltkriegs*, vol. 3: *Geschichte der Stadt Wien*. Vienna and Munich 1988.

Hahn, Alois. "Geheim," in *Das Geheimnis am Beginn der Moderne*, ed. Gisela Engel, et al. Frankfurt am Main 2002, 21–42.

Hahn, Peter Michael, and Ulrich Schütte (eds.). *Zeichen und Raum: Ausstattung und höfisches Zeremoniell in den deutschen Schlössern der Frühen Neuzeit*. Munich and Berlin 2006.

Haider-Pregler, Hilde. "Entwicklungen im Wiener Theater zur Zeit Maria Theresias," in *Österreich im Europa der Aufklärung: Kontinuität und Zäsur zur Zeit Maria Theresias und Josephs II.*, ed. Richard Georg Plaschka and Grete Klingenstein. Vienna 1985, 701–16.

Hammer, Elke. "Mariazeller Mirakelliteratur der frühen Neuzeit," in *Mariazell—Schatz und Schicksal. Katalog der Steirischen Landesausstellung*, ed. Helmut Eberhart und Heidelinde Fell. Graz 1996, 193–208.

Hammerstein, Notker, and Ulrich Herrmann (eds.). *Handbuch der deutschen Bildungsgeschichte*, vol. 2: *18. Jahrhundert*.Munich 2005.

Hanke, Gerhard. "Das Zeitalter des Zentralismus (1740–1848)," in *Handbuch der Geschichte der böhmischen Länder*, vol. 2: *Die böhmischen Länder von der Hochblüte der Ständeherrschaft bis zum Erwachen eines modernen Nationalbewußtseins*, ed. Karl Bosl. Stuttgart 1974, 413–645.

Hanzl-Wachter, Lieselotte (ed.). *Schloss Hof. Prinz Eugens tusculum rurale und Sommerresidenz der kaiserlichen Familie: Geschichte und Ausstattung eines barocken Gesamtkunstwerks*. St. Pölten 2005.

Harrasowsky, Philipp Harras Ritter von. *Geschichte der Codifikation des österreichischen Civilrechtes*. Vienna 1868; reprinted Frankfurt am Main 1968.

Härter, Karl. "Soziale Disziplinierung durch Strafe? Intentionen frühneuzeitlicher Policeyordnungen und staatliche Sanktionspraxis." *Zeitschrift für Historische Forschung* 26 (1999): 365–79.

Hartmann, Peter Claus. *Karl Albrecht—Karl VII: Glücklicher Kurfürst, Unglücklicher Kaiser*. Regensburg 1985.

Haslinger, Ingrid. *Ehemalige Hofsilber & Tafelkammer: Der kaiserliche Haushalt*. Vienna / Munich 1997.

————. *Küche und Tafelkultur am kaiserlichen Hofe zu Wien: Zur Geschichte von Hofküche, Hofzuckerbäckerei und Hofsilber- und Tafelkammer*. Bern 1993.

Hassenpflug-Elzholz, Eila. *Böhmen und die böhmischen Stände in der Zeit des beginnenden Zentralismus*. Munich 1982.

Hassler, Eric. *La cour de Vienne, 1680–1740: Service de l'empereur et stratégies spatiales de l'élite nobiliaire dans la monarchie des Habsbourg*. Strasbourg 2013.

Haug, Christine. "'In Frankreich verboten, sehr rar': Zu den Distributions- und Vermarktungsstrategien von Geheimliteratur in der Habsburgermonarchie zur Zeit der Aufklärung," in Kommunikation und Information *im 18. Jahrhundert. Das Beispiel der Habsburgermonarchie*, ed. Johannes Frimmel and Michael Wörglbauer. Wiesbaden 2009, 227–44.

Haug-Moritz, Gabriele. "Corpus evangelicorum und deutscher Dualismus," in *Alternativen zur Reichsverfassung in der Frühen Neuzeit*, ed. Volker Press. Munich 1995, 189–208.

————. *"Des Kaysers rechter Arm": Der Reichshofrat und die Reichspolitik des Kaisers, in Das Reich und seine Territorialstaaten im 17. und 18. Jahrhundert: Aspekte des Mit- Neben- und Gegeneinander*, ed. Harm Klueting and Wolfgang Schmale. Münster 2004, 23–42.

————. "Die Krise des Reichsverbands in kaiserlicher Perspektive (1750–1790)," in *Krisenbewusstsein und Krisenbewältigung in der Frühen Neuzeit: Festschrift für Hans-Christoph Rublack*, ed. Monika Hagenmaier, et al. Frankfurt am Main, et al. 1992, 73–80.

————. "Kaisertum und Parität: Reichspolitik und Konfessionen nach dem Westfälischen Frieden," in *Zeitschrift für Historische Forschung* 19 (1992): 445–82.

Haug-Moritz, Gabriele, and Sabine Ullmann (eds.). *Frühneuzeitliche Supplikationspraxis und monarchische Herrschaft in europäischer Perspektive.*Vienna 2015.

Hausen, Karin. "Die Polarisierung der Geschlechtscharaktere: Eine Spiegelung der Dissoziation von Erwerbs- und Familienleben," in *Sozialgeschichte der Familie in der Neuzeit Europas*, ed. Werner Conze. Stuttgart 1976, 363–93.

Hausenstein, Wilhelm. *Europäische Hauptstädte: Ein Reisetagebuch (1926–1932)*, 2nd rev. ed. Munich 1954.

Hausmann, Friederike. *Herrscherin im Paradies der Teufel: Maria Carolina, Königin von Neapel: Eine Biographie*. Munich 2014.

Haussherr, Hans. *Verwaltungseinheit und Ressorttrennung vom Ende des 17. bis zum Beginn des 19. Jahrhunderts*. Berlin 1953.

Hawlik-van de Water, Magdalena. *Die Kapuzinergruft*. Vienna 1987.

————. *Der schöne Tod: Zeremonialstrukturen des Wiener Hofes bei Tod und Begräbnis 1640–1740*. Vienna 1989.

Heartz, Daniel. *Music in European Capitals: The Galant Style, 1720–1780*. New York and London 2003.

Heer, Friedrich. *Das Glück der Maria Theresia*. Vienna and Munich 1966.

————. *Der Kampf um die österreichische Identität*, 2nd ed. Vienna / Cologne / Weimar 1996.

Heigel, Karl Theodor von. *Der Österreichische Erbfolgekrieg und die Kaiserwahl Karls VII.* Nördlingen 1877.

Heindl, Waltraud. "Bildung und Recht: Naturrecht und Ausbildung der staatsbürgerlichen Gesellschaft in der Habsburgermonarchie," in *Geschichte und Recht: Festschrift für Gerald Stourzh zum 70. Geburtstag*, ed. Thomas Angerer et al. Vienna 1999, 183–206.

————. "Caroline Pichler oder der bürgerliche Fortschritt: Lebensideale und Lebensrealität von österreichischen Beamtenfrauen," in *Von Bürgern und ihren Frauen. Bürgertum in der Habsburgermonarchie*, ed. Margret Friedrich and Peter Urbanitsch. Vienn / Cologne / Weimar 1996, 197–208.

————. "Marie-Thérèse, la Magna Mater Austriae," in *Austriaca: Cahiers universitaires d'information sur l'utriche* 35 (2010): 11–27.

————. "Mythos Nation: Geschichte und Geschlecht in der österreichischen Monarchie," in *Nationalgeschichte als Artefakt. Zum Paradigma "Nationalstaat" in den Historiographien Deutschlands, Italiens und Österreichs*, ed. Hans Peter Hye et al. Vienna 2009, 201–8.

Heindl, Waltraud, and Edith Saurer (eds.). *Grenze und Staat: Paßwesen, Staatsbürgerschaft, Heimatrecht und Fremdengesetzgebung in der österreichischen Monarchie 1750–1865*. Vienna / Cologne / Weimar 2000.

Heiss, Gernot, and Grete Klingenstein (eds.). *Das Osmanische Reich und Europa 1683–1789: Konflikt, Entspannung und Austausch*. Munich 1983.

Helfert, Joseph Alexander. *Die österreichische Volksschule*, vol. 1: *Die Gründung der österreichischen Volksschule durch Maria Theresia*. Prague 1860.

Hellmuth, Eckhart. *Naturrechtstheorie und bürokratischer Werthorizont: Studien zur preußischen Geistes- und Sozialgeschichte des 18. Jahrhunderts.* Göttingen 1985.

Helmedach, Andreas. "Bevölkerungspolitik im Zeichen der Aufklärung: Zwangsumsiedlung und Zwangsassimilierung im Habsburgerreich des 18. Jahrhunderts—eine noch ungelöste Forschungsaufgabe." *Comparativ* 6 (1996): 41–62.

Helmedach, Andreas, et al. (eds.). *Das Osmanische Europa: Methoden und Perspektiven der Frühneuzeitforschung zu Südosteuropa.* Leipzig 2014.

Hengerer, Mark. "Die Abrechnungsbücher des Hofzahlmeisters und die Zahlamtsbücher im Wiener Hofkammerarchiv," in *Quellenkunde der Habsburgermonarchie (16.-18. Jahrhundert): Ein exemplarisches Handbuch,* ed. Josef Pauser, Martin Scheutz, and Thomas Winkelbauer. Vienna / Cologne / Weimar 2004, 128–43.

———. "Die Zeremonialprotokolle und weitere Quellen zum Zeremoniell des Kaiserhofs im Wiener Haus- Hof- und Staatsarchiv," in *Quellenkunde der Habsburgermonarchie (16.-18. Jahrhundert): Ein exemplarisches Handbuch,* ed. Josef Pauser, Martin Scheutz, and Thomas Winkelbauer. Vienna / Cologne / Weimar 2004, 76–93.

———. "The Funerals of the Habsburg Emperors in the Eighteenth Century," in *Monarchy and Religion: The Transformation of Royal Culture in Eighteenth-Century Europe,* ed. Michael Schaich. Oxford / New York 2007, 367–94.

———. "Hofzeremoniell, Organisation und Grundmuster sozialer Differenzierung am Wiener Hof im 17. Jahrhundert," in *Hofgesellschaft und Höflinge an europäischen Fürstenhöfen in der Frühen Neuzeit (15–18. Jh),* ed. Klaus Malettke et al. Münster 2001, 337–68.

———. *Kaiserhof und Adel in der Mitte des 17. Jahrhunderts: Eine Kommunikationsgeschichte der Macht in der Vormoderne.* Constance 2004.

Hennings, Fred. *Und sitzet zur linken Hand: Franz Stephan von Lothringen.* Vienna 1961.

Heppner, Harald. "Die österreichische Militärgrenze im 18. Jahrhundert zwischen Krieg und Frieden," in *Krieg und Frieden im 18. Jahrhundert: Kulturgeschichtliche Studien,* ed. Stefanie Stockhorst. Hannover 2015, 287–304.

Heppner, Harald, and Eva Posch. *Encounters in Europe's Southeast. The Habsburg Empire and the Orthodox World in the Eighteenth and Nineteenth Centuries.* Bochum 2013.

Heppner, Harald, Peter Urbanitsch, and Renate Zedinger (eds.). *Social Change in the Habsburg Monarchy.* Bochum 2011.

Herre, Franz. *Maria Theresia: Die grosse Habsburgerin.* Cologne 1994.

Hersche, Peter. *Der Spätjansenismus in Österreich.* Vienna 1977.

———. *Muße und Verschwendung: Europäische Gesellschaft und Kultur im Barockzeitalter.* 2 vols. Freiburg 2006.

———. "War Maria Theresia eine Jansenistin?" *Österreich in Geschichte und Literatur* 15 (1971): 14–25.

Hertel, Sandra. "Kontinuität und Wandel: Der habsburgische Totenkult bei Maria Theresia," in *Multiple kulturelle Referenzen in der Habsburgermonarchie des 18. Jahrhunderts,* ed. Wolfgang Schmale. Bochum 2010, 251–81.

———. *Maria Elisabeth: Österreichische Erzherzogin und Statthalterin in Brüssel (1725-1741).* Cologne / Weimar / Vienna 2014.

Hintze, Otto. "Der österreichische und der preußische Beamtenstaat im 17. und 18. Jahrhundert: Eine vergleichende Betrachtung." *Historische Zeitschrift* 86 (1901): 401–44.

Hitzel, Frédéric. "*Sefâretnâme*: Comptes rendus des ambassadeurs ottomans à l'Europe," in *Turcs ert turqueries, XVIe–XVIIIe siècles*, ed. Association des historiens modernistes des universités francaises. Paris 2009, 97–110.

Hochedlinger, Michael. *Austria's Wars of Emergence 1683–1797*. Harlow 2003.

———. "Der gewaffnete Doppeladler: Ständische Landesdefension, Stehendes Heer und 'Staatsverdichtung' in der frühneuzeitlichen Habsburgermonarchie," in *Die Habsburgermonarchie 1620–1740: Leistungen und Grenzen des Absolutismusparadigmas*, ed. Petr Mat'a and Thomas Winkelbauer. Stuttgart 2006, 217–50.

———. "Der König und die Habsburgermonarchie. Oder: Wie preußisch war Österreich im 18. Jahrhundert?" URL: http://www.perspectivia.net/content/publikationen/friedrich300 -colloqien/friedrich-bestandsaufnahme/hochedlinger_habsburgermonarchie (01.02.2016).

———. "Mars Ennobled: The Ascent of the Military and the Creation of a Military Nobility in Mid-Eighteenth Austria." *German History* 17 (1999): 141–76.

———. *Österreichische Archivgeschichte: Vom Spätmittelalter bis zum Ende des Papierzeitalters*. Cologne / Weimar / Vienna 2013.

———. "Political History," in *18th Century Studies in Austria 1945–2010*, ed. Thomas Wallnig, Johannes Frimmel, and Werner Telesko. Bochum 2011, 13–32.

———. "Rekrutierung—Militarisierung—Modernisierung: Militär und ländliche Gesellschaft in der Habsburgermonarchie im Zeitalter des Aufgeklärten Absolutismus," in *Militär und ländliche Gesellschaft in der frühen Neuzeit*, ed. Stefan Kroll and Kersten Krüger. Hamburg 2000, 327–75.

———. "Stiefkinder der Forschung: Verfassungs-, Verwaltungs- und Behördengeschichte der frühneuzeitlichen Habsburgermonarchie," in *Herrschaftsverdichtung, Staatsbildung, Bürokratisierung. Verfassungs-, Verwaltungs- und Behördengeschichte der Frühen Neuzeit*, ed. Thomas Winkelbauer and Michael Hochedlinger. Vienna 2010, 293–394.

Hock, Carl Freiherr von, and Hermann Ignaz Bidermann. *Der österreichische Staatsrath: Eine geschichtliche Studie*. Vienna 1879, reprinted 1972.

Hofmann, Christina. *Das spanische Hofzeremoniell von 1500–1700*. Frankfurt am Main, et al. 1985.

Hofmannsthal, Hugo von. "Maria Theresia: Zur zweihundertsten Wiederkehr ihres Geburtstages im Jahre 1917, wieder," in *Maria Theresia und ihre Zeit*, ed. Walter Koschatzky. Salzburg / Vienna 1979, 11–16.

Holcik, Stefan (ed.). *Krönungsfeierlichkeiten in Pressburg/Bratislava 1563–1830*. Bratislava 1992.

Hollerweger, Hans. *Die Reform des Gottesdienstes zur Zeit des Josephinismus in Österreich*. Regensburg 1976.

Holzmair, Eduard. "Maria Theresia als Trägerin männlicher Titel." *MIÖG* 72 (1964): 122–34.

Honegger, Claudia. *Die Ordnung der Geschlechter: Die Wissenschaften vom Menschen und das Weib 1750–1850*. Frankfurt am Main and New York 1991.

Horn, Sonia. "Wiener Hebammen 1643–1753." *Studien zur Wiener Geschichte* 59 (2003): 35–102.

Hrazky, Josef. "Die Persönlichkeit der Infantin Isabella von Parma." *MÖStA* 12 (1959): 174–239.

Hunt, Lynn. *The Family Romance of the French Revolution*. Berkeley 1992.

Husslein-Arco, Agnes, and Georg Lechner (eds.). *Martin van Meytens der Jüngere*. Exhibition catalog. Vienna 2014.

Hüttl, Ludwig. *Marianische Wallfahrten im süddeutsch-österreichischen Raum: Analysen von der Reformations- bis zur Aufklärungsepoche*. Cologne and Vienna 1985.

Hye, Hans Peter, et al. (eds.). *Nationalgeschichte als Artefakt: Zum Paradigma "Nationalstaat" in den Historiographien Deutschlands, Italiens und Österreichs*. Vienna 2009.

Iby, Elfriede. "Schönbrunn als Residenzschloss Maria Theresias: Zur Raumdisposition der kasierlichen Appartements und der Repräsentationsräume." URL: http://www.perspectivia.net /publikationen/friedrich300-colloquien/friedrich_friderizianisch/galerie/iby_schoenbrunn (15.04.2016).

Iby, Elfriede, and Alexander Koller. *Schönbrunn*, 2nd ed. Vienna 2007.

Iby, Elfriede, et al. (eds.). *Maria Theresia 1717–1780: Strategin—Mutter—Reformerin*. Exhibition catalog. Vienna 2017.

Ilic, Tanasije Z. "Der Sanitätskordon an der österreichischen Militärgrenze und seine Funktionen zur Zeit Maria Theresias," in *Maria Theresia als Königin von Ungarn*, ed. DerBurgenländischen Landesregierung, Eisenstadt 1984, 339–53.

Imbruglia, Girolamo (ed.). *Naples in the Eighteenth Century: The Birth and Death of a Nation State*. Cambridge 2000.

Ingendahl, Gesa. *Witwen in der Frühen Neuzeit: Eine kulturhistorische Studie*. Frankfurt am Main 2006.

Ingrao, Charles W. The Habsburg Monarchy, 1618–1815, Cambridge 2000.

———. (ed.). *State and Society in Early Modern Austria*. West Lafayette 1994.

Ingrao, Charles W., and Andrew L. Thomas. *Piety and Power: The Empress-Consort of the High Baroque, in Queenship in Europe 1660–1815. The Role of the Consort*, ed. Clarissa Campbell Orr. Cambridge 2004, 107–31.

Jaeger, Stephan. "Multiperspektivisches Erzählen in der Geschichtsschreibung des ausgehenden 20. Jahrhunderts: Wissenschaftliche Inszenierungen von Geschichte zwischen Roman und Wirklichkeit" in *Multiperspektivisches Erzählen*, ed. Vera Nünning and Ansgar Nünning. Trier 2000, 323–46.

Jahn, Wolfgang, Evamaria Brockhoff, and Elisabeth Vavra (eds.). *Verbündet—Verfeindet— Verschwägert: Bayern und Österreich. Katalog der Bayerisch-Oberösterreichischen Landesausstellung*, vol. 2: *Habsburger und Wittelsbacher*. Stuttgart 2012.

Jansen, Sharon L. *The Monstrous Regiment of Women. Female Rulers in Early Modern Europe*. New York 2002.

Jesner, Sabine. "Die siebenbürgisch-sächsische Nation und die Einrichtung der Siebenbürgischen Militärgrenze." *Danubiana Carpathica* 53 (2012): 237–54.

Jordan, Sonja. *Die kaiserliche Wirtschaftspolitik im Banat im 18. Jahrhundert*. Munich 1967.

Kaduk, Svenja. *Maria Theresia und ihre Brüder. 'Weiblichkeit' und 'Männlichkeit' bei Ranke, Droysen und Treitschke*. URL: http://biecoll.ub.uni-bielefeld.de/volltexte/2009/2011/pdf /Kaduk (05.07.2015).

Kägler, Britta. "'so lang diese Frau die Hände in denen Regierungsgeschäften haben. . . .' Maria Amalia von Österreich als machtbewusste Kaiserin(witwe) in München," in *Nur die Frau des Kaisers? Kaiserinnen in der Frühen Neuzeit*, ed. Bettina Braun, Katrin Keller, and Matthias Schnettger. Cologne / Weimar / Vienna 2016, 193–209.

Kaiser, Thomas E. "Ambiguous Identities: Marie-Antoinette and the House of Lorraine from the Affair of the Minuet to Lambesc's Charge," in *Marie Antoinette: Writings on the Body of a Queen*, ed. Dena Goodman. New York and London 2003, 171–98.

———. "Who's Afraid of Marie-Antoinette? Diplomacy, Austrophobia, and the Queen." *French History* 14 (2000): 241–71.

Kalipke, Andreas. *Verfahren im Konflikt: Konfessionelle Streitigkeiten und Corpus Evangelicorum im 18. Jahrhundert*. Münster 2015.

Kallbrunner, Josef. "Zur Geschichte der Theresianischen Polizei," in *Monatsblatt des Altertums-Vereins zu Wien* 12 (1917): 142–45.

Kammerhofer, Leopold. "Die Gründung des Haus- Hof- und Staatsarchivs 1749," in *Speicher des Gedächtnisses: Bibliotheken, Museen, Archive*, vol. 2., ed. Moritz Csáky, et al. Vienna 2001, 81–99.

Kann, Robert A. *A Study in Austrian Intellectual History from Late Baroque to Romanticism*. New York 1960.

Kantorowicz, Ernst H. *The King's Two Bodies: A Study in Mediaeval Political Theology*. Princeton 1957.

Kaps, Klemens. *Ungleiche Entwicklung in Zentraleuropa: Galicien zwischen überregionaler Arbeitsteilung und imperialer Politik (1772–1914)*. Vienna 2014.

———. "Zwischen Emanzipation und Exklusion. Fortschrittsdenken und die Wahrnehmung kultureller Differenz in der europäischen Aufklärung," in *Europa als Weltregion: Zentrum, Modell oder Provinz?*, ed. Thomas Ertl, et al. Vienna 2014, 66–79.

Karajan, Theodor Georg von. *Maria Theresia und Graf Sylva-Tarouca: Feierliche Sitzungsberichte der Kaiserlichen Akademie der Wissenschaften*. Vienna 1859.

———. *Maria Theresia und Joseph II. während der Mitregentschaft: Feierliche Sitzungsberichte der Kaiserlichen Akademie der Wissenschaften*. Vienna 1865.

Karmasin, Matthias / Christian Oggolder (eds.). *Österreichische Mediengeschichte*, vol.1: *Von den frühen Drucken zur Ausdifferenzierung des Mediensystems (1500–1918)*. Wiesbaden 2016.

Karniel, Josef. *Die Toleranzpolitik Kaiser Josephs II.* Gerlingen 1985.

Karstens, Simon. *Lehrer—Schriftsteller—Staatsreformer. Die Karriere des Joseph von Sonnenfels (1733–1817)*. Vienna / Cologne / Weimar 2011.

Kauffmann, Kai. *"Es ist nur ein Wien!" Stadtbeschreibungen von Wien 1700 bis 1873: Geschichte eines literarischen Genres der Wiener Publizistik*. Vienna / Cologne / Weimar 1994.

Kaser, Karl. *Freier Bauer und Soldat: Die Militarisierung der agrarischen Gesellschaft an der kroatisch-slawonischen Militärgrenze (1535–1881)*. Vienna / Cologne / Weimar 1997.

Keller, Katrin. "Frauen und dynastische Herrschaft. Eine Einführung." In Bettina Braun, Katrin Keller, and Matthias Schnettger (eds.), *Nur die Frau des Kaisers? Kaiserinnen in der Frühen Neuzeit*. Cologne / Weimar / Vienna, 13–26.

———(ed.). *Gynäkokratie: Zu politischen Handlungsmöglichkeiten von Frauen in der höfischen Gesellschaft der Frühen Neuzeit*. Zeitenblicke 8 (2009). URL: http://www.zeitenblicke.de /2009/2/ (01.02.2015).

———. *Hofdamen: Amtsträgerinnen im Wiener Hofstaat des 17. Jahrhunderts*. Vienna, 2005.

Kernbauer, Eva, and Aneta Zahradnik (eds.). *Höfische Porträtkultur: Die Bildnissammlung der österreichischen Erzherzogin Maria Anna*. Berlin and Boston 2016.

Khavanova, Olga. "Die enge Einverständnuß beeder kaiserlichen Höfe": Österreichische Botschafter in St. Petersburg in der zweiten Hälfte des 18. Jahrhunderts," in *Politische Kommunikation zwischen Imperien. Der diplomatische Aktionsraum Südost- und Osteuropa*, ed.

Gunda Barth-Scalmani, Harriet Rudolph, and Christian Steppan. Innsbruck 2013, 193–208.

Kleinmann, Hans-Otto. *Die Politik des Wiener Hofes gegenüber der spanischen Monarchie unter Karl III. (1759–1788).* Cologne 1967.

Klingenstein, Grete. *Der Aufstieg des Hauses Kaunitz: Studien zu Herkunft und Bildung des Staatskanzlers Wenzel Anton.* Göttingen 1975.

———. "Institutionelle Aspekte der österreichischen Außenpolitik im 18. Jahrhundert," in *Diplomatie und Außenpolitik Österreichs: Elf Beiträge zu ihrer Geschichte,* ed. Erich Zöllner. Vienna 1977, 74–93.

———. "Kaunitz contra Bartenstein: Zur Geschichte der Staatskanzlei 1749–1753," in *Beiträge zur neueren Geschichte Österreichs,* ed. Heinrich Fichtenau and Erich Zöllner. Vienna 1974, 243–63.

———. "Modes of Religious Tolerance and Intolerance in Eighteenth Century Habsburg Politics." *Austrian History Yearbook* 24 (1993): 1–16.

———. *Staatsverwaltung und kirchliche Autorität im 18. Jh: Das Problem der Zensur in der theresianischen Reform.* Vienna 1970.

———. "Van Swieten und die Zensur," in *Gerard van Swieten und seine Zeit,* ed. Erna Lesky and Adam Wandruszka. Vienna / Graz / Cologne 1973, 93–106.

———. "Was bedeuten 'Österreich' und 'österreichisch' im 18. Jahrhundert? Eine begriffsgeschichtliche Studie," in *Was heißt Österreich? Inhalt und Umfang des Österreichbegriffs vom 10. Jahrhundert bis heute,* ed. Richard Georg Plaschka. Vienna 1995, 149–220.

Klingenstein, Grete, and Franz A. J. Szábo (eds.). *Staatskanzler Wenzel Anton von Kaunitz-Rietberg 1711–1794: Neue Perspektiven zu Politik und Kultur der europäischen Aufklärung.* Graz, et al. 1996.

Kleuting, Harm (ed.). *Das Reich und Österreich 1648–1740.* Münster 1999.

———(ed.). *Katholische Aufklärung—Aufklärung im katholischen Deutschland.* Hamburg 1993.

Klueting, Harm, and Wolfgang Schmale (ed.). *Das Reich und seine Territorialstaaten im 17. und 18. Jahrhundert Aspekte des Mit-, Neben- und Gegeneinander.* Münster 2004.

Knall, Dieter. *Aus der Heimat gedrängt: Letzte Zwangsumsiedlungen steirischer Protestanten nach Siebenbürgen unter Maria Theresia.* Graz 2002.

Knofler, Monika J. *Das Theresianische Wien: Der Alltag in den Bildern Canalettos.* Vienna 1979.

Koch, Rainer, and Patricia Stahl (eds.). "Wahl und Krönung in Frankfurt: Kaiser Karl VII. 1742–1745," in *Katalog der Ausstellung im Historischen Museum Frankfurt.* Frankfurt am Main 1986.

Kocher, Gernot. *Höchstgerichtsbarkeit und Privatrechtskodifikation: Die Oberste Justizstelle und das allgemeine Privatrecht in Österreich von 1749–1811.* Graz 1979.

———. "Rechtsverständnis und Rechtsreformen im aufgeklärten Absolutismus Österreichs," in *Österreich im Zeitalter des aufgeklärten Absolutismus,* ed. Erich Zöllner. Vienna 1983, 54–70.

König, Matthias. "'. . . wegen künftiger besserer und würthschaftlicher Besorgung der erkrankten und blessirten Soldaten, . . .' Die Reform der österreichischen Feldsanität zwischen 1748 und 1785," in *Multiple kulturelle Referenzen in der Habsburgermonarchie des 18. Jahrhunderts,* ed. Wolfgang Schmale. Bochum 2010, 283–94.

Körper, Gerlinde. "Studien zur Biographie Elisabeth Christines von Braunschweig-Lüneburg-Wolfenbüttel." Phd diss. Vienna 1975.

Koller, Markus. "Grenzwahrnehmung und Grenzmacht. Einleitende Bemerkungen zu den osmanisch-habsburgischen Grenzräumen (16.–18. Jh)," in *Ein Raum im Wandel: Die osmanisch-habsburgische Grenzregion vom 16. bis zum 18. Jahrhundert*, ed. Norbert Spannenberger and Szabolcs Varga. Stuttgart 2014, 9–24.

Kollmer, Gert. *Die Familie Palm: Soziale Mobilität in ständischer Gesellschaft*. Ostfildern 1983.

Komlosy, Andrea. *Grenze und ungleiche regionale Entwicklung: Binnenmarkt und Migration in der Habsburgermonarchie*. Vienna 2003.

Koos, Marianne. *Haut, Farbe und Medialität: Oberfläche im Werk von Jean-Étienne Liotard (1702–1789)*. Paderborn 2014.

Koschatzky, Walter. "Jean-Etienne Liotard in Wien," in *Maria Theresia und ihre Zeit*, ed. Walter Koschatzky. Salzburg / Vienna 1979, 308–19.

———(ed.). *Maria Theresia und ihre Zeit: Eine Darstellung der Epoche von 1740–1780 aus Anlaß der 200. Wiederkehr des Todestages der Kaiserin*. Salzburg / Vienna 1979.

———(ed.). *Maria Theresia und ihre Zeit: Zur Wiederkehr des 200*. Exhibition catalog. Todestages, Vienna 1980.

Kosean-Mokrau, Alfred. "Die gefälschten Memoiren des Pandurenobristen Franz von der Trenck." *Jahrbuch des Instituts für Deutsche Geschichte an der Universität Tel Aviv* 4 (1975): 13–51.

———. "Der Streit um das Erbe des Pandurenobristen Franz von der Trenck," in *Jahrbuch des Instituts für Deutsche Geschichte an der Universität Tel Aviv* 6 (1977).

Kovács, Elisabeth. "Einflüsse geistlicher Ratgeber und höfischer Beichtväter auf das fürstliche Selbstverständnis, auf Machtbegriffe und politische Entscheidungen österreichischer Habsburger während des 17. und 18. Jahrhunderts." *Cristianesimo nella storia* 4 (1983): 79–102.

———. "Die ideale Erzherzogin: Maria Theresias Forderungen an ihre Töchter." *MIÖG* 94 (1986): 49–80.

———(ed.). *Katholische Aufklärung und Josephinismus*. Munich 1979.

———. "Kirchliches Zeremoniell am Wiener Hof des 18. Jahrhunders im Wandel von Mentalität und Gesellschaft." *MÖStA* 32 (1979): 109–42.

———. "Spätmittelalterliche Traditionen in der österreichischen Frömmigkeit des 17. und 18. Jahrhunderts," in *Volksreligion im hohen und im späten Mittelalter*, ed. Peter Dinzelbacher et al. Paderborn 1990, 397–417.

Krajasich, Peter. "Die österreichische Militärgrenze unter Maria Theresia," in *Maria Theresia als Königin von Ungarn*. Exhibition catalog, Schloss Halbthurn. Eisenstadt 1980, 52–62.

Krajewski, Markus. *Der Diener: Mediengeschichte einer Figur zwischen König und Klient*. Frankfurt am Main 2010.

Kretschmayr, Heinrich. *Maria Theresia*. Gotha 1925.

Kreuter, Peter M. *Der Vampirglaube in Südosteuropa: Studien zur Genese, Bedeutung und Funktion*. Rumänien und der Balkanraum, Berlin 2001.

Krischer, André. "Das Gesandtschaftswesen und das vormoderne Völkerrecht," in *Rechtsformen Internationaler Politik: Theorie, Norm und Praxis vom 12. bis 18. Jahrhundert*, ed. Michael Jucker, Martin Kintzinger, and Rainer Christoph Schwinges. Berlin 2010, 197–240.

———. "Souveränität als sozialer Status. Zur Funktion des diplomatische Zeremoniells in der Frühen Neuzeit," in *Diplomatisches Zeremoniell in Europa und dem Mittleren Osten in der Frühen Neuzeit*, ed. Jan Paul Niederkorn, Ralf Kauz, and Giorgio Rota. Vienna 2009, 1–32.

Krömer, Ulrich. *Johann Ignaz von Felbiger: Leben und Werk*. Freiburg and Breisgau 1966.

Krueger, Rita. *Czech, German, and Noble: Status and National Identity in Habsburg Bohemia*. New York 2009.

Kubiska, Irene. "Zwischen Anspruch und Gnade: Die Altersversorgung Wiener Hofbediensteter und ihrer Witwen und Waisen im 18. Jahrhundert," in *Frühneuzeitforschung in der Habsburgermonarchie. Adel und Wiener Hof—Konfessionalisierung—Siebenbürgen*, ed. István Fazekas et al. Vienna 2013, 33–49.

Kubiska-Scharl, Irene. "Formalisierte Gnade: Das Supplikationswesen am Wiener Hof im 18. Jahrhundert am Beispiel supplizierender Reichshofräte," in *Frühneuzeitliche Supplikationspraxis und monarchische Herrschaft in europäischer Perspektive*, ed. Gabriele Haug-Moritz and Sabine Ullmann. Vienna 2015, 297–308.

Kubiska-Scharl, Irene, and Michael Pölzl. *Die Karrieren des Wiener Hofpersonals 1711–65*. Vienna 2013.

Kühl, Stefan. *Organisationen: Eine sehr kurze Einführung*. Wiesbaden 2011.

Kühn, Sebastian. "Die Gräfin, die Gouvernante und der König: Perspektiven auf Dienstleute als Boten in einem aristokratischen Haushalt des 18. Jhs.," in *Historische Anthropologie* 20 (2012): 58–75.

Kühnel, Florian. "Westeuropa und das Osmanische Reich in der Frühen Neuzeit: Ansätze und Perspektiven aktueller Forschungen," in *Zeitschrift für Historische Forschung* 42 (2015): 251–83.

Kühnel, Harry. *Die Hofburg zu Wien*. Graz and Cologne 1964.

Küster, Sebastian. *Vier Monarchien—vier Öffentlichkeiten: Kommunikation um die Schlacht bei Dettingen*. Münster 2004.

Kulenkampff, Angela. *Österreich und das Alte Reich: Die Reichspolitik des Staatskanzlers Kaunitz unter Maria Theresia und Joseph II*. Cologne / Weimar / Vienna 2005.

Kunisch, Johannes. "Der Ausgang des Siebenjährigen Krieges: Ein Beitrag zum Verhältnis von Kabinettspolitik und Kriegführung im Zeitalter des Absolutismus." *Zeitschrift für Historische Forschung* 2 (1975): 173–222.

———(ed.). *Der dynastische Fürstenstaat: Zur Bedeutung von Sukzessionsordnungen für die Entstehung des frühmodernen Staates*. Berlin 1982.

———. *Friedrich der Große: Der König und seine Zeit*. Munich 2004.

———. *Der Kleine Krieg: Studien zum Heerwesen im Absolutismus*. Wiesbaden 1973.

———. *Das Mirakel des Hauses Brandenburg: Studien zum Verhältnis von Kabinettspolitik und Kriegführung im Zeitalter des Siebenjährigen Krieges*. Berlin 1978.

———. *Staatsverfassung und Mächtepolitik: Zur Genese von Staatenkonflikten im Zeitalter des Absolutismus*. Berlin 1979.

Küntzel, Georg. "Über den Plan einer Begegnung Friedrichs des Großen und Josephs zu Torgau 1766," in *Forschungen zur brandenburgischen und preußischen Geschichte* 15 (1902): 507–19.

Kurz, Marlene, et al. (eds.). *Das Osmanische Reich und die Habsburgermornarchie*. Munich 2005.

Kwiatkowski, Ernest. *Die Constitutio Criminalis Theresiana: Ein Beitrag zur theresianischen Reichs- und Rechtsgeschichte*. Innsbruck 1903.

Labouvie, Eva. *Andere Umstände: Eine Kulturgeschichte der Geburt.* Cologne / Weimar / Vienna 1998.

Lachmayer, Herbert (ed.). "Mozart: Experiment Aufklärung im Wien des 18. Jahrhunderts," in *Katalogbuch und Essayband zur Ausstellung des Da Ponte Instituts in der Albertina.* Ostfildern 2006.

Landes, Joan. "Marie Antoinettes Remise und das Geschlecht der Diplomatie im späten 18. Jahrhundert," in *Das Geschlecht der Diplomatie: Geschlechterrollen in den Außenbeziehungen vom Spätmittelalter bis zum 20. Jahrhundert*, ed. Corina Bastian, et al. Cologne / Weimar / Vienna 2013, 115–29.

Landon, Else. *In der Gunst der Kaiserin: Karrieren unter Maria Theresia.* Vienna 1997.

Lang, Helmut Walter. "Die österreichische Tagespublizistik im Barockzeitalter," in *Öffentliche Meinung in der Geschichte Österreichs*, ed. Erich Zöllner. Vienna 1979, 39–52.

———. "Die Zeitschriften in Österreich zwischen 1740 und 1815," in *Jahrbuch für österreichische Kulturgeschichte* (1979): 203–27.

Laqueur, Thomas. *Auf den Leib geschrieben: Die Inszenierung der Geschlechter von der Antike bis Freud.* Frankfurt am Main 1992.

Lau, Thomas. *Die Kaiserin: Maria Theresia.* Vienna / Cologne / Weimar 2016.

Laube, Volker. "Geheimnisverrat in Wien," in *Internationale Beziehungen in der Frühen Neuzeit. Ansätze und Perspektiven*, ed. Heidrun Kugeler, Christian Sepp, and Georg Wolf. Hamburg, 212–36.

Lavandier, Jean-Pierre. *Le Livre au temps de Marie-Thérèse: Codes des lois de censure du livre pour les pays austro-bohemiens (1740–1780).* Bern 1993.

Lebeau, Christine. *Aristocrates et grands commis à la cour de Vienne, 1748–1791: Le modèle français.* Paris 1996.

———. "Finanzwissenschaft und diplomatische Missionen: Machtstrategien und Ausbildung der Staatswissenschaften in Frankreich und der österreichischen Monarchie," in *Akteure der Außenbeziehungen: Netzwerke und Interkulturalität im historischen Wandel*, ed. Hillard von Thiessen and Christian Windler. Cologne / Weimar / Vienna 2010, 151–72.

———. "Verwandtschaft, Patronage und Freundschaft: Die Rolle des Buches im Kreis um Kaunitz," in *Staatskanzler Wenzel Anton von Kaunitz-Rietberg 1711–1794: Neue Perspektiven zu Politik und Kultur der europäischen Aufklärung*, ed. Grete Klingenstein and Franz A. J. Szábo. Graz 1996, 291–304.

Leeb, Rudolf, Susanne C. Pils, and Thomas Winkelbauer (eds.). *Staatsmacht und Seelenheil: Gegenreformation und Geheimprotestantismus in der Habsburgermonarchie.* Vienna 2007.

Leeb, Rudolf, Martin Scheutz, and Dietmar Weikl (eds.). *Geheimprotestantismus und evangelische Kirchen in der Habsburgermonarchie und im Erzbistum Salzburg (17./18. Jahrhundert).* Vienna / Cologne / Weimar 2009.

Lehner, Ulrich. "What is 'Catholic Enlightenment'?" *History Compass* 8 (2010): 166–78.

Lehner, Ulrich, and Michael Printy (eds.). *A Companion to Catholic Enlightenment in Europe.* Leiden and Boston 2010.

Lemberg, Hans. "Imperien und Grenzregionen im Europa des 18. und 19. Jahrhunderts: Einige einführende Beobachtungen," in *Grenzregionen der Habsburgermonarchie im 18. und 19. Jahrhundert: Ihre Bedeutung und Funktion aus der Perspektive Wiens*, ed. Hans-Christian Maner. Münster 2005, 25–36.

Lembke, Katja (ed.). *Als die Royals aus Hannover kamen: Hannovers Herrscher auf Englands Thron 1714–1837.* Dresden 2014.

Lesky, Erna. "Die österreichische Pestfront an der k.k. Militärgrenze." *Saeculum* 8 (1957): 86–106.

———. "Österreichisches Gesundheitswesen im Zeitalter des aufgeklärten Absolutismus." *Archiv für österreichische Geschichte* 122 (1959): 1–228.

Lesky, Erna and Adam Wandruszka (eds.). *Gerard van Swieten und seine Zeit.* Vienna / Graz / Cologne 1973.

Lettner, Gerda. *Das Spannungsfeld zwischen Absolutismus und Aufklärung: Die Ära Kaunitz* (1749–1794). Göttingen 2016.

Lever, Evelyne. *Marie Antoinette: Die Biographie.* Düsseldorf 2004.

Lhotsky, Alphons. "Apis Colonna: Fabeln und Theorien über die Abkunft der Habsburger, in Lhotsky, Aufsätze und Vorträge." *Vienna* 1971, 7–102.

Liebel-Weckowicz, Helen, and Franz Szábo. "Modernization Forces in Maria Theresa's Peasant Policies, 1740–1780." *Histoire sociale / Social History* 15 (1982): 301–31.

Liebmann, Maximilian. "Mariazell im Spiegel kirchlich-religiösen und politischen Lebens von Mitteleuropa," in *Ökumene Symposion: Die Last der Geschichte—Mariazell und Marialogie von der Reformation bis ins 20. Jahrhundert.* URL: http://www.professor-liebmann.at/pdf /MariazellDruck.pdf (02.03.2014).

Link, Edith Murr. *The Emancipation of the Austrian Peasant 1740–1798.* New York 1949.

Link, Christoph. "Die habsburgischen Erblande, die böhmischen Länder und Salzburg," in *Deutsche Verwaltungsgeschichte,* vol. 1: *Vom Spätmittelalter bis zum Ende des Reiches,* ed. Kurt G. A. Jeserich, Hans Pohl, Georg Christoph von Unruh. Stuttgart 1983, 468–551.

Lobenwein, Elisabeth. "'Je gresser die lieb der eltern gegen ihren kündern ist, umb so gresser auch die betriebnus und schmerzen, wann solche in högster todts gefahr komben': Kinder im Zentrum der Wunderberichte von Maria Luggau/Kärnten," in *Forschungswerkstatt: Die Habsburgermonarchie im 18. Jahrhundert,* ed. Gunda Barth-Scalmani, et al. Bochum 2012, 143–55.

Loesche, Georg. "Aus der Endzeit des Geheimprotestantismus in Innerösterreich: Archivalische Ergänzungen." *Zeitschrift des Historischen Vereins Steiermark* 18 (1923): 124–34.

———. "Maria Theresias letzte Maßnahmen gegen die 'Ketzer.' Mit Benutzung archivalischer Quellen." *Zeitschrift des deutschen Vereins für die Geschichte Mährens und Schlesiens* 20 (1916): 198–219.

Lohrmann, Klaus. *Zwischen Finanz und Toleranz: Das Haus Habsburg und die Juden.* Graz / Vienna / Cologne 2000.

Lorenz, Hellmut. "The Imperial Hofburg: The Theory and Practice of Architectural Representation in Baroque Vienna," in *State and Society in Early Modern Austria,* ed. Charles W. Ingrao. West Lafayette 1994, 93–109.

Lorenz, Hellmut, and Anna Mader-Kratky (ed.). *Die Wiener Hofburg 1705–1835: Die kaiserliche Residenz vom Barock bis zum Klassizismus.* Vienna 2016.

Lorenz, Hellmut, and Huberta Weigl (eds.). *Das barocke Wien: Die Kupferstiche von Joseph Emanuel Fischer von Erlach und Johann Adam Delsenbach (1719).* Vienna 2007.

Lorenz, Matthias. *Der Jansenismus in der Habsburgermonarchie: Ein Forschungsüberblick.* Saarbrücken 2009.

Loupès, Philippe. "Telle mère, tel fils? Le bilan du règne de Marie-Thérèse au miroir des oraisons funèbres et des éloges en France," in *Josephinismus—eine Bilanz: Échecs et réussites du Joséphisme*, ed. Wolfgang Schmale, Renate Zedinger, and Jacques Mondot. Bochum 2008, 117–26.

Löwenstein, Uta. "Voraussetzungen und Grundlagen von Tafelzeremoniell und Zeremoientafel," in *Zeremoniell als höfische Ästhetik in Spätmittelalter und Früher Neuzeit*, ed. Jörg Jochen Berns and Thomas Rahn. Tübingen 1995, 266–78.

Lucassen, Leo. "Zigeuner im frühneuzeitlichen Deutschland: Neue Forschungsergebnisse, -probleme und -vorschläge," in *Policey und frühneuzeitliche Gesellschaft*, ed. Karl Härter. Frankfurt am Main 2000, 235–61.

Luebke, David M. "'Naive Monarchism' and Marian Veneration in Early Modern Germany." in *Past & Present* 154 (1997): 71–106.

Luh, Jürgen. *Kriegskunst in Europa 1650–1800*. Weimar / Vienna 2004.

Luhmann, Niklas. *Liebe als Passion: Zur Codierung von Intimität*. Frankfurt am Main. 1982.

Lukowski, Jerzy. *The Partitions of Poland, 1772, 1793, 1795*. London / New York 1999.

Maasburg, Friedrich von. *Geschichte der obersten Justizstelle in Wien*, 2nd ed. Prague 1891.

———. *Zur Entstehungsgeschichte der Theresianischen Halsgerichtsordnung*. Vienna 1880.

Maaß, Ferdinand. *Der Frühjosephinismus*. Vienna 1969.

———. "Maria Theresia und der Josephinismus." i*Zeitschrift für Katholische Theologie* 79 (1957): 201–13.

Macek, Bernhard A. *Die Krönung Josephs II. zum Römischen König in Frankfurt am Main*. Frankfurt am Main 2010.

———. "Der Krönungszyklus aus der Meytens-Werkstatt." *Das Achtzehnte Jahrhundert und Österreich* 27 (2012): 213–26.

Macek, Ondrej. "Geheimprotestanten in Böhmen und Mähren im 17. und 18. Jahrhundert," in Leeb, Rudolf, Martin Scheutz, and Dietmar Weikl (eds.). *Geheimprotestantismus und evangelische Kirchen in der Habsburgermonarchie und im Erzbistum Salzburg (17./18. Jahrhundert)*. Vienna / Cologne / Weimar 2009.

Maddalena, Aldo de, et al. (eds.) *Economia, istituzioni, cultura nell'età di Maria Teresa*. Bologna 1982.

Mader-Kratky, Anna. "Modifizieren oder 'nach alter Gewohnheit'? Die Auswirkungen des Regierungsantritts von Maria Theresia auf Zeremoniell und Raumfolge in der Wiener Hofburg," in *Im Dienste einer Staatsidee. Künste und Künstler am Wiener Hof um 1740*, ed. Elisabeth Fritz-Hilscher. Vienna / Cologne / Weimar 2013, 85–106.

Maner, Hans-Christian (ed.). *Grenzregionen der Habsburgermonarchie im 18. und 19. Jahrhundert: Ihre Bedeutung und Funktion aus der Perspektive Wiens*. Münster 2005.

Mansel, Philip. *Dressed to Rule: Royal and Court Costume from Louis XIV to Elizabeth II*. New Haven and London 2005.

———. *Prince of Europe. The Life of Charles Joseph de Ligne, 1735–1814*. London 2003.

Maria Theresia und Tirol. Exhibition catalog. Innsbruck 1958.

Marin, Louis. *Das Porträt des Königs, Aus dem Französischen von Heinz Jatho*. Original French edition Paris 1981. Berlin 2005.

Martus, Steffen. *Aufklärung: Das deutsche 18. Jahrhundert, ein Epochenbild*. Berlin 2015.

Mat'a, Petr. "Landstände und Landtage in den böhmischen und österreichischen Ländern (1620–1740)," in *Die Habsburgermonarchie 1620–1740: Leistungen und Grenzen des Absolutismusparadigmas*, ed. Petr Mat'a and Thomas Winkelbauer. Stuttgart 2006, 345–400.

Mat'a, Petr, and Thomas Winkelbauer (eds.). *Die Habsburgermonarchie 1620–1740: Leistungen und Grenzen des Absolutismusparadigmas*. Stuttgart 2006.

Matis, Herbert (ed.). *Von der Glückseligkeit des Staates: Staat, Wirtschaft und Gesellschaft in Österreich im Zeitalter des Aufgeklärten Absolutismus*. Berlin 1981.

Matsche, Franz. "Die Kunst im Dienst der Staatsidee Kaiser Karls VI," in *Ikonographie, Ikonologie und Programmatik des "Kaiserstils."* Berlin and New York 1981.

———. "Maria Theresias Bild als Herrscherin in der Kunst ihrer Zeit," in *Maria Theresias Kulturwelt*, ed. Pierre Béhar, Marie-Thérèse Mourey, and Herbert Schneider. Hildesheim / Zürich / New York 2011, 195–245.

Mauser, Wolfram. "Maria Theresia: 'Mutter der Völker,'" in *Konzepte aufklärerischer Lebensführung: Literarische Kultur im frühmodernen Deutschland*, ed. Wolfram Mauser. Würzburg 2000, 137–47.

———. "Maria Theresia. Mütterlichkeit: Mythos und politisches Mandat (Hofmannsthal, Sonnenfels, Wurz)," in *Mutter und Mütterlichkeit*, ed. Irmgard Roebling and Wolfram Mauser. Würzburg 1996, 77–97.

Mayerhofer, Claudia. *Dorfzigeuner: Kultur und Geschichte der Burgenland-Roma von der Ersten Republik bis zur Gegenwart*. Vienna 1987.

Maza, Sara. *Private Lives and Public Affairs: The Causes Célèbres of Prerevolutionary France*. Berkeley / Los Angeles / London 1993.

Mazura, Silvia. *Die preußische und österreichische Kriegspropaganda im Ersten und Zweiten Schlesischen Krieg*. Berlin 1996.

Meier, Christian. *Die Faszination des Biographischen*, in *Interesse an der Geschichte*, ed. Frank Niess. Frankfurt a.M. and New York 1989, 100–111.

Meisenburg, Friedrich. *Der Deutsche Reichstag während des Österreichischen Erbfolgekrieges (1740–1748)*. Dillingen 1931.

Meisner, Heinrich Otto. "Das Regierungs- und Behördensystem Maria Theresias und der preußische Staat," in *Die Entstehung des modernen souveränen Staates*, ed. Hanns Hubert Hofmann. Berlin 1967, 209–27.

———. *Urkunden- und Aktenlehre der Neuzeit*. Leipzig 1950.

Mell, Anton. *Die Anfänge der Bauernbefreiung in Steiermark unter Maria Theresia und Joseph II: Nach den Akten dargestellt*. Graz 1901.

Mertens, Bernd. *Gesetzgebungskunst im Zeitalter der Kodifikationen: Theorie und Praxis der Gesetzgebungstechnik aus historisch-vergleichender Sicht*. Tübingen 2004.

Mevorach, Barouh. "The Imperial Court-Jew Wolf Wertheimer as Diplomatic Mediator during the War of the Austrian Succession." *Hierosolymitana* 23 (1972): 184–213.

Meynert, Hermann. *Das königliche Krönungsceremoniel in Ungarn*. Vienna 1867.

Michalik, Kerstin. *Kindsmord: Sozial- und Rechtsgeschichte der Kindstötung im 18. und beginnenden 19. Jahrhundert am Beispiel Preußen*. Pfaffenweiler 1997.

Michaud, Claude. "Laudatio et Carmen port mortem: Nachrufe auf Maria Theresia in Frankreich und Belgien," in *Österreich im Europa der Aufklärung. Kontinuität und Zäsur in Europa zur Zeit Maria Theresias und Josephs II*, ed. Bundesministerium für Wissenschaft und Forschung and Österreichische Akademie der Wissenschaften. Vienna 1985, 673–700.

Midelfort, H. C. Erik. *Exorcism and Enlightenment: Johann Joseph Gassner and the Demons of Eighteenth Century Germany*. New Haven and London 2005.

Mikoletzky, Hanns Leo. "Der Haushalt des kaiserlichen Hofes zu Wien (vornehmlich im 18. Jahrhundert)." *Carinthia I*, 146 (1956): 658–83.

———. *Hofreisen unter Kaiser Karl VI. MIÖG* 60 (1952): 265–85.

———. *Kaiser Franz I: Stefan und der Ursprung des habsburgisch-lothringischen Familienvermögens*. Munich 1961.

———. "Die privaten 'geheimen Kassen' Kaiser Franz I. und Maria Theresias." *MIÖG* 71 (1963): 380–94.

Mitterauer, Michael. "Bedeutsame Orte: Zur Genese räumlicher Bezugspunkte österreichischer Identität," in *Memoria Austriae II: Bauten, Orte, Regionen*, ed. Emil Brix, Ernst Bruckmüller, and Hannes Stekl. Vienna 2005, 19–39.

Moraw, Peter. "Das Reich und Österreich im Spätmittelalter," in *Sacrum Imperium: Das Reich und Österreich 996–1806*, ed. Wilhelm Brauneder andLothar Höbelt. Vienna 1996, 92–130.

Mourey, Marie-Thérèse. "Tanz- und Ballettkultur unter Maria Theresia," in *Maria Theresias Kulturwelt*, ed. Pierre Béhar, Mare-Thérèse Mourey, and Herbert Schneider. Hildesheim, Zürich, New York 2011, 171–93.

Mraz, Gerda. "Anekdoten über Maria Theresia und Joseph II." *Österreich in Geschichte und Literatur* 33 (1989): 1–12.

Mraz, Gerda, and Gottfried Mraz. *Maria Theresia: Ihr Leben und ihre Zeit in Bildern und Dokumenten*. Munich 1979.

Müller, Herta. "Die k. k. Nadelburger Fabrik zu Lichtenwörth: Ihre Geschichte von 1751 bis 1815." Phd diss. Vienna 1941.

Müller, Michael G. *Die Teilungen Polens, 1772, 1793, 1795*. Munich 1984.

Müller, Matthias F. "Der Orden vom Goldenen Vlies und das Haus Habsburg im Heiligen Römischen Reich—Ein (kultur-) geschichtlicher Rückblick, in Mitteilungen der Gesellschaft für vergleichende Kunstforschung," *Wien* 61 (2009): 1–21.

Müller-Guttenbrunn, Adam (ed.). *Ruhmeshalle deutscher Arbeit in der österreichisch-ungarischen Monarchie*. Stuttgart and Berlin 1916.

Neugebauer, Wolfgang. "Niedere Schulen und Realschulen." *Handbuch der deutschen Bildungsgeschichte*. Vol. 2: *18. Jahrhundert*, ed. Notker Hammerstein and Ulrich Herrmann. Munich 2005, 213–61.

Neuhaus, Helmuth. "'Supplizieren und Wassertrinken sind jedem gestattet': Über den Zugang des Einzelnen zum frühneuzeitlichen Ständestaat," in *Staat—Souveränität—Verfassung. Festschrift für Helmut Quaritsch zum 70. Geburtstag*, ed. Dietrich Murswiek and Ulrich Storost. Berlin 2000, 475–92.

Niederhauser, Emil. "Maria Theresia in der ungarischen Geschichtsschreibung." *Ungarn und Österreich unter Maria Theresia und Joseph*, vol. 2: *Neue Aspekte im Verhältnis der beiden Länder*, ed. Anna M. Drabek, Richard G. Plaschka, and Adam Wandruszka. Vienna 1982, 29–41.

Nietzsche, Friedrich. *Untimely Meditations*, translated by R. J. Hollingdale. Cambridge 1997.

Novotny, Alexander. *Staatskanzler Kaunitz als geistige Persönlichkeit.* Vienna 1947.

Nowosadtko, Jutta. "Der 'Vampyrus Serviensis' und sein Habitat. Impressionen von der österreichischen Militärgrenze." *Militär und Gesellschaft in der Frühen Neuzeit* 8 (2004): 151–67.

Nubola, Cecilia (ed.). *Bittschriften und Gravamina: Politik, Verwaltung und Justiz in Europa (14.–18. Jahrhundert).* Berlin 2005.

Obersteiner, Gernot Peter. *Theresianische Verwaltungsreformen im Herzogtum Steiermark: Die Repräsentation und Kammer (1749–1763) als neue Landesbehörde des aufgeklärten Absolutismus.* Graz 1993.

O'Brian, Charles H. "Jansenists and Josephinism: 'Nouvelles Ecclesiatiques' and Reform of the Church in Late Eighteenth-Century Austria." *MÖStA* 32 (1979): 143–64.

Ogris, Werner. "Staats- und Rechtsreformen," in *Maria Theresia und ihre Zeit,* ed. Walter Koschatzky. Salzburg and Vienna 1979, 56–66.

Opitz, Claudia. "Pflicht-Gefühl: Zur Codierung von Mutterliebe zwischen Renaissance und Aufklärung." *Querelles* 7 (2002): 154–70.

———. "Von Frauen im Krieg zum Krieg gegen Frauen. Krieg, Gewalt und Geschlechterbeziehungen aus historischer Sicht." *L'Homme* 3 (1992): 31–44.

Ortlieb, Eva, and Gert Polster. "Die Prozessfrequenz am Reichshofrat (1519–1806)." *Zeitschrift für Neuere Rechtsgeschichte* 26 (2004): 180–215.

Osterloh, Karl-Heinz. *Joseph von Sonnenfels und die österreichische Reformbewegung im Zeitalter des aufgeklärten Absolutismus.* Lübeck and Hamburg 1970.

Österreich zur Zeit Josephs II: Mitregent Kaiserin Maria Theresias, Kaiser und Landesfürst. Exhibition catalog. Lower Austria State Museum, Vienna 1980.

Otruba, Gustav. *Die Wirtschaftspolitik Maria Theresias.* Vienna 1963.

Ottillinger, Eva B. "Das Paradebett Maria Theresias im 'Reichen Schlafzimmer' in der Wiener Hofburg." *Österreichische Zeitschrift für Kunst und Denkmalpflege* 51 (1997): 648–55.

Ottomeyer, Hans, and Michaela Völkel (eds.). *Die öffentliche Tafel: Tafelzeremoniell in Europa 1300–1900.* Exhibition catalog. Wolfratshausen 2002.

Pammer, Michael. *Glaubensabfall und Wahre Andacht: Barockreligiosität, Reformkatholizismus und Laizismus in Oberösterreich 1700–1820.* Vienna and Munich 1994.

Pangels, Charlotte. *Die Kinder Maria Theresias.* Munich 1980.

Pangerl, Irmgard, Martin Scheutz, and Thomas Winkelbauer (eds.). *Der Wiener Hof im Spiegel der Zeremonialprotokolle (1652–1800): Eine Annäherung.* Innsbruck / Bolzano / Vienna 2007.

Papp, Julia. "Reflexionen zur Ikonografie von Maria Theresia im Spiegel der Wiener Biografiesammlungen um 1810." *Wiener Geschichtsblätter* 65 (2010): 91–104.

Parvev, Ivan. "'Du, glückliches Österreich, verhandle' Militär versus Diplomatie in der habsburgischen Südosteuropa-Politik 1739–1878," in *Das Osmanische Reich und die Habsburgermonarchie,* ed. Marlene Kurz, et al. Munich 2005, 539–50.

———. "'Enemy Mine': Das osmanische Feindbild und seine Wandlung in der Habsburgermonarchie der späten Frühneuzeit," in *Friedens- und Konfliktmanagement in interkulturellen Räumen: Das Osmanische Reich und die Habsburgermonarchie,* ed. Arno Strohmeyer and Norbert Spannenberger. Stuttgart 2014, 371–83.

Pastor, Ludwig Freiherr von. *Geschichte der Päpste seit dem Ausgang des Mittelalters. Geschichte der Päpste im Zeitalter des fürstlichen Absolutismus von der Wahl Benedkts XIV. bis zum Tode Pius' VI. (1740–1799).* Freiburg / Br. 1931.

Pauser, Josef, Martin Scheutz, and Thomas Winkelbauer (eds.). *Quellenkunde der Habsburgermonarchie (16.–18. Jahrhundert): Ein exemplarisches Handbuch*. Vienna / Cologne / Weimar 2004.

Pečar, Andreas. "Gab es eine höfische Gesellschaft des Reiches? Rang- und Statuskonkurrenz innerhalb des Reichsadels in der ersten Hälfte des 18. Jahrhunderts," in *Das Reich und seine Territorialstaaten im 17. und 18. Jahrhundert: Aspekte des Mit- Neben- und Gegeneinander*, ed. Harm Klueting and Wolfgang Schmale. Münster 2004, 183–205.

———. *Die Masken des Königs: Friedrich II. von Preußen als Schriftsteller*. Frankfurt am Main and New York 2016.

———. *Die Ökonomie der Ehre: Der höfische Adel am Kaiserhof Karls VI. (1711–1740)*. Darmstadt 2003.

Pečar, Andreas, and Damien Tricoire. *Falsche Freunde: War die Aufklärung wirklich die Geburtsstunde der Moderne?* Frankfurt am Main and New York 2015.

Peper, Ines. *Konversionen im Umkreis des Wiener Hofes*. Vienna 2010.

Peper, Iris, and Thomas Wallnig. "Ex nihilo nihil fit: Johann Benedikt Gentilotti und Johann Christoph Bartenstein am Beginn ihrer Karrieren," in *Adel im "langen" 18. Jahrhundert*, ed. Gabriele Haug-Moritz. Vienna 2009, 167–86.

Petrat, Gerhardt. *Die letzten Narren und Zwerge bei Hofe: Reflexionen zu Herrschaft und Moral in der frühen Neuzeit*. Bochum 1998.

Petritsch, Ernst Dieter, "Interkulturelle Diplomatie zwischen Habsburgern und Osmanen: Fragen und Probleme," in *Audienzen und Allianzen: Interkulturelle Diplomatie in Asien und Europa vom 8. bis zum 18. Jahrhundert*, ed. Birgit Tremml-Werner and Eberhard Crailsheim. Vienna 2015, 184–200.

———. "Erziehung in guten Sitten, Andacht und Gehorsam: Die 1754 gegründete Orientalische Akademie in Wien," in *Das Osmanische Reich und die Habsburgermornarchie*, ed. Marlene Kurz, et al. Munich 2005, 491–502.

Pfeisinger, Gerhard. *Arbeitsdisziplinierung und frühe Industrialisierung 1750–1820*. Vienna / Cologne / Weimar 2006.

Plachta, Bodo. *Damnatur—Toleratur—Admittitur: Studien und Dokumente zur literarischen Zensur im 18. Jahrhundert*. Tübingen 1994.

———. "Zensur: Eine Institution der Aufklärung?" in *Das Achtzehnte Jahrhundert und Österreich*, vol. 17: *Strukturwandel kultureller Praxis. Beiträge zu einer kulturwissenschaftlichen Sicht des theresianischen Zeitalters*, ed. Franz M. Eybl. Vienna 2002, 153–66.

Plaggenborg, Stefan. "Maria Theresia und die böhmischen Juden." *Bohemia* 39 (1998): 1–16.

Plaschka, Richard Georg (ed.). *Was heißt Österreich? Inhalt und Umfang des Österreichbegriffs vom 10. Jahrhundert bis heute*. Vienna 1995.

Plaschka, Richard Georg, and Grete Klingenstein (eds.). *Österreich im Europa der Aufklärung. Kontinuität und Zäsur zur Zeit Maria Theresias und Josephs II.* Vienna 1985.

Pohlig, Matthias. "Vom Besonderen zum Allgemeinen? Die Fallstudie als geschichtstheoretisches Problem." *Historische Zeitschrift* 297 (2013): 297–319.

Polleroß, Friedrich. "Austriacus Hungariae Rex; Zur Darstellung der Habsburger als ungarische Könige in der frühneuzeitlichen Graphik," in Orsolya Bubryák (ed.), *"Ez világ, mint egy kert...": Tanulmányok Galavics Géza tiszteletére*. Budapest 2010, 63–78.

———. "'Pro Deo, Caesare et Patria'": Zur Repräsentation der Stände in Österreich vom 16. bis zum 18. Jahrhundert," in *Bündnispartner und Konkurrenten der Landesfürsten? Die Stände in der Habsburgermonarchie,* ed. Gerhard Ammerer, et al. Vienna / Munich 2007, 479–532.

Pölzl, Michael. "Die Kaiserinnen Amalia Wilhelmina (1673–1742) und Elisabeth Christine (1691–1750): Handlungsspielräume im Spannungsfeld dynastischer und persönlicher Interessen," in *Nur die Frau des Kaisers? Kaiserinnen in der Frühen Neuzeit,* ed. Bettina Braun, Katrin Keller, and Matthias Schnettger. Cologne / Weimar / Vienna 2016, 175–92.

———. "Kaiserin-Witwen in Konkurrenz zur regierenden Kaiserin am Wiener Hof 1637–1750." *Wiener Geschichtsblätter* 67 (2012): 165–89.

Pons, Rouven. *Die Kunst der Loyalität: Ludwig VIII. von Hessen-Darmstadt (1691–1768) und der Wiener Kaiserhof.* Marburg 2009.

Popelka, Liselotte. "Freuden- und Trauerzurüstungen in Wien und den Erblanden," in *Maria Theresia und ihre Zeit,* ed. Walter Koschatzky. Salzburg / Vienna 1979, 355–62.

———. "Martin Engelbrecht und die Hilfsvölker Maria Theresias," in *Maria Theresia als Königin von Ungarn,* ed. Der Burgenländischen Landesregierung. Eisenstadt 1980, 45–51.

Popitz, Heinrich. *Phänomene der Macht,* 2nd ed. Tübingen, 999.

Pörtner, Regina. "'De crimine magiae': Das Verbrechen der Zauberei im theresiansichen Strafrecht nach Akten des Diözesanarchivs Graz." *Zeitschrift des Historischen Vereins Steiermark* 94 (2004): 149–59.

———. "Die Kunst des Lügens. Ketzerverfolgung und geheimprotestantische Überlebensstrategien im theresianischen Österreich," in *Kommunikation in der Frühen Neuzeit,* ed. Johannes Burkhardt and Christine Werkstetter. Munich 2005, 385–408.

———. "Propaganda, Conspiracy, Persecution: Prussian Influences on Habsburg Religious Policies from Leopold I. to Joseph II.," in *Orte des Wissens: Jahrbuch der Österreichischen Gesellschaft zur Erforschung des 18. Jahrhunderts 18/19,* ed. Martin Scheutz, et al. Vienna 2004, 457–76.

Preradovich, Nikolaus von. *Das seltsam wilde Leben des Pandurenoberst Franz von der Trenck.* Graz 1980.

Press, Volker. "Bayern am Scheideweg: Die Reichspolitik Kaiser Josephs II. und der Bayerische Erbfolgekrieg 1777—1779," in Volker Press, *Das Alte Reich: Ausgewählte Aufsätze,* ed. Johannes Kunisch. Berlin 1997, 289–325.

———. "Das wittelsbachische Kaisertum Karls VII: Voraussetzungen von Entstehung und Scheitern," in Volker Press, *Das Alte Reich: Ausgewählte Aufsätze,* ed. Johannes Kunisch. Berlin 1997, 223–59.

———. "Friedrich der Große als Reichspolitiker," in Volker Press, *Das Alte Reich. Ausgewählte Aufsätze,* ed. Johannes Kunisch. Berlin 1997, 260–88.

———. "The Habsburg Court as Center of the Imperial Government." *Journal of Modern History* 58 (1986): 23–45.

———. "Patronat und Klientel im Heiligen Römischen Reich," in *Klientelsysteme im Europa der Frühen Neuzeit,* ed. Antoni Maczak. Munich 1988, 19–46.

Pribram, Karl. *Geschichte der österreichischen Gewerbepolitik.* Leipzig 1907.

Prinz Eugen und das barocke Österreich: Katalog zur niederösterreichischen Landesausstellung 1986. Schlosshof 1986.

Probst, Christian. "Gerard van Swieten als Arzt und Forscher," in *Gerard van Swieten und seine Zeit*, ed. Erna Lesky and Adam Wandruszka. Vienna / Graz / Cologne 1973, 80–92.

Puppel, Pauline. "Gynäcocratie: Herrschaft hochadeliger Frauen in der Frühen Neuzeit," in *Geschlechterstreit am Beginn der europäischen Moderne: Die Querelle des Femmes*, ed. Gisela Engel. Königstein im Taunus 2004.

———. "'Virilibus curis, faeminarum vitia exuerant': Zur Konstruktion der Ausnahme," in *Lesarten der Geschichte: Ländliche Ordnungen und Geschlechterverhältnisse: Festschrift für Heide Wunder*, ed. Jens Flemming et al. Kassel 2004, 356–76.

Quakatz, Manja. "'Conversio Turci': Konvertierte und zwangsgetaufte Osmanen, religiöse und kulturelle Grenzgänger im Alten Reich (1683–1710)," in *Ein Raum im Wandel: Die osmanisch-habsburgische Grenzregion vom 16. bis zum 18. Jahrhundert*, ed. Norbert Spannenberger and Szabolcs Varga. Stuttgart 2014, 215–34.

Ranke, Leopold von. *Sämtliche Werke*. Vol. 30: *Zur Geschichte von Österreich und Preußen zwischen den Friedensschlüssen von Aachen und Hubertusburg*. Leipzig 1875.

Raponi, Nicola. "Il mito del buongoverno teresiano nella Lombardia preunitaria," in *Economia, istituzioni, cultura nell'età di Maria Teresa*, ed. Aldo de Maddalena, et al. Bologna 1982, 269–306.

Rasche, Ulrich. "Urteil versus Vergleich? Entscheidungspraxis und Konfliktregulierung des Reichshofrats im 17. Jahrhundert im Spiegel neuerer Aktenerschließung," in *Mit Freundschaft oder mit Recht? Inner- und außergerichtliche Alternativen zur kontroversen Streitentscheidung im 15.-19. Jahrhundert*, ed. Albrecht Cordes. Cologne / Weimar / Vienna 2015, 199–231.

Rathkolb, Oliver (ed.). *250 Jahre: Von der Orientalischen zur Diplomatischen Akademie in Wien*. Innsbruck 2004.

Rauscher, Franz. "Die Bauernrevolte im Gföhlerwald anno 1765." *Das Waldviertel* 5 (1956): 41–64.

Rauscher, Peter. "Krieg—Steuern—Religion—Recht. Staatsgewalt und bäuerlicher Protest in Österreich ob und unter der Enns (16.–18. Jahrhundert)," in *Die Stimme der ewigen Verlierer? Aufstände, Revolten und Revolutionen in den österreichischen Ländern (ca. 1740–1815)*, ed. Peter Rauscher and Martin Scheutz. Munich 2013, 237–72.

Rauscher, Peter, and Martin Scheutz (eds.) *Die Stimme der ewigen Verlierer? Aufstände, Revolten und Revolutionen in den österreichischen Ländern (ca. 1740–1815)*. Munich 2013.

Redlich, Oswald. "Die Tagebücher Kaiser Karls VI.," in *Gesamtdeutsche Vergangenheit: Festgabe für Heinrich Ritter von Srbik*. Munich 1938, 141–51.

Reinalter, Helmut. *Aufklärung, Absolutismus, Reaktion: Die Geschichte Tirols in der zweiten Hälfte des 18. Jahrhunderts*. Vienna 1974.

———(ed.). *Aufklärung und Geheimgesellschaften: Zur politischen Funktion und Sozialstruktur der Freimaurerlogen im 18. Jahrhundert*. Munich 1989.

———(ed.). *Josephinismus als Aufgeklärter Absolutismus*. Vienna 2008.

———(ed.). *Joseph von Sonnenfels*. Vienna 1988.

Reinalter, Helmut, and Harm Klueting (eds.). *Der Aufgeklärte Absolutismus im europäischen Vergleich*. Vienna / Cologne / Weimar 2002.

Reinhardt, Rudolf. *Zur Kirchenreform unter Maria Theresia: Zeitschrift für Kirchengeschichte* 77 (1966): 105–19.

————. *De Sade oder die Vermessung des Bösen: Eine Biographie.* Munich 2014.

Reiniger, Alice. *Wolfgang von Kempelen: Eine Biographie.* Vienna 2007.

Reinöhl, Fritz. "Die Übertragung der Mitregentschaft durch Maria Theresia an Großherzog Franz Stephan und Kaiser Joseph II.," in *MIÖG* 11 (suppl. vol. 1929): 650–61.

Reisner, Andrea, and Alfred Schiemer. "Das Wien(n)erische Diarium und die Entstehung der periodischen Presse," in *Österreichische Mediengeschichte*, vol. 1: *Von den frühen Drucken zur Ausdifferenzierung des Mediensystems (1500–1918)*, ed. Matthias Karmasin and Christian Oggolder. Wiesbaden 2016, 87–112.

Reissenberger, Friedrich. "Das Corpus evangelicorum und die österreichischen Protestanten (1685–1764)," in *Jahrbuch der Gesellschaft für die Geschichte des Protestantismus in Österreich* 17 (1896): 207–22.

Reitböck, J. "Das Altarbild in der k.k. Nadelburg." *Berichte und Mittheilungen des Altertums-Vereins zu Wien* 27 (1891): 21–25.

Ribeiro, Aileen. *Dress in Eighteenth Century Europe, 1715–89.* New Haven and London 1984.

Riedel, Julia Anna. *Bildungsreform und geistliches Ordenswesen im Ungarn der Aufklärung.* Stuttgart 2012.

Rink, Martin. "Die noch ungezähmte Bellona: Der Kleine Krieg und die Landbevölkerung in der Frühen Neuzeit," in *Militär und ländliche Gesellschaft in der frühen Neuzeit*, ed. Stefan Kroll and Kersten Krüger. Hamburg 2000, 165–89.

————. *Vom "Partheygänger" zum Partisanen: Die Konzeption des kleinen Krieges in Preussen 1740–1813.* Frankfurt/Main 1999.

Robertson, John. *The Case for the Enlightenment: Scotland and Naples 1680–1760.* Cambridge 2005.

Robertson, Ritchie, and Edward Timms (eds.). *The Austrian Enlightenment and its Aftermath.* Edinburgh 1991.

Roche, Daniel. *The Culture of Clothing: Dress and Fashion in the Ancien Régime.* Cambridge 1994.

Roethlisberger, Marcel, and Renée Loche. *Liotard: Catalogue, sources et correspondance.* Doornspijk 2008.

Rohrschneider, Michael. *Österreich und der Immerwährende Reichstag: Studien zur Klientelpolitik und Parteibildung (1745–1763).* Göttingen 2014.

Roider, Karl A., Jr. *Austria's Eastern Question 1700–1790.* Princeton 1982.

Römer, Christof. "Der Kaiser und die welfischen Staaten 1679–1755: Abriß der Konstellationen und der Bedingungsfelder," in *Das Reich und seine Territorialstaaten im 17. und 18. Jahrhundert: Aspekte des Mit- Neben- und Gegeneinander*, ed. Harm Klueting and Wolfgang Schmale. Münster 2004, 43–67.

Roth, Erik. *Die planmäßig angelegten Siedlungen im Deutsch-Banater Militärgrenzbezirk 1765–1821.* Munich 1988.

Rothenberg, Gunther E. *Die österreichische Militärgrenze 1522–1881.* Vienna 1970.

Royal Academy of Arts London (ed.). *Jean-Étienne Liotard 1702–1789.* Exhibition catalog. London and New York 2015.

Ruzicka, Dagmar. *Friedrich Graf von Haugwitz (1702–1765): Weg, Leistung und Umfeld eines österreichisch-schlesischen Staatsmannes.* Frankfurt 2002.

Sacher-Masoch, Leopold von. "Maria Theresia als Sultanin," in Leopold von Sacher-Masoch, *Silhouetten: Novellen und Skizzen.* Leipzig 1879, 47–62.

Samerski, Stefan. "Hausheilige statt Staatspatrone: Der misslungene Absolutismus in Österreichs Heiligenhimmel," in *Die Habsburgermonarchie 1620–1740: Leistungen und Grenzen des
Absolutismusparadigmas*, ed. Petr Mat'a and Thomas Winkelbauer. Stuttgart 2006, 251–78.

Sandgruber, Roman. *Ökonomie und Politik. Österreichische Wirtschaftsgeschichte vom Mittelalter
bis zur Gegenwart*. Vienna 1995.

Sanger, Erneste. *Isabelle de Bourbon-Parme: La Princesse et la Mort*. Brussels 2002.

Sauer, Walter. "Angelo Soliman: Mythos und Wirklichkeit," in *Von Soliman zu Omofuma: Afri-
kanische Diaspora in Österreich, 17.-20. Jahrhundert*, ed. Walter Sauer. Innsbruck 2007,
59–96.

Saurer, Edith. "Frauengeschichte in Österreich: Eine fast kritische Bestandsaufnahme."
L'Homme 4 (1993): 37–63.

Schattkowsky, Martina (ed.). *Witwenschaft in der Frühen Neuzeit: Fürstliche und adlige Witwen
zwischen Fremd- und Selbstbestimmung*. Leipzig 2003.

Schennach, Martin Paul. "'ist das gaismarsch exempel noch in gedechtnus': Unruhen in den
oberösterreichischen Ländern," in *Die Stimme der ewigen Verlierer? Aufstände, Revolten und
Revolutionen in den österreichischen Ländern (ca. 1740–1815)*, ed. Peter Rauscher and Martin
Scheutz. Munich 2013, 39–66.

———. "Supplikationen," in *Quellenkunde der Habsburgermonarchie (16.–18. Jahrhundert): Ein
exemplarisches Handbuch*, ed. Josef Pauser, Martin Scheutz, and Thomas Winkelbauer.
Vienna / Cologne / Weimar 2004, 572–84.

Scheutz, Martin. "'Der vermenschte Heiland.': Armenspeisung und Gründonnerstags-
Fußwaschung am Wiener Kaiserhof," in *Ein zweigeteilter Ort? Hof und Stadt in der Frühen
Neuzeit*, ed. Susanne C. Pils and Jan P. Niederkorn. Innsbruck 2005, 189–253.

———. "Die fünfte Kolonne Geheimprotestanten in 18. Jahrhundert in der Habsburgermonarchie und deren Inhaftierung in Konversionshäusern (1752–1775)." *MIÖG* 114 (2006):
329–80.

———. "Fasching am frühneuzeitlichen Wiener Hof: Zur Domestizierung der 'verkehrten
Welt' in einem höfischen Umfeld," in *Wien und seine Wienerinnen: Ein historischer Streifzug
durch Wien über die Jahrhunderte: Festschrift für Karl Vocelka*, ed. Martin Scheutz, et al.
Vienna 2008, 125–55.

———. "Legalität und unterdrückte Religionsausübung: Niederleger, Reichshofräte, Gesandte
und Legationsprediger," in *Geheimprotestantismus und evangelische Kirchen in der Habsburgermonarchie und im Erzbistum Salzburg (17./18. Jahrhundert)*, ed. Rudolf Leeb, Martin Scheutz,
and Dietmar Weikl. Vienna / Cologne / Weimar 2009, 209–36.

———. "'Der vermenschte Heiland.': Armenspeisung und Gründonnerstags-Fußwaschung am
Wiener Kaiserhof," in *Ein zweigeteilter Ort? Hof und Stadt in der Frühen Neuzeit*, ed. Susanne C. Pils and Jan P. Niederkorn. Innsbruck 2005, 189–253.

Schilling, Heinz. *Das Reich un die Deutschen*, vol. 5: *Höfe und Allianzen: Deutschland 1648–1763*.
Berlin, n.d.

———. "Formung und Gestalt des internationalen Systems in der werdenden Neuzeit: Phasen
und bewegende Kräfte," in *Kontinuität und Wandel in der Staatenordnung der Neuzeit: Beiträge
zur Geschichte des internationalen Systems*, ed. Peter Krüger. Marburg 1991, 19–46.

Schilling, Lothar. *Kaunitz und das Renversement des alliances: Studien zur außenpolitischen Konzeption Wenzel Antons von Kaunitz*. Berlin 1994.

———. "Ohne Leidenschaft und Vorurteil? Prämissen außenpolitischer Urteilsbildung bei Kaunitz," in *Staatskanzler Wenzel Anton von Kaunitz-Rietberg 1711–1794: Neue Perspektiven zu Politik und Kultur der europäischen Aufklärung,* ed. Grete Klingenstein and Franz A. J. Szábo. Graz et al. 1996, 142–67.

Schindling, Anton. "Theresianismus, Josephinismus, katholische Aufklärung." *Würzburger Diözesangeschichtsblätter* 50 (1988): 215–24.

Schlögl, Rudolf. *Anwesende und Abwesende: Grundriss für eine Gesellschaftsgeschichte der Frühen Neuzeit.* Constance 2014.

Schmal, Kerstin. *Die Pietas Maria Theresias im Spannungsfeld von Barock und Aufklärung: Religiöse Praxis und Sendungsbewusstsein gegenüber Familie, Untertanen und Dynastie.* Frankfurt am Main et al. 2001.

Schmale, Wolfgang (ed.). *Das achtzehnte Jahrundert and Österreich,* vol. 24: *Multiple kulturelle Referenzen in der Habsburgermonarchie des 18. Jahrhunderts / Références culturelles multiples dans la monarchie des Habsbourgau dix-huitième siècle / Multiple Cultural References in 18th-Century Habsburg Monarchy.* Bochum 2010.

Schmale, Wolfgang, Renate Zedinger, and Jacques Mondot (eds.). *Das achtzehnte Jahrhundert und Österreich,* vol. 22: *Josephinismus—eine Bilanz: Échecs et réussites du Joséphisme.* Bochum 2008.

Schmid, Alois. "Franz I. Stephan von Habsburg-Lothringen (1745–1765): Der unbekannte Kaiser," *Eichstätter Hochschulreden:* 77 (1991): 1–28.

———. "Franz I. und Maria Theresia.," in *Die Kaiser der Neuzeit, 1519–1918: Heiliges römisches Reich, Österreich, Deutschland,* ed. Anton Schindling and Walter Ziegler. Munich 1990, 232–48.

Schmidt, Georg. *Wandel durch Vernunft: Deutsche Geschichte im 18. Jahrhundert.* Munich 2009.

Schmidt, Leopold (ed.). *Historische Volkslieder aus Österreich vom 15. bis zum 19. Jahrhundert.* Vienna 1971.

Schmidt-Haberkamp, Barbara (ed.). *Europa und die Türkei im 18. Jahrhundert / Europe and Turkey in the 18th Century,* Bonn 2011.

Schmitt, Carl. *Gespräch über die Macht und den Zugang zum Machthaber* (1st ed. 1954). Stuttgart 2008.

Schmitt-Vorster, Angelika. "Pro Deo et Populo. Die Porträts Josephs II. (1765–1790): Untersuchungen zu Bestand, Ikonografie und Verbreitung des Kaiserbildnisses im Zeitalter der Aufklärung." PhD diss. Munich 2006.

Schneider, Herbert. "Durazzo und Favart im Dialog: Die Erneuerung des Theaters in Wien im Spannungsfeld verschiedener Kulturen," in *Maria Theresias Kulturwelt,* ed. Pierre Béhar, Marie-Thérèse Mourey, and Herbert Schneider. Hildesheim / Zürich / New York 2011, 123–48.

Schnettger, Matthias. *Der Spanische Erbfolgekrieg 1701–1713/14.* Munich 2014.

——— (ed.) *Imperium Romanum—irregulare corpus—Teutscher Reich-Staat: Das Alte Reich im Verstännis der Zeigenossen und der Historiographie.* Mainz 2002.

———. "Ist Wien eine Messe wert? Protestantische Funktionseliten am Kaiserhof im 17. und 18. Jahrhundert," in *Grenzen und Grenzüberschreitungen: Bilanz und Perspektiven der Frühneuzeitforschung,* ed. Christine Roll, Frank Pohle, and Matthias Myrczek. Cologne / Weimar / Vienna 2010, 599–633.

———. *"Principe sovrano" oder "Civitas imperialis"? Die Republik Genua und das Alte Reich in der frühen Neuzeit (1556–1797)*. Mainz 2006.

Schnitzer, Claudia. *Höfische Maskeraden: Funktion und Ausstattung von Verkleidungsdivertissements an deutschen Höfen der Frühen Neuzeit*. Tübingen 1999.

Schort, Manfred. *Politik und Propaganda: Der Siebenjährige Krieg in den zeitgenössischen Flugschriften*. Frankfurt am Main 2006.

Schroeder, Aribert. *Vampirismus: Seine Entwicklung vom Thema zum Motiv*. Frankfurt am Main 1973.

Schulte, Regina (ed.). *Der Körper der Königin: Geschlecht und Herrschaft in der höfischen Welt seit 1500*. Frankfurt am Main and New York 2002.

———. "'Madame, ma Chère Fille'–'Dearest Child': Briefe imperialer Mütter an königliche Töchter," in *Der Körper der Königin: Geschlecht und Herrschaft in der höfischen Welt seit 1500*, ed. Regina Schulte. Frankfurt am Main and New York 2002, 162–95.

Schulze, Winfried. "Hausgesetzgebung und Verstaatlichung im Hause Österreich vom Tode Maximilians I. bis zur Pragmatischen Sanktion," in *Der dynastische Fürstenstaat: Zur Bedeutung von Sukzessionsordnungen für die Entstehung des frühmodernen Staates*, ed. Johannes Kunisch. Berlin 1982, 253–71.

Schumacher, Andreas (ed.). *Canaletto: Bernardo Bellotto malt Europa*. Exhibition catalog, Alte Pinakothek Munich. Munich 2014.

Schünemann, K. "Die Wirtschaftspolitik Josephs II. in der Zeit seiner Mitregentschaft." *Mitteilungen des österreichischen Instituts für Geschichtsforschung* 47 (1933): 13–56.

Schunka, Alexander. "Irenicism and the Challenges of Conversion in the Early Eighteenth Century," in *Conversion and the Politics of Religion in Early Modern Germany*, ed. David M. Luebke, et al. New York / Oxford 2012, 102–18.

Schütte, Ulrich. "Höfisches Zeremoniell und sakraler Kult," in *Zeremoniell als höfische Ästhetik in Spätmittelalter und Früher Neuzeit*, ed. Jörg Jochen Berns and Thomas Rahn. Tübingen 1995, 410–31.

Schwicker, Johann Heinrich. *Geschichte der österreichischen Militärgrenze*. Vienna and Teschen 1883.

Scott, Hamish M. "Reform in the Habsburg Monarchy, 1740–1790," in *Enlightened Absolutism. Reform and Reformers in Later Eighteenth Century Europe*, ed. Hamish M. Scott. London and Ann Arbor 1990, 145–87.

Seidel, Hans-Christoph. *Eine neue "Kultur des Gebärens": Die Medikalisierung von Geburt im 18. und 19. Jahrhundert in Deutschland*. Stuttgart 1998.

Seidler, Andrea. "Zur Entwicklung des Wiener Zeitschriftenwesens in der zweiten Hälfte des 18. Jahrhunderts," in *Österreichische Mediengeschichte*, vol. 1: *Von den frühen Drucken zur Ausdifferenzierung des Mediensystems (1500–1918)*, ed. Matthias Karmasin and Christian Oggolder. Wiesbaden 2016, 139–65.

Seidler, Andrea, and Wolfram Seidler. *Das Zeitschriftenwesen im Donauraum zwischen 1740 und 1809: Kommentierte Bibliographie der deutsch- und ungarischsprachigen Zeitschriften in Wien, Pressburg und Pest-Buda*. Vienna 1988.

Seidler, Wolfram. *Buchmarkt und Zeitschriften in Wien 1760–1786: Studie zur Herausbildung einer literarischen Öffentlichkeit im Österreich des 18. Jahrhunderts*. Szeged 1994.

Seitschek, Stefan. "Karussell und Schlittenfahrten im Spiegel der Zeremonialprotokolle—nur eine höfische Belustigung?" in *Der Wiener Hof im Spiegel der Zeremonialprotokolle (1652–1800): Eine Annäherung*, ed. Irmgard Pangerl, Martin Scheutz, and Thomas Winkelbauer. Innsbruck / Bozen / Vienna 2007, 357–434.

———. "Religiöse Praxis am Wiener Hof: Das Beispiel der medialen Berichterstattung," in *Frühneuzeitforschung in der Habsburgermonarchie: Adel und Wiener Hof—Konfessionalisierung—Siebenbürgen*, ed. István Fazekas, et al. Vienna 2013, 71–99.

Selb, Walter, and Herbert Hofmeister (eds.). *Forschungsband Franz von Zeiller (1751–1828): Beiträge zur Gesetzgebungs- und Wissenschaftsgeschichte*. Vienna / Cologne / Graz 1980.

Sicker, Martin. *From the Treaty of Karlowitz to the Disintegration of the Ottoman Empire*. London 2001.

Sikora, Michael. *Der Adel in der Frühen Neuzeit*. Darmstadt 2009.

Silva-Tarouca, Egbert. *Der Mentor der Kaiserin: Der weltliche Seelenführer Maria Theresias*. Vienna 1960.

Simmel, Georg. "Das Geheimnis und die geheime Gesellschaft," in Georg Simmel, *Soziologie*, 4th ed. Berlin 1958, 256–304.

Solf, Elisabeth. *Die Reichspolitik des Mainzer Kurfürsten Johann Friedrich Karl von Ostein von seinem Regierungsantritt (1743) bis zum Ausbruch des Siebenjährigen Krieges*. Berlin 1936.

Solomon, Maynard. *Mozart: A Life*. New York 1994.

Sommer, Monika (ed.). *Hieronymus Löschenkohl: Sensationen aus dem alten Wien*. Vienna 2009.

Sommer-Mathis, Andrea. "Theatrum und Ceremoniale: Rang- und Sitzordnungen bei theatralischen Veranstaltungen am Wiener Kaiserhof im 17. und 18. Jahrhundert," in *Zeremoniell als höfische Ästhetik in Spätmittelalter und Früher Neuzeit*, ed. Jörg Jochen Berns and Thomas Rahn. Tübingen 1995, 511–33.

———. *"Tu felix Austria nube": Hochzeitsfeste der Habsburger im 18. Jahrhundert*. Vienna 1994.

Spannenberger, Norbert, and Szabolcs Varga (eds.). *Ein Raum im Wandel: Die osmanisch-habsburgische Grenzregion vom 16. bis zum 18. Jahrhundert*. Stuttgart 2014.

Spies, Hans-Bernd / Helmut Winter (eds.). *Die Schlacht bei Dettingen 1743: Beiträge zum 250. Jahrestag*. Aschaffenburg 1993.

Srbik, Heinrich Ritter von. *Gestalten und Ereignisse aus Österreichs Vergangenheit*. Leipzig 1942.

Stadelmann, Christian. "Mariazell," in *Memoria Austriae II: Bauten, Orte, Regionen*, ed. Emil Brix, Ernst Bruckmüller, and Hannes Stekl. Vienna 2005, 304–35.

Stangl, Waltraud. "Tod und Trauer bei den österreichischen Habsburgern 1740–1780, dargestellt im Spiegel des Hofzeremoniells." PhD diss. Vienna 2001.

Stanzel, Josef. *Die Schulaufsicht im Reformwerk des Johann Ignaz von Felbiger (1724–1788): Schule, Kirche, und Staat in Recht und Praxis des aufgeklärten Absolutismus*. Paderborn 1976.

Starkenfels, Victor Weiß von. *Die Kaiserlich-königliche Orientalische Akademie zu Wien: Ihre Gründung, Fortbildung und gegenwärtige Einrichtung*. Vienna 1839.

Stauber, Reinhard. *Der Zentralstaat an seinen Grenzen: Administrative Integration, Herrschaftswechsel und politische Kultur im südlichen Alpenraum, 1750–1850*. Göttingen 2001.

———. "Vaterland—Provinz—Nation: Gesamtstaat, Länder und nationale Gruppen in der österreichischen Monarchie 1750–1800," in Nationalismus vor dem Nationalismus?" Aufklärung 10 (1998): 55–72.

Steidele, Angela. *"Als wenn Du mein Geliebter wärest": Liebe und Begehren zwischen Frauen in der deutschsprachigen Literatur 1750–1850*. Stuttgart 2003.

Steiner, Stephan. *Rückkehr unerwünscht: Deportationen in der Habsburgermonarchie der Frühen Neuzeit und ihr europäischer Kontext*. Vienna / Cologne / Weimar 2014.

———. "Schnepfenjagd im Wien des 18. Jahrhunderts," in *Hieronymus Löschenkohl: Sensationen aus dem alten Wien*, ed. Monika Sommer. Vienna 2009, 128–37.

———. "Transmigration: Ansichten einer Zwangsgemeinschaft," in *Geheimprotestantismus und evangelische Kirchen in der Habsburgermonarchie und im Erzbistum Salzburg (17./18. Jahrhundert)*, ed. Rudolf Leeb, Martin Scheutz, and Dietmar Weikl. Vienna / Cologne / Weimar 2009, 331–60.

———. "Wien—Temesvar und retour: Der Wasserschub unter Maria Theresia," in *Wien und seine Wienerinnen: Ein historischer Streifzug durch Wien über die Jahrhunderte, Festachrift für Karl Vocelka*, ed. Martin Scheutz, et al. Vienna 2008, 203–19.

Stekl, Hannes. *Österreichische Zucht- und Arbeitshäuser 1671–1920*. Munich 1978.

Steppan, Christian. "Kaiserliche Gesandte und ihre Annäherungspolitik durch die Kraft der Gesten: Der symbolische Startschuss zum österreichisch-russischen Bündnis von 1726," in *Forschungswerkstatt: Die Habsburgermonarchie im 18. Jahrhundert*, ed. Gunda Barth-Scalmani et al. Bochum 2012, 27–41.

Stevens, Maryanne. "Still-life, Trompe l'oeil and Genre Painting," in *Jean-Étienne Liotard 1702–1789*, ed. Royal Academy of Arts London. Exhibition catalog. London and New York 2015, 162–81.

Stöckelle, Angela. "Taufzeremoniell und politische Patenschaften am Kaiserhof." *MIÖG* 90 (1982): 271–337.

———. "Über Geburten und Taufen der Habsburger am Kaiserhof in Wien von Leopold I. bis Maria Theresia." PhD diss. Vienna 1971.

Stolberg, Michael. *Homo patiens: Krankheits- und Körpererfahrung in der Frühen Neuzeit*. Cologne 1971.

Stollberg-Rilinger, Barbara. "The Baroque State," in *The Oxford Handbook of the Baroque*, ed. John Lyons. Oxford 2019, 825–46.

———. *Das Heilige Römische Reich deutscher Nation: Vom Ende des Mittelalters bis 1806*, 5th ed. Munich 2013.

———. *Der Staat als Maschine: Zur Metaphorik des absoluten Fürstenstaats*. Berlin 1986.

———. "Die Frühe Neuzeit—eine Epoche der Formalisierung?," in *Die Frühe Neuzeit: Revisionen einer Epoche*, ed. Andreas Höfele, Jan-Dirk Müller, and Wulf Österreicher. Berlin and Boston 2013, 3–27.

———. *The Emperor's Old Clothes: Constitutional History and the Symbolic Language of the Holy Roman Empire*. New York / Oxford 2015.

———. "Maria Theresa and the Love of Her Subjects." *Archiv für österreichische Geschichte* 51 (2020): 1–12.

———. "Ordnungsleistung und Konfliktträchtigkeit der höfischen Tafel," in *Zeichen und Raum: Ausstattung und höfisches Zeremoniell in den deutschen Schlössern der Frühen Neuzeit*, ed. Peter-Michael Hahn and Ulrich Schütte. Munich and Berlin 2006.

———. *Rituale*. Frankfurt am Main 2013.

————. "Väter der Frauengeschichte? Das Geschlecht als historiographische Kategorie im 18. und 19. Jahrhundert." *Historische Zeitschrift* 262 (1996): 39–71.

————. "Vom Volk übertragene Rechte? Zur naturrechtlichen Umdeutung ständischer Verfassungsstrukturen im 18. Jahrhundert," in *Naturrecht und Staat: Politische Funktionen des europäischen Naturrechts (17.—19. Jahrhundert)*, ed. Diethelm Klippel. Munich 2006, 103–17.

————. *Vormünder des Volkes? Theorien landständischer Repräsentation in der Spätphase des Alten Reiches*. Berlin 1999.

————. "Zur moralischen Ökonomie des Schenkens bei Hof," in *Luxus und Integration. Materielle Hofkultur Westeuropas vom 12. bis zum 18. Jahrhundert*, ed. Werner Paravicini. Munich 2010, 187–202.

Stourzh, Gerald. "Vom Umfang der österreichischen Geschichte," in Gerald Stourzh, *Vom Umfang der Geschichte. Ausgewählte Studien 1990–2010*. Vienna / Cologne / Graz 2011, 11–37.

Strakosch, Henry. *Absolutism and the Rule of Law: The Struggle for the Codification of Civil Law in Austria 1753–1811*. Sydney 1967.

Strohmeyer, Arno, and Norbert Spannenberger. *Friedens- und Konfliktmanagement in interkulturellen Räumen: Das Osmanische Reich und die Habsburgermonarchie*. Stuttgart 2014

Suppanz, Werner. "Maria Theresia," in *Memoria Austriae I: Menschen, Mythen, Zeiten*, ed. Emil Brix, et al. Vienna 2004, 26–47.

————. *Österreichische Geschichtsbilder: Historische Legitimationen in Ständestaat und Zweiter Republik*. Cologne / Weimar / Vienna 1998.

Sutter Fichtner, Paula. "Habsburg Household or Habsburg Government? A Sixteenth-Century Administrative Dilemma." *Austrian History Yearbook* 26 (1995): 45–60.

————. *Terror and Toleration: The Habsburg Empire Confronts Islam, 1526–1850*. London 2008.

Swoboda, Gudrun (ed.). *Die kaiserliche Gemäldegalerie in Wien und die Anfänge des öffentlichen Kunstmuseums*, vol. 1: *Die kaiserliche Galerie im Belvedere (1776–1837)*. Vienna / Cologne / Weimar 2013.

Szábo, Franz A. J. *Between Privilege and Professionalism: The Career of Wenzel Anton Kaunitz, in Social Change in the Habsburg Monarchy*, ed. Harald Heppner, Peter Urbanitsch, and Renate Zedinger. Bochum 2011, 137–52.

————. "The Cultural Transformation of the Habsburg Monarchy in the Age of Metastasio, 1730–1780." *Studies in Music* 16 (1997): 27–50.

————. "Favorit, Premierminister oder 'drittes Staatsoberhaupt'? Der Fall des Staatskanzlers Wenzel Anton Kaunitz-Rietberg," in *Der zweite Mann im Staat: Oberste Amtsträger und Favoriten im Umkreis der Reichsfürsten in der Frühen Neuzeit*, ed. Michael Kaiser and Andreas Pečar. Berlin 2003, 345–62.

————. *Kaunitz and Enlightened Absolutism 1753–1780*. Cambridge 1994.

————. *The Seven Years War in Europe 1756–1763*. Harlow 2008.

Szijártó, István. "Der ungarische Landtag und seine Entscheidungsprozeduren im 18. Jahrhundert. Von der Institutionsgeschichte zur Kulturgeschichte. Methodologische Überlegungen," in *Geteilt—Vereinigt. Beiträge zur Geschichte des Königreichs Ungarn in der Frühneuzeit (16.-18. Jahrhundert)*, ed. Krisztián Csaplár-Degovics and István Fazekas. Berlin 2011, 356–68.

————. "The Diet: The Estates and the Parliament of Hungary, 1708–1792," in *Bündnispartner und Konkurrenten der Landesfürsten? Die Stände in der Habsburgermonarchie*, ed. Gerhard Ammerer, et al. Vienna and Munich 2007, 151–71.

Tamussino, Ursula. *Des Teufels Großmutter: Eine Biographie der Königin Maria Carolina von Neapel-Sizilien*. Vienna 1991.

――――. *Isabella von Parma: Gemahlin Joseph II*. Vienna 1989.

Tantner, Anton. *Ordnung der Häuser, Beschreibung der Seelen: Hausnummerierung und Seelenkonskription in der Habsburgermonarchie*. Innsbruck / Vienna / Bozen 2007.

Tanzer, Gerhard. *"Spectacle müssen seyn": Die Freizeit der Wiener im 18. Jahrhundert*. Vienna 1992.

Tapié, Victor Lucien. *Maria Theresia: Die Kaiserin und ihr Reich*. Graz / Vienna / Cologne 1980.

Tautscher-Gerstmeyer, Doris. *Die geschriebenen Zeitungen des 18. Jahrhunderts in Wien*. Vienna 1982.

Telesko, Werner. "'Die Erbinn so vieler Länder und Reiche': Zu Ausstattung und Programmatik der beiden Galerien in Schloss Schönbrunn unter Maria Theresia." *MIÖG* 124 (2016): 82–103.

――――. "Die Maria-Theresia-Krypta (1754) in der Wiener Kapuzinergruft: Dynastische Repräsentation als multimediale Inszenierung." *Geistes-, sozial- und kulturwissenschaftlicher Anzeiger* 149 (2014): 25–60.

――――. "Herrschaftssicherung mittels visueller Repräsentation: Zur Porträtkultur Maria Theresias." In Eva Kernbauer and Aneta Zahradnik (eds.), *Höfische Porträtkultur. Die Bildnissammlung der österreichischen Erzherzogin Maria Anna*. Berlin / Boston 2016, 37–47.

――――. "'Hier wird einmal gutt ruhen sey': Balthasar Ferdinand Molls Prunksarkophag für Franz Stephan und Maria Theresia in der Wiener Kapuzinergruft (1754)." *Wiener Jahrbuch für Kunstgeschichte* 59 (2010): 103–26.

――――. *Maria Theresia: Ein europäischer Mythos*. Vienna / Cologne / Weimar 2012.

――――. "Maria Theresias 'Familia Augusta' Zur Programmatik des 'Riesensaals' in der Innsbrucker Hofburg," in *Innsbruck 1765: Prunkvolle Hochzeit, fröhliche Feste, tragischer Ausklang*, ed. Renate Zedinger. Bochum 2015, 349–62.

Telesko, Werner, Sandra Hertel, and Stefanie Linsboth (eds.). *Die Repräsentation Maria Theresias: Herrschaft und Bildpolitik im Zeitalter der Aufklärung*. Vienna / Cologne / Weimar 2020.

――――(eds.). "Zwischen Panegyrik und Tatsachenbericht: Zu Struktur und Zielsetzung von 'Medienereignissen' zur Zeit Maria Theresias." *Zeitschrift für Historische Forschung* 44 (2017): 441–86.

Terlinden, Charles de. *Der Orden vom Goldenen Vlies*. Vienna 1970.

Thadden, Franz Lorenz von. *Feldmarschall Daun: Maria Theresias größter Feldherr*. Vienna 1967.

Thiessen, Hillard von. "Diplomatie vom type ancien: Überlegungen zu einem Idealtypus des frühneuzeitlichen Gesandtschaftswesens," in *Akteure der Außenbeziehungen: Netzwerke und Interkulturalität im historischen Wandel*, ed. Hillard von Thiessen and Christian Windler. Cologne / Weimar / Vienna 2010, 471–503.

Thiessen, Hillard von, and Christian Windler (eds.). *Akteure der Außenbeziehungen: Netzwerke und Interkulturalität im historischen Wandel*. Cologne / Weimar / Vienna 2010.

Tomenendal, Kerstin. *Das türkische Gesicht Wiens: Auf den Spuren der Türken in Wien*. Vienna 2000.

Trapp, Oswald. "Maria Theresia und Tirol," in *Maria Theresia und ihre Zeit*, ed. Walter Koschatzky. Salzburg / Vienna 1979, 131–37.

Tropper, Peter G. *Staatliche Kirchenpolitik, Geheimprotestantismus und katholische Mission in Kärnten (1752–1780)*. Klagenfurt 1989.

————. "Von der katholischen Erneuerung bis zur Säkularisierung, 1648–1815," in *Öster-reichische Geschichte*, vol. 3: *Geschichte des Christentums in Österreich: Von der Spätantike bis zur Gegenwart*, ed. Rudolf Leeb, et al. Vienna 2003, 181–360.

Urbanski, Hans. "Unveröffentlichte Aufzeichnungen Karls von Lothringen," in *Maria Theresia und ihre Zeit*, ed. Walter Koschatzky. Salzburg and Vienna 1979, 91–96.

Vajnági, Márta. "The Habsburgs and the Imperial Crown in the Eighteenth Century," in *Forsc-hungswerkstatt: Die Habsburgermonarchie im 18. Jahrhundert*, ed. Gunda Barth-Scalmani et al. Bochum 2012, 91–102.

Vallotton, Henry, *Maria Theresia: Die Frau, die ein Weltreich regiert*. Original French edition Paris 1963. Munich 1978.

Vann, James Allen, "Mapping under the Austrian Habsburgs," in *Monarchs, Ministers, and Maps: The Emergence of Cartography as a Tool of Government in Early Modern Europe*, ed. David Buisseret. Chicago 1992, 153–67.

Vasold, Manfred. "Die Hunger- und Sterblichkeitskrise von 1770/73 und der Niedergang des Ancien Régime." *Saeculum* 59 (2008): 107–42.

Vehse, Eduard. *Maria Theresia und ihr Hof*. Munich 1924.

Venturi, Franco. *Italy and the Enlightenment*. London 1972.

Vigarello, Paul. *Wasser und Seife, Puder und Parfum: Geschichte der Körperhygiene seit dem Mit-telalter*. Frankfurt am Main 1988.

Vilfan, Sergij. "Die Agrarsozialpolitik von Maria Theresia bis Kudlich," in *Der Bauer Mittel- und Osteuropas im sozio-ökonomischen Wandel des 18. und 19. Jahrhunderts*, ed. Dan Berindei, et al. Cologne and Vienna 1973, 1–52.

Vinken, Barbara. "Marie Antoinette oder Das Ende der Zwei-Körper-Lehre," in *Das Politische. Figurenlehren des sozialen Körpers nach der Romantik*, ed. Uwe Hebekus, Ethel Matala de Mazza, and Albrecht Koschorke. Munich 2003, 86–105.

Vismann, Cornelia. *Akten: Medientechnik und Recht*. Frankfurt am Main 2000.

Vocelka, Karl. *Glanz und Untergang der höfischen Welt: Repräsentation, Reform und Reaktion im habsburgischen Vielvölkerstaat (Österreichische Geschichte, 1699–1815)*. Vienna 2001.

Vocelka, Karl, and Lynne Heller. *Die private Welt der Habsburger: Leben und Alltag einer Familie*. Graz 1998.

Vocelka, Karl, and Anita Traninger (eds.). *Wien: Geschichte einer Stadt*, vol. 2: *Die frühneuzeitliche Residenz (16.–18. Jahrhundert)*. Vienna / Cologne / Weimar 2003.

Vogel, Christine. *Der Untergang der Gesellschaft Jesu als europäisches Medienereignis (1758–1773):Publizistische Debatten im Spannungsfeld von Aufklärung und Gegenaufklärung*. Mainz 2006.

————. *Die Aufhebung der Gesellschaft Jesu (1758–1773)* 2010. URL: http://www.ieg-ego.eu /vogelc-2010-de (24.06.2016).

Völkel, Michaela. "Der Tisch des Herrn: Das gemeinsame Zeichensystem von Liturgie und Tafelzeremoniell in der Frühen Neuzeit," in *Zeichen und Raum: Ausstattung und höfisches Zeremoniell in den deutschen Schlössern der Frühen Neuzeit*, ed. Peter-Michael Hahn and Ul-rich Schütte. Munich / Berlin 2006, 83–102.

Volkmer, Gerald. *Siebenbürgen zwischen Habsburgermonarchie und Osmanischem Reich*. Munich 2015.

Wacha, Georg. *Spatzenvertilgung unter Maria Theresia.* URL: http://www.zobodat.at/pdf /NKJB_6_0021-0053.pdf (20.09.2016).

Wachter, Friederike. "Die Erziehung der Kinder Maria Theresias." PhD diss. Vienna 1969.

Wagner, Hans. "Das geheime Kammerzahlamt und die Pensionszahlungen Maria Theresias," in *Maria Theresia und ihre Zeit,* ed. Walter Koschatzky. Salzburg / Vienna 1979, 170–75.

———. "Die Zensur in der Habsburger Monarchie (1750–1810)," in *Buch- und Verlagswesen im 18. und 19. Jahrhundert: Beiträge zur Geschichte der Kommunikation in Mittel- und Osteuropa,* ed. Herbert Göpfert, et al. Berlin 1977, 28–75.

———. "Fürstengnade und Rechtsspruch: Die Pensionszahlungen Maria Theresias und ihre Aufhebung durch Joseph II.," in Hans Wagner, *Salzburg und Österreich: Aufsätze und Vorträge.* Salzburg 1982, 297–360.

———. "Royal Graces and Legal Claims: The Pension Payments of Maria Theresa and Their Withdrawal by Joseph II.," in *Intellectual and Social Developments in the Habsburg Empire from Maria Theresa to World War I,* ed. Stanley B. Winters, et al. New York and London 1975, 5–29.

Wallnig, Thomas, Johannes Frimmel, and Werner Telesko (eds.) *18th Century Studies in Austria 1945–2010.* Bochum 2011,

Walter, Friedrich. *Die Geschichte der österreichischen Zentralverwaltung in der Zeit Maria Theresias (1740–1780).* Vienna 1938.

———. *Die Paladine der Kaiserin: Ein Maria-Theresien-Buch.* Vienna 1959.

———. "Die religiöse Stellung Maria Theresias." *Theologisch-praktische Quartalschrift* 105 (1957), 34–47.

———. *Die theresianische Staatsreform von 1749.* Munich 1958.

———. "Die zensurierten Klassiker: Neue Dokumente theresianisch-josephinischer Zensur." *Jahrbuch der Grillparzer-Gesellschaft* 29 (1930): 142–47.

———. "Kaiserin Maria Theresia," in *Gestalter der Geschicke Österreichs,* ed. Hugo Hantsch. Innsbruck / Vienna / Munich 1962, 235–52.

———. "Kaunitz' Eintritt in die innere Politik." *MIÖG* 46 (1932): 37–79.

———. *Männer um Maria Theresia.* Vienna 1951.

———. *Österreichische Verfassungs- und Verwaltungsgeschichte von 1550–1955.* Vienna / Cologne / Graz 1972.

Wandruszka, Adam. "Die Historiographie der theresianisch-josephinischen Reformzeit," in *Ungarn und Österreich unter Maria Theresia und Joseph II: Neue Aspekte im Verhältnis der beiden Länder,* ed. Anna M. Drabek, Richard G. Plaschka, and Adam Wandruszka. Vienna 1982, 13–27.

———. "Die Religiosität Franz Stephans." *MIÖG* 12 (1959): 162–73.

———. "Im Urteil der Nachwelt," in *Maria Theresia und ihre Zeit,* ed. Walter Koschatzky. Salzburg and Vienna 1979, 457–61.

———. *Leopold II.* 2 vols. Vienna and Munich 1963.

Wandruszka, Adam. *Maria Theresia: Die große Kaiserin.* Göttingen / Zürich / Frankfurt am Main 1980.

———. *Österreich und Italien im 18. Jahrhundert.* Vienna 1963.

Wangermann, Ernst. "Maria Theresia: A Reforming Monarchy," in *The Courts of Europe: Politics, Patronage / Royality, 1400–1800,* ed. Arthur Geoffrey Dickens. London 1977, 283–304.

———. "Matte Morgenröte: Verzug und Widerruf im späten Reformwerk Maria Theresias," in *Maria Theresia und ihre Zeit*, ed. Walter Koschatzky. Salzburg and Vienna 1979, 67–71.

———. *Mit den Waffen der Publizität: Zum Funktionswandel der politischen Literatur unter Joseph II.* Vienna and Munich 2004.

———. "Reform Catholicism and Political Radicalism in Austrian Enlightenment," in *The Enlightenment in National Context*, ed. Roy Porter and Mikulas Teich. Cambridge 1981, 127–40.

———. "Zur Frage der Kontinuität zwischen den theresianischen und josephinischen Reformen," in *Österreich im Europa der Aufklärung: Kontinuität und Zäsur zur Zeit Maria Theresias und Josephs II.*, ed. Richard Georg Plaschka and Grete Klingenstein. Vienna 1985, 943–54.

Was von den Türken blieb. Exhibition catalog. Perchtoldsdorf 1983.

Weber, Annemarie. "Der österreichische Orden vom Goldenen Vlies: Geschichte und Probleme." PhD diss. Bonn 1971.

Weber, Johannes. *Avisen, Relationen, Gazetten: Der Beginn des europäischen Zeitungswesens.* Oldenburg 1997.

Weber, Nadir. "Zwischen Arkanum und Öffentlichkeit: Der Brief als Medium politischer Kommunikation im 18. Jahrhundert," in *Politische Kommunikation von der klassischen Rhetorik zur Mediendemokratie*, ed. Felix Heidenreich and Daniel Schönpflug. Berlin 2012, 63–74.

Weinzierl-Fischer, Erika. "Die Bekämpfung der Hungersnot in Böhmen, 1770–1772." *MÖStA* 7 (1954): 478–514.

Welke, Martin. "'. . . zu Österreichs Gloria und Publicität mitzuwürcken':. Zur Pressepolitik des Kaiserhofes im Reich im 18. Jahrhundert," in *Mediengeschichte. Forschung und Praxis*, ed. Wolfgang Duchkowitsch. Vienna / Cologne / Graz 1985, 173–92.

Wiesinger, Peter. "Die Reform der deutschen Schriftsprache unter Maria Theresia: Ziele— Durchführung—Wirkung." *Das Achtzehnte Jahrhundert und Österreich*, vol. 17: *Strukturwandel kultureller Praxis: Beiträge zu einer kulturwissenschaftlichen Sicht des theresianischen Zeitalters*, ed. Franz M. Eybl. Vienna 2002, 131–40.

Wimmer, Johannes. *Gesundheit, Krankheit und Tod im Zeitalter der Aufklärung: Fallstudien aus den habsburgischen Erbländern.* Vienna and Cologne 1991.

Winkelbauer, Thomas. "Der Adel in Ober- und Niederösterreich in der Frühen Neuzeit: Versuch eines Literaturüberblicks." *Opera Historica* 2 (1992): 13–33.

———. *Robot und Steuer: Die Untertanen der Waldviertler Grundherrschaften Gföhl und Altpölla zwischen feudaler Herrschaft und absolutistischen Staat vom 16. Jahrhundert bis zum Vormärz.* Vienna 1986.

Winkelbauer, Thomas, and Michael Hochedlinger (eds.). *Herrschaftsverdichtung, Staatsbildung, Bürokratisierung. Verfassungs-, Verwaltungs- und Behördengeschichte der Frühen Neuzeit.* Vienna 2010.

Winter, Eduard. *Der Josephinismus: Die Geschichte des österreichischen Reformkatholizismus 1740–1848*, 2nd ed. Berlin 1962.

Winter, Gustav. "Die Gründung des kaiserlichen und königlichen Haus-, Hof- und Staatsarchivs 1749–1762." *Archiv für österreichische Geschichte* 92 (1903): 1–82.

Winterling, Aloys. "Die frühneuzeitlichen Höfe in Deutschland." *Internationales Archiv für Sozialgeschichte der deutschen Literatur* 21 (1996): 181–89.

———. "'Hof': Versuch einer idealtypischen Bestimmung anhand der mittelalterlichen und frühneuzeitlichen Geschichte," in *Hof und Theorie: Annäherungen an ein historisches Phänomen*, ed. Reinhard Butz, Jan Hirschbiegel, and Dietmar Willoweit. Cologne / Weimar / Vienna 2004, 77–90.

Wolf, Adam. *Aus dem Hofleben Maria Theresia's: Nach den Memoiren des Fürsten Joseph Khevenhüller.* 2nd edition. Vienna 1859.

———. *Fürstin Eleonore Liechtenstein 1745–1812: Nach Briefen und Memoiren ihrer Zeit.* Vienna 1875.

———. *Marie Christine, Erzherzogin von Österreich.* 2 vols. Vienna 1863.

Wolf, Adam, and Hans von Zwiedineck-Südenhorst. *Österreich unter Maria Theresia, Josef II. und Leopold II.* Vienna 1855.

Wolf, Hubert. "Katholische Aufklärung?," in *Religion und Aufklärung*, ed. Albrecht Beutel and Martha Nooke. Tübingen 2016, 81–95.

Wolf, Michaela. "'Diplomatenlehrbuben' oder angehende 'Dragomane'? Zur Rekonstruktion des sozialen 'Dolmetschfeldes,'" in *Das Osmanische Reich und die Habsburgermornarchie*, ed. Marlene Kurz, et al. Munich 2005, 503–14.

Wolff, Larry. "Hapsburg [sic] Letters: The Disciplinary Dynamics of Epistolary Narrative in the Correspondence of Maria Theresa and Marie-Antoinette," in *Marie Antoinette: Writings on the Body of a Queen*, ed. Dena Goodman. New York and London 2003, 25–43.

Wrede, Martin. *Ohne Furcht und Tadel—Für König und Vaterland: Frühneuzeitlicher Hochadel zwischen Familienehre, Ritterideal und Fürstendienst.* Stuttgart 2012.

Wührer, Jakob. "Ein teilgebautes Haus ohne Fundament? Zum Forschungsstand des frühneuzeitlichen Wiener Hofes am Beispiel der Organisationsgeschichte." *MIÖG* 117 (2009): 23–50.

———. "Um Nutzen zu fördern und Schaden zu wenden: Entstehung, Verwendung und Wirkung von Instruktionen und das Ringen um gute Ordnung am frühneuzeitlichen Wiener Hof," in *Ordnung durch Tinte und Feder? Genese und Wirkung von Institutionen im zeitlichen Längsschnitt vom Mittelalter bis zum 20. Jahrhundert*, ed. Anita Hipfinger, et al. Vienna / Cologne / Weimar 2012, 107–59.

Wührer, Jakob, and Martin Scheutz. *Zu Diensten ihrer Majestät: Hofordnungen und Instruktionsbücher am frühneuzeitlichen Wiener Hof.* Vienna 2011.

Wunder, Bernd. "Die Institutionalisierung der Invaliden-, Alters- und Hinterbliebenenversorgung der Staatsbediensteten in Österreich (1748–1790)." *MIÖG* 92 (1984): 341–406.

Wunder, Heide. *"Er ist die Sonn, sie ist der Mond": Frauen in der Frühen Neuzeit.* Munich 1992.

———. "Herrschaft und öffentliches Handeln von Frauen in der Gesellschaft der Frühen Neuzeit," in *Frauen in der Geschichte des Rechts. Von der Frühen Neuzeit bis zur Gegenwart*, ed. Ute Gerhard. Munich 1997, 27–54.

Wurzbach, Constant von (ed.). *Biographisches Lexikon des Kaiserthums Österreich, 1750–1850.* Vienna 1856–91.

Wuthenow, Ralph-Rainer. *Das erinnerte Ich. Europäische Autobiographie und Selbstdarstellung im 18. Jahrhundert.* Munich 1974.

Yonan, Michael. "Conceptualizing the Kaiserinwitwe: Empress Maria Theresa and Her Portraits," in *Widowhood and Visual Culture in Early Modern Europe*, ed. Allison Levy. Aldershot 2003, 109–125.

———. *Empress Maria Theresa and the Politics of Habsburg Imperial Art*. University Park, PA 2011.

———. "Modesty and Monarchy: Rethinking Empress Maria Theresa at Schönbrunn." *Austrian History Yearbook* 35 (2004): 25–47.

———. "Nobility and Domestic Conviviality in the Paintings of Archduchess Maria Christina." *Theatrum Historiae* 4 (2009): 135–54.

———. "Portable Dynasties: Imperial Gift-Giving at the Court of Vienna in the Eighteenth Century." *The Court Historian* 12 (2009): 177–88.

Zahirovic, Nedim. "Bemerkungen Friedrich Wilhelm von Taubes über Grenzleben und Grenzhandel in Slawonien und Syrmien in den Jahren 1776 und 1777," in *Europa und die Türkei im 18. Jahrhundert*, ed. Barbara Schmidt-Haberkamp, Bonn 2011, 277–85.

Zechmeister, Gustav. *Die Wiener Theater nächst der Burg und nächst dem Kärntnerthor von 1747 bis 1776*. Vienna 1971.

Zedinger, Renate. *Die Verwaltung der Österreichischen Niederlande in Wien (1714–1795): Studien zu den Zentralisierungstendenzen des Wiener Hofes im Staatswerdungsprozess der Habsburgermonarchie*. Vienna / Cologne / Weimar 2000.

———. "Erziehung in Wien Zum Aufenthalt des Erbprinzen Franz (Anton) Stephan von Lothringen am Hof Kaiser Karls VI. in den Jahren 1723 bis 1729." *Jahrbuch des Vereins für Geschichte der Stadt Wien* 50 (1994): 83–104.

———. *Franz Stephan von Lothringen (1708—1765): Monarch, Manager, Mäzen*. Vienna 2008.

———. *Hochzeit im Brennpunkt der Mächte: Franz Stephan von Lothringen und Maria Theresia*. Vienna / Cologne / Weimar 1994.

———(ed.). *Innsbruck 1765: Prunkvolle Hochzeit, fröhliche Feste, tragischer Ausklang*. Bochum 2015.

Zedinger, Renate, and Wolfgang Schmale (eds.). *Franz Stephan von Lothringen und sein Kreis / L'empereur François Ier et le réseau lorrain / L'imperatore Francesco I e il circolo lorenese*. Bochum 2009.

Zelepos, Ioannis. "Vampirglaube und orthodoxe Kirche im osmanischen Südosteuropa: Ein Fallbeispiel für die Ambivalenzen vorsäkularer Rationalisierungsprozesse," in *Das osmanische Europa: Methoden und Perspektiven der Frühneuzeitforschung zu Südosteuropa*, ed. Andreas Helmedach, et al. Leipzig 2014, 363–81.

Zimmermann, Christian von. "'Mit allen seinen Saiten schlaff geweint'"? Zur poetischen Form und politischen Funktion der dichterischen Denkmäler auf den Tod Maria Theresias," in *Oratio Funebris: Die katholische Leichenpredigt der frühen Neuzeit. Zwölf Studien*, ed. Birgit Boge and Ralf Georg Bogner. Amsterdam and Atlanta 1999, 275–315.

Žolger, Ivan Ritter von. *Der Hofstaat des Hauses Österreich*. Vienna and Leipzig 1917.

Zollinger, Manfred. "Das Glücksspiel in Wien im 18. Jahrhundert," in *Homo ludens: Der spielende Mensch*, vol. 1 (1991), 149–70.

————. *Geschichte des Glücksspiels vom 17. Jahrhundert bis zum Zweiten Weltkrieg.* Vienna 1997.

Zöllner, Erich (ed.). *Die Quellen der Geschichte Österreichs.* Vienna 1982.

————. *Österreich im Zeitalter des aufgeklärten Absolutismus.* Vienna 1983.

Zwiedineck-Südenhorst, Hans von. "Geschichte der religiösen Bewegung in Inner-Österreich im 18. Jahrhundert." *Archiv für österreichische Geschichte* 53 (1875): 460–546.

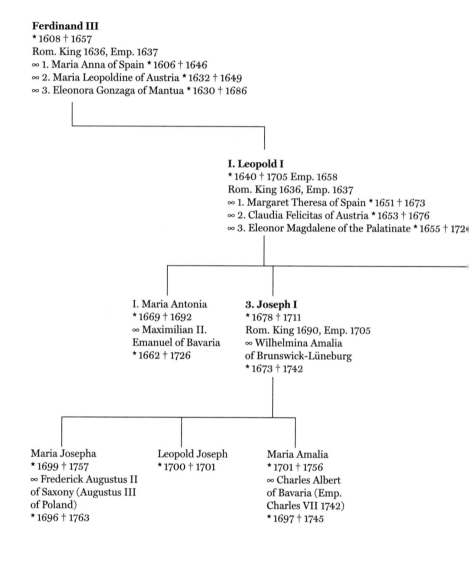

Table I: *House of Habsburg, Maria Theresa's ancestors*

Ferdinand III
* 1608 † 1657
Rom. King 1636, Emp. 1637
∞ 1. Maria Anna of Spain * 1606 † 1646
∞ 2. Maria Leopoldine of Austria * 1632 † 1649
∞ 3. Eleonora Gonzaga of Mantua * 1630 † 1686

I. Leopold I
* 1640 † 1705 Emp. 1658
Rom. King 1636, Emp. 1637
∞ 1. Margaret Theresa of Spain * 1651 † 1673
∞ 2. Claudia Felicitas of Austria * 1653 † 1676
∞ 3. Eleonor Magdalene of the Palatinate * 1655 † 172⬦

I. Maria Antonia
* 1669 † 1692
∞ Maximilian II.
Emanuel of Bavaria
* 1662 † 1726

3. Joseph I
* 1678 † 1711
Rom. King 1690, Emp. 1705
∞ Wilhelmina Amalia
of Brunswick-Lüneburg
* 1673 † 1742

Maria Josepha
* 1699 † 1757
∞ Frederick Augustus II
of Saxony (Augustus III
of Poland)
* 1696 † 1763

Leopold Joseph
* 1700 † 1701

Maria Amalia
* 1701 † 1756
∞ Charles Albert
of Bavaria (Emp.
Charles VII 1742)
* 1697 † 1745

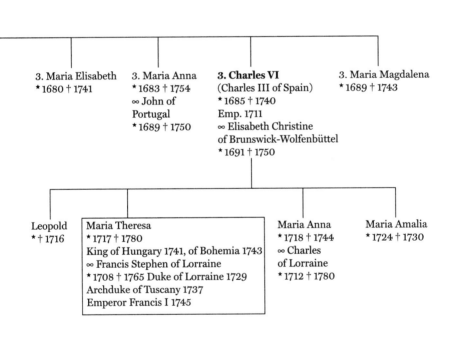

3. Maria Elisabeth
* 1680 † 1741

3. Maria Anna
* 1683 † 1754
∞ John of
Portugal
* 1689 † 1750

3. Charles VI
(Charles III of Spain)
* 1685 † 1740
Emp. 1711
∞ Elisabeth Christine
of Brunswick-Wolfenbüttel
* 1691 † 1750

3. Maria Magdalena
* 1689 † 1743

Leopold
* † 1716

Maria Theresa
* 1717 † 1780
King of Hungary 1741, of Bohemia 1743
∞ Francis Stephen of Lorraine
* 1708 † 1765 Duke of Lorraine 1729
Archduke of Tuscany 1737
Emperor Francis I 1745

Maria Anna
* 1718 † 1744
∞ Charles
of Lorraine
* 1712 † 1780

Maria Amalia
* 1724 † 1730

Table II: House of Lorraine, Francis Stephen's ancestors

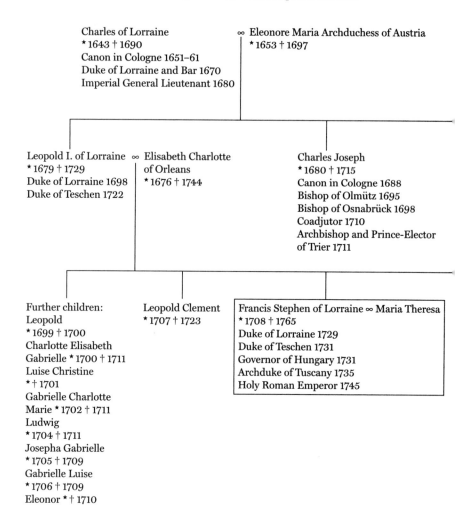

Charles of Lorraine
* 1643 † 1690
Canon in Cologne 1651–61
Duke of Lorraine and Bar 1670
Imperial General Lieutenant 1680

∞ Eleonore Maria Archduchess of Austria
* 1653 † 1697

Leopold I. of Lorraine
* 1679 † 1729
Duke of Lorraine 1698
Duke of Teschen 1722

∞ Elisabeth Charlotte
of Orleans
* 1676 † 1744

Charles Joseph
* 1680 † 1715
Canon in Cologne 1688
Bishop of Olmütz 1695
Bishop of Osnabrück 1698
Coadjutor 1710
Archbishop and Prince-Elector
of Trier 1711

Further children:
Leopold
* 1699 † 1700
Charlotte Elisabeth
Gabrielle * 1700 † 1711
Luise Christine
* † 1701
Gabrielle Charlotte
Marie * 1702 † 1711
Ludwig
* 1704 † 1711
Josepha Gabrielle
* 1705 † 1709
Gabrielle Luise
* 1706 † 1709
Eleonor * † 1710

Leopold Clement
* 1707 † 1723

Francis Stephen of Lorraine ∞ Maria Theresa
* 1708 † 1765
Duke of Lorraine 1729
Duke of Teschen 1731
Governor of Hungary 1731
Archduke of Tuscany 1735
Holy Roman Emperor 1745

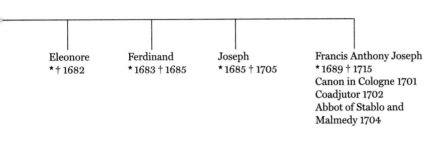

Eleonore
* † 1682

Ferdinand
* 1683 † 1685

Joseph
* 1685 † 1705

Francis Anthony Joseph
* 1689 † 1715
Canon in Cologne 1701
Coadjutor 1702
Abbot of Stablo and
Malmedy 1704

Elisabeth Therese
* 1711 † 1791
∞ Charles Emmanuel III
* 1701 † 1773
King of Sardinia 1730

Charles Alexander
* 1712 † 1780
Governor of the Austrian
Netherlands 1761
Grand Master of the
Teutonic Order 1761
∞ Maria Anna Archduchess
of Austria
* 1718 † 1744

Anna Charlotte
* 1714 † 1773
Abbess of Remiremont
1738
Abbess of Mons 1754

Table III: *House of Habsburg-Lorraine,*
Descendants of Maria Theresa
and Francis Stephen

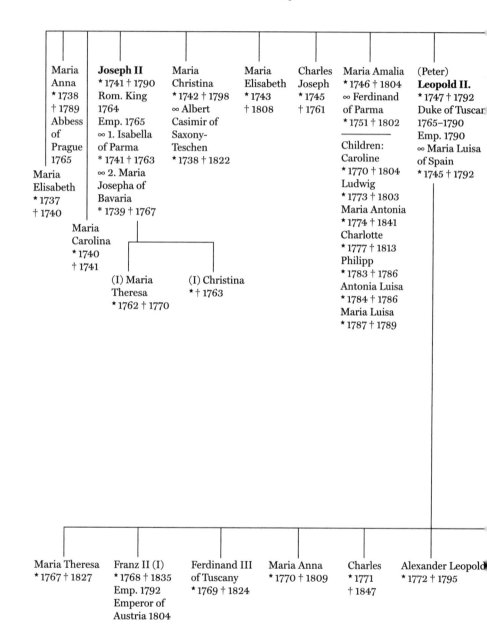

Maria
Anna
* 1738
† 1789
Abbess
of
Prague
1765

Maria
Elisabeth
* 1737
† 1740

Joseph II
* 1741 † 1790
Rom. King
1764
Emp. 1765
∞ 1. Isabella
of Parma
* 1741 † 1763
∞ 2. Maria
Josepha of
Bavaria
* 1739 † 1767

Maria
Carolina
* 1740
† 1741

Maria
Christina
* 1742 † 1798
∞ Albert
Casimir of
Saxony-
Teschen
* 1738 † 1822

(I) Maria
Theresa
* 1762 † 1770

(I) Christina
* † 1763

Maria
Elisabeth
* 1743
† 1808

Charles
Joseph
* 1745
† 1761

Maria Amalia
* 1746 † 1804
∞ Ferdinand
of Parma
* 1751 † 1802
—————
Children:
Caroline
* 1770 † 1804
Ludwig
* 1773 † 1803
Maria Antonia
* 1774 † 1841
Charlotte
* 1777 † 1813
Philipp
* 1783 † 1786
Antonia Luisa
* 1784 † 1786
Maria Luisa
* 1787 † 1789

(Peter)
Leopold II.
* 1747 † 1792
Duke of Tuscan
1765–1790
Emp. 1790
∞ Maria Luisa
of Spain
* 1745 † 1792

Maria Theresa
* 1767 † 1827

Franz II (I)
* 1768 † 1835
Emp. 1792
Emperor of
Austria 1804

Ferdinand III
of Tuscany
* 1769 † 1824

Maria Anna
* 1770 † 1809

Charles
* 1771
† 1847

Alexander Leopold
* 1772 † 1795

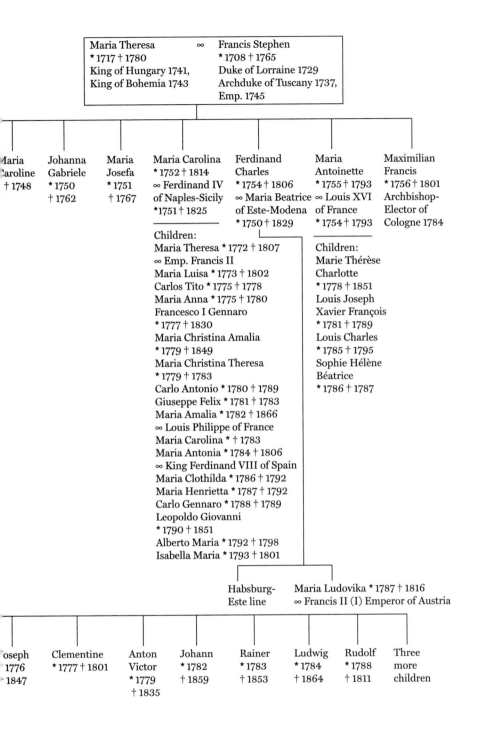

Maria Theresa
*1717 † 1780
King of Hungary 1741,
King of Bohemia 1743

∞ Francis Stephen
*1708 † 1765
Duke of Lorraine 1729
Archduke of Tuscany 1737,
Emp. 1745

Maria
Caroline
† 1748

Johanna
Gabriele
*1750
† 1762

Maria
Josefa
*1751
† 1767

Maria Carolina
*1752 † 1814
∞ Ferdinand IV
of Naples-Sicily
*1751 † 1825
——————
Children:
Maria Theresa *1772 † 1807
∞ Emp. Francis II
Maria Luisa *1773 † 1802
Carlos Tito *1775 † 1778
Maria Anna *1775 † 1780
Francesco I Gennaro
*1777 † 1830
Maria Christina Amalia
*1779 † 1849
Maria Christina Theresa
*1779 † 1783
Carlo Antonio *1780 † 1789
Giuseppe Felix *1781 † 1783
Maria Amalia *1782 † 1866
∞ Louis Philippe of France
Maria Carolina * † 1783
Maria Antonia *1784 † 1806
∞ King Ferdinand VIII of Spain
Maria Clothilda *1786 † 1792
Maria Henrietta *1787 † 1792
Carlo Gennaro *1788 † 1789
Leopoldo Giovanni
*1790 † 1851
Alberto Maria *1792 † 1798
Isabella Maria *1793 † 1801

Ferdinand
Charles
*1754 † 1806
∞ Maria Beatrice
of Este-Modena
*1750 † 1829

Maria
Antoinette
*1755 † 1793
∞ Louis XVI
of France
*1754 † 1793
——————
Children:
Marie Thérèse
Charlotte
*1778 † 1851
Louis Joseph
Xavier François
*1781 † 1789
Louis Charles
*1785 † 1795
Sophie Hélène
Béatrice
*1786 † 1787

Maximilian
Francis
*1756 † 1801
Archbishop-
Elector of
Cologne 1784

Habsburg-
Este line

Maria Ludovika *1787 † 1816
∞ Francis II (I) Emperor of Austria

Joseph
1776
1847

Clementine
*1777 † 1801

Anton
Victor
*1779
† 1835

Johann
*1782
† 1859

Rainer
*1783
† 1853

Ludwig
*1784
† 1864

Rudolf
*1788
† 1811

Three
more
children

ILLUSTRATION CREDITS

Color Insert

Plate 1, 15, 20: KHM-Museumsverband, Vienna

Plate 2: Elisabethinenkonvent Klagenfurt

Plate 3: © Nationalmuseum Stockholm / Bridgeman Images

Plate 4: From Koschatzky, Maria Theresia und ihre Zeit, 99, fig. 30

Plate 5: akg-images / Fototeca Gilardi

Plate 6, 14, 24, 25, 26, 28: akg-images

Plate 7: From z-Arco, Agnes / Georg Lechner (eds.), *Martin van Meytens der Jüngere*, 66–67. (Private collection, Vienna)

Plate 8: MAK—Österreichisches Museum für angewandte Kunst / Gegenwartskunst, Photos: © MAK / Mika K. Wisskirchen (above), © MAK / Georg Mayer (below)

Plate 9: Albertina, Vienna. www.albertina.at

Plate 10: Owned by Suermondt- Ludwig-Museums, © Anne Gold, Aachen

Plate 11: Schloss Schönbrunn Kultur- und Betriebsgesellschaft / Collection: Bundesmobilienverwaltung / Location: Schloss Schönbrunn / Photo: Edgar Knaack

Plate 12: Belvedere, Vienna

Plate 13: Wikimedia Commons, Wolfgang Sauber

Plate 16: akg-images / Erich Lessing

Plate 17: © Wien Museum

Plate 18: Wikimedia Commons, rollroboter

Plate 19: Nadelburg Museum / Photo: Robert Bachtrögl

Plate 21: ÖNB, Vienna, Handschriftensammlung, cod. min. 33a

Plate 22: Schloss Schönbrunn Kultur- und Betriebsges.mbH / Photo: Alexander Eugen Koller

Plate 23: Erzbischöfliche Diözesanbibliothek Eger, Inv. No. Ms. 2056 (K2.I.I). Reproduced in Elfriede Iby, et al. (ed.), *Maria Theresia 1717–1780. Strategin—Mutter—Reformerin*, Vienna 2017, 291 No. HM 24.4

Plate 27: Wikimedia Commons, Ludmila Pilecka

Plate 29: akg-images / Erich Lessing

Plate 30: From Koschatzky, *Maria Theresia und ihre Zeit*, 28, fig. 6

Scattered Images

Fig. 1: www.in-arcadia-ego.at

Fig. 2, 43: KHM-Museumsverband, Vienna

Fig. 3: ÖNB, Vienna, 128 866—B

Fig. 4: ÖNB, Vienna, Sign. 44.O.4 Alt

Fig. 5: From Mraz/Mraz, *Maria Theresia*, 33

Fig. 6: Budapest History Museum, Inv No. II, 216, Photo: József Szabolcs Csörge, Public Art Multimedia

Fig. 7, 29: akg-images

Fig. 8: Gartmann Sammel-Album 21 (1924), 6095

Fig. 9, 10, 11: Rijksmuseum Amsterdam

Fig. 12: From: Bressan / Grassi, *Maria Teresa*, 50 ff.

Fig. 13: LWL-Museum für Kunst und Kultur (Westfälisches Landesmuseum), Münster/Porträtarchiv Diepenbroick; Photo: LWL-Museum für Kunst und Kultur (Westfälisches Landes-museum), Münster, Hanna Neander

Fig. 14: From Mraz/Mraz, *Maria Theresia*, 73

Fig. 15: From Gerda Mraz (ed.), *Maria Theresia als Königin von Ungarn* (*Jahrbuch für österreichische Kulturgeschichte* 10), Eisen-stadt 1984, 179

Fig. 16: Historisches Museum Frankfurt (Inv.-No. C01192), Photo: Horst Ziegenfusz

Fig. 17, 27, 41: Albertina, Vienna; www.albertina.at

Fig. 18: From Koschatzky, *Maria Theresia*, 438

Fig. 19: Vienna, Österreichisches Staatsarchiv, Kriegsarchiv, HKR 1771, 98–136 (fol. 8v).

Fig. 20: De Agostini Picture Library / A. Dagli Orti / Bridgeman Images

Fig. 21: Photo: Erik Cornelius / Nationalmuseum Stockholm

Fig. 22 a. b, 42: akg-images

Fig. 23: From Johann Storch, *Weiberkrankheiten*, Vienna 1747

Fig. 24: © Burghauptmannstadt Österreich / Photo Bunge

Fig. 25: ÖNB, Vienna, Pk 3003, 530

Fig. 26: akg-images / Erich Lessing

Fig. 28: From Koschatzky, *Maria Theresia*, 417

Fig. 30: Hungarian National Gallery, Budapest / Bridgeman Images

Fig. 31: Belvedere, Vienna

Fig. 32: bpk / Staatsbibliothek zu Berlin

Fig. 33: Schloss & Park Eggenberg / Universalmuseum Joanneum GmbH, Graz

Fig. 34: Lars-Holger Thümler (ed.) (1993): *Die Österreichische Armee im Siebenjährigen Krieg. Die Bautzener Bilderhandschrift aus dem Jahre 1762* (facsimile), No. 70

Fig. 35: Private collection, © Luisa Riccarini / Leemage / Bridgeman Images

Fig. 36: ÖNB, Vienna, NB 500.160-C

Fig. 37: © Deutsches Historisches Museum, Berlin (Inv.-No. Gm 2004 / 20)

Fig. 38a. b: Office of Graphic Arts Museums of Art and History, Geneva, property of the Swiss Confederation, Gottfried Keller Foundation, Berne. Photo: ville-geneve.ch

Fig. 39: De Agostini Picture Library / Bridgeman Images

Fig. 40: © IMAGNO / Gerhard Trumler

Fig. 44: ÖNB, Vienna, E 6858-D

Fig. 45: © Deutsches Historisches Museum, Berlin (Inv.-No. 1988 / 613)

Fig. 46 a–d: René & Peter van der Krogt, http: // statues .vanderkrogt.net

Fig. 47: From Koschatzky, *Maria Theresia*, 316, fig. 149

Fig. 48: From *Prinz Eugen und das barocke Österreich*, Ausstellungs-katalog des Niederösterreichischen Landesmuseums, Vienna, 1986, FB 80.

Fig. 49: © Wien Museum

Fig. 50: Bayerische Staatsbibliothek Munich

Fig. 51: akg-images / Imagno

Fig. 52: ÖNB, Vienna, PORT_00047656

Unfortunately, it was not possible in all cases to determine the owner of the image rights. The publisher is of course ready to settle justified claims.

INDEX OF NAMES

A NOTE ON THE TYPE

This book has been composed in Arno, an Old-style serif typeface in the classic Venetian tradition, designed by Robert Slimbach at Adobe.